The LAW *of* TORTS *in* AUSTRALIA

The LAW *of* TORTS *in* AUSTRALIA

Second Edition

FRANCIS TRINDADE
Sir Owen Dixon Professor of Law, Monash University
Barrister and Solicitor, Victoria

PETER CANE
Fellow of Corpus Christi College, Oxford
Solicitor, New South Wales

Melbourne
OXFORD UNIVERSITY PRESS
Oxford Auckland New York

OXFORD UNIVERSITY PRESS AUSTRALIA

Oxford New York Toronto
Delhi Bombay Calcutta Madras Karachi
Kuala Lumpur Singapore Hong Kong Tokyo
Nairobi Dar es Salaam Cape Town
Melbourne Auckland Madrid
and associated companies in
Berlin Ibadan

First edition, 1985
Reprinted 1986, 1988, 1990

Second edition, 1993

National Library of Australia
Cataloguing-in-Publication data:

Trindade, F. A. (Francis Anthony), 1937-
The law of torts in Australia.

2nd ed.
Includes index.
ISBN 0 19 553316X.

1. Torts—Australia. I. Cane, Peter, 1950- . II. Title.

346.9403

Typeset by Solo Typesetting, South Australia
Printed by Australian Print Group, Victoria
Published by Oxford University Press,
253 Normanby Road, South Melbourne, Australia

CONTENTS

PREFACE

In the Preface to the first edition we said that 'the purpose of this book is to examine and present the law of torts from a truly Australian perspective. The emphasis in the work is therefore on the decisions of Australian courts and the enactments of Australian legislatures in the area of torts, though material from other jurisdictions is used where it is necessary or particularly helpful in explaining the law in Australia'. That purpose and that emphasis are continued in the second edition, and they have been clearly vindicated. As Brennan J., of the High Court of Australia, recently reminded us in *Mabo* v. *Queensland* (1992) 66 A.L.J.R. 408, 416 (in a context outside the law of torts), 'the law which governs Australia is Australian law'; and that increasingly since 1968, when the progressive abolition of appeals to the Privy Council began, the common law of Australia has been substantially in the hands of the High Court of Australia. Brennan J. acknowledged, however, that 'Australian law is not only the historical successor of, but is an organic development from, the law of England'.

The second edition, like the first, is directed principally to students in Australian law schools. However, we have also been encouraged by the reception and support given to the first edition by legal practitioners. They can be assured that they will find much in this book which will be useful and interesting to them.

The responsibility for writing Chapter 1 is joint and several. Francis Trindade is responsible for Chapters 2 to 8, and Peter Cane for Chapters 9 to 23. Each of us has, however, read the contribution of the other and made suggestions, not always acted upon, for improvement. We are grateful for the generosity and kindness of the many reviewers of the first edition, and hope that we have successfully dealt with their many constructive comments and suggestions in a satisfactory way.

A few major changes in this edition deserve specific mention. The chapter in the first edition dealing with occupiers' liability has been assimilated into the general negligence chapters in recognition of the decision in *Australian Safeway Stores* v. *Zaluzna*. There is a new section in Chapter 2 on malicious prosecution and abuse of process, a recent growth area within the law of torts. There is an expanded discussion of the economic torts in Chapter 5 as well as a discussion of the significant change in the way that some of these torts, and actions under ss.52, 53 and 55 of the Trade Practices Act 1974, are being litigated and will be litigated in the future as a result of recent cross-vesting legislation in Australia. Chapter 15 contains a discussion of the new Federal products liability law; and considerable rewriting has been necessary to deal with the new conceptual structure which a majority of members of the High Court has imposed on the law of negligence. In order to create enough space for discussion of these and other important developments, we have decided to omit from this edition the chapters on no-fault compensation schemes and on economic analysis of the law of torts; but this should not be taken to indicate any belief on our part that these topics are unimportant. We had planned to include a new chapter on defamation, but continuing uncertainty about the prospects for legislative reform caused us to abandon this plan.

Our thanks are due to Keith Akers for his research assistance and general helpfulness again in relation to this edition, and particularly for his help with the Index and Tables of Cases and Legislation; and to Anne Naidoo for her secretarial assistance with the manuscript.

In this edition, as in the first, the masculine forms 'he', 'his' etc., are not gender-restrictive. We have tried to take into account in this edition developments in the law of torts that have occurred up to 31 July 1992.

Oxford
October 1992

Francis Trindade
Peter Cane

ABBREVIATIONS

Entries marked with an asterisk are Nominate Reports, which can be found most easily in the series called the English Reports (E.R.).

A.	Atlantic Reporter (U.S.A.)
A.C.	Appeal Cases
A.C.L.R.	Australian Company Law Reports
A. Crim R.	Australian Criminal Reports
A.C.T.R.	Australian Capital Territory Reports
*Ad. & E.	Adolphus & Ellis
Adel. L.R.	*Adelaide Law Review*
A.I.R.	All India Reporter
A.J.R.	Australian Jurist Reports (Victoria)
All E.R.	All England Reports
A.L.J.	*Australian Law Journal*
A.L.J.R.	Australian Law Journal Reports
A.L.R.	Australian Law Reports
A.L.R.C.	Australian Law Reform Commission
A.P.R.	Atlantic Provinces Reports (Canada)
A.S.L.	Annual Survey of Law (Australia)
A.T.C.	Australian Tax Cases
A.T.L.A.L. Rep	American Trial Lawyers Association Law Reports
A.T.P.R.	Australian Trade Practices Reports
Am. J. Comp. L.	*American Journal of Comparative Law*
App. Cas.	Appeal Cases
Arg.L.R.	Argus Law Reports (Victoria)
Aronson & Whitmore	M. Aronson & H. Whitmore, *Public Torts and Contracts* (Sydney, 1982)
Atiyah's Accidents	P. Cane, *Atiyah's Accidents, Compensation and the Law* (4th edn, London, 1987)
Atiyah, Vicarious Liability	P.S. Atiyah, *Vicarious Liability in the Law of Torts* (London, 1967)
Auckland L.R.	*Auckland Law Review*
Aust. Torts Reports	Australian Torts Reports (CCH)
*B. & Ad.	Barnewall & Adolphus
*B. & C.	Barnwall & Creswell

*B. & P. (N.R.)	Bosanquet & Puller (New Reports)
*Barn. & Ald.	Barnewall & Alderson
*Barn. & Cress.	Barnwall & Cresswell
*Bing	Bingham
Brit. J. Law	*British Journal of Law and Society & Soc.*
Ch. (D)	Chancery (Division)
*C. & P.	Carrington & Payne
*C.B.	Common Bench
*C.B. (N.S.)	Common Bench (New Series)
C.L.J.	*Cambridge Law Journal*
C.L.P	*Current Legal Problems*
C.L.R.	Commonwealth Law Reports
C.L.Y.	Current Law Yearbook
*C.M. & R.	Crompton, Meeson & Roscoe's English Exchequer Reports (1834-6)
California L.R.	*California Law Review*
Camb. L.R.	*Cambrian Law Review*
*Camp.	Campbell
*Car. & K.	Carrington & Kirwan
*Car. & P.	Carrington & Payne
Can. B.R.	*Canadian Bar Review*
*Co. Rep.	Coke's Reports
Col. L.R.	*Columbia Law Review*
Conv.	*Conveyancer*
C.P.R.	Canadian Patent Reports
Cr. App. R.	Criminal Appeal Reports
*Cr. & M.	Crompton & Meeson
*Cro. Eliz.	Croke, Elizabeth
*Cro. Jac	Croke, James
Crim L.R.	*Criminal Law Review*
Cwth	Commonwealth (of Australia)
*D. & C.	Dean & Chapter
D.L.R.	Dominion Law Reports (Canada)
*Dow	Dow
*E. & B.	Ellis & Blackburn
E.A.C.A.	East African Court of Appeal
E.R.	English Reports
Ex. D.	Exchequer Division
Exch. Rep.	Exchequer Reports
*F. & F.	Foster & Finlason
F.L.C.	Family Law Cases
F.L.R.	Federal Law Reports
F.S.R.	Fleet Street Reports
Fifoot	C.H.S. Fifoot, *History and Sources of the Common Law* (London, 1949)
Fleming	J.G. Fleming, *The Law of Torts*
*H. & C.	Hurlstone & Coltman
*H. & N.	Hurlstone & Norman
H.L.	House of Lords
Harv. L.R.	*Harvard Law Review*

I.C.L.Q.	*International and Comparative Law Quarterly*
I.C.R.	Irish Circuit Reports
I.R.	Irish Reports
I.R.L.R.	Industrial Relations Law Reports
Ir. Jur. Rep.	Irish Jurist Reports
Ill.	Illinois
Ill. App.	Illinois Appeals
Ind. L.J.	*Indiana Law Journal*
Indust. L.J.	*Industrial Law Journal*
Int. Rev. of Law & Econ.	*International Review of Law and Economics*
I.P.R.	Intellectual Property Reports
*J. & H.	Johnson & Hemming
*J.P.	Justice of the Peace Reports
J. of Contract Law	*Journal of Contract Law*
J. of Leg. Stud.	*Journal of Legal Studies*
J.S.P.T.L.	*Journal of the Society of Teachers of Public Law*
K.B.	King's Bench
*Ld. Raym.	Lord Raymond
Law Inst. J.	*Law Institute Journal* (Victoria)
*Lev.	Levinz
*Lew.	Lewin's Crown Cases on the Northern Circuit
L.G.R.	Local Government Reports
L.G.R.A.	Local Government Reports of Australia
Lloyd's Rep.	Lloyd's Reports
L.Q.R.	*Law Quarterly Review*
L.R. (N.S.W.)	Law Reports (New South Wales)
L.R. Ir. (Ireland)	Law Reports: Chancery and Common Law
L.S.	*Legal Studies*
L.S.J.S.	Law Society Judgment Scheme (South Australia)
L.T.	Law Times
L.T.N.S.	Law Times Reports, New Series
Luntz, Hambly & Hayes	H. Luntz, A.D. Hambley & R. Hayes, *Torts: Cases and Commentary*
*M. Rob.	Moody & Robinson
*M. & W.	Meeson & Welsby
*Man. & G.	Manning & Granger
*Mer.	Merivale
*Mod. Rep.	Modern Reports
M.L.R.	*Modern Law Review*
M.U.L.R.	*Melbourne University Law Review*
Mal. L.R.	*Malaya Law Review*
McGregor	*McGregor on Damages*
Mon. U.L.R.	*Monash University Law Review*
M.V.R.	Motor Vehicle Reports
*N.C.	Notes of Cases (English Ecclesiastical and Maritime)
N.E.	North Eastern Reporter (U.S.A.)
N.I.L.Q.	*Northern Ireland Legal Quarterly*
New L.J.	*New Law Journal*

N.S.R.	Nova Scotia Reports (Canada)
N.S.W.L.R.	New South Wales Law Reports
N.S.W.L.R.C.	New South Wales Law Reform Commission
N.S.W.R.	New South Wales Reports
N.T.R.	Northern Territory Reports
N.W.	North Western Reporter (U.S.A.)
N.Y.S.	New York Supplement (U.S.A.)
N.Z.L.R.	New Zealand Law Reports
N.Z.U.L.R.	*New Zealand Universities Law Review*
O.H.L.J.	Osgoode Hall Law Journal
O.J.L.S.	Oxford Journal of Legal Studies
O.R.	Ontario Reports
Ottawa L.R.	*Ottawa Law Review*
P.	Probate (preceded by date in square brackets); Pacific Reporter (preceded by date in parentheses) President (preceded by surname)
P. & C.R.	Property and Compensation Reports
P.L.	*Public Law*
P.N.	*Professional Negligence*
Pearson Commission	Royal Commission on Civil Liability and Compensation for Personal Injury (London, 1978)
Q.B.	Queen's Bench
Q.B.D.	Queen's Bench Division
Q.J.P.R.	Queensland Justice of the Peace Reports
Q.S.R.	Queensland State Reports
Q.W.N.	Queensland Weekly Notes
Qd. R.	Queensland Reports
Qd. St. R.	Queensland State Reports
*Rol. Abr.	Rolle's Abridgment
R.C.C.	Rules of the County Court
R.P.C.	Reports of Patent Cases
R.S.C.	Rules of the Supreme Court
Restatement	Restatement of the Law of Torts (2d) (U.S.A.)
S.A.L.R.	South Australian Law Reports
S.A.S.R.	South Australia State Reports
S.C.R. (N.S.W.)	Supreme Court Reports (New South Wales)
S.C.R.	Supreme Court Reports (Canada)
S.E.	South Eastern Reporter (U.S.A.)
S.L.T.	Scottish Law Times
S.R. (N.S.W.)	State Reports (New South Wales)
S.R. (W.A.)	State Reports (Western Australia)
S.W.	South Western Reporter (U.S.A.)
Salmond & Heuston	J. Salmond & R.F.V. Heuston, *Law of Torts*
So.	Southern Reporter (U.S.A.)
Sol. Jo.	*Solicitors Journal*
St.R.Qd.	State Reports Queensland
*Stra.	Strange
Street	H. Street, *The Law of Torts*
*Sty.	Style
Syd. L.R.	*Sydney Law Review*

T.L.R.	Times Law Reports
Tas.L.R.	Tasmanian Law Reports
Tas. R.	Tasmanian Reports
Tas. S.R.	Tasmanian State Reports
*Term Rep.	Term Reports
Texas L.R.	*Texas Law Review*
Tulane L.R.	*Tulane Law Review*
U. Chi. L.R.	*University of Chicago Law Review*
U.N.S.W.L.J.	*University of New South Wales Law Journal*
U. Pa. L.R.	*University of Philadelphia Law Review*
U. Qld L.J.	*University of Queensland Law Journal*
U. Tas L.R.	*University of Tasmania Law Review*
U.T.L.J.	*University of Toronto Law Journal*
U.W.A.L.R.	*University of Western Australia Law Review*
V.L.R.	Victorian Law Reports
V.M.A.C.	Victorian Motor Accident Cases
Virginia L.R.	*Virginia Law Review*
V.R.	Victorian Reports
W.A.L.R.	Western Australia Law Reports
W.A.R.	Western Australian Reports
W.L.R.	Weekly Law Reports
W.N.	Weekly Notes
W.W. & a'B.	Wyatt, Webb and a'Beckett Reports (Victoria)
W.W.R.	Western Weekly Reports (Canada)
Weir	T. Weir, *A Casebook on Tort*
Williams & Hepple	G. Williams & B.A. Hepple, *Foundations of the Law of Tort*
*Wils.	Wilson
*Wm. Bl.	William Blackstone
*Wms Saund.	Williams' Saunders
Yale L.J.	*Yale Law Journal*

CASES

LEGISLATION

COMMONWEALTH OF AUSTRALIA STATUTES

NEW SOUTH WALES REGULATIONS

NORTHERN TERRITORY STATUTES

VICTORIA
RULES OF THE SUPREME COURT

VICTORIA
RULES OF THE COUNTY COURT

WESTERN AUSTRALIA
STATUTES

UNITED KINGDOM
STATUTES

UNITED KINGDOM
RULES OF THE SUPREME COURT

NEW ZEALAND
STATUTES

INTERNATIONAL AGREEMENTS

1

INTRODUCTION

1. What is a Tort?

The word 'tort', unlike the words 'contract' or 'crime', is not one in everyday use. And yet rules and principles of the law of torts deal with a very wide range of common occurrences as diverse as industrial disputes, libellous newspaper articles, road accidents, noisy neighbours, dangerous pharmaceutical drugs, vicious dogs, and so on. The word 'tort' is, by origin, a French word meaning 'wrong' or 'injury'; but in modern Australian law it has come to have a narrower meaning. In the first place, the law of torts is made up of a considerable number of torts, that is, separate wrongs with different characteristics or 'elements'—for example, trespass, negligence and nuisance—and because these torts together deal with such a wide range of situations, the differences between them are often more important than the similarities. But sometimes one and the same act can constitute more than one tort; and because different torts have different elements, parties may argue about which tort (if any) the defendant has committed.

Secondly, torts are *civil* wrongs as opposed to *criminal* wrongs. The most obvious consequences of this distinction relate to *procedure* (crimes are dealt with by the legal system according to procedures rather different from those applying to civil wrongs) and to the way the perpetrator of the wrong is dealt with (most commonly, persons convicted of crimes are 'sentenced' to pay a fine to the state, or to be imprisoned or subjected to some other reduction in their freedom of action; whereas a person who has committed a tort is usually ordered, by way of 'remedy', to pay a sum of money to the victim of the tort, or may be ordered to commit no further torts in the future). But the categories of civil and criminal wrongs are not mutually exclusive—some crimes are also torts (physically attacking a person, for example, or stealing their property).

Thirdly, torts are not the only civil wrongs: breaches of contracts or breaches of trusts are also civil wrongs. Furthermore, although many wrongs fall into only one legal category of wrongs, one and the same act can fall into more than one category; for example, some breaches of contract are also torts. Where an act constitutes more than one legal wrong, it may be easier for a plaintiff to get a remedy, or to get a better remedy, by choosing to treat the act as being one type of legal wrong rather than another.[1] In general, in such a situation Australian law allows the plaintiff a free choice as to how to treat the act—for example, whether as a tort or a breach of contract.[2]

So, it may be of practical importance[3] to decide whether an act constitutes a tort, either because it constitutes no other legal wrong, or because the plaintiff would be better off if it was dealt with as a tort rather than some other legal wrong; and it may be of practical importance to decide which tort or torts the defendant has committed. But in some contexts it may also be of practical importance to know whether the plaintiff has an 'action in tort'.[4] To decide this it may be necessary to identify the common features shared by all torts. Admittedly, this is a very difficult thing to do because the individual torts which make up the law of torts are extremely heterogeneous. We could, perhaps, start with a judicial definition of a tort (given by Murphy J. of the Victorian Supreme Court) as a breach of a duty 'owed generally to one's fellow subjects, the duty being imposed by law and not as a consequence of duties fixed by the parties themselves'.[5]

First, then, torts are breaches of duties—for example, the duty to take care not to injure other people. But, of course, many other legal wrongs also consist of breaches of duties, and so this element of the definition does not get us very far.

Secondly, it is usually said that torts are breaches of duties imposed by law (whether statute law or common law) as opposed to duties 'fixed by the parties themselves' (or, as it is often put, 'voluntarily assumed'). This distinction between duties imposed by law and duties voluntarily assumed is an extremely complex and difficult one which has generated a large literature.[6] But we can content ourselves with three observations. First, in one sense, all *legal* duties are imposed by law; breach of a voluntarily assumed duty will not constitute a legal wrong unless the law recognizes that duty. But the law sometimes imposes duties on people even if they deny that they have any such duty. Secondly, it is not only tort duties which may be imposed by law on a person who denies that there is any such duty. For example, some contractual duties, and many of the duties imposed by the law of trusts, are imposed in this strong sense. But, thirdly, sometimes (although rarely) a tortious duty will be imposed on a person only if, by words or conduct, the actor can be said to have bound himself to act in a certain way. For example, sometimes a duty to take positive

---

1 The same is true, *mutatis mutandis*, where the same act constitutes more than one tort.
2 See p. 10 below.
3 All of these matters are also of considerable theoretical interest.
4 e.g. *Blomme* v. *Sutton* (1989) 52 S.A.S.R. 76.
5 *MacPherson & Kelley* v. *Kevin J. Prunty & Associates* [1983] 1 V.R. 573, 587 *per* Murphy J.
6 The classic discussion is by P.S. Atiyah *Essays on Contract* rev. edn (Oxford, 1990) Ch. 1. See also P. Cane and J. Stapleton eds *Essays for Patrick Atiyah* (Oxford, 1991) Ch. 15.

action will be imposed only if a person has undertaken to act in a particular way.[7]

Finally, Murphy J. says that tortious duties are owed to persons generally, as opposed to specified individuals. By contrast, contractual duties, for example, are usually owed to specified persons or groups of persons. But it should be noted that while many tort duties are owed to persons generally or to groups of unspecified individuals, it is also sometimes true that a tort duty will be owed by A to B only if there is a 'special relationship' between A and B; and this usually means that A must be identifiable, whether individually or as a member of a specified and relatively small class of persons.[8]

There are two other characteristics of torts not mentioned by Murphy J. which need to be noted. The normal remedy for breach of a tortious duty is damages (that is, monetary compensation). Such damages are said to be 'unliquidated', which means that when a tort claim is actually tried in a court,[9] the amount of the damages is fixed by the court[10] and that the amount awarded depends on all the circumstances of the case. But claims for unliquidated damages are also very common in, for example, contract actions. Conversely, unliquidated damages is not the only remedy available for torts. In particular, an injunction may be awarded to restrain the threatened commission of torts such as trespass to land[11] or nuisance. Indeed, where the defendant's threatened action will interfere with the plaintiff's rights over land, the plaintiff is entitled to an injunction unless the injury can be easily compensated for in money and it would be unfair to the defendant to award an injunction. But in other cases, where injunctions are available, they may be awarded only if damages would not be an adequate remedy.[12]

Finally, although we have so far defined a tort in terms of breach of duty, it is also helpful to note that the corollary of a breached duty is an infringed right or interest. Duties protect rights and interests. An important way of distinguishing between the law of torts and other areas of the law of obligations is by specifying which legally recognized rights or interests are protected by the law of torts. Briefly, the law of torts protects the individual's interest in physical and mental integrity; it also protects interests in land and interests in goods or chattels. The law of torts also (but to a somewhat limited extent) protects a person against the infliction

---

7 See p. 383 below.

8 See, for example, p. 355 below.

9 Most tort claims are settled out of court.

10 This does not mean that in an action in tort the plaintiff cannot and does not, in the pleadings, specify a sum of money claimed as damages. He may, and often does, do so, and any such specified sum will provide an upper limit to the damages the court may award. In *Aaron* v. *Aaron* (1944) 61 W.N.(N.S.W.) 93, 95 Street J. (incorrectly) regarded a claim for unliquidated damages as an *essential* feature of a claim in tort.

11 Note also that an injunction may be granted to restrain threatened trespasses to the person, such as assault and battery, but only very reluctantly: *Parry* v. *Crooks* (1982) 27 S.A.S.R. 1, 8; *Corvisy* v. *Corvisy* [1982] 2 N.S.W.L.R. 557.

12 The law also tolerates self-help in some circumstances.

of purely economic loss, that is, financial loss which is not also accompanied by personal injury to the plaintiff or physical damage to his land or goods.

On the other hand, it follows from the fact that some acts can constitute more than one legal wrong that some interests are protected by more than one body of legal rules or by more than one branch of the law. Analysis of the law of torts in terms of protected interests is particularly important in relation to torts which protect 'property interests', because it leads us to consider which interests count as property interests for the purposes of the law of tort. For example, in *Victoria Park Racing and Recreation Grounds Ltd* v. *Taylor*[13] it was held that the plaintiff racecourse owner was not entitled to an injunction to restrain the defendants from broadcasting accounts of the races from a high tower erected on land belonging to one of the defendants and overlooking the racecourse, because the law recognized no interest in not being overlooked and observed in the use of one's land. Dixon J. reached this conclusion by examining the law as it stood at the time of the decision, and he found therein no support for recognizing the alleged right not to be overlooked.[14] But, of course, unless the law is to be treated as incapable of further development, it must be possible for the law to extend protection to interests not hitherto protected.

Another context in which analysis of the law of torts in terms of protected interests has become very important is that of liability for negligently inflicted, purely economic loss. For example, English courts have now reached the position that if a plaintiff complains that land or goods which he has acquired are defective as a result of alleged negligence on the part of the defendant, he can recover damages for such negligence only if, as a result of the defect, he has suffered some personal injury or physical damage to property other than the defective property. But it seems that the Australian law of negligence would, in certain circumstances, allow such a plaintiff to recover the cost of repairing the defective property, even if he has suffered no personal injury or property damage as a result of the alleged negligence.[15] Underlying such differences of approach is a wider issue about whether courts should take an essentially conservative attitude to the recognition of new interests or whether, by contrast, the law of torts in general[16] and the law of negligence in particular should be seen as a mechanism for adapting to changing expectations concerning the proper role of the law in protecting what people value.[17]

The view of the authors of this book is that it is a proper function of the law of torts to offer protection to hitherto unprotected interests either by including them in an existing category of protected interests or by creating a new category. What Lord Simonds said of the law of contract

---

13 (1937) 58 C.L.R. 479.

14 (1937) 58 C.L.R. 479, 505, 509-10.

15 See p. 594 below.

16 *Motherwell* v. *Motherwell* (1976) 73 D.L.R. (3d) 62, 68 *per* Clement J.A.:'it is not only in the field of negligence that the common law demonstrates its continuing ability to serve the changing and expanding needs of our present society'.

17 D. Howarth [1991] *C.L.J.* 58.

applies with equal force to the law of torts: 'It is . . . essential to the life of the common law that its principles should be adapted to meet fresh circumstances and needs'.[18]

2. The Relationship Between Tort Law and Other Legal Categories

Now that we have made some attempt to explain what a tort is, it may be useful to explore in a little more detail the relationship between tort law and some other areas of the law with which tort law is connected.

(a) Tort and crime We have already noted two differences between civil wrongs and criminal wrongs: first, the procedure for criminal trials is different from that for civil trials. One aspect of this is that the enforcement of the criminal law is usually left to state prosecution authorities (although in many cases prosecution by a private citizen is not ruled out), while the law of torts is normally activated by the victim of the tort. But there are some cases in which the Attorney-General may bring an action in his own right to restrain a public nuisance[19] or a breach of statutory duty;[20] and in other cases an action (called a 'relator action') may be brought in the Attorney-General's name, although the proceedings will be conducted and financed by the individuals on whose behalf the action is brought.[21]

Secondly, the sanctions most commonly imposed by the criminal law are different from those usually imposed by the law of torts: imprisonment and non-custodial sentences and fines paid to the state as opposed to monetary compensation and injunctions.[22] From this it is often deduced that the law of torts is primarily concerned with compensation whereas the criminal law is primarily concerned with punishment and deterrence. But this is an over-simplification. In the first place, there is a difference between punishing someone for having acted in a certain way and seeking to deter them from acting in that way in the future. An award of monetary compensation *may* have a deterrent effect, and deterrence of tortious conduct is usually seen as (at least) a subsidiary function of tort law. Also, the law of torts is sometimes prepared to require a defendant to pay to the plaintiff damages representing some gain or benefit derived from committing the tort, even though this gain does not represent a loss to the plaintiff, so that the damages cannot be said to be *compensating* the plaintiff. Such awards of 'restitutionary damages' can be seen as designed to deter tortious conduct.

Furthermore, in certain cases a plaintiff can be awarded what are called

---

18 *British Movietonews Ltd* v. *London & District Cinemas Ltd* [1952] A.C. 166, 188.
19 See p. 626 below.
20 See p. 662 below.
21 See p. 626 below.
22 Injunctions are rarely available to restrain threatened breaches of the criminal law because of the basic principle that a person is presumed innocent until it has been proved that he *has committed* a criminal offence.

'exemplary' (or 'vindictive', 'penal' or 'punitive') damages.[23] The explicit aim of such damages is to punish and deter the defendant and other would-be tortfeasors. The court may award damages

> over and above those required to compensate the plaintiff for the injury suffered by him if it forms the opinion . . . that the defendant's conduct in committing the wrong was so reprehensible as to require that he should not only compensate the plaintiff for what he has suffered but should be punished for what he has done in order to discourage him and others from acting in such a fashion.[24]

Such damages are not available in all tort actions, but chiefly in actions such as trespass and defamation where the defendant has acted deliberately and outrageously in defiance of the rights of the plaintiff. The fact that exemplary damages perform a quite different function from compensatory damages is illustrated by a New Zealand case in which it was held that although compensatory damages cannot be awarded for assault and battery because of the statutory compensation scheme embodied in the Accident Compensation Act 1972, nevertheless there is 'no reason in principle why a plaintiff should not sue in battery for exemplary damages *alone*'.[25] Another illustration is the case of *XL Petroleum (N.S.W.) Pty Ltd* v. *Caltex Oil (Australia) Pty Ltd*[26] in which it was held that in a case against more than one defendant, exemplary damages may be awarded against one, even though they are not awarded against the other(s).

Conversely, the criminal law is not solely concerned with punishment of the offender. There are statutory provisions in all Australian jurisdictions which enable courts in criminal proceedings to make orders requiring the offender to compensate the victim.[27] There are also publicly funded criminal injuries compensation schemes which operate outside the law of torts and which provide significant compensation to the victims of violent crimes. The importance of these two types of provision is that they show that the *state's* interest in crime extends beyond punishing and deterring offenders.

As we noted earlier, some crimes are also torts, and a question which this fact raises is whether the wrongdoer can be both prosecuted and

---

23 A distinction is drawn between exemplary and 'aggravated' damages. The latter are said to be compensatory because they are awarded where the effect of the tortious conduct on the plaintiff is particularly insulting or humiliating: see p. 288 below. But ordinary compensatory damages can contain an element for such insult and humiliation, and it is hard to see what the term 'aggravated' adds unless it be some extra element of disapproval of the defendant's conduct. See further H. Luntz *Assessment of Damages for Personal Injury and Death* 3rd edn (Sydney, 1990) pp. 68-72.

24 *Uren* v. *John Fairfax & Sons Pty Ltd* (1966) 117 C.L.R. 118, 158 *per* Owen J.

25 *Donselaar* v. *Donselaar* [1982] 1 N.Z.L.R. 97; see also *Auckland City Council* v. *Blundell* [1986] 1 N.Z.L.R. 732; S.M.D. Todd *et al.*, *Law of Torts in New Zealand* (Sydney, 1991) p. 873.

26 (1985) 155 C.L.R. 448.

27 See, for example, s. 546 of the Crimes Act 1958 (Vic.). In *R.* v. *Braham* [1977] V.R. 104, 112 the Victorian Full Court said that 'the objective of providing compensation to the victim dominates the provision of s.546'.

convicted for the criminal offence and also held liable in tort. The answer is that he can be, but there used to be a rule, called the 'felonious tort rule', which, in the case of a felony, prevented the plaintiff from bringing an action in tort until the wrongdoer had been dealt with by the criminal law. The status of that rule is now in doubt in Australia.[28]

In many cases, criminals are not worth suing in tort because they lack the resources to meet any judgment given against them. But in some contexts, the law of torts and the criminal law may play complementary roles in sanctioning and deterring undesirable conduct—although tort law is usually very much the junior partner in any such collaboration. This is especially true in relation to what is often called 'regulatory law'. For example, the law of torts, by imposing liability for accidents at work, plays some part in regulating industrial safety; but much more important are safety regulations backed up by licensing of certain activities, inspection of industrial sites and ultimately, in many instances, criminal sanctions for non-compliance with safety regulations. A similar pattern can be seen in the relationship of tort law and regulatory law in the areas, for example, of road safety, regulation of land-use[29] (to which the law of nuisance is relevant),[30] and regulation of the marketing of securities (to which the law of deceit and negligent misrepresentation is relevant). In such areas unlawful conduct may constitute both an offence against a regulatory regime and a tort.

But very often tortious conduct will not attract criminal liability.[31] For example, suppose that a police officer shoots a person under the mistaken impression that the person is a wanted criminal. The police officer might escape liability under the criminal law,[32] but it is doubtful that he would escape tortious liability for battery (that is, trespass to the person).[33] Similarly, a person who walks on to another's land mistakenly thinking that it is his own may be guilty of no criminal offence in so doing, but he has committed the tort of trespass to land.[34]

(b) Tort and contract The relationship between tort law and the law of contract is very complex, and this is not the place to examine it at length. It is the subject of detailed consideration at various points in this book. But some general comments may be helpful at this stage.

Contractual obligations can be distinguished from tortious obligations in a number of ways (but it must be stressed that none of these differences is universally true). First, many contractual obligations are 'productive' in the sense that they are obligations to produce advantageous outcomes, whereas the law of torts is predominantly 'protective' in the sense that the

---

28 See p. 25-7 below.
29 By means, for example, of zoning law and anti noise-pollution regulations enforced by local authorities.
30 See p. 597 below.
31 The converse is also true: not all crimes are torts.
32 In 1983 in England two detectives were acquitted of all criminal charges in just such circumstances. See *The Times* (of London), 20 October 1983.
33 F.A. Trindade (1982) 2 *O.J.L.S.* 211, 219-20.
34 *Basely* v. *Clarkson* (1681) 3 Lev. 37.

obligations it imposes are usually obligations to avoid disadvantageous outcomes. Secondly, a person will normally be under a contractual obligation to do X only if he has received some payment in return for doing it (the technical term for such payment is 'consideration'). By contrast, a person may be under a tortious obligation not to do Y (or, sometimes, to do X) even if he has received no payment.[35] Thirdly, most contractual obligations are owed to identified and specified individuals who have had dealings with the person subject to the obligation before the obligation arises; whereas tortious obligations may arise between 'strangers', by which we mean persons who are unknown to or unidentified by each other, or who may have had no dealings with each other before the tort occurs. Fourthly, the content of contractual obligations is often defined quite specifically and in some detail so that it is possible to know, in advance of performance, what will count as compliance with the contract, and when and how breaches of it might occur. By contrast, many tortious obligations are 'unfocused' in the sense that it is difficult to specify in advance the conduct which they proscribe and the circumstances in which proscribed conduct may occur.

Fifthly, the typical justification for imposing a contractual obligation is the fact that the person subject to the obligation has done some 'voluntary' act such as making a promise, giving an undertaking, executing a deed, signing a document containing promissory statements or undertakings, boarding a bus, borrowing money, taking goods from the shelf of a supermarket. By contrast, although a few tortious obligations result from such conduct (for example, a tortious obligation to do X may result from the giving of an undertaking to do X), the typical justification for tortious obligations is not that the person obliged has voluntarily engaged in some course of conduct (such as driving a car, or pursuing some profession), but that in so doing he has acted in a way which the law considers unacceptable and has damaged some protected interest of the plaintiff.

Two propositions are fundamental to understanding the relationship between tort law and the law of contract. The first is the so-called 'contract fallacy' which is said to have arisen from the case of *Winterbottom* v. *Wright*.[36] In that case A hired a carriage from D; P, a servant of A, was injured as a result of a defect in the condition of the carriage. P sued D but the action failed because the basis of P's claim was that D owed a contractual duty to A; but since P was not a party to that contract, the case was said to stand for the proposition that since a person cannot sue on a contract to which he is not a party, he should not be allowed to evade this rule by bringing an action in tort (this proposition is the contract fallacy). The effect of this proposition, if applied literally, would be to prevent a person recovering damages for personal injury (and so on) except from another with whom he had a contract under which the latter

35 But in some cases the fact that the defendant has received payment may strengthen the case for imposing a tortious obligation. See, for example, *Smith* v. *Eric S. Bush* [1990] 1 A.C. 831.

36 (1842) 10 M. & W. 109; 152 E.R. 402.

was liable for the damage suffered. This proposition was exposed as a 'fallacy'[37] and rejected in the famous 1932 case of *Donoghue* v. *Stevenson*[38] in which the plaintiff's friend bought for her in a café a bottle of ginger beer which allegedly contained the decomposed remains of a snail. It was held that the plaintiff could sue the manufacturer of the ginger beer in the tort of negligence for personal injury and shock even though she had no contract with the manufacturer (or indeed with anybody). This case clearly established that the tortious obligation not to injure others by carelessness can arise independently of contract and that tortious obligations can be owed to strangers. More particularly, the case forms the basis of the modern law of products liability.

But there are limits to these independent tort duties to take reasonable care. Courts have been rather wary of imposing tort liability for negligently caused, purely economic loss (as opposed to personal injury or physical damage to tangible property and economic loss consequential upon such injury or damage). In England there are some contexts in which economic loss in this sense is not recoverable at all in a negligence action; and in both England and Australia the class of persons who can recover for economic loss is more narrowly defined than the class of persons who can recover for other losses in the tort of negligence. One of the arguments used to suppport this reluctance to allow recovery in tort for negligently inflicted, purely economic loss is that if a person could have protected his economic interests by making a contractual arrangement with the defendant or with some third party, then he should have done so and should not be allowed to use the law of tort to make good the lack of such contractual protection.[39]

The independence of tort law from contract law was, however, established in one area long before 1932. At least by 1853[40] it was clear that if D intentionally induced C not to perform a contractual obligation owed by C to P, P could sue D *in tort* in respect of loss suffered by P as a result of C's breach of contract. Indeed, the law of tort plays a significant part in protecting a person's right to have existing contracts performed and the interest in making advantageous contracts in the future. Two examples of situations in which a person may incur tort liability for interfering with another's interest in making an advantageous contract are where D by threats or other unlawful conduct causes C not to make a contract with P, thus causing P loss;[41] and where D fraudulently or negligently tells P that C is creditworthy (when he is not), with the result that P makes a contract with C and loses money as a result.

A second proposition relevant to the relationship between tort and contract law concerns what is called 'concurrent liability'. Concurrent liability is possible where the same conduct amounts to more than one

---

37 It is not, of course, a logical fallacy but simply a proposition which, if generally applied, would produce results which the courts have found unacceptable.

38 [1932] A.C. 562.

39 For detailed analysis of this approach see Cane *Tort Law and Economic Interests* (Oxford, 1991) pp. 332-4, 336-52.

40 In *Lumley* v. *Gye* (1853) 2 E. & B. 216.

41 See pp. 218-22 below.

legal wrong. Here we are concerned with conduct which is both tortious and a breach of contract. Suppose D breaches a contract with P, and that the breach also amounts to a tort. It could be argued that since there is a contract between P and D, the legal rights of P and D arising out of the breach should be determined solely by rules of contract law; in other words, that D should not be concurrently liable in contract *and* tort. On the other hand, it could be argued that if D's conduct amounts to a tort as well as a breach of contract, P should be allowed to choose whether to sue D in tort or in contract. Those who support this argument are in favour of concurrent liability in tort and contract.

As we have already noted, Australian law allows concurrent liability: if the defendant's act constitutes both a breach of a contractual term and a tort,[42] he can be sued either in tort or in contract. For example, if a solicitor handles a client's affairs negligently, the client may sue the solicitor either in contract or tort. The concurrent liability principle also applies where a person has been induced to enter a contract by a false statement (a 'misrepresentation') negligently or fraudulently made by the other contracting party. If the defendant is held to have *warranted* the truth of the statement (or, in other words, if the statement is a term of the contract), then the plaintiff may choose between suing in contract or in tort for negligence or deceit (as the case may be).[43] But the defendant's liability in tort will be limited by any terms of the contract which effectively exclude or limit any tort liability that might otherwise have arisen. Indeed, D's tort liability may in some circumstances be limited by terms in a contract between P and C to which D is not a party, or by terms in a contract between D and C to which P is not a party.[44]

The reason why the choice between suing in contract and tort may be important is that the rules governing such matters as remoteness and assessment of damages, the defence of contributory negligence, contribution between wrongdoers and limitation periods may differ according to whether the action is brought in contract or tort. The concurrent liability principle is controversial because it allows a plaintiff to choose that cause of action which is more advantageous to himself (and correspondingly more disadvantageous to the defendant). Of course, a contracting party can usually insert terms in the contract designed to exclude or limit tort liability; and this is not infrequently done. But some would argue that where parties are in a contractual relationship, their respective rights and obligations should be governed by the contract and by relevant rules of contract law without the plaintiff having the option of by-passing

---

42 Not all breaches of contract are also torts. The typical example of conduct which constitutes both is negligent infliction of damage or loss (as opposed to failure to take positive action). See further Cane *Tort Law and Economic Interests* pp. 136-40.

43 The law is otherwise in New Zealand where tort remedies for pre-contractual misrepresentation have generally been abolished: Contractual Remedies Act 1979 (N.Z.) s.6. See S.M.D. Todd *et al.*, *The Law of Torts in New Zealand* (Sydney, 1991) pp. 159-61.

44 See p. 550 below.

the contract and those rules. The issues underlying this controversy are complex and cannot be pursued here.[45]

(c) Tort and the law of restitution[46] The law of restitution deals with obligations resting on one person (A) to restore to another person (B) benefits which A received from B, and with obligations resting on A to pay over to B benefits acquired by A from some third person at B's expense. An example of the first type of obligation is the obligation of a person who converts another's goods to restore those goods or their value to their true owner. An example of the second type of obligation is the obligation of a person who passes his goods off as being those of another to pay damages representing profits made as a result of the passing off which the latter could otherwise have made for himself.

It is now common[47] to draw a distinction between 'autonomous' (or 'independent') restitutionary obligations and 'restitution for wrongs'. An example of an autonomous restitutionary obligation is the (limited) obligation to return money or property transferred by B to A as a result of a mistaken belief on B's part that A was entitled to receive the money or property. Such obligations can arise even though A may have committed no legal wrong in acquiring the benefit which he is required to restore or pay over to B. In this book we are, of course, concerned with restitution for wrongs and, in particular, for torts.

There are two main contexts in which the law of torts imposes restitutionary obligations on tortfeasors. First, where the defendant has misappropriated the plaintiff's property the latter is entitled to damages based on the value of the property; or, exceptionally, to an order for the return of the property. Where the defendant has used or exploited the plaintiff's property without the plaintiff's consent, the latter may recover damages representing the value to the defendant of the use, even if the benefit which the defendant has thereby acquired represents no loss to the plaintiff because the plaintiff could not or would not have used the property in the way the defendant did. Secondly, an award of exemplary (or 'punitive') damages may contain an element representing profits made by the defendant at the plaintiff's expense (as well as an element of fine).

3. Conduct Regarded as Tortious

As we have seen, not all interests are protected by the law of torts. But it is also true that not all conduct which interferes with an interest protected by tort law counts as tortious conduct. In the first place, it is sometimes said that the law of tort never imposes 'absolute liability'. The meaning of this phrase is not clear; but it indicates, at least, that there are no cases in which the fact that the defendant interfered with some interest of the

45 For discussions see Cane *Tort Law and Economic Interests* (1991) pp. 328-32, 334-6; and in M. Furmston ed. *The Law of Tort* (London, 1986) Ch. 6.

46 See also Cane *Tort Law and Economic Interests* pp. 314-26.

47 Following P. Birks *An Introduction to the Law of Restitution* rev. edn (Oxford, 1989).

plaintiff *by itself* justifies the imposition of tort liability. Either the plaintiff will have to establish that the interfering conduct was of a certain sort or quality, or the defendant will be allowed to plead some justification, excuse or defence. The phrase also indicates that there can be no tort liability for 'involuntary' conduct. Involuntary conduct is conduct over which the actor had no control: so, for example, a sleepwalker could not be liable in tort for acts done in a state of sleep;[48] a person could not be liable for trespass to land if he was physically overpowered and thrown on to the land by another;[49] or for assault if he was overpowered and used as a projectile to injure another;[50] nor would a person be liable for negligent driving if he caused an accident as a result of having an unexpected[51] heart attack or epileptic fit while driving.[52]

Very often, tort liability will not be imposed unless the plaintiff can prove that the defendant was at *fault*; hence the (inaccurate) aphorism 'no liability without fault'. 'Fault', as is explained in greater detail below, involves either intentional (or reckless) conduct, or negligent conduct. Sometimes, however, it will not be for the plaintiff to prove that the defendant *was* at fault, but for the defendant to prove that he was *not* at fault. In general, it is harder to establish the truth of this negative proposition than of its positive equivalent; and so it is often said that casting the burden of proof on the defendant in this way has the effect of imposing liability without (proof of) fault. Furthermore, in a few types of case the plaintiff is not required to prove fault nor can the defendant escape liability by proving lack of fault. Liability without (proof of) fault is usually called 'strict liability'.

Strict liability for the infliction of physical injury or damage is very rare in the common law of torts. But there is one very important and extreme instance of strict tortious liability in the shape of vicarious liability: in certain circumstances, A can be held liable for the torts committed by B simply because B is A's employee or agent or independent contractor and despite the fact that injury or damage caused by B's tort may not have been the result of any fault on the part of A.

As already noted, 'fault' for the purposes of the law of torts is either 'intentional' conduct or 'negligent' conduct. Sometimes a person will be liable in tort *only* if his conduct was intentional (in the sense defined below), but often a person can be liable if his conduct was *either* intentional or negligent.[53] The words 'intention' and 'intentional' are used in a number of different senses in the law of torts. First, if a person 'meant to' invade the plaintiff's interests or to inflict injury or damage on him, then he will be said to have acted intentionally, to have intended the

---

48 See p. 30 below.

49 See p. 110 below.

50 See p. 31 below.

51 But he might be liable if, despite knowing of the risk of a heart attack or of epilepsy, he nevertheless chose to drive.

52 See p. 421 below.

53 Contrary to what one might at first expect, a person can be liable for intentional conduct in the tort of negligence. This is because conduct which satifies the definition of 'intentional' will usually also satisfy the definition of 'negligent'.

result of his conduct. Secondly, 'if A, intending to hit B unlawfully, in fact hits C, there is no doubt as to A's liability to C'.[54] In other words, if A intends to injure B but injures C instead, A may be held to have intentionally injured C. Thirdly, if a person acts 'recklessly' in the sense that he foresees that certain adverse consequences might follow from his conduct but does not care whether they do or not, he may be treated as having acted intentionally. Fourthly, a person may also be treated as having intended a result if that result was substantially certain to follow from what he did. In this case a person may be treated as having acted intentionally even though he neither willed the adverse result of his conduct nor actually realized that it might eventuate. This last meaning of 'intention' actually involves a form of liability for negligence.

This complex concept of intention will be discussed in greater detail later. But here it should be noted that there is a difference between intention and motive. The word 'motive' is used to refer to 'ends or purposes beyond the immediately obvious'.[55] So, for example, a person's immediate aim may be to inflict physical injury on another but his motive in doing so may be to 'punish' the other for some past action. The fact that the defendant acted against the plaintiff out of ill-will or spite or from some other bad motive does not *by itself* make the defendant liable in tort. So, for example, in the famous case of *Bradford Corporation* v. *Pickles*[56] it was held that it is not tortious to interfere with the supply of water which flows under the land of another in undefined channels, even if this is done with the motive of forcing the other landowner to sell his land to the defendant or to pay the defendant for the continuation of an uninterrupted supply. On the other hand, in some torts (such as malicious falsehood or malicious prosecution) one of the things the plaintiff has to prove is that the defendant acted 'maliciously' or out of a bad motive. Again, in the tort of nuisance, the fact that the defendant acted maliciously may be one factor to be taken into account in deciding whether his action was unreasonable and, therefore, an actionable nuisance. Finally, in the tort of defamation, proof that the defendant acted maliciously can deprive him of a defence of fair comment or qualified privilege.

In a colloquial sense, 'negligence' means 'carelessness'; but in a more technical sense it means something like 'failure to take reasonable precautions to avoid foreseeable and significant risks of injury'. Negligent conduct forms the basis of the tort of negligence, but it (or some version of it) also figures in many other torts which contain a requirement of fault. Negligence is not a state of mind. Rather, it is failure to measure up to a particular standard of conduct; and that standard of conduct is not normally measured according to the abilities of the individual defendant but according to an objective standard of reasonable conduct. This means that a person may be held to have acted negligently even though, in the circumtances with which he was faced at the time he acted, he could not have done otherwise. In other words, the definition of fault in the law of

54 *Bunyan* v. *Jordan* (1937) 57 C.L.R. 1, 12 *per* Latham C.J.
55 See G. Fridman (1958) 21 *M.L.R.* 484, 488.
56 [1895] A.C. 587.

torts allows a person to be held liable for doing that which he could not have avoided doing because of ignorance, lack of resources, inexperience or lack of skill.[57] So, on analysis, there is not as sharp a contrast between fault liability and strict liability as might at first appear. Indeed, it is often said that in some contexts the standard of care which the law specifies is so demanding that the liability it imposes approaches strict liability in its practical operation.

4. ALTERNATIVES TO THE TORT SYSTEM

In practice, perhaps the most important function of tort law is as a mechanism for dealing with the effects of traumatic injuries (as opposed to illnesses and diseases)[58] caused at work and on the roads. Unfortunately, the law of torts suffers from serious defects as a compensation system. This is not the place to examine these defects in detail,[59] but it is worth noting the main shortcomings of the tort system. The first arises out of the concept of fault (by which, in this context, we mean 'negligence'). As we will see, the concept of negligence is a vague one, and it is often very difficult for the plaintiff to establish; moreover, many accidents on the roads and at work are not caused by negligence in the sense in which this term is used in the law of torts. The result is that only a relatively small proportion of victims of road and work accidents receive compensation through the tort system. The number of victims of accidents occurring in other contexts who successfully invoke the law of torts is totally insignificant.

Secondly, even in theory the tort system only compensates for injuries which were caused in particular ways; it is, in other words, a 'cause-based' system of compensation. A basic problem with all cause-based systems[60] is that they discriminate between people with precisely the same *needs* for compensation and treat some better than others. Indeed, the level of compensation provided by the tort system is, in general terms, quite high relative to that provided by other compensation systems. In other words, it treats a small proportion of accident victims very generously. Many people now think that the difference between being injured tortiously and being injured in circumstances which fall outside the tort system does not justify this difference of treatment. It is not, of course, a defect of the tort system that it treats some people generously; the problem is that others with like needs are treated by the law much less generously.

Thirdly, the tort system is extremely expensive to operate. Leaving aside court costs (because only a tiny fraction of tort claims are ever tried in court), the administrative costs of delivering a dollar of tort compensation

---

57 Although there are exceptional cases, as we shall see in Chapter 10, in which lack of resources or inexperience can be taken into account in the defendant's favour.

58 J. Stapleton *Disease and the Compensation Debate* (Oxford, 1986).

59 See generally *Atiyah's Accidents*. See also I. Malkin (1990) 17 *M.U.L.R.* 685.

60 This problem is much more pronounced in the case of limited compensation schemes such as workers' compensation, no-fault road accident or no-fault medical accident compensation schemes.

are very much higher than the costs of delivering, for example, a dollar of social security benefit. So the tort system is an inefficient and wasteful way of compensating accident victims.

These and other criticisms have led to the enactment in a number of jurisdictions of limited replacements for or complements to the tort system.[61] Indeed, the oldest of such schemes—workers' compensation schemes—date from early this century and operate in all Australian jurisdictions. Typically, workers' compensation schemes supplement rather than replace the tort system, and they dispense with the need for the worker to show that his injuries were caused by anyone's fault: the employer is made strictly liable for work injuries.

Strict liability schemes are similar to the traditional tort system in that they involve the injured person suing an individual defendant. More radical departures from the tort system allow injured plaintiffs to recover compensation from a fund financed by levies on, for example, motor vehicle owners. The most extensive of such schemes is the New Zealand accident compensation scheme which was enacted in 1972 and which has replaced the tort system so far as it deals with accidental injuries (but, with a few exceptions, not diseases or illnesses).[62] The scheme provides compensation for all accident victims whether they would have previously been entitled to tort compensation or not, and so it is called a 'no-fault' scheme. Several Australian jurisdictions have now also adopted no-fault compensation schemes, but (with the exception of the Northern Territory road accident scheme) they only supplement the tort system and do not replace it. Most of these no-fault schemes are concerned with road accidents but some jurisdictions have schemes covering sporting accidents, for example. But in Australia the legislative approach to no-fault schemes has been very piecemeal, and an attempt in the 1970s to set up a national scheme along the lines of the New Zealand scheme foundered on the rocks of financial stringency and lack of political will. A recent proposal for a no-fault scheme for medical accidents[63] seems destined for a similar fate.

There seems little chance that new large-scale no-fault compensation schemes will eventuate in the foreseeable future. The New South Wales transport accidents scheme was in operation for only two years before being dismantled. A more likely pattern for the future is retention of the tort system with increasing and increasingly restrictive statutory control over the mode of assessment and the levels of compensation (as, for example, under the Motor Accidents Act 1988 (N.S.W.));[64] increasing use in serious cases of periodical payments provided by way of annuities purchased from private insurers; and an expansion in the market for first-party insurance to cover economic losses resulting from personal injury.

---

61 R.P. Balkin and J.L.R. Davis *Law of Torts* (Sydney, 1991) Ch. 12.

62 See Todd *et al., The Law of Torts in New Zealand* Ch. 2 (M. Vennell).

63 D. Marshall (1991) 21 *W.A.L.R.* 336.

64 Such controls may well also be imposed in cases not involving personal injuries. A N.S.W. bill designed to limit the liability of professionals for economic loss is, at the time of writing (October 1992), in limbo.

Another important type of non-tort compensation scheme is the criminal injury compensation scheme. Such schemes now exist in all Australian jurisdictions, and they provide a very important supplement to the tort system because perpetrators of violent crimes are typically not worth suing. Compensation is paid out of a fund financed by general taxation, but the schemes are not no-fault schemes because the applicant must establish that he has been the victim of a violent crime; and most violent crimes are torts as well.

Because very many accident victims who could, in theory, utilize the tort system receive nothing by way of tort compensation, many accident victims rely very heavily on social security for financial support; and we will see in Chapter 12 that a complex set of rules has developed concerning the relationship between social security benefits and tort compensation. In our terms, social security benefits are no-fault benefits.

The existence of these various alternatives to the tort system shows that tort law must be seen as only one part of a complex network of arrangements for dealing with the financial effects of personal injuries; and because the proportion of victims of personal injuries who receive compensation through the tort system is very small, the law of torts is correspondingly of limited practical importance. But it must be said that the legislative response to the shortcomings of the tort system has been extremely patchy, and is largely the result of the operation of political forces rather than of any principled approach to the serious social problems generated by personal injuries.

Of course, the law of torts deals with many things other than accidental personal injuries. In some cases there is no real alternative to tort litigation (or the threat thereof) as a means of protecting the interests involved; protection of business goodwill by the tort of passing off is an example. But in other cases, the law of torts plays a very marginal role: for example, the tort of nuisance is, in practice, little used to regulate land-use. In some areas the role which the law of torts plays is problematic and controversial: for example, the use of the 'economic torts' to deal with industrial disputes has been a matter of vigorous political debate ever since it became important in the late nineteenth century; and many people consider that the availability of tort damages as the chief means of vindicating reputation (through the tort of defamation) operates as an encouragement to fortune-hunting and court-endorsed mud-slinging. Once again, the reason for raising these points is simply to alert the reader to the fact that tort law is one, but in many cases only one, means for protecting a range of human interests; that the protection it provides is often limited and unsatisfactory; and that tort law is not a politically neutral set of legal rules but a complex institutional arrangement which needs to be examined in a wider context and subjected to critical analysis if its strengths and weaknesses are to be understood properly.

This book is primarily intended as an exposition of the rules of tort law. Space does not permit a full analysis of the social role and functions of tort law. But it is of crucial importance that the reader should avoid approaching tort law as if it were a self-contained and self-validating set of internally consistent propositions. It is, in fact, an imperfect attempt to deal with a very diverse and extremely complex set of social and human problems.

5. THE SOURCES OF AUSTRALIAN TORT LAW

Tort law consists largely of judge-made or 'common law' rules and principles. Under the doctrine of precedent, lower courts in any particular jurisdiction are, as a general rule, under an obligation to follow relevant decisions of higher courts in that jurisdiction but not their own decisions or decisions of courts at the same level in the judicial hierarchy. In Australia, too, courts in all jurisdictions are bound by decisions of the High Court of Australia. But courts are not bound to follow decisions of courts in other jurisdictions. However, although there may be no obligation to follow a particular decision, a court is free to consider and apply that decision provided it does not conflict with any decision which the court is bound to follow.

In fact the style adopted by judges of higher Australian courts in writing their judgments often involves extensive and detailed consideration of relevant decisions of courts in other Australian jurisdictions and in foreign common law jurisdictions. Because the Australian legal system (like all other so-called 'common law' legal systems) is ultimately derived from the English legal system, decisions of English courts (and of the Privy Council)[65] are referred to in Australian judgments much more than decisions from any other foreign jurisdiction are; but decisions from New Zealand are often given serious attention, as are some Canadian decisions and, to a lesser extent, decisions of United States courts.

This balance of sources is roughly maintained in this book. We have tried always to cite Australian authority where it is available; but we also make frequent reference to relevant English case law and, to a very much lesser extent, cases from New Zealand[66] and Canadian and U.S. cases. As far as possible, we have tried to give an account of the *Australian* law of torts; but there are many issues on which there is little or no relevant Australian case law, and there are some very important areas of uncertainty in Australian law which we have tried to illuminate by reference to relevant overseas decisions. Since the first edition of this book was written, Australian common law in general and Australian tort law in particular have become much more independent of foreign influence, and Antipodean tort law has, in important respects, diverged from its English sources. But Australian courts are still very respectful of English judicial decisions, and it is impossible to give a satisfactory account of Australian tort law without looking abroad in the process.

There are, of course, quite a few statutes relevant to different areas of tort law. Statutes of the United Kingdom Parliament were received into

65 Until recently, Australian courts were bound by decisions of the Privy Council on appeal from Australian courts.

66 The law of torts in New Zealand is now comprehensively dealt with in Todd *et al.*, *The Law of Torts in New Zealand* (Sydney, 1991).

Australian law when the colonies were established, but nearly all of the relevant statutes have ceased to have any operation in Australia.[67] Courts are, of course, bound to apply statutes in force in their own jurisdiction, but doing so often requires them to interpret the words of the statute before it can be applied. Decisions interpreting statutes in force in a particular jurisdiction are used by other courts in that jurisdiction in much the same way as decisions concerned with common law rules which we have just considered. However, a decision interpreting the words of a particular statute will only be of relevance in a different jurisdiction if there is a corresponding statute in that jurisdiction which uses the same or very similar words as were the subject of interpretation in the decision under consideration. It so happens that some of the Australian statutes relevant to the law of torts (those concerned with fatal accidents, for example) are modelled more or less closely on earlier U.K. statutes. So decisions of English courts interpreting U.K. statutes are sometimes relevant to the interpretation of Australian statutes.

The reader should be alert to the diversity of the sources of Australian tort law, not least because this raises the interesting and important question of the extent to which differences between physical, economic, social and cultural conditions in different countries justify or demand differences as between jurisidictions in rules dealing with similar issues. The reader should not view tort law simply as a set of arbitrary rules, but as a mechanism for dealing with social problems. Both the nature of those problems and the appropriate solutions to them may vary from one country (or jurisdiction) to another.

---

67 But until as late as 1985 the law of limitation of actions in the A.C.T. was based on ancient U.K. statutory provisions (see first edition of this book p. 632).

2

INTENTIONAL TORTS TO THE PERSON

I: SOME GENERAL COMMENTS

Protecting the physical and mental integrity of a person is an important function of the law. Today, in the law of torts, it is done essentially in four ways. First, by an action in intentional trespass, simply called trespass,[1] which is reserved[2] for acts both direct[3] (immediate) and intentional.[4] Developed from the writ of trespass *vi et armis*, which in medieval times was used for protecting people from forcible direct wrongs, trespass to the person has now come to mean the three nominate torts of battery, assault and false imprisonment. Secondly, by an action in negligent trespass, which, despite the efforts of Lord Denning M.R. in *Letang* v. *Cooper*[5] (and the efforts of Kirby P. in *Platt* v. *Nutt*[6]) to destroy it as a tort, continues to have a healthy existence in Australia. Though its use is rather limited, the action for negligent trespass is still appropriate and useful for some direct acts which are unintentional or careless and also where the plaintiff does not know if the act of the defendant is intentional or unintentional, for example, where a plaintiff who is shot in the back by

1 Although Fifoot (*History and Sources of the Common Law* (London, 1949) Ch. 3) says that 'the origin of Trespass is to be sought among the dark places of the law, and the search is complicated by the ambiguity of the word', F.W. Maitland in *The Forms of Action at Common Law* (Ed. A.H. Chaytor and W.J. Whittaker) (London, 1936) Lecture VI p. 65 says: '*Trespass* appears *circ.* 1250 as a means of charging a defendant with violence but no felony . . . There is a trifurcation, the writ varying according as the violence is done (1) to land, (2) to the body, or (3) to chattels . . . Trespass to the body [assaults and batteries] covered the whole ground of personal injury . . .' See also S.F.C. Milsom, *Historical Foundations of the Common Law* (London, 1969) Ch. 11.

2 It has been argued, particularly by Lord Denning M.R., that today the action in trespass is reserved for direct, intentional acts—see *Letang* v. *Cooper* [1965] 1 Q.B. 232, 239 and *Gray* v. *Barr* [1971] 2 Q.B. 554, 569.

3 For the meaning of 'direct' in trespass see pp. 28-30 below.

4 For the meaning of 'intentional' in trespass see pp. 30-6 below.

5 [1965] 1 Q.B. 232, 237-42. This point and other matters concerning negligent trespass are discussed at some length in F.A. Trindade (1971) 20 *I.C.L.Q.* 706-31.

6 (1988) 12 N.S.W.L.R. 231, 238-9.

a duck shooter does not know whether the act is deliberate, careless or just an inevitable accident.[7] Thirdly, we have the action on the case[8] for damages, which is used when the act in question is an intentional (wilful) act which is indirect or consequential as, for example, the act of the defendant in *Bird* v. *Holbrook*[9] in setting a spring gun which went off injuring the plaintiff when the plaintiff activated it by chasing a straying peahen on to the defendant's property. The act of the defendant in setting the spring gun was intentional but as it required an act of the plaintiff to activate it, the act of the defendant in relation to the injury was regarded as indirect or consequential. Finally, there is the tort of negligence, which is most appropriately used in relation to acts which are both unintentional and indirect. However, this tort of relatively recent origin has so quickly acquired such immense stature and strength that, as one writer puts it, 'one could be forgiven for wondering whether there was room left for any other tort at all'.[10]

In this chapter our attention will be concentrated on intentional or wilful invasions of the physical and mental integrity of a person, leaving for later consideration the question of negligent or careless invasions. So this chapter will deal with trespass to the person and the action on the case for damages, excluding for the moment discussion of the tort of negligent trespass[11] and the tort of negligence.[12]

An initial question, however, needs to be raised and answered. Are these four torts exclusive of each other in the sense that the plaintiff (more usually his lawyer) having made a careful assessment of the factual situation must choose to bring his action in only *one* of these torts, or can the plaintiff use the factual situation to base several causes of action,[13] i.e. to rely on several of the torts?

Those with a penchant for history will easily discover that even until the nineteenth century the plaintiff had to choose the most appropriate tort—in fact he had to choose the most appropriate form of action or writ—and failure to make the right choice would result in a total failure

---

7 An inevitable accident is one which occurs 'utterly without fault on the part of the defendant' *per* Cohen L.J. in *National Coal Board* v. *Evans* [1951] 2 K.B. 861, 874. Where the defendant is entirely without fault, he would have a good defence to an action in trespass.

8 The development of the action on the case has been described as 'perhaps the most important single achievement of English Common Law'; see A.K.R. Kiralfy, *The Action on the Case* (London, 1951). See also pp. 62-82 below.

9 (1828) 4 Bing. 628.

10 *Weir* (4th edn, 1979), p. 257.

11 See pp. 311-24 below.

12 See chapters 9-15 below.

13 'A cause of action is simply a factual situation the existence of which entitles one person to obtain from the court a remedy against another person. Historically, the means by which the remedy was obtained varied with the nature of the factual situation and causes of action were divided into categories according to the "form of action" by which the remedy was obtained in the particular kind of factual situation which constituted the cause of action.' *Letang* v. *Cooper* [1965] 1 Q.B. 232, 242-3 *per* Diplock L.J. 'When you speak of a cause of action you mean the essential ingredients in the title to the right which it is proposed to enforce' (*Williams* v. *Milotin* (1957) 97 C.L.R. 465, 474).

of the claim. Thus, if the contact between the plaintiff and the defendant had been caused by a direct (immediate) act, for example, a blow to the face, the plaintiff was required to bring his action in trespass for, 'if he sued in case, he was liable to be told that he had made a fatal blunder'.[14] It was only in *Williams* v. *Holland*[15] in 1833 that the Court of Common Pleas permitted a plaintiff to bring an action on the case even though the act that occasioned the contact was direct (immediate).[16] There, the defendant had through his carelessness driven his gig and horse into a horse and cart carrying the plaintiff's children so that they were thrown out of the cart on to the road and severely injured. The defendant argued that the plaintiff's action could be brought only in trespass but Tindal C.J. held that 'a plaintiff is at liberty to bring an action on the case, notwithstanding the act is immediate, so long as it is not a wilful act'.[17]

But even after *Williams* v. *Holland* in 1833 there was a restriction on the joinder of different forms of action. The plaintiff could not bring both trespass and case in the one action on a single set of facts. This only became possible as a result of statutory reform from the mid-nineteenth century when first, by the Common Law Procedure Act 1852,[18] joinder of trespass and case became possible because s.41 of the Act allowed causes of action, of whatever kind, to be joined in the same suit; and secondly, by the Supreme Court of Judicature Act 1875[19] which purported to abolish completely the different forms of action themselves.

What is still not clear, however, is whether an action in negligence can be brought for a direct intentional act. In *Letang* v. *Cooper* in 1964, Lord Denning M.R. in dealing with the application of force directly to another said: 'if intentional it is the tort of assault and battery. If negligent and causing damage, it is the tort of negligence'.[20] Williams and Hepple in their *Foundations of the Law of Tort* specifically refer to this statement and say 'this should not be taken to mean that an intentional tort cannot be pleaded as negligence'.[21] However, they appear to have overlooked the statement by Lord Denning M.R. in *Gray* v. *Barr* in 1971—seven years after *Letang* v. *Cooper*—where he said:

> Whenever two men have a fight and one is injured, the action is for assault, not for negligence. If both are injured, there are cross-actions for assault. The idea of negligence—and contributory negligence—is quite foreign to men grappling in a struggle.[22]

On the other hand, we have the more recent decision of Talbot J. in *Williams* v. *Humphrey*:

---

14 M.J. Prichard [1964] *Camb.L.J.* 234, 241.
15 (1833) 10 Bing. 112.
16 The words 'direct' and 'immediate' appear to be interchangeable.
17 (1833) 10 Bing. 112, 117-18.
18 15 & 16 Vict., c.76.
19 38 & 39 Vict., c.77.
20 [1965] 1 Q.B. 232, 239-40.
21 *Williams & Hepple*, p. 44, fn. 3.
22 [1971] 2 Q.B. 554, 569.

The plaintiff had taken the defendant to a swimming pool which both families frequented. The plaintiff was standing at the edge of the pool when the defendant deliberately and without warning pushed the plaintiff into the swimming pool as a joke. Unfortunately the plaintiff's left foot hit the concrete edge of the pool as he fell in and the result was that he sustained very serious injuries to his left ankle and foot and he was crippled.[23]

Talbot J. allowed the plaintiff's claim to be pleaded both in negligence and intentional trespass (battery), and found for the plaintiff on both counts. The question whether an intentional trespass can be pleaded as negligence was not specifically raised. The matter, it is suggested, is not as clear as Williams and Hepple imply and Australian courts may well take the view, if the question is specifically raised, that for an *intentional* direct act trespass is the *only* action that *should* be brought, just as the English Court of Appeal decided in *Letang* v. *Cooper* that for a negligent direct act the tort of negligence and not the tort of trespass is the *only* remedy. It seems, therefore, that it is possible for a plaintiff to base several causes of action on one factual situation and join those causes of action in the same suit. The only doubt that remains is whether an intentional trespass can be pleaded as negligence.

It must not be thought, however, that because these four torts are not today necessarily exclusive of each other, that it is sufficient to describe the factual situation in the writ (and the relief and remedy sought) leaving it to the court to decide the case on the basis of whatever tort it thinks fit. The Court of Appeal in England has decided in *Sterman* v. *E.W. & W.J. Moore Ltd (a firm)*[24] that a writ *must* mention a cause of action. It is, therefore, plainly necessary that the ingredients of the various torts be studied with some degree of particularity.

Sometimes, of course, intentional trespass is the *only* action that *can* be brought. Unfortunately there is no decision from the British Commonwealth to illustrate this proposition, but the American case, *Mink* v. *University of Chicago*, is an excellent illustration:

The plaintiffs while students at the University of Chicago between 1950–52 were given a drug ('DES') in the University's pre-natal clinic as part of a medical experiment conducted by the defendants, the University of Chicago and Eli Lilly & Co. The plaintiffs were not told that they were part of an experiment nor were they told that the pills administered to them were DES. Some twenty years later in 1971 the relationship between DES and cancer was established but the defendants made no efforts to notify the plaintiffs until 1975 when the University sent letters to the women in the experiment informing them of the possible relationship between the use of DES in pregnant women and abnormal conditions in the genital tracts of their offspring. The plaintiffs' suit was based on three causes of action. Battery, by conducting a medical experiment on them without their knowledge or consent. Products liability against the manufacturer for the manufacture of DES as a defective and unreasonably dangerous drug. And breach of

---

23 *The Times*, 13 February 1975. We are grateful to L. Bingham & Co., Solicitors, for providing us with the transcript of the judgment delivered by Talbot J. on 12 February 1975.

24 [1970] 1 All E.R. 581.

duty against the University in failing to notify the plaintiffs and their children of the experiment and of the precautions which the children should take to minimise the risk of contracting cancer as soon as they became aware of the relationship between DES and cancer in 1971.[25]

The defendants moved to dismiss the plaintiffs' suit for failure to state a claim. The court decided that the action for battery (intentional trespass) should proceed but that the actions for products liability and breach of duty should be dismissed 'since the plaintiffs have not alleged physical injury to *themselves*'.[26]

This leads us to consider very briefly the question of damage. In an action for the tort of negligence, damage is the gist of the action. The tort is not complete until damage occurs. Trespass, on the other hand, is actionable *per se*. It is not necessary to prove any actual damage. Of course in the absence of actual damage a plaintiff would not generally bring an action in trespass for, if he did, he would probably be penalized in costs. But the rule that trespass is actionable without proof of damage has the advantage over negligence in allowing a person to sue when he suffers an injury which cannot be described as 'damage' or as legally recognizable 'damage' for the purposes of the tort of negligence. Take the factual situation in *R.* v. *George*.[27] The defendant on two separate occasions attempted forcibly to remove a girl's shoe from her foot. He did this because it gave him a perverted sexual gratification. If it was necessary to prove actual damage the girl would surely have failed in any action, as the only 'damage' she suffered was indignity and humiliation. However, in an action for intentional battery, the trespass would be actionable *per se* and the court would take into account the indignity and humiliation which the girl had to suffer in order to satisfy the perverted sexual desires of the defendant. Trespass, by not insisting on damage as a necessary ingredient of the tort, helps to protect some interests not protected by the other torts which insist on damage as a requirement. The rule also provides a threshold on to which damages for insult and humiliation can be heaped. *Fogg* v. *McKnight* provides an admirable example where a judge using a technical assault (battery) with no physical hurt as the threshold awarded three times as much by way of damages to the plaintiff for 'the injury to his feelings'.[28] This traditional rule of the common law, that trespass is actionable *per se*, is particularly useful in providing

---

25 (1978) 460 F.Supp. 713 (U.S. District Court, N.D. Illinois, E.D. Grady, District Judge).
26 ibid., 723 (emphasis added).
27 [1956] *Crim.L.R.* 52 (a criminal case).
28 [1968] N.Z.L.R. 330, 332. See also H. Luntz, *Assessment of Damages* (2nd edn, Sydney, 1983) pp. 68-72. In *Kuchenmeister* v. *Home Office* [1958] 1 Q.B. 496, 513, Barry J. said: 'No pecuniary damage has been suffered but the very precious right of liberty . . . is one which must be protected. I think that a fair figure which will vindicate the plaintiff's rights without amounting to a vindictive award would be £150. I should have felt fully entitled to increase that amount to a very great extent if there had been any suggestion here that the plaintiff was being ill-treated by any of the immigration officials . . .'.

compensation for insult and humiliation, which is otherwise not compensated under our law of torts.

There is another traditional rule of the common law that requires comment. It is now generally accepted that fault is an essential element in determining liability in an action in trespass.[29] In an action in intentional trespass an intentional or wilful act is required; in negligent trespass, a negligent or careless act suffices. If neither an intentional nor negligent act is present the defendant is said to be without fault and the action in trespass will not succeed. But if fault is an essential element in determining liability in trespass does the burden of proving fault lie on the plaintiff (as in an action for the tort of negligence) or does the burden of disproving fault lie on the defendant? The traditional rule of the common law is that in actions of trespass, whether intentional or negligent, the burden of proving absence of intention or absence of negligence shifts to the defendant once the plaintiff proves a direct trespassory act on the part of the defendant.[30] In *Fowler* v. *Lanning*[31] in 1959, however, Diplock J., in an action where there was a bare allegation that 'the defendant shot the plaintiff', held that the statement of claim disclosed no cause of action, that the onus of proof of intention or negligence on the part of the defendant lay upon the plaintiff, and that under the modern rules of pleading, the plaintiff must allege either intention on the part of the defendant or, if he relies upon negligence, he must state the facts which he alleges constitute negligence. This attempt by Diplock J. to alter the burden of proof in actions of trespass has not been accepted or followed in Australia[32] and in two decisions delivered after *Fowler* v. *Lanning*, Windeyer J. in the High Court in *McHale* v. *Watson*[33] and Walters J. in the Supreme Court of South Australia in *Tsouvalla* v. *Bini*[34] have both taken the view that in an action of trespass, whether intentional or negligent, the burden of proving absence of intention or absence of

---

29 See *Holmes* v. *Mather* (1875) L.R. 10 Ex. 261; *Stanley* v. *Powell* [1891] 1 Q.B. 86; *National Coal Board* v. *J.E. Evans & Co.* [1951] 2 K.B. 861; *McHale* v. *Watson* (1964) 111 C.L.R. 384; *Venning* v. *Chin* (1974) 10 S.A.S.R. 299 and *Cowell* v. *Corrective Services Commission of N.S.W.* (1988) 13 N.S.W.L.R. 714.

30 The traditional rule of the common law is well stated in Bacon's *Abridgment* (7th edn, London, 1832) Vol. 7, 706 under the heading of 'Trespass' as follows: 'If the circumstance which is specially pleaded in an action of trespass do not make the act complained of lawful, and only make it excusable, it is proper to plead this circumstance in excuse; and it is in this case necessary for the defendant to shew not only that the act complained of was accidental [i.e. not intentional], but likewise that it was not owing to neglect, or want of due caution.' See also the judgment of Bray C.J. in *Venning* v. *Chin* (1974) 10 S.A.S.R. 299, 310-16.

31 [1959] 1 Q.B. 426.

32 In addition to *McHale* v. *Watson* and *Tsouvalla* v. *Bini* see also *Blacker* v. *Waters* (1928) 28 S.R.(N.S.W.) 406; *Venning* v. *Chin* (1974) 10 S.A.S.R. 299; and *Timmins* v. *Oliver* (Court of Appeal, N.S.W.), 12 October 1972 (unreported).

33 (1964) 111 C.L.R. 384.

34 [1966] S.A.S.R. 157.

negligence shifts to the defendant once the plaintiff proves a direct act on the part of the defendant. Windeyer J.[35] clearly indicated that he did not agree with the proposition put forward by Diplock J. in *Fowler* v. *Lanning*, and Walters J. put it even more clearly when he said:

> There is no onus upon the plaintiff to establish that the defendant threw the lime with intent to hit him, or so negligently that it did so. The burden rests upon the defendant to show absence of intent and negligence on his part, and in this case that onus has not been discharged.[36]

It is true, as Windeyer J. said in *McHale* v. *Watson*, that adjudication is not likely often to depend upon which side has the onus of proof but in cases like *Tsouvalla* v. *Bini* it did make a difference. It is, therefore, as well to know that the English and Australian rules in relation to the burden of proof of fault in actions of trespass have diverged considerably since Diplock J.'s judgment in *Fowler* v. *Lanning* in 1959.

As the three nominate torts of assault, battery and false imprisonment which now constitute the tort of intentional trespass to the person are also crimes, a question which has arisen is whether the plaintiff can have resort to a civil action against the defendant before criminal proceedings have been commenced or concluded against him. The matter was said to depend very much on whether or not the act in question was a felony committed by the defendant against the plaintiff. If it was a felony then the principle in *Smith* v. *Selwyn* applied. The principle (called the felonious tort rule) as enunciated by Kennedy L.J. in that case was as follows:

> This, however, is certain, that the Court has a right, if not an imperative duty, to stay the proceedings in a civil action for damages, if it is clear that that which is the basis of the claim in the action is a felony committed by the defendant against the plaintiff.[37]

The rule was accepted and acted upon in Australia.[38] The court not only looked at the pleading but also at all the circumstances to see whether the action was based on a felonious act. If it was, the civil action was suspended. But suspended for how long? Pape J. in *Wonder Heat Pty Ltd* v. *Bishop* in 1960 rather reluctantly held that the civil remedy in cases of injury by a felonious act could not be pursued until the completion of the prosecution of the alleged felon, though he would permit civil proceedings to be commenced if there had been a delay in the *completion*

---

35 'But the question remains, is it for the plaintiff to establish that the missile with which she was hit was thrown with intent to hit her or so negligently that it did so—or is it for the defendant who threw it to prove an absence of intent and negligence on his part? I think the latter view is correct.' (1964) 111 C.L.R. 384, 388.

36 [1966] S.A.S.R. 157, 158.

37 [1914] 3 K.B. 98, 103.

38 See *Wonder Heat* v. *Bishop* [1960] V.R. 489; *Henry Haskin* v. *Hooke* [1954] V.L.R. 300; *Hatherley & Horsfall* v. *Eastern Star Mercantile* [1965] V.R. 182; *Thomas* v. *High* [1960] S.R.(N.S.W.) 401; *Ricketts* v. *Ingersoll* (1930) 47 W.N.(N.S.W.) 56 and *Rochfort* v. *John Fairfax & Sons Ltd* [1972] 1 N.S.W.L.R. 16. See also C.L. Pannam (1965) 39 *A.L.J.* 164.

of the criminal proceedings. In *Oloro* v. *Ali* in 1965 Milmo J. said it was a sufficient compliance with the rule if 'the matter had been reported to the C.I.D., who investigated it, and . . . did not think it right to prosecute'.[39] He added that the usual and wisest course 'is to report the facts to the police and leave the matter in their hands'[40]—that would provide a reasonable excuse for not prosecuting and would exclude the rule that a prosecution for the felony must precede the civil action. The debate on whether the *institution* of criminal proceedings rather than the *completion* of the prosecution is required by the rule in *Smith* v. *Selwyn* is neatly sidestepped by Milmo J. by regarding reporting to the police as sufficient compliance with the rule. Of course, the rule in *Smith* v. *Selwyn* never applied to crimes other than felonies and this more than anything else is leading to its demise. As the distinctions between felonies and misdemeanours are abolished[41] there are no felonies left for the felonious tort rule to operate on, and so the rule in *Smith* v. *Selwyn* is gradually disappearing as statutes such as the Crimes (Classification of Offences) Act 1981 (Vic.) come on to the statute books. This Act not only abolishes the distinction between felonies and misdemeanours in Victoria but the rule in *Smith* v. *Selwyn* is also specifically abrogated.[42] The recent decision in *Halabi* v. *Westpac Banking Corporation*[43] shows, however, that there are differences among the members of the judiciary in New South Wales as to whether the felony–tort rule still exists in that State. Kirby P. in his judgment declared that the rule was obsolete and no longer part of the law of that State. McHugh J.A., while reluctant to declare the rule obsolete, was prepared to hold that 'the rule which was once applicable to felonies is now superseded by and is expressed in terms of the principles expounded in *McMahon* v. *Gould*. That is, the power to stay civil proceedings based on felonious conduct will only be exercised so as to achieve justice between the competing rights of the plaintiff and the defendant'.[44] Samuels J.A., however, regarded the felony–tort rule as neither obsolete nor anachronistic though he accepted the position that the rule could be avoided if 'a reasonable excuse is shown for the fact that the offender has not been prosecuted to conviction or acquittal'.[45] He regarded that excuse as established 'once it is shown that the person injured by the felonious tort made a proper complaint and, by that means, did all that he or she could do to initiate criminal process against the offender'.[46] Not much earlier two judges of the Supreme Court of New South Wales[47] had declared that the rule no longer exists, while Hunt J.,

39 [1965] 3 All E.R. 829, 830.
40 ibid., 831.
41 The distinction has been discarded in the Criminal Codes States of Queensland, Western Australia and Tasmania, and in Victoria.
42 See ss.2 and 10 of the Act and also s.322B of the Crimes Act 1958 (Vic.) and s.63B of the Supreme Court Act 1958 (Vic.).
43 (1989) 17 N.S.W.L.R. 26.
44 ibid., 58.
45 ibid., 47.
46 ibid., 48.
47 Roden J. in *Ceasar* v. *Sommer* [1980] 2 N.S.W.L.R. 929 and Rogers J. in *Halabi's* case at first instance.

also of the Supreme Court, in an *obiter dictum* in *Gypsy Fire* v. *Truth Newspaper Pty Ltd.*[48] had expressed the view that the rule does exist and is not the subject of any discretion. It is time for the matter to be dealt with by the legislature of New South Wales.

As plaintiffs in actions for the tort of intentional trespass to the person are also victims of crime they are entitled to and do rely upon the various criminal injuries compensation schemes which have come into existence in Australia in recent years.[49] It is premature, however, to suggest that 'the law relating to intentional torts to the person has already been superseded'[50] for it is becoming increasingly clear that it is not always possible to rely upon these schemes or to rely upon them to advantage for several reasons. First, no compensation is provided under the various schemes unless there is bodily harm or death. So the victim in *R.* v. *George* would not be able to recover under the criminal injuries compensation schemes but would have to rely on the tort action. Secondly, it would appear that the schemes will not avail an applicant where there is no violent crime even though there may be a civil battery, as in *Mink* v. *University of Chicago*, or false imprisonment, as in *Cowell* v. *Corrective Services Commission of N.S.W.*[51] Thirdly, though they seek to compensate victims on the basis of tort damages the victim compensation schemes in Australia are all subject to statutory maximum awards, the highest of which is $50 000.[52] Victims whose claims justify higher awards will have to rely upon the tort action in trespass. Fourthly, awards in actions in tort for intentional battery and assault are not subject to reduction (at least of compensatory damages) even where there has been provocation, whereas all the victim compensation schemes in Australia must consider any conduct of the victim 'which directly or indirectly contributed to his injury or death'. Fifthly, some of the Australian schemes 'give the appearance of a cumbersome *ad hoc* arrangement for compensation which cannot respond rapidly to meet victim needs'.[53] And sixthly, compensation is not payable by way of exemplary, punitive or even aggravated damages under the various criminal injuries compensation schemes whereas, as we shall see later, these different types of damages are all available in actions for intentional trespass to the person in Australia. We can see, therefore, that the intentional torts of trespass to the person still have a useful function to perform and that they have not been superseded by the coming into existence of the various criminal injuries compensation schemes for victims of crime in Australia.

---

48 (1987) 9 N.S.W.L.R. 382.

49 See Balkin and Davis, *Law of Torts* (Sydney, 1991) pp. 404-7. See also the A.L.R.C.'s proposals for a new Federal victim compensation scheme in *Sentencing of Federal Offenders* (Report No. 15) Interim (1980) Part IV pp. 279-302.

50 See E. Veitch & D.L. Meirs (1975) 38 *M.L.R.* 139, 152.

51 (1988) 13 N.S.W.L.R. 714. Clarke J.A. at p.743 regarded it as an intentional false imprisonment.

52 The lowest statutory maximum is $5000 (Queensland).

53 *Sentencing of Federal Offenders* at p. 294 (see fn.49).

II: TRESPASS TO THE PERSON

The intentional tort of trespass to the person, as we have said, consists of three nominate torts: battery, assault and false imprisonment, and it is to these intentional torts that we now turn our attention.

1. Battery

> A battery is a direct act of the defendant which has the effect of causing contact with the body of the plaintiff without the latter's consent. At the present time battery is usually brought only for intentional acts though actions for reckless or even careless[54] acts are not precluded.

It is felt that comment is necessary on at least five matters. First, what is meant by a direct act? Secondly, what is meant by an intentional act? Thirdly, what sort of contact is sufficient for the purposes of the tort of battery? Fourthly, we will comment on the question of the knowledge of the contact, both the knowledge of the plaintiff and the knowledge of the defendant. And fifthly, we shall comment briefly on the question of consent.

(a) Direct act The first ingredient of the tort of battery is that whatever has to be done to the plaintiff by the defendant to make the activity actionable as a battery must be done *directly*. It is an ingredient which is common to all three torts of trespass to the person—assault, battery and false imprisonment—but it is not sufficiently emphasized in the text-books.[55] But what is a 'direct' act? The example given by Fortescue C.J. in *Reynolds* v. *Clarke*[56] of tumbling over a log left unlawfully on a highway (consequential) and being hit by a log being thrown unlawfully on to the highway (direct) emphasized the element of immediate contact with which 'direct' acts came to be associated. But it was not only a hit by something thrown at you which was regarded as 'direct'. An act which set in motion an unbroken series of continuing consequences, the last of which ultimately caused contact with the plaintiff, was still regarded as sufficiently 'direct' for the purposes of trespass. So when the defendant rode his motorcycle into B who collided with the plaintiff who was thrown to the ground it was held that the facts constituted a 'direct' act for an action in trespass.[57] To turn over a chair or carriage in which another person is sitting is to commit 'a *direct* trespass against the person of him who is sitting in that carriage or chair'.[58] To set a mad ox loose in a crowd makes the person who turns him loose answerable in trespass (battery) for

---

54 Direct careless acts are dealt with under the head of 'negligent trespass'.

55 *Street* (7th edn) p. 20: 'although this requirement is not usually stated in the text-books it seems clear that . . . the act must be a "direct" one'.

56 (1725) 2 Ld.Raym. 1399.

57 *Hillier* v. *Leitch* [1936] S.A.S.R. 490.

58 *Hopper* v. *Reeve* (1817) 7 Taunt 698, 700 (*per* Gibbs C.J.). To pull a chair out deliberately from under the plaintiff while she is in the act of sitting down is definitely a battery. *Garratt* v. *Dailey* (1955) 279, P. 2d 1091, 1094.

any contact that is made with any plaintiff.[59] To set a dog upon a plaintiff is a sufficiently 'direct' act to constitute a trespass against the defendant who gives the dog the order. If D strikes a horse on which P is sitting and the horse throws P off, there is a sufficiently 'direct' act by D to constitute a battery.[60] Even if P jumps off the runaway horse, D will still be liable in battery.[61] But the flexibility of the doctrine of 'directness' in trespass is perhaps best illustrated by *Scott* v. *Shepherd*:

> The defendant threw a lighted squib made of gunpowder on to the stall of Y whereupon W instantly and to prevent injury to himself picked up the lighted squib and threw it across the market-house upon the stall of R who instantly to save his goods picked up the still lighted squib and threw it to another part of the market-house where it struck the plaintiff and the combustible matter bursting put out one of the plaintiff's eyes.[62]

The defendant was held liable in trespass (battery) to the plaintiff and the injury to the plaintiff was held to be from a 'direct' act of the defendant. It should be noticed that the acts of intervention by W and R were not regarded as breaking the chain of directness, for W and R were not regarded as free agents but as acting under a compulsive necessity for their own safety and preservation.[63] What if a plaintiff is given pills, which he takes, without knowing about their dangerous qualities? In *Mink's* case the judge said:

> The act of administering the drug supplies the contact with the plaintiff's person . . . had the drug been administered by means of a hypodermic needle, the element of physical contact would clearly be sufficient. We believe that causing the patient to physically ingest a pill is indistinguishable in principle.[64]

But in America,[65] there is not the same necessity for a 'direct' act as there is in England and Australia—so the matter is not so clear. In *Hutchins* v. *Maughan*[66] the Chief Justice of Victoria thought that trespass would lie against a defendant who threw poisoned meat to a dog which subsequently ate it. He thought the injury to the dog could properly be regarded as 'directly' occasioned by the act of the defendant.

---

59 An example given by Nares J. in *Scott* v. *Shepherd* (1773) 2 Wm.Bl. 892.
60 *Dodwell* v. *Burford* (1670) 1 Mod.Rep. 24.
61 *Leame* v. *Bray* (1803) 3 East 593.
62 (1773) 2 Wm.Bl. 892.
63 ibid., 900 *per* De Grey C.J.
64 (1978) 460 F.Supp. 713, 718.
65 The American (Second) *Restatement* in 1965 indicates that in America the element of 'directness' is no longer necessary for the intentional torts of assault, battery or false imprisonment. W. L. Prosser, *Handbook of the Law of Tort* (4th edn, St Paul, Minn., 1971) p. 30, says 'the shift was a gradual one and the courts seem to have been quite unconscious of it'.
66 [1947] V.L.R. 131: 'Had the baits been thrown by the defendant to the complainant's dog, then no doubt the injury could properly have been regarded as directly occasioned by the act of the defendant, so that trespass would lie' (*per* Herring C.J. at p. 134).

The requirement of a 'direct' act certainly causes many problems,[67] and it would simplify many actions of trespass to the person if we could somehow get rid of that traditional requirement of the common law.[68] In *Chic Fashions (West Wales) Ltd* v. *Jones*, Salmon C.J. (as he then was) said: 'the common law is not static . . . it is a growing organism which continually adapts itself to meet the changing needs of time'.[69] Perhaps the time has come to abolish the requirement of a 'direct' act in actions for intentional trespass to the person.

The doctrine of *directness* does, however, serve one particular purpose and that is that it sometimes removes the necessity to invoke the doctrine of '*transferred intent*',[70] which has been developed in America. In *Scott* v. *Shepherd*, which was discussed earlier,[71] it was not necessary for the court to transfer the intent to injure Y (the first stall-holder) to the plaintiff because the court was able to say that there was a 'direct' act from the defendant to the plaintiff.

(b) Intentional act At the present time, for a battery, the act must not only be 'direct', it must also be an 'intentional' act. But before we consider the various acts which are considered by the courts as 'intentional', we should point out that the courts will only go on to consider whether there has been an 'intentional' act if there is a 'voluntary' act on the part of the defendant. Voluntary here means that the defendant must consciously bring about the bodily movement for which he is being held liable. Though an impaired or clouded consciousness will, it seems, suffice, acts done in a state of automatism are regarded as 'involuntary'.[72] So if a sleepwalker stepped on your face while you were lying on the floor he would not be liable in battery as there would not be a voluntary act.[73] Similarly, if you are asleep on the back seat of a car and in your sleep you push the front seat forward so that the driver is thrown into the steering wheel or runs into P because he loses control of the car, neither will be

---

67 e.g. (i) An old woman of 83 is about to get off a bus at a bus-stop when the defendant, another passenger on the platform behind the woman, intentionally presses the bell so that the bus starts to move causing her to fall on to the road. Is there a 'direct' act for battery? (ii) Defendant adds methyl alcohol to home-made beer. A young woman suffers severe brain damage as a result of drinking, at a party, the home-made beer laced with methyl alcohol. Is there a 'direct' act for battery? The examples are from the English Criminal Injuries Compensation Board's 11th and 9th Reports.

68 The English Law Reform Committee on Conversion and Detinue has expressed the view that: 'the requirement under the existing law of trespass that the interference must be direct could, we think, with advantage be abolished. Such distinctions as that between giving poisoned meat to a dog (trespass) and leaving poisoned meat for a dog (case) do not seem to us to have any place in a rational system of law and, in our view, if an intentional act causes injury to a chattel it ought not to matter whether the result is brought about by direct or indirect means'. One could say the same thing in relation to trespass to the person.

69 [1968] 2 Q.B. 299, 319.

70 The doctrine of 'transferred intent' is discussed below at pp. 35-6.

71 At p. 29.

72 See *Roberts* v. *Ramsbottom* [1980] 1 All E.R. 7 where in a negligence case Neill J. suggests that automatism means a total loss of consciousness.

73 See *Morris* v. *Marsden* [1952] 1 All E.R. 925, 927.

successful in an action in battery against you.[74] It goes without saying that if A takes B's hand forcibly and strikes C with it, B is not liable because B has done no voluntary act.[75] But assuming you have done a voluntary act, when is the act for the purposes of the tort of battery said to be *intentional*?

If the act is deliberate or wilful, if the defendant 'meant to do it',[76] it will be regarded as intentional, as when D punches P in the face with his fist because P has insulted him, or when D takes a gun, points it at P, fires and hits him. But cases are not always as simple as that. For example, D throws a stone at P meaning to hit him in the eye, but either because D's aim is bad or because P moves at the vital moment P is struck on the ear and not the eye. There is little doubt that despite what D meant to do, D will be regarded as having committed an intentional battery against P. Again, if D under the mistaken impression that P has a wooden left leg strikes him deliberately on that leg there will be a battery if P has no wooden leg.[77] In America, D was held liable in trespass for shooting P's dog, believing it to be a wolf.[78] So a defendant would be liable in battery if he runs over the plaintiff under the mistaken impression that he was 'a bundle of rags, a dead dog or a dead kangaroo'[79] or a large piece of brown paper[80] or if he fires at and hits a moving object in long grass thinking it is a rabbit he had just lost sight of and it turns out to be a couple engaged in sexual intercourse in the long grass.[81] Take another situation: if D intends to shoot O but instead shoots P, who is wearing O's distinctive suit at the time, there is little doubt that there will be an intentional battery, and D's mistake will not prevent him being held liable for the contact which he intended. In battery, what is required is an intention to make contact, not an intention to do harm—and it is not correct to say that trespass can be brought 'only for the direct physical infliction of *harm*'.[82] As Talbot J. said in *Williams* v. *Humphrey*:

> It was argued that for the act to be a battery there must be an intent to *injure*. I do not accept this contention. The intention goes to the commission of the act of force. This seems to be the principle in the many cases of trespass to the person.[83]

More recently, Clarke J.A. in *Cowell* v. *Corrective Services Commission of N.S.W.* reiterated this point when he said:

---

74 See *Stokes* v. *Carlson* (1951) 240 S.W. 2d 132.

75 *Weaver* v. *Ward* (1616) Hob. 134.

76 *Per* Fox J. in *McNamara* v. *Duncan* (1979) 26 A.L.R. 584, 587.

77 Perhaps even if he has. See below p. 39.

78 *Ranson* v. *Kitner* (1888) 31 Ill.App. 241.

79 *Law* v. *Visser* [1961] Q.S.R. 46—a case brought in negligence: 'The defendant Visser cannot escape liability on the ground that he did not know the nature of the large object he made no attempt to avoid' (*per* Mack J. at p. 58).

80 *Public Transport Comm.* v. *Perry* (1976-77) 14 A.L.R. 273 (a case in occupier's liability and negligence).

81 The case is *Hammerton* v. *Darienza* (unreported). It is a decision of Bristow J. Regretfully we are obliged to rely upon a report in the Melbourne *Herald* of July 1978 in relation to this English decision.

82 See *Williams & Hepple*, p. 36: 'The plaintiff could not have brought an action for trespass, which lay only for the direct physical infliction of *harm*' (emphasis added).

83 See fn. 23 above at p. 20.

> [I]t is not a necessary element of assault (and battery) that the defendant intended to injure the plaintiff. It is sufficient if he intended to strike him.[84]

What if a defendant can foresee a risk of contact but does not necessarily desire contact with anyone? Can an *intentional* act still be imputed to him if contact takes place? A boy of 13 pushed a television set from the tenth floor of a tower block of flats and killed an 8-year-old girl who was struck by the set 20 metres below. The girl had run out from beneath the flats as the set was falling. As reported, the boy said in his statement: 'I know what I did was bad and someone might be hurt or killed, but I didn't mean to hurt anyone' and 'I wouldn't have pushed it over if there was somebody there, honestly'.[85] The judge directed the jury to return a verdict of not guilty of manslaughter. Would the girl have succeeded in a civil action in battery if she had survived the impact? Could it be said that the direct act was *intentional*? Unfortunately there are no authoritative decisions to guide us, but in America cases such as this one would be decided by what might be called for convenience the doctrine of substantial certainty. Prosser describes it in the following way:

> The man who fires a bullet into a dense crowd may fervently pray that he will hit no one, but since he must believe and know that he cannot avoid doing so, *he intends it.* The practical application of the principle has meant that where a reasonable man in the defendant's position would believe that a particular result was substantially certain to follow, he will be dealt with by the jury, or even by the Courts, *as though he had intended it.*[86]

The doctrine has been applied in *Garratt* v. *Dailey*:

> A boy who moved a chair in which the plaintiff, a heavy arthritic person, had formerly been sitting, was held liable in intentional battery when the plaintiff returned a few minutes later and in attempting to sit down at the place where the chair formerly had been, fell to the ground sustaining serious injuries.[87]

In coming to this conclusion the court said:

> A battery would be established if, in addition to the plaintiff's fall, it was proved that, when [the defendant] moved the chair, he knew with substantial certainty that the plaintiff would attempt to sit down where the chair had been . . . The

---

84 (1988) 13 N.S.W.L.R. 714, 743. See also *Wilson* v. *Pringle* [1987] Q.B. 237, 249: 'It is the act and not the injury which must be intentional. An intention to injure is not essential to an action for trespass to the person. It is the mere trespass by itself which is the offence' (*per* Croom-Johnson L.J.).

85 The *Guardian*, 31 October and 1 November 1979. See also *R.* v. *Franklin* (1883) 15 Cox C.C. 163, where the defendant took up a good sized box from a refreshment stall on Brighton pier and wantonly threw it into the sea. Unfortunately the box struck the deceased, who was at that moment swimming underneath the pier, and so caused his death. The jury returned a verdict of guilty of manslaughter.

86 W.L. Prosser, *Law of Torts* (4th edn, 1971) p. 32.

87 (1955) 279 P. 2d 1091 (Supreme Court of Washington).

mere absence of any intent to injure the plaintiff or to play a prank on her or to embarrass her, or to commit an assault and battery on her would not absolve him from liability if in fact he had such knowledge.[88]

There is some support for the doctrine in England. Glanville Williams says, 'there is one situation where a consequence is deemed to be intended though it is not desired. This is where it is foreseen as substantially certain'.[89] And Street writes: 'if in the circumstances [a defendant] had knowledge that his conduct was substantially certain to result in that act (not merely that he might have foreseen the result) his act would still be deemed to be intentional'.[90] It seems, therefore, that actions in *intentional* battery will succeed if plaintiffs can persuade the court that contact with their person was substantially certain to follow from the acts of the defendant. In the law of torts that test must surely be objective, and so the test would be not whether the defendants recognized that their acts were substantially certain to result in contact but whether all sober and reasonable people would recognize those acts to be substantially certain to result in contact. Using that test, a defendant who, on being refused service, fires through the window of a restaurant wounding a customer in the face, would be liable in intentional battery even though he does not know the customer is there.[91] Similarly, a defendant who, while standing on a parapet of a bridge crossing a railway line, pushes a piece of paving stone over the parapet on to the front part of an approaching train, would be liable in intentional battery if the stone crashes through the glass window of the train driver's cab and strikes the guard.[92] In both cases, the contact which in fact occurs is substantially certain to occur and the acts in both cases would, therefore, be regarded as *intentional* even though the defendant may not have known of the existence of the plaintiffs until after the contact had occurred. Using the same test, in *Bolton* v. *Stone*, if Miss Stone, who was struck by a cricket ball which had been hit by a visiting batsman out of the defendant's cricket ground, had brought an action in intentional battery against the batsman who hit the ball,[93] she would not have succeeded because although there was 'a conceivable possibility that someone would be hit'[94] it was a bare possibility and not a substantial certainty.

What about *reckless* acts? Could they be regarded as 'intentional' acts

---

88 ibid., 1094.

89 Glanville Williams, *Criminal Law: The General Part* (2nd edn, London, 1961) p. 38. He goes on: 'It may be objected that certainty is a matter of degree. In a philosophical view, nothing is certain; so-called certainty is merely high probability . . . We do in fact speak of certainty in ordinary life; and for the purpose of the present rule it means such a high degree of probability that common sense would pronounce it certain. Mere philosophical doubt, or the intervention of an extraordinary chance, is to be ignored' (at pp. 38-40).

90 *Street* (7th edn, 1983) p. 16.

91 *R.* v. *Holder* [1967] *Crim.L.R.* 66.

92 *D.P.P.* v. *Newbury* [1976] 2 All E.R. 365.

93 *Bolton* v. *Stone* [1951] A.C. 850. The question is posed in *Weir* (4th edn, 1979) p. 266.

94 *Bolton* v. *Stone* [1951] A.C. 850, 858, *per* Lord Porter.

for the purpose of the tort of battery? Fleming[95] says that *battery* is reserved for *intentional* wrongs, but the English decision in *R.* v. *Venna*, though a criminal case, shows that the dividing line between intention and recklessness is sometimes barely distinguishable:

The defendant while resisting arrest, and after he knew he was being arrested, continued to kick, to 'lash out' wildly with his legs, and in doing so kicked the hand of a police officer who came to the aid of two colleagues to assist in picking up the defendant from the ground. The kick caused a fracture of a bone and was the subject of a charge of assault occasioning actual bodily harm.[96]

The Court of Appeal in England upheld a conviction for assault on the basis that a reckless application of unlawful physical force was sufficient to constitute criminal assault, and added:

Insofar as the editors of text-books commit themselves to an opinion on this branch of the law they are favourable to the view that recklessness is or should logically be sufficient to support the charge of assault or battery . . . in our view the element of *mens rea* in the offence of battery is satisfied by proof that the defendant intentionally or recklessly applied force to the person of another . . . we see no reason in logic or in law why a person who recklessly applies physical force to the person of another should be outside the criminal law of assault.[97]

If there is no reason in logic or in law why a person who recklessly applies force to the person of another should be outside the criminal law of assault and battery, there is surely no reason in logic or in law why a person who recklessly applies force to the person of another should be outside the civil law of battery (or assault). There is a good case for regarding reckless acts of a defendant which have the effect of causing contact with the body of the plaintiff without his consent as constituting the intentional tort of battery, and it may be a better way of dealing with some defendants than using the doctrine of substantial certainty. There is even some authority for suggesting that the courts are prepared to treat *reckless* acts as *intentional* acts. In *Beals* v. *Hayward*, McGregor J. said:

Now deliberately firing a gun in the direction of another person is presumably done intentionally or recklessly, not caring whether the person was hurt or not, and if an act of this nature is done recklessly, that would itself amount to sufficient intention to commit an assault.[98]

A reckless act therefore which is sufficient to amount to an *intentional* act, for the purposes of the tort of battery, is any act where the defendant knowing that bodily contact with the plaintiff might ensue from his act has yet gone on to take the risk of it, not caring whether the contact took place or not. It is further submitted that 'deliberately closing his mind to

95 *Fleming* (6th edn, 1983) p. 24, fn. 23.
96 [1976] 1 Q.B. 421.
97 ibid., 428-9.
98 [1960] N.Z.L.R. 131.

the obvious' will not allow a defendant to escape the obvious consequences of his action, for as the Court of Appeal said in *R.* v. *Parker*:

. . . that type of action, that type of deliberate closing of the mind, is the equivalent of knowledge and a man cannot escape the consequences of his action . . . by saying, 'I never directed my mind to the obvious consequences'. . .[99]

The great value of treating *reckless* acts as *intentional* acts is seen particularly when one deals with those types of cases which in criminal law are called cases of transferred malice,[100] and in tort (at least in America) are called cases of *transferred intent.* Thus, when the defendant chased an adversary into a supermarket, picked up a bottle from a shelf and, in attempting to strike the adversary over the head with the bottle in the supermarket, missed and instead hit the plaintiff, an ordinary shopper, a painful blow to the elbow, the defendant was held liable in a civil action of intentional battery, and the court said that the defendant was liable to the plaintiff 'to the same extent as if he had been the intended victim'.[101] The intent was 'transferred', the court approving the statement in the 1932 decision in *Carnes* v. *Thompson*:

If one person intentionally strikes at, throws at, or shoots at another, and unintentionally strikes a third person, he is not excused, on the ground that it was a mere accident, but it is an assault and battery of a third person. Defendant's intention, in such a case, is to strike an unlawful blow, to injure some person by his act, and it is not essential that the injury be to the one intended.[102]

There do not appear to be any reported cases of transferred intent in tort in Australia. However, in *Bunyan* v. *Jordan*[103] Latham C.J. suggested that

---

99 (1976) 63 Cr.App.R. 211, 214. Both these uses of the word 'reckless' (i.e. deciding to ignore a risk of bodily contact or closing one's mind to the obvious consequences of one's acts) were approved by Lord Diplock in the House of Lords decision in *R.* v. *Caldwell* [1981] 1 All E.R. 961, 966, where he said that 'reckless' was an ordinary English word and that the meaning it bore in ordinary speech '. . . surely includes not only deciding to ignore a risk of harmful consequences resulting from one's acts that one has recognized as existing, but also failing to give any thought to whether or not there is any such risk in circumstances where, if any thought were given to the matter, it would be obvious that there was . . .'. In the later case of *R.* v. *Lawrence* [1981] 1 All E.R. 974, 982, Lord Diplock suggests that the consequences must be both obvious and serious: 'Recklessness on the part of the doer of an act does presuppose that there is something in the circumstances that would have drawn the attention of an ordinary prudent individual to the possibility that his act was capable of causing the kind of *serious* harmful consequences that the section which creates the offence was intended to prevent, and that the risk of those harmful consequences occurring was not so slight that an ordinary prudent individual would feel justified in treating them as negligible. It is only when this is so that the doer of the act is acting "recklessly" if, before doing that act, he either fails to give any thought to the possibility of there being any such risk or having recognized that there was such risk he nevertheless goes on to do it.'

100 See A. Ashworth, 'Transferred Malice and Punishment for Unforeseen Consequences' in *Reshaping the Criminal Law* (ed. P.R. Glazebrook) (London, 1978) pp. 77-94.

101 *Fordyce* v. *Montgomery* (1968) 424 S.W. 2d 746, 751.

102 (1932) 48 S.W. 2d 903, 904.

103 (1937) 57 C.L.R. 1, 12.

the doctrine of transferred intent is part of the law of Australia: 'If A, intending to hit B unlawfully, in fact hits C, there is no doubt as to A's liability to C'. Apart from *Scott* v. *Shepherd*, which has been described as 'the first case of transferred intent in tort',[104] there are only two other cases in English law where it could be said that the doctrine has been applied, though in neither case was there any indication that it was being consciously applied. In *James* v. *Campbell*[105] the defendant, who was fighting with a third party, swung his hand and unintentionally hit the plaintiff. The defendant was held liable in battery.[106] And in *Ball et Uxor* v. *Axten*[107] the defendant was attempting to strike at the plaintiff's dog with the handle of his riding whip when one of the blows fell upon the plaintiff's wife, who had come up to the spot and was trying to shield her dog from the blows. The report indicates that Cockburn C.J. told the jury that, 'even though the defendant had not aimed the blow at the woman, there was no doubt an assault'.[108] All of these cases, it is suggested, could be more easily decided on the basis of a *reckless*, therefore *intentional*, act of the defendant rather than by relying upon the fiction of 'transferred' intent. The doctrine of transferred intent would then become unnecessary.

Finally, there is another shade of meaning that the word 'intentional' conveys. It appears that infants can *intend* an act for the purposes of the tort of intentional battery even though they may not have the mental capacity for negligent conduct. In the American case of *Ellis* v. *D'Angelo*,[109] a 4-year-old boy violently impelled the adult baby-sitter on to the floor causing her to break bones in both arms and wrists. The court held that the boy was capable of intending and had intended the battery even though he lacked the mental capacity to recognize the wrongfulness of his conduct. A writer who has examined this question in some detail has come to the conclusion that in the intentional tort of battery 'the defence of incapacity to have the requisite intention is confined to very young children . . . [and] that somewhere about the age of four a child is capable of the intention necessary to commit this tort'.[110]

It should be added, before we move on to consider the next ingredient of the tort of battery, that in Australia (unlike the situation in England) there is no onus upon a plaintiff to establish that the defendant *intentionally* made direct contact with the body of the plaintiff. Once the plaintiff proves a direct contact proceeding from the defendant to the body of the plaintiff the burden is on the defendant to show absence of intent.[111]

(c) **Contact with the body of the plaintiff** One of the essential ingredients of the tort of intentional battery is contact with the body of the plaintiff by

---

104 W.L. Prosser (1967) 45 *Texas L.R.* 650, 654.
105 (1832) 5 Car. & P. 372.
106 Though that might have been a case of negligent battery.
107 (1866) 4 F. & F. 1019.
108 No doubt a battery, as the woman was struck. Note, however, that *Weir* (4th edn, 1979) at p. 286 places the case under assault and not battery. Why?
109 (1953) 253 P. 2d. 675.
110 Alexander, *Studies in Canadian Family Law* (1972) Vol. 2, 845, 854.
111 See pp. 24-5 above.

the defendant. Originally, of course, this contact would have been 'hand to hand' e.g. by the defendant striking the plaintiff or hitting him with a stick. But in 1838 Lord Denman pointed out that 'a battery does not necessarily mean something done cominus'.[112] In the well-known case of *Leame* v. *Bray*,[113] where the defendant ran against the plaintiff's curricle causing the horses to run away with the curricle so that the plaintiff, in order to preserve his life, jumped out of the curricle and fractured his collarbone, it was held that there was sufficient contact with the body of the plaintiff by the defendant to maintain an action in battery. But is any contact, however slight, enough to constitute a battery? Everyone is familiar with the *dictum* of Holt C.J. in *Cole* v. *Turner*[114] that 'the least touching of another *in anger* is a battery', but one might well ask whether the qualification implied by the words 'in anger' truly represents the legal position today, for Street says that kissing a sleeping lady in the presence of her friends would be a battery[115] and the editor of Salmond reinforces this opinion.[116] In America a 'friendly unsolicited hug' was held to be a battery.[117]

Quite recently, however, in *Wilson* v. *Pringle*,[118] the English Court of Appeal held that in a battery 'there must be an intentional touching or contact in one form or another of the plaintiff by the defendant' and that 'that touching must be proved to be a *hostile* touching'. The element of hostility was not clearly defined in the judgment though we are told that it 'cannot be equated with ill-will or malevolence'[119] and that the conduct of the police officer in *Collins* v. *Wilcock*[120] who touched a woman deliberately but without an intention to do more than restrain her temporarily was nevertheless 'acting unlawfully and in that way was acting with hostility'.[121] It is not surprising therefore that Wood J. in *T* v. *T and Another*[122] had grave reservations as to whether the requirement of a hostile touching was a necessary element of a battery. And in *In re F. (Mental Patient: Sterilisation)* Lord Goff in the House of Lords expressed the opinion that it was not correct to say that a touching must be 'hostile' to amount to a battery.[123] It is unlikely that courts in Australia will insist

112 i.e. hand to hand, in *Pursell* v. *Horn* (1838) 8 Ad. & E. 602, 604.
113 (1803) 3 East 593.
114 (1704) 6 Mod.Rep. 149. See also *Campbell* v. *Samuels* (1980) 23 S.A.S.R. 389, 392: 'The least touching, if intentional, and done in a hostile manner, is an assault' (*per* Zelling J.).
115 *Street* (7th edn, 1983), 20, fn. 1.
116 *Salmond & Heuston* (18th edn, 1981) p. 113: 'Nor is anger or hostility essential to liability; an unwanted kiss may be a battery'.
117 *Spivey* v. *Battaglia* (1972) 258 So. 2d 815.
118 [1986] 3 W.L.R. 1, 11 (emphasis added).
119 ibid.
120 [1984] 1 W.L.R. 1172.
121 [1986] 3 W.L.R. 1, 11.
122 [1988] 2 W.L.R. 189, 203 'The incision made by the surgeon's scalpel need not be and probably is most unlikely to be hostile, but unless a defence or justification is established it must in my judgment fall within the definition of a trespass to the person'.
123 [1990] 2 A.C. 1, 73.

that a battery must involve a hostile contact with the body of the plaintiff.[124]

Some contacts, however, do not attract any liability. One must put up with the everyday unintentional and even intentional jostling which is part of our ordinary life. As Holt C.J. said in *Cole* v. *Turner*, 'if two or more meet in a narrow passage, and without any violence or design of harm the one touches the other gently, it will be no battery'[125] but 'if any of them use violence against the other to force his way in a rude inordinate manner, it will be a battery'.[126] Again, in some sports forcible body contact is often part of the rules of the game, and such contacts will not lead to liability in battery if they find justification in the rules and usages of the game. Contacts which are prohibited or acts not within the rules and usages of the game will be regarded as unpermitted contacts.[127] Thus the defendant footballer in *McNamara* v. *Duncan*,[128] who deliberately 'felled' the plaintiff footballer during a game but after the plaintiff had parted with possession of the ball, was held liable to the plaintiff in an action of intentional battery. The question of unpermitted contacts also arises in relation to surgical and dental treatment. A patient might consent to a certain operation but not to another[129] or to the removal of a certain tooth but not another. This last matter will be dealt with later in relation to the question of consent.

For a battery, the contact must be *active* and *not passive*. As Denman C.J. said in *Innes* v. *Wylie*,[130] if a defendant is 'entirely passive like a door or wall put to prevent the plaintiff from entering the room' and simply obstructs the entrance of the plaintiff then no battery has been committed on the plaintiff by the defendant. This active contact, however, can take many forms. Not only is spitting on the plaintiff,[131] pulling away the chair he is about to sit on so that he falls to the ground,[132] forcibly taking a

---

124 See *Cowell* v. *Corrective Services Commission of N.S.W.* (1988) 13 N.S.W.L.R. 714, 744 where Clarke J.A. rejected the submission that hostility was an essential ingredient of false imprisonment, one of the three nominate torts of trespass to the person.

125 (1704) 6 Mod.Rep. 149.

126 ibid.

127 *Hilton* v. *Wallace* (1989) Aust. Torts Reports 8-231 suggests that even some contacts not strictly within the rules of the game might not constitute a battery.

128 (1979) 26 A.L.R. 584.

129 In *Schweizer* v. *Central Hospital* (1975) 53 D.L.R. (3d) 494 the plaintiff went into hospital for an operation on his toe and a spinal operation was performed instead. The consent to the toe operation did not mean he consented to the spinal fusion. In *Chatterton* v. *Gerson* [1981] 1 All E.R. 257, 256, Bristow J. mentions a case of a boy admitted to hospital for tonsillectomy who, due to administrative error, was circumcised instead. Bristow J. thought trespass would be the appropriate cause of action against the doctor.

130 (1844) 1 Car. & K. 257.

131 *R.* v. *Cotesworth* (1704) 6 Mod.Rep. 172; *Alcorn* v. *Mitchell* (1872) 63 Ill. 553.

132 *Garratt* v. *Dailey* (1955) 279 P. 2d 1091. Where American cases such as this one are used, it is submitted that they are persuasive and that there are no doctrinal differences which would preclude their use as persuasive authorities in Australia.

blood test[133] and firing a gun so close to his face as to burn him[134] a battery but it is also suggested that the transmission of any force to the body of the plaintiff will constitute a battery. Thus to forcibly X-ray a person would be a battery, and it has been so held in America.[135] If a bright light is deliberately shone into another person's eyes this may constitute a battery.[136] To snatch a book from a person[137] or to grab a plate from his hand[138] would also constitute a battery and the argument for regarding it as a battery is that 'the intentional snatching of an object from one's hand is as clearly an offensive invasion of his person as would be an actual contact with his body'.[139] So, in addition to actual bodily contact with the plaintiff, it is suggested that either contact with the clothing of the plaintiff[140] or with an object closely identified with the body of the plaintiff[141] will suffice to constitute contact for the purposes of the tort of battery.

If the contact is reasonably necessary for a purpose recognized by the courts then there will be no battery. In *Donelly* v. *Jackman*[142] the defendant struck a police officer when he touched the defendant on the shoulder intending to stop him for questioning. It was held that the defendant had committed an assault (battery) on the police officer while in the execution of his duty but that there was no battery by the police officer. Similarly, where a minor plaintiff persistently told the defendant doctor that 'his role in society could best be described by the sound of a duck' and the defendant intentionally and gently touched the plaintiff to call attention to his dislike of the plaintiff's repeated suggestions, a finding by the jury that there was not that kind of intentional touching which would amount to a battery, was held to be perfectly good.[143] In *Collins* v. *Wilcock*,[144] Robert Goff L.J. drew a distinction between a touch to draw a person's attention which is generally acceptable and a physical restraint which is not and came to the conclusion that the police officer's action in taking

133 See, e.g., *S.* v. *McC.*; *W.* v. *W.* [1972] A.C. 24 (at least in relation to an adult); *Rossell* v. *City and County of Honolulu* (1978) 579 P. 2d 663; and *Bednarik* v. *Bednarik* (1940) 16 A. 2d 80, 90.

134 *R.* v. *Hamilton* (1891) 12 L.R.(N.S.W.) 111, 114 *per* Windeyer J.

135 See *Irwin* v. *Arrendale* (1967) 159 S.E. 2d 719. An injury to sensitive eyes caused by floodlights used by a television crew can also be a battery. See *Stafford* v. *Hayes* (1976) 327 So. 2d 871.

136 See *Kaye* v. *Robertson* [1991] F.S.R. 62, 68.

137 See *S.H. Kress* v. *Brashier* (1932) 50 S.W. 2d 922.

138 See *Fisher* v. *Carousel Motor Hotel Inc.* (1967) 424 S.W. 2d 627. The defendant's employee grabbed the plate from the plaintiff's hand while the plaintiff was standing in a luncheon queue, because the plaintiff was black.

139 ibid., 629.

140 e.g. defendant putting his hand in the pocket of plaintiff woman's dress. See *Piggly-Wiggly Alabama Co.* v. *Rickles* (1925) 103 So. 860. Or on clothing covering the private parts of the plaintiff, *Skonson* v. *Nidy* (1961) 367 P. 2d 248.

141 See the examples in fns 137 and 138 above. Also see *Siegel* v. *Long* (1910) 53 So. 753.

142 [1970] 1 W.L.R. 562. In *Collins* v. *Wilcock* [1984] 1 W.L.R. 1172, 1179 Robert Goff L.J. indicated that *Donelly* v. *Jackman* should be regarded as 'an extreme case'.

143 *Morgan* v. *Pistone* (1970) 475 P. 2d 839. See also *Wiffin* v. *Kincard* (1807) 2 B. & P. (N.R.) 471.

144 [1984] 1 W.L.R. 1172, 1180.

hold of a woman's arm, when the woman walked away refusing to answer the police officer's questions, constituted a battery. But to hold down a motorist who is about to attack another motorist after an accident or to hold back a person from running into his burning house would, it is suggested, be regarded by the courts as contacts which are reasonably necessary to the common intercourse of life. This further category of permissible contacts, however, should be narrowly confined to those intentional and forcible contacts which are reasonably necessary to assist public officials in the execution of their duties[145] and to those contacts which are necessary to prevent a breach of the peace from occurring.

(d) Knowledge of the contact Knowledge of the contact either by the defendant or the plaintiff (at least at the time of contact) is not a necessary requirement for the tort of battery. Usually, of course, both the plaintiff and the defendant will have knowledge of the contact but there will be circumstances when this will not be so.

There will be liability for a battery even though at the time of contact the plaintiff is unaware of the contact. The woman who is kissed while she is asleep, the man who is punched while he is in a drunken stupor and the person who while under an anaesthetic has a different operation performed from that consented to will all be able to bring successful actions in battery. The plaintiff need not know of the contact at the time of the contact but he will need to show evidence of contact, e.g. a broken jaw, or provide evidence of those who have seen the contact take place.

The defendant will usually have knowledge of the contact for which he is being held responsible but there may be circumstances where the defendant has no knowledge that a contact with the plaintiff has taken place. For example, a defendant may run over the plaintiff under the mistaken impression that he is 'a bundle of rags, a dead dog or a dead kangaroo'.[146] Or a defendant might throw a stone to frighten X and the plaintiff, of whose presence the defendant is unaware, might be struck by the stone.[147] Or the defendant might recklessly throw a television set from the top of a block of flats and it might injure the plaintiff walking below.[148] In all these cases even though the defendant is unaware of the identity or even of the presence of the plaintiff he will be liable in battery. His lack of knowledge of the plaintiff will not affect his liability.

(e) Consent There is little doubt that if there is consent to the acts of the defendant then an action of trespass to the person, whether battery, assault or false imprisonment, will not succeed. An important question, however, on which there is some doubt is whether it is for the plaintiff to prove

---

145 *Rose* v. *Kempthorne* (1910) 103 L.T. 730. And also, perhaps, to those contacts which good medical practice 'demands' as in the exceptional circumstances prevailing in *T* v. *T* [1988] 2 W.L.R. 189.

146 See *Law* v. *Visser* (1961) Q.S.R. 46.

147 See *Alteiri* v. *Colasso* (1975) 362 A. 2d 798. Also *White* v. *Sander* (1897) 47 N.E. 90. Where applying the doctrine of recklessness, it is submitted, there would be success.

148 See fn. 85 above.

absence of consent or whether it is for the defendant to exculpate himself by alleging and proving consent to the act in question.

Several writers take the view that the onus of proving absence of consent is upon the plaintiff. The authors of one of the Australian casebooks[149] on the law of torts are of the view that 'lack of consent is the very gist of trespass and that the plaintiff must plead and prove that the defendant's direct contact with the plaintiff's person . . . occurred without consent'. Fleming takes the same view: 'strictly speaking, consent is not a privilege at all, because lack of it is the very gist of assault, battery [and] false imprisonment . . .'.[150] And Street has consistently maintained that 'on principle it would seem that the absence of consent is so inherent in the notion of a tortious invasion of interests in the person that the absence of consent must be established by the plaintiff'.[151]

There is no authoritative decision of the courts in Australia on the question but in a ruling given in *Hart* v. *Herron*, Fisher J. of the Supreme Court of New South Wales held that, in the intentional torts, the onus of proving consent is upon the defendant.[152] A similar opinion was expressed by Miles C.J. of the Supreme Court of the A.C.T. in *Sibley* v. *Milutinovic*[153] and more recently by McHugh J. of the High Court of Australia in *Department of Health & Community Services (N.T.)* v. *J.W.B. and S.M.B.*[154] The Canadian courts have on three recent occasions, in *Schweizer* v. *Central Hospital*,[155] in *Kelly* v. *Hazlett*,[156] and in *Allan* v. *New Mount Sinai Hospital*,[157] held that the onus of establishing a sufficient and effective consent in actions for trespasses to the person rests upon the defendant and that he can discharge that onus by proving facts that indicate a valid consent. These decisions have been subjected to some academic criticisms[158] but they correctly represent the law in Australia for the following reasons.

First, the courts in Australia have repeatedly held in recent years that in an action for trespass to the person, once the plaintiff proves a direct act on the part of the defendant, the burden of proving absence of intention or negligence shifts to the defendant. The plaintiff has done enough by

---

149 *Luntz, Hambly & Hayes* (1992) p. 680. *See also* Balkin & Davis *Law of Torts* (Sydney, 1991) pp. 38-9 and Blay (1987) 61 *A.L.J.* 25.

150 *Fleming* (6th edn, 1983) p. 73. Though in the 7th edn (1987) at p. 72 Fleming's view is somewhat changed.

151 Street's position has not changed from his first edition in 1955 (pp. 16-17) to his seventh edition in 1983 (p. 18).

152 (1984) Aust. Torts Reports 80-201. 'The onus is upon the defendant to prove an absence of intent to cause injury which in this case, upon the pleadings, he seeks to do by proving that he had the plaintiff's consent to the course of treatment and its necessary physical application' (at 67, 814).

153 (1990) Aust. Torts Reports 81-013 at 67, 688-9.

154 (1992) 66 A.L.J.R. 301, 337.

155 (1974) 6 O.R. (2d) 606, 53 D.L.R. (3d) 494 (Ont.H.C.).

156 (1976) 75 D.L.R. (3d) 536 (Ont.H.C.).

157 (1980) 109 D.L.R. (3d) 634.

158 See M.T. Hertz & E. Picard (1979) 17 *Alberta L.R.* 318-22. The contribution by Hertz is critical. E. Picard supports the decisions and so does A.M. Linden; see *Canadian Tort Law* (1977) 58.

proving a direct act, it is for the defendant to exculpate himself. In view of this, to require the plaintiff to prove absence of consent is much too onerous a requirement, particularly as it involves proving a negative, and it is very doubtful if Australian courts would agree to impose such a requirement upon a plaintiff in an action for trespass to the person. At the very most, courts here might insist that there be an *allegation* (not proof) of *no consent* in the pleadings but even that is doubtful. Secondly, if the facts sufficient to constitute an intentional trespass were pleaded in the tort of negligence (if it is possible to do so[159]) the defendant would have to allege and prove the defence of consent or *volenti non fit injuria*. In view of this, there is no reason why the onus of proving no consent in an action of trespass should be on the plaintiff. The whole thrust of the intentional torts to the person is to make it easier[160] for a plaintiff to succeed when the plaintiff can show a direct invasion of his person by the defendant. To put the onus of proving absence of consent to the trespass on the plaintiff would run counter to that thrust. Thirdly, such Australian authority as there is suggests that consent is a defence and like all defences in the law of torts must be raised and substantiated by the defendant. Fox J. in *McNamara* v. *Duncan* referred to consent as 'the defence of consent'[161] and that is what it really is. It will be treated in this book as a defence and dealt with later together with the other defences to the intentional torts.

2. ASSAULT

> An assault is any direct threat by the defendant which places the plaintiff in reasonable apprehension of an imminent contact with his person either by the defendant or by some person or thing within the defendant's control. At the present time assault is usually brought for intentional threats though actions for reckless[162] or even careless threats are not precluded.

Three matters need closer examination. First, what threats are sufficient to constitute the tort of assault? Secondly, what is meant by reasonable apprehension of imminent contact? Thirdly, we will comment on the question of knowledge of the threat.

'Assault' is often used to describe what is essentially a 'battery'. This is because most assaults often culminate in contact and therefore a battery, and the result is often described as an 'assault and battery' or simply as an 'assault'. An example of this is provided by the decision in *Butchard* v. *Barnett*:

Where a judge found that the defendant deliberately kicked the plaintiff in the head whilst the plaintiff was on the ground, that the blow was not by any means

---

159 See pp. 21-2.
160 i.e. easier than in an action for the tort of negligence.
161 (1979) 26 A.L.R. 584, 588. Followed in *Sibley* v. *Milutinovic* (1990) Aust. Torts Reports 81-013 at 67, 688.
162 See *Hall* v. *Fonceca* [1983] W.A.R. 309, 313.

an accidental blow occurring in a normal passage of play and that the kick was administered some appreciable time after the plaintiff had punched the ball away, he said he was satisfied that the defendant did *assault* the plaintiff.[163]

Without any attempt at pedantry, it should be said that the distinction between assault and battery is quite clear. Assault is the threat of force to the person of another, while battery is the actual application of that force. Strictly speaking, therefore, the word 'assault' should be reserved for those threats which, though they do not end up in contact with the person of the plaintiff, nevertheless place the plaintiff in reasonable apprehension of receiving an imminent contact with his person. The confusion between assault and battery is not peculiarly Australian. Quite recently a Canadian judge expressed the view that 'the distinction between assault and battery had been blurred, and that when we now speak of an assault, it may include a battery'.[164] And in an even more recent case, where the defendant threw the plaintiff down the stairs, the plaintiff framed his action in assault. The judge said that 'battery should properly have been pleaded' but held that a failure to do so was not fatal to the claim.[165]

In the vast majority of cases assault and battery usually go together but you can get a battery without an assault and an assault without a battery. An example of the first is provided by the decision in *Gambriell* v. *Caparelli* where the defendant swiftly and silently crept up to the plaintiff and struck him. As the judge said:

It is clear on the facts of the case with which I am dealing that, prior to the actual striking of the plaintiff by the defendant, there was no immediate apprehension of violence by the plaintiff as far as the defendant was concerned, for the simple reason that the plaintiff had not seen the defendant, as he was struck from behind, and the act of the defendant, if not justified, was a battery.[166]

There are several examples of an assault without a battery.[167] A good example is provided by *Stephens* v. *Myers*:

During a parish meeting it was resolved by a large majority to eject the defendant who was constantly interrupting the proceedings. The defendant advanced in a threatening manner towards the plaintiff, who was acting as chairman of the meeting, to strike him but was stopped by the Churchwarden before he was near enough to strike the plaintiff. It was held that the act of the defendant amounted to an assault in law.[168]

The definition of 'assault' will now be examined in greater detail.

---

163 (1980) 86 L.S.J.S. 47, 53.

164 *Gambriell* v. *Caparelli* (1975) 54 D.L.R. (3d) 661, 664.

165 *Doyle* v. *Garden of the Gulf Security & Investigation Inc. and Gallant* (1980) 65 A.P.R. 123.

166 (1975) 54 D.L.R. (3d) 661, 664.

167 See e.g. *Mortin* v. *Shoppee* (1828) 3 C. & P. 373 and *Read* v. *Coker* (1853) 13 C.B. 850.

168 (1830) 4 C. & P. 350.

(a) The meaning of direct threats Threats which constitute assaults are usually by acts accompanied by words, for example, in *Stephens* v. *Myers* (discussed above) the defendant said he would rather pull the chairman out of the chair than be turned out of the room, and immediately advanced with his fist clenched towards the plaintiff chairman. But words are not necessary for an assault if the act clearly places the plaintiff in reasonable apprehension of receiving a battery. Thus, where the defendant went riding after a person with an uplifted whip so as to compel him to run into his garden for shelter to avoid being beaten, this was adjudged to be an assault.[169] If words are not necessary for an assault can words alone without any act or gesture be sufficient to constitute an assault? In *Mead's and Belt's Case* in 1823, Holroyd J. in his direction to the jury said that 'no words or singing are equivalent to an assault'[170] but in *Barton* v. *Armstrong*[171] Taylor J., in the Supreme Court of New South Wales, held that threats made over the telephone were capable in law of constituting an assault. He accepted, however, that it was 'clear from the many authorities cited on this subject that mere words themselves are not sufficient to constitute an assault' but he felt that it would be open to a jury to take the view that there was more involved in the threats made over the telephone than mere words. As he said:

> I am not persuaded that threats uttered over the telephone are to be properly categorized as mere words. I think it is a matter of the circumstances. To telephone a person in the early hours of the morning, not once but on many occasions, and to threaten him, not in a conversational tone but in an atmosphere of drama and suspense, is a matter that a jury could say was well calculated to not only instil fear into his mind but to constitute threatening acts, as distinct from mere words . . .[172]

One of the difficulties with threatening words (whether they be words uttered *inter praesentes* or over the telephone) is that they might threaten an indirect act. For example, D might say to P, 'I shall tell TP [a third party] that you have seduced his daughter and he will then surely beat you up', or D might telephone P and say, 'I have set up a trap for you and as soon as you leave the room you will set off my carefully set spring gun'. Now both these examples are, in a sense, offers of bodily contact, imminent bodily contact if you like, but they are offers of *indirect* bodily contact and could only come within the description of assault if the threatening words themselves or the threatening telephone call itself were regarded as the *direct threat* necessary for the tort of assault. To treat the threatening message as the direct threat, however, involves an illogicality, for one would have to say that to set a spring gun which injures the plaintiff is

---

169 *Mortin* v. *Shoppee* (1828) 3 C. & P. 373 *per* Lord Tenterden C.J. See also *Vaughn* v. *Baxter* (1971) 488 P. 2d 1234 (chase with automobile). See also *Tuberville* v. *Savage* (1669) 1 Mod.Rep. 3: 'So if he hold up his hand against another in a threatening manner and say nothing, it is an assault'.

170 (1823) 1 Lew. 184, 185.

171 [1969] 2 N.S.W.R. 451.

172 ibid., 455.

not a trespass (battery) because the act is indirect as the contact has been held to be indirect or consequential (see *Bird* v. *Holbrook*[173]) but to *tell* the plaintiff that one has set up a spring gun would be trespass (assault) because the threatening speech (message) has been conveyed directly to the plaintiff. And what if the threat is conveyed by a recorded message or by a note left for the plaintiff? Obviously, the requirement of a *direct* threat causes serious problems and it would be preferable if directness was no longer required by the courts in actions of trespass.

Until that traditional requirement of the common law disappears, however, it is submitted that the only threats which can be classified as *direct threats* for the purposes of the tort of assault are, first, those threats which by some act alone or by some act coupled by words place the plaintiff in reasonable apprehension of an imminent and direct bodily contact,[174] and secondly, those threats by words alone which lead the plaintiff reasonably to apprehend an imminent and direct contact to his person by the defendant or by some person or thing within the defendant's control. For example, a telephone call by the defendant telling the plaintiff that he is telephoning from just outside his office and that as soon as he puts the telephone down (imminent) he will come around and shoot him (direct bodily contact) would be an assault. So would a statement, 'You're next', by the defendant, who proceeds immediately to beat up a father in the presence of his daughter.[175] Though the only threat to the daughter is by words, it would be sufficient to constitute an assault as the threat raises in the mind of the plaintiff daughter a reasonable apprehension of imminent bodily contact.[176] But if a defendant in a telephone call threatens a contact which is not imminent (e.g. the defendant telephones and threatens to beat up the plaintiff some time next year) then it will not be an assault. If the threatening words threaten an *indirect* contact (e.g. when the defendant telephones the plaintiff and says that he has set up a spring gun which the plaintiff is bound to set off if he moves from the room) then it will not be an assault because, being a trespass, assault requires a direct threat which means a threat of imminent and direct bodily contact.

When considering the nature of threats which constitute an assault, the distinction today, it is submitted, depends not so much upon the difference between threats by positive acts and threats by words but on whether the threat conveys the apprehension of an imminent and direct bodily contact. If the threat does convey the apprehension of an imminent and direct

---

173 (1828) 4 Bing. 628.

174 The same direct bodily contact required for the tort of battery.

175 See e.g. *Purdy* v. *Woznesensky* [1937] 2 W.W.R. 116. See also Glanville Williams [1957] *Crim.L.R.* 219 and P.R. Handford (1976) 54 *Can.B.R.* 563.

176 Even if the imminent bodily contact was to be effected by the defendant's burly servant acting under his orders or by a dog acting under the defendant's control, that would not make the direct threat in any way indirect.

bodily contact then it is an assault whether the threat is by deed, by deed and words, or by words alone.[177]

Sometimes words have the effect of unmaking or neutralizing a threat made by a positive act. In *Tuberville* v. *Savage*, T, after an exchange of words with S, put his hand upon his sword and said, 'If it were not assize-time, I would not take such language from you'.[178] These words were held to prevent what would otherwise be an assault (putting his hand upon his sword) from coming into being. The court took the view that T was in effect saying that he would not assault S as the judges were in town.[179]

Statements like the one in *Tuberville* v. *Savage* must, however, be distinguished from what are called *conditional* threats. If D gets a gun and says to P, 'I'll shoot you if you turn off the water' or 'if you cut off the electricity' then there is clearly an assault if P has authority to turn off the water or cut off the electricity. The fact that D makes it clear to P that no bodily contact will ensue if he obeys his instructions and does what he requires him to do will not prevent it from being an assault for it is no different from the threat of the highwayman, 'Your money or your life' which both Taylor J. in *Barton* v. *Armstrong*[180] and North P. in *Police* v. *Greaves*[181] thought would clearly be an assault. To threaten to shoot a trespasser or a burglar who refuses to leave your property would not, it is submitted, be an assault. They are examples of what might be described as lawful threats of force. But a threat of force made by a defendant in response to an original threat of force by the plaintiff, even though it may be classed as a conditional threat, will be actionable as an assault if it exceeds what is reasonably necessary to defend oneself against the original threat.[182]

It should be added that for a direct threat there must be a positive offer of imminent bodily contact whether by deed or word. No amount of preparation for an imminent bodily contact, such as purchasing a gun, sharpening a knife, hiring a thug etc., will constitute an assault unless the defendant follows it up by an offer of imminent bodily contact and makes

---

177 'In the age in which we live threats may be made and communicated by persons remote from the person threatened. Physical violence and death can be produced by acts done at a distance by people who are out of sight and by agents hired for that purpose. I do not think that these, if they result in apprehension of physical violence in the mind of a reasonable person, are outside the protection afforded by the civil and criminal law as to assault' (*per* Taylor J. in *Barton* v. *Armstrong* [1969] 2 N.S.W.R. 451, 455). In appropriate cases, the Supreme Court has jurisdiction to grant injunctions to restrain apprehended or threatened assaults. See *Corvisy & Another* v. *Corvisy* [1982] 2 N.S.W.L.R. 557.

178 (1669) 1 Mod.Rep. 3.

179 In fact, T was the plaintiff because S on hearing T's remarks actually drew his sword and poked T in the eye. The success of T's action in battery depended on whether T was guilty of assault. *Weir* (4th edn, 1976, p. 260) points out that 'in these cases one justifies self-defence by calling the other party a wrongdoer'.

180 [1969] 2 N.S.W.R. 451.

181 [1964] N.Z.L.R. 295.

182 See *Rozsa* v. *Samuels* [1969] S.A.S.R. 205.

an attempt towards a battery or exhibits an intention to assault, as in *Read* v. *Coker*.[183]

It should be added that in Australia (unlike the situation in England) there is no onus upon a plaintiff to establish that the defendant *intentionally* made a direct threat which placed the plaintiff in reasonable apprehension of an imminent bodily contact. Once the plaintiff proves a direct threat proceeding from the defendant the burden is on the defendant to show that he did not intend to threaten imminent bodily contact or that he did not intend to create a reasonable apprehension in the plaintiff of an imminent bodily contact. The decision of the Full Court of the Supreme Court of Western Australia in *Hall* v. *Fonceca* confirms the necessity of an intention on the part of a defendant to create a reasonable apprehension of imminent bodily contact in the plaintiff by use of a direct threat, but the decision says nothing about the burden of proof of intention in actions for intentional assaults.[184]

(b) Reasonable apprehension The word 'apprehension' has two meanings, anticipate with fear and knowledge, and both of them are relevant to the tort of assault. When we say that the plaintiff must be placed in reasonable apprehension of an imminent contact with his person it is not necessary (though it usually is the case) that he must anticipate with fear or be frightened by the possible contact, it is sufficient if he just knows and expects that it is about to take place. As Chubb J. said in *Brady* v. *Schatzel*:

> In my opinion, it is not material that the person assaulted should be put in fear . . . if that were so, it would make an assault not dependent on the intention of the assailant, but upon the question whether the party assaulted was a courageous or timid person.[185]

It should be noticed that because fear of imminent bodily contact is not necessary for the tort of assault, the tort also protects individuals from those threats which are more in the nature of insulting interferences or even annoyances. The various criminal injuries compensation schemes compensate persons only for those intentional assaults which are serious and cause fear and shock, but the tort of assault can perform an additional different role.

The apprehension of imminent contact must be *reasonable*. If it is quite clear that the person making the threat has the present actual ability to carry out that threat then the apprehension is reasonable, but if D who is in a train moving out of the station shakes his fist in a threatening manner at P who is standing on the platform there will be no assault as there is no actual ability to carry out the threat. If the defendant has a present actual ability to carry out the threat but is prevented from carrying

183 (1853) 13 C.B. 850.
184 [1983] W.A.R. 309. Note, however, that this was a case of civil assault where the Criminal Code defence of self-defence was relied upon.
185 [1911] St.R.Qd. 206, 208 (a case of criminal assault).

it out by a third party it would still be an assault, as in *Stephens* v. *Myers*.[186] If the defendant exaggerates his present actual ability he alone is to blame if it raises in the mind of a plaintiff a reasonable apprehension of imminent contact. Thus if D points a gun at P and says that it is loaded when it is not or points a toy replica of a gun at P which P does not recognize to be a toy replica it will be an assault in both cases[187] if P does not know or has no reason to believe that the gun is not loaded or that it is a toy replica. It seems, therefore, that apart from present actual ability even apparent present ability to carry out the threat will suffice. So, if on a lonely street, X walks towards Y with his hand in his pocket and a protruding bulge aimed in Y's direction, it is submitted that Y would be entitled to commit a battery on X on the ground that he thinks that X is pointing a gun at him.[188] It must be acknowledged, however, that to accept apparent ability as sufficient to raise a reasonable apprehension of contact transfers the relevant inquiry from the actual conduct of the defendant to the mental state of the plaintiff or victim and that this is done in respect of an intentional tort, which is supposed to be concerned with the conduct of the defendant.

We have said that for assault the contact apprehended must be imminent. How immediate in time must that be? Taylor J. offered an answer to this question in *Barton* v. *Armstrong*:

> In my opinion the answer is it depends on the circumstances. Some threats are not capable of arousing apprehension of violence in the mind of a reasonable person unless there is an immediate prospect of the threat being carried out. Others, I believe, can create the apprehension even if it is made clear that the violence may occur in the future, at times unspecified and uncertain. Being able to immediately carry out the threat is but one way of creating the fear of apprehension, but not the only way. There are other ways, more subtle and perhaps more effective.[189]

This seems to leave the question of time rather open, and the most that can be said is that it may still be reasonable to apprehend a bodily contact even though it is not to take place at once. This is particularly so if the defendant is in a position of dominance over the plaintiff at the time when the threat of future harm is made. In *Zanker* v. *Vartzokas*[190] (a case of criminal assault) White J. of the Supreme Court of South Australia held in a situation where the defendant was in a position of dominance (as a driver of a moving car in which he was falsely imprisoning the plaintiff) that a threat by the defendant that when they arrived at his 'mate's house.

---

186 (1830) 4 C. & P. 350.

187 See *R.* v. *St George* (1840) 9 C. & P. 483. *Street* (6th edn, 1976, p. 22) says that the ratio of this criminal case is that to point an unloaded gun at the plaintiff is an assault. In 1977, in Melbourne, a 19-year-old youth was convicted of assault when he aimed an imitation .38 snub-nosed revolver out of a car window at a police officer. See the *Age*, 22 March 1977. See also *Lowry* v. *Standard Oil Co.* (1944) 146 P. 2d 57, 60, and *State* v. *Machmuller* (1976) 246 N.W. 2d 69.

188 See *Anthony* v. *U.S.* (1976) 361 A. 2d 202. See now, *Hall* v. *Fonceca* [1983] W.A.R. 309, 314.

189 [1969] 2 N.S.W.R. 451, 455.

190 (1988) 34 A. Crim. R. 11.

He will really fix you up' was sufficient to constitute an assault even though the threat of violence was to be carried out in the future.

(c) **Knowledge of the threat** In an action for an assault the plaintiff must have knowledge of the threat at the time it is made, unlike battery where a plaintiff can bring an action in respect of a contact even though he was unaware of the contact at the time it was made.[191] As you cannot fear an imminent bodily contact unless you know about it, the plaintiff's knowledge of the threat is essential for the tort of assault. Subsequent knowledge of the threat will not avail a plaintiff because then there would not be an apprehension of imminent contact. So if D walks behind P with an uplifted stick to beat him but before P sees him D changes his mind and walks away there will be no assault even if a third party sees the whole incident and accurately informs P of what has happened. If D shoots at a wax image of P[192] or strikes at a dummy placed in the bed by P who anticipates an attack by D, it is suggested that there would be no assault as P knows there is no possibility of an imminent bodily contact and therefore cannot fear one. There might be a statutory offence of some kind (e.g. discharging a firearm with intent to endanger life) but there would be no tort of trespass to the person.

The knowledge of the plaintiff is also relevant to the question of actual and apparent ability to carry out the threat. In *Logdon* v. *D.P.P.*[193] (a criminal case) the defendant was convicted of assault because while holding a tax inspector hostage he opened the drawer and showed her a pistol. When she asked if the pistol was loaded the defendant answered in the affirmative. Not only was the pistol not loaded but it was a toy replica of a pistol. Dismissing the defendant's appeal against the conviction for assault the court held that the offence was committed when by some physical act the threatener intentionally or recklessly caused the other to believe that unlawful force was about to be inflicted on her. It was the knowledge of the inspector that mattered, not the knowledge of the defendant. If the inspector had known that the gun was not loaded or had recognized it as a toy replica, there would be no assault. Certainly this would be the position in tort. This leads us to consider the question of the knowledge of the defendant.

In *MacPherson* v. *Brown*[194] a university lecturer while in the university grounds was surrounded by a group of student demonstrators, including the defendant, who for some time prevented the lecturer from passing and caused him to be in fear of physical danger from the group, even though no actual physical contact was made. The Full Court of the Supreme Court of South Australia decided that the lecturer had not been assaulted by the defendant. The defendant had been convicted of assault by a magistrate who had taken the view that if a defendant indulges in conduct

---

191 See the examples at p. 40 above.

192 In *The Empty Room*, Sherlock Holmes' enemy, Colonel Maron, was induced to fire at a wax image of the detective silhouetted in the window.

193 [1976] Crim.L.R. 121.

194 (1975) 12 S.A.S.R. 184.

which he knows or ought to know may harm or give cause for belief of imminent harm he is deemed to have the necessary intention for assault. But the Full Court felt that 'actual knowledge is necessary' on the part of the defendant to constitute the offence.[195] There is of course no authority in tort. Smith and Hogan[196] indicate that the factual situation in *MacPherson* v. *Brown* would probably warrant a civil action in negligent assault but it is arguable that it is an intentional assault if it is reckless.[197]

Suppose D rushes into a crowded lecture theatre brandishing a gun and shouting 'I have come to kill Dick Lee'. If there are two students called Dick Lee would both have an action in assault against D if they reasonably apprehend contact with their person?[198] If the answer to that question is in the affirmative then a defendant may be liable in assault even in the absence of knowledge of the plaintiff and, at least in relation to one of them, even though he did not intend to threaten him. If, as in battery,[199] we can say that a man must be regarded as *intending* his reckless acts then it is certainly arguable that the courts should impose liability in the case of reckless assaults, treating them as intentional assaults. So both Dick Lees would be able to recover in assault. Again, if when D's progress is blocked by a group of demonstrators, he reverses his car and then at full speed drives into the group, would not D be liable in assault to any one of the group who apprehended imminent bodily contact? Or must D know about the existence and identity of each member of the group before they can bring an action for assault? It is suggested that at least in relation to reckless (intentional) assaults, the knowledge by the defendant of the existence of the plaintiff is not a necessary requirement.

3. FALSE IMPRISONMENT

> A false imprisonment is a wrongful total restraint on the liberty of the plaintiff which is directly brought about by the defendant. This action is usually brought for an intentional restriction on the freedom of movement of the plaintiff though actions for reckless and negligent false imprisonments are not precluded.

There are several matters that require comment and elucidation. First, what is meant by a total restraint? Secondly, must the total restraint required for false imprisonment be brought about by an act or by an act coupled with words or can it be brought about by words only? Thirdly, must the act (or words) and intention of the defendant coincide in an

---

195 In *MacPherson* v. *Beath* (1975) 12 S.A.S.R. 174 it was held that the conviction for assault was justified because the defendant was a *knowing* party to the physical and mental pressure which was brought on the university lecturer.

196 See *Criminal Law* (3rd edn, 1973) 284.

197 See pp. 33-6 above. See also *Hall* v. *Fonceca* [1983] W.A.R. 309, 313.

198 See *Lee* v. *Wilson* (1934) 51 C.L.R. 276 (a case in defamation) where a defamatory statement about one 'Detective Lee' enabled another to sue in relation to the defamatory statement.

199 See pp. 33-6 above.

action for false imprisonment? Fourthly, we shall consider the question of knowledge of the confinement or restraint.

(a) Total restraint If an action in false imprisonment is to succeed there must be a wrongful total restraint. The word 'wrongful' here simply means without lawful justification. Thus a person who is totally deprived of his liberty by a lawful order of a court sentencing him to a term of imprisonment or a person detained in a mental hospital under the properly invoked provisions of a Mental Health Act cannot complain of a false (wrongful) imprisonment. But what does total restraint mean?

In *Bird* v. *Jones*, a majority of the court drew a distinction between a total restraint of the liberty of a person and a partial obstruction of his will. The plaintiff was prevented by the defendant from using part of a bridge which was normally used as a footway because the defendant had put some seats there to view a regatta on the river. The plaintiff was told he could use the other part of the bridge but he declined and when he endeavoured to force his way through and assaulted the defendant he was taken into custody by policemen who were stationed there to prevent the plaintiff from using that part of the bridge.[200] The court held that the plaintiff had not been wrongfully imprisoned. It was true that his passage was obstructed in one direction but he was at liberty to stay where he was or to go in any other direction he pleased. That could not be described as total restraint which was necessary for false imprisonment.

If liberty to go in one direction rather than another implies lack of total restraint, can a person who is locked in a room be said to be totally restrained if there is a means of escape? The answer to that question seems to be, only if the means of escape is a reasonable one. In *R.* v. *Macquarie*, Hargraves J. expressed the opinion that where a person is set afloat alone in a vessel that he does not know how to control, and his only way of escape is by jumping into the water, he is clearly imprisoned because the means of escape is not a reasonable one.[201] And in *Burton* v. *Davies*, Townley J. said:

> If I lock a person in a room with a window from which he may jump to the ground at the risk of life and limb, I cannot be heard to say that he was not imprisoned because he was free to leap from the window.[202]

Again the emphasis is on a reasonable means of escape. If the plaintiff does not know about the existence of a way of escape and it is not apparent, then it will clearly not be regarded as a reasonable means of

200 (1845) 7 Q.B. 742.
201 (1875) 13 S.C.R.(N.S.W.) 264.
202 [1953] Q.S.R. 26.

escape, e.g. a trap-door which leads to the outside which is hidden under a carpet.[203]

In *R.* v. *Macquarie*, Sir James Martin C.J. felt that 'to constitute an imprisonment there must be an actual detention of the person in some place'.[204] The prison must have its limits, he suggested. Nowadays, the emphasis is slightly different and instead of concentrating on whether there is an actual detention in some place the question which is more often asked is whether the plaintiff 'submitted himself to the defendant's power, reasonably thinking that he had no way of escape which could reasonably be taken by him'. That is considered to be total restraint even though the plaintiff cannot be shown to be in 'actual detention' in 'some place' and even though it might not be apparent to others that the plaintiff is being falsely imprisoned. This point is well illustrated by the decision in *Symes* v. *Mahon*:

The defendant police officer thought that a warrant had been issued in Adelaide for the arrest of the plaintiff. He visited the plaintiff and despite the plaintiff's denial that he was the wanted man, the defendant required him to come to Adelaide the next day. The following morning they met at the station and travelled to Adelaide in different compartments. On arrival at Adelaide, although a police vehicle was waiting for them at the station they decided to walk. On the way to the police station the plaintiff checked into the Grosvenor Hotel where he left his luggage and the plaintiff and defendant then took a tramcar to the police station. At the police station the mistake was discovered, the defendant said 'I am very sorry, but don't forget I told you all along you were not under arrest'. The plaintiff replied 'Yes, you told me when I was getting on the electric car that I was not under arrest'.[205]

The plaintiff was held to be falsely imprisoned by the defendant (despite their peregrinations) from the time he met him at the station to catch the train to Adelaide because it could properly be inferred that from that time he submitted himself to the defendant's power. There was a total restraint without any reference to a place of detention.[206]

Can a person who goes into a particular place (e.g. a room that he knows is going to be locked, a ship, an aeroplane, a coal mine, etc.) of his own free will ever complain of false imprisonment, a total restraint of his liberty? The question was raised in *R.* v. *Macquarie* by counsel for the

---

203 See *Talcott* v. *National Exhibition Co.* (1911) 128 N.Y.S. 1059. The plaintiff, who went into an enclosure of a football ground to buy some tickets and was unable to get out of the ground because of the huge crowd (even though he could not get tickets for the game), was held to be falsely imprisoned. The court felt that the defendants should have helped him to get out of the ground: '. . . defendant owed him an active duty to point out the other existing methods of egress. It could not stand idly by, and simply detain and imprison the plaintiff against his will . . .'.

204 (1875) 13 S.C.R.(N.S.W.) 264, 273.

205 [1922] S.A.S.R. 447.

206 In *Louis* v. *Commonwealth of Australia* (1987) 87 F.L.R. 277 it was held that the plaintiffs who were forcibly carried from Hong Kong to Australia were falsely imprisoned on board the aircraft but not falsely imprisoned in Australia as they were at perfect liberty to move around Australia even though financial constraints might have prevented them from leaving Australia.

defendant as the man allegedly falsely imprisoned had gone on to the launch of his own free will. Faucett J.'s reply to the question was:

> So long as he was able to exercise that will, there would be no imprisonment, but the moment that will was interfered with, or any restraint placed upon him, an imprisonment commenced.[207]

But can that *dictum* be taken literally? Every year on Budget Day, financial journalists are locked up in a room in Canberra and given an advance copy of the Budget so that they might be ready with their analysis as soon as the Treasurer has delivered his Budget Speech. Can a journalist ask to be released as soon as he has finished reading his advance copy? Can a hitchhiker insist on being dropped off on a freeway or can a passenger on a direct flight from Melbourne to Perth demand to be let out at Adelaide as the aircraft is flying over that city? If there is a reasonable and pressing necessity, for example, if the passenger suffers a heart attack, and his demand for release can reasonably be met, then it must be immediately acceded to.[208] But what if there is nothing that can be described as a reasonable and pressing necessity? Take the case of *Herd* v. *Weardale*:

> The plaintiff, who was a miner, descended the mine shaft for the purpose of working a shift. A dispute having arisen, the plaintiff refused to undertake the task assigned to him and claimed the right to be hauled to the surface before the normal time. His involuntary detention at the bottom of the mine shaft for several hours was however held not to constitute false imprisonment.[209]

Street regards *Herd* v. *Weardale* as a case of a pure omission. While the example he gives—'if A falls down the mine of B while trespassing it is not false imprisonment should B refuse to bring him to the surface in his lift'[210]—might be a case of pure omission, it is suggested that *Herd* v. *Weardale* is in a different category. For example, would the pilot of an aircraft be able to claim that it is a mere omission not to open the door of an aircraft after it has landed[211] and would it be a pure omission for a ship's captain not to put down the gangway after the ship has berthed?[212] Surely not. The reason for that is that as soon as the defendant enters into

---

207 (1875) 13 S.C.R.(N.S.W.) 264, 277.

208 There is support for this view in Lord Moulton's speech in *Herd* v. *Weardale Steel, Coal and Coke Co.* [1915] A.C. 67 where he suggests that it would be acceded to because of 'the generous loving kindness of mankind'.

209 [1915] A.C. 67.

210 *Street* (7th edn, 1983) p. 25.

211 The captain of a TAA jet refused to land at Launceston Airport on 23 March 1978 after an incident when a beer can was thrown in the main passenger cabin. The captain radioed Launceston Airport, asking police to come to the airport, then refused to land until he saw the flashing light of the police vehicle waiting. What if he landed and refused to open the doors? See the *Australian*, 25 March 1978. See also s.25(2), Crimes (Aircraft) Act 1963 (Cwth).

212 Glanville Williams writes that Dr Johnson is credited with the remark that being in a ship is being in jail, with the chance of being drowned. See Glanville Williams, 'Two Cases on False Imprisonment' in *Law, Justice and Equity* (eds R.H.C. Holland & G. Schwarzenberger) (London, 1967).

a contractual relationship[213] with a plaintiff which either requires or results in his total confinement of the plaintiff at any time during the period of the contractual relationship then the defendant is under an obligation to secure his release from that confinement at the end of the contractual period[214] or even sooner if he knows that the plaintiff desires release from the confinement and it does not involve the defendant in significant inconvenience, substantial expense or grave risk. Not to accede to that request except in the circumstances indicated would result in the plaintiff's total restraint being regarded as wrongful and would subject the defendant to an action in false imprisonment. Under this approach, the defendants in *Herd* v. *Weardale*[215] would be liable for a false imprisonment. So would the defendants in *Robinson* v. *The Balmain New Ferry Co. Ltd*,[216] because to accede to the plaintiff's request for release from the confinement[217] would not have involved the defendants in any significant inconvenience, substantial expense or grave risk. *Herd* v. *Weardale* and *Robinson* v. *The Balmain New Ferry Co. Ltd* are decisions of the House of Lords and Privy Council respectively and are therefore entitled to some respect. It is suggested, however, that those decisions were given in an age when the sanctity of contract was thought to prevail over principles of liberty and freedom. It would be difficult today to support a decision that a contractual consent to deprivation of liberty, once given, cannot be revoked (*Herd* v. *Weardale*) or to find support for a decision that a creditor can deprive a debtor of his liberty in order to compel him to pay his debt (*Robinson* v. *The Balmain New Ferry Co. Ltd*)[218] 'even where the purpose of the detention is the reasonable one of ascertaining the debtor's name and address'.[219] The more recent Canadian decision in *Bahner* v. *Marwest Hotel Co.*[220] lends support to the view that the courts today will not tolerate an imprisonment by a creditor for failure to pay a debt (in this case the cost of a bottle of wine) even where the plaintiff is wrong in

---

213 Or a relationship akin to contract as in the case of the journalists and the Budget Speech.

214 i.e. end of flight, end of voyage, end of shift in mine etc.

215 [1915] A.C. 67.

216 [1910] A.C. 295. See also the High Court decision in the same case, *The Balmain New Ferry Co. Ltd* v. *Robertson* [1906] 4 C.L.R. 379. (The Privy Council mistakenly called Robertson Robinson, which accounts for the two spellings of his name.) Also the amusing account of the case in George Blaikie, *Scandals of Australia's Strange Past*, 62-7 ('The Expensive Penny').

217 It is not known when the next ferry would depart. Certainly Robertson was not keen to catch it. It is accepted that to jump into the sea and swim to another point is not a reasonable means of escape. It is arguable that Robertson was confined. See K.F. Tan (1981) 44 *M.L.R.* 166.

218 Glanville Williams (see fn. 212 above) argues that this was not the ratio of Robinson's case and that 'the reason, or an important reason, why Robinson failed in his claim for damages was that the contractual path of escape was never closed to him'. He also pointed out that it was held as early as 1838 in *Sunbolf* v. *Alford* (1838) 3 M. & W. 248 that an innkeeper had no right to imprison his guest until the latter had paid his bill.

219 Glanville Williams (see fn. 212 above) p. 55. In *Jacques* v. *Childs Dining Hall Co.* (1923) 138 N.E. 843 it was held that the defendant 'undoubtedly had the right, if apparently she had not paid, to detain her [the plaintiff] for a *reasonable* time to investigate the circumstances'.

220 [1970] 6 D.L.R. (3d) 322; affirmed [1970] 12 D.L.R. (3d) 646.

thinking that the sum is not owed. The plaintiff succeeded in false imprisonment.

A voluntary accompanying or stay will not be regarded as a total restraint. Thus if D suspects P of shoplifting and asks him to accompany him to the store manager's office and to stay there while he investigates the situation, P will not be falsely imprisoned if he goes voluntarily to clear his name.[221] But if P is *charged* by D with shoplifting and he goes voluntarily into the store manager's office in order to prevent force being used on him or in order to avoid creating an embarrassing scene in a crowded store, there will be a false imprisonment. As Alderson B. said in *Peters* v. *Stanway*:

> There is a great difference between the case of a person who volunteers to go in the first instance, and that of a person who, having a charge made against him, goes voluntarily to meet it. The question therefore is, whether you think the going to the station-house proceeded originally from the plaintiff's own willingness, or from the defendant's making a charge against her; for if it proceeded from the defendant's making a charge, the plaintiff will not be deprived of her right of action by her having willingly gone to meet the charge.[222]

And it will certainly be a false imprisonment if D at any time indicates that if P does not comply with his request, force will be brought to bear upon P to secure compliance with D's request.[223] That will be a sufficient total restraint for the tort of false imprisonment. This is well illustrated by the recent decision of the Supreme Court of Victoria in *Myer Stores Ltd* v. *Soo*.[224]

The plaintiff while in the defendant's store was told by the store's detective and two police officers that he matched the description of a shoplifter recorded a few days earlier on a television monitoring device within the store. They requested the plaintiff to accompany them to the security office 'to sort the matter out'. The plaintiff's request to be interviewed where he stood was denied and the plaintiff was then escorted to the security office where he was interviewed for an hour before being allowed to leave. A week later, after a fruitless search of the plaintiff's dwelling for the stolen goods (conducted under a search warrant) by another two police officers, the plaintiff was asked by those officers to come to a police station for the purpose of being further interviewed. The plaintiff went to the police station a couple of days later and at the conclusion of the interview the plaintiff was told that he was completely exonerated. The Supreme Court of Victoria (Appeal Division) agreed with the trial judge that the plaintiff had been falsely imprisoned from the moment he was actively escorted to the store's security office to the time when the interview ended because during that period the plaintiff was

---

221 See *Fogg* v. *McKnight* [1968] N.Z.L.R. 330. But it must be truly voluntary. See *Myers Stores Ltd & Ors* v. *Soo* (1991) Aust. Torts Reports 81-077.

222 (1835) 172 6 Car. & P. 737, 739-40. See also *Sinclair* v. *Woodwards Store Ltd* [1942] 2 D.L.R. 395 and *Conn* v. *David Spencer Ltd* [1930] 1 D.L.R. 805.

223 *Symes* v. *Mahon* [1922] S.A.S.R. 447.

224 (1991) Aust. Torts Reports 81-077.

justified in concluding that 'if he did not submit to do what was asked of him, he would have been compelled by force to do so'.[225] Therefore a restraint was imposed upon the plaintiff which amounted to an 'imprisonment' of him by the defendant. But the court also upheld the decision of the trial judge that the plaintiff was not unlawfully detained or imprisoned at any time while he was at the police station; no doubt because it was felt, on the facts, that the plaintiff had voluntarily gone to the police station to clear his name.

What if the compliance with the defendant's will or wish is brought about by a threat of force to another or by an even more subtle form of pressure? For example, D tells P that if he leaves the room within the next three hours he will beat up P's girlfriend or mother. P stays. Is that false imprisonment? Or if D tells P that if he leaves the room within the next three hours he will tell P's employer that P was convicted of a serious criminal offence several years ago or that P was a member of the Communist Party? P stays because he knows that he will surely be dismissed by his employer if he gets the information which D has threatened to convey to him. Is that false imprisonment? Or if D (a store detective) takes away P's handbag for examination of its contents? Although P is at liberty to leave the store at any time, she is reluctant to do so without her handbag (and is afraid that something might be inserted in her handbag in her absence), so she stays in the store. The handbag is only returned to her an hour later. Is she falsely imprisoned for that hour? Unfortunately there are no English or Australian decisions to guide us but in *Ashland Dry Goods Co.* v. *Wages*,[226] on which our last example is based, the court came to the conclusion that the retention of the purse (handbag) constituted an unlawful detention of the plaintiff without her consent and against her will.

This type of imprisonment, described by Dunfield J. in *Chaytor* v. *London, N.Y. & Paris Association*[227] as a 'psychological type of imprisonment', can only be held to be false imprisonment if it can be said that the total restraint has been secured *directly*, for, as false imprisonment is a trespass to the person, directness is an essential ingredient of the tort. In principle, however, if the tort of false imprisonment is intended to protect our interest in personal liberty and freedom of movement there is no reason why the total restraint in the situations described above should not be regarded as false imprisonments and the tort extended to cover these situations.

There is a recent indication that Australian courts might be prepared to make that extension. In *R.* v. *Garrett* von Doussa J. of the Supreme Court of South Australia expressed the view that there was no arbitrary rule 'that the threat which causes the person to submit to confinement against his will must be a threat of physical force to his person. The will of a person

---

225 ibid., at p. 68, 623. See also *Watson* v. *Marshall and Cade* (1971) 124 C.L.R. 621, 626.
226 (1946) 195 S.W. 2d 312.
227 (1962) 30 D.L.R. (2d) 527.

may be at least as effectively overborne by threats of physical force to other people, or even by threats of damage to valuable personal property'.[228]

While this extension is to be applauded, an unsatisfactory recent development in the law of false imprisonment should not go unnoticed. In *Hague* v. *Deputy Governor of Parkhurst Prison*[229] and *Weldon* v. *Home Office*,[230] the House of Lords decided that prisoners lawfully committed to prison under the relevant legislation did not have a residual liberty, *vis-à-vis* the governor, which would entitle them to sue the Secretary of State or a governor of a prison if the prisoners were unlawfully confined in a strip cell or unlawfully segregated in the prison. Such an alteration of the conditions of detention, said Lord Jauncey, 'did not deprive them of any liberty which they had not already lost when initially confined'.[231] Lord Jauncey rejected Ackner L.J.'s view in *Middleweek* v. *Chief Constable of Merseyside Police*[232] that if the conditions of detention become intolerable a detention initially lawful could be rendered unlawful and thereby provide a remedy to a prisoner in damages for false imprisonment. As Lord Jauncey put it, 'an alteration of conditions deprives a person of no liberty because he has none already'.[233] The House of Lords appear to have read the words 'may be lawfully confined in any prison' in the Prisons Act 1952 to mean 'may be confined in any prison and that any way the confinement takes place will be lawful'. It would be wise for Australian courts to avoid such an interpretation in similar legislation concerning lawful confinement of prisoners.

(b) Acts and words In the most simple case of false imprisonment there will usually be an assault or battery or both, preliminary to the false imprisonment. For example, D will advance towards P in a threatening manner (assault), grab him and push him into a room (battery) and lock the door (false imprisonment). There is a direct, intentional act which brings about the total confinement of the plaintiff and for however short a time the restraint continues there is a false imprisonment. Of course, there can be a false imprisonment without an assault or a battery; for instance, when D slips a note under the door of P's study (which P immediately finds) informing P that D has just locked him in.

The locking of the door in both our examples above are acts which have brought about the confinement of the plaintiff *directly*. This is necessary for false imprisonment as this tort is one of trespass to the person and all actions in trespass require the element of directness. If D digs a deep pit into which he intends P to fall and P does so subsequently and is unable to get out for several hours or even days there would be no false imprisonment as the total confinement of P would have been brought about

228 (1988) 50 S.A.S.R. 392, 405.
229 [1991] 3 All E.R. 733.
230 [1991] 3 All E.R. 733.
231 ibid., 755.
232 See [1990] 3 W.L.R. 481, 487. Lord Ackner in *Hague's* case indicated that he regarded his own view in *Middleweek* as erroneous. See [1991] 3 All E.R. 733, 747.
233 See [1991] 3 All E.R. 733, 756.

indirectly.[234] The proper action on these facts would be an action on the case.[235]

Physical contact with the plaintiff is not necessary for false imprisonment, and indeed in the majority of cases in false imprisonment there is no physical contact between the defendant and the plaintiff.[236] But there is usually some intentional *act* which directly brings about the total restraint necessary for the tort. In the majority of cases, too, these acts are accompanied by words. But what if there are words only, that is to say, the total restraint of the plaintiff is brought about merely by words? Take the following situation:[237] D, a store detective, says to P, a 10-year-old boy whom he suspects of shoplifting, 'If you don't go to the manager's office and turn out your pockets, I will have a police officer down here in a minute and he will arrest you'. P goes to the office of the manager, who after about an hour tells P that he is satisfied that the goods in his pockets were purchased elsewhere. D makes no effort to accompany P to the manager's office nor does he do any act to indicate that he would bring physical force to bear upon P if he does not go to the manger's office, apart from the words above. Could P bring an action for false imprisonment? There is little doubt that even though there is no act, the words uttered by D would have been sufficient to make P believe that if he left the store without a visit to the manager's office there would be some physical restraint, albeit by a third party. Should that not be sufficient for the tort of false imprisonment?

There are two difficulties with words only and false imprisonment. First, unlike acts, words may convey a threat of future action which may not be sufficient to constitute a present total restraint. For example, D says to P, 'if you leave this room I shall beat you up in *two years*' time'. If P stays in the room for some time because of the threat of future action the court might well say that P's stay should not be regarded as a total restraint. There is no authority. The second difficulty with mere words is that they might bring about a total restraint of the plaintiff but by the threat of indirect or consequential harm. For example, D might telephone P and say, 'I have laid booby traps all around your house and if you attempt to leave it today, you will surely be blown to bits'. P stays. Is a total restraint brought about by the threat of consequential harm sufficient to constitute false imprisonment? Again, there is no authority. It is suggested, however, that just as in an assault by words only the threat must convey an apprehension of imminent and direct bodily contact[238] so, for false imprisonment by words only, the total restraint must be brought

234 See *Bird* v. *Holbrook* (1828) 4 Bing. 628.

235 See *De Freville* v. *Dill* (1927) 96 L.J.K.B. 1056 where McCardie J. said that an action against a doctor for negligence in certification which resulted in the plaintiff being confined for one night involuntarily in a mental hospital should be regarded as an action on the case for damages.

236 See *Myer Stores Ltd* v. *Soo* (1991) Aust. Torts Reports 81-077 'Actual physical force does not have to be proved' *per* O'Bryan J.

237 The situation is based upon *Sweeney* v. *F.W. Woolworth Co.* (1924) 142 N.E. 50.

238 See pp. 44-6 above.

about by the threat of the use of imminent and direct force by the defendant to the plaintiff.

A false imprisonment, therefore, can be brought about not only by acts but also by words unaccompanied by acts, provided that the total restraint is procured by the threat of the use of imminent and direct force to get the plaintiff to submit himself to the defendant's power.

(c) **Coincidence of act and intention** Must the act[239] which brings about the total restraint of the liberty of the plaintiff coincide with the intention of the defendant to deprive the plaintiff of his liberty or can the act and intention occur at different times? Imagine the following situation: D invites P to dinner at his home. After dinner D takes P to his study. D suggests they lock the door to ensure their privacy. Later on in the evening they have a quarrel and when P expresses a desire to leave D refuses to unlock the door and says to P, 'You will have to stay here until you see sense'. P is detained for several hours against his wishes. Can P bring an action for false imprisonment? Certainly D has done all that is necessary for the tort of false imprisonment. He has done a direct act which results in the plaintiff's confinement (locking the door) and he has displayed an intention to detain the plaintiff. But the act and the intention did not coincide. Indeed, when D did the act, i.e. locking the door, he did not have any intention to confine the plaintiff. It was only done to ensure their privacy.

Should the fact that the act and intention do not coincide prevent D's behaviour from being regarded as false imprisonment? In *Mee* v. *Cruickshank*[240] a governor of a prison was held liable in false imprisonment when, due to the act of a warder, a prisoner was detained beyond the day when he should properly have been released. A similar situation arose recently in *Cowell* v. *Corrective Services Commission of New South Wales*[241] where a prisoner had been confined in prison for a period longer than the law provided because his entitlement to remissions had been miscalculated. The Court of Appeal of New South Wales (by a majority) held that the Corrective Services Commission had falsely imprisoned the prisoner from the date when he should have been released to the date when he actually was released. These two decisions illustrate the proposition that an imprisonment which begins lawfully can become a false imprisonment even though there is no further act on the part of the defendant. Besides, in *Fagan* v. *Metropolitan Police Commissioner*[242] where a motorist who accidentally drove his car on to a police constable's foot while parking his car ignored the plea of the constable to 'Get off my foot', it was held that it was not necessary that the *mens rea* be present at the inception of the *actus reus*.

It could be argued, therefore, that the *act* which brings about the total restraint of the plaintiff and the *intention* of the defendant to deprive him

---

239 Or words.
240 (1902) 86 L.T. 78.
241 (1988) 13 N.S.W.L.R. 714.
242 [1969] 1 Q.B. 439.

of his liberty need not coincide in an action for false imprisonment. If such an approach is accepted, we can look at *Herd* v. *Weardale* again.[243] The defendants certainly imprisoned the plaintiff by taking him down the mine shaft (a lawful act). If from the subsequent conduct of the defendants an 'intention' to deprive the plaintiff of his liberty can be gleaned, then, as the act and intention need not coincide, the defendant could be said to have falsely imprisoned the plaintiff in that case.

(d) Knowledge Must the plaintiff have knowledge of the confinement or the total restraint in order to bring an action in false imprisonment? The two cases usually contrasted when the question is discussed are *Herring* v. *Boyle*[244] and *Meering* v. *Graham-White Aviation Co.*[245] In *Herring* v. *Boyle,* the headmaster of a boarding school refused to let the mother of the plaintiff (child) take him home during the Christmas holidays unless she paid certain school fees which he alleged were owed to him. It was held that an action for false imprisonment could not be maintained against him on behalf of the child in the absence of proof that the child was against its will restrained from going with its mother, or at least that the refusal to surrender the child was made in its presence. In *Meering* v. *Graham-White Aviation Co.*, on the other hand, the plaintiff, at his employers' (the defendants) request, went to his employers' office because they said that they wanted him to give evidence in relation to certain thefts of the employers' property which had occurred. Unknown to the plaintiff, three detectives were stationed outside the room where he was being questioned, with instructions to stop him from leaving if he attempted to do so. It was held by a majority of the judges that the jury was right in finding that the plaintiff was falsely imprisoned by the defendants in their office. Atkin L.J. in dealing with the question of knowledge of the confinement said: 'It is perfectly possible for a person to be imprisoned in law without his knowing the fact and appreciating that he is imprisoned . . .'[246] And in a later passage:

> It appears to me that a person could be imprisoned without his knowing it. I think a person can be imprisoned while he is asleep, while he is in a state of drunkenness, while he is unconscious, and while he is a lunatic . . . the person might properly complain if he were imprisoned, though the imprisonment began and ceased while he was in that state. Of course, the damages might be diminished and would be affected by the question whether he was conscious of it or not . . . So a man might in fact . . . be imprisoned by having the key of a door turned against him so that he is imprisoned in a room in fact although he does not know that the key has been turned.[247]

---

243 [1915] A.C. 67.
244 (1834) 1 C.M. & R. 377.
245 (1919) 122 L.T. 44.
246 ibid., 53.
247 ibid., 53-4.

It has been very persuasively argued that the views of Atkin L.J. in *Meering's* case should be the law.[248] One example from that argument will suffice:

> Suppose A abducts B, a wealthy lunatic, and holds him for ransom for a week. B is unaware of his confinement, but vaguely understands that he is in unfamiliar surroundings, and that something is wrong. He undergoes mental suffering affecting his health. At the end of the week he is discovered by police and released without ever having known that he has been imprisoned. Has he no action against B?[249]

The rule in *Herring* v. *Boyle,* however, is preferred in America and 'to constitute false imprisonment under American law the one confined must be conscious of the confinement'.[250] However, in Australia, it would appear that the views expressed by Atkin L.J. in *Meering's* case on this question are preferred to the rule in *Herring* v. *Boyle.* As O'Bryan J. of the Supreme Court of Victoria said in *Myer Stores Ltd* v. *Soo,* 'it is not an essential element of the tort of false imprisonment that the victim should be aware of the fact of denial of liberty'.[251] Earlier, in *Murray* v. *Ministry of Defence*[252] the House of Lords had also espoused the same position. It is therefore safe to say that knowledge of the confinement will not be regarded in Australia or England as an essential element of false imprisonment.

Should the defendant know that he has confined the plaintiff before his acts will attract liability in false imprisonment? In most cases, the defendant will of course know of the presence of the plaintiff and that he is being detained but what if the defendant recklessly deprives a plaintiff of his liberty? In *MacPherson* v. *Brown,*[253] Zelling J. pointed out that nowadays it is possible quite easily to effect a false imprisonment by mechanical means:

> For example, one may arrange doors which open by means of sensors as a person approaches them, so that the sensors operate on one side only. Accordingly, when the victim goes through the door and essays to return, the doors stay closed. There is no doubt he is falsely imprisoned . . .[254]

If a defendant has an arrangement of the kind described by Zelling J. to imprison T and P innocently walks into the trap, it is submitted that both T and P will have an action in false imprisonment; T because he has been intentionally falsely imprisoned, and P because he has been recklessly falsely imprisoned. We have suggested earlier that recklessness can amount

---

248 W.L. Prosser (1955) 55 *Columbia L.R.* 847-50.
249 ibid., 849.
250 A.L. Goodhart (1935) 83 *U. Pa.L.R.* 411, 418. See also (Second) *Restatement,* Section 42.
251 (1991) Aust. Torts Reports 81-077 at p. 68, 634.
252 [1988] 2 All E.R. 521, 528, *per* Lord Griffiths.
253 (1975) 12 S.A.S.R. 184.
254 ibid., 209.

to intention in the law of torts.[255] The fact that D did not know that P would fall into the trap set for T or that D did not know about P's detention will not, it is suggested, prevent an action in false imprisonment from arising in those circumstances. If an action in intentional false imprisonment does not succeed, an action in negligent false imprisonment surely will. But that will be discussed later.

It should be noted that in *Cowell* v. *Corrective Services Commission of New South Wales*[256] the defendants were held liable in false imprisonment even though they did not realise, due to an error in calculating the remissions due to the plaintiff, that they were detaining the plaintiff beyond the period permitted by law. The lack of awareness that the detention was unlawful was considered irrelevant.[257]

III: THE ACTION ON THE CASE FOR DAMAGES FOR PHYSICAL INJURY

So far we have considered the tort of trespass which is reserved for acts which are both direct and intentional. But there are many situations where although the act of the defendant is intentional the contact with the plaintiff (which results in the physical harm) is caused indirectly or consequentially. Take the following example: P walks into and is injured by a trap set by D and which is activated by an act of P, such as stepping upon a doormat. In this case, although P has been injured by an intentional act of D (setting the trap) trespass would not be available as a remedy as the contact (injury) having been activated not by D's but by P's act would not be the direct but the consequential result of D's intentional act. In this sort of case, as trespass is not available, the injured plaintiff must rely upon another tort. Several other examples of factual situations where an action of trespass to the person would not be available even though there was an 'intention' to cause harm can be given.[258] Unknown to P, D puts some poison in a cup of tea which is about to be drunk by P and P then drinks it with consequential injury; D intentionally hides the key to P's medicine chest and P consequentially suffers severe physical distress as a result of a lack of medication; D deliberately digs a pit or deliberately leaves an object in the path of P, who is blind, so that P is injured by falling into the pit or by colliding with the object. Or D deliberately presses the bell of a bus just as P, an old lady, is about to get off, with the result that the bus starts to move causing P to fall on to the road.[259] In all these cases, it is suggested, trespass would not be available and the appropriate action would be an action on the case for damages for

---

255 See pp. 33-6 above.
256 (1988) 13 N.S.W.L.R. 714.
257 ibid., 743.
258 See *Street* (7th edn, 1983) pp. 22-3, and *Fleming* (7th edn, 1987) p. 37.
259 This example is from the English Criminal Injuries Compensation Board's 11th *Report*. The injury was held not to be compensable by the Board.

physical injury. The action should not be framed in the tort of negligence as that tort is totally inappropriate for situations involving conduct which is deliberate or intentional.

We do not here consider how the various gaps in the law of trespass were filled from the fourteenth century onwards by actions on the case—that particular shadowy development is best left to the writers of our legal history.[260] For our purposes, however, one thing is clear and that is that the courts were prepared to grant a remedy to a plaintiff in an action on the case for damages where it could be shown that the defendant albeit indirectly had done an intentional act for the express purpose of doing physical harm to the plaintiff and had in fact succeeded in causing physical injury to the plaintiff. The clearest evidence of this remedy which we call an action on the case for damages for physical injury is found in the decision of the Court of Common Pleas in *Bird* v. *Holbrook* in 1828.[261] The defendant who grew tulips and valuable flower-roots in a walled garden some distance from his dwelling-house was robbed of flowers and roots from his garden. With the assistance of another man he placed in his garden a spring gun which was set to go off if a person entered his summer-house or tulip beds. A peahen belonging to an occupier of a house in the neighbourhood escaped into the defendant's garden, and the plaintiff at the request of a female servant of the owner of the bird climbed over the walled fence and jumped into the garden to retrieve the bird. His foot came into contact with one of the wires attached to the gun and it discharged large swan shot into the body of the plaintiff causing him severe physical injury. The plaintiff brought an action against the defendant in respect of his injuries. The third count stated that the defendant 'contriving and intending to injure the plaintiff, wrongfully and injuriously permitted the gun to remain so loaded and set with a wire, by means of which it might be let off and discharged without any notice or warning'. The Court of Common Pleas held in favour of the plaintiff, Best C.J. saying that he was 'clearly of opinion that he who sets spring guns, without giving notice, is guilty of an inhuman act, and that, if injurious consequences ensue, he is liable to yield redress to the sufferer'.[262] But Best C.J. also pointed out quite clearly that the reason for the success of the plaintiff was not only because the defendant had committed an intentional act of setting up the spring gun but also because 'the defendant placed his spring gun for the express purpose of doing injury'.[263] As he said in a later passage: 'He intended therefore that the gun should be discharged and that the contents should be lodged in the body of his victim, for he could not be caught in any other way. On these principles the action is clearly maintainable and particularly on the latter ground'.

The decision in *Blyth* v. *Topham*[264] was referred to in argument. In that

260 See e.g. C.H.S. Fifoot, *History and Sources of the Common Law* (London, 1949) Ch. 4. See also S.F.C. Milsom, *Historical Foundations of the Common Law* (2nd edn, London, 1981) Ch. 11, especially pp. 300-13.

261 (1828) 4 Bing. 628.

262 ibid., 641.

263 ibid., 641-2.

264 (1607) 1 Rol.Abr. 88 Cro.Jac. 158.

case the plaintiff, an owner of a mare, brought an action against the defendant for digging a pit in a common, which his mare, having strayed, fell into and perished. As the pit was dug not for doing mischief but for the necessary cultivation and enjoyment of the defendant's property, the action on the case for damages was not successful. If the principle in *Blyth* v. *Topham* was carried over from the injury to animals situation to the physical injury to the person situation we could say that if D digs a pit intending P to fall into it then D would be liable in an action on the case for damages for physical injury, but if D digs a pit to plant a tree and P falls into it injuring himself then an action on the case for damages for physical injury would not be available.

Bird v. *Holbrook* and *Blyth* v. *Topham* would then seem to indicate that an action on the case for damages for physical injury is only available when in addition to doing an intentional act it can also be said of the defendant that the physical harm which resulted from the intentional act was also intended. As Best C.J. said in *Bird* v. *Holbrook*, the defendant must do the intentional act 'for the express purpose of doing injury'. This further distinguishes the action on the case for damages for physical injury from the action for trespass to the person. While both trespass and an action on the case for damages for physical injury are available for intentional acts, in an action for trespass (e.g. battery or assault) what is required is an intentional act (contact or threat) not an intention to do harm, but in an action on the case for damages for physical injury, in addition to an intentional act there must also be an 'intention' to inflict physical harm. Intention here not only means that the defendant meant to do it, it could also mean that the defendant knew that the physical injury was certain or substantially certain to follow from his conduct.[265] Not only must there be an intention to inflict physical harm but also the intended physical harm must in fact be caused to the plaintiff, in other words, there must be damage, whereas, as we know, in an action for trespass to the person, the tort is actionable *per se*, that is, without proof of any harm or damage.

The action on the case for damages for physical injury is available not only in relation to intentional acts but also in relation to intentional statements which are intended to cause physical harm to the plaintiff. That this is so is well illustrated by the decision of Wright J. in *Wilkinson* v. *Downton*[266] in 1897. The defendant, in the execution of what he seems to have regarded as a practical joke, told the plaintiff that her husband had been seriously injured in an accident and that she should go at once in a cab to fetch him home. That statement was totally false. As a result of the statement, the plaintiff suffered 'a violent shock to her nervous system, producing vomiting and other more serious and permanent physical consequences at one time threatening her reason, and entailing weeks of physical suffering and incapacity to her as well as expense to her husband for medical attendance'.[267] The plaintiff brought an action to recover the

---

265 It could also include 'recklessness'. See the discussion of this matter at pp. 32-6 above.
266 [1897] 2 Q.B. 57.
267 ibid., 58.

cost of the railway fares of persons sent by the plaintiff in obedience to the false message and also to recover compensation for her illness and suffering. The jury assessed the expenses of the railway fares at 1s. 10½d. and the damages for the physical injury to the plaintiff at £100. It was contended on behalf of the defendant that the verdict for the £100 could not be supported. Wright J., however, decided that the defendant had 'wilfully done an act calculated to cause physical harm to the plaintiff... and has in fact thereby caused physical harm to her . . .'.[268] He felt that this, without more, appeared to state a good cause of action.

The decision in *Wilkinson* v. *Downton* is one which shows quite clearly that a plaintiff can succeed in an action on the case for damages for physical injury in respect of a *statement* which is intentionally made and which is 'calculated' to cause physical harm to the plaintiff. It is difficult to know how the word 'calculated' was used by Wright J. in *Wilkinson* v. *Downton*. It could be a synonym for the word 'intended' or it could mean 'likely' (the likelihood being so great that an intention to do harm could be imputed to the defendant as indeed it was in *Wilkinson* v. *Downton*). So if D deliberately tells P that it is safe to eat some particular food, which D knows is dangerous, intending P to suffer physical harm, or if D deliberately tells P that he can safely enter a particular place when he clearly knows that a dangerous animal is loose there, intending P to be savaged by that animal, or if D deliberately tells P that it is perfectly safe to drive a particular vehicle which he knows is dangerous, intending P to be injured by the driving of that vehicle, then P can recover damages in an action on the case for damages for physical injury if he actually suffers physical harm as a result of acting upon any of those statements. In all these cases the action for deceit would probably also be available, though that action seems to be brought nowadays mainly for the protection of business interests and it is best dealt with when considering the intentional infliction of purely economic loss.[269] It is useful here, however, to refer briefly to the Canadian decision in *Graham* v. *Saville*[270] where the defendant, a married man, falsely told the plaintiff, a spinster, that he was a bachelor, as a result of which she went through a form of marriage with him and as a result of this union bore a child. Soon after the alleged marriage the defendant deserted the plaintiff. In an action by the plaintiff, the Court of Appeal of Ontario decided that the plaintiff was entitled to $1860 by way of damages because 'the defendant's fraudulent misrepresentation was plainly and wickedly calculated to bring about acts of coition with the plaintiff which he knew might result in physical harm and detriment to her'[271] and also for the 'physical injury, pain and suffering in consequence of her pregnancy and the birth of a child'.[272] The damages were awarded both on the basis of the tort of deceit and on

268 ibid., 58-9.
269 See the discussion at pp. 171-9 below.
270 [1945] O.R. 301.
271 ibid., 310.
272 ibid., 309.

reliance upon *Wilkinson* v. *Downton*, i.e. an action on the case for damages for physical injury.

The decision in *Wilkinson* v. *Downton* is also of great interest because Wright J. was prepared in that case to impute to the defendant an intention to cause physical harm to the plaintiff even though there was obviously some evidence that the statement was intended as a practical joke. Wright J. dealt with this matter in the following words:

> One question is whether the defendant's act was so plainly calculated to produce some effect of the kind which was produced that an intention to produce it ought to be imputed to the defendant, regard being had to the fact that the effect was produced on a person proved to be in an ordinary state of health and mind.[273]

So, a person is liable in an action on the case for damages not only for intentional acts and statements which are intended to cause damage and which in fact do cause damage to the plaintiff, but also in respect of intentional acts and statements from which (whether actually intended to cause harm to the plaintiff or not) the court can impute an intention on the part of the defendant to produce physical harm to the plaintiff if the acts or statements actually cause harm to the plaintiff, as in *Wilkinson* v. *Downton*.

IV: THE ACTION ON THE CASE FOR DAMAGES FOR NERVOUS SHOCK

The action on the case for damages, as we have seen, is available for the intentional infliction of physical harm which is caused indirectly or consequentially—the intention being actual or, as in *Wilkinson* v. *Downton*, imputed. It is also available for the intentional infliction of nervous shock which is caused indirectly or consequentially. What is 'nervous shock'? Lord Denning M.R. in *Hinz* v. *Berry* described it as 'any recognizable psychiatric illness'[274] and Windeyer J. of the High Court of Australia in *Mount Isa Mines* v. *Pusey* described it as a lasting disorder of the mind or body, some form of psychoneurosis or a psychosomatic illness, the starting point of which is usually emotional distress.[275] In *McLoughlin* v. *O'Brian*, Lord Wilberforce in the House of Lords described it as 'that recognizable and severe physical damage to the human body and system which is caused by the impact, through the senses, of external events on the mind'.[276] And more recently Deane J. in *Jaensch* v. *Coffey* said that the term was imprecisely used by lawyers to describe some forms of psychoneurosis and mental illness.[277]

---

273 [1897] 2 Q.B. 57, 59.
274 [1970] 2 Q.B. 40, 42.
275 (1970) 125 C.L.R. 383, 394.
276 [1982] 2 All E.R. 298, 301.
277 [1984] 58 A.L.J.R. 426, 433.

If D tells P that if he does not hand over certain documents he will beat him up and P suffers nervous shock as a result of the direct and immediate threat the proper action to bring is an action for trespass to the person (assault). But if D tells P falsely that he is a detective from Scotland Yard and that unless he hands over certain documents he will be charged with espionage by the military authorities and P suffers nervous shock as a result of the false statements and threats then the proper action to bring is an action on the case for damages for nervous shock, as there is no threat of imminent and direct bodily contact which is a necessary requirement of the tort of trespass (assault). The factual situation in the latter example is taken from the English case of *Janvier* v. *Sweeney*.[278] The plaintiff worked as a maid for a lady in whose house she resided. She had a German fiancé who was interned. The defendant, a private detective, who was anxious to retrieve some letters which were in the possession of the plaintiff's employer, called at the house and told the plaintiff that he was a detective inspector from Scotland Yard representing the military authorities and that she was a woman they wanted as she was corresponding with a German spy. The statements were false. The plaintiff was extremely frightened and claimed that, as a result, she suffered from a severe nervous shock including neurasthenia, shingles and other ailments. The jury found that the statements were calculated to cause physical injury to the plaintiff and that the illness from which the plaintiff suffered was caused by the utterance of the statements. On these findings Avory J. entered judgment for the plaintiff, basing his decision on *Wilkinson* v. *Downton*. The Court of Appeal in dismissing an appeal from the decision of Avory J. not only specifically approved of the decision in *Wilkinson* v. *Downton* but also Duke L.J. said *Janvier* v. *Sweeney* was a much stronger case than *Wilkinson* v. *Downton* because 'in [the latter] case there was no intention to commit a wrongful act; the defendant merely intended to play a practical joke upon the plaintiff. In the present case there was an intention to terrify the plaintiff for the purpose of attaining an unlawful object'.[279]

1. Must the Statement be Made To or In the Presence of the Plaintiff?

In order to succeed in an action on the case for damages for nervous shock it seems that it is necessary that the defendant's intentional act be done or the words uttered to the plaintiff or at least in his presence. In *Bunyan* v. *Jordan*,[280] the plaintiff, who was 22 years of age at the date of the incident, was employed as a clerk in a general store kept by the defendant. On the day of the incident the plaintiff came into the store and found the defendant, rather the worse off for alcohol, seated at a table with a revolver in front of him and a bottle marked 'Poison' on the table. The plaintiff

278 [1919] 2 K.B. 316.
279 ibid., 326.
280 (1937) 57 C.L.R. 1.

later overheard the defendant tell another employee that he was going to shoot himself. The plaintiff then went into an adjoining building and heard the report of a firearm. Apparently the defendant had fired the shot at himself after putting on an armour plated vest. He did this, he said, 'with the idea of putting the wind up the boys'—his sons. The plaintiff saw the defendant unharmed some minutes after the shooting, but later when she took the day's takings to the defendant he tore up the pound notes and said that he would not be there in the morning to mend them and to have them banked and that she would 'hear of a death before morning'. The plaintiff was shaken by the whole incident. A doctor who attended the plaintiff said that the facts which he observed as to her nervous condition could have been brought about by a shock. The plaintiff's attempt to bring an action on the case on the basis of *Wilkinson* v. *Downton* and *Janvier* v. *Sweeney* failed because, as Latham C.J. said, 'the acts of the defendant, taken all together, cannot be said to be calculated or likely to cause harm to any person—even to his sons, if they were normal persons'[281] and Dixon J. agreed when he said 'it is, of course, quite clear that the defendant did not intend to bring upon the plaintiff a nervous breakdown or any physical harm'.[282] But a major reason for the plaintiff's failure was that, as Latham C.J. said, 'the words were not uttered to the plaintiff and they were not even uttered in her presence',[283] to which he added that 'none of the cases has gone so far as to suggest that a man owes a duty to persons who merely happen to overhear statements that are not addressed to them'.[284]

It should be noticed in passing that even though the plaintiff did not succeed in *Bunyan* v. *Jordan* for the reason stated above, Dixon J. made it quite clear that an action on the case for damages for nervous shock is available in Australia if a defendant by his act or statement intends to cause nervous shock to a plaintiff and succeeds in doing so. As he said:

> I have no doubt that such an illness [i.e. a sufficiently emotional condition to lead to a neurasthenic breakdown amounting to an illness] without more is a form of harm or damage sufficient for the purpose of any action on the case in which damage is the gist of the action, that is, supposing that the other ingredients of the cause of action are present.[285]

There are two decisions, however, which seem to suggest that a defendant may be liable in an action on the case for damages in respect of a statement even when it is not made to the plaintiff or in his presence. In the New Zealand decision in *Stevenson* v. *Basham*,[286] the defendant's statement, 'I'll have you out within twenty-four hours. If I can't get you

---

281 ibid., 12.
282 ibid., 17.
283 ibid., 11.
284 ibid., 12.
285 ibid., 16.
286 [1922] N.Z.L.R. 225. The action was in negligence and in an action on the case for damages for nervous shock, though as Herdman J. points out at p. 232, 'the physical harm was so closely bound up with the shock which Mrs Basham suffered that it may be said that shock was accompanied by actual physical injury'.

out I'll burn you out', was made to the plaintiff's husband in an effort to get him to surrender the premises to the defendant. The plaintiff, who was pregnant at the time, was in bed. She overheard the statement and being genuinely afraid that the defendant would carry his threat into execution, suffered hysteria and a miscarriage. Herdman J. found for the plaintiff both in negligence and on the basis of *Wilkinson* v. *Downton*. The other decision is the Canadian decision in *Bielitzki* v. *Obadisk*.[287] In this case the defendant falsely stated to a third party that the plaintiff's son, who was temporarily absent from home, had hanged himself. After a series of repetitions the story was told to the plaintiff who, believing the report to be true, sustained a violent shock and mental anguish which brought on physical illness and incapacitated her for some time. The Saskatchewan Court of Appeal held that the plaintiff had a good cause of action under *Wilkinson* v. *Downton*. Lamont J. said that the defendant had deliberately originated the report and given it currency, and that:

> the conclusion should be drawn that he did it with the intention that it should reach the plaintiff . . . [as] any reasonable man would know that the natural and probable consequence of spreading such a report would be that it would be carried to the plaintiff and would, in all probability, cause her not only mental anguish but physical pain.[288]

It would seem, therefore, that there is some authority for saying that a statement not made to a plaintiff or in his presence might still attract liability in an action on the case for damages if the plaintiff can show that the statement was calculated to cause harm (physical harm or nervous shock) to him as a person, who the defendant knew or ought to have known would be likely to overhear it, and that such a statement will also attract a similar liability if the defendant originated and published the statement with the intention that it should come to the ears of the plaintiff or if that is a natural and probable consequence.

2. Must the Statement be False?

In most of the decisions where the action on the case for damages has been successful liability has been imposed in relation to a false statement. But is it necessary for liability that the statement be false? In *Stevenson* v. *Basham*,[289] for all we know, the statement might well have been true. The important criterion is not, it is suggested, whether the statement is false or true but whether the defendant had any business to be making the statement and whether the statement was intended or could reasonably be said to have been intended to cause harm (physical harm or nervous shock) to the plaintiff. Suppose D telephones P and tells her that her son, who is on a scientific expedition in South America, has been eaten by cannibals. A week later P hears from the expedition leader that her son is

287 [1922] 2 W.W.R. 238.
288 ibid., 242.
289 [1922] N.Z.L.R. 225 discussed above at pp. 68-9.

missing in jungle territory said to be inhabited by cannibals. At the time of the making of the statement by D, P's son was working safely at the base camp. Could P successfully bring an action on the case for damages for nervous shock against D? The answer to that question depends upon whether D's statement was calculated to cause nervous shock to P rather than upon the fact that the statement was false when made, possibly true a few days later and true at the time of the action.

If actions can be brought even in relation to true statements, would the bearer of bad news be at some disadvantage? The answer to that question is well put by Windeyer J. in *Mount Isa Mines* v. *Pusey*: 'There is no duty in law to break bad news gently or to do nothing which creates bad news . . . unless there be an intention to cause a nervous shock'.[290]

It should perhaps be added that in relation to acts, truth or falsity appears to be of little significance. If D cuts his throat in P's house, D (or his estate) would be liable to P in an action on the case for damages for nervous shock to P.[291] If D fakes suicide in similar circumstances he will be no more liable or no less liable to P in an action on the case.

3. THE POSITION OF PARTICULARLY SENSITIVE PLAINTIFFS

In order to recover damages for nervous shock in an action on the case for damages the plaintiff must show that such a consequence is within the scope of reasonable anticipation. Among the many reasons why the plaintiff did not succeed in *Bunyan* v. *Jordan* was the fact that the court thought that the plaintiff's reaction in suffering a nervous breakdown from the circumstances of that case was not that expected of an ordinary person. As Latham C.J. put it: 'in the case of ordinary persons, if a man said to them that he was going to shoot somebody and they then heard a shot or even saw the speaker shoot himself or someone else, they would be disturbed or upset in varying degrees, but they would not suffer from illness producing a nervous breakdown'.[292] As this view represents the majority view in *Bunyan* v. *Jordan*, it follows that the courts will not allow recovery in an action on the case for nervous shock if the plaintiff is a particularly sensitive person or suffers reactions which would not be suffered by ordinary persons. This view requires reconsideration.

If a defendant intentionally chooses to carry out an act or make a statement which is calculated to cause physical injury or nervous shock to the plaintiff it is difficult to see why a particularly sensitive plaintiff who suffers physical injury or nervous shock should not succeed in an action on the case. Why should the defendant not be required to take the plaintiff as he finds him? The better view, it is submitted, is the view of Evatt J.

---

290 (1970) 125 C.L.R. 383, 407. See also *D.* v. *N.S.P.C.C.* [1978] A.C. 171, 188-9.

291 See *Blakeley* v. *Shortal's Estate* (1945) 20 N.W. 2d 28—the plaintiff recovered for nervous shock and resulting serious illness from the estate of the deceased when the deceased who was a visitor at her house committed suicide by cutting his throat in her kitchen while she was out. On her return she was confronted with his corpse and blood all over the kitchen.

292 (1937) 57 C.L.R. 1, 14.

(dissenting) in *Bunyan* v. *Jordan*. Evatt J. thought that the particularly sensitive plaintiff should be able to succeed and that it should not be an answer to such an action for the defendant to say 'that many persons, or a majority of persons, or even that especially formidable person "the ordinary normal human being" would not be alarmed or terrified, or have suffered illness as a result of the defendant's action'.[293] That view is gradually gaining acceptance.[294]

If the defendant *knows* that the plaintiff is a particularly sensitive person then the plaintiff might be able to recover even in respect of a nervous shock which might not have been suffered by a person of an ordinary robust disposition. This much can be deduced from the judgments of the High Court in *Bunyan* v. *Jordan*. Dixon J. said 'there is . . . no evidence that, if the plaintiff was peculiarly susceptible to nervous shock, the defendant was aware that that was the case'[295] and McTiernan J. said 'there is no evidence that he knew that the plaintiff was so delicately constituted that she would be injured by his peculiar conduct'.[296] The implication is that if he knew she was particularly sensitive he might have been held liable.

4. Vicarious Liability and the Action on the Case for Damages

In an action in trespass it was formerly not possible for a plaintiff to bring an action against an employer in respect of acts done or statements made by the employee in the course of his employment because it was felt that there was not a sufficient element of directness, which is an essential ingredient of the tort of trespass.[297] An action on the case for damages can, however, be brought against an employer in respect of intentional acts or statements which are calculated to cause physical harm or nervous shock to the plaintiff and which in fact do cause such harm or shock. In *Janvier* v. *Sweeney*[298] the action was brought against both the private detective who made the threat, Barker, and his employer, Sweeney. It was argued that the action should not have been brought against Sweeney, but Bankes C.J. said that as Sweeney's object was to retrieve the letters and he had put

293 ibid., 18.

294 Windeyer J. in *Mount Isa Mines Ltd* v. *Pusey* (1970) 125 C.L.R. 383, 405, said that he regarded the position of particularly sensitive plaintiffs as an 'open question' and added: 'I am not to be taken as assenting to the proposition that nervous shock caused to a man who is prone to such shock is not compensable when a similar occurrence harming a "normal" man would be'.

295 (1937) 57 C.L.R. 1, 17.

296 ibid., 18.

297 See *Williams* v. *Milotin* (1957) 97 C.L.R. 465, 470. Nowadays this restriction appears to be somewhat eased and, depending on the facts, an employer can be held vicariously liable for an intentional assault, battery or false imprisonment committed by his employee. See *Atiyah, Vicarious Liability*, pp. 276-80. For three cases where there was no liability see *Deatons Pty Ltd* v. *Flew* (1949) 79 C.L.R. 370; *Warren* v. *Henlys* [1948] 2 All E.R. 935; and *Keppel Bus Co. Ltd* v. *Sa'ad bin Ahmad* [1974] 1 W.L.R. 1082.

298 [1919] 2 K.B. 316.

Barker in his place to do that, Sweeney must be answerable for the manner in which Barker conducted himself in doing the business entrusted to him. Sweeney was held vicariously liable for the threats made by Barker to the plaintiff, which were calculated to cause nervous shock to the plaintiff and which did in fact cause nervous shock to her.

V: THE INTENTIONAL INFLICTION OF MENTAL DISTRESS

We have just considered the action on the case for damages for nervous shock, which is available when a defendant, whether by an intentional act or statement calculated to cause nervous shock to the plaintiff, succeeds in causing nervous shock to the plaintiff. But the ordinary defendant knows little about nervous shock—which we have said is 'any recognizable psychiatric illness'—or how to cause it intentionally. What usually happens is that the ordinary defendant intends to cause purely mental distress[299] in the form of fright, fear, horror, grief, shame, anger, embarrassment, disappointment, humiliation, injured pride or wounded feelings which in some circumstances causes nervous shock or even physical illness, and the courts, to assist recovery on the part of the plaintiff, then impute to the defendant an intention to cause that nervous shock or that

---

299 The connection between mental distress and physical harm is well summarized in (1971) 59 *Georgetown L.J.* 1237, 1248-63 and the summary is approved of in the decision of the Supreme Court of Hawaii in *Leong* v. *Takasaki* 520 P. 2d 758, 766-7 (1974) (a case of negligently inflicted mental distress): 'From a medical perspective . . . mental distress may be characterized as a reaction to a traumatic stimulus which may be defined as an impact, force or event which acts upon an individual for a brief or extended period of time and can be either physical or purely psychic. Medical science has shown that a traumatic situation causes two types of mental reactions—an immediate automatic response designed to protect the individual from harm or unpleasantness and a secondary, longer-lasting reaction caused by the individual's inability to cope with the traumatic event. The primary response constitutes the individual's attempt to combat the stress . . . and is exemplified by such emotional responses as fear, anger, grief, shock, humiliation or embarrassment. These reactions occur automatically and instinctively . . . Secondary reactions, which may be termed traumatic neuroses . . . are caused by an individual's continued inability to adequately adjust to a traumatic event. Medical science has identified three types of neuroses which frequently occur from traumatic occurrence. In the anxiety reaction, the trauma produces severe tension, resulting in such physiological and psychological symptoms as nervousness, nausea, weight-loss, pains in the stomach, genito-urinary distress, emotional fatigue, weakness, headaches and backaches . . . A second common neurosis is the conversion reaction . . . where the individual converts consciously disowned wishes or impulses into a variety of physiological symptoms, such as paralysis, loss of hearing or sight, pain or muscular spasms . . . however, these symptoms should be distinguished from true physical injuries since they cannot be explained by an actual physical impairment . . . the third common neurosis, the hypochondriasis reaction, is characterized by an overconcern with health, a fear of illness, or other unpleasant sensations'.

physical injury. Thus in *Wilkinson* v. *Downton*,[300] even though there was considerable evidence that the statement was intended as a practical joke, the court was prepared to impute to the defendant an intention to cause physical harm to the plaintiff. Similarly in *Janvier* v. *Sweeney*[301] and *Stevenson* v. *Basham*,[302] where the defendants intended to frighten the plaintiff into giving up possession of certain letters and a house respectively, the courts were prepared to impute to the defendants an intention to cause nervous shock to the plaintiffs. And in *Bielitzki* v. *Obadisk*,[303] where the defendant originated a false rumour that the plaintiff's son had hanged himself, the court concluded that the defendant's statement was intended to come to the ears of the plaintiff and to 'cause her not only mental anguish but physical pain'.

Why have the courts engaged in what can only be described as a 'fiction' in relation to the intentional infliction of mental distress? There appear to be two reasons. On the one hand, the courts clearly wish to discourage the intentional infliction of mental distress. Whatever view they might take about the negligent infliction of mental distress there is little reason to sympathize with the defendant when he *intends* to inflict mental distress upon the plaintiff.[304] Prosser describes this as 'the natural tendency of the courts . . . in the field of torts, to extend liability as the moral guilt of the defendant increases'.[305] On the other hand, it would appear that there is no clear authority, at least in the Australian and English law of torts,[306] that an action on the case for damages is available for the intentional infliction of *purely* mental distress or, as it is sometimes described, mental distress *simpliciter*. Certainly, where the mental distress is inflicted in the course of commission of another tort such as battery,[307] assault,[308] false

---

300 [1897] 2 Q.B. 57. See also *Johnson* v. *The Commonwealth* (1927) 27 S.R.(N.S.W.) 133, 137 *per* Ferguson J.: 'I think the nervous shock and resulting physical illness complained of by the plaintiff might fairly and reasonably have been anticipated as a consequence of the assault committed upon her husband in her presence'.

301 [1919] 2 K.B. 316.

302 [1922] N.Z.L.R. 225.

303 [1922] 2 W.W.R. 238, 242. See also *Purdy* v. *Wosnesensky* [1937] 2 W.W.R. 116 where the defendant assaulted the plaintiff's husband in her presence. The court said that she had at least an action on the case for a severe shock she suffered as 'an intention to produce such an effect must be imputed' to the defendant.

304 See, for example, the judgment of Wright J. in *Wilkinson* v. *Downton* where he refused to follow *Victorian Railways Commissioner* v. *Coultas* (1888) 13 App.Cases 222 (where the Privy Council held that damages for negligently caused illness which was the effect of shock caused by fright were not recoverable) on the basis that 'there was not in that case any element of wilful wrong'.

305 W.L. Prosser (1939) 37 *Michigan L.R.* 874, 878.

306 Even in Canada and New Zealand.

307 *Johnstone* v. *Stewart* (1968) S.A.S.R. 142 (outrage and humiliation); *Henry* v. *Thompson* (1989) Aust. Torts Reports 80-265 (great emotional hurt, insult and humiliation).

308 *Fogg* v. *McKnight* [1968] N.Z.L.R. 330 (insult and injury to feelings).

imprisonment,[309] trespass to land,[310] defamation,[311] etc., damages have been awarded for the infliction of the mental distress but there have been no decisions where the courts in Australia and in England have awarded damages in tort where the only injury inflicted is mental distress, even where the injury has been intentionally inflicted by the defendant. So the courts have resorted to the fiction of imputing to a defendant an intention to cause physical injury or nervous shock in order to enable a plaintiff to recover damages, even though the defendant might have done the act or made the statement only with the intention of causing mental distress.

In the United States many courts have recognized the right to recover damages for mental distress alone without consequent physical harm or nervous shock[312] but only in cases involving 'extreme and outrageous intentional invasions of one's mental and emotional tranquility'.[313] This requirement of outrageous conduct, it is said, serves to ensure that the plaintiff experienced serious mental suffering and convinces the court of the validity of the claim.[314] In the United States the reason for allowing recovery in damages for the intentional infliction of severe mental distress unaccompanied by physical harm or nervous shock is that 'the interest in freedom from severe emotional distress is regarded as of sufficient importance to require others to refrain from conduct intended to invade it'.[315] Despite the apparent lack of litigation in Australia in relation to the intentional infliction of mental distress it is suggested that we need a tort which protects us against the intentional infliction of purely mental distress. There is no authoritative decision, binding on Australian courts, which lays down that damages are not available for the intentional infliction of purely mental distress. Street has suggested that there was no liability in *Bunyan* v. *Jordan* because the defendant intended merely to frighten the plaintiff[316] but the better explanation of that decision is that the plaintiff failed because the statement was not directed at the plaintiff—

---

309 *Hook* v. *Cunard Steamship Co.* [1953] 1 All E.R. 1021; *Myer Stores Ltd* v. *Soo* (1991) Aust. Torts Reports 81-077 (indignity, mental suffering, disgrace and humiliation).

310 *Greig* v. *Greig* [1966] V.R. 376 (injured feelings); *Johnstone* v. *Stewart* [1968] S.A.S.R. 142 (outrage and humiliation).

311 *Uren* v. *John Fairfax & Sons Pty Ltd* (1966) 117 C.L.R. 118 (injury to feelings and dignity).

312 See P.R. Handford (1979) 8 *Anglo-American L.R.* 1 and Handford (1982) *U.N.S.W.L.J.* 291. See also the American (Second) *Restatement* (1965) s.46 which is as follows:

(1) One who by extreme and outrageous conduct intentionally or recklessy causes severe emotional distress to another is subject to liability for such emotional distress, and if bodily harm results from it, for such bodily harm.

(2) Where such conduct is directed at a third person, the actor is subject to liability if he intentionally or recklessly causes severe emotional distress

(a) to a member of such person's immediate family who is present at the time, whether or not such distress results in bodily harm, or

(b) to any other person who is present at the time, if such distress results in 'bodily' harm.

For some fairly modern cases, see *Halio* v. *Lurie* (1961) 222 N.Y.S. 2d 759 and *Alsteen* v. *Gehl* (1963) 124 N.W. 2d 312.

313 See *Alcorn* v. *Anbro Engineers Inc.* (1970) 468 P. 2d 216, 218.

314 See *Molien* v. *Kaiser Foundation Hospitals* (1980) 616 P. 2d 813.

315 *State Rubbish Association* v. *Siliznoff* (1952) 240 P. 2d 282, 285.

316 *Street* (7th edn, 1983) p. 23.

'the words were not uttered to the plaintiff and they were not even uttered in her presence'.[317] It should be noted that when *Bunyan* v. *Jordan* was before the Court of Appeal in New South Wales, Jordan C.J. clearly indicated that an action would be available for *intentionally* inflicted alarm or fright: 'Apart however, from any intention to alarm, a person may be otherwise liable for injurious fright which he has in fact caused to another'.[318] Earlier Jordan C.J. had proposed a test for determining liability in connection with intentionally inflicted alarm or fright:

> It is established by the authorities that a person is liable for any act of his which has so terrified another person as to injure him, if the act was done with the intention of alarming the other, and was either of a kind reasonably capable of so terrifying a normal human being, or was known or ought to have been known to the doer of the act to be likely to terrify the person injured for reasons special to that person.[319]

He did not specifically mention that the plaintiff's 'injury' must be physical harm or nervous shock but the authorities he relied upon for his proposed test were *Wilkinson* v. *Downton* and *Janvier* v. *Sweeney*. We might well speculate whether Jordan C.J. regarded physical harm or nervous shock as absolutely essential for recovery for damages for alarm and fright or whether he was suggesting that an action on the case for purely mental distress was available where the defendant did an act or made a statement with the intention of inflicting alarm or fright on the plaintiff.

It was indicated earlier that there does not appear to be much litigation in Australia, at least by way of decided cases, involving the intentional infliction of mental distress, and certainly no decision one way or the other involving the infliction of purely mental distress. In the United States the tort of intentional infliction of mental distress is flourishing and there are several decisions where recovery has been allowed for the intentional infliction of purely mental distress. Three possible reasons might be offered for the almost complete absence of litigation in Australia in relation to the intentional infliction of purely mental distress. First, that Australians are a less litigious people than Americans; secondly, that situations do not arise in Australia which require such actions to be brought; and, thirdly, though these situations do arise and there are willing litigants, there is an unwillingness on the part of those who offer legal advice to advise that an action is available for the intentional infliction of purely mental distress. The first reason does not stand scrutiny. Though it is true that Australians are, or would appear to be, less litigious than Americans that would not explain the almost complete absence of litigation in this area. In relation to the second reason, it is difficult to maintain that Australians are any less inventive when it comes to the intentional infliction of mental distress and again it would be difficult to explain the almost complete absence of litigation in this area.

---

317 (1937) 57 C.L.R. 1
318 (1936) 36 S.R.(N.S.W.) 350, 353.
319 ibid.

The third reason is probably the explanation, and it is therefore necessary to devote more space than would otherwise be warranted in order to show that the tort of intentional infliction of purely mental distress is available, or would be available in appropriate circumstances, in Australia. The remaining discussion, therefore, focuses on three matters. We first look at various factual situations to see why we need a tort for the intentional infliction of mental distress. Secondly, we discuss whether there is anything to prevent the courts in Australia from granting recovery in an action on the case for damages for the intentional infliction of purely mental distress on the basis of *Wilkinson* v. *Downton* and *Janvier* v. *Sweeney*. And, thirdly, we consider what, if any, limits should be imposed by Australian courts in relation to recovery in that tort.

1. The Need for a Tort for the Intentional Infliction of Purely Mental Distress

Of course, the law of torts does offer protection against the intentional infliction of purely mental distress through various torts other than the action on the case for damages. Thus an action in trespass (assault) is available against a defendant for purely mental distress such as fright or fear or terror caused by a direct threat of imminent and immediate bodily contact with the plaintiff.[320] The tort of defamation is available where the defendant causes purely mental distress (humiliation, injured pride, wounded feelings) to the plaintiff by lowering his reputation in the eyes of right-thinking members of society generally.[321] And the tort of nuisance has been used to protect a plaintiff against intentional acts of the defendant which are intended to vex and harass the plaintiff.[322] But these actions will not be available if there is, for example, no direct threat of bodily contact (assault); no publication to a third party (defamation); or no interference in the use or enjoyment of land (nuisance). It is here that the action on the case for damages comes into its own. We have already discussed *Wilkinson* v. *Downton*, *Janvier* v. *Sweeney*, *Stevenson* v. *Basham* and *Bielitzki* v. *Obadisk*, where in each case the plaintiff succeeded in an action on the case for damages but in all these cases there was either physical injury or nervous shock to the plaintiff. Should not the plaintiff be able to succeed in all those factual situations if the only injury suffered was severe mental distress rather than physical injury or nervous shock? And what about the following situations?

(a) The police are making inquiries into a particularly gruesome murder. When asked by the police whether he saw anyone entering or leaving the house of the victim, D falsely says that he saw P leaving the victim's house at the time of the murder. P suffers severe mental

320 See e.g. *Barton* v. *Armstrong* [1969] 2 N.S.W.R. 451.
321 See e.g. *Hook* v. *Cunard Steamship Co.* [1953] 1 All E.R. 1021. See also fn. 328 below.
322 See e.g. *Christie* v. *Davey* [1893] 1 Ch. 316, and *Stoakes* v. *Brydges* [1958] Q.W.N. 15.

distress as a result of the statement and the subsequent inquiries which the police quite naturally make.[323]

(b) P is a very active anti-drugs campaigner. D plants some drugs in the schoolbag of P's son, and when P's son gets home D anonymously telephones the police and asks them to investigate the presence of drugs in P's home. The police find the drugs and P is very acutely embarrassed and suffers severe mental distress as a result.[324]

(c) D, a doctor, falsely tells W that she has syphilis and that she should have her husband P examined for the disease. This produces anxiety, suspicion and hostility on the part of W towards P and the consequent marital discord results in severe emotional distress to P.[325]

(d) D, the owner of a health studio, on several occasions in front of several persons tells P that she is 'revoltingly fat' and that she should come to his studio. D knows that P's obesity is due to a hormonal imbalance.[326] P suffers severe mental distress as a result of D's statements.

(e) P, an Aboriginal shop steward, tells D, the foreman, that he has advised T, another employee, that he should not drive a certain truck as he is not a member of the relevant union. D shouts at P in a rude, violent and insolent manner in front of several employees as follows: 'You bloody "abos" are not going to tell me about the rules. I don't want any "abos" working for me. I am getting rid of all the "abos". Go get your pay cheque. You're fired.' P suffers severe mental distress because of the humiliation and mental anguish.[327]

(f) P breaks off her engagement to D. In retaliation, D inserts the following advertisement in a newspaper: 'Attractive Young Woman Looking for Mr Right—Wonderful Opportunity for Someone Here'. P's home address and telephone number are given in the advertisement. As a consequence of the advertisement P receives a number of obscene telephone calls, several obscene and suggestive letters and some rather dubious proposals of marriage. She suffers severe mental

323 D might of course be committing a criminal offence like causing a public mischief but that is not much solace to P.

324 Again D might be subjecting himself to some criminal charge but without an action on the case P's chances of tort recovery are non-existent.

325 W might have some recovery in contract but does P (her husband) have any action in tort?

326 Presumably, if D's statement causes P to suffer from anorexia nervosa there would be liability for 'physical injury'. What about purely mental distress?

327 See *Alcorn* v. *Anbro Engineering Inc.* (1970) 468 P. 2d 216, 217: 'You goddam "niggers" are not going to tell me about the rules. I don't want any "niggers" working for me. I am getting rid of all the "niggers"; go . . . get your pay check; you're fired'. Plaintiff recovered for the humiliation, mental anguish and emotional physical distress he suffered.

distress (anger, embarrassment and humiliation) as a result of the various communications.[328]

(g) P's adult son, who is no longer living with her, is indebted to D Co. An employee of D Co. telephones P, represents himself as a solicitor, and in a conversation laced with profanity and insults, threatens to place both mother and son in jail if she does not pay the son's debt. P correctly informs the employee that she does not even know where her son is but a few days later the employee again telephones and makes the same threat. P suffers severe mental distress as a result of the telephone calls.[329]

(h) D falsely tells P, a young girl, that her mother is sleeping with another man and will be punished by God. P is extremely upset and suffers severe mental distress.[330]

(i) D is a visitor to P's house. While P is out shopping D cuts his own throat in P's bathroom in a suicide attempt. On her return, P goes to the bathroom to find D almost dead and the bathroom looking like a slaughter house. P suffers severe mental distress as a result of the horrific sight.[331]

There might be some difference of opinion as to whether the plaintiff ought to recover in *all* the situations above but many would agree that in most of the situations the plaintiff should be able to recover for the purely mental distress suffered. In the United States the plaintiff would probably recover in all the situations above but in Australia, unless we rely on an action on the case for damages for the intentional infliction of purely mental distress, the mental distress suffered would not be compensable on the present state of the law of torts. It is suggested, therefore, that the courts consider the granting of an action on the case for damages for the intentional infliction of purely mental distress on an analogy with *Wilkinson* v. *Downton* and *Janvier* v. *Sweeney*.

---

328 See *Novakovic* v. *Gorki Pty Ltd*, the *Age*, 9 October 1980, where the plaintiff, a woman, was awarded $8000 for her distress, embarrassment and humiliation and for the lowering of her standing in the Yugoslav community in Melbourne after an advertisement for male companionship appeared in her name in a local Yugoslav newspaper. She did not know about the advertisement. She received about 50 letters (some of them containing photographs of scantily clad men) and 400 telephone calls in the fortnight after the advertisement appeared. She had to take the telephone off the hook at night to get some sleep.

329 See *Lyons* v. *Zale Jewelry Co.* (1963) 150 So. 2d 154 from which this factual situation is taken. In England, the Administration of Justice Act 1970 s.40 makes it an offence to indulge in behaviour calculated to subject a debtor or members of his family or household to alarm, distress or humiliation—there is no mention of a civil claim.

330 See *Korbin* v. *Berlin* 177 So 2d 551 (1965) from which the factual situation is taken.

331 There are two decisions very similar to this factual situation: *Blakeley* v. *Shortal's Estate* (1945) 20 N.W. 2d 28 from the U.S. and *A. & Another* v. *B's Trustees* (1906) 13 S.L.T. 830 from Scotland. In both these cases the suicide attempt was successful and in both cases the plaintiff succeeded.

2. An Action on the Case for Damages for the Intentional Infliction of Purely Mental Distress

In the great majority of cases involving severe mental distress, the severity of the mental distress will be evidenced either by physical injury or by nervous shock. But there will be cases where there is severe mental distress alone and it is for those cases that we need the action on the case for damages as well. At the time of *Wilkinson* v. *Downton* (1897) medical science had not progressed sufficiently in recognizing mental injuries (even such mental injuries as nervous shock) so the courts demanded evidence of mental distress in the form of physical injuries even going so far as to say that there must be an intention to cause physical injury. By the time *Janvier* v. *Sweeney* was decided (1919) medical science had progressed sufficiently for the courts to say that an action on the case for damages would be available for the intentional infliction of nervous shock. Now, as one writer puts it, 'medical science is capable of satisfactorily establishing the existence, seriousness and ramifications of emotional harm'[332] and there is no reason why the courts should not extend the availability of the action on the case for damages to the intentional infliction of severe mental distress alone. It has also been suggested that 'it would be a reproach to the law if physical injuries [and nervous shock] might be recovered for and not those incorporeal injuries which would cause much greater suffering and humiliation'.[333]

It is not difficult to calculate damages for the intentional infliction of purely mental distress. As we have pointed out, courts have been used to granting damages for purely mental distress in the torts of assault, defamation, nuisance etc. and they have also been used to granting damages for purely mental distress as 'parasitic' damages in various other torts. Outside the law of torts damages have been awarded for mental distress in actions for breach of contract,[334] and in response to the comment that damages for mental distress for a spoilt holiday were difficult to assess, Singleton L.J. in *Stedman* v. *Swan's Tours* said it was 'no more difficult than to assess the amount to be given for pain and suffering in a case of personal injuries'.[335]

It was also thought that to allow an action for the intentional infliction of purely mental distress would lead to an irrepressible flood of litigation, but as one commentator who has examined the United States position in

332 See 'Comment' (1971) 59 *Georgetown L.J.* 1237, 1253.

333 ibid., fn. 92.

334 See *Jarvis* v. *Swan Tours* [1978] 1 Q.B. 233; *Jackson* v. *Horizon Holidays* [1975] 1 W.L.R. 1468 and the South Australian decision in *Athens-MacDonald Travel Service* v. *Kazis* [1970] S.A.S.R. 264. See also *Ichard* v. *Frangoulis* [1977] 2 All E.R. 461 where Peter Pain J. took into account, in assessing damages for personal injury, the loss of enjoyment of the plaintiff's holiday which had been ruined by the defendant's negligence in causing the accident. See also *Heywood* v. *Wellers (a firm)* [1976] Q.B. 446, where damages were awarded for 'vexation, anxiety and distress'. See generally P. Clarke (1978) 52 *A.L.J.* 626.

335 (1951) 95 *Sol.Jo.* 727.

some detail has said, 'in fact the fears of a flood of litigation have not proved well founded'.[336]

It has been urged that the law of torts should provide a remedy for the intentional infliction of purely mental distress:

> otherwise the tendency would be for the victim to exaggerate symptoms of sick headaches, nausea, insomnia etc. to make out a technical basis of bodily injury [or nervous shock] upon which to predicate a parasitic recovery for the more grievous disturbance, the mental and emotional distress . . . suffered.[337]

Of course, protection against the intentional infliction of purely mental distress can be afforded by the creation of a statutory tort, but it is difficult to imagine that legislative time will be found for that. The development by the courts of the decisions in *Wilkinson* v. *Downton* and *Janvier* v. *Sweeney* and the extension of the action on the case to cover the intentional infliction of purely mental distress appears to be the easiest and best solution at the present time.

3. Limits on the Recovery for the Intentional Infliction of Purely Mental Distress

If the Australian courts are to grant a remedy for the intentional infliction of purely mental distress by way of an action on the case for damages should there be any limits on that recovery? Obviously there will be no requirement of duty as this is an intentional tort where duty of care requirements have no place. But the plaintiff will have to prove that the defendant did the act or made the statement with the intention of causing mental distress to the plaintiff. As with the action on the case for physical harm and for nervous shock, 'intention' means not only that the defendant meant to do it but it could also mean that the defendant knew that mental distress was certain or substantially certain to follow from his conduct. The courts can also impute an intention on the part of the defendant to cause mental distress in the same way as the courts in *Wilkinson* v. *Downton* imputed an intention on the part of the defendant to cause physical harm, and in *Janvier* v. *Sweeney* and *Stevenson* v. *Basham* imputed an intention on the part of the respective defendants to cause nervous shock. Whether the intention of the defendant be actual or imputed, the act or statement must in fact produce mental distress in order to be actionable. The mental distress produced must be *serious* mental distress, substantial and enduring rather than transient. It is difficult to define serious mental distress, but that should emerge in time from the cases. But it should not be necessary that the mental distress produce physical harm or nervous shock in order to be labelled 'serious'. As was

---

336 See Handford (see fn. 312 above) p. 11.

337 Magruder, 'Mental and Emotional Disturbance in the Law of Torts' (1936) 49 *Harv.L.R.* 1033, 1057. See also *Bond* v. *Chief Constable of Kent* [1983] 1 All E.R. 456 where the plaintiff who suffered distress and anxiety when the defendant threw a stone through the window of his house was held to have suffered either 'personal injury' or 'damage'. Is this not a case of purely mental distress?

said in one American decision, 'Serious mental distress may be found where a reasonable man, normally constituted, would be unable to adequately cope with the mental distress engendered by the circumstances of the case'.[338]

Another limit on recovery besides the seriousness of the mental distress might be that the act or statement must be of a kind reasonably capable of causing mental distress to a normal human being. As Jordan C.J. said of the act in *Bunyan* v. *Jordan*, to attract liability it should be 'of a kind reasonably capable of . . . terrifying a normal human being'.[339] Prosser points out that an American court 'quite properly refused to allow recovery for the silly fright of a hysterical woman at the sight of a man dressed in female clothing'.[340] The courts in Australia would probably take the same view in similar circumstances. We have suggested earlier that in the case of acts and statements which are intended to cause physical harm or nervous shock the defendant may reasonably be required to take the plaintiff as he finds him. It may be that in the case of intentional infliction of purely mental distress we should take the same view, though one can understand the courts being rather hesitant to accept that view in relation to purely mental distress, which is much less capable of proof than physical harm or nervous shock. However, if a defendant knows of a particular sensitivity or peculiar susceptibility of a particular plaintiff and works upon it then he cannot complain that the mental distress would not be caused to an ordinary person or normal human being. The judgments in *Bunyan* v. *Jordan* both in the New South Wales Court of Appeal and in the High Court make it clear that a defendant would be liable in such a case for the mental distress that he has caused to the particularly sensitive or peculiarly susceptible plaintiff.

Should liability for purely mental distress be confined to false statements or should true statements also attract liability in some circumstances? There is no reason why a person who deliberately uses a true statement to inflict mental distress should escape liability. Thus, to take the example given earlier, if D, the owner of a health studio, on several occasions in front of several persons tells P that she is 'revoltingly fat' and that she should come to his studio and D knows that P's obesity is due to an hormonal imbalance and that she is very sensitive about her obesity, then D should be liable for the intentional infliction of purely mental distress if P suffers serious mental distress as a result of his statement. The truth of the statement should make no difference to liability if D intended to cause such mental distress.

Should liability be confined to acts or statements made to or in the presence of a plaintiff? Or should it extend also to cover third persons who might, for example, overhear the statements? Ordinarily, it is suggested, recovery of damages for the intentional infliction of purely mental distress should be confined only to those persons in whose presence the act is done

---

338 *Rodrigues* v. *State* (1970) 472 P. 2d 509, 520.

339 (1936) 36 S.R.(N.S.W.) 350, 353.

340 (1956) 44 *Californian L.R.* 40, 53. The decision is *Nelson* v. *Crawford* (1899) 81 N.W. 335.

or the statement is made which causes the mental distress. However, where the defendant knows, or should have known, that his behaviour would cause severe mental distress to persons not in his presence (as in *Stevenson* v. *Basham*[341]), or where the defendant does an act (as in *Blakeley* v. *Shortal's Estate*[342]), or makes a statement (as in *Bielitzki* v. *Obadisk*[343]) with the intention that the act or statement should come to the knowledge of the plaintiff reasonably quickly, then, it is suggested, there will be liability in respect of intentional behaviour not in the presence of the plaintiff which causes him severe mental distress.

Finally it should be pointed out as Jordan C.J. did in *Bunyan* v. *Jordan* that 'in this class of action as in any other, it is the function of the Judge to say whether the facts proved are capable of founding the cause of action; and it is only if they are so capable that it falls to the jury to determine whether they do'.[344] Whether a judge is sitting with a jury or not he determines the limits of the cause of action. The foregoing discussion attempts to suggest what those limits might be if, and when, an action on the case for damages for the intentional infliction of purely mental distress comes before the courts in Australia.

VI: MALICIOUS PROSECUTION AND ABUSE OF PROCESS

There are two other torts which must be considered before we conclude our discussion of the intentional torts to the person. These are the tort of malicious prosecution and the tort of abuse of process of the court. These two torts are actions on the case for damages, like the actions on the case just discussed, the characteristics of which are an intentional act on the part of the defendant which indirectly causes damage to the plaintiff, an intention (actual or imputed) on the part of the defendant to cause such damage and actual damage suffered by the plaintiff. The development of these two actions on the case was somewhat late and relatively slow and the elements of the tort of malicious prosecution, as the High Court of Australia pointed out in *Commonwealth Life Assurance Society Ltd* v. *Smith*,[345] did not become definite and certain before the nineteenth century and the requirements of the tort of abuse of process of the court did not emerge clearly until the decision of the Court of Exchequer Chamber in *Grainger* v. *Hill*[346] in 1838.

It should be pointed out here that these two torts are capable of protecting much more than interferences with the physical and mental integrity and freedom of movement of the person, and that it is clear from the many decisions involving these two torts that the protection afforded

---

341 [1922] N.Z.L.R. 225.
342 (1945) 20 N.W. 2d 28.
343 (1922) 2 W.W.R. 238.
344 (1936) 36 S.R.(N.S.W.) 350, 355.
345 (1938) 59 C.L.R. 527, 535.
346 (1838) 4 Bing. N.C. 212.

by these torts extends also to the protection of one's reputation, property and economic interests.[347]

Nevertheless, the actual or threatened loss of liberty has been the foundation of most of the actions for malicious prosecution, until recently, even though as long ago as 1698 Holt C.J. in *Savile* v. *Roberts*[348] held that damages in an action for malicious prosecution might be claimed under three heads: damage to the person, damage to property and damage to reputation. The actual loss of liberty was also the foundation of the leading case of *Grainger* v. *Hill*.[349] It is not, therefore, inappropriate to consider the torts of malicious prosecution and of abuse of process of the court at this particular point, just after the discussion of the tort of false imprisonment.

There are, of course, distinctions between the torts of false imprisonment and malicious prosecution, and between circumstances which might make it necessary to rely upon the tort of malicious prosecution rather than the tort of false imprisonment. No doubt it was the incapacity of the tort of false imprisonment to deal with all the situations of deprivation of liberty without lawful cause that led to the establishment of the tort of malicious prosecution.

Just what are the distinctions between the torts of false imprisonment and malicious prosecution? The first distinction is that in false imprisonment the deprivation of liberty of the plaintiff can only be brought about by a direct act of the defendant, while in malicious prosecution the deprivation of liberty by the defendant can be brought about indirectly. This might happen, for example, when the defendant improperly uses the judicial process by bringing an unjustifiable charge against the plaintiff and 'the opinion and judgment of a judicial officer are interposed between the charge and the imprisonment'.[350] The tort of false imprisonment cannot be used for indirect deprivations of liberty. Secondly, false imprisonment can be brought only for an actual and total deprivation of liberty for a particular period whereas malicious prosecution is available not only for actual but also for threatened total deprivations of liberty. Thirdly, in false imprisonment the actual deprivation of liberty is wrongful from the start because, for example, the wrong person has been arrested on a valid warrant[351] or a person has been arrested on a defective warrant,[352] but in malicious prosecution the right person might have been arrested and the proper legal procedures followed but the plaintiff claims that this has been done maliciously and without reasonable and probable cause. Malicious prosecution is one of the very few torts where the motive of the defendant in initiating or continuing unjustifiable litigation is deemed to be relevant. Finally, false imprisonment, as one of the nominate

347 See *Bond Brewing Holdings Ltd* v. *National Australia Bank Ltd* (1991) 1 V.R. 386.
348 (1698) 1 Ld. Raym. 374, 378.
349 (1838) 4 Bing. N.C. 212.
350 See *Austin* v. *Dowling* (1870) L.R. 5 C.P. 534, 540.
351 See *Symes* v. *Mahon* [1922] S.A.S.R. 447.
352 See e.g. *Marriner* v. *Smorgon* [1989] V.R. 485.

torts of trespass to the person,[353] is actionable without proof of actual damage but in an action for malicious prosecution, as it is an action on the case, actual damage must be pleaded and proved.

A definition of the torts of malicious prosecution and abuse of process of the court will now be offered, followed by comments on some of the matters in the definitions.

1. Malicious Prosecution

> The tort of malicious prosecution is committed when a person institutes legal proceedings against another maliciously and without reasonable and probable cause and the proceedings though they have terminated in favour of that person nevertheless cause damage to his person, property or reputation.

It is necessary to comment further on the following matters. First, does the tort apply to the institution of only criminal proceedings or does the tort extend to civil proceedings as well? Secondly, what is meant by the word 'maliciously' in this context? Thirdly, what is meant by the words 'without reasonable and probable cause'? Fourthly, when can it be said that the proceedings had terminated in favour of the person seeking to bring an action for malicious prosecution? Finally, what are the sorts of damage which will provide the foundation for an action of malicious prosecution?

(a) Institution of legal proceedings The foundation of the action for malicious prosecution 'lies in abuse of the process of the court by wrongfully setting the law in motion' and the action 'is designed to discourage the perversion of the machinery of justice for an improper purpose'.[354] Until recently it was thought that the action for malicious prosecution would only lie for the malicious initiation and continuance of criminal proceedings and only two forms[355] of civil proceedings, namely, the malicious presentation of a bankruptcy petition and the malicious presentation of a petition to wind up a solvent trading company.[356] In the recent decision of the Supreme Court of Victoria in *Little* v. *Law Institute of Victoria & Others (No. 3)*,[357] however, Kaye and Beach JJ. took the view that there is no longer any justification for confining the remedy of malicious prosecution to criminal proceedings and the civil proceedings of bankruptcy petitions and applications to

---

353 The other nominate torts are battery and assault.

354 *Mohamed Amin* v. *Jogendra Kumar Bannerjee* [1947] A.C. 322 (Privy Council).

355 See *Coleman* v. *Buckingham's Ltd* [1963] S.R. (N.S.W.) 171 for a third exception.

356 In reliance on the following decisions: *Barker* v. *Sands & McDougall Co. Ltd* (1890) 16 V.L.R. 719; *Quartz Hill Consolidated Gold Mining Co.* v. *Eyre* (1883) 11 Q.B.D. 674; *Wiffen* v. *Bailey and Romford Urban District Council* [1915] 1 K.B. 600; *Mohamed Amin* v. *Jogendra Kumar Banerjee* [1947] A.C. 322 and *Fenn* v. *Paul* (1932) 32 S.R. (N.S.W.) 315.

357 [1990] V.R. 257.

wind up a company[358] and Ormiston J. held that 'the policy of the law no longer would deny a party the right to assert that he has suffered damage to his reputation by reason of the wrongful and malicious institution or continuation of [any] civil proceedings'.[359] It would seem, therefore, that not only the malicious institution of criminal proceedings which threaten loss of liberty, which cause scandal to reputation or which require expenditure to be incurred in defending oneself in the proceedings will provide the foundation for an action in malicious prosecution, but also that the malicious institution of civil proceedings which cause damage to a person's reputation will provide a sufficient basis for an action in malicious prosecution.[360]

In determining whether the defendant *instituted* the legal proceedings which form the basis of the action for malicious prosecution Isaacs A.C.J. in *Davis* v. *Gell* expressed the view that 'the substance and not the legal form must in all cases govern . . . while, on the one hand, a person giving information to the police is not necessarily the prosecutor yet, on the other, the mere fact that the police conduct the prosecution does not exclude him from that position'.[361] Dixon J. in *Commonwealth Life Assurance Society Ltd* v. *Brain* said it was clear that 'no responsibility is incurred by one who confines himself to bringing before some proper authority information which he does not disbelieve, even although in the hope that a prosecution will be instituted, if it is actually instituted as the result of an independent discretion on the part of that authority'.[362] But, 'if the discretion is misled by false information, or is otherwise practised upon in order to procure the laying of the charge, those who thus brought about the prosecution are responsible'.[363] If a prosecution already instituted is 'adopted and carried on by a stranger to its institution, he may be civilly liable for doing so if it is unsuccessful and he acts maliciously and without reasonable and probable cause'.[364] A person who is thoroughly justified in bringing proceedings and who discovers facts during the proceedings which show the prosecution to be in fact groundless will be

358 ibid., 267.

359 ibid., 289. Ormiston J. persuasively argues that the factors inhibiting pre-trial publicity of allegations in civil proceedings in the nineteenth and earlier part of the twentieth century no longer apply today and therefore that it would not be true to say today that in civil proceedings the poison and the antidote are presented simultaneously and that the publicty of the proceedings is accompanied by the refutation of the unfounded charge. This appears to have been the reason for excluding the malicious initiation and continuance of ordinary civil proceedings from the ambit of the tort of malicious prosecution.

360 This might not be the position in England. See *Metall & Rohstoff A.G.* v. *Donaldson Lufkin & Jenrette Inc.* [1989] 3 W.L.R. 563, 614. 'There are dicta suggesting that in the case of an ordinary civil action, however maliciously and unjustifiably brought, the successful defendant has no action in tort.' *Per* Slade L.J.

361 (1924) 35 C.L.R. 275, 282-3.

362 (1935) 53 C.L.R. 343, 379. See also *Danby* v. *Beardsley* (1880) 43 L.T. 603 and *Fanzelow* v. *Kerr* (1896) 14 N.Z.L.R. 660.

363 (1935) 53 C.L.R. 343, 379.

364 ibid., 378. See also *Fitzjohn* v. *Mackinder* (1861) 9 C.B. N.S. 505 and *Daniels* v. *Telfer* (1933) 34 S.R. (N.S.W.) 99.

liable in malicious prosecution for *continuing* the proceedings if he does not inform the court of the facts which he has since discovered.[365]

The decision that the defendant in an action for malicious prosecution has instituted or continued legal proceedings will not be made unless the court concludes that the defendant has been 'actively instrumental in setting the law in motion'[366] or played 'a sufficient role in the institution of proceedings as to be regarded as setting them in motion'.[367] The courts are concerned to find the 'real prosecutor'.[368] This might be the person actually laying the information or making the charge,[369] the person who instigates[370] the proceedings by a concocted story designed to bring about the laying of the information,[371] the person who counsels and persuades the actual prosecutor to institute proceedings or procures him to do so by dishonestly prejudicing his judgment[372] or the person who has procured the institution of criminal proceedings by the police.[373]

The mere giving of false information to the police may not be sufficient to regard the giver of the information as the real prosecutor unless that information has had a substantial influence on the police decision to prosecute. As Richardson J. in *Commercial Union Assurance Co. of NZ* v. *Lamont* has reminded us, the police these days 'have the professionalism to critically weigh and test the reliability of complaints and information which may be affected by self-interest or ill-will'.[374] Besides, there is the public policy consideration that members of the community should be encouraged to aid the police in their function of investigating and prosecuting breaches of the criminal law and, therefore, 'the circumstances in which they are to be regarded as having instigated a prosecution should be rare and exceptional'.[375]

(b) Maliciously In order to succeed in an action of malicious prosecution the plaintiff must show that the legal proceedings, which are the subject of the complaint, were brought maliciously. He must also show that the proceedings were brought without reasonable and probable cause. The decision of the Supreme Court of New South Wales in *Rapley* v. *Rapley*[376] shows that malice and want of reasonable and probable cause are two separate elements of the tort of malicious prosecution and that the plaintiff must prove the existence of both these requirements if he is to succeed in an action of malicious prosecution.

---

365 See *Tims* v. *John Lewis & Co. Ltd* (1951) 2 K.B. 459, 472.
366 See *Danby* v. *Beardsley* (1880) 43 L.T. 603, 604.
367 See *Commercial Union Assurance Co. of NZ Ltd* v. *Lamont* [1989] 3 N.Z.L.R. 187, 193.
368 See *Davies* v. *Gell* (1924) 35 C.L.R. 275, 282.
369 See *Sharp* v. *Biggs* (1932) 48 C.L.R. 81 and *Commercial Union Assurance Co. of NZ Ltd.* v. *Lamont* [1989] 3 N.Z.L.R. 187, 204.
370 See *Commonwealth Life Assurance Society Ltd* v. *Brain* (1935) 53 C.L.R. 343, 379-80.
371 See *Gell* v. *Davis* [1934] V.L.R. 315.
372 See *Commonwealth Life Assurance Society Ltd.* v. *Brain* (1935) 53 C.L.R. 343, 379.
373 See *Commercial Union Assurance Co. of NZ Ltd.* v. *Lamont* [1989] 3 N.Z.L.R. 187, 196.
374 ibid., 199.
375 ibid.
376 (1930) 30 S.R. (N.S.W.) 94.

The issue of whether the defendant instituted or continued the proceedings maliciously is a question of fact to be determined by the jury. As Street C.J. said in *Rapley* v. *Rapley*: 'It is well settled that in actions of this kind what is meant by malice is malice in fact, and that is a matter to be determined by the jury on a consideration of all the circumstances of the case'.[377] That determination, however, must be made 'in accordance with the trial judge's direction concerning what on the evidence might constitute malice'.[378]

The classic definition of the malice required for the tort of malicious prosecution is found in the judgment of Hawkins J. in *Hicks* v. *Faulkner*: 'The malice necessary to be established is not even malice in law such as may be assumed from the intentional doing of a wrongful act . . . but malice in fact—*malus animus*—indicating that the party was actuated either by spite or ill-will towards an individual, or by indirect or improper motives, though these may be wholly unconnected with any uncharitable feeling towards anybody'.[379] Malice covers not only spite or ill-will but also any motive other than a desire to bring a criminal to justice.[380] If the plaintiff in attempting to prove malice is basing his case on evidence that the defendant was influenced by some other motive than to bring the plaintiff to justice then he must show that that other motive was an improper motive if he is to succeed in proving malice. In *Rapley* v. *Rapley*[381] the defendant took proceedings against the plaintiff, his mother, charging her with being a person deemed to be insane wandering at large. The defendant admitted that he took these proceedings to stop the plaintiff from disposing of her property and the plaintiff argued that the defendant, therefore, had an indirect and improper motive for taking the proceedings. Street C.J., however, said 'if he had no motive in acting as he did except a filial desire to do what was best in the circumstances how can it be said that he was acting maliciously and in bad faith'.[382] It follows, therefore, that if the defendant has some motive for instituting or continuing the proceedings other than to bring the plaintiff to justice that motive must be both indirect and improper—'some wrong or sinister motive, some other motive or desire . . . than to do what the moving party *bona fide* believed to be right in the interests of justice'.[383]

The indirect and improper motive must also be the predominant motive of the defendant if the plaintiff is to succeed in showing that the defendant acted maliciously.[384]

Just as a prosecution can be instituted maliciously it can be continued maliciously if the malicious motive arises at any time during the

377 ibid.
378 *Little* v. *Law Institute of Victoria & Others (No. 3)* [1990] V.R. 257, 265.
379 (1878) 8 Q.B.D. 167, 174-5.
380 See *Glinski* v. *McIver* [1962] A.C. 726, 766.
381 (1930) 30 S.R. (N.S.W.) 94.
382 ibid., 99.
383 ibid.
384 See *Abbott* v. *Refuge Assurance Co. Ltd* [1962] 1 Q.B. 432.

prosecution, which is the subject of the complaint, from the time of the original arrest or the laying of the charge up to the dismissal.[385]

(c) Without reasonable and probable cause As we said earlier, if a plaintiff is to succeed in an action for malicious prosecution he must not only show that the defendant in launching the prosecution was actuated by malice, in the sense just discussed, but he must also show that the prosecution was instituted or continued without reasonable and probable cause.

There is no better statement of what is meant by the words 'reasonable and probable cause', in an action for malicious prosecution, than that of Hawkins J. in *Hicks* v. *Faulkner*:

> I should define reasonable and probable cause to be, an honest belief in the guilt of the accused based upon a full conviction, founded upon reasonable grounds, of the existence of a state of circumstances, which, assuming them to be true, would reasonably lead any ordinarily prudent and cautious man, placed in the position of the accuser, to the conclusion that the person charged was probably guilty of the crime imputed.[386]

It can be seen from this definition, which has been approved both by the House of Lords[387] and the High Court of Australia,[388] that the question of reasonable and probable cause appears to be a double one. Did the prosecutor actually believe *and* did he reasonably believe that he had cause for prosecution?

The issue of whether there is an absence of reasonable and probable cause, though a question of fact, is to be decided by a judge, unlike the question of whether the defendant instituted or continued the proceedings maliciously, which is left to the jury to determine. As Starke J. said in *Commonwealth Life Assurance Society* v. *Brain*:

> The question whether there is an absence of reasonable and probable cause is for the judge and not for the jury and if the facts on which that depends are not in dispute there is nothing for him to ask the jury and he should decide the matter himself. If there are facts in dispute upon which it is necessary he should be informed in order to arrive at a conclusion on this point, those facts must be left specifically to the jury, and when they have been determined by the jury the judge must decide as to the absence of reasonable and probable cause . . .[389]

Why is the question of absence of reasonable cause left to the judge and not the jury? The answer given by Lord Devlin in *Glinkski* v. *McIver* is that the history of the action for malicious prosecution shows undoubtedly that juries are prone to favour a plaintiff and that, therefore, judges 'have taken the extraordinary course of reserving to themselves at a jury trial the

---

385 See *Cliff* v. *Birmingham* (1901) 4 W.A.L.R. 20.
386 (1878) 8 Q.B.D. 167, 171.
387 See *Herniman* v. *Smith* [1938] A.C. 305, 316.
388 See *Sharp* v. *Biggs* (1932) 48 C.L.R. 81, 109.
389 (1935) 53 C.L.R. 343, 352.

decision on a pure question of fact'.[390] Judges feel that they are better able to provide a balance where on the one side the liberty of the subject is involved and on the other the risk that the citizen in the performance of his duty may be embarrassed if a jury too readily gives a verdict in favour of a plaintiff who has been prosecuted and acquitted.[391]

Central to the question of whether the defendant acted without reasonable and probable cause is the question of whether the defendant had 'a genuine belief that the proceedings were justified'[392] or an honest belief in the guilt of the accused.[393]

If there is any evidence given or elicited by the plaintiff of lack of a genuine belief that the proceedings were justified or any evidence of lack of honest belief in the guilt of the accused on the part of the person launching the proceedings, 'the fact whether he honestly believed or not is a disputed but essential fact on which the judge is to draw his conclusion and is a question for the jury'.[394] But, as Evershed M.R. pointed out in *Tempest* v. *Snowden*, where the question of honest belief is an issue in the case 'the form of the question [to be put to the jury] should be "Did the defendant honestly believe in the plaintiff's guilt" or "Did the defendant honestly believe in the charges he was preferring", and that it is better not to put into the question a reference to reasonable grounds'.[395] This is because the reasonableness of the prosecutor's belief in the existence of facts on which he acted, together with the question of whether the facts so believed amount to reasonable cause for believing the accused to be guilty or the launching of the proceedings justified, are questions for the judge and not the jury.[396]

The facts upon which the prosecutor acted should be ascertained. When the judge knows the facts operating on the prosecutor's mind, he must then decide whether they afford reasonable and probable cause for launching the prosecution.[397] The facts which operate on the prosecutor's mind must be facts which were in the knowledge of the defendant at the time he launched the prosecution.[398] It goes without saying that if the plaintiff in an action for malicious prosecution places before the court evidence of the nature of the whole of the information which the defendant had 'it is for the judge and not the jury to determine whether it was reasonable for the defendant to believe in the accuracy of the information . . . and also to determine whether it was reasonable for him to act on it, i.e. whether it was sufficient to justify a man of ordinary prudence and caution in believing that the plaintiff was probably guilty'.[399] It is only when the

---

390 [1962] A.C. 726, 777.
391 ibid., 741.
392 See *Little* v. *Law Institute of Victoria & Others (No. 3)* [1990] V.R. 257, 262. This is described as 'an honest belief' in *Hicks* v. *Faulkner* (1878) 8 Q.B.D. 167, 171.
393 See *Hicks* v. *Faulkner* (1878) 8 Q.B.D. 167, 171. Approved by the House of Lords in *Herniman* v. *Smith* [1938] A.C. 305, 316 and *Glinski* v. *McIver* [1962] A.C. 726.
394 See *Herniman* v. *Smith* [1938] A.C. 305, 316.
395 [1952] 1 K.B. 130, 137.
396 See *Herniman* v. *Smith* [1938] A.C. 305, 317.
397 ibid.
398 See *Delegal* v. *Highley* (1837) 3 Bing. N.C. 950.
399 See *Mitchell* v. *John Heine and Son Ltd* (1938) 38 S.R. (N.S.W.) 466, 471.

plaintiff has given or elicited evidence of a lack of genuine or honest belief and that evidence is disputed by the defendant that the procedure of requiring disputed issues of fact of importance to be determined by the jury comes into play.[400] In *Glinski* v. *McIver*, Lord Devlin said that this extremely difficult division of functions between judge and juries will produce a sound result 'only when the utmost skill is exercised by the trial judge'.[401] The recent decision in *Hatzinikolaou* v. *Snape & Others*[402] points to difficulties caused by this division of functions. Perhaps the time has come to place within the province of the judge alone the whole question of want of cause, whether it involves disputed issues of fact or not, but such a great change may need to be effected by the legislature rather than the courts.[403]

It is difficult to give a comprehensive account of the factors which the judge takes into account in deciding whether there was reasonable and probable cause, but a few of those factors might be mentioned. If a defendant acts on the advice of counsel or takes other competent advice in launching the prosecution, that will be regarded as reasonable and probable cause, but only if the defendant 'lays all the facts of his case fairly before counsel, and acts bona fide upon the opinion given by that counsel (however erroneous that opinion may be)'.[404] Failure on the part of the prosecutor to call on the accused for an explanation of the offence does not constitute absence of reasonable and probable cause. Such a call may only cause material evidence to disappear or be manufactured. Besides, the prosecutor's duty is not to ascertain whether there is a defence, but whether there is reasonable and probable cause for the prosecution.[405] It is a necessary part of the question of whether there was an absence of reasonable and probable cause to determine whether reasonable care was taken by the prosecutor to inform himself of the true state of the facts.[406] Proof that the defendant, when he instituted the prosecution, knew the plaintiff was innocent may supply evidence of absence of reasonable and probable cause, but proof that the defendant was animated by a desire to injure the plaintiff would not supply evidence of absence of reasonable and probable cause.[407] Lastly, it is relevant whether the defendant's mistake in proceeding against the plaintiff is one of fact or law. A mistake of law on a difficult and doubtful question of law will not be regarded as evidence of absence of reasonable and probable cause[408] but prosecution of the plaintiff for a non-existent offence is evidence of absence of reasonable and probable cause.[409]

---

400 Ibid. See also *Hatzinikolaou* v. *Snape & Another* (1989) Aust. Torts Reports 80-262 at 68, 809.
401 [1962] A.C. 726, 778.
402 (1989) Aust. Torts Reports 80-262.
403 See *Glinski* v. *McIver* [1962] A.C. 726, 778.
404 See *Glinski* v. *McIver* [1962] A.C. 726, 745 and *Ravenga* v. *MacKintosh* (1824) 2 B. & C. 693, 697.
405 See *Herniman* v. *Smith* [1938] A.C. 305, 319.
406 See *Abrath* v. *North Eastern Railway Co.* (1883) 11 Q.B.D. 440, 450.
407 See *Mitchell* v. *John Heine & Son Ltd* (1938) 38 S.R. (N.S.W.) 466, 474.
408 See *Phillips* v. *Naylor* (1859) 4 H. & N. 565.
409 See *Mackenzie* v. *Hyam* (1908) 8 S.R. (N.S.W.) 587.

(d) Termination in favour of plaintiff In addition to showing that proceedings were instituted or continued maliciously and without reasonable and probable cause the plaintiff must also show that the proceedings have terminated in the plaintiff's favour, if from their nature they were capable of such a termination. It follows, therefore, that a plaintiff cannot succeed in an action for malicious prosecution if he has been convicted.[410] The three explanations for the requirement that the proceedings must have terminated in the plaintiff's favour, repeatedly stated in the decided cases, are to be found in the decision of the High Court of Australia in *Commonwealth Life Assurance Society Ltd* v. *Smith*.[411] They are, first, that 'otherwise the propriety of a conviction for crime might be drawn in question collaterally';[412] secondly, the requirement is regarded as an example of 'a general rule which prevents imputations in one proceeding against the justice of the other proceeding already pending or of a judicial determination still standing';[413] and, thirdly, because the final termination of the proceedings in favour of the plaintiff provides evidence that 'the proceedings (whether the proceedings be in bankruptcy or by indictment) were really without foundation'.[414]

The requirement of a termination in favour of the plaintiff is satisfied if the plaintiff has had his conviction quashed on appeal,[415] if he has been acquitted[416] (even though this might be on a technicality), if the defendant has discontinued the proceedings[417] and even when the plaintiff has been convicted of a lesser offence than the one with which he was charged.[418] Although it is not entirely clear from the decision of the High Court of Australia in *Davis* v. *Gell*[419] whether the entry of a *nolle prosequi* is a sufficient termination of the proceedings in favour of the plaintiff to found an action for malicious prosecution, several decisions of courts in Australia have established that in an action for malicious prosecution, the entry of a *nolle prosequi* is sufficient proof that the proceedings have terminated in the plaintiff's favour.[420]

Despite the earlier decision of the High Court of Australia in *Davis* v. *Gell*[421] that in an action of malicious prosecution the plaintiff is required to prove not only that the proceedings terminated in his favour but also that he was innocent of the charge, this latter requirement, after the decision of the High Court of Australia in *Commonwealth Life Assurance*

410 See *Soare* v. *Ashley* [1955] V.L.R. 438, 440.
411 (1938) 59 C.L.R. 527, 539-40.
412 See *Commonwealth Life Assurance Society Ltd* v. *Smith* (1938) 59 C.L.R. 527, 539. See also *Basébé* v. *Matthews* (1867) L.R. 2 C.P. 684, 687.
413 ibid. See also *Gilding* v. *Eyre* (1861) 10 C.B.N.S. 592, 604.
414 ibid. See also *Johnson* v. *Emerson* (1871) L.R. 6 Ex. 329, 344.
415 See *Reynolds* v. *Kennedy* (1748) 1 Wils. 232.
416 See *Wicks* v. *Fentham* (1791) 4 Term Rep. 247.
417 See *Watkins* v. *Lee* (1839) 5 M. & W. 270.
418 See *Boaler* v. *Holder* (1887) 51 J.P. 277.
419 (1924) 35 C.L.R. 275.
420 See *Mann* v. *Jacombe* (1961) N.S.W.R. 273; *Taylor* v. *Shire of Eltham* (1922) V.L.R.1 and *Hill* v. *Varley* (1923) Q.W.N. 23.
421 (1924) 35 C.L.R. 275.

Society Ltd v. *Smith*,[422] is unlikely to be demanded by a court in Australia.

If from either the nature or the course of the proceedings a termination is impossible the requirement of termination of the proceedings in favour of the plaintiff will not be insisted upon by the court.[423] As Isaacs J. said in *Varawa* v. *Howard Smith & Co.*, 'the plaintiff is absolved from showing the termination of the former proceedings in his favour where such an event is not legally possible'.[424]

(e) **Damage** As indicated earlier, the tort of malicious prosecution, as it is an action on the case, requires the plaintiff to prove actual damage suffered by him, in addition to the other four requirements discussed. It is not, however, any kind of damage that will provide the foundation for an action in malicious prosecution. As Kaye and Beach JJ. pointed out in *Little* v. *Law Institute of Victoria & Others (No. 3)*,[425] it is settled law that no action will lie for malicious legal proceedings unless the plaintiff has suffered damage of a form within the three heads of damage which were laid down by Holt C.J. in *Savile* v. *Roberts*[426] in 1698. In that decision Holt C.J. set out the three forms of damage, any one of which would support an action in malicious prosecution. They are: first, damage to a man's fame as where the matter of which he is accused is scandalous; secondly, damage to the person as where a man is put in danger of losing his life, limb or liberty; and, thirdly, damage to a man's property, as where he is forced to expend his money in necessary charges to acquit himself of the crime of which he is accused.[427] It would appear that one of these three forms of damage is still required if an action for malicious prosecution is to succeed, and there is no indication of a relaxation of this requirement. In the recent decision in *Little* v. *Law Institute of Victoria & Others (No. 3)*, Kaye and Beach JJ. confirmed the requirement that the damage suffered by the plaintiff must come within the three categories when they pointed out that 'clearly the appellant's claim for damages for mental and bodily pain and anguish suffered by him is not within the categories prescribed by Holt C.J.'.[428]

In relation to these categories or heads, the word 'scandalous' was very likely used by Holt C.J. 'as a synonym for "slanderous" in the sense of the kind of imputation which, if spoken, was [in 1698] slander actionable *per se*',[429] but in *Wiffen's* case the English Court of Appeal imposed a test of 'whether the institution of [the] proceedings necessarily and naturally conveyed an imputation affecting the plaintiff's fair fame'.[430] This was

422 (1938) 59 C.L.R. 527.
423 See *Davis* v. *Gell* (1924) 35 C.L.R. 275, 289.
424 (1911) 13 C.L.R. 35, 89. See also *Little* v. *Law Institute of Victoria & Others (No. 3)* [1990] V.R. 257, 277.
425 [1990] V.R. 257, 265.
426 (1698) 1 Ld. Raym. 374.
427 See also the statement of those three heads of damage by the High Court of Australia in *Commonwealth Life Assurance Society Ltd* v. *Smith* (1938) 59 C.L.R. 527, 544.
428 See [1990] V.R. 257, 265-6.
429 See *Berry* v. *British Transport Commission* [1961] 1 Q.B. 149, 161.
430 [1915] 1 K.B. 600, 608.

interpreted by Diplock J. to mean: 'Was the charge one which necessarily and naturally is defamatory of the plaintiff?',[431] and by Ormiston J. in *Little* v. *Law Institute of Victoria & Others (No. 3)* to mean an allegation in a civil proceeding 'such as to injure a person in his reputation'.[432] In *Assheton* v. *Merrett* Richards J. of the Supreme Court of South Australia held that the plaintiff was 'entitled to compensation for the indignity he has suffered and for the injury to his fame or credit caused by the prosecution'.[433] In relation to damage under the second head, not only is actual deprivation of liberty sufficient to constitute damage but also even a threatened loss of liberty suffices.[434] The deprivation of liberty, however, must flow directly from the proceedings which have been maliciously instituted and not, for example, from a later instituted contempt application for failure to abide by the order made in the earlier proceedings.[435] It should be noted that 'mental and bodily pain and anguish' was held not to fall within this head in *Little* v. *Law Institute of Victoria & Others (No. 3)*.[436] In relation to the third head of damage, it would appear that the recovery of costs of defending the proceedings depends on whether the malicious proceedings which are the subject of the complaint are civil or criminal. In *Berry* v. *British Transport Commission*[437] the English Court of Appeal decided that extra costs over and above the amount recovered in taxed costs in a civil action do not constitute expenses sufficient to support an action for malicious prosecution, but that expenses incurred by a plaintiff in defending criminal proceedings, over and above the sum which might be awarded as costs, are sufficient to support an action for malicious prosecution.

The measure of damages in an action for malicious prosecution is 'incapable of any precise limitation'[438] but 'there must be some reasonable relation between the wrong done and the solatium applied'.[439] The court will have regard to the seriousness of the charge and the ruinous effect which it is likely to have on the plaintiff's reputation.[440] If a prosecution is spiteful or shameful, exemplary damages may be awarded.[441] The

---

431 See *Berry* v. *British Transport Commission* [1961] 1 Q.B. 149, 166.

432 [1990] V.R. 257, 281.

433 [1928] S.A.S.R. 11, 15.

434 See *Wiffen* v. *Bailey Romford Urban Council* [1915] 1 K.B. 600, 615.

435 See *Little* v. *Law Institute of Victoria & Others (No. 3)* [1990] V.R. 257, 280.

436 ibid., 265. See, however, *White* v. *Metropolitan Police Commissioner, The Times*, 24 April 1982, where the plaintiffs were awarded £2500 for the distress, anxiety and damage to reputation which the malicious prosecution caused the plaintiffs.

437 [1962] 1 Q.B. 306, 338.

438 See *Commonwealth Life Assurance Society Ltd* v. *Brain* (1935) 53 C.L.R. 343, 354. In *Wentworth* v. *Rogers* (1985) Supreme Court (N.S.W.), unreported, the defendant in a cross-claim for malicious prosecution was awarded a sum of $571 000 against the plaintiff who maliciously brought criminal proceedings against the defendant. See the *Australian* 18 December 1985.

439 See *Greenlands Ltd* v. *Wilmhurst and the London Association for the Protection of Trade* [1913] 3 K.B. 507, 532, 533.

440 See *Commonwealth Life Assurance Society Ltd* v. *Brain* (1938) 53 C.L.R. 343, 402.

441 See *Assheton* v. *Merrett* [1928] S.A.S.R. 11, 15 and *White* v. *Metropolitan Police Commissioner, The Times*, 24 April 1982.

provocative conduct of the plaintiff can be taken into account in reducing those damages.[442]

(f) Vicarious liability A servant or agent who institutes or continues an action for malicious prosecution may make the master or principal liable also for the tort if the servant acts within the scope of his employment and the agent within the scope of his authority in initiating or continuing the action.[443]

2. Abuse of Process

> The tort of abuse of process of the court is committed when a person uses the process of the court, although regular in form, predominantly for an ulterior and improper purpose,[444] entirely outside the ambit of the legal claim upon which the court is asked to adjudicate, and thereby causes damage to the plaintiff.

The decision which is generally regarded as founding this tort is the decision of the Exchequer Chamber in *Grainger* v. *Hill*.[445] In that case the plaintiff had borrowed £80 from the defendants on the mortgage of a ship of which he was owner as well as captain. The debt was repayable on 28 September 1837. Under some apprehension as to the sufficiency of their security the defendants decided in November 1836, several months before the debt was repayable, to possess themselves of the ship's register without which the plaintiff could not go to sea. In order to achieve this purpose, after threatening to arrest the plaintiff unless he repaid the money lent, they made an affidavit of debt and sued out a writ of *capias* in the sum of some £95 and sent two sheriff's officers with the writ to the plaintiff, who was lying ill in bed from the effects of a wound and attended by a surgeon. When told by the surgeon that the plaintiff could not be removed the officers told the plaintiff that they had not come to take him but to get the ship's register, but that if he failed to deliver the register, or to find bail, they must either take him or leave one of the officers with him. The plaintiff, being unable to procure bail, and being much alarmed, gave up the register. The plaintiff claimed damages for the loss of voyages which he could not undertake because of the loss of the register and for the recovery of the register.

The plaintiff succeeded at the trial, and there was an appeal to the Exchequer Chamber, which dismissed it. In delivering judgment Tindal C.J. said:

---

442 See *Bishop* v. *Commissioner of Police of the Metropolis, The Times*, 5 December 1989.

443 See *Lennox* v. *Langdon* (1872) 3 A.J.R. 25 and *Little* v. *Law Institute of Victoria & Others (No. 3)* [1990] V.R. 257, 262.

444 Mahoney J.A. in *Spautz* v. *Gibbs* (1990) 21 N.S.W.L.R. 230, 234 prefers the phrase 'unacceptable object' to the phrase 'improper purpose'. See, however, *Williams* v. *Spautz* (1992) 107 A.L.R. 635, 648.

445 (1838) 4 Bing. N.C. 212.

The second ground urged for a nonsuit is, that there was no proof of the suit commenced by the Defendants having been terminated. But the answer to this, and to the objection urged in arrest of judgment, namely, the omission to allege want of reasonable and probable cause for the Defendants' proceeding, is the same: that this is an action for abusing the process of the law, by applying it to extort property from the Plaintiff, and not an action for a malicious arrest or malicious prosecution, in order to support which action the termination of the previous proceeding must be proved, and the absence of reasonable and probable cause be alleged as well as proved.[446]

Tindal C.J. went on to say that the plaintiff's complaint being that the process of the law had been abused, to effect an object not within the scope of the process it was 'immaterial whether the suit which that process commenced has been determined or not, or whether or not it was founded on reasonable and probable cause'.[447]

The action for abuse of process is different from the action for malicious prosecution in several ways. As explained in *Grainger* v. *Hill*[448] and the early decision of the High Court of Australia in *Varawa* v. *Howard Smith Co. Ltd*,[449] in a declaration founded on the cause of action for abuse of process of the court the plaintiff would not need to allege absence of reasonable and probable cause nor would it be necessary for him to prove that the previous proceedings had terminated in his favour. This difference between the action for abuse of process and the older action for malicious prosecution has recently been reiterated by the High Court of Australia in *Williams* v. *Spautz*.[450] This gives the action for abuse of process some advantages over the action for malicious prosecution. In *Hanrahan* v. *Ainsworth*,[451] for example, the plaintiff sued the first defendant for damages for abuse of process for bringing an action in defamation against him. The plaintiff alleged that the defamation proceedings were instituted by the first defendant for the real purpose of interfering, hindering and preventing the plaintiff from carrying out his duties as a police officer, investigating corruption in the poker machine industry and proceeding with criminal charges against the first defendant and not for the purpose of vindicating the first defendant's reputation or to obtain damages for defamation. There had been no decision in the defamation proceedings but Hunt J. nevertheless held that the action for abuse of process could proceed as 'the difference principally relevant here is the need in the action for malicious prosecution but not in the action for abuse of process for the plaintiff to plead and to prove that the earlier proceedings have terminated in his favour'.[452]

As the action for malicious prosecution and the action for abuse of process are both actions on the case, actual damage must be pleaded and proved in both. In an action for malicious prosecution, however, the

446 ibid., 221.
447 ibid.
448 (1838) 4 Bing. N.C. 212.
449 (1911) 13 C.L.R. 35, 55-6, 69-70, 91.
450 (1992) 107 A.L.R. 635, 643.
451 [1985] 1 N.S.W.L.R. 370.
452 ibid., 375.

damage suffered by the plaintiff must come within the three heads of damage laid down by Holt C.J. in *Savile* v. *Roberts*[453] in 1698, while in an action for abuse of process any special damage suffered by the plaintiff might be sufficient. In *Hanrahan* v. *Ainsworth* expenses incurred by the plaintiff in travelling to see his legal advisers and anxiety, worry and nervous upset suffered by the plaintiff were all held to be capable of constituting damage for the purposes of the tort of abuse of process.[454]

The nature of the motive which the plaintiff must prove in order to establish an abuse of process is also arguably easier to prove than the requirements of instituting proceedings 'malicously' and without 'reasonable and probable cause' which are necessary for the tort of malicious prosecution. In an action for abuse of process, as Hunt J. pointed out in *Spautz* v. *Williams*,[455] the *dominant*[456] motive must be one 'to exert pressure to effect an object not within the scope of the process' or one 'other than that for which the proceedings are properly designed and exist' or one 'seeking some collateral advantage beyond what the law offers'. Hunt J. said that the plaintiff need not establish a 'malicious motive' provided he can prove one of these 'ulterior' motives. But he also went further and said that it does not matter that the defendant

> genuinely believed that his motive was a proper one for invoking the criminal law. What must be proved is not that [the defendant] subjectively intended his prosecutions to amount to an abuse of process, but rather that his prosecutions objectively are in fact such an abuse of process because of the ulterior motive with which they were brought.[457]

Hunt J. was concerned not to 'unduly narrow the tort of abuse of process' which has been fashioned to prevent damage caused by the unnecessary invocation of the process of the court and to compensate for it. In the recent decision in *Williams* v. *Spautz*[458] the High Court of Australia indicated that the criterion for abuse of process is not whether the improper purpose of the moving party in using the legal process was his *sole* purpose, but whether the improper purpose was his predominant purpose. The court approved of the *dictum* of Slade L.J. of the English Court of Appeal in the *Metall* case that a person alleging an abuse of process 'must show that the predominant purpose of the other party in using the legal process has been one other than that for which it was designed'.[459] Is it essential to the exercise of the jurisdiction of the court in an action for abuse of process that there should be an improper act as well

---

453 (1698) 1 Ld. Raym. 374.
454 [1985] 1 N.S.W.L.R. 370, 373.
455 [1983] 2 N.S.W.L.R. 506, 543-4.
456 See *Metall & Rohstoff A.G.* v. *Donaldson, Lufkin & Jenrette Inc.* [1990] 1 Q.B. 391, 469 'a person alleging such an abuse must show that the predominant purpose of the other party in using the legal process has been one other than that for which it was designed and that as a result he had caused him damage' *per* Slade L.J.
457 [1983] 2 N.S.W.L.R. 506, 544.
458 (1992) 107 A.L.R. 635, 648-9.
459 [1990] 1 Q.B. 391, 469.

as an improper purpose? In *Williams* v. *Spautz*[460] the High Court of Australia said that neither the authorities in Australia nor those in England insist on the need for an improper *act* as an essential ingredient in the concept of abuse of process.

Finally, it should be noted that the tort of malicious prosecution was originally confined to the malicious institution of criminal proceedings and only two forms of civil proceedings, namely, the malicious presentation of a bankruptcy petition and the malicious presentation of a petition to wind up a solvent trading company. The action for abuse of process could be used in relation to both criminal and ordinary civil process, as the High Court of Australia has recently affirmed in *Williams* v. *Spautz*.[461] However, the recent decision in *Little* v. *Law Institute of Victoria & Others (No. 3)*[462] appears to extend the tort of malicious prosecution to other forms of civil proceedings which cause damage to a person's reputation because, as Ormiston J. stressed, many civil proceedings containing serious allegations at the present time receive publicity virtually from the day they have been issued (in the same way as criminal proceedings have done for a long time past). This decision would appear to remove this particular advantage which actions for abuse of process had over actions for malicious prosecution.

The action for abuse of process can be used not only for the purpose of obtaining compensation by way of damages but also for the purpose of terminating proceedings which have commenced.[463] Thus, 'existing proceedings may be stayed or dismissed, or documents delivered as a step in the proceedings may be struck out'.[464] If a stay is sought to stop a prosecution which has been instituted and maintained for an improper purpose, it is not necessary, before granting a stay, for the court to satisfy itself in such a case that unless the prosecution is stopped, an unfair trial will ensue.[465] Though usually a court acts against abuse of its process *after* proceedings have been commenced it can act *before*, for example, when a court restrains the presentation or advertising of a winding up petition.[466] The decisions of the courts have established the principle that a court in its inherent jurisdiction to prevent an abuse of process of the court may restrain, by an injunction, the presentation of a winding up petition where its presentation would amount to an abuse of the process of the court.[467] This principle enables companies to be protected from threatened or apprehended oppression and damage from abuse of court process.

Can the tort of abuse of process be used to debar a litigant with a genuine cause of action from proceeding if it can be shown that he had an

---

460 (1992) 107 A.L.R. 635, 647.
461 ibid. 640.
462 [1990] V.R. 257.
463 See *Herron* v. *McGregor* [1986] 6 N.S.W.L.R. 246 and *Cox* v. *Journeaux [No. 2]* (1935) 52 C.L.R. 713.
464 See *Fortuna Holdings* v. *Deputy Commissioner of Taxation* [1978] V.R. 83, 87.
465 See *Williams* v. *Spautz* (1992) 107 A.L.R. 635, 640-1.
466 See *Mann* v. *Goldstein* [1968] 1 W.L.R. 1091, 1093-4 especially if a debt is disputed. See also *Fortuna Holdings* v. *Deputy Commissioner of Taxation* [1978] V.R. 83, 87.
467 See *Mann* v. *Goldstein* [1968] 1 W.L.R. 1091, 1093-4.

ulterior purpose in view as a byproduct of the litigation? In *Williams* v. *Spautz*,[468] the High Court of Australia indicated that the power of the court 'must extend to the prevention of an abuse of process resulting in oppression, even if the moving party has a prima facie case or must be assumed to have a prima facie case'. So even if a moving party who commences criminal proceedings can establish a prima facie case against the defendant but has no intention of prosecuting the proceedings to a conclusion because, for example, he wishes to use them only as a means of extorting a pecuniary benefit from the defendant, the court would have the power to prevent the abuse of process in these circumstances.[469] However, if the ultimate and ulterior purpose in bringing proceedings is to take advantage of an entitlement, benefit or result which the law provides in the event that the proceedings terminate in the litigant's favour, the existence of that ultimate and ulterior purpose cannot constitute an abuse of process.[470]

It may be useful to conclude this discussion on abuse of process by mentioning some recent decisions in which abuse of process has been raised. Reference has already been made to the decision in *Hanrahan* v. *Ainsworth*.[471] In *Spautz* v. *Williams*[472] and in *Williams* v. *Spautz*[473] it was held that it was an abuse of process to commence and continue prosecutions against the applicants for criminal defamation because the dominant motive or predominant purpose with which the defendant prosecuted the applicants had been to pressure the University of Newcastle through its officers to reinstate the defendant or to agree to a favourable settlement of his claim for wrongful dismissal. In *Packer* v. *Meagher*[474] the court held that the plaintiff's purpose in bringing defamation proceedings against the defendant was not to vindicate his own reputation by an award of compensatory damages but rather it was to canvass or investigate the conduct of the Royal Commission which the defendant was appointed to assist. That purpose, it was held by Hunt J., was not a proper purpose for commencing defamation proceedings and the defamation proceedings should be dismissed as an abuse of the process of the court. And in *Speed Seal Products Ltd* v. *Paddington*[475] the English Court of Appeal held that there was an arguable case that there had been an actionable abuse of the process of the court if the defendant in an action for breach of confidential information could prove that the action was brought by the plaintiff to damage the defendant's business interests and not for the protection of any legitimate interest of the plaintiff.

It should be pointed out that the adduction of false evidence and the submission of a false case for the purpose of sustaining or defending a claim in legal proceedings does not expose the guilty plaintiff or defendant

468 (1992) 107 A.L.R. 635, 643.
469 ibid.
470 ibid., 646.
471 [1985] 1 N.S.W.L.R. 370.
472 [1983] 2 N.S.W.L.R. 506.
473 (1992) 107 A.L.R. 635.
474 [1984] 3 N.S.W.L.R. 486.
475 [1985] 1 W.L.R. 1327. See also *Goldsmith* v. *Sperrings Ltd* [1977] 1 W.L.R. 478.

to an action for damages in tort for abuse of process, even though it might subject him to sanctions by way of a penal order for costs or even a prosecution for perjury. As the English Court of Appeal stated recently in *Metall & Rohstoff* v. *Donaldson, Lufkin & Jenrette Inc.*: 'Relief in tort under the principle of *Grainger* v. *Hill* [i.e. the tort of abuse of legal process] is not, in our judgment, available against a party who, however dishonestly, presents a false case for the purpose of advancing or sustaining his claim or defence in civil proceedings. This may well cause hardship to an injured party who cannot be sufficiently compensated by an appropriate order for costs'.[476]

The action on the case for abuse of process is beginning to be used more often, and not only in situations involving the deprivation of liberty as in *Grainger* v. *Hill*. It is a tort gaining in importance and could well be used, for example, by borrowers against lenders who seek the appointment of receivers by the court, perhaps prematurely, as was argued in *National Australia Bank Ltd* v. *Bond Brewing Holdings Ltd*.[477] The action for abuse of process could be used by applicants who merely want the proceedings, which are an abuse of the process, stayed or dismissed. However, as Hunt J. noted in *Packer* v. *Meagher*, 'the court should act to stay or to dismiss proceedings as an abuse of process only in exceptional cases'.[478] In *Williams* v. *Spautz* the High Court of Australia adverted to the 'risk that the exercise of the jurisdiction to grant a stay may encourage some defendants to seek a stay on flimsy grounds for tactical reasons'. The court, however, went on to say that that risk and other policy considerations are not so substantial 'as to outweigh countervailing policy considerations and deter the courts from exercising the jurisdiction in appropriate cases'.[479]

The onus of satisfying the court that there is an abuse of process lies upon the party alleging it.[480] The onus is 'a heavy one'.[481]

---

476 [1989] 3 W.L.R. 563, 612-13.

477 [1991] 1 V.R. 386. See especially the judgment of Brooking J. at 592.

478 [1984] 3 N.S.W.L.R. 486, 500, approving the dictum of Lord Denning M.R. in *Goldsmith* v. *Sperrings Ltd* [1977] 1 W.L.R. 478, 490, 498. See also *Spautz* v. *Williams* [1983] 2 N.S.W.L.R. 506, 540.

479 (1992) 107 A.L.R. 635, 641.

480 ibid., 649.

481 See *Goldsmith* v. *Sperrings Ltd* [1977] 1 W.L.R. 478, 490 *per* Scarman L.J.

3

INTENTIONAL TORTS TO LAND

I: SOME GENERAL COMMENTS

In the previous chapter we considered how the law of torts protects the physical and mental integrity of a person against intentional interferences. We now consider how the law of torts protects a person's interests in land against similar interferences. There are, of course, several ways by which the law protects a person's interests in land. In many of the Australian States and Territories a person who wrongfully enters upon or remains on the land of another commits not only a tort but also a statutory offence punishable by fine or imprisonment.[1] In the law of torts, a person who has had his interests in land invaded has access to several causes of action: trespass, nuisance, negligence, *Rylands* v. *Fletcher* and the action on the case for damages. The discussion of several of these torts will be found elsewhere in this book. In this chapter, the discussion is confined to two torts which are available when there has been an *intentional* interference with another's interests in land.

The first is the tort of trespass to land. It is sometimes called 'trespass *quare clausum fregit*' because the words of the writ from which this tort is derived commanded the defendant to show cause why he had 'broken and

---

1 Vic.: Summary Offences Act 1966 ss.9(1)(d) & 50A; N.S.W.: Inclosed Lands Protection Act 1901 s.4; Qld: Vagrants, Gaming and Other Offences Act 1931, s.4A; Tas.: Police Offences Act 1935 ss.14B-14D & 19A; S.A.: Summary Offences Act 1953 s.17a; Cwth: Crimes Act 1914 s.89(1), Public Order (Protection of Persons and Property) Act 1971 ss.11, 12 & 20 [also operates in the A.C.T. & N.T.]; W.A.: Land Act 1933 s.164(2)(a); A.C.T.: Trespass on Territory Land Act 1932 s.4 and N.T.: Trespass Act 1987 ss.5-9.

In addition, criminal penalties are provided by the Statutes of Forcible Entry of the U.K. which have modern equivalents in Australia. See R. Sackville & M.A. Neave *Property Law: Cases and Materials* (4th edn, Sydney, 1988) pp. 109-10.

Also, under the Family Law Act 1975 (Cwth) a person can be restrained from going on to freehold property owned by him but such restraining orders are generally only made when the court is satisfied that people (generally wives or children) are under a real and imminent threat of harm from the person against whom the order is made. See *Cooper* v. *Pryce* (1984) 28 N.T.R. 10, 18.

entered the close' of the plaintiff[2]—or, in modern terminology, why he had invaded the land of the plaintiff. This tort is the appropriate remedy when a defendant interferes directly with the exclusive possession of land of the plaintiff either by entering on or by placing things upon land in the possession of the plaintiff. It is available even when the plaintiff cannot show any actual damage to his land; in other words, the tort is actionable *per se*. The second tort considered in this chapter is the action on the case for damages. This cause of action, based on the principle in *Beaudesert Shire Council* v. *Smith*,[3] is available when the defendant intentionally does some positive act forbidden by law which indirectly interferes with the land of the plaintiff or directly interferes with the land of a third party, and inevitably causes damage to the plaintiff. It is essential in such an action that the plaintiff prove damage, though it is not necessary for him to prove that there was an intention on the part of the defendant to cause harm or damage.[4] It is sufficient (the other elements being present) that the act is intentional and its inevitable consequence is to cause loss to the plaintiff.

The distinction between the two torts considered in this chapter can be best illustrated by an example. Suppose P grows cabbages on his land which adjoins a stream owned by a third party (T). P's land is irrigated by water from T's stream with T's permission and licence. Now if D comes on to P's land without permission and tramples on his crop of cabbages the appropriate remedy for this direct intentional act would be an action for trespass to land. But if D unlawfully takes away a large quantity of gravel from T's stream with the result that the flow of water to P's land is drastically reduced with the inevitable consequence that P's crop of cabbages fails due to a lack of water, the remedy for this intentional indirect interference with P's land would be an action on the case for damages against D, on the *Beaudesert* principle. Of course T would have an action in trespass to land against D and probably also an action in conversion for the taking of the gravel but P could not bring an action for trespass to land as D's act only indirectly interferes with P's land.

Before we consider the elements of these two torts in greater detail, however, it should be pointed out that in an age when people are less dependent on land for their living the tort of trespass to land has declined in importance. The emphasis has shifted from a concern with direct interferences with one's possession of land, with which the tort of trespass to land is concerned, to a concern for maximizing a person's use and enjoyment of his land with which the tort of nuisance is concerned. The courts seem much more occupied these days with balancing the rights and duties of owners or occupiers of neighbouring properties (which is done

---

2 See e.g. *Street* (6th edn, 1976) Ch. 5 where he heads the section on trespass to land as trespass *quare clausum fregit*. For some examples of the writ, see C.H.S. Fifoot *History and Sources of the Common Law* (London, 1949) p. 65.

3 (1966) 120 C.L.R. 145.

4 See Mason J. in *Kitano* v. *The Commonwealth* (1974) 129 C.L.R. 151, 174.

in cases of nuisance) than with preventing persons coming on to, remaining on or placing things upon another's land.[5]

We do not deal in this book, in any detail, with the action for recovery of possession of land. Even though the action has been described by Goddard L.J. in *Bramwell* v. *Bramwell* as the 'modern equivalent of the old action of ejectment' and as 'a species of the action of trespass',[6] and, more recently, as an action which should 'be treated as an action in tort',[7] it is perhaps more appropriately dealt with in books on property law and is, in fact, rather extensively dealt with there.[8] The action for recovery of possession of land is a remedy which allows a person with a superior title to recover possession of land and which prevents a person with an inferior title from remaining in possession of land. In such proceedings, the plaintiff can, and usually does, claim compensation for being deprived of the use of his land. This is described as a claim for mesne profits and is usually joined with an action for recovery of possession of land. The measure of damages is a reasonable sum in the nature of rent for the user during the period of the defendant's trespass. There is, however, a conflict of views as to whether the plaintiff can, in such an action, further claim the profits which the defendant has received from his use of the plaintiff's land. If a plaintiff can recover these further profits then he would be better off bringing an action for the recovery of possession of land rather than an action for trespass to land.[9] Though there is no clear authority, the decision in *Bilambil-Terranova Pty Ltd* v. *Tweed Shire Council* seems to suggest that Australian courts might allow plaintiffs to recover these profits on the ground that a defendant ought not to derive an advantage from his own wrong.[10] As Mahoney J.A. said, 'whether the law of unjust enrichment forms part of Australian law as such, the influences which inform it are not without effect in our law'.[11] The recovery of such profits is much more likely in an action for mesne profits joined with an action for recovery of possession of land rather than an action for trespass to land, where such profits would have to be given to the plaintiff by way of exemplary or punitive damages.[12]

---

5 See, however, the recent attempts to prevent unlawful intrusions on privacy by using the tort of trespass to land in *Lincoln Hunt Australia Pty Ltd* v. *Willesee* (1986) 4 N.S.W.L.R. 457 and *Emcorp Pty Ltd* v. *A.B.C.* [1986] Aust. Current Law 27.1. See also Handley (1988) 62 *A.L.J.* 216.

6 [1942] 1 K.B. 370, 373.

7 *Serbian Orthodox Ecclesiastic School Community 'Saint Nikolas'* v. *Vlaislavijevic* [1970] Qd.R. 386, 391, per W.B. Campbell J.

8 See R. Sackville & M.A. Neave *Property Law* (4th edn, Sydney, 1988) pp. 103-4, 106 ff; P. Brooking & A. Chernov *Tenancy Law and Practice*, Victoria (1980) Ch. 24 etc.

9 This was suggested in *Street* (6th edn, 1976) pp. 71-2.

10 [1980] 1 N.S.W.L.R. 465.

11 ibid., 495.

12 See *Austin* v. *Rescon Construction (1984) Ltd.* (1989) 57 D.L.R. (4th) 591 where this was done. See also *L.J.P. Investments Pty Ltd* v. *Howard Chia Investments Pty Ltd* (1991) Aust. Torts Reports 80-070.

II: TRESPASS TO LAND

Trespass to land is a direct physical interference by a defendant of a plaintiff's exclusive possession of land. The tort of trespass to land is usually brought only for intentional interferences, though actions for reckless and even careless interferences are not precluded.

There are at least six matters which require elaboration in relation to this tort.

1. What is 'Land'?

Blackstone, in his *Commentaries on the Laws of England*, 'an important 18th century legal treatise that all legal scholars have heard of but practically no one knows anything about',[13] wrote that 'the word "land" includes not only the face of the earth, but everything under it, or over it'.[14] It included not only 'any ground, soil or earth whatsoever . . . [but] also castles, houses and other buildings'. It had 'an indefinite extent, upwards as well as downwards', the owner of the surface owning everything to the heavens above and to the centre of the earth below. For this definition of 'land' Blackstone relied on the thirteenth-century maxim *cujus est solum ejus est usque ad coelum et ad inferos*. It should not, however, be assumed that the maxim states a definition of 'land' for, as Lord Wilberforce said more recently, there was no authoritative pronouncement that "land" means the whole of the space from the centre of the earth to the heavens: so sweeping, unscientific and impractical a doctrine is unlikely to appeal to the common law mind'.[15] Certainly there is an attempt by the courts, at the present time, to restrict the amount of airspace which can be the subject of an action for trespass to land and this matter is therefore discussed separately below. The ordinary legal meaning of 'land' today must take into account these decisions.[16]

In relation to the law of torts in general, and the law of trespass in particular, therefore, we can say that the word 'land' means not only the surface of any ground, soil or earth but also any buildings or structures that might be affixed to it or any mines sunk under it. The word includes both things growing on the surface such as trees and grass as well as minerals under the surface. A defendant who excavates for minerals or cuts down trees on the plaintiff's land not only commits a trespass to land but he could also be liable for the tort of conversion (discussed below) if he carries away the minerals or trees. The word 'land' includes the sub-soil to any depth and the airspace above the surface to a reasonable height. Easements and rights in the nature of *profits á prendre* such as exclusive

---

13 See D. Kennedy (1979) 28 Buffalo L.R. 209 where it is also described as 'the single most important source on English legal thinking in the 18th century'.

14 Blackstone *Commentaries on the Laws of England* (1st edn, London, 1766) Vol. 2, pp. 16-19.

15 See *Commissioner for Railways* v. *Valuer-General* [1974] A.C. 328, 351.

16 See *Bernstein (Baron)* v. *Skyviews Ltd* [1977] 3 W.L.R. 136 and *Sovmots Investments Ltd* v. *Secretary of State for the Environment* [1977] Q.B. 411.

fishery rights,[17] shooting or sporting rights,[18] rabbiting rights,[19] rights to fell timber etc. are interests in land[20] and are sufficient to confer a right to bring an action for trespass to land upon the person in exclusive possession of such rights. It could, therefore, be said that such rights, often described as 'incorporeal hereditaments', can also properly be described as 'land', at least for the purpose of the tort of trespass to land.

2. The Nature of the Plaintiff's Interest in Land

In order to maintain an action for trespass to land, the plaintiff must show that at the time of the interference by the defendant he was entitled to exclusive possession of the land. The court is not concerned with ownership but with possession. As Hodges J. said in *Rodrigues* v. *Ufton*, 'an action of trespass is an action for the disturbance of possession, and . . . the persons who can maintain it are those whose possession is disturbed'.[21] Thus, a tenant who acquires an exclusive right to possession of land under a lease can bring an action for trespass to land not only against third parties who unlawfully enter upon, remain on, throw things on or place things upon the land but also against the landlord who is the owner of the land, which is the subject of the lease, if he does any of those things. The landlord (or owner), on the other hand, cannot bring an action for trespass against a third party who, for example, comes on to the land and cuts down some trees. His only cause of action is an action on the case for damages for what is described as damage to his reversion.[22] It is also important to remember that land is very much like a layer cake, with each layer representing different proprietary interests, and that though the owner is usually in actual and exclusive possession of all the layers (airspace, buildings, surface soil, *profits á prendre*, sub-soil etc.), he is able to grant to others the right to exclusive possession of any of those layers. This right to exclusive possession is a sufficient interest to bring an action for trespass to land. The action can be brought even by a person who has exclusive possession of one layer against a person who has exclusive possession of another layer. This is well illustrated by the House of Lords decision in *Mason* v. *Clarke*,[23] where the plaintiff who was granted a *profit á prendre* (in this case, the exclusive right to enter upon certain farm land and to kill and take the rabbits there) was able to bring an action for trespass to land against the defendant who had interfered

17 See *Nicholls* v. *Ely Beet Sugar Factory* [1931] 2 Ch. 84.
18 See *Peech* v. *Best* [1931] 1 K.B. 1.
19 See *Mason* v. *Clarke* [1955] A.C. 778.
20 See the statement by Lord Morton of Henryton in *Mason* v. *Clarke* [1955] A.C. 778, 798: 'A *profit á prendre* is an interest in land'. See also the statement by Rigby L.J. in *Fitzgerald* v. *Firbank* [1877] 2 Ch. 96, 104: 'I hold that the grantees of an incorporeal hereditament have a right of action against any person who disturbs them by trespass or by nuisance, or in any other substantial manner'.
21 (1894) 20 V.L.R. 539, 543-4.
22 i.e. the land which will revert to the landlord on the determination of the lease.
23 [1955] A.C. 778.

and damaged the plaintiff's snares even though the defendant had been granted an exclusive tenancy of the farm on a lease from the landowner.

In order to succeed in an action for trespass to land the plaintiff must not only be entitled to exclusive possession of the land, he must also be in actual (or constructive)[24] exclusive possession of the land. In the absence of evidence to the contrary, the law will, without reluctance, ascribe possession either to the owner of the land with the paper title or to persons who can establish a title through the paper owner.[25] But a plaintiff who has no paper title to possession must show both factual possession and the requisite intention to possess in order to get the courts to attribute possession of the land to him.[26] Whether a plaintiff is in actual exclusive possession of land is usually a question of fact and in determining this question the courts take into account two matters. First, has the plaintiff the legal right to use the land to the exclusion of all others, and, secondly, has he physically displayed in some way an intention to exercise that right (the *animus possidendi*)?[27] If a person who is entitled to exclusive possession of land enters the land in the assertion of that possession, the law immediately vests actual exclusive possession of that land in the person who has so entered[28] and this actual exclusive possession of land is not lost simply because, for example, he is on holiday or even if he ceases to be in actual physical occupation of the land for a longer period because, for example, he decides to let his land lie fallow for a few years. The attitude of the courts has been that 'the type of conduct which indicates possession must vary with the type of land'[29] and that it is not necessary, in order to establish possession, that the plaintiff take some active step in relation to the land such as enclosing the land, cultivating it or living on it. As the Privy Council put it in *Ocean Estates Ltd* v. *Pinder*, 'it is clear law that the slightest acts by the person having title to the land or by his predecessor in title, indicating his intention to take possession, are sufficient to enable him to bring an action for trespass against a defendant entering upon the land without any title unless there can be shown a subsequent intention on the part of the person having the title to abandon the constructive possession so acquired'.[30]

If there is a dispute as to which of two persons is actually in possession

---

24 The words 'constructive possession' are used to describe situations where even though the plaintiff is not in actual physical occupation of the premises or land the courts are prepared to say that he is in actual exclusive possession of the land, e.g. while the land is lying fallow for a few years.

25 See *Powell* v. *McFarlane & Another* (1979) 38 P. & C.R. 452, 470 *per* Slade J. In *Whitehouse* v. *Remme* (1988) 64 L.G.R.A. 375 the Director of the National Parks and Wildlife Service was held entitled to sue in respect of trespasses committed within the Blue Mountains National Park.

26 See *Powell* v. *McFarlane & Another* (1979) 38 P. & C.R. 452, 470.

27 ibid., 471: 'The *animus possidendi* involves the intention, in one's own name and on one's own behalf, to exclude the world at large, including the owner with the paper title if he be not himself the possessor, so far as is reasonably practicable and so far as the processes of the law will allow' (*per* Slade J.).

28 *Jones* v. *Chapman* (1849) 2 Exch.Rep. 803, 821 *per* Maule J.

29 See *Wuta-Ofei* v. *Danquah* [1961] 3 All E.R. 596, 600; [1961] 1 W.L.R. 1238 (P.C.).

30 [1969] 2 A.C. 19, 25. See also *Bristow* v. *Cormican* (1878) 3 App.Cases 641, 657.

of certain premises or land, the law considers that one to be in possession who has the superior right to the land. This is described as the legal title. As Owen C.J. said in *The Baker's Creek Consolidated Gold Mining Co.* v. *Hack*, 'the law considers that one to be in possession who has the legal title'.[31] This legal title can be either a *documentary* (or paper) title to the land such as a lease, grant, gift, conveyance, transfer etc. or a *possessory* title to the land which is acquired when a trespasser has been in *adverse* possession[32] of land for a certain number of years.[33] Though a trespasser 'cannot by the very act of trespass, immediately and without acquiescence, give himself what the law understands by "possession" against the person whom he ejects, and drive the latter to produce his title',[34] it is possible for a trespasser to acquire a possessory title after adverse possession for the requisite period. During the period of adverse possession, however, the person who is in actual (or constructive) possession of the land under a claim of title and who is in the process of being dispossessed by the adverse possessor or trespasser can sue the adverse possessor or trespasser for trespass to land even though the adverse possessor or trespasser might himself be able to bring an action for trespass against a subsequent trespasser. There is no legal requirement that a plaintiff's exclusive possession of land be by lawful claim to title and it is not open to the subsequent trespasser to argue that the adverse possessor (or first trespasser) has no title to sue in trespass, for, as Lord Campbell is reported to have said in *Jeffries* v. *Great Western Railway*, 'the law is that a person possessed of [land] as his property has a good title as against every stranger'.[35] If 'any possession is a legal possession against a wrong-doer' according to Lord Kenyon C.J. in *Graham* v. *Peat*, then surely any possession is legal possession against a subsequent wrong-doer.[36] Nor can the subsequent trespasser argue that the person whose exclusive possession of land he has interfered with cannot bring an action in trespass because the lawful claim to title was in some third person. Such a defence, known as the *jus tertii*, cannot be raised unless the defendant also argues that the interference which is regarded by the plaintiff as a trespass has been committed with the authority and consent of the third party or as his agent, for, as Lord Davey said in *Glenwood Lumber Co.* v. *Phillips*, 'it is a well-established principle in English law that possession is good against a

---

31 (1894) 15 N.S.W.R. 207, 226. '"Title" is a shorthand term used to denote the facts which, if proved, will enable a plaintiff to recover possession or a defendant to retain possession of a thing.' (F.H. Lawson *Introduction to the Law of Property* (Oxford, 1958) p. 1).

32 See the statement by Lord Denning M.R. in *Wallis's Holiday Camp* v. *Shell-Mex* [1975] 1 Q.B. 94, 103 on the possession required to constitute adverse possession: 'Possession by itself is not enough to give a title. It must be *adverse* possession. The true owner must have discontinued possession or have been dispossessed and another must have taken it adversely to him. There must be something in the nature of an ouster of the true owner by the wrongful possessor'.

33 The period of adverse possession required to acquire a possessory title is twelve years in N.S.W., Qld, W.A. and Tas. and fifteen years in Vic.. and S.A.

34 *Nowland* v. *Humphrey* (1859) 2 Legge, 1167, 1169 *per* Dickinson J.

35 (1856) 5 E. & B. 802, 805.

36 (1801) 1 East 244, 246.

wrong-doer, and the latter cannot set up a *jus tertii* unless he claims under it'.[37] This statement also accurately represents the law in Australia.[38]

What is the position of the squatter[39] in relation to trespass? Obviously, the person who was in exclusive possession of the land before the trespass by the squatter will be able to bring an action in trespass against the squatter, but will the squatter himself be able to bring an action in trespass against a subsequent trespasser? Whether or not the squatter becomes an 'adverse possessor' or remains a 'trespasser' it would appear that he has a sufficient interest in the land to bring an action in trespass against a subsequent trespasser who interferes with his possession.[40] Once this is accepted, however, the requirement of 'exclusive' possession in relation to trespass becomes a trifle complicated, because it becomes difficult to understand how the squatter can have actual exclusive possession of the land which is necessary to bring his action in trespass against the subsequent trespasser while at the same time maintaining that the squatter can have an action in trespass brought *against* him by the person who was in exclusive possession of the land before the trespass by the squatter. Can actual 'exclusive' possession of land reside both in the squatter and in the person who was in actual exclusive possession of the land before the trespass by the squatter? The answer to this dilemma appears to be that the courts are sometimes prepared to accept something less than actual exclusive possession as a sufficient interest to sue in trespass to land.[41] Apart from the situation of the squatter, discussed above, licensees in some circumstances might also be considered to have sufficient possession to maintain an action for trespass to land, even though that possession is something less than actual 'exclusive' possession.

In *Vaughan* v. *Shire of Benalla*, Hood J. thought that it was a contradiction in terms to say that a man who has a licence to use land has exclusive possession of it.[42] All the cases which he had considered were in his opinion 'opposed to the view that a licensee had exclusive possession or may maintain an action for trespass to land'. This would certainly be true, even today, of a purely gratuitous licensee, for example, a Boy Scout who is given permission to put up a tent on a farmer's land. But if the

---

37 [1904] A.C. 405, 410.

38 See *Coles-Smith* v. *Smith & Others* [1965] Qd.R. 494, 501.

39 In *McPhail* v. *Persons (Names Unknown)* [1973] Ch. 447, 456 Lord Denning M.R. defines a squatter as 'one who, without any colour of right, enters an unoccupied house or land, intending to stay there as long as he can'.

40 See *R.* v. *Edwards* [1978] Crim.L.R. 49 (a criminal case). See also *Haddrick* v. *Lloyd* [1945] S.A.S.R. 40, 43-4: 'A trespasser in possession has the same right to use force to remove another trespasser as that to which one lawfully in possession is entitled' (*per* Reed J.). See also *Newington* v. *Windeyer* (1985) 3 N.S.W.L.R. 555, 563.

41 See *Greig* v. *Greig* [1966] V.R. 376 where damages for trespass to land were given in respect of a trespass by one co-tenant against another co-tenant even though the plaintiff did not plead that he was in exclusive possession of the land. But in *Proprietor of the C.B.U.P. No. 343* v. *Bourne* [1984] 1 Qd. R. 613, 620, Derrington J. of the Supreme Court of Queensland held that where possession of co-owners of common property is not exclusive to that of other co-owners trespass could not be brought for an interference (not amounting to ouster) by one co-owner with the rights of the other co-owners.

42 (1891) 17 V.L.R. 129, 135.

licensee has a licence for value is he in a different position? In *Hounslow L.B.C.* v. *Twickenham G.D. Ltd,* Megarry J. said that in the light of the *Winter Garden* case[43] a contractual licensee could not be treated as a trespasser so long as his contract entitles him to be on the land and that this was so whether or not his contract was specifically enforceable.[44] He went on to say that the licence could not be detached from the contract and separately revoked and that the licensee was in such a case on the land by contractual right and not as a trespasser. In *Verrall* v. *Great Yarmouth Borough Council* Lord Denning M.R. went even further and said that 'once a man has entered [land] under his contract of licence, he cannot be turned out. An injunction can be obtained against the licensor to prevent his being turned out.'[45] What if the licensee has not yet entered the land and the licensor was refusing to let him come in? In this case, Lord Denning suggested that the licensee could come to court and get an order for specific performance to allow him to come in. However, if the licensee is entitled to be on the land, he must be able to protect that entitlement against interferences by third parties, and, whether or not he has a sufficient interest to maintain an action in trespass against the licensor, it is suggested that he has a sufficient 'exclusive' possession to maintain an action of trespass against third parties who interfere with that possession. The earlier case of *Verrall* v. *Farnes*[46] also suggests that a plaintiff might even have sufficient possession to maintain an action for trespass to land if he is in occupation of land under a licence to occupy land which, under a legally enforceable contract, can be converted into a tenancy from year to year. In addition to contractual licensees there are other licensees who might have sufficient possession to maintain an action for trespass to land. In *Errington* v. *Errington and Woods,*[47] the deserted wife, although a licensee, was held to be entitled to retain possession of the matrimonial home and no doubt entitled to sue in trespass to land for interference with that possession. In *National Provincial Bank* v. *Ainsworth,* Lord Upjohn went so far as to say that even though the deserted wife's occupation of the matrimonial home was not exclusive against the deserting husband she was nevertheless in 'exclusive possession' of the home and could clearly bring proceedings against trespassers.[48] And in *Taylor* v. *Rees,*[49] a deserted wife, though a licensee, was held entitled to sue the landlady and the landlady's husband for trespass to land when they entered the house, without consent, during the currency of a contractual tenancy even though the lease was between the landlady and the plaintiff's husband and even though the plaintiff's right to occupy the house was not exclusive as against her husband unless she sought an injunction against him.

It is suggested, therefore, that apart from mere gratuitous licensees who

---

43 *Winter Garden Theatre (London) Ltd* v. *Millenium Productions Ltd* [1948] A.C. 173.
44 [1971] 1 Ch. 233, 254-5.
45 [1980] 1 All E.R. 839, 844.
46 [1966] 1 W.L.R. 1254.
47 [1952] 1 K.B. 290.
48 [1965] A.C. 1175, 1232.
49 [1979] C.L.Y. 2733

do not appear to be able to maintain an action for trespass to land, other licensees may perhaps in certain circumstances have a sufficient interest in land to be able to sue third parties (not the licensor) for trespass. This will be when a licensor will not be permitted by the courts to eject a licensee,[50] when a licensor will not be permitted by the courts to prevent a licensee from continuing to occupy the land,[51] and where the licensor will be stopped by the courts from denying the licensee's equitable right to possession of the land.[52] In all these cases, the licensee will have a sufficient interest to sue third parties in trespass if they interfere with his possession of land. But the licensee may not be able to sue the licensor in trespass, except where the licensee has succeeded in obtaining an injunction to exclude the licensor from the land.

3. The Nature of the Defendant's Acts and the Kinds of Interference Sufficient to Constitute Trespass

As trespass to land is a species of trespass, a necessary requirement of that tort is that whatever is done to the plaintiff's land by the defendant must be done *directly* to make the activity actionable as a trespass. As Denning L.J. (as he then was) said in *Southport Corporation* v. *Esso Petroleum Co. Ltd*, 'in order to support an action for trespass to land the act done by the defendant must be an act done by him directly on to the plaintiff's land'.[53] As actual damage is not necessary for an action of trespass to land,[54] it appears that all that is necessary is that there be contact with the land of the plaintiff and that that contact be direct. So a person who enters upon land in the exclusive possession of another or places or throws any object thereon or brings any animal upon that land commits a sufficiently 'direct' act to constitute a trespass to land. The nineteenth-century case of *Gregory* v. *Piper*[55] suggests that if a necessary and natural consequence of the act of the defendant is contact with the land of the plaintiff then the defendant can be sued for trespass to land, but Denning L.J. in *Southport Corporation* v. *Esso Petroleum Co. Ltd*[56] thought that to discharge oil in an estuary which was carried by the action of the tide on to the plaintiff's foreshore was not a direct act sufficient to constitute trespass to land. He regarded the contact as consequential. However, Morris L.J. in the same case thought that if a defendant deliberately employs the force of the wind or of moving water 'to cause a thing to go on to land' the act would be sufficiently direct to constitute trespass.[57] The view of Morris L.J. is to be preferred, for, if a person who sets a mad ox loose is answerable in trespass for whatever mischief the ox might do, as Nares J. held in *Scott* v.

50 See *Errington* v. *Errington and Woods* [1952] 1 K.B. 290.
51 As in *Verrall* v. *Farnes* [1966] 1 W.L.R. 1254.
52 See, e.g., *E.R. Ives Investment Ltd* v. *High* [1967] 2 Q.B. 379. See also F.R. Crane (1967) 31 *Conv.* (N.S.) 332.
53 [1954] 2 Q.B. 182, 195.
54 See *Dumont* v. *Miller* (1873) 4 A.J.R. 152.
55 (1829) 9 Barn. & Cress. 591.
56 [1954] 2 Q.B. 182.
57 ibid., 204.

Shepherd[58] (the leading case on directness), there is no reason why a person who uses natural forces such as the wind or the tide should be placed in any different position. It is suggested, therefore, that any act which sets in motion an unbroken series of continuing consequences, the last of which ultimately causes contact with the land of the plaintiff, will be regarded as sufficiently 'direct' for the purposes of the tort of trespass to land and that the deliberate employment of natural forces will not necessarily make the ultimate contact 'consequential'.

The defendant's act must not only be direct, it must also be a voluntary act. It will not be voluntary if the defendant is forcibly carried upon the land of the plaintiff by the force and violence of others,[59] if the defendant suffers an epileptic fit and falls unconsciously on to the land of the plaintiff[60] or if the defendant having been startled inadvertently steps on to the land of the plaintiff.[61] However, if the defendant does an act in relation to land in the mistaken belief that the land interfered with is in his exclusive possession that will not be regarded as an involuntary act. Thus in *Basely* v. *Clarkson*[62] the defendant, who while mowing his own land mowed down some grass on the plaintiff's land mistakenly thinking it was his, was held liable in trespass. The defendant argued that the act was an involuntary one, but the court regarded it as a voluntary act.

In addition to being direct and voluntary, the act of the defendant must be intentional (or reckless) for the tort of intentional trespass to land or negligent (or careless) for negligent trespass to land.[63] This is clear from the decision of Park J. in *League against Cruel Sports* v. *Scott*.[64] But the onus of proof in relation to these matters is not so clear. Though a statement by Park J. in *League against Cruel Sports* v. *Scott*[65] might suggest otherwise, the position in Australia, it is suggested, is that it is for the defendant to prove that his act was neither intentional nor negligent once the plaintiff proves that there has been direct contact with his land by a voluntary act of the defendant.[66] The act is intentional when the defendant deliberately or wilfully interferes with the land, for example, by deliberately chopping down the door of shop premises in the possession of the plaintiff[67] or if a defendant in control of a bulldozer deliberately and directly propels earth and rocks on to the plaintiff's land.[68] The act is also intentional if the contact or interference with the land is substantially certain to follow from the defendant's act, as when a defendant rolls a

58 (1773) 2 Wm.Bl. 892.
59 See *Smith* v. *Stone* (1647) Sty. 65.
60 See *Public Transport Commission of N.S.W.* v. *Perry* (1977) 14 A.L.R. 273.
61 See *Braithwaite* v. *South Durham Steel Co.* [1958] 1 W.L.R. 986.
62 (1681) 3 Lev. 37.
63 Negligent trespass to land is not dealt with further in this chapter. See, however, Chapter 8 on negligent trespass.
64 [1985] 3 W.L.R. 400, 408.
65 ibid., 408.
66 See *Cook* v. *Lewis* [1952] 1 D.L.R.1; *Goshen* v. *Larin* [1975] 56 D.L.R. (3d) 719 and *Kitchen* v. *Lorimer* (1988) 87 N.S.R. (2d) 18. The Canadian position is likely to be followed in Australia.
67 See *Pollack* v. *Volpato* [1973] 1 N.S.W.L.R. 653.
68 See *Watson* v. *Cowen* [1959] Tas.S.R. 194, 199.

boulder down a hill and it comes to rest on the plaintiff's land or damages his greenhouse. It is not open to the defendant to say that he did not intend it to come on to the plaintiff's land if that result is substantially certain to follow from the defendant's act. It is also now clear that the act will be regarded as intentional if it is reckless.[69] Thus a defendant who in the course of levelling his land with a bulldozer pushed earth over a steep slope on to the plaintiff's boat-shed was held liable in intentional trespass to land.[70] It was held that the work contracted to be done involved inevitably the fall of earth down the steep slope, with the probability of damage to the shed and there was evidence that 'it was obvious that some of the earth which came down as a result of the bulldozing would go over the side of the cliff'.[71] A defendant who recklessly fires a bullet in the direction of several houses or a balloonist who drops a soft-drink bottle while flying over a cluster of houses will be liable in intentional trespass to land to the person who is in exclusive possession of the house which the bullet hits or on which the soft-drink bottle lands. Similarly, a defendant who, in reckless pursuit of a hare or fox, enters the plaintiff's land will be liable for an intentional trespass to land.[72] Indifference to the risk of trespass might well amount to an intention to commit a trespass, as the decision in *League against Cruel Sports* v. *Scott* illustrates. There Park J. held that a master of hounds who knows that whatever precautions he takes will not prevent his hounds from entering the plaintiff's land and who despite this persists in hunting in the vicinity of the land with the result that the hounds trespass on the plaintiff's land would be liable in intentional trespass to land because 'the inference might well be drawn that [the master of hounds'] indifference to the risk of trespass amounted to an intention that the hounds should trespass on the land'.[73]

In describing the nature of the defendant's acts we have already dealt with some of the kinds of interferences which are sufficient to constitute trespass. The following is, however, a more complete list of those interferences.

One of the clearest cases of interference which amounts to trespass is entry on to the plaintiff's land without his express or implied consent.[74] Though there is an implied or tacit licence in favour of any member of the public to go upon the path or driveway to the entrance of any dwelling for the purpose of lawful communication with any person in the dwelling (until such licence is expressly or impliedly revoked)[75] and a similar tacit licence in favour of any potential customer to enter the premises of a firm for the purpose of bona fide seeking information or doing business with

69 See *League against Cruel Sports* v. *Scott* [1985] 3 W.L.R. 400, 409. For what are 'reckless' acts, see pp. 33-6 above.

70 *Watson* v. *Cowen* [1959] Tas.S.R. 194.

71 ibid., 200.

72 See *Dumont* v. *Miller* (1873) 4 A.J.R. 152.

73 [1985] 3 W.L.R. 400, 409.

74 See *Schumann* v. *Abbott* [1961] S.A.S.R. 149; *Greig* v. *Greig* [1966] V.R. 376 and *Coles-Smith* v. *Smith & Others* [1965] Qd.R. 494. See also *Halliday* v. *Nevill* (1984) 155 C.L.R.1 and *Plenty* v. *Dillon* (1991) 65 A.L.J.R. 231.

75 See *Halliday* v. *Nevill* (1984) 155 C.L.R. 1, 7.

it,[76] such a tacit licence will not permit, for example, a television reporter with cameras and associated equipment to enter the premises to harass the inhabitants by asking questions which would be televised throughout the State.[77] It is not necessary, however, to come physically on to the plaintiff's land and the defendant can commit a trespass by contact with the plaintiff's land even without coming on to it; for example, by leaving a pile of leaves on his own land which when it dries falls over on to the plaintiff's land,[78] by breaking the plaintiff's fence,[79] by growing a creeper on the plaintiff's wall,[80] by leaning a ladder against his wall,[81] by allowing a ventilation pipe to protrude over the plaintiff's land[82] or by throwing things over the wall on to the plaintiff's land.[83] If, however, a defendant takes a photograph of the plaintiff's land or objects on his land when standing on a public street or on adjoining land this does not amount to any trespass either to land or to airspace.[84]

It is trespass to place things on the land of the plaintiff or to cause any object (e.g. rocks, stones etc.),[85] substance (e.g. effluent, gases, water etc.), person[86] or animal[87] to go on to the plaintiff's land. To underpin the walls of another's building without his consent is a trespass.[88] The interference must be direct. If a spout is built in such a way that it conveys rainwater directly on to the plaintiff's land that is trespass (it is almost as if the defendant poured the water on to the land of the plaintiff), but if the rainwater is directed into storm water drains on the defendant's own land and some of the water drops or overflows on to the plaintiff's land that is not trespass and an action on the case would be the appropriate remedy if the plaintiff can show damage.

It is also trespass to dig a pit on the plaintiff's land, to go on to the plaintiff's property and dig and remove the soil,[89] to enter the plaintiff's land and extract gravel,[90] to depasture cattle on land belonging to the plaintiff[91] or to mine coal from the plaintiff's land.[92] If the extraction or mining is done furtively no length of time will be a bar to relief.[93]

A plaintiff who is in exclusive possession of land and who is refused

---

76 See *Lincoln Hunt Australia Pty Ltd* v. *Willesee* (1986) 4 N.S.W.L.R. 457.

77 ibid., 460 (per Young J.) See also *Church of Scientology Inc.* v. *Transmedia Productions Pty Ltd* (1987) Aust. Torts Reports 80-101.

78 *Gregory* v. *Piper* (1829) 9 Barn. & Cress. 591.

79 *Hogan* v. *A.G. Wright Pty Ltd* [1963] Tas.S.R. 44.

80 *Simpson* v. *Weber* (1925) 41 T.L.R. 302; 133, L.T. 46.

81 *Westripp* v. *Baldock* [1938] 2 All E.R. 779.

82 *Lawlor* v. *Johnston* [1905] V.L.R. 714.

83 See *Watson* v. *Cowen* [1959] Tas.S.R. 194.

84 See *Bathurst City Council* v. *Saban* (1985) 2 N.S.W.L.R. 704, 706 *per* Young J.

85 ibid.

86 *Smith* v. *Stone* (1647) Sty. 65.

87 *Beckwith* v. *Shordike* (1767) 4 Burr. 2092. See also *Yakamia Dairy Pty Ltd* v. *Wood* [1976] W.A.R. 57.

88 *Stoneman* v. *Lyons* [1974] V.R. 797.

89 *Minter* v. *Eacott* (1952) W.N.(N.S.W.) 93.

90 *Bilambil-Terranova Pty Ltd* v. *Tweed Shire Council* [1980] 1 N.S.W.L.R. 465.

91 *Yakamia Dairy Pty Ltd* v. *Wood* [1976] W.A.R. 57.

92 *In re the Bulli Coal Company* (1899) 20 L.R.(N.S.W.) Eq. 91.

93 ibid.

permission to enter and is prevented from entering his own land can bring an action for trespass to land against a defendant who refuses him admission.[94]

If a tenant in possession of land refuses to go out of possession at the end of the tenancy the plaintiff landlord should bring an action for recovery of possession of land against the overholding tenant and not trespass, because an act of overholding will not be regarded as a trespass.[95] Nor will a person who goes into possession of land under an agreement be regarded as a trespasser if he remains in occupation for several months after the date of the rescission of the agreement; though in such a case the courts will insist that he pay a sum of money in the nature of rent from the date of the rescission.[96]

A person who places rubbish on the land of another or builds a wall on the land of another not only commits a trespass but also the trespass continues until the rubbish or the wall is removed. Anyone in exclusive possession of the land can sue for the trespass as long as the rubbish or wall is there, even if the plaintiff acquires exclusive possession of the land after the rubbish was placed there or the wall built.[97] There is what is described as a continuing trespass, and anyone with exclusive possession of the land can sue in relation to that continuing trespass.[98] But a defendant who digs a pit on the plaintiff's land or who cuts down a tree on the plaintiff's land does not commit a continuing trespass. His trespass ceases when the act is done because there is nothing that the defendant can do to prevent further interference with the exclusive possession of the plaintiff or to put the plaintiff back in the same position as he was before the trespass.

In relation to the highway, members of the public are entitled to use the highway for the purpose of passing and repassing along the highway and for such other reasonable purposes for which the highway has been constructed.[99] The dedication of land as a public highway necessarily carries with it a grant of a public right to use also the airspace to a reasonable height above the surface of the highway.[100] If the highway is used for other purposes, the person using it will lay himself open to an action in trespass at the suit of the person who is in exclusive possession of the land over which the highway passes. However, as Collins L.J. pointed out in *Hickman* v. *Maisey*, 'it is not very easy to draw an exact line between the legitimate user of a highway as a highway and user which goes beyond the right conferred upon the public by its dedication'.[101]

---

94 See *Waters* v. *Maynard* (1924) 24 S.R.(N.S.W.) 618.

95 *Falkingham* v. *Fregon* (1899) 25 V.L.R. 211. See also *The Commonwealth* v. *Anderson* (1960) 105 C.L.R. 303 (successful action in ejectment by the Crown in right of the Commonwealth against an overholding tenant).

96 *Sommerhalder* v. *Burjan and Feigl* [1962] S.A.S.R. 271, 276-8.

97 See *Hudson* v. *Nicholson* (1839) 5 M. & W. 437.

98 See *Konskier* v. *B. Goodman Ltd* [1928] 1 K.B. 421.

99 See *Harrison* v. *Duke of Rutland* [1893] 1 Q.B. 142 and *Hickman* v. *Maisey* [1900] 1 Q.B. 752.

100 See *Prentice* v. *Mercantile House Pty Ltd* (1991) A.L.R. 107, 117.

101 [1900] 1 Q.B. 752, 757.

Paull J. in *Iveagh* v. *Martin*[102] gives some examples which might help to draw the line. A person can stand still on the highway for a reasonably short time but he must not put his bed upon the highway and permanently occupy a portion of it. He may stoop to tie his shoelace but he cannot place a chair on a portion of the highway and invite people to have their hair cut. And, though he can let his van stand long enough to deliver and load goods, he cannot turn his van into a permanent stall. *Hickman* v. *Maisey*[103] and *Harrison* v. *Duke of Rutland*[104] are further examples where the user of the highway was held to be a trespass to land.

If a defendant does not instigate or authorize a trespass by a third party but merely takes advantage of it, he is not liable in trespass. Thus if a defendant believes that he is entitled to certain goods on the plaintiff's premises but the plaintiff denies him access to those goods and a third party, without the defendant's authorization or instigation, removes the goods from the plaintiff's premises and places them on the road, the defendant can take advantage of the trespass by the third party and take the goods without being held liable himself for trespass to land.[105]

It goes without saying that if the plaintiff has consented to the entry of the defendant on to the land or to the interference in question then no action for trespass to land can be brought by him against the defendant.[106] This matter will be dealt with further when the defences to intentional torts are discussed.

4. Trespass to Airspace[107]

In discussing what the word 'land' means in connection with the tort of trespass to land, it was suggested that the word also includes the airspace above the surface of the soil. Certainly an action for trespass can be brought by a plaintiff in exclusive possession of land if a structural projection or fixture attached to the defendant's land protrudes into the plaintiff's airspace. Where an advertising sign projected a few inches into the plaintiff's airspace he was able to bring a successful action in trespass, as the leading decision in *Kelsen* v. *Imperial Tobacco Co. (of Great Britain and Ireland) Ltd*[108] illustrates. The Supreme Court of Victoria came to a similar decision in 1905 in the case of *Lawlor* v. *Johnston*[109] where Madden C.J. held that the defendant, who had erected ventilation pipes on the outside of his building in such a way that they protruded into the plaintiff's airspace, had committed a trespass of a continuing character. More recently, in *L.J.P. Investments Pty Ltd* v. *Howard Chia Investments*

102 [1961] 1 Q.B. 232, 273.
103 [1900] 1 Q.B. 752.
104 [1893] 1 Q.B. 142.
105 See *Doolan* v. *Hill* (1879) 5 V.L.R. 290.
106 See *Amess* v. *Hanlon* [1873] 4 A.J.R. 90.
107 See J. Richardson (1953) *Can. B.R.* 117 and P. Butt (1978) 52 *A.L.J.* 160.
108 [1957] 2 Q.B. 334.
109 [1905] V.L.R. 714.

Pty Ltd[110] a successful action in trespass was brought in the Supreme Court of New South Wales when the defendant, who was carrying out a commercial development of its property, built scaffolding which intruded about 5 feet (1.5 metres) into the airspace above the plaintiff's adjoining property at a height of about 15 feet (4.5 metres) above ground level.

It is usually presumed that the person who is in exclusive possession of the soil,[111] premises,[112] forecourt[113] etc. is also in exclusive possession of the airspace above[114] and the courts will make that assumption unless it is shown that the exclusive possession of the airspace has been given to another.[115] Not only is this the case in relation to persons whose exclusive possession of the land derives from ownership of the land, but even in the case of tenants there is a *prima facie* assumption that the tenancy of the land or premises carries with it the exclusive possession of the airspace above[116] and the right to bring an action in trespass for an incursion into that airspace. But is an incursion into the airspace at any height capable of constituting a trespass? In *Woollerton and Wilson Ltd* v. *Richard Costain Ltd*[117] the defendants were held liable in trespass when the jib of the defendant's tower crane swung over the plaintiff's premises and into its airspace at a height of 50 feet (15 metres) above roof level. Similarly, in *Graham* v. *K.D. Morris & Sons Pty Ltd*[118] the defendants were held liable in trespass when a jib of a crane encroached 62 feet (19 metres) over the plaintiff's land and was suspended over the roof of her house. In *Davies* v. *Bennison,*[119] Nicholls C.J. of the Supreme Court of Tasmania held that a bullet fired across the plaintiff's land could be a trespass even if it did not fall on any ground in the plaintiff's possession, but in *Bernstein of Leigh (Baron)* v. *Skyviews & General Ltd*[120] the defendants were held not liable in trespass when their aircraft flew 'many hundreds of feet' above the plaintiff's land taking aerial photographs of the plaintiff's house. Griffiths J. found that the defendant's aircraft 'did not infringe any rights in the plaintiff's airspace' and he further declared that he could find 'no support in authority for the view that a landowner's rights in the airspace above his property extend to an unlimited height'.

---

110 (1989) Aust. Torts Reports 80-269. See also *Didow* v. *Alberta Power Ltd* [1988] 5 W.W.R. 606 where the defendants were held liable in trespass when their power lines protruded six feet into the air space above the plaintiff's land.

111 See *Barker* v. *The Corporation of the City of Adelaide* [1900] S.A.L.R. 29 and *Lewvest Ltd* v. *Scotia Towers Ltd* (1982) 126 D.L.R. (3d) 239.

112 *Woollerton and Wilson Ltd* v. *Richard Costain Ltd* [1970] 1 W.L.R. 411 and *Graham* v. *K.D. Morris & Sons Pty Ltd* [1974] Qd.R. 1.

113 *Gifford* v. *Dent* [1926] W.N. 336.

114 See *Kelsen* v. *Imperial Tobacco Co. Ltd* [1957] 2 Q.B. 334, 339.

115 It appears that the New South Wales Government has been selling the airspace above many of its properties as a major revenue-generating exercise. See *Australian Financial Review,* 31 May 1982.

116 *Gifford* v. *Dent* [1926] W.N. 336 and *Kelsen* v. *Imperial Tobacco Co. Ltd* [1957] 2 Q.B. 334.

117 [1970] 1 W.L.R. 411.

118 [1974] Qd.R. 1.

119 [1927] Tas.L.R. 52.

120 [1977] 3 W.L.R. 136, 141.

We are left, therefore, with the situation that the common law accepts that the exclusive possession of land and premises carries with it exclusive possession of the airspace above and that an action for trespass to that airspace will succeed if the trespass is caused by structural projections or fixtures which intrude into the neighbouring airspace at whatever height the intrusion takes place. There is no suggestion in any of the decided cases that such intrusions are not trespasses beyond a certain height. In the case of overhanging cranes the same principle should apply and intrusions into neighbouring airspace at whatever height should be regarded as a trespass. The passage of projectiles such as bullets, rockets, missiles etc. and the transient use of the airspace by balloonists, hang-gliders and aircraft must be treated differently and it is suggested that these intrusions into the airspace of a plaintiff should only be treated as a trespass if the intrusion into the airspace is made at a height where it seriously interferes with the plaintiff's ordinary use and enjoyment of his land.[121] The rights of a person in exclusive possession of land should be balanced against the rights of the general public to take advantage of all that science offers in the use of airspace, as Griffiths J. pointed out in *Bernstein's* case, and the best way of achieving that balance in our present society is:

> by restricting the rights of an owner in the airspace above his land to such height as is necessary for the ordinary use and enjoyment of his land and the structures upon it, and declaring that above that height he has no greater rights in the airspace than any other member of the public.[122]

One other matter must be discussed. Under the Civil Aviation (Damage by Aircraft) Act 1958 (Cwth) it would appear that no person in Australia can bring an action for trespass to land if the only interference in respect of which the action is being brought is the passage of an aircraft[123] through the airspace in his exclusive possession. The Act gives legislative force in Australia to the Rome Convention of 1952,[124] Article 1 of which specifies that 'there shall be no right to compensation . . . if the damage results from the mere fact of passage of the aircraft through the airspace in conformity with existing air traffic regulations'. It should be noted that the immunity from an action for compensation for damage only arises if

---

121 In *L.J.P. Investments Pty Ltd* v. *Howard Chia Investments Pty Ltd* (1989) Aust. Torts Reports 80-269 (a case of an intrusion into the airspace of the plaintiff by the defendant's scaffolding) this distinction between a trespass caused by structural projections (or fixtures) which intrude into the airspace and a trespass caused by projectiles was blurred. Hodgson J., however, rejected the defendant's submission that entry into airspace is a trespass only if it occurs at a height and in a manner which actually interferes with the occupier's actual use of land at the time of the intrusions. Hodgson J. held that the relevant test for trespass was whether the intrusion was 'of a nature and at a height which *may* interfere with any ordinary uses of the land which the occupier *may* see fit to undertake' (at 68, 871).

122 [1977] 3 W.L.R. 136, 141.

123 The word 'aircraft' includes not only foreign aircraft but also aircraft registered in Australia in the circumstances described in Part III of the Act. See (1978) 52 *A.L.J.* 467.

124 *The Convention on Damage caused by Foreign Aircraft to Third Parties on the Surface.* The Convention opened for signature at Rome on 7 October 1952.

the flight is in conformity with existing air traffic regulations. Another aspect to note about this provision of Commonwealth legislation is that a person is deprived of the right to compensation for damage. The action for trespass to land, however, as we know, requires no damage. Is that action still available, therefore, to plaintiffs in respect of the mere passage of aircraft through the airspace? This question has been unambiguously dealt with in Victoria,[125] New South Wales,[126] Tasmania[127] and Western Australia,[128] where legislation patterned on section 40(1) of the Civil Aviation Act 1949 (U.K.) provides that:

> no action shall lie in respect of trespass or nuisance by reason only of the flight of an aircraft over any property at a height above the ground which having regard to the wind, the weather and all the circumstances is reasonable, or the ordinary incidents of such flight, so long as the provisions of the Air Navigation Regulations are duly complied with.[129]

In these four States, therefore, no action for trespass to land (airspace) can be brought if the plaintiff in exclusive possession of the land 'relies solely upon the flight of the aircraft above his property as founding his cause of action', but if he 'can point to some activity carried on by or from the aircraft that can properly be considered a trespass' then Griffiths J. in *Bernstein's* case suggests that an action in trespass can be brought.[130]

Finally, it should be noted that the Civil Aviation (Damage by Aircraft) Act 1958 (Cwth)[131] and the legislation in the four States mentioned above impose upon the owner of an aircraft a strict liability[132] to pay damages for any material loss or damage that may be caused 'to any person or property on land or water by or by a person in or by an article or person falling from an aircraft while in flight taking off or landing'.[133] In *Weedair (N.Z.) Ltd* v. *Walker*,[134] the Court of Appeal of New Zealand held that the word 'article' in similar legislation was not confined to solid objects and embraced a liquid spray and that the word was intended to apply comprehensively to things that might fall from an aircraft.

---

125 Wrongs Act 1958, s.30.
126 Damage by Aircraft Act 1952, s.2(1).
127 Damage by Aircraft Act 1963, s.3.
128 Damage by Aircraft Act 1964, s.4.
129 The wording chosen is from the Victorian Wrongs Act 1958, s.30. The wording of the legislation in the other three States is very similar.
130 [1977] 3 W.L.R. 136.
131 See Article 1 of the Schedule to the Act where the Rome Convention is set out.
132 In *Southgate* v. *Commonwealth of Australia* (1987) 13 N.S.W.L.R. 188 Brownie J. of the Supreme Court of N.S.W. held that s.2(2) of the Damage by Aircraft Act 1952 (N.S.W.) imposed an absolute liability on a defendant where damage is caused to a plaintiff on the ground by an aircraft.
133 See Victorian Wrongs Act 1958, s.31. The legislation in the other States is very similar though the West Australian and Tasmanian legislation refer to 'an article, *animal* or person falling from, an aircraft' etc.
134 [1961] N.Z.L.R. 153, 156.

5. Trespass Ab Initio and Trespass Pro Tanto

If a person comes on to land with the consent of the person in exclusive possession of land he can become a trespasser if he remains on the land after the permission to be on the land is revoked[135] and a reasonable period to withdraw from the land has elapsed.[136] This is certainly the case with the purely gratuitous licensee. In the case of a licensee for value, it has been suggested,[137] despite the opinion of the majority of the High Court of Australia in *Cowell* v. *Rosehill Racecourse Co. Ltd*,[138] that the licensee may be considered to have a right to remain on the land until the period of the licence is exhausted.[139] Even in the case of a licensee for value, the courts imply a condition that the licensee 'will behave in an orderly manner'.[140] If the licensee does not behave in an orderly manner the licence can be withdrawn and the licensee will become a trespasser after a reasonable period for withdrawal has elapsed.[141]

But what if persons come on to land not at the invitation of the person in exclusive possession of the land but by virtue of an authority given by law, for example, police officers with a warrant, food inspectors, factory inspectors, council inspectors, persons authorized to enter land to read gas, electricity and water meters etc. under the appropriate statutory authority? If such persons abuse their authority and commit an unlawful act after entry, the person in possession of the land is not in a position to revoke his consent and to treat them as trespassers as he did not consent to their entry in the first place. It is to meet this situation that the doctrine of trespass *ab initio* was created. The doctrine allows a plaintiff to treat as a trespasser a person whose entry on to the land was lawful, if he does something while on the land which can be regarded as an abuse of the authority to enter. The defendant is then treated as a trespasser *ab initio*, i.e. from the time of the original entry. As the court declared in the *Six Carpenters' Case*, 'where an entry, authority or licence is given to any one by the law, and he doth abuse it, he shall be a trespasser ab initio: but where an entry, authority or licence, is given by the party, and he abuses it, there he must be punished for his abuse, but shall not be a trespasser *ab initio*'.[142] The doctrine, therefore, only applies when the entry on to land has been made by authority of law and not at the invitation of the person in possession of land. Thus a police officer who enters premises under a search warrant, or a council inspector who enters premises to determine whether council regulations have been complied with, becomes a trespasser *ab initio* if he steals goods from the premises, unlawfully damages the

---

135 *Wood* v. *Leadbitter* (1845) 13 M. & W. 838. See also *Halliday* v. *Nevill* (1984) 155 C.L.R.1 and *Plenty* v. *Dillon* (1991) 65 *A.L.J.R.* 231.
136 *Robson* v. *Hallett* [1967] 2 Q.B. 939 and *Cowell* v. *Rosehill Racecourse Co. Ltd* (1937) 56 C.L.R. 605.
137 See pp. 107-8 above.
138 (1937) 56 C.L.R. 605.
139 See *Winter Garden Theatre (London) Ltd* v. *Millenium Productions Ltd* [1948] A.C. 173 and *Verrall* v. *Great Yarmouth Borough Council* [1980] 1 All E.R. 839, 844.
140 See *Cowell* v. *Rosehill Racecourse Co. Ltd* (1937) 56 C.L.R. 605, 633 *per* Dixon J.
141 See *Duffield* v. *Police* [1971] N.Z.L.R. 381.
142 (1610) 8 Co.Rep. 146a.

premises or makes a personal long distance call without the occupier's consent.

However, in *Canadian Pacific Wine Co.* v. *Tuley,*[143] the Privy Council decided that police officers who lawfully entered the premises and seized goods which they were entitled to do, did not become trespassers *ab initio* as to the land if they also seized goods which they were not lawfully entitled to seize. They were only trespassers in relation to the goods unlawfully seized. The effect of this decision and the decision in *Elias* v. *Pasmore*[144] is that the plaintiff cannot recover damages for the actions of the police officers from the time of the entry on to the land but only for the trespass to goods that they have unlawfully seized. It makes a difference to the amount of damages that the plaintiff will recover. Of course, if the original entry was unlawful because the defendant thought that he had an authority to enter land when in fact he did not, he will be regarded as a trespasser from the time when he entered the land and the doctrine of trespass *ab initio* will have no relevance.[145]

The application of the doctrine also requires an act of positive misfeasance. Mere nonfeasance, such as failure to pay for the food and wine consumed at an hotel or restaurant, will not make the person who fails to pay a trespasser *ab initio.*[146]

In *Chic Fashions (West Wales) Ltd* v. *Jones*[147] the English Court of Appeal was critical of the doctrine of trespass *ab initio* and Lord Denning M.R. even went so far as to suggest that the doctrine could not be applied at the present time.[148] The increase in the powers of entry by public officials and police officers, however, has given the doctrine 'some considerable surviving utility'[149] and even Lord Denning M.R. seems to have changed his mind and applied the doctrine in *Cinnamond* v. *British Airports Authority.*[150]

If a person is entitled to come on to the plaintiff's land to take some goods and he uses the entry also to take goods of the plaintiff which he is not entitled to take or to do other unlawful acts not connected with the entry, can he be treated as a trespasser in relation to the unlawful acts? In other words, can trespass be committed *pro tanto*? In *Inglis Electrix Pty Ltd* v. *Healing (Sales) Pty Ltd,*[151] the defendants were entitled to come on to the premises of the plaintiff to remove goods under a 'display plan' agreement but while they were on the premises they also removed the plaintiff's own goods. A majority of the Court of Appeal of New South

---

143 [1921] 2 A.C. 417.
144 [1934] 2 K.B. 164.
145 See *O'Brien* v. *President, Councillors and Ratepayers of the Shire of Rosedale* [1969] V.R. 845 and *Amstad & Another* v. *Brisbane City Council and Ward* (No. 1) [1968] Qd.R. 334.
146 See the *Six Carpenters' Case* (1610) 8 Co.Rep. 146a.
147 [1968] 2 Q.B. 299.
148 ibid., at 313: 'I know that at one time a man could be made a trespasser *ab initio* by the doctrine of relation back. But that is no longer true'.
149 *Clerk & Lindsell on Torts* (16th edn, London, 1989) para. 23-9.
150 [1980] 2 All E.R. 368, 373.
151 (1968) 69 S.R.(N.S.W.) 311.

Wales held that trespass can be committed *pro tanto* but Sugerman J.A. (dissenting) felt that it was 'difficult to grasp the notion of a person who at the same time is both a trespasser and not a trespasser which is implicit in the doctrine . . . of trespass *pro tanto*'.[152] When the matter came before the High Court,[153] Barwick C.J. and Menzies J. held that the defendants were not liable for trespass to land and they, at least by implication, rejected the doctrine of trespass *pro tanto*. Kitto J. specifically approved of the doctrine[154] and Windeyer and Owen JJ. did not advert to the doctrine. The doctrine has been used in at least two cases. In *Bond* v. *Kelly*[155] the defendant was given permission, under an agreement, to come on to the plaintiff's land to cut sufficient timber to enable him to obtain fifteen short and two long pieces of wood. When he cut more timber than he was entitled to do under the agreement he was held to be a trespasser on land in relation to the excess. And in *Singh* v. *Smithenbecker*[156] the defendant, who was given permission to enter the property to see if the plaintiff was there to give delivery of sheep, was held liable for trespass to land *pro tanto* when instead of confining his entry to the permitted purpose he mustered certain sheep, drove them across the plaintiff's land, took a gate off its hinges and drove the sheep off the land.

It should be noted that in *Inglis Electrix Pty Ltd* v. *Healing (Sales) Pty Ltd*[157] in *Bond* v. *Kelly*[158] and in *Singh* v. *Smithenbecker*[159] the defendant could not be treated as a trespasser *ab initio* by reason of his subsequent unlawful conduct because the entry was not made under an authority conferred by the general law but at the invitation of the person in possession of the land. The doctrine of trespass *pro tanto* is, therefore, useful in such situations and it acts as a deterrent to those who, on lawfully entering land at the invitation of the person in possession, conduct themselves in an unlawful manner. The doctrine ensures that such persons can be liable for trespass to land in addition to being liable for such other unlawful acts that they might do subsequent to their lawful entry. Of course, if a person given permission to enter land enters solely for a purpose which exceeds his licence he becomes a trespasser upon the land from the moment of entry.[160]

6. The Injuction as a Remedy for the Tort of Trespass to Land

If a person interferes with the plaintiff's exclusive possession of land by coming on to the land the plaintiff can eject him.[161] If the defendant has

152 ibid., 330.
153 *Healing (Sales) Pty Ltd* v. *Inglis Electrix Pty Ltd* (1968) 42 A.L.J.R. 280.
154 ibid., 286-7.
155 (1873) 4 A.J.R. 153.
156 (1923) 23 S.R.(N.S.W.) 207.
157 (1968) 69 S.R.(N.S.W.) 311 (C.A., N.S.W.); (1968) 42 A.L.J.R. 280 (H.C.).
158 (1873) 4 A.J.R. 153.
159 (1923) 23 S.R.(N.S.W.) 207.
160 See *Inglis Electrix Pty Ltd* v. *Healing (Sales) Pty Ltd* (1968) 69 S.R.(N.S.W.) 311, 330. See also *Barker* v. *The Queen* (1983) 57 A.L.J.R. 426.
161 See *Tullay* v. *Reed* (1823) 1 Car. & P.6.

entered forcibly, for example, by breaking down the door and entering the premises, he can be ejected forcibly and without any request to leave. But if the defendant's entry has been made quietly and peaceably, a request to leave is necessary after which the plaintiff can forcibly eject him if he does not depart within a reasonable time.[162] In either case, the force used must be reasonable,[163] though the courts, recognizing the frailties of excitable human nature and the necessity for quick action, will not 'strain to confine too closely the conception of reasonable force'.[164] If a person remains on land after permission to stay on the land is withdrawn he also can be ejected by the person entitled to exclusive possession of the land, after a reasonable time to withdraw from the land has elapsed and provided no more force is used than is reasonably necessary.[165] Even where a plaintiff invokes the process of the law by commencing an action for recovery of possession of land and obtaining a judgment against the defendant he can still exercise his common law right of self-help and eject the defendant because, as Harman J. said in *Aglionby* v. *Cohen*, 'a man does not lose his common law rights because he invokes the law up to a certain point'.[166]

If a person does not wish to resort to self-help, he can rely upon the action for recovery of possession of land making at the same time a claim for mesne profits if he has been dispossessed of the land. This matter has been discussed earlier.[167]

The person in exclusive possession of the land can also recover damages for the trespass. These can be nominal,[168] compensatory (including aggravated) damages[169] where appropriate and even exemplary or punitive damages.[170] Even though no recognizable damage may have occurred by virtue of the trespass, the person in exclusive possession of the land is entitled to damages assessed on the opinion and judgment of a reasonable man as the tort is actionable *per se*. An assessment arrived at by 'the exercise of a sound imagination and the practice of the broad axe' and within reasonable limits will not be disturbed on appeal.[171] There is further discussion in relation to the measure of damages for trespass to land in Chapter 7.

There are times, however, when the proper remedy for a trespass is not a remedy in damages but a remedy by way of an injunction. This might be the case where, as in *Kelsen* v. *Imperial Tobacco Co. Ltd*,[172] or *L.J.P.*

162 See *Polkinhorn* v. *Wright* (1845) 8 Q.B. 197, 206 and *Hemmings* v. *Stoke Poges Golf Club* [1920] 1 K.B. 720.
163 See *Hemmings* v. *Stoke Poges Golf Club* [1920] 1 K.B. 720.
164 See *Greenbury* v. *Lyon; Ex parte Lyon* [1957] Qd.R. 433, 439, per Stanley J.
165 *Hemmings* v. *Stoke Poges Golf Club* [1920] 1 K.B. 720.
166 [1955] 1 Q.B. 558, 563.
167 See p. 102 above.
168 See *Waters* v. *Maynard* (1924) 24 S.R.(N.S.W.) 618, 622 where it is pointed out that 'nominal damages does not mean small damages'.
169 See *Greig* v. *Greig* [1966] V.R. 376.
170 See *Pollack* v. *Volpato* [1973] 1 N.S.W.L.R. 653; *Coles-Smith* v. *Smith & Others* [1965] Qd.R. 494; *Johnstone* v. *Stewart* [1968] S.A.S.R. 142 and *L.J.P. Investments Pty Ltd* v. *Howard Chia Investments Pty Ltd. (No. 3)* (1991) Aust. Torts Reports 81-070.
171 See *Waters* v. *Maynard* (1924) 24 S.R.(N.S.W.) 618, 623 *per* Campbell J.
172 [1957] 2 Q.B. 334.

Investments Pty Ltd v. *Howard Chia Investments Pty Ltd*,[173] the remedy by way of damages would be a small money payment of nominal damages and the defendant would therefore be able to violate the plaintiff's airspace with impunity. In such circumstances, the injunction, developed by the courts of equity in England and available now in all courts of law in Australia, can be used not only to enjoin threatened trespasses to land but also to restrain the continuation or the repetition of such trespasses.[174] As Young J. of the Supreme Court of New South Wales pointed out in *Lincoln Hunt Australia Pty Ltd* v. *Willesee*,[175] : 'If a trespass to land is threatened it can be enjoined if it appears that the defendant is likely to carry out his threat and that the plaintiff will suffer irreparable damage if he does. If a defendant has once trespassed and appears likely to repeat his trespass then an injunction can be granted either at common law or in equity'. An injunction granted against an apprehended threat of a trespass is called a *quia timet* injunction and injunctions granted to restrain the continuation or repetition of a trespass can be either *negative* or *prohibitory* (those which forbid an act) or *positive* or *mandatory* (those which order an action to be done).[176]

The injunction is, however, an equitable remedy and, as such, is only available at the discretion of the court. It is useful, therefore, to consider in what circumstances the court will exercise its discretion to grant an injunction. The following are some tentative conclusions. First, if the court comes to the conclusion that if the plaintiff had applied for a *quia timet* injunction the defendant would have been unable to put forward any conceivable ground in answer to the claim for such an injunction, then the court will not put the defendant in any better position because he has committed a trespass and will grant an injunction to restrain the continuation or repetition of the trespass.[177] Secondly, the court will grant an injunction if it considers that damages will not be an adequate remedy. The court will more readily come to this conclusion if the defendant has made no reasonable offer of monetary compensation for the trespass[178] or where it believes that the defendant will gain a considerable economic advantage by trespassing on the property of the plaintiff.[179] It was suggested in argument in *John Trenberth Ltd* v. *National Westminster*

---

173 (1989) Aust. Torts Reports 80-269.

174 See R.P. Meagher, W.M.C. Gummow & J.R.F. Lehane, *Equity—Doctrine and Remedies* 2nd edn. (Sydney, 1984) para. 2121.

175 (1986) 4 N.S.W.L.R. 457, 462.

176 See J.D. Heydon, W.M.C. Gummow & R.P. Austin *Cases and Materials on Equity and Trusts* (3rd edn, Sydney, 1989) para. 3901; *Reliance Finance Corporation Pty Ltd* v. *Orwin, Walshe and Ward* [1964-65] N.S.W.R. 970, and *L.J.P. Investments Pty Ltd* v. *Howard Chia Investments Pty Ltd* (1989) Aust. Torts Reports 80-269.

177 See *John Trenberth Ltd* v. *National Westminster Bank Ltd* (1980) 39 P. & C.R. 104, 108.

178 See *Graham* v. *K.D. Morris* [1974] Qd.R. 1 and *Tipler* v. *Fraser* [1976] Qd.R. 272.

179 See *Lewvest Ltd* v. *Scotia Towers Ltd* (1982) 126 D.L.R. (3d) 239, 241 and *John Trenberth Ltd* v. *National Westminster Bank Ltd* (1980) 39 P. & C.R. 104, 106. See also *Caprino Pty Ltd* v. *Gold Coast City Council* (1982) 53 L.G.R.A. 243 and *L.J.P. Investments Pty Ltd* v. *Howard Chia Investments Pty Ltd (No. 3)* (1991) Aust. Torts Reports 81-070.

Bank Ltd that as the actual damage caused by the trespass was comparatively slight no injunction should be granted as the plaintiff would be obtaining an injunction for an injunction's sake. Walton J. in rejecting the argument said that 'far from that being a reason why an injunction should not be granted . . . the fact that any damage would be trifling is the very reason why the injunction should be granted'.[180] A similar point was made by Stamp J. in *Woollerton & Wilson Ltd* v. *Richard Costain Ltd* when he said:

> It is in my judgment well established that it is no answer to a claim for an injunction to restrain a trespass that the trespass does no harm to the plaintiff. Indeed, the very fact that no harm is done is a reason for rather than against the granting of an injunction: for if there is no damage done the damage recovered in the action will be nominal and if the injunction is refused the result will be no more nor less than a licence to continue the tort of trespass in return for a nominal payment.[181]

On the other hand, if the defendant has offered the plaintiff a substantial sum of money for the trespass the court will take this into account in considering whether an immediate injunction ought to be granted and, if so, on what terms.[182] Thirdly, the court will grant an injunction if it can be persuaded that irreparable damage will be suffered by the plaintiff if an injunction is not given and the balance of convenience favours the grant of an injunction. This might occur, for example, where the damages are virtually impossible to quantify.[183] Fourthly, the courts do take into account the behaviour of the parties in considering whether or not an injunction should be granted. Not only do they take into account whether the defendant has made an offer of a substantial sum of money for the trespass but they also consider whether the defendant sought the prior permission of the plaintiff for the trespass or whether the defendant has acted in flagrant disregard of the plaintiff's proprietary rights or by inadvertence. Where a defendant has acted in flagrant disregard of the plaintiff's rights (even though he might only have acted after he knew that he was not likely to get permission to trespass upon the plaintiff's land), it is more likely that the plaintiff will be granted an injunction, for, as Walton J. said in *Trenberth* v. *National Westminster Bank*, 'if flagrant invasion of another's rights of property of that nature is not sufficient to call forth the interposition of a court of equity, I do not know what invasion ever could be said so to do'.[184] The court, however, will refuse a mandatory injunction if it is satisfied that the plaintiff's conduct in refusing an offer by the defendant to pay for the use of the plaintiff's land,

---

180 (1980) 39 P. & C.R. 104, 107. See also *Spearwater* v. *Seaboyer* (1984) 65 N.S.R. (2d) 280; 147 A.P.R. 280 where although nominal damages were given it was felt to be an appropriate case for the exercise of discretion to issue a permanent injunction.

181 [1970] 1 W.L.R. 411, 413. See also *Patel* v. *W.H. Smith (Eziot) Ltd* [1987] 1 W.L.R. 853. For exceptional circumstances when the court will not think it appropriate to grant an injunction see *Behrens* v. *Richards* [1905] 2 Ch. 614.

182 ibid., 415.

183 See *Lincoln Hunt Australia Pty Ltd* v. *Willesee* (1986) 4 N.S.W.L.R. 457, 464.

184 (1980) 39 P. & C.R. 104, 106.

which offer bears a reasonable relationship to the gains or savings made by the defendant in using the plaintiff's land, has been unreasonable.[185]

Once it has been decided that an injunction should be granted the court can in a proper case suspend the operation of the injunction. It is difficult, however, to imagine that there would be many good reasons which would justify suspending the injunction for any length of time.[186] The injunction was suspended in *Woollerton* v. *Richard Costain Ltd*[187] in order to enable the defendants to have 'a proper opportunity of finishing the job', but the decision has not been followed in Australia[188] and even in England it has not received 'universal approbation', at least in relation to the question of the suspension of the injunction.[189] Of course, in some circumstances, the granting of an injunction might cause hardship to the defendant who might, for example, have to dismantle his projecting crane or use a different type of crane. In all these cases, the sensible answer which the courts should give is that the defendant should seek the prior permission of the plaintiff and negotiate with him before the commission of the act of trespass. Otherwise, by suspending the injunction the courts, in reality, give the defendant 'a licence to continue the tort of trespass in return for a nominal payment'.[190] Where a social need arises which requires the sanctioning of a trespass to land, for example, to allow building contractors to use the airspace over neighbouring land, the proper way to deal with that situation is by appropriate legislation and not by refusing or suspending an injunction which would otherwise be granted.[191]

III: THE ACTION ON THE CASE FOR DAMAGES

It was suggested earlier that if D commits a trespass to T's land by taking a large quantity of gravel from T's stream, with the result that the flow of water to P's land is drastically reduced with the inevitable consequence that P's crops fail due to a lack of water, P could not bring an action for trespass to land as D's act only indirectly interferes with P's land (crops). What action then can P bring against D? In *Beaudesert Shire Council* v. *Smith*,[192] the High Court of Australia decided that the action on the case

185 See *L.J.P. Investments Pty Ltd* v. *Howard Chia Investments Pty Ltd* (1989) Aust. Torts Reports 80-269 at 68, 872-3

186 See, however, *Tipler v. Fraser* [1976] Qd.R. 272 where the injunction was suspended for six months to enable the defendants to execute the necessary works upon their own land. In *L.J.P. Investments Pty Ltd* v. *Howard Chia Investments Pty Ltd* (1989) Aust. Torts Reports 80-269 Hodgson J. proposed an injunction which would enable completion of an amended development which involves the absolute minimum of trespass on the plaintiff's property (at 68, 873).

187 [1970] 1 W.L.R. 411.

188 See *Graham* v. *K.D. Morris & Sons Pty Ltd* [1974] Qd.R. 1.

189 See *Charrington* v. *Simons & Co. Ltd* [1971] 1 W.L.R. 598, 603 and *John Trenberth Ltd* v. *National Westminster Bank Ltd* (1980) 39 P. & C.R. 104, 107-8.

190 See G. Dworkin (1970) 33 *M.L.R.* 552, 555.

191 ibid., 556-7.

192 (1966) 120 C.L.R. 145.

for damages was available in these circumstances. As the High Court put it, 'independently of trespass, negligence or nuisance but by an action for damages upon the case, a person who suffers harm or loss as the inevitable consequence of the unlawful, intentional and positive acts of another is entitled to recover damages from that other'.[193] In that case, the Beaudesert Shire Council by taking, without any authority, 12000 yards (10975 metres) of gravel from the bed of the Albert River in the vicinity of Smith's farm destroyed the natural water-hole from which he used to pump water, under a licence, for the irrigation of his farm. This resulted in a loss of some crops due to a lack of water, for which the High Court awarded Smith the sum of £1000.

The decision has come in for some academic criticism[194] and in *Elston* v. *Dore* three judges of the High Court of Australia referred to 'the much criticized principle of *Beaudesert Shire Council* v. *Smith*'.[195] The Privy Council in *Dunlop* v. *Woollahra Municipal Council* did point out that the *Beaudesert* decision 'has never been applied in Australia in any subsequent case' and that there is difficulty 'in ascertaining what limits are imposed upon the scope of this innominate tort by the requirements that in order to constitute it the acts of the tortfeasor must be "positive", having as their "inevitable consequence" harm or loss to the plaintiff and, what . . . must be "unlawful"'.[196]

Meanwhile, judicial exegesis in the Australian courts, in relation to the action on the case for damages based on *Beaudesert*, continues. In *Kitano* v. *The Commonwealth*, Mason J. reaffirmed that 'the existence of an intention on the part of the defendant to cause harm to the plaintiff' is not necessary to found liability in that tort.[197] There was also an attempt in that decision to explain the meaning of loss as an 'inevitable consequence' of the defendant's act.[198] The meaning of 'unlawful' act has been considered in *Grand Central Car Park Pty Ltd* v. *Tivoli Freeholders*[199] and in *Dunlop* v. *Woollahra Municipal Council*.[200] It apparently does not include cases 'where the unlawfulness arose merely by virtue of the fact that [a] trade was one being carried on without a permit from the local authority'[201] nor does it include acts which are null and void as opposed to acts which are forbidden by law.[202] In *Beaudesert* itself the High Court had restricted the meaning of 'unlawful' to exclude any act which had no other element of 'unlawfulness' than that of being in breach of a statute and Mason J. in *Kitano* v. *The Commonwealth* reiterated this restriction when he said that for a plaintiff to succeed in an action on the case 'he must show something

193 ibid., 156.
194 See G. Dworkin & A. Harari (1967) 40 *A.L.J.* 296 and 347. See also M.J. Standish (1967) 6 *M.U.L.R.* 225 and R.J. Sadler (1984) 58 *A.L.J.* 38.
195 (1983) 57 A.L.J.R. 83, 87-8.
196 [1981] 1 N.S.W.L.R. 76, 82.
197 (1974) 129 C.L.R. 151, 174.
198 See also *Freedman* v. *Petty* [1981] V.R. 1001, 1032.
199 [1969] V.R. 62.
200 [1981] 1 N.S.W.L.R. 76.
201 *Grand Central Car Park Pty Ltd* v. *Tivoli Freeholders* [1969] V.R. 62, 64 *per* McInerney J.
202 *Dunlop* v. *Woollahra Municipal Council* [1981] 1 N.S.W.L.R. 76.

more than a mere breach of the statute and consequential damage; he must show something over and above what would ground liability for breach of statutory duty if the action was available'.[203]

This discussion on the *Beaudesert* principle can be concluded by saying that there are some intentional interferences with land for which the nominate torts of trespass, nuisance and *Rylands* v. *Fletcher* cannot provide a remedy. When this happens, the innominate tort of the action on the case for damages might be available as a remedy. The *Beaudesert* decision itself at least stands for the proposition that if a defendant intentionally commits a trespass on the land of a third party, a plaintiff who suffers damage to his land as the inevitable consequence of that tortious act can recover damages in an action on the case in respect of that damage. It is desirable, however, that the scope of this innominate tort be better delineated by the High Court of Australia at the first opportunity.[204]

Irrespective of the *Beaudesert* principle, it has been held that an owner of land which is in occupation of a tenant who might not be able to bring an action for trespass to land, because the exclusive possession of the land is in the tenant, can nevertheless bring an action on the case for damages against the trespasser if the act of trespass causes damage of a permanent character to the reversion.[205] This action can be brought immediately the damage is done and it is not necessary for the owner of the land to wait until the tenancy has come to an end. *Mayfair Property Co.* v. *Johnston*[206] and *Jones* v. *Llanrwst Urban Council*[207] suggest that an action of trespass can also be brought by an owner in such circumstances but in *Rodrigues* v. *Ufton*,[208] Hodges J. in the Supreme Court of Victoria held that an action on the case for damages was the appropriate remedy. As he said, 'I entertain no doubt that a reversioner cannot bring an action of trespass. He can bring an action, and can recover damages, if a trespass will injure his reversion'.[209]

An action on the case for damages might also be brought by a licensee against a trespasser if the act of the trespasser causes damage to the interest which the licensee has acquired under the licence.[210]

---

203 (1974) 129 C.L.R. 151, 174-5.

204 In *Elston* v. *Dore* (1983) 57 A.L.J.R. 83, 86, three judges of the High Court suggested that when the question whether the *Beaudesert* decision should be followed arises for decision 'it will be desirable that a court of seven justices should consider it'. This might soon happen. See *Hospitals Contribution Fund of Australia* v. *Hunt* (1982) 44 A.L.R. 365.

205 See *Rodrigues* v. *Ufton* (1894) 20 V.L.R. 539.

206 [1894] 1 Ch. 508.

207 [1911] 1 Ch. 393.

208 (1894) 20 V.L.R. 539.

209 ibid., 546.

210 Thus, if contrary to the views expressed above, a deserted wife or a contractual licensee cannot bring an action in trespass there is always the action on the case to fall back on. The plaintiff would, of course, have to prove damage to rely upon this innominate tort.

4

INTENTIONAL TORTS TO GOODS

I: SOME GENERAL COMMENTS

We now turn our attention to how the law of torts protects a person's interests in his goods or chattels (an archaic expression for the word 'goods') against intentional interferences. In England an attempt has been made to deal with many of these interferences statutorily and the Torts (Interference with Goods) Act 1977 has been enacted. But in Australia these interferences are dealt with almost entirely by the common law and we therefore have to consider several torts, most of which have an ancient origin. There are four torts that are considered in this chapter: trespass to goods, conversion (formerly called trover), detinue and the action on the case for damages. These separate civil remedies for intentional interferences with goods each have their separate incidents, but there is also a certain amount of overlap, and in many instances two or more of these torts can be brought in relation to the same set of facts. It is said that, apart from a single exception, a wrong which gives rise to a right of action in detinue now also gives rise to an action in conversion.[1] The exception is the case of a bailee who allows goods to be lost or destroyed by sheer carelessness in breach of his duty to the bailor. This has prompted the legislature in England to abolish the tort of detinue and to allow an action in conversion 'for loss or destruction of goods which a bailee has allowed to happen in breach of his duty to his bailor'.[2] There are, of course, many forms of conversion which do not amount to detinue. The legislative changes in England might eventually find acceptance in Australia, but until that happens we will continue to have several separate civil remedies which protect a person against intentional and negligent wrongful interferences with his goods. In this chapter, which is concerned only with intentional wrongful interferences, we deal with trespass to goods, conversion, detinue and the action on the case for damages.

1 See English Law Reform Committee, 18th *Report (Conversion and Detinue)* 1971, Cmnd. 4774, para. 8.

2 See s.2, Torts (Interference with Goods) Act 1977.

Before we do that, however, let us examine briefly the right of recaption of chattels. This common law right allows a person who has been deprived of the possession of his goods to recover those goods immediately and without recourse to the various actions in tort which have just been mentioned. Not only can a person defend his possession of goods but, in the absence of statutory provisions which prevent the recovery of certain goods except by following certain procedures,[3] he can also peaceably retake his goods from any person who is unlawfully in possession of them, just as the person whose exclusive possession of land is interfered with can resort to self-help to recover possession of it.

If a person in actual possession of goods loses possession of those goods as a result of a trespass, he can regain possession of those goods by the use of reasonable force. No prior demand for the return of the goods appears necessary, particularly where the interval of time between the trespassory taking and the attempt to regain possession is brief. A person entitled to possession of goods but not in possession is in no different position, as the decision in *Blades* v. *Higgs*[4] suggests, and such a person can also exercise his right of recaption using reasonable force. It may be that in this case a prior demand for the delivery up of the goods should be made but it is not always necessary. For example, it would not be necessary to request a poacher to refrain from carrying away the dead rabbits which he has just shot on your property, it would be permissible just to take them away from him. In the case of a bailment, a bailor who wishes to regain possession of the goods should make a demand for the return of the goods, before he attempts to retake them, in order to make quite clear to the bailee that the bailment is at an end. If such a demand is made and the bailee refuses to return the goods the bailor can regain possession of the goods, even by the use of reasonable force.[5]

A person can also go on to another's land to regain possession of his goods.[6] If fruit or a tree belonging to A falls on to the land of B, A can go on to B's land to regain his property if the fruit or the tree have fallen on to B's land by accident but not if the falling of the goods on to B's land has been brought about by A's design.[7] If B has placed A's goods on B's land, A can also go on to B's land to regain his goods.[8] It was suggested in *Patrick* v. *Colerick*[9] that B's act would give A an implied licence to enter to exercise his right of recaption. But if A's goods are placed upon B's land by a third party then A cannot enter B's land for the purpose of recaption except when B has connived with or given active assistance to the third

---

3 e.g. in the case of goods on hire-purchase. See Hire-Purchase Act 1959 (Vic.), s.13. There are Hire-Purchase Acts in every State and Territory of Australia.

4 (1861) 10 C.B.(N.S.W.) 713, 720.

5 If A has made a gratuitous bailment of a valuable painting to B and some months later A wishes to sell it to an art dealer who is in Melbourne only for a day and B refuses to return it, A can exercise his right of recaption in order to regain possession of the painting in order to sell it. See also *De Lambert* v. *Ongley* [1924] N.Z.L.R. 430 (recaption of a receipt).

6 See *Cox* v. *Bath* (1893) 14 L.R.(N.S.W.) 263, 266.

7 See *Anthony* v. *Haney & Harding* (1832) 8 Bing. 186, 191.

8 ibid.

9 (1838) 3 M. & W. 483, 485.

party[10] or where the goods have been placed on B's land as the result of an indictable offence.[11]

In retaking his goods a person must act in a reasonable manner. What is a reasonable manner will vary according to the circumstances of the case but generally the courts will require that the force used to retake the goods must not be more than is reasonably necessary to wrest the goods from the control of the person who is in unlawful possession of them. A person is not entitled to wound or inflict serious injury on another in order to regain his goods but he can, apparently, resort to a trick to regain his goods.[12] The common law right to recaption of chattels and the limits on the right are given statutory recognition in several of the Australian States.[13] The entry upon land for the purpose of recaption of chattels must also be reasonable. The courts will more readily acquiesce in entry upon land where the 'land' entered is a field, yard, garden or outhouse rather than an occupied dwelling-house, but 'it is not impossible to imagine circumstances in which entry even into a dwelling-house may be reasonable'.[14]

The right of recaption of chattels will be available as a defence to actions in tort such as assault, battery or trespass to land which might be brought against a person who commits these torts while attempting to retain possession of his goods or while attempting to regain possession of them.

We will now consider the torts of trespass to goods, conversion, detinue and the action on the case for damages.

II: TRESPASS TO GOODS

Trespass to goods is a direct interference by a defendant of a plaintiff's possession of goods. The tort of trespass to goods is usually brought for wrongful intentional interferences, though actions for reckless and even careless interferences are not precluded.

There are at least four matters that require elaboration in relation to this tort. First, we consider the nature of the plaintiff's interest and the kind of possession that he must have in order to sue for trespass to goods. Secondly, we examine the nature of the defendant's act and the kinds of interferences which are sufficient to constitute a trespass to goods. Thirdly,

---

10 See *Huet* v. *Lawrence* [1948] St.R.Qd. 168.

11 In *Anthony* v. *Haney and Harding* (1832) 8 Bing. 186 the word 'felonious' act was used. Now that 'felonies' have been abolished, it might be better to exclude the right of recaption in these cases, leaving the police to recover the goods and to return them to the persons entitled to possession. The exercise of the right of recaption in these circumstances might destroy valuable evidence of the criminal offence committed.

12 *Sutton Motors (Temora) Pty Ltd* v. *Hollywood Motors Pty Ltd* [1971] V.R. 684.

13 See Qld: Criminal Code Act 1899, ss.274 and 276; Tas.: Criminal Code Act 1924, ss.43 and 45; W.A.: Criminal Code 1913, ss.251 and 253. See also *R.* v. *Timmins* [1913] Q.W.N. 44; 7 Q.J.P.R. 61 and *Mitchell* v. *Norman; Ex parte Norman* [1965] Qd.R. 587.

14 English Law Reform Committee, 18th *Report (Conversion and Detinue)* 1971, Cmnd. 4774, para. 124.

we consider the question whether these interferences are actionable *per se* or whether the tort of intentional trespass to goods requires proof of damage. And finally there is a brief discussion on whether the *jus tertii* can be raised as a defence to an action for trespass to goods.

1. THE NATURE OF THE PLAINTIFF'S INTEREST

Trespass is a wrong to possession;[15] therefore, a plaintiff who is to succeed in an action for trespass to goods must be able to show that he was in possession of the goods at the time of the act of interference by the defendant. While it may not be possible to give a completely logical and exhaustive definition of 'possession',[16] in determining who has the possession of goods the courts generally take into account who has physical control of the goods and whether he has displayed an intention to exercise that control on his own behalf. The possession which a plaintiff must have at the time of the trespass must be either 'actual or constructive or a legal right to the immediate possession' of the goods.[17] If A is driving his car or wearing his watch he is in actual possession of those goods, but if A's car accidentally runs off the wharf into the sea or if A accidentally drops his watch overboard into the sea, he will not have actual possession of his car or watch but only constructive possession of them; he will, however, be able to bring an action of trespass if B attempts wrongfully to interfere with those goods.[18] If A keeps racing pigeons locked in his dovecote he is in actual possession of them, but if he sets them free, either for the purpose of exercise or for a race, though he may not have actual possession of the pigeons, he would have constructive possession of them and would be able to bring an action of trespass against anyone who shoots them.[19] When is 'a legal right to the immediate possession' of goods a sufficient interest to sue for trespass to goods? In *Penfolds Wines Pty Ltd* v. *Elliott* Dixon J. approved of the opinion expressed by Sir Frederick Pollock in 1888[20] that the right to immediate possession as a title for maintaining an action for trespass to goods is merely a right in one person to sue for a trespass done to another's possession, and that this right only exists when the person whose actual (or constructive) possession was violated held as servant, agent or bailee

---

15 *Penfolds Wines Pty Ltd* v. *Elliott* (1946) 74 C.L.R. 204, 224.

16 See D.R. Harris, 'The Concept of Possession in English Law' in *Oxford Essays in Jurisprudence* (ed. A.G. Guest) (Oxford, 1961) p. 69. See also F. Pollock & R.S. Wright, *An Essay on Possession in the Common Law* (Oxford, 1888).

17 See *Johnson* v. *Diprose* [1893] 1 Q.B. 512, 515.

18 In *Wilson* v. *Lombank Ltd* [1963] 1 All E.R. 740 the plaintiff left his car with a garage for repairs. When the repairs were completed the car was placed on the forecourt of the garage from where it was wrongfully taken away by the defendants. Hinchcliffe J. in holding that the defendants were liable to the plaintiff in trespass said that he did not think that the plaintiff had ever lost possession of the car. So, in such circumstances, the plaintiff had either actual or constructive possession of the car.

19 See *Hamps* v. *Darby* [1948] 2 K.B. 311, 322-3. The action of trespass would also be available against a person who catches the racing pigeons by standing on top of a hill with a big net. See the *Age*, 10 May 1983.

20 F. Pollock & R.S. Wright, *Possession in the Common Law* (Oxford, 1888) p. 145.

under a bailment determinable at will for or under or on behalf of the person having the immediate right to possession.[21] So a person without actual or constructive possession cannot maintain an action for trespass to goods except where he brings an action for the violation of the actual (or constructive) possession of his servant, agent or bailee at will. In the *Penfolds* case itself the majority of the High Court held that there was no trespass to goods when the defendant filled the plaintiffs' bottles with bulk wines produced by another vigneron because the bottles had been given to the defendant by the plaintiffs' bailee. As there had been no violation of the actual or constructive possession of the bailee there was no trespassory act in respect of which the plaintiffs, who as bailors of the bottles had the right to immediate possession of the bottles, could sue for trespass to the bottles. Apart from being able to sue the trespasser in respect of a violation of the actual or constructive possession of goods bailed to his bailee, a bailor can also sue his bailee for trespass if the goods are completely destroyed by the bailee. But this is an exceptional case.

There appear to be three exceptions to the general rule that either actual or constructive possession or the right to immediate possession of the goods is required to bring an action in trespass.[22] They are that trustees may sue for trespass to goods in the hands of the beneficiary,[23] that executors and administrators of an estate may sue for trespass to goods of the estate committed between the date of the death and that of the grant[24] and that an owner of a franchise in wrecks can sue in trespass for interference with the wrecks.[25] These authorities are not recent and they are not Australian decisions but there is no reason to assume that they will not be followed here.

2. The Nature of the Defendant's Acts and the Kinds of Interference Sufficient to Constitute Trespass

As it is a species of trespass, a necessary requirement of the tort of intentional trespass to goods is that the interference by the defendant, if it is to be actionable as a trespass, must be 'directly' occasioned by an act of the defendant. Acts of the defendant which make immediate contact with the goods of the plaintiff, without any voluntary human intervention, are regarded as 'direct'. Thus to smash the windscreen of the plaintiff's car with a hammer or to fire a bullet into the plaintiff's cat is a direct act and a trespass to the plaintiff's goods.[26] But to lock a room in which the plaintiff has left some of his goods is not a trespass as there is no direct contact with the plaintiff's goods.[27] Also, as with trespass to the person

21 *Penfolds Wines* v. *Elliott* (1946) 74 C.L.R. 204, 228 *per* Dixon J.

22 See *Street* (6th edn, 1976) pp. 33-4. The number of exceptions has not expanded since the first edition (London, 1955) p. 32.

23 Reasoning from *Barker* v. *Furlong* [1891] 2 Ch. 172 (a case on conversion of chattels).

24 *Tharpe* v. *Stallwood* (1843) 5 Man. & G. 760.

25 See *Dunwich Corporation* v. *Sterry* (1831) 1 B. & Ad. 831.

26 See *Davies* v. *Bennison* (1927) 22 Tas.L.R. 52.

27 See *Hartley* v. *Moxham* (1842) 3 Q.B. 701. The plaintiff would have to bring an action in detinue.

and to land, any act which sets in motion an unbroken series of continuing consequences, the last of which ultimately causes contact with the goods of the plaintiff, will be regarded as sufficiently 'direct' for the purposes of the tort of trespass to goods. Thus if D intentionally pushes P who is carrying a crystal decanter causing P to drop it, P can sue D for trespass to goods (the decanter) even though D does not himself touch the decanter. And in *Hutchins* v. *Maughan*,[28] Herring C.J. of the Supreme Court of Victoria thought that trespass would lie against a defendant who threw poisoned meat to a dog which subsequently ate it. In both these situations, the damage to the decanter and the injury to the dog would, it is suggested, properly be regarded as directly occasioned by the act of the defendant.

The act of the defendant must also be voluntary. As McGregor J. pointed out in *Beals* v. *Hayward*,[29] a sleepwalker would not be liable for trespass to goods if he broke a valuable vase while sleepwalking. But if D, for example, mistakenly carries away a sofa belonging to P together with other furniture purchased by D, an action for trespass to goods will lie against D in respect of the asportation of the sofa. The mistake will not make the act in any sense involuntary.[30]

In addition to being direct and voluntary, the act of the defendant must be intentional (or reckless) for the tort of intentional trespass to goods, or negligent (or careless) for the tort of negligent trespass to goods.[31] The act is intentional when the defendant deliberately or wilfully interferes with the plaintiff's goods and it is also intentional if the contact or interference with the goods is substantially certain to follow from the defendant's act. It is also suggested that the act will be regarded as intentional if it is reckless.[32]

The kinds of interferences which constitute a trespass to goods are many and varied. Latham C.J. in the *Penfolds* case gives several examples of such interferences.

> A mere taking or asportation of a chattel may be a trespass without the infliction of any material damage. The handling of a chattel without authority is a trespass . . . Unauthorised user of goods is a trespass; unauthorised acts of riding a horse, driving a motor car, using a bottle, are all equally trespasses . . .[33]

In *Kirk* v. *Gregory*,[34] moving some valuable objects from one place to another in the same house was regarded as a trespass to those goods. Any intentional unpermitted contact by the defendant with the plaintiff's goods is actionable as a trespass provided it is direct. Scratching the paintwork of a car is a trespass.[35] Painting slogans on it or even writing in

---

28 [1947] V.L.R. 131, 134.
29 [1960] N.Z.L.R. 131, 137.
30 See *Colwill* v. *Reeves* (1811) 2 Camp. 575.
31 For negligent trespass to goods, see pp. 323-4 below.
32 For what are 'reckless' acts, see pp. 33-6 above.
33 (1946) 74 C.L.R. 204, 214-15.
34 (1876) 1 Ex.D. 55.
35 See *Fouldes* v. *Willoughby* (1841) 8 M. & W. 540, 549 *per* Alderson B.

chalk upon it is a trespass. The fact that no material damage is done to the goods does not prevent the cause of action from arising. To beat or strike an animal[36] or to shoot a bird[37] in the possession of the plaintiff is a trespass to goods. And it is also a trespass to chase an animal in another's possession over a cliff,[38] though it is not clear whether it would be a trespass to chase an animal in another's possession until it dies of exhaustion.[39] It has already been pointed out that to throw poisoned meat to a dog which subsequently eats it has been regarded as a trespass in Australia but that to leave poisoned meat for an animal which might come on to your land is not regarded as a trespass because the contact with the animal is brought about by indirect means. These distinctions do not have much to commend them and 'the requirement under the existing law of trespass that the interference must be direct could . . . with advantage be abolished'.[40]

3. Does the Tort of Intentional Trespass to Goods Require Proof of Actual Damage?

There is little doubt that an intentional trespass to the person and an intentional trespass to land are actionable *per se* and that proof of actual damage is not required. Is this true also of an intentional trespass to goods? If there has been an asportation of the goods, *Kirk* v. *Gregory*[41] is an authority for the proposition that an intentional trespass to goods is actionable *per se*. *Demers* v. *Desrorier*[42] shows, however, that a plaintiff will succeed in an action for intentional trespass even where there has been no asportation of the goods and no actual damage. In that case, goods belonging to the plaintiff had been seized by the sheriff in execution of an irregular default judgment obtained by the defendant, which judgment was later set aside. The goods were not removed from the plaintiff's premises or moved in any way, because the plaintiff agreed to become the bailiff of the sheriff and responsible for the safe keeping of the goods under the seizure. Nevertheless, the action in trespass was successful, even though the plaintiff could show no actual damage, because Ford J. held that the 'owner was dispossessed of the chattels notwithstanding that they were never actually out of his custody'.[43] But what if there has been no asportation of the goods and no dispossession? Is an intentional touching of goods without any actual damage actionable as a trespass? The opinion of most writers on the law of torts suggests that it is. But such slender judicial authority as there is suggests that the matter is not

36 See *Wright* v. *Ramscot* (1665) 1 Wms. Saund. 84.
37 See *Hamps* v. *Darby* [1948] 2 K.B. 311.
38 On an analogy with *Leame* v. *Bray* (1803) 3 East 593.
39 See B. McMahon & D.W. Binchy, *Irish Law of Torts* (Oxford, 1981) p. 536.
40 English Law Reform Committee, 18th *Report (Conversion and Detinue)* 1971, Cmnd. 4774, para. 20.
41 (1876) 1 Ex.D. 55.
42 [1929] 3 D.L.R. 401. See also *William Leitch & Co.* v. *Leydon* [1931] A.C. 90, 106 *per* Lord Blanesburgh.
43 [1929] 3 D.L.R. 401, 405.

free from doubt. In *Everitt* v. *Martin*, F.B. Adams J. said that there was no right of action 'for the mere touching of another's goods without damage or asportation' though that statement, he felt, could more confidently be applied to 'mere accidental contacts' than 'intentional contacts'.[44] There are several situations where it would be most useful to have an intentional touching of goods without any actual damage actionable as a trespass. Not only should persons be prevented from touching museum exhibits with impunity[45] but they should also be prevented from touching objects which are worn by others, such as jewellery or even a hearing aid, and they should also be prevented from touching corpses whether by way of an unauthorized post-mortem examination or for other purposes.[46] If the tort of intentional trespass to goods is available in all these situations, the courts will be using that tort not only to protect the plaintiff against damage to his goods but they will also be protecting him against interfering annoyances with his possession of the goods and interferences with his goods which cause him indignity, humiliation or distress. That the tort of intentional trespass to goods performs this additional function is more reason for taking the view that the tort of intentional trespass to goods is actionable *per se*.

4. The Jus tertii and Trespass to Goods

It appears to be a well-established principle that a person who is in actual or constructive, albeit wrongful, possession of goods can bring an action for trespass to goods against anyone except the rightful owner who interferes with his possession and that it is no answer to such an action that someone else is rightfully entitled to the possession of those goods. In other words, a defendant who violates the actual or constructive possession of the plaintiff cannot plead the defence of *jus tertii* in relation to that trespass. There appear to be only two exceptions to that principle.[47] The first is when the defendant defends the action on behalf and by authority of the person rightfully entitled to possession of the goods and the second is when the defendant commits the act complained of by the authority of the person rightfully entitled to possession of the goods. In these cases the *jus tertii* can properly be pleaded. If a defendant wrongfully takes goods out of the actual or constructive possession of the plaintiff and later returns them to the true owner he will still be liable to an action in trespass at the suit of the plaintiff who was in actual or constructive possession of the goods.[48]

---

44 [1953] N.Z.L.R. 298, 302-3.

45 See *Street* (6th edn, 1976) p. 31.

46 See *Gonzalez* v. *Sacramento Memorial Lawn* (1982) 25 A.T.L.A. L.Rep. 348 where a 21-year-old woman employee of a mortuary admitted to committing some 20 to 40 acts of necrophilia on the corpse of the plaintiff's son.

47 These exceptions were enumerated by *Salmond* and approved by Henchman J. in *Henry Berry & Co. Pty Ltd* v. *Rushton* [1937] St. R.Qd. 109, 119 and by Hinchcliffe J. in *Wilson* v. *Lombank Ltd* [1963] 1 All E.R. 740, 742.

48 See *Wilson* v. *Lombank Ltd* [1963] 1 All E.R. 740.

The position when the plaintiff is not in actual or constructive possession is more difficult to state with confidence, but it would appear that the *jus tertii* can properly be pleaded. As Henchman J. said in *Henry Berry & Co. Pty Ltd* v. *Rushton*,[49] if the plaintiff is not in actual possession when the wrongful act is done but relies upon his right to possession, 'he must recover on the strength of his title, and the defendant may, under a plea of not guilty or not possessed, show that the plaintiff has no right to immediate possession, because that right is in some other person'.[50] In other words, in the case of a plaintiff who is not in actual or constructive possession of the goods at the time of the trespass, the *jus tertii* may be pleaded by the trespasser.

III: CONVERSION

The tort of conversion is an ancient one:[51] it has its beginnings in the old common law action of trover. Though there is 'some doubt both as to the precise circumstances surrounding its appearance and as to the chronology of its early development',[52] it has been suggested that conversion (trover) 'emerged late in the fifteenth century as a branch of the action on the case . . . [and] was invented through the ingenuity of some long forgotten common law pleader, to fill the gaps left by the actions of trespass, which lay for the wrongful taking of a chattel, and detinue, which lay for its wrongful detention'.[53]

Today, the tort of conversion is committed when a defendant by his intentional conduct and without lawful justification, deals with goods in a manner repugnant to the plaintiff's possession (actual or constructive) or immediate right to possession of those goods.

There are at least five matters that require elaboration in relation to this tort. First, the subject-matter of conversion. Obviously, conversion is concerned with goods, but are negotiable instruments, such as cheques, treated by the courts as goods for the purposes of the tort of conversion? Secondly, we consider the nature of the plaintiff's interest, i.e., the interest in the goods which the plaintiff must show if he is to succeed in an action for conversion. Thirdly, we discuss the kind of intentional conduct which is sufficient to constitute conversion. Fourthly, we examine the kinds of dealings with goods or chattels which have been held by the courts to amount to conversion. And fifthly, there is a brief discussion as to whether the plea of *jus tertii* can be raised as a defence to an action in conversion.

---

49 [1937] St.R.Qd. 109.

50 ibid., 119.

51 Though not as ancient an origin as trespass and detinue, which 'date from the beginning of our legal system'. See J.W. Salmond (1905) 21 *L.Q.R.* 43, 44.

52 See A.W.B. Simpson (1959) 75 *L.Q.R.* 364.

53 See W.L. Prosser (1957) 42 *Cornell L.Q.* 168, 169.

1. The Subject-matter of Conversion

The subject-matter of conversion is goods. But what are 'goods' for the purposes of the tort of conversion? No complete definition can be offered, though the following points may be helpful. The first is that a thing which is incapable of being property cannot be the subject-matter of conversion.[54] Secondly, any tangible movable object which is in, or is capable of being in, the actual possession of a person can be the subject-matter of conversion.[55] Thus bottles,[56] motor-cars,[57] machinery and plant,[58] yachts[59] and business papers[60] are all capable of conversion; so are title deeds[61] and mortgage documents;[62] trees cut down and carried away may be converted;[63] domestic animals such as horses,[64] sheep[65] and cows[66] can be converted and so can animals *ferae naturae* if they have been reduced into possession by the plaintiff. Thirdly, in the case of money, it too can be the subject-matter of conversion provided the plaintiff can show that the money in question was a specific tangible, movable object and not money simply as currency. Thus if a defendant steals specific coins,[67] specific banknotes,[68] money lying in a specific receptacle such as a bag or wallet or in a drawer of the plaintiff's desk, an action in conversion will lie in relation to that money, but a person who borrows $100 and refuses to repay the debt cannot be sued in conversion because the money was

---

54 See *Doodeward* v. *Spence* (1908) 6 C.L.R. 406 where it was suggested by both Griffith C.J. and Higgins J. that 'a mere corpse awaiting burial' was incapable of being the subject of property. However, the majority of the High Court (Higgins J. dissenting) thought that the corpse of a still-born two-headed child preserved in a bottle of spirits was capable of being the subject-matter of conversion.

55 See D.C. Jackson, *Principles of Property Law* (Sydney, 1967) Ch. 2. *Clerk & Lindsell on Torts* (16th edn, 1989) at paras 22-36 describe the subject-matter of conversion as any 'corporeal personal property'.

56 See *Penfolds Wines Pty Ltd* v. *Elliott* (1946) 74 C.L.R. 204; *Model Dairy Pty Ltd* v. *White* (1935) A.L.R. 432; and *Milk Bottles Recovery Ltd* v. *Camillo* [1948] V.L.R. 344.

57 See *Foster* v. *Franklin* [1924] V.L.R. 267; *Motor Dealers Credit Corporation Ltd* v. *Overland (Sydney) Ltd* (1931) 31 S.R.(N.S.W.) 516; and *Gurr* v. *Esanda Ltd* (1981) 28 S.A.S.R. 297.

58 See *Kidd* v. *McCrae* (1921) 23 W.A.L.R. 98 and *Craig* v. *Marsh* (1935) 35 S.R.(N.S.W.) 323.

59 See *McKeown* v. *Cavalier Yachts Pty Ltd* (1988) 13 N.S.W.L.R. 303 and *King* v. *Bulli Coal Mining Co.* (1877) Knox 389 (N.S.W. Sup.Ct., F.C.).

60 *Turner* v. *N.S.W. Mont de Piete Deposit and Investment Co.* (1910) 10 C.L.R. 539.

61 *Kay* v. *Barnett* (1909) Q.W.N. 39.

62 *Heavener* v. *Loomes* (1924) 34 C.L.R. 306 (detinue).

63 *The Tinaroo Shire Council* v. *Purcell* [1904] St.R.Qd. 186.

64 *Talbett* v. *Chrystall* (1862) 1 S.C.R.(N.S.W.) 86 and *Ryan* v. *Vince* (1962) 9 L.G.R.A. 253.

65 *Bennett* v. *Flood* (1864) 3 S.C.R.(N.S.W.) 158 and *Roache* v. *Australian Mercantile Land & Finance Co. Ltd* (1966) 67 S.R.(N.S.W.) 54.

66 *Owen* v. *Turner* [1939] Q.W.N. 23.

67 See *Orton* v. *Butler* (1822) 5 Barn. & Ald. 652, 654.

68 See *Burn* v. *Morris* (1834) 2 Cr. & M. 579.

money as currency.[69] Fourthly, in the case of negotiable instruments such as cheques, insurance policies, shares etc., the courts have overcome the problem that intangible rights cannot be converted, by treating the documents which evidence or embody those rights, i.e. the pieces of paper in question, as the goods which are converted.[70] The conversion of the goods (cheque, insurance policy, share certificate etc.) is then treated as the conversion of the money the documents (pieces of paper) represent. It is only in this way that negotiable instruments have been made the subject-matter of conversion in relation to the money that those instruments represent. It should be noted, however, that a forged cheque has been held not to be a negotiable instrument and therefore not the subject-matter of conversion, at least in relation to the money that it purports to represent.[71]

2. The Nature of the Plaintiff's Interest in Goods

(a) In general It is well established that to maintain an action in conversion the plaintiff must show that he had either actual possession of the goods or the immediate right to possession of the goods at the time of the conversion.[72] What is actual possession has already been considered when discussing the tort of trespass to goods. All that need be said here is that if a defendant interferes with the actual possession of the plaintiff's goods, for example, by stealing them, then the plaintiff has an action in both trespass to goods and conversion. As in trespass, it is not necessary for the plaintiff to have ownership of the goods, actual possession of the goods being sufficient title to sue in conversion.[73] As Green C.J. pointed out in *Perpetual Trustees & National Executors of Tasmania Ltd* v. *Perkins*, 'a possessory title derived from the fact of possession is sufficient to give the right to bring an action for conversion or wrongful detention'.[74]

---

69 He would have to be sued in contract or in a restitutionary action for 'money had and received'. See R. Goff & G. Jones, *The Law of Restitution* (3rd edn, London, 1986). See also *Thomas* v. *High* (1960) 60 S.R.(N.S.W.) 401, 403 where money left by the plaintiff in the defendant's safe was regarded as a bailment of specific notes and not one of money lent.

70 See *Lloyds Bank Ltd* v. *Chartered Bank of India, Australia and China* [1929] 1 K.B. 40, 56. See also *Wilton* v. *Commonwealth Trading Bank of Australia; Model Investments Pty Ltd* [1973] 2 N.S.W.L.R. 644; *McClintock* v. *Union Bank of Australia Ltd* (1920) 20 S.R.(N.S.W.) 494; *Grantham Homes Pty Ltd* v. *Interstate Permanent Building Society Ltd* (1979) 37 F.L.R. 191 (cheques); *Haddow* v. *The Duke Company No Liability* (1892) 18 V.L.R. 155; and *Gorman* v. *H.W. Hodgetts & Co.* [1932] S.A.S.R. 394 (shares); *Canadian Imperial Bank of Commerce* v. *Federal Business Development Bank* [1985] 3 W.W.R. 318 (accounts receivable).

71 *Koster's Premier Pottery Pty Ltd* v. *The Bank of Adelaide* (1981) 28 S.A.S.R. 355.

72 See *Wilbraham* v. *Snow* (1669) 2 Wms.Saund. 47 and *Gordon* v. *Harper* (1796) 7 Term Rep. 9, 12. See also *Associated Midland Corporation Ltd* v. *Bank of New South Wales* [1983] 1 N.S.W.L.R. 533, 549. It is also suggested that 'constructive possession' is a sufficient interest to sue in conversion. For what is meant by the terms 'actual possession' and 'constructive possession', see pp. 130-1 above.

73 See *Armory* v. *Delamirie* (1722) 1 Stra. 505.

74 (1989) Aust. Torts Reports 80-295.

A plaintiff who does not have actual possession of goods can also have a sufficient title to sue in conversion if he has an immediate right to possession of those goods. In *Penfolds Wines Pty Ltd* v. *Elliott*,[75] the High Court, by a majority, decided that the plaintiff, who had parted with the actual possession of some wine bottles (on certain conditions including retention of the property in the bottles) when they were sold to purchasers of the plaintiff's wines, was nevertheless entitled to sue the defendant in conversion when he filled the empty wine bottles with wine other than the plaintiff's wines. This act was considered as entirely inconsistent with the terms of the bailment and, the lawful bailment coming to an end, the immediate right to possession revested in the plaintiff entitling him to sue the defendant in conversion. So, a plaintiff who does not have actual possession can nevertheless have a sufficient interest to sue in conversion if he has an immediate right to possession of the goods.

In two recent decisions of the Supreme Court of Victoria[76] it has been held that a drawer of a cheque who gave it to a broker to be handed over to the payee of the cheque remained the true owner of the cheque and entitled to immediate possession of it until it was delivered to the payee or to some other person with the plaintiff's authority and that the drawer of the cheque had sufficient title to sue in conversion the defendant bank which collected the proceeds of the cheque and credited it to the account of a third party who had nothing to do with the payee named on the cheque.[77]

(b) Bailment A bailee of goods, as one who usually has actual possession of the goods, has a sufficient interest to sue in conversion. In the case of a bailment which is terminable at the bailor's will, both the bailee and the bailor have a right to sue in conversion—the bailee because of his actual possession and the bailor because of his right to immediate possession.[78] If, however, the bailment is for a term, then only the bailee can sue for conversion during the period of the term and the bailor cannot,[79] unless there is an act or disposition by the bailee which is so repugnant to the bailment as to amount to an absolute disclaimer of the holding as bailee.[80] Not only can a bailor not sue in conversion before the period of the term has ended but also a bailee wrongfully dispossessed by the bailor during the term can sue him either for trespass to goods, or in conversion, or in detinue.[81] On the other hand, where goods have been placed in the hands

---

75 (1946) 74 C.L.R. 204.

76 See *Australian Guarantee Corporation Ltd* v. *Commissioners of the State Bank of Victoria* [1989] V.R. 617 and *Hunter BNZ Finance Ltd* v. *Australia and New Zealand Banking Group Ltd* [1990] V.R. 41.

77 A similar decision was arrived at in *Harrison Group Holdings Ltd* v. *Westpac Banking Corporation* (1989) 51 S.A.S.R. 36 where the cheque was obtained by fraud of the payee. The defendant collecting bank was held liable in conversion to the drawer of the cheque.

78 See *Kahler* v. *Midland Bank Ltd* [1950] A.C. 24, 56.

79 See *Gordon* v. *Harper* (1796) 7 Term Rep. 9. See also *Glen* v. *Abbott* (1880) 6 V.L.R. 483.

80 See *North Central Wagon & Finance Co. Ltd* v. *Graham* [1950] 2 K.B. 7, 15.

81 See Windeyer J. in *City Motors (1933) Pty Ltd* v. *Southern Aerial Super Service Pty Ltd* (1961) 35 A.L.J.R. 206, 212.

of a bailee for a limited purpose and he deals with them in a manner wholly inconsistent with the terms of the bailment, the immediate right to possession revests in the bailor who can then sue the bailee or third parties in conversion.[82]

It has been pointed out that where there is a bailment for a limited purpose or a bailment for a term and the bailee acts in a way which destroys the basis of the contract of bailment, the common law rule is that the bailor becomes entitled at once to bring that contract to an end and therefore the immediate right to possession in relation to the article bailed is acquired by the bailor. But what if a contract specifies that the bailor may only resume possession of the goods on the giving of notice to the bailee of the goods or on the performance of some other act by way of voluntary termination of the bailment?[83] If the provisions of the contract displace the common law rule then the revesting of the immediate right to possession would be postponed until the notice is given or until the act which is required to be done under the agreement is done. There is no authoritative decision of the courts of Australia, but the decision of the English Court of Appeal in *Union Transport Finance Ltd* v. *British Car Auctions Ltd*[84] is useful in the discussion of this question. In that case, Roskill L.J. decided that the common law rule had not been displaced by the hire-purchase agreement in question and that 'it would require very clear language to deprive the bailor of his common law rights'[85] and Bridge L.J. said that while 'in theory it would be perfectly possible to introduce into a contract of bailment a term expressly limiting the manner in which the bailee's right to possession as against the bailor could be terminated . . . it would require the clearest express terms to have that effect'.[86]

The common law rule concerning the revesting of the immediate right to possession can also be affected by statute. In *Citicorp Australia Ltd* v. *B.S. Stillwell Ford Pty Ltd*[87] it was argued that the provisions of the Consumer Transaction Act 1972–73 (SA) operated to prevent the revesting of the right to immediate possession in the bailor. But the Supreme Court of South Australia (*in banco*) decided that the provisions of the Act, which required the mortgagee of goods to give seven days' notice in writing to the mortgagor prior to repossession of the goods, were 'designed to protect a consumer mortgagor in default from the harsh consequences of an unfettered power of repossession [and not] to deprive the mortgagee of his title to sue for conversion of the goods, or indeed, of his right to retake

82 See *Milk Bottles Recovery Ltd* v. *Camillo* [1948] V.L.R. 344, 346; *Penfolds Wines Pty Ltd* v. *Elliott* (1946) 74 C.L.R. 204 and *Plasycoed Collieries Co. Pty Ltd* v. *Partridge, Jones & Co. Ltd* [1912] 2 K.B. 345, 351. See also *Rick Cobby Haulage Pty Ltd* v. *Simsmetal Pty Ltd* (1986) Aust. Torts Reports 80-026 which involved the conversion of goods entrusted to a bailee by a sub-contractor employed by the bailee.

83 This question is discussed in some detail in W.L. Morison et al., *Torts Commentary and Materials* (7th edn, Sydney, 1989) pp. 118 ff.

84 [1978] 2 All E.R. 385.

85 ibid., 390.

86 ibid., 391.

87 (1979) 21 S.A.S.R. 142.

possession without delay, where the mortgagor has fraudulently disposed of them'.[88] It seems, therefore, that statutory provisions will not affect the common law rule concerning the revesting of the immediate right to possession in the bailor unless the statute does so in the clearest express terms.

(c) **Lien** A lien is a right of a creditor to retain goods until the debt is paid. A person who has a lien over goods therefore has a limited interest in the goods. Nevertheless, it has been held that he has a sufficient interest to sue in conversion in respect of his interest in the goods. In *Standard Electronics Apparatus Laboratories Pty Ltd* v. *Stenner*[89] the plaintiff, who had assembled certain 'medical units' under an arrangement with the defendant, and who had not received remuneration for his work, was held, as lienor, to have a sufficient interest to sue the defendant in conversion when the defendant removed the 'medical units' from the plaintiff's premises. This was despite the fact that the defendant, under the arrangement with the plaintiff, remained at all times the owner of the 'medical units'. So a person who has a lien over goods can not only sue third parties but also he can even sue the owner of those goods for a conversion of those goods. On the other hand, if the lienor, for example, sells the goods, he (and possibly third parties) will be liable in conversion to the owner of the goods because, as *Mulliner* v. *Florence*[90] illustrates, the doing of an act repugnant to the bailment destroys the lien and revests the immediate right to possession of the goods in the bailor (owner).

(d) **Mortgage** There is some authority to suggest that a mortgagor may bring an action in conversion either against a third party or against the mortgagee himself if he became a wrongdoer by entering and taking the goods without having given the proper notice.[91] But a mortgagee who has never had possession of the mortgaged goods does not appear to have such title as is required to support an action for conversion.[92]

(e) **Sale** In the case of a sale of goods the question of whether the buyer has a sufficient interest to sue in conversion will depend very much on the terms of the sale concerning the passing of the property in the goods and how those terms are construed by the courts. In *Healing (Sales) Pty Ltd* v. *Inglis Electrix Pty Ltd*[93] the defendant was held liable in trespass to goods and conversion when the defendant seized certain goods which the defendant had sold to the plaintiff. The goods had been sold to the plaintiff on terms that the property in the goods should pass to the plaintiff upon delivery and that payment should be made within sixty days thereafter. The sixty-day period had not expired at the time of the

88 ibid., 146-7.
89 [1960] N.S.W.R. 447.
90 (1878) 3 Q.B.D. 484.
91 See *Brierly* v. *Kendall* (1852) 17 Q.B. 937 and *Standard Electronic Apparatus Laboratories Pty Ltd* v. *Stenner* [1960] N.S.W.R. 447, 450.
92 See *White* v. *Elder, Smith and Company Ltd* [1934] S.A.S.R. 56, 61.
93 (1968) 121 C.L.R. 584.

seizure of the goods. The plaintiff succeeded in the action for conversion, even though the purchase price was still owed by the plaintiff to the defendant, mainly because the property in the seized goods had, under the terms of the agreement, passed to the plaintiff at the time of the delivery of the goods.

In *Healing (Sales)*, the defendant (seller) had delivered the goods to the plaintiff (buyer) and so the plaintiff had actual possession of the goods at the time of the conversion. But can the buyer have a sufficient interest to sue in conversion if there has been no delivery of the goods to the buyer by the seller? In *Chinery* v. *Viall*,[94] the judge directed the jury that the property in the goods (sheep) had passed to the plaintiff (buyer) even without delivery and that the buyer had therefore an immediate right to possession of the goods. He was therefore able to maintain an action for conversion against the seller, who had sold the sheep again to a third party.

(f) Contract 'It is clear law that a contractual right to have goods handed to him by another person is not in itself sufficient to clothe the person who has the right with power to sue in conversion.' The clear law that Sir David Cairns was referring to was the decision of the English Court of Appeal in *Jarvis* v. *Williams*.[95] The matter, however, is less clear since the recent decision of the English Court of Appeal in *International Factors Ltd* v. *Rodriguez*,[96] where Buckley L.J. even went so far as to say that the plaintiffs' contractual right to demand immediate delivery of a cheque to them under an agreement gave them 'a sufficient right to possession to give them a status to sue in conversion'[97] in relation to a wrongful disposal of the cheque in question. So whether a plaintiff under a contract has a sufficient interest to sue in conversion will depend upon the terms of the contract and whether the plaintiff has a contractual right to demand immediate delivery of the goods under the contract.

(g) Statute Sometimes a statute might divest goods from A and absolutely vest those goods in B; B would then have ownership of the goods and an immediate right to possession of those goods sufficient to sustain an action in conversion. This is what happened in *Egg Marketing Board (N.S.W.)* v. *Graham*,[98] where the Marketing of Primary Products Act 1927–56 (N.S.W.) divested producers of eggs of the property in those eggs and vested the property in the eggs in the Egg Marketing Board, which was able to bring an action in conversion against a producer of eggs who sold the eggs to a third party.

(h) Estoppel Sometimes a person who would otherwise have a good title to goods is estopped from asserting his title. This situation is brought

---

94 (1860) 5 H. & N. 288.
95 [1955] 1 W.L.R. 71.
96 [1979] 1 Q.B. 351.
97 ibid., 360.
98 (1961) S.R. (N.S.W.) 952.

about not only by decisions of the courts[99] but also by statutory provisions.[100] The decision of the House of Lords in *Moorgate Mercantile Co. Ltd* v. *Twitchings*,[101] however, suggests that a person will not be estopped from asserting his title if all that he has done can be described as 'mere inaction or silence'. What is required to validate a claim of estoppel is positive conduct or a statement by the person who is to be estopped from asserting his title which conduct or statement creates 'a situation of ostensible ownership' in another.[102]

(i) Co-owners The common law rule appears to be that a co-owner has no right to sue in conversion (or trespass) if the other co-owner uses the goods, takes the goods or keeps the goods, but he would have a right to sue in conversion if the other co-owner destroys the goods or sells the goods in market overt.[103] The rule has been criticized[104] but it has been applied in Australia in *Parr* v. *Ash*,[105] where it was held that no action would lie in trespass or conversion when one co-owner seized and took possession of an unfinished ship, there being no evidence that the goods had been destroyed or that the goods had been sold in market overt.[106] However, in *Kitano* v. *The Commonwealth* Mason J. held that 'conversion may be brought at the instance of a co-owner of a ship'.[107] The plaintiff did not, however, succeed in conversion in that case.

What if one co-owner, without the consent of the other co-owner, sells the commonly owned goods otherwise than in market overt? Would such a sale give a co-owner a right to sue in conversion the co-owner who sells the goods? In *Coleman* v. *Harvey* the Court of Appeal of New Zealand held that 'the limitation on the right of a co-owner to bring an action for conversion upon the sale of commonly owned goods by another co-owner save where the right of property is lost ought no longer to be sustained [as] it rests upon an historical basis not now consonant with the requirements of society or of justice'[108]. There is no reason to suppose that courts in Australia will take a different view.

---

99 See the discussion by Devlin J. in *Eastern Distributors Ltd* v. *Goldring (Murphy, Third Party)* [1957] 2 Q.B. 600.

100 See e.g. s.27, Goods Act 1958 (Vic.). Similar provisions derived from s.21, Sale of Goods Act 1893 (Imp.) are found in every State and Territory of Australia.

101 [1977] A.C. 890.

102 See *Eastern Distributors Ltd* v. *Goldring* [1957] 2 Q.B. 600; *Motor Credits (Hire Finance) Ltd* v. *Pacific Motor Auctions Pty Ltd* (1963) 109 C.L.R. 87, 98-9; and *Saltoon* v. *Lake and Others* [1978] 1 N.S.W.L.R. 52, 59.

103 *Fennings* v. *Lord Grenville* (1808) 1 Taunt 241. See also *Parr* v. *Ash* (1876) 14 S.C.R.(N.S.W.) 352, 357.

104 See D.P. Derham (1952) 68 L.Q.R. 507.

105 (1876) 14 S.C.R.(N.S.W.) 352.

106 In some of the Australian States provisions in statutes have the effect of divesting title in goods if the sale is in market overt. The provisions usually state that 'where goods are sold in market overt according to the usage of the market, the buyer acquires a good title to the goods, provided he buys them in good faith and without notice of any defect or want of title on the part of the seller'. See, generally, K.C.T. Sutton, *Sales and Consumer Law in Australia and New Zealand* (3rd edn, Sydney, 1983) pp. 355-9.

107 (1973) 129 C.L.R. 151, 172.

108 [1989] 1 N.Z.L.R. 723, 731.

(j) **Finders** The question whether the finder of goods has a sufficient interest to sue in conversion is a complicated one. It depends upon whether the finder of goods acquires a better title than the occupier of land upon which the goods are found. This in turn depends upon various circumstances, such as who the defendant is, where the goods were found, whether the goods were attached to realty (land or buildings) when they were found, whether the finder found the goods in the course of his employment or agency, etc.

The following comments are intended to state the general principles of law which it is felt the courts would apply when, in a particular case, they are asked to consider whether the finder of goods has acquired a sufficient interest in the goods to sustain an action in conversion:

(i) The finder of goods will never acquire a better title than the true owner of the goods or one who claims through the true owner.[109]

(ii) The finder of goods acquires no interest in the goods unless the goods have been actually abandoned or lost.[110]

(iii) The finder of goods is less likely to acquire an interest in the goods if he takes control of the goods with dishonest intent or if he finds the goods as a result of being a trespasser on land or premises.[111]

(iv) The finder of goods which at the time of finding are beneath the surface of the soil,[112] embedded in the soil,[113] attached to land or buildings[114] or completely buried in the land,[115] will not acquire an interest in the goods sufficient to sustain an action in conversion but the interest will instead be acquired by the occupier of the land or the premises on which the goods are found.[116]

(v) The finder of goods which are lying on the floor of part of a shop to which the public normally have access,[117] lying on the floor of a departure lounge at an airport,[118] lying loosely on top of a window-frame[119] or lying loose on the surface of land forming part of the public exit of a drive-in theatre[120] will acquire an interest in the goods sufficient to sustain an action in conversion in preference to the occupier of the shop, lounge, house or drive-in.

(vi) The finder of goods will not acquire a sufficient interest in the goods to sustain an action in conversion if the finder as an employee

---

109 See *Moffat* v. *Kazana* [1969] 2 Q.B. 152.
110 See *In re Cohen, decd., National Provincial Bank Ltd* v. *Katz* [1953] Ch. 88, 92.
111 *Hibbert* v. *McKiernan* [1948] 2 K.B. 142.
112 *Elwes* v. *Brigg Gas Co.* (1886) 33 Ch.D. 562.
113 *South Staffordshire Water Co.* v. *Sharman* [1896] 2 Q.B. 44.
114 *City of London Corporation* v. *Appleyard* [1963] 1 W.L.R. 982.
115 *Ranger* v. *Giffin* (1968) 87 W.N.(N.S.W.) 531.
116 See, however, *Tamworth Industries Ltd* v. *Attorney-General* [1988] 1 N.Z.L.R. 296 where the Court of Appeal of New Zealand expressed the view that it was arguable that an occupier of property on whose property the proceeds of drug transactions were found might in certain circumstances not acquire a sufficient title to the goods to sue in conversion.
117 *Bridges* v. *Hawkesworth* (1851) 21 L.J.Q.B. 75.
118 *Parker* v. *British Airways Board* [1982] 2 W.L.R. 503.
119 *Hannah* v. *Peel* [1945] 1 K.B. 509.
120 *Byrne* v. *Hoare* [1965] Qd.R. 135.

or agent acquires custody of the goods by reason of his employment.[121] Instead his employer or principal will acquire the interest. But a finder will acquire a sufficient interest in the goods if the employment merely provides the occasion of the finding but was not the effective cause.[122]

3. The Kind of Intentional Conduct Sufficient to Constitute Conversion

It is a requirement of the tort of conversion that there be *intentional* conduct on the part of the defendant, which conduct, if it is regarded as a 'dealing' with goods in a manner repugnant to the plaintiff's actual or immediate right to possession, would make him liable to an action in conversion. Although it might appear from some decisions on conversion, such as the auction cases,[123] that a *voluntary* dealing with goods is, without more, sufficient to constitute conversion,[124] this is not the case in another set of decisions involving involuntary bailees,[125] which appear to require something more than a mere voluntary dealing with the goods. This additional requirement is described in this chapter as intentional conduct or an intentional dealing with the goods in a manner repugnant to the plaintiff's actual or immediate right to possession of the goods. This intentional conduct could be by way of an actual denial of the plaintiff's actual or immediate right to possession or by way of an assertion of an inconsistent right.[126] What kind of intentional conduct is sufficient to constitute the tort of conversion? The courts appear to have given a wide meaning to the words 'intentional conduct'. Not only is a deliberate and wilful 'dealing' with goods in a manner inconsistent with the right of the true owner regarded as intentional conduct amounting to conversion, but a reckless 'dealing' or a 'dealing' with goods which is substantially certain to result, or which in all probability would result, in the owner's being deprived of his goods, will also be regarded as intentional conduct sufficient to constitute conversion. Thus in *Moorgate Mercantile Co. Ltd* v. *Finch and Read*[127] the second defendant, who borrowed a car from the first defendant (who had hired it from the plaintiff under a hire-purchase agreement) and used it to smuggle watches, was held liable in conversion when the customs authorities seized, forfeited and sold the car under the provisions of the Customs and Excise Act on discovering that it was used for the purposes of smuggling. It was argued by the second defendant that 'he did not intend, as a matter of conscious volition, to set up a title in the Customs authorities' but Danckwerts L.J.

121 *Willey* v. *Synan* (1937) 57 C.L.R. 200; *South Staffordshire Water Co.* v. *Sharman* [1896] 2 Q.B. 44; and *Grafstein* v. *Holme and Freeman* (1958) 12 D.L.R. (2d) 727.
122 *Byrne* v. *Hoare* [1965] Qd.R. 135, 149.
123 See *Barker* v. *Furlong* [1891] 2 Ch. 172 and *Consolidated Co.* v. *Curtis & Son* [1892] 1 Q.B. 495.
124 See also P. Cane, *Tort Law and Economic Interests* (Oxford, 1991) Ch. 2 esp. 30-1.
125 See *Elvin and Powell Ltd* v. *Plummer Roddis Ltd* (1933) 50 T.L.R. 158.
126 See *Cuff* v. *Broadlands Finance Ltd* [1987] 2 N.Z.L.R. 343, 346.
127 [1962] 1 Q.B. 701.

rejected this argument on the ground that 'whether the second defendant intended that consequence to follow or not . . . he must be taken to intend the consequences which were likely to happen from the conduct of which he was guilty, and which did in fact result in the loss of the car to the plaintiffs'.[128] Danckwerts L.J. had no doubt whatever that this was *intentional* conduct sufficient for conversion.

A negligent dealing with a chattel resulting in its loss does not constitute conversion and this is one explanation of the decision in *Ashby* v. *Tolhurst*,[129] where the negligence of the attendant of a private parking ground in allowing a stranger to take the plaintiff's car from the car park was not regarded as a conversion by misdelivery as there was no intentional conduct on the part of the attendant. On the other hand, it is clear law that an auctioneer who sells goods at an auction and thereafter delivers them to the purchaser will be liable in conversion to the true owner if the vendor has no title. The purchaser will also be liable in conversion to the true owner and it will not matter that the auctioneer is an 'innocent handler' and the purchaser an 'innocent acquirer' of the goods. They are both regarded as engaging in intentional conduct sufficient to constitute conversion.[130] Similarly, a bank which presents a cheque for payment and collects the proceeds of a cheque for a customer who is not the true owner or entitled to immediate possession of the cheque will be liable in conversion to the true owner or the person entitled to immediate possession of the cheque. The bank will be held to have intentionally, albeit innocently, converted the cheque.[131]

The intentional conduct must also be a positive act of misconduct to constitute conversion.[132] So if a bailee, such as a carrier, loses the goods entrusted to him this is not a conversion, but if he delivers the goods to the wrong person it is. In the latter case, by delivering the goods to someone else the bailee has done a positive act of misconduct which, by depriving the owner of the goods of his dominion over them, amounts to an interference with his ownership sufficient to constitute conversion. However, in the case of involuntary bailees, even delivery to the wrong person will not be regarded as an act of *intentional* conduct amounting to conversion, because, as Hawke J. said in *Elvin and Powell Ltd* v. *Plummer Roddis Ltd*, 'if persons were involuntary bailees and had done everything reasonable they were not liable to pay damages (in conversion) if something which they did resulted in the loss of the property'.[133] In that case,

128 ibid., 706.

129 [1937] 2 K.B. 242.

130 See *R.H. Willis & Son* v. *British Car Auctions Ltd* [1978] 1 W.L.R. 438, 442. See also *Barker* v. *Furlong* [1891] 2 Ch. 172, 181 and *Consolidated Co.* v. *Curtis & Son* [1892] 1 Q.B. 495.

131 See *National Commercial Banking Corporation of Australia* v. *Batty* (1986) Aust. Torts Reports 80-013; *Australian Guarantee Corporation Ltd* v. *Commissioners of the State Bank of Victoria* [1989] V.R. 617; *Hunter BNZ Finance Ltd* v. *Australia and New Zealand Banking Group Ltd* [1990] V.R. 41; *Harrison Group Holdings* v. *Westpac Bank Corporation* (1989) 51 S.A.S.R. 36 and *Associated Midland Corporation Ltd* v. *Bank of New South Wales* [1983] 1 N.S.W.L.R. 533.

132 See *Joule Ltd* v. *Poole* (1924) 24 S.R.(N.S.W.) 387, 390.

133 (1933) 50 T.L.R. 158, 159.

the fact that the defendants had *voluntarily* handed over the goods to a rogue (albeit as a result of a trick) was not sufficient to make the act one of conversion, as there was no *intentional* dealing with the goods in a manner repugnant to the plaintiff's actual or immediate right to possession.

It should also be noted that the tort of conversion 'does not involve any element of dishonesty in the tortfeasor'. In *Rendell* v. *Associated Finance Pty Ltd*[134] the defendant repossessed a truck under a claim of right for the person whom he believed to be the true owner but, unknown to the defendant, the truck had an engine installed in it which belonged to the plaintiff. The Full Court of the Supreme Court of Victoria decided that the defendant was liable for the conversion of the engine. The court said that it did not matter that the defendant was mistaken as to what engine was attached to the truck or that he wrongly believed the finance company, on whose behalf he was acting, to be the owner of that engine. As he intended to repossess the truck, it could be inferred that he intended to repossess the whole vehicle including the engine and there was therefore intentional conduct in relation to the engine sufficient to constitute a conversion. This case suggests that reckless 'dealing' with goods could well be regarded as intentional conduct. It also illustrates the very broad meaning given by the courts to *intentional* conduct in the tort of conversion.

4. Dealings with Goods that Amount to Conversion

In *Penfolds Wines Pty Ltd* v. *Elliott,* Dixon J. said that 'the essence of conversion is a *dealing* with a chattel in a manner repugnant to the [actual possession or the] immediate right of possession of the person who has the property or special property in the chattel'.[135] He then went on to give several examples of interferences with chattels which would amount to a 'dealing' sufficient to constitute conversion: 'it may take the form of a disposal of the goods by way of sale, or pledge or other intended transfer of an interest followed by delivery, of the destruction or change of the nature or character of the thing, as for example, pouring water into wine or cutting the seals from a deed, or of an appropriation evidenced by refusal to deliver or other denial, of title'. He also gave several examples of interferences which would not amount to conversion: 'damage to the chattel is not conversion, nor is use, nor is a transfer of possession otherwise than for the purpose of affecting the immediate right to possession, nor is it always conversion to lose the goods beyond hope of recovery'.

We now consider the kinds of interferences with chattels which the courts have held to be 'dealings' in chattels sufficient to amount to conversion. It should be noted that these interferences can be actionable in the tort of conversion even when they are only 'indirectly' occasioned by

134 [1957] V.R. 604.
135 (1946) 74 C.L.R. 204, 229.

an act of the defendant, unlike the tort of trespass to goods where the interferences must be 'directly' occasioned by an act of the defendant.

(a) Disposing of goods If a defendant disposes of the plaintiff's goods by sale and delivery, there is a dealing in the goods sufficient to constitute conversion.[136] Collins J. put it very clearly in *Consolidated Company* v. *Curtis & Son*: 'a sale and delivery with intent to pass the property in chattels by a person who is not the true owner and has not got his authority is a conversion'.[137] It does not matter that the purported disposition does not operate to transfer the title in the goods: the sale, accompanied by delivery, is sufficient to make both the seller and the buyer liable in an action for conversion. Nor does it matter that neither the seller nor the buyer knew that the person offering the goods for disposal was not entitled to dispose of the goods. A 'mere bargain of sale' without delivery is not conversion.[138] In this context, the word 'delivery' covers not only the situation where the seller gives the buyer 'possession of a chattel with his own hands' but also the case where the seller points out the chattel and tells the buyer that he can take it away.[139] If a sale and delivery takes place in market overt, the buyer acquires a good title to the goods if 'he buys them in good faith and without notice of any defect or want of title on the part of the seller'[140] and the buyer will therefore not be liable in an action for conversion in such situations, even though the seller continues to be liable in conversion to the person who had the title to the goods at the time of the conversion.

If a seller uses an agent such as a broker[141] or an auctioneer[142] to effect the sale and delivery of the goods then that agent will also be liable in conversion in respect of the disposition of the goods that he has effected. In *National Mercantile Bank* v. *Rymill*[143] and *Turner* v. *Hockey*,[144] the auctioneers were held not liable in conversion because, it was said, the sales were effected by the parties themselves and the auctioneers had merely delivered the goods to the buyers. In the relatively recent decision in *R.H. Willis & Son* v. *British Car Auctions Ltd*,[145] Lord Denning M.R. said that he doubted the correctness of those decisions because he felt that although the auctioneers in each of those cases 'had not actually effected

136 See *Foster* v. *Franklin* [1924] V.L.R. 269, 273.

137 [1892] 1 Q.B. 495, 498.

138 See *Douglas Valley Finance Co. Ltd* v. *S. Hughes (Hirers) Ltd* [1969] 1 Q.B. 738, 751 and *Consolidated Company* v. *Curtis & Son* [1892] 1 Q.B. 495, 498. See also *Australian Provincial Assurance Co. Ltd* v. *Coroneo* (1938) 38 S.R.(N.S.W.) 700, 717.

139 See *Foster* v. *Franklin* [1924] V.L.R. 269, 273.

140 See s.27(1) Sale of Goods Act 1896 (Tas.); s.22 Sale of Goods Act 1895-1952 (S.A.) and s.22 Sale of Goods Act 1895 (W.A.). For a discussion of what is a sale in market overt, see K.C.T. Sutton, *Sales and Consumer Law in Australia and New Zealand* (3rd edn, Sydney, 1983) pp. 355-9.

141 See *Hollins* v. *Fowler* (1875) L.R. 7 H.L. 757.

142 See *Barker* v. *Furlong* [1891] 2 Ch. 172, 181 and *Consolidated Company* v. *Curtis & Son* [1892] 1 Q.B. 495.

143 (1881) 44 L.T.N.S. 767.

144 (1887) 56 L.J.Q.B. 301.

145 [1978] 1 W.L.R. 438.

the sale, his intervention in each case was an efficient cause of the sale and he got his commission for what he did'.[146] If this interesting doctrine receives acceptance in Australia then agents such as auctioneers, brokers etc. will not only be liable when they actually effect the sale and delivery of the goods, but they will also be liable in conversion if their intervention is an effective cause of the sale.

Apart from sale and delivery, other dispositions of goods can also amount to a dealing sufficient to constitute conversion. In *Parker et al.* v. *Godin*[147] a pledger of goods which did not belong to him was held liable in conversion notwithstanding that he delivered the money received as a result of the pledge to the wife of the bankrupt who owned the goods.[148] In *Singer Manufacturing Co.* v. *Clark*[149] the pledgee of goods was held liable in conversion when on coming into possession of the goods by a wrongful act of the pledger he refused to return the goods to the plaintiff, who was the true owner of the goods, but instead returned the goods to the pledger. This act was regarded as a denial of the plaintiff's title to the goods sufficient to constitute conversion. But in *Spackman* v. *Foster*[150] Grove J. suggested that a pledgee of certain title deeds who received the deeds with no knowledge that the person who pledged them had no title to them would not have been liable in conversion if he had handed the title deeds to the true owner on demand. If this decision is correct, the pledgee as an 'innocent handler' of goods is treated differently from, and more favourably than, the auctioneer or the buyer or seller of goods who is also an innocent handler of goods. There appears to be no rational basis for this distinction.

(b) Taking possession of goods To take goods without lawful justification out of the possession of anyone with the intention of exercising dominion over them is a dealing with goods sufficient to constitute conversion and it does not matter whether the goods were taken for the use of the defendant or a third person. As Alderson B. pointed out in *Fouldes* v. *Willoughby*, the person entitled to possession of the goods 'is entitled to the use of it at all times and in all places. When, therefore, a man takes that chattel, either for the use of himself or of another, it is a conversion'.[151] This statement of the law was accepted by the House of Lords in *Hollins* v. *Fowler*[152] and, more recently, by the Full Court of the Supreme Court of Victoria in *Rendell* v. *Associated Finance Pty Ltd.*[153] The mere taking or asportation of goods, however, without any intention of exercising dominion over them, is not a conversion though it may be a trespass to

146 ibid., 443.
147 (1728) 2 Stra. 813.
148 See also *McCombie* v. *Davies* (1805) 7 East 5.
149 (1879) 5 Ex. D. 37.
150 (1883) 11 Q.B.D. 99.
151 (1841) 8 M. & W. 540, 548-9. See also *Cuff* v. *Broadlands Finance Ltd* [1987] 2 N.Z.L.R. 343.
152 (1875) L.R. 7 H.L. 757.
153 [1957] V.R. 604.

goods.[154] So in *Fouldes* v. *Willoughby*[155] where the defendant took horses belonging to the plaintiff and put them ashore in the hope that the plaintiff, who was misconducting himself, would leave the boat to be with the horses, the defendant's taking of the horses was held not to be a dealing with the goods of the plaintiff sufficient to constitute conversion.

A taking of goods even for a very short period will be regarded as a conversion if the defendant has taken the goods as his own or used the goods as his own. Thus in *Aitken Agencies Ltd* v. *Richardson*,[156] when the defendant wrongfully and intentionally took the plaintiff's motor vehicle and used it for his own purposes to have a 'joy-ride', McGregor J. of the Supreme Court of New Zealand held that the taking of the goods out of the possession of the plaintiff was 'clearly a positive wrongful act in dealing with the goods in a manner inconsistent with the owner's rights and an intentional assertion of a right inconsistent with the rights of the owner'[157] and that the plaintiff's claim was rightly brought as an action for conversion. In *Schemmel* v. *Pomeroy*, however, White J. of the Supreme Court of South Australia expressed the view that not every joy-rider who takes a car without authority is guilty of conversion. It would, he said 'only be trespass in the absence of serious damage. The position will be different and the tort of conversion will probably be committed where the joyrider takes the owner's car in complete disregard for the owner's right to possession and for the chances of recovery of possession or recovery of the car in one piece'.[158]

In *Model Dairy Pty Ltd* v. *White* Gavan Duffy J. in the Supreme Court of Victoria expressed the view that 'a slight deprivation of possession is not in itself sufficient for conversion'[159] and *Fleming* suggests that to constitute conversion the taking must have '*resulted in a major interference* with the owner's rights so serious as to warrant a forced sale'.[160] These views would be much more acceptable if the defendant, on being held liable in conversion, was forced to purchase the goods and required to pay the full value of the goods as damages. But, if the defendant has the option to return the goods and the owner must give credit for the value of the goods at the time when he receives them back,[161] then there is no reason why a taking of goods which results in something less than a major interference with the owner's rights should not be regarded as a

154 'A mere taking or asportation of a chattel may be a trespass without the infliction of material damage' (*Penfolds Wines Pty Ltd* v. *Elliott* (1946) C.L.R. 204, 214-15 *per* Dixon J.).

155 (1841) 8 M. & W. 540.

156 [1967] N.Z.L.R. 65.

157 ibid., 66.

158 (1989) 50 S.A.S.R. 450, 452.

159 (1935) 41 Arg.L.R. 432, 433.

160 *Fleming* (7th edn, 1987) p. 52. This view has also been expressed by W.L. Prosser (1957) 42 *Cornell L.Q.* 168 who would limit conversion to important and serious interferences with chattels.

161 See *Aitken Agencies Ltd* v. *Richardson* [1967] N.Z.L.R. 65, 67 and *Solloway* v. *McLaughlin* [1938] A.C. 247, 257-8.

conversion. It is interesting to note that in *Lord Petre* v. *Heneage*[162] Holt C.J. held that the taking and wearing of a pearl necklace belonging to the estate of the late Lord Petre by the executor's wife was a conversion.

(c) Abusing possession of goods There are many situations where a person can be liable in conversion because he has abused the possession of goods, even though that possession may have been rightfully acquired. This type of dealing with goods finds its clearest expression in the words of the Supreme Court of New South Wales in *McKenna & Armistead Pty Ltd* v. *Excavations Pty Ltd*:

> it is clear that a bailor is entitled to sue a bailee for damage resulting from any use by the bailee of the goods or any dealing with the goods going outside or beyond the terms upon which he has become bailee. An unauthorised departure from the terms of the bailment renders the bailee liable for damage which results from it.[163]

In *Craig* v. *Marsh*[164] the defendant, who used certain articles which had been left on the premises by the plaintiff when he vacated the premises, was held liable in conversion—he had abused his possession of those articles by using the articles for his own purposes in connection with his business. There have been several cases of persons who though lawfully in possession of bottles (milk and wine) have been held liable in conversion because they used those bottles in a manner repugnant to the terms of the bailment.[165] This has been so even though in most cases no actual damage to the bottles could be shown.

The intentional destruction of the goods of another which are in one's possession is an abuse of possession and clearly a conversion. To change the nature or character of the goods, for example, by pouring water into wine or cutting the seals from a deed, is also an abuse of possession which will be regarded as a conversion.[166]

In *Moorgate Mercantile Co. Ltd* v. *Finch and Read*[167] the second defendant was held liable in conversion because he abused his possession of the plaintiff's car by using it to smuggle watches—an act which led to the forfeiture of the car by the customs authorities.

A bailee of goods who sells the goods,[168] a person who has a lien over goods who sells the goods[169] and a bailee of goods who pledges the

---

162 (1701) 12 Mod. Rep. 519.

163 [1957] 57 S.R.(N.S.W.) 515, 518.

164 (1935) 35 S.R.(N.S.W.) 323.

165 See *Penfolds Wines Pty Ltd* v. *Elliott* (1946) 74 C.L.R. 204; *Model Dairy Pty Ltd* v. *White* (1935) 41 Arg.L.R. 432; and *Milk Bottles Recovery Ltd* v. *Camillo* [1948] V.L.R. 344.

166 The examples are given by Dixon J. in *Penfolds Wines Pty Ltd* v. *Elliott* (1946) 74 C.L.R. 204, 229.

167 [1962] 1 Q.B. 701.

168 See *Glass* v. *Hollander* (1935) 35 S.R.(N.S.W.) 304.

169 *Mulliner* v. *Florence* (1878) 3 Q.B.D. 484 and *Bolwell Fibreglass Pty Ltd* v. *Foley* [1984] V.R. 97, 117 *per* Brooking J.: 'It is clear that an artificer's lien gives no power of sale at common law'.

goods[170] will all be regarded as having abused their possession of the goods and therefore liable to an action in conversion.

Although common carriers are not liable in conversion for the loss of goods consigned to them for carriage, they will be liable in conversion if they abuse their possession by some act of misfeasance, for example, by delivering those goods to a wrong person or by refusing to hand over the goods at a time when it is shown they had them in their possession.[171] They may even be liable in conversion if they deviate unnecessarily from the usual course and this results in the loss of the goods.[172]

Where goods have been deposited with a warehouseman, he is not liable in conversion if he merely keeps the goods for the person who deposited them; nor will he be liable in conversion if he restores them to that person even though it turns out that that person had no authority from the true owner to deposit the goods with the warehouseman.[173] But if the warehouseman contracts to warehouse the goods of the plaintiff at a particular place and without authority from the plaintiff he warehouses them at another place he may be liable in conversion if the goods are lost or destroyed even without negligence on his part. As Grove J. said in *Lilley* v. *Doubleday*: 'if a bailee elects to deal with the property entrusted to him in a way not authorised by the bailor, he takes upon himself the risks of so doing, except when the risk is independent of his acts and inherent in the property itself'.[174]

(d) **Transferring of possession** Another kind of dealing with goods which is sufficient to constitute conversion is where the defendant by some act transfers or assists in transferring the right or title to possession of the goods from the plaintiff to a third person.

A recent example of such a dealing is provided by *Wilson* v. *New Brighton Panelbeaters Ltd.*[175] Walters, a rogue, claimed to have bought a vehicle from the plaintiff and asked the defendants to collect the vehicle from the plaintiff's home and to tow it to an address in Christchurch. An employee of the defendants collected the vehicle from the carport of the plaintiff's home and delivered it to Walters, who paid $40 and then disappeared together with the vehicle. Tipping J. of the Supreme Court of New Zealand held that the defendants had 'undoubtedly committed conversion by handing the car to Walters in return for the towing fee of $40, thereby transferring possession to Walters and in the event rendering it impossible to return the car to the [plaintiff]'.[176]

In *Hiort* v. *Bott*[177] the plaintiffs by mistake sent goods to the defendant with an invoice and delivery order. G, a rogue, induced the defendant to indorse the delivery order to him on the pretext that that was the least

170 *Parker* v. *Godin* (1728) 2 Stra. 813.
171 See *Joule Ltd* v. *Poole* (1924) 24 S.R.(N.S.W.) 387, 395.
172 See *Davis* v. *Garrett* (1830) 6 Bing. 716.
173 See *Hollins* v. *Fowler* (1875) L.R. 7 H.L. 757, 767 *per* Blackburn J.
174 (1881) 7 Q.B.D. 510, 511.
175 [1989] 1 N.Z.L.R. 74.
176 ibid., 80.
177 (1874) L.R. 9 Exch. 86.

expensive way to get the goods back to the plaintiff. But when the defendant indorsed the delivery order, G took it to the station, collected the goods from the railway company and absconded with the goods. The defendant was held liable in conversion because he had transferred title to possession of the goods so as to cause them to be lost to the true owner.

It is interesting to compare *Hiort* v. *Bott* with the comparatively recent decision of the High Court of Australia in *Kitano* v. *The Commonwealth*.[178] The plaintiff and three companions sailed from Japan to Darwin in a yacht of which they were all co-owners. On arrival in Australia they had a dispute. The plaintiff and M (one of his co-owners) independently applied for a certificate of clearance under the Customs Act 1906–68 (Cwth) so as to enable the yacht to leave Darwin. M was given a certificate of clearance and he sailed the yacht away without the plaintiff. The plaintiff brought an action in conversion against the Commonwealth for the acts of the customs authorities but Mason J. in the High Court (in its original jurisdiction) held that the issue of the certificate of clearance did not amount to a transfer of title to possession and that 'the deprivation sustained by the plaintiff was his exclusion from possession which was effected, not by the issue of the certificate, but by the action of his companion in sailing the boat away'.[179] The fact that the certificate of clearance facilitated the companion in excluding the plaintiff from possession of his yacht was not considered relevant. On appeal, all the judges of the High Court expressed their agreement with Mason J.'s judgment.[180]

It would seem, therefore, that in Australia, at least, an act which it is alleged transfers possession must be an act which in actual fact excludes the plaintiff from possession of his goods if it is to be regarded as a dealing in goods sufficient to constitute conversion, and that an act will not be regarded as transferring possession and therefore will not be regarded as an act of conversion if it merely facilitates a third party in excluding the plaintiff from possession of his goods.

(e) Withholding of possession In the absence of any lawfully asserted right, an intention to withhold or detain goods in defiance of the person who is entitled to possession of them is a conversion of those goods—a conversion by detention.[181] But not every withholding of goods from the person entitled to possession of the goods is a conversion. A brief withholding of goods made merely in order that the defendant may verify the plaintiff's title to the goods or to confirm that delivery to the plaintiff would be proper is not a dealing in goods which amounts to conversion.[182] On the other hand, an unqualified refusal to return goods which belong

---

178 (1973) 129 C.L.R. 151.
179 ibid., 173.
180 (1973) 129 C.L.R. 176.
181 See *Upton* v. *TVW Enterprises Ltd* (1985) A.T.P.R. 40-611.
182 See *Craig* v. *Marsh* (1935) 35 S.R.(N.S.W.) 323, 326. Though 'a long delay made under the guise of seeking legal advice could, in some circumstances, amount to a denial of a claimant's rights.' *Crowther* v. *Australian Guarantee Corp. Ltd.* (1985) Aust. Torts Reports 80-709 at 69, 103 per Bollen J.

to the plaintiff is almost always conclusive evidence of a conversion.[183] If a qualification is annexed to the refusal, for example, if the defendant says that he will need an order from his employer before he returns the goods, then the refusal to return the goods will not be a conversion if the courts take the view that the qualification is a reasonable one.[184] In *Howard E. Perry & Co. Ltd* v. *British Railways Board*,[185] however, where the defendants withheld delivery of the plaintiffs' steel to the plaintiffs because they feared that delivery of the goods would result in industrial action by the defendants' employees, Sir Robert Megarry V.-C. held that the defendants, by withholding delivery of the plaintiffs' goods until their fears of industrial action had been removed, had committed an act of conversion. As he said: 'There is a detention of the steel which is consciously adverse to the plaintiffs' rights and this seems to me to be the essence of at least one form of conversion'.[186] The genuine and reasonable fear for the refusal to release the goods did not prevent the withholding of the goods from being regarded as an act of conversion. It may be that Sir Robert Megarry was influenced by the fact that the defendants did not indicate how long they would withhold the goods for.[187] It is suggested, therefore, that where there is a withholding of goods for a reasonable reason it might still be regarded as a conversion unless the period for which the goods are withheld is also a reasonable and definite period.

Where a defendant has come into possession of goods by an unauthorized act of the plaintiff's servant or agent, he commits an act of conversion if he withholds the goods and refuses to deliver them to the plaintiff after notice and a demand for the return of the goods.[188] The defendant is also liable in conversion if, having come into possession of the plaintiff's goods by a wrongful act of a third party, e.g. a wrongful sale or wrongful pledge, he refuses to return the goods to the plaintiff; he would even be liable if he delivers the goods back to the third party who sold or pledged the goods to the defendant.[189]

If goods are bailed to a person under a contract to do certain work on them, is the bailee entitled to keep the goods and continue to work on them until the work is completed or can the bailor at any time countermand the order for the doing of the work and require that the goods be delivered up to him? In *Bolwell Fibreglass Pty Ltd* v. *Foley*[190] Brooking J. of the Supreme Court of Victoria thought that the bailee was entitled to retain possession of the goods and complete the work (the subject of the agreement) even though this view seems contrary to the decision in *Lilley*

183 See *Eason* v. *Newman* (1596) Cro. Eliz. 495.
184 See *Alexander* v. *Southey* (1821) 5 Barn. & Ald. 247.
185 [1980] 1 W.L.R. 1375.
186 ibid., 1380.
187 ibid., 'The defendants are denying the plaintiffs most of the rights of ownership, including the right to possession, for a period which clearly is indefinite. It may be short, or it may be long; but it is plainly uncertain'.
188 See *McCombie* v. *Davies* (1805) 7 East 5.
189 See *Singer Manufacturing Co.* v. *Clark* (1879) 5 Ex.D. 37.
190 [1984] V.R. 97, 112.

v. *Barnsley*.[191] He also thought that a workman has a lien (an artificer's lien) on the goods and can withhold the goods not only when the work contracted to be done is actually completed but also where the work has not been finished. The artificer's lien in the latter case is for 'the fair and reasonable price of the work actually done'.[192]

It is not a conversion for an unpaid seller to withhold the goods until the purchase price is paid. This is referred to as the unpaid seller's lien. Where an unpaid seller has still to do some work on the goods he can withhold the goods until the process of manufacturing is complete. In both these situations, if the buyer does not pay the purchase price the unpaid seller can not only withhold the goods but also, on giving notice to the buyer, exercise the statutory power of sale given to an unpaid seller in the various States and Territories of Australia.[193]

(f) Denial of plaintiff's right If a defendant denies or repudiates the plaintiff's right to goods and the plaintiff is entitled to those goods then that denial or repudiation is an act of conversion if it can be regarded as an 'absolute denial of the plaintiff's right'.[194] It is not necessary that the defendant be in physical possession of the goods to deny the plaintiff's right to goods. When the plaintiff carriers wrongly delivered goods to M and the defendant's managing director on happening to see the goods claimed them as belonging to his firm and promptly sold them to M, the defendant was held liable in conversion because what it had done was a denial of the plaintiff's right to the goods even though the firm was not in physical possession of the goods at any time.[195] In *Motor Dealers Credit Corporation Ltd* v. *Overland (Sydney) Ltd*[196] the Supreme Court of New South Wales held that the defendant, who, after notice of the plaintiff's claim to a car nevertheless carried the sale of the car to completion, by authorizing delivery of the car from a third party who had possession of the car to a fourth party, was exercising dominion over the car inconsistent with the plaintiff's right. Street C.J., pointing out that 'there could hardly be a more absolute denial of the plaintiff's right', went on to say that he did not think that 'it was essential that the plaintiff should prove that the defendant company had actual possession of the car'.[197]

A mere assertion of right is not, however, a sufficient dealing to constitute a conversion when the defendant is not in actual possession of

---

191 (1844) 2 M. & Rob. 548.

192 *Bolwell Fibreglass Pty Ltd* v. *Foley* [1984] V.R. 97, 114.

193 See e.g. s.54(3), Goods Act 1958 (Vic.).

194 See *Motor Dealers Credit Corporation Ltd* v. *Overland (Sydney) Ltd* (1931) 31 S.R.(N.S.W.) 516.

195 *Van Oppen & Co. Ltd* v. *Tredegars Ltd* (1921) 37 T.L.R. 504. See *Oakley* v. *Lyster* [1931] 1 K.B. 148 where the English Court of Appeal held that there may be a conversion of goods even though the defendant has never been in physical possession of them, if his act amounts to an absolute denial and repudiation of the plaintiff's right. See also *Douglas Valley Finance Co. Ltd* v. *S. Hughes (Hirers) Ltd* [1969] 1 Q.B. 738.

196 (1931) 31 S.R.(N.S.W.) 516.

197 ibid., 519.

the goods,[198] but if the defendant *is* in actual possession of the plaintiff's goods a mere assertion of a right or claim to the goods may be sufficient to constitute conversion, particularly if it is made to the person entitled to the goods. In *Short* v. *The City Bank,* Street J. said: 'no case can be found where a man not in possession of the property has been held liable in trover, unless he has absolutely denied the plaintiff's right, although, if in possession of the property, any dealing with it inconsistent with the true owner's right would be a conversion'.[199] However, in *Perpetual Trustees & National Executors of Tasmania Ltd* v. *Perkins*[200] the Supreme Court of Tasmania decided that a mere statement by a bailee in possession that he intended to give the goods to his son was an insufficient 'dealing' with the goods to constitute conversion in the absence of delivery of the goods to the son. And in *Crowther* v. *Australian Guarantee Corp. Ltd*[201] the defendant's solicitor's expression of his client's present intention to sell the (plaintiffs') cars was not regarded by a majority of the Full Court of the Supreme Court of South Australia as an assertion of dominion over the cars or as an act in relation to the cars in a way which was inconsistent with the plaintiffs' rights. This conclusion was no doubt assisted by the court's earlier conclusion that the defendant was never in possession of the cars.

(g) Statutory provisions for uncollected and unsolicited goods There are statutory provisions in every State and Territory of Australia which allow bailees who have accepted goods for repair or other treatment to dispose of the goods without being liable to an action in conversion if upon completion of the repair or treatment the bailor fails both to pay the bailee his charges in relation to the goods and to take delivery (or arrange for redelivery) of the goods.[202]

In relation to unsolicited or unordered goods, statutory provisions both of the Commonwealth[203] and the States[204] allow a recipient of unsolicited goods to acquire the property in the goods after a specified period if the recipient has given notice to the sender or owner of the goods that he has the goods and he has not unreasonably refused to allow the sender or owner to take possession of the goods. The provisions also give the recipient immunity from any action in relation to any loss or injury to the goods before he acquires the property in the goods except for loss or damage resulting from the doing by him of a wilful and unlawful act in

---

198 See *Short* v. *The City Bank* (1912) 12 S.R.(N.S.W.) 186. See also *Short* v. *The City Bank of Sydney* (1912) 15 C.L.R. 148, 158: 'It was not really contended that an assertion of right by the Bank—apart from its actual or constructive possession—would amount to conversion. Such a position would be manifestly untenable' (*per* Isaacs J.).

199 (1912) 12 S.R.(N.S.W.) 186, 200.

200 (1989) Aust. Torts Reports 80-295.

201 (1985) Aust. Torts Reports 80-709.

202 See e.g. s.2, Disposal of Uncollected Goods Act 1961 (Vic.).

203 See s.65, Trade Practices Act 1974 (Cwth).

204 See e.g. ss. 29-30 Fair Trading Act 1985 (Vic.) and J. Goldring, *Consumer Protection Law in Australia,* 3rd ed. pp. 307-16.

relation to the goods, such as unlawful disposal, unlawful destruction or unlawful damaging of the goods.

5. The Jus Tertii and Conversion

A plaintiff in actual or constructive possession of goods can succeed in bringing an action in conversion against a defendant who interferes with that possession by dealing with the goods in a manner repugnant to his possession of those goods, even though the defendant can show that someone else is rightfully entitled to the possession of those goods. The *jus tertii* cannot be pleaded against a plaintiff who has actual possession at the time of conversion unless the defendant is defending the action on behalf of and by the authority of the person rightfully entitled to possession of the goods.[205] But if the plaintiff does not have actual or constructive possession but only the immediate right to possession of the goods at the time of the conversion, then, it would appear that the *jus tertii* can be pleaded by the converter of the goods. He will be able to avoid liability in conversion by showing that someone else is rightfully entitled to the possession of those goods.[206] This rule, that a plaintiff with only an immediate right to possession of goods can have the *jus tertii* pleaded against him, is subject to only one exception, i.e. 'a bailee is not entitled to dispute his bailor's title' and therefore the *jus tertii* cannot be pleaded by a bailee against his bailor even though the bailor only has the immediate right to possession of the goods. It is also no defence for the bailee to assert that the goods have been handed over to a third party even if it should appear that, as between the bailor and the third party, the latter had a contractual right to possession of the goods.[207] However, as Herron J. pointed out in *Edwards* v. *Amos & Others*, a bailee is not estopped from pleading the *jus tertii* if he has already on the demand of the true owner given up possession to him, or if, having retained the goods he defends the action on his behalf and by his authority.[208]

The common law rules in Australia in relation to the *jus tertii* can lead, at the present time, to a multiplicity of actions because the converter can not only be sued in conversion by the bailor in the circumstances outlined above but also he can once again be sued by a third party who might be rightfully entitled to possession of the goods. The Torts (Interference with Goods) Act 1977 in England attempts to avoid this situation by providing that, in an action for wrongful interference with goods (principally

---

205 See *Standard Electronic Apparatus Laboratories Pty Ltd* v. *Stenner* [1960] N.S.W.R. 447, 451. In the case of joint owners with actual joint possession it is possible for the defendant to plead *jus tertii* if he has authority from one of the joint owners to possess the goods with the other joint owner. See *Cuff* v. *Broadland Finance Ltd* [1987] 2 N.Z.L.R. 343, 346.

206 See *Henry Berry & Co. Pty Ltd* v. *Rushton* [1937] St.R.Qd. 109; *Leake* v. *Loveday* (1842) 4 Man. & G. 972; *Butler* v. *Hobson* (1838) 4 Bing. N.C. 290 and *Edwards* v. *Amos & Others* (1945) W.N.(N.S.W.) 204.

207 See *Elkin & Co. Pty Ltd* v. *Specialised Television Installations Pty Ltd* (1960) 77 W.N.(N.S.W.) 844, 849.

208 (1945) W.N.(N.S.W.) 204, 207.

trespass to goods and conversion), 'the defendant shall be entitled to show . . . that a third party has a better right than the plaintiff as respects all or any part of the interest claimed by the plaintiff'.[209] Rules of court which have been drawn up as a result of the Act[210] now require the plaintiff to give particulars of his title, require the plaintiff to identify any person who, to his knowledge, has or claims any interest in the goods and even allow a bailee who is sued by his bailor to have a third party with a better title than the bailor to be joined in.

IV: DETINUE

The tort of detinue, like the tort of conversion, also has an ancient origin, but its usefulness today is rather limited. In England, it has been abolished as a tort by the Torts (Interference with Goods) Act 1977. At one time, detinue was thought to be an action in contract[211] and, because one of the two ancient writs of detinue provided a proprietary remedy, i.e. a remedy which allowed the plaintiff to recover the goods themselves, it was also thought by some to partake of the nature of an action *in rem*[212] rather than a purely personal action like all actions in tort.[213] There was some doubt, therefore, as to whether an action in detinue was an action in tort. The matter now appears to be settled[214] and nobody today in Australia would question the existence of the tort of detinue as a remedy for the wrongful detention of goods. In a typical modern claim in detinue, the plaintiff claims the return of the chattel or its value and damages for its detention.

Many interferences with goods, particularly the withholding of goods from the person entitled to immediate possession of the goods, do create a cause of action in both conversion and detinue but the principal reason why an action in detinue would be brought at the present time, rather than an action in conversion, is because detinue allows a court in appropriate circumstances to direct the defendant to return the plaintiff's goods which the defendant is detaining: a form of judgment which is not available in conversion even where damages do not provide adequate satisfaction to the plaintiff. In fact, detinue is the only intentional tort to goods in which the plaintiff can claim not only damages but also the recovery of the goods themselves. The Common Law Procedure Act 1854 (s.78) gave the courts in England power to order delivery up of the chattel by the defendant without giving him the option to pay the value of the

---

209 Section 8(1).

210 Section 8(2). See also R.S.C. Ord. 15, r. 10A & 11A.

211 See J.B. Ames, *Lectures on Legal History* (Harvard, 1913) Ch. VI. See also *Pizer* v. *Pizer* [1926] V.L.R. 231, 233.

212 An action *in rem* is one in which the plaintiff seeks specific restitution of his chattel. See *General & Finance Facilities Ltd* v. *Cooks Cars (Romford) Ltd* [1963] 1 W.L.R. 644, 650.

213 A purely personal action is one in which the plaintiff seeks a judgment for pecuniary damages only. Almost all actions in tort are purely personal actions.

214 See *Bellinger* v. *Autoland Pty Ltd* [1962] V.R. 514, 520-1. See also C.H.S. Fifoot, *History and Sources of the Common Law* (London, 1949) Ch. 2.

chattel as assessed and this power has now been given to courts in Australia by the Rules of Court made by the Supreme Courts of the various States and Territories.[215]

Apart from an action in detinue there are two other ways in which a plaintiff can recover goods of his which a defendant is detaining. The action of replevin[216] can be used by a person who has been deprived of his possession of goods to obtain delivery up of his goods as interim relief until the question of who is entitled to the goods is determined at the trial of the action. It is only available when the defendant is wrongfully detaining the plaintiff's goods after taking them out of the plaintiff's possession by judicial process or by a trespassory taking. The plaintiff in an action of replevin must apply to an officer of the court who, upon receiving security (by way of a deposit of money or a bond) that the plaintiff will prosecute the action of replevin and, if unsuccessful, return the goods to the defendant, will by a writ of replevin directed to the sheriff require him to recover the goods and to restore them to the plaintiff.

In addition to the action of replevin there are statutory provisions in most of the Australian States and Territories under which summary proceedings can be brought for the detention of goods of a limited value.[217] In situations where these provisions apply, the court of summary jurisdiction is given the power to order the return of the goods and by the same order to direct payment of their value in the event of the order not being obeyed. But the court can order only that the value of the goods be paid and no compensation or damages for wrongful detention can be given by the court. The court also seems to have the power under these provisions merely to order the return of the goods to the complainant and is not bound to make a further order for payment of the value of the goods in default of their return.[218] These statutory provisions are not an enactment of the action in detinue though there are many points of resemblance with that common law action.[219] The action in detinue is now considered in some detail.

The tort of detinue is committed when a defendant who is, or has been, in possession of goods detains them after a proper demand has been made for their return by the person who has an immediate right to possession of the goods. There are five matters which are discussed further in relation to this definition.

1. The Subject-matter of Detinue

The subject-matter of detinue, like the subject-matter of conversion, is

215 See e.g. R.S.C. (Victoria) r. 21.03(1)(d). This matter is discussed further on pp. 164-6 below. See also *McKeown* v. *Cavalier Yachts Pty Ltd* (1988) 13 N.S.W.L.R. 303.

216 See R. Sutton, *Personal Actions at Common Law* (London, 1929) pp. 66-71.

217 See e.g. s.131, Local and District Criminal Courts Act 1926-75 (S.A.); s.78, Police Act 1892-78 (W.A.); s.12, Local Courts (Civil Claims) Act 1970 (N.S.W.).

218 See *Wood* v. *Wood* [1944] V.R. 64.

219 See *Bellinger* v. *Autoland Pty Ltd* [1962] V.R. 514, 520-1. See also *Pizer* v. *Pizer* [1926] V.L.R. 231.

goods, and the earlier discussion of what 'goods' are should be referred to.[220]

2. THE NATURE OF THE PLAINTIFF'S INTEREST

The interest which the plaintiff must have to bring an action in detinue is that he must have an immediate right to possession of the goods detained. As the action in detinue is for the wrongful detention of the plaintiff's goods, the plaintiff will normally not have actual possession of the goods[221] but the right to have the goods handed over to him immediately on demand. An immediate right to possession of the goods is sufficient title to sue in detinue.[222]

3. DETENTION OF GOODS WHICH AMOUNTS TO DETINUE

The action in detinue is not to be used for damage done to a chattel, it is only to be used for its detention. The essential element in the tort of detinue is the 'detention' of the plaintiff's goods by the defendant. But not every withholding of goods is a detention for the purposes of the tort of detinue. As already indicated, a brief withholding of goods made merely so that the defendant may verify the plaintiff's title to the goods or to confirm that delivery to the plaintiff would be proper does not amount to conversion and it does not amount to 'detention' for the purposes of the tort of detinue. On the other hand, if the plaintiff has made a proper demand for the return of the goods and in response to that demand the defendant either refuses or neglects to return the goods, then the withholding of those goods in those circumstances will amount to a detention sufficient for the tort of detinue.

It should be noted that the 'intentional' conduct required for the tort of detinue relates to the refusal to return the chattel when a proper demand for its return is made. If goods have been bailed by a bailor to a bailee it does not matter that the goods have been lost or destroyed by the intentional, reckless or even negligent conduct of the bailee.[223] It is the deliberate refusal to return the goods (even though the return may be

220 See pp. 136-7 above. Perhaps the only point worthwhile adding is that goods which belong to P which are fitted to goods belonging to D can be the subject-matter of detinue if, as a matter of practicality, the goods can be detached by D and returned to P. See *Lewis* v. *Andrews & Rowley Pty Ltd* (1956) S.R.(N.S.W.) 439 and *Rendell* v. *Associated Finance Pty Ltd* [1957] V.R. 604.

221 See, however, *Metals & Ropes Co. Ltd* v. *Tattersall* [1966] 3 All E.R. 401, 403 where the plaintiff, who was suing in detinue, was said to be in actual (or constructive) possession of the boilers.

222 The discussion on the plaintiff's title to sue in conversion should also be referred to. See pp. 137-44 above.

223 See *Reeve* v. *Palmer* (1858) 5 C.B.(N.S.) 84, 90-1. Though if the defendants are disabled from delivering the goods through destruction or loss of the goods which reasonable care and skill on their part could not avoid, there could be no detinue. See *John F. Goulding Pty Ltd* v. *Victorian Railway Commissioner* (1932) 48 C.L.R. 157, 166. See also *W.L. Mack Engineering Pty Ltd* v. *Australasian Pipe & Tube Pty Ltd* (Federal Court, Sydney, Lockhart J.) 21 June 1991 (unreported).

impossible because the goods are lost or destroyed) that is the gist of the action in detinue. But the goods must have been in the possession of the defendant at some time, even though they may not be in his possession at the time the action is brought, if the action in detinue is to succeed against the defendant. As Parke B. said in *Jones* v. *Dowle*: 'Detinue does not lie against him who never had possession of the chattel, but it does against him who once had, but has improperly parted with the possession of it'.[224] To a certain extent the court is not concerned with the motive of the defendant. A withholding of goods by the defendant because of a fear of unpleasant industrial consequences if the goods are delivered to the plaintiff will still be regarded as an intentional detention sufficient to constitute detinue,[225] though, as indicated earlier, a brief withholding of the plaintiff's goods so that the defendant can verify the plaintiff's title to the goods is regarded as permissible and not a deliberate detention sufficient to amount to detinue.

In determining whether there has been a detention the courts usually ask whether there has been a proper demand by the plaintiff for the return of his goods and a clear refusal on the part of the defendant to return them.[226] In *Lloyd* v. *Osborne*, Darley C.J. of the Supreme Court of New South Wales said: 'I am quite clearly of opinion that the law is . . . that there must be a demand for the return of goods and a refusal to comply with that demand before an action can be brought for detainer of them'.[227]

What is a proper demand? It is important that the demand indicate with clarity that the plaintiff is requesting the return of the goods, and it must also give sufficiently clear instructions regarding delivery of the goods, if it is to be regarded as a proper demand. In *Lloyd* v. *Osborne*, where the plaintiff's solicitor wrote to the defendant that he had been instructed by his client 'to demand that you will at once deliver to her or to her agent all sheep branded F. or F.G. (tar brand) which you unlawfully withhold from her . . . '[228] the Supreme Court of New South Wales regarded the demand as not a proper one because the instructions concerning delivery were insufficient. The Chief Justice said that the letter did not say where the sheep were to be delivered, nor did it say who the agent was; as he put it, 'this demand was insufficient, in that it does not state where the sheep are to be delivered or to whom'.[229] It is also not a proper demand if the plaintiff demands that the defendant return the goods to a particular place unless there is some contractual obligation on the defendant to do so. In *Capital Finance Co. Ltd* v. *Bray*[230] the plaintiff demanded delivery up of

---

224 (1841) 9 M. & W. 19, 20.
225 See *Howard Perry & Co. Ltd* v. *British Railways Board* [1980] 1 W.L.R. 1375.
226 The reason for the demand and refusal is stated in *Clayton* v. *Le Roy* [1911] 2 K.B. 1031, 1048: 'If there is a demand by the owner from the person in possession of the chattel and a refusal on the part of the latter to give it up, then in six years the remedy of the owner is barred; it is therefore very important for the owner that the law should lay down the principle that some clear act of that kind (i.e. a demand and a refusal) is required to constitute a cause of action in detinue' (*per* Fletcher Moulton L.J.).
227 (1899) 20 L.R.(N.S.W.) 190, 193.
228 ibid., 194.
229 ibid.
230 [1964] 1 All E.R. 603.

the goods by the hirer at his own expense to one of three named places: Edinburgh, Waterloo Place in London or Stone Buildings, Lincoln's Inn. The English Court of Appeal decided that the demand was not a proper demand. Lord Denning M.R., after pointing out that the defendant was 'not bound to be active and send the goods back unless there is an obligation by contract to do so', went on to say that the demand 'was not a good demand such as to found a claim in detinue. It did not merely demand delivery up. It demanded the hirer should take the car back to one of these three addresses. He was under no obligation to do so'.[231] On the other hand, if the plaintiff does not demand delivery up but writes instead to say that he will come and remove his goods from the defendant's land on a certain date and the defendant writes back to say that he will resist any attempt on the plaintiff's part to remove the goods, there is a sufficiently proper demand and refusal to amount to a detention.[232] It has recently been suggested that 'where the defence of a defendant shows clearly that if a demand had been made on him for possession of the property, he would have refused delivery, then it should no longer be a defence to an action in detinue that no demand was made'.[233] This is a sensible approach to the question of a proper demand, and it seems likely that if a plaintiff clearly shows that if the demand had been made it would have been futile, that courts in Australia will dispense with the requirement of a proper demand. There might, however, be some problem in determining when the original act of detention could be said to have taken place. This approach was echoed by Bollen J. in *Crowther* v. *Australian Guarantee Corporation Ltd*, where he expressed the view that it was not an immutable rule that there must be a demand for and refusal of the return of goods before an action in detinue would lie. As he said: 'A man may demonstrate that he intends not to deliver up goods come what may. If that intent be proved, absence of demand will not defeat the plaintiff's claim'.[234]

When can it be said that there has been a refusal to return the goods? The first point that should be made is that the refusal need not be an express one. If a proper demand has been made, taking no notice of it may be regarded as a refusal. As Darley C.J. said in *Lloyd* v. *Osborne*: 'if the demand was sufficient, taking no notice of it might be equivalent to a refusal'.[235] On the other hand, *Nelson & Another* v. *Nelson*[236] shows that a failure to send a reply cannot always be construed as a refusal. In that case, the solicitors for the plaintiff wrote to the defendant demanding that the plaintiff be allowed to remove certain goods that were then in the defendant's possession. The defendant did not reply to that letter. The Supreme Court of Queensland decided that there was no legal obligation to send a reply to that letter and that a failure to send a reply cannot be construed as a refusal to allow the plaintiff to remove the goods. Where,

231 ibid., 607.
232 See *Caley & Others* v. *Rogers* [1938] St.R.Qd. 25.
233 See *Baud Corporation N.V.* v. *Brook* (1970) 40 D.L.R. (3d) 418, 423.
234 (1985) Aust. Torts Reports 80-709 at 69, 102.
235 (1899) 20 L.R.(N.S.W.) 190, 194.
236 [1923] St.R.Qd. 37, 40.

however, the plaintiff has obtained an order for delivery up of the goods, it is not sufficient, in order to establish delivery of the goods to the plaintiff, that the defendant should do nothing at all and merely wait and remain inert in all respects. The English Court of Appeal decided in *Metals & Ropes Co. Ltd* v. *Tattersall*[237] that the defendant should take some steps to make it clear to the plaintiff that the defendant regards the property in the goods as now being entirely in the plaintiff and that the goods are entirely at the disposal of the plaintiff. Otherwise, the defendant will still be regarded as refusing to return the goods to the plaintiff. What if the defendant writes to the plaintiff in the following terms? 'We admit that the goods are yours and that you are entitled to the possession of them. Yet because we fear that industrial action may be taken against us if we permit you to remove them, we have refused to allow you to collect them for some weeks now, despite your demands, and we will continue to refuse to allow you to collect them until our fears have been removed.' In *Howard Perry & Co.* v. *British Railways Board*,[238] Sir Robert Megarry V.-C. regarded a refusal couched in such terms as a conversion. It would also be detinue. The fact that the refusal to return the goods is accompanied by a statement that the plaintiff is entitled to the possession of the goods and that the goods are not being returned only because of the fear of industrial action will not prevent the refusal from being regarded as a detention of the goods sufficient for the purpose of the tort of detinue.

Not being able to explain the loss of the plaintiff's goods will not prevent the defendant from being held liable in detinue. In *Houghland* v. *R.R. Low (Luxury) Coaches Ltd*[239] the plaintiff, who was travelling in one of the defendant's coaches, deposited her suitcase with the coach driver who put it in the boot which was then locked. After a stop for tea, the coach engine would not start again and a relief coach was sent for. When the relief coach arrived the luggage was transferred to it but on arrival at her destination the plaintiff could not find her suitcase and nobody could say what had happened to it. The plaintiff sued the defendants in detinue for the delivery up of the suitcase and its contents or their value. The plaintiff succeeded in detinue and when the matter went on appeal Willmer L.J. in the Court of Appeal said that the plaintiff by proving delivery of the suitcase to the coach driver at Southampton and its non-return on the arrival of the coach at Hoylake had made out a *prima facie* case. The defendants could avoid liability in detinue by proving what in fact did happen to the suitcase and by showing that what did happen happened without any default on their part. Otherwise, they would be regarded as detaining the goods and therefore liable in detinue. So, a bailee of goods who cannot explain the loss of the goods can nevertheless be held liable in detinue for their detention.

One further point should be mentioned. In many cases the loss of the

---

237 [1966] 3 All E.R. 401, 403.
238 [1980] 1 W.L.R. 1375, 1380.
239 [1962] 1 Q.B. 694. See also *John F. Goulding Pty Ltd* v. *Victorian Railways Commissioners* (1932) 48 C.L.R. 157 and *A. Abrahams & Sons Pty Ltd* v. *Commissioner for Railways* (1958) S.R.(N.S.W.) 134.

goods will be both a breach of contract and a detention sufficient for the purposes of detinue. Is the plaintiff in such circumstances under any restraint to choose one or other of these remedies? Further, the same act may be both a conversion and an act which may form the basis of an action in detinue. Is the plaintiff free to choose which action to bring? The answer to both these questions is that the plaintiff is free to bring detinue even though he may have an action in contract or an action in conversion and even where he has discontinued the action in contract.[240] As the High Court pointed out in *John F. Goulding Pty Ltd* v. *Victorian Railways Commissioners*,[241] the wrong of detinue, apart from being distinguished in point of legal conception from conversion and breach of contract, might actually take place at a different time and upon a different occasion. Detinue, as we have seen, only arises when a proper demand has been made and there has been a refusal by the defendant to return the goods. This being so, detinue may be available even when the period of limitation for bringing the action for breach of contract or conversion has expired. However, as has been pointed out,[242] modern statutes of limitiation sometimes 'adopt the view that it is wrong for a plaintiff, whose real grievance is that the defendant has wrongly parted with his goods, to allow himself an indefinite time to sue by delaying making a demand until it suits him' and that these statutes of limitation might 'set out to prevent an action being brought in detinue based upon such a demand after the time for an action for conversion has expired'.[243] In cases where these statutes of limitation apply, the date of detention, i.e. the date on which the defendant refused to return the goods after a proper demand was made, might sometimes be irrelevant.

4. The Forms of Judgment in an Action in Detinue

If a plaintiff has succeeded in persuading the court that the defendant is wrongfully detaining his goods and that after a proper demand made by the plaintiff the defendant is refusing to deliver them up, he must then decide what form of judgment he will seek in his action of detinue. If the goods are no longer in the possession of the defendant, for example, because they have been lost or destroyed while in his possession, the only form of judgment that the plaintiff can reasonably seek will be one for the value of the chattel as assessed and damages for its detention. But if the goods detained are still in the possession of the defendant or thought to be in his possession then the plaintiff can seek a judgment in one of three different forms as Diplock L.J. explained so clearly in his judgment in

240 See *A. Abrahams & Sons Pty Ltd* v. *Commissioner for Railways* (1958) S.R.(N.S.W.) 134 and *John F. Goulding Pty Ltd* v. *Victorian Railways Commissioners* (1932) 48 C.L.R. 157. See also *W.L. Mack Engineering Pty Ltd* v. *Australasian Pipe & Tube Pty Ltd* (Federal Court, Sydney, Lockhart J.) 21 June 1991 (unreported).

241 ibid., 170.

242 See W.L. Morison et al. *Torts Commentary and Materials* (7th Edn, Sydney, 1989) p. 144.

243 For examples of such statutes of limitation, see s.6, Limitation of Actions Act 1958 (Vic.) and s.21, Limitation Act 1969 (N.S.W.).

General Finance Facilities Ltd v. *Cooks Cars (Romford) Ltd.*[244] Those three forms of judgment are available in Australia both as a result of the common law and as a result of Rules of Court[245] made by the Supreme Courts of the various Australian States and Territories which have followed section 78 of the Common Law Procedure Act 1854 in England.[246] This section gave the court or a judge, in any action for the detention of any chattel, the power to order the return of the chattel detained without giving the defendant the option of retaining such chattel upon paying the value assessed. We now consider the three forms of judgment.

(a) Judgment for the value of the chattel as assessed and damages for its detention If the chattel detained is an ordinary article in commerce, with no special value or interest, whether to the plaintiff or others, the court will not normally order specific restitution of the chattel unless damages would not be an adequate remedy.[247] The defendant, of course, can return the goods to the plaintiff at any time, but once the time for judgment has arrived and the defendant has not returned the goods, the plaintiff, if he chooses to do so, can ask for a judgment in this form as of right.[248] If a judgment in this form is given, it deprives the defendant of the option of returning the chattel after the judgment is given.

(b) Judgment for the return of the chattel or recovery of its value as assessed and damages for its detention In this second form of judgment the defendant is given the option of returning the chattel but the plaintiff is also given the right to apply to the court to enforce specific restitution of the chattel. It is essential that the judgment should specify separate amounts for the assessed value of the chattel and damages for its detention so as to give the plaintiff the option of distraining for the assessed value of the chattel if it is not recovered by the sheriff. In *Juhlinn-Dannfelt* v. *Crash Repairs Pty Ltd,*[249] where the plaintiff claimed the return of a vintage Horch motor car, Hoare J. of the Supreme Court of Queensland thought that a judgment in this form was appropriate. This was also the form of the judgment in *W.L. Mack Engineering Pty Ltd* v. *Australasian Pipe & Tube Pty Ltd.*[250]

(c) Judgment for the return of the chattel and damages for its detention A judgment in this third form is for the specific restitution of the chattel itself. Under such a judgment the only pecuniary sum which is recoverable

---

244 [1963] 1 W.L.R. 644, 650-2.

245 See e.g. Ord. 22 r.13 (Vic.); Ord. 53 r.1 (Tas.); Ord. 52 r.1 (Qld); Supreme Court Act 1970 s. 93(1).(N.S.W.).

246 17 & 18 Vict., c.125.

247 *See Whiteley* v. *Hilt* [1918] 2 K.B. 808, 819; *General and Finance Facilities Ltd* v. *Cooks Cars (Romford) Ltd* [1963] 1 W.L.R. 644, 649-50; and *Howard Perry & Co.* v. *British Railways Board* [1980] 1 W.L.R. 1375, 1382-3.

248 *General and Finance Facilities Ltd* v. *Cooks Cars (Romford) Ltd* [1963] 1 W.L.R. 644, 650.

249 [1969] Q.W.N. 1.

250 Federal Court, Sydney, Lockhart J. 21 June 1991 (unreported).

is damages for the detention of the chattel. The value of the chattel need not be assessed because the plaintiff is in effect seeking the return of the chattel which he obtains by a writ of delivery, attachment or sequestration.[251] A judgment of this kind could not be obtained at common law because the defendant had to be given an option to return the chattel or to pay its value. Now, as a result of s.78 of the Common Law Procedure Act 1854 in England, Rules of Court have been made by the Supreme Courts of the various States and Territories of Australia which give power to courts in Australia, in appropriate cases, to order the return of the chattel by the defendant without giving him the option of retaining it and paying its value.[252] An application for such an order can be made *ex parte*. A judgment which orders specific restitution of the chattel is rare, but it has been given.[253] In two recent decisions orders for specific restitution of a family portrait[254] and a yacht[255] have been made in Australia. As the giving of a judgment of this kind is entirely discretionary the court should not order specific restitution of goods which are ordinary articles in commerce, particularly when damages are an adequate remedy.[256] As Sir Robert Megarry V.-C. put it in *Howard Perry & Co.* v. *British Railways Board*:

> If a plaintiff can easily replace the goods detained by purchasing their equivalent on the market, then the payment of damages out of which the price of the equivalent may be paid is adequate compensation to the wronged plaintiff, and there is little or no point in making an order for the delivery of the goods. Far better to let the plaintiff fend for himself with the defendant's money.[257]

But goods which are ordinary articles in commerce may nevertheless be the subject of an order for specific restitution if they are 'obtainable on the market only with great difficulty', as was the steel in *Howard Perry & Co.* v. *British Railways Board.* Specific restitution of a chattel, even if it is an ordinary article in commerce, may also be ordered if it can be shown that the defendant is insolvent and therefore unable to pay any damages that may be awarded against him.

The power to order delivery up of goods has been held to be wide enough to cover an order requiring a defendant to allow the plaintiff to

---

251 *General and Finance Facilities Ltd* v. *Cooks Cars (Romford) Ltd* [1963] 1 W.L.R. 644, 651. See also *Linke* v. *Schramm* [1932] V.L.R. 352, 354.

252 See e.g. Ord. 22 r.13 (Vic.); Ord. 53 r.1 (Tas.); Ord. 52 r.1 (Qld); and Supreme Court Act 1970 s. 93(1) (N.S.W.).

253 See *Hymas* v. *Ogden* [1905] 1 K.B. 246 and *General Motors Acceptance Corporation of Australia* v. *Davis* [1971] V.R. 734. See also *Howard Perry & Co. Ltd* v. *British Railways Board* [1980] 1 W.L.R. 1375.

254 See *Perpetual Trustees & National Executors of Tasmania Ltd* v. *Perkins* (1989) Aust. Torts Reports 80-295.

255 See *McKeown* v. *Cavalier Yachts Pty Ltd* (1988) N.S.W.L.R. 303.

256 In *General Motors Acceptance Corporation of Australia* v. *Davis* [1971] V.R. 734 the judgment was for the specific restitution of a motor car merely described as 'motor vehicle registered No. JFT 843'. It is not clear from the report of the case why it was not regarded as an ordinary article in commerce or why specific restitution of the motor car was ordered.

257 [1980] 1 W.L.R. 1375, 1383.

come and collect the goods himself. If the circumstances require it, the court can devise a form of wording which will allow 'delivery up' to the plaintiff and which will not require the defendant to take any physical step to move the goods. Such an order was made in *Howard Perry & Co.* v. *British Railways Board.*

Finally, it would appear that a court, in an action in detinue, may decline to order specific restitution of goods if it would be unjust to do so or if it would give the plaintiff some benefit more than he was entitled to or perhaps deserved. In an appropriate case, such as *McKeown* v. *Cavalier Yachts Pty Ltd,*[258] a court may require the plaintiff to compensate the defendant for work done on the goods (if the work has conferred an incontrovertible benefit on the plaintiff) as a prerequisite to obtaining an order for specific recovery of the goods.

5. THE JUS TERTII AND DETINUE

It has been suggested in relation to the *jus tertii* that the rules are the same as in conversion.[259] It is true that a defendant who detains goods will be able to avoid liability in detinue by showing that someone else, other than the plaintiff, is rightfully entitled to possession of the goods. This is because by showing this, the defendant will in effect have destroyed the plaintiff's title to sue in detinue as the third party would have the immediate right to possession of the goods. In this respect, perhaps, the rules of *jus tertii* in detinue are the same as in conversion because, as we have seen, in conversion a plaintiff who is relying on his immediate right to possession of the goods at the time of the conversion can have the *jus tertii* pleaded by the converter of the goods who will be able to avoid liability in conversion by showing that someone else is rightfully entitled to the possession of those goods.

In the case of a bailment we have pointed out that in conversion, despite the rule that 'a bailee is not entitled to dispute his bailor's title', a bailee is not estopped from pleading the *jus tertii* if he has already on the demand of the true owner given up possession to him, or if, having retained the goods, he defends the action on his behalf and by his authority.[260] Where an action was brought in detinue by a bailor against his bailee, it was decided recently that a bailee can only plead the *jus tertii* if he defends his possession of the goods 'upon the right and title and by the authority of the tertius *from whom he himself obtained the property in the [goods]*'.[261] The rules in relation to the *jus tertii* are therefore very similar in conversion and detinue, but it is difficult to say with any degree of confidence that they are the same.

In any case, a defendant bailee who is faced with a claim by a person purporting to be the true owner should bear in mind the words of Herron

---

258 (1988) 13 N.S.W.L.R. 303.

259 See *Street* (6th edn, 1976) pp. 58-9, who relies upon the decision in *Rogers, Sons & Co.* v. *Lambert & Co.* [1891] 1 Q.B. 318 for that suggestion.

260 *Edwards* v. *Amos & Others* (1945) W.N. (N.S.W.) 204, 207.

261 *Horne* v. *Richardson* [1970] 64 Q.J.P.R. 47, 48 (emphasis added).

J. in *Edwards* v. *Amos & Others* that he would be 'very foolish indeed if he yields to a demand by anyone except that of his own client. He may, without any risk whatever, take the attitude that he will interplead in an action between the two contesting parties, and . . . that is his proper duty, and it is his proper duty in all such cases at least to notify his bailor of the claim of the opposing party'.[262]

V: THE ACTION ON THE CASE

In addition to the torts of trespass, conversion and detinue there is also a remedy for intentional interferences with goods called the action on the case. In *Penfolds Wines Pty Ltd* v. *Elliott,* Dixon J. referred to it as 'a special action on the case'.[263] In this action, while the plaintiff must show damage he need not show that the damage or injury was direct and he also need not show that he had actual or constructive possession or even an immediate right to possession of the goods. It is therefore useful for those situations where damage is inflicted by a defendant on a chattel which is not in the owner's possession and particularly so when the owner's right to possession is suspended, because, for example, the chattel is held by a third party upon a bailment for a term, which term has not yet expired. The foundation of the action is 'permanent' damage to the chattel, that is, damage which would enure to the 'reversioner'.[264]

Mears v. *The London and South Western Railway Company*[265] is an example of a successful action on the case of this kind. The plaintiffs, who were owners of a barge, let the barge to a third party for a term which had not yet expired when the defendants' servants, while lifting a boiler from the barge, dropped it, severely damaging the barge. The plaintiffs brought an action against the defendants for damage to the barge. Counsel for the defendants argued that there was no precedent to be found for an action by a reversioner for any injury to a chattel while out of his possession, but the court found in favour of the plaintiffs, Williams J. saying: 'It seems to me . . . to be clear that, though the owner cannot bring an action where there has been no permanent injury to the chattel, it has never been doubted that, where there is a permanent injury, the owner may maintain an action against the person whose wrongful act has caused that injury'.[266] Though the damage in *Mears* was caused by negligence, the principle of that case extends to intentional damage as well. So, a defendant who causes intentional permanent damage to a chattel can be sued not only by the bailee but also by the bailor in an action on the case, even where the bailment is for a term and the term has not expired.

The decision in *Mears* has been applied by the Supreme Court of

262 (1945) W.N.(N.S.W.) 204, 206.
263 (1946) 74 C.L.R. 204, 230.
264 ibid.
265 (1862) 11 C.B.(N.S.) 850.
266 ibid., 854-5.

Victoria in *The Dee Trading Co. Pty Ltd* v. *Baldwin*[267] where an owner of a motor-car was held entitled to sue the defendant who was responsible for permanent damage to the car, even though the owner did not have possession or the immediate right to possession of the car at the time the car was damaged by the defendant. This was despite the fact that the owner of the car had a right to insist that the bailee of the car (who had possession of the car under a hire-purchase agreement) make good the damage.[268] The fact that a plaintiff can recoup his losses from another source will not prevent him from suing a defendant who is responsible for permanent damage to goods in which the plaintiff has a reversionary interest in an action on the case. But the plaintiff must clearly show the nature of such interest.[269]

267 [1938] V.L.R. 173.
268 ibid., 178.
269 *Wertheim* v. *Cheel* (1885) 11 V.L.R. 107.

5

THE INTENTIONAL INFLICTION OF PURELY ECONOMIC LOSS

I: SOME GENERAL COMMENTS

We have now discussed the ways in which the law of torts protects a person against intentional interferences with his person, his land and his goods. This chapter discusses the ways in which the law of torts protects a person against the intentional infliction of purely economic loss, that is, financial loss which is not also accompanied by personal injury to the plaintiff or physical damage to his land or to his goods. It has been said with a good deal of truth that:

> Our law remedies intentional injuries to the plaintiff's body, to his nervous system, to his land and chattels; it is anomalous that a general theory of intentional tortious liability has developed for injuries to all those interests, but not for injuries to the plaintiff's financial interests. The generalising tendency of the twentieth century common lawyer has passed the economic torts by.[1]

What we have today, instead, is a collection of torts which in a variety of ways protect a person (usually a business) against intentional interferences which inflict purely economic loss. Most of these torts are called 'economic torts' or 'industrial torts', principally because they are most often used to protect the commercial and business interests of traders and because the interferences very often occur in the context of a trade or industrial dispute. There is no equivalent in Australia to the Trade Disputes Act 1906 in England, which gave immunity in tort both to individuals and unions for acts done 'by two or more persons . . . in contemplation or furtherance of a trade dispute'.[2] The Act also removed liability for interfering with another person's business, for example, by inducing

1 J.D. Heydon, *Economic Torts* (2nd edn, London, 1978) p. 130.
2 6 Edw. 7, C.47, s.1. No such legislation has been enacted by the Commonwealth Parliament and the only State equivalent found in s.72 of the Industrial Conciliation and Arbitration Act 1961 (Qld) was repealed in 1976.

some other person to break a contract of employment etc.[3] The common law development of these economic and industrial torts in Australia has been greatly influenced by the development of these torts in England because of the early reliance by Australian courts on English decisions in these areas. It is possible, therefore, though the matter has not been closely examined, that some small measure of this immunity was reflected in early Australian decisions because the English decisions were arrived at in the shadow of the Trade Disputes Act 1906. On the other hand, the fact that these torts are available for use in Australia not only against other individuals and traders but also against unions and their officials, when their interferences result in purely financial loss, has meant that the study of some of these torts is relevant not only to torts lawyers but also to those with an interest in industrial law. Indeed, it is true to say that the economic and industrial torts are examined much less cursorily in courses in industrial law than in courses in the law of torts in Australia.

Another point must be mentioned by way of general comment. Not every tort, from the collection of torts available for intentional interferences which result in purely financial loss to the plaintiff, is properly called an economic tort or an industrial tort. The tort of deceit, for example, is more often than not treated separately from those torts, as deceit is not only available when the defendant's fraudulent misrepresentation is intended to cause and does cause purely financial loss to the plaintiff but it is also available when, for example, 'the defendant's fraudulent misrepresentation was plainly and wickedly calculated to bring about acts of coition with the plaintiff which he knew might result in physical harm and detriment to her'[4] or when the defendant's false representation that a car had new tyres resulted in physical damage to the car and personal injury to the plaintiff when he drove the car and one of the tyres which had a rubber strip vulcanized on it burst owing to the loosening of the vulcanized strip.[5] So, even though not strictly an 'economic tort', we deal with the action of deceit in this chapter as, nowadays, it is brought mainly for the protection of business interests. We have already seen that the action on the case for damages can be used to protect a plaintiff against intentional interferences with his person, his land and his goods. It can also be used to protect a person against intentional interferences which cause him purely financial loss. So we deal with that innominate tort in this chapter as well. There is yet another tort which is dealt with in this chapter. It is the tort of misfeasance in a public office, which lies against a public officer whose intentional act amounts to an abuse of his office and results in purely financial loss to the plaintiff. This, again, is not an economic tort or an industrial tort but it properly finds its place in a chapter concerned with the intentional infliction of purely economic loss.

---

3 See now s.13(1), Trade Union and Labour Relations Act 1974 as amended by the Trade Union and Labour Relations Act 1976 and the Employment Act 1982.

4 *Graham* v. *Saville* [1945] O.R. 301, 310. See also *Garnaut* v. *Rowse* (1941) 43 W.A.L.R. 29. In very similar circumstances general damages for deceit were held to be not recoverable in *Smythe* v. *Reardon* [1949] St.R.Qd. 74.

5 *Nicholls* v. *Taylor* [1939] V.L.R. 119.

We first deal with the tort of deceit, then the economic and industrial torts of injurious falsehood, passing off, interference with contractual relations, intimidation, conspiracy and causing loss by unlawful means. We then deal briefly with the action on the case for damages and the actions for malicious prosecution and abuse of process before considering the requirements of the tort of misfeasance in a public office. Space does not permit a detailed consideration of the statutory provisions in Australia which intrude into the area occupied by some of these torts. These statutory provisions, particularly ss.52, 53 and 55 of the Trade Practices Act 1974 (Cwth), which prohibit 'misleading or deceptive conduct', 'false representations', 'false and misleading statements' and 'conduct that is liable to mislead the public' in relation to goods and services,[6] are assuming increasing importance and over the next decade or two may well be relied upon as possible alternatives to the common law torts of deceit, injurious falsehood and passing off.[7]

II: DECEIT

The origin of the common law action of deceit as a separate tort is generally attributed to the decision in *Pasley & Another* v. *Freeman*[8] in 1789. The plaintiffs approached the defendant and told him that they were going to deal with a third party and wanted to know about his credit worthiness. The defendant 'falsely, deceitfully and fraudulently' told the plaintiffs that the third party was a person safely to be trusted and given credit and so the plaintiff sold goods to the third party on credit with a consequent loss of £2634. The Court of King's Bench decided by a majority that the plaintiffs were entitled to recover the value of the goods from the defendant on the basis of an action on the case for deceit. As Lord Kenyon C.J. said: 'I am of opinion that the action is maintainable on the grounds of deceit in the defendant, and injury and loss to the plaintiffs'.[9] The tort of deceit was, however, confined to fraudulent representations such as those in *Pasley* v. *Freeman* and, until recently, there was no liability in tort for negligent representations which resulted in purely

---

6 There is also legislation in the several States of Australia which provides that 'a person shall not, in trade or commerce, engage in conduct that is misleading or deceptive or is likely to mislead or deceive'. See s.11(1) Fair Trading Act 1985 (Vic.); s.42(1) Fair Trading Act 1987 (N.S.W.); s.38(1) Fair Trading Act 1989 (Qld); s.56(1) Fair Trading Act 1987 (S.A.); s.10(1) Fair Trading Act 1987 (W.A.) and s.14 Fair Trading Act 1990 (Tas.).

7 Although s.52 of the Trade Practices Act 1974 has spawned a great deal of litigation, the recent decision of the High Court of Australia in *Concrete Constructions (N.S.W.) Pty Ltd* v. *Nelson* (1990) 64 A.L.J.R. 293 suggests that the court might rein in the use of s.52 in commercial litigation. McHugh J. (at p. 304) reminds us of the *dictum* of Mason J. (as he then was) in *Parkdale Custom Built Furniture Pty Ltd* v. *Puxu Pty Ltd* (1982) 149 C.L.R. 191, 203, that for s.52 to apply 'it is not enough that conduct damages a rival trader; it must mislead or deceive or be likely to mislead or deceive members of the public in their capacity as consumers'.

8 (1789) 3 Term Rep. 51.

9 ibid., 65

economic loss. But, as we shall see in Chapter 9, as a result of the decisions of the House of Lords in *Hedley Byrne & Co. Ltd* v. *Heller & Partners Ltd*[10] in 1964 and the decision of the High Court of Australia in *Caltex Oil (Australia) Pty Ltd* v. *Dredge 'Willemstad'*[11] in 1976, it is now possible to impose liability on a defendant for negligently inflicted purely economic loss. Further, as a result of those decisions, persons who suffer purely economic loss because of the fraudulent statements or conduct of others may prefer to bring an action in the tort of negligence rather than an action for deceit, as fraud is more difficult to prove than negligence because of the heavy onus which a party alleging fraud bears. As we shall discover, however, deceit retains two advantages over the tort of negligence. It is not necessary for the plaintiff in deceit to show any 'special relationship'[12] or 'proximity'[13] between himself and the defendant as he must show if he is to bring an action in the tort of negligence for the infliction of purely economic loss, and the plaintiff in deceit can recover all the actual damages directly flowing from the fraudulent representation[14] whereas in the tort of negligence the plaintiff can only recover the damage which is 'reasonably foreseeable'. It is these advantages which might ensure the continued use of the action for deceit despite the availability of the tort of negligence for fraudulent representations which result in purely economic loss.

The tort of deceit is committed when a defendant makes a false representation to the plaintiff knowingly, or without belief in its truth, or recklessly, not caring whether it be true or false, with the intention that the plaintiff should believe and act on the false representation. To be actionable, the plaintiff's reliance on the false representation must result in actual damage to the plaintiff. So there are basically five requirements for the tort of deceit.

1. THE FALSE REPRESENTATION

If a defendant makes a representation which he does not in fact honestly believe to be true, it is a false representation. Representations are usually made by statements, orally or in writing, but sometimes conduct without any statement is sufficient.[15] As Franki J. said in *Given* v. *C.V. Holland (Holdings) Pty Ltd*, 'the step of placing the car on display for sale with a mileage shown on the odometer in a used car dealer's yard, where the vehicle is placed with the intention that it will be inspected by prospective purchasers is, in the absence of any special circumstances, *a representation*

10 [1964] A.C. 465.
11 (1976) 136 C.L.R. 529.
12 See below pp. 363.
13 See below pp. 354.
14 See *Doyle* v. *Olby (Ironmongers) Ltd* [1969] 2 Q.B. 158, 167. See also *State of South Australia* v. *Johnson* (1982) 42 A.L.R. 161 and *Yorke* v. *Ross Lucas Pty Ltd* (1983) 45 A.L.R. 299, 320-1.
15 It is also sufficient if the defendant has manifestly approved and adopted a false representation made by some third person. See *Bradford Third Equitable Benefit Building Society* v. *Borders* [1941] 2 All E.R. 205, 211.

by the used car dealer that the car has travelled the number of miles shown on the odometer'.[16]

Although 'mere silence' or 'mere non-disclosure of material facts' is not a sufficient foundation for an action in deceit,[17] it has also been said that 'half a truth will sometimes amount to a real falsehood'.[18] Thus in *Bristow & Anor.* v. *Moffat-Virtue (Qld) Pty Ltd,* the Full Court of the Supreme Court of Queensland held that in the circumstances of that case it was not sufficient for the defendant to tell the plaintiff the price for its engine but that the defendant owed a clear duty to the plaintiff 'to amplify his offer by telling him that the engines were not new'.[19] The representation in order to sustain an action of deceit need not be made in actual terms because words may be used in such a way as 'to convey to the person to whom they are addressed a meaning or inference beyond what is expressed; and if it appears that the person employing them knew this, and also knew that such meaning or inference was false, there is sufficient proof of fraud'.[20] So if a car is described as a 'demonstration model' or 'a good demo' there is a false representation if the car has been used as a rental car, even though there might have been small use as a demonstration model, or if the car is not still within the new car warranty.[21]

A false representation is a misstatement of an existing and specific fact but a misstatement by a person as to his state of mind is also a representation of fact sufficient to found an action for damages for deceit. As Bowen L.J. said in *Edgington* v. *Fitzmaurice,* 'the state of a man's mind is as much a fact as the state of his digestion'.[22] So a misstatement of opinion or belief or even of desire, intention or purpose can be regarded as a false representation for the purposes of the tort of deceit. If D tells P that he desires and intends to purchase P's shares in X Co. so that the business could be developed for the benefit of D's family, but D's desire and intention, either at the time of making the statement or subsequently but before the time of purchase, is to purchase the shares to realize a profit by reselling them, there is a false representation by D sufficient to found an action in deceit.[23]

If a person honestly and bona fide makes a representation in order to

---

16 (1977) 15 A.L.R. 439, 443.

17 *Peek* v. *Gurney* (1873) L.R. 6 H.L. 377, 403 *per* Lord Cairns. See also *Scott, Fell & Co. Ltd* v. *Lloyd* (1906) 4 C.L.R. 572 and (1907) 7 S.R.(N.S.W.) 512.

18 *Peek* v. *Gurney* (1873) L.R. 6 H.L. 377, 392 *per* Lord Chelmsford. See also the *dictum* of Lord Cairns at p. 403: 'There must in my opinion be some active misstatement of fact, or, at all events, such a partial and fragmentary statement of fact, as that the withholding of that which is not stated makes that which is stated absolutely false'.

19 [1962] Qd.R. 377, 391 *per* Stanley J. A duty to volunteer further information also arises when there is a fiduciary relationship between the parties.

20 *Delany* v. *Keogh* [1905] 2 I.R. 267, 286-7 *per* Holmes L.J.

21 See *Thompson* v. *J.T. Fossey Pty Ltd* (1978) 20 A.L.R. 496—a decision under s.53(a), Trade Practices Act 1974 (Cwth).

22 (1885) 29 Ch.D. 459, 483. See also *Nicholas* v. *Thompson* [1924] V.L.R. 554 and *Bisset* v. *Wilkinson* [1927] A.C. 177, 182.

23 See *Jones* v. *Dumbrell* [1981] V.R. 199. The judgment was delivered in 1968 but the decision was not reported until 1981. See also *Commercial Banking Co. of Sydney Ltd* v. *Brown & Co.* (1972) 126 C.L.R. 337 (opinion not honestly held).

induce a contract but before the contract is made discovers the representation to be false, he would be liable in an action in deceit if he does not disclose the falsity of the representation to the other party.[24] Even a representation which is not shown to have been false when made but which subsequently becomes false to the knowledge of the representor can found an action for deceit. This was decided by Smith J., in *Jones* v. *Dumbrell*, when he held that the representor's 'liability in deceit is the same as if the representation had been false to his knowledge when originally made'.[25]

If there is a doubt whether a fraudulent representation sufficient to found an action in deceit has been made, the judge should discharge his responsibility to find that a fraudulent misrepresentation has been made 'only when he feels persuaded clearly on the balance of probabilities that representations have been made which are false'.[26]

2. Knowledge of Falsity

The second requirement for the tort of deceit is that the false statement must be made by the defendant knowingly or recklessly. The courts do not seem to make a distinction between the two types of conduct. As Bowen L.J. said in *Edgington* v. *Fitzmaurice*: 'it is immaterial whether the defendants made the statement knowing it to be untrue, or recklessly, without caring whether it was true or not, because to make a statement recklessly for the purpose of influencing another person is dishonest'.[27] The statement by Lord Herschell in *Derry* v. *Peek* is regarded as the classical exposition of this requirement:

> I think the authorities establish the following propositions: First, in order to sustain an action of deceit, there must be proof of fraud, and nothing short of that will suffice. Secondly, fraud is proved when it is shewn that a false representation has been made (1) knowingly, or (2) without belief in its truth, or (3) recklessly careless whether it be true or false . . . To prevent a false statement being fraudulent, there must, I think, always be an honest belief in its truth.[28]

In *Derry* v. *Peek* itself the defendants who were directors of a company were held not liable in deceit. They had issued a prospectus saying that their company had the right to use steam or mechanical motive power for their trams instead of horses. In fact, the company had the right only to use animal power (horses) though they fully expected that the Board of Trade would give them their consent to use steam and other mechanical power. The Board of Trade, however, refused their consent and the company was wound up. The plaintiff who was induced to take shares in the company on the strength of the statements in the prospectus brought

---

24 *Robertson & Moffatt* v. *Belson* [1905] V.L.R. 555, 563.
25 [1981] V.R. 199, 204.
26 See *Smith* v. *Madden* (1945) Q.W.N. 33, 42. The judgment is that of Dixon J. of the High Court. The decision does not appear to be reported anywhere else.
27 (1885) 29 Ch.D. 459, 481.
28 (1889) 14 App.Cases 337, 374.

an action in deceit against the defendants but the House of Lords (reversing the decision of the Court of Appeal) held that the defendants were not liable in deceit because the statement as to steam and mechanical power was made by them in the honest belief that it was true. As Lord Herschell said, 'making a false statement through want of care falls far short of, and is a very different thing from, fraud, and the same may be said of a false representation honestly believed on insufficient grounds'.[29] So a party alleging fraud bears a very heavy onus.

3. The Defendant Must Have Intended the Plaintiff to Act upon the False Representation

To sustain an action of deceit it is essential that the defendant must have intended the plaintiff to act upon the false representation. As Bowen L.J. put it, 'it is wholly immaterial with what object the lie is told . . . but it is material that the defendant should intend that it should be relied on by the person to whom he makes it'.[30] In the leading case of *Peek* v. *Gurney*[31] the House of Lords decided that a person who purchased shares from an allottee of shares could not sue the directors of the company in deceit, in relation to false representations in the company's prospectus, because the prospectus was only intended for original shareholders or persons invited to become allottees of shares and not for persons who bought shares on the stock-market. The principle derived from that decision and followed by the High Court of Australia in *Commercial Banking Co. of Sydney Ltd* v. *R.H. Brown & Co.* is that 'a person who makes a false and fraudulent misrepresentation is only liable to the persons to whom it is made, i.e. to the persons whom it is intended should act upon it'.[32] But there is no necessity for the plaintiff to show that the defendant made the false representation directly to the plaintiff himself:[33] 'it can be made to one, to be passed on to another; it can be made to a group to which the plaintiff belongs so that the plaintiff is one of those intended to be deceived. The representation must, however, in one way or another, be made to the plaintiff to induce him to act upon it'.[34] In *Commercial Banking Co. of Sydney Ltd* v. *R.H. Brown & Co.*[35] the plaintiffs were woolgrowers who had sold wool to a buyer. Before delivery, they requested their own bank (the first defendant) to make inquiries about the buyer's financial standing.

---

29 ibid., 375.

30 *Edgington* v. *Fitzmaurice* (1885) 29 Ch.D. 459, 482.

31 (1873) L.R. 6 H.L. 377.

32 (1972) 126 C.L.R. 337, 343 *per* Menzies J.

33 See *Bradford Third Equitable Benefit Building Society* v. *Borders* [1941] 2 All E.R. 205, 211; *Swift* v. *Winterbotham* (1873) L.R. 8 Q.B. 244, 253; *Langridge* v. *Levy* (1837) 2 M. & W. 519; *Barry* v. *Croskey* (1861) 2 J. & H. 1, 23; *Peek* v. *Gurney* (1873) L.R. 6 H.L. 377, 412-13; *Richardson* v. *Silvester* (1873) L.R. 9 Q.B. 34, 36; *Robinson* v. *National Bank of Scotland* [1916] S.C. 46 (H.L.) and *Pilmore* v. *Hood* (1838) 5 Bing. N.C. 97.

34 *Commercial Banking Co. of Sydney Ltd* v. *R.H. Brown & Co.* (1972) 126 C.L.R. 337, 343 *per* Menzies J.

35 ibid. The matter first came before the Supreme Court of Western Australia in *R.H. Brown & Co.* v. *Bank of New South Wales and Commercial Banking Company of Sydney Ltd* [1971] W.A.R. 201.

The bank sought this information from the second defendant (the buyer's bank). The second defendant's manager wrote to the plaintiff's bank saying that the buyer was 'capably managed by directors well experienced in the wool trade. The company has always met its engagements, is trading satisfactorily and we consider that it would be safe for its trade engagements generally. This opinion is confidential and for your private use and without responsibility on the part of this bank or its officer'. The trial judge found that the opinion conveyed was not honestly held by the second defendant's manager and that it misrepresented the buyer's financial position. He found the second defendant liable in deceit in respect of the manager's report even though the opinion was only conveyed to the plaintiff's bank, and not to the plaintiff directly, and despite the existence of the disclaimer of responsibility. As he said, of the false representation, 'I conclude that it was made with intent to deceive and with intent that it should be acted on by the first defendant *and any customer of the first defendant concerned in obtaining the opinion*, and that the plaintiff was such a person'.[36]

Can a defendant who fraudulently makes a false representation to a third party with the intention that the plaintiff will act upon it protect himself from liability for damages for deceit by telling the third party that the information or opinion is for his use only or that the information or opinion is given without responsibility? The question was raised in *Commercial Banking Co. of Sydney Ltd* v. *Brown* and given a very clear answer by Menzies J.: 'in so far as the disclaimer could protect the defendant, it would, but it could not protect it against fraud'.[37] So, whatever the position in the tort of negligence,[38] such a disclaimer will not avail a defendant in an action in deceit.

4. THE PLAINTIFF MUST HAVE ACTED UPON THE FALSE REPRESENTATION

In order to sustain an action of deceit, a plaintiff must be able to show that he relied upon the defendant's false representation in acting as he did to his own detriment.

If the plaintiff acts in the manner contemplated by the defendant who makes the false representation, for example, by buying the business, buying the shares, entering into the contract etc. or in a manner which is manifestly probable[39] or most natural[40] then the court will infer that the plaintiff has acted upon the false representation.

If the plaintiff can show that the false representation was either 'the sole cause of the plaintiff's act or materially contributed to his so acting'[41] that

---

36 ibid., 213 *per* Virtue S.P.J.
37 (1972) 126 C.L.R. 337, 344.
38 See *Hedley Byrne & Co. Ltd* v. *Heller & Partners Ltd* [1964] A.C. 465.
39 *Graham* v. *Saville* [1945] O.R. 301, 309.
40 *Nicholls* v. *Taylor* [1939] V.L.R. 119, 122.
41 *Edgington* v. *Fitzmaurice* (1885) 29 Ch.D. 459, 482. See also *Clarke* v. *Dickson* (1858) 6 C.B. (N.S.) 453.

will be sufficient proof that the plaintiff has acted upon the false representation. In *Edgington* v. *Fitzmaurice*[42] the plaintiff was induced to advance money to a company both by his own mistake and by a misstatement in the defendant's prospectus. It was held, by the English Court of Appeal, that the false representation in the prospectus influenced the conduct of the plaintiff and rendered the directors of the company liable to an action in deceit even though the plaintiff's conduct was also influenced by his own mistake. But the courts will not assume that every false representation influenced the conduct of the plaintiff and materially contributed to his acting to his detriment. In *Alati* v. *Kruger*[43] an agent of the vendor of a business made a false representation to the plaintiff that the average takings of the business were £130 per week. The vendor subsequently made a statement to the plaintiff that the average takings of the business were £100 per week and this sum appeared in the contract of sale. The High Court of Australia found that, in those circumstances, it was difficult to come to the conclusion that the conduct of the plaintiff had been influenced by the false representation of the agent in entering into the contract. The action in deceit against the agent of the vendor therefore failed.

If the defendant can show that the plaintiff knew the facts[44] or that the plaintiff acknowledged that he did not rely on the false representation whether he knew the facts or not,[45] or, in the case of goods, that the purchaser could have seen the defect in the goods[46] then in all these cases there can be no action in deceit because the plaintiff has not relied upon the false representation. In *Commercial Banking Co. of Sydney Ltd* v. *Brown*[47] the defendant argued that the false and fraudulent misrepresentation that a buyer was credit-worthy was not acted upon by the plaintiffs because they were already under a contractual duty to deliver their wool to the buyer. Both Virtue S.P.J. in the Supreme Court of Western Australia and the High Court of Australia dismissed this argument by saying that the plaintiffs would not have delivered their wool, notwithstanding their contract, had they not had the defendant's opinion that the buyer could be expected to pay for wool delivered. Both courts, therefore, held that the plaintiffs had in fact acted upon the false representation irrespective of their contractual obligations.

If, however, all that the plaintiff can show is a false representation made to a third party which has induced the third party to act to the plaintiff's detriment there can be no action in deceit. In *T.J. Larkins & Sons* v. *Chelmer Holdings Pty Ltd and Van den Broek*[48] an architect's failure to give the plaintiffs, a firm of builders, a notice of practical completion prevented the plaintiffs from collecting their money from the company for whom they had built a block of flats. An action in deceit against the

42 (1885) 29 Ch.D. 459.
43 (1955) 94 C.L.R. 216, 226-7.
44 *Alati* v. *Kruger* (1955) 94 C.L.R. 216, 226-7.
45 See *Arnison* v. *Smith* (1889) 41 Ch.D. 348, 369.
46 *Horsfall* v. *Thomas* (1862) 1 H. & C. 90, 102.
47 (1972) 126 C.L.R. 337.
48 [1965] Qd.R. 68.

architect failed. As Lucas J. said, 'what is alleged is a fraudulent misrepresentation, not to the plaintiffs, but to the building owner: not made with the intention that the plaintiffs should in any way act upon it, but made with the result that the building owner acted upon it to the detriment of the plaintiffs; no doubt, it is implied that this result was intended'.[49] He regarded these actions as laying 'a strange foundation for an action for damages for deceit'. This decision illustrates most clearly the requirement that in an action in deceit it is the plaintiff who must have acted upon the false representation if the action is to succeed.

There seems little doubt that the ultimate onus of proving that he was induced to act upon the the false representation rests upon the party seeking relief in respect of the fraudulent misrepresentation.[50]

5. DAMAGE

To succeed in an action in deceit the plaintiff must also prove that he has sustained actual damage as a result of acting upon the false representation. The damage is generally a pecuniary or money loss, though as we have indicated earlier, the action in deceit is also available for personal injuries and property damage. The onus of establishing his damage lies upon the plaintiff and if, upon the evidence, it is impossible to say whether or not he has suffered a loss his claim in deceit must fail.[51] What is the measure of damages in an action in deceit? In *McAllister* v. *Richmond Brewing Company (N.S.W.) Pty Ltd* Jordan C.J. referred to the well-established rule of practice that 'where a person complains that he has been induced by deceit to buy something and pay more for it than it was worth, the amount of damages which he is entitled to recover is restricted, *prima facie* at any rate, to the amount by which the price which he paid exceeds the true value of the thing bought at the time when he bought it'.[52] But Jordan C.J. did indicate that the measure of damages ought never to be governed by mere rules of practice and it now seems that the courts are prepared in actions in deceit to award more than the difference between the real value of the property and the sum which the plaintiff was induced to give for it by the deceit. The decision of the High Court of Australia in *State of South Australia* v. *Johnson*[53] suggests that in actions in deceit the damages which are recoverable will include the whole loss directly flowing from the fraudulent inducement. Even those losses not reasonably foreseeable are recoverable, because, as Lord Denning M.R. said in *Doyle* v. *Olby (Ironmongers) Ltd*, 'it does not lie in the mouth of fraudulent persons to say that they could not reasonably have been foreseen'.[54] So a

---

49 ibid., 70.
50 See *Gould* v. *Vaggelas* (1984) 56 A.L.R. 31, 47. See also *Holmes* v. *Jones* (1907) 4 C.L.R. 1692, 1706 and *Potts* v. *Miller* (1940) 64 C.L.R. 282, 296.
51 *De Vries* v. *Wightman* [1961] Qd.R. 196, 201.
52 (1942) 42 S.R.(N.S.W.) 187, 192.
53 (1982) 42 A.L.R. 161, 169-70. See, however, *Toteff* v. *Antonas* (1952) 87 C.L.R. 647 and *Alati* v. *Kruger* (1955) 94 C.L.R. 216.
54 [1969] 2 Q.B. 158, 167.

plaintiff is entitled not only to those losses which are the immediate result of the fraudulent act of the defendant but also to those direct *consequential* losses which are not rendered too remote by the plaintiff's own conduct. It is not necessary for recoverability that the defendant should have foreseen such consequential loss. Thus the measure of damages to be recovered in an action in deceit can exceed the difference in value between the amount paid by the plaintiff as a result of the deceit and the true value of the property or the business at the time of the purchase. If a plaintiff suffers losses in carrying on the business those losses are also recoverable, provided they are actual losses flowing directly from the fraudulent inducement. The plaintiff can also recover expenses reasonably and properly incurred, including bank interest on any money borrowed as a result of the deceit.[55]

The question of the measure of damages in deceit when the victim is not the purchaser but, for example, a lender or guarantor, was raised for decision in *Gould* v. *Vaggelas*.[56] The High Court of Australia held that the measure of damages in these circumstances is the sum which represents the loss suffered because of altering his position in reliance on the fraudulent misrepresentation. As Brennan J. said: 'A sum representing his net prejudice or disadvantage is recoverable as damages in deceit'.[57] Where a plaintiff has been permanently deprived of his goods as a result of the defendant's deceit, the correct measure of the plaintiff's damages is the same as in the tort of conversion, namely, the market value of the goods and not the cost of replacing them and the market price is ascertained by asking the question: what price would the plaintiff have been able to obtain for the goods if he had not been deceived into selling them to the defendant?[58]

The decision in *Archer* v. *Brown*[59] suggests that aggravated damages may be awarded in an action in deceit and in Australia, at least, there is no reason why exemplary damages may not be awarded in appropriate circumstances. In the recent decision in *Musca* v. *Astle Corporation*,[60] French J. in the Federal Court of Australia awarded one of the plaintiffs $1200 by way of exemplary damages in an action for the tort of deceit.

III: INJURIOUS FALSEHOOD

The tort of injurious falsehood is essentially an action on the case for words which disparage the plaintiff's goods. At different times and in different places this tort has been given different names: 'slander of title', 'slander of goods', 'disparagement of property' and 'injurious falsehood'. Today it is generally accepted that the tort of injurious falsehood embraces

55 See *Archer* v. *Brown* [1984] 2 All E.R. 267.
56 (1984) 56 A.L.R. 31.
57 ibid., 60.
58 See *Smith Kline & French Laboratories Ltd* v. *Long* [1988] 3 All E.R. 887, 895.
59 See *Archer* v. *Brown* [1984] 2 All E.R. 267, 283..
60 (1988) 80 A.L.R. 251, 269.

all these actions on the case for words which disparage the plaintiff's goods and we shall, therefore, use the words 'injurious falsehood' to describe comprehensively all those other actions.

A definition of the tort which is usually referred to is that given by Bowen L.J. in *Ratcliffe* v. *Evans*.[61] In that case, the plaintiff, who had for many years carried on the business of an engineer and boiler-maker under the name of 'Ratcliffe & Sons', and who was entitled to the goodwill of the business, brought an action against the defendant, who published a weekly newspaper, when the defendant published a story in the newspaper which implied that the plaintiff had ceased to carry on his business of engineer and boiler-maker and that the firm of 'Ratcliffe & Sons' did not then exist. The jury thought that the plaintiff's business suffered injury to the extent of £120 from the publication of that statement and judgment was given for the plaintiff for that sum. In dismissing an appeal from that judgment the English Court of Appeal confirmed that the tort of injurious falsehood was well established. As Bowen L.J. put it:

> That an action will lie for written or oral falsehoods, not actionable per se nor even defamatory, where they are maliciously published, where they are calculated in the ordinary course of things to produce, and where they do produce, actual damage, is established law. Such an action is not one of libel or of slander, but an action on the case for damage wilfully and intentionally done without just occasion or excuse, analogous to an action for slander of title. To support it, actual damage must be shown, for it is an action which will only lie in respect of such damage as has actually occurred.[62]

Though in 1892 the action of injurious falsehood was described as 'analogous to an action for slander of title', the tort of injurious falsehood today seems to cover those situations for which the action on the case for slander of title or slander of goods was developed.[63]

Early acceptance of the decision in *Ratcliffe* v. *Evans* and of the tort of injurious falsehood in Australia is to be found in the decision of the High Court of Australia in *Hall-Gibbs Mercantile Agency Ltd* v. *Dun*.[64] The defendants, in a newspaper published by them, published a notification which led the public to believe that the plaintiffs had ceased to carry on their business and that such business had been acquired and absorbed by the business of the defendant firm. Relying on *Ratcliffe* v. *Evans*, the High Court decided that if the plaintiffs could show actual damage they would be able to succeed in what today would be described as an action for injurious falsehood. However, as the plaintiffs had not led any evidence to show actual damage they had to rely upon another cause of action. This cause of action was defamation and the High Court decided that the untrue statement that the plaintiffs had ceased to carry on business and which the jury found was likely to injure the plaintiffs in their business

61 [1892] 2 Q.B. 524.
62 ibid., 527.
63 See, however, the remarks of Mason J. in *Sungravure Pty Ltd* v. *Middle East Airlines Airliban S.A.L.* (1975) 134 C.L.R. 1, 21.
64 (1910) 12 C.L.R. 84.

was defamatory matter coming within the words of s.4 of the Defamation Law of Queensland 1889 and actionable without proof of damage. It should be added that the plaintiffs in *Hall-Gibbs* by basing their cause of action in defamation rather than injurious falsehood had two advantages. They did not have to show damage and they did not have to show that the imputation was a disparaging one.[65] This interpretation of s.4 of the Defamation Law of Queensland 1889 was confirmed by the High Court in *Sungravure Pty Ltd* v. *Middle East Airlines*[66] when it considered the effect of s.5 of the Defamation Act 1958 (N.S.W.).[67] A majority of the High Court held that a statement that 'potential air travellers by Arab aircraft to wit by plaintiffs' Middle East Airlines faced a serious risk of hijacking by Israelis with attendant danger of death, grievous injury, suffering, inconvenience and loss' was defamatory even though the statement could not be considered as a 'disparaging imputation' as the plaintiffs' condition of being especially prone to hijacking by reason of its nationality was unconnected with any conduct on the plaintiffs' part. Mason J. thought there was no *a priori* reason why such a statement about the plaintiff, though it may also be a statement about his goods, 'should not be actionable as defamation rather than as an injurious falsehood'. He went on to say: 'Whether statements of this kind should be actionable in defamation rather than as injurious falsehoods is a matter on which there may be differences of opinion but this consideration cannot influence the construction of the section [i.e. s.5 of the Defamation Act 1958]'.[68]

Section 5 of the Defamation Act 1958 (N.S.W.) has now been repealed by the Defamation Act 1974 (N.S.W.) and there are therefore only two such provisions in existence in Australia at the present time.[69] There is no immediate fear, therefore, that the tort of injurious falsehood will be rendered otiose by statutory defamation provisions. However, it should be pointed out that in the Unfair Publications Act[70] proposed by the Australian Law Reform Commission, s.9(1)(c) makes it defamatory to publish 'matter concerning a person which tends . . . to injure that person in his occupation, trade, office or financial credit'. This provision would, therefore, treat as defamatory any false statement about a person which is likely to injure him in his profession or trade. Thus to say of a trader that he has

---

65 See *Sungravure Pty Ltd* v. *Middle East Airlines Airliban S.A.L.* (1975) 134 C.L.R. 1, 10 *per* Gibbs J.

66 (1975) 134 C.L.R. 1.

67 Section 5 of the Defamation Act 1958 (N.S.W.) had repeated almost verbatim the words of s.366 of the Criminal Code (Qld) which itself was a re-enactment of s.4 of the Defamation Law of Queensland 1889. The Defamation Act 1974 (N.S.W.), has repealed the Defamation Act 1958 (N.S.W.) s.5 of which was in issue in *Sungravure Pty Ltd* v. *Middle East Airlines.* There are still two equivalent statutory defamation provisions in existence in Australia: see s.366, Criminal Code (Qld) and s.5, Defamation Act 1957 (Tas.). Section 346, Criminal Code (W.A.), though it looks as if it is an equivalent provision, does not apply to civil proceedings.

68 (1975) 134 C.L.R. 1, 23.

69 See fn. 67 above.

70 See A.L.R.C. *Unfair Publication: Defamation and Privacy* Report No. 11 (1979) Appendix C. See also s.4(1)(a) of the uniform Defamation Act 1984 proposed by the Standing Committee of Attorneys-General as a result of that report.

ceased to carry on business would be defamatory;[71] to say of a shopkeeper that he has tuberculosis would also be an imputation capable of being defamatory as he is likely to be injured in his trade—and this would be so even though the condition imputed to him is one for which he is not himself responsible.[72] It would also be defamatory to say of a trader that through no fault on his part he will be unable to do business with members of the public henceforth because a certain trade union is picketing his premises so as to put him out of business.[73] Even statements made about goods which cast a reflection on a person would be defamatory and only those statements confined to 'goods alone' in the sense that they do not cast any reflection on the person would remain exclusively the subject of injurious falsehoods.[74] The enactment of s.9(1)(c) of the Unfair Publications Act in its present form would, therefore, render injurious falsehood near to superfluous because a person would much prefer to rely upon the remedy in statutory defamation, which, according to the interpretation of the High Court in *Hall-Gibbs* and *Sungravure Pty Ltd* v. *Middle East Airlines,* requires no disparaging imputation, no malice or any actual damage to be shown by the plaintiff in order to recover in respect of a statement which is likely to injure him in his profession or trade. But the enactment of the Unfair Publications Act may be some time away[75] and a brief look at some of the elements of the tort of injurious falsehood may, therefore, be useful.

In *Swimsure (Laboratories)* v. *McDonald* Hunt J. pointed out that the elements of a cause of action in injurious falsehood 'consist of a statement of and concerning the plaintiff's goods which is false (whether or not it is also defamatory of the plaintiff) published maliciously and resulting in actual damage . . . The actual damage done is said to be the very gist of the action'.[76] These three elements require some further consideration.

1. FALSE STATEMENT

The requirement for injurious falsehoods that there must be a false statement merely means that the oral or written statement which is disparaging of the plaintiff's property or business must be untrue.[77] While

---

71 *Hall-Gibbs Mercantile Agency Ltd* v. *Dun* (1910) 12 C.L.R. 84.

72 See *Sungravure Pty Ltd* v. *Middle East Airlines* (1975) 134 C.L.R. 1, 10.

73 ibid., 24.

74 ibid., 23: 'Thus, for a newspaper to observe in the course of a published report on the performance of a particular model of a car that it was unsafe would be to make a statement likely to injure the distributors of that car in their business; yet it would not be a statement about the distributors and would therefore not defame them. Conversely, it could well be regarded as a statement about the manufacturer of the car, viz. that it produced an unsafe product, likely to injury it in its business and therefore actionable by it' (*per* Mason J.).

75 In this connection see the criticism of s.9(1)(c) by Mr Justice Hunt in 'The Reform of Defamation', an address presented on 5 July 1983 at the Twenty-Second Australian Legal Convention, in Brisbane.

76 [1979] 2 N.S.W.L.R. 796, 799.

77 *Royal Baking Powder Co.* v. *Wright, Crossley & Co.* (1901) 18 R.P.C. 95 and *Roberts* v. *Gray* (1897) 13 W.N.(N.S.W.) 241, 242.

it is usual only to talk about false 'statements' it should be noticed that conduct can also be regarded as an injurious falsehood. Thus in *Wilts United Dairies Ltd* v. *Thomas Robinson Sons & Co. Ltd*[78] where the defendant put old stock of the plaintiff's condensed milk tins in circulation as being the plaintiff's normal standard stock, Stable J. held that the defendant's act amounted not only to passing off but also to an injurious falsehood. The conduct of the defendant was regarded as the falsehood. A statement by D to a third party that D's goods are better than P's goods has been regarded as a puffing advertisement and not as a false statement.[79] If a trader turns from puffing his own goods to denigrating the goods of his rival, the test of actionability will be 'whether a reasonable man would take the claim being made as being a serious claim or not'.[80] The courts are reluctant to go into the question of whether one product is better than another because then 'the Courts of law would be turned into a machinery for advertising rival productions by obtaining a judicial determination which of the two was the better'.[81] But a factual assertion that D's airline carries more passengers than P's airline or that D's newspaper has a bigger circulation than P's newspaper will be actionable as an injurious falsehood if the statement can be shown to be untrue.[82]

As the essence of the tort is that the falsehood deceives others about the plaintiff's property or business so as to cause the plaintiff loss, it is essential that the falsehood be communicated to a third party other than the plaintiff. In deceit, on the other hand, the falsehood which causes the plaintiff the loss is communicated to the plaintiff himself. This distinction is well brought out in *T.J. Larkins & Sons* v. *Chelmer Holdings Pty Ltd and Van den Broek*.[83] The plaintiffs, a firm of builders, sued the defendant, a company's architect, for failure to give a notice of practical completion which would have enabled them to collect their money from the company for whom they had built a block of flats. The action in deceit by the builders against the architect failed because, as Lucas J. of the Supreme Court of Queensland said, the architect's failure to give the certificate of practical completion, if it could be regarded as a misrepresentation, is alleged to have induced a third party to act to the detriment of the plaintiffs. Such a misrepresentation he thought was not a 'sufficient basis

---

78 [1957] R.P.C. 220.

79 See *De Beers Abrasive Products Ltd* v. *International General Electric Co. of New York* [1975] 1 W.L.R. 972, 978.

80 ibid.

81 *White* v. *Mellin* [1895] A.C. 154, 165 *per* Lord Herschell L.C. But see *Insurance Commissioner* v. *Australian Associated Motor Insurers Ltd [No. 1]* [1982] 1 T.P.R. 458. If a defendant says the plaintiff's methods are 'inadequate' the court will examine the question. See *The London Ferro-Concrete Co. Ltd* v. *Justicz* (1951) 68 R.P.C. 65, 68. See also *De Beers Ltd* v. *International Co. Ltd* [1975] 1 W.L.R. 972, 982.

82 See *Australian Ocean Line Pty Ltd* v. *West Australian Newspapers Ltd* [1983] 5 T.P.R. 265, 267. Though there is no admission there that it would be a case of injurious falsehood. In view of *De Beers Ltd* v. *International Co. Ltd* [1975] 1 W.L.R. 972, 978, the court may well ask whether a reasonable man would take the claim being made as being a serious claim or not.

83 [1965] Qd.R. 68.

for an action of deceit, although it is possible that it may give rise to an action for injurious falsehood'.[84]

It is for the plaintiff to satisfy the court about the untruth of the statements made by the defendant.[85]

2. PUBLISHED 'MALICIOUSLY'

It is not enough that the statement should be untrue, there must be some evidence either from the nature of the statement itself or otherwise to show that the statement was published 'maliciously'.[86] It has been suggested that this meant merely that the plaintiff had to prove that the defendant intended to disparage the plaintiff's goods by his false statement to a third party,[87] but the decisions which have considered the ingredient of malice in injurious falsehood present a different and, perhaps, confusing picture. In *Clarke* v. *Meigher*[88] Cullen J. of the Supreme Court of New South Wales said that malice could not be implied from the fact of publication, it is necessary for the plaintiff to prove malice. But what must be proved to prove malice?

In *Greers Ltd* v. *Pearman & Corder Ltd*[89] Bray J. at first instance thought that if a person says something that he knows to be untrue it is malicious *ipso facto,* because he has said something that is false and something that he knows to be false, regardless of whether his object in making the false statement was his own advantage or the detriment of someone else. In the Court of Appeal, Bankes L.J. thought the word maliciously meant 'with some indirect object' and Scrutton L.J. thought it meant 'with some indirect or dishonest motive'.[90] In *Joyce* v. *Motor Surveys Ltd* Roxburgh J. thought that 'if a person in pursuing an improper objective . . . publishes falsehoods he . . . publishes them maliciously'.[91] In *White* v. *Mellin*[92] Lord Herschell L.C. in the House of Lords thought that the word 'maliciously' meant either with an intention to injure the plaintiff or published with a knowledge of its falsity. He went on to say: 'one or other of those elements . . . must be intended by the addition of the word "maliciously"'. And in the recent decision in *Schindler Lifts Australia Pty Ltd* v. *Debelak,* Pincus J. in the Federal Court of Australia thought that the necessary mental element for the tort of injurious falsehood is either knowledge of falsity of the statement or reckless indifference as to whether it is true or false.[93]

---

84 ibid., 70.
85 *Roberts* v. *Gray* (1897) 13 W.N.(N.S.W.) 241, 242.
86 *Halsey* v. *Brotherhood* (1881) 19 Ch.D. 386, 388.
87 See F. Newark (1944) 60 L.Q.R. 366, 376. See also *Western Counties Manure Co.* v. *Lawes Chemical Manure Co.* (1874) L.R. 9 Ex. 218, 222.
88 (1917) 17 S.R.(N.S.W.) 617.
89 (1922) 39 R.P.C. 406 and 416. See also *Schindler Lifts Australia Pty Ltd* v. *Debelak* (1989) 89 A.L.R. 275, 290-1.
90 See also *Joyce* v. *Motor Surveys Ltd* [1948] 1 Ch. 252, 255 and *London Ferro-Concrete Co. Ltd* v. *Justicz* (1951) 68 R.P.C. 65, 66.
91 [1948] 1 Ch. 252, 257.
92 [1895] A.C. 154, 160-1.
93 (1989) 89 A.L.R. 275, 291. See also *Shapiro* v. *La Morta* (1923) 40 T.L.R. 201, 203.

In view of this confusing array of judicial pronouncements the following propositions of law, it is suggested, might be helpful in determining whether a statement has been published maliciously for the purposes of the tort of injurious falsehood.

If a statement is made by a defendant which he honestly believes to be true and the statement is made for the purpose of protecting or advancing his own interests and not for the purpose of injuring the plaintiff's property or business interests, then the statement is not published maliciously even though it is false and even though it is in fact injurious to the plaintiff's property or business interests.[94]

If a statement is made by a defendant which he honestly believes to be true but the statement is made not for the purpose of protecting or advancing his own interests but solely or primarily for the purpose of injuring the plaintiff's property or business interests then the statement, if it turns out to be false, is published maliciously notwithstanding the bona fides of the belief of the defendant.[95]

If a statement is made by a defendant which he knows to be false and the statement is one which either the defendant knows is likely to injure the plaintiff's property or business interests or one which he should know is likely to injure those interests, because the statement is intrinsically injurious,[96] then the statement is published maliciously even if the object of making the statement was not to injure the plaintiff's property or business interests but only to protect and advance the defendant's own interests.[97]

If a statement is made by a defendant who, though he does not know the statement is false, nevertheless makes it recklessly,[98] not caring whether it is true or false and the statement is one which either the defendant knows is likely to injure the plaintiff's property or business interests or one which he should know is likely to injure those interests because the statement is intrinsically injurious, then the statement is published maliciously.[99]

If a statement critical of a competitor or his goods is false and the statement was made by the defendant purely as an attempt to attract

---

94 *Clarke* v. *Meigher* (1917) 17 S.R.(N.S.W.) 617; *Mentone Racing Club* v. *Victorian Railways* (1902) 28 V.L.R. 77; *Balden* v. *Shorter* [1933] 1 Ch. 427; *Shapiro* v. *La Morta* (1923) 40 T.L.R. 201 and *Schindler Lifts Australia Pty Ltd* v. *Debelak* (1989) 89 A.L.R. 275, 291.

95 *Wilts United Dairies Ltd* v. *Thomas Robinson Sons & Co. Ltd* [1957] R.P.C. 220 and *The Royal Baking Powder Co.* v. *Wright, Crossley & Co.* (1901) 18 R.P.C. 95, 99.

96 That is, where injury to the plaintiff's property or business is 'inherent in the statement itself' (*per* Stable J. in *Wilts United Dairies Ltd* v. *Thomas Robinson Sons & Co. Ltd* [1957] R.P.C. 220, 237).

97 *Joyce* v. *Motor Survey Ltd* [1948] 1 Ch. 252, 255-6; *Shapiro* v. *La Morta* (1923) 40 T.L.R. 201, 203; *London Ferro-Concrete Co. Ltd* v. *Justicz* (1951) 68 R.P.C. 65 and 261; *Wilts United Dairies Ltd* v. *Thomas Robinson Sons & Co. Ltd* [1957] R.P.C. 220, 237; *Swimsure (Laboratories) Pty Ltd* v. *McDonald* [1979] 2 N.S.W.L.R. 796, 802; and *Grappelli* v. *Derek Block (Holdings) Ltd* [1981] 2 All E.R. 272, 274.

98 But it is not sufficient to prove that the false statement was negligently made. See *Mentone Racing Club* v. *Victorian Railways* (1902) 28 V.L.R. 77.

99 *Clarke* v. *Meigher* (1917) 17 S.R.(N.S.W.) 617, 622 and *Shapiro* v. *La Morta* (1923) 40 T.L.R. 201, 203.

business, then the defendant will be held to have made the statement 'maliciously' whether he knew that the disparaging statement was false or whether he had a reasonable basis for believing the statement to be true.[100]

It is for the plaintiff to satisfy the court that the false statement was published maliciously.

3. Actual Damage

It is well-established law that an action in injurious falsehood cannot be maintained without proof of actual damage.[101] As Tindal C.J. said in *Malachy* v. *Soper*, there must be 'an express allegation of some particular damage resulting to the plaintiff' from the injurious falsehood.[102] In *Burns* v. *Mellor*[103] the Supreme Court of New South Wales held that in an action of injurious falsehood it was necessary to allege not only the actual damage but also the circumstances out of which it is possible that actual damage may arise. And in *Lauchame* v. *Broughton* Stephen A.C.J., also in the Supreme Court of New South Wales, said: 'It has been laid down over and over again in the clearest possible way, first of all in *Malachy* v. *Soper* . . . and also in *Ratcliffe* v. *Evans* . . . that [any statement of claim in injurious falsehood] must be accompanied, not only by particulars of alleged loss, but of "actual loss" . . . It must be some loss *actually sustained*'.[104] The actual damage which is required by the courts must be a pecuniary loss.[105] In injurious falsehood a plaintiff can recover for any money loss such as the cost of circulars or advertisements to correct the falsehood, or the cost of getting an expert to reassure a third party that the aspersions cast on the plaintiff's specifications and designs are unjustified.[106] But a plaintiff cannot recover for injured feelings in an action of injurious falsehood.[107]

What if the only loss that the plaintiff has suffered is a general loss of custom? Is it sufficient to allege a general loss of business? If the nature of the business is such that it is impossible for the plaintiff to point to the loss of identifiable customers then damages in injurious falsehood will be recoverable even though all that the plaintiff can show is a general loss of business.[108] But, of course, his position would be much strengthened if he could show the existence of identifiable customers who have stopped trading with him as a result of the injurious falsehood.

---

100 See *Schindler Lifts Australia Pty Ltd* v. *Debelak* (1989) 89 A.L.R. 275, 290-1.
101 *Hall-Gibbs Mercantile Agency Ltd* v. *Dun* (1910) 12 C.L.R. 84.
102 (1836) 3 Bing. N.C. 371, 383.
103 (1892) 9 W.N.(N.S.W.) 38, 39. (The action was one for slander of title.)
104 (1903) 3 S.R.(N.S.W.) 475, 479 (emphasis added).
105 *Malachy* v. *Soper* (1836) 3 Bing. N.C. 371, 382; *Fielding* v. *Variety Incorporated* [1967] 2 Q.B. 841, 850 and *Jervois Sulphates (N.T.) Ltd* v. *Petrocarb Explorations NL & Others* (1974) 5 A.L.R. 1, 32.
106 *London Ferro-Concrete Co. Ltd* v. *Justicz* (1951) 68 R.P.C. 65, 69.
107 *Fielding* v. *Variety Incorporated* [1967] 2 Q.B. 841, 850.
108 *George* v. *Blow* (1899) 20 L.R.(N.S.W.) 395, 399-400 and *Ratcliffe* v. *Evans* [1892] 2 Q.B. 524, 533.

Even though there might be no evidence of actual loss suffered by the plaintiff a court will grant an injunction against continued publication of an injurious falsehood if there is a 'reasonable probability that actual damage will result to the plaintiff from the continued publication of the statements in question'.[109] This is one advantage which an action of injurious falsehood has over an action in defamation, where the power to grant interlocutory injunctions is exercised with great caution.[110]

IV: PASSING OFF

The action for deceit is available for the intentional infliction of economic loss which is inflicted when a defendant makes a false representation to a plaintiff who acts upon it to his detriment. The action of injurious falsehood is available when a plaintiff suffers economic loss because the falsehood deceives *others* about the plaintiff's property or business. The action for passing off, however, is intended to prevent economic loss by protecting the property in the goodwill of a business[111] which is likely to be injured by the misrepresentation made by passing off one person's goods or services as the goods or services of another.[112] The 'goodwill' of a business is 'the benefit and advantage of the good name, reputation and connection of a business . . . the attractive force which brings in custom'.[113] The economic loss which is suffered by the plaintiff, where there is a passing off, might be of two kinds. First, the plaintiff may suffer financial loss because on the strength of the defendant's misrepresentation the plaintiff's customers actually purchase the goods and services of the defendant instead of the goods and services of the plaintiff.[114] Secondly, the plaintiff may also suffer financial loss because, after having purchased the defendant's goods or services on the strength of the defendant's misrepresentation, potential customers of the plaintiff might be so disappointed with the defendant's goods or services that they stop purchasing

---

109 See *Swimsure (Laboratories) Pty Ltd* v. *McDonald* [1979] 2 N.S.W.L.R. 796, 802 where Hunt J. in the Supreme Court of New South Wales refused to follow the decision of the House of Lords in *White* v. *Mellin* [1895] A.C. 154, which held that absence of evidence of actual loss suffered by the plaintiff precluded the grant of an injunction, on the ground that the New South Wales Supreme Court had wider power to grant interlocutory injunctions than the House of Lords had in 1895. *Fleming* (7th edn, 1987) p. 673, however, suggests that in the absence of damage, even an injunction against repetition of the falsehood will be refused.

110 See *Stocker* v. *McElhinney (No. 2)* (1961) 79 W.N.(N.S.W.) 541, 544 and *Crescent Sales Pty Ltd* v. *British Products Pty Ltd* [1936] V.L.R. 336, 339.

111 The goodwill can extend to a religious organisation. See *The Holy Apostolic and Catholic Church of the East (Assyrian) Australia NSW Parish Association* v. *Attorney General; Ex rel Elisha* (1989) 16 I.P.R. 619

112 See *A.G. Spalding & Brothers* v. *A.W. Gamage Ltd* (1915) 32 R.P.C. 273 and *Star Industrial Co. Ltd* v. *Yap Kwee Kor* [1976] F.S.R. 256, 259.

113 *Taco Bell Pty Ltd* v. *Taco Co. of Australia Ltd* (1982) 40 A.L.R. 153, 169 *per* Ellicott J. See also *Inland Revenue Commissioners* v. *Muller & Co.'s Margarine Ltd* [1901] A.C. 217, 223-4.

114 See *CPC (United Kingdom) Ltd* v. *Keenan* [1986] F.S.R. 527.

goods or services of that type altogether, whether from the plaintiff or the defendant.[115] It is to protect the plaintiff against both these kinds of purely economic loss that the tort of passing off exists.

The action for passing off will only be available when the plaintiff has acquired a trader's goodwill in relation to the name, mark, get-up[116] etc. of his goods or services because they have become *distinctive* in the market or, as Ellicott J. said in *Taco Bell*, because they have 'come to mean *his* goods or services'.[117] It should be noted, however, that the common law action for passing off is, in a sense, only an additional remedy in Australia because trade names, trade marks, get-ups, designs, copyright etc. are today the subject of statutory protection in Australia by virtue of both Commonwealth and State legislation.[118] But trade names, trade marks, get-ups, designs etc. may for some reason or another not be registered,[119] be not registrable[120] or wrongly registered under the various Acts; in these cases the action for passing off will be a useful remedy. However, in addition to the legislation mentioned above, there is also in Australia the Trade Practices Act 1974 (Cwth).[121] Sections 52 and 53 of this Act attempt to prohibit 'misleading or deceptive conduct' and 'false representations' and 'false and misleading statements' in relation to goods and services. Certainly, s.52 has been used in addition to or as a substitution for the common law action for passing off.[122] What does that do to the common law action for passing off? In *Hornsby Building Information Centre Pty Ltd* v. *Sydney Building Information Centre Ltd*[123] it was argued that s.52 should not be allowed to be used by traders to enforce rights and protect interests more usually enforced and protected by recourse to a passing off action and that it should only be used for the protection of consumers as

---

115 See e.g. *Lloyds* v. *Lloyds (Southampton) Ltd* (1912) 29 R.P.C. 433; *Totalizator Agency Board* v. *Turf News Ltd* [1967] V.R. 605; *Henderson & Another* v. *Radio Corporation Pty Ltd* (1960) 60 S.R.(N.S.W.) 576; *Flamingo Park Pty Ltd* v. *Dolly Dolly Creation Pty Ltd* (1986) 65 A.L.R. 500 and *Sabazo Pty Ltd* v. *Ruddiman* (1987) 8 I.P.R. 599.

116 'The "get-up" of a product is the dress in which it is presented for sale, that is the shape, size and colouring of the container or packaging, the design of the label, and to some extent, the design of the product itself.' (D.R. Shanaghan, *Australian Law of Trade Marks and Passing Off* (2nd edn. Sydney, 1990) p. 408). See also *Reckitt & Colman Products Ltd* v. *Bordern Inc.* [1990] 1 All E.R. 873 (the *Jif Lemon* case).

117 (1982) 40 A.L.R. 153, 164.

118 See Designs Acts 1906 (Cwth) (as amended); Copyright Act 1968 (Cwth) (as amended); Trade Marks Act 1955 (Cwth) (as amended); Patents Act 1990 (Cwth) (as amended) and the Business Names Acts in the various States and Territories of Australia, e.g. Business Names Act 1962 (N.S.W.); Business Names Ordinance 1963 (N.T.) etc.

119 The design of the Contour suite which was in dispute in *Parkdale Custom Built Furniture Pty Ltd* v. *Puxu Pty Ltd* (1982) 56 A.L.J.R. 715 was not registered under the Designs Act 1906 (Cwth) (as amended).

120 See e.g. *Imperial Group Ltd* v. *Philip Morris & Co. Ltd* [1980] F.S.R. 146 where the word 'MERIT' being merely a word with a laudatory meaning was not registrable as a trade mark.

121 There are also various State laws relating to consumer protection. See fn. 461 at p. 293 below.

122 See e.g. *Taco Bell* (1982) 40 A.L.R. 153 and (1982) 42 A.L.R. 177 (Fed. Court, F.C.); *Hornsby Building Information Centre Pty Ltd* v. *Sydney Building Information Centre Ltd* (1978) 140 C.L.R. 216 and *Puxu* (1982) 56 A.L.J.R. 715.

123 (1978) 140 C.L.R. 216.

s.52 appears in a part of the Trade Practices Act 1974 (Part V) headed 'Consumer Protection'. The majority of the High Court of Australia rejected the contention that s.52 should be concerned only with the protection of consumers and not with the protection of traders who complain of the effect upon their business of the conduct of a competitor. Stephen J. thought it was inappropriate that 'the unambiguous words of s.52 should be given some unnaturally confined meaning because of the heading to Part V'.[124] Stephen J. then adverted to the possible effect that the jurisdiction conferred by s.52 of the Trade Practices Act might have on the common law action for passing off.

> If . . . the legislative prohibition can be enforced by an injunction which 'any other person' may seek (see s.80(1)), it then becomes possible for a trader, injured by the competition of his trade rival, to gain a remedy under the Act instead of having recourse to civil action by way of proceedings for passing off. The remedy in such a case will not, as in passing off, be founded upon any protection of the trader's goodwill but, being directed to preventing that very deception of the public which is injuring his goodwill, it will nevertheless be an effective remedy for that of which he complains. The provisions of s.82 . . . which allow a person who suffers loss by another's act which is contravention of s.52 to recover by action the amount of his loss, may render the statutory remedy even more complete.[125]

It is likely that the provisions of the Trade Practices Act 1974, particularly s.52, will make the action for passing off somewhat irrelevant in the next few years but meanwhile a consideration of some of the important aspects of passing off may be useful,[126] particularly as some plaintiffs continue to base their primary case upon the law of passing off.[127]

The tort of 'passing off' is committed when a trader[128] by an act or by a statement made to prospective customers of his or to ultimate consumers of goods or services supplied by him either misrepresents his own goods or services as being those of somebody else, or attaches to his goods a name or description with which it has no natural association, in order to take advantage of the goodwill attaching to goods genuinely indicated by that name or description. The action for passing off can be brought either when the act or statement causes actual damage to the business or goodwill of the plaintiff or in the case where an injunction is sought, where it will probably do actual damage to the business or goodwill of the plaintiff if the injunction is not granted to stop the conduct of the defendant.

---

124 ibid., 225.

125 ibid., 226.

126 See generally W.L. Morison (1956) 2 *Syd. L.R.* 50; W.M.C. Gummow (1974) *Syd. L.R.* 224; D.R. Shanaghan, *Australian Law of Trade Marks and Passing Off* (2nd edn. Sydney, 1990) Chs 20-2 and C. Wadlow, *The Law of Passing Off* (London, 1990).

127 See *Conagra* v. *McCain Foods* (1991) 101 A.L.R. 461, 470.

128 See *Australian Society of Accountants* v. *Federation of Australian Accountants Inc.* (1987) A.T.P.R. 40-796 where Woodward J. in the Federal Court applied the principles of passing off to persons who provided services in the form of a qualification at a price rather than being involved in trade, properly so called.

This definition might not embrace all the situations in which an action of passing off has been held to exist but it attempts to take account of most of those situations. Some matters in the definition require further explanation.

1. THE KIND OF CONDUCT REQUIRED FOR AN ACTION OF PASSING OFF

While a deliberate intention to deceive prospective customers of the plaintiff is usually present in passing off actions, the conduct which is required in actions of passing off is a representation, that is, an act or statement by the defendant 'which is calculated to injure the business or goodwill'[129] of the plaintiff by leading customers of the plaintiff or ultimate consumers of his goods or services to mistake the defendant's goods or services for the goods or services of the plaintiff. Lord Diplock in *Erven Warnink BV* v. *J. Townend & Sons (Hull) Ltd* (the 'Advocaat' case) further stated that if the injury was 'a reasonably foreseeable consequence' then it could also be regarded as 'calculated' or 'intended'.[130] So, the tort of passing off embraces not only deliberate and wilful conduct but also conduct which is substantially certain and even conduct which is likely to injure the business or goodwill of the plaintiff. As was pointed out by Gibbs J. (as he then was) in *B.M. Auto Sales* v. *Budget Rent A Car*, in an action of passing off 'fraud is not a necessary ingredient of the cause of action'.[131] It is, therefore, not necessary for the plaintiff to show that the defendant's act or statement actually deceived anyone or that it was intended to deceive prospective customers of the plaintiff or ultimate consumers of goods or services supplied by the plaintiff,[132] it is sufficient if the plaintiff can show that such customers or consumers were, as a result of the defendant's conduct, likely to be misled or even confused into believing that the defendant's goods and services were goods and services of the plaintiff or associated with the plaintiff.[133] If the plaintiff can show an intention on the part of the defendant to deceive prospective customers of the plaintiff or ultimate consumers of the plaintiff's goods or services or if he can show that members of the public have actually been deceived[134] by the defendant's representation into believing that the defendant's goods are the goods of the plaintiff that evidence will immeasurably

---

129 *Erven Warnink BV* v. *J. Townend & Sons* (Hull) Ltd [1979] 2 All E.R. 927, 933 *per* Lord Diplock. The decision is referred to as the 'Advocaat' case.

130 ibid.

131 (1977) 51 A.L.J.R. 254, 258.

132 See *Reddaway* v. *Bentham Hemp-Spinning Co.* [1892] 2 Q.B. 639; *Millington* v. *Fox* (1838) 3 My.&Cr. 333, 352 and *Australian Woollen Mills Ltd* v. *F.S. Walton & Co. Ltd* (1937) 58 C.L.R. 641, 657.

133 *Reddaway* v. *Bentham Hemp-Spinning Co.* [1892] 2 Q.B. 639, 644 *per* Lindley L.J. See also *Erven Warnink BV* v. *J. Townend & Sons (Hull) Ltd* [1979] 2 All E.R. 927 and *Cadbury-Schweppes Pty Ltd* v. *The Pub Squash Co. Ltd* (1980) 32 A.L.R. 387.

134 'Evidence of actual cases of deception, if forthcoming, is of great weight.' (*per* Dixon and McTiernan JJ. in *Australian Woollen Mills Ltd* v. *F.S. Walton & Co. Ltd* (1937) 58 C.L.R. 641, 658).

strengthen his case[135]—just as failure to show that anyone has been misled will be some evidence to show that no one is likely to be misled.[136] The fact that the act of passing off was done honestly or innocently will not assist the defendant if there is a probability of injury to the business of the plaintiff[137] and it certainly will not assist the defendant if on realizing that there is a passing off he persists in conduct which was originally honest or innocent.[138]

2. GOODS OR SERVICES

If a plaintiff is to succeed in an action of passing off he must establish that his goods or services have acquired a certain goodwill or reputation and that the defendant has misrepresented his goods or services as goods or services of the plaintiff. If a plaintiff has never had a trade or business it is difficult to use the tort of passing off even though the defendant might be exploiting the plaintiff's reputation as an Olympic champion in order to sell the defendant's goods.[139] The decision in *Henderson* v. *Radio Corporation Pty Ltd*,[140] however, shows that there can be passing off even where the defendant, in order to sell his goods, states or suggests that the plaintiff 'recommends or approves the defendant's goods or has had or has some concern or connexion with their manufacture or sale'. In that case the defendant, who was a maker and distributor of gramophone records, put a photograph of the plaintiffs, who were well-known professional ballroom dancers, on the cover of an instructional record, 'Strictly for Dancing'. This was done without the plaintiffs' knowledge or permission. The Supreme Court of New South Wales held that the plaintiffs were entitled to an injunction to restrain the defendants from disposing of any further record covers bearing a visual representation of the plaintiffs. The basis for granting this injunction to restrain the passing off was that, as Manning J. put it:

> The plaintiffs . . . had acquired a reputation which placed them in a position to earn a fee for any recommendation which they might be disposed to give to aid the sale of recorded dance music . . . The result of the defendant's action was to give the defendant the benefit of the plaintiffs' recommendation and the value of such

---

135 See *Parker Knoll Ltd* v. *Knoll International Ltd* [1962] R.P.C. 265, 278. See also *Conagra* v. *McCain Foods* (1991) 101 A.L.R. 461, 476. It should, perhaps, be noted here that in *10th Cantanae Pty Ltd* v. *Shoshana Pty Ltd* (1988) 79 A.L.R. 299 and in *Telmak Teleproducts (Australia) Pty Ltd* v. *Coles Myer Ltd* (1988) 84 A.L.R. 437, 466 Gummow J. argues that 'fraud is a concept of continued significance in the substantive law of passing off' but that view has not found acceptance in Australia.

136 *Reddaway* v. *Bentham Hemp-Spinning Co.* [1892] 2 Q.B. 639, 644 *per* Lindley L.J.

137 *F.M.C. Engineering Pty Ltd* v. *F.M.C. (Australia) Ltd* [1966] V.R. 529. See also *Baume & Co. Ltd* v. *A.H. Moore Ltd* [1958] 1 Ch. 907, 916; *Parker Knoll Ltd* v. *Knoll International Ltd* [1962] R.P.C. 265 and *Henderson* v. *Radio Corporation Pty Ltd* (1960) S.R.(N.S.W.) 576.

138 See *B.M Auto Sales* v. *Budget Rent A Car* (1977) 51 A.L.J.R. 254.

139 See *Wickham* v. *Associated Pool Builders* (1988) 12 I.P.R. 567, 577. The plaintiff succeeded, however, under ss.52 and 53 of the Trade Practices Act 1974 (Cwth).

140 (1960) 60 S.R.(N.S.W.) 576.

recommendation and to deprive the plaintiffs of the fee or remuneration they would have earned if they had been asked for their authority to do what was done. The publication of the cover amounted to a misrepresentation of the type which will give rise to the tort of passing off, as there was implied in the acts of the defendant an assertion that the plaintiffs had 'sponsored' the record.[141]

So, in an action of passing off, a plaintiff can protect not only his goods and services against passing off but also his 'right to recommend' goods and services. But this latter 'expansion of the protection given by the law of passing off'[142] will only enable an action in passing off to succeed provided the court is satisfied that the advertisement published by the defendant would be read as containing a representation that the plaintiff endorsed or was otherwise associated with the product of the defendant.[143] The protection also appears to be limited to persons 'engaged in business, using that expression in its widest sense to include professions and callings'.[144]

3. What Kinds of Misrepresentations Can Amount to Passing Off?

In an action of passing off the plaintiff will need to show that the defendant's acts or statements (his representations or, more correctly, his misrepresentations) have caused, or will in all probability cause, prospective customers of the plaintiff or ultimate consumers of goods or services supplied by him, to believe that the defendant's goods or services are those of the plaintiff or that the defendant's business is in some way associated with the plaintiff. It is the making of a misrepresentation to consumers, not damage to a rival trader, which is the critical consideration in actions in passing off (as well as in actions under s.52 of the Trade Practices Act).[145] These misrepresentations are many and varied and it might be useful to look at some of them.

(a) Misrepresenting that defendant's goods are products of the plaintiff

If a defendant tries to sell his goods with a statement that the goods are the products of the plaintiff then this is a clear case of passing off.[146] In the recent decision of the House of Lords in *Reckitt & Colman Products Ltd* v. *Borden Inc.*, however, Lord Jauncey said 'it is not essential to the success of a passing-off action that the defendant should misrepresent his goods

---

141 ibid., 603.

142 See *10th Cantanae Pty Ltd* v. *Shoshana Pty Ltd* (1988) 79 A.L.R. 299, 300 *per* Wilcox J.

143 ibid. The word 'associated' is here used as meaning a connection other than one relating to quality or endorsement. See *Hogan* v. *Koala Dundee Pty Ltd* (1988) 83 A.L.R. 187, 198.

144 See *Henderson* v. *Radio Corp. Pty Ltd* (1960) S.R. (N.S.W.) 576, 590.

145 See *Sitmar Cruises Ltd* v. *Carnival Cruise Lines Inc.* (1986) A.T.P.R. 40-728 at 47, 951. *Telmak Teleproducts (Australia) Pty Ltd* v. *Coles Myer Ltd* (1989) A.T.P.R. 40-966 and *TV-am p.l.c.* v. *Amalgamated Television Services Pty Ltd (ATN Channel 7)* (1988) A.T.P.R. 40-891.

146 *Byron (Lord)* v. *Johnston* (1816) 2 Mer. 29.

as those of the plaintiff. It is sufficient that he misrepresents his goods in such a way that it is a reasonably foreseeable consequence of the misrepresentation that the plaintiff's business or goodwill will be damaged'.[147]

(b) Misrepresenting one class of plaintiff's products as another If a defendant attempts to sell goods of the plaintiff of a particular class or quality as goods of another class or quality that can amount to passing off.[148] In *Hennessy* v. *White*[149] the defendants sold the plaintiff's cask brandy as the plaintiff's bottled brandy (the latter being of superior quality). The Supreme Court of Victoria decided that the plaintiff was entitled to an injunction to restrain the passing off. In *Hennessy* v. *White* the defendants were passing off the plaintiff's inferior goods for the superior goods of the plaintiff but in the later case of *Ingram & Sons* v. *The India Rubber Gutta Percha, and Telegraph Co. Ltd*[150] the Supreme Court of Victoria held that there can be a passing off even if the two brands of the plaintiff's goods are in all respects practically equal. If the distinction between the two classes of goods is recognized only by the trade and not by members of the public that is sufficient for establishing passing off of one class of the plaintiff's goods for another class.[151]

(c) Misrepresentation by using plaintiff's name If a defendant uses a name which is not his but which is identical to or so nearly resembles the name of the plaintiff as to be calculated or likely to mislead or deceive the public into the belief that his business is the same as the plaintiff's then the use of that name can be restrained by an action in passing off. Even if the name is his own name it may not be used, for, as Swinfen Eady C.J. said in *Teofani & Co. Ltd* v. *A. Teofani*, 'a man may not by the use of his name or otherwise pass off his goods as and for the goods of another'.[152] Thus in *Jenyns* v. *Jenyns & Others*,[153] the defendant, who was the husband of the plaintiff, was restrained from passing off certain goods under the name 'Jenyns' even though it was his own name. As Woolcock J. said:

> Where two persons have the same name, one of whom has, for many years, traded in a certain well-known class of goods and those goods have, under that name, established a considerable reputation, and the other of such persons commences to trade in that class of goods, it is the duty of such last-mentioned person to exercise great care so that his goods may be clearly distinguishable from those of the first-mentioned person. It is quite hopeless to say that a man may so use his name

147 See [1990] 1 All E.R. 873, 890.

148 See *A.G. Spalding & Bros.* v. *A.W. Gamage Ltd* (1915) 32 R.P.C. 273. See also *Gillette Safety Razor Co. & Gillette Safety Razor Ltd* v. *Franks* (1924) 20 T.L.R. 606.

149 (1869) 6 W.W. & a'B 216.

150 (1903) 29 V.L.R. 172.

151 See *Wilts United Dairies Ltd* v. *Thomas Robinson Sons & Co. Ltd* [1957] R.P.C. 220.

152 [1913] 2 Ch. 545, 565. See also *Gollel Holdings Pty Ltd* v. *Kenneth Maurer Funerals Pty Ltd* (1987) A.T.P.R. 40, 790 at 48, 618 and the cases there cited and *Boswell-Wilkie Circus Pty Ltd* v. *Brian Boswell Circus Pty Ltd* [1986] F.S.R. 479. See, however, *Cameron Real Estate Pty Ltd* v. *D.J. Cameron* (1984) 73 F.L.R. 99.

153 [1927] St.R.Qd. 313.

as to take away or to appropriate . . . to himself the business or the goods of another person of the same name. He must be prevented from carrying on a practice which is alike against law and against fairness.[154]

In *Parkdale Custom Built Furniture Pty Ltd* v. *Puxu Pty Ltd* Murphy J. gave the following example:

if a publisher puts out novels authored by Jane Austen, although the Jane Austen concerned (using her real name) is not the Jane Austen of *Sense and Sensibility* fame, unless a clear distinction between the well-known and the other is drawn, this conduct would be misleading or deceptive.[155]

It would also be actionable as passing off.

(d) Misrepresentation by using the plaintiff's trade name One of the ways in which passing off may be committed is that the defendant by the adoption[156] or use[157] of a name similar to the plaintiff's trade name may deceive or confuse members of the public into thinking that the business of the defendant is in some way associated with the business of the plaintiff and this might undermine the plaintiff's goodwill. Such a claim was made in two recent cases in the Federal Court of Australia: *Taco Bell Pty Ltd* v. *Taco Company of Australia Ltd*[158] and *Cue Designs Pty Ltd* v. *Playboy Enterprises Pty Ltd.*[159] In the *Taco Bell* case Ellicott J. granted injunctions pursuant to s.52 of the Trade Practices Act and the general law of passing off to restrain the defendant from operating any restaurants in the Sydney metropolitan area under the name 'Taco Bell' or under any name similar thereto. But in *Cue Designs* the plaintiffs, who manufactured and sold female apparel, failed to get an injunction to restrain the defendants from operating a restaurant named 'The Cue Restaurant'. Fisher J. decided that there was no passing off because the plaintiff had not acquired a significant reputation or goodwill in Adelaide in respect of their business and that they had not established some actual or probable damage.

These two cases show that while the courts are prepared in actions of passing off to restrain the defendant from using the plaintiff's trade name, or one similar to it, if it undermines the plaintiff's goodwill by deceiving or confusing members of the public into thinking that the business of the

---

154 ibid., 341-2.

155 (1982) 56 A.L.J.R. 715, 723.

156 See *Fletcher Challenge Ltd* v. *Fletcher Challenge Pty Ltd* [1981] 1 N.S.W.L.R. 196; *Harrods Ltd* v. *R. Harrod Ltd* (1923) 40 T.L.R. 195; *Australian Marketing Development Pty Ltd* v. *Australian Interstate Marketing Pty Ltd* [1972] V.R. 219; *Westpac Banking Corporation* v. *Goodmaker Leasing Corporation Berhad* (1986) 8 I.P.R. 9 and *Burswood Management Ltd* v. *Burswood Casino View Motel/Hotel Pty Ltd* (1987) A.T.P.R. 48, 911.

157 See *Whatmore* v. *General Transport Co. Ltd* [1947] St.R.Qd. 219. See also *Australian National Airlines Commission* v. *Trans-Australia Transport Pty Ltd* [1961] Q.W.N. 16; *Maxim's Ltd* v. *Dye* [1977] 1 W.L.R. 1155 and *10th Cantanae Pty Ltd* v. *Shoshana Pty Ltd* (1988) 79 A.L.R. 299.

158 (1981) 40 A.L.R. 153; (1982) 42 A.L.R. 177 (Fed. Court, F.C.).

159 (1983) 45 A.L.R. 535.

defendant is in some way associated with the business of the plaintiff,[160] they will only do so if the plaintiff has acquired a significant local reputation or goodwill in respect of that trade name. It would appear that if the misrepresentation gives people who might be expected to buy or use the goods cause to wonder whether the two products come from the same source that is sufficient confusion for an action in passing off, though it would not be sufficient for an action under s.52 of the Trade Practices Act.[161] Even though it is not necessary for the plaintiff to establish any overlapping of the fields of activity to succeed in an action of passing off,[162] nevertheless, as the plaintiff must establish actual or probable damage to succeed, the chances of success will not be great where the parties are operating different businesses totally dissociated from each other, such as the Cue Shop and the Cue Restaurant.[163]

The use by a defendant of a descriptive name which is similar to the plaintiff's trade name will not usually cause an action in passing off to arise. If A describes his art gallery as A's Art Gallery there will be no passing off if B describes his art gallery as B's Art Gallery but there would be passing off if B describes his art gallery as A's Art Gallery.[164] This approach is taken 'because everyone has the privilege to use words which belong to the common stock of language' and because the courts are reluctant to create monopolies (by creating a monopoly in the use of descriptive words) which would have the effect of deterring new entrants into a field which ought to be open to legitimate competition. A similar approach to descriptive names was taken in relation to words which are descriptive, such as 'The Zoo', even though the words were not strictly descriptive of the place to which they were applied, namely, a discotheque.[165]

However, as Gibbs J. indicated in *Budget Rent A Car*, even *descriptive* words might sometimes become *distinctive* of the plaintiff's business and

---

160 See *Lloyd's Shipping Holdings Pty Ltd* v. *Davros Pty Ltd* (1987) 72 A.L.R. 643, 673-4; *INXS* v. *South Sea Bubble Co. Pty Ltd* (1986) A.T.P.R. 40-667 and *Ocean Pacific Sunwear Ltd* v. *Ocean Pacific Enterprises Pty Ltd* (1990) A.T.P.R. 41-027. See, however, *Barry* v. *Lake Jindabyne Reservation Centre Pty Ltd* (1985) A.T.P.R. 40-613.

161 See *Southern Cross Refrigerating Co.* v. *Toowoomba Foundry Pty Ltd* (1954) 91 C.L.R. 592 and *Parkdale Custom Built Furniture Pty Ltd* v. *Puxu Pty Ltd* (1982) 56 A.L.J.R. 715, 717.

162 See *Annabel's (Berkeley Square) Ltd* v. *G. Schock* [1972] R.P.C. 838 and *Fido Dido Inc.* v. *Venture Stores (Retailers) Pty Ltd* (1988) 16 I.P.R. 365, 370-71.

163 *Cue Designs Pty Ltd* v. *Playboy Enterprises Pty Ltd* (1983) 45 A.L.R. 535, 541. See also *Chase Manhattan Overseas Corp.* v. *Chase Corp. Ltd* [1986] 8 I.P.R. 69.

164 See *Hornsby Building Information Centre Pty Ltd* v. *Sydney Building Information Centre* (1978) 140 C.L.R. 216, 231.

165 See *United Telecasters Sydney Ltd* v. *Pan Hotels International Pty Ltd* [1978] 3 T.P.R. 220, 226 where Franki J. said that the discotheque presented 'some of the features which persons associate with a zoo, such as animals and reptiles, even though only of a simulated nature'. Although this was a decision under s.52 of the Trade Practices Act the courts have considered it appropriate in applying s.52 to have regard to the principles relating to the action of passing off. See e.g. *Taco Bell Pty Ltd* v. *Taco Co. of Australia Ltd* (1982) 40 A.L.R. 153, 165 'it is appropriate, in applying s.52 to have regard to the principles relating to the action of passing off' (*per* Ellicott J.). Cf. *Taco Co. of Australia Ltd* v. *Taco Bell Pty Ltd* (1982) 42 A.L.R. 177, 197 *per* Deane & Fitzgerald JJ.

when this happens the defendant will be liable for passing off unless he clearly distinguishes his business, which uses those descriptive words in his trade name, from the business of the plaintiff. As Gibbs J. said:

It is true that 'budget' is an ordinary word, which nowadays is sometimes used to mean 'inexpensive'. The phrase 'rent a car' contains three ordinary words, and is commonly used to describe a business of a particular kind. However, it is clear law that a name composed of descriptive words may become distinctive of the business of a particular person, and if a plaintiff shows that the name in fact distinguishes his business and that the use of the name by the defendant is calculated to deceive persons into supposing that the business carried on by the defendant is that of the plaintiff, and is likely to cause damage to the plaintiff's business, he will be entitled to relief.[166]

The difficulty of distinguishing between words which are descriptive and those which are distinctive must be acknowledged, because words 'shade gradually and almost imperceptibly from one type into another'. It is for the plaintiff, whose trade name consists of descriptive words, to show that the words have become so associated in the public mind with his business that they have acquired a special and secondary meaning[167] distinct from their descriptive meaning. The defendant, on the other hand, can avoid liability in passing off by showing clear, even though slight, differences between the plaintiff's trade name and his own.[168] As Lord Simonds said in *Office Cleaning Services Ltd* v. *Westminster Window and General Cleaners Ltd*, 'the Court will accept comparatively small differences as sufficient to avert confusion'.[169]

When descriptive words in a trade name acquire a secondary meaning distinct from their descriptive meaning that trade name can be protected by an action of passing off.[170] But it does not mean that that situation will remain for all time. This secondary meaning can be lost. Thus in *South Australian Telecasters Ltd* v. *Southern Television Corporation Ltd* Walters J. of the Supreme Court of South Australia held that although the words 'New Faces' may have had a secondary meaning when the plaintiffs chose the title for its programme it was clear that 'by the overlay of promotional publicity and advertising, when the programme "New Faces" began, the words had ceased to have any distinctive signification identifying them with [the plaintiffs'] programme, and that to the ordinary member of the

---

166 (1977) 51 A.L.J.R. 254, 257-8. See also *James Watt Construction Pty Ltd* v. *Circle-E Pty Ltd* [1970] 3 N.S.W.R. 481.

167 See *Cut Price Stores Pty Ltd* v. *Nifty Thrifty Self Service Stores Pty Ltd* [1967] Q.W.N. 13.

168 See *South Australian Telecasters Ltd* v. *Southern Television Corporation* [1970] S.A.S.R. 207, 220-1; *Australian National Airlines Commission* v. *Trans-Tasman Transport Pty Ltd* [1961] Q.W.N. 16 and *The Australian Telecommunications Corporation* v. *Hutchison Telecommunications (Australia Ltd)* (1990) A.T.P.R. 41-008.

169 (1946) 63 R.P.C. 39, 43.

170 See *Reckitt & Colman Products Ltd* v. *Borden Inc.* [1990] 1 All E.R. 873, 885. See also *L.S.K. Microwave Advance Technology Pty Ltd* v. *Rylead Pty Ltd* (1989) A.T.P.R. 40-958.

public they were descriptive of a talent quest'.[171] This secondary meaning, it is suggested, can be lost not only by descriptive words but also by fancy words,[172] e.g. gramophone.[173]

(e) **Misrepresentation by using the plaintiff's trade mark** In *Schweppes Ltd* v. *E. Rowlands Pty Ltd*[174] Isaacs J. referred to the well-established rule at common law that no trader is justified in taking the peculiar symbol, device or mark, or any 'accompaniment', by which another man distinguishes his goods in the market, and so attract to himself the custom which would otherwise flow to his rival.

At the present time the best way to protect a trade mark is to register it under the Trade Marks Act 1955, but if the mark is not registered or registrable then the action for passing off will be useful. In order to succeed in an action for passing off, however, it is necessary for the plaintiff to prove a misrepresentation, but under the Trade Marks Act there is no requirement that there should be a misrepresentation in fact before an action can be brought. 'Once the trade mark is registered, it is an infringement for another person to use the trade mark or a mark which is substantially identical with it or deceptively similar to it in the course of trade in relation to goods or services in respect of which the trade mark is registered'.[175]

Cadbury Schweppes Pty Ltd & Others v. *Pub Squash Co. Pty Ltd*[176] illustrates that if a defendant sufficiently distinguishes his products from the plaintiff's products an action for passing off will fail even though the defendant fully intends to and does take advantage of the market developed by the plaintiff's advertising campaign for its own product—in that case the soft drink 'Solo'. The issue in that case was whether the defendant, by promoting its product 'Pub Squash', so confused or deceived the market that it passed its product off as the product of the plaintiff. The Privy Council in upholding the decision of the trial judge that no passing off had occurred said that the action would only be available if the defendant had invaded the plaintiff's 'intangible property right' in his product 'by misappropriating descriptions which have become recognised by the market as distinctive of the product'.[177] As the defendant 'never went so far as to suggest that Pub Squash was the product of the [plaintiff], or merely another name for Solo' the Privy Council agreed with the trial judge that there was no 'relevant misrepresentation', no deception or probability of deception sufficient to found an action of passing off even though the defendant took advantage of the plaintiff's promotion of its own product.

---

171 [1970] S.A.S.R. 207, 219.
172 Fancy words are invented words or words having no reference to the character or quality of the goods, not being a geographical name.
173 See *In re Gramophone Company's Application* [1910] 2 Ch. 423.
174 (1910) 11 C.L.R. 347, 357.
175 See Emmerson, 'Trade Marks in *Protecting Your Business Reputation*', proceedings of a seminar held in Melbourne on 13 September 1982 by the Business Law Section of the Intellectual Property Committee of the Law Council of Australia.
176 (1980) 32 A.L.R. 387.
177 ibid., 399.

(f) Misrepresentation by imitating the get-up or design of the plaintiff's goods In *Parkdale Custom Built Furniture Pty Ltd* v. *Puxu Pty Ltd*[178] Brennan J. of the High Court of Australia approved of the following passage from the judgment of Graham J. in *Benchairs Ltd* v. *Chair Centre Ltd*:

> The mere copying of the shape of the plaintiffs' article is not in itself such a representation [i.e. a representation by the defendant that his goods are those of the plaintiff]. Anyone is entitled, subject to some monopoly or statutory right preventing him, to copy and sell any article on the market, and false representation and passing off only arise when a defendant does something further which suggests that the article which he is selling is that of the plaintiff. This he may do by a direct representation to that effect such as by the use of the plaintiff's name or mark, or by an indirect representation such as by imitation of get-up by enclosing the article in a distinctive package which is similar to that used by the plaintiff.[179]

In the *Puxu* case the High Court of Australia decided that Parkdale, who had made a lounge suite called Rawhide, which was almost an exact copy of a Contour lounge suite which was designed and manufactured by Puxu, had not engaged in misleading or deceptive conduct contrary to s.52 of the Trade Practices Act because Parkdale had labelled the Rawhide suite in accordance with the practice of the trade and the label clearly distinguished that suite from the Contour suite. Brennan J., however, discussed the question of passing off.

> Of course, Parkdale was not free to pass off the Rawhide suite as a Contour suite, but there is no evidence that it did so. It used its own trade name; it affixed its own distinguishing label. Nor did Parkdale get up the Rawhide suite for sale in a way which would induce anybody to think that it was the Contour suite.[180]

Brennan J. then went on to point out that in passing off a distinction is drawn between the get-up of goods and the copying of the actual goods. 'Similarity in get-up may evidence passing off, but (statutory monopoly apart) all are free to copy the goods themselves'.[181] So a distinction is drawn between an imitation of the get-up of the goods and an imitation of the design of the goods. The former would, in the absence of some clearly distinguishing label, wrongly imply that the defendant's goods were goods put out by the plaintiffs and, therefore, constitute passing off.[182] But an imitation of the design of an article will not in itself be sufficient to found an action for passing off. If the shape, pattern, design or configuration of the goods has acquired a secondary meaning in the sense that the shape, pattern, design etc. indicates to a sufficient section of the relevant community that the goods made according to that shape, pattern or design come from a particular source, whether the name of the source is

---

178 (1982) 56 A.L.J.R. 715, 726-7.
179 [1974] R.P.C. 429, 435.
180 (1982) 56 A.L.J.R. 715, 727.
181 ibid., 727-8. See *Telmak Teleproducts (Australia) Pty Ltd* v. *Coles Myer Ltd* [1989] A.T.P.R. 40-966.
182 See *William Edge & Sons Ltd* v. *William Niccolls & Sons Ltd* [1911] A.C. 693.

known or not, then there might be a passing off to imitate those goods. It is not easy, however, to show that the shape, pattern, design etc. has acquired a sufficient reputation associated with the plaintiff. In *Starcross* v. *Liquidchlor*[183] Franki J. held that the apparatus in question had not acquired a sufficient reputation which resided in the plaintiff, even though the plaintiff had won an Australian design award for the piece of apparatus in question. However, in the recent decision in *Reckitt & Colman Products Ltd* v. *Borden Inc.*[184] (the *Jif Lemon* case) the House of Lords decided that the plaintiffs, who had been marketing lemon juice in the United Kingdom for over thirty years in convenient plastic squeeze packs of a colour, shape and size of a natural lemon (the *Jif Lemon*), could get an injunction to restrain the defendants from passing off their lemon juice as that of the plaintiffs by marketing their lemon juice in a get-up deceptively similar to that of the plaintiffs' goods (namely plastic lemon-shaped squeeze containers albeit with a different label). Lord Jauncey while acknowledging that a plastic lemon was a common shape which it was open to anyone who trades in lemon juice to use nevertheless said that he saw 'no reason why a trader should not obtain protection for a get-up whose shape and colour ingeniously alluded to its contents'.[185] Lord Oliver felt that the defendants' deception was not in selling plastic lemons but in selling lemon juice in containers so fashioned as to suggest that the juice emanates from the source with which the containers of those particular configurations have become associated in the public mind.[186] He held that the distinguishing label put by the defendants on their lemons did not sufficiently and effectively distinguish their goods from those of the plaintiffs and that it was 'no answer, in a case where it is demonstrable that the public has been or will be deceived, that they would not have been if they had been more careful, more literate or more perspicacious. Customers have to be taken as they are found'.[187] The effect of the decision in the *Jif Lemon* case is that the shape and configuration of a product where it is part of the get-up can be protected against deception by an action in passing off if the product has acquired a secondary meaning and the defendant in promoting or selling his own products with a similar get-up has not sufficiently and effectively distinguished his own products from that of the plaintiff.

(g) Misrepresentation that defendant's goods come from a particular geographical region In the usual case of passing off the defendant is held liable because he has by various misrepresentations, many of which we have considered, either deceived or confused potential customers of a particular trader (the plaintiff) into thinking that the goods of the defendant are the goods of the plaintiff. But what if the defendant misrepresents his goods as coming from a particular geographical region,

---

183 [1982] 1 T.P.R. 103.
184 [1990] 1 All E.R. 873.
185 ibid., 896.
186 ibid., 884.
187 ibid., 888.

which has acquired a high reputation for goods of a particular kind and quality, without necessarily implying that the goods are from a particular source, that is, a particular trader? Can this be regarded as passing off? In *J. Bollinger* v. *Costa Brava Wine Co. Ltd*[188] the plaintiffs were twelve producers of champagne who carried on business in the Champagne district of France and who sold champagne in England and Wales. They brought an action in passing off against the defendants, who were wine and spirit merchants in London, for selling in England wine made in Spain which they sold as 'Spanish Champagne'. The action was brought on behalf of themselves and of all other persons who produced wine in the Champagne district of France and supplied it to England and Wales. Danckwerts J. held that the defendants should be restrained from describing the wine made in Spain as 'champagne'.[189] As he put it:

> There seems to be no reason why such licence should be given to a person, competing in trade, who seeks to attach to his product a name or description with which it has no natural association so as to make use of the reputation and goodwill which has been gained by a product genuinely indicated by the name or description.[190]

There are three significant points about this decision. First, it extends the tort of passing off to misrepresentations made by a defendant that goods of his come from a particular geographical region when in fact they do not. The defendant does not have to misrepresent his goods as being that of another particular or specific trader; it is now sufficient for passing off if he misrepresents his goods as coming from a particular geographical region with which his goods have no natural association in order to take advantage of the reputation or goodwill which attaches to products which come from that particular geographical region.[191] Secondly, after *Bollinger* v. *Costa Brava* it would seem that a plaintiff who sues in passing off in respect of such misrepresentations need not have an exclusive reputation in relation to goods coming from that particular geographical region; it is sufficient if he is one of several producers of such goods in that region. Thirdly, as a result of the decision in *Bollinger* v. *Costa Brava* a passing off action can be brought by several plaintiffs[192] if all of them are in fact producers of goods in the particular geographical region in relation to which the defendant is attempting to pass off his goods; the goodwill attaches to all the traders who are able to say that their goods come from

---

188 [1960] 1 Ch. 262; see also *J. Bollinger* v. *Costa Brava Wine Co. Ltd (No. 2)* [1961] 1 All E.R. 561 (trial of the action).

189 A different approach has been taken in other jurisdictions. See the decisions mentioned in footnotes 197 and 198 below.

190 [1960] 1 Ch. 262, 283-4.

191 In *Vine Products Ltd* v. *Mackenzie & Co.* [1969] R.P.C. 1, 29 Cross J. described this misrepresentation as 'quite a different sort of deception from that usually relied on in passing off actions'. Earlier he had described the passing off in *Bollinger* v. *Costa Brava* as a 'special type of passing off'.

192 Until *Bollinger* v. *Costa Brava* cases where more than one party could sue for passing off were rare and usually involved two separate businesses derived from a common predecessor using the one name which name the defendant was attempting to use. See *Dent* v. *Turpin* (1861) 2 J. & H. 139 and *Southorn* v. *Reynolds* (1865) 12 L.T.(N.S.) 75.

that geographical region. In *Bollinger* v. *Costa Brava* there were twelve named plaintiffs bringing the passing off action on behalf of themselves and another 140 producers of champagne in the Champagne district of France. The decision in *Bollinger* v. *Costa Brava* has been followed in *Vine Products Ltd* v. *Mackenzie & Co.*,[193] *John Walker & Sons Ltd* v. *Henry Ost & Co. Ltd*[194] and *John Walker & Sons Ltd* v. *Douglas McGibbon & Co. Ltd*,[195] but the ramifications of that decision are yet to be worked out.[196] In Australia, for example, where the word 'champagne' means more often a product made by the *méthode champenoise* in Australia rather than wine from the Champagne district of France, it is unlikely that the producers of French champagne would be able to restrain Australian producers from calling wines made in Australia by the *méthode champenoise* 'champagne'.[197] It is perhaps for that reason that the applicants in *Comité Interprofessionel du Vin de Champagne* v. *N.L. Burton Pty Ltd*[198] 'made it perfectly clear that they do not seek to restrict the use of the word "champagne" by Australian manufacturers manufacturing wine by the "méthode champenoise"'.[199]

(h) Misrepresentation that the defendant's goods which contain different ingredients from the plaintiff's goods are the same This method of passing off is well illustrated by *Erven Warnink BV* v. *Townend & Sons* (the 'Advocaat' case).[200] The plaintiffs in that case were the manufacturers in Holland and their distributors in England of an alcoholic drink known in England and Holland as 'advocaat'. The principal ingredients of their 'advocaat' were eggs and spirits but no wine. The plaintiff Warnink together with a small number of Dutch manufacturers were, for all practical purposes, the only manufacturers of 'advocaat' which, as Goulding J. at first instance held, had acquired over a long period a substantial reputation and goodwill as a drink with 'recognisable qualities of appearance, taste, strength and satisfaction'.[201] The defendants produced an alcoholic egg drink made from a mixture of dried eggs and a Cyprus sherry and marketed it as 'Keeling's Old English Advocaat'. As it attracted

193 [1969] R.P.C. 1 ('Sherry').
194 [1970] 2 All E.R. 106 ('Scotch Whisky').
195 [1972] S.L.T. 128 ('Scotch Whisky').
196 See W.M.C. Gummow (1974) *Syd. L.R.* 224, 232-4.
197 Nor Canadian producers of 'champagne'. See *Institut National des Appellations d'Origine des Vins et Eaux-de-Vie* v. *Andres Wines Ltd* (1990) C.P.R. (3d) 279.
198 (1981) 38 A.L.R. 664, 666. The applicants' attempt to prohibit the use of the words 'champagne', 'imported champagne', 'Spanish champagne' or 'imported Spanish champagne' in relation to the wine Freixenet failed because Franki J. decided that the applicants had not made out a prima facie case of misleading or deceptive conduct under s.52, Trade Practices Act 1974. See also *Weitman* v. *Katies Ltd* (1977) 29 F.L.R. 336 and *Snoid* v. *C.B.S. Records Australia Ltd* (1981) 38 A.L.R. 383.
199 Legislation with regard to labels in various States of Australia prohibit the use of the word 'champagne' in the label attached to any package of wine 'when the wine is not produced by the traditional method of fermentation in a bottle'. See Food Regulations 1937 (NSW) r.63A(5) made under the Food Act 1989 (N.S.W.). Similar provisions exist in Victoria, Queensland, South Australia and Tasmania.
200 [1979] 2 All E.R. 927.
201 ibid., 937.

a lower rate of excise duty (being wine based rather than spirit based) the defendants were able to undersell the plaintiffs and capture a considerable share of the English market for 'advocaat'. The plaintiffs were granted an injunction to restrain the defendants from calling their alcoholic drink 'advocaat'. Lord Diplock thought that the same principle should apply to cases where the defendant misrepresents that his goods contain the same ingredients as the plaintiffs' goods (when in fact they contain different ingredients) as applies to cases where the defendant misrepresents his goods as coming from a particular geographical region.

> It cannot make any difference in principle whether the recognisable and distinctive qualities by which the reputation of the type of product has been gained are the result of its having been made in, or from ingredients produced in, a particular locality or are the result of its having been made from particular ingredients *regardless of their provenance.*[202]

It follows, therefore, that if a plaintiff manufactures goods with a certain set of ingredients and the goods being marketed under a descriptive or distinctive name acquire after a time a substantial reputation or goodwill it will not be possible for a defendant to market goods under the same name if his goods in fact contain different ingredients. This will be a misrepresentation sufficient to constitute the tort of passing off. The persons who can sue in relation to such passing off will be all the members of the class entitled to share in the goodwill and will include all those traders who have supplied and still supply to the relevant market goods which possess those ingredients. Any individual member of the class is entitled to sue in his own name.[203]

(i) Misrepresenting plaintiff's goods as defendant's goods Although in passing off the defendant normally attempts to pass off his own goods as those of the plaintiff, passing off can also occur when the defendant attempts to pass off the plaintiff's goods as his own. So, if a defendant buys goods from the plaintiff, who has an exclusive agency in those goods, removes the label and resells the goods in order to induce others to believe that he also is an agent of the manufacturer of those goods, then there is a passing off which has been described as a 'reverse' or 'inverse' passing off.[204] There is also a passing off if the defendants use the plaintiff's publications for the purpose of obtaining business for themselves without at the same time clearly stating that such publications have not been produced by the defendants.[205]

---

202 ibid. (emphasis added). 'The fact that the name advocaat differs from champagne in respect that it has no geographical significance seems to me neither here nor there. It does have a definite meaning . . . and the misrepresentation here was I think of exactly the same kind as in the Champagne case.' (*per* Lord Fraser at p. 942).

203 See *Scott* v. *Tuff-Kote (Australia) Pty Ltd* [1975] 1 N.S.W.L.R. 537.

204 See *Dwarkadas* v. *Lalchand* (1932) A.I.R. Sind 222 and *Bullivant* v. *Wright* (1897) 13 T.L.R. 201. See also *British Conservatories Ltd* v. *Conservatories Custom Built Ltd* [1989] R.P.C. 455.

205 See *Testro Bros* v. *Tennant* (1984) 2 I.P.R. 469.

(j) Misrepresentation must be in the course of trade In order to succeed in an action of passing off the misrepresentation must be in the course of trade.[206] The courts do not interfere to protect a non-trader. But, as Ackner L.J. said in the English Court of Appeal in *Kean* v. *McGivan*, 'the word "trade" is widely interpreted and includes persons engaged in a professional artistic or literary occupation'.[207] In that case the plaintiffs failed in an action of passing off to stop the defendants from using the name 'Social Democratic Party' even though the plaintiff had begun to use that name nearly two years before the defendants' political party came into existence. The court held that despite the possibility of confusion between the plaintiffs' political party and the later political party, neither was engaged in commercial activity and, therefore, there was no real possibility of damage to some business or trading activity. Such a misrepresentation could not, therefore, amount to passing off.

4. Must the Plaintiff Trade Within the Jurisdiction in Order to Bring an Action in Passing Off?

It sometimes happens that a plaintiff has a substantial foreign reputation in relation to his goods and services which he wants to protect in Australia. To what extent can he protect that reputation and, more specifically, must he trade within the jurisdiction in order to be able to bring an action in passing off? In the *Athletes Foot*[208] case in England, Walton J. indicated that there were two schools of thought about these questions: the 'hardline' school of thought, which maintains that it is essential for the plaintiff to have carried on a trade within the jurisdiction,[209] and a much less demanding approach, which suggests that something less than that will do.[210] In the *Athletes Foot* case itself the action in passing off failed because the plaintiffs could not show even 'one single solitary transaction by way of trade with anybody in England'.[211] However, in *Maxim's Ltd* v. *Dye*, Graham J. said that it was not correct in law to say that 'a plaintiff cannot establish that he has goodwill in England which will be protected by our courts without actually showing that he has a business in England'.[212] He held that the plaintiff, who owned a world-famous restaurant in Paris known as 'Maxim's', could restrain the defendant from opening a restaurant named 'Maxim's' in Norwich, England. The goodwill which the plaintiff had was in a sense a

206 See, however, *British Association of Aesthetic Plastic Surgeons* v. *Cambright Ltd* [1987] R.P.C. 548.
207 [1982] F.S.R. 119, 120.
208 *The Athletes Foot Marketing Associates Inc.* v. *Cobra Sports Ltd* [1980] R.P.C. 343.
209 Walton J. said this approach was best exemplified by *A. Bernadin et Cie* v. *Pavilion Properties Ltd* [1967] R.P.C. 581: the 'Crazy Horse' case.
210 Walton J. thought this appraoch was exemplified by *Maxim's Ltd* v. *Dye* [1977] 1 W.L.R. 1155.
211 [1980] R.P.C. 343, 357.
212 [1977] 1 W.L.R. 1155, 1159.

prospective goodwill 'none the less real in relation to any future business which may later be set up by the plaintiff in this country'.[213]

What is the position in Australia? There has been no authoritative pronouncement by the High Court of Australia on the matter, though there was a reference to it in the judgment of Gibbs J. in *B.M. Auto Sales Pty Ltd* v. *Budget Rent A Car System Pty Ltd.*[214] The position being open it is suggested that the courts in Australia should not adopt the 'hardline' approach, which maintains that it is essential for the plaintiff, in an action of passing off, to have carried on a trade within the jurisdiction, and that the relevant test which should be applied is 'does the plaintiff have the necessary reputation within the jurisdiction?' rather than 'does the plaintiff itself carry on business here?'.[215] In a sense this suggested test was applied in the *Budget Rent A Car* case even though the High Court found the plaintiff 'had commenced business activities in the Northern Territory'[216] before the defendant began to use the name Budget Rent A Car which the plaintiff was anxious to protect against passing off. In the *Taco Bell* case,[217] however, Ellicott J. in the Federal Court at first instance and Franki J. in the Full Court of the Federal Court preferred, it would seem, to ask whether the plaintiff itself carried on business within the jurisdiction, though Ellicott J. seemed to concede that a business could have a goodwill within the jurisdiction even though it has itself no place of business there.[218] Of course, in determining the question whether the

---

213 ibid., 1160. In a later passage Graham J. explains further what he means by 'prospective' goodwill: 'There ought to be no requirement that he must trade in England in order to prevent his reputation there being tarnished or stolen. If, in fact, it is permissible for a third party to steal his reputation and start a business ahead of him under the same name in England it may be very difficult, if not impossible for him to start trading in England when, as he may, he later decides to do so. It is in this sense and for the above reasons that earlier in this judgment I used the adjective "prospective" as applied to his English goodwill in such circumstances.' (per Graham J. at 1161-2). See however, *Ritz Hotel Ltd* v. *Charles of the Ritz (No.1)* (1987) 14 N.S.W.L.R. 95.

214 (1977) 51 A.L.J.R. 254, 258. Reference is there made to the rather inconclusive views, on this matter, of the High Court of Australia in *Turner* v. *General Motors (Australia) Pty Ltd* (1920) 42 C.L.R. 352.

215 This is the approach suggested by Powell J. in *Fletcher Challenge Ltd* v. *Fletcher Challenge Pty Ltd* [1981] 1 N.S.W.L.R. 196, 205. See also *Ramsay* v. *Nichol* [1939] V.L.R. 330, 342.

216 (1977) 51 A.L.J.R. 254, 258.

217 (1981) 40 A.L.R. 153 and (1982) 42 A.L.R. 177 (F.C.).

218 'Even if it has no place of business there people residing there may, nevertheless, be attracted to do business with it. For example, by buying goods which it produces and are sold there by importers, or by ordering goods from it by mail or by travelling from their residence to its place of business in an adjoining country. This "attractive force" is usually created because there has been some business activity in that place on the part of the owner of the business or those dependent on it, intended to so attract people. One cannot, in logic, exclude the possibility that it could exist because people who live there are prompted to seek out the business by a knowledge gained by them whilst travelling or living in another country where the place of business exists (e.g. a Hong Kong tailor). However, one thing, in my opinion, is clear, namely, knowledge by people in Sydney that a successful business is being conducted in the United States under a distinctive name does not give that business a reputation or goodwill here unless people in Sydney are attracted to do business with it despite the distance separating them' (1981) 40 A.L.R. 153, 169 *per* Ellicott J.

plaintiff does have the necessary reputation within the jurisdiction the question of its business activity within the jurisdiction will be relevant, but it is suggested that the fact that the plaintiff does not have a place of business within the jurisdiction or that it cannot show a single solitary transaction by way of trade with anybody in the jurisdiction should not be the only determining factor or factors in deciding whether an action in passing off is available or not. In the recent decision in *Conagra* v. *McCain Foods* Hill J. in the Federal Court of Australia expressed the view that 'the time has come to recognise that, although the tort of passing off is based upon the existence of a business or trade, it does not matter whether that trade or business is in fact itself carried on in the jurisdiction, provided that there is in respect of that trade or business, extant, a reputation in the jurisdiction'.[219] He recognized, however, that neither the decisions of the High Court nor the Full Federal Court had presently gone so far and he felt constrained, therefore, to decide that 'the tort of passing off requires the existence of a business in Australia (albeit slight activities will suffice)'.[220]

The plaintiff would, of course, need to establish the necessary reputation in each jurisdiction where it seeks to bring an action of passing off but whether this reputation is proved would be a question of fact and what is sufficient to prove the necessary reputation would vary from case to case.[221] In The *Cricketer Ltd* v. *Newspress Pty Ltd & David Syme & Co. Ltd*[222] the plaintiff, a company incorporated in the United Kingdom, which was the proprietor and publisher of a monthly magazine known as *The Cricketer*, was able to establish the necessary reputation in Victoria in relation to the name of its magazine by proving that during one month 123 copies of the plaintiff's magazine had been distributed by retailers in Victoria and that an undisclosed number of copies were despatched monthly by the plaintiff from London direct to subscribers in Victoria.[223]

Establishing the necessary reputation in one State will not, however, enable Australia-wide protection to be provided by the courts. In *Snoid* v. *Handley*[224] Ellicott J. granted the plaintiffs an Australia-wide injunction preventing the defendants from using the name POPULAR MECHANICS or the name POP MECHS or any other colourable imitation of those names, such as POP MECHANIX, POP MEX, or POP MX. But on appeal to the Full Court of the Federal Court, that court decided that the plaintiffs had not established the necessary reputation outside the cities of Sydney and Canberra and that, therefore, they were not entitled to injunctions restraining any conduct outside those cities. It follows, therefore, that in an action of passing off a plaintiff who seeks to protect his reputation or goodwill

---

219 (1991) 101 A.L.R. 461, 474.

220 ibid., 476. See also *Miki Shoko Co Ltd* v. *Merv Brown Pty Ltd* (1988) A.T.P.R. 40-858.

221 See *Paracidal Pty Ltd* v. *Herctum Pty Ltd* (1983) 4 I.P.R. 201.

222 [1974] V.R. 477.

223 In *Conagra* v. *McCain Foods* (1991) 101 A.L.R. 461, 483 the evidence of reputation took two forms: evidence of the plaintiff's advertisements in magazines with sales in Australia and evidence from persons presently in Australia who were aware of the plaintiff's product.

224 (1981) 38 A.L.R. 383 (a case under s.52, Trade Practices Act 1974).

in Australia must at least establish the necessary reputation in the jurisdiction where he wants it protected and that the necessary reputation in one State or city of Australia will not automatically guarantee protection in another State or city of Australia.[225]

5. REMEDIES FOR PASSING OFF

If a plaintiff can persuade the court that the misrepresentations of the defendant constitute a passing off there are several remedies which he can seek.

First of all a plaintiff can claim damages. In an action of passing off 'damage is presumed on proof of passing off and therefore a nominal sum by way of damages follows as a matter of course. General damages may, however, only be awarded if there is evidence of damage'.[226] As the law presumes that if the goodwill of a person's business has been interfered with by the passing off of goods, damage results therefrom; there seems no good reason why the right to nominal damages should not be available even where there has been an innocent passing off. In the recent decision in *Petersville Sleigh Ltd* v. *Sugarman*,[227] however, the Supreme Court of Victoria took the view that the only cases of passing off in which the courts have been prepared to presume damage are 'classic passing off cases of rival traders where the plaintiff suffers damage immediately the offending sale is made in that his goodwill in his trade is inevitably injured'[228] and that in cases of innocent passing off the courts are reluctant to presume damage.[229] Apart from nominal damages, actual damage which can be proved, such as loss of profits resulting from diversion of custom, damage to the plaintiff's trade reputation etc. can also be recovered. 'The more he can show that he has suffered damage in fact, the larger the damages he can recover.'[230] The weight of authority favours the view that 'fraud' is necessary to support a claim for damages (other than nominal damages), in passing off, but what fraud means in this connection is unsettled.[231] It might consist in persisting in the same conduct after notice from the plaintiff that the defendant's conduct amounts to passing off.[232]

Secondly, the equitable remedy of account of profits is also available to a plaintiff. This remedy requires the defendant to disclose and enables the plaintiff to recover whatever profits were made by the defendant as a direct result of the passing off. In appropriate cases a plaintiff may be given the

---

225 See also *Dairy Vale Metro Co-operative Ltd* v. *Browne's Dairy Ltd* (1981) 35 A.L.R. 494.
226 *Henderson* v. *Radio Corporation Pty Ltd* (1960) 60 S.R.(N.S.W.) 576, 594 *per* Evatt C.J. & Myers J. See also *Sabazo Pty Ltd* v. *Ruddiman* (1987) 8 I.P.R. 599, 607.
227 [1988] V.R. 426.
228 ibid., 442.
229 ibid., 430.
230 *Draper* v. *Trist* [1939] 3 All E.R. 513, 526.
231 See *Hogan* v. *Koala Dundee Pty Ltd* (1988) 83 A.L.R. 187, 201.
232 See *B.M. Auto Sales Pty Ltd* v. *Budget Rent A Car System Pty Ltd* (1977) 51 A.L.J.R. 254, 258.

choice to pursue a claim for damages for passing off or for an account of profits in respect of the passing off.[233]

Thirdly, the plaintiff can seek an injunction to restrain the passing off. In order to obtain a final injunction which prohibits, in the future, the conduct which is complained of as passing off, the plaintiff must be able to show irreparable injury, 'that is that he has suffered injury which cannot be properly compensated by damages, or that he will probably suffer such injury'.[234] But the injunction which is most often sought in passing off cases and which is the subject of some controversy is the interlocutory or interim injunction which can be granted at any time between the date of the issue of the writ until the final decision of the question by the court. In *Beecham Group Ltd* v. *Bristol Laboratories Pty Ltd* the High Court of Australia considered the two inquiries which must be made by a court before an interlocutory injunction is granted:

> The first is whether the plaintiff had made out a *prima facie* case, in the sense that if the evidence remains as it is there is a probability that at the trial of the action the plaintiff will be held entitled to relief. How strong the probability needs to be depends . . . upon the nature of the rights he asserts and the practical consequences likely to flow from the order he seeks. Thus, if merely pecuniary interests are involved, 'some' probability of success is enough.[235]

In *World Series Cricket Pty Ltd* v. *Parish*,[236] Bowen C.J. in the Federal Court pointed out that if the facts were seriously in dispute the court would not undertake a preliminary trial of the action in order to forecast a probable result, but instead would ask whether the plaintiff 'has a fair chance of success'. What is required for a fair chance of success will of course vary according to the nature of the case.[237] If the court comes to the conclusion that the plaintiff has made out a *prima facie* case for an interlocutory injunction the court embarks on the second inquiry, which is 'whether the inconvenience or injury which the plaintiff would be likely to suffer if an injunction were refused outweighs or is outweighed by the injury which the defendant would suffer if an injunction were granted'.[238] In deciding whether, on the balance of convenience, injunctive

---

233 See *Hogan* v. *Pacific Dunlop Ltd* (1988) 83 A.L.R. 403, 432.

234 *Henderson* v. *Radio Corporation Pty Ltd* (1960) 60 S.R.(N.S.W.) 576, 594 *per* Evatt C.J. & Myers J.

235 (1968) 118 C.L.R. 618, 622.

236 (1977) 16 A.L.R. 181. See also *Commercial Bank of Australia* v. *Insurance Brokers' Association of Australia* (1977) 16 A.L.R. 161, 168 and *Victorian Egg Marketing Board* v. *Parkwood Eggs Pty Ltd* (1978) 20 A.L.R. 129, 145.

237 In *American Cyanamid* v. *Ethicon Ltd* [1975] A.C. 396 the House of Lords thought that the first inquiry should be whether there is a *serious question to be tried*. In several cases after the *American Cyanamid* case Australian courts have decided that if there was a divergence between the views of the High Court and of the House of Lords as to the strength of the case which an applicant for an interlocutory injunction must make out, viz. whether it is necessary to establish a *prima facie* case in the *Beecham* sense or a serious question to be tried in the *American Cyanamid* sense, then it is proper for Australian courts to follow the judgment of the High Court in the *Beecham* case. See *World Series Cricket Pty Ltd* v. *Parish* (1977) 16 A.L.R. 181, 186 and the authorities there cited; cf. *The Cricketer Ltd* v. *Newspress Pty Ltd* [1974] V.R. 477, 483.

238 *Beecham Group Ltd* v. *Bristol Laboratories Pty Ltd* (1968) 118 C.L.R. 618, 623.

relief should be granted the court particularly takes into account any undertakings offered by the defendant in relation to his future conduct[239] and may take into account the laches of the plaintiff, especially if the delay has caused the defendant to alter his position to his detriment.[240]

If an interlocutory injunction is granted it is usual for the court to impose terms upon the plaintiff requiring him, in the event that his claim for passing off ultimately fails, to submit to such order as to damages as the court may make in order to compensate the defendant for any injury caused by the injunction. Likewise, if the interlocutory injunction is refused the court may require the defendant to keep an account of the profits he makes from the alleged passing off so that if he loses the case the plaintiff will be able to ascertain readily the amounts of profits in case the plaintiff wishes to resort to the remedy of an account of profits.[241]

V: INTERFERENCE WITH CONTRACTUAL RELATIONS

A knowing and intentional interference by the defendant with the plaintiff's contractual rights without justification is an actionable tort if the interference causes damage to the plaintiff.[242] The existence of the tort of interference with contractual relations, as a separate tort, is probably due to the decision in *Lumley* v. *Gye*.[243] In that case, the Court of Queen's Bench held that an action would lie in tort against the defendant for maliciously procuring a breach of contract between the plaintiff and a singer (Miss Wagner) who had agreed under a valid contract with the plaintiff to give her services exclusively to him for a period of three months, if it could be shown that the defendant had maliciously persuaded Miss Wagner to refuse to perform for the plaintiff and to abandon her contract with him during the contractual period. The broad principle enunciated in *Lumley* v. *Gye*, that an interference with any contract which causes damage to the plaintiff is an actionable tort, was affirmed by the House of Lords in *Quinn* v. *Leathem*[244] in 1901, though in the latter case the requirement stated in *Lumley* v. *Gye*, that the interference with the contract be done maliciously, was repudiated and substituted with the requirement that the interference with the contract must be done knowingly.

For an actionable interference with contractual relations to take place there must usually be a contract which is already in existence and which is interfered with by the defendant, either by inducing one of the parties to break the contract or by interfering in some way with its performance.

---

239 *Comité Interprofessionel du Vin de Champagne* v. *N.L. Burton Pty Ltd* (1981) 38 A.L.R. 664, 671.
240 *World Series Cricket Pty Ltd* v. *Parish* (1977) 16 A.L.R. 181, 190.
241 *Beecham Group Ltd* v. *Bristol Laboratories Pty Ltd* (1968) 118 C.L.R. 618, 623.
242 See *Davies* v. *Nyland* (1975) 10 S.A.S.R. 76, 98.
243 (1853) 2 E. & B. 216.
244 [1901] A.C. 495, 510.

The tort cannot usually be brought against a defendant who persuades other people *not* to enter into contracts or deal with the plaintiff.[245] But if there is a *regular course of dealing* between two contracting parties then the tort of interference with contractual relations may extend not only to existing contracts but also to those contracts yet to come into existence as a result of the regular course of dealing.[246] If a defendant induces another not to contract with the plaintiff that might attract tortious liability but only if unlawful means are used or threatened.[247]

The tort of interference with contractual relations can be used not only against a union official who persuades or procures workers to walk off the job in breach of their contracts of employment,[248] but it can also be used if the union official induces or procures the members of his union, by a directive, to work only from 9 a.m. to 5 p.m. in a job which is a 24-hours-a-day operation, for example, an airline.[249] It can also be used, and has been used, to bring to an end what is described as a 'secondary boycott'. In a secondary boycott situation a defendant union official may, as in *Torquay Hotel Co. Ltd* v. *Cousins,*[250] induce a supplier not to supply the plaintiff with a commodity until the dispute between the union and the plaintiff is settled. If there is a contract or a course of dealing between the supplier and the plaintiff, the court could hold the defendant liable for interference with that contractual relationship and order him not only to pay for any damage caused by that interference but also it can enjoin him from interfering with that relationship.[251]

The tort, therefore, covers not only interferences with contracts of service or contracts of employment, it also extends to interferences with commercial contracts, such as contracts for the supply of goods and services both with local and overseas suppliers.[252]

It does not seem to matter that the party induced to break the contract cannot be sued by the other party for breach of the contract. Nor does it seem to matter that the party induced to break the contract was 'even before the supposed inducement or procurement, very willing to break his contract'.[253] The person inducing or procuring the breach can still be sued for an interference with the contractual relations of the parties concerned. But it is not an actionable interference to interfere with a contract that is void.[254]

---

245 See *Midland Cold Storage Co. Ltd* v. *Steer* [1972] Ch. 630, 645.

246 See *Brekkes* v. *Cattel* [1972] Ch. 105, 114. See also *Torquay Hotel Co. Ltd* v. *Cousins* [1969] 2 Ch. 106.

247 See pp. 231-5 below.

248 See *Falconer* v. *A.S.L.E.F. and N.U.R.* [1986] I.R.L.R. 331.

249 See *Ansett Transport Industries (Operations) Pty Ltd* v. *Australian Federation of Air Pilots* [1991] 1 V.R. 637.

250 [1969] 2 Ch. 106.

251 See *Woolley* v. *Dunford* (1972) 3 S.A.S.R. 243.

252 See *Schindler Lifts Australia Pty Ltd* v. *Debelak* (1989) 89 A.L.R. 275.

253 See *Ansett Transport Industries (Operations) Pty Ltd* v. *Australian Federation of Air Pilots* [1991] 1 V.R. 637, 659 and *Woolley* v. *Dunford* (1972) 3 S.A.S.R. 243, 290-1.

254 See *Said* v. *Butt* [1920] 3 K.B. 497.

1. Interferences Which Attract Liability

There are three types of interference with contractual relations which would appear to attract liability in tort if the interference causes purely economic loss to the plaintiff.

(a) Directly persuading one of the parties to a contract to break it This form of interference takes place when the defendant directly persuades or induces a party who has a contract with the plaintiff to break it, as in *Lumley* v. *Gye*. It is not necessary, in the case of such direct interferences, for the plaintiff to show that the defendant used unlawful means such as a coercive threat to persuade or induce a party who had a contract with the plaintiff to break it—the persuasion or inducement is regarded as wrongful in itself.[255] In *Delphic Wholesalers Pty Ltd* v. *Elco Food Co. Pty Ltd*[256] it was argued that it was necessary to show that the conduct of the defendant amounted to coercion in the sense that it conveyed a threat to the person who had a contract with the plaintiff, but McGarvie J. rejected the argument, saying that a coercive threat is necessary to constitute the tort of intimidation but not the tort of inducing breach of contract. Even if the party induced cannot be sued by the plaintiff for the breach of the contract there can still be an actionable interference for which the defendant can be held liable.[257] And in *Falconer* v. *A.S.L.E.F. and N.U.R.* the plaintiff succeeded against the defendants in an action for interference with contractual relations, even though the defendants did not know of the existence of the plaintiff when they called an unlawful withdrawal of labour by British Rail employees and thus prevented the British Rail Board from fulfilling its contractual obligations to its passengers, of which the plaintiff was one.[258]

Though the distinction between persuasion and advice is a fine one, it should be pointed out that it is only the former that is regarded as an actionable interference. If a union official informs an employer that the plaintiff is not a member of the union and that he should therefore be dismissed in accordance with a current agreement between the employer and the union, the union official's action will not be regarded as an actionable interference with the contractual relationship between the plaintiff and the employer. It is 'no more than telling the employer the attitude which the union was taking up'.[259] Nor is it an actionable interference 'to use one's best endeavours to persuade somebody else to terminate lawfully a contractual arrangement'.[260] But a defendant who has persuaded one of the parties to a contract to break it cannot excuse

---

255 See *Woolley* v. *Dunford* (1972) 3 S.A.S.R. 243, 267 and *Davies* v. *Nyland* (1975) 10 S.A.S.R. 76, 98.
256 (1987) 8 I.P.R. 545, 552.
257 See *Torquay Hotel Co. Ltd* v. *Cousins* [1969] 2 Ch. 106 and *Davies* v. *Nyland* (1975) 10 S.A.S.R. 76.
258 See *Falconer* v. *A.S.L.E.F. and N.U.R.* [1986] I.R.L.R. 331.
259 See *Hymes* v. *Conlon* [1939] Ir.Jur.Rep. 49, 51 *per* Hanna J.
260 See *Emerald Construction Co. Ltd* v. *Lowthian* [1966] 1 W.L.R. 691, 695.

that conduct on the ground that it was open to that party lawfully to bring the contract to an end.[261]

So far as direct persuasion or inducement to break a contract is concerned, it does not matter that the breach was induced by *lawful* means. It will still be an actionable interference with contractual relations. So, if A persuades B by lawful means not to perform his contract with C, C can sue A for the tort of interference with contractual relations. The commission of this tort may also provide the *unlawful* means necessary if a plaintiff who is alleging an *indirect* interference with a contract between him and a third party, as in *Davies* v. *Nyland,*[262] is to succeed in bringing an action in this tort.

The party who is persuaded or induced to break a contract cannot, however, sue the person who persuades or induces him to do so; his only recourse is to withstand the persuasion or inducement.[263]

(b) Direct action not amounting to persuasion Another form of actionable interference with contractual relations occurs when a defendant directly prevents one of the parties to a contract, against his will, from performing his part of the contract.[264] This might happen, for example, when D physically detains a contracting party, T, or deprives him of his essential tools, so that he cannot perform his part of the contract with the other contracting party, P. Or if D physically prevents persons and vehicles from approaching and entering P's premises to fulfil their contractual obligations to P.[265] In these cases, there is no question of persuasion or inducement but the defendant is nevertheless liable for an actionable interference with contractual relations. The traditional view is that for these direct interferences to be actionable, the means of interference must be unlawful. So, if D hires all the available equipment in town, or buys up all the goods from a sole supplier, so that T is unable to perform his contract with P, D would not be liable for an actionable interference with P's contract with T as D has not committed any unlawful act. There are, however, some recent decisions which suggest that it is not necessary for these direct interferences to be unlawful.[266]

(c) Indirectly procuring the breach of a contract by another party If the interference with the performance of a contract is indirect it is generally accepted that for the interference to be actionable in such a case 'the means by which the interference is effected must be, or include, an unlawful act, that is to say an act which the law does not permit the defendant to

---

261 ibid., 701.

262 (1975) 10 S.A.S.R. 76, 100.

263 See *Williams* v. *Hursey* (1959) 103 C.L.R. 30, 77.

264 See *Ranger Uranium Mines Pty Ltd* v. *Federated Miscellaneous Workers' Union of Australia* (1987) 89 F.L.R. 349, 350-1.

265 See *Dollar Sweets Pty Ltd* v. *Federated Confectioners Association of Australia* [1986] V.R. 383, 388.

266 See J.D. Heydon, 'Interference with Contractual Relations: Recent Developments' in *Negligence and Economic Torts: Selected Aspects* (ed. T. Simos) (Sydney, 1980) 139, 142-3.

commit'.[267] This is the accepted view,[268] though as Bray C.J. pointed out in *Davies* v. *Nyland*, the distinction between direct and indirect interferences 'may have to be more thoroughly explored'.[269] A good illustration of this form of actionable interference is provided by the decision of the House of Lords in *Merkur Island Shipping Corporation* v. *Laughton*.[270] In that case certain union officials declared a ship under charter 'black', as a result of which tugmen employed by tugowners refused to move the ship, in breach of their contracts of employment, and the shipowners were unable to fulfil their contractual obligations under the charter. The House of Lords held that the shipowners had a cause of action at common law which was the tort of interfering by unlawful means with the performance of a contract. Lord Diplock said:

> The contract of which the performance was interfered with was the charter, the form the interference took was by immobilising the ship in Liverpool to prevent the captain from performing the contractual obligation of the shipowners under . . . the charter . . . The unlawful means by which the interference was effected was by procuring the tugmen and the lockmen to break their contracts of employment by refusing to carry out the operations on the part of the tugowners and the port authorities that were necessary to enable the ship to leave the dock.[271]

In addition to the requirement that the means by which the interference is effected must be, or include, an unlawful act, an indirect interference with the performance of a contract is only actionable if the breach of contract which the plaintiff is complaining about is a *necessary* consequence of the defendant's interference.[272]

2. CONDUCT OF THE DEFENDANT

For the conduct of the defendant to be regarded as an actionable interference, the plaintiff must show that the defendant *knowingly* induced or procured a breach of the contract. In order that the defendant may be said to have acted knowingly it would have to be shown by the plaintiff that the defendant had knowledge of the existence of the contract and had also an intention to interfere with its performance. Questions of knowledge and intention, however, often become inevitably intertwined in this area.

If a defendant knows of the contract and deliberately seeks to procure its breach he has acted knowingly, and that is an actionable interference with

---

267 See *Davies* v. *Nyland* (1975) 10 S.A.S.R. 76, 110. See also *Building Workers' Industrial Union of Australia* v. *Odco Pty Ltd* (1991) 99 A.L.R. 735, 770.

268 See *Woolley* v. *Dunford* (1972) 3 S.A.S.R. 243, 267; *Davies* v. *Nyland* (1975) 10 S.A.S.R. 76, 98; *D.C. Thomson & Co. Ltd* v. *Deakin* [1952] Ch. 646, 694-6; *Torquay Hotel Co. Ltd* v. *Cousins* [1969] 2 Ch. 106, 139; *J.T. Stratford & Son Ltd* v. *Lindley* [1965] A.C. 269, 324 and *Shipping Company Uniform Inc.* v. *International Transport Workers Federation* [1985] I.C.R. 245.

269 (1975) 10 S.A.S.R. 76, 99.

270 [1983] 2 W.L.R. 778.

271 ibid. 785.

272 See *J.T. Stratford & Son Ltd* v. *Lindley* [1965] A.C. 269, 333 and *Davies* v. *Nyland* (1975) 10 S.A.S.R. 76, 98-9.

contractual relations.[273] Even if the defendant does not know of the actual terms of the contract but had the means of knowledge it would be an actionable interference, because, as Lord Denning M.R. said in *Emerald Construction Co. Ltd* v. *Lowthian,* 'it is unlawful for a third person to procure a breach of contract knowingly, or recklessly, indifferent whether it is a breach or not'.[274] However, in the recent decision in *Schindler Lifts Australia Pty Ltd* v. *Debelak* Pincus J. in the Federal Court held that an alternative supplier of maintenance services is not obliged to infer, from the mere fact that a potential customer is already having its lifts serviced, that there is a continuing contract whose breach he must be careful not to induce.[275] In *Woolley* v. *Dunford* Wells J. of the Supreme Court of South Australia thought it was right to take into account not only what the plaintiff proved the defendant to have known or to have learnt about the contractual relationship between the plaintiff and third parties but also what 'he must actually have worked out for himself'.[276] There is a suggestion in *D.C. Thomson & Co. Ltd* v. *Deakin* that 'common knowledge about the way business is conducted' might be enough to establish knowledge.[277] This kind of 'constructive knowledge', which the courts are now prepared to accept, makes considerable inroads into the requirement of knowledge of the contract which the courts had earlier insisted that the defendant must have if he was to be held liable. And in *Falconer* v. *A.S.L.E.F. and N.U.R.* as we have seen the plaintiff succeeded against the defendants in an action for interference with contractual relations, even though the defendants did not know of the existence of the plaintiff when they called an unlawful withdrawal of labour by British Rail employees and thus prevented the British Rail Board from fulfilling its contractual obligations to its passengers of which the plaintiff was one.[278]

Although a defendant's conduct is considered to be *intentionally* interfering with contractual relations if it is deliberate or even reckless[279]—and such conduct is actionable under the tort of interference with contractual relations—negligent interferences with contractual relations which cause damage are only actionable, if at all, under the tort of negligence.[280]

It is not necessary for a plaintiff to prove that the defendant's conduct was aimed at the plaintiff nor is it necessary for the plaintiff to prove that the defendant desired to injure him in order to establish the necessary intention to interfere with the plaintiff's contractual relations.[281]

---

273 See *Quinn* v. *Leathem* [1901] A.C. 495, 510 and *Emerald Construction Co. Ltd* v. *Lowthian* [1966] 1 W.L.R. 691, 700.

274 [1966] 1 W.L.R. 691, 701. See also *Carlton & United Breweries Ltd* v. *Tooth & Co. Ltd* (1986) 7 I.P.R. 581, 625; *Delphic Wholesalers Pty Ltd* v. *Elco Food Co. Pty Ltd* (1987) 8 I.P.R. 545, 552, 553 and *Greig* v. *Insole* [1978] 1 W.L.R. 302.

275 [1989] 89 A.L.R. 275, 294.

276 (1972) 3 S.A.S.R. 243, 282.

277 [1952] Ch. 646, 687. See also *Schindler Lifts Australia Pty Ltd* v. *Debelak* (1989) 89 A.L.R. 275, 293.

278 See *Falconer* v. *A.S.L.E.F. and N.U.R.* [1986] I.R.L.R 331.

279 ibid., 333-4.

280 See *Caltex Oil (Australia) Pty Ltd* v. *The Dredge 'Willemstad'* (1976) 136 C.L.R. 529.

281 See *Edwin Hill & Partners (a firm)* v. *First National Finance Corp. p.l.c.* [1989] 1 W.L.R. 225, 234. See also *Falconer* v. *A.S.L.E.F. and N.U.R.* [1986] I.R.L.R. 331.

If a defendant reasonably entertains a bona fide belief that what he was inducing or procuring was not a breach of contract he cannot be liable under this tort. As Isaacs J. of the High Court of Australia put it in *Short* v. *City Bank of Sydney*:

If the defendant did not know of the existence of the contract, he could not induce its breach; if he reasonably believed it did not require a certain act to be performed, his inducing a party to the contract to do something inconsistent with it could not be regarded as an inducement or procurement knowingly to break the contract; if he believed on reasonable grounds that the contract had been rescinded, or performance waived, when in fact it had not, he could not be said to knowingly procure its breach. If this were not so, no man would be safe in the ordinary transactions of life, because he might find contrary to his knowledge or belief and expectation that some contract or enterprise he entered into was inconsistent with the contractual or other obligation of the party with whom he was agreeing or dealing. No doubt every man must be understood to intend the natural consequences of his acts; but that means having regard to the circumstances with which he is or is assumed to be acquainted. And the terms of an agreement and its true construction, for it may be very complicated, and the acts of the parties in relation to it are circumstances without knowledge of which reasonably brought home to the mind no man can be said to intend consequences regarding the breach of the agreement.[282]

In the more recent case of *Woolley* v. *Dunford* Wells J. of the Supreme Court of South Australia considered the question of the sort of proof which is required in relation to the conduct of the defendant in actions of this kind and came to the conclusion that:

When the claim is based on induced breach of contract, the relevant question is whether the defendant had sufficient knowledge of the terms to know he was inducing a breach of contract, the relevant question, when the claim is based on an interference with its performance, should be whether the defendant had sufficient knowledge of the contract to know he was hindering, or preventing, its performance.[283]

3. JUSTIFICATION

We have seen that an interference with contractual relations recognized by law is actionable 'if there be no sufficient justification for the interference'.[284] But what constitutes justification?[285] In *Brimelow* v. *Casson* Russell L.J. thought that 'no general rule can be laid down as a general guide in such cases'[286] and in *Whitfeld* v. *De Lauret & Co. Ltd* Isaacs J. felt that it should be left to each tribunal to analyse the circumstances of each particular case and discover whether a justification exists or not.[287] The problem is made more difficult, as the Full Court of the Federal Court

282 (1912) 15 C.L.R. 148, 160.
283 (1972) 3 S.A.S.R. 243, 270.
284 See *Quinn* v. *Leathem* [1901] A.C. 495, 510.
285 See generally J.D. Heydon (1970) 20 *U.T.L.J.* 139, 161-71.
286 [1924] 1 Ch. 302, 313.
287 (1920) 29 C.L.R. 71, 83.

pointed out in the *Odco* case, by the fact that 'the tort of intentional interference with contractual relations may be established either by the proof of conduct, the only unlawful element in which is the intentional procurement of a breach of contract, or by conduct which has the additional quality of being independently unlawful'.[288] The Full Court felt that if justification is a defence in both cases 'it does not seem right that circumstances capable of justifying an interference with contractual relations which is not otherwise unlawful should necessarily justify also an interference by means that are independently unlawful'.[289] It may perhaps be this kind of reasoning that inclined Brooking J. in the *Ansett* case to the view that justification is no defence to a claim for interference with contractual relations by *unlawful means*,[290] contrary to the view expressed by Nagle J. in *Latham* v. *Singleton* that a defendant in an action for interference with contractual relations even by unlawful means can avoid a verdict if he can establish a defence of 'justification'.[291]

Though the decisions of the courts do not offer very clear guidance as to what might amount to justification, the following discussion might be helpful in indicating what matters might be regarded by the courts as sufficient and what not sufficient to constitute justification. It would appear that a defendant is justified in interfering with the contractual relations of others to protect his own existing contracts if the later contract is inconsistent with his earlier contract.[292] An interference with contractual rights, it seems, may also be justified if the defendant has equal or superior rights to those of the plaintiff and acts reasonably to protect his own interests in accordance with those rights.[293] A defendant is also justified in interfering with contractual relations of others if he has statutory authority to do so[294] or if it is otherwise in the public interest.[295] An interference with contractual relations may also be justified if the defendant has a personal relationship with one of the parties and the interference is regarded as a moral duty. As Viscount Simon L.C. said in *Crofter Hand Woven Harris Tweed Co.* v. *Veitch* 'a father may persuade his daughter to break her engagement to marry a scoundrel' without being liable for an actionable interference.[296] And a medical practitioner might properly advise a patient to withdraw from a contract in the interests of his health.[297] What matters will not amount to justification?

288 See *Building Workers' Industrial Union of Australia* v. *Odco Pty Ltd* (1991) 99 A.L.R. 735, 771.
289 ibid.
290 See *Ansett Transport Industries (Operations) Pty Ltd* v. *Australian Federation of Air Pilots* [1991] 1 V.R. 637, 678.
291 [1981] 2 N.S.W.L.R. 843, 869.
292 See *Smithies* v. *National Association of Operative Plasterers* [1909] 1 K.B. 310, 337 and *Read* v. *Friendly Society of Operative Stonemasons* [1902] 2 K.B. 88, 95.
293 See *Edwin Hill & Partners (a firm)* v. *First National Finance Corp. p.l.c.* [1989] 1 W.L.R. 225, 233.
294 See *Stott* v. *Gamble* [1916] 2 K.B. 504.
295 See *Brimelow* v. *Casson* [1924] 1 Ch. 302.
296 [1942] A.C. 435, 442-3.
297 See *Building Workers' Industrial Union of Australia* v. *Odco Pty Ltd* (1991) 99 A.L.R. 735, 772-3.

The commercial or other best interests of the interferer or the contract breaker will not be sufficient to constitute justification.[298] As Brooking J. said in the *Ansett* case:

'Authorities I should follow establish that a trade union and its officials cannot set up as a defence of justification in an action for interference with contractual relations the suggestion that what they did was by way of performance of a duty to advise members of the union and protect their interests in relation to an industrial dispute . . . '[299]

Brooking J. went on to say that the view expressed by him has prevailed since the turn of the century and can only be challenged in the High Court of Australia.[300] Though Zelling J. (dissenting) in *Davies* v. *Nyland* suggested that the defendants in that case 'might well have had justification for what they were doing in that they were promoting their own interests and were not activated by a simple desire malevolently to injure the respondents',[301] that view might not receive universal acceptance in Australia[302] and union officials might well have to rely on legislation rather than the common law to justify interferences with contractual relations in furtherance of their own legitimate economic interests. It should also be noted that absence of malice or ill-will or intention to injure the person whose contract is broken will not amount to justification. As Slade J. emphasized in *Greig* v. *Insole*: 'it is quite irrelevant that the [defendant] may have acted in good faith and without malice or under a mistaken understanding as to his legal rights; good faith, as such, provides no defence to a claim based on this tort'.[303]

The onus of proving justification to the satisfaction of a court lies upon the party who has interfered in the contractual relations of another.[304]

---

298 See *Edwin Hill & Partners (a firm)* v. *First National Finance Corp. p.l.c.* [1989] 1 W.L.R. 225, 230 and the authorities there cited.

299 See *Ansett Transport Industries (Operations) Pty Ltd* v. *Australian Federation of Air Pilots* [1991] 1 V.R. 637, 677.

300 ibid.

301 (1975) 10 S.A.S.R. 76, 113.

302 See e.g. *Trident Constructions Pty Ltd* v. *The Australian Builders' Labourers' Federated Union of Workers—Western Australian Branch* [1984] W.A.R. 245, 251. Note also that *Glamorgan Coal Co.* v. *South Wales Miners' Federation* [1905] A.C. 239 suggests that pursuit of a legitimate self-interest is not sufficient justification for an interference with the contractual relations of others. See, however, (1975) 38 *M.L.R.* 217, 220 where it is suggested that a distinction should be drawn between union action aimed at *furthering* the interests of its members and that which is designed to *protect* their interests. See also *Northern Drivers Union* v. *Kawau Island Ferries Ltd* [1974] 2 N.Z.L.R. 617 where the Court of Appeal of New Zealand thought that it might be permissible to take into account a moral duty resting on an industrial union to protect its members.

303 [1978] 1 W.L.R. 302, 332.

304 See *Building Workers' Industrial Union of Australia* v. *Odco Pty Ltd* (1991) 99 A.L.R. 735, 770 and *Edwin Hill & Partners (a firm)* v. *First National Finance Corp. p.l.c.* [1989] 1 W.L.R. 225, 228.

4. Remedies

(a) Injunction In most cases of actionable interferences with contractual relations the remedy sought by the plaintiff is an injunction to stop the defendant from further interfering with the contractual relations between the plaintiff and a third party. If a *prima facie* case for relief is made out by the plaintiff, and it should be a strong case, the court might grant an interlocutory injunction after it weighs the balance of convenience to the parties. In doing so, the court assesses 'the nature of the injury that is likely to be suffered by the defendants if the injunction was granted and they should be ultimately successful on the principal hearing, and that which is likely to be suffered by the plaintiffs if the injunction was refused and they should finally establish their claim'.[305] The burden of proof of greater inconvenience is on the plaintiff.

If a final injunction is sought, the court considers whether the tort can be fairly compensated by the payment of money, whether there is any adequate remedy in law other than the injunction and whether the grant of the injunction would result in such hardship to the defendant that unreasonable oppression would be caused by the court's intervention. These were the matters considered by Wells J. in *Woolley* v. *Dunford.*[306] In that case the form of injunction granted was based upon the order proposed in *J.T. Stratford & Son Ltd* v. *Lindley*[307] and *Torquay Hotel Co. Ltd* v. *Cousins*[308] and it provides a useful precedent if such an order is being sought, particularly in cases of industrial disputes.

If there is an alternative and particularly suitable tribunal with authority to deal with the dispute between the parties an injunction is likely to be refused.[309]

(b) Damages The plaintiff must show damage to succeed in the tort of intentional interference with contractual relations. But if he can show damage, how much can he recover of the purely economic loss that he suffers? In *Whitfeld* v. *De Lauret & Co. Ltd* Knox C.J. of the High Court of Australia thought that the plaintiff should be given such a sum as would 'compensate the plaintiff for the material loss suffered by it by reason of the wrongful acts of the defendant which constituted the cause of action, taking into consideration that the defendant is only responsible for damage which was intended and for damage which is the natural and probable consequence of the wrongful acts'.[310]

In the usual case, the damage suffered is most likely to be loss of profits which the plaintiff would have made out of the contract if it had not been interfered with. The damages are calculated from the date of the breach. Apart from loss of profits, expenses incurred in combating the effects of

305 See *Davies* v. *Nyland* (1975) 10 S.A.S.R. 76, 95.
306 (1972) 3 S.A.S.R. 243, 296.
307 [1965] A.C. 269.
308 [1969] 2 Ch. 106.
309 See *Harry M. Miller Attractions Pty Ltd* v. *Actors and Announcers Equity Association of Australia* [1970] 1 N.S.W.R. 614, 615.
310 (1920) 29 C.L.R. 71, 77.

the tort can also be recovered[311] but the courts are reluctant to compensate a plaintiff for a non-pecuniary loss unless there is also some pecuniary loss.[312]

It would seem that aggravated damages can be recovered in this tort[313] as well as exemplary damages in appropriate circumstances.[314]

(c) Account of profits Although the plaintiff in *Schindler Lifts Australia Pty Ltd* v. *Debelak*[315] did not succeed in getting this remedy the decision would seem to suggest that in an appropriate case the court might order that the defendant account for any profits earned as a result of his actionable intentional interference with the contractual relations of the plaintiff.

VI: INTIMIDATION

Another tort which can be used by a plaintiff who suffers purely economic loss as a result of an intentional act of the defendant is the tort of intimidation. This tort is available when a plaintiff suffers a loss because the defendant has threatened a third party with an unlawful act as a result of which the third party acts to the financial detriment of the plaintiff. Intimidation was firmly established in England as a separate tort by the decision of the House of Lords in *Rookes* v. *Barnard*[316] in 1964 and it has now been used in Australia in *Latham* v. *Singleton,*[317] *Sid Ross Agency Pty Ltd* v. *Actors and Announcers Equity Association of Australia*[318] and *Dollar Sweets Pty Ltd* v. *Federated Confectioners Association of Australia.*[319]

In *Rookes* v. *Barnard,* the defendants, who were union officials, threatened B.O.A.C. (now British Airways) that unless the plaintiff was dismissed they would go on strike in breach of their contracts of service (two of the defendants were employees of B.O.A.C.). Afraid that other union employees would also go on strike in sympathy, B.O.A.C. dismissed the plaintiff in accordance with the terms of his contract. In an action to recover damages for this loss, the House of Lords held that the tort of intimidation was available to the plaintiff in such circumstances and that it extended not only to threats to commit criminal or tortious acts but also to threats to break a contract. Lord Reid said that he could 'see no

311 See *British Motor Trade Association* v. *Salvadori* [1949] Ch. 556. See also *Falconer* v. *A.S.L.E.F. and N.U.R* [1986]. I.R.L.R. 331.
312 See *McGregor on Damages* (15th edn, 1988) para. 1696. See also *Pratt* v. *British Medical Association* [1919] 1 K.B. 244.
313 See *Nash* v. *Copeland* (1887) 4 W.N.(N.S.W.) 41, 43.
314 ibid. See also *Whitfeld* v. *De Lauret & Co. Ltd* (1920) 29 C.L.R. 71, 77.
315 (1989) 89 A.L.R. 275, 300-2.
316 [1964] A.C. 1129.
317 [1981] 2 N.S.W.L.R. 843.
318 [1971] 1 N.S.W.L.R. 760. See also *Pierce* v. *Annis-Brown* (Bourke District Court, Judge Newton, 1971, unreported).
319 [1986] V.R. 383.

difference in principle between a threat to break a contract and a threat to commit a tort'.[320] One of the difficulties raised by *Rookes* v. *Barnard* is why a third party who suffers purely economic loss as a result of a threat by A to break his contract with B can sue A for that loss whereas a third party who suffers purely economic loss when A simply breaks his contract with B cannot sue A for that loss. Lord Reid in *Rookes* v. *Barnard* attempts to resolve the difficulty by saying that the reason for the distinction is that in the first case the third party is suing for the loss caused to him 'by the use of an unlawful weapon against him—intimidation of another person by unlawful means',[321] adding that if the defendant 'only threatens to do what he has a legal right to do he is on safe ground'.[322] Some remain unconvinced by Lord Reid's reasoning.

Can the person threatened himself bring an action for intimidation? There is no Australian authority on this point, though in *Ansett Transport Industries (Operations) Pty Ltd* v. *Australian Federation of Air Pilots*, Brooking J. of the Supreme Court of Victoria indicated that there is authority from other jurisdictions suggesting that he may. Brooking J. preferred to express no opinion on this point.[323]

1. INTENTION TO HARM THE PLAINTIFF

A necessary ingredient of the tort of intimidation is the intention to harm the plaintiff. Without such an intention, the action will not succeed. However, in many industrial disputes, there are many objects which the actors might hope to attain of which the harm to the plaintiff might just be one. What is the position then? In *Latham* v. *Singleton*, Nagle C.J. felt that provided the intention to harm the plaintiff could be shown to be the predominant object of the actor, that was sufficient, whatever other secondary objects were hoped to be attained.[324] It was also sufficient if the harm sought to the plaintiff was only 'a stepping stone to an ultimate objective'. But if the harm to the plaintiff was a 'result foreseen but not aimed at', that is not enough for the tort of intimidation.

2. THE KIND OF THREAT NECESSARY FOR INTIMIDATION

A bare threat without a demand does not amount to the tort of intimidation.[325] It must be a coercive threat coupled with a demand which is intended to force a person to do something which he does not want to do or to refrain from doing something which he actually wishes to do.[326]

320 [1964] A.C. 1129, 1168.
321 ibid.
322 ibid.
323 See [1991] 1 V.R. 637, 687 and the authorities there cited.
324 [1981] 2 N.S.W.L.R. 843, 872.
325 See *J.T. Stratford & Son Ltd* v. *Lindley* [1965] A.C. 269, 284.
326 ibid., 283-4.

Such a coercive threat is a necessary ingredient of the tort of intimidation.[327] In order for a plaintiff to sue in intimidation it is also necessary for him to show that the person threatened by the defendant complied with the demand, otherwise there will be no cause of action as the plaintiff would have suffered no damage from the threat.[328]

It is also now clear that the threat, if it is to be actionable under the tort of intimidation, must be a threat to do an unlawful act.[329] This unlawful act might be a crime, a tort or, as in *Rookes* v. *Barnard*, a threatened breach of contract.[330] If a threat to do any of these things is used by A, to compel B to do something which he does not want to do or to refrain from doing something that he wishes to do, with the intention of harming C, and B complies with the demand rather than risk the threat being carried into execution, then C if he suffers economic loss as a result of the compliance by B can sue A for damages by using the tort of intimidation. In *Morgan* v. *Fry*[331] a majority of the English Court of Appeal decided that a 'strike notice' of proper length (that is, of a period equivalent to the period of notice required by either party to terminate the contract of employment) was not a breach of contract and hence not a threat of an unlawful act sufficient to constitute intimidation. However, Nagle C.J. in *Latham* v. *Singleton* took the view that although 'it is correct to assert that in the practical realities of industrial practice a strike notice is rarely, if ever, acted upon as a breach of contract that does not mean that it is not one',[332] even though he assumed for the purposes of the judgment in that case that a 'strike notice' of itself is not to be taken as a breach of contract.[333]

What if A threatens to break his contract with B with the intent of harming B, and B complies with the demand and does an act which leads him to suffer economic loss? Can B bring an action in intimidation against A? Although there is some authority for the view that the tort can be used in these two-party situations,[334] it is arguable that B should either stand up to the threat or be confined to his remedy in contract.

If two or more persons acting in concert walk off a job when a third party appears at the place of employment, a court can conclude that they present a 'threat' to the employer which is intended to act to the detriment of the third party. Their actions can be regarded as a 'threat' of an unlawful or illegal breach of contract and the third party's cause of action based on intimidation would succeed if the employer in compliance with

327 See *Delphic Wholesalers Pty Ltd* v. *Elco Food Co. Pty Ltd* (1987) 8 I.P.R. 545, 552.
328 See *Rookes* v. *Barnard* [1964] A.C. 1129, 1208.
329 See *Sid Ross Agency Pty Ltd* v. *Actors and Announcers Equity Association of Australia* [1971] 1 N.S.W.L.R. 760.
330 ibid.
331 [1968] 2 Q.B. 710.
332 [1981] 2 N.S.W.L.R. 843, 863.
333 ibid.
334 See *D. & C. Builders* v. *Rees* [1966] 2 Q.B. 617, 625 and *Cory Lighterage Ltd* v. *T.G.W.U.* [1973] 2 All E.R. 341 and 558. See also G. Dworkin (1974) 1 *Mon. U.L.R.* 4, 22.

the 'threat' suspends or dismisses the third party.[335] Such a threat is sufficient for the tort of intimidation.

3. Justification

In *Rookes* v. *Barnard* the issue of justification was not raised and so the House of Lords did not have to consider what part, if any, justification plays in the tort of intimidation. However, in *Latham* v. *Singleton* the issue was raised and Nagle C.J. came to the conclusion that '[t]o permit a plea of justification would mitigate some of the harsher results which text writers and others have stated could flow from the decision of *Rookes* v. *Barnard*'.[336] He went on to say that although 'in principle it may sound odd that an "illegal act" can ever be justified, such an approach would appear to be oversimplistic and the better view seems . . . that defendants should be able to avoid a verdict if they can establish a defence of "justification"'.[337] Nagle C.J. suggested that we should look at 'the predominant motive' for the actions of those involved and the fact that those actions are mistaken or ill-conceived should not necessarily be a bar to a successful defence based on justification.[338] He then considered the circumstances in which the defence of justification would be available. 'If what the defendant did was genuinely considered by him to be for proper union purposes it should normally be accepted as justification'[339] but the defence of justification is not established merely by a claim that the action attacked by the defendant might have some remote connection with union interests.[340] If the actions of the defendant are actuated by feelings of spite, ill-will or malice towards the plaintiff then the defence of justification is unlikely to succeed as the decisions against at least three of the defendants in *Latham* v. *Singleton* itself illustrate.[341] It is doubtful whether the defence of justification is available to an action in intimidation in England.[342]

4. Damages

There is no doubt that in an action for intimidation the plaintiff is entitled to receive substantial damages for any actual pecuniary damage suffered by him which is not too remote.[343] But the plaintiff is not limited to claiming actual pecuniary damage. Once some actual financial loss is proved, the court or jury may award a sum appropriate to the whole

335 See *Latham* v. *Singleton* [1981] 2 N.S.W.L.R. 843.
336 ibid., 869.
337 ibid., 869.
338 ibid., 870.
339 ibid., 873.
340 ibid., 874.
341 ibid., 872, 874.
342 See *Lonrho p.l.c.* v. *Fayed* [1989] 3 W.L.R. 631, 637 and 640 *per* Dillon and Ralph Gibson L.JJ.
343 See *Latham* v. *Singleton* [1981] 2 N.S.W.L.R. 843 and also *Coal Miners Industrial Union of Workers of Western Australia, Collie* v. *True* (1959-60) 33 A.L.J.R. 224, 228.

circumstances of the tort. Thus a plaintiff can claim not only damages for 'past, present and future economic loss', but also damages for 'the pain, suffering and distress caused to the plaintiff by the defendant's actions'.[344] The damages are at large and the court can, after a consideration of the various headings under which damages are claimed, fix an overall sum as damages which it thinks will be proper to compensate the plaintiff.

Aggravated and exemplary damages can also be awarded in an action of intimidation. In *Pratt* v. *British Medical Association*,[345] McCardie J. said that he could not ignore the deliberate and relentless vigour with which the defendants by means of threats and widely extended coercive action sought to achieve the infliction of complete ruin of the plaintiffs and felt that he 'must regard not merely the pecuniary loss sustained by the plaintiffs, but the long period for which they respectively suffered humiliation and menace'.[346] So aggravated damages have been available for intimidation for a long time. This has now been affirmed in *Latham* v. *Singleton*, which also decided that exemplary damages can be awarded in the tort of intimidation.

VII: CONSPIRACY

Yet another tort which can be used by a person who suffers purely economic loss as the result of an intentional act of another is the tort of conspiracy.[347] This tort can be used when two or more persons combine to effect some economic loss on the plaintiff. The tort has often been used (not always successfully) against trade unionists who have combined to pressure others to act in a way which leads to the financial detriment of the plaintiff but that is not the only situation in which it is used and there are other situations, such as where one set of traders combine to injure another set of traders and cause them economic loss,[348] which might also be actionable in the tort of conspiracy.

There are two ways in which the tort of conspiracy can be committed at the present time. Two or more persons can combine to injure a plaintiff by lawful means and cause him economic loss, and two or more persons can combine to commit an unlawful act and cause the plaintiff economic loss by that unlawful act. Both these combinations can result in successful actions in conspiracy against the persons involved in the combinations.

1. Conspiracy by Lawful Means

The decision of the House of Lords in *Crofter Hand Woven Harris Tweed Co. Ltd* v. *Veitch*[349] clearly established conspiracy (by lawful and unlawful

344 [1981] 2 N.S.W.L.R. 843, 875.
345 [1919] 1 K.B. 244.
346 ibid., 282.
347 See generally P. Heffey (1975) 1 *Mon. U.L.R.* 136.
348 See *Mogul Steamship Co.* v. *McGregor, Gow & Co.* [1892] A.C. 25 where the action failed.
349 [1942] A.C. 435.

means) as a separate tort, though the foundations of the tort were laid in three cases about the end of the last century: *Mogul Steamship Co.* v. *McGregor, Gow & Co.*,[350] *Allen* v. *Flood*[351] and *Quinn* v. *Leathem*.[352] In the *Crofter* case, the appellants (plaintiffs) were manufacturers of a cloth known as Harris tweed. This cloth was hand-woven for them by crofters on the island of Lewis in Scotland from yarn obtained from the mainland where it was cheaper. Harris tweed was also manufactured by mills on the island from yarn spun on the island and hand-woven by the crofters. The respondents (defendants) were union officials who represented most of the workers on the island. When negotiating for improved wages for employees of the mills on the island they were told by the mill owners that no increase was possible because of the competition provided by the appellants who bought their yarn more cheaply on the mainland. The respondents, in combination with others, then imposed a ban on the importation of yarn from the mainland and instructed members of their union who were dockers not to handle yarn shipped from the mainland. The dockers complied with the ban without breaking their contracts of employment so the carrying out of the ban involved no unlawful act. The appellants sought an injunction to put an end to the ban but the House of Lords held unanimously that the appellants had no cause of action because, the predominant purpose of the combination being the legitimate promotion of the interests of the persons combining and the means employed by them to achieve their object being neither criminal nor tortious in themselves, the combination was not unlawful and therefore not actionable as a conspiracy. Even though the appellants did not succeed in the conspiracy action in the *Crofter* case, the decision is important because the judgments in that case discuss the various elements necessary if an action in conspiracy (whether by lawful or unlawful means) is to succeed. But the decision is particularly important in relation to conspiracy by lawful means because it clearly established that two or more persons who combine together with the intention of injuring another, even by lawful means, commit a tortious conspiracy if damage results to the other unless the predominant purpose of the combination is the lawful protection or promotion of any lawful interest of the combiners.[353]

One of the problems with the tort of conspiracy by lawful means is why an act which is not actionable if done by one person should become actionable if done by two or more persons. As Lord Diplock put it in *Lonrho Ltd* v. *Shell Petroleum Co. Ltd (No. 2)* (the *Lonrho* case): 'Why should an act which causes economic loss to A but is not actionable at his suit if done by B alone become actionable because B did it pursuant to an agreement between B and C?'[354] When the *Mogul* case was before the Court of Appeal, Bowen L.J. offered an explanation for the distinction:

---

350 [1892] A.C. 25.
351 [1898] A.C. 1.
352 [1901] A.C. 495.
353 [1942] A.C. 435, 445 (Viscount Simon L.C.).
354 [1982] A.C. 173, 188.

'The distinction is based on sound reason, for a combination may make oppressive or dangerous that which if it proceeded only from a single person would be otherwise'.[355] But, as Lord Diplock pointed out in the *Lonrho* case,

to suggest today that acts done by one street-corner grocer in concert with a second are more oppressive and dangerous to a competitor than the same acts done by a string of supermarkets under a single ownership . . . is to shut one's eyes to what has been happening in the business and industrial world since the turn of the century and, in particular, since the end of World War II . . . [though] the civil tort of conspiracy to injure the plaintiff's commercial interests where that is the predominant purpose of the agreement between the defendants and of the acts done in execution of it which caused damage to the plaintiff, must . . . be accepted . . . as too well-established to be discarded however anomalous it may seem today.[356]

It is perhaps time to consider again the wise words of Evatt J. in *McKernan* v. *Fraser* in 1931: 'It may be that if A, inspired by bad motives, does an act which is not unlawful but which designedly causes injury to B, a proper system of jurisprudence should hold A liable'.[357]

It is not unthinkable that this matter might be reconsidered; after all, it was for many years thought that a husband and wife acting in concert were incapable of committing an actionable conspiracy, because they were treated as one in law, though they could each be liable if they jointly conspired with other persons. Yet, in *Midland Bank Trust Co. Ltd* v. *Green (No. 3)* in 1979, Oliver J. held that there was 'no good logical or historical reason for slavishly applying to the law of tort, simply because the tort is called the "tort of conspiracy", the primitive and inaccurate maxim that spouses are one, so as to confer on them an immunity from civil liability not accorded to the unmarried',[358] and in the Court of Appeal, Lord Denning M.R. said that he could 'see no good reason for applying the doctrine of unity [between husband and wife] to the modern tort of conspiracy'.[359]

Another matter that should be mentioned is that although criminal conspiracy and the tort of civil conspiracy may to some extent have shared a common origin, they are quite different in their modern forms. 'The essence of the crime is agreement—execution of the agreement is not necessary. The position is quite different in the law of tort. In tort . . . although the agreement is necessary, intention to injure and actual injury are also both necessary'.[360]

There is some doubt whether the tort of conspiracy by lawful means serves any useful purpose today. Lord Denning M.R. in *Midland Bank*

355 (1889) 23 Q.B.D. 598, 616.
356 [1982] A.C. 173, 189.
357 (1931) 46 C.L.R. 343, 410.
358 [1979] 2 All E.R. 193, 218.
359 [1982] 1 Ch. 529, 539.
360 See *Midland Bank Trust Co. Ltd* v. *Green (No. 3)* [1982] 1 Ch. 529, 541 *per* Fox L.J.

Trust Co. Ltd v. *Green (No. 3)* felt that it might serve some purpose. As he said:

> It is of use primarily when the act which causes damage would not be actionable if done by one alone (as in *Bradford Corporation* v. *Pickles* [1895] A.C. 587 and *Allen* v. *Flood* [1898] A.C. 1), because it is then the only way in which the injured person can recover damages for the wrong done to him.[361]

But as we shall see when we consider the question of justification, those combining are usually able to satisfy the court that they are acting for the lawful protection and promotion of their lawful interests and so the chances of a successful action for conspiracy by lawful means are remote unless the predominant purpose of those combining is to injure the plaintiff.[362]

2. Conspiracy by Unlawful Means

The other kind of conspiracy which attracts liability is one where the conspirators agree to do an unlawful act (that is, an act independently unlawful apart from the conspiracy) or to use unlawful means to attain their object. We refer to this as a conspiracy by unlawful means. As Dixon C.J. pointed out in *Coal Miners' Industrial Union of Workers of Western Australia, Collie* v. *True* a 'combination to threaten and if necessary carry out an unlawful act as a means of securing an end is actionable as a civil conspiracy'.[363]

What is an unlawful act or what are 'unlawful means' for the purposes of the tort? These are many and varied and include not only crimes and torts but also breaches of statutory provisions.[364] A strike in breach of a statute and a threat of such a strike can also constitute unlawful means.[365] In *Williams* v. *Hursey*[366] the question of whether or not the means agreed upon and used by the defendants to prevent the plaintiffs from presenting themselves for obtaining work were unlawful was debated at length, and in their decisions several judges adverted to the means used which they regarded as unlawful and sufficient for the tort of conspiracy by unlawful means.[367] Probably a combination to commit an actual breach of a contract would constitute unlawful means for the purposes of the tort of conspiracy though the question was left open in *Rookes* v. *Barnard*.[368] But

---

361 ibid., 539.
362 See *Street* (8th edn, 1988) p. 136.
363 (1959) 33 A.L.J.R. 224, 227.
364 See *Daily Mirror Newspapers Ltd* v. *Gardner* [1968] 2 Q.B. 762. See also *Galea* v. *Cooper* [1982] 2 N.S.W.L.R. 411.
365 See *Williams* v. *Hursey* (1959) 103 C.L.R. 30; *Southan* v. *Grounds* (1916) 16 S.R.(N.S.W.) 274; *Coffey* v. *Geraldton Lumpers Union* (1928) 31 W.A.L.R. 33; and *Coal Miners' Industrial Union of Workers of Western Australia, Collie* v. *True* (1959) 33 A.L.J.R. 224.
366 (1959) 103 C.L.R. 30.
367 See e.g. (1959) 103 C.L.R. 30, 78-9; 108-9 and 125-6.
368 [1964] A.C. 1129, 1210.

a threat of a breach of contract by a combination would constitute an unlawful act sufficient for conspiracy.[369]

In many of the cases of conspiracy by unlawful means another tort might also be committed. What purpose then is served by alleging a conspiracy? It looks as if some purpose may be served by alleging a conspiracy. As Burt C.J. of the Supreme Court of Western Australia pointed out in *Galland* v. *Mineral Underwriters Ltd*: 'Once an agreement to commit a tort is found and it is found that the tort has been committed pursuant to and in the execution of that agreement then *all* the parties to that agreement . . . are joint tortfeasors and it matters not that one party was not actively engaged in the commission of the tort'.[370] So, by bringing the action in conspiracy the plaintiff can choose the conspirator he wishes to pursue and he can even choose as a defendant one of the conspirators against whom he might not otherwise have succeeded in tort because the tortious act, for example, was committed *only* by a fellow conspirator of the defendant.[371] The decision in *Galland* v. *Mineral Underwriters Ltd* also suggests another advantage in suing in conspiracy, and that is that 'the conspiracy may aggravate the damage'.[372]

3. INTENTION TO INJURE

In the *Lonrho* case, Lord Diplock pointed out that in the *Crofter* case 'it was made clear that injury to the plaintiff and not the self-interest of the defendants must be the predominant purpose of the agreement in execution of which the damage-causing acts were done'[373] if the agreement is to be actionable as a conspiracy. The *Crofter* case was of course concerned with conspiracy by lawful means but in the *Lonrho* case in 1982 the House of Lords decided that even in the case of conspiracy by unlawful means it is necessary for the plaintiff to show that there was an intention to injure the plaintiff on the part of the defendants if the agreement is to be actionable as a conspiracy. There is, therefore, now no distinction, in relation to the requirement of an intention to injure the plaintiff, between a conspiracy by lawful and a conspiracy by unlawful means; both require an intention to injure the plaintiff on the part of the defendant. Whether the intention to injure the plaintiff must be the predominant purpose of the conspiracy in both types of conspiracy to injure (by lawful and unlawful means) is a different question, and in relation to that question the two types of conspiracy to injure differ. The 1982 decision of the House of Lords in *Lonrho* was, however, misinterpreted by the English Court of Appeal in the *Metall* case[374] as laying down a rule of law that the tort of conspiracy to injure (whether by lawful or unlawful means) required proof in every case not merely of an intention to injure the

---

369 ibid.
370 [1977] W.A.R. 116, 123 (emphasis added).
371 See *Galea* v. *Cooper* [1982] 2 N.S.W.L.R. 411, 417.
372 See [1977] W.A.R. 116, 121.
373 See [1982] A.C. 173, 189.
374 See *Metall & Rohstoff A.G.* v. *Donaldson, Lufkin & Jenrette Inc.* [1989] 3 W.L.R. 563.

plaintiff but also that injury to the plaintiff was the *predominant* purpose of the conspiracy. This interpretation of the 1982 decision of the House of Lords in *Lonrho* was held, in the 1991 decision of the House of Lords in *Lonrho p.l.c.* v. *Fayed*,[375] to be wrong and the decision of the Court of Appeal in *Metall* on this aspect was overruled, the House of Lords deciding that in an action for conspiracy to injure by unlawful means it was *not* necessary for the plaintiff to prove that the intention on the part of the defendant to injure the plaintiff was the *predominant* purpose of his alleged unlawful action and that it was sufficient to show that the defendant had an intention to injure the plaintiff by the alleged unlawful act. It would seem, therefore, after the 1991 decision of the House of Lords in *Lonrho p.l.c.* v. *Fayed*, that for the tort of conspiracy to injure by a lawful act it is necessary for the plaintiff to prove not merely that there was an intention to injure the plaintiff but also that injury to the plaintiff (rather than advancement of the defendant's own interests) was the *predominant* purpose of the conspiracy, but that for the tort of conspiracy to injure by an unlawful act (or unlawful means) it is only necessary to prove an intention to injure the plaintiff and it is not necessary to go further and prove that injury to the plaintiff (rather than the advancement of the defendant's own interests) was the *predominant* purpose of the conspiracy.[376] There is, therefore, a significant distinction between the tort of conspiracy to injure by a lawful act, and the tort of conspiracy to injure by an unlawful act and decisions such as that of Hirst J. in *Allied Arab Bank Ltd* v. *Hajjar*[377] limiting the scope of the tort of conspiracy 'exclusively to cases where the *predominant* purpose of the defendants' agreement is to injure the plaintiffs' interests' must now clearly be regarded as wrongly decided.

The distinction between the two types of conspiracy to injure is well illustrated by the decision of the Supreme Court of Victoria in *Ansett Transport Industries (Operations) Pty Ltd* v. *Australian Federation of Air Pilots* (the *Ansett* case).[378] When the defendants conspired to procure mass resignations of airline pilots and that alleged conspiracy did not involve an unlawful act or unlawful means it was necessary for the plaintiffs to prove not only an intention to injure the plaintiffs but also that the sole or predominant purpose of the conspiracy was to injure the plaintiffs. This the plaintiffs were unable to do (as the court found that the predominant purpose of the conspiracy was to protect the pilots against claims for damages by the plaintiffs) and the action for conspiracy did not succeed. But in relation to the conspiracy to issue a directive to the pilots to work only from 9 a.m. to 5 p.m., in breach of their contracts of employment, it was only necessary as this was an unlawful act, to prove an intention on the part of the defendants to injure the plaintiffs, and as the plaintiffs were able to do that the action for conspiracy succeeded.

---

375 [1991] 3 W.L.R. 188, 198.
376 ibid.
377 [1988] 3 W.L.R. 533.
378 [1991] 1 V.R. 637. The distinction between the two types of conspiracy is blurred in *Little* v. *Law Institute of Victoria & Others (No. 3)* [1990] V.R. 257.

An inquiry into the defendant's intention to injure is inextricably bound up with the 'object' or 'purpose' of the infliction of the harm and leads inevitably to the question of whether the combination must possess the additional character or quality of being 'malicious'. Evatt J. pointed out in *McKernan* v. *Fraser* that 'no recognised formula has yet been adopted by the Courts in order to ascertain such character or quality'.[379] The position has not changed in recent years and Evatt J.'s analysis of what can be regarded as 'malicious' in any inquiry as to intention to injure is still the best treatment of this difficult topic. According to that analysis, if the agreement to cause damage or loss is made 'solely with the object or motive of causing such damage' or if the agreement is 'stamped with wantonness, almost with absence of meaning or significance'[380] the necessary intention to injure will be presumed. If the common object or motive is 'the satisfaction of a personal hatred or grudge by means of the ruin or impoverishment of the plaintiff, liability is clear'; but if the common object or motive is 'the protection or advancement of trading, professional or economic interests common to the defendants, there is no liability'.[381] If the common object or motive is the carrying out of 'some religious, social or political object, the law prefers to examine the motive or object in each case before pronouncing an opinion. The pursuit of economic ends is most favoured'.[382]

Where there are two or more possible common objects or motives, the court inquires into the predominant object or motive. Any proved hostility or dislike of the plaintiff does not automatically imply an intention to injure and therefore liability. The hostility or dislike must be further analysed 'in order to ascertain whether it is a motive related to a clash of economic or professional interests and arises from strong opinions as to the plaintiff's own conduct in relation thereto [or] whether . . . [it] has its true source in personal hatred or bitterness'.[383]

What if there are three parties to a combination and A and B have a wrongful or unjustifiable object or motive whereas C has a justifiable object or motive? Can all three be liable in conspiracy? The answer appears to be no. As Evatt J. said in *McKernan* v. *Fraser*: 'hatred or grudge does not, on any principle of law, become a motive imputable to those who are either unaware of it or who, being aware of it, condemn'.[384] But if A and B communicate the existence of their 'malice' to C and he continues to combine with them then all three will have committed an actionable conspiracy. If A and B have agreed between themselves to injure the plaintiff and have procured the services of C to achieve their object, A and B will be liable for the separate conspiracy between the two of them even when it cannot be said that there was a conspiracy between the three of them.

---

379 (1931) 46 C.L.R. 343, 398.
380 ibid., 399.
381 ibid., 400.
382 ibid., 400.
383 ibid., 403.
384 ibid., 408.

4. JUSTIFICATION

If the conspiracy is by lawful means it is possible to avoid liability by showing that the common object or motive of the conspirators was the protection or advancement of the legitimate trading, professional or economic interests common to the defendants,[385] and by showing that those matters were the predominant object or motive of the conspirators.[386] This is described by the courts as 'justification of the conspiracy'. As Nader J. said in *Ranger Uranium Mines Pty Ltd* v. *Federated Miscellaneous Workers' Union of Australia* (the *Ranger Uranium Mines* case): 'the fact that the combination is predominantly inspired by self interest will amount to justification'.[387]

It is not very easy to give a precise and exhaustive definition of the interests that the courts will regard as 'legitimate' for the purpose of justifying a conspiracy.[388] As Romer L.J. said in *Gibland* v. *National Amalgamated Labourers' Union of Great Britain and Ireland*: 'in ascertaining what is a "justification" . . . regard must be had to the circumstances of each case as it arises'.[389] In addition to trading, professional and economic interests (including the furtherance of trade union objects) other interests which 'cannot be positively translated into or shown to be reflected in detailed financial terms'[390] have also been regarded as legitimate interests. And in the *Ranger Uranium Mines* case Nader J. thought that the health and safety of the defendants and fellow workmen could well be regarded as a 'legitimate' interest for the purpose of justifying a conspiracy.[391]

If the conspiracy is by unlawful means, justification, it seems, cannot be used to avoid liability. As Viscount Simon L.C. said in the *Crofter* case, '[i]f the predominant purpose is the lawful protection or promotion of any lawful interest of the combiners (*no illegal means being employed*), it is not a tortious conspiracy even though it causes damage to another person'.[392] This would seem to suggest that a pursuit of even a lawful interest by the participants to a conspiracy affords them no protection or justification if unlawful means are used.[393] This view has been confirmed recently by the House of Lords in *Lonrho p.l.c.* v. *Fayed.* As Lord Bridge said, 'when conspirators intentionally injure the plaintiff *and use unlawful means to do so,* it is no defence for them to show that their primary

385 ibid., 400.

386 See *Crofters'* case [1942] A.C. 435, 445. See also *Lonrho p.l.c.* v. *Fayed* [1991] 3 W.L.R. 188 (House of Lords).

387 (1987) 89 F.L.R. 349, 354.

388 See, however, P. Heffey (1975) 1 *Mon. U.L.R.* 136, 157-66 and J.D. Heydon, *Economic Torts* (2nd edn, London, 1978) pp. 16-28.

389 [1903] 2 K.B. 600, 618.

390 See *Scala Ballroom (Wolverhampton) Ltd* v. *Ratcliffe* [1958] 1 W.L.R. 1057, 1063 *per* Morris L.J.

391 (1987) 89 F.L.R. 349, 353-4.

392 [1942] A.C. 435, 445. Note, however, the view of Lord Porter at pp. 495-6 of the judgment.

393 See also *Scala Ballroom (Wolverhampton) Ltd* v. *Ratcliffe* [1958] 1 W.L.R. 1057, 1058-59.

purpose was to further or protect their own interests; it is sufficient to make their action tortious that the means used were unlawful'.[394]

Who has the burden of proof in relation to justification? In a case of conspiracy by lawful means there is some authority to suggest that the plaintiff must establish 'that there was a wilful and concerted intention to injure without just cause, and consequent damage. The plaintiff has to prove the wrongfulness of the defendants' object'.[395] Lord Buckmaster put the matter more plainly in *Sorrell* v. *Smith* when he said that 'the onus is not on the defendant to justify but on the plaintiff to prove that the act was spiteful and malicious'.[396] It may be desirable for the courts to take the view that once the plaintiff establishes that the defendants deliberately interfered with his trade or business and caused him loss then the burden of excusing their actions should shift to the defendants,[397] but there is no evidence that the courts presently take that view. In view of the decision of the House of Lords in *Lonrho p.l.c.* v. *Fayed* it is extremely doubtful whether a conspiracy by unlawful means can ever be justified. But if it can be,[398] then the burden of justifying such a conspiracy would rest on the defendants.

5. Damages

If a conspiracy on the part of the defendants is proved and there are continuing acts on the part of the defendants, an injunction will of course be granted.[399] But how are the damages calculated in an action in conspiracy?

It is, of course, essential that the plaintiff should have sustained some damage which he can prove. But if he can do this he is not limited only to special damage that he can prove. There is no reason why the damages should not be at large and the court can therefore award the plaintiff such sum as it thinks proper to compensate him. The damages are likely to be mainly loss of profits or salary or wages, but in addition any expenses incurred in unravelling the conspiracy are also recoverable.[400] If parties to a conspiracy succeed in seriously impairing the plaintiff's opportunity to retain and regain a considerable number of profitable clients, expenses incurred in mounting a 'rescue operation' to regain those clients can be claimed in the action in conspiracy against the conspiring parties.[401]

---

394 [1991] 3 W.L.R. 188, 195 (emphasis added). If Nader J. is suggesting at (1987) F.L.R. 349, 355 that a conspiracy to injure by unlawful means can be justified that proposition must be regarded as doubtful.

395 See *Crofters'* case [1942] A.C. 435, 471-2 *per* Lord Wright.

396 [1925] A.C. 700, 748.

397 The suggestion is mentioned by Lord Sumner in *Sorrell* v. *Smith* [1925] A.C. 700, 742.

398 See *Crofters'* case [1942] A.C. 435, 495-6. See also *Ranger Uranium Mines Pty Ltd* v. *Federated Miscellaneous Workers' Union of Australia* (1987) 89 F.L.R. 349, 355.

399 See *British Motor Trade Association* v. *Salvadori* [1949] 1 Ch. 556, 572.

400 ibid., 568-9.

401 See *Lintas (S.S.C. & B:) New Zealand Ltd* v. *Murphy* (1986) Aust. Torts Reports 80-008 at 67, 552.

In an action of conspiracy a plaintiff can also recover aggravated damages[402] and there is no reason why, in Australia, exemplary damages should not also be awarded in appropriate circumstances for an actionable conspiracy.[403] In *Lintas (S.S.C. & B.:)* v. *Murphy*, Prichard J. in the High Court of New Zealand decided that the conduct of the parties to the conspiracy was deserving of censure and awarded exemplary damages.[404]

VIII: THE ACTION FOR INTERFERENCE WITH TRADE OR BUSINESS BY UNLAWFUL MEANS

So far we have dealt with three recognized individual economic torts—interference with contractual relations, intimidation and conspiracy—which can be brought by a plaintiff who has suffered intentionally inflicted economic loss at the hands of a defendant or defendants. But apart from these known and specific economic torts is there a general tort of causing economic loss by unlawful means? In *Acrow (Automation) Ltd* v. *Rex Chainbelt Inc.*, Lord Denning M.R. suggested that there was such a general tort:

> I take the principle of law to be that which I stated in *Torquay Hotel Co. Ltd* v. *Cousins* [1969] 2 Ch. 106, 139, namely, that if one person, without just cause or excuse, deliberately interferes with the trade or business of another, and does so by unlawful means, that is, by an act which he is not at liberty to commit, then he is acting unlawfully. He is liable in damages: and, in a proper case, an injunction can be granted against him.[405]

Earlier, in *J.T. Stratford & Son Ltd* v. *Lindley*[406] in 1965, Lord Reid and Viscount Radcliffe had adverted to the tort of causing loss by unlawful means in a manner which suggested that this tort was already in existence.[407] More recently, in *Hadmor Productions Ltd* v. *Hamilton*[408] and in *Merkur Island Shipping Corporation* v. *Laughton*,[409] Lord Diplock in the House of Lords seemed unequivocally to accept the existence of the tort of interference with trade or business by unlawful means. And in *Lonrho p.l.c.* v. *Fayed* in 1989 the English Court of Appeal confirmed the existence of the tort while pointing out that 'the detailed limits of it have

---

402 See *Clarke et al.* v. *Urquhart* [1930] A.C. 28, 50. See also *Denison* v. *Fawcett* (1958) 12 D.L.R. (2d) 537, 543 where Schroeder J.A. refers to the element of conspiracy as 'another circumstance of aggravation of weighty import'.

403 See *Denison* v. *Fawcett* (1958) 12 D.L.R. (2d) 537 and *Klein* v. *Jenoves & Varley* [1932] 3 D.L.R. 571. See also *Nauru Local Government Council* v. *New Zealand Seamen's Industrial Union of Workers*, High Court, Wellington, 27 July 1982 (A.583/73) (unreported).

404 (1986) Aust. Torts Reports 80-008 at 67,554.

405 [1971] 1 W.L.R. 1676, 1682.

406 [1965] A.C. 269.

407 ibid., 324, 328.

408 [1982] 2 W.L.R. 322, 333.

409 [1983] 2 A.C. 570, 609-10.

to be refined'.[410] The tort has formed the basis of the decision in *Mintuck* v. *Valley River Band No. 63A*[411] in Canada where the tort was used against defendants who engaged in a programme of harassment of the plaintiff and interfered with his farming operations in order to get him to abandon his rights to a lease, and the existence of the tort was recognised in New Zealand in *Van Camp Chocolates Ltd* v. *Auslebrooks Ltd.*[412]

The existence of this general tort of interference with trade or business by unlawful means appears to be recognized in Australia in the decision in *Sid Ross Agency Pty Ltd* v. *Actors and Announcers Equity Association of Australia* where Else-Mitchell J. said:

> There can, I think, be no doubt in the light of authorities that have been referred to such as *Rookes* v. *Barnard* . . . *J.T. Stratford & Son Ltd* v. *Lindley* . . . *Daily Mirror Newspapers Ltd* v. *Gardner* . . . [and] *Morgan* v. *Fry* . . . that a right of action is available to a person who suffers damage as a result of interference by another with his trade or business by unlawful means and that this may be so even though the interference does not entail the procurement or inducement of an actual breach of contract.[413]

But Else-Mitchell J. went on to say that 'it is not every use of an unlawful means which will allow of, justify or support an action for unlawful interference with economic or business interests'.[414] More recently, in *Ansett Transport Industries (Operations) Pty Ltd* v. *Australian Federation of Air Pilots*[415] the action for interference with trade or business by unlawful means was not only recognized but also applied by Brooking J. in the Supreme Court of Victoria.

> The defendants had issued a directive to their members that they should only work from 9 a.m. to 5 p.m. even though the job at which they worked, piloting aircraft for the plaintiffs' airlines, was a 24 hours a day operation. Brooking J. decided that in giving that directive the defendants had committed the tort of interference with trade or business by unlawful means because they had wrongfully interfered with contractual relations between the plaintiffs and their employees (the pilots) and others (those with whom the plaintiffs had contracts for the carriage of passengers and goods) and because they had incited members of the union to refrain from working in accordance with the relevant award, contrary to s.312 of the Industrial Relations Act 1988 (Cwth) and that these unlawful acts had resulted in damage to the plaintiffs.

Why is such a general tort of interference with trade or business by unlawful means necessary? It is possible that the known individual economic torts which we have already discussed may not always be appropriate or applicable to the circumstances of the case. For example, the defendant might cause the plaintiff loss by unlawful means without in

---

410 [1989] 3 W.L.R. 631, 638 *per* Dillon L.J.
411 [1977] 2 W.W.R. 309. The plaintiff also succeeded in the tort of intimidation.
412 [1984] 1 N.Z.L.R. 354, 359.
413 [1970] 2 N.S.W.R. 47, 52. The action finally succeeded on the basis of the tort of intimidation (see [1971] 1 N.S.W.L.R. 760).
414 [1970] 2 N.S.W.R. 47, 52.
415 [1991] 1 V.R. 637.

any way interfering with the plaintiff's existing contractual relations with a third party.[416] The plaintiff would not be able to bring an action for interference with contractual relations but he could bring an action for interference with trade or business by unlawful means because the tort of causing loss by unlawful means does not require proof that existing contracts have been broken or interfered with.[417] Again, the defendant might cause the plaintiff loss by unlawful means which do not necessarily involve the kinds of threats (and responses to those threats) necessary for the tort of intimidation.[418] For the tort of causing loss by unlawful means, threats are not necessary. Besides, the tort of intimidation might not be 'wide enough to cover all the cases which could reasonably be said to involve causing loss by unlawful means'.[419] The tort of causing loss by unlawful means will also be useful in those situations where an act which if done by two or more persons, acting in concert, would be actionable as a conspiracy by unlawful means, is in fact done by only one person.

It can be seen, therefore, that the general tort of interference with trade or business by unlawful means is very useful to supplement some of the deficiencies of the presently known and specific economic torts. In the *Merkur* case,[420] Lord Diplock not only recognized the existence of this general tort but he described the specific torts, such as interference with contractual relations, intimidation and conspiracy, as species of this wider genus of tort.[421] If the development of this general tort continues one might wonder if the species will, or should, continue to exist; though in this connection it should be noted that the tort of conspiracy by *lawful means* remains outside this general tort, which is only available for interferences with trade or business by *unlawful means*. It may even be that it is now time for this more general tort to become the subject of legislation—the common law moves much too slowly in this important and rapidly developing area of interferences with trade and business interests. If this happens, several matters will have to be clarified. The notion of 'unlawful means' will need to be considered and more logically defined[422] and the meaning of 'trade'[423] and 'business'[424] elaborated. The tort appears to be confined at the present time to 'intended' economic harm which results in damage to the plaintiff,[425] but it is not absolutely

---

416 See *Hadmor Productions Ltd* v. *Hamilton* [1982] 2 W.L.R. 322 and *Acrow (Automation) Ltd* v. *Rex Chainbelt Inc.* [1971] W.L.R. 1676.

417 See *Merkur Island Shipping Corp.* v. *Laughton* [1983] 2 All E.R. 189, 196-7 *per* Lord Diplock.

418 See *Acrow (Automation) Ltd* v. *Rex Chainbelt Inc.* [1971] 1 W.L.R. 1676.

419 See L. Hoffman (1965) 81 *L.Q.R.* 116, 121.

420 [1983] 2 A.C. 570.

421 ibid., 609-10.

422 See H. Carty (1983) 3 *Legal Studies* 193, 206-7.

423 See *R.C.A. Corporation* v. *Pollard* [1982] 3 W.L.R. 1007 and *Ex parte Island Records Ltd* [1978] Ch. 122.

424 See *Lonrho p.l.c.* v. *Fayed* [1989] 3 W.L.R. 631, 641-2.

425 See *Mintuck* v. *Valley River Band etc.* [1977] 2 W.W.R. 309. In *Copyright Agency Ltd* v. *Haines* [1982] 1 N.S.W.L.R. 182, 194-5 McLelland J. decided that in this tort 'the existence in the mind of the wrongdoer of a purpose or intention of inflicting injury on the plaintiff' was 'an essential criterion of its application'.

clear whether this tort requires an intention to inflict economic harm on the plaintiff (as in the torts of interference with contractual relations, intimidation and conspiracy) or whether it is sufficient merely to show that the defendant intended to do the act which resulted in economic harm to the plaintiff (as in the action on the case for damages based on *Beaudesert Shire Council* v. *Smith*,[426] which is discussed next). If Lord Diplock's view in the *Merkur* case, that the tort of interference with trade or business by unlawful means is the genus of which the specific torts of interference with contractual relations, intimidation and conspiracy are the species, is correct then the tort of interference with trade or business by unlawful means would seem to require an intention to cause economic harm to the plaintiff as one of its necessary ingredients. This was the view taken by McLelland J. in *Copyright Agency Ltd* v. *Haines*[427] and endorsed by Dillon L.J. in the English Court of Appeal in *Lonrho p.l.c.* v. *Fayed* by requiring those who rely on this tort to prove that 'the unlawful act was in some sense directed against the plaintiff or intended to harm the plaintiff'.[428] But in *Acrow (Automation) Ltd* v. *Rex Chainbelt Inc.*,[429] where the plaintiffs (Acrow) successfully used the tort of interference with trade or business by unlawful means against the defendants (Rex Chainbelt), it was clear that Rex Chainbelt had no intention whatever of causing economic harm to Acrow when they deliberately refused to supply Acrow with the special chainbelt which was necessary for Acrow to be able to manufacture their special automatic equipment for conveying goods. This was, in fact, made very clear in the letter which the solicitors for Rex Chainbelt wrote to Acrow's solicitors:

> the business relationship between your clients and ours has hitherto been friendly, and our clients would be more than willing to supply your clients with chainbelt if they were not prevented by their contractual arrangements with W.I. Inc. from doing so.[430]

So, in *Acrow (Automation) Ltd* v. *Rex Chainbelt Inc.* the plaintiffs succeeded in this tort even though the defendants did not intend to cause economic harm to the plaintiff. If this tort is to become the subject of legislation, as is suggested above, the legislature will have to decide whether the statutory tort of interference with trade or business by unlawful means should be confined only to those cases where the defendant intends to cause economic harm to the plaintiff or whether it should also extend to those cases where the defendant intends to do the act which in fact causes economic harm to the plaintiff even though he does not intend

---

426 (1966) 120 C.L.R. 145. For discussion of the action on the case for damages based on the *Beaudesert* case, see pp. 235-6 below.

427 [1982] 1 N.S.W.L.R. 182, 194-5.

428 [1989] 3 W.L.R. 631, 637. The view of the English Court of Appeal was followed by Brooking J. in *Ansett Transport Industries (Operations) Pty Ltd* v. *Australian Federation of Air Pilots* [1991] 1 V.R. 637, 668.

429 [1971] 1 W.L.R. 1676.

430 ibid., 1681.

the economic harm which in fact ensues.[431] In the 1991 decision of the House of Lords in *Lonrho p.l.c.* v. *Fayed*,[432] Lord Templeman indicated that the ambit and ingredients of the tort of interference with trade or business by unlawful means (and the tort of conspiracy) requires further analysis and reconsideration by the courts.

Finally, in relation to the defence of justification, the authorities favour the view that justification is no defence to a claim for interference with trade or business by unlawful means,[433] though Nagle C.J. in *Latham* v. *Singleton* thought that the better view was that defendants should be able to avoid a verdict in an action for interference with trade or business by unlawful means if they can establish a defence of justification.[434] In the 1989 decision of the English Court of Appeal in *Lonrho p.l.c.* v. *Fayed*[435] at least two of the judges specifically indicated that it is not an essential element of the tort of interference with trade or business by unlawful means that there must be a predominant intention to injure the plaintiff on the part of the defendant. In England, therefore, an intention to injure the plaintiff would be sufficient for the tort of interference with trade or business by unlawful means and the defendant would not justify the commission of the tort by proving that the unlawful act was done for the predominant purpose of furthering his own commercial interests. Justification would not, therefore, be regarded in England as a defence to the tort of interference with trade or business by unlawful means.

IX: THE ACTION ON THE CASE FOR DAMAGES (BEAUDESERT)

It has been suggested in the previous discussion that the specific torts of interference with contractual relations, intimidation and conspiracy and the general tort of interference with trade or business by unlawful means all require, as an essential ingredient of those torts, an intention to inflict economic harm on the plaintiff. What if there is no such intention but there is instead an intentional *act* which, in fact, causes economic harm to the plaintiff? The remedy for such economic harm, it is suggested, is an action on the case for damages based upon the decision in *Beaudesert Shire Council* v. *Smith*.[436] In that case, the High Court of Australia decided that an action on the case to recover damages from another was available, independently of trespass, negligence or nuisance, to 'a person

431 This is now dealt with, in some cases, by the action on the case for damages based on the *Beaudesert* case.

432 [1991] 3 W.L.R. 188, 200.

433 See *Ansett Transport Industries (Operations) Pty Ltd* v. *Australian Federation of Air Pilots* [1991] 1 V.R. 637, 677. See also *Read* v. *Friendly Society of Operative Stonemasons of England, Ireland and Wales* [1902] 2 K.B. 732, 739; *Brisbane Shipwrights' Provident Union* v. *Heggie* (1906) 3 C.L.R. 686, 702; *Camden Nominees Ltd* v. *Forcey* [1940] Ch. 352, 362 and *Posluns* v. *Toronto Stock Exchange* (1964) 46 D.L.R. (2d) 210, 285-7.

434 [1981] 2 N.S.W.L.R. 843, 869.

435 [1989] 3 W.L.R. 631, 637 and 640 *per* Dillon and Ralph Gibson L.JJ.

436 (1966) 120 C.L.R. 145. See also pp. 124-6 above.

who suffers harm or loss as the inevitable consequence of the unlawful, intentional and positive acts' of the other.

In *Kitano* v. *The Commonwealth*, Mason J. indicated that in an action on the case for damages based on *Beaudesert* 'the existence of an intention on the part of the defendant to cause harm to the plaintiff' was not necessary to found liability in that tort.[437] It was sufficient to found liability, provided that the other elements were present, that the *act* was intentional and its inevitable consequence was to cause loss to the plaintiff. Expressed, as it is, in such general terms, the potential use of this tort, in cases of intentional interferences which inevitably result in purely economic losses, is very great. But no such action has succeeded since the decision in the *Beaudesert* case, even though several attempts have been made to base a claim on this tort.[438] In *Macksville & District Hospital* v. *Mayze* Kirby P. of the Court of Appeal of New South Wales regarded the decision in the *Beaudesert* case as binding on the Court of Appeal.[439] As suggested earlier,[440] it is desirable that the scope of this innominate tort be better delineated by the High Court of Australia, and preferably by a court of seven justices as suggested in *Elston* v. *Dore*.[441]

But until that happens it may be useful to know that an action on the case based on *Beaudesert* is available to a person for the recovery of economic losses which flow inevitably as a consequence from the intentional acts of another even though there may be no intention on the part of the defendant to injure the plaintiff financially. To take the *Beaudesert* case itself as an example, it could hardly be said that any intention to wreak economic damage on the plaintiff was present in that case yet the plaintiff was able to recover the damage that he suffered from the defendant because it was the inevitable consequence of the unlawful, intentional and positive act of the defendant, namely, its unlawful trespass in removing gravel from the river-bed which was in the exclusive possession of a third party.

X: MALICIOUS PROSECUTION AND ABUSE OF PROCESS

There are two other actions on the case which can be used by a plaintiff to recover purely economic loss which he has suffered as a result of an intentional act on the part of the defendant. These are the tort of

---

437 (1973-74) 129 C.L.R. 151, 174.

438 See *Kitano* v. *The Commonwealth* (1973-74) 129 C.L.R. 151; *Dunlop* v. *Woollahra Municipal Council* [1981] 1 N.S.W.L.R. 76; *Copyright Agency Ltd* v. *Haines* [1982] 1 N.S.W.L.R. 82; *Elston* v. *Dore* (1982) 43 A.L.R. 577; *Hospitals Contribution Fund of Australia* v. *Hunt* (1982) 44 A.L.R. 365; *Grand Central Car Park Pty Ltd* v. *Tivoli Freeholders* [1969] V.R. 62 and *Chan Yee Kin* v. *Minister for Immigration, Local Government and Ethnic Affairs* (1991) 103 A.L.R. 499.

439 (1987) 10 N.S.W.L.R. 708, 724.

440 See p. 126 above.

441 (1983) 57 A.L.J.R. 83, 86.

malicious prosecution and the tort of abuse of process. Recent developments in the tort of malicious prosecution suggest that the tort might be used by a plaintiff to recover purely economic loss when the defendant has instituted legal proceedings against the plaintiff maliciously and without reasonable and probable cause and those proceedings, though they have terminated in the plaintiff's favour, have nevertheless caused him some purely economic loss particularly in the form of expenses in defending those legal proceedings. More detailed discussion of the requirements of this tort and its possible extension to protect economic interests is to be found in Chapter 2. The tort of abuse of process can also be used by a plaintiff to recover purely economic loss which is caused to him when a defendant uses the process of the court, although in its regular form, for a purpose other than that for which the process was properly designed and exists or with the dominant motive of exerting pressure to effect an object not within the scope of the process. More detailed discussion of the possible role of the tort of abuse of process in protecting economic interests is also found in Chapter 2.

XI: THE ACTION FOR MISFEASANCE IN A PUBLIC OFFICE

There is yet another common law tort which is available to a person who suffers purely economic loss. This is the tort of misfeasance in a public office, which is available as a result of the intentional and wrongful conduct on the part of some public officials. The tort appears to be well established in Australia[442] and its existence was recognized by the Privy Council in *Dunlop* v. *Woollahra Municipal Council.*[443] The existence of the tort has also been recognized in New Zealand.[444]

The best definition of this tort is, perhaps, that of Smith J. of the Supreme Court of Victoria in *Farrington* v. *Thomson and Bridgland* where he said:

> If a public officer does an act which, to his knowledge, amounts to an abuse of his office, and he thereby causes damage to another person, then an action in tort for misfeasance in a public office will lie against him at the suit of that person.[445]

No detailed treatment of the precise requirements or limits of this tort is offered here, but it should be noted that the tort is only available against a holder of a public office, that is, generally speaking, a person who is paid out of public funds and who 'owes duties to members of the public as to

---

442 See *Farrington* v. *Thomson and Bridgland* [1959] V.R. 286; *Tampion* v. *Anderson* [1973] V.R. 715; *Pemberton* v. *Attorney-General* [1978] Tas.S.R. 1; and *Campbell* v. *Ramsay* (1968) 70 S.R.(N.S.W.) 327.

443 (1981) 33 A.L.R. 621, 630. The decision of the Supreme Court of Tasmania in *Poke* v. *Eastburn* [1964] Tas.S.R. 98 which seemed to doubt the existence of the tort can now safely be ignored.

444 See *Takaro Properties Ltd* v. *Rowling* [1978] 2 N.Z.L.R. 314.

445 [1959] V.R. 286, 293.

how the office shall be exercised',[446] if the holder of that office abuses that office. The plaintiff must show 'not only damage from the abuse; he must also show that he was the member of the public, to whom the holder of the office owed a duty not to commit the particular abuse complained of'.[447]

What kind of wrongful intentional conduct on the part of a public officer is necessary to establish liability in the tort of misfeasance in a public office? Again, the words of Smith J. in *Farrington's* case offer us some guidance in the matter:

> Some of the authorities seem to assume that in order to establish a cause of action for misfeasance in a public office it is, or may be, necessary to show that the officer acted maliciously, in the sense of having an intention to injure . . . It appears to me, however, that this is not so and that it is sufficient to show that he acted with knowledge that what he did was an abuse of his office.[448]

In *Farrington's* case itself, the defendants (two police officers) entered the plaintiff's hotel and *ordered* the plaintiff (licensee) to close the bar and to cease trading in liquor as a result of certain convictions under the Licensing Act. The defendants purported to exercise and threatened to exercise 'powers which they were well aware that they did not possess'.[449] The plaintiff obeyed the order and as a result suffered damage through the closure of the hotel. Smith J. decided that the giving of the order to close the hotel constituted a tort of misfeasance in a public office (even though the jury found that the defendants were acting honestly in the belief that the plaintiff's licence had terminated) and he awarded damages against the defendants for amounts assessed by the jury. So it seems that the tort can be committed when a public officer acts maliciously[450] or when he deliberately exceeds his power.[451] But in the absence of either malice or deliberate acts in excess of power, there will be no wrongful intentional conduct which 'is capable of amounting to such "misfeasance" as is a necessary element in this tort'.[452] This view has been affirmed by the Privy Council in *Dunlop* v. *Woollahra Municipal Council*[453] and more recently by the Appeal Division of the Supreme Court of Victoria in *Little* v. *Law Institute of Victoria & Others (No. 3)*.[454]

The plaintiff must prove damage in order to succeed in this tort. As Smith J. said in the *Farrington* case, 'proof of damage is, of course,

---

446 See *Tampion* v. *Anderson* [1973] V.R. 715, 720.
447 ibid.
448 [1959] V.R. 286, 293.
449 ibid., 290.
450 For a discussion of the requirement of malice in this tort, see R. Evans (1982) 31 *I.C.L.Q.* 640, 649-54.
451 In *Calveley* v. *Chief Constable of the Merseyside Police* [1989] 2 W.L.R. 624, 632, Lord Bridge in the House of Lords indicated that the act must at least be 'done in bad faith or (possibly) without reasonable cause'.
452 See *Dunlop* v. *Woollahra Municipal Council* (1981) 33 A.L.R. 621, 630. See also *Pemberton* v. *Attorney-General* [1978] Tas.S.R. 1, 29-31.
453 (1981) 33 A.L.R. 621, 630.
454 [1990] V.R. 257, 269-71. See also *Bourgoin S.A.* v. *Ministry of Agriculture, Fisheries and Food* [1986] 1 Q.B. 716, 775-7 *per* Oliver L.J.

necessary in addition'.[455] There is a suggestion in that case that exemplary damages cannot be awarded in this tort[456] but it is doubtful whether that view is correct. Even in England, where the categories of cases in which exemplary damages can be awarded are restricted, it is recognized that an award of exemplary damages can be made in cases of 'oppressive, arbitrary or unconstitutional action by servants of the government'.[457] In Australia, where the categories of cases in which an award of exemplary damages may be made are much wider[458] than the three categories postulated by Lord Devlin in *Rookes* v. *Barnard*,[459] it is more than likely that an award of exemplary damages can properly be made in an appropriate case in relation to conduct which amounts to the tort of misfeasance in a public office.

XII: STATUTORY PROVISIONS

No discussion of the intentional infliction of economic loss in Australia today can be complete without at least a brief mention of some of the statutory provisions which attempt in various ways to prevent persons, particularly traders, from inflicting economic loss on others in the course of business. It is important to realize that the conduct regulated by such common law torts as deceit, injurious falsehood and passing off is also regulated by Federal legislation[460] and legislation of the States and Territories.[461]

Among the most important statutes of this vast amount of legislation is the Trade Practices Act 1974 (Cwth) which, principally by ss.52, 53 and 55 of that Act, proscribes 'misleading or deceptive conduct', 'false representations', 'false and misleading statements' and 'conduct that is liable to mislead the public' in relation to goods and services. The Act was probably intended to supplement some of the common law torts discussed in this chapter, but more and more tort actions are being brought as proceedings under the Trade Practices Act 1974, (particularly under s.52

---

455 [1959] V.R. 286, 293.
456 ibid., 291.
457 See *Rookes* v. *Barnard* [1984] A.C. 1129, 1226.
458 See *Uren* v. *John Fairfax & Sons Pty Ltd* (1966) 117 C.L.R. 118.
459 [1964] A.C. 1129.
460 Principally the Trades Practices Act 1974 (Cwth) (as amended).
461 The relevant legislation is as follows: Fair Trading Act 1987 (NSW) Part 5—Fair Trading; Fair Trading Act 1989 (Qld) Part III—Trade Practices, Division I—General Rules; Fair Trading Act 1987 (SA) Part X, Division II—Trade Practices; Fair Trading Act 1987 (WA) Part II—Unfair Practices, Division 1—Misleading Conduct and False Representations; Fair Trading Act 1990 (Tas.) Part 2—Fair Trading; Fair Trading Act 1985 (Vic.) Part II—Unfair Practices, Division 1—Misleading Conduct and False Representation. Consumer Affairs and Fair Trading Act 1990 (N.T.) Part V Fair Trading, Division I—Prohibition of Unfair Trade Practices. Law Reform (Misrepresentation) Act 1977 (N.T.) ss.7, 8 and 9. It is not proposed to discuss this legislation in the various States and Territories any further.

of that Act)[462] and the common law torts of deceit, injurious falsehood and passing off, may well decline in importance in the future as ss.52, 53 and 55 are relied upon, increasingly, in addition to or as a substitution for these torts. In this connection it should be noted that s.52 goes further than the torts of deceit, injurious falsehood and passing off, for it not only proscribes misleading or deceptive conduct but it also makes liable those persons who unwittingly contravene s.52 'by engaging in conduct which was at least *likely* to mislead'.[463]

It may be an exaggeration to say that no important discussion of the torts of deceit, injurious falsehood and passing off can be undertaken today without a consideration of s.52 of the Trade Practices Act 1974 but it is also quite obvious that many actions which could have been brought in deceit, injurious falsehood and passing off have also been brought under s.52 of the Trade Practices Act 1974. This has happened in many cases since the introduction of the Act.[464]

Until recently, when proceedings under s.52 of the Trade Practices Act were brought, they were heard in the Federal Court. This ensured such proceedings a much more speedy hearing than proceedings in a State Supreme Court. The High Court of Australia decided in *Fencott* v. *Muller*[465] that the Federal Court had jurisdiction to hear common law claims (such as claims in tort) if those claims are associated with claims under the Trade Practices Act. This is commonly described as the pendant or accrued jurisdiction of the Federal Court. As a result of that decision many claims in tort, particularly in the areas which we are now considering, ended up in the Federal Court either as proceedings under s.52 of the Trade Practices Act or as claims associated with claims under the Trade Practices Act. When these proceedings were brought in the Federal Court there was a variety of remedies available to an applicant which would not be available to him if the action was being brought as a tort action in the Supreme Court of a State. Apart from being able to grant an injunction under s.80 of the Trade Practices Act and to award damages under s.82, the Federal Court is also empowered under s.87 to make a variety of ancillary orders. The common law remedies by comparison would have seemed rather feeble to an applicant. There was also the possibility, in some cases,

---

462 See also F.A. Trindade, 'Section 52 as an Alternative to Remedies in Tort' in *Practical Uses of Section 52 of the Trade Practices Act*, Monash Continuing Legal Education Transcripts, Faculty of Law, Monash University, 1984, pp. 49-64.

463 Italics added. See *Yorke* v. *Ross Lucas Pty Ltd* (1983) 45 A.L.R. 299, 314 and *Hornsby Building Information Centre Pty Ltd* v. *Sydney Building Information Centre Ltd* (1978) 140 C.L.R. 216, 228.

464 See *Yorke* v. *Ross Lucas Pty Ltd* (1983) 45 A.L.R. 299, *Frith* v. *Gold Coast Minerals Springs Pty Ltd* (1983) A.T.P.R. 40-339 and *Fencott* v. *Muller* (1983) 46 A.L.R. 41 (deceit); *Hanimex Pty Ltd* v. *Kodak (Australasia) Pty Ltd* (1982) 1 T.P.R. 1; *Commercial Bank of Australia Ltd* v. *Insurance Brokers Association of Australia* (1977) 16 A.L.R. 161; *Calsil Ltd* v. *TVW Enterprises Ltd* (1984) decision of Jenkinson J., 11 April 1984 (unreported) and *Schindler Lifts Australia Pty Ltd* v. *Debelak* (1989) 89 A.L.R. 275 (injurious falsehood); and *Hornsby Building Information Centre Pty Ltd* v. *Sydney Building Information Centre Ltd* (1978) 140 C.L.R. 216; *Parkdale Custom Built Furniture Pty Ltd* v. *Puxu Pty Ltd* (1982) 56 A.L.J.R. 715 and *Taco Company of Australia Ltd* v. *Taco Bell Pty Ltd* (1982) 42 A.L.R. 177 (passing off).

465 (1983) 152 C.L.R. 570, 608.

that a successful claim under s.52 of the Trade Practices Act might yield more by way of damages than a tort action at common law as Fisher J. in *Yorke* v. *Ross Lucas Pty Ltd* suggested.[466] In *Musca* v. *Astle Corporation*, French J. in the Federal Court decided that exemplary damages were not recoverable under ss.82 and 87 of the Trade Practices Act but that s.22 of the Federal Court of Australia Act 1976 (Cwth) empowered the court to award exemplary damages in the disposition of a cause of action raised under the accrued jurisdiction of the court, where such relief would be available at common law and that the tort of deceit, with its essential element of fraud, was a paradigm case for an award of exemplary damages.[467]

Even a cursory glance at the decisions involving the torts of deceit, injurious falsehood and passing off suggest that there was a widespread and frequent resort to the use of ss.52, 53 and 55 of the Trade Practices Act in order to ensure that the proceedings were heard in the Federal Court.

The position has changed somewhat with the coming into operation of the cross-vesting legislation of the Commonwealth[468] and the States.[469] As a result of this legislation (and amendments to the Trade Practices Act 1974) actions for deceit, injurious falsehood and passing off and actions under ss.52, 53 and 55 of the Trade Practices Act 1974 can now be brought either in the Federal Court or the Supreme Court of a State or Territory at the choice of the plaintiff.[470] The jurisdiction of the Federal Court in relation to matters arising under ss.52, 53 and 55 of the Trade Practices Act 1974 is no longer exclusive and s.86(2) of the Trade Practices Act 1974 (by an amendment to the Act effected in 1987) invests the several courts of the States and the several courts of the Territories with Federal jurisdiction to determine these matters 'within the limits of their several jurisdictions'. The cross-vesting legislation and amendments made in 1987 to the Trade Practices Act 1974 empower the court in which these actions are brought to transfer the proceedings to another court if it appears more appropriate that the relevant proceeding be determined by the other court or if it is in the interests of justice to effect such a transfer.[471] Actions for deceit, injurious falsehood and passing off and actions under ss.52, 53 and 55 of the Trade Practices Act which are brought in the Federal Court could

---

466 See (1983) 45 A.L.R. 299, 319 where Fisher J., while accepting that a guide to the relevant measure of damages to be awarded in that case should be the approach generally adopted in tort, and more particularly in an action in deceit, nevertheless felt that he should not confine himself to the principles accepted in actions in deceit and that there was no bar to his 'making an assessment of all the loss suffered by the applicants in consequence of their purchase'.

467 (1988) 80 A.L.R. 251, 268.

468 See Jurisdiction of Courts (Cross-vesting) Act 1987 (Cwth).

469 See the Jurisdiction of Courts (Cross-vesting) Act 1987 enacted in all the States and the Northern Territory.

470 See s.4 of the Jurisdiction of Courts (Cross-vesting) Act 1987 of the Commonwealth, the States and the Northern Territory and ss.86(1) and 86(2) of the Trade Practices Act 1974 (the amendments to the Trade Practices Act 1974 were also enacted in 1987).

471 See s.5 of the Jurisdiction of Courts (Cross-vesting) Act 1987 of the Commonwealth, the States and the Northern Territory and s.86A of the Trade Practices Act 1974 (s.86A was inserted by an amendment in 1987 to the Trade Practices Act 1974).

therefore be transferred to the Supreme Court of a State or Territory or vice versa. While s.10 of the Jurisdiction of Courts (Cross-vesting) Act 1987 of the Commonwealth and the States and the Northern Territory allows the Federal Court, the Supreme Court, or the Supreme Court of another State or a Territory where such an action is pending, to transfer the proceeding even to an inferior court of a State or Territory, s.86A of the Trade Practices Act 1974 imposes the condition that the court concerned cannot transfer the proceeding to another court unless that other court has power to grant the remedies sought before the transferring court in the matter and the transferring court is satisfied that the matter arises out of or is related to a proceeding that is pending in that other court or it is otherwise in the interests of justice that the matter be determined by that other court.[472] The cross-vesting legislation does not allow an appeal against a decision of a court, which is seized of the matter, to transfer the matter to another court.[473] A decision given by a single judge of the Federal Court cannot be made the subject of an appeal to the Full Court of a Supreme Court nor can a decision given by a single judge of a Supreme Court be the subject of an appeal to the Full Federal Court.[474] The cross-vesting legislation has, therefore, effected a significant change in the way that the torts of deceit, injurious falsehood and passing off and actions under ss.52, 53 and 55 of the Trade Practices Act are being litigated and will be litigated in the future.

Torts lawyers in Australia, particularly in view of the cross-vesting legislation, must therefore familiarize themselves with all the statutory provisions in the area of consumer protection and in particular with ss.52, 53 and 55 of the Trade Practices Act 1974. It may well be that in the years ahead we shall see these provisions being used as much more effective remedies for the recovery of intentionally inflicted economic losses than the traditional common law torts of deceit, injurious falsehood and passing off and we shall also see those provisions being used not only in the Federal Court but also in the Supreme Courts of the States and Territories, and perhaps even in the inferior courts of the States and Territories.

472 See s.86A(6) of the Trade Practices Act 1974 which was enacted in 1987.
473 See s.13 of the Jurisdiction of Courts (Cross-vesting) Act 1987 of the Commonwealth, the States and the Northern Territory.
474 ibid., s.7.

6

DEFENCES TO INTENTIONAL TORTS

I: SOME GENERAL COMMENTS

Normally, the intentional (or even reckless) conduct of the defendant described in the preceding chapters should result in liability in tort where the plaintiff's physical and mental integrity, land or goods have been interfered with by that intentional conduct. Over the years, however, the courts have developed certain situations of immunity from actions in tort in relation to what would otherwise be actionable intentional conduct. Where such a situation of immunity from tort action exists, the defendant is said to have a defence to an action in tort.

Some of these defences apply not only to the intentional torts but can also be raised in relation to other torts, but in this chapter we are only concerned with the defences as they relate to the intentional torts which have been considered in the previous chapters.

Why have these defences to actions in tort been created and developed by the courts? The answer in relation to most of these defences is that public policy requires that immunity from an action in tort be accorded to persons in certain circumstances as it is in the interest of society generally that their conduct be encouraged and not discouraged by making them pay damages to the plaintiff in respect of that conduct. Thus, if D sees P about to run into his burning house in order to rescue some valuable paintings and D forcibly restrains P from entering his own house because he believes P will be in imminent peril if he does enter, P's actions in trespass to the person (battery or false imprisonment) or trespass to land (preventing the plaintiff from entering his own house[1]) would be met by the defence of necessity. It is in the interest of all of us that D should be immune from actions in tort if P decides to sue him when D's interference was both necessary and reasonable. Similarly, if D interferes with P's chattel in order to prevent damage to the chattel itself or damage to chattels of another, an action of trespass to goods brought by P would be

1 *Waters* v. *Maynard* (1924) 24 S.R. (N.S.W.) 618.

met with the defence of necessity. The existence of any other rule, said Hannan A.J. of the Supreme Court of South Australia in *Proudman* v. *Allen*,[2] would only encourage on the part of the community generally 'an attitude of callous indifference to the imminent destruction of property which might be easily prevented' and 'the common law, for reasons of public policy' would not, therefore, recognize any other rule.

The rest of the discussion in this chapter is devoted to a consideration of the decisions of the courts and legislation in Australia which together have created and developed these situations of immunity from actions in tort which today are described as defences to actions in tort. Each of these defences will be described in turn and if the defence is specifically applicable or not applicable to some torts then this will be pointed out.

II: DEFENCES TO INTENTIONAL TORTS TO THE PERSON AND PROPERTY

1. Necessity

The defence of necessity creates an immunity from liability in tort for a defendant who intentionally interferes with the person or property of another if the interference is reasonably necessary as a means of protecting either persons or property from the threat of real and imminent harm. Thus, a defendant who *prima facie* committed a trespass to the person (battery) by forcibly feeding a suffragette prisoner, sometimes through the mouth and sometimes through the nose, because he felt that it was necessary to save her life,[3] a defendant who committed a trespass to land in order to preserve his master's sporting rights[4] and a defendant who committed a trespass to the plaintiff's goods in order to protect the plaintiff's and others' property from the imminent risk of damage and destruction[5] were all held not liable, using the defence of necessity, for what would otherwise clearly have been intentional tortious conduct. The decisions were based on the ground that the various acts were necessary to preserve life or protect property from real and imminent harm.

If the defence of necessity is to be successfully raised the defendant must prove that it was reasonably *necessary* to do the act, in respect of which the action is brought, to preserve life or protect property from a situation of great danger or harm.[6] It is not sufficient to show that it was *convenient* to do it.[7] Secondly, the defendant must prove that the situation of great danger or harm from which the defendant attempted to preserve life or

2 [1954] S.A.S.R. 336.

3 See *Leigh* v. *Gladstone* (1909) 26 T.L.R. 139. See also s.463B, Crimes Act 1958 (Vic.) which allows any person to use such force as is necessary to prevent another person from committing suicide.

4 See *Cope* v. *Sharpe (No. 2)* [1912] 1 K.B. 496.

5 See *Proudman* v. *Allen* [1954] S.A.S.R. 336.

6 See *Kirk* v. *Gregory* (1876) 1 Ex.D. 55 and *Proudman* v. *Allen* [1954] S.A.S.R. 336, 340.

7 See *Murray* v. *McMurchy* [1949] 2 D.L.R. 442, 445.

protect property was one which created 'an urgent situation of imminent peril'.[8] Thirdly, the defendant must also prove that such an urgent situation of imminent peril '*existed actually*, and not merely in the belief of the defendant'.[9] It is not necessary for the defendant to prove that the means adopted to preserve life or to protect property in an urgent situation of imminent peril actually succeeded in preserving life or in protecting property.[10] Nor is it necessary for the defendant to prove that the person or property sought to be protected would, but for the interference complained of, have suffered injury or destruction.[11] And, fourthly, the defendant must show that it was not any act of negligence on his part which created or contributed to the occasion of necessity if he is to rely successfully on the defence of necessity.[12]

While the state undoubtedly has a strong interest in protecting and preserving the health of its citizens, this interest, it would appear, does not prevent a competent adult from refusing even life-preserving medical treatment. If this refusal is clear, those who perform medical treatment, even in the justifiable belief that the treatment was necessary to save the life or to preserve the health of the person refusing treatment, will incur tortious liability and will not be able to avail themselves of the defence of necessity. In the recent decision in *Malette* v. *Shulman*[13] the Court of Appeal of Ontario held that a medical practitioner who had administered blood transfusions to an unconscious accident victim who was carrying a Jehovah's Witness card requesting that no blood or blood products be administered to her under any circumstances had committed a battery even though his honest and justifiable belief was that the administration of the blood transfusions was medically essential and may well have been responsible for saving her life. The defence of necessity was unsuccessful.

The defence of necessity when successfully raised allows the defendant to escape liability in the tort action which is being brought by the plaintiff. But should the defendant nevertheless be required to compensate the plaintiff for the damage that he has suffered as a result of the act done under the defence of necessity so that an innocent plaintiff who does not derive any benefit from the act does not have to bear this loss? It has been suggested that there should be quasi-contractual liability resting not upon the doer of the act as such but upon the person whose interests are advanced by the act.[14] But there are problems 'when we try to make the law of torts redress unjust enrichment as well as remedy wrongs'.[15] After all, the situations in which the defence of necessity may be successfully raised are many and varied. The act of necessity might be done by the

---

8 See *Southwark London Borough Council* v. *Williams* [1971] 1 Ch. 734, 746.
9 See *Cope* v. *Sharpe (No. 2)* [1912] 1 K.B. 496, 508.
10 ibid., 502.
11 ibid., 508.
12 See *Rigby* v. *Chief Constable of Northamptonshire* [1985] 1 W.L.R. 1242, 1254.
13 (1990) 72 O.R. (2d) 417. See also Human Tissue Act 1982 (Vic.) and Medical Treatment Act 1988 (Vic.).
14 See F.H. Bohlen (1926) *Harv. L.R.* 307, 316.
15 See Glanville Williams (1953) 6 *C.L.P.* 216, 231.

defendant for the plaintiff's own benefit, as in *Leigh* v. *Gladstone*;[16] it might be done for the benefit of a third party, as in *Proudman* v. *Allen*;[17] or it might be done for the defendant's own benefit, as in *Greyvensteyn* v. *Hattingh*.[18] It might also be done for the plaintiff's benefit, the defendant's benefit and the benefit of many others, as is shown by *Mouse's* Case[19] where the defendant threw a casket belonging to the plaintiff (Mouse) overboard so as to lighten a barge which had on board the plaintiff, the defendant and forty-seven passengers (other passengers threw things overboard as well). It was proved that if the various things had not been thrown overboard all the passengers would have drowned. The defence of necessity prevailed to relieve the defendant of liability in tort. Whose interests could it be said were advanced by the defendant's act and in what proportions should the liability be apportioned? As the question of compensation for damage done by acts of necessity is not likely to be easily resolved it is important that the defence of necessity be carefully circumscribed. There is some evidence that this is being done.[20]

Whatever the position in relation to acts done because of private necessity, do the courts take a different view in relation to innocent victims of acts done because of a public necessity? What about the plaintiff whose house is pulled down in time of fire, by order of an officer of the Fire Brigade, in order to stop the fire from spreading?[21] In *Southwark London Borough Council* v. *Williams*, Lord Denning M.R. said that such an act 'has always been justified *pro bono publico*'.[22] And in *Shaw Savill and Albion Co. Ltd* v. *The Commonwealth*, Dixon J. pointed out that 'the law has always recognized that rights of property and of person must give way to the necessities of the defence of the realm'.[23] It is not clear that Dixon J. was here necessarily referring to any prerogative of the Crown nor is it clear from his judgment whether he thought any compensation should be payable in respect of any such damage in any circumstances. Counsel for the Commonwealth of Australia argued, however, that '[t]he King may destroy property of the subject for the national good and the subject is not entitled to any compensation therefor. If anything were done intentionally and it were urgently required in the operation, then clearly no right to compensation for the damage

---

16 (1909) 26 T.L.R. 139.
17 [1954] S.A.S.R. 336.
18 [1911] A.C. 355. In this case the defendant diverted locusts from his own land with the result that they damaged the plaintiff's crops.
19 (1609) 12 Co. Rep 63.
20 See *Southwark London Borough Council* v. *Williams* [1971] 1 Ch. 734.
21 Authority to do this is given by statute in every State and Territory of Australia. See e.g. Metropolitan Fire Brigade Act 1958 (Vic.), s. 33.
22 [1971] 1 Ch. 734, 743.
23 (1940) 66 C.L.R. 344, 362.

would arise'.[24] In 1984 several members of the Australian Security Intelligence Service (ASIS) caused injury to several persons and damage to property during what is now commonly described as a 'bungled ASIS exercise' at the Sheraton Hotel in Melbourne. In the High Court of Australia,[25] Dawson J. refused to grant an application by the Commonwealth to be released from undertakings earlier given and injunctions earlier granted in the High Court permanently restraining the Commonwealth from releasing the names of the ASIS officers. The undertakings and injunctions which were granted on the basis of national security have the effect of preventing the plaintiffs from bringing actions for intentional trespass to the person, land and goods because the identities of the defendants have not been disclosed. The Commonwealth Government, however, made a substantial offer of compensation to the parties who suffered loss or damage as a result of the incident. It is suggested that this example should be followed and innocent victims of acts done because of a public necessity should receive offers of compensation from the government concerned commensurate with the losses suffered by them. In the alternative, the defence of public necessity should also be very strictly circumscribed.

2. INCAPACITY

It has already been pointed out that the courts will only go on to consider whether there has been an intentional act on the part of the defendant if there is a voluntary act on his part.[26] So there will be no liability for an involuntary act, for example, for a battery committed in a state of automatism or for a trespass to land if the defendant is involuntarily carried on to the land of the plaintiff.[27] But if the act is voluntary can the defendant raise the defence of incapacity in relation to what *prima facie* looks like his intentional conduct, by alleging either insanity or infancy, and avoid liability on that account?

(a) Insanity In *White* v. *Pile*[28] where the defendant, who was a lunatic, committed a battery upon the plaintiff, O'Sullivan D.C.J. felt that it was 'more in accord with reason and the common sense of the thing to allow immunity from the civil consequences of the tort of [battery] committed by an insane person where the nature and degree of his insanity are such

---

24 ibid., 350. Note, however, that in *Burmah Oil Co. Ltd* v. *Lord Advocate* [1965] A.C. 75 the House of Lords decided that while no compensation was payable for damage, whether accidental or deliberate, actually done in the course of fighting operations (battle damage), the Crown had no prerogative to take or destroy property, which was not battle damage, without the payment of compensation. The United Kingdom Parliament in the War Damage Act 1965 reversed, with retroactive effect, the decision in that case by legislating to the effect that no compensation was payable in the circumstances of that case which the House of Lords had held was not battle damage.

25 See the *Age* (Melbourne), 3 May 1984 p.6.

26 See pp. 30-1, 110 and 132 above.

27 See *Smith* v. *Stone* (1647) Sty. 65.

28 (1951) 68 W.N.(N.S.W.) 176.

as would establish a defence if the [battery] were the subject of a criminal charge'.[29] But in *Morris* v. *Marsden*[30] where Stable J. found that at the time of the attack on the plaintiff the defendant's mind 'directed the blows he struck',[31] the defence of insanity was held not to be available to the defendant even though he was a certifiable lunatic. Stable J. said that he had come to the conclusion that 'knowledge of wrongdoing is an immaterial averment, and that, where there is the capacity to know the nature and quality of the act, that is sufficient although the mind directing the hand that did the wrong was diseased'.[32] The decision of Stable J. in *Morris* v. *Marsden* is to be preferred to the decision in *White* v. *Pile*. If a court has to choose where to place the loss for the actions of a lunatic defendant there is no good reason why it should not place it upon the lunatic defendant rather than his innocent victim, the plaintiff.[33] This is particularly so if it can be shown, as it was in *Morris* v. *Marsden*, that the defendant knew the nature and quality of his act even though he did not appreciate that what he was doing was wrong.[34] However, if a defendant by reason of insanity is incapable of appreciating the nature and quality of his acts, then in such circumstances the insanity of the defendant would be available to him as a defence, either on the ground that the act cannot be described as voluntary or on the basis that the defendant is incapable of forming the necessary intention for intentional conduct.[35] The onus of proving insanity is on the party alleging it.

The decision in *Morris* v. *Marsden* is not necessarily confined to cases of trespass to the person but also applies to the other intentional torts. As Stable J. said in *Morris* v. *Marsden*:

> I cannot think that, if a person of unsound mind converts my property under a delusion that he is entitled to do it or that it was not property at all, that affords a defence. I can bring an action against him for the recovery of my property, or, if it has been converted and destroyed, for its value.[36]

(b) Infancy To what extent is infancy a defence to an intentional tort? In *Smith* v. *Leurs*[37] Mayo J. of the Supreme Court of South Australia held the defendant, a 13-year-old boy, liable for an intentional battery when he discharged a stone from a 'shanghai' and struck the plaintiff. Mayo J. was of the view that '[a] boy of the age of seven years and upwards is in general

---

29 ibid., 180.
30 [1952] 1 All E.R. 925.
31 ibid., 926.
32 ibid., 928.
33 See E.C.E. Todd (1952) 26 *A.L.J.* 299, 303 who suggests that in the law of torts, evidence of insanity should be considered as a subsidiary factor in mitigation of damages but not as excluding liability.
34 The decision in *Morris* v. *Marsden* has been approved in *Beals* v. *Hayward* [1960] N.Z.L.R. 131, *Phillips* v. *Soloway* (1957) 6 D.L.R. (2d) 570 and *Lawson* v. *Wellesley Hospital* (1976) 61 D.L.R. (3d) 445. See also *Beale* v. *Beale* (1982) 106 A.P.R. 550.
35 See *Lawson* v. *Wellesley Hospital* (1976) 61 D.L.R. (3d) 445, 452.
36 [1952] 1 All E.R. 925, 927.
37 [1944] S.A.S.R. 213. The decision of the High Court of Australia reported at (1945) 70 C.L.R. 256 is concerned only with the liability of the parents for the tort of their child.

liable for his own wrongs'.[38] In *McHale* v. *Watson,* however, Windeyer J. said:

> A child is personally liable for the consequences of his wrongful acts. This is certainly so if he was old enough to know that his conduct was wrongful—that is to say if, in the common phrase, he was old enough to know better.[39]

This *dictum* of Windeyer J. should not be used to suggest that there will be no liability in the intentional torts if an infant knows the nature and quality of his act but does not appreciate that the act is wrong. As pointed out earlier,[40] in the American case of *Ellis* v. *D'Angelo,*[41] a 4-year-old boy who violently impelled the adult baby-sitter on to the floor causing her to break bones in both arms and wrists was held liable in the intentional tort of battery. The court held that the infant was capable of intending and had intended the battery even though he lacked the mental capacity to recognize the wrongfulness of his conduct. A similar decision has been arrived at in Tasmania in *Hart* v. *Attorney-General for Tasmania and Pascoe.*[42]

In the intentional tort of battery 'the defence of incapacity to have the requisite intention is confined to very young children [and] somewhere about the age of four a child is capable of the intention necessary to commit this tort'.[43] This might also be true in relation to the other intentional torts discussed above.

3. MISTAKE

It is no defence in the intentional torts for a defendant to plead that he did the act under a mistake of fact or law. If D intends to shoot O but instead shoots P who is wearing O's distinctive suit at the time, there is little doubt that there will be an intentional battery and D's mistake will not prevent him from being held liable for the contact which he intended.[44] The only occasion on which mistake may be relevant is in cases of mistaken self-defence. Thus, if D, erroneously but reasonably believing that P is about to attack him, uses force to defend himself there will be no liability provided that D uses no more force than he believed on reasonable grounds to be necessary.[45] If D who has a warrant for T's arrest asks P to come with him to the police station because he mistakenly thinks that P is

---

38 [1944] S.A.S.R. 213, 217.
39 (1964) 111 C.L.R. 384, 386.
40 See p. 36 above.
41 (1953) 253 P.2d 675.
42 The decision is unreported. See *Fleming* (7th edn, 1987) p. 22, fn. 58.
43 See Alexander *Studies in Canadian Family Law,* Vol. 2 (1972) 845, 854.
44 See F.A. Trindade (1982) 2 *O.J.L.S.* 211, 220. In the *Waldorf* case (*The Times,* 20 October 1983) two detectives who shot Waldorf because they had mistaken him for a dangerous fugitive were acquitted of all criminal charges, but the civil action against the detectives was settled by the payment of £100 000 (almost $250 000).
45 See *Hall* v. *Fonceca* [1983] W.A.R. 309.

T, there is no doubt that D will be liable in an action for false imprisonment brought by P.[46] A defendant who walks on to another's land mistakenly thinking it is his own will certainly be liable in an action for trespass to land.[47] A defendant who shot the plaintiff's dog under the mistaken impression that it was a wolf was held liable in trespass to goods,[48] and so was the defendant who mistakenly carried away a sofa belonging to the plaintiff together with other furniture that the defendant had purchased at an auction.[49] In *Rendell* v. *Associated Finance Pty Ltd*[50] the defendant, who repossessed a truck, was held liable for the conversion of an engine which belonged to the plaintiff. The engine had been installed in the truck without the knowledge of the defendant. The Full Court of the Supreme Court of Victoria decided that it did not matter that the defendant was mistaken as to what engine was attached to the truck nor did it matter that the defendant wrongly believed the finance company, on whose behalf he was acting, to be the owner of the engine. Neither mistake was held to be a defence to an action in conversion.

However, in *Elvin & Powell Ltd* v. *Plummer Roddis Ltd*[51] where the defendant, who was an involuntary bailee of goods, mistakenly delivered the goods, to the wrong person, the court held that he was not liable in conversion because 'if persons were involuntary bailees and had done everything reasonable they were not liable to pay damages [in conversion] if something which they did resulted in the loss of the property'.[52] Finally, in *Egan* v. *State Transport Authority*[53] where the defendants seized and detained the plaintiff's plant and materials under the mistaken belief that they had some legal or equitable justification for doing so, they were held liable in both conversion and detinue.

It will be seen, therefore, that mistake of the defendant, except perhaps in the instances mentioned above, will not be able to be raised by the defendant as a defence in any of the intentional torts so far discussed.

4. DISCIPLINE

It is generally accepted that a parent has a right to discipline his or her child and, in the course of exercising that discipline, to inflict bodily punishment on the child. As Sholl J. put it in *R.* v. *Terry*: 'A parent has a lawful right to inflict reasonable and moderate corporal punishment on his or her child for the purpose of correcting the child in wrong behaviour.'[54] But as Sholl J. went on to point out in that case, there are exceedingly strict limits to that right. The punishment must be moderate and reasonable, it must have a proper relation to the age, physique and

---

46 See *Symes* v. *Mahon* [1922] S.A.S.R. 447.
47 See *Basely* v. *Clarkson* (1681) 3 Lev. 37.
48 See *Ranson* v. *Kitner* (1888) 31 Ill.App. 241.
49 See *Colwill* v. *Reeves* (1811) 2 Camp. 575.
50 [1957] V.R. 604.
51 (1933) 50 T.L.R. 158.
52 ibid., 159.
53 [1982] 31 S.A.S.R. 481.
54 [1955] V.L.R. 114, 116.

mentality of the child and it must be carried out with a reasonable means or instrument.[55] The reasonableness of the punishment is a question of fact depending on the circumstances of the case.[56] If the punishment meted out is reasonable and moderate it will provide the parent with a defence to any action for trespass to the person that might be brought by the child. Instances where such actions have been brought are rare, but in a rather ancient case a child successfully brought an action for assault, battery and false imprisonment against her mother.[57]

In the course of disciplining a child a parent can also reasonably deprive the child of his liberty for a reasonable duration or confiscate property of the child such as an air-gun or cigarettes without being liable for false imprisonment or trespass to goods, conversion or detinue.

In addition to parents there are others who, due to the circumstances in which they find themselves, may need to exercise discipline in relation to a child. These persons might be schoolteachers, school bus-drivers, school-crossing supervisors etc. What is their position? It seems to be well established that persons in such positions have the right to discipline a child and that the defence of discipline would be available in an action in tort if a schoolteacher or a school bus-driver applied reasonable and moderate force to compel a schoolboy to stay seated,[58] if a teacher detained a pupil during the lunch break or even after school hours (commonly described as detention or 'det') for a breach of school discipline by the pupil or if a teacher confiscated an air-gun, cigarettes or unsuitable reading material. Although Cullen C.J. of the Supreme Court of New South Wales in *Hole* v. *Williams*[59] suggested that a teacher has a common law right to discipline a pupil simply because the teacher 'exercises an authority delegated to him by the parents of his pupils', the better view is that a teacher's right to discipline a pupil exists, at least under a system of compulsory education, 'not by virtue of a delegation by a parent at all, but by virtue of the nature of the relationship of [teacher] and pupil and the necessity inherent in that relationship of maintaining order in and about the school'.[60] If this view is accepted, the right to discipline would reside in the teacher, school bus-driver etc. because of the supervisory status of these persons and not because of any authority delegated to them by the parent. This would enable the teacher to exercise discipline which might even be contrary to the wishes of the parent of the pupil. Thus, a teacher would be able to confiscate an air-gun given to a pupil by his parent because he believed that it would be a danger to the pupil or others and he would be able to confiscate cigarettes which the pupil has on his person even though the parent of the pupil might not object to the child

---

55 ibid. See also *Smith* v. *O'Byrne* (1894) 5 Q.L.J.R. 127.

56 See *R.* v. *Terry* [1955] V.L.R. 114 and *R.* v. *Trynchy* (1970) 73 W.W.R. 165, 168.

57 *Ann Ash* v. *Lady Ash* (1696) Comb. 357.

58 See *R.* v. *Trynchy* (1970) 73 W.W.R. 165. See also *Craig* v. *Frost* (1936) 30 Q.J.P. 140, 142.

59 (1910) 10 S.R.(N.S.W.) 638, 649.

60 See *Ramsey* v. *Larsen* (1964) 111 C.L.R. 16, 29 where Kitto J. suggested that *Hole* v. *Williams* should be overruled. See also *Hansen* v. *Cole* (1890) 9 N.Z.L.R. 272 and *Murdock* v. *Richards* [1954] 1 D.L.R. 766, 769.

smoking.[61] The right to discipline which the common law gives to teachers is not confined only to the conduct of the pupil within the school but can also extend to conduct outside the school and in relation to conduct outside school hours.[62] School rules are not unreasonable merely because they may extend beyond the actual precincts of the school.[63]

Even where there are regulations (school or governmental) prohibiting certain methods of discipline, for example, corporal punishment, or regulations restricting a method of discipline only to a particular individual, for example, a regulation which restricts the administration of corporal punishment only to the headmaster, it will still be possible for a teacher who acts in breach of those regulations to rely upon the defence of discipline.[64] If a teacher has chastised a pupil contrary to regulations the real questions with which the courts should concern themselves on this occasion, as indeed on all occasions when the defence of discipline is raised, is not whether the act was contrary to regulations but whether it was a reasonable means of preserving discipline, whether the punishment was both moderate and reasonable[65] and whether it was dictated by a genuine motive of chastisement and correction rather than by feelings of spite, rage, fury, anger or ill-will.[66] If the answers to all those questions are in the affirmative then the defence of discipline should be available to the defendant even though it might not be strictly allowed by the regulations of the school or of the Department of Education. It would be wise, however, for a teacher to abide by such regulations as exist in relation to discipline, as a breach of those regulations may lay him open to dismissal for failure to observe the regulations.

Can adults also be subject to the discipline of others so that the defence of discipline can be raised by a defendant in relation to conduct which would otherwise be tortious? There are some decisions which suggest that a ship's captain (and, by analogy, the captain of an aircraft) has a common law right to arrest and confine in a reasonable manner and for a reasonable duration any person on board his ship, whether a passenger or a member of his crew, provided that the arrest and confinement are necessary for either the preservation of order on the ship or the safety of one or more of its passengers or crew (an objective requirement). The ship's captain must also, in fact, believe that the arrest and confinement are necessary for either of those purposes (a subjective requirement).[67] In *Hook* v. *Cunard Steamship Co. Ltd*, Slade J. indicated that the arrest and confinement must comply 'not only with the objective but also with the

---

61 See *Craig* v. *Frost* (1936) 30 Q.J.P. 140.
62 See *Cleary* v. *Booth* [1893] 1 Q.B. 465, 468.
63 See *R.* v. *Newport (Salop) Justices* [1929] 2 K.B. 416.
64 See *King* v. *Nichols* (1939) 33 Q.J.P. 171. See also *Mansell* v. *Griffin* [1908] 1 K.B. 160 and 947.
65 See *Byrne* v. *Hebden* [1913] Q.S.R. 233, 235 and *Ryan* v. *Fildes* [1938] 3 All E.R. 517, 520.
66 See *R.* v. *Terry* [1955] V.L.R. 114, 117 and *Mansell* v. *Griffin* [1908] 1 K.B. 160, 168.
67 See *Hook* v. *Cunard Steamship Co. Ltd* [1953] 1 All E.R. 1021. See also s. 463A, Crimes Act 1958 (Vic.) which allows the person in command of an aircraft in cases of necessity to place a person who is on board the aircraft under restraint or in custody or, if the aircraft is not in the course of flight, to remove a person from the aircraft.

subjective requirements in that respect'.[68] In the interesting case of *Aldworth* v. *Stewart*[69] an Australian passenger on an Australian ship on a voyage from London to Melbourne was forcibly pushed into and confined to his cabin by the captain for seven days 'for his insolence in putting his hand to his nose to the captain'.[70] Channell B. thought that this was probably a case for excluding the plaintiff from the dinner-table rather than imprisoning him and the jury agreed by awarding the plaintiff £25 (in 1866) for the assault and imprisonment.

A husband no longer has any right to discipline his wife, whether his wife is separated or not. Although a decision from the mid-nineteenth century allowed a husband legally to confine his wife within his own dwelling in order to prevent her from eloping,[71] the late nineteenth-century decision in *R.* v. *Jackson*[72] held that a husband could not keep his wife in confinement even in order to enforce a decree of restitution of conjugal rights. More recently, in *R.* v. *Reid,* Cairns L.J. in the English Court of Appeal said that the notion that 'a husband can, without incurring punishment, treat his wife, whether she be a separated wife or otherwise, with any kind of hostile force is obsolete'.[73] So discipline is unlikely to be available as a defence to a husband for a trespass to his wife.

Other adults in relation to whom the defence of discipline might be raised are patients in mental institutions. Their position is now almost entirely dealt with by statute.[74]

5. EX TURPI CAUSA

The defence of *ex turpi causa,* or the defence of illegality, as it is sometimes called, once again illustrates the effect of public policy in this area of the defences to the intentional torts. The defence has been recognized in the law of torts for over a hundred years and was successfully raised in *Hegarty* v. *Shine*[75] in 1878. In that case the plaintiff was a woman who became infected with venereal disease as a result of sexual intercourse with the defendant. The plaintiff did not know of the defendant's condition when she permitted him to have intercourse with her. The Queens Bench Division of Ireland decided that an action of assault (battery) brought by the plaintiff could not be sustained because it arose *ex turpi causa,* having originated in an immoral arrangement. The decision of the Divisional Court was upheld by the Irish Court of Appeal.[76] The best modern description of the defence of *ex turpi causa* is perhaps that of Kitto J's. in *Smith* v. *Jenkins* where he described it as a general principle of law 'that persons who join in committing an illegal

68 ibid., 1023.
69 (1866) 4 F. & F. 957.
70 ibid., 959.
71 *In re Cochrane* (1840) 8 Dowl. 630.
72 [1891] 1 Q.B. 671.
73 [1973] 1 Q.B. 299, 303.
74 See e.g. Mental Health Act 1959 (Vic.).
75 (1878) 2 L.R. Ir. 273.
76 (1878) 4 L.R. Ir. 288.

act which they know to be unlawful or . . . which they must be presumed to know to be unlawful . . . have no legal rights *inter se* by reason of their respective participations in that act'.[77] This suggests that the fact that the plaintiff and the defendant are participating in an illegal course of conduct in which both parties are jointly engaged will afford the defendant a *complete* defence in relation to any tort which arises from that course of conduct. While no doubt this complete immunity from tort action is to discourage persons generally from engaging in illegal conduct it does no credit to the law that an intentional tortfeasor is able to rely upon the illegal nature of the transaction with the victim to escape liability for his own intentional and tortious conduct. Thus, in *Thomas Brown & Sons Ltd* v. *Fazal Deen*[78] the plaintiff, who had deposited nineteen bars of gold with the defendants under a contract of bailment in breach of the National Security (Exchange Control) Regulations in force at the time of the deposit, was held unable to recover the gold from the defendants in an action in detinue as he would be obliged to rely upon the illegal contract of bailment to recover the gold even though it was quite clear that the gold had been given to the defendants by the plaintiff for safekeeping and had been converted by them. This case shows quite clearly that the High Court of Australia has accepted the defence of *ex turpi causa* in relation to the intentional torts. In *Bowmakers Ltd* v. *Barnet Instruments Ltd*[79] the English Court of Appeal did attempt to mitigate the harshness of the application of the principle of *ex turpi causa* by expressing the opinion that:

> [A] man's right to possess his own chattels will as a general rule be enforced against one who, without any claim of right, is detaining them, or has converted them to his own use, even though it may appear from the pleadings, or in the course of the trial, that the chattels in question came into the defendant's possession by reason of an illegal contract between himself and the plaintiff, provided that the plaintiff does not seek, and is not forced, either to found his claim on the illegal contract or to plead its illegality in order to support his claim.

But, unfortunately for the plaintiff in *Thomas Brown & Sons Ltd* v. *Fazal Deen*, the right of action in conversion was time barred and he was therefore obliged to prove the illegal contract of bailment, and the failure of the defendants to redeliver the gold in accordance with that contract, to support his claim in detinue. Quite recently, the High Court of Australia in *Jackson* v. *Harrison*[80] had occasion to consider the defence of *ex turpi causa* and the majority of the court came to the conclusion that the principle denying a remedy to a plaintiff who is a participant in a joint illegal enterprise need not be applied with such rigidity that, in every case in which the parties have been in some respect in breach of the law, the relationship between them must be regarded in the same way. And one of

---

77 (1970) 199 C.L.R. 397, 403.

78 (1962) 108 C.L.R. 391.

79 [1945] K.B. 65.

80 (1978) 138 C.L.R. 438. The defence of *ex turpi causa* was in this case considered in the context of an action in negligence. It could be argued, however, that what the judges had to say about the defence could be applied with equal force to the intentional torts.

the judges expressed the view that the defence of *ex turpi causa* 'should be confined strictly'.[81]

What then is the present position in Australia in relation to the defence of *ex turpi causa* in relation to the intentional torts? The defence of *ex turpi causa,* it would appear, cannot be successfully raised in a tort action to put the plaintiff out of court *merely* because the plaintiff and the defendant were engaged in some common illegal enterprise at the time of the commission of the tort. To take an example: 'if A and B are proceeding to the premises which they intend burglariously to enter and before they enter them, B picks A's pocket and steals his watch',[82] A could sue B in trespass to goods or conversion and B would not be able to raise successfully the defence of *ex turpi causa* in relation to those actions in tort. In order that the defence of *ex turpi causa* can apply, to prevent the plaintiff from recovering from the defendant for an intentional tort, it must be shown by the defendant that the injury or loss was caused as part and parcel of the common illegal enterprise in which both were jointly engaged. Thus, a plaintiff who is party to an illegal prize fight would not be able to recover damages for battery from the defendant who inflicts the injury during the course of the conflict, because the defendant would be able to raise the defence of *ex turpi causa*. Similarly, if P, in pursuance of a pre-arranged scheme, admits D to premises of a bank to enable him to steal the contents of safe deposit boxes from the bank and D, in addition to stealing the contents from the safe deposit boxes of third parties, also steals the contents of P's safe deposit box at the bank, P would not be able to bring an action for trespass to goods or conversion against D because the stealing of P's goods was part and parcel of the illegal course of conduct in which both parties were jointly engaged.[83] Further, if the plaintiff is obliged to prove the illegal transaction or enterprise in order to support his claim in tort, even though the tort is not committed as part and parcel of the illegal course of conduct in which both parties were jointly engaged, then the defence of *ex turpi causa* will apply to defeat the plaintiff's claim as it did in *Thomas Brown & Sons Ltd* v. *Fazal Deen.*[84]

Apart from these situations where the tort is committed during the course of an illegal enterprise or transaction in which both the plaintiff and the defendant are jointly engaged, the defence of *ex turpi causa* might also possibly be raised in some other situations. If a burglar breaks into a house and the householder, finding him there, picks up a gun and shoots him, causing personal injury and property damage (e.g. damage to his expensive watch), the householder might well have a defence on the ground of *ex turpi causa* as Lord Denning M.R. suggested in *Murphy* v. *Culhane.*[85]

---

81 (1978) 138 C.L.R. 438, 465 *per* Murphy J.

82 This example is given by Lord Asquith in *National Coal Board* v. *England* [1954] A.C. 403, 429. Lord Asquith goes on to say, 'I cannot prevail on myself to believe that A could not sue in tort.'

83 See *Saqui and Lawrence* v. *Stearns* [1911] 1 K.B. 426.

84 (1962) 108 C.L.R. 391.

85 [1977] 1 Q.B. 94, 98.

Recently, the defence of *ex turpi causa* arose in two novel situations. In *Gollan* v. *Nugent & Ors*[86] the defendants who were police officers acting under a search warrant seized 'documents, books, posters, tape recordings, photographs, puppets and other things' on premises of the Australian Pedophile Support Group. The plaintiffs, the owners of the goods, alleged that the warrant and seizure were invalid and demanded the return of the goods, but the defendants refused the demand. The plaintiffs' claim for damages in trespass, conversion and detinue was met with the defence that the goods in question were indecent, obscene, immoral or otherwise of such a nature that the court's assistance in recovering them from the defendants should not be given on the grounds of public policy. The plaintiffs' response was that the defence was not arguable, but the High Court came to the conclusion that as a defence it *was* arguable. And in *Tamworth Industries Ltd* v. *Attorney-General*[87] the Court of Appeal of New Zealand held that in an action for conversion and detinue brought against the Crown for retention of certain money found by the Crown on the land of the plaintiff occupier it was an arguable defence that the money was probably the proceeds of a crime of which the plaintiff occupier might have had some knowledge even though not himself guilty of the crime. These then are other situations where the defence of *ex turpi causa* might be used and where public policy plays an important role.

6. Self-defence

A person who is threatened or attacked by another and who reasonably believes that he is in danger of death or serious injury can act in order to protect his right of personal safety. The act which is done in self-defence, however, must be reasonably necessary[88] and it must not be excessive,[89] that is, it must not be out of all reasonable proportion to the emergency confronting the person threatened or attacked. In *McClelland* v. *Symons*[90] the plaintiff loaded and pointed a rifle at the defendant, these actions being accompanied by an oral threat. The defendant picked up a metal crowbar and struck the plaintiff a heavy blow causing him serious injury which included a fractured skull and concussion. The plaintiff's action in assault and battery was not successful because Sholl J. of the Supreme Court of Victoria felt that the blow could be justified as having been struck in self-defence. There was conflicting evidence in that case as to whether a second blow had been struck by the defendant when the plaintiff had been disarmed and was lying helpless on the ground. In relation to such a blow, Sholl J. said:

86 (1988) 82 A.L.R. 193.
87 [1988] 1 N.Z.L.R. 296.
88 See *Fontin* v. *Katapodis* (1962) 108 C.L.R. 117, 181. See also *Bennett* v. *Dopke* [1973] V.R. 239, 240.
89 ibid., 182.
90 [1951] V.L.R. 157.

The authorities on the right of a person assaulted to resort to a battery in self-defence, even though they admit the right so to resort before the person threatened is himself struck, limit his right to strike a blow to the period within which he is in danger from the assault i.e. the period when assault or further assault is threatened. The law denies to a person assaulted the right to strike a further blow by way of revenge. Nor does it permit a defendant to absolve himself in such a case on the ground that, in the excitement of the moment or by reason of provocation, he went on to inflict blows which without such excitement or provocation he would not have been moved to inflict.[91]

In *Fontin* v. *Katapodis*[92] the High Court of Australia had to deal with a claim that the defendant had exceeded his right of self-defence. After an exchange of words between the plaintiff and the defendant, the plaintiff grabbed a wooden T-square and hit the defendant with it once on the arm and once on the shoulder. When he raised the T-square to hit the defendant again the defendant picked up an off-cut of louvre glass and threw it at the plaintiff's face. The plaintiff raised one of his hands to fend off the piece of glass which cut the socket of the plaintiff's thumb and severed the ulna nerve. The plaintiff's action in assault and battery succeeded and the plea of self-defence was rejected, because, as McTiernan J. said, 'to throw the piece of glass at the [plaintiff] as a means of self-defence was out of all reasonable proportion to the emergency confronting [the defendant]'.[93]

Not only can a person who is actually threatened or attacked resort to the plea of self-defence but also any person who on reasonable grounds believes that he is likely to be the subject of an imminent attack can take reasonable steps to defend himself.[94] So, a person who while walking on a lonely road on a dark night is approached by a stranger, whom he reasonably suspects is going to attack and rob him, is entitled to take reasonable measures for his self-protection. He does not have to wait for the stranger to attack him before he acts in self-defence, provided his suspicion of being attacked is a reasonable belief or a belief based on reasonable grounds. The measures taken to ward off the suspected attack must also be reasonable.

In both the case of an actual attack and a suspected attack, the question of whether the measures taken in self-defence were reasonably necessary and the question of whether the defendant had exceeded the limits of self-defence are questions of fact and the decision will depend very much upon the circumstances of the case. In deciding these questions the court considers, for example, whether it was necessary for the defendant to stand his ground or whether the defendant could easily have used a means of escape and avoided the necessity for any act of self-defence; whether it was necessary for the defendant to use the weapon, missile or object that he actually used in his self-defence etc. It also seems that the court will not forget that an 'action in self-defence is instinctive and does not wait upon

---

91 ibid., 162.
92 (1962) 108 C.L.R. 177.
93 ibid., 182.
94 See *Hall* v. *Fonceca* [1983] W.A.R. 309.

a precise appreciation of the exigencies of the occasion or upon the formation of a belief concerning the precise measures which are necessary'.[95] If a defendant raises the plea of self-defence in an action in tort the onus of proving that he committed the intentional tort in self-defence lies upon him.[96]

To detain a person against his will without arresting him is an unlawful act and a serious interference with his liberty, and the person detained is entitled to take such steps as are reasonably necessary against the person detaining him to extricate himself from such detention, including the use of reasonable force.[97] However, in *Albert* v. *Lavin*[98] the House of Lords decided that 'every citizen in whose presence a breach of the peace is being, or reasonably appears to be about to be, committed has the right to take reasonable steps to make the person who is breaking or threatening to break the peace refrain from doing so; and those reasonable steps in appropriate cases will include detaining him against his will'.[99] So, a person who is detained, whether by a police officer or a private citizen, because he is breaking or threatening to break the peace cannot use force to free himself from such a detention, and a person who does use force to free himself from such a detention will therefore lay himself open to an action of trespass to the person by the person detaining him. He will not be able to rely upon the plea of self-defence as justifying his conduct.

7. DEFENCE OF ANOTHER

If a person can act in order to protect his own right of personal safety, can he also act in order to protect the personal safety of another? Certainly if the person being attacked is a relative or friend, the plea of defence of another would be available to a defendant who strikes a plaintiff in coming to the aid of his relative or friend he believes on reasonable grounds is in danger of death or serious injury from the plaintiff. In *Gambriell* v. *Caparelli*[100] the defendant on hearing an altercation in the street came on to the scene to find the plaintiff with his hands about her son's neck. She picked up a garden fork and struck the plaintiff, who sustained severe lacerations to his head. The defendant was held not liable in an action of assault (battery) because, as the judge said, '[s]he held an honest belief that her son was in danger, and she was justified in protecting him as an extension of the defence of self-defence'.[101] Decisions from the seventeenth and eighteenth centuries had already accepted the fact that the plea of defence of another would be available in the case of

---

95 See *R.* v. *Howe* (1958) 100 C.L.R. 448, 468.
96 See *McClelland* v. *Symons* [1951] V.L.R. 157. See also *Pearce* v. *Hallett* [1969] S.A.S.R. 423, 428-9.
97 See *Albert* v. *Lavin* [1982] A.C. 546, 564-5.
98 ibid., 564-5.
99 ibid., 565 *per* Lord Diplock.
100 (1975) 54 D.L.R. (3d) 661. See also *Pearce* v. *Hallett* [1969] 423.
101 (1975) 54 D.L.R. (3d) 661, 666 *per* Carter Co. Ct. J.

servants who came to the aid of their masters[102] and in the case of masters who came to the aid of their servants.[103]

What if the person being attacked or about to be attacked is not a relative or friend and not a master or servant? Can the plea of defence of another be raised in relation to a complete stranger? In *Goss* v. *Nicholas*, Crawford J. of the Supreme Court of Tasmania said:

> After considering the various text books and authorities I take the law to be that a person is entitled to use force to prevent a stranger from being assaulted if he has reasonable grounds for believing that an assault upon that stranger is about to take place.[104]

And in the earlier case of *Saler* v. *Klingbiel* Richards J. of the Supreme Court of South Australia thought that there was a 'general principle recognized in the authorities that a man may intervene, in such manner as the circumstances reasonably appear to call for, in order to prevent, or to stop, serious personal injury to third persons'.[105]

What if the defendant who intervenes thinks the third person (whether a relative or a stranger) is in immediate danger from the plaintiff but in actual fact he is not? Suppose P and T are locked in a rather loving but nevertheless forceful embrace and D, mistakenly thinking that P is attempting to rape T, strikes him rather violently. Can D raise the plea of defence of another in those circumstances? In *Gambriell* v. *Caparelli*, the judge thought that the defence could successfully be raised. As he said:

> [W]here a person in intervening to rescue another holds an honest (though mistaken) belief that the other person is in imminent danger of injury, he is justified in using force, provided that such force is reasonable.[106]

Just as in self-defence, the question of whether the measures used by the defendant to defend another were reasonably necessary and whether the force used exceeded the limits which the occasion demanded are questions to be decided by the trier of fact and will be determined by the circumstances of the case. The onus of proof in relation to this defence is on the defendant.[107]

8. Defence of Property

A person may use reasonable force to defend his property, whether it be his land or his goods. Sometimes this right and the limits to its exercise find expression in a statute,[108] but generally the matter is left to the

---

102 See *Barfoot* v. *Reynolds* (1733) 2 Stra. 953.
103 See *Seaman* v. *Cuppledick* (1615) Owen 150.
104 [1960] Tas.S.R. 133, 144.
105 [1945] S.A.S.R. 171, 174. Although this was a case of criminal assault the principle applied should not differ in an action in tort.
106 (1975) 54 D.L.R. (3d) 661, 666 *per* Carter Co.Ct.J.
107 See *Pearce* v. *Hallett* [1969] S.A.S.R. 423, 429.
108 See e.g. *Greenbury* v. *Lyon* [1957] St. R. Qd. 433 and the provisions of the Queensland Criminal Code mentioned in that case.

common law. A person who interferes with another's exclusive possession of land by coming on to the land can be ejected.[109] If the entry has been made peaceably a request to leave is usually necessary but if the entry on to the land has been made forcibly, for example, by breaking down the door and entering the premises, then the person entering can be ejected forcibly and without any request to leave. Whether the entry is peaceable or forcible, the force used to eject the trespasser must be reasonable,[110] though the courts recognizing the frailties of excitable human nature and the necessity for quick action will not 'strain to confine too closely the conception of reasonable force'.[111] A person may also use force in defence of his goods if another interferes with them, for example, by attempting to take them or destroy them.[112]

If in attempting to defend his property against acts of the plaintiff the defendant commits a trespass to the person or a trespass to goods of the plaintiff, he will be able to plead the defence of property in any action brought by the plaintiff. The measures taken by the defendant to defend his property must be reasonably necessary and the force used must not be excessive. In *Shaw* v. *Hackshaw*[113] Southwell J., the trial judge, gave the jury the following example of what he considered to be the use of excessive force in the defence of one's property:

> [I]f you saw someone stealing your motor mower and you picked up a gun, and without any warning fired to kill him, and killed him you would be guilty of murder, because the infliction of intentional death or serious harm would be quite out of proportion to the harm you were trying to avoid, that is the loss of your motor mower.[114]

When the matter went up to the Full Court of the Supreme Court of Victoria, McInerney J. expressed disagreement with the view that the use of deadly force is not justifiable in the protection of one's property unless one's life is threatened.[115] McInerney J. felt that, in the circumstances of the case, the defendant was entitled to resort to the kind of deadly force that he resorted to in the defence of his property. As McInerney J. put it: 'If the State cannot provide an adequate law enforcement or crime prevention agency, it is almost inevitable that private citizens will resort, as the [defendant] did, to self-help'.[116] However, on appeal, the High Court in reversing the judgment of the Full Court of the Supreme Court of Victoria

---

109 See *Tullay* v. *Reed* (1823) 1 Car. & P. 6 and *Haddrick* v. *Lloyd* [1945] S.A.S.R. 40, 44.
110 See *Hemmings* v. *Stoke Poges Golf Club* [1920] 1 K.B. 720.
111 See *Greenbury* v. *Lyon, Ex parte Lyon* [1957] St. R. Qd. 433, 439 *per* Stanley J.
112 See *Seaman* v. *Cuppledick* (1615) Owen 150. See also *Shaw* v. *Hackshaw* [1983] 2 V.R. 65.
113 See [1983] 2 V.R. 65, 105.
114 ibid.
115 McInerney J. specifically disagreed with Fleming's view that the use of deadly force is not justifiable at the present time because of 'modern police force, speedy remedy for recovery of possession and the prevailing belief in precedence for sanctity of life over property'.
116 [1983] 2 V.R. 65, 101.

delivered a warning against the use of firearms by occupiers of property even against trespassers on the property.[117]

In *Shaw* v. *Hackshaw* Cox, the plaintiff's boyfriend, drove the plaintiff on to the defendant's property to steal petrol from a bowser on the defendant's property. The defendant fired a number of shots at Cox's car in an attempt to make it undriveable because the police had told the defendant, when he had reported previous thefts of petrol to them, that he would have to get better evidence of the thefts of his petrol, such as a description of any car involved in the theft. Unfortunately, the shots fired by the defendant injured the plaintiff, who brought actions in both trespass and negligence against him. The plaintiff succeeded at first instance, but on appeal a majority of the Full Court of the Supreme Court of Victoria decided that the plaintiff should not succeed because she was a trespasser of whose presence the defendant was not aware and that the defendant had not been negligent towards her. The High Court allowed the plaintiff's appeal and reinstated the decision at first instance. It should be noted, however, that the trial judge and the Full Court were all agreed that if the defendant's firing of the shots had injured Cox rather than the plaintiff, the defendant would have been able to raise the plea of defence of property and that Cox would not have been able to succeed in an action of trespass against the defendant unless he was able to show that the firing of the shots, to disable the car, involved the use of more force than was reasonably necessary in the circumstances. As McInerney J. put it: 'Had Cox sued [the defendant] for damages, either for trespass to the person or trespass to goods [the car], Cox's action would have been maintainable by him only on proof that [the defendant] had used excessive force in seeking to detain him or his vehicle'.[118]

It seems, as a result of the decision in *Shaw* v. *Hackshaw*, that a person can use such force as is reasonably necessary in the circumstances to defend his property and that the use of deadly force, such as that used in *Shaw* v. *Hackshaw*, is not necessarily ruled out. It also seems that the onus of proving that the measures taken by the defendant to defend his property were reasonably necessary in the circumstances and the onus of proving that the force used was not excessive in the circumstances both lie upon the defendant, even though McInerney J. suggested in *Shaw* v. *Hackshaw* that the onus of proving that the defendant had used excessive force in the circumstances lies upon the plaintiff who alleges that the force used was excessive.[119]

9. Recaption of Chattels

The common law right which allows a person who has been deprived of the possession of his goods to recover those goods immediately and without recourse to the various actions in tort available for interferences with goods is called the right of recaption of chattels. The right of

117 See *Hackshaw* v. *Shaw* (1984) 155 C.L.R. 614.
118 [1983] 2 V.R. 65, 100.
119 ibid.

recaption has already been discussed in some detail.[120] Here, it is only necessary to point out that the right of recaption will be available as a defence to actions in tort such as assault, battery, false imprisonment, trespass to land or trespass to goods which might be brought against a person who commits those torts while attempting to retain possession of his goods or while attempting to regain possession of them. Thus in *Huet* v. *Lawrence*[121] the plaintiff's action in trespass to land against the defendant, for entering upon the plaintiff's land and removing the gates erected thereon, failed because the court decided that the defendant in trespassing upon the plaintiff's land was acting as an agent of a third party, who had been deprived of his possession of a motor truck, which was on the plaintiff's land by the connivance of the plaintiff and a fourth party. The defendant was therefore entitled, as agent of the third party, to come on to the plaintiff's land to exercise the right of recaption of the chattel in question and that was a complete defence to the action for trespass to land.

10. Re-entry on Land

The right of re-entry on land is nothing more than the common law remedy of self-help which allows a person who is entitled to exclusive possession of land to come on to the land and to eject the person who is no longer entitled to be there without incurring any liability in tort, if no more force is used than is reasonably necessary. As Harman J. pointed out in *Aglionby* v. *Cohen*,[122] '[I]t has been well known to be the law ever since the celebrated case of *Hemmings* v. *Stoke Poges Golf Club*,[123] that if no more force be used than is necessary a man may turn a trespasser off his property and put his chattels out of the house', without incurring any liability in tort for his actions. In *Haniotis* v. *Dimitriou*,[124] a decision of Brooking J. of the Supreme Court of Victoria, there is a reminder of the requirement, first enunciated in *Polkinhorn* v. *Wright*[125] in 1845, that a landlord who intends to exercise his right of re-entry and eject his tenant should not only give him notice to leave but also a reasonable opportunity to pack up and go. As Brooking J. put it: 'once he re-enters, he can use whatever force is reasonably necessary to expel his former tenant without becoming liable to an action for assault and battery, provided that he first asks the tenant to leave and gives him a reasonable opportunity of doing so'.[126] Though a person exercising his right of re-entry can put the trespasser's own chattels out of the house or premises if the trespasser does not remove the goods after receiving reasonable notice requiring removal of the goods,[127] it is doubtful if he can do this if the resulting loss to the

120 See pp. 128-9 above.
121 [1948] St.R.Qd. 168. See also *Cox* v. *Bath* (1893) 14 L.R.(N.S.W.) 263.
122 [1955] 1 Q.B. 558, 562.
123 [1920] 1 K.B. 720.
124 [1983] 1 V.R. 498.
125 (1845) 8 Q.B. 197, 206-7.
126 [1983] 1 V.R. 498, 500.
127 See *Haniotis* v. *Dimitriou* [1983] 1 V.R. 498.

trespasser would be wholly disproportionate to the inconvenience or 'encumbering' of the premises that the goods cause by being left there by the trespasser.[128] So a landlord who exercises a right of re-entry cannot take the tenant's Stradivarius from the house and put it out on the footpath even though the tenant has not made any arrangements to collect the instrument after receiving reasonable notice from the landlord that he ought to do so.

11. Abatement by Self-help

The common law, in certain circumstances, recognizes a right in a person to remedy a situation by a resort to self-help which is called a right of abatement by self-help. When this right of abatement exists, the person who has the right of abatement can, for example, enter the defendant's land and put an end to a nuisance without incurring liability for the trespass.[129] It is for this reason that the right of abatement by self-help is considered among the defences available in relation to the intentional torts. The right of abatement, if it is exercised at all, is usually exercised in cases of nuisance and the circumstances in which the right of abatement by self-help can be exercised are dealt with in Chapter 16 below.[130] However, it may be necessary to point out here, as Martin J. indicated in *Traian* v. *Ware*, that '[T]he law does not favour the remedy of abatement in preference to legal action' and 'requires strong reason to justify it when it involves entering upon the land of another'.[131] The onus of justifying the abatement would rest upon the defendant committing the trespass to land.

The right of abatement by self-help not only arises in the context of the tort of nuisance. In *R.* v. *Chief Constable of Devon and Cornwall, Ex parte Central Electricity Generating Board*[132] where protesters frustrated the work of the Central Electricity Generating Board, which was surveying the property of a third party in order to determine whether it was a suitable site for a possible nuclear power station, by lying down in front of moving vehicles, chaining themselves to equipment and by sitting down where the work had to be done, the English Court of Appeal decided that the Central Electricity Generating Board (which was a statutory body) could use the minimum of force reasonably necessary to remove those persons who were obstructing the Board in its exercise of its statutory powers from the area where the work had to be carried out, even though this might involve a trespass to the person. Lawton L.J. described this right to use force as the 'common law remedy of abatement by self-help'.[133] However, it should be pointed out that Lawton L.J. felt that the

---

128 ibid., 502.
129 See *Jones* v. *Williams* [1843] 11 M. & W. 176.
130 See pp. 612-13 below.
131 [1957] V.R. 200, 207.
132 [1982] 1 Q.B. 458.
133 ibid., 473.

use of the remedy of abatement by self-help should be discouraged and that it should not be used if any other remedy could be used effectively.[134]

12. DISTRESS

The common law right of distress is nothing more than the right of a person, in certain circumstances, to seize and detain the goods of another person in order to force the other to perform some obligation or to punish him for the non-performance of an obligation. Where the right exists the distrainor, that is, the person exercising the right of distress, can enter the plaintiff's premises and commit what in anyone else would be both a trespass to land and a trespass to goods (perhaps even conversion and detinue) without incurring any liability in tort. So, where the right of distress exists,[135] and is properly exercised, it will provide the distrainor with a complete defence to any action in tort which might be brought in respect of acts committed while the defendant was distraining on the goods of the plaintiff.

The right of distress is used not only for the purpose of recovering rent which is in arrear, by seizing goods which are on the premises and detaining them until the rent is paid,[136] but it can also be used to recover compensation for damage done to land by trespassing cattle[137] (or even other objects[138]) by seizing and impounding the cattle (or other objects) until the owner pays compensation for the damage caused by the trespassing cattle (or other objects). When the right of distress is used to ensure that compensation is paid for the damage caused by cattle or by an object, it is described as distress damage feasant.[139]

The right of distress is dealt with in some detail in books on property law and further elaboration of this defence should be sought there.

13. PROVOCATION

Can the provocative conduct of the plaintiff be raised by the defendant as a defence to an action for assault and battery?

In two decisions, *Grehan* v. *Kann*,[140] and *White* v. *Connolly*,[141] the Supreme Court of Queensland has accepted provocation as a defence to an

---

134 ibid.

135 The landlord's right of distress for non-payment of rent has been abolished by legislation in some Australian States and drastically affected by legislation in other States. See generally E.I. Sykes, *The Law of Securities* (3rd edn, Sydney, 1978) pp. 75-6 and 156-8.

136 See *Wood* v. *Fetherston* (1901) 27 V.L.R. 492. Note, however, that the right of the landlord to distrain for rent in arrear has been abolished in New South Wales, Victoria, Queensland and Western Australia.

137 See *Swenson* v. *The Council of the Shire of Drayton* [1932] St.R.Qd. 98.

138 See *Street* (7th edn, 1983) p. 77.

139 It is doubtful whether the remedy of distress damage feasant can be used to prevent trespassory parking of motor vehicles unless the vehicle has actually caused some damage. See *R* v. *Howson* (1966) 55 D.L.R. (2d) 582.

140 [1948] Q.W.N. 40.

141 [1927] St.R.Qd. 75.

action in tort for assault and battery. There is no indication in the report of what the provocation was in *Grehan* v. *Kann* but in *White* v. *Connolly* the defendant discovered the plaintiff sexually embracing the defendant's wife in a bed in a bedroom of an hotel. In the course of the struggle that ensued the defendant struck the plaintiff. In an action by the plaintiff for assault (battery) the defendant pleaded provocation. By his reply the plaintiff pleaded that the defendant's plea of provocation should be struck out but Macnaughton J. refused, saying that it was his opinion that 'the defence of provocation as an excuse for assault may be pleaded in a civil action for damages for assault as well as in criminal proceedings for the offence of assault'.[142] In the more recent decision in *Love* v. *Egan*, McLoughlin D.C.J. felt that he was bound by the two decisions just mentioned to find that, in Queensland at least, conduct which amounts to provocation, as defined by s. 268 of the Criminal Code, 'can be pleaded as a defence to a civil action for assault if the response to the provocation is reasonable'.[143]

However, in *Fontin* v. *Katapodis*[144] where the plaintiff provoked the defendant by hitting him several times with a wooden T-square and the defendant responded to the provocation by picking up an off-cut of louvre glass and throwing it at the plaintiff's face, the High Court of Australia decided that the provocation of the plaintiff could not be used by the defendant to mitigate or reduce compensatory damages but that provocation 'operates only to prevent the award of exemplary damages or to reduce the amount of such damages which, but for the provocation, would have been awarded'.[145] McTiernan J. added that he was 'inclined to the view that there ought to be no reduction of actual or compensatory damages for provocation in the case of assault and battery'.[146] Though none of the judges of the High Court in *Fontin* v. *Katapodis* specifically indicated that provocation is not a defence to an action in intentional assault or battery, it is arguable that that view is implicit in their decision. For if the provocation of the plaintiff cannot be used by the defendant, even to mitigate or reduce compensatory damages, how can it be used to defeat the claim of the plaintiff completely? It is for this reason that Brooking J. in *Horkin* v. *North Melbourne Football Club Social Club* took the view that '[c]learly provocation is no defence to an action for battery'.[147] More recently, Young J. of the Supreme Court of New South Wales decided in *Plumb* v. *Breen*[148] that 'the law in New South Wales is that provocation is no defence to a battery'. He acknowledged that the situation in Queensland might possibly be different.

It would appear, therefore, that the courts have not thought things out very clearly in relation to this defence. For example, in *Lane* v. *Holloway*

142 ibid., 77.
143 (1971) 65 Q.J.P.R. 102, 104.
144 (1962) 108 C.L.R. 177.
145 ibid., 187.
146 ibid., 184.
147 [1983] 1 V.R. 153, 162.
148 Judgment of 13 December 1990 (Supreme Court of N.S.W.) p. 12 (unreported).

Lord Denning M.R. said that '[p]rovocation by the plaintiff can properly be used to take away any element of aggravation. But not to reduce the real damages'.[149] Lord Denning M.R. and the other judges of the English Court of Appeal relied upon the decision of the High Court of Australia in *Fontin* v. *Katapodis*. But in *Murphy* v. *Culhane*[150] Lord Denning M.R. said that the decisions in *Lane* v. *Holloway* and *Fontin* v. *Katapodis*, that 'provocation . . . can be used to wipe out the element of exemplary damages but not to reduce the actual figure of pecuniary damages',[151] should only be applied to those cases where the provocation offered by the plaintiff was trivial and the response of the defendant savage and entirely out of proportion to the occasion, so much so that the defendant could fairly be regarded as solely responsible for the damage done. He thought that those two decisions cannot or should not be applied 'where the injured man, by his own conduct, can fairly be regarded as partly responsible for the damage he suffered'.[152] So it looks as if Lord Denning did not rule out the possibility that even *compensatory* damages might be reduced if the provocative conduct of the plaintiff was more than trivial so that the plaintiff could fairly be regarded as partly responsible for the injury suffered or the damage done. Again, in *Horkin's* case Brooking J. took the view that provocation on the part of the plaintiff could 'prevent the award or reduce the amount of *aggravated* damages' even though he accepted the view that such damages are compensatory damages.[153] It is not without good reason, therefore, that McLoughlin D.C.J. expressed himself in the following way in *Love* v. *Egan*:

> It seems to me absurd that the Common Law should allow a person who is guilty of the most outrageously provoking conduct to recover full compensatory damages for any injuries occasioned by a reasonable response to his conduct. It seems to me even more absurd that if he claims only compensatory damages, the circumstances of his conduct are irrelevant and may not be pleaded or given in evidence.[154]

If this matter is reconsidered by the High Court of Australia at some time in the future it might be better if it took the view that provocation can, if the response to the provocation is reasonable, be pleaded as a complete defence to an action in assault or battery, for example, in the circumstances in *White* v. *Connolly*,[155] but that in other circumstances it can be taken into account in mitigation or reduction of exemplary damages and even compensatory damages, whether the latter amount includes an element of aggravated damages or not. The onus of proving the provocation and that the response to the provocation was reasonable would lie upon the defendant who is seeking to rely upon it as a defence.

---

149 [1968] 1 Q.B. 379, 387.
150 [1977] 1 Q.B. 94.
151 ibid., 98.
152 ibid.
153 [1983] 1 V.R. 153, 162 (emphasis added).
154 (1971) 65 Q.J.P.R. 102, 104.
155 [1927] St.R.Qd. 75.

14. Contributory Negligence

Whatever the correct view about provocation as a defence to the intentional torts of assault and battery, the next question which must be considered is whether a defendant in the case of an intentional tort can rely upon the contributory negligence of the plaintiff[156] as a defence, or at least to reduce the damages payable to the plaintiff. Again, the matter is one of some difficulty but several courts in Australia have now expressed the view that contributory negligence was not available at common law as a defence to an intentional tort and that it is not available today under the contributory negligence statutes (described in Chapter 13 as the apportionment legislation) as a ground of apportionment of damages.

In *Horkin* v. *North Melbourne Football Club Social Club*[157] the question of whether the contributory negligence of the plaintiff could be pleaded by the defendant either as a defence to an action in intentional battery or as a means of reducing the damages which would otherwise be payable for that intentional tort was considered by Brooking J. of the Supreme Court of Victoria. In that case, the plaintiff was forcibly thrown out of the defendant's club premises when he tried to stay after he was asked to leave and given a reasonable opportunity of doing so. Even though Brooking J. found that the plaintiff 'was guilty of contributory negligence in that he became intoxicated while on licensed premises and failed to leave when asked in a proper manner to do so, and given a reasonable opportunity of doing so . . . [and] created a situation in which the use of force to expel him was the natural and lawful consequence of his own misbehaviour',[158] nevertheless the judge held that the plaintiff was entitled to the full award of $9750 for the battery because he concluded that 'contributory negligence was not at common law and is not under the statute [that is, the apportionment legislation] available in an action in battery'.[159] There is no reason why this decision cannot be extended to the other intentional torts of trespass to the person, such as assault and false imprisonment, and indeed in *Venning* v. *Chin*[160] Bray C.J. of the Supreme Court of South Australia seemed to say as much when he said that it was clear that 'contributory negligence could never be a defence to an *intentional tort*'.[161] It seems, therefore, that the contributory negligence of the plaintiff cannot be raised as a defence to an action in intentional trespass either at common law or under the apportionment legislation. The contrary decision of Moller J. of the Supreme Court of New Zealand in *Hoebergen* v. *Koppens*,[162] that contributory negligence constituted by insulting words could lead to an apportionment in an action for battery, is not likely to be followed in Australia, though in the unreported decision in *Barley* v.

156 For a discussion of what is contributory negligence, see Chapter 13 below.
157 [1983] 1 V.R. 153.
158 ibid., 147.
159 ibid., 166.
160 (1974) 10 S.A.S.R. 299.
161 ibid., 317 (emphasis added).
162 [1974] 2 N.Z.L.R. 597.

Paroz[163] Sheahan J. of the Supreme Court of Queensland came to the conclusion that the apportionment legislation could be applied to reduce compensatory damages for assault where the plaintiff failed to have due regard for his own safety in the circumstances leading up to the assault.

The contributory negligence of the plaintiff has also been raised as a defence to an action in conversion. In *Helson* v. *McKenzies (Cuba Street) Ltd*[164] the New Zealand Court of Appeal allowed the defence to succeed in an action in conversion when the plaintiff, who had left her handbag on a counter of the defendant's store, sued the defendant for conversion when one of its servants handed the handbag over to an impostor who claimed it was hers. The plaintiff's damages were reduced for her contributory negligence in leaving the bag on the counter. This decision was followed by Donaldson J. in *Lumsden* v. *London Trustee Savings Bank.*[165] But there have now been several decisions in Australia, such as *Wilton* v. *Commonwealth Trading Bank of Australia: Model Investments Pty Ltd (Third Party),*[166] *Day* v. *The Bank of New South Wales*[167] and *Grantham Homes Pty Ltd* v. *Interstate Permanent Building Society Ltd,*[168] in which it has been held that the contributory negligence of the plaintiff was not at common law a defence to an action in conversion and that the contributory negligence of the plaintiff cannot be raised as a defence under the apportionment legislation in the various States of Australia. The view which the Australian courts have preferred to follow is the view put rather persuasively by Scrutton L.J. in *Lloyds Bank Ltd* v. *The Chartered Bank of India, Australia and China* where he said:

> If my butler for a year has been selling my vintage wines cheap to a small wine merchant I do not understand how my negligence in not periodically checking my wine book will be an answer to my action against the wine merchant for conversion.[169]

Contributory negligence is not in Australia a defence to an action in conversion, nor, presumably, to an action in detinue. Nor, for that matter, to an action for trespass to goods.

15. Inevitable Accident

In discussing the intentional torts of trespass to the person, trespass to land and trespass to goods we had occasion to point out that once the plaintiff proves a direct act on the part of the defendant which causes injury or damage to the plaintiff the burden rests on the defendant to disprove fault. This can be done by the defendant by showing that the act

163 See *Horkin* v. *N. Melb. Football C.S.C.* [1983] 1 V.R. 153, 163.
164 [1950] N.Z.L.R. 878.
165 [1971] Ll.L.R. 114.
166 [1973] 2 N.S.W.L.R. 644.
167 (1978) 18 S.A.S.R. 163. See also *Oxland Enterprises Pty Ltd* v. *Gierke* (1980) 91 L.S.J.S. 276.
168 (1979) 37 F.L.R. 191.
169 [1929] 1 K.B. 40, 60.

was not done intentionally and that it was done without negligence or carelessness on his part. If the defendant succeeds in showing this, then he has succeeded in disproving fault on his part and will escape liability in trespass—or more generally in tort. The injury or damage done to the plaintiff will be regarded by the courts as an inevitable accident. It is in this sense that inevitable accident is a defence to the intentional torts of trespass to the person, trespass to land and trespass to goods.

In *McHale* v. *Watson*[170] the defendant who was alleged to have thrown a metal dart in the direction of the plaintiff escaped liability in tort because he was able to show absence of intent to make contact with the body of the plaintiff and absence of negligence. The injuries to the plaintiff were regarded by the court as being caused by an inevitable accident.

Where a defendant having been startled inadvertently stepped on to the land of the plaintiff,[171] and where a defendant suffered an epileptic fit and fell unconsciously on to the land of the plaintiff,[172] there was no liability in trespass as the act in each case was not only not voluntary but also there was no fault on the part of the defendant. The acts were not regarded as being trespasses to land but were regarded instead as inevitable accidents.

Again, in *National Coal Board* v. *J.E. Evans & Co. (Cardiff) Ltd*[173] the defendant who damaged the plaintiff's underground cable in the course of digging with a mechanical excavator was held not liable for the damage. As the defendant showed that he had not acted intentionally or negligently in damaging the cable, the English Court of Appeal decided that the plaintiff could not recover for the inevitable accident. As Cohen L.J. observed, 'where the defendant was entirely without fault, he would have a good defence to an action in trespass'.[174]

16. Consent

It has already been suggested in Chapter 2 that consent should be treated as a defence to the intentional torts of trespass to the person rather than as an essential ingredient of those torts such as battery, assault and false imprisonment. It is not for the plaintiff to prove absence of consent but for the defendant to exculpate himself by alleging and proving consent to the acts in question.[175] This is also true in relation to the other intentional torts, such as trespass to land, trespass to goods, conversion and detinue. If, however, the defendant proves that the plaintiff has consented to the acts in question then an action for none of the torts considered in the previous chapters will succeed.[176]

170 (1964) 111 C.L.R. 384. See also *Weaver* v. *Ward* (1616) Hob. 134.
171 See *Braithwaite* v. *South Durham Steel Co.* [1958] 1 W.L.R. 986.
172 See *Public Transport Commission of N.S.W.* v. *Perry* (1977) 14 A.L.R. 273.
173 [1951] 2 K.B. 861.
174 ibid., 874.
175 See *Hart* v. *Herron* (1984) Aust. Torts Reports 80-201 at p. 67, 814 where Fisher J. of the Supreme Court of New South Wales endorses the view that the burden of proving consent is upon the defendant. See also *Sibley* v. *Milutinovic* (1990) Aust. Tort Reports 81-013 and *Department of Health* v. *J.W.B. and S.M.B.* (1992) 66 A.L.J.R. 300.
176 See *Maynegrain Pty Ltd* v. *Compafina Bank* [1984] 1 N.S.W.L.R. 258 (conversion).

A distinction should be drawn between the defence of consent which is discussed in this book, principally in relation to the intentional torts, and the defence of *volenti non fit injuria* which is discussed by us principally in relation to the tort of negligence. Where the defence of consent is available the defendant generally succeeds if he can show that the plaintiff agreed to the infliction of the injury, but for the defence of *volenti* to succeed the defendant need only show that the plaintiff assented to the *risk* of injury by the defendant's negligence. The courts, however, have not always made this distinction, or made it clearly enough, and in *Bain* v. *Altoft*,[177] for example, Gibbs J., in a case where the consent of the plaintiff was successfully raised as a defence to an action in intentional battery, described it as the defence of *volenti non fit injuria*. The defence of *volenti* is discussed in some detail in Chapter 13.[178] In this chapter we look at the defence of consent in greater detail, attempting to find out when, and in what circumstances, a court comes to the conclusion that consent has been established, that is, that the plaintiff has agreed to the intentional infliction of an injury by the defendant.

(a) **Consent obtained by duress or fraud** If the consent of the plaintiff to the intentional act has been obtained by duress or by fraud it will not be a valid consent and will not be available to the defendant as a defence to an intentional tort.

If the plaintiff's capacity to consent is overborne or inhibited in any way by the use or the threat of physical force then the consent of the plaintiff can be said to have been obtained by duress and it is no defence to an action in tort to say that the plaintiff has consented to the act in question. In *Freeman* v. *Home Office (No. 2)*[179] the plaintiff, who was a prisoner in an English prison, brought an action in battery against the defendants, alleging that a prison doctor had administered drugs to him by way of an injection, without his real consent. Counsel for the plaintiff argued that in a prison setting, where a doctor has the power to influence a prisoner's situation and prospects, what appears to be on the face of it a real consent might not in fact be so. In other words, counsel was alleging that the plaintiff's consent had been obtained by duress. McCowan J., while accepting that duress would vitiate consent pointed out that 'questions of duress and relative strength of bargaining power are always questions of fact'[180] and in the circumstances of the case he held that the consent of the plaintiff to the administration of the drugs was not given under duress. The decision was upheld by the English Court of Appeal.[181] In *Aldridge* v. *Booth* acts of sexual intercourse agreed to by the plaintiff under economic duress were held not to be consensual acts.[182]

---

177 [1967] Qd.R. 32.
178 See p. 540 ff. below.
179 [1984] 2 W.L.R. 130.
180 ibid., 145.
181 See *Freeman* v. *Home Office* [1984] 1 All E.R. 1036.
182 (1988) 80 A.L.R. 1. See also *Latter* v. *Braddell* (1880) 50 L.J.Q.B. 448, a decision which is unlikely to be followed today.

Consent obtained by fraud also raises difficult issues. In *Hegarty* v. *Shine*,[183] as we have seen,[184] the plaintiff's action in battery did not succeed, even though it was quite clear from the evidence that the plaintiff would not have consented to the act of sexual intercourse with the defendant if she knew that he was infected with venereal disease. On the other hand, if a defendant obtains the plaintiff's consent to an act of sexual intercourse, as in *R.* v. *Williams*,[185] by persuading her that what is being done to her is not the ordinary act of sexual intercourse but some medical or surgical procedure to improve her voice, there is little doubt that an action in battery would succeed. How are the two cases distinguished? Probably on the basis that in *Hegarty* v. *Shine* the plaintiff consented to the act of sexual intercourse albeit under the mistaken impression that it would be a disease-free activity, whereas in a case like *R.* v. *Williams* the plaintiff did not consent to an act of sexual intercourse at all but only to a medical or surgical procedure, so the consent to the act of sexual intercourse was therefore obtained by fraud which would vitiate the consent. This would mean that if the defendant fraudulently represents to the plaintiff that the ceremony which they have just gone through is a marriage ceremony and the plaintiff consequently agrees to an act of sexual intercourse there can be no action in battery, even though the plaintiff has only consented to an act of marital intercourse and not to one of fornication.[186] It is obvious that these cases cause some difficulty and it might be better if the courts were to hold that fraud vitiates consent if the fraud induces a mistake *either* as to the actual nature of the act (sexual intercourse or surgical procedure) *or* in relation to an extremely important incident of the act (marital intercourse or fornication).

(b) Consent to illegal acts If a person consents to injury or harm being inflicted on him which is really grievous as, for instance, in a case of maiming, 'the consent should be treated as nugatory'. This was the conclusion reached by McInerney J. in *Pallante* v. *Stadiums Pty Ltd (No. 1)*.[187] The reason for this conclusion is not only that the injured person is likely to become a burden on society but also because 'it injures society if a person is allowed to consent to the infliction on himself of such a degree of serious physical injury'.[188]

However, in *Bain* v. *Altoft*[189] the Full Court of the Supreme Court of Queensland came to the conclusion that the plaintiff who had consented to engage in a scuffle with the defendant and had instigated it could not sue the defendant for damages for personal injuries suffered by him as a result of the battery committed upon him by the defendant. Gibbs J. said

183 (1878) 2 L.R.Ir. 273.
184 See p. 253 above.
185 [1923] 1 K.B. 340.
186 See *R.* v. *Papadimitropoulos* (1957) 98 C.L.R. 249. The accused in this decision was found not guilty of rape.
187 [1976] V.R. 331, 340. See also *Reg.* v. *Brown (Anthony)* [1992] 2 W.L.R. 441 (criminal assault).
188 ibid. See also *Department of Health* v. *J.W.B. and S.M.B.* (1992) 66 A.L.J.R. 300, 303.
189 [1967] Qd.R. 32.

that he could see 'no reason of public policy that requires a consent to an illegal act to be treated as void in civil proceedings', and went on to hold that 'consent is a defence to an action of trespass to the person, notwithstanding that the act consented to was illegal'.[190]

(c) Consent to medical procedures It is well-established law that a medical practitioner must obtain the consent of the patient to any medical procedure (including surgical procedures) which is to be performed on a patient. In the absence of consent, the medical practitioner commits a battery and is liable for damages for trespass to the person.[191]

Consent to one medical procedure does not imply consent to another medical procedure and the patient who is admitted to a hospital for tonsillectomy and who, due to an administrative error, is circumcised instead will be able to bring an action in trespass to the person against the surgeon who performed the medical procedure.[192] If during the course of an operation the surgeon decides to adopt a medical procedure not authorized by the patient, as, for example, tying the Fallopian tubes of a patient during the course of a Caesarean operation to prevent her undergoing the hazards of a second pregnancy,[193] the surgeon will be liable in trespass unless he can show that the procedure was urgently necessary for the protection of the life or the preservation of the health of the patient. It is not sufficient for the surgeon to show that it was more *convenient* to carry out the unauthorized procedure at that time.[194]

If a person is brought to a medical practitioner in an unconscious state and that medical practitioner performs a medical procedure which is urgently necessary for the protection of the life or the preservation of the health of the person then even in the absence of consent no action in trespass can be brought. This is so because the necessity of the occasion overrides the absence of consent. Can a person refuse consent, in advance of an emergency, to medical treatment of any kind? In *Malette* v. *Shulman*[195] the Court of Appeal of Ontario held recently that a medical practitioner who administered blood transfusions to a patient, who was brought unconscious to the hospital after an accident, had committed a battery, because the patient had been carrying a card in her purse identifying her as a Jehovah's Witness and requesting on the basis of her religious convictions that she be given no blood transfusion under any circumstances. Robins J.A. held that as this card was discovered by the defendant's physician before the blood transfusions were administered he had no authorization under the emergency doctrine to override the plaintiff's wishes and that 'she was entitled to reject in advance of an

190 ibid., 41.
191 The medical practitioner may also in certain circumstances commit the offence of medical trespass. See Medical Treatment Act 1988 (Vic) s.6.
192 See *Chatterton* v. *Gerson* [1981] 1 All E.R. 257, 265. A patient in South Australia who injured his right knee but who by mistake had an operation performed by a surgeon on his undamaged left knee received an out of court settlement of $40 000 in May 1991.
193 See *Murray* v. *McMurchy* [1949] 2 D.L.R. 442.
194 ibid., 445.
195 [1990] 72 O.R. (2d) 417.

emergency a medical procedure inimical to her religious values'.[196] He added that 'by imposing civil liability on those who perform medical treatment without consent, even though the treatment may be beneficial, the law serves to maximise individual freedom of choice'.[197]

What if a patient is suffering from such mental abnormality as never to be able to give consent to a medical procedure to cure the mental disorder? In the case of such mentally ill patients medical procedures authorized by an authorized medical officer or the superintendent of a mental hospital where the patient is being held can be carried out without the consent of the patient, but legislation usually specifies that the 'authorized medical officer or superintendent shall before giving such consent satisfy himself that the operation or treatment is necessary or desirable for the safety or welfare of the person proposed to be operated upon or treated'.[198] Any person carrying out the medical procedure is then protected against any civil or criminal proceedings.[199] What if the medical procedure is not any medical or surgical treatment for the mental disorder but treatment for the patient's *physical* health? In *T* v. *T*[200] the patient was a severely mentally handicapped woman aged 19 years who, despite the excellent care of all those around her, was found to be pregnant. Her doctors wanted to terminate the pregnancy and at the same time to effect sterilization and her mother supported the doctors' views. The doctors, however, were reluctant to perform these procedures without a declaration by a court that no civil liability would be attracted by carrying out these procedures without the patient's consent. Wood J. (in the Family Division of the English High Court), while agreeing that the operative procedures proposed were *prima facie* acts of trespass, held that in the circumstances a medical practitioner was 'justified in taking such steps as good medical practice "demands"'[201] and granted the declaration. The House of Lords had approved the grant of such a declaration in the case of a minor[202] (a girl 17 years of age) but Wood J. was prepared to extend the principle to an adult.[203] It would seem, therefore, that medical procedures (both to cure mental disorders and in relation to the physical health of the patient) can be carried out by medical practitioners without the consent of those patients who are suffering from such mental abnormality as never to be able to give their consent even in the absence of legislation conferring immunity, but in such cases it would be prudent to seek a declaration by a court before carrying out such procedures. In the recent decision in *Department of Health* v. *J.W.B. and S.M.B.*[204] the parents of a 14-year-old intellectually disabled child who wanted a hysterectomy and ovariectomy performed on the child for the purpose of preventing pregnancy and

---

196 ibid., 433
197 ibid., 430.
198 See s.102, Mental Health Act 1959 (Vic.).
199 See s.103, Mental Health Act 1959 (Vic.).
200 [1988] 2 W.L.R. 189.
201 ibid., 204.
202 *In re B. (A Minor) (Wardship: Sterilisation)* [1987] 2 W.L.R. 1213.
203 See also *In re F. (Mental Patient: Sterilisation)* [1990] 2 A.C. 1.
204 (1992) 66 A.L.J.R. 300.

menstruation argued that provided such procedures were in the best interests of the child they as guardians of the child could give lawful consent to a sterilization on behalf of their mentally incompetent child. The High Court of Australia, however, by a majority decided that the parents could not lawfully authorize the carrying out of a sterilization procedure upon the child without an order of a court and that only the Family Court could authorize the carrying out of such a procedure (though in authorizing the carrying out of such a procedure, the court may, if necessary, permit the parents to give any requisite consent). In this type of case, therefore, the involvement of the court has been held by the High Court to be compulsory and not optional or a matter of prudence.

If a medical practitioner mistakenly thinks that he has got the consent of the patient when in fact he has not, the defence of consent will not be available to him.[205]

Is a consent to a medical procedure vitiated by a failure on the part of a medical practitioner to give the patient sufficient information about the medical procedure and its attendant risks? In other words, is a consent which on the face of it appears to be a true consent (for example, a consent form signed by a patient before an operation) not a consent at all unless it is also an 'informed consent'? And is a medical procedure performed in the absence of a fully informed consent a battery? The answers to these questions are different in the United States from those in Canada and in England. In the United States a medical practitioner to avoid liability for trespass to the person must show that the consent of the patient is based on knowledge of all the facts relevant to the formation of an intelligent and informed consent,[206] but in Canada[207] and England,[208] as Sir John Donaldson M.R. pointed out in *Sidaway* v. *Bethlehem Royal Hospital Governors*, 'a consent is not vitiated by a failure on the part of a doctor to give the patient sufficient information before the consent is given. It is only if the consent is obtained by fraud or by misrepresentation of the nature of what is to be done that it can be said that an apparent consent is not a true consent'.[209] So in Canada and in England the failure on the part of the medical practitioner to give the patient full and sufficient information about the medical procedure will not vitiate the consent, so that the patient can sue the medical practitioner in assault and battery. The proper cause of action, if any, in these cases is the action in negligence, which is discussed in Chapter 9. The position in Australia, if and when the matter arises, is likely to be the same as in England and Canada and a patient who undoubtedly gives his consent to the very medical procedure

---

205 See, however, Prisons (Medical Tests) Amendment Act 1990 (N.S.W.) which gives a defence to a person carrying out a medical test or examination on a prisoner if the person believed on *reasonable grounds* that the examination or test was authorized. This defence only applies to tests or examinations authorized by statute and not to mistakes about consent.

206 See *Canterbury* v. *Spence* (1972) 464 F. 2d 772.

207 See *Reibl* v. *Hughes* (1980) 114 D.L.R. (3d) 1.

208 See *Sidaway* v. *Bethlehem Royal Hospital Governors* [1984] 1 All E.R. 1018; *Chatterton* v. *Gerson* [1981] Q.B. 432; and *Hills* v. *Potter* [1983] 3 All E.R. 716.

209 [1984] 1 All E.R. 1018, 1026.

carried out will not be able to bring an action for trespass to the person on the ground that he was given insufficient information about the medical procedure. That sort of complaint should properly be laid in negligence.[210]

Medical procedures performed on animals without the consent of those entitled to exclusive possession of the animal will lay the person performing the procedure open to an action for trespass to goods. The owners of a cat which was neutered without the consent of the owners by a veterinary surgeon acting for the Cat Protection Society of New South Wales were able to bring a successful action for trespass to goods against both parties.[211]

(d) Consent by minors[212] In the case of very young children the usual practice is for the medical practitioner to seek the consent of the parent or guardian before embarking upon a medical procedure in relation to the child. Such a consent should be sufficient to protect the medical practitioner against any action of trespass that might be brought by a child and, 'if he has the consent of the parent or guardian, he may safely proceed regardless of the wishes of the infant'.[213] In *S.* v. *McC; W.* v. *W.*[214] Lord Reid in the House of Lords said that it was 'impossible to deny that a parent can lawfully require that his young child should submit to a blood test'. Presumably that applies to other medical procedures as well. However, as Lord Reid went on to say, as soon as a child understands something about medical procedures it would generally be unwise to subject him to a medical procedure against his will.[215] It is difficult to say at what age this understanding will come, it is really a question of fact and would largely depend on the circumstances of the case. There is no fixed age rule and as the High Court of Australia has recently pointed out in *Department of Health* v. *J.W.B. and S.M.B.* 'the capacity of a child to give (and consequently to refuse) informed consent to medical treatment depends on the rate of development of each individual'.[216] If in any doubt about the consent of the child to a medical procedure, the wise medical practitioner should seek an order or directions from a court.[217] This might happen, for instance, where it appears that a parent is forcing a 14-year-old daughter to have a therapeutic abortion or where a parent appears to be forcing one child to donate an organ for a transplant operation on

210 And it has been so laid. See *F.* v. *R.* [1982] 29 S.A.S.R. 437.

211 See the *Age* (Melbourne), 19 May 1984.

212 See P.D.G. Skegg (1973) 36 *M.L.R.* 370.

213 See N. O'Bryan (1961) 8 *Proc. Med.-Leg. Soc. Vic.* 138.

214 [1972] A.C. 24, 43.

215 ibid., 45.

216 (1992) 66 A.L.J.R. 300, 306. The High Court applied the decision of the House of Lords in *Gillick* v. *West Norfolk A.H.A.* [1986] A.C. 112, 183-4, 189.

217 Probably by an originating summons invoking the inherent jurisdiction of the appropriate court in the exceptional circumstances of the case. See *In re D. (Minors) (Wardship Jurisdiction)* [1973] 3 W.L.R. 53. See also *In re B. (A Minor) (Wardship: Sterilisation)* [1987] 2 W.L.R. 1213. This order or direction is now considered essential in those cases where the person is disabled both by age and mental capacity from giving consent and the proposed medical procedure is for non-therapeutic purposes. See *Department of Health* v. *J.W.B. and S.M.B.* (1992) 66 A.L.J.R. 300.

another child of the same family.[218] Such an order can also be sought where the parents are refusing their consent to a medical procedure to be performed on the child.[219]

Legislation in Australia[220] allows certain medical procedures to be performed on children without the consent of their parents or guardians. Where a medical practitioner acts in pursuance of such legislation the medical procedure is deemed to have been performed with the consent required for the performing of that procedure and no tortious or other liability will be attracted by the performance of the medical procedure.

(e) **Consent to medical research** In discussing consent to medical procedures we came to the conclusion that a patient who gives his consent to the very medical procedure carried out would not be able to bring an action for trespass to the person on the ground that he was given insufficient information about the medical procedure. We suggested that the complaint against the medical practitioner should properly be laid in negligence. What about the person who gives his consent to a medical researcher on the basis of insufficient information? Should the medical researcher be placed in the same position as the medical practitioner in relation to consent? The decision in *Halushka* v. *University of Saskatchewan*[221] suggests that they should be treated differently. In that case the plaintiff, a student, volunteered to undergo anaesthetic tests for the purposes of medical research in the department of anaesthetics in the University of Saskatchewan. Even though the plaintiff had signed a consent form the Court of Appeal of Saskatchewan decided that the consent was ineffective and that the defendants were liable in battery when as a consequence of the test the plaintiff suffered a heart stoppage and was unconscious for four days and hospitalized for ten days. It was held that the plaintiff was entitled to a 'full and frank disclosure of all the facts, probabilities and opinions which a reasonable man might be expected to consider before giving his consent'.[222] The court felt that there could be no exceptions to the ordinary requirements of disclosure in the case of medical research as there may well be in ordinary medical practice. Sometimes it might be necessary to hide some risks from a patient when it is important that he should not worry, but the court said that that consideration 'can have no application in the field of research'.[223] It is suggested, therefore, that the position of a medical researcher is different from a medical practitioner and that a failure to give sufficient information about the experiment might vitiate the consent and lay the medical researcher open to a successful action in trespass to the person, as it did in *Halushka's* case. This is important, as trespass casts upon the medical researcher the burden of proving consent to what was done.

218 See s.15, Human Tissue Act 1982 (Vic.).
219 See *In re B. (A Minor)* [1981] 1 W.L.R. 1421.
220 See e.g. s.3, Emergency Medical Treatment of Children Act 1960 (S.A.) and s.24, Human Tissue Act 1982 (Vic.).
221 [1966] 53 D.L.R. (2d) 436.
222 ibid., 444.
223 ibid.

(f) Consent to sporting contacts If persons are engaged in a game or sporting contest, to what contacts can they be said to have consented? In *Pallante* v. *Stadiums Pty Ltd (No. 1)* McInerney J. indicated that a person only consents to 'such violence as is ordinarily and reasonably to be contemplated as incidental to the sport in question' with the additional requirement that such violence must be inflicted 'within the spirit and intendment of the rules of that game or sporting contest'.[224] It is only if both these requirements are met that a defendant will be able to rely upon the consent of the plaintiff as a defence to an action for assault and battery brought by a plaintiff who is the victim of physical violence during a game or sporting contest. In *McNamara* v. *Duncan*[225] the defendant footballer who deliberately 'felled' the plaintiff footballer, during a game but after the plaintiff had parted with possession of the ball, was held liable to the plaintiff in an action of intentional battery. Counsel for the defendant put forward the thesis that 'a little bit of foul play is a common, if not invariable, concomitant of a game of football (or at least of Australian Rules Football)'[226] and the plaintiff should therefore be regarded as having consented to the act in question, but Fox J. in the Supreme Court of the Australian Capital Territory rejected the thesis saying that it could not 'reasonably be held that the plaintiff consented to receiving a blow such as he received in the present case. It was contrary to the rules and was deliberate'.[227] Fox J. agreed that forcible body contact was part of Australian Rules Football (and of some other games and sporting contests) and that a participant in such a game should be deemed to have consented to some forcible body contact. But he went on to say that the defence of consent will only be available if 'such contact finds justification in the rules and usages of the game'.[228] In *Giumelli* v. *Johnston*,[229] however, the Full Court of the Supreme Court of South Australia took the view that some bodily contact outside the rules of the game is to be expected as an ordinary incident of a football match and that the consent which a participant in a football match gives to the application of physical force to him extends to physical force of that kind even though it might involve some infringement of the rules.

Spectators who are injured might also bring an action in intentional trespass in some circumstances. Suppose a fielder in a cricket match, taunted by spectators on the boundary, picks up the ball and deliberately throws it into a group of spectators. There is no doubt that a spectator injured in such circumstances could bring a successful action in battery against the player and it would be no defence to such an action for the player to say that the spectator by coming to the cricket ground had consented to being hit by a cricket ball which might have been hit for a six

224 [1976] V.R. 331, 339.
225 (1971) 26 A.L.R. 584.
226 ibid., 587.
227 ibid., 588.
228 ibid.
229 Judgment delivered on 31 October 1989 (unreported) at pp. 4-5 *per* King C.J.

by a batsman. Actions for injuries to spectators are usually brought in negligence.[230]

(g) Withdrawal of consent Even though consent to the act in question may have been given to the defendant at some time, that consent will not be available to him as a defence to an action for an intentional tort if the plaintiff shows that the consent was withdrawn before the act in question was committed.[231] So, a plaintiff who had consented to an operation for the amputation of a limb and a few hours before the operation changed his mind and withdrew his consent was able to sue the defendant surgeon in battery when the defendant went ahead with the operation.[232] The withdrawal of the consent must be in very clear and unambiguous terms and it must also be communicated to the defendant if it is to be effective.

It should not be imagined, however, that the withdrawal of consent immediately makes the defendant liable in tort for any act that he does in relation to the plaintiff after the withdrawal of consent has been communicated to him by the plaintiff. If a surgeon is performing an operation on a patient's foot using a local anaesthetic and half-way through the operation the patient demands that the surgeon stop, the surgeon is entitled probably to finish the operation but certainly to continue with such surgical procedures as stitching up the wound left by the excision.

Can a person who has agreed to a deprivation of his liberty for a particular period, by contract or otherwise, withdraw that consent and demand to be released from the confinement immediately? The decision of the House of Lords in *Herd* v. *Weardale*[233] suggests that he cannot, unless there is what can be described as a reasonable and pressing necessity, for example, if he suffers a heart attack. However, as we have suggested in Chapter 2,[234] the withdrawal of consent should be effective not only where there is a reasonable and pressing necessity but also in situations where releasing the plaintiff from his confinement does not involve the defendant in significant inconvenience, substantial expenditure or grave risk.

A person who comes on to the land of another with his consent (express or implied) can become a trespasser if he remains on the land after the permission to be on the land is effectively revoked and a reasonable period to withdraw from the land has elapsed.[235] However, it has been suggested

230 See, generally, H. Luntz (1980) 54 A.L.J. 588.

231 See *R* v. *L.* (1992) 103 A.L.R. 577 where it was held that a husband who forces his wife to have sexual intercourse with him commits rape (and the tort of battery) because it was never the common law that by marriage a wife gave irrevocable consent to sexual intercourse by her husband.

232 See *Klovis Njareketa* v. *The Director of Medical Services, Entebbe* (1950) 17 E.A.C.A. 60 (Court of Appeal for Eastern Africa).

233 [1915] A.C. 67.

234 See pp. 52-5 above.

235 See *Horkin* v. *N. Melb. Football C.S.C.* [1983] 1 V.R. 153, 155 and *Mackay* v. *Abrahams* [1916] V.L.R. 681. See also *Plenty* v. *Dillon* (1991) 65 A.L.J.R. 231, 236 'A person who enters or remains on property after the withdrawal of the licence is a trespasser' *per* Gaudron and McHugh JJ.

in Chapter 3[236] that in the case of a licensee for value consent to remain on the land cannot be withdrawn until the period of the licence is exhausted provided that the licensee behaves in an orderly manner.

Also, in the recent decision in *Bolwell Fibreglass Pty Ltd* v. *Foley*,[237] Brooking J. expressed the view that:

> if goods are bailed to a person by an agreement under which he is to carry out certain work upon them and the bailor subsequently instructs him to stop work and to redeliver the goods, the bailee is . . . entitled to retain possession of the goods and complete the work the subject of the agreement.[238]

So, even though in general the withdrawal of consent would make the defendant liable in tort for any act which is done by the defendant after the withdrawal has been communicated to him, in the situations which we have just described the defendant is entitled to continue to perform certain acts without incurring liability in tort.

17. LAWFUL AUTHORITY

Apart from the defence of lawful arrest, which is considered separately as the next defence, there are many situations where a defendant can claim, in relation to what would otherwise be actionable tortious conduct, that he has acted under lawful authority in performing the act in question. The situations are too numerous to consider exhaustively but the following situations should convey some idea of the dimensions of this defence.

(a) Common law In *Albert* v. *Lavin*[239] the House of Lords pointed out that at common law every citizen has the right to detain another person, without necessarily arresting him, if the other person is either committing, or reasonably appears to be about to be committing, a breach of the peace. Such a detention would therefore be a defence to any action for trespass to the person.

Under common law a police officer or citizen also has a power of entry into premises and, if necessary, powers to break down doors to do so, in four cases without being subjected to an action for trespass to land. These four cases are conveniently set out by Donaldson L.J. (and affirmed as the law applicable in Australia by the High Court of Australia in *Plenty* v. *Dillon*[240]) in *Swales* v. *Cox*,[241] where it is suggested that the power of entry can be exercised (i) by a police officer or a citizen in order to prevent murder; (ii) by a police officer or a citizen if an arrestable offence had in fact been committed and the person who had committed the arrestable offence had been followed to a house; (iii) by a police officer or a citizen if

236 See pp. 107-9 above.
237 [1984] V.R. 97.
238 ibid., 112.
239 [1982] A.C. 546, 564-5.
240 (1991) 65 A.L.J.R. 231, 236. The four cases are those set out by Donaldson L.J. in *Swales* v. *Cox*.
241 [1981] Q.B. 849. See also *McLorie* v. *Oxford* [1982] 1 Q.B. 1290, 1296.

an arrestable offence was about to be committed, and would be committed, unless prevented; and (iv) by a police officer following an offender running away from an affray. In other circumstances there was no power at common law to enter premises without a warrant. Even in the four cases mentioned in *Swales* v. *Cox* 'it was an essential pre-condition that there should have been a demand and refusal by the occupier to allow entry before the doors could be broken'.[242] In *Lippl* v. *Haines & Ors.*[243] the Court of Appeal of New South Wales held that a police officer (or other person) entering a house forcibly to effect an arrest, whether in the exercise of a common law power or statutory power to arrest, could do so against the will of a householder only if there were reasonable and probable grounds for the belief that the person sought was within the premises and if a proper announcement was made before entry.[244] But according to the Court of Appeal there is no common law power to enter a house forcibly because it is believed that a fugitive *may* be in the house.[245] The court was prepared, however, not to insist on the proper announcement prior to entry in exigent circumstances e.g. where someone was at a window or other aperture with a gun, firing or ready to fire at police outside.

In *Halliday* v. *Nevill*[246] the High Court of Australia (by a majority) held that a police officer who in pursuit of an unlicensed driver entered an open driveway leading to the entrance of another's dwelling house, without the prior permission of the occupier, to arrest the unlicensed driver had lawful authority to do so because a member of the police force has an implied or tacit licence from the occupier to enter an open driveway for the purpose of questioning or arresting a person whom he has observed committing an offence on a public street in the immediate vicinity of the driveway. The High Court indicated, however, that there would be no lawful authority to enter the driveway if the driveway is closed off by a locked gate or any other obstruction or if there is a notice or other indication advising visitors (whether police officers or others) that intrusion upon the open driveway is forbidden.[247] Where there was such a notice or indication, as in *Plenty* v. *Dillon*,[248] police officers who entered the plaintiff's land for the purpose of serving a summons were held to have committed a trespass to land, as any implied or tacit licence to enter

---

242 [1981] Q.B. 849, 853.
243 (1989) Aust Torts Reports 80-302.
244 These two conditions on the powers of entry were imposed by the Supreme Court of Canada in *Eccles* v. *Bourque* and approved by Hope A.J.A. in *Lippl* v. *Haines* (1989) Aust. Torts Reports 80-302 at 69, 309.
245 ibid., at 69, 309-10. See also *Plenty* v. *Dillon* (1991) 65 A.L.J.R. 231, 236 'No public official, police constable or citizen has any right at common law to enter a dwelling house merely because he or she suspects that something is wrong' *per* Gaudron and McHugh J.J.
246 (1984) 155 C.L.R. 1. See also *Nevill* v. *Halliday* [1983] 2 V.R. 553.
247 (1984) 155 C.L.R. 1, 8.
248 (1991) 65 A.L.J.R. 231.

the land had expressly been revoked.[249] It would seem, therefore, that the maxim that every man's house is his castle is concerned only with dwelling-houses and that the common law right to enter another's land other than his dwelling-house might be somewhat wider than the four cases mentioned in *Swales* v. *Cox*.[250]

At common law a police officer also has power to seize and retain goods or documents in certain circumstances without being subjected to an action for trespass to goods, conversion or detinue. In *Chic Fashions (West Wales) Ltd* v. *Jones*[251] the English Court of Appeal held that a police officer who enters a house by virtue of a search warrant for stolen goods may seize not only goods covered by the warrant but also any other goods which he believes on reasonable grounds to be stolen. But in *Ghani* v. *Jones*[252] the Court of Appeal indicated that the police officer must not keep the goods or documents or prevent their removal for any longer than is reasonably necessary to complete his investigations or present them for evidence. This common law right to seize goods and documents is necessary not only to preserve material evidence but also to enable the goods to be restored to their rightful owner at the end of the trial.[253] And it is also necessary because it may not always be possible to obtain a search warrant in relation to some goods or documents.[254]

(b) Statutory authority In every State and Territory of Australia there are statutory provisions which allow an ordinary citizen,[255] a police officer[256] or others placed in a special position[257] to deprive a person of his liberty, with force if necessary, in certain circumstances. Where a person who is authorized to act under such a statute does so, he will not be liable in any action in tort.

Statutory provisions also allow a police officer to enter private property for the purpose of effecting an arrest[258] and they also give power to a local authority[259] or a statutory body[260] to enter upon private land for the purposes mentioned in the statute. The public official who is given this power of entry can exercise such reasonable force as is necessary in order

---

249 The position would be different if the police officers were entering the land for the purpose of arresting a person or for the purpose of execution of coercive process against the body of a person or against the goods of a person. See *Plenty* v. *Dillon* (1991) 65 A.L.J.R. 231, 238. In these cases the person effecting the arrest is entitled not only to enter as of right but also to break down the outer doors of the offender's house after making the customary demand. See *Halliday* v. *Nevill* (1984) 155 C.L.R. 1, 12.

250 [1981] Q.B. 849. See now *Hart* v. *Chief Constable of Kent, The Times*, 15 November 1982.

251 [1968] 2 Q.B. 299, 313 and 316.

252 [1970] 1 Q.B. 693, 709.

253 See *Chic Fashions (West Wales) Ltd* v. *Jones* [1968] 2 Q.B. 299, 316-17.

254 See e.g. *West Mercia Constabulary* v. *Wagener* [1981] 3 All E.R. 378.

255 See e.g. ss. 458 and 463B, Crimes Act 1958 (Vic.).

256 See e.g. s.459, Crimes Act 1958 (Vic.).

257 See e.g. s.463A, Crimes Act 1958 (Vic.).

258 See *Dinan* v. *Brereton* [1960] S.A.S.R. 101.

259 See *O'Brien* v. *Shire of Rosedale* [1969] V.R. 645 and *Amstad* v. *Brisbane City Council (No. 1)* [1968] Qd. R. 334.

260 See *Egg Marketing Board (N.S.W.)* v. *Cassar* [1978] 1 N.S.W.L.R. 90.

to effect an entry and the force may be used both to remove a physical barrier such as a locked door or to remove a person who obstructs the entry.[261] There will be no liability in tort for those acts because the defence of statutory authority would be available to the defendant as a defence to those acts. The general policy of the law, however, is against public officials having rights of entry upon private land without the consent of the occupier and unless a statutory provision expressly provides for such an entry the public official who enters upon land without the consent of the occupier would be committing a trespass to land.[262] As Lord Diplock said in *Morris* v. *Beardmore,* there is a presumption 'that in the absence of express provision to the contrary Parliament did not intend to authorise tortious conduct'.[263]

There are also statutory provisions in all the States and Territories of Australia which allow a member of the police force in certain circumstances not only to arrest persons and enter upon premises but also to seize and carry away goods without being subject to an action of trespass to goods, conversion or detinue.[264]

Since the power to act under statutory authority is usually an executive discretion conferred by statute on a public official, 'the lawfulness of the way in which [it is] exercised . . . in a particular case cannot be questioned in any court of law except on those principles laid down by Greene M.R. in *Associated Provincial Picture House Ltd* v. *Wednesbury Corporation*[265] . . . that have become too familiar to call for repetitious citation'.[266] The *Wednesbury* principles, as they are usually referred to, are applicable not only to determining the lawfulness of the exercise of the statutory discretion of police officers and other public officials in proceedings for judicial review, but also for the purpose of founding a cause of action in tort, as Lord Diplock recently pointed out in *Holgate-Mohammed* v. *Duke.*[267]

18. Lawful Arrest

The power to arrest[268] a person can be exercised either with a warrant or without a warrant. If a person is arrested with a warrant, and arrests by warrant are apparently the exception rather than the rule,[269] the police officer will escape any liability in tort unless the warrant is defective[270] in

261 ibid., 94. See also s.459 A, Crimes Act 1958 (Vic.)
262 See *Plenty* v. *Dillon* (1991) 65 A.L.J.R. 231.
263 [1981] A.C. 446, 455.
264 See e.g. ss.81-90, Drugs, Poisons and Controlled Substances (Amendment) Act 1983 (Vic.). See also s.465, Crimes Act 1958 (Vic.).
265 [1948] 1 K.B. 223.
266 *Holgate-Mohammed* v. *Duke* [1984] 1 All E.R. 1054, 1057 *per* Lord Diplock. The *Wednesbury* principles are to be found at [1948] 1 K.B. 223, 228-31.
267 [1984] 1 All E.R. 1054, 1057.
268 For an explanation of what the word 'arrest' means, see *Holgate-Mohammed* v. *Duke* [1984] 1 All E.R. 1054, 1056-7 per Lord Diplock.
269 See *Criminal Investigation*, A.L.R.C. Report No. 2 (1975) para. 25.
270 But what is the remedy if a warrant is irregular and should not have been issued but is in fact executed? See *Marriner* v. *Smorgon* (1989) 167 C.L.R. 368.

some way or the person arrested is not the person named in the warrant, that is, the wrong person is arrested.[271] The defence of a lawful arrest with a warrant is not, therefore, considered further. But what if the arrest is without a warrant? In what circumstances is an arrest without a warrant lawful so that it will enable the arrestor to avoid any liability in tort?

(a) Common law The common law does allow a private citizen (which term includes private detectives, nightwatchmen, security guards etc.) to arrest another person in certain circumstances. This power of arrest can be used by one person to arrest another person in the following circumstances: (i) if he finds that person in the act of committing or immediately after having committed an arrestable offence;[272] (ii) to prevent that person from committing an arrestable offence; (iii) if he reasonably suspects that person of having committed an arrestable offence and that offence, in respect of which the arrest is made, has in fact been committed by someone;[273] and (iv) if he finds that person committing a breach of the peace in his presence or it reasonably appears to him that that person is about to commit a breach of the peace in his presence.[274]

A member of the police force can, at common law, arrest a person without a warrant in all these circumstances but, in addition, a member of the police force can also arrest a person without a warrant if he reasonably suspects that person of having committed an arrestable offence even though in fact no arrestable offence, in respect of which the arrest is made, has been committed by anyone. In this respect, the powers of a member of the police force to arrest a person without a warrant are wider than the powers of arrest enjoyed by the ordinary citizen.

(b) Statutory powers of arrest The common law powers of arrest previously described have been altered by statute in almost every Australian jurisdiction. In some States, such as Victoria, no person can be arrested without a warrant except pursuant to the provisions of the Crimes Act 1958 (Vic.) or some other Act expressly giving power to arrest without a warrant.[275] It is difficult to deal with all this legislation in this book but the provisions of the Victorian Crimes Act 1958, which incorporates the provisions of the Crimes (Powers of Arrest) Act 1972 (Vic.),[276] are briefly as follows: (i) any person (whether a member of the police force or not) can, without a warrant, arrest another person whom he finds committing any offence (whether an indictable offence or an offence punishable on summary conviction) if he believes on reasonable grounds that the apprehension of that person is necessary either to ensure the appearance of the offender before a court of competent jurisdiction, to preserve public order, to prevent the continuation or repetition of the offence or the commission

---

271 See *Symes* v. *Mahon* [1922] S.A.S.R. 447.
272 See *Nolan* v. *Clifford* (1904) 1 C.L.R. 429, 445 *per* Griffith C.J.
273 See *Walters* v. *W.H. Smith & Sons Ltd* [1914] 1 K.B. 595, 602.
274 See *Nolan* v. *Clifford* (1904) 1 C.L.R. 429, 445. See also *Albert* v. *Lavin* [1982] A.C. 546, 564-5.
275 See s.457, Crimes Act 1958 (Vic.).
276 And also the Crimes (Classification of Offences) Act 1981 (Vic.).

of a future offence or for the safety or welfare of members of the public or of the offender;[277] (ii) any person can arrest another person without a warrant if he is instructed to do so by any member of the police force having power under the Act to apprehend that person;[278] (iii) any person can, without a warrant, arrest another person whom he believes on reasonable grounds is escaping from legal custody or avoiding apprehension by some person having authority to apprehend that person in the circumstances of the case;[279] and (iv) a member of the police force can at any time, without a warrant, arrest any person whom he believes on reasonable grounds has committed an indictable offence in Victoria or elsewhere.[280]

The provisions of the Victorian Crimes Act 1958 appear to protect both a private citizen and a police officer who effects an arrest of another person on reasonable grounds against any action for an unlawful arrest even if it 'subsequently appears or is found that the person apprehended did not commit the offence alleged'[281] and the meaning given to the words 'finds committing' by s. 462 of the Act is so extensive that it might even protect a private citizen who believing on reasonable grounds that a person is guilty of an offence (and it is necessary to arrest him) arrests him even though the offence, in respect of which the arrest is made, is subsequently discovered not to have been committed by anyone. If this is the case, then the statutory powers of arrest in Victoria are much wider, at least in relation to an arrest by a private citizen, than the powers of arrest at common law which those statutory powers are intended to replace.

(c) **Method of effecting an arrest** The statutory provisions in relation to arrests without a warrant in Victoria do not affect the common law rules in relation to the way in which an arrest must be effected if it is to be lawful. These rules require the arrestor not to use more force than is reasonably necessary to effect the arrest[282] and they require that the person being arrested must be notified at or within a reasonable time of his arrest of the grounds on which he is being taken into custody unless that is obvious from the circumstances[283] or the person arrested by his own acts produces a situation which makes it practically impossible to inform him of the offence in respect of which he is being arrested.[284] The rules also require that the arrested person be brought before a court as soon as practicable after he is taken into custody.[285] A failure to observe these

277 ibid., s.458(1)(a).
278 ibid., s.458(1)(b).
279 ibid., s.458(1)(c).
280 ibid., s.459.
281 ibid., s.461(1).
282 See *Wiltshire* v. *Barrett* [1965] 2 All E.R. 271, 277 and 280. See also s.462A, Crimes Act 1958 (Vic.).
283 See *Christie* v. *Leachinsky* [1947] A.C. 573. See also *Murray* v. *Ministry of Defence* [1988] 1 W.L.R. 692.
284 See *Hall* v. *Nuske* (1974) 8 S.A.S.R. 587, 594-5.
285 See *John Lewis & Co. Ltd* v. *Tims* [1952] A.C. 676. See also s.460(1), Crimes Act 1958 (Vic.).

common law rules in relation to the method of arrest might make the arrestor liable to actions in tort,[286] though as Connor J. pointed out in *McIntosh* v. *Webster*:

> [A]rrests are frequently made in circumstances of excitement, turmoil and panic [and it is] altogether unfair to the police force as a whole to sit back in the comparatively calm and leisurely atmosphere of the courtroom and there make minute retrospective criticisms of what an arresting constable might or might not have done or believed in the circumstances.[287]

The common law and statutory rules in relation to an arrest without a warrant represent a compromise which has been evolved for the accommodation of two rival public interests, that is, 'the public interest in preserving the liberty of the individual and the public interest in the detection of crime and the bringing to justice of those who commit it'.[288] It is therefore to be expected that adjustments will be made in relation to that compromise as circumstances change.

The burden of proving that the arrest was justified lies upon the arrestor. As Diplock L.J. (as he then was) said in *Dallison* v. *Caffery*:

> [S]ince arrest involves trespass to the person and any trespass to the person is *prima facie* tortious, the onus lies on the arrestor to justify the trespass by establishing reasonable and probable cause for the arrest. The trespass by the arrestor continues so long as he retained custody of the arrested person, and he must justify the continuance of his custody by showing that it was reasonable. What is reasonable conduct on the part of a police officer in this respect may not be the same as what would be reasonable conduct on the part of a private arrestor.[289]

III: DEFENCES TO INTENTIONAL TORTS INVOLVING THE INFLICTION OF PURELY ECONOMIC LOSS

The defences which are available to a defendant who intentionally inflicts purely economic loss on a plaintiff are discussed in Chapter 5 in the course of a consideration of the ways in which the law of torts protects a person against the intentional infliction of purely economic loss, and there is therefore no need for a separate discussion again of those defences.

---

286 See e.g. *Lindley* v. *Rutter* [1981] Q.B. 128. See also *Dallison* v. *Caffery* [1965] 1 Q.B. 348, 366-7.

287 (1980) 43 F.L.R. 112.

288 See *Holgate-Mohammed* v. *Duke* [1984] 1 All E.R. 1054, 1059 *per* Lord Diplock.

289 [1965] 1 Q.B. 348, 370-1.

7

DAMAGES IN INTENTIONAL TORTS

I: SOME GENERAL COMMENTS

When a tort is committed, the principal remedy which is sought by a plaintiff is usually damages, that is, monetary compensation for the wrong. But on what basis is that compensation given? What factors do the courts take into account in assessing the amount of monetary compensation which the plaintiff should receive from the defendant? A further question which is examined in this chapter is whether the courts in Australia, in assessing damages, can award sums of money to a plaintiff which are over and above those required to compensate him for the injury or loss suffered by him. These sums of money, which are called exemplary damages, are awarded when a court, particularly in the case of an intentional tort,[1] wants to punish the defendant for what he has done and to discourage others from acting in the same way as the defendant. In other words, the court wants to make an example of the defendant.

Damages which are awarded in the intentional torts can be nominal, substantial (or real), aggravated or exemplary damages. These various kinds of damages require further explanation.

The phrase 'nominal damages' appears to be used in two senses by the courts. In the first sense, the words 'nominal damages' are used to describe the monetary sum which is given to a plaintiff when a recognized interest (or legal right) of his is violated by the defendant but the plaintiff is unable to show (or there is no evidence of) any personal injury, property damage or monetary loss. Such situations arise particularly in the intentional torts such as trespass to the person, trespass to land or trespass to goods which are actionable *per se*. Thus, if a technical trespass is committed by the defendant by touching the plaintiff, moving his goods

---

1 In the recent decision in *Coloca* v. *BP Australia Ltd* (1992) Aust. Torts Reports 81-153, O'Bryan J. of the Supreme Court of Victoria held that in appropriate cases exemplary damages could be awarded in Victoria in actions for personal injuries caused by negligence.

or going on to his land, the plaintiff would be entitled to nominal damages even if he cannot show that he has suffered any actual or real damage. As Piper J. said in *Law* v. *Wright*: 'the mere assault without physical harm and monetary loss, entitles the assailed to a nominal sum'.[2] This sum can, of course, be increased by the judge or jury taking into account the conduct of the defendant and of the party aggrieved. If this is done, the case ceases to be one in which there is an award of nominal damages only.[3] The amount of damages awarded is, within reasonable limits, at the discretion of the judge or (if there is one) the jury.[4] The other sense in which the words 'nominal damages' are used is to describe an award which is small or modest in amount.[5] Thus in *Hill* v. *Cooke*,[6] where the plaintiff brought an action in battery against the defendant (a police constable) for striking him twice in the face while taking him to the police station after his arrest, the jury awarded the plaintiff only £1 ($2) by way of damages. The Supreme Court of New South Wales (*in banco*) decided that the case was one in which the damages awarded 'might range from a nominal amount to a substantial sum' and that the jury were fully entitled 'to award only the nominal amount of one pound'.[7]

Where nominal damages in the first sense are awarded they are non-compensatory but where nominal damages in the second sense are awarded they *are* compensatory, because even though the damages awarded are modest or small and amount to a nominal sum they are in fact an assessment by the judge or jury of the injury or loss suffered by the plaintiff.

An award of nominal damages enables a plaintiff to recover his legal costs from the defendant and this is one of the principal reasons why a plaintiff whose interest has been invaded by the defendant might bring an action and persist with his claim even though he may realize that all he is likely to get by way of an award of damages is a nominal sum. It should be noted, however, that the court has a discretion as to whether it will order the defendant to pay the plaintiff's costs and that an undeserving plaintiff may well find himself with an award of only nominal damages and the burden of paying his own legal costs.[8]

Substantial or real damages, as they are sometimes called, are an actual assessment in monetary terms, by the judge or jury, of the injury or loss suffered by the plaintiff as a result of the tort. The purpose of the assessment is to place the plaintiff in the same position, in so far as it is possible to do so by an award of money, as he was before the tort was committed by the defendant. It is generally recognized that a plaintiff cannot in most cases be placed in exactly the same position as he would

---

2 [1935] S.A.S.R. 20, 25.
3 See *Greig* v. *Greig* [1966] V.R. 376.
4 See *Turner* v. *N.S.W. Mont de Piete Co. Ltd* (1910) 10 C.L.R. 539, 548.
5 See, however, *Baume* v. *The Commonwealth* (1906) 4 C.L.R. 97, 116.
6 (1958) 58 S.R. (N.S.W.) 49.
7 ibid., 50 *per* Owen J. (Roper C.J. and Manning C.J. concurred).
8 See e.g. s.24(1) Supreme Court Act 1986 (Vic.) and also General Rules of Procedure in Civil Proceedings 1986 (Vic.) Ord. 63 r.02. In relation to the County Court, see County Court Rules of Procedure in Civil Proceedings 1989 (Vic.) Ord. 63A r.02.

have been if the tort had not been committed, but if the substantial damages that he recovers are a fair and reasonable estimate of his loss he is regarded as being adequately compensated for his loss. In this sense, awards of substantial or real damages are regarded as compensatory damages. The term 'substantial damages' covers two kinds of damages claimed by a plaintiff: 'general damages' and 'special damages'. The terms 'general damages' and 'special damages' are not very easily defined and the definitions offered sometimes overlap, but for our present purpose it is sufficient to say that the term 'general damages' is used for those damages which are not capable of precise calculation by the plaintiff and which are left to be estimated by the court. This kind of damage does not have to be specifically pleaded by the plaintiff. The other kind of damages are called 'special damages'. This term is used to describe damage which is capable of precise calulation, documentation and proof by the plaintiff. It must be specifically pleaded by the plaintiff.

In calculating general damages the court also takes into account the circumstances in which the tort was committed. If a trespass', as in *Henry* v. *Thompson*[9] where two police officers beat up the plaintiff and one of the officers urinated on him, is committed in particularly insulting or humiliating circumstances or where, for example, in the case of a battery the relationship between the tortfeasor and the victim is one of master and pupil, the court might feel that an award of a higher sum by way of damages is appropriate.[10] Where such a higher sum is awarded it is usually referred to as aggravated damages. This higher award, however, is made not to punish the defendant but because the court feels that the plaintiff is entitled to compensation for the aggravation suffered by him in various ways as a result of the tort. As Somers J.A. said in *Taylor* v. *Beere*: 'It is clear that aggravated damages are given to compensate the plaintiff when the injury or harm done to him by the wrongful act of the defendant is aggravated by the manner in which he did the act'.[11]

Exemplary damages are damages given to the plaintiff which are over and above those given to him as ordinary compensatory damages or aggravated compensatory damages. They are given to the plaintiff when the conduct of the defendant is so outrageous that it calls for an element of punishment of the defendant. As Lord Devlin said in *Rookes* v. *Barnard*:

> Exemplary damages are essentially different from ordinary damages. The object of damages in the usual sense of the term is to compensate. The object of exemplary damages is to punish and deter . . . Exemplary damages can properly be awarded whenever it is necessary to teach a wrongdoer that tort does not pay.[12]

However, in *Rookes* v. *Barnard* Lord Devlin also restricted the categories of cases in which exemplary damages would be awarded in England to

---

9 (1989) Aust. Torts Reports 80-265.

10 See *Costi* v. *Minister of Education* (1973) 5 S.A.S.R. 328. See also *Greig* v. *Greig* [1966] V.R. 376.

11 [1982] 1 N.Z.L.R. 81, 93.

12 [1964] A.C. 1129, 1221 and 1227.

three classes. First, where there has been oppressive, arbitrary or unconstitutional action by the servants of the government; secondly, where the defendant's conduct has been calculated by him to make a profit for himself which may well exceed the compensation payable to the plaintiff; and, thirdly, to those cases where exemplary damages are expressly authorized by statute. In *Uren* v. *John Fairfax & Sons Pty Ltd*[13] the High Court of Australia decided that the categories of cases in which an award of exemplary damages may be made in Australia was much wider than the three categories postulated by Lord Devlin in *Rookes* v. *Barnard*, and that the limiting circumstances of that decision should not be followed here.[14] This position has recently been strongly reaffirmed by the High Court of Australia in *Lamb* v. *Cotogno*.[15] A similar position has also been reached by the Court of Appeal of New Zealand in *Taylor* v. *Beere*.[16] So the courts in Australia and New Zealand are free to award exemplary damages in cases of conscious wrongdoing where there is outrageous conduct on the part of the defendant in contumelious disregard of the plaintiff's rights.[17]

Exemplary damages, also called 'punitive', 'vindictive' or 'retributory' damages, are not compensatory in nature. Instead they are intended to punish the defendant for his outrageous conduct and to make an example of him, thus deterring him and perhaps other like-minded persons from engaging in similar conduct in the future.[18] The decision of the Supreme Court of Tasmania in *Watts* v. *Leitch*[19] suggests that if a defendant has already been punished by a criminal court in respect of acts which are now the subject of an action in tort then no exemplary damages will be awarded against the defendant because, as Nettlefold J. said: 'To punish him again would be to punish him twice for the one act'.[20]

We now consider the basis on which the courts calculate the monetary compensation which the defendant is required to pay to the plaintiff in relation to the various intentional torts discussed in the preceding chapters.

13 (1966) 117 C.L.R. 118.

14 The Privy Council in *Australian Consolidated Press Ltd* v. *Uren* [1969] A.C. 590 decided that the High Court of Australia was free to decide whether it would follow the decision of the House of Lords in *Rookes* v. *Barnard* and it could not be said to be wrong in deciding not to follow that decision.

15 (1987) 164 C.L.R.1.

16 [1982] 1 N.Z.L.R. 81.

17 See *Whitfeld* v. *De Lauret & Co. Ltd* (1920) 29 C.L.R. 71, 77.

18 See *Lamb* v. *Cotogno* (1987) 164 C.L.R.1, 10. Even though the High Court acknowledged that an award of exemplary damages against a compulsorily insured motorist might have a limited deterrent effect upon him it took the view that 'the deterrent effect is undiminished for those minded to engage in conduct of a similar nature which does not involve the use of a motor vehicle'.

19 [1973] Tas.S.R. 16.

20 ibid., 24.

II: TRESPASS TO THE PERSON

1. Battery and Assault

As these torts are actionable *per se*, damage is presumed by the courts and even if the plaintiff cannot produce any evidence of real or actual damage at least an award of nominal damages will be made. If, however, the battery or assault results in any physical injury or nervous shock then the damages payable by the defendant will be calculated in the same way as they are calculated in personal injury cases in negligence or any other tort which results in personal injury. The calculation of damages in actions for personal injury is dealt with in some detail in Chapter 12.

Briefly, the recognized heads of damages in a tort action for personal injury are as follows. The courts first of all give damages to the plaintiff for economic loss, which includes compensation not only for loss of earning capacity caused by the injury but also damages for the cost of care, that is, the expenses incurred for medical, hospital and nursing care. The courts also award damages for non-economic loss such as pain and suffering, loss of amenities, loss of expectation of life and cosmetic disfigurement. Damages for pain and suffering include not only the pain caused by the injury but also the pain caused by treatment of those injuries and the plaintiff's suffering because of the awareness of his injuries and their consequences. Damages for loss of amenities are given to compensate the plaintiff where he is deprived of the ability to pursue his leisure activities and to enjoy life to the full. Where a person's expectation of life is curtailed or shortened by the injury a plaintiff is awarded damages for the fact of loss of expectation of life. Damages for cosmetic disfigurement are given when a person is left without a limb or an ear as a result of the injury or left badly scarred as a result of the injury.

In addition to the damages for personal injury discussed above, a plaintiff will also be able to recover damages for insult, indignity, disgrace or humiliation if the battery or assault is committed in circumstances which are humiliating and insulting. The damages are increased because the injury is aggravated by the circumstances in which the personal injury is inflicted. The increased damages, even though given for the injured feelings of the plaintiff, are nevertheless still described as compensatory damages. As the High Court of Australia stated in *Lamb* v. *Cotogno*: 'Aggravated damages, in contrast to exemplary damages, are compensatory in nature, being awarded for injury to the plaintiff's feelings caused by insult, humiliation and the like'.[21] In *Henry* v. *Thompson,* where the defendant, a police officer, beat up the plaintiff and then urinated on him, Williams J. of the Supreme Court of Queensland took the view that it was a classic case for a high award of aggravated damages because even though urinating on the plaintiff caused him no actual physical harm it did cause him 'great emotional hurt, insult and humiliation'.[22]

---

21 (1987) 164 C.L.R.1, 10; See also *Johnstone* v. *Stewart* [1968] S.A.S.R. 142.
22 (1989) Aust. Torts Reports 80-255 at 68, 826.

Apart from ordinary and aggravated damages which are compensatory in nature the courts may also, in cases of intentional battery and assault, award an additional sum by way of exemplary damages which goes beyond compensation.[23] This is done where the sum to be awarded, aggravated by the way in which the defendant has behaved to the plaintiff, is still inadequate to punish the defendant for his outrageous conduct. This additional sum is awarded to mark the disapproval and detestation of such conduct and to deter the defendant and others from engaging in such conduct in the future. If the outrageous conduct on the part of the defendant is provoked in some way by an act of the plaintiff the court may take this into account in refusing to award exemplary damages or to reduce the amount of such damages. But the High Court of Australia has held in *Fontin* v. *Katapodis* that provocation on the part of the plaintiff 'has no application to damages awarded by way of compensation'.[24] It would seem to follow, therefore, that neither ordinary nor aggravated damages can be reduced because of provocation on the part of the plaintiff.[25]

2. False Imprisonment

In many cases of false imprisonment, there will usually be no personal injury, though if there is the damages will be calculated on the same basis as that for battery and assault. If there is any deleterious effect on the plaintiff's health that will also be compensable.[26] The damages claimed in an action for false imprisonment are for the deprivation of the liberty of the plaintiff, for the injury to his feelings, including 'the loss of dignity, mental suffering, disgrace and humiliation' caused by that deprivation,[27] and, if the circumstances warrant it, for the effect that the false imprisonment might have upon his reputation.[28]

Though the basis on which damages are calculated in an action of false imprisonment has not been explicitly spelt out in the cases it can be asserted with some confidence that 'any evidence which tends to aggravate or mitigate the damage to a man's reputation which flows naturally from his imprisonment must be admissible up to the moment when damages are assessed'.[29] So regret or an apology expressed to the plaintiff in relation to the deprivation of liberty will tend to reduce the damages awarded in an action for false imprisonment in the same way as the damages are likely to be increased (aggravated) if the defendant fails to

23 See *Lamb* v. *Cotogno* (1987) 164 C.L.R.1, 8.
24 (1962) 108 C.L.R. 177, 187 *per* Owen J. See also *Lamb* v. *Cotogno* (1987) 164 C.L.R.1, 13.
25 The position in England might be different. Compare *Lane* v. *Holloway* [1968] 1 Q.B. 379 and *Murphy* v. *Culhane* [1977] Q.B. 94.
26 See *Myer Stores Ltd* v. *Soo* (1991) Aust. Torts Reports 81-077 at 68, 625.
27 See *Myer Stores Ltd* v. *Soo* (1991) Aust. Torts Reports 81-077 at 68, 625 and *McIntosh* v. *Webster* [1980] 43 F.L.R. 112. See also *Hook* v. *Cunard Steamship Co.* [1953] 1 W.L.R. 682.
28 See *Walter* v. *Alltools Ltd* (1944) 171 L.T. 371.
29 ibid., 372 *per* Lawrence L.J.

tender an apology[30] or persists in maintaining that the plaintiff's imprisonment was lawful or if the deprivation of the plaintiff's liberty was carried out in humiliating or in most unpleasant circumstances.[31] Exemplary damages can also be awarded in an action of false imprisonment in Australia[32] but only if they are specifically pleaded and claimed in the Statement of Claim together with the facts to be relied on to substantiate such claim.[33]

Any specific pecuniary loss which follows from the imprisonment can be claimed as special damage. Though a decision of some antiquity from the Supreme Court of New South Wales[34] has declared that in an action of false imprisonment the plaintiff cannot recover as damages the costs incurred in defending himself in respect of the charge which resulted in the false imprisonment, nevertheless the preferable view now is that such legal costs are recoverable as damages in an action of false imprisonment as they follow from the false imprisonment and are necessary to prevent its continuance.[35] These legal costs would have to be claimed as special damages in the action for false imprisonment.

III: TRESPASS TO LAND

In an action for trespass to land a plaintiff is entitled to recover damages for the trespass even though no actual damage to the land has been done by the trespass.[36] In such cases the plaintiff will only recover nominal damages[37] but this is not always the case. Thus in *Waters* v. *Maynard*[38] where the plaintiff was wrongfully prevented from entering his own premises on two occasions by the defendant the jury awarded the plaintiff £75 even though there was no evidence as to any or what damage had been suffered by him.

Where the defendant commits a trespass to the land of the plaintiff by occupying his premises or using his land it is not always easy to determine the measure of damages. The test of the measure of damages is not always what the plaintiff has lost but sometimes rather what the defendant would have to pay for the use of the premises or the land. Thus, in *Swordheath Properties* v. *Tabet*[39] where the plaintiff established that the defendant had occupied residential premises as a trespasser, the English Court of Appeal

30 See *Myer Stores Ltd* v. *Soo* (1991) Aust. Torts Reports 81-077 at 68, 637.
31 See *McIntosh* v. *Webster* (1980) 43 F.L.R. 112, 128 and *Myer Stores Ltd* v. *Soo* (1991) Aust. Torts Reports 81-077.
32 See *Burton* v. *Davies* (1953) St.R.Qd. 26, 30.
33 See *Myer Stores Ltd* v. *Soo* (1991) Aust. Torts Reports 81-077 at 68, 647.
34 See *Chippel* v. *Thomson* (1869) 8 S.C.R.(N.S.W.) 219.
35 See *Bahner* v. *Marwest Hotel Co. Ltd* (1969) 6 D.L.R. (3d) 322. See also *McGregor on Damages* (14th edn, 1980) para. 1359.
36 See *Dumont* v. *Miller* (1873) 4 A.J.R. 75.
37 See *Prentice* v. *Mercantile House Pty Ltd* (1991) 99 A.L.R. 107 and *Dehn* v. *Attorney-General* [1988] 2 N.Z.L.R. 564, 583.
38 (1924) 24 S.R.(N.S.W.) 618.
39 [1979] 1 W.L.R. 285.

held that the plaintiff was entitled to damages for the trespass calculated by reference to the ordinary letting value of the premises without the plaintiff adducing any evidence that he could or would have let those premises to someone else if the defendant had not been wrongfully in occupation. Similarly, where defendants for many years trespassed on the plaintiff's land by tipping soil on it from their colliery the Court of Appeal held that the defendants must not only pay damages to the plaintiff for diminishing the value of the land but that they should also pay the plaintiff a sum or charge for the use of the land.[40] In *Yakamia Dairy Pty Ltd* v. *Wood*[41] the Supreme Court of Western Australia decided that the defendant who depastured cattle belonging to his wife upon the plaintiff's land had intentionally and wrongfully made use of the land and that the plaintiff was entitled to recover for that trespass 'damages based upon the agistment fees which would have been payable had there been an agreement to allow the cattle to pasture on the land'.[42] And recently in *LJP Investments Pty Ltd* v. *Howard Chia Investments Pty Ltd*,[43] Hodgson J. in the Supreme Court of New South Wales decided that the defendant who initially sought the plaintiff's permission to enter its land to erect scaffolding, nevertheless erected scaffolding, which protruded over the plaintiff's property, without the consent of the plaintiff because the price sought by the plaintiff was thought by the defendant, though not by the judge, to be unreasonable, was liable to the plaintiff in trespass and that the proper measure of damages payable by the defendant was not confined to the compensatory damages for the actual trespass but also included additional compensatory damages (or 'restitutionary damages'[44]) equal to such sum as the defendant should reasonably pay for the use it made of the plaintiff's land. As Hodgson J. said: 'I think it should be made clear to developers that they cannot expect to do better by an unlawful trespass than by paying a price demanded by an adjoining owner, at least unless the price demanded is clearly unreasonable'.[45] A defendant who acts in this way may well find the courts prepared to allow a plaintiff to claim compensatory damages for loss of the right to bargain for the sale of rights of use of the plaintiff's land[46] and even perhaps to claim exemplary damages.[47]

If in committing the act of trespass the defendant severs part of the realty (land) and converts it into chattels (goods), as, for example, when he enters upon the land of the plaintiff and cuts down and carries away trees on the plaintiff's land or mines his minerals and takes them away, then the defendant has not only committed a trespass but also an act of conversion of the plaintiff's goods. In such cases, as actions in both

---

40 See *Whitwham* v. *Westminster Brymbo Coal and Coke Co.* [1896] 2 Ch. 538.
41 [1976] W.A.R. 57.
42 ibid., 58 *per* Jackson C.J.
43 (1991) Aust. Torts Reports 81-070.
44 ibid., at 68, 557.
45 ibid., at 68, 558.
46 See *LJP Investments Pty Ltd* v. *Howard Chia Investments Pty Ltd (No. 2)* (1991) Aust. Torts Reports 81-069 at 68, 550.
47 ibid.

trespass and conversion will be brought, the court should be careful to ensure that in the amounts awarded in the two actions there is no overlapping.[48] The method of calculating the damages for the conversion of the goods is discussed below.[49]

If the trespass to land consists of damage to or destruction of the soil or of premises on the land there are two methods by which the damages payable by the defendant can be assessed. The first is by establishing the reasonable cost of replacement or repairs to the premises or land to restore it to its original condition.[50] The second method is by calculating the diminution in the value of the premises or land occasioned by the trespass.[51] Which method is used is not necessarily at the election of the plaintiff but is determined by the circumstances of the case and the overriding requirement of what is reasonable. Sometimes the diminution in value basis might produce an award of little or no damages while the reinstatement or restoration basis might produce a substantial sum. This might happen, for example, when a house situated on land zoned for high-rise development is damaged or destroyed by the defendant. The defendant could argue that the improvements on the land (the house etc.) have no value on the market and that the plaintiff ought, therefore, to receive a modest sum by way of damages even though the cost to the plaintiff of reinstatement and repair of the house might be substantial. In such a case the court will inquire whether it is reasonable for the plaintiff to reinstate and restore his property. If the evidence suggests that there is something about the property personal to the plaintiff requiring restoration to the original condition, for example, if an ancestral family home is destroyed, then even though the cost of restoration is disproportionate to the diminution in value the plaintiff will be entitled to have as damages the cost of restoration. As Samuels J.A. put it in *Evans* v. *Balog*: if that course of action 'turns out to be more expensive than another, the wrongdoer has no one but himself to blame'.[52] But in the absence of such personal considerations the court will not award as damages the cost of restoration where it is out of proportion to the injury done to the land and, therefore, disproportionate to the diminution in the value of the land.[53]

Whether the cost of restoring land to its former condition or the diminished value of the land is used as the basis of assessing damages in an action for trespass to land, any expenses reasonably and properly incurred for professional fees payable to a surveyor, an architect or an engineer engaged to advise the plaintiff on remedial measures to restore

---

48 See *Bilambil-Terranova Pty Ltd* v. *Tweed Shire Council* [1980] 1 N.S.W.L.R. 465, 488.

49 See pp. 298-304 below.

50 See *Minter* v. *Eacott* (1952) 69 W.N.(N.S.W.) 93 and *Evans* v. *Balog* [1976] 1 N.S.W.L.R. 36.

51 See *Jones* v. *Shire of Perth* [1971] W.A.R. 56; *Bushells Pty Ltd* v. *Commonwealth* [1948] St.R.Qd. 79; and *Adams* v. *Mayor of Brunswick* (1894) 20 V.L.R. 455.

52 [1976] 1 N.S.W.L.R. 36, 40.

53 See *Jones* v. *Shire of Perth* [1971] W.A.R. 56; and *Public Trustee* v. *Hermann* (1968) 88 W.N.(N.S.W.) 422.

the land to its original state will be payable by the defendant as special damages to the plaintiff.[54]

The plaintiff will also be able to recover in an action for trespass to land damages in respect of any consequential loss which is a natural or reasonable consequence of the trespass.[55] Thus a plaintiff was able to recover, in an action of trespass to land, damages for the loss of a filly which escaped when the defendant trespassed on the plaintiff's land with a bulldozer and broke down his fence.[56] However, in *Mayfair Ltd* v. *Pears*[57] the Court of Appeal of New Zealand decided that where the defendant illegally parked his car on the plaintiff's premises and the car inexplicably caught fire and damaged the plaintiff's premises, that even though there had been an intentional trespass to land by the defendant he was not liable for the injury to the plaintiff's premises because that injury was caused without intent or negligence, was not foreseeable and could not reasonably be described as a direct or immediate result of the trespass.

If the defendant commits a trespass to land in such circumstances as would severely embarrass or outrage the plaintiff there is no doubt that an award of aggravated damages can be made.[58] Thus in *Greig* v. *Greig*[59] where the defendant's act of trespass consisted of entering the plaintiff's flat and installing a microphone to record the plaintiff's private conversations, Gillard J. of the Supreme Court of Victoria held that a case for aggravated damages had been made out.[60]

Exemplary damages, too, can be awarded in Australia against a defendant in an action for trespass to land.[61] These damages are intended to punish the defendant for his conduct, not to compensate the plaintiff for his loss. They are beyond the strict line of compensation. The availability of exemplary damages, however, could also overcome the problems which a plaintiff may sometimes have in quantifying the damages arising from the trespass.[62] The decision of the Court of Appeal of New South Wales in *Pollack* v. *Volpato*,[63] however, suggests that the award of exemplary damages must be reasonable. An award which, for example, would make a man lose his home would be regarded as excessive and, therefore, not reasonable. A plaintiff who claims exemplary damages would be well advised, therefore, to tender evidence of the resources of the defendant.[64]

---

54 *Jones* v. *Shire of Perth* [1971] W.A.R. 56, 61.

55 See *Svingos* v. *Deacon Avenue Cartage and Storage Pty Ltd* [1971] 2 S.A.S.R. 126.

56 See *Hogan* v. *A.G. Wright Pty Ltd* [1963] Tas.S.R. 44.

57 [1987] 1 N.Z.L.R. 459.

58 See *Plenty* v. *Dillon* (1991) 171 C.L.R. 635, 654-5.

59 [1966] V.R. 376, 378.

60 See also *Johnstone* v. *Stewart* [1968] S.A.S.R. 142 and *Drake* v. *Evangelou* [1978] 1 W.L.R. 455, 463.

61 See *Schumann* v. *Abbott Davis* [1961] S.A.S.R. 149; *Coles-Smith* v. *Smith* [1965] Qd.R. 494, 507; *Johnstone* v. *Stewart* [1968] S.A.S.R. 142; *Caltex-Oil (Australia) Pty Ltd* v. *XL Petroleum (N.S.W.) Pty Ltd* [1982] 2 N.S.W.L.R. 852; *Caprino Pty Ltd* v. *Gold Coast City Council* (1982) 53 L.G.R.A. 243 and *Amstad* v. *Brisbane City Council (No.1)* [1968] Qd.R.34.

62 See *Lincoln Hunt Australia Pty Ltd* v. *Willesee* (1986) 4 N.S.W.L.R. 457, 464.

63 [1973] 1 N.S.W.L.R. 653.

64 ibid., 657-8.

Finally, in relation to damages for trespass to land it should be noted that a plaintiff with a limited interest in the land will only be able to recover damages to the extent of his interest. Thus, a tenant will only be able to recover damages in respect of the interference with his possession of the land and not in relation to any permanent damage to the reversion, that is, the land which will revert to the landlord on the determination of the lease. The landlord not in possession of the property who suffers permanent damage to his reversion will, however, only be able to recover that damage in an action on the case for damages.[65]

IV: TRESPASS TO GOODS

It was pointed out in Chapter 4 that, though there is some doubt, the preferable view is that the tort of intentional trespass to goods is actionable *per se* and that proof of actual damage is not required. If the plaintiff can show a trespass to his goods he will receive at least nominal damages even though he cannot show any real damage to the goods.[66] But, if the circumstances warrant it, a judge or jury can award more than nominal damages even though no actual or real damage can be shown by the plaintiff as a result of the trespass.[67]

If goods are damaged or destroyed by an act of trespass the measure of damages will vary according to whether the goods are profit-earning chattels or not. If profit-earning chattels are damaged by the trespass the normal measure of damages which the plaintiff will receive will include not only the cost of repairing the chattel and any reduction in the market value of the goods as a result of the repairs effected[68] but also any consequential damage naturally and directly flowing from the wrongful act, such as loss of profits during the period the chattel was unable to be used in its profit-earning capacity. If the cost of repairs can be estimated by an expert with reasonable certainty the plaintiff must adduce evidence of such an estimate, but if a reasonably certain estimate cannot be given the court must assess the damages as best it can.[69] If the cost of repairing the chattel exceeds the market value of the chattel before the act of trespass was committed then the measure of damages is the market value of the chattel, that is, its replacement cost and not the cost of repairing the chattel. The onus is on the plaintiff to show which method of assessing damages is the more reasonable in the circumstances.[70]

If repair to the damaged chattel increases the value of the chattel to above what it was before the trespass was committed, the plaintiff would have to make an allowance to the defendant for the increase in value of the

---

65 See *Rodrigues* v. *Ufton* (1894) 20 V.L.R. 539 and pp. 309-10 below.
66 See *Dymocks Book Arcade Ltd* v. *McCarthy* (1966) 2 N.S.W.R. 411, 417.
67 See *Harvey* v. *Birrell* (1878) 12 S.A.L.R. 58.
68 See *Dryden* v. *Orr* (1928) 28 S.R.(N.S.W.) 216 and *Volker* v. *Frizzell* [1953] Q.W.N. 6.
69 See *Wheeler* v. *Riverside Coal Transport Co. Pty Ltd* [1964] Qd.R. 113, 124.
70 See *Jansen* v. *Dewhurst* [1969] V.R. 421, 427.

chattel.[71] If a profit-earning chattel is totally destroyed by the trespass or cannot be economically repaired the measure of damages is in general the market value of the chattel immediately before the act of trespass. No doubt in such cases the plaintiff can also claim for loss of profits during a reasonable period required to purchase a replacement or the cost of hiring a replacement.[72]

If a non-profit-earning chattel is damaged by an act of trespass the court must decide, as in the case of a profit-earning chattel, whether it will award the plaintiff the cost of repairing the chattel or its market value prior to the trespass. Again it is for the plaintiff to show which method of assessing damages is the more reasonable in the circumstances. If there is something unique about the chattel as, for example, in the case of a 'vintage car', replacement may be impossible and repair at very heavy cost, which may be the only course appropriate, will be ordered by the court.[73] Even though the chattel damaged is not profit-earning the plaintiff is still entitled to substantial damages for deprivation of its use and the court can give whatever it thinks is the proper equivalent for the fact that the trespass to the chattel has resulted in the withdrawal of the chattel from actual or possible use. If a non-profit-earning chattel is totally destroyed or cannot be economically repaired the measure of damages is the market value of the chattel immediately before the act of trespass. This should be roughly equivalent to the replacement cost of the chattel.[74]

There is no obligation on a plaintiff to repair a chattel, damaged as a result of a trespass, before selling it. The plaintiff can exercise his option to sell the damaged chattel without repairing it and then to claim as damages the difference between the market value of the chattel before the trespass and its market value when sold in its damaged condition.[75]

It should be noted that if the defendant has an interest in the goods then the measure of damages will not be the value of the goods but the value of the plaintiff's interest in the goods at the time of the trespass.[76]

If the trespass to the chattels has been committed in aggravating circumstances, such as, for example, by the defendant overturning the plaintiff's car while he is sitting in it, it is open to the court to award a sum by way of aggravated damages even though the plaintiff might not have suffered any personal injury. And it is certainly possible for an award of exemplary damages to be made if the trespass to the goods is made in circumstances in which exemplary damages are appropriate and the court wishes to express its assessment of the heinousness of the defendant's conduct.[77]

---

71 *Eastern Construction Co. Pty Ltd* v. *Southern Portland Cement Ltd* (1961) 78 W.N.(N.S.W.) 293. However, cf., *Anthoness* v. *Bland Shire Council* (1960) 60 S.R.(N.S.W.) 659.

72 See *The Liesbosch* [1933] A.C. 449. See also *Egan* v. *State Transport Authority* [1982] 31 S.A.S.R. 481.

73 See *Jansen* v. *Dewhurst* [1969] V.R. 421, 426.

74 ibid., 426-7 and *Van der Wal* v. *Harris* [1961] W.A.R. 124.

75 See *J.S. Gilbert Fabrications Pty Ltd* v. *Davidson* (1985) Aust. Torts Reports 80-725.

76 See *Dean* v. *T. Thomas & Son* [1981] Qd.R. 62, 67; and *Brierly* v. *Kendall* (1852) 17 Q.B. 937.

77 See *Healing (Sales) Pty Ltd* v. *Inglis Electrix Pty Ltd* (1968) 121 C.L.R. 584 and *Caltex Oil (Australia) Pty Ltd* v. *XL Petroleum (N.S.W.) Pty Ltd* [1982] 2 N.S.W.L.R. 852.

V: CONVERSION

If a defendant has converted the plaintiff's goods he must pay some damages but the damages awarded will sometimes be nominal as, for example, when the defendant delivers the plaintiff's goods to a third party just a day before he receives a proper delivery order requiring him to deliver the goods to the third party[78] or when the defendant immediately returns the goods which he has converted in exactly the same condition and the plaintiff accepts the goods. In these two cases, even though there has been a technical conversion of the goods the award made by the court is likely to be one of nominal damages.[79] However, if the conversion is more than merely technical substantial damages will be awarded.

Where substantial damages are sought the measure of damages in an action of conversion is usually the full market value of the goods converted at the time of the act of conversion[80] since that is usually the measure of the plaintiff's actual loss.[81] As the Privy Council indicated in *The Jag Shakti*, if A is deprived of the possession of his goods by an act of conversion by B 'the proper measure in law of the damages recoverable by A from B is the full market value of the goods at the time when and the place where possession of them should have been given . . . [T]he circumstance that, if A recovers the full market value of the goods from B, he may be liable to account for the whole or part of what he has recovered to a third party, C, is . . . irrelevant, as being *res inter alios acta*'.[82] Where goods are irreversibly converted and the plaintiff thus loses those goods the courts will hold that the plaintiff loses the value of those goods at the date of the conversion even though there might be no evidence that the plaintiff knew of the conversion or would have sold the goods at the date of the conversion but for the act of conversion. Thus in *BBMB Finance (Hong Kong) Ltd* v. *Eda Holdings Ltd*[83] the plaintiff whose shares were converted by the defendant at a time when their market price was $5.75 and replaced by the defendant at a time when their market price was $2.50 was able to recover as damages for conversion the difference between the value of the shares at the date of the conversion and the value of the replacement shares, even though there was no evidence that the plaintiff knew about the conversion of the shares at the time of the conversion or that he would have sold the shares at the market price of $5.25 but for the act of conversion by the defendant. However, if there are circumstances in a particular case which reduce the plaintiff's actual loss below the full market value of the goods at the time of the conversion then the measure of the plaintiff's damages will be reduced accordingly. As the High Court

---

78 See *Hiort* v. *L.N.W. Railway* (1879) 4 Ex.D. 188.

79 See *Associated Midland Corporation* v. *Bank of New South Wales* [1983] 1 N.S.W.L.R. 533, 547.

80 See *Ley* v. *Lewis* [1952] V.L.R. 119.

81 Unless the party complaining can allege and prove further special damage arising from the wrongful act of which he complains. *Haddow* v. *Duke Co. (N.L.)* (1892) 18 V.L.R. 155, 173 and 174.

82 [1986] 1 A.C. 337, 345.

83 [1991] 2 All E.R. 129 (Privy Council).

of Australia has reminded us in *Butler* v. *Egg & Egg Pulp Marketing Board*: 'the statement which appears so often in the books that the general rule is that the plaintiff in an action of conversion is entitled to recover the full value of the goods converted . . . should not be allowed to obscure the broad principle that damages are awarded by way of compensation'.[84]

What, then, are some of the circumstances in which the measure of damages in conversion will be less than the full market value of the goods converted? First, if the defendant as between himself and the plaintiff has an interest in the goods converted, as, for example, in the case of a bailor and bailee[85] or owner and lienor,[86] then the damages will not be the full market value of the goods but the value less the defendant's interest in the goods. In *Chinery* v. *Viall*[87] the unpaid seller of goods who had remained in possession of the goods by arrangement with the purchaser converted the goods by selling them again to a third party. The damages for the conversion were held to be the full market value of the goods at the time of the conversion less the price of the goods owed by the plaintiff to the defendant. But an unpaid seller who retains neither the property nor the possession of the goods will not have a sufficient interest in the goods to enable him to have the unpaid purchase price deducted from the full market value of the goods. So, if such an unpaid seller commits an act of conversion in relation to the goods the measure of damages will be the full value of the goods without any deduction for the unpaid purchase price.[88]

Secondly, if payment of the full market value by the defendant will result in the plaintiff making a profit at the expense of the defendant then the court will award less than the full value of the goods. In *Butler* v. *Egg & Egg Pulp Marketing Board*[89] legislation in the State of Victoria divested all producers of eggs in Victoria of property in the eggs and vested it in the Board. An egg producer did not deliver the eggs produced to the Board but sold them instead to a third party. In an action by the Board for conversion of the eggs, the High Court of Australia decided that the plaintiffs were entitled to the sale price of the eggs less such amount as the plaintiffs would have to pay to the defendant under the egg marketing scheme if the defendant had delivered the eggs to the Board instead of selling them to a third party. Taylor and Owen JJ. in a joint judgment agreed that the defendant had no interest in the eggs but only a claim for payment which was conditioned upon delivery of the eggs to the Board, a delivery which in fact had not been made. Nevertheless, Taylor and Owen JJ. decided that if the Board received the full sale price of the eggs as damages for the conversion they would be in a better position financially

---

84 (1966) 114 C.L.R. 185, 191.

85 See *City Motors (1933) Pty Ltd* v. *Southern Aerial Super Service Pty Ltd* (1961) 35 A.L.J.R. 206, 212.

86 See *Standard Electronics Apparatus Laboratories Pty Ltd* v. *Stenner* [1960] N.S.W.R. 447.

87 (1860) 5 H. & N. 288. See also *Johnson* v. *Stear* (1863) 15 C.B.(N.S.) 330; *Belsize Motor Supply Co.* v. *Cox* [1914] 2 K.B. 244, 252; and *Garven* v. *Ronald Motors Pty Ltd* [1938] Q.W.N. 74.

88 See *Healing (Sales) Pty Ltd* v. *Inglis Electrix Pty Ltd* (1968) 121 C.L.R. 584. See also J. Peden (1970) 44 A.L.J. 65.

89 (1966) 114 C.L.R. 185.

than they would have been if the defendant had delivered the eggs to the Board. They decided, therefore, that this was a case where payment of less than full value was the appropriate measure of damages for the conversion and made the deduction earlier mentioned.

Thirdly, where goods which have been let under a hire-purchase agreement by a finance company are converted, the normal measure of damages in an action in conversion brought by the finance company will not be the full market value of the goods but only the amount outstanding under the hire-purchase agreement, the 'payout figure' as it is called.[90] It should also be noted that the 'payout figure' which the defendant is required to pay is not the amount outstanding under the hire-purchase agreement at the time of the conversion but the amount outstanding at the *date of judgment.*[91] However, if the goods are worth less at the time of the conversion than the amount outstanding under the hire-purchase agreement at the date of judgment then the court will award the value of the goods at the time of the conversion as the proper measure of damages for the conversion rather than the 'payout figure'.[92]

Fourthly, where, for example, coal (or other minerals) or gravel are severed from the land by the defendant and subsequently converted by him there are two specific methods which have been used by the courts to calculate the measure of damages for the conversion of the goods. The first is by calculating the damages in the analogy of a royalty which the plaintiff might have demanded from the defendant if the latter had sought his permission to extract the coal or gravel.[93] The second is by calculating damages on the basis of the price of the coal on the site (at the pit's mouth) less the costs of severing and raising the goods in question.[94] Neither method is intended to give the plaintiff the 'full value' or the 'market value' of the goods converted. However, it is suggested that these two methods of calculating the measure of damages in conversion are only appropriate where the defendant has acted bona fide and in ignorance of the plaintiff's rights. If the act of conversion is done furtively, for example, by the defendant mining the plaintiff's coal by means of a secret underground trespass, then the measure of damages in conversion will be the full market value of the coal without any allowance being made for the cost of severing and raising it.[95]

Fifthly, if the value of the goods has been increased as a result of some work done on them by the defendant then the measure of damages will not be the full market value of the goods at the time of the conversion. In

---

90 See *Western Credits Pty Ltd* v. *Dragan Motors Pty Ltd* [1973] W.A.R. 184. See also *Wickham Holdings Ltd* v. *Brooke House Motors Ltd* [1967] 1 W.L.R. 293 and *Belvoir Finance Co. Ltd* v. *Stapleton* [1971] 1 Q.B. 210.

91 See *Western Credits Pty Ltd* v. *Dragan Motors Pty Ltd* [1973] W.A.R. 184. The amount owing to the finance company at the time of the conversion was $2295 but between then and the date of judgment this was reduced to $499. The Full Court of the Supreme Court of Western Australia held that the proper measure of damages was $499.

92 See *Pacific Acceptance Corp. Ltd* v. *Mirror Motors Pty Ltd* (1961) 61 S.R.(N.S.W.) 548. See also *Chubb Cash Ltd* v. *John Crilley & Son* [1983] 2 All E.R. 294, 297.

93 See *Livingstone* v. *Raywards Coal Co.* (1880) 5 App.Cases 25.

94 See *Bilambil-Terranova Pty Ltd* v. *Tweed Shire Council* [1980] 1 N.S.W.L.R. 465.

95 See *Bulli Coal Mining Co.* v. *Osborne* [1899] A.C. 351.

Munro v. *Willmott*[96] the defendant was the bailee of the plaintiff's motor car worth £20 to £25 as scrap. He spent £85 in making the car saleable and then sold the car for £110. In an action for conversion of the motor car the plaintiff was awarded as damages not £110 (the value of the motor car at the time of the conversion) but £35 because, as Lynskey J., said that was the value of the property which he had lost. Lynskey J. felt that the defendant was entitled to credit for £85 'not from the point of view of payment for what he has done, but in order to arrive at what is the true value of the property which the plaintiff has lost'.[97]

Sixthly, if a defendant who has converted the goods returns or delivers the goods back to the plaintiff then the measure of damages is likely to be less than the full value of the goods. As Bramwell L.J. said in *Hiort* v. *The London and North Western Railway Co.*, 'it is clear . . . that on the return of the goods the plaintiff would recover, not their value, but the damages he had sustained by the wrongful act, which was called the conversion'.[98] The measure of damages would vary according to the condition in which the goods were returned (unimpaired condition or seriously damaged) and the time at which they were returned (promptly after the conversion or just before the date of judgment). Though in *Kidman* v. *Farmers' Centre Pty Ltd*[99] it was held that the plaintiff could not be compelled to accept the defendant's offer to recover and return the goods converted, nevertheless, it is suggested, the court has a discretion as to whether it will order the plaintiff to take back the chattel converted from the defendant by ordering a stay of proceedings. It is much more likely to order a stay of proceedings if the offer to return the chattel is made promptly after the conversion rather than after the judgment in the action is given. Similarly, if a defendant who has converted a cheque by wrongfully depositing it in his account subsequently but deliberately makes payments to discharge a liability of the true owner of the cheque then the court may in some circumstances, in determining the damages payable to the owner for the conversion of the cheque, take those payments into account.[100] This will most likely be done if the payments made by the defendant converter to or for the benefit of the plaintiff have been made out of the proceeds of the conversion.[101] However, before a payment or benefit can be taken into account in reduction of damages for conversion it must be established that the payment or benefit was not made or received collaterally to the commission of the tort, or that it is not a *res inter alios acta*.[102] Payments made by a concurrent or subsequent converter, whether a party to the proceeding or not, might also be taken into account. But, as *Hunter BNZ Finance Ltd* v. *Australia and New Zealand Banking Group Ltd* illustrates,

---

96 [1949] 1 K.B. 295.

97 ibid., 299. See also *Dean* v. *J. Thomas & Son* [1981] Qd.R. 62.

98 (1879) 4 Ex.D. 188, 195. See also *Craig* v. *Marsh* (1935) 35 S.R.(N.S.W.) 323, 329-30.

99 [1959] Qd.R. 8.

100 See *Associated Midland Corp. Ltd* v. *Bank of N.S.W.* [1983] 1 N.S.W.L.R. 533.

101 [1990] V.R. 41. See also *Australia and New Zealand Banking Group Ltd* v. *AMEV Finance Ltd* (1989) Aust. Torts Reports 80-228.

102 See *Australia and New Zealand Banking Group Ltd* v. *Hunter BNZ Finance Ltd* [1991] 2 V.R. 406, 411.

the source or sources of the payments to the plaintiff on which the defendant relies must be exceedingly clear before the court will take those payments into account.[103]

Just as there are circumstances in which the measure of damages awarded in an action in conversion will be *less* than the full market value of the goods at the date of the conversion, so there are also circumstances where the measure of damages in conversion will be *more* than the full market value of the goods at the date of the conversion. First, in the case of goods which have risen in value since the date of the conversion there is authority which suggests that the plaintiff will be able to recover more than the market value of the goods at the date of the conversion if the plaintiff did not know about the conversion at the time it was committed and the goods have risen in value since the date of the conversion.[104] This rule is particularly useful where the goods which have been converted are, for example, shares which have a fluctuating value. The rise in value, to be recoverable, must not be due to any act on the part of the defendant.[105] There is some conflict of authority as to the date on which the subsequent increase in value should be calculated. *Sachs* v. *Miklos*[106] suggests that the date at which the increase in value must be calculated is the date on which the plaintiff knew of the conversion irrespective of the actual date of the conversion. *Aitken* v. *Gardiner*[107] decided that the relevant date was the date of the trial but in *Amoretty* v. *The City of Melbourne Bank*[108] A'Beckett J. of the Supreme Court of Victoria decided that the increase in value must be calculated on the date the plaintiff commenced the action, that is, the date on which the writ was issued.

It is suggested that in the case of goods which have increased in value since the date of the conversion the value on the date on which the writ was issued should be the proper measure of damages for the conversion of the goods. However, if there is evidence that the plaintiff has waited until the property of which he has been deprived has reached its highest point before he issues his writ then the court might make an allowance in calculating the value of the goods converted.[109] Although this does not appear to have been required in *Amoretty*, Wickham J. in *Western Credits Pty Ltd* v. *Dragan Motors Pty Ltd* suggests that the increase in value must be recovered as consequential damage.[110] Secondly, as we have noted in Chapter 4,[111] in the case of negotiable instruments such as cheques, insurance policies, shares etc. the conversion of the goods (cheque, insurance policy, share certificate etc.) is treated as conversion of the

---

103 See *Australia and New Zealand Banking Group Ltd* v. *Hunter BNZ Finance Ltd* [1990] V.R. 41, 48-9.

104 See *Sachs* v. *Miklos* [1948] 2 K.B. 23; *Aitken* v. *Gardiner* [1956] 4 D.L.R. (2d) 119; and *Amoretty* v. *The City of Melbourne Bank* (1887) 13 V.L.R. 431.

105 See *Graham* v. *Voight* (1989) A.C.T.R. 11.

106 [1948] 2 K.B. 23.

107 [1956] 4 D.L.R. (2d) 119.

108 (1887) 13 V.L.R. 431.

109 *Sachs* v. *Miklos* [1948] 2 K.B. 23, 41 and *Amoretty* v. *The City of Melbourne Bank* (1887) 13 V.L.R. 431, 433.

110 [1973] W.A.R. 184, 191.

111 See p. 137.

money the documents represent rather than the pieces of paper that they actually are. The damages for conversion of the piece of paper is assimilated to the value of the negotiable instrument.[112] Thirdly, where an owner of the copyright in a work or other subject-matter brings an action for conversion of the copyright in relation to an infringing copy or copies, the measure of damages, it was decided in *W.H. Brine & Co.* v. *Whitton*,[113] must be the full market value of the goods which are regarded as infringing copies rather than the value of the copyright. In that case, where the defendant sold a number of soccer balls imported from Korea which were marked with various marks and devices some of which were the property of the plaintiff, Fox J. in the Federal Court of Australia decided that the measure of damages was the full market value of the balls at the date of the conversion in Australia. Fox J. agreed that this was 'an unreasonably excessive amount if the aim is simply to compensate the [plaintiff] for loss and damage he suffered'[114] but he felt that the measure of damages for conversion of the copyright of the plaintiff contains also a penalty aspect which therefore gives more to the plaintiff than the full value of his loss.

In addition to the normal measure of damages it is also possible to recover damages in an action in conversion for what might be described as 'consequential damage' or 'consequential loss' which is reasonably foreseeable[115] and not too remote to be recoverable in law. As Bush J. stated in *Chubb Cash Ltd* v. *John Crilley & Son*, 'in all actions in conversion the plaintiff may recover any additional damage he may suffer which is not too remote'.[116] But, as the decision in *Chubb Cash Ltd* shows, the damage to be recoverable as consequential damage must actually flow from the act of conversion and not from some other act. In that case, the plaintiffs in consideration of receiving a cash sum assigned their right to receive hire-purchase instalments from the hire-purchaser (debtor), in respect of a cash register, to a credit company (Masterloan). The assignment provided that if the debtor defaulted on payment of an instalment then the plaintiffs would have to repay Masterloan the cash sum less any payment made by the debtor to Masterloan. The defendants (bailiffs), acting on behalf of the Commissioner of Customs and Excise, wrongly assumed that the cash register was the property of the debtor and distrained on it. They removed it to their own premises, stored it and subsequently had it sold at a public auction for £155 plus V.A.T. The debtor refused to pay any further instalments and the plaintiff had to pay Masterloan £951.55 under the terms of the assignment. The plaintiffs sued the defendants for this amount but the English Court of Appeal decided that the measure of

112 See *Kosters Premier Pottery Pty Ltd* v. *The Bank of Adelaide* [1981] 28 S.A.S.R. 355, 358. See also *Associated Midland Corp. Ltd* v. *Bank of N.S.W.* [1983] 1 N.S.W.L.R. 533, 536 and 550 and *Lloyds Bank Ltd* v. *The Chartered Bank of India, Australia and China* [1929] 1 K.B. 40, 55-6.

113 (1981) 37 A.L.R. 190.

114 ibid., 200.

115 See *Harrisons Group Holdings Ltd* v. *Westpac Banking Corporation* (1989) 51 S.A.S.R. 36, 40.

116 [1983] 2 All E.R. 294, 299.

damages for the conversion by the defendants was only £155 plus V.A.T., the amount realized at the auction sale. The argument by the plaintiffs that the measure of damages should be £951.55, the sum they had to pay Masterloan, was rejected by the court. As Bush J. said: 'This damage does not in this case flow from the conversion, but flows from the failure of the debtor to perform his obligations under the agreement'.[117]

Another type of consequential loss, in a sense unrelated to the value of the goods, which is recoverable in an action in conversion is loss of profits. There must, however, be a clear causal connection and a foreseeable connection between the act of conversion and the loss if it is to be recoverable.[118] The loss of profits must not arise from an independent cause.[119]

Although there is no decision of the courts in England or Australia which specifically decides that aggravated damages may be awarded in an action in conversion there are several decisions of the courts both in England and Australia which seem to imply that aggravated damages may be awarded in an action in conversion in appropriate circumstances.[120] And, if the circumstances indicate that there has been a cynical disregard for the plaintiff's rights by the defendant, there is now little doubt that the courts in Australia can award exemplary damages in an action in conversion.[121] However, in *Dymocks Book Arcade Ltd* v. *McCarthy* Jacobs J.A. suggested that exemplary damages in an action in conversion may properly be awarded only where the evidence in the action for conversion discloses a trespass to the goods and not where the wrong sued upon is a bare conversion.[122]

VI: DETINUE

Though there may be some cases where the measure of damages in conversion and detinue are the same this is not necessarily so in all cases and, therefore, it is better to deal with the measure of damages in detinue separately.

If the plaintiff's goods are no longer in the defendant's possession, for example, because they have been lost or destroyed while in his possession,

117 ibid.

118 See *Egan* v. *State Transport Authority* (1982) 31 S.A.S.R. 481, 526. See also *Bodley* v. *Reynolds* (1846) 8 Q.B. 779; *Brilawsky* v. *Robertson* (1916) 10 Q.J.P.R. 113; and *Howe* v. *Teefy* (1927) 27 S.R.(N.S.W.) 301.

119 See *Egan* v. *State Transport Authority* (1982) 31 S.A.S.R. 481, 526 and *The Liesbosch* [1933] A.C. 449.

120 See *Dymocks Book Arcade Ltd* v. *McCarthy* [1966] 1 N.S.W.R. 411; *Healing (Sales) Pty Ltd* v. *Inglis Electrix Pty Ltd* (1968) 121 C.L.R. 584; *Brewer* v. *Dew* (1843) 11 M. & W. 625; *Owen & Smith* v. *Reo Motors* (1934) 151 L.T. 274, 277 and *Williams* v. *Settle* [1960] 1 W.L.R. 1072. See also *Rookes* v. *Barnard* [1964] A.C. 1129.

121 See *Healing (Sales) Pty Ltd* v. *Inglis Electrix Pty Ltd* (1968) 121 C.L.R. 584 and *Dymocks Book Arcade Ltd* v. *McCarthy* [1966] 2 N.S.W.R. 411. See also *Eli* v. *Royal Bank of Canada* (1986) 24 D.L.R. (4th) 127 where exemplary damages of 10 per cent of the amount converted from the plaintiff's account were awarded.

122 [1966] 2 N.S.W.R. 411, 414-15.

the only form of judgment that the plaintiff can obtain will be one for the value of goods as assessed and damages for their detention. But if the goods are still in the defendant's possession then, as indicated earlier,[123] the plaintiff can seek a judgment in one of three different forms. Under the first form he can ask for the value of the chattel as assessed and damages for its detention, under the second form he can ask for the return of the chattel or recovery of its value as assessed and damages for its detention and under the third form he can ask for the return of the chattel and damages for its detention. The form of judgment which is most commonly sought is one in the second form, that is, one which asks for the return of the chattel or recovery of its value as assessed and damages for its detention.

How is the value of the chattel assessed in actions of detinue? If the chattel has not been returned before the date of judgment then obviously the tort of detinue is still being committed at the date of judgment. As the detention is a continuing wrong it is only appropriate that the time at which the value of the chattel is assessed is the *date of judgment* rather than the date on which the plaintiff demanded or the defendant first refused to return the chattel.[124] The value of the chattel at the date of judgment can be arrived at either by taking the market value of a chattel, in the same condition as the chattel detained, at the time of initial wrongful detention by the defendant and multiplying that figure by the relevant inflationary figure for the period between the initial wrongful detention and the date of judgment, or by estimating the cost to the plaintiff, at the time of judgment, of replacing the goods detained by comparable goods in a comparable condition.[125] In the absence of proof to the contrary the goods will be deemed to be in the best condition which could reasonably be expected of goods of that type and age.[126] If the defendant, as between himself and the plaintiff, has an interest in the chattel detained then the damages awarded for the assessed value of the chattel will be abated, in the nature of a set-off or a counter-claim, by the amount assessed for that interest.[127] If the value of the chattel has increased between the initial detention and the date of judgment because of improvements made to the chattel by the defendant then the costs of those improvements will be deducted from the value of the chattel at the date of judgment in arriving at its proper assessed value. As Lynskey J. said in *Munro* v. *Willmott*:

---

123 See pp. 163-6 above.

124 It should be noted, however, that in the recent decision of the English Court of Appeal in *IBL Ltd* v. *Coussens* [1991] 2 All E.R. 133, 143 (involving the detention of two cars) Nicholls L.J. said that there is no absolute rule regarding the date as to which the cars are to be valued and suggested that the measure of damages in that case should be calculated by reference to the value of the cars at such date as will fairly compensate the plaintiff for its loss if the defendant chooses to pay the sum and keep the cars. Despite the enactment of the Torts (Interference with Goods) Act 1977 in England this decision might be of relevance in Australia.

125 See *Egan* v. *State Transport Authority* (1982) 31 S.A.S.R. 481, 530.

126 See *Armory* v. *Delamirie* (1722) 1 Stra. 505.

127 See *Matthews* v. *Heintzmann & Co.* (1914) 16 D.L.R. 522 and *Egan* v. *State Transport Authority* (1982) 31 S.A.S.R. 481, 546.

> when I am asked to give damages in detinue for the value of a motor car as at today and when I find that a large sum of money has been spent upon it for the purpose of making it even saleable, I must take that into account in assessing what is the value of the property which the plaintiff has lost.[128]

But any increase in value between the initial detention and the date of judgment not due to anything done by the defendant will not be deducted from the value of the chattel at the date of judgment in arriving at the proper assessed value.[129]

What if the plaintiff seeks specific restitution of a chattel and the defendant has improved the chattel detained? In this type of case Young J. decided in *McKeown* v. *Cavalier Yachts Pty Ltd*[130] that if the plaintiff has given full and free acceptance to the work done then it is appropriate that the defendant should be compensated for the work done. What if the work done which has improved the value of the chattel has been carried out by an innocent third party? In this type of case Young J. decided that the question which must be asked is 'whether the work done conferred on the plaintiff an incontrovertible benefit. If it did, the plaintiff must pay compensation as a prerequisite to obtaining an order for specific recovery of the chattel and the measure of that compensation is the amount of incontrovertible benefit'.[131]

The normal measure of damages in an action of detinue, in addition to the assessed value of the chattel, also includes damages for the detention of the chattel. The basis on which these damages are calculated has not been spelt out in the decided cases but White J. in *Egan* v. *State Transport Authority*[132] in the Supreme Court of South Australia did attempt to deal with the matter in some detail. It should be pointed out, however, that White J. described these damages for the detention of the chattels as 'consequential loss in detinue'[133] while the learned author of *McGregor on Damages* describes these damages as the 'normal loss through the detention of the goods'.[134] Whatever the way these damages are described, it is clear that these damages are at large and that the court is free to award substantial damages if there has been a detention of the chattels even though no loss is alleged by the plaintiff.[135]

How are these damages for the detention of the chattels assessed? If the chattel detained is a profit-earning chattel and the defendant not only detains the chattel but also uses it during the period of detention then the measure of damages for the detention will be the reasonable cost of hiring the chattel or of hiring a chattel in the same condition. As Denning L.J. said in *Strand Electric and Engineering Co. Ltd* v. *Brisford Entertainments Ltd*: 'If a wrongdoer has made use of goods for his own purposes then he

---

128 [1949] 1 K.B. 295, 299.
129 See *Graham* v. *Voight* (1989) A.C.T.R. 11.
130 (1988) 13 N.S.W.L.R. 303.
131 ibid.
132 (1982) 31 S.A.S.R. 481.
133 ibid., 530.
134 *McGregor on Damages* (13th edn, 1972) para. 1033.
135 See *Strand Electric and Engineering Co. Ltd* v. *Brisford Entertainments Ltd* [1952] 2 Q.B. 246, 251.

must pay a reasonable hire for them, even though the owner has in fact suffered no loss'.[136] This reasoning was accepted by Giles J. in the recent decision in *Gaba Formwork Contractors Pty Ltd* v. *Turner Corporation Ltd*, though, as he pointed out in that case, it is confined to the situation where the defendant has used for his own purposes goods which the plaintiff would or might otherwise have hired out for reward.[137] If the plaintiff's chattel is detained by the defendant up to the date of judgment then the hiring charge runs up to that time and must be paid for the whole period with no deduction being made for the contingency that the plaintiff would not have been able to use the chattel himself or to hire it out to anyone else for the whole period.[138] The reason why no deduction is made is because the wrongdoer would have to pay the hire for the whole period if he sought the permission of the plaintiff to use his goods; 'he cannot be better off because he did not ask permission'.[139] There is no substantial difference between the measure of damages for the detention of a profit-earning chattel which could be hired *out* (as in the *Strand Electric* case) and the measure of damages for the detention of a profit-earning chattel which requires the plaintiff to hire *in* a substitute chattel, in order, for example, to continue working as a contractor (as in the *Egan* case). The damages for the detention will be the recognized hiring value of the chattel or the recognized hiring value of a reasonable substitute. There is no reason why these costs should not be the same.[140]

If a profit-earning chattel is detained by the defendant but not used by the defendant for his own purposes, the damages for the detention of the chattel should be based upon the loss of use of the chattel[141] or upon the loss of the chance to put the chattel to profitable use from the time of the detention to the date of judgment. This in turn is likely to be based on the hiring *out* or hiring *in* charge of the chattel,[142] even though Denning L.J. said in the *Strand Electric* case that 'the damages for detention recoverable against a carrier or warehouseman have never been measured by a hiring charge'.[143] If, however, the hiring charge is to be used, then at least an appropriate deduction should be made, from the damages for the detention, for the contingency that the chattel would not always be hired out during the period of the detention or appropriate credit should be given to the defendant for the expenses which the plaintiff would have incurred during that period in maintaining the chattel if he had not been deprived of it by the defendant.[144] These deductions are appropriate when a profit-earning chattel is detained but not used by the defendant for his own purposes. It should be emphasised that if a plaintiff is claiming damages

136 ibid., 254.
137 (1991) Aust. Torts Reports 81-138 at 69,314.
138 ibid., 253. See also *Hillesden Securities Ltd* v. *Ryjack Ltd* [1983] 1 W.L.R. 959.
139 See *Strand Electric and Engineering Co. Ltd* v. *Brisford Entertainments Ltd* [1952] 2 Q.B. 246, 254.
140 See *Egan* v. *State Transport Authority* (1982) 31 S.A.S.R. 481, 531.
141 See *Matthews* v. *Heintzmann & Co.* (1914) 16 D.L.R. 522, 524.
142 ibid.
143 [1952] 2 Q.B. 246, 254.
144 *Egan* v. *State Transport Authority* (1982) 31 S.A.S.R. 481, 531.

for the detention of a profit-earning chattel which has not been used by the defendant it is essential that the plaintiff provide proof of actual loss caused to the plaintiff by the detention of the chattel by the defendant.[145]

If the goods which are detained are raw materials which the plaintiff uses in his business, such as building materials which would have been incorporated into a structure if not detained[146] or copper which would have been refined and sold as cathodes if not detained,[147] then the damages for the detention of these raw materials will be based on the loss of a chance to put the materials to profitable use and the likely profit which the plaintiff would have made if he had not been hindered in incorporating those materials or refining them.[148] Though in *Egan's* case, White J. was content to leave these damages to be estimated by the Master of the Supreme Court, in *Brandeis Goldschmidt & Co. Ltd* v. *Western Transport Ltd*[149] the English Court of Appeal held that it was for the plaintiff to show that their business had been affected adversely by the detention of the raw materials and that they had suffered a properly quantifiable loss by reason of it.[150] In the absence of such proof, the plaintiffs were either entitled to no damages at all or to nominal damages at most.[151] The plaintiffs were awarded nominal damages of £5.

If a non-profit-earning chattel is detained then the proper measure of damages for the detention of the chattel is a sum payable by way of interest on the assessed value of the chattel from the date of wrongful detention to the date of judgment.

In addition to the assessed value of the chattel and damages for its detention, the plaintiff in an action of detinue can also recover damages for any consequential loss which flows directly from the detention and is not too remote. Thus in *Brilawsky* v. *Robertson*[152] the plaintiff, an artist, was able to recover damages for loss of profits, based on his average profits as an artist in Queensland, when the defendants wrongfully detained a wooden box containing his artist's materials. If the plaintiff's chattel has been damaged or has depreciated during the period of detention, more than the normal wear and tear expected during that period, then a claim for this loss can also be made. Again, if the plaintiff's chattel has been detained and the plaintiff cannot hire a substitute at the recognized hiring value but only at an increased cost, then the plaintiff can claim this increased cost. If a plaintiff has to incur expenses in recovering his own goods from the place where they are being detained those expenses would also be recoverable as consequential damage.[153] These damages would

145 See *Gaba Formwork Contractors Pty Ltd* v. *Turner Corporation Ltd* (1991) Aust. Torts Reports 81-138 at 69, 315.
146 ibid.
147 See *Brandeis Goldschmidt & Co. Ltd* v. *Western Transport Ltd* [1981] 3 W.L.R. 181.
148 *Egan* v. *State Transport Authority* [1982] 31 S.A.S.R. 481, 531.
149 [1981] 3 W.L.R. 181.
150 ibid., 186.
151 ibid., 185.
152 (1916) 10 Q.J.P.R. 113.
153 See *Howard Perry & Co.* v. *British Railways Board* [1980] 1 W.L.R. 1375.

have to be claimed as special damage and would have to be specifically pleaded.

There is no reason why aggravated damages should not be available in an action of detinue. In *Egan* v. *State Transport Authority* the plaintiff was awarded $25 000 by way of exemplary damages in an action of detinue for the unlawful seizure and detention of certain chattels because White J. felt that 'the ignominy surrounding the peremptory and overbearing exercise of contractual power (on an erroneous basis) justifies the award of a substantial, but not inflated, award of exemplary damages'.[154] The award seems very much like an award of aggravated damages, though White J. clearly labelled it as an award of exemplary damages. So there is some authority in Australia that exemplary damages can be awarded in an action of detinue.

VII: THE ACTION ON THE CASE FOR DAMAGES

If the tort action which is being brought is an action on the case for damages for physical injury or nervous shock, as in *Wilkinson* v. *Downton*[155] or *Janvier* v. *Sweeney*,[156] then the damages will be calculated in the same way as damages are calculated for physical injury and nervous shock in actions in trespass to the person or actions in negligence for personal injury. The plaintiff will be able to claim any damage that is not too remote a consequence of the defendant's act or statement.[157]

If the action which is being brought is an action on the case for damages for property damage then the plaintiff will be able to recover substantial damages from the defendant for all the harm or loss which is the 'inevitable consequence of the unlawful, intentional and positive act' of the defendant as the High Court of Australia decided in *Beaudesert Shire Council* v. *Smith*.[158] There is no further elaboration in that decision on the measure of damages in an action on the case for damages involving property damage or on how these damages should be calculated in such an action. Probably the calculation will be based on an analogy with actions for trespass to land[159] though, as we know, trespass to land is actionable without proof of any damage, whereas in an action on the case for damages, the damage actually done is the gist of the action and so some damage will have to be shown.

If the action which is being brought is an action on the case for damages for purely economic loss the plaintiff will also be able to recover substantial damages in that tort. In *Ratcliffe* v. *Evans*[160] the English Court of Appeal indicated that it was established law that an action on the case

154 [1982] 31 S.A.S.R. 481, 532.
155 [1897] 2 Q.B. 57. See also Chapter 2.
156 [1919] 2 K.B. 316. See also Chapter 2.
157 [1897] 2 Q.B. 57, 59.
158 (1966) 120 C.L.R. 145, 156.
159 See pp. 292-6 above.
160 [1892] 2 Q.B. 524.

for damages would lie for purely economic loss or damage 'wilfully and intentionally done without just occasion or excuse'. The Court of Appeal did not indicate with any degree of particularity what damage is recoverable or what damage the plaintiff must allege and prove, preferring to leave the matter to the circumstances of each case. As Bowen L.J. said:

> In all actions . . . on the case where the damage actually done is the gist of the action, the character of the acts themselves which produce the damage, and the circumstances under which these acts are done, must regulate the degree of certainty and particularity with which the damage done ought to be stated and proved. As much certainty and particularity must be insisted on, both in pleading and proof of damage, as is reasonable, having regard to the circumstances and to the nature of the acts themselves by which the damage is done. To insist upon less would be to relax old and intelligible principles. To insist upon more would be the vainest pedantry.[161]

In that case itself the plaintiff was able to recover substantial damages of £120 for a general loss in business as a result of a false and malicious publication about the trade and manufactures of the plaintiff, even without specific proof of the loss of any particular customers or orders. And in the earlier case of *Crouch* v. *The Great Northern Railway Company* Martin B. expressed the view that in an appropriate case it would even be possible for a plaintiff to recover exemplary damages in an action on the case for damages.[162] There is no reason why aggravated damages should not be available in appropriate circumstances in an action on the case for damages involving intentional conduct, particularly as these damages are available today in other actions involving intentional conduct, such as actions in deceit.[163]

If aggravated and exemplary damages are available in actions on the case for damages involving purely economic loss they should surely be available in actions on the case involving the intentional infliction of physical injury and nervous shock and in cases involving intentionally inflicted property damage, as intentional conduct which interferes with a person's physical and mental integrity or with a person's property ought to receive greater disapproval from the courts than intentional conduct which merely causes pecuniary loss to the plaintiff.

VIII: INTENTIONAL TORTS WHICH CAUSE PURELY ECONOMIC LOSS

Apart from the action on the case for damages for purely economic loss, such as the action in *Ratcliffe* v. *Evans* which has just been discussed, the measure of damages in the other intentional torts, which are brought for purely economic losses, is dealt with in the discussion of the essential ingredients of each of those torts and should be referred to accordingly.

161 ibid., 532-3.
162 (1856) 11 Ex. 742, 759.
163 See Chapter 5 pp. 178-9.

8

NEGLIGENT TRESPASS

I: SOME GENERAL COMMENTS

A chapter on negligent trespass perhaps sits unhappily among chapters on the intentional torts. It is, as its name implies, not an intentional tort but neither is it part of the tort of negligence which is discussed in succeeding chapters. The word 'negligence' is used in two senses in this book. It is used to describe a mode of committing a variety of torts and it is also used to describe the tort of negligence with its various requirements of duty, breach and damage.

Trespass is an ancient tort, which provided a remedy for direct and intentional injuries. It was only early in the nineteenth century that the courts allowed an action to be brought in trespass where the direct act which caused the injury was not intentional but negligent. This was the beginning of the tort of negligent trespass. Meanwhile the action on the case was developing rapidly into the modern tort of negligence. The two torts, however, never merged and, as the High Court said in their joint judgment in *Williams* v. *Milotin*, 'the two causes of action are not the same now and they never were'.[1]

In our earlier account of the tort of trespass we indicated that trespass could be committed either intentionally or negligently. In previous chapters we have dealt with the tort of trespass to the person, to land and to goods where intentional acts are involved;[2] in this chapter we deal with the tort of trespass where an unintentional (i.e. negligent or careless) act is involved. This is the tort of negligent trespass. It is difficult to know where exactly one should place the tort of negligent trespass in a textbook on the law of torts. In one sense negligent trespass displays all the characteristics of the tort of intentional trespass. Just as in the tort of intentional trespass, in an action of negligent trespass the plaintiff must be able to show a 'direct' act on the part of the defendant, there must be

1 (1957) 97 C.L.R. 465, 474.
2 Perhaps even 'reckless' acts.

'fault' on the part of the defendant and it is not necessary for the plaintiff to prove any actual damage. But unlike in the tort of intentional trespass, where the fault which is relied on is the intentional conduct of the defendant, in the tort of negligent trespass, the fault relied on is the unintentional (i.e. negligent or careless) act of the defendant. It is, therefore, appropriate that the discussion of the tort of negligent trespass should be placed at the end of our discussion of the intentional torts and just before our discussion of the tort of negligence.

II: NEGLIGENT TRESPASS TO THE PERSON

It is quite clear that in Australia both the action of intentional trespass and the action for negligent trespass are available, in appropriate circumstances, to a plaintiff who has been injured by a direct act of the defendant. Where the injury is occasioned by a direct intentional act the cause of action is in intentional trespass, but where the injury is occasioned by a direct, unintentional (negligent or careless) act the cause of action is in negligent trespass.

Leame v. *Bray*[3] in 1803 is one of the earliest cases of negligent trespass to the person. The plaintiff, who was negligently injured by a direct act of the defendant, brought an action of trespass. Counsel for the defendant argued that in order to maintain trespass the act must be intentional (wilful) but the Court of King's Bench[4] decided that where the injury was direct, trespass was the proper remedy whether the act was intentional or negligent.

However, in *Letang* v. *Cooper*[5] more than a century and a half after *Leame* v. *Bray*, the Court of Appeal in England decided[6] that there was no cause of action in negligent trespass for a direct unintentional (negligent) act. As Lord Denning M.R. put it:

> Instead of dividing actions for personal injuries into trespass (direct damage) or case (consequential damage), we divide the causes of action now according as the defendant did the injury intentionally and unintentionally. If one man intentionally applies force directly to another, the plaintiff has a cause of action in assault and battery, or, if you so please to describe it, in trespass to the person . . . If he does not inflict injury intentionally, but only unintentionally, the plaintiff has no cause of action today in trespass. His only cause of action is in negligence, and then only on proof of want of reasonable care. If the plaintiff cannot prove want of reasonable care, he may have no cause of action at all.[7]

In *Letang* v. *Cooper* the plaintiff, who was sunbathing in the carpark of an hotel, was injured when the defendant, who did not see her, drove his car over her legs while entering the carpark. The plaintiff brought an

---

3 (1803) 3 East 593; 102 E.R. 724.
4 Lord Ellenborough C.J. and Grose, Lawrence and Le Blanc JJ.
5 [1965] 1 Q.B. 232.
6 At least by a majority consisting of Lord Denning M.R. and Danckwerts L.J.
7 [1965] 1 Q.B. 232, 239.

action against the defendant more than three years after the accident. The action in negligence was statute-barred but the plaintiff claimed that on the same facts she could bring an action for negligent trespass and that that action was not barred as six years[8] had not elapsed since the date of the acccident. The trial judge agreed and awarded the plaintiff £575 damages for trespass to the person. The Court of Appeal was dismayed that on the same set of facts a plaintiff could succeed in an action in negligent trespass when the action in negligence would fail and that 'the plaintiff could get out of the three-year limitation by suing in trespass instead of in negligence'.[9] One way out of this dilemma was to say that whatever the historical position, the action of negligent trespass was no longer available at the present time for direct injuries caused by negligence or carelessness. So this is exactly what the Court of Appeal said, at least by a majority.

But *Letang* v. *Cooper* has not been accepted in Australia. Bray C.J. of the Supreme Court of South Australia in *Venning* v. *Chin*[10] thought that what the Court of Appeal was doing in *Letang* v. *Cooper* was 'judicial legislation' and that the courts did not have the power 'to legislate so as to deprive plaintiffs of a remedy which they have enjoyed for over a century and a half'. In any case, he thought that, in Australia, the matter had been concluded by the decision of the High Court in *Williams* v. *Milotin*.[11] In that case the High Court decided that the plaintiff, who was struck from behind by a motor truck while riding a bicycle along a public road and who relied upon the negligence of the defendant to bring an action, could lay his cause of action not only as a negligent trespass to the person but also as an action for the tort of negligence. It is clear that the High Court thought that the plaintiff, in the circumstances, had two causes of action, one in trespass and the other in the tort of negligence. As they said in the joint judgment delivered by the court:

> The two causes of action are not the same now and they never were. When you speak of a cause of action you mean the essential ingredients in the title to the right which it is proposed to enforce. The essential ingredients in an action of negligence for personal injuries include the special or particular damage—it is the gist of the action—and the want of due care. Trespass to the person includes neither. But it does include direct violation of the protection which the law throws around the person . . . It happens in this case that the actual facts will or may fulfil the requirements of each cause of action. But that does not mean that . . . only 'one' cause of action is vested in the plaintiff.[12]

---

8 The period of limitation for all actions founded 'on tort' was six years under the Limitation Act 1939. By s.2(1), Law Reform (Limitation of Actions etc.) Act 1954 the period of limitation for 'actions for damages for negligence, nuisance or breach of duty . . . where the damages claimed by the plaintiff for the negligence, nuisance or breach of duty consist of or include damages in respect of personal injuries to any person' was reduced to three years.

9 [1965] 1 Q.B. 232, 239, *per* Lord Denning M.R.

10 (1974) 10 S.A.S.R. 299, 307.

11 (1957) 97 C.L.R. 465.

12 ibid., 474.

Apart from *Williams* v. *Milotin* and *Venning* v. *Chin* there are other decisions of courts in Australia, such as *Elliott* v. *Barnes,*[13] *Kruber* v. *Grzesiak,*[14] *McHale* v. *Watson,*[15] *Tsouvalla* v. *Bini,*[16] *Timmins* v. *Oliver,*[17] *James* v. *Harrison & Another,*[18] *Horkin* v. *North Melbourne Football Club Social Club,*[19] *Shaw* v. *Hackshaw,*[20] *Ross* v. *Warwick Howard (Australia) Pty Ltd*[21] and *Platt* v. *Nutt,*[22] which indicate that trespass is still available for injuries which are caused directly and negligently. We must accept therefore, that there is now a clearly established divergence between Australian and English law on this matter, that *Williams* v. *Milotin* and *Letang* v. *Cooper* cannot stand together and that as far as Australian law is concerned, it is the decision of the High Court of Australia in *Williams* v. *Milotin,* that an action in negligent trespass is available as a remedy in appropriate circumstances, that is binding.

Granted that, however, it is still pertinent to ask why a plaintiff today should want to resort to an action in negligent trespass if the set of facts in the case is sufficient to found both an action in negligent trespass and an action in the tort of negligence. After all, did not Winfield and Goodhart suggest over fifty years ago that the tort of negligence had 'driven the action of trespass for personal injuries into the shade'?[23] The answer to these questions is that, even at the present time, there are still some situations where it would be advantageous to bring an action for negligent trespass rather than an action of negligence. Not only is this so, but there are also situations where the action of negligent trespass will sometimes be available when the action for the tort of negligence will not be available as a remedy. These are some of those situations.[24]

(a) When a plaintiff who has suffered a direct injury inflicted by the defendant cannot show a duty owed by the defendant to the plaintiff When we examine the tort of negligence in the next chapter we will see that an essential element of that tort is a duty to take reasonable care owed at the time of his act of negligence by the defendant to the plaintiff.[25] Unless the plaintiff can establish this duty of care, he will not succeed in an action of negligence. In negligent trespass, however, once the plaintiff shows the injury was directly occasioned by the defendant's act, the burden of disproving negligence, i.e. showing he was neither careless nor inadvertent,

13 (1951) 51 S.R.(N.S.W.) 179; 68 W.N. 133.
14 [1963] V.R. 621.
15 (1964) 111 C.L.R. 384.
16 (1966) S.A.S.R. 157.
17 (1972) Court of Appeal (N.S.W.) (12 October 1972) (unreported).
18 (1977) 18 A.C.T.R. 36, 38.
19 [1983] V.R. 153, 157.
20 [1983] 2 V.R. 65.
21 (1987) 4 S.R. (W.A.) 1.
22 (1988) 12 N.S.W.L.R. 231.
23 'Trespass and Negligence' (1933) 49 *L.Q.R.* 359.
24 For a detailed discussion on some of these situations, see F.A. Trindade (1971) 20 *I.C.L.Q.* 706. See also P.G. Heffey & H. Glasbeek (1966) *M.U.L.R.* 158 and R. Bailey (1976) 5 *Adelaide L.R.* 402.
25 See Chapter 9.

rests on the defendant[26] (at least in non-highway cases).[27] It is not necessary for the plaintiff to prove that the defendant owed him a duty of care. A 'trespasser'[28] or a criminal being pursued[29] may not be owed a duty of care, in which case they might be better off suing a defendant who injures them in negligent trespass where 'duty' questions are not relevant.

(b) Where the injury which the plaintiff has suffered has not yet been accepted by the courts as legally recognizable 'damage' In an action for the tort of negligence, damage is the gist of the action. The tort is not complete until actual damage occurs. Trespass, on the other hand, is actionable *per se*. Of course in the absence of actual damage a plaintiff would generally not bring an action in trespass for, if he did, he would probably be penalized in costs. But what if the plaintiff suffers an injury which cannot be described as 'damage' for the purposes of the tort of negligence? In such a situation it would be advantageous to bring an action in negligent trespass rather than negligence. As actual damage is not a necessary ingredient of trespass to the person a plaintiff will succeed in establishing the tort of negligent trespass even though he would probably fail in an action for the tort of negligence, where actual damage is an essential element of the tort. The following example will help to clarify this point.

Suppose D (a library attendant) negligently imprisons P (a student) for twenty minutes in the Law Library but instead of acknowledging his fault D heaps insult upon injury by telling P, at the time of his release, that he suspects that P had deliberately hidden himself in the Law Library to carry out various nefarious activities. In these circumstances, an action by P in negligent trespass (negligent false imprisonment) should yield a substantial sum in damages. As P has suffered a technical false imprisonment (albeit for twenty minutes) he can be awarded damages not only in respect of that minor interference with his liberty but also for the insult which has arisen from that interference and the injury to his feelings, that is, the indignity, mental suffering, disgrace and humiliation that may be

---

26 *Platt* v. *Nutt* (1988) 12 N.S.W.L.R. 231, however, shows quite clearly that the burden of disproving negligence only shifts to the defendant once the plaintiff proves a direct act by the defendant which *caused* the plaintiff's injuries.

27 The onus of proof in cases of negligent trespass occurring on the 'highway' is discussed below at pp. 319-20.

28 e.g. a thief or a peeping-tom. See *Woodward* v. *Begbie et al.* (1962) 31 D.L.R. (2d) 22 (negligent trespass to a peeping-tom by two police officers).

29 In *Marshall* v. *Osmond* [1982] 2 All E.R. 610, 614, Milmo J. said: '. . . in my judgment a police officer driving a motor car in hot pursuit of a person or persons whom he rightly suspects of having committed an arrestable offence does not owe that person the same duty of care which he owes to a lawful and innocent user of the highway going about his lawful occasions'. And in *Ashton* v. *Turner* [1981] 1 Q.B. 137 it was held that in certain circumstances, as a matter of public policy, the law might not recognize that a duty of care was owed by one participant in a crime to another in relation to an act done in the course of the commission of the crime.

caused by D's conduct.[30] P would, however, be unlikely to succeed in an action in negligence despite D's insulting behaviour as it is very doubtful if he has suffered anything which might be described as legally recognizable 'damage' for the purposes of the tort of negligence[31] and would not, therefore, have the initial 'damage' on which to base his action in negligence.

It will be seen, therefore, that by bringing the action in trespass (i.e. negligent false imprisonment) rather than negligence, the plaintiff has an advantage in not having to prove that he has suffered some legally recognizable 'damage'.[32] In addition, the plaintiff will be able to recover in his action for trespass, damages for insult, indignity, disgrace, humiliation etc. which he would not be able to recover in negligence as he would not have the initial 'damage' on which to base the action for the tort of negligence. *Fogg* v. *McKnight*[33] and *Kuchenmeister* v. *Home Office*[34] show that in an action for intentional trespass even where there is a mere technical trespass, damages may be awarded to a plaintiff by way of compensation for injury to his feelings. There is no reason to assume that any different principles should apply to an action for a negligent battery or a negligent false imprisonment which is followed by humiliating or insulting remarks as in the example we gave earlier. Both intentional and negligent trespass are actionable *per se* and in both intentional and negligent trespass damages for insult and humiliation can be awarded. It is difficult to maintain that the tort of negligence has developed to such an extent as to allow compensation for insult or humiliation in an action for that tort.

(c) Where the plaintiff can prove that he was directly injured by an act of the defendant but finds it difficult to prove fault in the defendant In an action for negligent trespass, once the plaintiff proves that he was directly injured by an act of the defendant, the onus of proving that the injury was

---

30 *Fogg* v. *McKnight* [1968] N.Z.L.R. 330, 331, *per* McGregor J.

31 In 1979 a man suffered great inconvenience when he was negligently falsely imprisoned in a Singapore bank's vault for eighteen hours. See Harding and Tan (1980) 22 *Mal.L.R.* 29. The authors suggest that a claim in the tort of negligence would have failed and argue that a claim in negligent false imprisonment should be available in the circumstances of that case. See also P.G. Heffey (1983) 14 *M.U.L.R.* 53, who argues that in a case of negligently inflicted imprisonment the loss of freedom of movement is itself sufficient damage to sustain an action in negligence.

32 The view of Diplock L.J. in *Letang* v. *Cooper* that 'actual damage is . . . a necessary ingredient in unintentional as distinct from intentional trespass to the person' is based on an erroneous view that negligent trespass involves a failure 'to take reasonable care to avoid causing actual damage [i.e. legally recognizable damage] to one's neighbour'. The better view is that negligent trespass is a careless but direct infliction of *injury* which may or may not involve actual damage, i.e. legally recognizable damage.

33 [1968] N.Z.L.R. 330.

34 [1958] 1 Q.B. 496.

inflicted without negligence rests on the defendant.[35] This is in contrast to the position in the tort of negligence where the onus of proving every element of that tort rests with the plaintiff. In what are described as 'highway' accidents,[36] however, the distinction between bringing an action in trespass or in negligence in relation to injuries suffered as a result of a collision on the highway is one without a difference. Even where the action is brought in negligent trespass the onus of proof is not reversed and the plaintiff is no better off bringing his action in trespass rather than in negligence. This is the present position in Australia in relation to the onus of proof in actions of negligent trespass. The view of Diplock J. (as he then was) in *Fowler* v. *Lanning*, that 'the onus of proving negligence, when the trespass is not intentional, lies upon the plaintiff whether the action be framed in trespass or in negligence',[37] has not received general acceptance in Australia. In several decisions delivered after *Fowler* v. *Lanning* courts all over Australia have taken the view that in an action of trespass, whether intentional or negligent, the burden of proving absence of intention or negligence rests on the defendant once the plaintiff proves that the defendant has directly injured him.[38] But, as Bray C.J. pointed out in *Venning* v. *Chin*, 'the weight of authority [also] favours the proposition that highway accidents are an exception to this rule and that in trespass for injury on the highway the onus is on the plaintiff to prove either intention or negligence on the part of the defendant'.[39]

If the burden of disproving fault immediately rests on the defendant once the plaintiff has shown that the defendant has directly injured him, it would be advantageous for a plaintiff (in a non-highway case) who has been directly injured by the defendant to sue in negligent trespass rather than negligence, particularly when the circumstances which surround the accident are better known to the defendant rather than the plaintiff. A good example of such a situation is one which occurred in Victoria. A and

35 It should be noted that this burden of disproving negligence only shifts to the defendant once the plaintiff proves a direct act on the part of the defendant which caused the plaintiff's injuries. In *Platt* v. *Nutt* (1988) 12 N.S.W.L.R. 231 where the defendant slammed a glass door shut in the vicinity of the plaintiff the majority of the Court of Appeal of New South Wales held that the plaintiff had not established on a balance of probabilities that the injuries to her hand were caused by a reflex action to a threatening situation rather than as a consequence of her own wilful act of thrusting out her arm to prevent the defendant from closing the glass door. The plaintiff therefore failed to prove a direct act by the defendant which was a cause of the injury to her.

36 What are 'highway' accidents is discussed at pp. 319-20 below.

37 [1959] 1 Q.B. 426, 439.

38 See Windeyer J. in *McHale* v. *Watson* (1964) 111 C.L.R. 384; Walters J. in *Tsouvalla* v. *Bini* [1966] S.A.S.R. 157; Hogarth J. in *Venning* v. *Chin* (1974) 8 S.A.S.R. 397; *West* v. *Peters* (1975) 18 S.A.S.R. 338 and *Lord* v. *The Nominal Defendant* (1980) 24 S.A.S.R. 458; the Full Supreme Court of South Australia in *Venning* v. *Chin* (1975) 10 S.A.S.R. 299 and *Lord* v. *The Nominal Defendant* (1980) 24 S.A.S.R. 467; and the Court of Appeal (N.S.W.) in *Timmins* v. *Oliver* (1972) judgment of Jacobs, Manning & Moffitt JJ.A. (12 October 1972) (unreported). See also Keall J. in *Ross* v. *Warwick Howard* (1987) 4 S.R. (W.A.) 1.

39 (1974) 10 S.A.S.R. 299, 316.

B were riding on a hay cart when A was suddenly shot in the back by a bullet from B's gun. A was unable to say how the accident happened. B's explanation was that he was holding the gun when his dog jumped on the trigger setting off the loaded gun.[40] As A can only prove that he was shot in the back by a bullet from B's gun, A would be in a much better position if he sued in negligent trespass rather than negligence, for, once he had proved that he had been directly injured by a bullet from B's gun, B would have to prove that the injury was done without intention or negligence on his part. This was the reason why the plaintiff in *Fowler* v. *Lanning* who was shot in the back in a hunting accident attempted to sue in trespass and not in negligence.

Difficulties arise if the plaintiff is injured by only one of two members of a shooting party and it is not known which of the two he was injured by. This was the situation in *Cook* v. *Lewis*,[41] where the court decided that if both members of the shooting party have directly invaded an interest of the plaintiff it is reasonable that each of them should prove that he was without fault. If, however, only one of them has directly injured the plaintiff should the burden of disproof rest on both of them anyway, so that both are asked to explain the accident and help exculpate one of them? As the members of the shooting party are in a better position to explain the accident than the plaintiff, one is tempted to suggest that both the defendants must disprove fault or be held liable in trespass. However, if only one defendant has directly injured the plaintiff then, at least in relation to one of them, the plaintiff has not proved direct injury or indeed any injury at all. We must conclude, therefore, that the decision in *Cook* v. *Lewis* is an extension of the law of trespass and an unwarranted extension at that.[42] The plaintiff had not proved that *both* defendants had directly injured him and yet in relation to both of them the burden of negativing fault was said to rest on the defendants.[43] The decision in *Cook* v. *Lewis* has been rightly criticized on the ground that it fails to give to the interests of the defendant the same consideration which it readily accords the plaintiff.[44]

There is also an advantage in bringing an action in negligent trespass rather than in negligence where there is the likelihood that the defendant while denying fault by his pleadings will fail to appear by counsel or in person. This is what happened in the South Australian case of *Tsouvalla* v. *Bini*.[45] The plaintiff, a boy aged 8, was being chased by the defendant, a boy aged 14. The defendant was holding in his cupped hands a substance of whitish colour. Whilst he was running, the plaintiff turned his head to

---

40 See *Wilson* v. *The Queen* (1970) 44 A.L.J.R. 221.

41 [1952] 1 D.L.R. 1.

42 *Query* whether all ten members of a shooting party would be made to disprove fault or else be held liable if it could be shown that only *one* of them directly injured the plaintiff but it is impossible to say which one.

43 Denning L.J. in *Roe* v. *Minister of Health* [1954] 2 Q.B. 66, 82 suggests that this happens even in the tort of negligence: 'If an injured person shows that one or other or both of two persons injured him, but cannot say which of them it was, then he is not defeated altogether. He can call on each of them for an explanation'.

44 T. Brian Hogan (1961) 24 *M.L.R.* 331.

45 [1966] S.A.S.R. 157.

look back at the defendant and as he did so, he saw the defendant throw his cupped hands in a forward movement and he was struck in the face and eyes by the white substance which the defendant had held in his hands. It was subsequently established that the substance was lime. The plaintiff suffered injuries to his eyes and face. When the action was brought on for trial the defendant, who had by then attained full age, did not appear by counsel or in person, though by his pleading he denied the alleged battery. On the facts given above, Walters A.J. had no hesitation in finding that the defendant committed a trespass to the person of the plaintiff. He then went on to discuss the onus of proof in a case such as this:

> There is no onus upon the plaintiff to establish that the defendant threw the lime with intent to hit him, or so negligently that it did so. The burden rests upon the defendant to show absence of intent and negligence on his part, and in this case that onus has not been discharged.[46]

It can be seen, therefore, that the plaintiff will, in such circumstances, be at some advantage in bringing an action in negligent trespass rather than negligence. In negligence, whether the defendant puts in an appearance or not, the plaintiff must allege and prove the facts which he alleges constitute the negligence. In negligent trespass, on the other hand, once the plaintiff proves a direct injury the onus of disproving negligence rests on the defendant. If the defendant fails to put in an appearance, he rather than the plaintiff is prejudiced, for, as he is not there to discharge the burden of disproof, the decision will almost certainly go against him, as in *Tsouvalla* v. *Bini*. It is more advantageous, therefore, to sue in negligent trespass rather than in negligence if there is the slightest doubt that the defendant will not appear either by counsel or in person.

We said earlier that 'highway' accidents were an exception to the rule that in actions of negligent trespass the onus of proving that the injury was inflicted without negligence rests on the defendant once the plaintiff proves that he was directly injured. It is difficult to explain this exception to the rule. As Jacobs J.A. put it in *Timmins* v. *Oliver*: 'a distinction which places vehicular collisions on the highway in a special category less favourable to a plaintiff could have no rhyme or reason except a tender care for the owners and drivers of motor vehicles and those who stand behind them'.[47] Hogarth J. in *Venning* v. *Chin,*[48] *West* v. *Peters*[49] and *Lord* v. *The Nominal Defendant*[50] has not accepted the existence of the 'highway' exception but the Full Court of the Supreme Court of South Australia, in both *Venning* v. *Chin*[51] and *Lord* v. *The Nominal Defendant,*[52] has accepted its existence, and it certainly is 'the assumption

46 ibid., 158.
47 (1972) Court of Appeal (N.S.W.) (12 October 1972) (unreported).
48 (1974) 8 S.A.S.R. 397.
49 (1975) 18 S.A.S.R. 338.
50 (1980) 24 S.A.S.R. 458.
51 (1974) 10 S.A.S.R. 299.
52 (1980) 24 S.A.S.R. 467.

on which thousands of collision cases have been conducted in Australia in recent years'.[53] So, in 'highway' cases, there is no advantage in bringing an action in negligent trespass rather than negligence because even when the plaintiff proves an injury by a direct act of the defendant the onus is on the plaintiff to prove negligence on the part of the defendant.

What is a 'highway' case has never been clearly defined but 'a collision between vehicles or between a vehicle and a pedestrian on the highway . . . is clearly covered'.[54] So are 'damage to property adjoining the highway caused by a vehicle running off the highway and contacts between things lowered or carried out of such property with people using the highway'.[55]

In *Timmins* v. *Oliver*[56] the Court of Appeal of New South Wales decided that the 'highway' exception would not be extended to a motor boat accident on a river and that it was sufficient for the plaintiff to allege and prove that the defendant had driven a motor boat against the plaintiff which has resulted in the plaintiff's injuries. It was then for the defendant to prove that this was done neither intentionally nor negligently.[57]

(d) Where the period of limitation for an action in negligent trespass is longer than in an action for the tort of negligence As we shall see later,[58] there are in the law of torts time limits within which proceedings must be brought otherwise the right to bring the action will be barred. These time limits are usually prescribed by statutes which are called statutes of limitation. On this ground alone there will only be an advantage in bringing an action in negligent trespass rather than negligence if the period of limitation for an action in negligent trespass is longer than the period of limitation for an action in negligence. Are there any jurisdictions in Australia where the period of limitation for an action in negligent trespass is longer than that for an action in negligence? Although there were several jurisdictions in Australia where it could have been argued that the period of limitation for an action in negligent trespass was longer than the period of limitation for an action in negligence,[59] legislative changes over recent years have changed the position so that now it is only in Tasmania[60] that it can reasonably be argued that the period of limitation for an action in negligent trespass is longer than the period of limitation for an action in negligence. In all the other jurisdictions in Australia,

---

53 (1975) 49 A.L.J.R. 378, 379 *per* Gibbs J.
54 (1974) 10 S.A.S.R. 299, 315 *per* Bray C.J.
55 ibid., 315-16.
56 (1972) Court of Appeal (N.S.W.) (12 October 1972) (unreported).
57 It is a matter of some surprise that this decision of the Court of Appeal of New South Wales was not referred to in *Platt* v. *Nutt* (1988) 12 N.S.W.L.R. 231.
58 See Chapter 23 below.
59 See the discussion in Trindade and Cane, *The Law of Torts in Australia* (1st edn, O.U.P., 1985) pp. 271-3.
60 Limitation Act 1974, No. 98, ss.4(1) and 5(1). The provision is virtually identical to the English provision discussed in *Letang* v. *Cooper* [1965] Q.B. 232 and to the old Victorian provision discussed in *Kruber* v. *Grzesiak* [1963] V.R. 621. See also *Carnegie* v. *State of Victoria* (1980) (15 December 1980) (unreported) F.C. of the Supreme Court of Victoria.

there is either a uniform period of limitation of six years[61] or three years[62] for all actions in tort or a shorter period of limitation for actions in negligent trespass.[63] In these jurisdictions there is obviously no advantage in bringing an action in negligent trespass rather than negligence on the basis that one gives more time to sue than the other. Whatever advantage there previously might have been has progressively been removed by legislative intervention.

(e) **When the plaintiff wants to prevent the defendant from cutting down the amount of the plaintiff's recovery by pleading contributory negligence on the part of the plaintiff** If a plaintiff has in any way contributed to a direct injury which has been inflicted upon him by the defendant he will be faced with the prospect that the defendant will raise the defence of contributory negligence and thus attempt to reduce the amount of damages that he will be required to pay to the plaintiff. If the action is brought in negligence, contributory negligence[64] will succeed as a defence and the damages will be reduced in accordance with the apportionment statutes in the various States and Territories.[65]

What happens if the plaintiff, instead of bringing his action in negligence, brings it instead in negligent trespass? Will the defendant still be able to raise the defence of contributory negligence? In other words, is contributory negligence a defence to an action in trespass as it is to an action in negligence? We can now say, with some degree of confidence, that contributory negligence is not, in Australia, a defence to an action in intentional trespass. In the decision of the Supreme Court of Victoria in *Horkin* v. *North Melbourne Football Club Social Club*[66] Brooking J. held that contributory negligence was not at common law or under the apportionment statute[67] available as a defence in an action for intentional battery. The High Court refused in *Fontin* v. *Katapodis*[68] to reduce compensatory damages in an action of intentional trespass even though there was a high degree of provocation on the part of the plaintiff. It is

61 Vic.: Limitation of Actions Act 1958, s.5 (six years for actions 'founded on tort'); N.S.W.: Limitation Act 1969, No. 31 s.14 (six years for all actions 'founded on tort'); A.C.T.: Limitation Act 1985, s.11 (six years for 'any cause of action').

62 N.T.: Limitation Act 1981 s.12(1)(b) (three years for all actions 'founded on tort'); S.A.: Limitation of Actions Act 1936 s.35 (six years for all actions 'founded on tort'. But s.36 provides that if the claim involves damages in respect of 'personal injuries to any person' the limitation period is shortened to three years); Qld.: Limitation of Actions Act 1974, s.10 (six years for all actions 'founded on tort'. But s.11 provides that any action for damages 'for negligence, trespass, nuisance or breach of duty' and which involves a claim for damages in respect of 'personal injury to any person' must be brought within three years).

63 W.A.: Limitation Act 1935, s.38 (the period of limitation is four years for 'actions for trespass to the person' and six years for 'all other actions founded on tort').

64 For a discussion of contributory negligence as a defence to an action in negligence, see pp. 531-40 below.

65 For a discussion of the apportionment legislation in the various States and Territories, see pp. 536-40 below.

66 [1983] V.R. 153.

67 Wrongs Act 1958 (No. 6420), s.25.

68 (1963) 108 C.L.R. 177.

unlikely, therefore, that they would allow contributory negligence to reduce those damages and the decision of Moller J. of the Supreme Court of New Zealand in *Hoebergen* v. *Koppens*,[69] that contributory negligence of the plaintiff can be used in an action based on trespass to reduce the damages payable by the defendant to the plaintiff, will not be followed here in preference to the decision of Brooking J. in *Horkin*. As Bray C.J. said in *Venning* v. *Chin*, 'it is clear that contributory negligence could never be a defence to an intentional tort'.[70]

What about negligent trespass? In *Venning* v. *Chin* the Full Court of the Supreme Court of South Australia held that the defence of contributory negligence of the plaintiff was available to a defendant in an action of negligent trespass arising out of a highway accident and the apportionment statutes were therefore applicable. As Bray C.J. said:

> On the whole I have come to the conclusion that before s.27A of the Wrongs Act [the apportionment legislation] came into operation the defence of contributory negligence would, in an action for trespass arising out of a highway accident, have been available to a negligent (though not to an intentional) defendant to the same extent . . . as in an action on the case for negligence, or, as it would have been called in later times, an action for negligence, simpliciter.[71]

The decision of the Full Court to apply the apportionment statute to the factual situation in the case was affirmed by the High Court in *Chin* v. *Venning*,[72] but the members of the High Court treated the case as one of negligence rather than negligent trespass and no member of the High Court specifically adverted to the point made by Bray C.J. that the defence of contributory negligence would be available to a defendant in an action of negligent trespass. In *Horkin*, Brooking J. expressed the view that the defence of contributory negligence of the plaintiff was available to a defendant in an action of negligent trespass and that it did not matter that the trespass occurred on or off the highway. As he said: 'It seems to me . . . that at common law contributory negligence was an answer in all cases of unintentional trespass to the person, *on or off the highway*'.[73]

The matter is beginning to get settled. If the decision of the Full Court of the Supreme Court of South Australia in *Venning* v. *Chin* and the *obiter dictum* of Brooking J. in *Horkin* that the defence of contributory negligence is available to a defendant in an action of negligent trespass, whether on or off the highway, is accepted in Australia then obviously there will be no advantage in suing in negligent trespass rather than negligence but, if it is not accepted, or if the defence of contributory negligence is confined only to highway cases, then a plaintiff who has in any way contributed to a direct injury which has been inflicted on him by

---

69 [1974] 2 N.Z.L.R. 597, 603: 'I have come to the conclusion that, in a proper case, it is open to a defendant in an action based on an assault to call in aid the provisions of the Contributory Negligence Act'.

70 (1974) 10 S.A.S.R. 299, 317.

71 ibid., 321.

72 (1975) 49 A.L.J.R. 378.

73 [1983] V.R. 153, 159 (emphasis added).

the defendant would be better off suing in negligent trespass rather than negligence. This might not be an altogether desirable state of affairs but it is necessary to point it out.[74]

III: NEGLIGENT TRESPASS TO PROPERTY

We have assumed in the previous discussion that the action of negligent trespass is available not only in relation to direct injuries to the person but also in relation to direct injuries to land and to goods. So there can be an action for negligent trespass to land[75] and an action for negligent trespass to goods.[76] In such actions, not only must the injury be direct but there must also be fault on the part of the defendant. In *National Coal Board* v. *J.E. Evans & Co. (Cardiff) Ltd*[77] the defendant was held not liable for damage to the plaintiff's electric cable, placed under land without the knowledge or consent of the landowner, because there was no negligence on the defendant's part and the injury was not intentional. The injury was held to be the result of an inevitable accident. The burden of disproving negligence (i.e. a negligent or careless act) in an action of negligent trespass to property (as in negligent trespass to the person) will rest upon the defendant once the plaintiff shows a direct act on the part of the defendant and the plaintiff will win unless the defendant can disprove negligence. This is what happened in *Bell Canada* v. *Bannermount Ltd.*[78] The plaintiff's buried cable was damaged when the defendant, while digging a hole with a 'jack-hammer', struck the cable. The Ontario Court of Appeal held that the burden of disproving negligence had not been discharged by the defendant and therefore found for the plaintiff. The burden of proof in actions in negligent trespass in Australia and Canada is exactly the same.[79] In relation to damage, we have said already that negligent trespass to the person is actionable *per se*. *Dumont* v. *Miller*[80] and *Demers* v. *Desrorier*[81] illustrate that an action in intentional trespass to land and goods respectively will lie without proof of actual damage.

---

74 *Williams & Hepple*, 45 fn. 2 regard a restrictive reading of the Law Reform (Contributory Negligence) Act as 'retrogressive'. This might well be so but it would be folly to discuss only the liberal construction of the provisions in question.

75 See e.g. *F.W. Jeffrey & Sons* v. *Copeland Flour Mills* [1923] 4 D.L.R. 1140, 1145: 'a trespass to land (at least if it is not excusable as being e.g. the result of inevitable accident) is actionable although it is unintentional' (*per* Rose J.).

76 See e.g. *Bell Canada* v. *Bannermount Ltd* (1973) 35 D.L.R. (3d) 367, where the plaintiff telephone company brought an action in negligent trespass to goods for damage to their underground cables caused by the negligent digging of the defendant.

77 [1951] 2 K.B. 861.

78 (1973) 35 D.L.R. (3d) 367.

79 See F.A. Trindade (1971) 21 *I.C.L.Q.* 706, 713-19. See also (1971) 49 *Can.B.R.* 612-19.

80 (1873) 4 A.J.R. 152. For a recent English decision that trespass to land (airspace) is actionable without proof of damage, see *Woollerton and Wilson Ltd* v. *Richard Costain Ltd* [1970] 1 W.L.R. 411.

81 [1929] 2 D.L.R. 401—even where there has been no asportation. If there has been an asportation of goods, *Kirk* v. *Gregory* (1876) 1 Ex.D. 55 is authority for the proposition that trespass is actionable *per se*.

There is no reason why the principle should not be extended to negligent trespass to land and to goods.[82] In Western Australia, the eyes were removed from the body of a heart attack victim without permission of the next of kin.[83] Is this a trespass and should it be actionable? If so, what is the damage? If corpses are treated, intentionally or negligently, in a manner which causes distress to the immediate family[84] there is, it is suggested, a tortious remedy in intentional or negligent trespass without the necessity of showing actual damage. If contributory negligence is a defence to an action for negligent trespass to the person then it will very likely be a defence to an action for negligent trespass to property, but, as we have indicated earlier, the matter is not beyond controversy and it is difficult to say categorically that the principle of contributory negligence will be applied to an action for negligent trespass to land or to goods. In relation to the periods of limitation, there will not be much difference between bringing an action in negligence and an action in negligent trespass to property unless the claim in negligence *includes* damages for personal injuries.[85]

---

82 See, however, the New Zealand case of *Everitt* v. *Martin* [1953] N.Z.L.R. 298, 303: 'there is no right of action in the case of merely accidental contacts where no damage is done' (*per* F.B. Adams J.).

83 See the *Age* (Melbourne), 20 February 1982.

84 See e.g. *Owens* v. *Liverpool Corporation* [1939] 1 K.B. 394.

85 See fn. 62 and 63 above.

9

NEGLIGENCE—THE DUTY OF CARE

I: GENERAL INTRODUCTION

In some torts the focus of attention is some right or interest of the plaintiff which the law seeks to protect from illegitimate interference or injury by the defendant—trespass to land and defamation are examples. Other torts focus on a specific act or type of conduct which the law seeks to discourage or sanction—inducing breach of contract and collecting dangerous substances on one's land (the tort generally called *Rylands* v. *Fletcher*) are examples. The tort of negligence, too, is concerned primarily with the defendant's conduct; but it is more concerned with the *way* he behaved rather than with exactly what he did. The admonition which is implied in the tort—not to behave carelessly or negligently—can be addressed to anyone who does anything. The tort of negligence is, therefore, potentially applicable across the whole range of human conduct. This is not to say that any negligent conduct which causes another injury or damage will attract liability: as we will see, there are some interests which are not protected by the tort of negligence, and negligently causing injury to such an interest is not actionable as such. English courts, in particular, have also become wary of allowing negligence principles to encroach upon or displace different (and narrower) principles of liability in other well-established areas of the law, such as the law of contract,[1] trusts and intellectual property.[2] But the principle of liability based on fault which the idea of negligence liability involves has always had considerable attraction, and because it can be applied to any type of

1 This is a very complex matter, detailed discussion of which is outside the scope of this book. See Cane *Tort Law and Economic Interests* (Oxford, 1991) pp. 326-52.

2 e.g. *C.B.S. Songs Ltd* v. *Amstrad Consumer Electronics p.l.c.* [1988] A.C. 1013; *China and South Sea Bank Ltd* v. *Tan* [1990] 1 A.C. 536; *Parker-Tweedale* v. *Dunbar Bank p.l.c.* [1991] Ch. 12; cf. *Fletcher* v. *National Mutual Life Nominees Ltd* [1990] 1 N.Z.L.R. 97. There are a number of relevant New Zealand cases: *Westpac Banking Corporation* v. *McCreanor* [1990] 1 N.Z.L.R. 580; *Shivas* v. *Bank of New Zealand* [1990] 2 N.Z.L.R. 327.

human activity, negligence has not only become the essence of a tort but has also become an element in a number of other torts of which it was not historically an element, such as trespass[3] and nuisance.[4]

II: SKETCH OF THE TORT OF NEGLIGENCE

The term 'negligence' is used in two senses in modern law. In one sense it refers to the tort of negligence. The birth of the modern tort of negligence is usually traced to the famous case of *Donoghue* v. *Stevenson*,[5] and in particular to Lord Atkin's judgment in that case. The tort consists of three elements (all of which must be established by the plaintiff in order to succeed in the action): a duty to take reasonable care owed at the time of the act of negligence by the defendant to the plaintiff; a breach of that duty by the defendant; and damage resulting to the plaintiff from that breach which is not too remote in law. 'Negligence' in its other sense refers to the second of these elements. Negligence in this sense is roughly synonymous with 'carelessness', but more technically it consists of failure to take reasonable care and precautions to guard against reasonably foreseeable and not insignificant risks of injury to the plaintiff. Whether a risk is significant or not is judged by weighing in the balance four factors: the likelihood of the risk materializing; the likely seriousness of its consequences if it does; the cost of guarding against it; and the social utility of the defendant's activity.

So far as the third element of the tort of negligence is concerned, the test of whether damage is too remote in law is basically whether it was a reasonably foreseeable consequence of the defendant's negligence, although there are qualifications to this principle which allow recovery for unforeseeable damage in many circumstances.

III: THE ANATOMY OF DUTY OF CARE

1. GENERAL PRINCIPLES OF DUTY

Because of the potentially unlimited application of the negligence principle and the desire of the courts not to subject every human activity to the regime of negligence liability,[6] the courts have developed 'control devices'[7] which serve to restrict or limit the circumstances in which a defendant can be held liable for careless conduct. The duty of care is one such device and it is used to specify the type of situations and activities to which the tort applies, and the sort of interests which the tort of negligence

---

3 *Fleming* 17-22; *Chin* v. *Venning* (1975) 49 A.L.J.R. 378, 379 *per* Gibbs J; R. Bailey (1976) 5 *Adelaide L.R.* 402.

4 See pp.619-22, 628-9 below.

5 [1932] A.C. 562; R.F.V. Heuston (1957) 20 *M.L.R.* 1.

6 *Hedley Byrne & Co. Ltd* v. *Heller & Partners Ltd* [1964] A.C. 465, 534 per Lord Pearce.

7 J.G. Fleming (1953) 31 *Can. B.R.* 470, 474.

protects; in other words, duty of care is concerned with the *scope* of the tort of negligence or with the *range of liability* for negligent conduct.

It is with the duty of care that the seminal case of *Donoghue* v. *Stevenson* is concerned. In that case a woman went into a restaurant with a friend who bought her a bottle of ginger beer in which, it was alleged, were the decomposed remains of a snail. The woman claimed that as a result of drinking some of the ginger beer she became ill and suffered shock. The House of Lords held by majority that on these facts the woman would be entitled to recover damages from the manufacturer if she could prove that the contamination of the drink was the result of negligence on the part of the manufacturer. The exact point of law involved will be discussed in the chapter on defective products. Our present concern is with Lord Atkin's attempt to formulate a general principle on the basis of which it could be decided whether the manufacturer owed a duty to consumers to be careful in manufacturing its products.

Before this case the question of whether a duty of care was owed in particular circumstances depended on whether the relationship between the plaintiff and the defendant fell into one of the categories to which the law recognized that a duty of care attached. There were many such relationships; for example, surgeon and patient, attorney and client, common carrier and owner of goods or passenger, occupier of land and visitor. But the list of duty relationships was not endless, and if the plaintiff's case did not fall within one of the categories he would have to persuade the court that his case was sufficiently analogous to other cases in which a duty was recognized to enable the court to extend a category to cover it.

In *Donoghue* v. *Stevenson* Lord Atkin laid down a principle designed both to state the factor common to all the existing categories of duty relationship and to enable new duty relationships to be generated in situations where a duty had not previously been held to arise. That principle, which has become known as the 'neighbour principle', was in these terms:

> You must take reasonable care to avoid acts and omissions which you can reasonably foresee would be likely to injure your neighbour. Who then, in law, is [your] neighbour? The answer seems to be persons who are so closely and directly affected by [your] act that [you] ought reasonably to have them in contemplation when [you] are directing [your] mind to the acts or omissions which are called in question.[8]

Lord Atkin went on to say that the term 'proximity' could be used to describe the relationship between an actor and persons whom he ought to know would be directly affected by his actions. Applying the neighbour principle to the case at hand, Lord Atkin held that because the manufacturer had intended that the drink should reach the consumer unopened and without being inspected by an intermediate person, it ought to have

8 [1932] A.C. 562, 580.

foreseen injury to the plaintiff if it did not take care; therefore the plaintiff was owed a duty of care.

Lord Atkin's enunciation of the neighbour principle started a debate (which has not yet ended) as to which of two methods of justifying the imposition of new duties of care is to be preferred. Should new duties of care be derived from some general principle in the way Lord Atkin suggested, or should they be developed by incremental extension of established duty relationships? Several of the current members of the High Court[9] favour the former approach, while the English position, as enunciated in recent judgments in the House of Lords,[10] is that the incremental approach championed by Brennan J. in the High Court[11] is better.

The main argument in favour of adopting a general principle of duty appears to be that this approach will inject an element of theoretical consistency and order into the law; whereas the main argument in favour of the incremental approach seems to be that it gives the courts more control over the development and expansion of negligence liability. The adoption of the incremental approach by the House of Lords is a reaction against a *dictum* of Lord Wilberforce in *Anns* v. *Merton L.B.C.*[12] to the effect that if, on the facts of any particular case, the injury to the plaintiff was foreseeable, then a duty of care ought to be imposed unless there was a good reason why it should not be. In some later cases this *dictum* was interpreted as raising a presumption in favour of imposing liability for negligent conduct unless the defendant could adduce policy reasons why he should not be held liable. This approach resulted in a number of decisions imposing new duties of care which the House of Lords came to view as mistaken; and in general it was thought that Lord Wilberforce's *dictum* had given courts too much freedom to impose liability for economic loss and to hold public authorities liable. We will examine these matters in more detail later. The main point to make at the moment is that in England the incremental approach is seen as a way of restricting negligence liability and the general principle approach is seen as dangerously expansionary.[13]

The High Court has also sought to weaken the expansionary tendencies inherent in the neighbour principle, but in a quite different way. We have

---

9 *San Sebastian Pty Ltd* v. *The Minister Administering the Environmental Planning and Assessment Act* (1986) 162 C.L.R. 340; *Australian Safeway Stores Pty Ltd* v. *Zaluzna* (1987) 162 C.L.R. 479.

10 See e.g. *Caparo Industries p.l.c.* v. *Dickman* [1990] 2 A.C. 605, 618 *per* Lord Bridge of Harwich; 379-80 per Lord Oliver of Aylmerton; *Murphy* v. *Brentwood D.C.* [1991] 1 A.C. 398, 461 *per* Lord Keith of Kinkel.

11 *Sutherland S.C.* v. *Heyman* (1985) 157 C.L.R. 424,481; *Hawkins* v. *Clayton* (1988) 164 C.L.R. 539, 555-6. A classic judicial exposition of how this approach might work is that of Lord Diplock in *Dorset Yacht Co. Ltd* v. *Home Office* [1970] A.C. 1004, 1058-9 (supported extrajudicially by McHugh J. in P.D. Finn (ed.) *Essays on Torts* (Sydney, 1989) pp. 39-42).

12 [1978] A.C. 728. Lord Wilberforce's approach is still in favour in New Zealand: *Mainguard Packaging Ltd* v. *Hilton Haulage Ltd.* [1990] 1 N.Z.L.R. 360, 364-8.

13 But the incremental approach has dangers of its own: J. Stapleton (1991) 107 *L.Q.R.* 249.

seen that Lord Atkin used two terms to describe the sort of relationship which would give rise to a duty of care: 'reasonable foreseeability' and 'proximity'. Opinions have differed as to whether Lord Atkin intended these two terms to be synonymous; but the view which has been approved by the High Court is that they do not mean the same thing, and that the term 'proximity' establishes a test which is harder for the plaintiff to satisfy than that based on the notion of reasonable foreseeability.[14] In other words, it may be that the defendant ought reasonably to have foreseen that negligence on his part would injure the plaintiff, but he may owe no duty of care to the plaintiff because there was not a sufficient relationship of proximity between them. So the Australian way of keeping the development of the tort of negligence under control is to insist that the general principle of duty is a restrictive one. This approach has also been adopted in England as an adjunct to the idea that new duties must be developed incrementally.

A major difficulty with both 'reasonable foreseeability' and 'proximity' as tests of duty is that they are extremely vague terms. What can we say about their meaning? Reasonable foresight is the foresight of the reasonable person:[15] the relevant question is not what could the defendant have foreseen, but what would a reasonable person in his position have foreseen. The reasonable person is the mythical personification of fairness.[16] Therefore, reasonable foresight is the foresight which justice and fairness requires. 'Reasonable' is a word used to express moral judgments about the extent to which a person ought to be expected to think of the likely effects of his conduct on others. 'Foreseeable' is a problematic word. In one sense its meaning is obvious—a foreseeable event is one which can be anticipated in advance of its occurrence. But this definition tells us no more than the word itself. It is very difficult to give a helpful account of what the word means except by giving examples of foreseeable events. The courts express this by saying that foreseeability as a test of the existence of a duty of care is a question of fact: the word cannot be defined in advance as a matter of law. All we can do is to say whether on particular facts the event was foreseeable or not.

Proximity obviously means 'nearness' in some sense.[17] This may be physical or temporal, and a good illustration of the use of proximity in a physical sense is *Home Office* v. *Dorset Yacht Co. Ltd*,[18] in which it was alleged that juvenile offenders who had been taken on a training exercise to an island had escaped through the negligence of the warders. The boys had stolen and damaged a yacht which they found nearby. The House of

14 The main proponent of this idea is Deane J. and the basic discussion is in *Jaensch* v. *Coffey* (1983-4) 155 C.L.R. 549, 578-87; see also his Honour's judgments in *Sutherland Shire Council* v. *Heyman* (1984-5) 157 C.L.R. 424, 495-8; *Stevens* v. *Brodribb Sawmilling Co. Pty Ltd* (1986) 160 C.L.R. 16. For more detailed consideration see S. Quinlan and D. Gardiner (1988) 62 *A.L.J.* 347.

15 *Vaughan* v. *Menlove* (1837) 3 Bing. N.C. 468, 475; *Hall* v. *Brooklands Club* [1933] 1 K.B. 205, 224; *Mt Isa Mines Ltd* v. *Pusey* (1970) 125 C.L.R. 383, 397-8.

16 *Fareham Contractors Ltd* v. *Fareham U.D.C.* [1956] A.C. 696, 728. The concept of the reasonable person is discussed in detail in Chapter 10.

17 *Jaensch* v. *Coffey* (1983-4) 155 C.L.R. 549, 584 *per* Deane J.

18 [1970] A.C. 1004.

Lords held that the Borstal officers could in certain circumstances owe a duty of care to the yacht owner. Lord Diplock thought that this duty was not based merely on foreseeability of damage; it was foreseeable that the boys on reaching the harbour shore might steal a car, drive many miles and damage property at their destination. But this would not justify holding the Home Office to be under a duty of care to those remote property owners because, by and large, individual citizens are expected to bear the costs of crime and cannot recover them from the government (as opposed to the criminal). His Lordship, therefore, held that the duty was owed only to persons whose property was in close proximity to the island and was, as a result, subject to special risk of damage when the escapees sought to evade immediate recapture.

But it is clear from *Donoghue* v. *Stevenson* itself that proximity need not be either physical or temporal.[19] The negligence of the manufacturer of a defective product is very often far removed in time and space from the effect of that negligence on the plaintiff. In that case the plaintiff was proximate to the defendant partly because the latter had marketed a product in a sealed container which enabled it to be consumed much later and far away without any intermediate inspection;[20] and partly because a majority of the court judged that, as a matter of fairness or social policy, manufacturers should bear the cost of injuries caused by their negligence.

From this it should be clear that both 'reasonable foreseeability' and 'proximity' are terms which express value judgments by courts as to when it is appropriate to impose liability for negligent conduct; and they are both concerned with the relationship between the two parties. But the two notions concentrate on different aspects of the parties' relationship. Foreseeability is concerned with the parties as persons (with interpersonal morality, if you like). Judgments of foreseeability are moral judgments about the degree of care for and awareness of others, and about the degree of sensitivity to their presence and vulnerability to injury, which it is reasonable and proper to expect people to display. Proximity is more concerned with factors such as nature of the injury inflicted (victims of purely economic loss are less likely to be held to be in a relationship of proximity with the defendant than victims of personal injury, for example), the nature of the plaintiff's interest (for example, property interests are much better protected by the tort of negligence than are contractual interests) and the circumstances in which the injury was inflicted. As we will see, the notion of proximity is also concerned with matters of social policy which are not specific to any particular case.

But it is most important to realize that these general tests of duty do not, by themselves, answer the question in any particular case of whether a duty ought to be imposed in circumstances where a duty has not hitherto been recognized. They are merely organizing concepts which courts use to express value judgments about whether liability ought to be imposed in

19 cf. *Hawkins* v. *Clayton* (1988) 164 C.L.R. 539, 577-8 *per* Deane J.
20 *Jaensch* v. *Coffey* (1983-4) 155 C.L.R. 549, 584-5 *per* Deane J.

particular circumstances.[21] Nor does the incremental approach tell judges whether to impose duties in particular cases; it only tells them to be cautious and conservative in deciding the issue. Indeed, there is no reason to think that judges will reach different results in particular cases simply by virtue of adopting one approach or the other to questions of duty. The only way properly to understand how the courts deal with questions of duty is to study the cases.

2. Duty of Care and the Foreseeability of the Plaintiff

As we have seen, the concept of reasonable foreseeability plays a role in all the elements of the tort of negligence. But we can distinguish the role it performs in the various elements of the tort by saying that duty is concerned (in part) with the foreseeability of the plaintiff; that breach is concerned with the foreseeability of the risk of injury; and that remoteness is concerned with the foreseeability of the damage actually suffered by the plaintiff. So far as duty is concerned, the fact that injury to the plaintiff was reasonably foreseeable by the defendant may not by itself establish a duty of care; but no duty will be owed unless injury to the plaintiff was reasonably foreseeable. The test of reasonable foreseeability does not mean that a person can be held liable in negligence only if he was in a position to foresee the plaintiff particularly or individually. It is often enough that the defendant ought to have foreseen injury to a class of persons of which the plaintiff was one. In *Chapman* v. *Hearse*[22] Chapman negligently collided with the car in front of him and was thrown onto the road. Dr Cherry, who was driving by, stopped to give aid to Chapman and while doing so was run down by the negligent driving of Hearse and killed. Dr Cherry's estate successfully sued Hearse for damages and Hearse sued Chapman to obtain a contribution from him to those damages on account of Chapman's original negligence. The High Court held that Chapman owed a duty of care to Dr Cherry even if he could not have been expected to foresee the precise chain of events which led to Dr Cherry's death. He could be expected to foresee that *someone* might come to his aid if he had an accident, and that in so doing that person might be injured or killed. From this case we can see that not only does the law expect of defendants a high degree of foresight of general classes of events and persons quite abstractly defined, but also that it is prepared to impose liability even when the details of what happened were quite bizarre.

However, there are limits to the degree of foresight by the defendant of the plaintiff which the law demands. For example, in the American case of *Palsgraf* v. *Long Island Railroad Co.*[23] the plaintiff was standing on the defendant's railway platform near some scales. Much further down the platform a man carrying a small package wrapped in newspaper was

---

21 *Sutherland S.C.* v. *Heyman* (1984-5) 157 C.L.R. 424, 497 *per* Deane J. ('a unifying rationale' not a 'criterion of liability'); *Stevens* v. *Brodribb Sawmilling Co. Pty Ltd* (1986) 160 C.L.R. 16, 52.

22 (1961) 106 C.L.R. 112; cf. *Eaton* v. *Pitman* (1991) 55 S.A.S.R. 386..

23 (1928) 162 N.E. 99.

having difficulty in boarding a train which had already started to move. A guard employed by the defendant, who was on the train, reached out to help him, and another guard pushed him from behind. In the process the package, which contained fireworks, fell between the platform and the train and exploded. The resulting vibrations allegedly dislodged some scales, which fell on the plaintiff, injuring her. The court held that the defendant was not liable to the plaintiff because 'life will have to be made over, and human nature transformed, before prevision so extravagant can be accepted as the norm . . . to which behaviour must conform'. The plaintiff was not a foreseeable victim of injury.

Windeyer J. pointed out in *Mt Isa Mines Ltd* v. *Pusey*[24] that the rule that foresight relates to classes of harms, events and persons leaves unsolved the question of the level of abstraction or particularity at which the class of harm, person or event is to be defined. For example, why did the court in *Chapman* v. *Hearse* choose to describe what had happened in such broad terms? It has often been noted that the choice of the level of description must be based on criteria which go beyond the idea of foreseeability because events can be more or less foreseeable depending on the degree of detail with which they are described.[25] In relation to personal injury, a duty will normally arise if the defendant ought to have foreseen injury to anyone; but, as we will see in more detail later, in order to restrict recovery for economic loss (for example), the law may not require that people foresee economic injury to anyone, but only to the plaintiff as an individual or to a limited class of persons of whom the plaintiff was one. So, by manipulating the definition of the class of persons who must be foreseeable, the courts can regulate the scope of liability for negligent conduct.

3. Duty of Care and Proximity

It is very difficult to say anything in general about the role of proximity in questions of duty because an assertion that the plaintiff and the defendant were not in a relationship of proximity seems to mean little more than that, in the light of all the relevant arguments of social, legal and economic policy, the defendant ought not to be held liable for negligently injuring the plaintiff. In other words, whether the parties were in a relationship of proximity depends on the facts of individual cases. But a couple of propositions seem to find support in the cases. First, where the alleged negligence consists of making a false statement, a relationship of proximity may exist if the plaintiff suffered loss by *relying* to his detriment on that statement. Detrimental reliance may establish proximity. On the other hand, there is, as we shall see, some authority for saying that reliance is not necessary in order to establish proximity in such cases; and it is clear that detrimental reliance by itself may not be sufficient to justify

24 (1971) 125 C.L.R. 383, 402.
25 e.g. G.H.L. Fridman & J.S. Williams (1971) 45 *A.L.J.* 117; D. Jackson (1965) 39 *A.L.J.* 3.

the imposition of liability. For example, it has been held in England that a company auditor does not owe a duty of care to prospective purchasers of shares in the company even if they rely on the audited accounts in deciding to purchase (or not to purchase) shares.[26] This is because the purposes for which the statutory functions of auditors exist do not include the protection of purchasers of shares.

Secondly, this question of statutory purpose has proved very important in a number of English cases concerning liability for alleged negligence in the performance of statutory powers. We will discuss these cases in more detail in Chapter 20. Here we should note that the notion of proximity has been used to express the idea that because, in the court's view, the statutory power in question was not, as a matter of interpretation of the statute, conferred in order to protect people such as the plaintiff, then no duty to take care in exercising the power was owed to the plaintiff. But the idea of purpose may extend beyond the realm of actions based on allegedly negligent performance of statutory powers. For example, in *Smith* v. *Eric S. Bush*[27] it was held that a surveyor employed by a prospective mortgagee owed a duty of care in valuing a house to the purchaser of the house (the mortgagor) because it was common knowledge that the vast majority of purchasers relied on the mortgagee's survey and did not commission an independent survey. In other words, the court considered that it was properly part of the surveyor's job in valuing the house to take care of the interests of the purchaser as well as those of the mortgagee who employed him, even though the two interests were rather different. There was, therefore, a sufficient relationship of proximity between the surveyor and the purchaser. This decision serves to define the purposes which mortgagees' surveys must serve.

4. ESTABLISHED CATEGORIES OF DUTY RELATIONSHIP

We have noted that the incremental approach to the 'invention' of new duties of care builds on already existing duty categories, that is, on relationships which have already been recognized as giving rise to a duty of care. But it should not be thought that the other approach to new duties (the general principle approach) has no place for established duty categories. Although Lord Atkin sought to generalize the idea of the duty relationship by establishing a general relationship of proximity or foreseeability, this did not mean that particular duty categories (such as surgeon and patient) were no longer of any importance. Indeed, *Donoghue* v. *Stevenson* itself established that a particular duty relationship existed between a manufacturer and a consumer of its goods even though there was no contract between them. The neighbour principle embodied a relationship of proximity of which the particular duty categories were examples or illustrations or sub-categories.[28]

---

26 *Caparo p.l.c.* v. *Dickman* [1990] 2 A.C. 605.
27 [1990] 1 A.C. 831.
28 Deane J. in *Jaensch* v. *Coffey* (1983-4) 155 C.L.R. 549, 584 refers to such categories by the phrase 'circumstantial proximity'.

Under the general principle approach to duty, the general principle only comes into play in cases not covered by any existing duty category.[29] And the result of applying the general principle is usually the creation of a new particular duty category. One of the most recently recognized categories is the one we noted above between mortgagees' valuers and prospective mortgagors. These particular duty categories are simply applications or illustrations of the general principle of proximity. Under the general principle approach, the function of such duty categories is to obviate the need to decide on the facts of particular cases whether there is a sufficient relationship of proximity between the parties. The creation of duty categories enables questions of duty to be decided as a matter of precedent or authority; and this reduces litigation and encourages settlement of disputes. If there is no authoritative decision on the question of whether a duty exists in the circumstances of a particular case, then the general principle approach can be used to decide the issue.

But what happens if there is authority to the effect that no duty is owed in the circumstances of a particular case? Depending on the strength of the authority, a plaintiff who wants to argue that a duty ought to be recognized may seek to persuade an appropriate court to overrule or ignore the authority on the ground that there are good reasons of justice or policy to recognize a duty of care on the facts of the case. It might be more difficult to recognize a new duty category in such circumstances if one adopts the incremental approach than if one adopts the general principle approach; but even the latter approach does not allow courts to ignore precedents entirely. There are cases in which courts have refused to go against existing authority, regardless of the existence of good arguments in favour of such an approach, simply because the authority existed and had stood for a long time. For example, in *Leigh & Sillavan Ltd* v. *Aliakmon Shipping Co. Ltd*[30] the House of Lords declined to overrule authorities to the effect that a plaintiff could not recover in the tort of negligence for economic loss suffered as a result of damage to goods belonging to another. One of the main reasons for this decision was that the relevant authorities were old and that traders had for very many years organized their affairs on the basis that they were correct. To change the law would create uncertainty and would upset established patterns of commerce; and this, the House thought, was a good reason not to change the law, regardless of whether good arguments in favour of change could be made.

So, authority plays an important part in questions of duty: not only may it establish the existence of a duty category, but it may also be used to justify a refusal to create a new duty category if the court thinks that changing the law would do more harm than good.

The relationship between the general principle of proximity and particular duty categories is complicated by the fact that particular duty categories may not be merely applications of the general relationship of

29 Deane J. in *Jaensch* v. *Coffey* (1983-4) 155 C.L.R. 549, 585; Gibbs C.J. in *Sutherland S.C.* v. *Heyman* (1984-5) 157 C.L.R. 424, 441-2.

30 [1986] A.C. 785.

neighbourhood or proximity. A good illustration is provided by the law of occupiers' liability. An occupier of land owes a duty to persons visiting his land to take care to protect them from suffering injury as a result of the existence of dangers on the land. Until recently the content of the obligations of the occupier varied according to the status of the visitor: visitors were divided into a number of categories (invitee, licensee, and so on), and the occupier's obligations to any particular visitor depended on the category into which the visitor fell. These particular duty categories were first established in the nineteenth century, and they continued to exist even after the enunciation of the neighbour principle by Lord Atkin. But recently the High Court has held that the old categories of visitor should be abolished and that the relationship of occupier and visitor should be treated as just an application of the general principle of proximity; so the obligation owed by the occupier to any particular visitor now depends on all the facts of the case rather than on the status of the visitor in terms of the old categories. Another duty category which was established in the nineteenth century is that of employer and employee. Unlike the law of occupiers' liability, the law of employers' liability, although part of the law of negligence, has retained certain distinctive features which justify giving it separate treatment: the category of employer/employee is still not treated as just an application of the general principle of proximity. The duty category of public authority and private individual also arguably possesses special features which demand separate treatment.

5. Duty and Policy Immunities

We have noted several times that considerations of policy play an important part in decisions about whether a duty of care exists in particular circumstances. But policy arguments (that is, arguments about community values, whether social, political, economic or whatever) can be used not only to justify establishing a particular duty category but also to justify holding that no duty exists even when there is a relationship of proximity between the parties.[31] For example, barristers are immune from liability to their clients in respect of court work and associated activities, despite close proximity between barrister and client, for reasons having to do with the proper functioning of the judicial system rather than the relationship of the parties. Again, the 'defence' of illegality may operate to prevent a duty of care arising even between parties who are in a relationship of proximity.

6. Summary

We have seen that decisions about duty of care depend on a number of factors: ought the defendant to have foreseen that the plaintiff (as a member of a broadly or narrowly defined class, or as an individual) would

31 Deane J. in *Jaensch* v. *Coffey* (1983-4) 155 C.L.R. 583, 586.

suffer injury if he did not take care? Was there a sufficient relationship of proximity between the parties? Are there any policy considerations which might demand refusal to impose a duty of care despite foreseeability and proximity? Is there strong authority against imposing a duty of care in this case? Ought any authority in favour of recognizing a duty of care be overruled or ignored? We have also noted that considerations of policy, in the broad sense of value judgments about the propriety or wisdom of imposing a duty, are relevant to answering all of these questions and not just the one which explicitly refers to policy.

These questions provide a framework for the court's consideration, in any particular case in which the parties contest the issue of duty, of whether a duty of care ought to be recognized. But they only provide a framework, and in order to fill in the structure of the law of duty of care we must examine cases in which duties have been held to exist or not. Our aim will be to discover the scope of the tort of negligence, the types of injury for which compensation can be obtained in the tort, and the types of interests which the tort protects.

IV: PHYSICAL DAMAGE

1. Duty Sometimes Superfluous

The vast majority of negligence claims concern the infliction of personal injury,[32] property damage[33] and financial loss consequential upon such injury and damage; and the great bulk of such claims arise out of either motor accidents or industrial accidents.[34] Because of the fact that in such cases any damages awarded to the plaintiff will be paid out of an insurance fund, the courts have placed very few limitations in terms of duty on recovery for personal injury or property damage inflicted on the road or at work. Further, because physical damage, particularly personal injury, is normally considered the most serious type of damage and most worthy of compensation, the courts have in fact placed very few limitations on recovery for physical damage in any context. If the damage was foreseeable it is usually recoverable; in other words, the requirement of proximity is normally satisfied by foreseeability.[35] One of the results of this is that in such cases the concept of duty adds nothing in theory to the concept of negligence, the second element of the tort, since it too contains the requirement of foreseeability. It is only if the defendant argues absence of proximity or that some precedent or policy is against the imposition of a duty that the questions of duty and breach of duty need separate

---

32 In this section this term refers to bodily injury. As to injury to the mind see the next section.

33 'Damage' here includes destruction and loss.

34 For a variety of reasons, it is much more difficult to obtain compensation through the tort system for illnesses and diseases which do not result from traumatic accidents. See generally J. Stapleton *Disease and the Compensation Debate* (Oxford, 1986).

35 *Jaensch* v. *Coffey* (1983-4) 155 C.L.R. 549, 581-2; *Hawkins* v. *Clayton* (1988) 164 C.L.R. 539, 576 *per* Deane J.

treatment.[36] For example, in *James* v. *Harrison*[37] the plaintiff, a customer, left a shop just behind an employee of the owner. The employee, who was hurrying along the pavement, suddenly turned to go back and knocked the plaintiff to the ground, injuring her. McGregor J. held that on these facts the employee both owed the plaintiff a duty of care and had breached it. Again, in *O'Connor* v. *South Australia*[38] a stenographer was injured when a door behind which she was standing was opened suddenly and forcefully. The case was decided simply on the basis that the injury was, under the circumstances, foreseeable.

However, even in cases of personal injury, a decision that the plaintiff's injury was foreseeable does not always obviate the need to decide whether the defendant was negligent by failing to take precautions against the foreseeable risk. Foreseeability of injury is part, but only part, of the definition of negligent conduct. In *Mazinska* v. *Bakka*[39] Bakka was slowly driving his car into his driveway just before dawn in poor visibility; he ran over a person, apparently drunk, lying in the driveway. It was held that the presence of the person was foreseeable so that the defendant owed him a duty of care. However, the possible presence of a person did not require the defendant to drive in such a manner as would have enabled him to see and avoid someone crouched or prone in the driveway—it only required him not to drive completely ignoring the possibility of a person's presence. So the plaintiff's claim was dismissed.

It should not be thought that in cases which are dealt with solely in terms of foreseeability no issues of policy are relevant, and that the only issue is a moral one about how aware of other people the defendant ought to have been. It is simply that in cases of road and industrial accidents, for example, the policy judgment involved in deciding that drivers or employers should pay the costs of foreseeable accidents negligently caused by them in conducting their activities is now so widely accepted that it goes unchallenged. But this is not so in every case of physical damage. For example, the extent to which defendants ought to be burdened with the cost of taking extra precautions to protect hypersensitive plaintiffs causes trouble in several areas of law. In *Levi* v. *Colgate-Palmolive Pty Ltd*[40] it was held that the manufacturer of a washing product owed no special duty to take precautions to a consumer particularly prone to dermatitis, but only the same duty as it owed to normal consumers. In *Nova Mink Ltd* v. *Trans Canada Airlines*[41] it was held that the defendant could not be expected to have foreseen that the ordinary noise of aircraft overflying the plaintiff's farm would upset female mink and cause them to eat their young. Although these decisions could be explained simply by saying that the statistical probability of abnormal persons in the population is too low to expect a defendant to foresee them and to take special precautions

---

36 *Richards* v. *State of Victoria* [1969] V.R. 136, 140.
37 (1977) 18 A.C.T.R. 36.
38 (1976) 14 S.A.S.R. 187.
39 (1979) 20 S.A.S.R. 350.
40 (1941) 41 S.R. (N.S.W.) 48.
41 [1951] 2 D.L.R. 241.

to protect them, it is helpful to explain them further in terms of an economic policy decision not to burden industry with the cost of protecting abnormally sensitive people or activities: the hypersensitive should take steps to protect themselves.

Furthermore, there are some cases in which foreseeability of injury does not, by itself, establish a duty of care even in relation to personal injury or property damage. For example, we have already noted Lord Diplock's *dictum* in *Home Office* v. *Dorset Yacht Co.*[42] to the effect that even if it was foreseeable that escaping prisoners might damage property remote from the prison, only persons who owned property in close proximity to the prison could claim damages from the prison authorities for negligently allowing the prisoners to escape. The policy behind this *dictum* is that in general, individuals should protect themselves against criminal damage. It has also been held in England that the police normally owe no duty of care in investigating crime to persons who suffer personal injury at the hands of a criminal whom the police are seeking to apprehend, because the duties of the police to investigate crime are owed to the public at large, and there is no sufficient relationship of proximity between the police and any individual victim of crime unless, perhaps, that individual is especially at risk of being injured by the criminal.[43] An important reason for this approach is that the courts are afraid that the threat of negligence actions might cause the police to be unduly cautious in investigating crime, to the detriment of society generally.

So, although personal injury or property damage can usually form the basis of a successful negligence action provided only that the injury or damage was foreseeable, this is not always the case: there is not always a duty of care to avoid foreseeable personal injury or property damage.

2. Foreseeability and Particular Duty Relationships

In *Richards* v. *State of Victoria*[44] the duty owed by a teacher to pupils in the classroom to protect them from the violence of other pupils was said to arise out of the relationship of teacher and pupil and not out of a general relationship of proximity. At the other extreme, in *Hahn* v. *Conley*[45] Barwick C.J. and Windeyer J. both said that the duty owed by a parent to its child to protect the latter from harm did not arise out of the relationship of the parties but was a factual question to be decided in terms of foresight and reasonable care. It is not clear what function the idea of relationship is serving in these cases or why it is thought important to assert or deny that the duty depends on the relationship. But it may be, especially in *Hahn* v. *Conley*, that the idea of relationship is being used to regulate the incidence of liability for failure to take positive steps to care

42 [1970] A.C. 1004.

43 *Hill* v. *Chief Constable of West Yorkshire* [1989] A.C. 53.

44 [1969] V.R. 136; cf. *Geyer* v. *Downs* (1977) 17 A.L.R. 408, 410 *per* Stephen J. See generally P.G. Heffey (1985) 11 *Mon. U.L.R.* 1; G. Lowe (1983-4) *U.Q.L.J.* 28.

45 (1971) 126 C.L.R. 276; cf. *McCallion* v. *Dodd* [1966] N.Z.L.R. 710. See also *Rogers* v. *Rawlings* [1969] Qd.R. 262.

for and protect children. Barwick C.J. in *Hahn* v. *Conley* went to great lengths to insist that the law should not be too ready to translate the moral duties of a parent into legal duties. Liability should be imposed only when the parent has assumed control of the child. This could explain *Richards* v. *Victoria*—a teacher could presumably be said to have assumed control over the children in the classroom in a way that the grandparent in *Hahn* had not.

3. Duty of Care, Relationships and the Scope of the Duty

The main function of the concept of duty of care is to determine whether the plaintiff is entitled to sue in negligence. The main function of the second element of the tort ('breach of duty') is to specify the sort of conduct which is actionable as 'negligence'; or, in other words, the sort of precautions which the defendant ought to have taken to avoid injury to the plaintiff. But the concept of duty is sometimes used to perform this latter function. This is well illustrated by the case of *Sydney County Council* v. *Dell'Oro*[46] in which a worker was fatally injured by contact with a high voltage link left uncovered by an employee of the council during a temporary absence from the job. The employee reasonably but wrongly thought that the worker was a qualified electrician to whom an uncovered link would present little danger. It was held that the council was not liable for the act of its employee. The court defined the relationship between the parties in terms of electricity authority and *qualified* electrical contractor, and in so doing it more or less decided the limits of the precautions which were required by stressing one feature of the facts (the reasonable belief that the contractor was qualified) at the expense of others, such as the extreme dangerousness of the situation. Thus Jacobs J. could say that the question of whether the council's employee had been negligent depended on whether he did or omitted to do anything which the reasonable person would not do or would do in circumstances *defined by* the duty of care.[47]

In *Bus* v. *Sydney County Council*[48] a majority of the High Court disapproved this use of the duty concept in *Dell'Oro*, apparently on the basis that it elevated what was essentially a question of fact (did the defendant's employer act negligently?) into a principle of law concerning the duty owed to a qualified worker (of the type enunciated by Gaudron J. in *Bus*). The basis of this objection is, as we shall see later, that decisions on duty create precedents which later courts may find unduly restricting.

A different use of the duty concept to define the scope of liability is seen in *Geyer* v. *Downs*.[49] The gates of a school were opened at about 8 a.m. but teachers were not rostered for playground duty until 9 a.m. It was held

---

46 (1975) 132 C.L.R. 97.

47 ibid, 119. Another illustration is *Haley* v. *London Electricity Board* [1965] A.C. 778. Cf *Cook* v. *Cook* (1986) 162 C.L.R. 376, 382.

48 (1989) 167 C.L.R. 78.

49 (1977-8) 138 C.L.R. 91.

that the headteacher had failed to exercise reasonable care for the safety of a girl injured at about 8.50 a.m.; the question before the High Court was whether the headteacher had owed any duty of care at this time. Stephen J. held that since the duty arose out of the relationship of teacher and pupil, the duty existed for as long as the relationship; and that the relationship came into existence when the gates opened, because the headteacher had asserted authority over the children by issuing instructions as to how they were to behave in the period before the arrival of teachers.

V: NERVOUS SHOCK

'Nervous shock' is injury caused by the impact on the mind, through the senses, of external events.[50] However, the law does not compensate for mere grief or sorrow caused, for instance, by the death of or injury to someone else.[51] Injury caused by the impact on the mind of external events, which is recognized by the law, is of three types: physical injury—a pregnant woman may suffer a miscarriage or a person may suffer a heart attack or a stroke; psychological injury, such as hysteria, neurosis, depression or any other 'recognized psychiatric illness';[52] and psychosomatic effects of psychological illnesses, such as paralysis.[53] The term 'nervous shock' is not a very satisfactory one to describe these various injuries, but it is still widely used.

Apart from an isolated *dictum* of Denning L.J. in *King* v. *Phillips*[54] to the effect that the duty owed by the driver of a motor vehicle did not differ according to whether the injury inflicted was physical injury or nervous shock, courts have usually distinguished between these two types of injury. The law has always displayed a reluctance to compensate as generously for nervous shock as for direct physical injury. A number of different arguments have been put forward to justify this different treatment.

1. POLICY ARGUMENTS FOR LIMITING RECOVERY

(a) The 'floodgates argument': this argument is often raised against extensions of legal liability as well as being used as a basis for restricting liability for certain types of loss, such as economic loss and nervous shock.

---

50 *McLoughlin* v. *O'Brian* [1983] 1 A.C. 410, 418 *per* Lord Wilberforce. See generally A.L. Goodhart (1944) 8 *Camb. L.J.* 478; J. Havard (1956) 19 *M.L.R.* 478; P.G. Heffey (1974) 48 *A.L.J.* 196; 240; F.A. Trindade [1986] *C.L.J.* 476; H. Teff (1983) 99 *L.Q.R.* 100; J. Swanton (1992) 66 *A.L.J.* 495.

51 *Mt Isa Mines Ltd* v. *Pusey* (1971) 125 C.L.R. 383, 394 *per* Windeyer J.; *Benson* v. *Lee* [1972] V.R. 879, 880; *Swan* v. *Williams (Demolition) Pty Ltd* (1987) 9 N.S.W.L.R. 172.

52 *Mt Isa Mines* v. *Pusey* (1971) 125 C.L.R. 383, 394 *per* Windeyer J. In a recent English case, four firefighters were awarded substantial compensation for 'post-traumatic stress' suffered as a result of attending a large fire in an underground railway station.

53 *McLoughlin* v. *O'Brian* [1983] A.C. 410, 431 *per* Lord Bridge.

54 [1953] 1 Q.B. 429, 440.

But not all judges find it equally compelling. The argument is based on a fear that if the scope of liability rules is too wide, 'the floodgates will open' and the court system will be swamped with cases, judicial resources will be overtaxed and there will be long delays in the hearing of cases. But it is likely that the cost and trouble of litigation are much more important regulators of the flow of litigation than liability rules.

(b) Nervous shock claims are difficult to prove and easy to fabricate. This argument has received a mixed reception from judges. Some judges have answered it by saying that the courts are equal to coping with evidentiary difficulties and weeding out fraudulent claims. But the law's chief response to this argument has been to deny recovery for mental distress which has no medically recognized and verifiable symptoms whether physical, psychiatric or psychosomatic. This does not solve all the problems because even experts often differ as to whether the symptoms were caused by witnessing the external event. But at least it forestalls a situation where the only possible witness to the effect of the event is the plaintiff himself.

(c) Once duty and breach have been established it is then necessary for the plaintiff to show that the defendant's negligence in injuring or endangering the victim actually caused the nervous shock. Expert evidence is usually called in order to enable the court to answer the causal question. This has led to the fear that if recovery for nervous shock was allowed in any but the most direct and clear cases, evidentiary difficulties would add greatly to the length and expense of trials. Some judges have expressed confidence in the ability of courts to cope with such complex questions. But the real loser here may be the plaintiff who might well find this complex question decided against him.

(d) It is sometimes argued[55] that because changes in the rules governing liability for road and industrial accidents will have an effect on large sections of the population via the medium of insurance premiums, any changes in the law should be made by Parliament after extensive research and wide consultation. This is a difficult argument to assess since almost every judicial decision has an impact beyond the immediate parties and there seems to be no particular pattern in the way the courts react to the argument.

(e) It is often argued that an extensive liability for nervous shock would be unfair to defendants because it would impose upon them a burden of damages out of proportion to the negligence complained of. This argument is part of a more general objection to the fault system. Under the rules about damages, once a defendant has been proved to be negligent he is liable for all the damage the act of negligence inflicted on the plaintiff, provided it is not too remote, however large that damage may be and however slight and insignificant or morally forgivable the defendant's carelessness might have been. If damages awarded are not proportioned to fault, how can they be said to be based on fault? The difficulty with using this argument in relation to one particular area of liability is that unless

55 e.g. as it was by Lord Scarman in *McLoughlin* v. *O'Brian* [1983] 1 A.C. 410. But the majority did not accept this argument.

we are prepared to abandon the '100 per cent principle' entirely and in some way make liability proportional to fault, there is little reason to deny a plaintiff recovery for any particular item of damage since any head of damage is liable to produce disproportion between fault and liability. This argument, therefore, gives no reason to deny or limit recovery for nervous shock rather than for any other head of damage.

(f) Another argument is that a limitation on liability for shock is needed because shock by its nature is capable of affecting a large number of people. Because shock operates through the mind, it is able to afflict people who are beyond the range of any physical effect of an act of negligence. Not only may a person who is present at the scene of an accident suffer shock, but so might a person who comes upon the scene some time later or who reads about it in a newspaper or perhaps sees it on television. Thus the range of potential victims of shock is much greater than the range of potential victims of physical injury. But why should this require a limitation of liability? Partly for reasons we have already considered—the floodgates argument and the desire not to burden defendants unfairly. But also, perhaps, there is a feeling that a line has to be drawn somewhere. There are some unpleasant things in life, including a certain amount of mental distress, which are just incidents of living and which sufferers have to bear as best they can. The law is only one technique for coping with and ameliorating the effects of life's adversities, and people should be discouraged from using it when some other way of coping would be just as good or better.

(g) In *Bourhill* v. *Young* Lords Wright and Porter[56] indicated that one reason why the plaintiff in that case should not recover was that, being pregnant, she was hypersensitive to nervous shock and that the defendant could not be expected to foresee that she would suffer shock which the normal person[57] would not. In that case the plaintiff heard a collision between a motor cycle and a car and suffered shock and a miscarriage when she saw the aftermath of the accident. She did not see the collision itself and at the time it occurred she was behind a tram and outside the range of physical injury. This aspect of *Bourhill* v. *Young* is out of step with *Dulieu* v. *White*[58] in which Kennedy J. held that the defendant could not avoid liability for nervous shock by pointing to the plaintiff's pregnancy—he had to take his victim as he found her. Similar is *Dooley* v. *Cammell Laird Ltd*[59] in which a crane driver suffered shock from fear for his colleagues' safety when a load fell off a crane he was driving. In deciding that the defendant ought to be liable Donovan J. ignored the fact that the shock had allegedly aggravated a pre-existing condition.

In *Mt Isa Mines* v. *Pusey* Windeyer J. made some *obiter* comments about hypersensitivity.[60] He thought that any principle denying a duty to avoid nervous shock to the abnormal plaintiff was undesirable for the

56 [1943] A.C. 92, 110 and 117 respectively.
57 J. Havard (1956) 19 *M.L.R.* 478, 482.
58 [1901] 2 K.B. 669.
59 [1951] 1 Lloyd's Rep. 271.
60 (1971) 125 C.L.R. 383, 406.

reason, first, that it is very difficult to draw a line between the mentally normal and the mentally abnormal because our concept of mental normality is rather unclear; and secondly, because a finding of no duty would be difficult to reconcile with the principle that the defendant must take his victim as he finds him. Regarding the second reason, in *Levi* v. *Colgate-Palmolive*[61] the two principles were reconciled by saying that although the defendant was under no duty to take special precautions to protect the abnormal, if an abnormal plaintiff suffered loss in circumstances in which a normal plaintiff would also have suffered loss, the fact that the abnormal plaintiff suffered more loss than the normal plaintiff would not prevent him recovering for all his loss. This argument has been applied to nervous shock[62] as well as to physical damage (as in *Levi*). So the law seems to be that if no normal person would have suffered any shock at all as a result of the defendant's negligence, then an abnormal plaintiff cannot recover for any of his shock; but if a normal person would have suffered some shock, an abnormal plaintiff can recover for all his shock, even if this is greater than the normal person would have suffered.

2. Principles of Recovery

First, a plaintiff can recover from a defendant for nervous shock resulting from physical injury to himself caused by the defendant's negligence. This statement follows from the wider principle that if a person suffers an actionable loss (such as personal injury or property damage), he can also recover damages for other losses which are a consequence of the initial loss. It also follows from the wider principle that a person may recover for psychological or mental injury which is a consequence of some other actionable loss even if the former does not satisfy the definition of nervous shock, but can only be described as 'vexation', 'worry', 'anxiety', 'distress' or 'inconvenience'.[63] In *Victorian Railways Commissioners* v. *Coultas*[64] the Privy Council held that a plaintiff could recover for nervous shock *only* if he also suffered physical injury. This decision was not well received in Australia. There are legislative provisions in several Australian jurisdictions which provide, in effect, that a plaintiff shall not be debarred from recovering damages merely because the injury complained of arose wholly or in part from mental or nervous shock.[65]

Secondly, a plaintiff can recover for nervous shock resulting from reasonable (and hence foreseeable) fear, generated by another's tortious

61 (1941) 41 S.R. (N.S.W.) 48.

62 *Beavis* v. *Apthorpe* (1964) 80 W.N. (N.S.W.) 852, 857 *per* Herron C.J.; cf. *Brice* v. *Brown* [1984] 1 All E.R. 997; *Jaensch* v. *Coffey* (1984) 155 C.L.R. 547, 556 *per* Gibbs C.J.; cf. Brennan J. at 568 (unless the defendant knew of the plaintiff's hypersensitivity).

63 *Brickhill* v. *Cooke* [1984] 3 N.S.W.L.R. 396; *Campbelltown C.C.* v. *Mackay* (1988) 15 N.S.W.L.R. 501; *Clarke* v. *Shire of Gisborne* [1984] V.R. 971, 997 (but note strictures in respect of 'inconvenience').

64 (1888) 13 App. Cas. 222.

65 Wrongs Act 1958 (Vic.), s.23; Law Reform (Miscellaneous Provisions) Act 1944 (N.S.W.), s.31(1); Wrongs Act 1936 (S.A.), s.28(1); Law Reform (Miscellaneous Provisions) Act 1955 (A.C.T.), s.23(1).

conduct, of physical injury or death to himself;[66] and, perhaps, for psychiatric illness resulting from exposure to circumstances to which the plaintiff would not have been exposed but for the defendant's tort.[67] Thirdly, a plaintiff can, in certain circumstances, recover for nervous shock resulting from reasonable fear, generated by another's tortious conduct, for the personal safety of another.[68] The person who suffers shock may recover even though he was in no physical danger himself and was not in the area of possible physical impact. But there would probably be no recovery unless the plaintiff's fear was generated by what the plaintiff saw or heard. This point will be discussed below. It is not necessary that the plaintiff be a close relative of the endangered person.[69] Nor is it necessary that someone actually was injured or put in peril: it is enough if the plaintiff suffered shock through reasonable fear for another's safety even if that fear was in fact groundless.

Suppose that the plaintiff's nervous shock arises not out of fear for the safety of another *person* but out of apprehension that property is in danger of being damaged, destroyed or lost. As we will see, damages can be recovered for nervous shock which results from witnessing damage to one's property, and there would seem no reason of principle why recovery should not extend to shock caused by apprehension of such damage. Of course, the plaintiff would have to prove that any shock suffered *was* a result of fear for the safety of property, and that such shock was foreseeable. Unless the plaintiff had a very significant interest in the property and unless the property was of a substantial nature, this might be very difficult to do.

The fifth principle of liability is that a plaintiff can, in certain circumstances, recover from a defendant for nervous shock caused by witnessing an accident or the aftermath of an accident in which another[70] was killed or injured[71] and which was caused by the defendant's tortious act. A number of issues arise here.

(a) It is clear that the plaintiff need not himself have been in any physical danger.[72]

(b) The plaintiff need not have been related to the injured person.[73] The general principle is that the closer the ties of love and affection between the plaintiff and the victim the stronger will be the plaintiff's

---

66 *Dulieu* v. *White* [1901] 2 K.B. 669; cf. *Stevenson* v. *Basham* [1922] N.Z.L.R. 225. But the fear itself is not compensatable: *Hicks* v. *Chief Constable of South Yorkshire* [1992] 2 All E.R. 65. The risk of injury or death must not be too hypothetical: *Wilks* v. *Haines* [1991] Aust. Torts Rep. 81-078.

67 *Gillespie* v. *Commonwealth of Australia* (1991) 104 A.C.T.R. 1.

68 *Hambrook* v. *Stokes* [1925] 1 K.B. 141. Contrast *King* v. *Phillips* [1953] 1 Q.B. 429; but this decision is generally regarded to be incorrect: *Alcock* v. *Chief Constable of South Yorkshire* [1992] 1 A.C. 310, 412 *per* Lord Oliver. *Query* including the defendant himself? See Trindade [1986] *C.L.J.* 476, 481-2; *Alcock* [1992] 1 A.C. 310, 401 *per* Lord Ackner; 418 *per* Lord Oliver. See also *Bunyan* v. *Jordan* (1936-7) 57 C.L.R. 1.

69 *Dooley* v. *Cammell Laird & Co. Ltd* [1951] 1 Lloyd's Rep. 271.

70 *Query*, including the defendant?

71 *Jaensch* v. *Coffey* (1983-4) 155 C.L.R. 549.

72 *Mt Isa Mines* v. *Pusey* (1971) 125 C.L.R. 383; *Jaensch* v. *Coffey* (1983-4) 155 C.L.R. 549.

73 e.g. *Mt Isa Mines* v. *Pusey* (1971) 125 C.L.R. 383.

case, but that in every case it is a question of whether the defendant ought to have foreseen that the plaintiff might suffer shock.[74] This might depend, for example, on the extent to which the plaintiff was involved in the distressing events and how shocking the events were. In *Chadwick* v. *British Transport Commission*[75] the plaintiff suffered shock as a result of rendering aid to the victims of a rail crash. One explanation of this case is that the courts are keen to protect rescuers.[76]

(c) If the plaintiff sees the aftermath of an accident, how soon afterwards must he see it? In both *Benson* v. *Lee*[77] and *Jaensch* v. *Coffey* the plaintiff recovered, having seen the aftermath within a couple of hours of the accident. But in *Alcock* v. *Chief Constable of South Yorkshire* Lord Ackner regarded a gap of eight hours between accident and seeing a corpse in a mortuary as too long to permit recovery.[78] Where is the line to be drawn? Certainly, if the plaintiff has time to 'prepare' himself, whether for the exact scene he is to see, or for 'the worst' if he does not know exactly what he will meet, then the courts are unlikely to allow recovery.

(d) What exactly is 'the aftermath?[79] In *Benson* v. *Lee* the mother actually saw her son lying on the road and accompanied him to hospital. In *McLoughlin* v. *O'Brian* the mother saw her family at the hospital in much the same state they had been in immediately after the accident. In *Pusey* the impact of seeing the workman 'just burnt up', as the plaintiff put it, was no doubt extremely traumatic. But suppose a parent sees his child cleaned and bandaged and lying sedately in a hospital bed? Probably the courts would want to draw the line somewhere and require that the scene be of a certain level of gruesomeness if shock is to be held foreseeable. It is also clear that mental illness suffered as a result of caring over a long period for a person disabled by negligence would not be compensatable.[80] In the words of Brennan J., injury to the psyche will be actionable only if it is the result of 'sudden sensory perception'.[81] An important result of these limitations is that nervous shock is unlikely to be recoverable in cases where a person is disabled by a negligently caused illness as opposed to a traumatic accident.[82]

---

74 *Alcock* v. *Chief Constable of South Yorkshire* [1992] 1 A.C. 310; H. Teff (1983) 99 L.Q.R. 100; *Jaensch* v. *Coffey* (1983-4) 155 C.L.R. 549, 569-70 *per* Brennan J.; 605, 610-11 *per* Deane J.

75 [1967] 2 All E.R. 945.

76 *McLoughlin* v. *O'Brian* [1983] A.C. 410, 419 *per* Lord Wilberforce.

77 [1972] V.R. 879.

78 [1992] 1 A.C. 310, 405. Cf. *Pratt* v. *Pratt* [1975] V.R. 378; see also *Jaensch* v. *Coffey* (1983-4) 155 C.L.R. 549, 570-1 *per* Brennan J.; 606-7 *per* Deane J.

79 *Jaensch* v. *Coffey* (1983-4) 155 C.L.R. 549, 607-8 *per* Deane J.

80 *Jaensch* v. *Coffey* (1983-4) 155 C.L.R. 549, 565 *per* Brennan J.; 606 *per* Deane J; *Spence* v. *Percy* [1991] Aust. Torts Rep. 81-116.

81 *Jaensch* v. *Coffey* (1983-4) 155 C.L.R. 549, 567. Cf. *Alcock* [1992] 1 A.C. 310, 400 *per* Lord Ackner.

82 But see *Gillespie* v. *Commonwealth of Australia* (1991) 104 A.C.T.R. 1. For a discussion of the 'accident preference' in tort law see J. Stapleton *Disease and the Compensation Debate* (Oxford, 1986) esp. Ch. 1.

(e) Must the plaintiff witness the accident or its aftermath with his own unaided senses, either sight or hearing? This raises two issues: first, what if the plaintiff suffers shock solely as a result of having been told of the accident?[83] Suppose he reads about it in a newspaper or is told by a friend? In *Pusey* Windeyer J. said that if the *sole* cause of the shock was being told about an accident, damages could not be recovered against the person who caused the event which the plaintiff has been told about.[84] But not all the cases support this *dictum*. In *Schneider* v. *Eisovitch*[85] both husband and wife were injured in an accident due to the defendant's negligence. The wife was rendered unconscious and only learnt later in hospital that her husband had been killed. Paull J. held that the plaintiff wife could recover not only for nervous shock resulting from her injuries but also for shock resulting from being told of the accident, because the defendant owed her a duty not to cause her physical injury, and she could add the nervous shock caused by the bad news on to the consequences of that breach of duty. This case has been applied in at least two Australian decisions.[86] These decisions are open to objection on technical grounds because it is clear that in order to be liable for nervous shock the defendant must owe the plaintiff a duty not to cause him *nervous shock* rather than a duty not to cause him physical damage. This is sometimes put by saying that the plaintiff cannot recover damages for nervous shock which is merely parasitic on some other injury suffered and recoverable by him. One thing seems clear: the requirement, if it be such,[87] that the plaintiff must have witnessed the accident or its aftermath personally cannot be justified solely in terms of foreseeability as that term is understood and applied in the law.

A second issue is this: suppose the plaintiff witnesses the accident or its aftermath on television. This possibility opens up the prospect of a very large number of potential plaintiffs and of people suffering shock as a result of watching replays of the harrowing events some considerable time after those events took place. The only direct authority on this point suggests that if what was seen on television was at least as distressing as what would have been witnessed by a person within natural sight or hearing of the accident or its aftermath, then the fact that the scene was mediated through television would not necessarily bar recovery.[88]

---

83 There is no problem if shock caused by being told of events adds to shock caused by observation: *Jaensch* v. *Coffey*.

84 (1971) 125 C.L.R. 383, 407; cf. *Jaensch* v. *Coffey* (1983-4) 155 C.L.R. 549, 567 *per* Brennan J; *Alcock* [1992] 1 A.C. 310, 398 *per* Lord Keith; 400-1 *per* Lord Ackner.

85 [1960] 2 Q.B. 430.

86 *Andrews* v. *Williams* [1967] V.R. 831; *Tsanaktsidis* v. *Oulianoff* (1980) 24 S.A.S.R. 500.

87 The requirement has been much criticized: e.g. Deane J. in *Jaensch* v. *Coffey* (1983-4) 155 C.L.R. 549, 608-9 and this dictum was applied by Kneipp J. in *Petrie* v. *Dowling* [1992] 1 Qd.R. 284. It is often suggested that provided the person suffering shock was in a close emotional relationship with the person injured, it should not matter how the shock was suffered.

88 *Alcock* [1992] 1 A.C. 310.

(f) Finally, what if the incident witnessed involves damage to property rather than injury to a person? As a general rule, if a plaintiff can sue in respect of property damage, then he will also be entitled to recover for injury consequential upon the property damage. This can explain *Attia* v. *British Gas*[89] in which it was held, as a preliminary point of law, that there could be liability for shock suffered as a result of witnessing a fire which damaged the plaintiff's house. More difficult are cases in which the person who suffers the shock could not sue in respect of the property damage. This seems to have been the case in *Owens* v. *Liverpool Corporation*[90] in which a tramcar collided with a hearse damaging the vehicle and causing the coffin inside to be overturned. Mourners in the funeral procession, relatives of the deceased, suffered nervous shock for which they were awarded damages. The things damaged in both of these cases were the sort of things to which most people attach great emotional significance. The more insignificant the property damaged or destroyed, the less likely it is that a court would hold that any shock suffered as a result of the damage or destruction was foreseeable.

The final principle of recovery concerns the liability of people who convey bad news. If the bearer of bad tidings acts with the intention of causing the plaintiff harm and distress the plaintiff can recover.[91] But there may also be liability for foreseeable shock caused by the *negligent* making of statements, whether true[92] or false.[93] So the negligence might consist in lack of reasonable care as to the truth of the statement or lack of care in making the statement even if true. Usually, no doubt, the media could not be sued for reporting bad news, provided they reasonably believed it to be true. But one can imagine situations where the media might convey bad news before it has been broken to relatives more gently, and it might be thought that the media should be under a legal duty to stay quiet until relatives have been informed.

It follows from the fact that a person may be liable for shock caused by a true statement that, although a person who suffers shock just as a result of being told of an accident or harrowing event, and without personally witnessing the accident or event, cannot recover for nervous shock from a person whose tort caused the accident or event, the sufferer of the shock may be able to sue the teller of the tale, even if the tale is true.

3. THE ROLE OF FORESEEABILITY IN RECOVERY FOR NERVOUS SHOCK

There are cases in which liability for nervous shock seems to have been imposed just on the ground that the nervous shock was foreseeable; but on

89 [1988] Q.B. 304.

90 [1939] 1 K.B. 394. But this decision has been disapproved: *Alcock* [1992] 1 A.C. 310, 412 *per* Lord Oliver.

91 *Janvier* v. *Sweeney* [1919] 2 K.B. 316; *Blakeney* v. *Pegus* (1885) 6 L.R.(N.S.W.) 223.

92 *Furniss* v. *Fitchett* [1958] N.Z.L.R. 396.

93 *Barnes* v. *Commonwealth* (1937) 37 S.R.(N.S.W.) 511; *Wilkinson* v. *Downton* [1897] 2 Q.B. 57.

analysis these appear to be cases in which none of the policy factors which support limiting liability for nervous shock was operative. In cases where one or more of these factors is seen to be operative, some qualification on the notion of foreseeability is likely to be introduced. One view, espoused for example by Brennan J. in *Jaensch* v. *Coffey*,[94] is that foreseeability is the sole test of liability for nervous shock, and that any desired limits on the scope of liability can be taken into account in applying the principles of foreseeability. On the other hand, there clearly are limitations on liability for nervous shock, such as the aftermath doctrine, which it is difficult to explain in terms solely of foreseeability.[95] The most common view appears to be that the scope of liability for nervous shock needs to be more limited than application of the foreseeability test alone would achieve; and such limitations can be seen as based directly on considerations of policy,[96] or as being part of the definition of 'proximity' as a requirement of the existence of a duty of care.[97]

4. STATUTORY PROVISIONS

In New South Wales and the Australian Capital Territory there are statutory provisions relating to recovery for nervous shock.[98] Under these provisions: (i) a parent (broadly defined) or husband or wife of a person killed, injured or put in peril by the defendant's (wrongful)[99] act, neglect or default may recover damages for nervous shock arising out of the accident regardless of whether it occurred within the sight or hearing of the person suffering the shock; (ii) other members of the family (broadly defined) of the victim may recover for nervous shock if the accident occurred within the sight or hearing of that member of the family.

The following points should be made about these provisions. First, they extend the common law in that it is not necessary for the plaintiff to show that shock to him was foreseeable. All he has to prove is that the defendant caused the accident and, under (ii), that the accident occurred in his sight and hearing; and, in both cases, that his shock resulted from the accident.[100] Secondly, under the Compensation to Relatives Act 1897 (N.S.W.) (and equivalent provisions in other jurisdictions) a relative of a dead person on whom the relative was financially dependent and who was killed by the wrongful act of the defendant can recover damages for loss of financial support. The cause of action under the provisions being currently

94 (1983-4) 155 C.L.R. 549.

95 See *Jaensch* v. *Coffey* (1983-4) 155 C.L.R. 549, 554-5 *per* Gibbs C.J.; 591-3 *per* Deane J.; 612 *per* Dawson J.

96 This was the approach of Lord Wilberforce in *McLoughlin* v. *O'Brian*.

97 As *per* Deane J. in *Jaensch* v. *Coffey* (1983-4) 155 C.L.R. 549, 592-3, 603.

98 Law Reform (Miscellaneous Provisions) Act 1944 (N.S.W.), s.4 as amended by Law Reform (Miscellaneous Provisions) (De Facto Relationships) Amendment Act 1984; Law Reform (Miscellaneous Provisions) Act 1955 (A.C.T.), s.24.

99 The provision does not contain this word but it has been held, obviously enough, that it must be read in.

100 *Anderson* v. *Liddy* (1949) 49 S.R. (N.S.W.) 320, 323 *per* Jordan C.J.; *Armytage* v. *Commissioner for Government Transport* [1972] 1 N.S.W.L.R. 331.

considered is additional to and quite distinct from that under the Compensation to Relatives Act.[101] Thirdly, damages for ordinary grief and anguish are not recoverable under the provisions.[102] Fourthly, the provisions do not apply where the person killed, injured or put in peril has inflicted injury or peril on himself.[103]

Fifthly, the cause of action of the relative under the provisions is separate from and independent of that of the injured person. So it is not necessary that the victim be able to sue the defendant. It is sufficient that the defendant's act was in some sense wrongful. For example, even if the victim could not recover from the defendant because he had accepted the risk, this would not stop the relative recovering if the defendant had acted negligently. The same is true of an action for nervous shock at common law.[104]

Finally, it is not clear whether the effect of the provision is to bar recovery for nervous shock by a person who is not related to the victim in the way required by the provision.[105] The likely position is that persons falling within the terms of the provision may recover even if they cannot prove that nervous shock to them was foreseeable, whereas persons not falling within the provision must satisfy all the common law requirements for recovery. However, this last statement must be qualified in relation to road and work accidents which, in New South Wales, are covered by restrictive provisions which confine liability for 'psychological or psychiatric injury' to certain categories of claimant.[106] There is also a restrictive provision dealing with motor accident cases in South Australia.[107]

VI: ECONOMIC LOSS

Economic loss[108] comes in a variety of forms: loss of wages; loss of profits; loss of an expected legacy by a beneficiary under a will; expenses incurred as a result of the defendant's act of negligence, such as hospital expenses; and so on. The law has not found any difficulty in compensating for negligently caused economic loss which is the immediate consequence of

---

101 *Anderson* v. *Liddy* (1949) 49 S.R.(N.S.W.) 320.

102 *Macpherson* v. *Commissioner for Government Transport* (1959) 76 W.N.(N.S.W.) 352.

103 *Ball* v. *Winslett* [1958] S.R.(N.S.W.) 149.

104 *Scala* v. *Mammolitti* (1965) 114 C.L.R. 153, 159 *per* Taylor J. For the common law position see *Chester* v. *Waverley Corporation* (1939) 62 C.L.R. 1, 21 *per* Evatt J. In South Australia a relative may recover both damages for shock under Wrongs Act 1939 (S.A.), s.28 and as a *solatium* under Wrongs Act 1936 (S.A.), ss.23a and b.

105 See *Mt Isa Mines* v. *Pusey* (1971) 125 C.L.R. 383, 408 *per* Windeyer J.

106 Motor Accidents Act 1988 s.77; Workers Compensation Act 1987 s.151P.

107 Wrongs Act 1936 s.35a(1)(c).

108 The literature on this topic is very large. The earliest important English article is P.S. Atiyah (1967) 83 L.Q.R. 248. In Cane *Tort Law and Economic Interests* (Oxford, 1991) this topic is dealt with in a very different way from the approach taken here. Readers referring to the book should be alert to relevant differences between the English and Australian law.

personal injury or property damage.[109] For example, in cases of serious personal injury, loss of wages and medical and hospital expenses are usually the largest items of loss for which damages are awarded. Again, the cost of repair is often the appropriate measure of damages in a case involving negligent damage to a chattel. The difficulties in this area have been felt to lie in compensating for economic loss which is not the result of physical damage, often called purely (or, less grammatically, pure) economic loss. Such loss can consist of loss arising from injury to or the death of another person. Actions for loss of services and consortium and for loss of support (or dependency) fall into this category. Such actions are usually dealt with in the context of the assessment of damages, and this purely conventional arrangement is adopted in this book. Such actions are limited exceptions to general rules denying recovery for loss arising out of injury to or the death of another; because the class of persons at whose suit such action will lie is limited and clearly defined, the policy arguments against allowing recovery for economic loss which will soon be considered are not relevant to them.

Secondly, purely economic loss can consist of loss arising out of damage to the property of a third party. *Caltex Oil (Australia) Pty Ltd* v. *Dredge 'Willemstad'*[110] provides an example. Oil products belonging to Caltex were carried in an underwater pipeline from a refinery owned and operated by Australian Oil Refining (A.O.R.) to a terminal belonging to Caltex. The pipeline, which was owned by A.O.R., was damaged by the dredge as a result of negligent navigation and the use of an inaccurate map. A small quantity of oil products belonging to Caltex was lost and Caltex had to arrange alternative means of transport for its products while the pipeline was out of operation. Caltex made no claim in respect of its lost products but did claim for its extra transport costs resulting from the damage to A.O.R.'s pipeline. Similar are cases in which gas pipes or telephone or electricity cables belonging to the utility supplier are damaged, thus cutting off an essential service and causing loss of production or other economic loss to a customer of the supplier.

Thirdly, purely economic loss can be suffered even where no damage is done to any person or property. For example, suppose that an auditor negligently certifies that a company is in a sound financial position, and as a result of reliance on that certificate a person buys shares in the company for more than they are worth.[111] Or suppose that the supply of gas, electricity or water to a factory is cut off (but without damage to the medium of supply), with the result that the factory is put out of operation for a period causing loss of production, and hence profits. Again, suppose that a person buys a defective building or product but discovers the defect before it causes physical damage to the building or product itself, or to

---

109 Negligence is by no means the only tort in which economic loss is recoverable. But here our attention is restricted to that tort.

110 (1976) 136 C.L.R. 529.

111 See *Scott Group Ltd* v. *McFarlane* [1978] 1 N.Z.L.R. 553; *Caparo Industries p.l.c.* v. *Dickman* [1990] A.C. 605

any person or other property. The cost of repair would be purely economic loss.[112]

1. Policy Arguments for Limiting Recovery

As in the case of nervous shock, the courts have not been willing to compensate as freely for purely economic loss as for physical damage. A number of reasons have been suggested. It should be noted, however, that not all of these arguments are (equally) relevant to all cases of economic loss.

(a) The floodgates argument.[113]

(b) In the scheme of values of most people, financial interests would rank rather lower than the interest in personal health and safety. If the world were a place of unlimited resources then we could afford to compensate everyone for all losses suffered (and not only as a result of negligence). But since resources are limited, money spent on compensation is that much money not available for some other purpose. Personal health and safety is so important that usually we are prepared to compensate for personal injury even if this means money is not available for other valued enterprises. But we are less prepared to compensate for economic loss.

(c) Insurance sometimes plays a role in arguments against imposing liability for economic loss, although Stephen J. in *Caltex* denied its relevance.[114] A distinction can be drawn between liability insurance and loss insurance.[115] A liability insurance policy covers the insured's legal liability to third parties, for example, in negligence. The most common example is a third-party motor vehicle policy. A loss insurance policy (or 'first-party' policy) covers loss suffered personally by the insured. Householders' fire and contents insurance, travel insurance and private health insurance are common examples. One argument against shifting at least some negligently caused economic losses from the plaintiff to the defendant is that the risk of economic losses is much more often and easily spread widely by loss insurance or other means than is the risk of physical injury.[116] Take, for example, profits lost by a company as a result of being shut down during a power failure. One of the arguments used by Lord Denning M.R. in *Spartan Steel* v. *Martin* against recovery for such loss was that power failures of relatively short duration are a common occurrence, the costs of which industries could easily absorb in a variety of ways—by installing a stand-by generator or by insurance against loss of profits.[117] The cost of such measures could then be spread very widely by being added to the price of the industry's goods or services. In the case of insurance, the burden of loss of profits would first be spread among all

---

112 *Sutherland S.C.* v. *Heyman* (1984-5) 157 C.L.R. 424, 504-5 *per* Deane J.; *D. & F. Estates Ltd* v. *Church Commissioners* [1989] A.C. 177.

113 See p. 340 above.

114 (1976) 136 C.L.R. 529, 580-1.

115 See further *Atiyah's Accidents* Ch. 10.

116 Atiyah (1967) 83 *L.Q.R.* 248, 270-3.

117 [1973] Q.B. 27, 38; cf. *Lamb* v. *Camden L.B.C.* [1981] Q.B. 625, 637-8.

policy holders, and then much more widely among all their customers if they pass on the costs of their premiums in the prices of their goods and services.

There is a related point which is particularly relevant to cases in which a large number of people suffer relatively small amounts of economic loss as a result, for example, of damage to infrastructure such as bridges. Compensating people (for economic loss) costs money: lawyers' fees, court costs, insurers' administrative costs and so on. If the result of allowing recovery were that a large number of small claims were made against a defendant who, by insurance or some other means, could spread the cost of liability among a large group of people, then very little might be achieved in the end, especially if there was a significant overlap between the class of claimants and the class among whom the losses were ultimately spread. A large amount of money would have been spent on shifting losses to a party who was then able to pass them on to a different group of people. It might well be cheaper in the long run for individuals simply to absorb losses of the type in question or to take out insurance against them. This sort of argument rests on two very important points: first, that the administrative cost of making tort claims should be taken into account in determining whether such claims ought to be allowed; and secondly, that we need to consider who, in the end, actually pays the damages before we can assess the desirability of awarding them.

But it is important to note that arguments such as these involve rejection of the idea that it is important and desirable that persons who cause loss by their negligence should compensate the sufferers of the loss (this is an aspect of the 'fault principle'). In other words, such arguments rest on the assertion that it is more important that losses be spread widely than that those who cause them by their negligence should be held responsible for them. This assertion, in turn, rests partly on a realization that if, as is often the case, the person who caused the loss can spread it by means of liability insurance, then being held liable may give that person very little incentive to take more care in the future. If this is so, little may be achieved by shifting the loss to that person.

(d) Just as in the area of nervous shock, an argument against extension of liability for economic loss is sometimes based on disproportion between the defendant's fault and the losses he is expected to bear. This argument rests on an assertion of the relative unimportance of economic losses and, as we saw in the context of nervous shock, on a more general criticism of the fault system. By contrast, in *Caltex* Stephen J.[118] thought it an argument against the alleged rule[119] that economic loss was recoverable only if it was the immediate consequence of physical damage, that it was 'quite unresponsive to the grossness of the wrongdoer's want of care in its exclusion of non-consequential economic loss'. The fact is that there is no yardstick by which we can measure whether damages awarded are proportional to fault; the best we can do is to assert, as did Stephen J. in

118 (1976) 136 C.L.R. 529, 568.
119 *Spartan Steel* v. *Martin* [1973] Q.B. 27.

Caltex, that community morality supports the rule we personally favour.[120]

(e) One of the most widely used arguments against recovery for purely economic loss is that by its nature it can spread widely, being subject to no physical limitations, and so the defendant's liability for it could be, in the now famous words of an American judge, 'in an indeterminate amount for an indeterminate time to an indeterminate class'.[121] If liability for purely economic loss were limited only by the test of foreseeability of purely economic loss, the defendant might be burdened not only with a very heavy liability but also one the extent of which it would be impossible to determine in advance with any degree of confidence. Suppose that, as a result of the negligent navigation of its master, a ship collides with a bridge which divides the business district from the residential area of a city and puts it out of action. A very large and unidentifiable class of businesses and workers may suffer economic loss in the form of lost wages and profits as a result of the accident. The defendant would have no way of calculating with any degree of accuracy, in advance of claims, how many plaintiffs there might be or the likely size of their claims. Suppose, again, that a newspaper negligently publishes a falsely optimistic report about the financial position of a company. As a result readers invest in the company and lose money. The size of the class of injured investors would be very difficult to calculate as would the sum of their losses. Further, different investors may well invest at different times and suffer loss at different times, so that it would be difficult for the defendant to be sure at any particular time that the last possible claim had been made. And yet in neither of these examples could it be said that the losses suffered by the victim were of an unforeseeable type.

But not only may economic loss spread widely, it may also have a 'snowballing' effect in the affairs of individual plaintiffs. A significant loss on the stockmarket may force the investor's family to lower its standard of living, it may cause loss to the investor's creditors whom he cannot pay in full; this may in turn lead to hardship for the creditor's family and creditors. In a complex chain of economic relations, weakness in one link can lead to disaster at other points along the chain. But the extent of such consequential loss would be very difficult to assess in advance of claims. Once again, however, it seems that such further losses would be foreseeable in the very broad sense in which that word is used in the law of negligence.

The basis of this concern with the potential indeterminacy of the loss is the judgment that a defendant is entitled to have a reasonable idea, in advance, of his likely liabilities so that he can plan his affairs accordingly and, if he wishes, insure against his liabilities. Liabilities are harder and more expensive to insure against the more uncertain they are. Of course, liability for personal injury may also be indeterminate: for example, a defendant will never know in advance whether his victim will be a high or low earner and so be entitled to a large or small amount of damages for lost earnings; and it will be impossible in some cases for a defendant to

---

120 (1976) 136 C.L.R. 529, 575.

121 *Ultramares Corporation* v. *Touche* (1931) 174 N.E. 441, 444 *per* Cardozo C.J.

predict in advance how many claims he may be faced with—liability for the effects of marketing an unsafe drug, or for colliding with an offshore oil-drilling platform provide examples. But uncertainty in this context worries us less because of the high value we put on personal safety.

(f) It is not infrequently said that compensating for economic loss is more properly the function of the law of contract than of the law of tort. What this argument seems to mean is that if the plaintiff could have protected himself from economic loss by entering into a suitable contract with someone then he should not be allowed to use the law of tort to recover for that economic loss.[122]

2. THE RANGE OF PLAINTIFFS

How has the law sought to limit liability for economic loss so as to meet arguments based on the potential size or indeterminacy of such liability? In general terms the law requires the plaintiff to show not just that the defendant ought to have foreseen that he would suffer economic loss, but that there existed between himself and the defendant a *special relationship* on the basis of which the defendant ought to have had him particularly in mind as likely to suffer economic loss. In other words, in this context, the requirement of proximity is *not* satisfied by ordinary reasonable foreseeability. A useful distinction can be drawn between special relationships which are continuing and special relationships which are *ad hoc*. The typical example of a continuing relationship is that between a professional, such as a solicitor, and his client. *Ad hoc* special relationships are relationships which arise out of isolated transactions or events. *Hedley Byrne & Co. Ltd* v. *Heller & Partners Ltd*[123] provides an example. In that case the plaintiffs, who were advertising agents, sought, through their bank, advice from the defendant bank about the financial soundness of a company on whose behalf the plaintiff had bought advertising space and which was a customer of the defendant. The defendant reported favourably but disclaimed responsibility for the advice which turned out to be inaccurate and was held to be negligent. The House of Lords held that, but for the disclaimer, the defendant could have been held liable for its negligent advice.

(a) Ad hoc relationships

(i) *Statements*:[124] The risk of a large or indeterminate number of claims is particularly acute in the case of the written or spoken word. It may be

---

122 For discussions of this argument, which has assumed great importance in the English case law, see Cane *Tort Law and Economic Interests* (Oxford, 1991) pp. 326-52; J. Stapleton (1991) 107 *L.Q.R.* 249.

123 [1964] A.C. 465.

124 Statements or representations may be express or implied from conduct. But, for example, making and publishing a development plan does not imply any statement that the plan will be applied and followed: *San Sebastian Pty Ltd* v. *Minister Administering the Environmental Planning and Assessment Act 1979* (1986) 68 A.L.R. 161. As this case shows, whether particular acts are treated as entailing representations is as much a question of policy as of fact.

very difficult for the maker of the statement to control its dissemination and it may be unreasonable to expect him to foresee who (or how many people) will rely on it and for what purposes. In cases where the statement in question was made to the plaintiff personally and to him alone, the problem of unforeseeable reliance does not arise, but the problem of reliance for an unforeseeable purpose may. In cases where the statement on which the plaintiff has relied was made to a large audience, or where it was not made to the plaintiff personally but to someone who has subsequently disseminated it, both problems may arise. In *Hedley Byrne* Lord Reid said that since the defendant knew that the inquiry was being made in connection with an advertising contract and it was at least probable that the information was wanted by an advertising agency, a special relationship arose between the agency and the defendant.[125] These two requirements, of knowledge of the person likely to rely on the statement, and knowledge of the transaction in connection with which he will rely on it, were laid down in 1952 by Denning L.J. dissenting in *Candler* v. *Crane Christmas & Co.*[126] In this case the accountant of a company carelessly prepared accounts and, at the request of the company, showed them to and discussed them with a person whom he knew proposed to invest in the company. Within a year the company was wound up and the plaintiff investor lost the whole of his money. Denning L.J. said that an accountant owed a duty not only to his clients but also to any third person to whom he himself might show the accounts[127] or to whom he knew his employer would show the accounts.[128] The question is whether the defendant either himself showed the plaintiff the accounts or knew they would be shown to him. Further, in his Lordship's view, the duty of care extended to use of the accounts for any transaction for which the accountant knew they were required. In short, the duty is owed to the very person[129] and in respect of the very transaction the defendant knows about or (in accordance with general principles) ought to know about. Denning L.J. declined to say whether it would be sufficient for the accountant to know that his accounts would be relied upon by a 'specific' or 'ascertainable' class of persons in a transaction of a particular or quite narrowly defined type, but it now seems accepted that it would be.[130]

Although Denning L.J. dissented in *Candler*, his approach was preferred to that of the majority by the House of Lords in *Hedley Byrne* and, more recently, in *Caparo Industries* v. *Dickman*;[131] and the principles which his Lordship enunciated have been applied in a number of other

125 [1964] A.C. 465, 482.
126 [1951] 2 K.B. 164.
127 cf. *Diamond Manufacturing Co. Ltd* v. *Hamilton* [1968] N.Z.L.R. 705.
128 [1951] 2 K.B. 164, 180-4.
129 But it is not necessary that the defendant knew of the plaintiff by name.
130 cf. *B.T. Australia Ltd* v. *Raine & Horne Pty Ltd* [1983] 3 N.S.W.L.R. 221, 234-5; the judgments in *Caparo* v. *Dickman* [1990] 2 A.C. 605 seem to support this view.
131 [1990] 2 A.C. 605.

cases.[132] These principles help to give content to the concept of 'proximity' in this context. The requirement of foreseeability as applied in cases of physical damage is very easily satisfied: it allows a defendant to be held liable to a person of whom he knew nothing in particular. By contrast, using Denning L.J.'s principles, a defendant is unlikely to be held liable for economic loss unless he had, or ought to have had, considerable knowledge of the plaintiff or persons like him.

The main difficulty in applying these principles is how to define 'specific' (classes of) persons and transactions. To some extent, this must depend on the facts of individual cases: for example, the maker of a statement is more likely to be held liable to the person(s) to whom it was made than to others. But it is inevitable that considerations of policy will enter here. Another way of putting this is to say that there may be insufficient proximity between the plaintiff and the defendant even if Denning L.J.'s stringent foreseeability requirements are met. Take the case of auditors: can the auditor of a company's accounts, who negligently certifies that the accounts accurately represent the company's financial position, be held liable (by virtue of being the company's auditor) to investors in the company, or only to the company itself and its current shareholders to whom the auditor is required by statute to report? In *Scott Group Ltd* v. *McFarlane*[133] it was held, by majority, that an auditor could owe a duty of care to a purchaser of a company who had relied to its detriment on false accounts; but in *Caparo* v. *Dickman* the House of Lords held that auditors could not be held liable to prospective purchasers of shares, whether or not they already owned shares. This difference of opinion is the result, partly at least, of different views about the proper scope of the responsibilities of auditors (and, technically, about the proper interpretation of the statutory provisions governing the duties of auditors). On one view, it is no part of the purpose of having auditors to protect prospective investors. Similarly, it has also been held that an auditor, by virtue of being an auditor, owes no duty of care to existing or prospective creditors of the company;[134] and that the directors of a company, by virtue of being directors, owe no duty of care to the company's creditors.[135] It does not follow from these decisions denying a duty of care that an auditor or director could never be held liable in negligence to a purchaser of shares or a creditor: liability might arise if, for example, the auditor or director had had dealings with the purchaser or creditor on the basis of which it would be reasonable to impose on the former a duty of care to the latter;[136] but the decisions do establish that auditors and directors owe no

132 *Haig* v. *Bamford* (1977) 72 D.L.R. (3d) 68; *JEB Fasteners Ltd* v. *Marks, Bloom & Co.* [1981] 3 All E.R. 289; *Scott Group Ltd* v. *McFarlane* [1978] 1 N.Z.L.R. 553 (auditors and prospective investors in or purchasers of company). But note that the reasoning in these last two cases was disapproved in *Caparo* v. *Dickman* [1990] 2 A.C. 605. See also *Punjab National Bank* v. *De Boinville* [1992] 1 Lloyd's Rep. 7.

133 [1978] N.Z.L.R. 553.

134 *Al Saudi Banque* v. *Clarke Pixley* [1990] Ch. 313.

135 *Kuwait Asia Bank E.C.* v. *National Mutual Life Nominees Ltd* [1991] 1 A.C. 187.

136 *Morgan Crucible Co. p.l.c.* v. *Hill Samuel & Co. Ltd* [1991] Ch. 295.

such duty merely by virtue of being and acting in their capacities as auditors or directors.

By contrast, it was held in *Smith* v. *Bush*[137] that a property valuer employed by a mortgagee may owe a duty of care to the mortgagor even though the valuer had had no direct dealings with the mortgagor; in that case the mortgagor had, in effect, paid for the valuation, and it was well known that the vast majority of purchasers of less expensive houses relied upon the mortgagee's valuation and did not commission an independent survey.[138] Moreover, the valuer was held liable despite the fact that it had expressly attempted to exclude liability to the mortgagor. Considerations of social policy played a very important role in justifying this decision, which shows that the court will ultimately decide for what purposes it thinks people ought to be able to rely on particular statements.

This concept of purpose is a central one because it can be used to control indeterminacy in the class of prospective plaintiffs[139] as well as indeterminacy in the use to which statements might be put.[140] Does the concept have any logical foundation? On the one hand, it may be seen as giving effect to the speaker's expectations: he might not have spoken at all if he had realized that the plaintiff would rely on what he said in the way he did; or he might have said something different; or he might have charged (more) for his advice.[141] Recipients of advice ought, perhaps, to be encouraged to enquire about the purposes which the speaker had in mind. On the other hand, if the use to which the recipient put the advice is a reasonable one, and if it was not clear from what the adviser said that he did not intend his advice to be relied upon for that purpose, there is no obvious reason why the plaintiff should not recover. At the end of the day, courts have to choose to favour one party or the other; and the concept of 'purpose' does not relieve them of this choice.

(ii) *Acts:* It was not until 1976 that the High Court held (in *Caltex Oil* v. *Dredge 'Willemstad'*)[142] that in certain circumstances a plaintiff can recover for purely economic loss caused by negligent acts or omissions. The reason for the late acceptance of this proposition was not that the issue had not arisen for decision earlier. There were a number of English and Australian cases decided after *Hedley Byrne* in which it was held that economic loss caused by negligent acts was only compensatable if it was

---

137 [1990] 1 A.C. 831.

138 It is relevant to ask whether the defendant ought to have foreseen that the plaintiff would rely on him *without taking independent advice: James McNaughton Paper Group Ltd.* v. *Hicks Anderson & Co.* [1991] 2 Q.B. 113.

139 *Pisano* v. *Fairfield C.C.* [1991] Aust. Torts Reports 81-126.

140 But its relevance is even wider: it may apply (1) to acts/omissions as well as to statements; (2) in cases where there is no threat of indeterminacy of liability; and it may (3) positively justify the imposition of liability as well as negatively justify refusal to impose liability (see *Hawkins* v. *Clayton* (1988) 164 C.L.R. 539, 551-5 *per* Brennan J.); or (4) justify the imposition of a duty to take positive action (see further p. 371 below).

141 As a result of *Hedley Byrne* v. *Heller*, a person can be liable in tort for gratuitous advice.

142 (1976) 136 C.L.R. 529.

the immediate consequence of damage to the plaintiff's person or property.[143] Rather it seems that judges found the precedents against recovery for purely economic loss caused by negligent acts more compelling or difficult to disregard than those concerning negligent statements. There were, perhaps, three main reasons for this, all of which arise from the fact that, in many cases, the act which causes the economic loss does so by causing physical damage to tangible property in which the plaintiff had no proprietary or possessory interest at the time the damage occurred. First, for a long time a sharp distinction has been drawn in the law of tort between owning something and merely having a contractual or other financial interest in it: the law of tort gives much more protection to proprietary and possessory interests than to other financial interests. But it has often been argued (in the *Caltex* case, for example) that from the plaintiff's point of view, if property is put out of action and has to be repaired, the financial loss caused by not being able to use the property and by having to repair it is the same regardless of whether the plaintiff incurs that loss because he *owns* the property or because he has some 'lesser' interest in it. Also, from the defendant's point of view, the precise nature of the plaintiff's interest in the property is of no real importance.

Secondly, sometimes the number of people who suffer economic loss as a result of physical damage to property is apt to be very large: for example, if the property damaged is a public bridge or an electricity cable. In such cases, the fear of multiple actions comes into play. But not all of the relevant cases raise the spectre of multiple actions: for example, in *Leigh & Sillavan Ltd* v. *Aliakmon Shipping Co. Ltd*[144] the fact that the plaintiff's interest in the damaged property was only contractual simply meant that the financial loss resulting from the physical damage was transferred from one person (the property owner) to another (the plaintiff).

The third reason for the courts' caution in these cases is the feeling that if a person has a financial interest (whether contractual or not) in someone else's property, he should protect that interest by insurance or by entering a contract with the property owner to shift the loss on to the latter. In this view, the law of tort is a last resort to be used only when no other means of protecting financial interests is reasonably available.

So it was not until some years after it had been decided (in *Hedley Byrne*) that economic loss caused by negligent words could be actionable, that it came to be argued that there is no important distinction between words and acts. It is true that a single statement can be disseminated in a way that a single product or an act cannot. But when words travel, the loss they cause is economic. When a statement does physical damage, for example in a case where an architect negligently advises that a building is safe,[145] the damage it does is unlikely to be any more widespread than the

---

143 e.g. *French Knit Sales Pty Ltd* v. *N. Gold & Sons Pty Ltd* [1972] 2 N.S.W.L.R. 132; *Spartan Steel and Alloys Ltd* v. *Martin & Co. (Contractors) Ltd* [1973] Q.B. 27.

144 [1986] A.C. 785.

145 *Voli* v. *Inglewood Shire Council* (1963) 110 C.L.R. 74; *Clay* v. *A.J. Crump & Sons Ltd* [1964] 1 Q.B. 533.

negligence of a builder in building an unsafe house. Again, wrong advice that a product is safe will not necessarily cause more physical damage than a design defect in a line of mass-produced products. Conversely, the economic loss caused by a negligent act, such as damage to a bridge, can be every bit as indeterminate and widespread as that caused by a statement.

Perhaps more importantly, in many cases it is unrealistic to distinguish between words and acts. Should there be any difference between the liability of a car mechanic who negligently states that a car needs no repair and that of one who negligently repairs it?[146] Is there any good reason to impose liability on the captain in *Caltex* for negligent navigation but not on the party who provided inaccurate navigation information?[147] If a council building inspector inspects foundations and then certifies that they comply with building regulations,[148] or if an auditor inspects a company's accounts then certifies that they are accurate,[149] has he done an act or made a statement? It seems he has done both, and the way the conduct is categorized does not affect the type of loss it is liable to cause. The important distinction is not between words and acts but between physical and economic loss. It is the nature of the loss which determines whether or not (any of) the policy arguments discussed above seem to be relevant.

There is, however, one factual difference between words and acts: a statement will only cause loss if it is relied upon (by someone).[150] At this point it is necessary to introduce a distinction between what might be called 'general' and 'specific' reliance.[151] 'Specific reliance' refers to some action (or inaction) of the plaintiff which causes him detriment or loss and which is a response to some conduct of the defendant, such as a statement or an act which leads the plaintiff to believe that the defendant will act in a particular way. 'General reliance' refers to a situation where a person reasonably expects that another will, for example, exercise a power or use skill or knowledge (which he has or is reasonably presumed to have) for the former's benefit, not as a result of anything said or done by that other, but merely because the other has (or is reasonably believed to have) that power, skill or knowledge.[152] Another way of putting this is to say that 'general reliance' exists where one person is dependent on another to exercise some power or to use some skill or knowledge in such a way as to protect him from injury or loss (or, in some cases, perhaps, to procure him some benefit). A person may rely on another in this sense even though he has neither acted nor refrained from action on account of the

146 *Hedley Byrne* [1964] A.C. 465, 516 *per* Lord Devlin.

147 *Caltex* (1976) 136 C.L.R. 529, 552 *per* Gibbs J.

148 e.g. *Anns* v. *Merton L.B.C.* [1978] A.C. 728; but see now *Murphy* v. *Brentwood D.C.* [1991] 1 A.C. 398.

149 e.g. *Scott Group* v. *McFarlane* [1978] 1 N.Z.L.R. 553.

150 e.g. *Stafford* v. *Conti Commodity Services Ltd* [1981] 1 All E.R. 961; but the reliance need not be the sole cause of the loss: *JEB Fasteners* v. *Marks, Bloom* [1983] 1 All E.R. 583.

151 See *Sutherland S.C.* v. *Heyman* (1984-5) 157 C.L.R. 424, 461-4 *per* Mason J.

152 McHugh J. decided in favour of the plaintiff in *Parramatta C.C.* v. *Lutz* (1988) 12 N.S.W.L.R. 293 on this basis.

other's skill, power or knowledge. When I say that a statement will cause loss only if it is relied upon, I am referring to specific reliance.

At first it was thought, on the basis of *Hedley Byrne*, that liability for economic loss would only arise if (specific) reliance *by the plaintiff* on a statement could be shown, even in cases where, as a matter of fact, the plaintiff had suffered loss despite lack of (specific) reliance by him.[153] But it now seems clear that if a causal link can be traced from a negligent act or statement of the defendant to the plaintiff's economic loss the fact that the plaintiff did not act to his detriment in reliance upon anything said or done by the defendant will not prevent his recovering for economic loss. So, P may recover for economic loss resulting from D's negligent statement or act even if the person who relied on the statement or act was C not P.[154] Furthermore, general reliance or dependence may justify the imposition of liability for economic loss caused by negligent acts or omissions.[155] Finally, *Caltex*[156] shows that economic loss caused by negligent acts may be recoverable in the absence of reliance in any meaningful sense of the word by P on D.[157]

How have Australian courts sought to limit liability for purely economic loss caused by negligent acts? In *Caltex*[158] a number of different approaches were taken. Gibbs and Mason JJ. were prepared to allow recovery because, on the facts, the defendant ought to have foreseen damage to the plaintiff individually and not merely as a member of a general or unascertained class of persons, as would be sufficient under Lord Atkin's neighbour principle. Stephen J. thought that what was required, and present in this

---

153 It may be that in some cases there could be no liability for economic loss in the absence of specific reliance. See *F.W. Neilsen (Canberra) Pty Ltd* v. *P.D.C. Constructions (A.C.T.) Pty Ltd* (1971) 71 A.C.T.R. 1; *Opat* v. *National Mutual Life Association of Australasia Ltd* [1992] 1 V.R. 283.

154 *Ministry of Housing and Local Government* v. *Sharp* [1970] 2 Q.B. 223 (but see *Murphy* v. *Brentwood D.C.* [1991] 1 A.C. 398, 486 *per* Lord Oliver of Aylmerton); *Ross* v. *Caunters* [1980] Ch. 297; P.F. Cane (1981) 55 *A.L.J.* 862, 863-4 (but see *Seale* v. *Perry* [1982] V.R. 193, 215-18 *per* Murphy J.); *B.T. Australia* v. *Raine & Horne* [1983] 3 N.S.W.L.R. 221. See also *Brown* v. *Heathcote C.C.* [1987] 1 N.Z.L.R. 720.

155 *Hawkins* v. *Clayton* (1988) 164 C.L.R. 539; *Cuckmere Brick Co. Ltd* v. *Mutual Finance Ltd* [1971] Ch. 949; *Standard Chartered Bank Ltd* v. *Walker* [1982] 1 W.L.R. 1410; *National Westminster Finance New Zealand Ltd* v. *United Finance and Securities Ltd* [1988] 1 N.Z.L.R. 226; *First City Corporation Ltd* v. *Downsview Nominees Ltd* [1989] 3 N.Z.L.R. 710. But contrast *China and South Sea Bank Ltd* v. *Tan* [1990] 1 A.C. 536; *Parker-Tweedale* v. *Dunbar Bank p.l.c.* [1991] Ch. 12.

156 (1976) 136 C.L.R. 529.

157 In one sense, we 'rely' on others to take reasonable care in daily life; in this way, the whole of the law of negligence could be said to rest on reliance. But to give the word such a wide connotation is to deprive it of any real explanatory power. Only certain relationships are relationships of dependence (general reliance). The essence of such relationships seems to be *inequality* resulting from an imbalance of power, skill or knowledge between the parties relevant to some transaction in which they are both involved. The most obvious examples of relationships of dependence involve the exercise of statutory powers by public authorities and the provision of professional services.

158 (1976) 136 C.L.R. 529. Cf. *New Zealand Forest Products Ltd* v. *Attorney-General* [1986] 1 N.Z.L.R. 14; *Williams* v. *Attorney-General* [1990] 1 N.Z.L.R. 646; *Mainguard Packaging Ltd* v. *Hilton Haulage Ltd* [1990] 1 N.Z.L.R. 360. But note *R.G. & T.J. Anderson Pty Ltd* v. *Chamberlain John Deere Pty Ltd* (1988) 15 N.S.W.L.R. 363

case, was a high degree of proximity between the defendant's act and the plaintiff's loss—there was a direct or foreseeable causal connection between the loss and the negligent act.[159] The difference between these two approaches seems to be that Gibbs and Mason JJ. required the plaintiff to be specifically foreseeable whereas Stephen J. seems to have required that the specific economic loss which he suffered (as opposed to economic loss generally) be foreseeable. The Gibbs/Mason test has been applied in a few Australian cases.[160] But the High Court has not yet had a chance to discuss the *Caltex* case in detail in the light of the rediscovery of the concept of proximity. It may be that when it does, the outcome in relation to economic loss caused by negligent acts will be analogous to the rules which apply to negligent statements:[161] in both cases the plaintiff will have to establish that the defendant ought to have foreseen injury to him in particular or to a small group of which he is a member; and that the economic loss suffered was of a particularly foreseeable type[162] (in cases concerning statements, this requirement is embodied in the rule that the defendant must have been able to foresee the particular purpose for which the statement would be used).

It has been suggested, partly on the basis of certain *dicta* in the *Caltex* case,[163] that liability for economic loss ought to be limited to expenses actually incurred and should not, except in certain exceptional cases, extend to profits or expectations not realized.[164] One of the grounds on which the Supreme Court of Victoria in *Seale* v. *Perry*[165] refused to follow *Ross* v. *Caunters*[166] was that a beneficiary under a will has, until the testator dies, no more than a *spes successionis* (or 'bare expectation of a legacy') because the testator can always change his will. Lush J. further supported the argument by saying that if, in *Caltex*, Caltex had been unable to procure alternative transport and had lost profits as a result, these would not have been recoverable.[167] The suggested limitation has the apparent advantage of simplicity and certainty and of being quite easy to apply. The specific foreseeability test, on the other hand, is vague and uncertain because its application is tied closely to the detailed facts of particular cases. But the suggested limitation is not tailored to meeting the objections to recovery for economic loss which the courts have been

---

159 Deane J. refers to this as 'causal proximity'. The more traditional term is 'remoteness of damage'. See also *Mainguard Packaging Ltd* v. *Hilton Haulage Ltd* [1990] 1 N.Z.L.R. 360.

160 *George Hudson Pty Ltd* v. *Bank of New South Wales* [1978] 3 A.C.L.R. 366; *Johns Period Furniture Ltd* v. *Commonwealth Savings Bank of Australia* (1980) 24 S.A.S.R. 224; *Millar* v. *Candy* (1981) 38 A.L.R. 299; *Ball* v. *Consolidated Rutile Ltd* [1990] Aust. Torts Reports 81-023.

161 Cf. *National Mutual Life Association of Australasia Ltd* v. *Coffey & Partners Pty Ltd* [1991] 2 Qd.R. 401; *Opat* v. *National Mutual Life Association* [1991] 2 V.R. 283.

162 *Canadian National Railway Co.* v. *Norsk Pacific Steamship Co. Ltd* (1990) 65 D.L.R. (4th) 321.

163 (1976) 136 C.L.R. 529, 577 *per* Stephen J.; 598-9 *per* Jacobs J.

164 (1979) 12 *M.U.L.R.* 79; for a detailed reply see Cane (1980) 12 *M.U.L.R.* 408.

165 [1982] V.R. 193.

166 [1980] Ch. 297.

167 [1982] V.R. 193, 201.

concerned with. There is no reason to think that liability for lost expectations is likely to be more indeterminate than liability for expenses. Also, in relation to other types of loss—personal injury and nervous shock—the courts have not shown much sympathy with dissections of types of loss into sub-types. At the moment, the most that can be said is that the courts have not yet properly addressed this issue and that the arguments on both sides are inconclusive. It should be noted, however, that it is by no means true that damages for unfulfilled expectations are irrecoverable in tort law. Apart from the fact that damages for lost earnings and profits are recoverable in cases where they are consequential upon injury or damage to person or property, damages for unrealized future gains can also sometimes be recovered even when they stand alone.[168]

The English case law has taken a quite different direction from the Australian. The Gibbs/Mason approach has not found favour. The only important case which could be seen as adopting something like it is *Junior Books Ltd* v. *Veitchi Co. Ltd*[169] in which it was held that a building owner could sue in negligence a sub-contractor who had laid a defective floor in the building because the flooring contractor had been nominated by the plaintiff to do the job and, presumably, knew the plaintiff's needs well. But this case has since been interpreted as involving reliance by the plaintiff on misrepresentations by the defendant of quality and fitness for purpose, and so as being a '*Hedley Byrne case*'.[170] The English cases dealing with negligent acts fall into two broad classes: first, those concerning accidental damage to property such as ships and electricity cables; and secondly, cases involving claims by purchasers of real property or chattels based on some defect in the property as acquired. In cases of the first type, the rule is that there can be no liability for negligently inflicting economic loss by causing physical damage to property in which, at the time of the damage, the plaintiff had no proprietary or possessory interest.[171] The main reasons for this rule are: (1) that it is well known and long-standing, and provides a clear and simple basis for the conduct of commercial activity; (2) a fear that any other rule would generate floods of litigation; and (3) that people who have non-proprietary interests in property should protect those interests themselves by contract or insurance.

In the cases involving the acquisition of property affected by a latent defect which is later discovered and needs to be repaired, English courts have taken the view that the plaintiff's claim is one for purely economic loss even if the defect (such as a weakness in the foundations of a building)

---

168 See pp. 525-9 below for further discussion.

169 [1983] 1 A.C. 520.

170 *Murphy* v. *Brentwood D.C.* [1991] 1 A.C. 398, 466 *per* Lord Keith; 441 *per* Lord Bridge.

171 *Spartan Steel* v. *Martin* [1973] Q.B. 27; *Candlewood Navigation Corporation Ltd* v. *Mitsui OSK Lines Ltd* [1986] A.C. 1 (this is a Privy Council decision on appeal from N.S.W. But the Privy Council declined to apply *Caltex*, apparently on the basis that their Lordships could not extract a ratio from it, and on the basis that the principles enunciated by Gibbs, Mason and Stephen JJ. were insufficiently precise. Of course, *Caltex* is binding on Australian courts whereas *Candlewood* is not); *Leigh & Sillavan* v. *Aliakmon Shipping* [1987] A.C. 728.

causes 'damage' to the property (such as cracks in the superstructure); and that such claims cannot be made in the tort of negligence, which is basically confined to personal injury and physical damage to property (other than the defective property).[172] There may be a couple of minor exceptions to this principle, but as yet the status of the suggested exceptions is unclear. A major defect in the conceptual basis of these cases is that they do not satisfactorily explain why purely economic loss should be recoverable in *Hedley Byrne*-type cases (which involve negligent financial advice and services) but not in cases involving negligence in the design and construction or production of property.[173]

(b) Continuing relationships Such relationships pre-exist the act of negligence and are typically contractual relationships between professionals and their clients—solicitors, accountants and so on. In this context, no distinction is drawn between words and acts. The relationship solves all problems of proximity and indeterminancy but leaves open, of course, the issue of whether there are any policy grounds not related to proximity for denying liability. So, for example, advocates acting as such are immune from tort liability to their lay clients for negligent conduct.

3. Other Conditions of Liability for Negligent Advice and Services[174]

(a) The *Hedley Byrne* principle This area of the law is largely a development of the principles laid down in *Hedley Byrne* v. *Heller*.[175] The basis of the decision was that there was a 'special relationship' between the parties; special in the sense that it was neither contractual nor fiduciary, and in the sense that it was not based simply on the concept of foreseeability as enunciated by Lord Atkin in *Donoghue* v. *Stevenson*.[176] The basis of the special relationship was that the defendant had 'voluntarily undertaken' to give advice in circumstances such that it ought to have realized that the plaintiff was relying on it to exercise care, and such that it was reasonable for the plaintiff so to rely. This principle was tailored to the facts of the case in that *Hedley Byrne* concerned the making of a statement in response to a request for advice by the plaintiff's bank[177] and detrimental reliance on that statement. But the requirement of reliance goes to causation rather than to liability, and it is this fact which has allowed the *Hedley Byrne* principle to be used as the basis for imposing liability in tort for professional negligence even in cases where the plaintiff has not relied on the defendant.

Liability under the *Hedley Byrne* principle can attach to the giving of

172 *D. & F. Estates Ltd* v. *Church Commissioners* [1989] A.C. 177; *Murphy* v. *Brentwood D.C.* [1991] 1 A.C. 398. See further pp. 529-30 below.

173 J. Stapleton (1991) 107 *L.Q.R.* 249.

174 See *San Sebastian* (1986) 162 C.L.R. 340, 356-7.

175 [1964] A.C. 465; D.M. Gordon (1964) 38 *A.L.J.* 39 and 79; A.M. Honore (1964-5) 8 *J.S.P.T.L.* 284; P.F. Cane (1981) 55 *A.L.J.* 862.

176 [1932] A.C. 562.

177 But request is not necessary: *San Sebastian* (1986) 162 C.L.R. 340,356-7.

information as well as to opinions or advice. In a New Zealand case it has been held, contrary to the weight of other authority, that the principle can also apply to statements of intention to act in a particular way in the future.[178] This decision tends to blur the distinction between tort and contract because breach of undertakings as to future action normally only gives rise to liability if the undertaking satisfies the requirements for the existence of a contract.

(b) *Ad hoc* relationships

(i) *Undertaking of responsibility*: The concept of 'voluntary assumption or undertaking of responsibility' is particularly important in relation to *ad hoc* special relationships which arise out of an isolated statement made or an isolated service done by the defendant for the plaintiff. *Hedley Byrne* was such a case. The point of the word 'voluntary' is to indicate that the liability is not being *imposed* by the law but is a product of the defendant's own free action in giving advice without disclaiming responsibility for its accuracy. In this way, liability under the *Hedley Byrne* principle is seen as being 'akin to' contractual liability, the main difference being that a contract requires consideration whereas gratuitously given advice can be actionable in tort. This analogy with contract was drawn in order to justify imposing liability in tort for purely economic loss, which was traditionally seen as being mainly within the province of the law of contract.

It has now been recognized by English courts that undertakings of responsibility are normally imposed by the law rather than assumed.[179] Advisers very rarely *expressly* accept legal responsibility for the accuracy of their advice, and *implied* undertakings are, in effect, *imposed by law*. If the adviser expressly disclaims responsibility for accuracy, as in *Hedley Byrne* itself, it seems accurate to say that the adviser has *not* voluntarily assumed such responsibility; but in such cases in England, statutory provisions may have the effect of rendering the disclaimer of no effect, and a defendant may be held liable despite his express attempts to prevent this happening. In other words, liability for *ad hoc* advice will be imposed if the court thinks that the adviser ought to bear legal responsibility for negligence in giving the advice. The only context in which express undertakings are at all common is when a person says he will perform some action or do some job.

(ii) *The skill principle*: In *Mutual Life and Citizens' Assurance Co. Ltd* v. *Evatt*[180] the Privy Council laid down what might be called the 'skill principle': a duty of care[181] will arise only if the giving of the advice required some special skill or competence, and if the adviser was in the business of giving advice of the type sought or held himself out as having and being willing to exercise the skill and competence appropriate to a

178 *Meates* v. *A.G.* [1983] 2 N.Z.L.R. 308.

179 See particularly *Smith* v. *Bush* [1990] 1 A.C. 831.

180 [1971] A.C. 793; C.S. Phegan (1971) 45 *A.L.J.* 20; K.E. Lindgren (1972) 46 *A.L.J.* 176.

181 Concerning the relevance of skill to the standard of care see p. 423 below.

person in that advice-giving business. Only in such cases can it be said that the defendant must have assumed responsibility for his statement.

The skill principle was applied in a variety of contexts, but it has now been very largely eroded.[182] English courts never accepted it, but rather preferred what might be called the 'course of business' principle to the effect that although the advice need not have been given by a professional adviser, it must at least have been given in a business context.[183] This principle does not seem to require that the defendant be in the habit of making statements of the type made in the course of business, only that he did so on this occasion. The relevance of the statement being made on a business occasion is that this ensures that it was meant to be taken seriously and that it was reasonable for the plaintiff to rely on it.

In *L. Shaddock & Associates Pty Ltd* v. *Parramatta City Council*[184] the plaintiff wished to purchase some land in the council's area. Their solicitor made a written application for a certificate under s.342AS of the Local Government Act 1919 (N.S.W.), appended to which was an inquiry as to whether the land was affected by any road-widening proposals. The council was under a statutory obligation to issue the certificate but not to answer the inquiry. However, it had adopted the practice of answering such inquiries by making an endorsement if the land was affected but by making no endorsement if it was unaffected. In this case the council failed to endorse, even though the land was affected. The High Court held the council liable to the purchaser. Gibbs C.J. doubted that correctness of the skill principle but did not decide the point because he thought that the council was, in effect, in the business of supplying information (even though it was under no statutory duty to do so); and, since the information was on a serious business matter, the council owed the inquirer a duty of care. It had voluntarily set up a system for the providing of information which it was in a better position than anyone else to gather,[185] of which it had a virtual monopoly, and which, moreover, concerned its own activities.[186] Furthermore, the gathering and collating of information can be a skilled activity (it was sometimes doubted whether the collecting and imparting of factual information was an activity in respect of which a person could profess or undertake to exercise skill); but even if it does not require special skill, a public authority might be thought more experienced or competent than others at supplying information in its possession for the purpose of its public functions.

---

182 *San Sebastian* (1986) 162 C.L.R. 340, 371 *per* Brennan J. But see *Mohr & Mohr* v. *Cleaver & Cleaver* [1986] W.A.R. 67 and *Norris* v. *Sibberas* [1990] V.R. 161, 171-2 (esp. points 1 and 5) *per* Marks J; *James* v. *Australia and New Zealand Banking Group Ltd* (1985-6) 64 A.L.R. 347, 384. See also M. Davies (1990) 17 *M.U.L.R.* 484.

183 *Esso Petroleum Co. Ltd* v. *Mardon* [1976] Q.B. 801; *Howard Marine and Dredging Co. Ltd* v. *A. Ogden & Sons (Excavations) Ltd* [1978] 1 Q.B. 574. It is normally assumed that there would be no liability for statements made in social situations; but see *Chaudhry* v. *Prabhakar* [1989] 1 W.L.R. 29 which may, however, rest on an unjustified concession: see May L.J. at pp. 38-9.

184 (1981) 150 C.L.R. 225; but see now Environmental Planning and Assessment Act 1979 (N.S.W.), s.149(5) and (6).

185 Cf *M.L.C.* v. *Evatt* (1968) 122 C.L.R. 556, 565-72 *per* Barwick C.J.

186 cf. *Brown* v. *Heathcote C.C.* [1987] 1 N.Z.L.R. 720.

Stephen J. distinguished *M.L.C.* by saying that it only concerned the liability of those in business or a profession in respect of their business or professional activities. Here the duty arose not out of the exercise of skill, but because the council had set itself up as a monopoly supplier of essential information in a quite formalized manner. Mason J., with whom Aickin J. agreed, went further and held that the *Hedley Byrne* principle is not restricted in the way suggested by *M.L.C.*, but that it applied quite generally to situations in which it was reasonable for the plaintiff to rely on the defendant, and in which the defendant ought to have realized that the plaintiff would rely on him.

Shaddock goes at least as far as establishing that there is no crucial distinction between information and advice[187] (although it may be less easy to found a duty on the giving of information because it will probably less often be reasonable to rely on another for information as opposed to advice or opinion,[188] since information gathering on the whole requires less special skill than advising), and that a person who is in a particularly good position to collect information, and has voluntarily made that information available to others, is under a duty to take care in the imparting of that information. It is safe to say that in a world increasingly dominated by information technology, the incidence of reliance on others for information will grow apace, and that the scope for the application of *Shaddock* principles will expand accordingly. It is, of course, the case that when a statutory authority makes some statement involving the imparting of advice or opinion as opposed to information, it can be held liable under *Hedley Byrne* principles.[189]

Further doubt is cast on both the skill principle and the 'business context' idea by *Meates* v. *A.G.*[190] in which the New Zealand government was held liable for negligent assurances that financial assistance would be given to an industrial venture even though the assurances were not given in any business or professional capacity but for political and social reasons. It may indeed be that the law is moving to a position where the only requirement will be that the statement was made in circumstances making it reasonable for the plaintiff to rely on it and it would be fair to hold the defendant responsible for its accuracy.

(iii) *Financial interest*: Another ground, suggested in *M.L.C.*, for the imposition of a duty of care is that the giver of the advice or information has a financial interest in the subject matter of the statement.[191] Thus, it has been held that company directors have a financial interest in advising the shareholders to accept a takeover offer[192] and that a retailer has a financial interest in advising prospective customers about the goods on

---

187 *San Sebastian* (1986) 162 C.L.R. 340, 356-7.

188 *M.L.C.* v. *Evatt* (1968) 122 C.L.R. 556, 572 *per* Barwick C.J.

189 *Hull* v. *Canterbury Municipal Council* [1974] 1 N.S.W.L.R. 300; *G.J. Knight Holdings Pty Ltd* v. *Warringah Shire Council* [1975] 2 N.S.W.L.R. 795; *Rutherford* v. *Attorney-General* [1976] 1 N.Z.L.R. 403.

190 [1983] 2 N.Z.L.R. 308.

191 e.g. *O'Leary* v. *Lensworth* (1974) 7 S.A.S.R. 159.

192 *Coleman* v. *Myers* [1977] 2 N.Z.L.R. 225.

display, at least in a case where a sale is almost certain.[193] But the interest of a local authority 'in promoting or encouraging development of its area would not ordinarily be classified as' a financial interest.[194]

The cases suggest that a financial interest will be relevant only if it is such that, by virtue of it, the speaker is in a better position than he would otherwise be to know the truth.[195] This interpretation of the financial interest principle might be thought to be suspect now, in that it seems to treat the interest as relevant to the question of possession or holding out of special skill. However, we could just say that it is only if the financial interest gives the speaker some special qualification that such interest makes it reasonable for the plaintiff to rely on him. In many cases the possession of a financial interest might make a reasonable plaintiff justifiably suspicious of anything said by the adviser.

(iv) *Relationships of dependence*: It will be recalled that another suggested basis for imposing liability for economic loss is 'general reliance', which arises where one party is in a relationship of dependence upon another. This notion of dependence is particularly helpful in explaining two types of case: first, cases where a public authority has statutory powers designed to enable it to protect individuals, with the result that individuals reasonably come to expect that those powers will be exercised for their protection. Although it was held in *Sutherland S.C.* v. *Heyman*[196] that the statutory provisions there in question did not justify holding that such a relationship of dependence existed between the council and the plaintiff, the judgments indicate that, on suitable facts, such a relationship could arise. Relationships of dependence between public authorities and individuals will often be *ad hoc* relationships.

Secondly, the idea of dependence is apposite in cases where negligence is alleged against a skilled professional such as a solicitor or accountant. Here, disparity of skill, knowledge and information between the professional acting as such and those whom his services are meant to benefit creates dependence. *Hawkins* v. *Clayton*[197] provides a good example of such a case. It is not clear which other sorts of case, if any, will be seen as giving rise to relationships of dependence in the relevant sense. Relationships of dependence between professionals and their clients are continuing relationships whereas such relationships with third parties may be *ad hoc*.

(v) *Reasonable reliance*: It is now clear that liability can be imposed under the *Hedley Byrne* principle even though the defendant did not voluntarily choose to make the statement but was under a statutory duty to do so or was performing a statutory function in doing so. Thus, statutory authorities have been held liable for carelessly giving false

---

193 *Jenkins* v. *Godfrey Hirst of Australia Pty Ltd* (1974) 3 D.C.R.(N.S.W.) 214; cf. *Capital Motors Ltd* v. *Beecham* [1975] 1 N.Z.L.R. 576.

194 *San Sebastian* (1986) 162 C.L.R. 340, 358.

195 *W.B. Anderson & Sons Ltd* v. *Rhodes (Liverpool) Ltd* [1967] 2 All E.R. 850; *Presser* v. *Caldwell Estates Pty Ltd* [1971] 2 N.S.W.L.R. 471; *Plummer-Allinson* v. *Ayrey* [1976] N.Z.L.R. 254.

196 (1984-5) 157 C.L.R. 424.

197 (1988) 78 A.L.R. 69.

information,[198] for negligently issuing a certificate falsely stating that a truck was roadworthy,[199] and for negligently representing that development consent granted was valid when it was really void.[200]

It can be argued that since (as was noted above) the proper question is not whether the defendant voluntarily assumed responsibility but whether it is fair and just to impose responsibiilty on him, then even in cases where the notion of a voluntary undertaking fits the facts it adds nothing to the idea of reasonableness of reliance. If it was reasonable for the plaintiff to rely on the defendant's statement, then the latter will be treated in law as having assumed responsibility even if in fact he did not do so.

The choice between voluntary assumption and reasonableness of reliance is relevant to the role of disclaimers. It will be recalled that it was held in *Hedley Byrne* that the fact that the defendant had expressly disclaimed responsibility for the accuracy of its statement prevented a duty of care arising. It has therefore been argued that assumption of responsibility and absence of a disclaimer are just two sides of the one coin.[201] But there are *dicta* in the cases which suggest that a disclaimer will not necessarily be effective to prevent a duty of care arising just because it has been uttered. If liability rests on reasonableness of reliance, there may be cases in which this objective principle will neutralize the effect of a disclaimer if, for example, there is great inequality between the maker and the recipient of the statement.[202]

(c) **Continuing relationships** As we have seen, the typical continuing relationship is based on the contract between a professional and his client. By means of the idea of the continuing special relationship and the relationship of dependence, the *Hedley Byrne* principle has been extended from statements to acts and omissions and from specific to general reliance. The job of the professional, for example, a solicitor, is often to 'advise' in a rather extended sense of carrying through a particular transaction or set of transactions. There may be no specific request for advice in the narrow sense and no advice given, but documents prepared, legal requirements met, signatures obtained, and so on. In such cases the immediate cause of the plaintiff's loss will often be an act or omission of the solicitor rather than a statement on which the plaintiff relies to his detriment. But from a wider perspective, it can be said that the plaintiff, by committing his affairs generally to the solicitor, has placed (general) reliance on him.

---

198 *Ministry of Housing and Local Government* v. *Sharp* [1970] 2 Q.B. 223.

199 *Rutherford* v. *A.G.* [1976] 1 N.Z.L.R. 403; cf. *Bruce* v. *Housing Corporation of New Zealand* [1982] 2 N.Z.L.R. 28 (negligent approval of house design).

200 *Hull* v. *Canterbury M.C.* [1974] 1 N.S.W.L.R. 300; *Knight* v. *Warringah S.C.* [1975] 2 N.S.W.L.R. 795.

201 Tony Weir [1963] *C.L.J.* 206, 217.

202 *M.L.C.* v.*Evatt* (1968) 122 C.L.R. 556, 570-1 *per* Barwick C.J.; *Scott Group* v. *McFarlane* [1978] 1 N.Z.L.R. 553, 569 *per* Richmond P., 580 *per* Cooke J.; see also *B.T. Australia Ltd* v. *Raine & Horne* [1983] 3 N.S.W.L.R. 221. In England, the Unfair Contract Terms Act 1977 can operate to deprive disclaimers of effect: see *Smith* v. *Bush* [1990] 1 A.C. 831.

The basic rule in England[203] and Australia[204] (but not in New Zealand)[205] is that professionals can be sued by their clients concurrently, in respect of the same conduct, in contract (for breach of a contractual obligation to take care, which is normally implied rather than express) and tort (for breach of a duty of care) for negligence in the performance of their contractual functions.[206] The contract between the parties is very important in the tort action because it helps to define what it was that the defendant was under an obligation to do,[207] and so what (in both contract and tort) he can be sued for not doing, or for doing badly. Why should a client want to sue his adviser in tort when he can sue him in contract? The main reason relates to limitation of actions: the limitation period in contract begins to run when the contract is breached, but in tort only when damage is suffered. The limitation period in tort may, therefore, be more generous to the plaintiff than that in contract.[208] There are, too, certain differences between the rules governing remoteness and measure of damages in contract and tort which may be of practical importance in some cases.

The contract is also very important because it has been held in a series of English cases that the obligations imposed on the defendant by the contract define the limits of his liability in tort. In other words, unless the contract expressly or impliedly requires the defendant to do (or to refrain from doing) X, he cannot be liable in tort for not doing (or for doing) X. This means that the law of tort cannot be used to fill gaps in contracts.[209]

However, it is not clear that the High Court would adopt a similar approach. In *Hawkins* v. *Clayton* Deane J. took the view that the law of tort could be used to impose obligations 'beyond the specifically agreed professional task or function' and that once it is accepted that

> the ordinary law of negligence can apply to render a solicitor liable for economic loss caused to a client by professional negligence, the content and incidence of the solicitor's common law[210] duty of care must be seen as representing the law's

---

203 e.g. *Midland Bank Trust Co. Ltd* v. *Hett Stubbs & Kemp* [1979] Ch. 384 (solicitor); *Batty* v. *Metropolitan Property Realizations Ltd* [1978] Q.B. 554 (building developer).

204 *MacPherson & Kelley* v. *Kevin J. Prunty & Associates* [1983] 1 V.R. 573; *Aluminium Products (Qld) Pty Ltd* v. *Hill* [1981] Qd.R. 33; *Vulic* v. *Bilinsky* [1983] 2 N.S.W.L.R. 472; *Brickhill* v. *Cooke* [1984] 3 N.S.W.L.R. 396; *Waimond Pty Ltd* v. *Byrne* (1989) 18 N.S.W.L.R. 642. But contrast *F.W. Neilsen (Canberra) Pty Ltd* v. *P.D.C. Constructions (A.C.T.) Pty Ltd* (1987) 71 A.C.T.R. 1.

205 e.g. *Bevan Investments Ltd* v. *Blackhall & Struthers (No. 2)* [1973] 2 N.Z.L.R. 45 (architect); *McLaren Maycroft & Co.* v. *Fletcher Development Co. Ltd* [1973] 2 N.Z.L.R. 100 ('professional men') not followed in *Rowlands* v. *Collow* [1992] 1 N.Z.L.R. 178; question left open is *Sutherland* v. *Public Trustee* [1980] 2 N.Z.L.R. 536.

206 There are New Zealand cases which also refuse to allow an action in tort concurrently with an action for breach of fiduciary duty: *Shivas* v. *Bank of New Zealand* [1990] 2 N.Z.L.R. 327; *Westpac Banking Corporation* v. *McCreanor* [1990] 1 N.Z.L.R. 580; but contrast *Shotter* v. *Westpac Banking Corporation* [1988] 2 N.Z.L.R. 316.

207 Midland Bank Trust Co. v. *Hett, Stubbs & Kemp* [1979] Ch. 384, 402-3.

208 See further p. 742 below.

209 Cane *Tort Law and Economic Interests* pp. 332-4.

210 That is, 'tortious'.

judgment of the extent to which it is reasonable and desirable to render a solicitor liable for loss or damage suffered by his client.[211]

In other words, although it may be open to contracting parties to modify or exclude the obligations imposed by the law of tort, tort law has a legitimate role to play in specifying the rights and obligations of contracting parties *inter se* by reference to what is just and fair in moral and policy terms.

When the plaintiff is not the client but a third party, such as an intended beneficiary under a will prepared by the solicitor for his client, the solicitor's liability can arise only in tort. In *Ross* v. *Caunters*[212] it was held that a disappointed beneficiary could sue in tort the solicitor whose negligence had led to the failure of the gift to the plaintiff. The duty owed to a third party is to use proper care in carrying out the client's instructions to benefit a third party. The solicitor owes third parties no duty to attempt to extract from his client instructions which will benefit them;[213] nor to take care in handling transactions concerning the testator's property during his lifetime.[214] In Victoria the approach in *Ross* v. *Caunters* was vigorously rejected by a majority of the Full Court in *Seale* v. *Perry*,[215] but this rejection is not easy to justify either in theoretical or policy terms. Furthermore, it seems inconsistent with the decision of the High Court in *Hawkins* v. *Clayton*[216] in which a solicitor was held liable for failure to notify the executor and beneficiary under a will which was in his possession that the testator had died. The consequent delay in administering the estate reduced its value.[217]

(d) Omissions Another major issue raised by the professional negligence cases is the extent to which liability for omissions may be imposed. From a technical point of view, it will usually be possible to say that any failure to act by a professional will not be a pure omission *vis-à-vis* his client because the continuing relationship between them imposes on the professional a positive duty to act. Thus a solicitor can be held liable for failure to register an option to purchase real estate[218] or for failure to ensure that a will has been properly executed.[219] Again, an insurance

---

211 (1988) 164 C.L.R. 539, 579 and 584 respectively. The approach of the minority in this case was similar to the English approach. Deane J.'s approach was applied in *Waimond Pty Ltd* v. *Byrne* (1989) 18 N.S.W.L.R. 642. See also *Foti* v. *Banque Nationale de Paris* (1989) 54 S.A.S.R. 354.

212 [1980] Ch. 297; applied in *Watts* v. *Public Trustee* [1980] W.A.R. 97; cf. *Gartside* v. *Sheffield, Young & Ellis* [1983] N.Z.L.R. 37.

213 *Sutherland* v. *Public Trustee* [1980] 2 N.Z.L.R. 536; cf. *Seale* v. *Perry* [1982] V.R. 193, 214 *per* Murphy J.

214 *Clarke* v. *Bruce Lance & Co.* [1988] 1 W.L.R. 881.

215 [1982] V.R. 193. For detailed discussion see Cane (1983) 99 *L.Q.R.* 346; H. Luntz (1983) 3 *O.J.L.S* 284.

216 (1988) 164 C.L.R. 539.

217 But note that the action was treated as one brought by the executor as personal representative of the deceased and not in his own right as beneficiary: see esp. Deane J. at (1988) 164 C.L.R. 539, 581.

218 *Midland Bank Trustee* v. *Hett Stubbs* [1979] Ch. 384.

219 *Ross* v. *Caunters* [1980] Ch. 297.

broker who normally renews his client's policy is under a positive duty either to ensure that the policy is kept current or to warn the client that he will not do so in a particular year.[220]

In *Hawkins* v. *Clayton*[221] Brennan and Deane JJ. both suggested that the content of the duty of care in any particular case depends on the reason why the duty is recognized. In that case it was recognized in order to ensure that the testator's wishes, as expressed in her will, were given effect to; and, in the circumstances of the case, this required the solicitor to take reasonable and reasonably prompt steps to locate the executor and inform him of the testator's death. In other words, if the *purpose* for which the defendant was employed requires, for its achievement, that he take positive action, then a duty to take such action can be recognized in tort.

(e) **When is the duty owed?** It is clear that, provided the conditions for the existence of a special relationship exist, a duty to take care can arise in relation to statements made in negotiations preceding the making of a contract.[222] But the contract may exclude liability for such statements or, by casting the burden of inquiry on one of the parties, relieve the other of liability to provide accurate information relevant to the making of the contract. An English decision holds that the writer of a reference may be liable in negligence for false statements made in the reference.[223] But it can be argued that to impose liability for negligence in such circumstances outflanks the rule of defamation law that statements protected by qualified privilege (such as those in a reference) are only actionable if made maliciously. So this decision might not be followed in Australia.[224]

In general, a duty will arise only if, in the circumstances, reliance by the plaintiff was reasonable. By and large, this will be so only if the statement was made or the service performed on a serious occasion or in the context of a serious business or other relationship. Statements made on social occasions or services performed in family contexts would not normally give rise to a duty.[225] Nor is it reasonable to rely on advice given 'off the cuff' or 'off the top of the head'[226] or in circumstances where it could not be said that the speaker ought to have realized he was being relied upon. Thus in *Shaddock*[227] the plaintiff's solicitor had made an initial inquiry over the telephone of an unidentified person in the town planning

---

220 *Morash* v. *Lockhart & Ritchie Ltd* (1978) 95 D.L.R. (3d) 647; see also *Norwest Refrigeration Services Pty Ltd* v. *Bain Dawes (W.A.) Pty Ltd* (1984) 157 C.L.R. 149.

221 (1988) 164 C.L.R. 539.

222 *Esso Petroleum Co. Ltd* v. *Mardon* [1976] Q.B. 801; *State of South Australia* v. *Johnson* (1982) 42 A.L.R. 161; but for New Zealand see Contractual Remedies Act 1979, s.6; S.M.D. Todd *et al., The Law of Torts in New Zealand* (1991) pp. 159-61.

223 *Lawton* v. *BOC Transhield Ltd.* [1987] 2 All E.R. 608.

224 See *Bell-Booth Group Ltd* v. *Attorney-General* [1989] 3 N.Z.L.R. 148; S. Todd (1992) 108 *L.Q.R.* 360.

225 *M.L.C.* v. *Evatt* (1968) 122 C.L.R. 556, 569 *per* Barwick C.J.; *Shaddock* v. *Parramatta C.C.* (1981) 150 C.L.R. 225, 231 *per* Gibbs C.J.; but see n. 183 above.

226 But see *James* v. *Australia and New Zealand Banking Group Ltd* (1985-6) 64 A.L.R. 347, 384.

227 (1981) 150 C.L.R. 225.

department. Since the inquiry was informal and oral and was not confirmed in writing, and since there was a formal procedure for making the inquiry in writing which the plaintiff then followed, it was held that no duty arose in relation to the negative answer given over the telephone.

A variety of circumstances can make it unreasonable for a party to rely on another. In *Allied Finance and Investments Ltd* v. *Haddow & Co.*[228] it was held that normally a party represented by a solicitor in dealings with another party represented by a solicitor may not sue the latter's solicitor for failure to disclose information relevant to the former's dealings with the latter. The solicitor's duty is to his client, not to a third party (to the extent that the two duties conflict). Again, in *Dominion Freeholders Ltd* v. *Aird*[229] the defendant, the plaintiff's auditor, sued the plaintiff's accountant for supplying it with inaccurate information about the company's financial position. It was held that the auditor (who had personal statutory duties to give an accurate report of the company's financial position) was owed no duty by the accountant because he was not entitled to rely on the accountant for the information which formed the basis of his report.

What is the relationship between saying that it was not reasonable for the plaintiff to rely on the defendant and saying that the plaintiff was contributorily negligent? The answer would appear to be that whereas a finding of unreasonable reliance completely debars recovery by the plaintiff, a finding of contributory negligence would allow the damages to be apportioned between the parties. This has been done in a number of Canadian cases[230] and it would seem fairer to the plaintiff.

4. Statutory Liability

By far the most important statutory source of liability for statements is s.52 of the Trade Practices Act 1974 (Cwth) and provisions modelled on it in several States and New Zealand.[231] It prohibits 'conduct which is misleading or deceptive or is likely to mislead or deceive'. The scope of application of the Commonwealth legislation is wide, but is confined by the limits of the legislative power of the Commonwealth. The State provisions are not so limited in their operation; but all the provisions apply only to conduct 'in trade or commerce'. The basic provision is

228 [1983] N.Z.L.R. 22; but on the facts it was held that the other party's solicitor did owe a duty of care to the plaintiff because the latter had specifically asked the former to certify that his client was the owner of a vessel offered as security for a loan; the court said that in the circumstances the solicitor ought to have realized that the plaintiff would rely on his certificate. Cf. *Business Computer International Ltd* v. *Registrar of Companies* [1988] Ch. 229. See also *Thors* v. *Weeks* (1990) 92 A.L.R. 131 and *Gran Gelato Ltd* v. *Richcliff (Group) Ltd* [1992] 2 W.L.R. 867.

229 [1966] 2 N.S.W.R. 293.

230 *Morash* v. *Lockhart* (1978) 95 D.L.R.(3d) 647; cf. *West Coast Finance Ltd* v. *Gunderson, Stokes, Walton & Co.* (1974) 44 D.L.R. (3d.) 232; *Grand Restaurants of Canada Ltd* v. *City of Toronto* (1981) 123 D.L.R. (3d) 349; *Spiewak* v. *251268 Ontario Ltd* (1987) 43 D.L.R. (4th) 554.

231 Fair Trading Act 1987 (N.S.W.) s.42; Fair Trading Act 1987 (S.A.) s.56; Fair Trading Act 1985 (Vic.) s.11; Fair Trading Act 1987 (W.A.) s.10; Fair Trading Act 1986 (N.Z.) s.9.

supplemented by a number of more detailed provisions dealing with particular types of misleading or deceptive conduct, but all the statutes provide that nothing in these supplementary provisions limits by implication the generality of the basic provision. In other words, *any* conduct which can be described in the words of the basic provision is caught by the statutes. Although s.52 of the 1974 Act was originally conceived as a consumer protection measure, it has generated more litigation on the part of businesses than of individuals. One area in which it has been much used is that covered by the tort of passing off, and it is discussed in that context;[232] it also deals with situations covered by the torts of deceit and injurious falsehood. Here we are concerned with the use of the provisions as an alternative to a cause of action for negligence.

It is beyond the scope of this book to examine these provisions in detail.[233] But their importance cannot be overestimated.[234] Mr Justice French of the Federal Court believes that because of 'the simplicity and strength of the prohibitions contained in [it] s.52 . . . will displace the existing torts in its area of operation'.[235] So we must note a few of the most important features of the statutory provisions. The first is that although misleading or deceptive *conduct* will often consist of, or at least imply, a false statement (a 'misrepresentation'), there are grounds for saying that the word *conduct* extends beyond misrepresentations narrowly defined.[236] But even so, the conduct must be capable of being described as 'misleading or deceptive or likely to mislead or deceive'; in this way, the provisions are not as wide in their reach as the principles developed out of *Hedley Byrne* v. *Heller*: it would, for example, be hard to describe the negligent conduct in either *Ross* v. *Caunters* or *Hawkins* v. *Clayton* as actually or potentially misleading or deceptive.[237] Secondly, because the statutory provisions only apply to conduct 'in trade or commerce' they are, in theory, narrower than the tort of negligence; however, in practice a private person is quite unlikely either to be sued or to be held liable under the principles derived from *Hedley Byrne* v. *Heller*.[238]

Thirdly, to the extent that the statutory provisions and the tort of negligence overlap, the former are much more advantageous to the

232 See p. 188-9 above.

233 Useful discussions are: A. Terry (1987) 10 *U.N.S.W.L.J.* 260; W. Pengilley [1987] *A.B.L.R.* 247; the Hon. Mr Justice R.F. French (1989) 63 *A.L.J.* 250 and Ch.8 of P.D. Finn (ed.) *Essays on Torts* (Sydney, 1989).

234 It has even been suggested that s.52 might, in certain circumstances, ground an action for personal injuries sustained in a road or industrial accident: S. Davis [1989] *Law Institute J.* 830. See also *Concrete Constructions (N.S.W.) Pty Ltd* v. *Nelson* (1990) 92 A.L.R. 193. Section 60 of the Commonwealth Act (and equivalents in other jurisdictions) explicitly covers situations dealt with by the torts of assault and battery.

235 Finn (ed.) *Essays on Torts* p. 202.

236 French (1989) 63 *A.L.J.* 250, 254-6. It is generally agreed that mere silence is more likely to be actionable under the statutes than in the common law of tort where the bias against imposing liability for omissions is operative. See generally on this point Finn in Finn (ed.) *Essays on Torts* pp. 179-82.

237 Similarly, simple breach of contract is not actionable under the statutes: French in Finn (ed.) *Essays on Torts* pp. 188-190.

238 On the application of the statutory provisions to commercial pre-contractual negotiations see A. Terry (1988) 16 *A.B.L.R.* 189.

plaintiff because: (a) the plaintiff does not have to prove that he was in any particular relationship with the defendant;[239] (b) whatever doubts there may be about the role of reliance in common law actions do not arise under the statutes, which do not require the plaintiff to show that he relied (in either sense) on the defendant;[240] but (c) in cases where the plaintiff can prove reliance, it is not necessary for him to show that the defendant knew or ought to have foreseen that he (the plaintiff) would rely on him (the defendant) for any particular purpose; and (d) most radically, except in relation to 'representations as to any future matter',[241] liability under the statutes is strict in the sense that they apply even if the person engaging in the conduct did not intend to mislead or deceive and was neither reckless nor negligent. Furthermore, (e) whereas a duty of care may be prevented from arising at common law by the use of a disclaimer, it would seem that a disclaimer could only be effective under the statutes if, and to the extent that, it prevented the conduct being misleading or deceptive or likely to mislead or deceive,[242] or if it broke the chain of causation between the defendant's conduct and the loss which is required by s.82 of the Commonwealth statute and its equivalents in other jurisdictions. Similarly, (f) whereas at common law a plaintiff might not recover if he acted unreasonably in relying on the defendant, under the statutes the plaintiff's conduct is relevant only to the extent that it prevents the defendant's conduct being described as misleading or deceptive: conduct which would only mislead a person careless of his own interests could not be so described.[243]

Fourthly, whereas in the tort of negligence the only available remedy is damages, under the statutes a variety of remedies can be had including damages, injunctions and orders avoiding or varying contracts or requiring corrective advertising. It has been held that damages under the Commonwealth statute should be assessed by analogy with the principles relevant to common law actions in the tort of deceit.[244]

One result of the breadth of these provisions is that whereas in England courts have been concerned to limit the scope of the tort of negligence so as to prevent it encroaching on the territory of other torts and of the law of contract, in Australia the common law of tort in general and of negligence

239 So, for example, there is nothing in the words of the statutes which would prevent actions being brought by, or even on behalf of, members of large or unascertained groups of persons.

240 Not only is there no mention of reliance, but also the words 'likely to mislead or deceive' make it clear that no one need actually have been misled or deceived. But, as at common law, reliance is an important causal factor in many cases: French in Finn (ed.) *Essays on Torts* p. 195.

241 Such a representation is deemed to be misleading unless the representor can prove that he had reasonable grounds for making it.

242 The statutes contain no provision similar to s.3 of the Misrepresentation Act 1967 (U.K.) or s.4 of the Contractual Remedies Act 1979 (N.Z.) to the effect that liability can be excluded or disclaimed provided the exclusion clause or disclaimer is, in all the circumstances, reasonable.

243 French (1989) 63 *A.L.J.* 250, 264. But the standard by which the plaintiff's conduct is evaluated is lower than the common law's 'reasonable person' yardstick: Pengilley [1987] *A.B.L.R.* 247, 254-5.

244 *Gates* v. *City Mutual Life Assurance Society Ltd* (1986) 160 C.L.R. 1.

in particular is the victim, not the predator.[245] The danger here is that the statutory provisions will 'sweep away painstakingly constructed principles and doctrines in the areas of tort and contract'.[246]

VII: SOME SPECIFIC DUTY ISSUES

We have so far considered general principles of duty of care and the way the duty concept operates in relation to different types of injury and loss. Now we examine some more specific issues relating to duty of care.

1. OMISSIONS

Although a defendant can be held liable in the tort of negligence for both acting (misfeasance) and failing to act (nonfeasance), it is not every omission which gives rise to liability.[247] The law draws a distinction between mere omissions and omissions in the course of some larger activity. For example, a failure to warn a fellow-picnicker that the bridge he is about to cross is dangerous[248] or to warn another that a fraud is being perpetrated upon him by a third party would be a mere omission; whereas failure, while driving, to stop at a red light would be an omission in the course of driving. Negligent omissions in the course of an activity are treated in the same way as negligent actions. Mere omissions are not actionable unless the defendant was under some legally recognized pre-existing duty to take positive action (as opposed to a duty to avoid harmful action).[249] A very large number of negligence actions are concerned with failure to take some precaution, but very few of them are treated as raising any issue about liability for omissions. For example, in *Bolton* v. *Stone*[250] a cricket ball was hit over a fence on to the road, injuring the plaintiff. The House of Lords treated the case not as involving an omission to provide an adequate fence but as involving the negligent playing of cricket without adequate precautions to prevent injury from stray balls.

In fact, it is very difficult analytically to draw a distinction between a mere omission and an omission in the course of conduct. It all depends on how we choose to define the defendant's activity—often it is only if we view the failure to act in isolation that it appears to be a mere omission. In one case a swimmer was injured by diving into shallow water and hitting a concealed rock. The swimmer sued the authority which controlled the

---

245 As to contract, see esp. A. Terry (1987) 10 *U.N.S.W.L.J.* 260.

246 French (1989) 63 *A.L.J.* 250, 251.

247 *Atiyah's Accidents* pp. 80-93; J.M. Ratcliffe (ed.) *The Good Samaritan and the Law* (1966); Marshall Shapo *The Duty to Act* (Austin, Texas and London, 1977); E.J. Weinrib (1980) 90 *Yale L.J.* 247; J.C. Smith & P. Burns (1983) 46 *M.L.R.* 47; B.S. Markesinis (1989) 105 *L.Q.R.* 104.

248 *Quinn* v. *Hill* [1957] V.R. 439, 445.

249 *Thomas* v. *Elder Smith Goldsborough Mort Ltd* (1982) 30 S.A.S.R. 592.

250 [1951] A.C. 850.

area. One of the judges agreed with the plaintiff's argument that the authority had been negligent not in failing to remove the rocks but in encouraging people to believe that the area was safe for swimming.[251]

There are several reasons underlying the view that in some cases it would be unfair to hold a person liable for inactivity. Sometimes we feel that it would be expecting too much of the defendant to require him to act like the Good Samaritan and take action. There is a limit to the burdens we think *the law* should impose upon individuals, no matter how harshly morality may judge them for doing nothing. This is not to say that the law is unconcerned with people who go out of their way to help others. The courts have gone to some lengths to ensure that rescuers have a right to recover damages from persons who create dangers for injury sustained in effecting a rescue.[252] But it is one thing not to discourage rescuers—it is another thing to require heroism. Again, while morality might lay upon us a general duty to be our 'brother's or sister's keeper', the law has been unwilling to impose a general duty to control the conduct of others. The law tends to treat every person as an individual responsible only for his own conduct.

A second reason for uneasiness about omissions arises out of the law's emphasis on proximity and relationship. A person expected to go to the aid of another might well ask 'Why me?'. We often feel that the mere fact that we are around when something goes wrong puts no burden on *us* rather than the next person to do something about it. Only if we are in some special relationship with the party in need do we feel that some special obligation rests on us. Where the law does recognize some special relationship, for example between employer and employee, it will often impose a duty to take positive steps to protect a person from danger in circumstances where, if there was no such relationship, failure to take the necessary precautions might be seen as a mere omission.[253] In many situations, however, where there is no 'special' relationship between parties the law is loath to impose duties to warn of or to prevent impending loss or danger.

A third ground of uneasiness about omissions relates to causation. In a negligence action it is necessary for the plaintiff to prove that the defendant's negligence caused his loss or damage. It is often much harder to establish that a failure to act caused an injury than to establish that a negligent act did so. For example, it is very difficult to say that a drowning person would have been saved if someone had gone to his rescue; or that a person would have used any safety device that might have been (but was not) provided. He might have been injured or killed even if the defendant had acted to assist him. But even in cases where we can be reasonably sure that if reasonable steps had been taken, loss or damage would not have occurred, we might still feel that a person who was in a

---

251 *Nagle* v. *Rottnest Island Authority* [1991] Aust. Torts Reports 68,752 68,761 *per* Wallace J. The majority held the defendant not liable.

252 See p. 409 below.

253 e.g. *Commissioner for Railways* v. *Halley* (1978) 20 A.L.R. 409; cf. *Paris* v. *Stepney Borough Council* [1951] A.C. 367.

position to but omitted to take those steps did not *cause* the loss or damage but only failed to prevent it. For example, suppose a local authority, in exercise of its statutory powers, negligently inspects the foundations of a house which is being constructed in its area and fails to notice that the builder has made them too shallow. We might want to say that while the local authority failed, by its negligence, to prevent the faulty foundations being laid, it was the builder who caused any loss to the owner resulting from the faulty foundations.

Despite these arguments and a general uneasiness about imposing legal duties to take positive action, it is by no means the case that failure to take reasonable steps to prevent other suffering injury or loss is never actionable in tort. But whether a person is under a pre-existing duty to take positive action is largely a matter of choice according to whether we think persons in that situation *ought* to do something. In order to say anything more specific, we need to examine the law in rather more detail.

(a) Economic loss In *Deyong* v. *Shenburn*[254] the English Court of Appeal held that the employer of an actor was under no duty of care to prevent the actor's clothes being stolen from his dressing room by providing a lock for the room. In *John's Period Furniture Pty Ltd* v. *Commonwealth Savings Bank of Australia*[255] it was held that the bank owed no duty of care to a trader, who was paid with a forged cheque, to warn that cheque forms drawn on it had been stolen from a post office. In both cases the loss was economic and the law seems particularly unwilling to impose positive duties to act to prevent such loss. Even the relationship of employer and employee (which is the foundation of many duties to prevent personal injury) was not regarded in *Deyong* as a ground for imposing liability.

This unwillingness to impose liability for failure to warn of or prevent economic loss is well illustrated by a series of recent English cases: in one case it was held that school authorities owed no duty in tort to advise parents of the wisdom of taking out insurance to cover the risk that their children might be injured while playing sport;[256] and in another that an employer who sent its employees abroad to work owed no tortious duty to take reasonable steps to advise them of the wisdom of taking out personal accident and medical insurance to cover them while overseas.[257] In two other cases it was held that although the parties to an insurance contract owe each other a duty (called a 'duty of utmost good faith') to disclose facts material to the insurance policy, breach of this duty does not give rise to a right to sue for damages but only to rescind the insurance contract; and, furthermore, that a person involved in commercial dealings with another does not owe any duty in tort to take reasonable steps to warn the other that a fraud is being perpetrated on him by a third party unless he is contractually bound to warn him or has undertaken (either expressly or

254 [1946] K.B. 227; cf. *P. Perl (Exporters) Ltd* v. *Camden L.B.C.* [198] Q.B. 342; contrast *Stansbie* v. *Troman* [1948] 2 K.B. 48; see also pp. 379, 384-6 below.
255 (1980) 24 S.A.S.R. 224.
256 *Van Oppen* v. *Clerk to the Bedford Charity Trustees* [1990] 1 W.L.R. 235.
257 *Reid* v. *Rush & Tompkins Group p.l.c.* [1990] 1 W.L.R. 212.

impliedly) to do so.[258] The courts seem particularly unwilling to turn commercial morality into commercial law, and they would, no doubt, treat with considerable caution any argument that a non-contractual undertaking to warn of impending financial loss should be implied from conduct. As between parties engaged in commerce, the current basic philosophy of the English courts is that the only legal obligations they owe to each other are those which are expressed in the contract between them or can be implied in accordance with the stringent 'necessity' and 'officious bystander' tests of contract law. The law of tort has little or no part to play in this context.

On the other hand, there are at least three types of case in which courts have been prepared to impose liability for economic loss resulting from failure to act. The first is illustrated by *Anns* v. *Merton L.B.C.*[259] in which the House of Lords had to decide whether the council could be held liable either for negligent failure to exercise a statutory power to inspect the foundations of houses under construction to ensure they complied with building by-laws, or for negligent inspection by its building inspector. It was held, *inter alia,* that if the council negligently failed to give proper consideration to the question whether to inspect or not it might be held liable to the owner of an affected dwelling for the cost of repairing the premises. This result arose from a consideration of rules of administrative law about the proper exercise of statutory powers. These impose on the holder of a power a duty to give due consideration to the question of whether the power ought to be exercised.

The House of Lords has since held that a local authority cannot normally be held liable for the cost of repairing defective premises;[260] and it has shown very considerable unwillingness to impose liability on regulatory authorities generally for failure to prevent loss occurring, especially economic loss. But the general principle that a body with a statutory power may, in certain circumstances, be liable in tort for failure to exercise that power still seems to be good law. However, *Sutherland S.C.* v. *Heyman*[261] suggests that liability would arise only if the plaintiff could show that he had relied on the authority (in either a specific or a general sense) to exercise its power.[262] It is not clear that a subsequent purchaser, such as the plaintiffs in *Heyman* and *Anns,* could satisfy this requirement. *Heyman* does not provide much guidance on this point because the council had not said or done anything on which specific

---

258 *Banque Keyser Ullman S.A.* v. *Skandia Insurance (U.K.) Ltd* [1990] 1 Q.B. 665 (C.A. affirmed on other grounds by H.L. [1991] 2 A.C. 249); *Bank of Nova Scotia* v. *Hellenic Mutual War Risks Association (Bermuda) Ltd* [1990] 1 Q.B. 818. Cf. *Cooper Henderson Finance Ltd* v. *Colonial Mutual General Insurance Co. Ltd* [1990] 1 N.Z.L.R. 1. But breach of an insurer's duty to act with good faith in processing insurance claims may sound in damages: *Gibson* v. *The Parkes District Hospital* [1991] Aust. Torts Rep. 81-140; J.G. Fleming (1992) 108 *L.Q.R.* 357.

259 [1978] A.C. 728.

260 *Murphy* v. *Brentwood D.C.* [1991] 1 A.C. 398.

261 (1984-5) 157 C.L.R. 424.

262 cf. *Parramatta C.C.* v. *Lutz* (1988) 12 N.S.W.L.R. 293 discussed by J. Keeler (1989) 12 *Adel. L.R.* 93,104-6. See also *Casley-Smith* v. *F.S. Evans & Sons Pty Ltd* (1988) 67 L.G.R.A. 108.

reliance was placed by the plaintiff, and no evidence or argument was presented on the issue of general reliance.

The second type of case is illustrated by *L. Shaddock & Associates Pty Ltd* v. *Parramatta C.C.*[263] There a formal inquiry was made on a standard form as to whether a property which the plaintiff wished to purchase was subject to road-widening proposals. The council had adopted the practice of only marking the appropriate part of the inquiry form if there was some proposal in existence. In this case the form was return unmarked, but there was a relevant proposal under consideration. In the New South Wales Court of Appeal Moffitt P. and Mahoney J.A. interpreted the failure to endorse as a positive giving of information (which the council had a duty to do carefully) because the council intended the absence of endorsement to stand as a reply, and this is the way a reasonable solicitor, knowing of the council's practice, would have taken it.[264] In the High Court Gibbs C.J. explicitly agreed with this.[265] It is also accepted that a duty to give information or a warning could arise if a person, by words or conduct, led another reasonably to believe that information or a warning would be relayed.

The idea of undertaking is important in this context: if a person agrees or undertakes to do X, this may provide a sound basis for the imposition of liability for failure to do X. Such undertakings may be contractual (as in the typical case where a professional fails to protect his client's interests),[266] but they need not be.[267] Such an undertaking may ground liability not only for failure to do a particular act, but also for failure to do it carefully.[268] Such undertakings may be express,[269] but they are often implied; and to imply an undertaking is often to impose an undertaking which was never actually made, on the ground that the defendant *ought* in the circumstances to be liable for his failure to act. So the use of the word 'undertaking' is sometimes fictional, and is designed to give greater weight to a judgment, made on other (often unexpressed) grounds, that the defendant ought to be liable.

Thirdly, we have already seen that the complementary ideas of the continuing professional relationship and the relationship of dependence have been used to justify the imposition of liability for failure to act. The leading case is *Hawkins* v. *Clayton*[270] in which a solicitor was held liable for failure to advise the executor of a will of the death of the testator. In

---

263 (1981) 150 C.L.R. 225.
264 [1979] 1 N.S.W.L.R. 566, 582, 595.
265 (1981) 150 C.L.R. 225, 230, 235.
266 And as, for example, in *Stansbie* v. *Troman* [1948] 2 K.B. 48.
267 See, for example, *Norwest Refrigeration Services Pty Ltd* v. *Bain Dawes (W.A.) Pty Ltd* (1984) 157 C.L.R. 149.
268 *Norwest Refrigeration* v. *Bain Dawes* (1984) 157 C.L.R. 149.
269 e.g. *Marac Finance Ltd* v. *Colmore-Williams* [1988] 1 N.Z.L.R. 625.
270 (1988) 164 C.L.R. 539. See also *Cornish* v. *Midland Bank p.l.c.* [1985] 3 All E.R. 513, 521-3 *per* Kerr L.J; but banks appear to be under no general duty to give their customers financial advice relevant to transactions being conducted by the bank for the customer: *James* v. *Australia and New Zealand Banking Group Ltd* (1985-6) 64 A.L.R. 347; *David Securities Pty Ltd* v. *Commonwealth Bank of Australia* (1990) 93 A.L.R. 271.

Barnes v. *Hay*[271] a solicitor was held liable for failing to warn a client that premises, a lease of which he was negotiating, were about to be sold, and of the desirability of obtaining a registered lease before this happened. Again, in *Ross* v. *Caunters*[272] liability was imposed on a solicitor for negligent failure to warn his client that his will should not be witnessed by the spouse of a beneficiary; and in *Midland Bank Trust Co.* v. *Hett, Stubbs & Kemp*[273] a solicitor was held liable in tort for negligent failure to register an option to purchase a farm. In these cases the relationship between the solicitor and the client imposes on the former a positive duty to do everything necessary to carry through the transactions which he has been instructed to effect. This duty is owed, in the first instance, to the client, but a derivative duty of similar content may be owed to third parties.

In *Waimond Pty Ltd* v. *Byrne*[274] the New South Wales Court of Appeal (by majority) went somewhat further and held that a solicitor could owe a duty to a client to warn the client that a fraud or a breach of trust was being perpetrated on him, even if this was not required by any instructions given by the client to the solicitor. But it seems that no such duty would be owed to a non-client. The solicitor in *Waimond* knew facts which ought to have alerted him to the fraud, and if he had not, he would probably not have been held liable for failure to discover the fraud. Some professional groups, most notably auditors and surveyors, are often employed exactly to take positive steps to discover and investigate facts which might indicate hidden problems or irregularities; in such cases the crucial question is not whether there can be liability for failure to investigate, but rather what steps must be taken to discharge the duty to take care in investigating.[275]

(b) Dangerous activities There are several cases which support the proposition that the conduct of an especially dangerous activity or the creation of a physically dangerous situation can impose positive duties to act in such a way as to obviate or warn of the danger.[276]

(c) Duties of physical protection There are a number of situations in which the law is prepared to impose duties of positive action on persons who are in a particularly good position to take steps to protect others from physical dangers and who, it might be thought, are under some moral obligation to do so by reason of their relationship with the person in

---

271 (1988) 12 N.S.W.L.R. 337.

272 [1980] Ch. 297.

273 [1979] Ch. 384.

274 (1989) 18 N.S.W.L.R. 642.

275 See, for example, *Pacific Acceptance Corporation Ltd* v. *Forsyth* (1970) 92 W.N.(N.S.W.) 29; *Arthur Young & Co.* v. *W.A. Chip & Pulp Co. Ltd* [1989] W.A.R. 100 (auditors); *Roberts* v. *J. Hampson & Co.* [1990] 1 W.L.R. 94.

276 e.g. *Smith* v. *Victorian Railway Commissioners* (1902) 28 V.L.R. 44; *Harrison* v. *Sydney M.C.* (1931) 10 L.G.R. 116; *McKinnon* v. *Burtatowski* [1969] V.R. 899; *Commissioner of Railways* v. *Halley* (1978) 20 A.L.R. 409; *Bird* v. *Pearce* [1979] R.T.R. 369; *Casley-Smith* v. *F.H. Evans & Sons Pty Ltd* (1988) 67 L.G.R.A. 108; *Arnold* v. *Teno* (1978) 83 D.L.R. (3d) 609.

danger. So, for example, employers owe their employees duties to provide safe tools, a safe workplace and safe working systems, on the basis that the individual employee often has little control over working conditions. Again, doctors and hospitals may be held liable for failure to provide treatment,[277] or for failure to warn patients of risks associated with particular treatments;[278] or for failure to give patients information about their health.[279]

Another relationship which has given rise to considerable litigation is that between parents (or persons *in loco parentis*) and teachers and children. There are cases which support the view that a parent owes no general duty to his child to take positive steps to supervise it and protect it from danger.[280] This appears to mean that a parent cannot, merely by reason of blood relationship with the child, be under any legal duty which any other person in similar circumstances would not be under.[281] Unfortunately, the leading case of *Hahn* v. *Conley*[282] is not clear as to what the exact basis of any duty might be. There are suggestions that the duty arises out of a relationship which comes into existence when an adult, whether parent or not, takes charge of or assumes control over the child.[283] On the other hand, *Hahn* v. *Conley* is also open to the interpretation that any duty arises out of the creation by the parent of a situation of foreseeable danger for the child. This approach now clearly represents the law in South Australia.[284] The difference between the two views is that a duty to take positive action is more easily imposed on the basis of a control relationship because it does not require the defendant to have acted negligently in creating the particular situation in which protection is needed. It might be thought that neither approach takes proper account of the dependence of the child or pupil on the parent or teacher, at least in cases where the child is quite young. (The older the child the more care it can be expected to take for itself.)

The good sense behind restricting the duty of parents (though not of teachers) may be that in normal circumstances there would be no advantage to the child in suing its parent unless the parent was insured against

---

277 *Barnett* v. *Chelsea and Kensington Hospital Management Committee* [1969] 1 Q.B. 428 (but the claim failed on the issue of causation).

278 See further p. 429 below.

279 e.g. *Thomson* v. *Davison* [1975] Qd.R. 93. A related, and highly contentious, issue is whether doctors should be under a duty to tell third parties that a patient has a communicable disease (most topically, that the patient is HIV positive, on which see M. Neave (1987) 9 *Tas. L.R.* 1, 23-30). And does a person who is diagnosed as HIV positive have a duty to warn his or her sexual partner? (see R. O'Dair [1990] *C.L.P.* 219, 220-31).

280 e.g. *Cameron* v. *Commissioner for Railways* [1964] Qd.R. 480; *Collett* v. *Hutchins* [1964] Qd.R. 495; *Rogers* v. *Rawlings* [1969] Qd R. 262.

281 See also *Posthuma* v. *Campbell* (1984) 37 S.A.S.R. 321.

282 (1971) 126 C.L.R. 276. Cf. Stephen J. in *Geyer* v. *Downs* (1977) 138 C.L.R. 91.

283 cf. *Anderson* v. *Nader* (1990) 101 F.L.R. 34.

284 *Robertson* v. *Swincer* (1989) 52 S.A.S.R. 356; *Towart* v. *Adler* (1989) 52 S.A.S.R. 373; in neither case was a duty imposed. In *Bye* v. *Bates* (1989) 51 S.A.S.R. 67 a duty was imposed, but the basis on which this was done is not entirely clear. This approach finds support in the judgment of Murphy and Aickin JJ. in *Geyer* v. *Downs*.

liability.[285] The point is even stronger in cases where the child sues a negligent third party who then seeks contribution from a negligent parent. In neither case will a finding of liability benefit the child financially.

Another type of case where issues of protection arise is that of gaolers and prisoners. In *Howard* v. *Jarvis*[286] it was held that a gaoler who deprives a prisoner of his liberty and assumes control of his person falls under a duty to take reasonable care for his safety. In another case in which a prisoner committed suicide, it was held that the police were under a duty to inform the prison authorities of the prisoner's suicidal tendencies when they handed him into the latter's custody.[287] On the other hand, in *Quinn* v. *Hill*[288] an elderly woman prisoner sued the prison authorities for alleged negligence by a wardress in allowing her to do a task beyond her physical capacity. It was held that prisoners are not in the same position as schoolchildren and that a wardress is under no duty to warn a prisoner of the dangers of her job, although she could be under a duty not to *allocate* a difficult job to a physically weak prisoner.[289]

It has also been held in a number of cases that prison authorities are under a duty of reasonable care to protect one prisoner from physical attack by other prisoners.[290] The best view may be that a gaoler is under a duty to protect prisoners from dangers to which imprisonment makes them particularly vulnerable, such as assault, suicide and being trapped in a burning cell, but not from dangers which are exactly similar to those met in the outside world and against which there is no general duty of protection.

The list of relationships which may give rise to duties of protection is not closed. In Canada, for example, it has been held that a hotel proprietor may owe a duty of reasonable protection to an intoxicated patron whom he turns out of the hotel and who is subsequently run down by a car;[291] and that vehicle owners owe a duty of protection to unlicensed and uninstructed persons whom they allow to use their vehicles. In another case it was held by the Supreme Court of Canada that a ski resort operator owed a duty to take reasonable steps to discourage an intoxicated patron from taking part in a dangerous competition run by the operator.[292]

Slightly different issues arise in rescue situations where the rescuer may not have any personal relationship with the person in danger and where he may himself be faced with physical risks in the process of helping the endangered person. In *Horsley* v. *McLaren (The Ogopogo)*[293] K was the

---

285 See *Robertson* v. *Swincer* (1989) 52 S.A.S.R. 356, 361 *per* King C.J.; but contrast Legoe J. at p. 370. See also Insurance Constracts Act 1984 (Cwth) s.65.
286 (1958) 98 C.L.R. 177.
287 *Kirkham* v. *Chief Constable of Manchester* [1990] 2 Q.B. 283.
288 [1957] V.R. 439.
289 cf. *Morgan* v. *Attorney-General* [1965] N.Z.L.R. 134.
290 *Hall* v. *Whatmore* [1961] V.R. 225; *Dixon* v. *State of Western Australia* [1974] W.A.R. 65; *L.* v. *Commonwealth* (1976) 10 A.L.R. 269.
291 cf. *Akers* v. *P* (1986) 3 M.V.R. 385.
292 *Crocker* v. *Sundance Northwest Resorts Ltd* [1988] 1 S.C.R. 1186.
293 [1972] S.C.R. 441.

owner and in charge of a motor vessel from which M fell overboard, through no fault of K, into very cold water. Another passenger, H, jumped in to assist M when it seemed that K's attempts to manoeuvre the boat into a suitable position to help M were going to fail. Both H and M died. The question before the court was whether the tactics adopted by K, which were the cause of H's death, were negligent. On this issue the court disagreed, but all judges were agreed that the relationship of boat owner and guest imposed a duty on K to exercise reasonable care in rescuing M, whether he had fallen overboard through his own carelessness or accidentally. Laskin J. went further and said that relationships such as that of employer and employee, carrier and passenger, could give rise to an affirmative duty to go to someone's rescue—in such cases the rescuer would not just be a Good Samaritan. The duty is, of course, not a duty to effect a successful rescue but just to exercise reasonable care in attempting a rescue; so the rescuer is entitled to weigh the potential danger to himself against the chance of a successful rescue. Another rescue situation which might generate a duty of positive action is this: a motorist comes across an injured person on an isolated stretch of road. He offers to fetch help but then fails to do so. He might well be held liable for that failure especially if, in reliance on it, the injured person declined an offer of help from someone else. This would be another example of liability for omissions based on failure to perform an undertaking to take positive action.

(d) Duties of landowners Traditionally the law of tort did not impose on property owners duties to take positive steps to ensure that the operation of nature on their land did not cause damage to others. The rationale for this approach was partly the supposed difficulty of framing a general duty which would take account of the different abilities and resources of those subject to it;[294] and partly that it was thought unfair to require a person to take action when he was not responsible for the creation of the danger. So the rule also applied to dangers created by the acts of third parties of whom the landowner had no knowledge and over whom he had no control.[295] But if the landowner did intervene he could be held liable if by his negligence he made matters worse.[296]

In *Goldman* v. *Hargrave*[297] a tree on the defendant's land was struck by lightning and caught fire. The landowner cut the tree down and cleared the area around it, but several days later the fire rekindled and spread to the plaintiff's land. It was held that if the defendant had exercised reasonable care the fire could have been entirely extinguished several days before it spread. But the defendant had not increased the danger of its spreading—in fact, he had diminished the danger; on the other hand, if he had taken all reasonable care he could have eliminated it. On these facts it could be argued for the defendant that since, according to the

294 *Havelberg* v. *Brown* [1905] S.A.L.R. 1, 11 *per* Way C.J.
295 ibid p. 10.
296 ibid pp. 12-13.
297 [1967] 1 A.C. 645; cf. *Leakey* v. *National Trust* [1980] Q.B. 485; *Bradburn* v. *Lindsay* [1983] 2 All E.R. 408.

relevant authorities, he was under no duty to take positive action, he would not be liable if, by his careless intervention, he failed to decrease the risk as much as he might have. The Privy Council countered this argument by denying the immunity of the landowner for failure to act at all. Clearly there would be no point holding that a landowner could be liable only if he intervened, because this might encourage people to stand by and watch other persons or their property being damaged (although in many cases the landowner would want to intervene to protect his own property as well). So, the landowner is under a duty to take reasonable care to prevent damage from hazards on his land, whether natural or created by third parties. Reasonable care is judged in light of the fact that the landowner was not responsible for creating the danger, and so is under a lesser obligation to take precautions against it than if he had created it. It is fair to expect the loss caused by natural disasters and the acts of anti-social citizens to be spread around and, to some extent at least, to lie where it falls. So, for example, a landowner who sets a fire to burn off stubble is rightly held to a higher standard of care than the farmer whose stubble is set alight by a flash of lightning or the cigarette butt of a picnicking traveller.

Further, the burden of taking positive action is lightened by the principle that what is required of the defendant is to be judged in the light of his own particular physical abilities and financial resources. As we will see later, in general the law judges reasonable care objectively according to the standard of the reasonable person and not according to the subjective characteristics of the defendant. The law does not require the defendant to take precautions which are so costly or difficult as to be quite out of proportion to the damage likely to be prevented; but once the appropriate precautions have been established, it is usually no answer for the defendant to say that he was not able or could not afford to take them. The subjective principle recognized in this area also acknowledges the fact that the hazard is not of the landowner's making.

(e) Duties to control others To what extent must a person who has control of another person take steps to prevent that other person causing injury or damage to some third person? There seems no doubt in this area that liability depends not on the existence of any particular relationship between controller and controlled, but on a failure in all the circumstances to exercise a reasonable degree of control over a person whom one ought to have controlled. So, not only may parents or school authorities owe a duty to control young children, and prison authorities a duty to control inmates,[298] but it has also been held that a hotel manager may owe a duty to his patrons to supervise or eject an intoxicated or dangerous customer;[299] that the owner of a roller-skating rink may be under a duty to take steps to control deliberate and repeated dangerous conduct by skaters, especially if

298 See generally *Home Office* v. *Dorset Yacht Co. Ltd* [1970] A.C. 1004; *Thorne* v. *W.A.* [1964] W.A.R. 147.

299 *Chordas* v. *Bryant (Wellington) Pty Ltd* (1989) 91 A.L.R. 149.

complaints about it have been made;[300] that a local authority which establishes a system for regulating the use of surfboards on a beach owes a duty to swimmers to take reasonable care in policing the system;[301] and that the owner of a car may owe a duty not to allow an incompetent or incapacitated person to drive his car.[302] In the case of children the duty to control is sometimes related to the duty to protect since steps taken to protect the child may also be adequate to protect third parties.[303] But in other cases the child will not be in danger itself, but will simply present a danger to others; for example, where it is wielding a shanghai.[304]

By contrast, in England it seems that public regulatory and law-enforcement agencies are very unlikely to be held to owe a duty of care to third parties injured by conduct of a regulated person or a law-breaker to exercise their powers in such a way as to prevent the injury occurring. This appears to be true of physical injury as well as economic loss. So, for example, in England the police generally owe no duty of care to victims of law-breaking. It is not clear to what extent this principle represents Australian law.[305]

It is necessary to distinguish between liability to control and vicarious liability.[306] Vicarious liability is liability imposed on one person for a *tort* committed by another. On the other hand, a person may be liable for negligently failing to control another even if the conduct of that other which caused the injury was not itself tortious.[307]

In the absence of an obligation to control, a person is unlikely to be held liable for injury or damage caused by another unless, to the knowledge of the defendant, it was *highly* likely (and hence highly foreseeable) that injury or damage would result if the defendant did not take some precaution against the adverse effects of the third party's action. A common situation is where a property owner allows the property to stand empty and dilapidated with the result that vandals use it for access to other contiguous properties which they damage or break into, or where vandals set property alight with the result that neighbouring properties are damaged.[308] Similarly, in *Lamb* v. *Camden L.B.C.*[309] workmen of the council negligently broke a water main. Escaping water undermined the foundations of a house forcing the tenants to leave. Squatters broke into the now derelict house and did more damage. It was held that the houseowner could not recover against the council for the damage caused by the squatters; Oliver L.J. thought that the criminal acts of the squatters were not foreseeable enough.

---

300 *Maynard* v. *Glideway* (1985) 3 S.R.(W.A.) 154.
301 *Glasheen* v. *Waverley M.C.* [1990] Aust. Torts Reports 81-016.
302 *Harris* v. *Van Spijk* [1986] 1 N.Z.L.R. 275, 278.
303 *Carmarthenshire County Council* v. *Lewis* [1955] A.C. 549.
304 *Smith* v. *Leurs* (1945) 70 C.L.R. 256.
305 See, e.g., *Ticehurst* v. *Skeen* (1988) 3 M.V.R. 307.
306 See Chapter 21 below.
307 *Haines* v. *Rytmeister* (1986) 6 N.S.W.L.R. 529.
308 *Perl (P.) Exporters Ltd* v. *Camden L.B.C.* [1984] Q.B. 342; *King* v. *Liverpool C.C.* [1986] 1 W.L.R. 890; *Smith* v. *Littlewoods Ltd* [1987] A.C. 241.
309 [1981] Q.B. 625; B.S. Markesinis (1989) 105 *L.Q.R.* 104.

In a case like *Lamb* v. *Camden L.B.C.* this rule arguably produces a fair result: perhaps absent owners should take steps to protect their property against squatters while it is empty, or at least take out adequate insurance. But the rule seems less satisfactory in cases where vandals gain access to property through neighbouring premises: why should the neighbour have to take steps to neutralize the indolence of the defendant, or suffer because he has not insured his own property (especially if insurance is not available at all or at an affordable price)?

2. The Liability of Occupiers of Land to Visitors

In this section we are concerned with the liability of occupiers of land for loss, injury or damage suffered by people visiting the land as a result of dangers arising on the land. Occupiers' liability (as this area of the law is called) provides example of tortious liability for omissions: occupiers can be held liable not only for creating dangers on their land but also for failing to remove them,[310] and they can also be held liable for failure to exercise reasonable control over activities of their visitors which endanger others on the premises.[311]

(a) Background to the current law In the first edition of this book, a separate chapter was devoted to the law of occupiers' liability. This was because although the liability of occupiers to their visitors is basically liability for negligence, the rules governing occupiers' liability were well developed before *Donoghue* v. *Stevenson*,[312] and for a long time remained relatively unaffected by Lord Atkin's general-principle approach to questions of duty. Those rules distinguished between different classes of visitor (invitees, licensees, contractual entrants, trespassers and so on), and the duty of the occupier varied according to the status of any particular visitor. In other words, the general duty category of occupier and visitor was divided into a number of duty sub-categories. It might have been expected that the general principle of liability for negligently caused physical injury laid down by Lord Atkin would soon have caused the sub-categories of visitor to be assimilated into one general category. But in Australia this did not happen until 1987 when the High Court decided, in *Australian Safeway Stores Pty Ltd* v. *Zaluzna*,[313] that the old duty sub-categories were just applications of the general duty to take care to avoid

---

310 The occupiers' liability statutes (Wrongs Act 1936 (S.A.) s.17d; Wrongs Act 1958 (Vic.) s.14B(3); Occupiers' Liability Act 1985 (W.A.) s.5(1)) all apply to things done or *omitted to be done* by the occupier to ensure that the premises are reasonably safe, and this reflects the common law.

311 e.g. *Glasgow Corporation* v. *Muir* [1943] A.C. 448; *Hislop* v. *Mooney* [1968] N.S.W.R. 559; *Wilkinson* v. *Joyceman* [1985] 1 Qd.R. 567; *Maynard* v. *Glideway* (1985) 3 S.R.(W.A.) 154. Cf. *De Jager* v. *Payneham and Magill Lodges Hall Incorporated* (1984) 36 S.A.S.R. 498.

312 [1932] A.C. 562.

313 (1987) 162 C.L.R. 479.

physical injury which was embodied in the neighbour principle.[314] As might be expected, Brennan J. dissented, mainly on the ground that the old sub-categories injected an element of certainty and predictability into the law which would be lacking if they did not exist. But the history of this area of the law in England, where the old sub-categories were abolished by the Occupiers' Liability Act 1957,[315] suggests that Brennan J.'s apparent fear that the majority's decision would generate excessive litigation seems unfounded.

One result of *Zaluzna* is that much of the old law discussed in Chapter 14 of the first edition is now of doubtful relevance or importance. Indeed, even before 1987 this was the position in several Australian jurisdictions where legislation designed to achieve much the same effect as the decision in *Zaluzna* had already been enacted.[316] In jurisdictions where wide-ranging legislation on occupiers' liability exists, questions may arise as to the relationship between the statutory regime of liability and the common law: in all cases the legislation replaces the common law in the area of its operation, so that cases which fall within it are governed by it while cases which fall outside it are governed by the common law. Given that the basic effect of all the statutes is to extend the principles of the common law of negligence to occupiers' liability, it may not matter in most cases whether the statute or the common law applies. But, as we will see, there are uncertainties as to the scope of the various statutes, and so there will be room for various technical arguments about which set of rules should apply to certain cases. This unfortunate situation can only benefit lawyers' pockets.

(b) Who is an occupier? If the logic of *Zaluzna* were followed rigorously, this question would not deserve separate treatment because the liability of an occupier in negligence would simply be an illustration of the operation of principles of duty of care. Nor would the question of what are 'premises', which we will consider in a moment. Only if there are rules of law which apply exclusively to occupiers of premises does one need to define these terms; and the thrust of *Zaluzna* is that there are no such rules. However, the law is not as neat as this. In the first place, *Zaluzna* only decides that the liability of occupiers does not depend on the old sub-categories of visitor; it leaves open the question of whether there are *any* rules of negligence law which apply to 'occupiers' but not to other defendants. Secondly, all of the relevant statutes apply only to 'occupiers of premises' and they all adopt the pre-*Zaluzna* definition of 'occupier' as

314 The concept of proximity has little relevance here, partly because occupiers' liability is mainly liability for personal injury, and partly because the relationship of occupier and lawful visitor (but, perhaps, not that of occupier and trespasser) is a relationship of close proximity.

315 The Occupiers' Liability Act 1962 (N.Z.) is modelled on the English Act.

316 In the light of *Zaluzna* the Australian Law Reform Commission recommended that legislation to reform the law of occupiers' liability was not needed in the A.C.T.: A.L.R.C. 42.

the starting point for the statutory definition.[317] So we must first discuss what the terms 'occupier' and 'occupation' mean at common law.

The leading case on the meaning of the term 'occupation' is *Wheat* v. *E. Lacon & Co. Ltd.*[318] There the licensee of a public house owned by the defendant occupied a flat above the public house. His wife was permitted by the defendant to have paying guests, one of whom was killed when descending the staircase to the flat, which was badly lit and had a handrail for only part of its distance. It was held that the defendant was in occupation of the premises in the relevant sense. Lord Denning said that a person is in occupation if he has a sufficient degree of control over the premises that he ought to realize that any failure of care on his part may result in injury to a person coming there. The test is, therefore, a factual one: does the person have some control, any control, over the premises such that he can prevent injury to visitors? It would seem to follow from this that any person in physical occupation of the premises would be an occupier for the purposes of occupiers' liability since he will always have power to do something, even, for example, if only to turn on a light at night. But it also follows that someone may be an occupier even though he is not in physical occupation: for example, the brewery company in *Wheat* v. *Lacon* which was a licensor, or the owner of a building site on which an independent contractor is working. The independent contractor[319] and the licensee would also be in occupation since the control test allows that more than one person can be in occupation at the same time.[320] Joint occupiers can each be in control of the whole or the same part of the premises—as in *Wheat* v. *Lacon*; or of different parts of the same premises—as where a landlord lets flats[321] but retains control of the common areas such as stairs and lifts. A person is, then, an occupier of premises or parts of premises if he has any degree of control over them, and his duty as an occupier is relative to the degree of control.

It should be noted, however, that a person who is in physical occupation or control of premises merely as a servant of someone else is not an occupier for the purposes of liability.[322] (This is not true, as we saw above, of an independent contractor.) On this basis Viscount Dilhorne held in *Wheat* v. *Lacon* that the licensee of the public house was not an occupier since he had control over the premises merely as a servant of the brewery

---

317 The Wrongs Act 1958 (Vic.) does this silently by not defining 'occupier'; the Wrongs Act 1936 (SA) s.17b and the Occupiers' Liability Act 1985 (W.A.) s.2 define 'occupier' in terms of occupation and control of premises.

318 [1966] A.C. 552. This was a case under the Occupiers' Liability Act 1957 (U.K.) but in the Act the word 'occupies' is used in the same sense as it bore at common law (s.1(2)).

319 *Hartwell* v. *Grayson, Rollo and Clover Docks Ltd* [1947] K.B. 901; *Blackman* v. *M. & D.J. Bossie Pty Ltd* [1968] W.A.R. 97; *Canberra Formwork Pty Ltd* v. *Civil & Civic Ltd* (1982) 41 A.C.T.R. 1.

320 cf. *Burton* v. *Melbourne Harbour Trust Commissioners* [1954] V.L.R. 353; *Smith* v. *Yarnold* (1969) 90 W.N.(Pt.1)(N.S.W.) 316; *Thompson* v. *The Commonwealth* (1969) 70 S.R.(N.S.W.) 398.

321 At common law a lease is regarded as involving a complete relinquishment of control even though the landlord undertakes (or has a right) to repair. This seems inconsistent with the control test.

322 *Smith* v. *Yarnold* (1969) 90 W.N.(Pt.1)(N.S.W.) 316; *Stone* v. *Taffe* [1974] 1 W.L.R. 1575.

which owned it. The licensee had some control over the state of premises, but was not responsible for their condition. It is not easy to reconcile this principle with the control test since the licensee in *Wheat* v. *Lacon* and, no doubt, the club secretary in *Smith* v. *Yarnold,*[323] enjoyed a degree of autonomy in the day-to-day running of the premises. The test introduces the idea of where legal responsibility for exercising control ought to lie to overcome the fact of where physical power to act does lie. This has led to approval of Viscount Dilhorne's approach on the ground that it places the liability on the party best able to bear or insure against it.[324]

A particular application of the control test is seen in cases where the defendant has the right to admit or exclude visitors. Control sufficient to entitle a person expressly or impliedly to invite persons on to premises is control sufficient (but not necessary) to make a person an occupier.[325] The right to admit can override arrangements between the invitor and third parties concerning which of them is obliged to keep the premises in repair. In *Kevan* v. *Commissioners for Railways*[326] the plaintiff was injured while using steps in the entrance to a station. The area was owned by the A.M.P. Society; the defendant had a right of way over it, and under the agreement between it and A.M.P. the latter was obliged to keep the area in good repair. It was held that as between the plaintiff and the defendant the obligation of A.M.P. to repair was irrelevant because the defendant's right to invite persons into the area made it an occupier. Further, A.M.P.'s obligation to repair did not prevent the defendant from repairing or relieve it of a duty to see that A.M.P. repaired or, in default of this, to repair the area itself.

Finally, it has been held that a person may be an occupier if he has an immediate right to exercise control, even though he may never enter into actual physical possession.[327]

As noted earlier, the occupiers' liability statutes take the common law definition of 'occupier' as their starting point.[328] Section 14A(a) of the Victorian statute extends the common law definition to cover a lessor who has an obligation under the lease to repair or maintain the premises or who has (or could have put himself in a position to have) a right to enter and carry out maintenance or repairs. Section 17b of the South Australian statute defines 'occupier' to include 'landlord'; but s.17d provides, in effect, that a landlord who is not in occupation is only liable for injury, loss or damage arising from negligence in carrying out or failing to carry out an obligation[329] to maintain or repair the demised premises. The net effect of these somewhat confusing South Australian provisions seems to be that the liability to visitors of a landlord who satisfies the control test of

---

323 (1969) 90 W.N.(Pt.1)(N.S.W.) 316.

324 H. Luntz, D. Hambly, R. Hayes *Torts: Cases and Commentary* (Sydney, 1980) at p. 472.

325 *Burton* v. *Melbourne Harbour Trust Commissioners* [1954] V.L.R. 353.

326 [1972] 2 N.S.W.L.R. 710.

327 *Harris* v. *Birkenhead Corporation* [1976] 1 All E.R. 341.

328 And, in the case of the Western Australian statute, the ending point: Occupiers' Liability Act 1985 s.4(2); cf. Occupiers' Liability Act 1962 (N.Z.) s.3(2).

329 The words 'under the lease' are, presumably, to be understood.

occupation is to be decided according to the principles of the law of negligence (s.17c(1)), while the liability of a landlord who does not satisfy that test depends on the terms of the lease.

Section 9 of the Western Australian statute imposes on a landlord,

> a duty . . . to show towards any persons who may from time to time be on the premises the same care in respect of dangers arising from any failure on his part in carrying out his responsibilities of maintenance and repair of the premises [under the tenancy] as is required under this Act to be shown by an occupier of premises towards persons entering on those premises.

As we have seen, at common law a landlord is not treated as occupying the demised premises (although he may be in occupation of common parts of a building which are not subject to a lease). Furthermore, at common law a landlord, as such, cannot be sued in tort in respect of the state of the demised premises.[330] The combined effect of these common law rules is that landlords can only be sued in respect of the condition of the demised premises by the tenant (and not, for example, other people living in the premises or guests) and that they can only be sued in contract. Australian Capital Territory legislation provides that a lessor is not exempt from owing a duty of care to visitors by reason only that the lessor is not an occupier of the premises.[331]

Under the Victorian statute a landlord who falls within the terms of s.14A(a) owes the same duty of care to visitors as any other occupier;[332] as, under the South Australian statute, does a landlord who is in occupation of the demised premises. But the Western Australian statute, and the South Australian provision dealing with landlords who are not in occupation, limit the landlord's liability to failure to perform such obligations of maintenance or repair as the lease of the demised premises imposes on him. Both the Western Australian and the South Australian statute allow exclusion of an occupier's obligations by contract as against the other party to the contract but forbid such exclusion as against third parties;[333] but these provisions do not seem to apply to landlords in respect of their obligations under the lease, so that a landlord is free, by limiting his obligations under the lease, indirectly to limit his liability to third parties.[334]

In 1988 the Tasmanian Law Reform Commission recommended that a statute should be passed dealing with the liability of 'occupiers' as defined

---

330 See *Cavalier* v. *Pope* [1906] A.C. 428; and p. 593 below. The Full Court of South Australia declined to apply this rule in *Parker* v. *South Australian Housing Trust* (1986) 41 S.A.S.R. 493 to which the new legislation did not apply; see N. Seddon (1987) 61 *A.L.J.* 653. The Australian Law Reform Commission has recommended reversal of the rule in *Cavalier* v. *Pope* for the A.C.T.: see A.L.R.C. 42, paras 62-82, which contain a careful discussion of the whole issue of landlords' liability.

331 Law Reform (Miscellaneous Provisions) Act 1955 s.29.

332 The effect of s.4 of the Defective Premises Act 1972 (U.K.) is similar to that of the Victorian statute. Section 8 of the Occupiers' Liability Act 1962 (N.Z.) is somewhat narrower.

333 Section 17c(4) of the South Australian statute; s.7(1) of the Western Australian statute.

334 But in South Australia the landlord of residential premises has obligations under the Residential Tenancies Act 1978 (S.A.).

at common law, but also that the liability of landlords should be considered further.

(c) **What are premises?** Occupiers' liability is liability in respect of *premises*. First, the common law: the basic example of premises is land and immovable structures on land including bridges,[335] lifts[336] and escalators,[337] flagpoles,[338] wharves[339] and diving towers.[340] But the concept has also been applied to a wide variety of movable structures such as ladders,[341] scaffolding,[342] ships and the means of boarding them,[343] and even motor vehicles.[344] Even before the decision in *Zaluzna*, these extensions of the notion of premises raised the question of the rationale for having special rules governing the liability of occupiers. The inclusion of movable chattels not used on the defendant's land seems to rule out the idea that the principles of occupiers' liability are designed to express the freedom of the occupier to use his land as he wills. But if the notion of premises is extended to cover any object over which the defendant exercises control and which a person can come on or into, then it ceases to be clear why most car accidents involving the owner as defendant and passengers as plaintiffs are not treated according to the rules of occupiers' liability. It is clear that in the case of car accidents the occupiers' liability rules will apply only if the accident is the result of the defect in the car as opposed to negligent driving of the owner,[345] but even so it is apparently the case that most car accidents, even those involving defects in the vehicle, are dealt with in terms of general negligence principles.[346]

The liability of an occupier can extend to the means of access to the premises even if the occupier has no legal right of control over them and only the most minimal factual control.[347]

The Victorian and Western Australian statutes define 'premises' to include 'any fixed or movable structure, including any vessel, vehicle or aircraft', and the Tasmanian Law Reform Commission adopted this formula in its legislative proposals. The South Australian statute in addition specifically mentions 'land',[348] 'buildings' and 'boats'. There is no reason to think that there is any significant divergence between the common law and statutory definitions of 'premises'.

---

335 *Bulmer* v. *Ryde Municipal Council* (1976) 34 L.G.R.A. 300.
336 *Haseldine* v. *C.A. Daw & Son Ltd* [1941] 2 K.B. 343.
337 *David Jones (Canberra) Pty Ltd* v. *Stone* (1970) 123 C.L.R. 185.
338 *Introvigne* v. *The Commonwealth* (1980) 32 A.L.R. 251; affirmed (1982) 56 A.L.J.R. 749.
339 *Aiken* v. *Kingborough Corporation* (1939) 62 C.L.R. 179.
340 *James* v. *Kogarah Municipal Council* [1961] S.R. (N.S.W.) 129.
341 *Woodman* v. *Richardson and Concrete Ltd* [1937] 3 All E.R. 866.
342 *London Graving Dock Co. Ltd* v. *Horton* [1951] A.C. 737.
343 *Swinton* v. *China Mutual Steam Navigation Co. Ltd* (1951) 83 C.L.R. 553.
344 *Dolbel* v. *Dolbel* (1962) 80 W.N.(N.S.W.) 1056; *Conway* v. *George Wimpey & Co. Ltd* [1951] 1 All E.R. 363.
345 *Dolbel* v. *Dolbel* (1962) 80 W.N.(N.S.W.) 1056.
346 *Meth* v. *Moore* (1983) 44 A.L.R. 409.
347 *Bulmer* v. *Ryde M.C.* (1976) 34 L.G.R.A. 300.
348 cf. Occupiers' Liability Act (N.Z.) s.2.

(d) Classes of visitors As already noted, the basic thrust of both *Zaluzna* and the various occupiers' liability statutes is to abolish the old sub-categories of visitors. So, s.14B(3) of the Victorian statute speaks of 'any person on the premises'[349] and the South Australian and Western Australian statutes apply to 'persons entering on(to) the premises'. But matters are not quite as simple as they might initially appear. In the first place, if the logic of *Zaluzna* were applied strictly, there would be no reason (at least for the purposes of negligence liability) to distinguish between persons *on* the premises who suffer injury, damage or loss as a result of some danger there, and persons *off* the premises who suffer injury, damage or loss as a result of some such danger. But both the common law and the statutes are limited in their operation to persons on the premises. Secondly, at common law visitors who are injured on their employer's premises in their capacity as employees are normally dealt with according to rules governing employers' liability,[350] and not according to occupiers' liability rules, although there is no rule requiring this. Section 8(2) of the Western Australian statute expressly provides that the Act does not apply as between employers and employees; but the relationship between these two sets of rules is not mentioned in either of the other two statutes.

Thirdly, before *Zaluzna* there were, at common law, six sub-categories of visitor: invitees, licensees, persons entering under contract, persons entering in exercise of a legal power of entry,[351] persons entering as of public right (all of whom were lawfully on the land) and trespassers (that is, unlawful entrants). While these sub-categories no longer determine the content of the duty of care owed to any particular visitor, it was said in *Zaluzna* that the content of the duty owed 'will vary with the circumstances of the plaintiff's entry upon the premises'.[352] The old sub-categories referred to the basis on which the visitor came to be upon the premises, and so although the precise categories may no longer be relevant to the liability of the occupier, the essential ideas underlying them still are.[353] This is equally true under the statutes, all of which lay down factors to be taken into account in determining whether the occupier discharged the duty of care: one of these factors refers to the circumstances of the plaintiff's entry. So we should examine briefly the basic principles underlying the old sub-categories.

For a long time the common law drew a distinction between lawful visitors and trespassers, that is, respectively, persons on the land with and

---

349 The recommendations of the Tasmanian L.R.C. use the same phrase.

350 It seems unlikely that this position will be changed as a result of *Zaluzna*. The obligations of employers as occupiers will continue to be governed by a separate set of rules: *Seeley* v. *Gray* (1987) 48 S.A.S.R. 130,147 *per* White J.

351 See Occupiers' Liability Act 1962 (N.Z.) s.4(9); Occupiers' Liability Act 1957 (U.K.) s.2(6).

352 (1987) 162 C.L.R. 479, 488.

353 *Phillis* v. *Daly* (1988) 15 N.S.W.L.R. 65, 67-8 *per* Samuels J.A..

without the permission of the occupier.[354] At first the duty owed to the trespasser was minimal: not to cause him injury or loss intentionally or recklessly. In a series of cases the High Court found a way around this ungenerous rule by holding that in suitable circumstances an occupier could be concurrently subject to an ordinary duty of care towards a trespasser which would override the narrower duty.[355] The last High Court case in which this approach was adopted was *Hackshaw* v. *Shaw*.[356] At the same time, an alternative approach was developed by the House of Lords and the Privy Council according to which trespassers were not owed the ordinary duty of care but a somewhat lower 'duty of common humanity'.[357] Under this approach, occupiers would not be liable to trespassers simply because their presence was foreseeable, but only if the occupier ought to have realized that their presence was 'quite likely'; secondly, occupiers were not necessarily required to take the same precautions to protect trespassers as to protect lawful visitors; and thirdly, the physical abilities and financial resources of the occupier were relevant in deciding what precautions should have been taken to protect trespassers, whereas this is irrelevant in ordinary negligence cases.

The duty of common humanity was really just an application of ordinary negligence principles to the case of trespassers. The crucial characteristic of a trespasser which justifies treating him less generously is, of course, that the trespasser forces his presence on an unwilling occupier. But not all trespassers are equally undeserving of sympathy (consider burglars on the one hand and straying children on the other), and the duty of common humanity was a flexible one which enabled distinctions to be drawn between trespassers. In *Zaluzna* the High Court rejected the concurrent duties approach and opted for a single formula to express the duty owed to visitors of all types, including trespassers. But, of course, that formula is flexible in its application, and the sort of factors which led to the invention of the duty of common humanity will, no doubt, continue to be relevant in deciding in particular cases whether an occupier has exercised reasonable care towards a trespasser.

Among the statutes, only the Victorian provisions fully assimilate trespassers to lawful visitors. In Western Australia persons who are 'on the premises with the intention of committing, or in the commission of an offence punishable by imprisonment' are singled out for special treatment: the duty owed to such persons is 'not to create a danger with the deliberate intent of doing harm or damage to the person or his property and not to act with reckless disregard of the presence of the person or his

354 A person may be a trespasser even though he originally enters with the permission of the occupier if he disregards any valid limitation or condition placed by the occupier on the entry. For example, entry may be allowed for a limited time or to a specified part of the premises. If the visitor outstays the specified time or wanders beyond the permitted area, he becomes a trespasser.

355 For an acccount of this technique, see first edition of this book pp. 454-6.

356 (1984) 155 C.L.R. 614.

357 See first edition of this book pp. 456-7.

property'.[358] Under the South Australian statute (s.17c(6)) the duty owed to trespassers is separately specified but seems, in essence, to be an ordinary duty of care; however, the relevant provision seems to create a presumption against a duty arising, and this may be taken to indicate that a duty is less likely to be owed to a trespasser than to a lawful visitor.

So far as lawful entrants are concerned, under the pre-*Zaluzna* law the duty owed by the occupier to invitees was more stringent that that owed to licensees. This can be explained by the fact that whereas licensees were persons who entered with the consent or permission of the occupier, invitees were persons who entered at the occupier's invitation or request and for his benefit.[359] Persons who entered as of public right (for example, people using public parks, wharves and so on) were unlike invitees in that their presence did not usually confer any material benefit on the occupier, but were also unlike licensees in that they did not need the permission of the occupier to enter (although the occupier could normally[360] refuse entry or impose conditions on visitors).[361] The duty owed to such persons was much the same as that owed to invitees; as was the duty owed to persons who entered in exercise of a legal (that is, common law or statutory) power of entry. But this latter group differed from all other categories of lawful entrant in that the occupier would not be able to refuse entry. The power to refuse entry carries with it the subsidiary power to allow entry only on certain conditions: for example, that the occupier's liability to the entrant for personal injury would be limited. So, whereas an occupier might, by posting a suitable notice, exclude or limit his liability to an invitee or a licensee, for example,[362] this might not be possible in the case of a person exercising a legal power of entry.[363] In the case of a statutory power, any attempt to place conditions on entry would, in order to succeed, have to be consistent with the terms of the statute.

The last sub-category of visitors comprised persons entering under the terms of a contract. A person could be a contractual entrant even if he was not a party to the relevant contract, provided the contract obliged the

---

358 Occupiers' Liability Act 1985 s.5(2) and (3). Note that the provision is not limited to criminal *trespassers*. For arguments against this type of provision see A.L.R.C. 42 paras 57-60. For the law in England see Occupiers' Liability Act 1984 (U.K.).

359 Employees entering their employer's business premises usually fall into this category but, as we have already noted, the duties of employers to employees are governed by special rules which are dealt with in Chapter 14.

360 But common carriers are entitled to refuse to carry a passenger only on certain grounds. The obligations of common carriers (and bailees) are expressly preserved by s.8(1) of the Western Australian statute to the extent that they are more onerous than the obligations imposed by the Act. It is likely that the common law rules governing these groups in their capacity as occupiers will also survive *Zaluzna*.

361 *Aiken* v. *Kingborough Corporation* (1939) 62 C.L.R. 179.

362 *Ashdown* v. *Williams* [1957] 1 Q.B. 409.

363 Section 17c(4) of the South Australian statute expressly allows exclusion or limitation of liability by contract, but 'subject to any Act or law to the contrary'. Section 5(1) of the Western Australian statute allows the occupier to limit his liability 'in so far as he is entitled to'.

occupier to admit that person to the premises.[364] If (unusually) the terms of the contract made provision as to the duty owed by the occupier, this governed the situation.[365] Otherwise, the law implied into the contract a duty of reasonable care; but this implied term was peculiar in that it made the occupier liable not only for negligence on his part or that of his employees, but also for negligence of independent contractors.[366] The occupier was liable to the contractual entrant not only for dangers arising out of the state of the premises but also for dangers resulting from the conduct on the premises of activities such as sports and entertainments. Thus, the duty owed to the contractual entrant was high; and this was justified by the fact that the occupier had received payment for allowing entry.

What relevance are these distinctions likely to have after *Zaluzna*? Three points seem to stand out. First, although the relationship between an occupier and his lawful visitors is often not contractual, if there is a contract between them concerning the visitor's presence on the land, both its existence and its terms may have an impact on the application and operation of the general rules of occupiers' liability.[367] The fact that an occupier has been paid to allow entry could justify imposing a stricter duty on him than on occupiers who have received no payment even if the contract does not expressly provide for a higher standard of care. Secondly, it seems reasonable that the obligations of the occupier to his lawful visitors should be decided in the light of whether the visitor was entitled or empowered by law to enter, whether he entered at the invitation or request of the occupier or merely with his permission, and whether or not his entry benefited the occupier. Thirdly, it will continue to be arguable that if the occupier was not in a position to refuse entry, he might not be

---

364 But the contract had to be one for *entry*: first edition of this book p. 453; and there may have been other requirements as well: see Swanton (1989) 15 *M.U.L.R.* 69, 74. It is to be hoped that the courts will now take a less technical approach to the question of whether the fact that the occupier has received payment should affect his obligations to any particular visitor. If the visitor is not a party to the contract, his only claim will be in tort; but if he is a party, he may sue in tort or contract: see generally Swanton (1989) 15 *M.U.L.R.* 69.

365 The contract might provide for a higher or lower duty than would otherwise have applied.

366 And perhaps even of previous occupiers: *Frances* v. *Cockrell* (1870) L.R. 5 Q.B. 501, 507. On the vicarious liability of occupiers see further p. 710 below.

367 It is a possible interpretation of s.14B(5) of the Victorian statute that s.14B does not apply at all to contractual entrants; but its intended effect may be to give precedence to contractual provisions imposing higher duties than the statute does. (Read strictly, this subsection seems inconsistent with s.14A.) Section 8(1) of the Western Australian statute expressly gives 'any enactment or rule of law imposing special liability or standards of care on particular classes of persons' precedence over the statutory regime. It is not clear whether this formulation is apt to include contractual provisions, but the later reference to 'common carriers and bailees' perhaps suggests that it is limited to rules of law which themselves impose liability on occupiers. Section 17c(5) of the South Australian statute removes any doubt by expressly mentioning contracts which impose higher standards of care than does s.17c. In *Morawski* v. *State Rail Authority* (1988) 14 N.S.W.L.R. 374 Kirby P. said that despite *Zaluzna*, the contractual entrant had not been assimilated into the general category of entrant. See also *Calin* v. *Greater Union Organisation Pty Ltd* (1991) 100 A.L.R. 746, 749.

in a position to impose conditions on that entry or to limit or exclude his liability to the visitor.

(e) Exclusion of liability This is a convenient place to say a few more words about attempts by occupiers to exclude or limit their liability to visitors. Take the common law first: if the visitor enters the premises under a contract between him and the occupier, and this contract contains a clause purporting to exclude or limit the occupier's liability to the visitor, the effectiveness of this clause will depend on relevant rules of contract law. If the visitor enters under a contract to which he is not a party, the ordinary rules of privity of contract would suggest that he would not be bound by any exclusion or limitation clause in the contract; but there is some authority to the contrary.[368] It might be argued that since the visitor takes the benefit of the contract, he should also accept its burdens.

In cases where the visitor does not enter under a contract the occupier may nevertheless exclude or limit his liability to the visitor either orally or by means of a written notice. As we have already seen, an occupier can do this on the basis, and to the extent that, he is free to exclude the visitor entirely from his land: the power to exclude entirely implies the power to attach conditions to entry. However, such conditions will be binding on the visitor only if he was aware of them at or before the time of entry, or if he ought to have been aware of them because the occupier took reasonable steps to bring them to his notice. Furthermore, it seems that such conditions will bind an entrant only if he had a genuine and realistic choice whether or not to enter the premises on those conditions.[369]

Finally, although there is no authority on the point, it has often been argued that there is a certain irreducible minimum duty (that is, the duty to the trespasser, which is the 'lowest' of the occupier duties) liability for breach of which cannot be excluded. In other words, a notice excluding or limiting liability would not bind a trespasser. It would also follow that an exclusion notice would be of no effect as against a lawful visitor in a case where, if the lawful visitor had been a trespasser, he would have been able to recover.

The Victorian statute contains no provision about exclusion of liability. Section 7(1) of the Western Australian statute provides that an exclusion or limitation clause in a contract does not bind a visitor who is not a party to the contract even if the occupier was bound by the terms of the contract to permit him to enter. But the effect of s.5(1) of the Act is to allow the occupier to exclude or limit his liability to contracting parties 'to the extent that he is entitled to'. Section 5(1) also allows, to the same extent, the exclusion or limitation of liability by means of non-contractual notices of the type we discussed above, and s.7(1) does not deal with such notices.[370] The words 'to the extent that he is entitled to' mean that any

---

368 *Fosbroke-Hobbes* v. *Airwork Ltd* [1937] 1 All E.R. 108.

369 *Burnett* v. *British Waterways Board* [1973] 1 W.L.R. 700; *White* v. *Blackmore* [1972] 2 Q.B. 651,677 *per* Roskill L.J.

370 See Handford (1987) 17 *U.W.A.L.R.* 182, 204-5.

exclusion or limitation clause or notice will be effective unless there is some rule of statute or common law to the contrary. We noted relevant common law restrictions above. In England there are relevant statutory restrictions contained in the Unfair Contract Terms Act 1977, but there is no equivalent of these provisions in Western Australia. The effect of s.17c(4) of the South Australian statute is similar to that of the Western Australian provisions.

(f) Types of dangers Before *Zaluzna* a distinction was often drawn between dangers arising out of the static condition of premises and dangers arising out of activities being conducted on the land. It was widely thought that the rules of occupiers' liability applied only to the static condition of the land, and that liability for activities was governed by the ordinary rules of negligence. This distinction was also relevant to the theory of concurrent duties: if the injury to the visitor was the result of some activity being conducted by the occupier on the premises, then the relationship between them was not simply that of occupier and visitor; and on this basis, an ordinary duty of care could be imposed on the occupier in respect of the activity.

As has already been noted, the theory of concurrent duties was rejected in *Zaluzna*; and since the old occupiers' duties are now seen as applications of ordinary negligence principles, the distinction between the static condition of the land and activities being conducted on it would seem to have no part to play in the common law. In other words, the ordinary common law of negligence will apply to all actions brought by visitors against occupiers in respect of injury or damage suffered on the land.

The position under statute is less straightforward. The Western Australian statute applies to 'dangers which are due to the state of the premises or to anything done or omitted to be done on the premises'. This provision seems to achieve the same effect as *Zaluzna*. The Victorian statute applies to injury or damage which results from 'the state of the premises or things done or omitted to be done in relation to the state of the premises'. This is a narrower formulation under which, it seems, the common law, not the statute, will apply to many activities on the land. The South Australian statute applies to 'injury, damage or loss attributable to the dangerous state or condition of the premises'; this wording seems to preserve the distinction between static condition and activities. Thus, both the Victorian and the South Australian statutes may give rise to disputes about whether the statute or the common law should apply to particular cases. Since the broad effect of both statutes is to assimilate occupiers' liability to ordinary negligence liability, it may not matter in many cases which regime of rules is applied. But the statutes do, for example, list factors to be taken into account in deciding whether the occupier has discharged the duty of care; and they do alter the common law in various ways. So the issue of whether the statute applies to any particular case may sometimes be an important one. It is highly unfortunate, to say the least, that legislation designed to simplify the law should generate such complications.

(g) Recoverable loss Occupiers' liability is primarily concerned with personal injury; but at common law, visitors can recover for damage to their personal property which they bring on to the premises with them, if the invitation or permission to enter expressly or impliedly contemplated that the visitor would bring his belongings with him. Furthermore, if a visitor brings someone else's property on to the land, the owner may be able to recover for damage to it. For example, in *Drive-Yourself Lessey's Pty Ltd* v. *Burnside*[371] a person hired a car from the plaintiff and parked it in a carpark run by the defendant. The car was damaged, and a majority of the court held, in effect, that since the invitation to the hirer to enter the land extended to bringing the car as well, damages could be recovered by the plaintiff (even though it was not the visitor) because the invitation was not limited to the visitor's property.[372]

In *A.M.F. International Ltd* v. *Magnet Bowling Ltd* it was held that financial loss consequential upon damage to property can be recovered, subject to the ordinary rules of remoteness of damage, in any case where the occupier's duty extends to prevention of damage to property.[373] As for purely economic loss, if one assumes that recovery depends on there being a very close relationship of proximity between the plaintiff and the defendant, this requirement would, no doubt, be satisfied in many cases by the relationship of invitation or permission between the occupier and the visitor. But it might be harder to satisfy if the plaintiff entered as of public right, for example.

There is no reason to think that these common law rules will not continue to apply in the post-*Zaluzna* era. So far as the legislation is concerned, s.4(1)(b) of the Western Australian statute expressly states that it applies, *in place of* the common law, to 'property brought on to the premises by, and remaining on the premises in the possession and control of [the visitor], whether it is owned by that person or by any other person'. This provision is narrow in requiring that the property remain in the possession and control of the visitor; and it does not advert to the question of whether the owner could sue in cases where the property did not belong to the visitor—but the wording of the Act generally seems to assume that only visitors can sue under its provisions. The statute does not mention economic loss. The words 'injury, damage or loss' in the South Australian statute are wide enough to cover property damage or economic loss; but it

---

371 [1959] S.R.(N.S.W.) 390.

372 There is some doubt about the extent to which an occupier can be held liable for theft of property brought on to the premises by the visitor. In *Tinsley* v. *Dudley* [1951] 2 K.B. 18 it was held that where an invitation extends to the visitor's goods, the occupier is under a duty to protect them from damage caused by defects in the premises but not from theft by third parties. Cf. *Ashby* v. *Tolhurst* [1937] 2 K.B. 242. However, in *Eggins* v. *Canberra Enterprises Pty Ltd* (1974) 2 A.C.T.R. 66 Connor J. held that an occupier could be liable for personal injury caused to a visitor by the criminal acts of third parties. It seems a short extension to impose liability for theft if the invitation or permission covers goods.

373 [1968] 1 W.L.R. 1028. This case was decided under the Occupiers' Liability Act 1957 (U.K.) but on the assumption that the rules governing liability for property damage were the same under the Act as at common law. On purely economic loss see ibid. pp. 1049-51.

is not clear whether they cover damage to property owned by someone other than the visitor, or, indeed, whether anyone other than the visitor can sue under the occupiers' liability provisions.[374] The Victorian statute is even unclear on whether property damage (let alone economic loss) falls within its terms, although on balance it appears that property damage is covered.[375]

(h) Content of the duty This is really a question of standard of care, and is discussed in the next chapter.[376]

(i) Conclusion The reader will have observed that the various occupiers' liability statutes are, in certain respects, not very clearly drafted; and that their provisions raise a number of difficult issues as to the scope and interpretation of the legislation. Since the main aim of the legislation was simply to abolish the special rules governing occupiers' liability and to put the ordinary law of negligence in their place, it is a pity (to say the least) that this was not done in so many words. In the light of *Zaluzna,* there is an argument for repealing these statutory provisions and for leaving the common law to develop along the lines suggested by the High Court.

3. JUDICIAL PROCESS IMMUNITY

(a) Liability for statements made in court The law goes to considerable lengths to protect participants in the judicial process from actions for torts committed in the course of their duties. Thus, statements made in preparation for[377] or in the course of judicial proceedings by judges,[378] counsel, witnesses, jurors and parties are protected by absolute privilege in the law of defamation. Nor can statements made in court form the basis of actions for deceit, conspiracy[379] or negligence.[380] This means that the maker of the statement cannot be successfully sued even if he spoke out of malice, with a view to injuring the plaintiff. The justification for this privilege and immunity is obvious—it is of the utmost importance in an adversary system of court procedure that no unnecessary constraints be put on freedom of speech before a court. The possibility of being sued, even if unsuccessfully, might not only inhibit witnesses and others from appearing in court, but also might undermine the credibility of what they say, if it were thought that the fear of being sued might cause them to 'hold back'.

---

374 The only mention of the visitor in the provisions is contained in one of the guidelines for determining whether the occupier has taken reasonable care: s.17c(2)(e).
375 See Johnstone (1984) 14 *M.U.L.R.* 512, 516.
376 See p. 431 below.
377 *Evans* v. *London Hospital Medical College* [1981] 1 All E.R. 715.
378 *Scott* v. *Stansfield* [1868] L.R. 3 Ex. 220.
379 *Cabassi* v. *Vila* (1940) 64 C.L.R. 130.
380 But on expert witnesses and the law of negligence see T. Hervey [1985] *P.N.* 102.

(b) Liability for court orders The law also accords to judges considerable immunity from actions in tort arising out of things done in the course of judicial proceedings.[381] The common law traditionally drew a distinction in this area between inferior courts of limited jurisdiction and superior courts, such as the English High Court. Judges of inferior courts were immune from liability provided they were acting within their powers and provided they did not act maliciously (that is, out of an improper motive);[382] whereas judges of superior courts, acting as such, were immune from liability even for acts done maliciously, provided they did not knowingly exceed their powers.[383]

The main argument for judicial immunity goes as follows: the proper course for a party aggrieved by a court decision is to challenge the *decision* by ordinary means, such as appeal, rather than to sue the judge, even if he acted out of malice, envy or hatred. It is not that judges should be entitled to engage in unseemly behaviour, but that the threat of such attacks on judges personally might open them to corrupt outside influences, which could threaten their impartiality and independence. Actions for damages would also bypass the established means of correcting judicial errors, such as appeals and applications for habeas corpus. Actions for damages for negligence against a judge would in effect involve a rehearing of the original action by another court at the same level in the judicial hierarchy, and this would run counter to the law's proper concern with securing finality of litigation[384] and might generate an unhealthy lack of confidence in the competence of the judiciary.[385]

Immunity from liability for negligence also extends to other persons and bodies exercising judicial functions, such as administrative tribunals and officials, and arbitrators.[386] The difficulty in applying this immunity is to distinguish between judicial and other functions. For example, it has been held that an architect employed by a building owner to value and certify work done by a builder, or an auditor employed by a vendor of shares to value them for the purposes of sale, is not performing a judicial

---

381 See generally *Rajski* v. *Powell* (1987) 11 N.S.W.L.R. 522.

382 In respect of magistrates, this rule is embodied in statute: Court of Petty Sessions Act 1930 (A.C.T.) ss.231, 241; Justices Act 1928 (N.T.) ss.190, 191; Justices Act 1921 (S.A.) ss.190, 191; Justices Act 1902 (N.S.W.) ss.135, 136; Justices of the Peace Act 1975 (Qld) s.24; Justices Act 1959 (Tas) ss.126, 127; Justices Act 1902 (W.A.) s.230. But in Victoria, magistrates enjoy the same immunity as judges of the Supreme Court: Magistrates' Court Act 1989 s.14. See also Court and Legal Services Act 1990 (U.K.) s.75; R.J. Sadler (1982) 13 *M.U.L.R.* 508.

383 *Rajski* v. *Powell* (1987) 11 N.S.W.L.R. 522, 529-30 *per* Kirby P.

384 For a general consideration of all these arguments see *Nakhla* v. *McCarthy* [1978] 1 N.Z.L.R. 291.

385 For a contrary view see M. Brazier [1976] *P.L.* 397, 408-9.

386 *Sutcliffe* v. *Thackrah* [1974] A.C. 727; *Arenson* v. *Casson, Beckman, Rutley & Co.* [1977] A.C. 430 (arbitrators); *Partridge* v. *The General Council of Medical Education of the United Kingdom* (1890) 25 Q.B.D. 90 (tribunals). But public bodies may be held to owe no duty of care in performing their functions even if they are not judicial: e.g. *Calveley* v. *Chief Constable of Merseyside Police* [1989] A.C. 1228, and see further Ch. 20 below. Court-appointed sequestrators are not immune from liability for negligence at the suit of the owner of the sequestrated property: *Inland Revenue Commissioners* v. *Hoogstraten* [1985] Q.B. 1077.

function even though he has to make a decision on an issue (that is, the value of goods or services) in relation to which the two parties involved have conflicting interests. The most widely accepted reason is that the architect or auditor does not, while the arbitrator does, settle a *dispute* between the parties. But as Lord Kilbrandon said in *Arenson,* the distinction between an actual dispute and a situation of potential dispute between parties with conflicting interests is not very satisfying.[387]

A viable distinction might be based on the fact that judges and arbitrators are empowered to apply the law of the land and to decide disputed questions of law. In this sense they form part of the machinery of government, whereas architects and auditors perform no such governmental function.[388] It is to ensure the impartial administration of *the law* that judicial independence is maintained; it is not only the parties who have an interest in the due administration of law. The independence of private arbitrators is not as well protected as that of judges, in that they are appointed by the parties in dispute and have no security of tenure. However, this fact provides no reason not to attempt to make their position in relation to particular decisions as impregnable as possible, by immunizing them from actions in respect of them. This explanation has the advantage both that it explains why the line is drawn where it presently is and that it rests on the idea of impartiality and independence from control by private citizens.

(c) **Liability of lawyers for negligent conduct of litigation**[389] In *Giannarelli* v. *Wraith*[390] a majority of the High Court held that, at common law, an advocate is immune from being sued in negligence in respect of the performance of his functions as an advocate.[391] In light of the fact that no other professional group enjoys such immunity in respect of the conduct of their professional duties, this might seem like an extreme example of partiality on the part of judges who know from long experience what it is like to be a barrister.[392] However, the immunity is limited to what can be loosely described as the conduct of the case in court and to other out-of-court work which is 'so intimately connected with the conduct of the cause in court that it can fairly be said to be a preliminary decision affecting the way that cause is to be conducted when it comes to a hearing'.[393] On the basis of this principle, immunity has been held to attach to advice as to the plea to be entered by the defendant to a criminal prosecution;[394] to advice that there is no evidence to support a claim of

---

387 [1977] A.C. 405, 430.
388 *O'Reilly* v. *Mackman* [1983] 2 A.C. 237 (C.A.).
389 P.C. Heery (1968) 42 *A.L.J.* 3; P. Sutherland (1979) 5 *Mon. U.L.R.* 271.
390 (1988) 165 C.L.R. 543.
391 Cf. *Rondel* v. *Worsley* [1969] 1 A.C. 191; *Saif Ali* v. *Sydney Mitchell & Co.* [1980] A.C. 198.
392 [1980] A.C. 198, 223 *per* Lord Diplock.
393 *Rees* v. *Sinclair* [1974] 1 N.Z.L.R. 180, 187 *per* McCarthy P.
394 *Somasundaram* v. *M. Julius Melchior & Co.* [1988] 1 W.L.R. 1394.

misconduct by a wife made in maintenance proceedings on the part of a husband;[395] to a refusal by counsel to ask all the questions or lead all the evidence suggested by his client;[396] to settlement of an action by compromise in court after oral evidence;[397] to failure to advise a client that he has a good defence to a prosecution and failure to object to inadmissible evidence.[398] Immunity has been held not to apply to a failure by a barrister at an early stage to advise the joining of certain parties to an action[399] or to the entering into of a compromise of appeal proceedings before the appeal was heard.[400]

The immunity is potentially very wide. It is apt to cover anything done in court in the conduct of a case, and any advice about what ought or ought not to be done in court or as to the way the case ought to be conducted in court. It would also, presumably, cover advice as to the conduct of a trial which never takes place. So what is left outside the immunity? Decisions about whether to institute proceedings at all or against particular parties might seem well outside the immunity, and *Saif Ali* has held the latter to be so. But are these not direct counterparts of decisions made in court not to pursue an action further or not to do so against a particular party? In fact, it might be thought that the only activities of advocates which are not caught by the principle in its terms are non-litigious activities. This is not to say that the immunity will not be interpreted more narrowly than the terms in which it is stated could justify, but only that the present formulation of the immunity seems very wide.

None of the arguments in favour of the immunity is entirely convincing. The main argument is that a barrister has a duty not only to his client but also to the court, and that these duties may conflict. Since the duty to the court is higher, the barrister might be required to do something which could adversely affect his client's case. But the mere doing of one's duty to the court to the detriment of one's client could never be called negligent—liability could only be justified where the barrister wrongly and negligently reached the conclusion that his duty to the court required him to act to his client's detriment.[401] So the basis of the argument must be that the *fear* of actions, even unfounded ones,[402] might cause advocates to be unduly cautious and long-winded in presenting their client's case,[403] and might lead them, when in doubt, to prefer the interests of their clients to their duty to the court.

The argument from conflict of duties is sometimes bolstered by saying that counsel would be hindered in doing their duty to the court when

395 *Rees* v. *Sinclair* [1974] 1 N.Z.L.R. 180.
396 *Rondel* v. *Worsley* [1969] 1 A.C. 191.
397 *Biggar* v. *McLeod* [1978] 2 N.Z.L.R. 9.
398 *Giannarelli* v. *Wraith* (1988) 165 C.L.R. 543.
399 *Saif Ali* v. *Mitchell* [1980] A.C. 198.
400 *Donnellan* v. *Watson* (1990) 21 N.S.W.L.R. 335.
401 *Giannarelli* v. *Wraith* (1988) 165 C.L.R. 543, 572 *per* Wilson J; 594 *per* Dawson J.; but see 555-7 *per* Mason C.J.
402 cf. *Giannarelli* v. *Wraith* (1988) 165 C.L.R. 543, 573 *per* Wilson J.; 596 *per* Dawson J.
403 *Rondel* v. *Worsley* [1969] 1 A.C. 191, 229 *per* Lord Reid.

forced to make a quick decision in court in the heat of the moment and without the benefit of calm reflection, if they operated under the fear of being sued (even if unsuccessfully) by their clients. Supported in this way, the argument would not seem to justify immunity in any case where there was time for reflection, even if it was on a matter to which immunity would attach in court.

A second argument in favour of immunity is that since a barrister is not free to refuse a brief in the area of his competency, immunity protects him from the fear of action at the suit of a disgruntled client with a bad case which, given the choice, the barrister may not have taken on. But barristers are not uniquely placed in this respect: doctors in hospital emergency departments, for example, are not free to turn away a patient who has a condition which is difficult to treat.[404] It is not clear why the advocate deserves an immunity which the doctor is denied; such immunity seems a high price to pay for protection from what in practice must be the very small risk of being subjected to vexatious litigation (which is, anyway, unlikely to get very far).

A final argument[405] is similar to one used in support of the immunity accorded to judges: an action in negligence against a barrister would only succeed if it could be proved that, but for his negligence, his client would have won. Such proof would require a retrial of the issues and would undermine the finality of judicial decisions and create an unhealthy and, in our society, unjustified, disrespect for the competence of judges. This 'collateral challenge' argument would, however, not apply in cases where there was no court decision: for example, where a barrister negligently advises submission to a default judgment or negligently compromises an appeal from an admittedly correct first instance decision.[406] Nor would it apply to advice not to institute proceedings or not to join parties. The argument is, anyway, not as strong in this context as in the case of judges. It might be thought that the exposure of incompetence among advocates would strengthen the judicial system, not weaken it: judges in our system rely very heavily on counsel to present their cases fully and in the best possible way,[407] and a finding that a decision of a court *might*, on the balance of probabilities, have been different if an advocate (not the judge) had acted differently, would not seem likely to undermine (legitimate) public confidence in the system as a whole.

We might conclude that, even taken together, the justifications adduced for the immunity hardly support it. This conclusion is reinforced when the position of solicitors is examined. In *Saif Ali* Lords Wilberforce, Diplock and Salmon said that a solicitor *acting as an advocate* enjoyed the same immunity as a barrister/advocate.[408] It is clear that a solicitor is not

---

404 *Barnett* v. *Chelsea and Kensington Hospital Management Committee* [1969] 1 Q.B. 428.

405 And the one which received the greatest support in *Giannarelli* v. *Wraith*.

406 *Donnellan* v. *Watson* (1990) 21 N.S.W.L.R. 335.

407 But this has been used as an argument to support the immunity: *Giannarelli* v. *Wraith* (1988) 165 C.L.R. 543, 595-6 *per* Dawson J.

408 [1980] A.C. 198 at pp. 215, 224 and 227 respectively; approved by Mason C.J. in *Giannarelli* v. *Wraith* (1988) 81 A.L.R. 417, 423.

protected simply by reason of the fact that the allegedly negligent conduct is such that, if it had been done by an advocate in the same circumstances, it would have fallen within the immunity. So, a solicitor instructing a barrister is not protected even in circumstances where the barrister would be.[409] The solicitor's only protection lies in the possibility of a plea that the advice he gave had been approved by counsel, so that the solicitor was not negligent in giving it; or that the barrister's negligence broke the chain of causation between the solicitor's advice and the plaintiff's loss. On the other hand, solicitors, like barristers, are 'officers of the court' and, as such, owe duties to the court as well as to their clients. In this light, the relative positions of barristers and solicitors as regards liability in tort is extraordinarily anomalous, and throws considerable doubt on the justifiability of the barrister's immunity.

So far as concerns solicitors in jurisdictions where the two sides of the profession are fused, it has been held in South Australia and New Zealand that a solicitor who is also on the roll of barristers enjoys the immunity in respect of his work (such as pre-trial work) done as a solicitor.[410] The position of a person in a fused profession who is only on the roll of solicitors but acts as an advocate has not been decided, but there seems no reason why the immunity should not extend to him. If anything, the fact of fusion should reduce the significance of the distinction between barristers and solicitors.

4. Military and Police Operations[411]

Actions for negligence cannot be brought either by civilians or service personnel in respect of damage or injuries suffered as a result of anything done in the course of actual operations of war or in the course of warlike operations short of official war.[412] The reasons are straightforward—war cannot be conducted according to standards of reasonable care. Courts of law are not equipped for judging the quality of fighting operations.[413] Also, the maintenance of internal discipline within the armed forces could be seriously hindered if actions taken in compliance with orders could be challenged in the courts. The criterion of non-actionability is not whether the act was done in wartime, but whether it was an act of war. Not everything done in wartime is done in war.[414] This immunity has also been held to extend to military exercises, at least so far as concerns injuries to other service personnel, even though the injuries result from horseplay.[415] The argument that negligence actions, if allowed, would undermine discipline and obedience to lawful orders might justify immunity in

409 *Somasundaram* v. *M. Julius Melchior & Co.* [1988] 1 W.L.R. 1394.

410 *Rees* v. *Sinclair* [1974] 1 N.Z.L.R. 180; *Feldman* v. *A Practitioner* (1978) 18 S.A.S.R. 238.

411 R.S. Ashton (1978) 10 *U.Q.L.J.* 157.

412 *Shaw Savill and Albion Co. Ltd* v. *The Commonwealth* (1940) 66 C.L.R. 344; *Parker* v. *Commonwealth of Australia* (1965) 112 C.L.R. 295.

413 cf. *Rootes* v. *Shelton* (1967) 116 C.L.R. 383, 389 *per* Kitto J.

414 *Shaw Savill* v. *Commonwealth* (1940) 66 C.L.R. 344, 353-4 *per* Starke J.

415 *Connell* v. *The Commonwealth* (1979) 37 F.L.R. 95; *Commonwealth* v. *Jenner* (1989) 9 M.V.R. 387. Contrast *Johnstone* v. *Woolmer* (1977) 16 A.C.T.R. 6.

respect of acts done in the course of exercises in pursuance of orders, but it seems hard to justify immunity for acts not done in pursuance of orders.[416]

In *Hill* v. *Chief Constable of West Yorkshire*[417] the House of Lords held that the police normally owe no duty to take care in investigating crime or seeking to apprehend criminals to members of the public who suffer injury or damage at the hands of a criminal. One of the reasons given for this conclusion was that the investigation of crime is not normally an appropriate subject for scrutiny by a court of law: the police need to be left free to get on with the job without the fear of being sued if things go wrong. The result might be different if, as in *Dorset Yacht Co.* v. *Home Office*,[418] injury or damage was caused by a criminal who had negligently been allowed to escape from custody, or if the risk of injury or damage to the plaintiff was significantly greater than that to other members of the public. This decision is an illustration of a wider unwillingness on the part of English courts to impose negligence liability on public bodies performing regulatory and investigative functions.

5. Duties of Care in Relation to Conception and Birth

(a) Injuries to unborn children The basic theoretical difficulty involved in compensating for pre-natal injuries is that at the time of the injuries the plaintiff is not a legal person.[419] The position at common law has always been that legal personality begins at birth.[420] It follows that until birth a child cannot possess legal rights or be owed legal duties, including a duty to take reasonable care. However, it seems clear that, if it can be shown that while *en ventre sa mere* a foetus suffered injury as the result, for example, of a car accident caused by the negligence of the defendant, or of the ingestion by its mother of a drug negligently marketed by the defendant for use by pregnant mothers, there is no good policy reason why the child when born should not recover damages for its injuries, even though these were suffered before it attained legal personality by being born alive.

In *Watt* v. *Rama*[421] it was alleged that physical disabilities suffered by the plaintiff at and after her birth were the result of the negligence of the defendant causing a collision between his car and a car in which the plaintiff's mother was travelling. It was held that the allegations gave rise to a good cause of action. The crucial feature of the reasoning in *Watt* v. *Rama* is that a cause of action accrues only if and when the child is born alive with injuries or disabilities caused by the defendant's negligence. So

---

416 cf. *Groves* v. *Commonwealth of Australia* (1982) 40 A.L.R. 193, 211 *per* Brennan J. In the U.K. the immunity of the Crown from tort liability in relation to the armed forces has been abolished subject to revival in time of war or emergency: Crown Proceedings (Armed Forces) Act 1987 (U.K.). See also D. Brahams (1989) *New L.J.* 1371.

417 [1989] A.C. 53.

418 [1970] A.C. 1004.

419 P. Cane (1977) 51 *A.L.J.* 704; R. Hayes and S.C. Hayes (1982) 56 *A.L.J.* 643.

420 J.V. Barry (1941) 14 *A.L.J.* 351, 353-5.

421 [1972] V.R. 353; cf. Congenital Disabilities (Civil Liability) Act 1976 (U.K.) s.1(1) and (2).

it is not necessary to decide whether the foetus is a legal person because the basis of the award of damages is the injuries which the live plaintiff suffers at and after birth. The general principle enunciated in *Watt* v. *Rama* has been held to extend to acts of negligence occurring before the child's conception,[422] such as the marketing of damaging contraceptive pills, or acts causing injury to the mother's pelvis, or exposure of the genitals of the parents to radiation thus causing gene mutation.

A number of important questions were left unanswered by *Watt* v. *Rama*. First, should a child be able to recover damages against either of its parents? A child might, for example, be injured by the negligent driving of one of its parents, or an allegation might be made that the mother had done damage to her foetus by smoking or taking drugs while pregnant. The main argument advanced for parental immunity is the emotional upheaval which litigation between members of the same family can cause, especially if one parent wishes to be vindictive towards the other. On the other hand, if, as would be the case in relation to motor accidents, the parent is insured against liability to the child, it seems hard to justify denying the child access to the insurance funds; and if the main aim of an action against a parent is to tap insurance funds, the litigation might well not cause much emotional tension. Both considerations could be given effect by immunizing parents from liability except in cases where insurance is compulsory. An action by a child against its mother in respect of negligent driving has succeeded in New South Wales.[423]

A second issue is the extent to which defences available to the defendant against the mother should also be available against the child. It could be argued that since the child is so physically identified with the mother at the date of the tort, it would be unfair to the defendant not to allow him to plead such defences against the child. So the English legislation allows the defendant to plead against the child contributory negligence on the part of the mother, and any exclusion or limitation of liability agreed to between the mother and the defendant.[424] On the other hand, this position does seem hard on the child: if it were injured while lying in a crib on the back seat of a car just after birth, rather than in the womb of its mother sitting in the front seat just before birth, it would not be saddled with these defences. In this instance, the fact of birth seems relatively insignificant, and does not justify the radical change in the defendant's liability to the child. It would be preferable to deny the defendant the right to plead such defences against the child.

So far we have been dealing with claims by an injured child, but it should be noted that there is authority for allowing a pregnant woman to recover damages for nervous shock associated with injury to or miscarriage of an unborn child, or the fear of such an occurrence.[425] Furthermore, there is, perhaps, no reason why a father should not recover for nervous

---

422 *X* v. *Y* (1991) 23 N.S.W.L.R. 26.
423 *Lynch* v. *Lynch* [1991] Aust. Torts Reports 69,335.
424 Congenital Disabilities (Civil Liability) Act 1976 (U.K.) s.1(6) and (7).
425 *Dulieu* v. *White* [1901] 2 K.B. 669; *Stevenson* v. *Basham* [1922] N.Z.L.R. 225.

shock caused by fear for the safety of his unborn child or by witnessing an accident in which his pregnant wife is involved.

(b) Actions for wrongful life Suppose that, as the result of a negligently performed sterilization, or as the result of failure to warn of the risk that a competently performed sterilization operation might not be successful, a healthy but unplanned or unwanted child is conceived and born; or that, as a result of a negligently performed abortion, a healthy but illegitimate child is born. Or suppose that a deformed or disabled child is born to a woman whom a doctor has failed to warn of the risk of her bearing such a child, thus depriving her of information relevant to the choice of whether or not to conceive a child or to have her foetus, once conceived, aborted;[426] or that a doctor negligently performs an unsuccessful operation to abort a deformed foetus. In any of these cases can either the child or its parents recover damages from the negligent defendant?[427] The American cases, of which there are quite a few, have almost universally rejected the claim of the child. The basic reason for this rejection is that the child's claim has been interpreted as one for having been born at all, rather than as one for having been born illegitimate, or unwanted, or disabled: in none of these cases is the defendant's negligence the cause of the child's disadvantage, whether it be illegitimacy, unwantedness or disability; the result of the negligence is that the child is conceived or born at all.

Two main objections have been raised to such claims. The first is a policy argument based on the sanctity of human life: human life, however disadvantaged, is always something of positive value, and if damages are to be awarded for the fact of life this must be done by legislative act, not judicial decision. On the other hand, it might be thought that, in the light of the increasing use of artificial contraception, the legalization of abortion in certain circumstances and the sympathy which many feel for mercy-killing of severely disabled children, the force of the 'sanctity of human life' argument would vary according to the nature of the child's disadvantage. Whereas we might not have much sympathy for the claim of the illegitimate or unwanted child that the burdens of life outweigh its benefits, such an argument might seem more plausible in the case of a severely disabled child. But, on the whole, courts have been unwilling to make such discriminations. The second objection rests on the difficulty of assessing damages: damages are designed to put the plaintiff in the position he would have been in had the tort not been committed; but in that case the plaintiff would not have been alive, and since we have no experience of non-existence there is no way we can value non-existence and determine by how much its value exceeds (or falls short of) that of life. These two arguments also weighed heavily with the English Court of

426 *Salih* v. *Enfield Health Authority* [1991] 3 All E.R. 400. But damages would not be recoverable if abortion would have been unlawful: *Rance* v. *Mid-Downs Health Authority* [1991] 2 W.L.R. 159.

427 D.J. Mark (1976) 76 *Col.L.R.* 1187; G. Robertson (1983) 23 *Med., Sc. and the Law* 2; A.C. Reichman (1983-5) 10 *Syd.L.R.* 568. For New Zealand see C.J. O'Neill (1985) 5 *Auckland L.R.* 180.

Appeal in *McKay* v. *Essex Area Health Authority*.[428] In that case a child was born disabled as a result of her mother contracting rubella during pregnancy. One of the allegations made by the child was that the defendant had been careless in not telling the mother of the advisability of an abortion. This was interpreted as a wrongful life claim and rejected both as a matter of common law and by virtue of a provision of the Congenital Disabilities (Civil Liability) Act 1976 (U.K.). One Australian court has reached a similar conclusion as a matter of common law.[429]

But courts have been much less hostile to claims by parents in such cases. In England, parents have recovered in cases where the child was healthy but illegitimate,[430] healthy but unplanned,[431] planned but disabled,[432] unplanned and disabled.[433] Damages have been awarded under various heads: loss of parental earnings (actual and prospective), pain and suffering, mental anxiety and distress, and impairment of marriage prospects. Damages are also available for the cost of rearing an unwanted child and for the extra costs of rearing a disabled child; in one case, the father of a healthy unplanned child was even awarded the cost of educating the child privately on the ground that the parents believed in educating their children privately.[434] In a South Australian case,[435] the mother of an unwanted child born after an unsuccessful sterilization operation was awarded damages for pain and suffering associated with a Caesarean section operation and a second sterilization operation. Her husband was awarded a small amount for loss of consortium. Damages were not awarded for the cost of rearing the child (obviously a very substantial amount), not, apparently, for any reason of principle, but simply because it had not been proved that the family was any worse off financially as a result of the birth of the child.

However, it seems inconsistent to allow a claim by the parents while that of the child, whether healthy or disabled, is rejected. Surely the parents' claim is equally repugnant to ideas of the sanctity and value of human life and rests, like that of the child, on a comparison between a situation where a human being exists and one where it does not.[436] Admittedly, we have experience of what the alternatives are to having unwanted or disabled children, but how is the difference between having a

---

428 [1982] Q.B. 1166.

429 *Bannerman* v. *Mills* [1991] Aust. Torts Reports 81-079.

430 *Sciuriaga* v. *Powell* (unreported) noted in (1982) 44 *M.L.R.* 215.

431 *Udale* v. *Bloomsbury Area Health Authority* [1983] 1 W.L.R. 1098; *Thake* v. *Maurice* [1986] Q.B. 644.

432 *Salih* v. *Enfield Health Authority* [1991] 3 All E.R. 400.

433 *Emeh* v. *Kensington and Chelsea and Westminster Area Health Authority* [1985] Q.B. 1012.

434 *Benarr* v. *Kettering Health Authority* [1988] *New L.J.* 179.

435 *F.* v. *R.* (1982) 29 S.A.S.R. 437; reversed on appeal on grounds that doctor had not been negligent; but possibility of liability in appropriate circumstances not questioned: (1983) 33 S.A.S.R. 189.

436 P.R. Glazebrook ([1992] *C.L.J.* 226) is prepared to contemplate claims based on negligent failure to prevent conception, but finds totally unacceptable claims based on negligent deprivation of the chance to have an abortion.

child, however disadvantaged, and having no child, to be valued in money terms?

In cases where the parents argue that the defendant negligently failed to warn them of the risk of conceiving a disabled child, they would also have to prove that if they had been warned, the woman would have undergone a (legal) abortion. Conversely, it is often argued, in cases where unplanned children are conceived, that the woman's failure to have an abortion broke the chain of causation between the negligence and the birth of the child; but this argument has received short shrift on the basis that the courts should not give any encouragement to women to seek abortions.

6. Rescuers

At one stage the law seems to have taken the view that since there is, under normal circumstances, no positive duty to go to the rescue of someone in danger, there is also no duty owed to a person who is injured while rescuing a person in peril.[437] Now, however, so as not to discourage rescuers, and to express approval of heroism, the law recognizes that a person who, by his negligence, creates a situation of danger which imperils another can be held liable to a person who comes to the rescue.[438] Professional rescuers, such as firefighters, can take advantage of this principle as much as anyone else.[439] The duty to the rescuer is independent of any duty to the person put in peril, and is based on the foreseeability that if a danger is created, someone is likely to come to the rescue.[440] Indeed, it may be that a duty could be owed even if the dangerous situation was created in a very remote area where it was highly unlikely that anyone would be around who could effect a rescue: the duty is based on the foreseeability that *if* someone is in a position to attempt a rescue, the creation of a danger will invite rescue; and if a rescue is in fact attempted, it may not matter that the presence of a rescuer was highly unlikely.

The independence of the duty owed to the rescuer means that the creator of the danger can be liable to the rescuer even if the person put in peril was contributorily negligent; or if for some reason no duty was owed to the person put in peril;[441] or if the person being rescued is the person

437 J. Tiley (1967) 30 *M.L.R.* 25.

438 Related issues are whether a rescuer can be liable for injury or damage inflicted in the course of rescuing, and whether the rescuer can recover costs incurred by him in assisting the victim. On these issues see Cane *Tort Law and Economic Interests* (Oxford, 1991) pp. 234-8.

439 *Ogwo* v. *Taylor* [1988] A.C. 431.

440 *Baker* v. *T.E. Hopkins & Son Ltd* [1959] 3 All E.R. 225, 241-2 *per* Willmer L.J.; *Haynes* v. *G. Harwood & Son* [1935] 1 K.B. 146, 156 *per* Greer L.J.

441 *Videan* v. *British Transport Commission* [1963] 2 All E.R. 860. The reasoning in this case, based on the fact the child was a trespasser, is now outdated.

who has created the situation of danger and so is the defendant;[442] or if the imperilled person in fact suffers no injury.[443]

The rescuer must act reasonably, but since he acts under the pressure of emergency the courts will tend to be lenient in judging the reasonableness of his conduct—only if he acted in an extremely foolhardy way will the damages be reduced.[444] A duty can be owed to a person who attempts to rescue imperilled property,[445] but clearly it would be unreasonable to take some risks for the sake of property which it would be perfectly justifiable to incur for the sake of a person. The fact that there was actually no danger would not make a rescue unreasonable, provided it was reasonable for the rescuer to think there was a danger.

A rescuer can recover damages not only for physical injury but also for nervous shock, even if this is the only injury suffered, and even if the rescuer was in no way related to the victim.[446]

---

442 *Harrison* v. *British Railways Board* [1981] 3 All E.R. 679. Concerning nervous shock see *Alcock* v. *Chief Constable of South Yorkshire* [1992] 1 A.C. 310, 401 *per* Lord Ackner; 418 *per* Lord Oliver.

443 *Horsley* v. *McLaren (The Ogopogo)* [1971] 2 Lloyd's Rep. 410, 418 *per* Laskin J.

444 *Baker* v. *Hopkins* [1959] 3 All E.R. 225, 244 *per* Willmer L.J.

445 *Hyett* v. *Great Western Railway Co.* [1948] 1 K.B. 345.

446 *Mt Isa Mines Ltd* v. *Pusey* (1970) 125 C.L.R. 383; *Chadwick* v. *British Transport Commission* [1967] 2 All E.R. 945.

10

NEGLIGENCE: STANDARD OF CARE

Once it has been decided that the defendant owed the plaintiff a duty of care it is then necessary for the plaintiff to prove that the defendant committed a breach of that duty. But 'breach of duty' is a rather misleading title for the second element of the tort. It is better to refer to it as concerning the standard of care required of the defendant or the question of whether the defendant's conduct was careless. This is because it is possible for a defendant to be held to have been careless or negligent even though, for some policy reason, he was under no duty to the plaintiff to take care. It is perfectly possible for this second requirement of the tort to be satisfied and yet for the plaintiff to escape liability.

I: FORESEEABILITY, PROXIMITY AND STANDARD OF CARE

Carelessness for the purposes of the tort of negligence can be defined as failure to take necessary steps to eliminate reasonably foreseeable and significant risks of injury to the plaintiff.[1] The reasonable person takes precautions against such risks. Alternatively, whether the defendant was careless or not may be said to depend on whether he did or omitted to do any act which a reasonable person would not do or omit to do, whereby injury was likely to be caused to the plaintiff.[2] '[T]he measure for determining what constitutes reasonable care is an objective and impersonal one';[3] in other words, the appropriate standard is not that which the defendant *could* have reached, but rather the standard which the law says *should* have been reached.

1 *Overseas Tankship (U.K.) Ltd* v. *The Miller Steamship Co. Ltd (The Wagon Mound) (No.2)* [1967] A.C. 617, 643.

2 *Sydney County Council* v. *Dell'Oro* (1974) 132 C.L.R. 97, 119 *per* Jacobs J.; *State Electricity Commission of Victoria* v. *Gay* [1951] V.L.R. 104.

3 *Cook* v. *Cook* (1986) 162 C.L.R. 376, 382.

As in the context of duty, the concept of foreseeability of risk is essentially a moral concept, and the reasonable person, who is the standard against which the conduct of the defendant is measured, is a personification of supposed community standards of justice and fairness. Foreseeability is related to probability in the sense that what we can foresee depends largely on our knowledge of the way things happen in the world, of what causes what and of how likely one thing is to follow another. The leading case on the meaning of foreseeability in the context of breach and its relationship to probability is *Wyong Shire Council* v. *Shirt.*[4] In this case a water-skier was injured when he interpreted a sign saying 'Deep Water' as indicating that the area beyond the sign was deep water, whereas in fact it only indicated the presence of a deep dredged channel. It was argued that it was not reasonably foreseeable that any reasonable skier would be misled in this way. The question in the case boiled down to whether the law expects defendants to foresee only risks which are 'real' or 'not unlikely to occur' (as opposed to being 'mere possibilities') or whether defendants are required to foresee any risk, however unlikely, provided only that it is not 'far-fetched' or 'fanciful'. By majority (Wilson J. dissenting) the High Court held that the latter view was correct. The law therefore requires of the defendant a very high degree of perspicacity and it may not be unfair to say, as Wilson J. did in *Shirt*, that the law 'tends to credit [the reasonable] man with an extraordinary capacity for foresight, extending to "possibilities" which are highly speculative and largely theoretical'.[5]

There are, however, two important qualifications which must added to this account of the role of foreseeability in questions of standard of care. First, it is clear from Mason J.'s judgment in *Shirt* that while foreseeability of risk is a necessary condition of liability it is not a sufficient condition.[6] It is not every risk against which the defendant is required to take precautions, only risks which we might call 'significant'. According to Mason J. the question of whether the defendant *ought* to have taken some precaution that he did not take 'calls for a consideration of the magnitude of the risk[7] and the degree of probability of its occurrence, along with the expense, difficulty and inconvenience of taking alleviating action, and any other conflicting responsibilities which the defendant may have'. The classic source of this sort of 'calculus of negligence' is *Bolton* v. *Stone.*[8] In this case Stone was injured by a cricket ball which was hit out of a cricket ground on to the adjacent road where she was standing. There was evidence that balls were very rarely hit over the two-metre-high fence around the ground, on which cricket had been played for nearly 100 years. The House of Lords held that the risk of an accident of the type Stone suffered was so small that it could not be said that the cricket club had been negligent in not taking further precautions against it. The two

---

4 (1980) 146 C.L.R. 40; cf. *Haileybury College* v. *Emanuelli* [1983] V.R. 323.
5 (1980) 146 C.L.R. 40, 53.
6 (1980) 146 C.L.R. 40, 47; cf. *Webb* v. *State of South Australia* (1982) 43 A.L.R. 465.
7 Or, in other words, the likely seriousness of its consequences if it does materialize.
8 [1951] A.C. 850.

factors which figured most in the reasoning of their Lordships were the slight probability, on the evidence, of a ball escaping from the ground, and the impracticality of any precaution other than ceasing to play cricket on the ground. Lord Reid would have been prepared to ignore the draconian nature of such a solution had the risk been greater, but in the circumstances his Lordship clearly felt that the club should not be put in a financial position where the threat of damages awards against it might force it to give up its sport.[9] We will examine the various elements of the negligence calculus a little later.

The second qualification on the concept of foreseeability as a measure of standard of care is a product of the development by the High Court of the notion of 'proximity'. We saw in the last chapter that a duty of care will arise only if there is a sufficient relationship of proximity between the plaintiff and the defendant; in some cases this requirement of proximity is satisfied by reasonable foreseeability of injury, damage or loss to the plaintiff, but in other cases something more is needed. The notion of proximity, as a test of duty of care, is a restrictive one which may justify refusal to impose liability for foreseeable injury; and, as we saw, it operates basically as a conceptual basket into which can be placed policy considerations which count against the imposition of a duty of care in cases where the court thinks no duty ought to be imposed.

The notion of proximity as a measure of standard of care operates in a related but rather different way. In *Cook* v. *Cook*[10] the question was whether an inexperienced driver owes the same standard of care to a passenger as an experienced one. We will consider the answer to this question in more detail later; here we are concerned with the way the majority of the High Court went about answering it. Their Honours took as a starting point the 'ordinary relationship of driver of a motor vehicle and passenger' and asked whether the standard of care which would normally be expected of the driver was appropriate given the facts of the case before them or, on the contrary, whether the facts revealed 'special and exceptional circumstances which would transform the ordinary relationship of driver and passenger into a special one so that it would be plainly unreasonable for the standard of care owed by the driver to the passenger to be what could reasonably be expected of an experienced, skilled and careful driver'.[11] The contrast between ordinary cases and exceptional cases which is inherent in this approach is a slightly curious one in that the court seems to have assumed that the 'ordinary' description of the 'driver/passenger' relationship is somehow given, and that any departure from that description makes the case special. But the truth appears to be that the special description is simply more detailed than the ordinary description; and, as we saw in the last chapter, the degree of detail with which any particular relationship is described is a matter of choice for the court. In fact, the only idea which the concept of proximity,

9 [1951] A.C. 850, 867-8.
10 (1986) 162 C.L.R. 376.
11 This passage is not an exact quote but an amalgam of relevant phrases from the majority's judgment.

as used in this context, seems to encapsulate is the absolutely basic one that the standard of care appropriate in any particular case has to be judged in the light of the facts of that case. As we will see later, it is not true to say that *all* the facts of every case are relevant to setting the standard of care: some facts are simply ignored for what can be called (for want of a better term) 'policy reasons'. The concept of proximity is just as empty of content in this context as in the duty context; and the appearance of conceptual unity which its use in both contexts is meant to generate is illusory. As with duty, the only way of understanding the law is to examine the cases in some detail; concepts as abstract as 'proximity' are of almost no value.

II: THE NEGLIGENCE CALCULUS

1. PROBABILITY

As with all the factors in the negligence calculus, low probability of an accident is not conclusive against liability. All the factors in the calculus have to be taken into account. Thus in *Goode* v. *Nash*[12] a doctor gave his services gratuitously at a free public screening for glaucoma. This involved placing a tonometer on the eye. To avoid cross-infection between patients it was sterilized over an open flame. The plaintiff's eye was burned and permanently injured when the tonometer was put on his eye before it had properly cooled down. It was held that the doctor had been negligent and the fact that such a thing had never happened to the defendant before was irrelevant; the activity was so dangerous and the consequences of negligence so grave that the defendant ought to have taken precautions to ensure that it never happened.

The way the probability question is asked affects the question of whether evidence of earlier occurrences is relevant. In *Bolton* v. *Stone* the risk was defined quite narrowly (the risk of a ball escaping from *this* ground on to *this* road), whereas in *Goode* v. *Nash* the risk was defined more generally (the risk of a patient's eye being injured by a hot instrument). If the court defines the question in general terms it will probably not require evidence of probability but simply decide the question on its own knowledge of the world.[13] But if the question is couched narrowly the court will feel the need to call evidence, as was done in *Bolton* v. *Stone*. Thus, much depends on the way the parties present their case and on the way the court frames the issue; and this, in turn, seems to depend on how crucial the issue of probability is seen as being. In *Bolton* v. *Stone* the whole case was seen to turn on probability. In *Goode* v. *Nash* the seriousness of the risk was more important. This approach is clearly affected by circularity.

---

12 (1979) 21 S.A.S.R. 419; cf. *Webb* v. *South Australia* (1982) 43 A.L.R. 465.

13 cf. *Carmarthenshire C.C.* v. *Lewis* [1955] A.C. 549 where no evidence as to the propensity of children generally or of the children in question to wander was called.

2. Seriousness of Risk

The basic principle here is that the more serious the likely injury to the plaintiff if the risk materializes the more significant or substantial the risk and the greater the precautions which the defendant must take. In *Paris* v. *Stepney Borough Council*[14] the plaintiff had lost the effective sight of one eye in the war. He worked as a motor mechanic and this often involved him in lying under vehicles from which dust and other particles frequently fell. The plaintiff lost the sight of his other eye when a chip from a rusty bolt which he had struck with a steel hammer lodged in his eye. It was held that even if the failure to provide goggles for motor mechanics generally was not negligent, failure to provide them for the plaintiff was, since the defendant knew that he had only one eye and that the loss of his second eye would be particularly serious for him. This case shows how important the classification of the risk is—if the court had classified the risk simply as that of *a worker* losing an eye it may not have held the defendant negligent. In this case it was no doubt prompted to characterize the risk as it did because the defendant knew the plaintiff had the sight of only one eye—a fact which an employer might often not know.[15]

More often the question of seriousness arises in relation to the activity carried on by the defendant rather than the effect of that activity on the particular plaintiff. Thus the running of railways over level crossings,[16] the unloading of drums of mustard gas[17] and more recently the driving of cars[18] have been held to be dangerous activities which require a very high standard of care in their practitioners.

3. Practicability of Precautions

This consideration takes into account the expense of the precautions which the plaintiff alleges ought to have been taken, the difficulty of taking them and the inconvenience they would cause. The most extreme case would be one in which the precautions required to reduce the risk of injury to an acceptable level were so expensive or inconvenient that if the defendant were required to take them he would have to give up the activity entirely. In less extreme cases the precautions might just make the activity less efficient or easy to run, or less profitable or more of a drain on the public purse.[19] The courts are sometimes unwilling to impose liability if the result is likely to be that an activity will stop (as in *Bolton* v. *Stone*), especially if the risk generated by it is small; or to hold that the defendant was negligent in not closing down his operation on the occurrence of some event, such as a flood, until its dangerous effects were removed.[20] On

---

14 [1951] A.C. 367.
15 cf. *Brkovic* v. *Clough (J.O.) & Son Pty Ltd* (1983) 49 A.L.R. 256.
16 *Caledonian Collieries Ltd* v. *Speirs* (1956-7) 97 C.L.R. 202, 225.
17 *Swinton* v. *The China Mutual Steam Navigation Co. Ltd* (1951) 83 C.L.R. 553, 566-7.
18 *Leahy* v. *Beaumont* (1981) 27 S.A.S.R. 290, 294 *per* White J.
19 *Cekan* v. *Haines* (1990) 21 N.S.W.L.R. 296.
20 *Latimer* v. *A.E.C. Ltd* [1953] A.C. 634.

the other hand, if the danger to be guarded against is significant and the precaution easy to take, the courts have no hesitation in holding the defendant negligent,[21] even if the resulting burden of precautions might put the defendant out of business.[22]

The question of practicability tends to raise more problems where the question is whether the whole system under which an activity is operated ought to have been designed differently, than where the question is whether some precaution ought to have been taken in the doing of a more narrowly defined act. A clear example is *Caledonian Collieries Ltd* v. *Speirs*[23] where the question was whether the defendant ought to have installed catch-points on its railway line to prevent runaway trucks careering across a level crossing by derailing them before they reached the crossing. A majority of the court were unconvinced by the evidence of impracticality of catch-points partly because the witness giving it had assumed that if catch-points were to be installed at this crossing they would have to be installed at every other level crossing in the State. The judges thought that the particular crossing involved was sufficiently unique to justify holding the defendant liable for not having installed catch-points without thereby implying that every level crossing in the country should be equipped with them. Similarly, in *Paris* v. *Stepney B.C.* Lord MacDermott was prepared to accept the judge's view that it might not be negligent not to provide goggles for all motor mechanics even though it was negligent not to provide them for one particular motor mechanic.[24]

4. THE IMPORTANCE OR UTILITY OF THE DEFENDANT'S CONDUCT

Mason J. in *Shirt* spoke of 'any other conflicting responsibilities which the defendant may have'. By this he indicated that in deciding what precautions the defendant ought to have taken to protect the plaintiff, it is necessary to decide whether the taking of those precautions was compatible with the defendant's responsibilities to other people and the community at large. Some activities are more worth taking risks for than others—an individual plaintiff may be required to submit to a risk for the sake of some greater good which he would not be required to accept if some lesser interest were at stake. The most common situation in which precautions which would normally be thought reasonable can be waived is that where a fire engine is racing to a fire or an ambulance is speeding an injured or sick person to hospital.[25] As Denning L.J. pointed out in *Watt* v.

---

21 e.g. *Baggermaayschappij Boz & Kalis B.V.* v. *Australian Shipping Commission* (1980) 30 A.L.R. 387.

22 *Arnold* v. *Teno* (1978) 83 D.L.R. (3d) 609.

23 (1957) 97 C.L.R. 202; *Pilon* v. *Commissioner for Railways* [1963] S.R.(N.S.W.) 845.

24 [1951] A.C. 367, 390; see also *Mercer* v. *Commissioner for Road Transport and Tramways* (1936) 56 C.L.R. 580 esp. at p. 596.

25 e.g. *Daborn* v. *Bath Tramways Motor Co. Ltd* [1946] 2 All E.R. 333; *South Australian Ambulance Transport Inc.* v. *Wahlheim* (1948) 77 C.L.R. 215; *Blight* v. *Warman* [1946] S.A.S.R. 163; cf. *Marshall* v. *Osmond* [1983] 2 All E.R. 225 (police car).

Hertfordshire C.C., it is one thing to take risks when driving for some commercial purpose with no emergency, but quite another to take risks to save life and limb.[26] This is usually recognized by statutory provisions or regulations relieving drivers of emergency vehicles of criminal liability for disobedience of traffic rules such as speed limits, the requirement to stop at red lights and to drive on the left. The cases make it clear that the driver of an emergency vehicle is under a duty of care in the same way as any other driver. But whether such a driver has been negligent must be judged by taking into account the special circumstances in which he was driving and the important purpose which he was pursuing.

But it is not only in these obviously emergency situations that the negligence calculus requires or implies a judgment about the value of the defendant's conduct. The classic example goes something like this: if *all* vehicles travelled at ten kilometres an hour nearly all road accidents would be avoided. However, we put such value on faster travel that we are prepared to accept that it is not *per se* negligent to drive at any speed from 60 to 100 kilometres per hour or more according to driving conditions, even though this greatly increases the risk of collisions.[27] Less far-fetched examples are not difficult to find. It is often suggested that if the sport being played in *Bolton* v. *Stone*[28] had been anything other than cricket, the result might have been different. Again, it is often suggested that courts show too great an unwillingness to hold doctors' mistakes to be the result of negligence as opposed to mere non-negligent errors of judgment.[29] The accusation being made in both these instances is that improper value has been placed on the defendant's activity; but even ignoring this point, the examples do show how implicit valuations often underlie judgments about negligence. The law's concern with the social value of activities is partly based on a desire to achieve a fair result as between the plaintiff and the defendant. But it is perhaps more concerned with the deterrent effect of negligence judgments. If the burden of precautions placed on an activity is 'too heavy' then that activity may cease and if the burden is 'too light' the activity may increase. But to decide whether the burden is too heavy or too light or just right we have to make a decision about how much of the activity we want.

---

26 [1954] 2 All E.R. 368, 371.

27 *Daborn* v. *Bath Tramways* [1946] 2 All E.R. 333, 336 *per* Asquith L.J.; *Mercer* v. *Commissioner for Road Transport* (1937) 56 C.L.R. 580, 589 *per* Latham C.J.

28 [1951] A.C. 850.

29 Indeed, in the case of doctors, the legal rules themselves contain a bias against findings of negligence; the question, in a negligence action against a doctor, is not whether the defendant acted reasonably, but whether a responsible body of medical opinion supports acting as he did, even if a majority of doctors would have acted differently. In other words, a doctor will be acquitted of negligence unless he acted so unreasonably that *no* responsible body of medical opinion can be found to back him up. See generally *Maynard* v. *West Midlands Regional Health Authority* [1984] 1 W.L.R. 634. It is not clear whether this rule applies to other professional groups as well. *Edward Wong Finance Co. Ltd* v. *Johnson Stokes & Master* [1984] A.C. 296 suggests that it does not apply to solicitors. Judges are, no doubt, more willing to decide how lawyers should behave than how doctors should behave. Much less clear is why skilled but non-professional service providers should not also have the benefit of the generous rule.

5. COMPLETING THE EQUATION

How do the factors relevant to the calculus of negligence fit together? Somehow or other the disparate elements of probability and seriousness of risk, practicability of precautions and social value have to be put together to produce a judgment about reasonable precautions. The ultimate test is always, 'what precautions would the reasonable person have taken?'.

The chief difficulty is that the negligence calculus requires us to compare things which cannot really be compared because they are so unlike one another in nature. If courts were prepared to make extensive use of statisticians and actuaries they might be able to give reasonably accurate numerical values to the probability of the risk and its likely consequences; although even here, as we have seen, much depends on how the risk is defined. But the real difficulty is with the cost of precautions. The relevant cost of precautions is not just their economic cost to the defendant. It may be thought right also to take into account the cost to society as a whole of certain precautions (which it may be very difficult to quantify), or even to discount or inflate the economic cost of precautions to take account of the intangible, non-economic value (or disvalue) of the defendant's activity.[30] It would seem, therefore, that at best the negligence calculus can only work in a rather imprecise and impressionistic way. The court in some vague way constructs a balance with the probability and gravity of the risk on one side, and the practicability of the precautions which the plaintiff alleges the defendant ought to have taken and judgments of social value on the other. If this metaphysical balance shows that the first two elements are 'heavier' than the latter two then the plaintiff wins; otherwise the defendant wins.

There are, of course, many cases of negligence where the court decides the issue of carelessness without explicitly using the significant risk calculus. It is probably true to say that the main use of the calculus is to concentrate attention upon that one of the factors relevant to carelessness which 'may be determinative in any given situation'.[31] This point can be illustrated by *Bolton* v. *Stone*.[32] The evidence in that case suggested that the chance of someone on the road being hit by a cricket ball was very slight. It was this factor of the low probability of risk which seems to have prompted enunciation by the House of Lords of the significant risk calculus. But unless a particular issue is made of one element of the calculus, explicit reference to it will probably not be made. The court will simply ask whether the defendant acted reasonably.

A question which needs to be considered here is how the risk against which the defendant is required to take precautions is to be defined. This question is very important because the degree of detail in which the risk is described affects its probability (the probability of a water-skiing accident is higher than that of a water-skier being injured by misreading a sign), its gravity (the loss of an eye is more serious to a one-eyed motor mechanic than to an ordinary (two-eyed) motor mechanic), and the practicability of

30 e.g. the activity of saving the life of a disabled, non-wealth-creating person.
31 *Moisan* v. *Loftus* (1947) 178 F. 2d 169, 173 *per* Judge Learned Hand.
32 [1950] A.C. 850.

precautions (it costs less to provide goggles for one-eyed motor mechanics than for all motor mechanics). Since fact situations can be described at many different levels of generality (just as can classes of plaintiffs or types of loss), the best we can do is to look behind the classification adopted for some clue as to why the court decided the way it did, because usually the classification chosen will determine or help to determine the result. Sometimes the explanation will lie in some value judgment about the defendant's activity or the plaintiff's moral right to be compensated, or the relative abilities of the parties to pay. Sometimes the motivation may be the effect the decision will have on people's future conduct. Classification can be used to all these ends.

III: NEGLIGENCE AS AN OBJECTIVE STANDARD

Whether the defendant took the precautions he ought to have, given the result of the negligence calculus, is a question to be decided objectively according to the standards of the reasonable person. This means, in effect, that it is no answer for the defendant to say that he did his best given his particular abilities, resources and circumstances.[33] If the defendant was not in a position to take the precautions which the court decides were reasonable then he ought not to have engaged in the activity. On the other hand, whether a person was negligent or not must depend on what he did or failed to do in the circumstances in which he found himself. To take a very obvious example: a doctor's conduct must be measured by the standards of a reasonable doctor, not of a reasonable layman. The same applies to persons generally who perform skilled tasks. In other words, the reasonable person test only tells us that certain circumstances of the defendant's position and certain of his personal characteristics ought to be ignored in deciding what he ought to have done, but by itself it does not tell us which ones. The basic position is that unless the law specifically allows a particular characteristic to be taken into account in the defendant's favour it must be ignored. So which characteristics will the law allow the defendant to plead in his defence?

1. Financial Resources

There are only two areas in which the law may take account of the financial resources of the defendant. They are, first, where a landowner is faced with a natural hazard on his land, and secondly, when determining what precautions an occupier must take to protect trespassers on his land from injury.[34] Both of these areas were discussed in Chapter 9.[35] A general point should be made at this stage about the meaning of the words 'objective' and 'subjective' in this context. It is often said that to take

---

33 *Herrington* v. *British Railways Board* [1972] A.C. 877, 898G-H *per* Lord Reid.
34 *PQ* v. *Australian Red Cross Society* [1992] V.R. 19.
35 See pp. 383 and 392 above; see also p. 431 below.

resources (or physical ability, etc.) into account is to subjectivize the standard of care. This is true in the sense that in determining what the reasonable person in the position of the defendant would have done, these characteristics are usually ignored. But the standard of the reasonable person is still applied. The question becomes what the reasonable person in the position of the defendant, including his financial and physical position, would have done. The defendant's answer is not that he acted as he did because of his resources or ability but that the reasonable person with his resources and ability would have acted as he did.

2. Physical and Intellectual Ability

Once again, the only areas in which it has been specifically held that the defendant's physical strength or ability (or rather lack of it) may be relevant to liability are the two mentioned above in relation to financial resources. But there are other areas where the physical strength of the defendant might seem particularly relevant. Would a 60-kilogram woman schoolteacher be expected to take personal physical steps to prevent two burly teenage lads engaging in a classroom fight? Would a prison warder of medium build be expected to protect a prisoner from assault by a determined heavy-weight cell-mate? These examples concern cases where the defendant is required to take positive steps, and it may be that in this area lack of physical ability would be relevant in a way it would not be when the defendant is expected to avoid negligent conduct. In these cases, too, the liability rests on a legal or moral *right* to control a person or thing rather than on *ability* to control, and it is this which makes us think that lack of physical ability should be an answer. But in some situations the liability itself may rest on physical ability to act. For example, if the principle enunciated by Laskin J. in *The Ogopogo*[36] represents the law, liability under that principle is based in some cases at least on the ability of the rescuer to help the person in danger. The master of a ship is clearly in a position, at little or no risk or effort to himself, to take positive steps to help the man overboard. But it is highly unlikely that the law would require a person to go to the rescue if this would involve him in grave risk of injury or death.

It has been held that insanity is not a defence to a claim in negligence; in other words, it is not permissible to judge whether the defendant's conduct was negligent in light of the fact that for psychological reasons he was not in normal control of his actions. In *Adamson* v. *Motor Vehicle Insurance Trust*[37] the defendant driver was acting under a compulsion to flee quickly to save his life which he irrationally believed was in danger from his workmates. The judge held that he knew he had ignored a traffic signal and run down the plaintiff, but that he felt that he had to save his life at all costs. It is clearly difficult in such a situation not to feel sympathy for the plaintiff even if it is also difficult to attribute moral fault

---

36 See p. 382 above.
37 (1957) 58 W.A.L.R. 56.

to the defendant. In situations where there is an insurance fund to meet the damages there seems little reason not to hold the defendant liable. On the other hand, there seems something rather strange in asking what the reasonable insane person would have done—in this context the idea of fault simply breaks down. Cases where the defendant's physical incapacity is self-inflicted or the result of some sudden traumatic occurrence are different. The case of the drunken driver is an example. Here, clearly, it can be no answer to a claim of negligent driving for a driver to say that he was under the influence of alcohol (or drugs). He may have behaved as carefully as his condition permitted, but his real negligence consists in driving while drunk rather than in any precise failure of care in driving. Other examples are provided by cases in which the defendant was stung by a bee, or had a coughing fit or a heart attack while driving.[38] A driver who knows he might suffer some illness at the wheel which will render him unfit to drive might be held negligent in driving at all,[39] but if a driver is overcome by an unexpected illness while driving which renders him physically incapable of taking care, he is not liable in negligence for resulting damage.[40]

The law, in many of these cases, concerned with disability faces a dilemma: on the one hand the courts are concerned not to allow the gap between moral culpability and legal liability to become too wide. On the other hand, given the dangerousness of driving and the universal presence of third-party liability insurance, there seems little reason not to impose very strict standards of conduct on drivers regardless of their ability to meet those standards.[41] The prime role of the law of torts, at least in the motor accident area, has changed from sanctioning and discouraging faulty conduct to compensating injured plaintiffs; but the law of tort, with its emphasis on moral fault, and the case-by-case method of allocating losses on the basis of responsibility, is a very inefficient way of compensating victims, many of whom are injured without fault or find it difficult to prove fault.[42]

3. Age

It was held in *McHale* v. *Watson*[43] that where the defendant is a child, it is no more permissible to take account of his personal peculiarities than it is in the case of an adult. But it is necessary to take into account the fact that

---

38 e.g. *Billy Higgs & Sons Ltd* v. *Baddeley* [1950] N.Z.L.R. 605; cf. *Waugh* v. *James K. Allan Ltd* [1964] 2 Lloyd's Rep. 1; *Robinson* v. *Glover* [1952] N.Z.L.R. 669.

39 *Higgs* v. *Baddeley* [1950] N.Z.L.R. 605; cf. *Jones* v. *Dennison* [1971] R.T.R. 174.

40 cf. *Scholz* v. *Standish* [1961] S.A.S.R. 123; but contrast *Roberts* v. *Ramsbottom* [1980] 1 W.L.R. 823. The plea that the accident was caused by factors completely outside the defendant's control is sometimes referred to as the defence of inevitable accident. In *Jockel* v. *Jockel* [1963] S.R.(N.S.W.) 230 it was held that a plea of inevitable accident is not a separate defence but simply a denial of negligence. (If it were a proper defence the onus of proof would rest on the defendant, not the plaintiff.)

41 See *Leahy* v. *Beaumont* (1981) 27 S.A.S.R. 290 *per* White J.

42 For a general discussion see *Atiyah's Accidents* esp. Chapter 19.

43 (1966) 115 C.L.R. 199.

children as a group have less foresight, experience and prudence than adults; and the younger the child the less its ability to exercise the care and foresight which is attributed to the reasonable person. It appears from *McHale* v. *Watson* that the characteristics of children which the court had in mind were mental (that is, basically, ability to appreciate and foresee risks) rather than physical; it is not clear from the case to what extent the fact that children may be weaker or physically less co-ordinated than adults can be taken into account. In the context of deciding whether a plaintiff has been guilty of *contributory* negligence and, if so, by how much his damages should be rescued, there are a number of cases which indicate not only that the mental and physical capabilities of a child plaintiff ought to be considered[44] but even that the *particular* child's intelligence, knowledge and educational level and attainments should be taken into account.[45] Hence a child educated in road sense would be treated differently from one not so educated.[46] This difference of approach may spring from a desire not to deprive negligent plaintiffs of compensation which will usually be provided by an insurer.

Should the age of the defendant normally be relevant to liability? If youth is relevant, why should old age not be? And if the mental immaturity of youth is relevant, should its physical immaturity also be relevant? But if it is, why should the infirmity of age be ignored? Leaving aside insurance arguments, and assuming that the defendant (or plaintiff) is not in some sense responsible for the disability he has, we might say that the law should try to reflect morality. We might then argue that morality would never condemn a person who could not help doing what he did. This might suggest that the law should take account of every feature of the plaintiff's personality and make-up. But, on second thoughts, it is not so clear that this is what our morality requires at all. We often judge as morally at fault people who have acted in ways commensurate with the nature that they have acquired through birth or upbringing. The rude or the heedless, the selfish or the rapacious are not thought any the better of because we can trace their character to forces inside themselves which they find it difficult to control. Adults should adjust their behaviour to take account of their weaknesses and foibles. And this is perhaps the crux of the matter. Children are not and are not expected to be as responsible as adults. Adults who are suddenly attacked by illness or bees can be forgiven because and to the extent that they have no chance to exercise responsible control over their actions. On this basis the insane should be excused too, unless we see insanity as some sort of wages of sin. The fault principle must, at bottom, be a principle which expresses a person's responsibility for his own actions. Morality, as much as law, makes demands which we

---

44 e.g. *Aubrey* v. *Carter* [1962] W.A.R. 51; *Griffiths* v. *Doolan* [1959] Qd. R. 304; *Ralph* v. *Henderson and Pollard Ltd* [1968] N.Z.L.R. 759. The fact that the plaintiff is a child can also be relevant to the question of whether the defendant has been negligent: *Yachuk* v. *Oliver Blais Co.* [1949] A.C. 386.

45 e.g. *Cotton* v. *Commissioner for Road Transport and Tramways* (1942) 43 S.R.(N.S.W.) 66; *Farrall* v. *Stokes* (1954) 54 S.R.(N.S.W.) 294.

46 *Bassani* v. *Mudge* [1964] S.A.S.R. 56.

sometimes find difficult to meet or, at least, the fulfilment of which requires conscious effort.[47]

4. Experience and Skill

The function of the law, however, is not primarily to make moral judgments but to decide when damages ought to be paid. There are circumstances where, even though the defendant cannot be said to have been morally culpable, or even though his conduct can be said to have been morally excusable, it is fair that he should pay compensation. This idea of fairness is usually associated with torts of strict liability—because the defendant has created a risk it is fair that he should pay compensation if the risk materializes, even though the accident occurred through no fault of the defendant. But the idea of fairness can also go a long way to explaining why, for example, we require drivers to exercise quite unrealistically high standards of care—driving is a very risky activity and, especially when the defendant is insured, it is fair that he should bear the costs of driving by paying damages. Again, in *Bolton* v. *Stone* Lord Radcliffe thought that it would be fair for the cricket club to pay compensation to Stone even though they were not strictly at fault.[48]

The cases on skill and experience can be seen as an application of this idea. There are at least some cases where lack of skill or experience is no answer to a claim of negligence: the greenest learner driver owes the same standard of care to passengers and other road users as the most experienced;[49] the newest doctor owes the same duty to his patients as the most seasoned.[50] However, both these statements need immediate qualification. There are circumstances in which the inexperienced driver is allowed to plead inexperience;[51] doctors are only required to display the degree of skill which is appropriate to their position—for example, as general practitioner or specialist;[52] the home carpenter is not expected to display the skill of a professional.[53] A player of sports is only required to display the skill that an ordinary person would acquire before playing the sport for the first time in public competition, not the skill of an experienced player.[54]

---

47 For a similar, but much more philosophically sophisticated, argument see Tony Honoré (1988) 104 *L.Q.R.* 530.

48 [1950] A.C. 850; cf. *Mercer* v. *Commissioner for Road Transport* (1936) 56 C.L.R. 580.

49 *Nettleship* v. *Weston* [1971] 2 Q.B. 691; *Cook* v. *Cook* (1986) 68 A.L.R. 353.

50 *Jones* v. *Manchester Corporation* [1952] 2 Q.B. 852; *Wilsher* v. *Essex A.H.A.* [1987] Q.B. 730 (C.A. reversed on other grounds [1988] A.C. 1074).

51 *Cook* v. *Cook* (1986) 68 A.L.R. 353; *Walker* v. *Turton-Sainsbury* [1952] S.A.S.R. 159; *Chang* v. *Chang* [1973] 1 N.S.W.L.R. 708.

52 *Whitehouse* v. *Jordan* [1981] 1 W.L.R. 246; see also *Luxmoore-May* v. *Messenger May Baverstock* [1990] 1 W.L.R. 1009 (auctioneers; criticized N. Mullaney (1991) 107 *L.Q.R.* 28); *Knight* v. *Home Office* [1990] 3 All E.R. 237, 243 (hospitals).

53 *Wells* v. *Cooper* [1958] 2 Q.B. 265.

54 *Wooldridge* v. *Sumner* [1963] 2 Q.B. 43, 68 *per* Diplock L.J.; but the level of competition may affect the standard of care required: *Condon* v. *Basi* [1985] 1 W.L.R. 866.

Is there any explanation of these apparent inconsistencies? In *The Insurance Commissioner* v. *Joyce* Dixon J. suggested that if a plaintiff accepted a lift from a driver whom he knew had lost a limb or an eye, or was deaf or drunk, he was only entitled to expect a degree of care commensurate with the driver's condition.[55] This *dictum* has since been generalized to produce the idea of variable standards of care according to which the standard of careful conduct varies according to the plaintiff's knowledge or reasonable assessment of the skill and experience of the defendant. This approach came under considerable attack in *Nettleship* v. *Weston*[56] on several grounds. First, it would be very difficult to apply; for example, as the skill and experience of a learner driver increased so would the standard of care expected of him; but his actual skill and experience would be relevant only to the extent that the plaintiff knew or ought to have known of his current abilities; and, anyway, how could a court work out the standard of care required of people who fell short in various ways and in an infinite range of degrees from the norm of the reasonable person? Secondly, Lord Denning M.R. thought it unacceptable in days of compulsory third-party motor insurance that insurance funds should be protected at the cost of injured plaintiffs by requiring of learners and other deficient drivers a lower standard of care.

On the other hand, Salmon L.J. in *Nettleship* broadly accepted Dixon J.'s approach with the qualification that, in the case of disabilities, as opposed to inexperience, the disability must be one which is generally known to affect the ability to execute the task in question; for example, having only a right leg would not impair one's ability to drive an automatic car with reasonable care.[57] The basis of Salmon L.J.'s approach was that there is no 'special relationship' between a driver and a member of the public, and so a plea of inexperience would never succeed against a stranger. But if the plaintiff knows that the defendant is incapable of measuring up to the standard of the reasonable experienced driver and nevertheless travels with him, he cannot demand that the driver reach that standard and claim damages if he does not. This is especially true of a driving instructor—if the instructor was a professional and there was a contract between the instructor and the pupil, a court would not imply into that contract a promise on the part of the pupil to drive with the skill of an experienced driver, since such a promise would be inconsistent with the very purpose of the contract; the fact that there is no contract between the instructor and the driver cannot give the instructor a right to expect a degree of care which he could not expect if there were a contract.

An approach very similar to that of Salmon L.J. was adopted by the High Court in *Cook* v. *Cook*.[58] and it was, as we saw above, related by the court to the concept of proximity. The High Court stressed, however, that it would only be in exceptional cases that the standard of the person of

55 (1948) 77 C.L.R. 39, 56.
56 [1971] 2 Q.B. 691.
57 ibid 703-4.
58 (1986) 162 C.L.R. 376. Some of the difficulties of this decision are explored in *Radford* v. *Ward* [1990] Aust. Torts Reports 68,361.

ordinary skill and experience could be displaced, and the court thought that this fact overcame the main perceived difficulty of Dixon J.'s approach. However, the High Court gave no real guidance as to how exceptional cases were to be identified, and *Cook* v. *Cook* gives very little help in dealing with the most commonly litigated cause of driving incompetence: intoxication. The court rejected Lord Denning's insurance-based argument on the ground that it was for the legislature and not the courts to give effect to such an argument. The High Court also held that if, for example, the standard of care was lowered to take account of the defendant's inexperience, this would only prevent liability arising from actions fairly seen as resulting from inexperience, and not from actions which not even a reasonably careful inexperienced driver would have done.[59] In other words, whatever the standard of care, the legal concept of negligence is objective: did the defendant act reasonably given the characteristics which the court considers, in the circumstances of the particular case, to be relevant to the question of negligence?

This idea of a special relationship based on the plaintiff's knowledge of the defendant's inexperience or lack of skill helps to explain the results in some of the cases mentioned earlier. In *Walker* v. *Turton-Sainsbury*[60] the plaintiff not only knew that the defendant was not used to driving high-powered sports cars but also actually encouraged her to take him for a drive. The language of special relationship is also present in *Whitehouse* v. *Jordan* where Lord Fraser of Tullybelton spoke of the doctor being held to the standard and type of skills which the defendant 'held himself out' as having.[61] This seems to assume that the patient has some sort of reasonable expectation, based on knowledge, of the standard of treatment he can expect. This can be compared with *Philips* v. *William Whitely Ltd*[62] where it was held that a woman who goes to a jeweller to have her ears pierced cannot expect the same degree of cleanliness as she could expect of a doctor doing the same operation. In the case of competitive sports, the whole notion of competition is based on differences of skill and experience, and participants in such sports can be expected to realize that not all players will be equally skilled and experienced. All these cases assume a certain knowledge on the part of the plaintiff of the degree of skill and experience possessed by the defendant, and that the plaintiff had some choice whether or not to expose himself to the risk posed by the defendant's lack of skill or experience. But in many cases, where, for example, a patient is treated in a public hospital, a plaintiff will not in any sense have chosen his defendant. It is to such situations that statements in cases such as *Jones* v. *Manchester Corporation*[63] are directed.

We might conclude from all this that in cases involving acts or activities requiring experience or acquired skill for their proper execution, the courts consider it fair that the risks of lack of skill or inexperience should

---

59 cf. *Ricketts* v. *Laws* (1988) 14 N.S.W.L.R. 311.
60 [1952] S.A.S.R. 159.
61 [1981] 1 W.L.R. 246, 263.
62 [1938] 1 All E.R. 566.
63 [1952] 2 Q.B. 852; see text to n. 50 above. But contrast *Knight* v. *Home Office* [1990] 3 All E.R. 237.

rest on the learner or inexperienced defendant rather than on stranger plaintiffs even though the defendant may not, because of inexperience or non-culpable lack of skill, have been at fault. However, where the plaintiff is in some special relationship with the defendant based on knowledge and choice, or on the nature of the activity in which they are engaged, it may be fair to demand of the defendant only an objectively determined degree of care commensurate with his skill and experience. The principle may also operate in the converse: suppose a doctor or a driver is more highly skilled or more experienced than the ordinary driver or doctor of his rank. A plaintiff who knew this and consulted this particular doctor because of his great skill, or only agreed to drive with this driver who intended to perform some dangerous manoeuvre because he was very experienced, might be entitled to hold the defendant to a higher than usual standard of care. But could a plaintiff who knew nothing of the defendant's special skill or experience complain if he did not exercise it in relation to him? If he could, this would be a variety of liability for omission and it may be that the law would shrink from imposing liability for it in the absence of a special relationship.[64]

Despite all this, however, there is a serious objection to the whole approach in *Cook* v. *Cook* of variable standards of care based on the plaintiff's knowledge of the defendant's lack of skill and experience. The effect of lowering the standard of care may be that the defendant will be held not liable. But there are other ways of dealing with the sort of case we are considering. If, instead of asking whether the defendant's conduct ought to be judged according to a lower than usual standard of care, the court were to ask whether the plaintiff ought to be held to have been contributorily negligent, then the court could adopt the more flexible and arguably fairer approach of reducing the plaintiff's damages to reflect his contributory negligence. Alternatively, the court could ask whether the plaintiff had *voluntarily assumed the risk* presented by the plaintiff's lack of skill or experience; if it held that he had, the effect would be the same as lowering the standard of care—namely, to deprive the plaintiff of any damages at all. But courts seem prepared to reach this conclusion in only the most extreme cases, and certainly not just because the plaintiff knew of the risk and could have avoided it. In other words, the variable standard of care approach is more likely to work against plaintiffs than other applicable doctrines. To the extent that the prime aim of the law of tort is to compensate injured plaintiffs, there is an argument against the variable standards of care approach. We will discuss the defences of contributory negligence and voluntary assumption of risk in more detail in Chapter 13.

64 *Rust* v. *Needham* (1974) 9 S.A.S.R. 510, 523 *per* Bray C.J.

IV: EXTERNAL FACTORS RELEVANT TO STANDARD OF CARE

Now we must consider certain other factors relevant to standard of care which operate outside of the negligence calculus which we have just considered.

1. Custom and Accepted Standards

Defendants often argue that they were not negligent because they acted in the way that people in their position normally act. Evidence of normal or customary commercial, industrial or professional practice is commonly called in a wide variety of contexts—in actions against solicitors, doctors, engineers, manufacturers and so on. The basic rule is that compliance with custom or standard practice is not conclusive evidence of due care, nor is departure from it conclusive that the defendant has been negligent.[65] If all or the bulk of the evidence of custom or practice on a particular point is favourable to the defendant the court will usually accept the practice as being reasonable.[66] But the court is entitled to decide that the prevailing practice is negligent if it believes that the degree of risk involved in the practice is socially or morally unacceptable;[67] although a court would probably not adopt this course except in what it saw as a very extreme case. If the evidence of accepted practice is significantly divided (that is, if it shows that some people would have acted as the defendant did but that others would have acted differently) the court is placed in a difficult position. The whole point of calling evidence of customary practice is to inform the court about technical matters (often involving opinion or judgment) of which judges typically have little knowledge; how then can the court resolve disputes between technically expert witnesses?

In actions against doctors in respect of clinical decisions about treatment the law appears to be that a court should not attempt to choose between conflicting expert evidence as to how the defendant ought to have acted. A doctor will not normally[68] be held negligent provided he acted 'in accordance with a practice accepted at the time as proper by a responsible body of medical opinion even though other doctors adopt a different practice'.[69] In other words the standard of care in medical negligence cases

65 See e.g. *Mercer* v. *Commissioner for Road Transport* (1937) 56 C.L.R. 580.

66 e.g. *Chin Keow* v. *Government of Malaysia* [1967] 1 W.L.R. 813, 817.

67 *Sidaway* v. *Governors of Bethlem Royal Hospital and the Maudsley Hospital* [1985] 2 W.L.R. 480, 504-5 *per* Lord Bridge; *F* v. *R* (1983) 33 S.A.S.R. 189, 194 *per* King C.J.; *Battersby* v. *Tottman* (1985) 37 S.A.S.R. 524, 537 *per* Zelling J. See also *Informed Decisions about Medical Procedures* (V.L.R.C. 24; A.L.R.C. 50; N.S.W.L.R.C. 62, 1989) pp. 15-16.

68 But just as the courts retain a residual power to castigate widely accepted practices as negligent so, *a fortiori*, there must be a power to hold a contested practice negligent.

69 The advantage of this approach is said to be that it does not penalize medical experimentation, which often produces beneficial advances in treatment techniques: *Sidaway* v. *Bethlem Royal Hospital* [1985] A.C. 871, 893 *per* Lord Diplock.

is basically 'a matter of medical judgment'.[70] But it is by no means clear that this approach applies to cases other than medical cases.[71] If it does not, then the court may attempt to choose between the rival bodies of evidence on the basis of the relative credibility, qualifications or numbers of the two bodies of experts giving it.[72] But if this is not possible, it either has to choose, itself, between the two conflicting views (presumably on non-technical grounds) or it will refuse to choose and will dismiss the plaintiff's claim for lack of evidence of negligence.

From one point of view this position seems most unsatisfactory—how can we justify setting a lay tribunal over an expert defendant to judge him in the conduct of his profession when professionals themselves disagree as to what constitutes good practice? The answer to this question must be along the following lines: one function of the law of negligence is, in relation to risks generated by any particular activity, to specify which risks are socially acceptable and which are not. It should not be left to those engaged in an activity to decide which risks should be removed and which should be allowed to remain. At the end of the day this is a social question which the courts must play a part in answering.

It is often argued that courts should be slow to hold professionals negligent because of the serious negative impact such a holding might have on the professional reputation and career of the defendant;[73] and because professional groups may be led by the risk of liability to engage in 'defensive' practices, that is, 'unnecessary' precautions designed not to protect their clients from loss but to protect themselves from allegations of negligence.[74] But this argument is weak on both grounds: why should the reputations and careers of professionals be more protected than those of any other group in society which is potentially subject to negligence liability? As for defensive practices, these are an irrational reaction to the fear of liability: a court is very unlikely to hold anyone negligent for failing to take a precaution which could not reasonably be said to be for the real benefit of the patient or client; moreover, even in the case of professionals other than doctors, in practice the normal benchmark of reasonable conduct is accepted practice within the profession. Courts are

---

70 *Sidaway* v. *Bethlem Royal Hospital* [1985] A.C. 871, 881 *per* Lord Scarman (who, however, dissented in this case). Cf. *Maynard* v. *West Midlands Regional Health Authority* [1984] 1 W.L.R. 634. This is often called 'the *Bolam* rule' because it was first enunciated by Mc Nair J. in *Bolam* v. *Friern Hospital Management Committee* [1957] 1 W.L.R. 582, 587. On medical treatment given by first-aid volunteers see G. Griffiths (1990) 53 *M.L.R.* 255.

71 The Privy Council seems not to have adopted it in *Edward Wong Finance Co. Ltd* v. *Johnson Stokes & Master* [1984] A.C. 296 in a case against a solicitor. But Lloyd L.J. in *Gold* v. *Haringey H.A.* [1988] Q.B. 481, 488-9 said that it applied to any case involving the application of 'special skill'; and it was adopted in relation to fine art auctioneers in *Luxmoore-May* v. *Messenger May Baverstock* [1990] 1 W.L.R. 1009. See also *Z.W. Pty Ltd* v. *Peter R. Hughes & Partners Pty Ltd* [1992] 1 Qd.R. 352.

72 *Bolam* v. *Friern Hospital* [1957] 1 W.L.R. 582, 587 *per* McNair J.

73 See *Willcox* v. *Sing* [1985] 2 Qd.R. 66.

74 For empirical evidence on this issue see D. Tribe and G. Korgaonkar [1991] *Prof. Neg.* 2. Studies in the U.S. suggest that 'unnecessary' medical procedures are often the result of patients being charged *per* procedure performed rather than of fear on the part of doctors of being sued.

wary of finding negligence against professionals in the absence of weighty expert evidence against the defendant, and of evidence that additional precautions or alternative procedures were practicable and not too costly. This is particularly so where a question of negligence in design of a system of working is in issue. This caution, it might be thought, amply protects professional defendants.

So far as doctors are concerned, the lenient approach to standard of care has come under recent attack in cases involving allegations of failure to warn patients of risks inherent in particular treatments or procedures. The argument in such cases is not that the treatment or procedure was negligently carried out, but rather that if the plaintiff had known of the risk which in fact materialized (and which was inherent in the procedure or treatment however carefully executed) he would not have agreed to the treatment or procedure. It is often argued that patients should not be subjected to treatments or procedures to which they have not given their 'informed consent', because everyone has the right to determine what shall be done with their own body.[75] According to this view, whether a doctor ought to warn a patient of any particular risk depends not on whether a reasonable body of medical opinion would favour its disclosure, but whether the 'prudent patient' would regard it as a significant or material factor to take into account in deciding whether to consent. However, even under this approach, medical opinion plays a part: a doctor may be justified in concealing even material risks if, in the opinion of responsible doctors, knowledge of it would do the patient more harm than good. Under this approach, doctors would be held to a higher standard of care in giving information to patients than in treating them, on the ground that technical expertise is less relevant to the former than to the latter, and in order to promote better communication between doctors and patients.

There is authority, both English[76] and Australian,[77] rejecting the informed consent principle and applying the same rule both to the treatment of and to the giving of information to patients.[78] However, the New South Wales Court of Appeal has recently held that if a patient asks questions about the risks attendant upon particular treatment (so that the issue is not simply whether the doctor ought to have volunteered information) the court might decide for itself whether failure to give relevant information was negligent, even in the face of evidence that a responsible

---

75 Lord Scarman (dissenting) accepted this argument in *Sidaway* v. *Governors of Bethlem Royal Hospital* [1985] A.C. 871.

76 *Sidaway* v. *Governors of Bethlem Royal Hospital* [1985] A.C. 871; the test applies to 'non-therapeutic' as well as to 'therapeutic' advice: *Gold* v. *Haringey H.A.* [1988] Q.B. 481. For a different view of the effect of *Sidaway* see N. Iles (1987) 11 *Adel. L.R.* 88.

77 *Battersby* v. *Tottman* (1985) 37 S.A.S.R. 524. See also D.I. Cassidy (1992) 66 *A.L.J.* 67.

78 Special problems arise where the patient is not able to give consent because he is unconscious or mentally incompetent or below the age of understanding. In such cases the question would be whether some other person (such as a parent (J. Devereux (1991) 11 *O.J.L.S.* 283) or other relative, or a court in the case of wards of court (see, for example, *Re F* [1990] 2 A.C. 1)) should be given information on the basis of which they could decide whether the proposed treatment was in the best interests of the patient.

body of doctors would not have given the information in the circumstances of the particular case.[79]

There is legislation dealing with consent to medical and dental procedures in South Australia,[80] but the definition of consent in the legislation does not discriminate between the informed consent approach and the ordinary negligence approach. There are also statutes in Victoria[81] and New South Wales[82] requiring patients to be given very full information prior to the administration of certain treatments for mental illness. In a 1989 joint report the Australian, Victorian and New South Wales Law Reform Commissions recommended that the common law test of reasonable care should not be replaced by legislative provisions, but that guidelines should be issued by the National Health and Medical Research Council; failure to comply with the guidelines could be taken into account by a court in deciding whether a doctor had been negligent in withholding information. There is a considerable body of academic opinion in favour of greater disclosure than the current law requires.[83]

2. Statutory Rules and Regulations

Sometimes actions in tort can be brought for failure to comply with statutory duties. We will examine the action for breach of statutory duty in greater detail later. But also in an ordinary action for negligence the question may arise of whether compliance with some statute or regulation is a sufficient answer on the defendant's part, or conversely, whether failure to comply with a statute or regulation is conclusive evidence of negligence. The basic rule is that compliance or non-compliance is relevant to but not conclusive of the question of negligence.[84] The apparent basis of this principle is that statutory regulations usually fix minimum standards of acceptable conduct rather than a standard of reasonable conduct in all the circumstances. Facts alter cases, and to treat failure to comply with a regulation as negligence *per se* would turn the action from one for negligence into one for breach of statutory duty.

---

79 *Rogers* v. *Whitaker* (1991) 23 N.S.W.L.R. 600. But it is very difficult to discern from the judgments any principle governing when the *Bolam* test will apply and when it will not. Perhaps it is best to treat the case as involving an exercise of the court's residual power to hold an accepted practice negligent (see now decison of H.C.).

80 Consent to Medical and Dental Procedures Act 1985 (S.A.). Section 8 is relevant to the present discussion, but it may only apply to emergency treatment and treatment of minors: K. Mack (1988) 11 *Adel. L.R.* 448.

81 Mental Health Act 1986 (Vic.).

82 Mental Health Act 1983 (N.S.W.).

83 e.g. G. Robertson (1981) 97 *L.Q.R.* 102; M.A. Jones (1984) 100 *L.Q.R.* 355; H. Teff (1985) 101 *L.Q.R.* 432; M. Brazier (1987) 7 L.S. 169. D. Manderson (1988) 62 *A.L.J.* 430 is sceptical of how much can be achieved by law in increasing the flow of information. Some very tricky issues arise out of the AIDS epidemic: should a patient be told that his blood will be tested for HIV? (see J. Keown (1989) 52 *M.L.R.* 790); when should a doctor warn B that A is HIV positive? (see M. Neave (1987) 9 *U. Tas. L.R.* 1, 23-30; R. O'Dair [1990] *C.L.P.* 219, 232-41). As to consent to participation in randomized clinical trials see A. Whitfield and D. Brahams (eds) *Medicine and the Law* (London, 1990) pp. 7-8.

84 *Sibley* v. *Kais* (1967) 118 C.L.R. 424.

Indeed, it has been said that sometimes obedience to a regulation can be the worst course to take.[85] On the other hand, if there is no other evidence of negligence than a breach of regulation, and if there is no reason to doubt the evidence, it may be proper for the court to find negligence on the basis of the breach.[86] These principles well illustrate the way in which the compensatory and deterrent functions of the law of negligence interact. Regulations are aimed at deterrence of particular types of conduct regardless of whether, in a particular case, the conduct causes an accident or not. The aim of reducing potentially accident-causing behaviour is worthwhile in itself. But the tort of negligence is primarily concerned with compensation on the basis of fault, and deterrence is secondary to this. So a breach of regulation is only actionable in negligence if it was faulty and caused damage.

In the area of occupiers' liability, the relevant Australian legislation[87] explicitly lays down factors to be taken into account in deciding whether the occupier has discharged the duty of care resting on him. Once again, the ultimate question is whether the occupier acted negligently as this term is understood at common law, and the statutory factors have the status of guidelines. As one writer puts it, the factors 'merely draw the attention of the court to considerations already prominent in any formulation of the standard of care in negligence cases'.[88] On the other hand, it has also been argued that this explicit laying-down of factors to be taken into account may 'give rise to arguments about whether the legislature intended them to be a subtly different standard of care in cases coming within the legislation'.[89] It can only be hoped that this does not happen.

So far as the common law of occupiers' liability is concerned, the standard of care laid down in *Australian Safeway Stores Pty Ltd* v. *Zaluzna*[90] is the reasonable person test applicable in negligence cases generally. But 'what is reasonable, of course, will vary with the circumstances of the plaintiff's entry upon the premises'.[91] So a trespasser may be owed a lower standard of care than a lawful visitor;[92] a contractual entrant may be owed a higher duty of care than a person for whose entry the occupier was not paid; and so on. In this way, the old categories of entrant may continue to exercise an influence on the question of standard of

---

85 *Tucker* v. *McCann* [1948] V.L.R. 222, 225-6 *per* Herring C.J.

86 ibid., p. 237 *per* Gavan Duffy J.

87 Wrongs Act 1936 (S.A.) s.17c.(2); Wrongs Act 1958 (Vic.) s.14B(4); Occupiers' Liability Act 1985 (W.A.) s.5(4).

88 R. Johnstone (1984) 14 *M.U.L.R.* 512, 516.

89 ALRC 42 (1988) p. 16.

90 (1987) 162 C.L.R. 479.

91 (1987) 162 C.L.R. 479, 488.

92 Prior to *Zaluzna*, the duty owed to trespassers (as expounded in *Herrington* v. *British Railways Board* [1972] A.C. 877 and *Cooper* v. *Southern Portland Cement Ltd* (1973) 129 C.L.R. 295) differed from that owed to lawful visitors in important respects: for example, the precautions which the occupier could be required to take had to be judged (contrary to normal principle) in the light of his physical and financial resources; and he could not be required to make inquiries or inspections to discover sources of danger which had arisen without his knowledge. The precise status of these limitations (particularly the first) in the post-*Zaluzna* world is unclear.

care.[93] But there are no longer any rigid rules relevant to the standard of care owed by occupiers. The only question is, did the occupier act reasonably in all the circumstances of the case? It should be remembered, however, that the relationship of occupier and visitor (but not, perhaps, that of occupier and trespasser) is one of those on the basis of which courts are willing to impose duties to take positive steps to remove and to warn of dangers and even, perhaps, in some cases to ascertain whether dangers exist.[94]

3. EMERGENCIES

Another external factor which is relevant to judging negligence is whether the defendant acted in the face of an emergency. If so, allowance can be made for the fact that under pressure and 'in the heat of the moment' less care and foresight can reasonably be expected than when there is ample time for reflection and planning.[95] This principle applies both to negligence of a defendant and contributory negligence of a plaintiff.[96] But if the emergency is created by the plaintiff's or defendant's own negligence, no allowance will be made.[97] The principle does not mean that what a party does in an emergency created by another can never be negligent. All it means is that a person faced with an emergency is only required to exercise such care and skill as a person of ordinary prudence, firmness and experience might have exhibited in the circumstances of the emergency.[98] The principle applies to any emergency situation created by another, whether that person is the other party to the litigation or not.[99]

A related question arises out of the playing of sports and games. Participants in sporting activities must exercise reasonable care not to injure fellow players. But in many sports, some injuries are the result of playing the game in the way it is meant to be played. Some games involve inherent risks.[100] What these inherent risks are is a question of fact on which the rules of the game are relevant but not conclusive evidence. The ultimate question is always whether the defendant (or plaintiff if the issue is contributory negligence) acted as the reasonable player would.[101] The spectator at a sporting fixture may also have to accept certain risks as inherent to the game, for example, being hit by a six at a cricket match.[102]

---

93 *Phillis* v. *Daly* (1988) 15 N.S.W.L.R. 65.
94 cf. *Western Suburbs Hospital* v. *Currie* (1987) 9 N.S.W.L.R. 511.
95 *Leishman* v. *Thomas* (1958) 75 W.N.(N.S.W.) 173; *Latimer* v. *A.E.C.* [1953] A.C. 643; *Marshall* v. *Osmond* [1983] 2 All E.R. 225; *Antonow* v. *Leane* (1989) 53 S.A.S.R. 60.
96 *Shelly* v. *Szelly* [1971] S.A.S.R. 430, 431 *per* Bray C.J.
97 *Purdon* v. *Scott* [1968] N.Z.L.R. 83; *Municipal Tramways Trust* v. *Ashby* [1951] S.A.S.R. 61.
98 *Cortis* v. *Baker* [1968] S.A.S.R. 367.
99 *Upward* v. *Tomkinson* [1954] Tas. S.R. 60.
100 *Rootes* v. *Shelton* (1967) 116 C.L.R. 383.
101 ibid.; *Evans* v. *Waitemata District Pony Club* [1972] N.Z.L.R. 773; *Johnston* v. *Frazer* (1990) 21 N.S.W.L.R. 89; G.M. Kelly (1992) 66 *A.L.J.* 329.
102 *Evans* v. *Waitemata District Pony Club* [1972] N.Z.L.R. 773; *Wooldridge* v. *Sumner* [1963] 2 Q.B. 43; *Murray* v. *Harringay Arena* [1951] 2 K.B. 529; *Hall* v. *Brooklands Auto Racing Club* [1933] 1 K.B. 205.

Provided the competitor exercised a degree of care consistent with the nature of the game and which is reasonable judged by the standards of the reasonably killed competitor, he will not be held negligent.[103]

4. Time for Assessing Negligence

The question of whether the defendant was negligent is to be assessed at the time of the act of alleged negligence because the question is what precautions it would have been reasonable to expect the defendant to take against the accident before it occurred. Thus, in *Roe* v. *Minister of Health*[104] two patients were paralyzed as a result of being given an anaesthetic contaminated with phenol which seeped into glass ampoules of nupercaine through cracks undetectable by ordinary examination. Apparently the cracks were caused by the submersion of the ampoules in phenol to disinfect them. It was held that since at the time of the accident no one realized the possibility of undetectable cracks it could not be said that the injury was foreseeable; it was theoretical only.

V: NEGLIGENCE AS A QUESTION OF FACT

It is usually said that the standard of care question is a question of fact, while whether a duty exists is a question of law. This apparently simple statement is actually a very complex one. An attempt will be made to elucidate it in a number of propositions.

a) Where a case is tried by judge and jury, questions of law are for the judge, questions of fact are for the jury. Where the case is tried by judge alone this distinction between questions of law and fact is generally unimportant except on appeal.[105] For the sake of clarity it is better to refer to 'judge's questions' and 'jury questions' respectively rather than 'questions of law' and 'questions of fact'.
b) Only decisions on questions of law can create precedents; decisions on questions of fact cannot.[106] This distinction is important even where there is no jury. Once again, for the sake of clarity, it is often better to refer to questions which do or do not create precedents than to questions of law and fact. It is best for present purposes to define questions of fact as questions as to what actually happened.[107]

---

103 *Wooldridge* v. *Sumner* [1963] 2 Q.B. 43, as glossed in *Wilks* v. *The Cheltenham Home Guard Cycle and Light Car Club* [1971] 2 All E.R. 369, 374 *per* Edmund Davies L.J. But the original principle was restated in *Harrison* v. *Vincent* [1982] R.T.R. 8.

104 [1965] 2 Q.B. 66; cf. *Footner* v. *Broken Hill Associated Smelters Pty Ltd* (1983) 33 S.A.S.R. 58.

105 It is much harder successfully to challenge on appeal answers to jury questions than answers to judge's questions.

106 R. Cross and J.W. Harris *Precedent in English Law* 4th edn (Oxford, 1991) pp. 222-4.

107 The question of whether the defendant was negligent is not a question of what actually happened but an 'inference' or value judgment based on what happened.

c) Answers to jury questions never create precedents. Answers to judge's questions can create precedents but not all do so. It is for the judge to decide in a particular case whether there is any evidence on which the jury could decide a jury question in a particular way (for example, whether there is sufficient evidence to justify a finding that the defendant was negligent; if so, the jury then decides whether he was negligent); but the answer to this question creates no precedent.

d) We can say whether the defendant acted negligently[108] only if we know, as a matter of fact, what happened and how he behaved. Thus, evidence must be called on this question.

e) Once any disputes of fact have been resolved by the jury (or by the judge, if there is no jury), the question of whether the plaintiff was foreseeable for the purposes of deciding whether a duty existed is a question for the judge; but the answer to it does not create a precedent because, as we have seen, the question of foreseeability is one that can only be decided on the basis of particular facts. The foreseeability aspect of the breach question is a jury question. In cases in which the issue of duty receives no separate consideration but is merged with the foreseeability aspect of the standard of care question, the foreseeability question is a jury question.

f) Questions of policy and particular duty relationships relevant to duty are judge's questions, the answers to which create precedents. So the issue of proximity may be a judge's issue, and the resolution of it in a particular case may create a precedent.

g) The significant risk calculus and the standard of the reasonable person are established as a matter of precedent. They apply to all cases whatever their facts.

h) Certain broad propositions about the characteristics of the reasonable person are established by authority and precedent and are in this sense propositions of law. The judge is entitled (and obliged) to direct the jury (if there is one) in general terms about the standard of reasonableness, for example, about the relevance of age or skill or experience.[109] The detailed filling out and application of these principles is a jury task.[110] The question of what the reasonable person would do is a value question about right conduct which is answered in the light of the facts as found. The answer is sometimes called an 'inference from the facts' or an 'inference of fact'. Both of these phrases are misleading in that they disguise the essentially evaluative nature of a 'finding' of negligence. The significant risk calculus is a more detailed criterion of negligence which has developed more for use by judges than juries. It has been said that the first three elements of the calculus, that is, probability, seriousness of risk and cost of precautions, are matters to be established by evidence and not by 'the

---

108 Or whether the plaintiff was contributorily negligent.

109 *Nova Mink Ltd* v. *Trans Canada Airlines* [1951] 2 D.L.R. 241, 254 per MacDonald J.; J.G. Fleming (1953) 31 *Can. B.R.* 471, 475.

110 *Qualcast (Wolverhampton) Ltd* v. *Haynes* [1959] A.C. 743, 757 *per* Lord Somervell of Harrow.

fertile but unqualified imagination of counsel or judge'.[111] Questions of the social utility or value of the defendant's conduct are sometimes a matter of precedent—for example, the special position of emergency vehicles. These are questions on which the judge should direct the jury (if there is one). The final assessment of the balance of the calculus, assuming the jury to have been directed in terms of it, is a jury task.

Now that juries are uncommon in negligence actions in Australia, judges increasingly indulge in detailed filling out of the standard of reasonableness. Whereas juries never give reasons for their decisions, judges usually do; and whereas judges' directions to the jury in negligence actions were rarely reported, decisions of single judges in negligence actions more often are. So it has become much more common for detailed standards of conduct to appear in the law reports and, hence, it is easier for them to be taken into the law as statements of legal principle. These developments have led appeal courts[112] to deprecate the making of detailed statements about standards of conduct in such a way as to encourage their generalization and repeated use as precedents, that is, by putting them forward as statements of duty or as general propositions about reasonableness.

There appear to be two reasons for this concern about the legalization of negligence. One is fear of being drowned by a flood of authorities. The other is that certainty and predictability in the law can be taken too far; the reasonable person should not be given such a detailed biography that very little account can be taken of the circumstances of particular cases. Of course, no test can be laid down in general terms about how detailed or general binding statements of conduct should be. The appropriate level of generality can only be set by appeal courts as a matter of quite arbitrary fiat.

i) The question of reasonable foreseeability is usually decided retrospectively with the benefit of hindsight.[113] Explicit statements that it should be decided prospectively can be found[114] but perhaps only when some reason for denying liability is being positively searched for. In many cases the courts impose liability for the taking of risks which would, in prospect, be present only to the mind of a defendant who was much more averse to taking risks than many would consider normal or practical. This element of retrospectivity removes the question of reasonable foreseeability even further from the realm of facts, since the question asked is not really tied to the factual position the defendant was actually in before the accident.

---

111 *Maloney* v. *Commissioner for Railways* (1978) 18 A.L.R. 147, 148 *per* Barwick C.J.

112 e.g. *Qualcast (Wolverhampton) Ltd* v. *Haynes* [1959] A.C. 743, 757-8 *per* Lord Somervell of Harrow; 759-61 *per* Lord Denning; *Teubner* v. *Humble* (1963) 108 C.L.R. 491, 503 *per* Windeyer J.

113 *Sydney County Council* v. *Dell'Oro* (1974) 132 C.L.R. 97, 106 *per* McTiernan J.

114 *Maloney* v. *Commissioner for Railways* (1978) 18 A.L.R. 147, 148 *per* Barwick C.J.; *Glasgow Corporation* v. *Muir* [1943] A.C. 448, 455 *per* Lord Thankerton; *Morris* v. *West Hartlepool Steam Navigation Co. Ltd* [1956] A.C. 552, 568 *per* Lord Porter.

VI: PROOF OF NEGLIGENCE

1. Inferences and Credibility

The issues with which we are concerned here can be best illustrated by an example. Suppose a collision between two cars occurs and both cars come to rest entirely on one side of the road. Three questions might arise: first, was one of the cars wholly or partly on the wrong side of the road immediately before the collision? If so, secondly, why was it on the wrong side of the road—was it because of carelessness on the defendant's part? Thirdly, did the fact that it was on the wrong side of the road cause the accident? The second question, as we have seen, has two aspects: what did the defendant do (a factual issue), and was his conduct negligent (an evaluative issue)? As we will see in due course, the third question also has two aspects: a factual one (would the accident have happened but for the defendant's act?) and an evaluative one (was the defendant's act the effective or real cause of the accident, or was the plaintiff's injury a foreseeable result of the defendant's act?). The first question is a purely factual one. It is with the factual aspects of these questions that we are here concerned.

Facts are established by evidence. There is often cause for grave doubts about the accuracy of evidence—the passage of time, the fading of memory and the conscious or unconscious motivations of witnesses, to say nothing of possible distortions caused by the pressure of a courtroom appearance and the skill of examining and cross-examining counsel, can all affect the witnesses' ability to give an accurate account of what they witnessed.[115] But even if individual witnesses give internally coherent and apparently accurate accounts it does not follow that their accounts tell the court all it needs to know. In the first place, no witness may be able to answer the exact question which the court needs to ask. In our example, no witness may be able to say whether either of the cars was wholly or partly on the wrong side of the road immediately before the collision. If witnesses, whom the court believes, are able to say that one of the cars was wholly or partly on the wrong side of the road, this enables the court to make a relevant finding of 'primary fact'. By this is meant that the fact found is exactly the fact to which the witnesses deposed. On the other hand, if the only relevant evidence is that the cars ended up both entirely on one side of the road, this evidence is only circumstantial evidence of the fact in issue and the question for the court is whether it can *infer* from the circumstances that one of the cars was on the wrong side of the road immediately before the accident. The need to draw inferences arises particularly in relation to the question of causation, because causal processes are often not physically observable. The first major problem of proof involves, therefore, the drawing of inferences as to what happened from circumstantial evidence, of bridging the gap between the facts deposed to by the witnesses and the facts the court needs to find in order to

---

115 e.g. *Broadhurst* v. *Millman* [1976] V.R. 208; Sir T. Bingham [1985] *C.L.P.* 1.

justify a decision for the plaintiff. This is essentially a problem of judging the probability of events and sequences of events.

The second problem which arises even with apparently accurate accounts is the problem of credibility. This problem may arise even where all the evidence on a particular point is one way, if the court does not believe the witnesses. But it arises more often when (as is frequently the case) there are conflicts of evidence and the court has to choose between the accounts. If a witness's evidence is internally inconsistent or inherently implausible this may be a reason for rejecting it, although, obviously, this does not necessarily follow. The inherently implausible does sometimes happen and internal inconsistency, which may be produced by lapse of memory or courtroom confusion, may only mean that part of the evidence is inaccurate.[116] Evidence may also be disbelieved if it is inconsistent with undisputed facts. But if the account fulfils all the criteria of coherence and plausibility, the court may still reject it if it does not trust the witness's truthfulness or reliability either because of evidence that the witness is mentally defective in a way which affects reliability, or is biased against a party, or has a reputation for mendacity; or as a result of observing the witness's behaviour and demeanour under examination. This second problem of proof is, therefore, essentially a psychological problem of belief.

2. Onus and Standard of Proof

The onus of proof in a negligence action is distributed as follows: the plaintiff must prove all the factual elements of his case whether these factual elements relate to duty, breach, causation or remoteness of damage. Thus, most importantly, the plaintiff must prove that the defendant was negligent and that his negligence caused the plaintiff's injury.[117] It is for the defendant to prove the elements of any defence raised by him, such as contributory negligence of the plaintiff or *volenti non fit injuria.*

The normal burden of proof of all issues in a negligence action is to prove on the balance of probabilities. This means that it must be 'more probable than not' that things happened the way the plaintiff says they did.[118] In numerical terms, this means that if the plaintiff is to succeed the balance of probabilities must weigh more than 50 per cent in his favour. If

---

116 cf. *Horton* v. *Byrne* (1957) 30 *A.L.J.* 583.

117 The only presently relevant exception to this rule is that in actions against bailees for negligent loss of or damage to goods, the bailee must prove that the loss or damage was not caused by his negligence: *Dalgety & Co. Ltd* v. *J.P. & C.J. Warden* [1954] St.R.Qd. 251; *Frankhauser* v. *Mark Dykes Pty Ltd* [1960] V.R. 376; *Port Swettenham Authority* v. *J.W. Wu & Co. (M) Snd Bhd* [1978] 3 All E.R. 337.

118 *Holloway* v. *McFeeters* (1956) 94 C.L.R. 470, 480-1 *per* Williams, Webb and Taylor JJ.; *Luxton* v. *Vines* (1952) 85 C.L.R. 352, 358 *per* Dixon, Fullagar and Kitto JJ.; *Maher-Smith* v. *Gaw* [1969] V.R. 371. This rule applies equally to any issue on which the onus of proof rests on the defendant.

the scales are evenly balanced then the plaintiff must lose.[119] The principles, as stated thus, assume that the choice is between two outcomes, that is, either the defendant's negligence caused the injury or it did not. But the principles apply similarly where there are three possible outcomes (that is, defendant responsible, plaintiff responsible or each party responsible).[120]

It should be noted, however, that very many of the issues of proof which arise in litigation, both questions of credibility and of whether inferences ought to be drawn, cannot in practice be reduced to precise mathematical probabilities. This means that a court's statement that an event more probably than not occurred will often not be a statement of probability but a statement of the court's judgment as to probability. A court may well be *satisfied* that an event was more probable than not even though *in fact* it was not; or fail to be satisfied of an event which more probably than not occurred. But in the absence of precise mathematical data, the question of whether the court's satisfaction or lack of it is justifiable is largely a matter for opinion or individual judgment. It does not follow from the fact that a court says an event more probably occurred than not that this is so. All it means is that the court was satisfied that it is so.

A final point should be made regarding the burden of proof. As noted above, questions of causation are very often matters of inference from circumstances rather than of direct proof of primary facts. A long-standing debate among philosophers is whether causation is just a matter of one thing (the thing caused) *regularly* following another (the cause) in a temporal sequence of events, or whether causation involves some greater link between events than mere contiguity in time. Regardless of the merits of either view, courts have adverted to the problem. Thus in *St George Club Ltd* v. *Hines*[121] it was said that 'proof of default followed by injury [does not] show that the default caused the injury'. On the other hand, of course, the fact that one event follows another in time is a precondition of a finding of causation. Where the events in issue are the subject of expert evidence, as in cases where the question is the causation of some disease, it has been said that even if the medical evidence only supports the view that the alleged causal link was possible (rather than more probable than not), the court may act on its own 'intuitive reasoning' and decide on all the evidence, including temporal sequence, that the allegation of causal link in this particular case is made out.[122] Such an approach is unjustifiable in theory because, in the absence of evidence based on direct observation, statistical evidence is the only rational basis on which judgments about

---

119 *Bell* v. *Thompson* (1934) 34 S.R.(N.S.W.) 431; *Maher-Smith* v. *Gaw* [1969] V.R. 371; contrast *Cook* v. *Lewis* [1951] S.C.R. 830 (Canada): where negligence of one (but not both) of two defendants must have caused plaintiff's injury, burden is on each defendant to exonerate himself; unlikely to be followed in Australia.

120 *Nesterczuk* v. *Mortimore* (1965) 115 C.L.R. 149; cf. *West* v. *Government Insurance Office of New South Wales* (1981) 35 A.L.R. 437.

121 (1961) 35 A.L.J.R. 106, 107 (workers' compensation case); *Commonwealth* v. *Butler* (1958-9) 102 C.L.R. 465, 476-7 *per* Taylor J.

122 *E.M.I. (Australia) Ltd* v. *Bes* [1970] 2 N.S.W.R. 238, 242 *per* Herron C.J. (workers' compensation case).

causation can be made; but it may be defensible in policy terms. We will consider the issue of proof of causation in much more detail in the next chapter.

3. Res Ipsa Loquitur

Loosely translated, this phrase means 'the event speaks for itself'. The event in question is the accident[123] causing injury to the plaintiff. The force of the phrase was stated succinctly by Barwick C.J. in *Lambos* v. *Commonwealth of Australia*:

> An accident will itself provide evidence of negligence where in the ordinary affairs of mankind such an incident is unlikely to occur without want of care on the part of the person sued.[124]

We are here concerned, therefore, with establishing that injuries were caused by the defendant's negligence. Sometimes the mere fact that an accident happened justifies a court in inferring, on the balance of probabilities, that it was the result of negligence on the part of the defendant even though the plaintiff cannot specify the particular act or acts of negligence of the defendant which caused[125] the accident.[126]

It must be admitted at the outset that there is a difficulty in explaining the operation of *res ipsa loquitur* as a distinct legal principle. This difficulty arises out of the accepted view of the way the principle operates. English courts have on the whole[127] taken the view that if something under the exclusive control of the defendant causes an accident which would not, in the ordinary course of things, happen without negligence on the defendant's part, then it is for the defendant to prove that he was not negligent.[128] In other words, the effect of the *res ipsa loquitur* principle is to shift the burden of proof on the issue of negligence from the plaintiff, who normally bears it, to the defendant. If the case is one in which the court decides that *res ipsa loquitur* then the defendant must explain how the accident happened without his negligence or, if he cannot do this, show that none of the possible causes of the accident was due to his negligence. It is not good enough for the defendant to give an explanation of how the accident *might* have happened consistently with due care on his part. Thus the English courts operate with a definite rule

123 In this context, this word is used in the sense of 'an unintentional infliction of loss'. So it includes illness and disease as well as traumatic injuries: see J. Stapleton *Disease and the Compensation Debate* (Oxford, 1986).

124 (1967-8) 41 A.L.R. 180, 182.

125 The relationship between *res ipsa loquitur* and causation is slightly tricky. Strictly, *res ipsa loquitur* is concerned with proof of *negligence*, not causation. But in most cases, the two questions are conflated so that if *res ipsa loquitur*, then it will be assumed that the negligence caused the plaintiff's loss. But see *Brady* v. *Girvan Bros Pty Ltd* (1986) 7 N.S.W.L.R. 241 *per* McHugh J.A. See further pp. 447-8 below.

126 In theory, it is possible for an accident to justify an inference of negligence on the part of twm (or more) persons.

127 But see *Ng Chun Pui* v. *Lee Chuen Tat* [1988] R.T.R. 298.

128 P.S. Atiyah (1972) 35 *M.L.R.* 337; *Clark* v. *McLennan* [1983] 1 All E.R. 416.

having an identifiable legal effect, and in this context it makes sense to ask when and under what conditions the principle operates.

Australian courts, on the other hand, have taken the view that the 'principle' of *res ipsa loquitur* just expresses a simple truth, namely that sometimes a court is justified in drawing an inference of negligence on the balance of probabilities, even though the evidence in support of it is very sparse, if such evidence as there is speaks loudly enough of negligence.[129] According to this view, *res ipsa loquitur* is just a special application of the ordinary rules of evidence—the plaintiff must prove his case on the balance of probabilities, and in deciding whether he has or not, all the evidence, including any given by the defendant, must be considered. If the defendant gives no evidence, or if his evidence is feeble or not believed, this may count against him,[130] but in the end it is all a question of whether on the whole of the evidence the plaintiff has proved his case. The plaintiff may lose even though the defendant remains silent if the *res* does not speak loudly enough to justify an inference of negligence on the part of the defendant. He may also lose if the defendant suggests a way the accident might have happened consistently with his not having been negligent if this throws sufficient doubt on the inference drawn from the *res* itself to lead the court to refuse to draw that inference on the balance of probabilities.

Taking this Australian view, the fact that the accident happened is just like any other fact relevant to the question of negligence. There is no reason to distinguish between the fact of the accident itself and evidence of specific acts or omissions said to have caused the accident or of detailed explanations of the accident. Taking the English view, if the plaintiff gives detailed explanations of causes or makes specific allegations of negligence the case is not one in which *res ipsa loquitur* applies, because it is not one in which the court is asked to infer negligence from the mere happening of the accident. The rationale for this is that *res ipsa loquitur* is designed to assist a plaintiff in cases in which the defendant is in a much better position to know what happened than the plaintiff; in such cases the defendant is forced to divulge his knowledge by being burdened with the onus of proof. But if the plaintiff puts forward detailed evidence of his own, this indicates that there is no great disparity of knowledge and so there is no justification for placing the onus of proof on the defendant. In the Australian view, on the other hand, there is no logical reason to distinguish between the accident itself and any other fact, because the burden of proof always rests on the plaintiff. Thus in *Public Trustee* v. *Western Hauliers Pty Ltd* Sangster J. said that the question whether, at the end of the evidence, the defendant has been shown by the plaintiff, on the balance of probabilities, to have been negligent could be answered by inference from the occurrence itself or from evidence of specific acts or

129 *Franklin* v. *Victorian Railways Commissioners* (1959-60) 101 C.L.R. 197, 201 *per* Dixon C.J.; *Anchor Products Ltd* v. *Hedges* [1967] A.L.R. 421, 424-5 *per* Windeyer J.; *Nominal Defendant* v. *Haslbauer* (1967) 117 C.L.R. 448, 461-3 *per* Kitto J.; *Government Insurance Office of New South Wales* v. *Fredrichberg* (1969) 118 C.L.R. 403, 413-15 per Barwick C.J.

130 e.g. *Brown* v. *Target Australia Pty Ltd* (1984) 37 S.A.S.R. 145.

omissions or from explanations by the defendant consistent with no negligence or from a combination of all or any of them.[131]

Consistent with this, it has been held that if a plaintiff offers detailed explanations of the accident or makes specific allegations of negligence but none of these is accepted by the court as more probably than not the cause, he may still rest his case simply on the fact of the accident. For example, in *Doonan* v. *Beecham*[132] the trial judge found for the defendant because in his view the evidence did not establish on the balance of probabilities which of four particular allegations of negligence was correct—speeding, failing to keep a proper lookout, driving on the wrong side of the road and failure to apply the brakes. The High Court reversed the decision on the ground that rejection of each of the detailed allegations did not justify a conclusion that the accident was not, on the balance of probabilities, the result of negligence on the part of the defendant. In fact, the very function of the *res ipsa loquitur* principle is to allow an inference of negligence to be drawn, where this seems right, even though the exact act of negligence cannot be specified.[133] In other words, the plaintiff does not at any stage have to elect whether he will rest his case solely on the fact of the accident or on more detailed allegations.[134]

In the light of all this, it seems that the only function performed by the principle of *res ipsa loquitur* is to serve as a reminder of what we might forget because of its apparent implausibility, namely that the mere fact that an accident happens can in certain circumstances justify an inference that it was more probably than not caused by someone's negligence.

As a result, we can say that the principle of *res ipsa loquitur* answers this question: suppose that all the plaintiff can prove is that an accident happened, but he cannot explain how it happened (or, at least, not in a way the court can accept). In what circumstances will it be open to a court to find for the plaintiff on the basis of evidence of the accident alone? There are two conditions: first, that the accident must be such as would not, in the ordinary course of things, happen without negligence; and secondly, that the accident must speak of negligence on the part of the defendant. These are not requirements of the accident speaking for itself; they are merely an explanation of what this means. If evidence is required to explain why, or in what way, the accident speaks of negligence then, logically, evidence of the accident by itself is not enough. And if the accident does not speak of negligence on the part of the defendant it is irrelevant to a claim against him. So decisions on whether *res ipsa loquitur* are no more than decisions on the facts of the case that an inference of negligence was justified.

(a) The *res* defined The first thing that the court must do is to define the accident. This, from one point of view, is the most crucial part of the

131 (1971) 1 S.A.S.R. 27.
132 (1953) 87 C.L.R. 346.
133 cf. *Kilgannon* v. *Sharpe Bros Pty Ltd* (1986) 4 N.S.W.L.R. 600, 625B, 629E-F *per* Hope J.A.
134 *Anchor Products Ltd* v. *Hedges* [1967] A.L.R. 421; *Whelan* v. *Padgett* [1969] Tas. S.R. 17.

whole process because it can predetermine whether the two above-mentioned conditions will be met. For example, suppose a car runs off the road because its steering fails. Is the accident the fact that the car ran off the road, or that its brakes failed and it ran off the road? In *Piening* v. *Wanless*[135] the court said that the fact of the steering failure was part of the explanation of the accident, not part of the accident itself. While the fact that a car runs off the road may speak of negligence on the part of the driver, a steering failure does not do so nearly as loudly.[136] Again, in *Nesterczuk* v. *Mortimore* Windeyer J. said that a head-on collision in broad daylight in the centre of a flat stretch of open road might speak of negligence on the part of both the drivers, but if the description of the accident was made more detailed so as to include the speed of the vehicles, the presence or absence of other traffic, the state of the road and the weather, the accident would speak much less loudly because so many possible causes other than negligence by either or both the drivers had been introduced.[137]

It does not follow from this, however, that the more sketchy the surrounding details in the plaintiff's description of the accident the better for him. In *Dulhunty* v. *J.B. Young Ltd*[138] the plaintiff slipped on a grape on the floor of the haberdashery department of the defendant's store. It was held that a finding that the accident had been caused by negligence on the part of the defendant could not be justified because there was nothing to link the presence of the grape to the defendant. There was no evidence as to how it got there or how long it had been on the floor when the plaintiff slipped on it.[139] It is clear, then, that the way the accident is described, or, in other words, the exact amount of detail the plaintiff can or should supply about it, is crucial. There is no clear line between the accident and detailed explanation of it. This is exactly what one would expect if *res ipsa loquitur* is just treated as an application of ordinary rules of evidence.

(b) The ordinary course of events The accident must be such as would not, in the ordinary course of events, occur without negligence on the part of the defendant. This means two things. First, the likely causation of the accident must be within the knowledge of the ordinary person untutored by expert evidence. Counsel may seek to convince the court of what happens in the ordinary course of things and it may, somewhat curiously, be the subject of evidence.[140] The following are examples of things which have been held to be beyond the understanding of the ordinary person: the

135 (1967-8) 117 C.L.R. 498.
136 cf. *Mummery* v. *Irvings* (1965) 96 C.L.R. 99.
137 (1965) 115 C.L.R. 140, 152.
138 (1974) 23 F.L.R. 212; (1975) 7 A.L.R. 409; see D.C. McKelvey (1977-8) 10 *U. Qld L.J.* 231.
139 cf. *Incorporated Nominal Defendant* v. *Knowles* [1987] V.R. 138.
140 *Piening* v. *Wanless* (1967-8) 117 C.L.R. 498, 508; *Lambos* v. *Commonwealth* (1967-8) 41 A.L.R. 180. From another point of view, the peculiarity is that evidence is not required: *Kilgannon* v. *Sharpe Bros Pty Ltd* (1986) 4 N.S.W.L.R. 600, 632 *per* Hope J.A.

steering mechanism of cars;[141] the habits of a circular wood-saw;[142] a washing machine 'energized partly by electricity and partly by compressed air';[143] the causation of AIDS.[144] In general, *res ipsa loquitur* is unlikely to apply cases in which the issue of negligence turns on expert evidence. On the other hand, in *Mahon* v. *Osborne*[145] it was held by majority that the ordinary person knows enough about abdominal operations to say that if a swab is left in the patient after the operation this is more likely than not the result of negligence by the surgeon. *Res ipsa loquitur* is unlikely to have much application to cases involving illnesses and diseases (as opposed to traumatic injuries) because of the complexity of the standard of care issues which typically arise in such cases.[146]

Second, the accident must be of a type which more often than not is caused by negligence since the maxim allows an inference that more probably than not the accident was caused by negligence. So, for example, in *Stafford* v. *Conti Commodity Services Ltd*[147] it was held that the *res ipsa loquitur* principle could not apply to a case involving loss suffered by investing in a commodities market in accordance with a broker's advice—the volatility of the market prevented the drawing of an inference of negligence from the mere fact of loss. Whether an inference of negligence will be drawn is said to depend on all the circumstances of the case. For example, it is easier to infer negligent failure to provide an adequate cleaning system from the presence of yoghurt on the floor of a supermarket[148] than from the presence of a grape on the floor of a shop which does not sell grapes.[149] Again, it is easier to infer negligence from the presence of a slippery substance on the floor of a common passageway of a busy shopping mall than on the pathway of a private dwelling.[150] This latter example shows the link between *res ipsa loquitur* and standard of care: the greater the care appropriate to the circumstances of the case, the easier it is to infer lack of care from the occurrence of foreseeable loss.

(c) **Defendant's negligence** The accident must speak of negligence by the defendant. An accident such as a head-on collision may speak of negligence on the part of both parties. The normal way of stating this principle is that the defendant must have been in control of the situation or thing which caused the accident. Thus, in *Kouris* v. *Prospector's Motel Pty Ltd*,[151] where an employee was injured when a fire started in a storage room of a service station owned by the defendant, it was held that the principle *res ipsa loquitur* did not apply because the storeroom was not in

141 *Piening* v. *Wanless* (1967-8) 117 C.L.R. 498.
142 *Mummery* v. *Irvings* (1956) 96 C.L.R. 99.
143 *Lambos* v. *Commonwealth* (1967-8) 41 A.L.R. 180.
144 *Dwan* v. *Farquhar* [1988] 1 Qd.R. 234.
145 [1939] 2 K.B. 14; cf. *Cassidy* v. *Ministry of Health* [1951] 2 K.B. 343.
146 J. Stapleton *Disease and the Compensation Debate* pp. 60-78.
147 [1981] 1 All E.R. 691.
148 *Ward* v. *Tesco Stores Ltd* [1976] 1 W.L.R. 810.
149 *Dulhunty* v. *Young* (1975) 7 A.L.R. 409.
150 *Brady* v. *Girvan Bros Pty Ltd* (1986) 7 N.S.W.L.R. 241.
151 (1978) 19 A.L.R. 343.

the sole control of the defendant. The fire was just as likely to have been started by some negligent act of the plaintiff.[152] On the other hand,

> The doctrine will apply notwithstanding that some possible causes of the occurrence could have been the responsibility of a person other than the defendant, so long as the evidence supports a rational inference that 'the fault lay somewhere within the control of' the defendant, its servants or agents.[153]

In cases involving multiple defendants it is not enough that the *res* points to one or another of them: the plaintiff must establish to the court's satisfaction that it points to one of them in particular,[154] unless one of them was responsible for the acts of the others.[155]

The question of control is of particular relevance in cases involving defective products. Unless the product can be shown to have been in the control of the manufacturer with no reasonable probability of intermediate inspection between the time of manufacture and the time of the accident, it will be extremely difficult to infer, merely on the basis of the accident itself, that negligence by the manufacturer was to blame.[156]

(d) The function of the *res ipsa loquitur* principle The principle of *res ipsa loquitur* serves to ease the burden of proof on the plaintiff by substituting general knowledge of the common causes of accidents for detailed evidence of the cause of a particular accident. In some cases, this may force a defendant to divulge what he knows about the cause of the accident; but in many cases, particularly road accidents, it will make good a lack of knowledge on the part of both parties as to what happened. The court can manipulate the outcome to some extent by deciding in how much detail to describe the accident, by decisions on what is within the experience of the ordinary person and by the way it deals with the issue of control. In these ways it can take advantage of the vagueness of the idea of the balance of probabilities and the difficulty in most cases of attaching mathematical values to the probability of particular events to reach a decision which the court feels is just. In theory, the principle is simply an application of ordinary rules of proof, but in practice it may well operate to justify decisions where the court is 'satisfied' the defendant was negligent but where this is very difficult to prove as rigorously as is normally required. In this way a defendant can be made liable for causing an accident even if it is very difficult to show that it was the result of negligence by the defendant. For this reason it is sometimes said that the principle goes some way to turning negligence into strict liability (that is, liability without proof of negligence).

---

152 cf. *Pemberton National Park Board* v. *Johnson* [1966] W.A.R. 61.

153 *Kilgannon* v. *Sharpe Bros Pty Ltd* (1986) 4 N.S.W.L.R. 600, 625 *per* Hope J.A.; cf. *Griffith District Hospital* v. *Hayes* (1962) 108 C.L.R. 50.

154 *Kilgannon* v. *Sharpe Bros* (1986) 4 N.S.W.L.R. 600.

155 As in *Cassidy* v. *Ministry of Health* [1951] 2 K.B. 343.

156 e.g. *Godfrey's Ltd* v. *Ryles* [1962] S.A.S.R. 33; *Kilgannon* v. *Sharpe Bros* (1986) 4 N.S.W.L.R. 600.

4. Expert Evidence

The function of expert evidence[157] is to inform the court about matters which are beyond the experience of the ordinary person (if the trial is by jury) or beyond the limits of what is called 'judicial notice' if the trial is by judge alone. A court should not decide an issue requiring expert knowledge without the benefit of expert evidence; if such evidence is lacking the party who bears the onus of proof on that issue will fail.[158] For example, a court could usually not decide an issue of negligence against a surgeon without the help of expert evidence as to the way in which surgeons of reasonable skill and experience would have acted in the defendant's position.[159] Conversely, 'expert' evidence should not be called on matters which lie within the area of the ordinary person's (or judge's) experience or knowledge.[160]

Expert evidence is called on two main issues: the practice or custom in a particular profession or industry and the question of causal link between events and injuries. An expert witness who deposes to the practice in an industry or profession is not entitled to say whether in his view the defendant acted negligently.[161] The question of negligence ultimately involves a value judgment which it is for the court to make. Further, common practice in a profession or industry is not conclusive one way or the other.[162]

The value of expert evidence as to causation is often problematic. The first difficulty is that in many cases there is conflicting expert evidence. The reason for the conflict may be that nobody knows enough about the matter in issue to give a definite answer, in which case it seems futile for the court to attempt to choose between the accounts on technical grounds. But even if there is a way of choosing on technical grounds between the accounts the court is, *ex hypothesi*, not equipped to do this.[163] The court may avoid the problem simply by holding that the plaintiff's case is not made out on the balance of probabilities. But it would make the plaintiff's burden of proof impossibly heavy if he could *never* succeed if well-qualified experts disagreed. The fact is that while expert witnesses can afford the luxury of doubt, a court's job is to make a decision whether or not to award compensation. All sorts of factors of justice, social policy and the function of tort law are relevant to the court's decision. Scientific truth is only one consideration, and it should not be thought that the purpose of expert evidence is necessarily to provide a clear answer to the

---

157 See generally I.R. Freckleton *The Trial of the Expert* (Melbourne, 1987).

158 *Neill* v. *N.S.W. Fresh Food & Ice Pty Ltd* (1962-3) 108 C.L.R. 362, 369 *per* Taylor & Owen JJ.; *Tubemakers of Australia Ltd* v. *Fernandez* (1976) 10 A.L.R. 303, 312 *per* Murphy J.; *Sweeney* v. *Boulton* (1984) 2 M.V.R. 124, 131.

159 *Albrighton* v. *Royal Prince Alfred Hospital* [1979] 2 N.S.W.L.R. 165, 173 *per* Yeldman J.

160 *Sweeney* v. *Boulton* (1984) 2 M.V.R. 124, 127.

161 *Weal* v. *Bottom* (1966) 40 A.L.J.R. 436; *Clark* v. *Ryan* (1960) 103 C.L.R. 486; *Dahl* v. *Grice* [1981] V.R. 513, 522-3.

162 See p. 427 above.

163 One suggestion is the greater use of expert assessors to assist the court: Bingham [1985] *C.L.P.* 1, 19-26; Freckleton *The Trial of the Expert* (Melbourne, 1987) pp. 224-32.

causation question. For one thing, experts may not function as disinterested participants in the forensic process.[164] In fact, it would be more accurate to say that their function is just to ensure that whatever decision the court makes is consistent with the views of the experts as to the possible causes of an accident.[165] If this is so, then the court can convert an inference of possible cause derived from the expert evidence into one of probable cause by having regard to non-expert evidence and to facts such as the sequence of events (i.e. the temporal element of causation) and the absence of any alternative explanation in the case before it.[166] Rich A.C.J. in *Adelaide Stevedoring Co. Ltd* v. *Forst* went so far as to say that the court can act on its own 'intuitive inferences'.[167] The notion of causation, as indeed every other element of the tort of negligence, is a sufficiently pliable concept to be manipulated to justify the result the court thinks right.[168]

There is a considerable case-law on the question of what 'expert' means in the context of road accidents. An expert is a person who has made a study of an area which can be described as an organized branch of knowledge or science.[169] Areas which cannot be so described are not outside the experience of the ordinary person. As science develops, areas which were once areas of common knowledge may become the subject of specialized study: for example, the effect of alcohol on driving capacity.[170] Whether an area is one of organized knowledge is a question of fact for the judge to decide,[171] and there has been much disagreement among judges as to whether the study of various aspects of road accidents is an area of expertise. No other area has generated quite the degree of discussion as this but one can imagine arguments, for example, about certain forms of 'alternative medicine'.

Finally, an important practical difficulty in the use of expert evidence is worthy of note. In cases in which the plaintiff wishes to establish by expert evidence that the defendant did not measure up to some professional standard he may find it extremely difficult to find experts willing to testify on his behalf. Professional people tend to stick together: doctors, lawyers, surveyors and so on rarely enjoy, and are often not even prepared to undertake the exercise of, exposing the failings of their fellows. Apart from feelings of solidarity, the realization that 'there but for the grace of God go I' is no doubt a powerful disincentive to assisting a plaintiff in obtaining an award of damages. On the other hand, there are well-known professionals who make it part of their business to act regularly as expert witnesses.

---

164 Freckleton *The Trial of the Expert* Ch. 8.
165 *Tubemakers of Australia* v. *Fernandez* (1976) 10 A.L.R. 303.
166 An alternative explanation was important in *X and Y* v. *Pal* (1991) 23 N.S.W.L.R. 26.
167 (1940) 64 C.L.R. 538, 564. Cf. *Holtman* v. *Sampson* [1985] 2 Qd.R. 472, 474. See also p. 438 above.
168 *Dahl* v. *Grice* [1981] V.R. 513, 522-3 *per* Gobbo J.
169 *Clark* v. *Ryan* (1960) 103 C.L.R. 486.
170 *Eagles* v. *Orth* [1976] Qd. R. 313, 319 *per* Dunn J.
171 ibid., 320.

11

CAUSATION AND REMOTENESS OF DAMAGE

I: CAUSATION

A cause of action in negligence is complete only if the plaintiff can prove, on the balance of probabilities, that some negligence on the part of the defendant caused him injury or damage.[1] Problems of causation arise, of course, throughout the law of tort but perhaps more often in the context of negligence actions than in other areas. In any negligence action the causation question is not 'What caused the plaintiff's loss?' but, more specifically, 'Was the defendant's act of negligence the (or a) cause of the plaintiff's loss?' It is for the plaintiff to prove that the defendant's act was a cause of the damage. However, this basic principle needs to be qualified in a number of ways. First, we have already noted cases in which courts have been prepared to find for the plaintiff on the issue of causation even though the only medical evidence was that a causal link was an acceptable hypothesis.[2] Secondly, a principle similar to *res ipsa loquitur* is applied

---

1 The word 'cause' is tricky. The most obvious sense of the word applies to positive acts which inflict injury: for example, when a car driver knocks down a pedestrian and causes him physical and mental injury; or when an assailant physically attacks his victim (in *Nader* v. *Urban Transit Authority of N.S.W.* Mahoney J.A. called this 'causation in the physical sense': (1985) 2 N.S.W.L.R. 501, 515). But there are several other less obvious uses of the word: (1) we say that a misstatement has caused loss even though this happened because someone relied upon it—the immediate cause of the loss was the reliance (see p. 359 above); (2) we may say that a person caused loss when, by failing to perform an obligation to take action, he failed to prevent it occurring (see p. 379 above); (3) a person can be said to cause loss if he gives another the opportunity to inflict it, or deprives another of the opportunity of taking action to prevent it occurring (as in cases where doctors fail to inform patients of risks inherent in treatment and so deprive them of the opportunity of refusing to be treated); (4) persuading another to inflict injury is sometimes equated with causing injury (for example, in the tort of inducing breach of contract). Cases where D's tort is held to be the cause of loss which is the immediate result of a willed act of another are sometimes called cases of 'interpersonal causation': *Nader* (1985) 2 N.S.W.L.R. 501, 516-18 *per* Mahoney J.A.

2 See p. 438 above.

here: a *prima facie* case of causal link will be made out by the plaintiff if he establishes that before the accident he was not disabled and that after it he was disabled in a way that could be the consequence of the accident. Such evidence can justify a finding in favour of the plaintiff on the issue of causation and so put the defendant in the tactical position of having to introduce some evidence which at least casts doubt on the proposition that his negligence caused the injury by establishing with some degree of precision some alternative causal factor and its likely effects.[3] In practice, once the plaintiff has proved that the defendant was negligent, then unless the defendant raises the issue of causation, it will be decided (often silently) in favour of the plaintiff. But the ultimate onus of proof rests on the plaintiff.

The causation question has two parts: what is usually called the issue of 'factual causation' and what might be called the question of 'attributive causation'.[4] Causes which satisfy the test of factual causation may be called 'causes in fact' or 'factual causes'; and causes which satisfy the test hf attributive causation may be called 'causes in law' or 'legal causes'.

1. Factual Causation

The defendant's act will be a factual cause of the plaintiff's loss if it was a necessary condition (or in Latin, *conditio sine qua non*) of that loss. This test is often called the 'but-for' test: would the plaintiff's loss have occurred but for the defendant's negligence? If not, then the defendant's negligence was a necessary condition of the plaintiff's loss. For example, in *Barnett* v. *Chelsea and Kensington Hospital Management Committee*[5] a nightwatchman presented himself to a hospital casualty department complaining that he had been vomiting for three hours after drinking tea. He was told to go home to bed and call his own doctor. Five hours later he died of arsenic poisoning. It was held that the negligent advice was not the cause of the death because even if the man had been admitted to hospital and cared for for five hours he still would have died. The same test applies to the question of whether the plaintiff's failure to take care for his own safety caused or materially contributed to his injuries.

The hypothetical question: 'What would have happened if the defendant had taken due care?' is particularly difficult to answer in cases where the answer depends on how the plaintiff would have reacted. For example, in employers' liability cases the issue often arises of whether the employee would have taken advantage of a particular safety device if the employer had provided it. In that context, English courts (at least) have adopted a

---

3 *Watts* v. *Rake* (1960) 108 C.L.R. 158; *Purkess* v. *Crittenden* (1965) 114 C.L.R. 164. See also *Clarke* v. *MacLennan* [1983] 1 All E.R. 416. Similarly, if P proves that D's negligence materially contributed to his injury or loss, it is then for D to adduce evidence that some pre-existing condition which afflicted P also made a contribution; and the evidence must be reasonably precise as to what that contribution was if D's negligence is to be held only partly the cause, thus justifying reduction of the damages payable by D: *Western Australia* v. *Watson* [1990] W.A.R. 248, 311.

4 *Chapman* v. *Hearse* (1961) 106 C.L.R. 112, 122.

5 [1969] 1 Q.B. 428.

somewhat 'objective' approach which is, in practice, quite favourable to plaintiffs.[6] But in cases where the plaintiff argues that if he had been warned of risks inherent in some medical treatment he would not have consented to the treatment, Australian courts have taken a line which may present plaintiffs with considerable problems of proof: the question is not whether the reasonable person would have refused consent, but whether *this* patient would have done so.[7] This so-called subjective' approach prevents the causation question becoming an evaluative one concerned with the risks it is reasonable for people to take with their own lives or safety.

The but-for test is very indiscriminate. In most cases it casts its net much too widely: every happening has an infinite number of necessary conditions, most of which are of no legal significance at all. To give a banal example: a necessary condition of a person being injured at the age of 20 is that he was born; but his having been born would not usually be called *the* cause, or even *a* cause, of his injury.[8] A more subtle example is where the necessary condition is itself a tortious act. Suppose a person is injured by another's negligence and while returning home from hospital some weeks later is shot by an escaping thief. He would not have been shot if he had not been where he was and he would not have been there but for the first accident. But we would not call the first tortious act *the* cause or even *a* cause of the person's being shot.[9] But sometimes, by contrast, instead of being over-inclusive, the but-for test is under-inclusive or, in other words, too selective. This happens where injury or death results from more than one factor, each of which was sufficient without the other(s) to cause the injury. For example, suppose that a person receives two gunshot wounds, either wound by itself being fatal; or that a pedestrian has a fatal stroke just as he is mortally injured by a car. In both these instances it is true of neither factor that the fatal injury would not have been suffered but for its occurrence, and so in this sense neither is a cause of the injury. But a good case could be made for calling both events in each case a cause of the death. Such causes are often referred to as multiple sufficient causes. We will examine the way in which the law deals with these shortcomings of the but-for test in the section below on attributive causation. In short, the law picks one or more of the factual causes to which legal responsibility is attributed; these we can call 'legal causes' or 'causes in law'.

One result of the fact that every event has a number of necessary causal conditions which combine to produce it is, of course, that a defendant can

---

6 See p. 565 below.

7 *Gover* v. *Perriam* (1985) 39 S.A.S.R. 543; *Ellis* v. *Wallsend District Council* (1989) 17 N.S.W.L.R. 553.

8 *National Insurance Co. of N.Z. Ltd* v. *Espagne* (1961) 105 C.L.R. 569, 590-2 *per* Windeyer J.

9 *Faulkner* v. *Keffalinos* (1970) 45 A.L.J.R. 80, 86 *per* Windeyer J. A real life example is *McKiernan* v. *Manhire* (1977) 17 S.A.S.R. 571. So, in *Baker* v. *Willoughby* [1970] A.C. 467 it was not suggested that the first tortfeasor was the cause of the loss of the plaintiff's leg even though the plaintiff would not have been shot if he had not been forced to change jobs as a result of the road accident.

be held liable for loss even though his tortious act operated in conjunction or combination (and more or less simultaneously)[10] with other causal factors (which may or may not be tortious) to produce the loss, provided only that the court is satisfied, on the balance of probabilities, that the loss would not have occurred but for the causal contribution made by the defendant's tort. Where there are two or more contributory *tortious* causal factors, then (provided both are held to be causes of the plaintiff's loss in law as well as in fact) each tortfeasor will be liable to contribute to the plaintiff's damages, and the contribution payable by a tortfeasor can, in theory, be anything greater than zero.[11] In practice, however, a tortfeasor is probably unlikely to be ordered to pay less than (say) 10 per cent of the damages. Similarly, where the plaintiff's negligence contributes to the loss, the damages payable by the defendant can be reduced proportionally to reflect the plaintiff's negligence. Where any contributory (and contemporaneous) causal factors (other than the defendant's negligence) are non-tortious, the defendant may be liable to pay the whole of the plaintiff's damages (provided the tort is held to be the legal as well as a factual cause of the loss). The fact that the defendant's tort caused the loss in combination with other factors does not reduce his liability to pay damages for the loss unless the defendant can adduce evidence which could establish with some precision what the contribution of those other factors was.[12]

In the last paragraph we considered cases where necessary conditions *combine* to produce the plaintiff's loss. A different situation arises where two or more causal factors operate *cumulatively* to produce the plaintiff's loss. This may happen where a plaintiff is exposed to different loss-causing factors at different times, or where several factors operate at the same time to produce in total more loss than any one of them operating alone would have produced. Suppose that a plaintiff suffers loss as a cumulative result of the operation of the defendant's tort and a non-tortious factor. If the plaintiff can prove, on the balance of probabilities, how much of the loss was caused by the defendant's tort, then the defendant will be held liable for that proportion of the loss. But suppose that the plaintiff can only prove that the two factors operated cumulatively, and cannot prove the relative contributions made by the two different causes to the loss. On a strict application of the balance of probabilities test, the plaintiff will lose because he cannot prove that the defendant caused the whole of the loss, nor can he prove which part of the loss the defendant caused. This situation not uncommonly arises in cases involving industrial and other diseases, the aetiology of which is imperfectly understood.

---

10 See p. 456 below.

11 On contribution see p. 737 below.

12 But even if the defendant cannot adduce evidence which could establish the relative contribution made by his tort, the effect of non-tortious causal factors can be taken into account in assessing damages by increasing the discount for contingencies (as to which see p. 488 below): *Western Australia* v. *Watson* [1990] W.A.R. 248, 312 citing *Wilson* v. *Peisley* (1975) 50 A.L.J.R. 207, 209.

In *Bonnington Castings Ltd* v. *Wardlaw*[13] the House of Lords overcame this problem by holding that it was enough for a plaintiff to prove that the defendant's tort had caused *or materially*[14] *contributed to* his loss. Again, in *Wilsher* v. *Essex A.H.A.*[15] the House of Lords held, in effect, that in cases involving cumulative causation, each tortious legal cause can be held responsible for the whole of the plaintiff's loss.[16] The curiosity of this principle is that a defendant can be held liable for the whole of a loss even though all that can be proved on the balance of probabilities is that he contributed to it. The principle allows the court simply to ignore the lack of evidence on the issue of which factor caused which part of the plaintiff's loss.[17]

Suppose, now, that the cumulative causal factors are both tortious. If the relative contribution of each can be proved on the balance of probabilities, the plaintiff will recover judgment against each representing the contribution of each to the total loss. But if the relative contributions cannot be established, it would seem to follow from *Bonnington Castings* and *Wilsher* that each tortfeasor could be held liable for the whole loss suffered. If this is correct, a plaintiff who cannot prove who caused what ends up in a better position than a plaintiff who can, because he has two sources from which he can seek to recover the whole of the loss. It is not clear how a court would deal with contribution proceedings between the two tortfeasors given the absence of evidence as to their relative contributions: it might simply split the damages 50/50 *faute de mieux*.[18] There is some authority for the proposition that the total loss in such a case can be divided between the tortfeasors on any basis not inconsistent with the evidence.[19]

As we have already noted, the plaintiff must prove that the defendant's tort was more probably than not a necessary condition of the occurrence of his loss.[20] In numerical terms, 'more probably than not' equates with a greater than 50 per cent chance. In theory this means that a defendant may be held liable for a loss provided only that the chance that his tortious conduct was not a necessary condition of its occurrence is anything less than 50 per cent. But in practice a court is unlikely to decide the causal question in favour of the plaintiff unless it is rather more satisfied of the causal relevance of the defendant's tort than this statement suggests. It should be noted, however, that provided the plaintiff proves causation 'more probably than not' (and provided the court decides that the defendant's negligence was the (or a) *legal* cause of the plaintiff's loss), he is entitled to judgment against the defendant for damages representing the whole of the loss which is the subject of his claim. The fact that it may be

---

13 [1956] A.C. 613.

14 Or 'not negligibly': *Western Australia* v. *Watson* [1990] W.A.R. 248, 286.

15 [1988] A.C. 1074.

16 See further J. Stapleton (1988) 104 L.Q.R. 398.

17 But it can make an adjustment by increasing the discount for contingencies used when assessing damages: *Western Australia* v. *Watson* [1990] W.A.R. 248, 312.

18 See further p. 737 below.

19 *Nilon* v. *Bezzina* [1988] 2 Qd.R. 420 esp. 242 *per* McPherson J.

20 Or, in cases of cumulative causation, of some part of it.

less than certain that the defendant's tort was a necessary condition of the plaintiff's loss does not mean that the plaintiff is not entitled to full compensation. In other words, the damages awarded in a tort action are not proportional to the probability that the defendant's tort was a necessary condition of the loss. The logic of this basic position is clear: it is often very difficult to be certain what happened in the past, and so we have to be satisfied with something less than certainty. Having been so satisfied, it would make no sense to penalize the plaintiff for our lack of certainty by reducing the damages representing his loss, which is the same no matter how uncertain we are as to what caused it.[21]

The rule that the plaintiff must prove on the balance of probabilities that the defendant's tort (either alone or in combination with other factors operating more or less simultaneously) caused the loss can be translated into saying that he must prove that the defendant's tortious act (either alone or in combination with other factors operating more or less simultaneously) *increased the risk* of the loss occurring by more than 50 per cent.[22] If the defendant's tort (either alone or in combination with other factors operating more or less simultaneously) increased the risk of the loss[23] by less than 50 per cent, it did not cause or materially contribute to that loss. This rule causes most difficulty in cases where the plaintiff suffers loss as a result of contracting some illness or disease as opposed to cases in which his loss is the result of a traumatic accident.[24] The aetiology of many diseases and illnesses is very imperfectly understood; and in the case of many conditions, background circumstances which are beyond the control of the defendant and the non-tortious behaviour of the sufferer play significant but ill-understood roles in the causation process. As a result, it is often difficult for expert witnesses to say that the plaintiff's condition was more probably than not the result of the

---

21 The impact of the basic rule is, however, diluted by the fact that in cases in which damages are awarded for loss likely to be incurred after the date of the trial as a result of the tort, a discount (the so-called 'discount for vicissitudes') is always made to take account of the chance that the plaintiff would have suffered equivalent loss as a result of some other event: see p. 488 below. But the discount is standard and is not meant to reflect accurately the chance that the defendant's tort might not be the cause of post-trial loss: the defendant does not have to prove that the plaintiff might have suffered a similar misfortune anyway. Of more importance, however, is that if the defendant can point to a specific misfortune which the plaintiff has suffered or may suffer as a result of the initial injuries and which might have overtaken the plaintiff even if he had not been injured, the court can reduce the plaintiff's damages proportionally to the chance that the misfortune would have so occurred regardless of whether the chance is more than 50 per cent. In other words, damages proportional to risk can be awarded in respect of events consequential upon the plaintiff's initial injuries but not in respect of events leading to those initial injuries. See generally *Malec* v. *J.C. Hutton Pty Ltd* (1990) 169 C.L.R. 638. This proposition assumes, of course, that we have some criterion for distinguishing between initial injuries and consequential misfortunes, but the line may not always be obvious. Nor is it obvious why liability for the initial injuries (however defined) is decided on the balance of probabilities whereas liability for subsequent misfortunes is proportional to the chance that they resulted from the defendant's negligence.

22 J. Stapleton (1988) 104 L.Q.R. 389. What follows depends heavily on this article.

23 Or, in cases of cumulative causation, some part of it.

24 J. Stapleton *Disease and the Compensation Debate* (Oxford, 1986) Ch. 3.

defendant's tort. In many cases, the most they can say is that the defendant's tort *might* have caused the condition, or that it (more probably than not) increased the risk of the condition by a specified or unspecified amount less than 50 per cent. In either case the plaintiff should, according to the basic rule, lose his case.

As we have seen, courts sometimes deal with such cases simply by saying that the medical evidence, taken together with all the other relevant evidence, 'satisfies' the court that the defendant's tort caused the plaintiff's loss.[25] But the House of Lords in *McGhee* v. *National Coal Board*[26] adopted a different approach. In that case the pursuer worked in a brick factory; during the day brick dust adhered to his skin and at the end of the working day he used to cycle home in that state because the defender provided no showers. No tort was established in relation to the working conditions, but the failure to provide showers was held to be tortious. Exposure to brick dust was a recognized cause of dermatitis, but the expert medical witnesses could not say that the provision of showers would probably have prevented the dermatitis, but only that it would have materially reduced the risk of contracting it. Nevertheless, the House of Lords held the defendant liable for the plaintiff's dermatitis, apparently on the basis that a person can be said to have caused a condition if his conduct increased the risk of its occurrence materially, even if by less than 50 per cent. But in *Wilsher* v. *Essex A.H.A.*[27] Lord Bridge said that the case did not create an exception to the normal balance of probabilites rule of causation because, taking a 'robust and pragmatic approach' to the evidence, the case was one of cumulative causation; and so it could be said that the defender's negligence had materially contributed to the pursuer's dermatitis. Lord Bridge was, perhaps, encouraged to reinterpret *McGhee* in this way by the fact that both of the sources of risk were under the control of the defendant and that it was at least possible that the dermatitis had been caused by the cumulative effect of both the sources of risk.[28] However, of the several possible causes of the plaintiff's condition in *Wilsher* itself, only one was under the control of the defendant, and there was no suggestion that the various sources had operated cumulatively; so the only question in that case was whether the evidence showed that that factor had more probably than not caused the condition.[29]

---

25 See p. 445 above.

26 [1973] 1 W.L.R. 1; E.J. Weinrib (1975) 38 *M.L.R.* 518. Cf. *Barker* v. *Permanent Seamless Floors Pty Ltd* [1983] 2 Qd.R. 561.

27 [1988] A.C. 1074.

28 But no evidence was given in *McGhee* which justified preferring this explanation to one which attributed the dermatitis to one or other of the factors but not both: Stapleton (1988) 104 *L.Q.R.* 389, 404. Moreover, the reinterpetation *does* involve a departure from normal principles (in the same way as does *Bonnington Castings* v. *Wardlaw*) because the plaintiff in *McGhee* was awarded full damages even though, on Lord Bridge's view, the defendant had only caused part of the loss.

29 *McGhee* (before being reinterpreted by the House of Lords in *Wilsher*) was applied in *Fitzgerald* v. *Lane* [1987] Q.B. 781. The House of Lords subsequently allowed an appeal on unrelated grounds ([1989] A.C. 328; see p. 738 below), but the Court of Appeal's decision on causation was not questioned. It is difficult to see how the Court of Appeal's decision can stand beside the House's decision in *Wilsher*.

It should be noted that in both *McGhee and Wilsher* the plaintiff did not claim damages proportional to increase of risk, but rather damages representing the loss suffered. Indeed, in neither case was any attempt made to quantify the increase in risk which the defendant's tort was alleged to have brought about. So it is not, perhaps, surprising that the House of Lords in *Wilsher* was not prepared to create an exception to the normal rule about burden of proof. On the other hand, in *Hotson* v. *East Berks A.H.A.*[30] the plaintiff did claim damages proportional to risk: he argued that the defendant's negligence had deprived him of a 25 per cent chance of avoiding a particular condition, and he claimed damages representing 25 per cent of what he would have recovered if he had been able to show that but for the defendant's negligence he would more probably than not have contracted the condition. It is important to notice that the plaintiff's argument in *Hotson* was *not* that the defendant's negligence had *increased the risk* of his contracting the condition by 25 per cent, but that (as the evidence established on the balance of probabilities) because of the defendant's negligence he had lost a one in four chance of getting better. In other words, Hotson was not claiming damages for the fact that he had contracted the condition, but rather damages for the *loss of the chance* of avoiding the condition. Hotson succeeded in the Court of Appeal, but the House of Lords reinterpreted his claim and then dismissed it: instead of treating the claim as one for the loss of a chance, the House of Lords treated it as a claim for damages on the ground that, one chance out of four, the defendant's negligence had caused *the condition*. But, the House of Lords said, it is not enough to prove that the defendant increased the risk of the condition by 25 per cent: it must be proved that he increased it by more than 50 per cent.

This result leaves open the question of how the House would have dealt with the plaintiff's claim if they had not reinterpreted it in this way. On the one hand, there are, as we shall see later,[31] certain circumstances in which damages are recoverable in tort for the loss of a chance of making a gain or avoiding a loss. Most of these cases are like *Hotson* in that at the time of the trial the plaintiff's loss had already occurred; and they suggest that the Court of Appeal may have been right to allow Hotson's claim in its original form.[32] Much more difficult would be cases in which, at the time of the trial, the outcome—of which the defendant was alleged to have increased the risk—had not yet occurred. Should a person be allowed to recover damages for the loss of a chance of avoiding an outcome which has not yet occurred and which may never occur? As we will see later,[33] English courts have, in some contexts, refused to award damages for the cost of avoiding losses which are either imminent or virtually certain to occur at some time in the future. The grounds on which this has been done are not entirely satisfactory, but they apply equally to any claim in

---

30 [1987] A.C. 750.

31 p. 526 below.

32 See also the inconclusive *dicta* of Lord Mackay and Lord Bridge in *Hotson* itself: [1987] A.C. 750, 768 and 782-3 respectively.

33 p. 585 below.

respect of the loss of a chance of avoiding a loss or making a gain in the future.

There is another context in which the issue of awarding damages proportional to risk has arisen: suppose a plaintiff suffers illness or injury as a result of taking a drug which is manufactured and marketed by a number of companies, and that the plaintiff is unable to prove which of those companies manufactured and marketed the particular doses he took. Suppose, too, that the plaintiff can prove that his illness or injury was more probably than not caused by taking the drug, and that the manufacturing or marketing of the drug by all of the companies involved was in some respect tortious; but that he cannot prove, in relation to any particular defendant, that his condition was caused by *that defendant's* tortious behaviour. Applying traditional causation principles, the plaintiff should not recover damages against any of the drug companies. But this seems unfair and undesirable. One way out of this problem is to require each company to pay damages proportional to its share of the drug market.[34] This seems reasonably fair to the drug companies but not to plaintiffs, unless they successfully sue all the companies involved. A different problem arises where a group of people contract a particular condition, and the medical evidence establishes that a certain number of them probably contracted it as a result of tortious behaviour on the part of a defendant, but does not indicate which ones because the condition has a number of possible causes.[35] A suggested solution here is to require the defendant to pay an amount proportional to the increase, attributable to his tort, in the incidence of the condition and to distribute it equally among all the members of the group of sufferers. Once again, this seems a fair result for the defendant but not for the plaintiffs, who either get some damages even though they were entitled to none, or inadequate damages for the loss which the defendant caused them.[36] It is problems such as these which have led some to argue that the tort system of compensating for personal injuries has outlived its useful life. But difficult problems of causation would arise in any compensation system in which entitlement was based on proving that the loss arose from a specific cause. Only if we adopted a system in which financial provision was made for everyone with particular needs, regardless of how they came to be in need, would these problems of causation be avoided.

Even if the court decides that the defendant's tort was, on the balance of probabilities, a *factual* cause of the plaintiff's loss, it does not follow that the defendant will be held liable *in law* for that loss. The court must still decide to which of the factual causes to attribute the loss as a matter of law and for the purposes deciding who, if anyone, is liable to pay compensation.

---

34 J.G. Fleming (1989) 68 *Can. B.R.* 661, 664-9.

35 This is the *Hotson* problem with the added complication of multiple plaintiffs.

36 Fleming (1989) 68 *Can. B.R.* 661, 679-80.

2. ATTRIBUTIVE CAUSATION

(a) Choosing among necessary conditions This part of the inquiry is often put in the form, 'What was the "real" or "effective" cause of the loss?' (or, in Latin, the *causa causans*). The relationship between the 'legal' cause(s) and the necessary conditions of a loss can be described by saying that the latter are the 'surrounding circumstances' or the 'circumstances in which, or on which' the effective cause(s) of the loss in question operated.[37]

In most cases the attributive causation question presents no real difficulty, partly because of the form in which it is asked: 'Was the defendant's negligence the (or a) cause of the loss?'. Putting the question in this way eliminates all but a very few of the necessary conditions as legally significant in that it leads us to concentrate on factors which stand out as being as important as human action and which were operating more or less at the same time as the defendant's act. It is important to realize, however, that no matter how obvious it might be that the defendant's act should be treated as the (or a) legal cause, picking out that act does require us to apply some test in addition to the but-for test.[38] For example, it is probably true that defects in the construction or lighting of roads are often a necessary condition of road accidents but they are rarely picked out as the legal cause. The question of whether the defendant's act ought to be singled out from among the mass of necessary causal conditions operating more or less at the same time we might call the question of 'initial causation'.

Sometimes, by contrast, the attributive causation issue arises in relation to events which were separated significantly in time. For example, suppose a person is badly injured in an accident and then negligently treated in hospital. The question will often arise as to whether his final state is to be attributed to the accident or to the treatment. In such a case the possible outcomes are that the driver will be held wholly responsible or that he will be held responsible for some of the loss and the doctor or the hospital (or both) for any additional loss caused by the bad treatment.[39] Other cases are slightly different in that the two causal factors, separated in time, both precede the infliction of any loss. For example, suppose an employer negligently sends an employee out late at night unescorted to deliver the day's takings to a safe deposit box. On the way, the employee is mugged. Is the mugging attributable to the negligence of the employer as well as to

---

37 *The Commonwealth* v. *Butler* (1958-9) 102 C.L.R. 465, 476 *per* Taylor J. See also *Parsons* v. *John Holland-Christiani and Nielson Joint Venture* [1991] 1 Qd.R. 137, 151.

38 This truth is sometimes concealed and even denied by saying that the 'but-for' test must be applied in 'a common-sense way', and by dealing with intervening causal factors in terms of remoteness of damage: see, for example, the judgments of Glass and McHugh JJ.A. in *Alexander* v. *Cambridge Credit Corporation* (1987) 2 N.S.W.L.R. 310. Mahoney J.A. in the same case adopts the view put in the text. But there seems to be no direct correlation between the theory adopted and the results reached: for example, in *Alexander* Glass J.A. dissented from the majority holding of McHugh and Mahoney JJ.A. on the causation issue.

39 *Liston* v. *Liston* (1982) 31 S.A.S.R. 245; *Lawrie* v. *Meggitt* (1974) 11 S.A.S.R. 5.

the crime of the muggers?[40] In both types of case we are concerned with whether the event which intervenes between the initial act of negligence and some or all of the loss should be treated as a legal cause. This is sometimes put by asking whether the intervening event 'broke the chain of causation' or was, in Latin, a *novus actus* (or *nova causa*) *interveniens*. If the chain of causation was broken then the intervening, not the initial, cause will be held responsible in law for the consequences of which it was a necessary condition.

Where an initial and an intervening cause are both held partly responsible for the plaintiff's loss, they are what might be called 'multiple contributing causes'. Sometimes multiple contributing causes occur more or less contemporaneously. For example, suppose a pedestrian is injured as a result of a collision between two cars which would not have happened without the negligence of both drivers. Both acts of negligence are necessary conditions of the loss which they combine to inflict. In such cases there will usually be no doubt that both drivers should be held liable, as what are called 'several concurrent tortfeasors', and each ordered to pay damages to the plaintiff. Another example of this situation is where a plaintiff's failure to take reasonable care for his own safety contributes to his loss. This is usually treated in terms of the defence of contributory negligence and the damages can be divided between the plaintiff and the defendant; but it is essentially a case of multiple contributing causes.

There are two main theories as to how the law picks out the legal cause from the mass of necessary conditions. The view most popular among judges is that the law makes use of the ordinary person's common-sense notions of causation and refers to the ordinary usage of causal language. The attributive causation question is a jury question;[41] it is one to which the answer of the ordinary person in the street is appropriate. Thus judges should be wary of discussing with juries philosophical or scientific or legal theories of the concept of causation.[42] Common-sense notions are not, however, sufficiently rich or detailed to solve every causal problem presented in litigation, since litigation sometimes throws up bizarre fact situations. When this happens, the causal question requires a policy answer, but this is only the case at the margin, as it were.[43] The two basic principles of causation said to be recognized by common sense are that voluntary human action tends to be treated as a cause in preference to natural events or circumstances; and that unusual combinations of causally

40 See *Chomentowski* v. *Red Garter Restaurant Pty Ltd* [1970] 92 W.N.(N.S.W.) 1070.

41 See p. 433 above for a definition of the term 'jury question'.

42 *Fitzgerald* v. *Penn* (1954) 91 C.L.R. 268, 276-8 *per* Dixon C.J., Fullagar & Kitto JJ.; *The Commonwealth* v. *Butler* (1958-9) 102 C.L.R. 465, 479 *per* Windeyer J.

43 H.L.A. Hart & A.M. Honoré *Causation in the Law* 2nd edn (Oxford, 1985) pp. 88-94 (for further discussion of this seminal work see J. Stapleton (1988) 8 O.J.L.S. 111); this approach forms the basis of the exposition of causation by Smith J. in *Haber* v. *Walker* [1963] V.R. 339, 357-8. See also *Nader* v. *Urban Transit Authority of N.S.W.* (1985) 2 N.S.W.L.R. 501, 509-10, 514-15 *per* Mahoney J.A; *March* v. *E.&M.H. Stramare Pty Ltd* (1991) 171 C.L.R. 506, 515-16 *per* Mason C.J. For an interesting example of the use of a policy argument to decide an issue of causation see *State Rail Authority (N.S.W.)* v. *Wiegold* [1991] 25 N.S.W.L.R. 500.

independent events (of which the wrongful act is one), which can be described as coincidences or quirks of chance, tend to be treated as causes in preference to the wrongful act which combined with the other events to produce the coincidence. The preference for voluntary human conduct explains why, in most cases where negligence of a party is proved, the attributive causation question presents so little difficulty.[44] Coincidence, too, can play a part in initial causation. For example, in an American case a cab driver was negligent in not sounding his horn or giving right of way to a pedestrian. As he passed the pedestrian the cab door flew open through no fault of the driver and injured the pedestrian. The injury was not treated as a consequence of the negligence.[45]

The second theory as to how the law picks out the legal cause says, contrary to the theory just discussed, that common use of causal language is an inappropriate standard for the solution of problems of attributive causation.[46] Several reasons are given. First, the way a causal question is answered depends partly on the reason why it is asked. The law is concerned with ascribing responsibility; the road engineer is concerned with improving road design; the motor vehicle manufacturer is concerned with improving his product. Each might give a different answer to the question of what caused a road accident. It is not clear, it is said, that the person in the street, and hence common-sense notions of causation, have the ascription of responsibility as their prime purpose. This is reflected in the way the law asks the causal question—not 'What was the cause?' but, 'Was the defendant's act the (or a) cause?'. Secondly, common-sense notions of causation are 'extraordinarily difficult to formulate and apply'.[47] Thirdly, what seems common sense to the 'untutored mind' might seem nonsense to the mind informed, for example, by relevant expert evidence.[48] Fourthly, causal language tends to conceal the policy choices presented by many difficult causal questions. For example, if the alternative to holding the defendant liable is to hold some third party liable, the policy arguments in favour of a finding against the defendant may be different from those which would be applicable if the alternative were to attribute the loss to a natural occurrence. This second theory,

44 It should be noted that I am using 'voluntary' in a different sense from that adopted by Hart & Honoré in *Causation in the Law.* They define 'voluntary' so as to exclude negligent acts (see pp. 41-2, 136-7). But even in the context of intervening causation, where they define the term in this way, it is not true, as we will see below, that negligent acts cannot break the chain of causation. It should also be noted that the preference for voluntary conduct, even if defined in Hart & Honoré's sense, only operates in cases where A directly inflicts loss on B. It does not operate in cases where A can be held liable for failing to act to prevent B causing loss (see e.g. *Barnes* v. *Hay* (1988) 12 N.S.W.L.R. 337); or for providing B with the opportunity to inflict loss; or for inducing B to inflict loss: in such cases, A can be held liable even if the direct cause of the loss was deliberate intentional action by B.

45 *Canada* v. *Royce* (1953) 257 P.2d 624.

46 *Atiyah's Accidents* at pp. 102-9. S. Lloyd Bostock (1979) 42 *M.L.R.* 143. For a strong judicial statement of the relevance of policy to the question of causation see the judgment of Samuels J.A. in *State Rail Authority of New South Wales* v. *Wiegold* (1991) 25 N.S.W.L.R. 500.

47 *Atiyah's Accidents* at p. 107.

48 *March* v. *E. & M.H. Stramare Pty Ltd* (1991) 171 C.L.R. 506, 533 *per* McHugh J.

therefore, says that attributive causation is essentially a question of legal policy.

There seem to be two main points at issue here. The first concerns the role of rules and principles in the law. The first theory favours the formulation of relatively fixed and clear rules and principles on the basis of which cases can be decided and the outcome of cases predicted. The second theory is more in favour of moulding the decision in a particular case to deal with the particular circumstances of that case. The inclinations of most Australian judges would seem to be in the direction of the first approach.[49] The first theory does not deny that principles of attributive causation are ultimately based on value (or policy) judgments about attribution of responsibility, but holds that the law should make use of causal principles which give expression to the value judgments of the ordinary person. The second point at issue is whether, even given that causal rules of relatively fixed formulation should be used, these should be formulated by courts with the particular aim of attributing legal responsibility or whether, on the contrary, the rules should be taken from ordinary language regardless of whether ordinary usages of causal words are directed to the attribution of responsibility to pay damages. This point is perhaps of less importance now because of the gradual demise of the civil jury. Although courts are keen to stress that the lawyer's idea of causation is different from the scientist's or philosopher's,[50] they do not seem particularly concerned to champion the ordinary person's answer to causal questions at the expense of the legal policy answer. This should become clear in the discussion which follows.

(b) Multiple sufficient causes The but-for test treats necessary conditions as causes. But what is to be done if the defendant's tort was a *sufficient* but not a *necessary* condition of the plaintiff's loss, because the loss would more probably than not have occurred even if the defendant had not committed a tort? There are a number of situations which need to be considered here.

(i) Alternative causes: Suppose that the defendant causes the death of a person who would probably have died anyway as the result of a pre-existing illness or condition (which we might call the 'hypothetical cause'); or that a person has an illness the operation of which the defendant's act accelerates thus causing death sooner than it would otherwise probably have occurred. In *Von Hartmann* v. *Kirk* Sholl J. held that where a defendant by negligence appreciably accelerates the death of a person who would anyway have died from a pre-existing illness at some later time, the defendant can be held liable for that death;[51] but he will only have to pay damages in respect of the period of acceleration.[52] If, on

49 *National Insurance Co. of N.Z. Ltd* v. *Espagne* (1961) 105 C.L.R. 569, 590-2 *per* Windeyer J.
50 G. Williams [1961] *C.L.J.* 62.
51 [1961] V.R. 544; but contrast *Commonwealth* v. *Butler* (1958-9) 102 C.L.R. 465.
52 Similarly, if the defendant accelerates the onset of an illness: *Hole* v. *Hocking* [1962] S.A.S.R. 128.

the other hand, death occurs as a result of the defendant's negligence no sooner than it would otherwise have done, then the defendant is not liable for the death, which would have occurred at the same time anyway as a result of the illness.

In some cases the defendant's act has the effect of necessitating some medical or surgical operation sooner than would otherwise have been the case by accelerating a condition needing attention. In *Zumeris* v. *Testa*[53] it was held that if an accelerated condition proves incapable of cure, the defendant can be held liable for the acceleration. But if the condition is capable of partial cure, the plaintiff will recover only if he can show that he has suffered injuries or losses as a result of the defendant's act greater than those he would have suffered eventually anyway; or that he is suffering ill-health now whereas otherwise he would only have suffered it later; or that if the condition had not been accelerated the treatment might never have been necessary, either because some vicissitude of life might have intervened and insulated the plaintiff from the condition or, perhaps, a cure might have been found before the operation was needed. If a total cure is available the plaintiff recovers nothing on account of the acceleration.[54] The important point to note about these cases is that the issue is not treated simply as whether the defendant's act or the pre-existing condition caused the death or injury. Both are treated as causally relevant, and the damages payable by the defendant to the plaintiff are calculated so as to reflect the temporal relationship between the two events.

If the hypothetical cause were another wrongful human act then the result might be different. For example, suppose if A had not killed B in a car accident he would have gone home and been killed in an explosion negligently caused by his next-door neighbour. Here, too, there is acceleration but it seems unlikely that a court would allow A to avoid liability for the full consequences of B's death by holding him responsible just for its acceleration. The difference of result is perhaps to be explained by the fact that in this case the alternative cause is not operative at the time of the defendant's negligence in the same way as it is in the pre-existing illness cases.

It is possible to imagine situations in which the alternative human act is operative at the time the later act of negligence causes the loss. For example, suppose a negligently lit fire spreads; by itself it is sufficient to destroy a house in its path, but before it reaches the house a flood of water from a negligently ruptured dam extinguishes the fire and sweeps away the house. Here questions of acceleration are non-existent or unimportant and so the question of causation has to be faced squarely. It seems likely that both negligent parties would be held liable.

(ii) Additional causes: Sometimes two sufficient causes combine to bring about damage. For example, if a fire negligently started by A combines with a fire negligently started by B and destroys C's house, both fires by themselves being sufficient to destroy the house, both A and B will be held

53 [1972] V.R. 839.
54 cf. *Cutler* v. *Vauxhall Motors Ltd* [1971] 1 Q.B. 418.

liable as concurrent tortfeasors. It is important to note that the causes are independent of one another. If one of the causes would not have occurred or would not have had the effect it did but for the occurrence of the other, they will not be multiple sufficient causes but multiple contributing causes.

In other cases the causes will not combine in this way but will operate independently but simultaneously: for example, if two people simultaneously deliver fatal blows to the plaintiff's body. Here, too, both would no doubt be held liable. If only one of the sufficient causes is tortious, for example if a pedestrian has a fatal stroke just as he is mortally injured by a car, the negligent driver would probably not be held liable. Where a negligent defendant accelerates death or illness attributable to no one's fault he is only liable for the acceleration. By analogy, where there is no acceleration he should not be held liable at all. Why does the law here, and elsewhere, draw this distinction between tortious and non-tortious causes? The answer would seem to be that where a person suffers injury or death as a result of two negligent acts he or his dependants should not be worse off than if he had been similarly injured by one such act, which they would be if both defendants were allowed to use the but-for argument. And since both defendants seem similarly placed from the causal point of view there seems no reason to discriminate between them by holding only one liable. But where the plaintiff or deceased would have suffered naturally anyway, he or his dependants are not being made worse off by not being allowed to sue—the negligent act is, as it were, a coincidence. The reason why we call the negligent act—rather than the disease or illness—the coincidence is probably because the latter is beyond human control in a way that the former is not.

More frequent in the cases are situations where the additional cause operates at some time later than the initial cause (these are not cases of intervening causation, which are examples of multiple contributing causes). In *Performance Cars Ltd* v. *Abraham*[55] the plaintiff's Rolls-Royce was hit twice by different cars within the space of two weeks. Each collision was solely the fault of the other driver. As a result of the first collision the whole of the lower section of the car needed respraying at a cost of £75. The plaintiff obtained judgment for this amount from the first driver but could not secure payment. The plaintiff then sued the second driver, the defendant, for an amount including the £75. The second collision had affected a different area of the lower part of the car and this, too, necessitated respraying of the whole of the lower part of the car. The loss suffered here for which compensation was sought was the cost of respraying; the second collision did not add to that cost even though it caused a separate dent. As a result, the defendant was able to argue successfully that his negligence in running into the car was not a necessary condition of the plaintiff having to pay the cost of respraying. So the case looks as if it was decided by applying the but-for test. However, the reasoning of the court ignored the fact that the first driver could also argue that his negligence was not a necessary condition of the

55 [1962] 1 Q.B. 33.

loss. The defendant seems to have benefited from the fact that he collided with the car some time after the first collision. If both collisions had occurred more or less simultaneously it is likely that both drivers would have been held liable, leaving it to them to sort out matters between themselves in contribution proceedings.

Much the same principle as was applied in *Performance Cars* was adopted in *Baker* v. *Willoughby.*[56] There the plaintiff's leg was injured in an accident caused by the negligence of the defendant; the plaintiff suffered loss of earning capacity, loss of amenities, and pain and suffering. Some time later a thief shot the plaintiff in the same leg which then had to be amputated, thus increasing the plaintiff's loss of amenities and earning capacity. The defendant was liable for the loss suffered by the plaintiff between the first and second 'accidents'; the defendant was not liable for the additional loss inflicted on the plaintiff by the thief over and above that which the plaintiff would have suffered if the second accident had never occurred. Although the plaintiff was shot while at work as a security officer, and although he only took the job as a security officer because the first accident had rendered him unfit to do his former job, this factual link was, in a legal sense, a coincidence, and so causally irrelevant. But the defendant argued that he ought not to be held liable for *any* of the loss suffered by the plaintiff after the date of the second accident: the thief's act had 'swallowed up' the effects of the defendant's negligence—the plaintiff no longer had a leg and so was no longer suffering any loss caused by having an injured leg. The plaintiff would have suffered this loss even if he had not been injured by the defendant. (But equally he would have suffered it even if he had not been shot by the thief.)

The House of Lords held the defendant liable for all but the additional loss inflicted by the thief over and above that which the plaintiff would have suffered if he had not been shot. He could only escape liability for the continuing effects of his tort after the second tort if the second event reduced the plaintiff's loss or reduced the period during which he would suffer it. But since what is compensated for is the loss caused by injuries and not the injuries themselves, the second event did not reduce the loss caused by the defendant's tort since, although the plaintiff no longer had a stiff leg, he was still suffering the loss resulting from having a stiff leg. The second event became a concurrent sufficient cause of part of the loss and a cause of some additional loss. And on the same principle as in *Performance Cars* v. *Abraham*, the thief would be allowed to argue that his act was not a necessary condition of the concurrently caused loss. In the language of the law of damages, the thief was entitled to take the victim as found—already injured. Once again, it is not clear why both tortfeasors should not be held liable for all the loss caused by each of two

---

56 [1970] A.C. 467 (applied in *Nicholson* v. *Walker and Wolf* (1979) 21 S.A.S.R. 481); D.M.A. Strachan (1970) 33 M.L.R. 378; but contrast *Griffiths* v. *Commonwealth* (1983) 50 A.C.T.R. 7 which applies the vicissitudes principle discussed below. See also *Nilon* v. *Bezzina* [1988] 2 Qd.R. 420 in which the two tortfeasors were treated as cumulative causes of the plaintiff's final condition after the second accident. In the two latter cases, unlike in *Performance Cars or Baker* v. *Willoughby*, both of the tortfeasors were sued; but this should make no difference to the principles applied.

independent sufficient tortious causes.[57] One advantage of this would be that it would give the plaintiff the maximum number of chances of finding a solvent defendant.

The distinction between subsequent events which on the one hand reduce losses and on the other merely add to losses was accepted by Windeyer J. in *Faulkner* v. *Keffalinos.*[58] But Windeyer J. also seems to have drawn a distinction between tortious and non-tortious subsequent events, the latter including, as in *Faulkner* v. *Keffalinos,* a subsequent accident caused by the plaintiff's own fault: a defendant *can* rely on a subsequent non-tortious event. Several other Australian cases support this approach.[59] Once again, here we can see the law requiring the plaintiff to bear the cost of non-tortious events. In *Jobling* v. *Associated Dairies Ltd*[60] the plaintiff fell at work and suffered a partially disabling back injury. Between the accident and the trial he developed a back condition (independently of the accident) which would within a few months anyway have proved totally disabling. The House of Lords held that the onset of this condition had to be taken into account in reduction of the damages recoverable by the plaintiff from his employer. The reasoning is based on two principles. The first might be called the 'vicissitudes' principle, which says that in assessing damages for future continuing loss the court must take account of factors (independent of the injuries) which might have inflicted such loss on the plaintiff even if he had not been injured. When a vicissitude is hypothetical the court makes a reduction of damages reflecting the chance of the event materializing. But when the event materializes before trial the court, following a principle that the law will not speculate when it knows, reduces the damages to take account of the event which has occurred and which would have inflicted loss on the plaintiff even if he had not been injured.

The second principle rests on the proposition that since the law of tort is only one of a complex network of systems for providing compensation, questions of tort liability cannot be decided in isolation from this wider context. This approach, which sees the role of tort law solely in terms of compensation and loss allocation, is most explicitly adopted by Lord Wilberforce.[61] He thought that in the absence of information as to how much the plaintiff would get by way of social security benefit in respect of his illness, the court would get closest to awarding the plaintiff the balance of his loss by taking full account of the effects of the supervening condition (that is, by assuming that the plaintiff would receive full compensation from other sources). Lord Wilberforce agreed with Lord Edmund-Davies[62] that the decision in *Baker* v. *Willoughby* was suspect because the court had not taken account of the fact that the plaintiff

---

57 This appears to have been done in *Commonwealth of Australia* v. *Martin* (1985) 59 A.L.R. 439 (fatal accident claim).

58 (1970) 45 A.L.J.R. 80, 85; cf. *Nicholson* v. *Walker* (1979) 21 S.A.S.R. 481.

59 *Leschke* v. *Jeffs* [1955] Q.W.N. 67; *Jaksic* v. *Cossar* (1966) 85 W.N.(Pt.1)(N.S.W.) 102; *Zeppos* v. *Pridue* (1967) 86 W.N.(Pt.1)(N.S.W.) 270.

60 [1982] A.C. 794; C.J.F. Kidd (1982) 56 *A.L.J.* 389.

61 [1982] A.C. 794, 803.

62 ibid., 807.

could, no doubt, have received partial compensation for the effects of the crime under the Criminal Injuries Compensation Scheme (of which there are Australian equivalents).[63] The force of this approach is not entirely clear. Taken to its logical conclusion it would mean that 'no general, logical, or universally fair rules [could] be stated which [would] cover . . . cases of supervening events whether due to tortious, partially tortious, non-culpable or wholly accidental events'.[64] The law of tort would become purely a mechanism for topping up the compensation received from other sources. To go as far as Lord Wilberforce requires being prepared to view the law of torts in a way very different from the way it has been traditionally viewed, and there must be a real question as to whether Australian or English judges generally are ready for such a change.

What of *Baker* v. *Willoughby* in the light of this decision? This depends on whether there is thought to be a relevant distinction between tortious and non-tortious supervening events. There is, as we have seen, Australian authority for this distinction. Against the distinction it could be argued that a criminal attack is just as much a vicissitude as is a disease. On the other hand, as we have noted before, since simultaneous sufficient tortfeasors are jointly liable there seems no reason why successive tortfeasors should not also be jointly liable for damage inflicted by them. There is no logical objection to such an outcome and it has the policy advantage of giving the plaintiff the maximum chance of being compensated.

What is the position if the non-tortious event precedes the tortious event? Suppose, for example, that a plaintiff is tortiously shot in a badly arthritic leg necessitating amputation. The implicit assumption in *Jobling* is that the tortfeasor would be liable only for the additional loss inflicted by him, and the analogy of the acceleration cases supports this. So, in summary, the position regarding additional causes appears to be that if both are tortious the first tortfeasor is liable for all the loss except that attributable solely to the second tort. If one of the causes is non-tortious then, whether it precedes or succeeds the tort, the tortfeasor is only liable for so much of the loss as is attributable solely to the tort.

3. Intervening Causation

It is now time to leave issues of multiple sufficient causation and return to consider the way the law deals with multiple contributing causes where those causes are separated in time. Intervening causes[65] are always causally related to the initial causal factor in that it can always be said of their consequences that not only would they not have occurred but for the intervening cause, but also they would not have occurred but for the

63 But in the English context, at least, this argument is circular because criminal injuries compensation would only be available if and to the extent that the injuries had been caused by the crime, and causation is defined in accordance with common law rules.

64 *Jobling* v. *Associated Dairies* [1982] A.C. 794, 804 *per* Lord Wilberforce.

65 The principles of intervening causation would appear to relate to Deane J.'s concept of 'causal proximity': *Jaensch* v. *Coffey* (1984-5) 155 C.L.R. 549, 584-5.

initial cause. However, a distinction is usually drawn between intervening causes which are in some sense sparked off by or a reaction to the initial cause and intervening causes which are independent but operate in and on the situation created by the initial cause. The former type of intervening cause is usually a human action; the latter type is more often some natural event. The latter are more often treated as consequences in the chain of consequences caused by the initial cause rather than as intervening causes (probably because we perceive of natural events not as acting, but as acting on situations[66]). Thus the defendant's liability for the consequences of such intervening events is judged according to the principles of remoteness of consequences. On the other hand, liability for the consequences of intervening human action is often treated in terms of causation—did the intervening event break the chain of causation between the initial act of negligence and the ultimate consequences?[67]

It is not easy to work out from the cases exactly what test is to be applied in deciding whether a human act has broken the chain of causation.[68] There is considerable authority for the view that it depends on whether the act was foreseeable by the initial tortfeasor; if so, the chain is not broken and the initial tortfeasor is responsible for the consequences of the intervening act.[69] On the other hand, in *Chapman* v. *Hearse*[70] the High Court said both that foreseeability is not a test of causation and that human action does not break the chain of causation if it is foreseeable. In *Haber* v. *Walker* Smith J. thought that these apparently inconsistent statements were reconcilable.[71] His Honour said that an event will break the chain of causation if it consists either of voluntary human action[72] or of a causally independent event, the conjunction of which with the negligent act being so unlikely as to be termed a coincidence. A foreseeable act of negligence would be neither a coincidence (because not improbable enough)[73] nor voluntary, because a voluntary act, in the sense in which it

---

66 cf. *Rowe* v. *McCartney* [1976] 2 N.S.W.L.R. 72, 82-3 *per* Glass J.A. (dissenting).

67 In most cases it does not matter much whether cases of intervening acts or events are dealt with in terms of causation or remoteness of damage. Some of the cases considered in this section (for example, *Lamb* v. *Camden L.B.C.* [1981] Q.B. 625) were reasoned in terms of remoteness of damage. But Mahoney J.A. of the N.S.W. Court of Appeal is a strong proponent of the causation approach: see, for example, his Honour's judgments in *Nader* v. *Urban Transit Authority* (1988) 2 N.S.W.L.R. 501; *Alexander* v. *Cambridge Credit Corporation* (1987) 9 N.S.W.L.R. 310; *Barnes* v. *Hay* (1988) 12 N.S.W.L.R. 337.

68 An intervening event, to be a cause, must, of course, be a necessary condition of loss: *Robinson* v. *Post Office* [1974] 2 All E.R. 737. As in the case of initial causation, policy can be relevant here: *State Rail Authority of New South Wales* v. *Wiegold* (1991) 25 N.S.W.L.R. 500. See also *Bennett* v. *Minister of Community Welfare* (1992) 107 A.L.R. 617.

69 This is particularly so where the intervening actor is the plaintiff. See e.g. *Mt Isa Mines Ltd* v. *Bates* [1972-3] A.L.R. 635, 638.

70 (1961) 106 C.L.R. 112, 122, 124-5; see also *Mahony* v. *J.K. Kruschich (Demolitions) Pty Ltd* (1985) 59 A.L.R. 722, 725.

71 [1963] V.R. 339, 356.

72 cf. *Havenaar* v. *Havenaar* [1982] 1 N.S.W.L.R. 626.

73 A coincidence might be defined as a combination of events so improbable as to be unforeseeable.

is being used here,[74] is an intentional act—that is, one the consequences of which are intended. By definition, the consequences of a negligent act are, at most, foreseen.

The principle that negligent acts cannot break the chain of causation because they are not intentional is not borne out by the cases.[75] Further, it does not seem correct to say that the reason why intentional acts break the causal chain is that they *are* intentional. For example, in *Lamb* v. *Camden L.B.C.*[76] employees of the council negligently ruptured a water main outside the plaintiff's house, flooding the house and undermining its foundations. The house began to crack and subside causing the tenants in it to leave. The plaintiff was overseas and the house, left vacant, was taken over by squatters who caused further extensive and deliberate damage to it. The plaintiff sought damages from the council, *inter alia* for the damage caused by the squatters. The Court of Appeal held the damage inflicted by the squatters to be irrecoverable because it was too remote; two of the judges reached this conclusion by applying the foreseeability principle. Conversely, intervening intentional acts do not necessarily break the chain of causation provided they are foreseeable.[77]

It would seem, therefore, that the basic test of whether intervening human action breaks the chain of causation is foreseeability: if the action was foreseeable by the initial tortfeasor it does not break the chain of causation; if it was unforeseeable the chain is broken. In theory, non-tortious as well as tortious conduct can break the chain of causation;[78] but non-tortious conduct is less likely to be unforeseeable than tortious conduct. Negligent action (such as negligent medical treatment of symptoms caused by an accident)[79] may be foreseeable, but the more

---

74 But see n. 44 above.

75 e.g. *Neall* v. *Watson* (1960) 34 A.L.J.R. 364 (cf. *Havenaar* v. *Havenaar* [1982] 1 N.S.W.L.R. 626 *per* Glass J.A.); *McKew* v. *Holland and Hannen & Cubitts (Scotland) Ltd* [1969] 3 All E.R. 1621. But this last case can be attacked on two grounds: first, there is other authority for the proposition that foreseeable acts of negligence on the part of the defendant will not normally break the chain of causation: *Mt Isa Mines* v. *Bates* [1972-3] A.L.R. 635 (see also *Wieland* v. *Cyril Lord Carpets Ltd* [1969] 3 All E.R. 1006); and secondly, that the fair way to deal with intervening negligence on the part of the plaintiff is to reduce his damages for contributory negligence, and not to treat him as the sole cause of the loss: cf. *Jacques* v. *Matthews* [1961] S.A.S.R. 205 and *Charlton* v. *Public Trustee for the Northern Territory* (1967) 11 F.L.R. 42. Other examples of negligent acts breaking the chain of causation are *Martin* v. *Isbard* (1946) 48 W.A.L.R. 52 (on which see *Mahony* v. *Kruschich* (1985) 59 A.L.R. 722, 726); *Clarke* v. *Damiani* (1973) 5 S.A.S.R. 427 and *Knightly* v. *Johns* [1982] 1 W.L.R. 349.

76 [1981] Q.B. 625.

77 e.g. *Hird* v. *Gibson* [1974] Qd.R. 14; *Chomentowski* v. *Red Garter Restaurant Pty Ltd* [1970] 92 W.N.(N.S.W.) 1070; *Stansbie* v. *Troman* [1948] 2 K.B. 48; *Ward* v. *Cannock Chase District Council* [1986] 1 W.L.R. 660.

78 See *Knightly* v. *Johns* [1982] 1 W.L.R. 349, 366-7 *per* Stephenson L.J.

79 *Vieira* v. *The Water Board* [1988] Aust. Torts Reports 80-166.

unreasonable[80] it is the more likely it will break the causal chain.[81] It may be expected, too, that an omission would be less likely to break the chain of causation than a positive act,[82] although this is not explicable in terms of foreseeability.

The only exceptions to the foreseeability principle seem to be cases involving causes of action in which recovery does not depend on foreseeability. In cases under fatal accidents legislation it has been held that, as a matter of statutory interpretation, the test of liability for intervening causes is 'direct causal link', not foreseeability. Thus, in *Haber* v. *Walker*[83] the deceased committed suicide while mentally unbalanced as a result of injuries received in an accident caused by the defendant's fault. It was held that since the suicide was not truly voluntary but committed under pressure of mental disturbance, it did not break the chain of causation between the defendant's act and the death. In the tort of deceit, too, the test of liability for consequences is not foreseeability but direct causal link.[84]

The shift from causal to foreseeability principles is well illustrated in cases concerning rescue. In early rescue cases it was held that the rescuer's 'voluntary' action in going to the rescue broke the chain of causation.[85] However, in later cases[86] it was recognized that action taken on the spur of the moment out of a sense of moral duty ought not to be held to be voluntary in the relevant sense. Now the only question is whether the intervention of the rescuer was foreseeable, and as a general principle it is held to be.[87]

What does 'foreseeable' mean in this context? It may be that a distinction has to be drawn between acts of the plaintiff and acts of third parties: there is an argument for saying, especially in cases where the defendant is insured or better able to bear the loss, that he should be liable (subject to apportionment of damages for contributory negligence) provided that the act of the plaintiff was foreseeable as that term is ordinarily understood.[88] But if the plaintiff behaves very unreasonably, his conduct may break the causal chain.[89]

In regard to acts of third parties,[90] there is some authority for the view

80 This appears to mean something like 'unacceptable' or 'outrageous' or 'unexpected'.

81 *Mahony* v. *Kruschich* (1985) 59 A.L.R. 722, 726-7. I am treating the notion of unreasonableness as relevant to foreseeability; but it can be, and often is, treated as an independent factor, so that foreseeable conduct can break the causal chain if it is unreasonable enough (see, for example, *Thorpe Nominees Pty Ltd* v. *Henderson & Lahey* [1988] 2 Qd R. 216). The cases are not clear on how it should be viewed.

82 *O'Brien* v. *Thorpe* [1987] Aust. Torts Reports 69,102 at 69,112 per Derrington J.

83 [1963] V.R. 339. See also *Commonwealth of Australia* v. *Martin* (1985) 59 A.L.R. 439.

84 *Doyle* v. *Olby (Ironmongers) Ltd* [1969] 2 Q.B. 158.

85 e.g. *Evenden* v. *Manning Shire Council* (1929) 30 S.R.(N.S.W.) 52.

86 *Haynes* v. *G. Harwood & Son* [1935] 1 K.B. 146; *Ward* v. *T.E. Hopkins & Son Ltd* [1959] 3 All E.R. 225.

87 *Chapman* v. *Hearse* (1961) 106 C.L.R. 112.

88 *Mt Isa Mines* v. *Bates* [1972-3] A.L.R. 635; *Shirt* v. *Wyong S.C.* [1978] 1 N.S.W.L.R. 631, 644 *per* Glass J.A.; M.A. Millner (1971) 22 *N.I.L.Q.* 168.

89 *McKew* v. *Holland* [1969] 3 All E.R. 1621 (apparently accepted in *Mahony* v. *Kruschich* (1985) 59 A.L.R. 722, 725); *Beard* v. *Richmond* [1987] Aust. Torts Reports 68,991.

90 Such cases are sometimes reasoned in terms of duty of care: see p. 385 above.

that it is not whether the act was foreseeable as a possibility, but whether it was the very kind of thing one would expect to happen.[91] In *Lamb* v. *Camden L.B.C.*[92] this supposed principle received a mixed reception. Lord Denning M.R. thought it inadequate because it would not exclude liability to the very persons whom it was designed to exclude (by Lord Reid who put it forward in the *Dorset Yacht* case[93]), namely faraway property owners. It was very likely that escaped prisoners would do damage a long way from the prison. Oliver L.J. thought that the proper test was ordinary reasonable foreseeability but that when it came to human acts these could often only be described as reasonably foreseeable if they were likely or in some cases almost inevitable. Since in this case it had been found at first instance that the incursion of squatters was unlikely, the damage caused by them was not reasonably foreseeable. Watkins L.J. also held that the test was reasonable foreseeability; but to avoid imposing liability for the acts of the squatters he held that sometimes the test has to be qualified if the intervening act is 'anti-social' and 'criminal'.

In *Thorpe Nominees* v. *Henderson & Lahey*[94] the Queensland Full Court held that the 'very likely' test applied only to the chance that a third party would intervene in the situation in such a way as to affect the plaintiff, and that it did not apply either to the precise part the third party in fact played or to the consequences of his intervention:[95] for example, a defendant could be held liable for the consequences of negligent third-party medical treatment if medical treatment was very likely, and he would not be relieved of liability just because the precise form the treatment took or its consequences were not very likely; he would be relieved of liability only if the precise treatment given or its consequences were not foreseeable as this term is used in the rules of remoteness of damage.[96]

It seems clear, then, that the foreseeability test by itself cannot bear all the weight of deciding when human action breaks the chain of causation. We need to look beneath the formula at the underlying value judgments. Thus in *Lamb* v. *Camden L.B.C.* Lord Denning M.R. decided against the property owner on the ground that there was no good policy reason to charge the depredations of the squatters to council revenue rather than to the insurance company with whom the plaintiff no doubt had a policy covering the damage; and all of the judges were clearly influenced by the fact that the damage done by the squatters was not just ordinary wear and tear but quite deliberate destruction. By contrast, in *Chapman* v.

---

91 *Haynes* v. *Harwood* [1935] 1 K.B. 146; *Home Office* v. *Dorset Yacht Co. Ltd* [1970] A.C. 1004, 1030 *per* Lord Reid; *Bohdal* v. *Streets* [1984] Tas. R. 82.

92 [1981] Q.B. 625. Cf. *Paterson Zochonis Ltd* v. *Merfarken Packaging Ltd* [1983] F.S.R. 273; *P. Perl (Exporters) Ltd* v. *Camden L.B.C.* [1984] Q.B. 342; see also *Candlewood Navigation Corporation Ltd* v. *Mitsui O.S.K. Lines Ltd* [1986] A.C. 1.

93 [1970] A.C. 1004.

94 [1988] 2 Qd R. 216.

95 This may explain *Nader* v. *Urban Transit Authority of N.S.W.* (1985) 2 N.S.W.L.R. 501.

96 cf. *Robinson* v. *Post Office* [1974] 1 W.L.R. 1176.

Hearse[97] where a rescuer was knocked down while helping an injured motorist, the High Court, probably in order not to discourage altruism, was prepared to hold foreseeable (by the driver being helped) not only the intervention of the rescuer but also the negligence of the second driver. It is, perhaps, in cases where one link in the causal chain is the conduct of someone other than the defendant that the evaluative component in the concept of attributive causation becomes most clear. The principle that very 'unreasonable' conduct can break the causal chain invites courts to classify behaviour in a value-laden ways.

II: REMOTENESS OF DAMAGE

A defendant will be liable only for those consequences of which his negligence is the factual and legal cause if they are not too remote.[98] The basic test of remoteness is foreseeability of consequences. In the leading case of *The Wagon Mound (No. 1)*[99] the defendant's employees negligently allowed a large quantity of oil to spill overboard when the ship was taking on furnace oil. The oil caught fire when a piece of molten metal produced by welding operations on the plaintiff's ship fell into the water on to a piece of cotton waste which acted as a wick and set the oil alight, doing great damage to the plaintiff's ship. Since the flashpoint of the oil was 1700F there was no chance of its igniting simply by virtue of being discharged on to the surface of the water. It was held that the damage by fire was not a foreseeable consequence of the negligence of the defendant's employees. The question of whether consequences are foreseeable is a jury question;[100] but in general terms, consequences are foreseeable if they are the result of the occurrence of a risk which the reasonable person would describe as 'real' (even if 'remote') rather than 'far-fetched'.[101] What has to be foreseeable is the type or kind of injury suffered[102] rather than its exact

---

97 (1961) 106 C.L.R. 112.

98 Deane J. would refer to rules of remoteness as principles of causal proximity: *Jaensch* v. *Coffey* (1984-5) 155 C.L.R. 549, 584-5. Rules of remoteness of damage are chiefly concerned with cases in which the damage suffered is of an unexpected or unusual nature, or where it occurs in a surprising or extraordinary way. But damage may be too remote just because it is too separated in time from the defendant's tort, or because the causal chain between the damage to the tort has many links (e.g. *Meah* v. *McCreamer* (No. 2) [1986] 1 All E.R. 943; but contrast *Versic* v. *Connors* (1969) 90 W.N.(Pt.1) (N.S.W.) 33; and see p. 476 below).

99 *Overseas Tankship (U.K.) Ltd* v. *Morts Dock & Engineering Co. Ltd, The Wagon Mound (No.1)* [1961] A.C. 388; R.W.M. Dias [1962] *C.L.J.* 178; A.M. Honoré (1961) 39 Can. B.R. 267.

100 *Richards* v. *State of Victoria* [1969] V.R. 136, 146; *Stephenson* v. *Waite Tileman Ltd* [1973] 1 N.Z.L.R. 152.

101 *Overseas Tankship (U.K.) Ltd* v. *Miller Steamship Co. Pty Ltd, The Wagon Mound (No. 2)* [1967] 1 A.C. 617 (*Wagon Mound (No.1)* reversed on different findings of fact; but discussion mainly in terms of breach not remoteness.)

102 *Wagon Mound (No. 1)* [1961] A.C. 388; *Chapman* v. *Hearse* (1961) 106 C.L.R. 112.

extent[103] or manner or occurrence.[104] The general approach of the courts is that 'kinds of injury' ought to be defined broadly: physical injury and nervous shock are often treated as kinds of injury, and the details of the injury or shock are subsumed under 'extent' or 'manner of occurrence'. We will return to this point below. The principle that the extent of the injury need not be foreseeable has two aspects. One is usually referred to as the 'thin-skull rule'.

1. THE THIN-SKULL RULE

An early statement of this rule is that of Kennedy J. in *Dulieu* v. *White & Sons*:

> If a man is negligently run over or otherwise negligently injured in his body, it is no answer to the sufferer's claim for damages that he would have suffered less injury, or no injury at all, if he had not had an unusually thin skull or an unusually weak heart.[105]

Another obvious example of physical hypersensitivity is haemophilia. The thin-skull rule is often put in terms that the defendant must take his victim as he finds him. We have already seen that while the fact that the plaintiff is hypersensitive may prevent there being a breach of duty because a defendant is not, by and large, expected to take any greater precautions to protect the hypersensitive than to protect the normal plaintiff,[106] if the defendant has breached a duty owed to the plaintiff he cannot complain if, because of his hypersensitivity, the plaintiff suffers more than a normal plaintiff would.[107]

A form of the thin-skull rule applies in two types of case: where the plaintiff suffers from some hypersensitivity which pre-dated or pre-existed the accident; and where the accident induces an abnormal sensitivity or susceptibility to further injury.

(a) Pre-existing susceptibility or sensitivity An example of the first type of case is *Smith* v. *Leech Brain & Co.*[108] where the plaintiff suffered a burn on the lip from which developed a malignant cancer which killed him. The risk of a burn was foreseeable in the ordinary course of the plaintiff's work as a galvanizer, but the risk of cancer, which developed in tissue which was in a pre-malignant condition, was not. The defendant was held liable for all the consequences of the burn, including the cancer.

---

103 *Smith* v. *Leech Brain & Co. Ltd* [1952] 2 Q.B. 405; *Stephenson* v. *Waite Tileman* [1973] 1 N.Z.L.R. 152; *Beavis* v. *Apthorpe* (1964) 80 W.N. (N.S.W.) 852.

104 *Hughes* v. *Lord Advocate* [1963] 2 Q.B. 405; *Doughty* v. *Turner Manufacturing Co. Ltd* [1964] 1 Q.B. 518.

105 [1901] 2 K.B. 669, 679. See generally P.J. Rowe (1977) 40 *M.L.R.* 377.

106 See p. 342 above.

107 Unless, perhaps, he was aware of the plaintiff's susceptibility: *Paris* v. *Stepney B.C.* [1951] A.C. 367.

108 [1952] 2 Q.B. 405; cf. *Warren* v. *Scrutton's Ltd* [1962] 1 Lloyd's Rep. 497; *Robinson* v. *P.O.* [1974] 2 All E.R. 737.

Viewed in terms of causation principles, this decision may appear troubling: if a person is more than usually susceptible to developing a particular condition, the most that can be said may be that but for the defendant's tort, the plaintiff would not have contracted the condition *at the time he did*, but that it was quite likely that even if the defendant's tort had not occurred, he would still have contracted the condition at some time. In this light, it may seem unfair that the defendant should have to pay damages representing the whole of the plaintiff's loss. So, in *Smith* v. *Leech Brain* itself, the plaintiff's damages were reduced to reflect the chance that he might have contracted cancer at some time even if the defendant had not injured him.[109] Alternatively, the defendant's act could be treated as merely having accelerated the condition suffered by the plaintiff, in which case the defendant would be required to pay damages only in respect of the period of acceleration.[110]

The principle that the defendant must take the victim as found apparently applies as much to psychological harm as to physical.[111] To what extent the principle applies to economic loss is not so clear. In *Owners of Dredger Liesbosch* v. *Owners of Steamship Edison*[112] the plaintiff's dredge was sunk by the negligence of the defendants. Because of lack of funds the plaintiffs could not afford to buy a new dredge immediately but only to hire a replacement. The total costs associated with hiring were greater than would have been the cost of buying a new dredge. The House of Lords held that the plaintiff could not recover damages for the loss attributable to its impecuniosity. The decision is open to two interpretations. One is that the plaintiff's impecuniosity was an 'extrinsic' factor which broke the causal chain between the defendant's negligence and the plaintiff's loss;[113] the other is that the principle that a defendant must take the victim as found does not apply to business losses. This decision perhaps reflects the law's unwillingness to compensate as freely for economic loss as for other types of injury.

---

109 J. Stapleton (1988) 104 *L.Q.R.* 389, 397-8. Cf. *Wilson* v. *Peisley* (1975) 7 A.L.R. 571 esp. Barwick C.J. at 571; *Western Australia* v. *Watson* [1990] W.A.R. 248, 312. See also *Meah* v. *McCreamer* [1985] 1 All E.R. 367 esp. 383b-e and p. 452 above.

110 See p. 459 above; *Negretto* v. *Sayers* [1963] S.A.S.R. 313.

111 *Malcolm* v. *Broadhurst* [1970] 3 All E.R. 508; *Stephenson* v. *Waite Tileman* [1973] 1 N.Z.L.R. 152; *Hoffmeuller* v. *Commonwealth* (1981) 54 F.L.R. 48; *Brice* v. *Brown* [1984] 1 All E.R. 997; *Meah* v. *McCreamer (No. 2)* [1986] 1 All E.R. 943, 946a-b. According to McHugh J.A. in *Nader* v. *Urban Transit Authority of N.S.W.* (1985 2 N.S.W.L.R. 501, 536-7), a defendant must take the victim as found, not only in respect of physical and psychological characteristics but also in respect of life circumstances (in that case the relevant circumstance was the fact that the plaintiff had over-protective parents).

112 [1933] A.C. 449; applied in *Copeland* v. *Stanthorpe S.C.* [1941] St.R.Qd. 86 and *Ramwade Ltd* v. *Emson & Co. Ltd* [1987] R.T.R. 72; *Companieria Financeria 'Soleada' S.A.* v. *Harmoor Tanker Corporation Inc.* [1981] 1 W.L.R. 274. *Liesbosch* was decided before *Wagon Mound (No. 1)* which decided that the test of remoteness was foreseeability. Before this case the remoteness rule was that laid down in *Re Polemis & Furness, Withy & Co. Ltd* [1921] 3 K.B. 560, namely direct causal link. The decision can be explained in modern terms by syaing that it was not foreseeable that the plaintiff would be put in the difficulties it was by the defendant's tort: *Perry* v. *Sidney Phillips & Son* [1982] 1 W.L.R. 1297, 1307 *per* Kerr L.J.

113 This ground was preferred by Lord Wright in *The Liesbosch* A.C. 449, 460.

On the other hand, in *Martindale* v. *Duncan*[114] it was held that a taxi driver who could not afford to pay to have his taxi repaired was justified in waiting until he had an authorization from an insurer for the repairs, and could recover for profits lost in the period before the repairs were begun. In *Perry* v. *Phillips*[115] the plaintiff was induced by a negligently prepared surveyor's report to purchase a house which needed major repairs. The repairs had not been done by the date of the trial and the plaintiff claimed, *inter alia,* damages for anxiety and inconvenience. The defendant argued that since the only reason why the repairs had not been done sooner was the plaintiff's lack of funds, the *Liesbosch* principle prevented his recovering such damages. Lord Denning M.R. met this argument by saying that, in the circumstances, the anxiety and inconvenience was a foreseeable result of the defendant's negligence and so damages for the effects of this on the plaintiff were recoverable. His Lordship also said that the *Liesbosch* was to be restricted to its own facts, but it is not entirely clear what this means for the future of the principle embodied in it. The *Liesbosch* was clearly a very different case from *Perry* v. *Phillips,* with which it is perhaps reconcilable by saying that where the plaintiff is an individual or a small business rather than a substantial business concern, impecuniosity and its associated effects are foreseeable. This explanation would fit *Martindale* v. *Duncan*[116] and it is supported by a recent New Zealand decision in which Cooke J. stressed that it was foreseeable that a *family* company would lack the resources to meet an unexpected major financial crisis.[117]

(b) Consequential susceptibility or sensitivity The other type of case in which a form of the thin-skull rule operates is where the injury or damage inflicted by the defendant also renders the plaintiff susceptible to further injury or damage. In some cases the further damage occurs as a result of the combination of some causally independent factor with the result of the defendant's act. For example, in *Stephenson* v. *Waite Tileman Ltd*[118] one hypothesis as to how the plaintiff reached his ultimate state was that a virus had entered his body through a cut inflicted by the defendant's negligence. Although these cases are factually rather different from the pre-existing hypersensitivity cases, they are similar in that the consequences of the defendant's act of negligence are much more serious than in the normal run of cases. Thus the principle applies here, too, that provided the kind of damage inflicted was foreseeable the defendant is

---

114 [1973] 2 All E.R. 355.

115 [1982] 1 W.L.R. 1297; but contrast *Westwood* v. *Cordwell* [1983] 1 Qd.R. 276.

116 And the *Harmoor Tanker* decision [1981] 1 W.L.R. 274. See also *Fox* v. *Wood* (1981) 55 A.L.J.R. 562. A difficult case which throws doubt on the validity of the *Liesbosch* principle is *Dodd Properties Ltd* v. *Canterbury City Council* [1980] 1 W.L.R. 433.

117 *Attorney-General* v. *Geothermal Produce N.Z. Ltd* [1987] 2 N.Z.L.R. 248.

118 [1973] 1 N.Z.L.R. 152; cf. *Neall* v. *Watson* (1960-1) 34 A.L.J.R. 364. See also *Beavis* v. *Apthorpe* (1964) 80 W.N.(N.S.W.) 852.

liable for the full extent of the loss suffered. The principle also applies to economic loss.[119]

In other cases the defendant's negligence renders the plaintiff more prone to accidents which happen without the intervention of any causally independent factor. For example, in *Pyne* v. *Wilkenfeld*[120] the plaintiff was injured in a car accident due to the defendant's negligence. This made it necessary for her to wear a cervical collar which restricted her vision so she could not see immediately in front of her. As a result the plaintiff fell on a footpath. It was held that the defendant was responsible for the second accident.

2. Extent of Harm

This second aspect of the principle that only the type or kind of injury and not its exact extent has to be foreseeable can easily be illustrated. In *Richards* v. *State of Victoria*[121] a boy received a blow on the temple in a classroom fight. The blow ruptured an artery from which blood escaped causing pressure on the brain resulting in spastic paralysis. It was held to be foreseeable that such a blow might cause concussion or contusion of the brain and that the defendant could not limit his liability simply because the injuries turned out to be more grave than could be expected. This principle also applies to property damage.[122]

3. Manner of Occurrence

Nor is it necessary that the exact manner in which the injury occurs be foreseeable. In *Hughes* v. *Lord Advocate*[123] the plaintiff was severely burned when he knocked a paraffin lamp into a manhole. It was foreseeable that if paraffin lamps were left lying around children might play with them and in the process be burned. But what happened was that the breaking of the lamp set off a very large explosion which knocked the plaintiff into the manhole from which flames were leaping ten metres into the air. It was held that injury by fire was foreseeable and it was irrelevant that the exact manner the injury occurred and its extent were unforeseeable. On the other hand, in *Doughty* v. *Turner Manufacturing Co. Ltd*[124] the plaintiff was injured when an asbestos cover fell into a cauldron of molten liquid. The cover reacted with the liquid to cause an eruption of the liquid. The state of knowledge at that time gave no reason to expect such an occurrence. It was argued that it was foreseeable that the

---

119 *Taupo B.C.* v. *Birnie* [1978] 2 N.Z.L.R. 397; cf. *Fox* v. *Wood* (1981) 55 A.L.J.R. 562; *Clearlite Holdings Ltd* v. *Auckland City Corporation* [1976] N.Z.L.R. 729; *Egan* v. *State Transport Authority* (1982) 31 S.A.S.R. 481.

120 (1981) 26 S.A.S.R. 441; cf. *Wieland* v. *Cyril Lord Carpets Ltd* [1969] 3 All E.R. 1006. See also *Jacques* v. *Matthews* [1961] S.A.S.R. 205.

121 [1969] V.R. 136. See also *Bradford* v. *Robinson Rentals Ltd* [1967] 1 All E.R. 267.

122 *Vacwell Engineering Co. Ltd* v. *B.D.H. Chemicals Ltd* [1971] 1 Q.B. 88.

123 [1963] A.C. 837.

124 [1964] 1 Q.B. 518. See also *Tremain* v. *Pike* [1969] 3 All E.R. 1303.

plaintiff might be injured by splashing and that what happened was just a variant of injury by splashing. But the court held that it was a quite different and unforeseeable type of injury.

4. Foreseeability in Perspective

It is clear from the foregoing that it is only in a very qualified sense that foreseeability is the test of remoteness of damage.[125] There are many situations in which damage is recoverable even though it is unforeseeable, provided it was caused by the defendant's negligence—in the sense that the defendant's negligence was a necessary condition of the damage occurring. It is possible to reconcile the above rules with the foreseeability principle by saying that the reasonable person ought to foresee that all sorts of people, including the highly susceptible, exist in the world and that the consequences of even the simplest accident are unpredictable.[126] But such reasoning removes the notion of foreseeability from the realm of practical calculation to the realm of purely theoretical possibilities.

In the end, it is a matter of policy how far we are prepared to trace the consequences of the defendant's negligence for the purpose of fixing him with liability for them.[127] In *The Wagon Mound (No. 1)*[128] one of the main arguments in favour of foreseeability as the test of remoteness was that it was unfair to hold the defendant liable for any consequences other than those which it was negligent of the defendant not to take steps to avoid. Since negligence is failure to guard against foreseeable risks, liability should be imposed only for foreseeable consequences. But the law's concern with fairness to the defendant is rather selective. We have seen many times that the law is prepared to hold defendants to quite unrealistically high standards of care; and we will see that in assessing the plaintiff's damages the law has adopted the principle that the plaintiff should be compensated for 100 per cent of his loss no matter how 'disproportionate' that loss might be to the gravity of the defendant's negligence.

The fact is that while the foreseeability test of remoteness may be a corollary of the fault principle, fault is only one of the factors which the law takes into account in imposing liability. The prevalence of liability insurance has no doubt played an important role in preserving the rules in *Smith* v. *Leech Brain* and *Hughes* v. *Lord Advocate* despite the decision in *Wagon Mound (No. 1)*. The predominant role of tort law in modern society is seen as compensation, not the enforcement of the notion of fault.

---

125 J.G. Merrills (1973) 6 *Ottawa L.R.* 18.

126 *Negretto* v. *Sayers* [1963] S.A.S.R. 313, 318 *per* Chamberlain J.; *Havenaar* v. *Havenaar* [1982] 1 N.S.W.L.R. 626, 631 *per* Glass J.A.

127 Sir R. Cooke [1978] *Camb. L.J.* 288; A.M. Linden [1969] *Can. B.R.* 545.

128 [1961] A.C. 388.

5. THE KIND OF DAMAGE

Perhaps the key concept used to manipulate the rules of remoteness to policy ends is that of the kind or type of damage suffered. There is no analytic way of deciding what type of damage has been suffered. An obvious starting point would be to divide injury into three types—physical, psychological and economic. We have seen that this is the division which the law adopts for the purposes of deciding whether a duty of care is owed. But it is clear that very often a more detailed description of the type of damage is utilized for the purposes of remoteness rules. The easiest cases are probably those where the plaintiff's injury occurs in two distinct stages. In these cases, it would seem, the foreseeability question should be asked in respect of the initial injury. So, in *Smith* v. *Leech Brain*[129] the question was whether a burn on the lip was foreseeable; in *Stephenson* v. *Waite Tileman*[130] the question was whether a cut on the hand was foreseeable; in *Pyne* v. *Wilkenfeld*[131] the question was whether an injury to the neck was foreseeable.

Much harder are cases where the loss is indivisible and the question is how to describe it. For example, in *Doughty* v. *Turner Manufacturing*[132] was the injury caused by splashing (foreseeable) or by an eruption resulting from a chemical reaction (unforeseeable)? A particularly clear illustration of this problem is *Rowe* v. *McCartney*.[133] The plaintiff allowed a friend to drive her car on condition he drove carefully. There was an accident caused by the friend's negligence in which the plaintiff was badly injured and the driver was rendered quadriplegic. As a result, the plaintiff developed a guilt complex for having let the friend drive. The question was whether this psychological condition ought to be classified as nervous shock (foreseeable) or as a guilt neurosis (unforeseeable).[134] A majority of the Court of Appeal opted for the latter classification. Although the judgments contain lengthy discussions of the problem of classification, the result adopted by each judge depends on a simple assertion that the level of abstraction or detail chosen by him to describe the injury is the proper one. The concept of kinds of damage is, once again, one which cannot be defined but only illustrated. A mere assertion that a particular item of damage is of a certain kind is unilluminating unless the value judgments which prompted the classification are made clear.

Underlying the distinction between type of injury on the one hand, and extent or manner of occurrence on the other, is an assumption that the foreseeability question is being asked as at the time of the act of negligence.

---

129 [1952] 2 Q.B. 405.
130 [1973] 1 N.Z.L.R. 152.
131 (1981) 26 S.A.S.R. 441.
132 [1964] 1 Q.B. 518.
133 [1976] 2 N.S.W.L.R. 72.
134 But contrast the obscure explanation of this case given by McHugh J.A. in *Nader* v. *Urban Transit Authority* (1985) 2 N.S.W.L.R. 501, 535-6. In that case a rare psychological condition was treated as a form of a foreseeable kind of loss, namely recognized psychiatric illness (nervous shock).

But not all cases adopt this approach. For example, in *Versic* v. *Connors*[135] the plaintiff's husband was drowned when his truck overturned as a result of the defendant's negligence. It was held that his death was a reasonably foreseeable result of the initial act of negligence. Jacobs J.A. said that the question whether the death was reasonably foreseeable should not be asked in an abstract way: is it foreseeable that a person might be drowned in a suburban street? Rather the question should be asked with reference to the specific events of that day; each step of the chain of events should be taken one by one, and only if, at each step, the next step was unforeseeable would the damage be too remote. So, it was foreseeable that negligent driving might cause another vehicle to overturn; and if this happened the driver of the overturned vehicle might be thrown out; he might end up in the gutter; the gutter might have water flowing in it; and the man might be lying in such a way as to be drowned by the water. Clearly, this technique would be most suited to cases in which an act of negligence sets off a bizarre train of events; and it shows how attenuated the idea of foreseeability becomes as a practical notion if the attempt is made to explain all decisions in terms of it. It might have been better if *Versic* had either been decided differently, or if the decision in favour of the plaintiff had been explained in terms other than foreseeability.

III: THE RELATIONSHIP BETWEEN CAUSATION AND REMOTENESS OF DAMAGE

It is now clear that the principles of attributive causation—both initial and intervening—and the principles of remoteness of damage are concerned with essentially the same issue, namely whether the plaintiff's loss ought to be treated in law as a consequence of the defendant's negligence, of which it is the factual consequence. Why, then, have two sets of principles? Could we not say that the defendant's act is the legal cause of all consequences not too remote in law? There seems no logical reason why we should not have just one unified test of liability for consequences. The explanation for the two concepts, causation and remoteness, seems to be simply that they differ in focus. Causal principles justify a court in denying liability for any of the consequences which follow an act held not to be a cause or intervening cause. On the other hand, remoteness principles allow the court to impose liability for some consequences but not others.

The relationship between causation and remoteness is particularly close in the context of intervening causes. The consequences of intervening causes are always on the same chain of factual causation as the defendant's negligence. It is thus always possible to treat the consequences of an intervening cause as consequences of the initial negligence—it would not have had the effect it did if the defendant had not been negligent. When

---

135 (1969) 90 W.N.(Pt.1)(N.S.W.) 33; cf. *Castellan* v. *Electric Power Transmission Pty Ltd* (1967) 69 S.R.(N.S.W.) 159, 170 and *Haileybury College* v. *Emanuelli* [1983] V.R. 323.

the test of remoteness was direct causal link the question of remoteness and intervening cause were one and the same—consequences were too remote if the causal chain had been broken.[136] When in *The Wagon Mound (No.1)* the test of remoteness was changed to foreseeability the principles of intervening causation were left somewhat out on a limb. Courts in some cases showed an unwillingness to hold defendants liable for intervening human acts which were merely foreseeable. Nevertheless, it now appears that the test of intervening causation is foreseeability. In some cases where the intervening cause is a human act the foreseeability test is applied generously to the plaintiff—for example, in cases of rescue or where the intervening actor is the plaintiff himself. But in other cases, for example where the intervening conduct is deliberate or criminal, the defendant may be held liable only if the conduct was highly likely or even almost inevitable. Another way of putting this is to say that in some cases, where the exact manner of occurrence of damage includes an intervening human act, not only must the kind of damage be foreseeable; the way it occurred—that is, via the medium of intervening human action—must also be foreseeable or even highly likely.

IV: FORESEEABILITY AS A TEST OF STANDARD OF CARE AND REMOTENESS

We have seen that duty and standard of care overlap to the extent that they both depend on the notion of foreseeability of risk of injury to the plaintiff. We have also seen that foreseeability plays a central role in questions of remoteness. This would suggest that there is a degree of overlap here as well. The reasoning in *The Wagon Mound (No. 1)* supports this view. If a defendant is to be held liable only for those consequences which make his act negligent, then surely there is no reason to ask 'Was he negligent?' and to ask 'In respect of which consequences is he to be made liable?' for the latter question must have been answered in the course of answering the former. A good illustration of the point is *Doughty* v. *Turner Manufacturing Co.*[137] There it was held that the eruption of the molten liquid was an unforeseeable consequence of the falling of the asbestos cover into the vat. But it was also held that since no one knew that the asbestos cover would react as it did, the defendant had not been negligent in not taking precautions to prevent it falling in. They might have been negligent in not taking precautions to prevent it falling in if this created a risk of splashing, but since it probably did not, they had not been negligent in this respect either.

On the other hand, we have seen that the rules of remoteness allow recovery for much damage that is unforeseeable. It is thus clear that the overlap between standard of care and remoteness principles cannot be complete. The relationship between them is perhaps best put by saying

136 *The Oropesa* [1943] P. 32; *The Liesbosch* [1933] A.C. 449.
137 [1964] 1 Q.B. 518.

that a defendant could not be held liable in negligence if all the damage inflicted by his acts was unforeseeable; but if some of the damage inflicted was unforeseeable then he might be liable, and not only to the extent of the foreseeable damage but also for some unforeseeable damage.

V: FORESEEABILITY AS A TEST OF DUTY, BREACH AND REMOTENESS

Because the factor of foreseeability is common in each of the elements of the tort there is a great deal of overlap between them. Often exactly the same issue can be decided in terms of different elements of the tort. For example in *Chapman* v. *Hearse*[138] it is extremely difficult to disentangle questions of duty, causation and remoteness. This interchangeability of the elements of the tort led Denning L.J. in *Roe* v. *Minister of Health* to say that instead of asking three questions it would in many cases be simpler to ask one—namely, was the injury suffered within the risk which the defendant ought to have guarded against?[139] Why, then, does the law continue to divide the tort into three elements as if each had an independent role to play? There has been a lot of academic discussion of this question as it relates to duty and standard of care. Several writers have taken the view that the duty concept is superfluous, a 'fifth wheel on the coach' incapable of sound analysis.[140] By the same token, there are very many judicial pronouncements to the effect that the duty concept is an essential part of the tort.[141] A number of arguments against the duty concept have been put forward and only a few will be considered here.

Perhaps the oldest argument against the duty concept is that it is tautologous with standard of care because both depend on the notion of a foreseeable risk of injury to the plaintiff. This, as we have seen, is true to an extent, but it is only part of the truth. The duty concept is used not only to give effect to foreseeability arguments but also to give effect to a variety of relationship, proximity and policy arguments.[142] Again, although foreseeability figures in questions of standard of care, so do issues of proximity of relationship, probability and seriousness of risk, cost of precautions and social utility. Finally, remoteness is by no means just a matter of foreseeability, although the policy issues at work here which dictate liability for unforeseeable damage have not often been articulated. So perhaps the simplest reason why the three elements survive as separate entities is that they do have separate characteristics even though they share the feature of foreseeability.

138 (1961) 106 C.L.R. 112.

139 [1954] 2 Q.B. 66, 85. See also Glanville Williams (1961) 71 *L.Q.R.* 179 and *March* v. *Stramare* (1991) 171 C.L.R. 506, 535-6 *per* McHugh J.

140 W.W. Buckland (1935) 51 *L.Q.R.* 637, 639. See also P.H. Winfield (1934) 34 *Columbia L.R.* 41 and *Atiyah's Accidents* Ch. 3. The main defender of the duty concept is F.H. Lawson (1947) 22 *Tulane L.R.* 111.

141 *Hedley Byrne* v. *Heller* [1964] A.C. 465 made it clear that in at least some cases the plaintiff, to succeed, would have to address positive argument to the question of duty.

142 C.R. Symmons (1971) 34 *M.L.R.* 394 and 528.

Another argument against the concept of duty is that it is 'simply co-extensive with the boundaries of liability once negligence in fact and damage in fact have been shown'.[143] This argument recommends that courts should state conditions of liability rather than stating that the defendant owed a duty and *therefore* that he is liable. The assumption underlying this seems to be that whereas duty embodies policy arguments which define the scope of liability, negligence and damage are factual concepts. But we have seen that this is far from the truth. The idea of negligence is itself value-laden, as are the concepts of causation and remoteness of damage. If we were to do away with all concepts which give expression to policy arguments we would, as Lord Denning often recommends, simply ask as a matter of policy whether the defendant ought to be liable. So if we are prepared to keep the value-laden concepts of causation, damage-not-too-remote-in-law and the objectively determined standard of reasonable care, why not keep the duty concept as well? The main advantage of the elements of the tort, in this view, is that they help to channel and categorize the information relevant to liability in a way which makes it manageable. The elements of the tort are useful organizing categories. They enable us to make sense of a mass of facts and relevant value judgments and to give an explanation of why a case was decided in the way it was. It is useful to be able to distinguish between reasons for decision which concern the relationship between the parties (duty), the nature of the defendant's conduct (standard of care) and the nature and extent of the damage inflicted (remoteness). The fact that all these considerations together add up to liability or no liability is no particular reason for eliminating the categories if they help in understanding and rationalizing results, which is, after all, the only function of any legal concept or category.

On the other hand, we should not fall into the opposite error of arguing in favour of the duty concept that there are matters of policy, such as those relating to omissions, purely economic loss and nervous shock, which dictate limitations on liability for negligent conduct which are expressed in terms of duty and for which no other suitable repository has been found. This does not show that duty is a necessary concept because the fact is that no one has ever thought it worthwhile to attempt to restate the law of negligence without recourse to the concept of duty. The argument for the duty concept, as for any other legal concept, must be that it is a useful tool of exposition and explanation; it cannot be that the concept is necessary.

A final argument against duty which is worth noting says that the duty concept is unnecessary because other torts manage without it.[144] For example, the tort of defamation has no separate element of a duty not to defame. This argument simply points out again that the duty concept is not necessary. But there is a good explanation of why it is more appropriate in the tort of negligence than in the tort of defamation: whereas the latter tort is designed primarily to protect the plaintiff's *rights,* the tort of

143 *Atiyah's Accidents* at p. 61.
144 ibid.

negligence focuses primarily on the defendant's *conduct* and asks whether it reached a particular standard. Standards of conduct are typically couched in the language of duty.

In summary, then, we can say that the elements of the tort of negligence are only useful to the extent that they help to explain and rationalize the decisions the courts reach. To the extent that they overlap, they are not very useful; to the extent that courts can, by the choice of concept, manipulate the result of a case they hide rather than explain what is done; to the extent that concepts are used to mask or as a substitute for value judgments they are a hindrance to good decisions and sound understanding. But if the elements of the tort are just used, metaphorically, as baskets in which to put principles and policies which relate to the same aspect of the case—the relationship of the parties, the required standard of conduct, the nature of the damage—they can assist rather than hinder analysis.

So far as foreseeability is concerned, it would seem to be quite unnecessary to ask the foreseeability question three times. In many cases the only necessary question is whether there was a foreseeable risk of the kind of injury suffered to a person of the same general class as the plaintiff. In some cases, for example cases of purely economic loss, it may be necessary to ask a different foreseeability question about—that is, apply a different foreseeability test to—the damage and the plaintiff: was the kind of damage foreseeable? was the plaintiff specifically or individually foreseeable? But it must be said that it is difficult to find cases in which the courts actually ask the foreseeability question more times than is necessary. The theoretical excess of foreseeability categories is dealt with in practice simply by eliminating some of the categories. What does happen is that the same sort of question is sometimes dealt with in one way, for example as a duty question, and at other times in another way, for example as a breach question. This can lead to confusion unless one is aware of the difficulty.

12

THE ASSESSMENT OF DAMAGES

We have already dealt in Chapter 7 with certain aspects of the assessment of damages in respect of intentional torts. In this chapter we will consider the assessment of damages for personal injuries, for loss arising out of the death of or injury to a person other than the plaintiff, for physical damage to chattels and land, and for certain interferences with economic interests. The principles discussed are relevant not only to actions in negligence but also to any tort action in which damages are sought for injury, damage or loss of any of the types discussed in this chapter.

I: TWO BASIC PRINCIPLES

1. THE ONCE-FOR-ALL RULE

In respect of the sorts of tortious injuries we will be considering in this chapter the plaintiff's cause of action for damages[1] is not complete until he has suffered actionable damage.[2] Once the damage has been suffered the cause of action crystallizes, as it were, and the plaintiff's damages are, with qualifications, assessed with reference to the date when the damage was inflicted. So if a plaintiff is injured in a car accident, damages are to be assessed with reference to the date of the accident. Furthermore, the common law rule is that once the damages have been assessed that is the end of the matter: even if the plaintiff's condition deteriorates much more than was anticipated at the time of trial and than was allowed for in the assessment of damages, the plaintiff cannot come back to the court and ask for more damages for injury inflicted by the same tortious act. Only if

1 'Damages' means the sum of money payable by the defendant to the plaintiff. The standard Australian work is H. Luntz *Assessment of Damages for Personal Injury and Death* (3rd edn, Sydney, 1990).

2 The meaning of the word 'damage' is by no means straightforward: J. Stapleton (1988) 104 *L.Q.R.* 213 and 389.

the defendant has committed a further tort against the plaintiff giving a fresh cause of action can the plaintiff bring another action. The major exception to this principle is the tort of nuisance, which is a continuing tort. For example, if a defendant creates a nuisance by emitting smoke or smells from its factory the plaintiff is entitled to seek damages in respect of every particular emission; he is not limited to a single award of damages to cover all emissions past and future.[3]

The once-for-all rule has very important consequences. The first is that where the plaintiff's injury has effects which will continue into the future (for example, continuing income loss, or pain and suffering) the court has to assess the appropriate amount of damages for that future loss before it occurs. This, as we will see, involves a great deal of speculation and uncertainty. Secondly, the damages awarded must be in a single lump sum. At common law, the court has no power to order the defendant to make periodical payments to the plaintiff. The first of these problems can only be fully solved by a system under which compensation takes the form of *reviewable* periodical payments; although a partial solution is to allow a first lump sum award to be followed some time later by an application for a further lump sum award.[4] But in respect of continuing economic losses in serious cases, periodical payments have considerable advantages over lump sums awards even if they are not reviewable.[5] A power to award periodical payments in motor accident cases has existed in Western Australia since 1966,[6] but it appears to be used very rarely, if at all. An important development of the last few years has been the use of 'structured settlements'[7] in serious cases which are settled out of court (as the vast majority of personal injury actions are). Under the typical structured settlement an agreed lump sum of damages is used by the insurance company which pays it to buy an annuity from a life insurer, the proceeds of which provide the plaintiff with periodical payments for an agreed period. Structured settlements are still rare in Australia, but the value of 'structuring' has been recognized in New South Wales, where, in motor and work accident cases, the court has power to order that the plaintiff's compensation be provided in periodical form.[8] But in the large majority of personal injury cases dealt with by the tort system, damages and settlements will continue to take the form of a once-for-all lump sum.

---

3 *Fetter* v. *Beal* (1701) Ld. Raym. 339; (1701) 12 Mod. 542.

4 Supreme Court Act 1981 (U.K.), s.32A; Supreme Court Act 1935 (S.A.), s.30b (which confers power to enter judgment on liability and leave assessment of damages until later, and to make an award of interim damages which may be in periodical form). See Luntz op. cit. pp. 31-4; N.S.W.L.R.C. Discussion Paper No. 25 (1992).

5 For a thorough discussion see Luntz op. cit. pp. 12-35.

6 ibid., pp. 29-31.

7 ibid., pp. 498-50.

8 Motor Accidents Act 1988 s.81; Workers Compensation Act 1987 s.151Q. See also Law Reform Commission of Tasmania Report No. 52 (1987), recommendations 1-8; and Report No. 67 (1991).

2. THE COMPENSATION PRINCIPLE

The basic function of the award of damages in a tort action is to compensate the plaintiff for his loss; the plaintiff is entitled to *restitutio in integrum*, that is, to be put in the position he would have been in had the tort not been committed.[9] Thus the common law imposes no ceilings[10] or thresholds[11] on the amount of damages awarded; and the defendant cannot complain if the plaintiff is a millionaire rather than a pauper—he must pay the plaintiff for the full extent of the loss however rich or poor the plaintiff might be.

The *restitutio* principle differs in its significance depending on the type of loss to which it is applied. The principle applies in its most straightforward way to pre-trial pecuniary (or 'economic') losses such as hospital and medical expenses or loss of income or profits. These losses can usually be quantified quite accurately in money terms. The application of the principle is more difficult in relation to future pecuniary losses, such as future loss of income or profits, or future nursing expenses. Since the award of damages is a once-for-all lump sum there are several sources of possible inaccuracy in putting a figure to what the plaintiff has lost. First, suppose that there is a reasonably quantifiable chance that at some time in the future the plaintiff will suffer a further misfortune as a result of the original injuries; or that there is a reasonably quantifiable chance that some further misfortune which has overtaken the plaintiff as a result of the original injuries would have occurred even if the plaintiff had not been injured by the defendant. The way the common law deals with such chances is to award the plaintiff a proportion of the damages which would be awarded if it was certain he would suffer the further misfortune or a proportion of the damages which would be awarded if a further misfortune actually suffered would certainly not have occurred but for the defendant's tort.[12] But such awards of proportional damages are bound either to under-compensate or to over-compensate the plaintiff because the plaintiff either will or will not suffer a further misfortune as a result of the defendant's negligence; or because the defendant's negligence either was or was not the cause of the further misfortune already suffered. Either way, the plaintiff will not receive *restitutio*. There is no way of solving this problem in a once-for-all lump sum system.

Secondly, since the plaintiff has to be put in the position he would have been in had the tort not been committed, the court must speculate about what the plaintiff's financial position would have been had he not been injured. Thirdly, since the court has to award damages for the future, it must speculate as to what the plaintiff's needs in the future will be.

9 *British Transport Commission* v. *Gourley* [1956] A.C. 185; H. McGregor (1965) 28 *M.L.R.* 629.

10 For example, that the plaintiff may recover a maximum of $X or may only recover Y% of the loss. But, as we will see later, in personal injury cases the courts do attempt to achieve as high a degree of consistency as possible (in terms of the severity of the injuries suffered) in the amounts awarded for non-pecuniary loss.

11 For example, that the plaintiff must bear the first $X of the loss.

12 *Malec* v. *J.C. Hutton Pty Ltd* (1990) 169 C.L.R. 638. But see *White* v. *Thiess Dampier Mitsui Coal Pty Ltd* [1991] 1 Qd.R. 97.

Fourthly, the law requires the court to discount the sum arrived at to take account of 'the vicissitudes of life', that is, to take account of the fact that even if the defendant had not injured the plaintiff, the latter might in the ordinary course of things have suffered income loss, for example, as a result of accident or unemployment. Fifthly, to the extent that the court takes account of the impact of future inflation or taxation on the plaintiff's award it will have to speculate about inflation and tax rates. All these factors create the possibility of inaccuracy which may be very considerable in some cases.

The application of the *restitutio* principle is even more problematic in relation to non-pecuniary losses such as pain and suffering and loss of the amenities of life. Here, most would agree that there is no possibility, even in theory, of expressing these losses in money terms, let alone with any semblance of 'accuracy'. In this context the *restitutio* principle gets watered down to something like 'fair recompense'.[13] These difficulties in applying the *restitutio* principle have produced the idea that although compensation must be 'full' it must also be 'fair' to the defendant; full so far as assessment in money terms is possible, fair to the extent that any money value is seen as arbitrary.[14] Moderation must be exercised in assessing damages for non-pecuniary losses because, since there is no rational relationship between the award and the loss, the court might easily be led to express its sympathy for the plaintiff in such an award, ignoring the rights of the defendant to fair treatment.[15]

As is noted later, the *restitutio* principle has been considerably modified by statute in several jurisdictions in recent years, particularly in respect of road and work accident cases (which represent the vast majority of tort actions) and particularly in relation to damages for non-pecuniary loss. Both thresholds and ceilings have been imposed with the aims of reducing the amount paid in tort compensation and, consequently, of keeping down insurance premiums. In relation to damages for non-pecuniary loss, another aim of some of the relevant provisions has been to promote consistency of awards in comparable cases. But the provisions vary considerably from one jurisdiction to another, and the result is a complex patchwork, more the result of local political expediencies than of any discernible common principles.[16] Some of the provisions also present difficult issues of interpretation which are likely to generate much litigation. Uniform and well-drafted legislation is badly needed in this area.

---

13 *Sharman* v. *Evans* (1977) 13 A.L.R. 59, 75 *per* Gibbs & Stephen JJ.

14 *Foulds* v. *Roach* (1955) 72 W.N.(N.S.W.) 105, 106; *Hately* v. *Allport* (1954) 54 S.R.(N.S.W.) 17.

15 *Pamment* v. *Pawelski* (1949) 79 C.L.R. 406, 410-11 *per* Dixon J.

16 A New South Wales bill (see Appendix A to N.S.W.L.R.C. Discussion Paper No. 25) to extend the limitations which apply in road and work accident cases to all personal injury cases is, at the time of writing (October, 1992), in limbo. So, too, is a bill designed to limit damages for economic loss in professional liability cases.

II: ASSESSMENT OF DAMAGES: GENERAL MATTERS

1. Division into Pre- and Post-trial

In cases where the loss to be assessed occurs both before and after the trial (for example, continuing income loss) the damages awarded may be divided into pre-trial and post-trial components. In strict theory the plaintiff's loss is one and indivisible; it accrues at the date of the accident (or the death in a fatal accident action) and should be assessed with reference to that date. In practice, however, the damages are assessed as at the date of trial and are often divided into pre-trial and post-trial components. Pre-trial losses are called 'special' and must be specifically pleaded, quantified and proved by the plaintiff.[17] Post-trial losses are called 'general' and need not be specifically pleaded except if the loss claimed is out of the ordinary.[18] General damages are 'at large'; they are for the tribunal of fact to quantify. There are two main reasons for dividing damages in this way. The first arises from the fact that, in theory, the whole of the plaintiff's loss accrues at the date of the accident and the whole amount should be discounted for vicissitudes. But the court will not speculate when it knows the truth, and so will take account of what actually has happened to the plaintiff up to the date of trial in assessing the damages.[19] Secondly, the award may have to be divided for the purposes of awarding interest, to which we now turn.

2. Interest

In theory the plaintiff has, from the date the cause of action accrues, a right to compensation for the whole of the loss. But in practice the award of compensation will not be made until some time later since there is always a greater or lesser gap of time between the date of the accident and the date of judgment. The plaintiff may therefore be entitled to interest[20] on account of the fact that he has been 'kept out of' or kept waiting for his damages. There is no power at common law to award such interest and not all Australian jurisdictions have statutory provisions giving power to award it.[21] The legislation which does exist is not uniform. In some States the power to award interest is discretionary[22] while in others the court is required to award interest unless good cause is shown why it should not.[23]

---

17 *Ilkiw* v. *Samuels* [1963] 1 W.L.R. 991, 1006 *per* Diplock L.J.; see generally J.A. Jolowicz [1960] *Camb. L.J.* 214; *Paff* v. *Speed* (1961) 105 C.L.R. 549, 558-9 *per* Fullagar J.

18 *Perestrello E. Companhia Limitada* v. *United Paint Co.* [1960] 1 W.L.R. 570.

19 *Jobling* v. *Associated Dairies Ltd* [1982] A.C. 794; *Australian Telecommunications Commission* v. *Parsons* (1985) 59 A.L.R. 535 (fatal accident claim).

20 D.I. Cassidy (1982) 56 *A.L.J.* 213; D. O'Connor (1982) 56 *A.L.J.* 456.

21 Supreme Court Act 1935 (W.A.) s.32 gives the power to award interest, but it does not apply to actions for personal injury or death (ss.(2)(aa)).

22 Supreme Court Act 1970 (N.S.W.), s.94.(1) (see generally *Pheeney* v. *Doolan* [1977] 1 N.S.W.L.R. 601), but note Workers Compensation Act 1987 (N.S.W.) s. 151M and Motor Accidents Act 1988 (N.S.W.) s.73; Common Law Practice Act 1867 (Qld), s.72.

23 Supreme Court Act 1958 (Vic.), s.79A; Supreme Court Act 1935 (S.A.), s.30c.

In Victoria the legislation fixes a maximum rate of interest while in New South Wales, Queensland and South Australia it is up to the court to fix the rate. In South Australia[24] and Victoria interest is to be awarded from the date the action is commenced until the entry of judgment, whereas in Queensland and New South Wales the interest period begins on the date when the cause of action arose.

It might be thought that since the plaintiff has a right at the date the cause of action accrues to compensation for the whole of the loss, he would be entitled to interest on the whole of that amount up till the date of trial. However, in Victoria and South Australia the legislation provides that interest is not to be awarded on compensation for loss or damage to be incurred or suffered after the date of the award. This provision has been interpreted to mean that damages for economic loss awarded in personal injuries actions[25] should be divided into pre- and post-trial components and interest only awarded on the former.[26] It has also been held that even in States without this provision damages both for economic loss[27] and for non-pecuniary loss[28] may be subjected to similar treatment.

3. Delay by the Plaintiff and Mitigation of Loss

As a general principle, the plaintiff in a tort action must take reasonable steps to mitigate (or 'minimize') the loss which he suffers as a result of the defendant's tort.[29] For example, if the defendant damages a profit-earning chattel, the plaintiff should take reasonable steps to repair or replace it (as appropriate) so as to mitigate loss of profits. This so-called 'duty' to mitigate loss is not really such. All it means is that if the plaintiff does not take all reasonable steps to reduce the loss to a minimum then the damages will be calculated as if he had taken those steps. This principle gives the plaintiff a desirable incentive to take steps to help himself. The plaintiff is entitled to recover the costs of mitigating his loss, provided the costs incurred were reasonable.

In personal injury cases, there are two types of situations in which a plaintiff's award of damages may be reduced because of his own conduct. The first situation involves a well-known phenomenon called compensation or litigation neurosis. This condition is generated by uncertainty and anxiety about the outcome of litigation. Since a successful outcome for the plaintiff in monetary terms depends to some extent on the degree of his injuries (entirely so if the dispute is only as to the quantum of damages, not as to liability) this may generate psychological or psychosomatic conditions which may moderate or disappear entirely after the litigation is concluded. If a plaintiff is known to be suffering from

24 But see Wrongs Act 1936 s.35a(1)(k) *re* motor accident cases.
25 Concerning fatal accident claims see p. 511 below.
26 *Thompson* v. *Faraonio* (1979) 24 A.L.R. 1.
27 *Fire and All Risks Insurance Co. Ltd* v. *Callinan* (1978) 52 A.L.J.R. 637.
28 *Cullen* v. *Trappell* (1980) 57 A.L.J.R. 295; cf. *Bennett* v. *Jones* (1977) 2 N.S.W.L.R. 355. *Re* interest on pre-trial non-pecuniary losses see *M.B.P (S.A.) Pty Ltd* v. *Gogic* (1991) 171 C.L.R. 657.
29 See also Workers Compensation Act 1987 (N.S.W.) s.151L.

pre-trial compensation neurosis, it has been held that he is under a duty to take all reasonable steps to bring the litigation to the earliest possible conclusion so as to minimize the effects of the neurosis.[30] Failure to do this may be penalized not only by a reduction of the award of interest[31] but also by a reduction of damages.

Secondly, in some cases it is successfully argued that the plaintiff should have had some treatment or operation as a result of which he could have returned to work (or returned to work sooner) or his total income loss would have been reduced. In such a case, if the operation or treatment would have had its beneficial effect at some date before the trial then the damages will be appropriately reduced from that date to reflect the position he would have been in if he had had the operation.

The onus of proof on issues of mitigation is on the defendant.[32] In personal injury actions, the question is not whether it would have been reasonable to have the treatment, but whether it was unreasonable of the plaintiff to refuse the operation.[33] It appears that this question, which is one of fact, is to be judged objectively but taking into account quite a few of the plaintiff's personal characteristics.[34] Thus, if the plaintiff has a pre-disposition to react neurotically to slight physical trauma, he is entitled to have this taken into account in assessing his response to mitigation opportunities.[35] It is also permissible to consider physical characteristics of the plaintiff which would make failure of the treatment more serious for him than for the normal person; and his ability to understand the advice.[36] It is also relevant to consider whether the plaintiff received conflicting or unanimous medical advice as to: the advisability of the treatment;[37] its chances of success;[38] and the likely degree of disability if the treatment is not administered.[39]

4. Method of Calculation of Damages for Future Losses

Future (that is, post-trial) losses can be divided into two categories: those which are assessed in one lump sum, such as non-pecuniary losses; and those which are assessed on a periodical basis before being reduced to a lump sum, such as loss of earnings or profits. The method for calculating

30 *Buczynski* v. *McDonald* (1971) 1 S.A.S.R. 569; *Bates* v. *Nelson* (1973) 6 S.A.S.R. 149.
31 But concerning interest in motor accident cases in South Australia see Wrongs Act 1936 s.35(1)(k).
32 *Munce* v. *Vindex Tubemakers Pty Ltd* [1974] 2 N.S.W.L.R. 235; *Plenty* v. *Argus* [1975] W.A.R. 155; *Dininis* v. *Kaehne* (1982) 29 S.A.S.R. 118; *Karabatsos* v. *Plastex Industries Pty Ltd* [1981] V.R. 675; *Lorca* v. *Holt's Corrosion Control Pty Ltd* [1981] .Qd.R. 261.
33 *Fazlic* v. *Milingimbi Community Inc.* (1982) 56 A.L.J.R. 211.
34 *Glavonjic* v. *Foster* [1979] V.R. 536; *Lorca* v. *Holt's* [1981] Qd.R. 261; *Hisgrove* v. *Hoffman* (1981) 29 S.A.S.R. 1.
35 *Donjerkovic* v. *Adelaide Steamship Industries Pty Ltd* (1979) 24 S.A.S.R. 347, 361 *per* White J.
36 *Karabatsos* v. *Plastex Industries* [1981] V.R. 675.
37 *Polidori* v. *Staker* (1973) 6 S.A.S.R. 273.
38 *Dininis* v. *Kaehne* (1982) 29 S.A.S.R. 118; *Plenty* v. *Argus* [1975] W.A.R. 155.
39 ibid.

periodical losses is called the multiplier method.[40] The way this method works can be represented by a formula: [(M x T) — V] *x* n%. In this formula, M stands for the multiplicand or net annual loss. In personal injury actions this will be made up of such wages as the plaintiff will lose and such recurrent expenses for medical, hospital and nursing care as he will incur. In fatal accident actions it will be made up of the dependants' loss of support. To the extent that the multiplicand is made up of amounts which would be taxable if they had been received periodically but will not be taxed when received as a lump sum, the multiplicand must be reduced by the amount of the avoided tax liability; otherwise the plaintiff will be over-compensated.[41] The multiplicand is then multiplied by T, which represents the term of the award. In the case of lost earnings this will be the period of the plaintiff's expected working life judged before the accident. In fatal accident claims T will represent the expected period of dependency; for example, in the case of children, up until they are likely to be self-supporting.

From this amount is then deducted V: an allowance for the vicissitudes (or contingencies) of life. Contingencies are the ups-and-downs of life which might have made the plaintiff better or worse off even if he had not suffered injury or damage. Contingencies are chances and risks which cannot be assessed with anything like mathematical accuracy.[42] Although contingencies are, in theory, ups as well as downs, contingencies are always allowed for by a discount, never by an increase of damages.[43] The reduction takes the form either of a lump sum or a percentage of (M x T).[44] The discount for contingencies is designed to take account of changes personal to the plaintiff and not, for example, general movements in wages throughout society. In fatal accident cases there are two relevant sets of contingencies: those affecting the dependants and those which would have affected the deceased's ability to go on providing for his dependants.

In the formula the sign *x* stands for 'discounted by'. This refers to what is usually called the discount for early receipt. The assumption made when awarding lump sum damages is that the plaintiff will invest the

---

40 The multiplier method operates rather differently in England and the following discussion will concern only the Australian method. So care has been taken in reading English cases on this topic: see *Beneke* v. *Franklin* [1975] 1 N.S.W.L.R. 571, 592 *per* Glass J.A.

41 *British Transport Commission* v. *Gourley* [1956] A.C. 185; *re* cases where lump sum taxable see *Shore* v. *Downs Surgical p.l.c.* [1984] 1 All E.R. 7. See also *State Government Insurance Office (Qld)* v. *Bull* (1987) 19 A.T.R. 37.

42 *General Motors-Holdens Pty Ltd* v. *Moularas* (1964) 111 C.L.R. 234, 258 *per* Windeyer J. If the chance of a relevant event occurring in the future can be calculated with some degree of accuracy, then it can be specifically allowed for in the assessment of damages.

43 But see *Black* v. *Motor Vehicle Insurance Trust* [1986] W.A.R. 32.

44 The conventional figure is 15 *per* cent according to Glass J.A. in *Burnicle* v. *Cutelli* [1982] 2 N.S.W.L.R. 26, 30; but see *Elia* v. *O'Byrne* [1990] Aust. Torts Rep. 68,177, 68,180-1.

lump sum.[45] Since the aim of the award is to provide the plaintiff with an amount equal to his net annual loss every year for the term of the award, and since at the end of the term it is usually reckoned that the lump sum should be exhausted, the expectation is that by drawing as the years go by on both interest and capital, the plaintiff will be put in the position he would have been in had the tort not been committed. Tables are available which show the lump sum which would be needed to produce a specified income over a specified period of years at a specified interest rate by exhaustion of both interest and capital. It is easy to see how the amount needed will vary according to the rate of interest which is chosen—the higher the rate of interest, the less will be the lump sum needed to produce a given income. The crucial point is that [(M x T)—V] is calculated as the amount which would be necessary to produce the required income just out of drawings on capital. This amount has, therefore, to be reduced, or discounted, to take account of the fact that it can be invested to produce income as well. The higher the interest rate it is assumed the plaintiff's lump sum will earn, the greater the discount has to be. The calculation of the appropriate interest (or discount) rate is a very complex operation. It requires account to be taken of the fact that the plaintiff's real return on his money is less than the nominal return because of the effects of inflation and taxation on his investment income. The High Court has set the discount rate for personal injury actions at 3 per cent.[46]

III: HEADS OF LOSS IN PERSONAL INJURY ACTIONS

1. Loss of Earning Capacity

The plaintiff is compensated, both in respect of pre-trial and of post-trial loss, for loss of earning capacity, not for loss of earnings as such.[47] Loss of

---

45 In some jurisdictions the cost of managing the damages fund may be awarded if, as a result of the tort, the plaintiff is unable to do this for himself: *Campbell* v. *Nangle* (1985) 40 S.A.S.R. 161 (but contrary rule applies in motor accident cases in S.A.: Wrongs Act 1936 s.35a(1)(f)); *Treonne Wholesale Meats Pty Ltd* v. *Shaheen* (1988) 12 N.S.W.L.R. 522; *Wegert* v. *Dittman* [1988] 2 Qd.R. 228; *Mullins* v. *Duck* [1988] 2 Qd.R. 674; *Farr* v. *Schultz* [1989] 1 W.A.R. 94. King C.J. in *Campbell* v. *Nangle* (at p. 172) goes further and would allow such an award even if the plaintiff's inability to manage his affairs predated the tort; but contrast *Fox* v. *Commissioner for Main Roads* [1988] 1 Qd.R. 120 (fatal accident claim by infant).

46 *Todorovic* v. *Waller* (1982) 150 C.L.R. 402; J.L.R. Davis (1982) 56 *A.L.J.* 168. As to other types of claim see p. 520 below. Statutory rules are: N.S.W.: Motor Accidents Act 1988 s.71 and Workers Compensation Act 1987 s.151J (prescribed rate or 5%); Qld: Common Law Practice Act 1867-1981, s.5 (5%), but *Todorovic* rule applies to fatal accident claims: *Gwydir* v. *Peck* [1983] 1 Qd.R. 351; S.A.: Wrongs Act 1936 s.35a(1)(e) (provision applies only to motor accident cases); Tas.: Common Law (Miscellaneous Actions) Act 1986 s.4 (prescribed rate or 7% in personal injury and death actions); Vic.: Transport Accident Act 1986 s.93(13) (6%); W.A.: Law Reform (Miscellaneous Provisions) Act 1941 s.5(1) (prescribed rate or 6% in personal injury and death actions).

47 e.g. *Paff* v. *Speed* (1961) 105 C.L.R. 549, 566 *per* Windeyer J; P.S. Atiyah (1971) 45 *A.L.J.* 228; M. Tilbury (1982) 14 *U.W.A.L.R.* 469.

earning capacity is compensated for only to the extent that it is likely to cause financial loss.[48] Thus the fact that the plaintiff did not before his accident exercise his earning capacity to the full, or that in the future he would probably not have exercised it at all or to the full, should be taken into account in assessing damages for loss of earning capacity.[49] But it does not follow from this that a plaintiff who has not exercised an alleged earning capacity before the trial may never be awarded damages for loss of the capacity. Most notably, plaintiffs who have not reached working age, or plaintiffs who are of working age but have never been able to find a job, or plaintiffs who have spent most of their adult life as domestic carers but plan to enter the workforce when circumstances allow, would not be disentitled from an award of damages representing the full value of their capacity by the fact that the capacity had never been exercised or not, at any rate, for a very long time, even though by choice.

Where the plaintiff is a young child not yet earning some judges have shown unwillingness to award large sums for future loss of earnings,[50] mainly because of the degree of speculation involved in deciding what the future would have held for the plaintiff. However, this attitude is not universal.[51] But courts often stress the even-more-than-usually imprecise nature of the process of arriving at a figure for damages in such cases.[52] Clearly much will depend on the age of the child: the older the child the more chance that it will be possible to adduce material on which a reasonable estimate of earning potential can be made. In *Connolly* v. *Camden & Islington A.H.A.*[53] Comyn J. said that he could envisage cases other than ones of children who already had careers, for example, as television stars, in which there would be an adequate basis for an award of damages for loss of earning capacity: for example, cases involving the only child of a parent who owns a prosperous business, or the child of a farmer who is able to leave him the estate.

Damages for loss of earning capacity can be awarded for what are called 'the lost years'.[54] If a plaintiff's life expectancy is reduced by the accident he can recover for loss of earnings not only in respect of the remainder of

---

48 *Graham* v. *Baker* (1961) 106 C.L.R. 340. But P does not have to make allowance for increased earnings after the accident: *G.M.H. Ltd* v. *Whetstone* (1988) 50 S.A.S.R. 199. Relevant statutory limitations are: N.S.W.: Workers Compensation Act 1987 ss.151H and 151I (damages for 'economic loss' only recoverable in 'serious' work accident cases and subject to a ceiling); S.A.: Wrongs Act s.35a(1)(d) (threshold on damages for loss of earning capacity in work injury cases); Vic.: Transport Accident Act 1986 s.93 (common law damages for transport accidents only available in 'serious' cases and subject to a threshold and a ceiling); W.A.: Limitation Act 1935 s.38A(3) (ceiling on damages for pecuniary loss in asbestos-related cases).

49 *Mann* v. *Ellbourne* (1973) 8 S.A.S.R. 298.

50 *Gammell* v. *Wilson* [1982] A.C. 27, 71 *per* Lord Edmund-Davies; 78 *per* Lord Scarman; *Pickett* v. *British Rail Engineering Ltd* [1980] A.C. 136, 150 *per* Lord Wilberforce; 153 *per* Lord Salmon.

51 See e.g. *Parker* v. *Parker* [1980] Qd.R. 50; *Masson* v. *Crook* (1979) 22 S.A.S.R. 473; *Hunt* v. *Johnson* [1962] W.A.R. 55; *Croke* v. *Wiseman* [1982] 1 W.L.R. 71.

52 *Martin* v. *Howard* [1983] Tas.R. 188; *D'Ambrosio* v. *De Suza Lima* (1985) 60 A.C.T.R. 18.

53 [1981] 3 All E.R. 250, 256.

54 J.G. Fleming (1962) 50 *California L.R.* 598; J. Mesher & S. Todd (1980) 29 *I.C.L.Q.* 719.

his life but also in respect of the period he would have remained alive and working had he not been injured in such a way as to reduce his life expectancy. However, since the plaintiff will not, by definition, have any living expenses in the lost years, these must be deducted from the damages for loss of earnings.[55] 'Living expenses' appears to mean subsistence costs; it does not include everything except what the plaintiff would have saved.[56] The main function of a lost years award is to enable the plaintiff to make provision for dependants and this end would be defeated if all amounts other than what the plaintiff would have saved were deducted from the damages.[57] But it has also been held that where the plaintiff has no dependants and, by reason of the seriousness of his injuries, will never or is unlikely ever to have any dependants, damages for loss of earnings should not include an amount for hypothetical support of dependants during the lost years.[58] But if it can be said with some certainty that the victim, if his life expectancy had not been shortened, would probably have married and had children, then it may be that his award should be sufficient to cover a substantial proportion of the cost of maintaining a family.[59]

2. Loss of Competitiveness in the Job Market

Compensation may be awarded for the fact that at some time in the future the plaintiff may have difficulty getting a job doing what he is capable of.[60] Under this head what is compensated for is the loss of a chance—that is, the estimated income loss if the risk that the plaintiff will not in the future be able to find a job at all (or one as remunerative as that which he has, or could get, at the date of trial) were to materialize, multiplied by the chance that it will materialize—capitalized to present value.

The fact that the plaintiff's employer has taken him back on to the job at the same wage does not necessarily mean that little or nothing should be awarded under this head. The re-employment may not be secure;[61] the plaintiff may be restricted in his freedom to move job or locality;[62] the employer may not continue to pay him his old wage indefinitely. All these are matters of fact which the plaintiff must prove if he is to be awarded a

55 *Skelton* v. *Collins* (1965-6) 115 C.L.R. 94; *Pickett* v. *British Rail Engineering Ltd* [1980] A.C. 136.

56 *Sharman* v. *Evans* (1977) 138 C.L.R. 563, 579-83 *per* Gibbs & Stephen JJ; *Fitch* v. *Hyde-Cates* (1982) 56 A.L.J.R. 270; see also *Adsett* v. *West* [1983] Q.B. 826.

57 *White* v. *London Transport Executive* [1982] Q.B. 489; *Government Insurance Office of N.S.W.* v. *Johnson* [1981] 2 N.S.W.L.R. 628 *per* Hutley J.A. But contrast *Skelton* v. *Collins* (1965-6) 115 C.L.R. 94, 114 *per* Taylor J.

58 *Croke* v. *Wiseman* [1982] 1 W.L.R. 71, 82 *per* Griffiths L.J., *Kandalla* v. *British European Airways Corporation* [1981] Q.B. 158.

59 *White* v. *London Transport Executive* [1982] Q.B. 489; but see *Harris* v. *Empress Motors Ltd* [1984] 1 W.L.R. 212, 231; perhaps a modest allowance should be made for the chance of having children: *Adsett* v. *West* [1983] Q.B. 826, 854ff.

60 *Moeliker* v. *A. Reyrolle & Co. Ltd* [1976] I.C.R. 253; *O'Brien* v. *Dunsdon* (1965) 39 A.L.J.R. 78; *Smith* v. *Australian Iron and Steel Ltd* (1960) 77 W.N.(N.S.W.) 889.

61 *Azzopardi* v. *Nicholson Bros and Lucas Pty Ltd* [1962] N.S.W.R. 1270.

62 *Breska* v. *Lysaght's Works Pty Ltd* (1957) 74 W.N.(N.S.W.) 168.

substantial sum under this head. There must be 'a real prospect' or 'a reasonable probability'[63] as opposed to a 'mere chance or risk' of unemployment in the future.[64]

3. Cost of Care

Damages for hospital and medical expenses, both pre-trial and post-trial, are awarded as compensation for the cost incurred and not for the need to incur it.[65] So in respect of pre-trial losses the plaintiff must prove either that he has paid out certain amounts or that he is liable to do so. Damages are awarded for the cost of *reasonable* care; so, for example, it may be right to award the cost of care in an institution rather than the (higher) cost of care in the plaintiff's own home, if the extra benefits of the latter do not justify the extra cost.[66] The defendant's liability for hospital and medical expenses is defined by what the hospital or medical practitioner is entitled to charge, not by what he or it claims to be entitled to charge.[67] If there are no legal rules relevant to the proper level of medical or hospital charges, the expenses claimed must be reasonable.[68]

This head covers not only expenses for specifically medical items but also general subsistence and accommodation to the extent that these are provided as part of the medical or nursing care. Where a claim is made for damages for both loss of earning capacity and cost of care it is necessary to avoid overlap between these two heads of damages leading to over-compensation; because, of course, one of the main items on which wages are spent is food and housing. In *Lim Poh Choo* v. *Camden A.H.A.*[69] Lord Scarman suggested that the easiest way to avoid over-compensation was not to deduct living expenses from the claim for loss of earnings, but to deduct the 'domestic element' from the claim for cost of care.[70]

4. Loss of Ability to Perform Housekeeping Functions

This head of damages has been recognized by the English Court of

---

63 See generally *Irkovic* v. *Australian Iron and Steel Ltd* [1963] S.R.(N.S.W.) 598; *Falcon Joinery Co.* v. *Maher* [1963] N.S.W.R. 354

64 *Victorian Stevedoring Pty Ltd* v. *Farlow* [1963] V.R. 594; *Irkovic* v. *Australian Iron and Steel* [1963] S.R.(N.S.W.) 598 especially 612 *per* Else-Mitchell J.

65 *O'Brien* v. *McKean* (1968) 42 A.L.J.R. 223. Such damages will not be awarded at the suit of a spouse against the other spouse when the latter has himself incurred the cost: *Jones* v. *Jones* [1982] Tas.S.R. 282.

66 *Farr* v. *Schultz* [1989] 1 W.A.R. 94. See also *Taccone* v. *Electric Power Transmission Pty Ltd* [1962] Qd.R. 545.

67 *Aitken* v. *Rowe* [1960] V.R. 343; *Lyons* v. *Lyons* [1981] V.R. 497.

68 *Beckmann* v. *Haddy* [1959] S.A.S.R. 11.

69 [1980] A.C. 174, 191.

70 But see J. Mesher and S. Todd (1980) 29 *I.C.L.Q.* 719, 728-30.

Appeal,[71] by the New South Wales Court of Appeal,[72] and in Queensland.[73] It was, no doubt, originally conceived as a replacement for the husband's common law action for loss of services,[74] the new theory being that the husband has not suffered by his wife's injuries but that she has suffered a loss in not being able to provide for her family, in the same way that a person can recover damages for loss of the earnings with which he provides for his family—a theory more in line with modern views of the family. But such damages can be recovered by anyone who performs housekeeping functions.

Compensation under this head is for loss of ability to perform services, not for the cost of substitute services, so that it does not matter whether the damages will actually be used for the hire of a housekeeper. In other words, damages can be recovered for loss of this ability even if it is not productive of actual financial loss, because, for example, a third party replaces the lost services gratuitously. The basic measure of damages appears to be the cost of hiring a domestic worker to do what the plaintiff can no longer do (the 'replacement cost' of the services) subject to a proviso that damages will only be awarded for so much of the loss as it would not be reasonable to expect other members of the household to absorb by doing more for themselves.[75]

5. Expenses Incurred by Third Parties

In *Wilson* v. *McLeay*[76] Taylor J. held that the plaintiff could be awarded a sum as general damages representing the reasonable cost of visits by her parents: she was in hospital many kilometres from her home and there was medical evidence that the attendance of her parents was important to her recovery. To recover under this head it must be established that the visiting is in some sense necessary for the alleviation of the plaintiff's suffering.[77] In one case[78] it was held that the cost of moving home to be nearer an injured child was reasonable and recoverable.

6. Services Rendered by Third Parties to the Injured Person

In *Blundell* v. *Musgrave* Dixon C.J. and Fullager J. said that a plaintiff could recover damages in respect of nursing services rendered gratuitously by a third party only if it was more or less certain that he would have to

71 *Daly* v. *General Steam Navigation Co. Ltd* [1980] 3 All. E.R. 696; K.A. Clarke & A.I. Ogus (1978) 5 *Brit.J. of Law & Soc.* 1.
72 *Burnicle* v. *Cutelli* [1982] 2 N.S.W.L.R. 26; but see *Maiward* v. *Doyle* [1983] W.A.R. 210 *contra*. See also R. Graycar (1983-5) 10 *Syd.L.R.* 528.
73 *Waters* v. *Mussiq* [1986] 1 Qd.R. 224.
74 On which see p. 506 below.
75 *Burnicle* v. *Cutelli* [1982] 2 N.S.W.L.R. 26; *Veselinovic* v. *Thorley* [1988] 1 Qd.R. 191, 207 *per* Derrington J. But see *Hodges* v. *Frost* (1984) 53 A.L.R. 373.
76 (1961) 106 C.L.R. 523. See also *Gow* v. *Motor Vehicle Insurance Trust* [1967] W.A.R. 55.
77 *Taccone* v. *Electric Power Transmission* [1962] Qd.R. 545.
78 *Timmins* v. *Webb* [1964] S.A.S.R. 250.

pay for them.[79] He could not recover if his liability to pay was conditional on his recovering damages. The best evidence of this would be a legal liability to pay, but something less might suffice in some cases. On the other hand, in *Donnelly* v. *Joyce*[80] it was held that an injured plaintiff could recover an amount in respect of gratuitous services rendered by a member of his family or a friend even though he was under no legal or moral obligation to pay for the services. Nor will the court impose on the plaintiff any obligation to pay over the amount awarded to the benefactor on the ground that what the plaintiff does with his damages is his own business.[81]

In *Griffiths* v. *Kerkemeyer*[82] Gibbs J. thought that *Blundell* v. *Musgrave* precluded unqualified acceptance of the principle in *Donnelly* v. *Joyce.* That principle, in effect, provides compensation for the creation of a need even though the plaintiff has suffered no financial loss in meeting that need. But a reconciliation of the conflict which allowed the desirable principle in *Donnelly* v. *Joyce* to be adopted was found by Gibbs J. in the following way—the relevant inquiry should be divided into two parts: (i) were the services which the plaintiff needed such that it would be reasonable to procure them at a cost? If so, the fulfilment of that need is likely to be productive of financial loss; (ii) if this loss does not occur, it is relevant to ask why this is so. If it is because of private benevolence then the value of the benevolence should be ignored in assessing damages and the plaintiff should be awarded the reasonable cost of meeting his need. But it is not clear how this approach overcomes the basic objection that the plaintiff has suffered no actual loss. At all events it would seem that, consistent or not with *Blundell* v. *Musgrave,* the *Donnelly* v. *Joyce* principle is part of Australian law,[83] and its application is not restricted to nursing services.[84] Where the provider of the services is himself a defendant it has been held that damages under this head ought not to be awarded to the plaintiff at his cost and effectively for his benefit.[85] But in New South Wales, *Griffiths* v. *Kerkemeyer* damages have been held recoverable from a compulsorily insured defendant who renders gratuitous services.[86]

Gibbs J.'s qualifications on the *Donnelly* v. *Joyce* principle have been used to impose a significant limitation on the sort of services for which

---

79 (1956) 96 C.L.R. 73; R. Parsons (1957) 30 *A.L.J.* 618.

80 [1974] Q.B. 454; cf. *Hay* v. *Hughes* [1975] Q.B. 790 (fatal accident claim).

81 This seems an unnecessary and wasteful application of the principle which is probably based in part on the supposed difficulty of enforcing on a plaintiff any obligation imposed as to how he will use the damages. However, an obligation simply to pay an amount of money to another person presents no such difficulty; on the contrary, it is the most common form of court order. Cf. J.G. Fleming (1966) 54 *California L.R.* 1478, 1527.

82 (1977) 139 C.L.R. 161, 166-9.

83 But see Common Law (Miscellaneous Actions) Act 1986 s.5 (Tas.) and Transport Accident Act 1986 (Vic.) s.93(10) (damages not recoverable unless the plaintiff has paid or is liable to pay for the services).

84 *O'Keefe* v. *Schulter* [1979] Qd.R. 224.

85 *Cowling* v. *Mercantile Mutual Insurance Co. Ltd* (1980) 24 S.A.S.R. 321.

86 *Lynch* v. *Lynch* [1991] Aust. Torts Reports 81-142, criticized by J.G. Fleming (1992) 66 *A.L.J.* 388.

compensation can be awarded under the *Griffiths* v. *Kerkemeyer* principle. If services are provided by a member of the plaintiff's household and are such as can be described as 'ordinary incidents of family life' which one member of a family would in the normal course perform for another disabled member whatever the source of his disablement, then the services are not such as it would be reasonable to procure at a cost and so not a proper subject for compensation. This is so particularly if the provision of the services causes no financial loss to the provider and if the injured person would change his lifestyle rather than buy the services if they were not provided by the other family member.[87]

Subject to statutory limitations,[88] the measure of damages under this head is the reasonable value of the services. Two possible yardsticks suggest themselves: either the market cost of hiring a carer, or the loss of wages which the provider of the services suffers (or the wages he could earn were he not caring for the plaintiff). The first is called replacement cost, the second opportunity cost (that is, the value of opportunities forgone). While courts have recognized the distinction between these two, they have often not been prepared to commit themselves to one or the other, leaving themselves the option of awarding whichever seems more appropriate on the facts.[89] Although from one point of view the *Donnelly* v. *Joyce* principle is a generous extension of the compensatory principle, from another point of view, since the plaintiff has suffered no financial loss and is under no obligation to reimburse the benefactor, the major justification for this head of damages, as for the previous one, must be to ensure that the costs generated by the defendant's activity are borne by it. This is one aspect of the concern with efficient loss allocation which is interested not only in spreading losses but also in reducing accidents and not encouraging activities by relieving them of their true social costs.[90]

7. NON-PECUNIARY LOSSES

(a) General theory There are three heads of non-pecuniary loss: pain and suffering, loss of amenities and loss of expectation of life. The view is now widely accepted that awards for non-pecuniary loss could be doubled or halved overnight and still be as defensible or indefensible as they are today.[91] The general judicial attitude would perhaps be that although there is an element of arbitrariness in picking a figure for individual cases,

---

87 *Kovac* v. *Kovac* [1982] 1 N.S.W.L.R. 656; *Settree* v. *Roberts* [1982] 1 N.S.W.L.R. 649; *Carrick* v. *Commonwealth* [1983] 2 Qd.R. 365; *Veselinovic* v. *Thorley* [1988] 1 Qd.R. 191. But contrast *Trevali Pty Ltd* v. *Haddad* [1989] Aust. Torts Reports 80-286. See also R. Graycar (1992) 14 *Syd. L.R.* 86.

88 Motor Accidents Act 1988 (N.S.W.) s.72 and Workers Compensation Act 1987 (N.S.W.) S.151K; Wrongs Act 1936 (S.A.) s.35a(1)(g),(h), s.35a(2).

89 *Donnelly* v. *Joyce* [1974] Q.B. 454, 462 *per* Megaw L.J.; *K.* v. *J.M.P. Co. Ltd* [1976] Q.B. 85, 96 *per* Stephenson L.J.; for awards of opportunity cost see *Mehmet* v. *Perry* [1977] 2 All E.R. 529; *Settree* v. *Roberts* [1982] 1 N.S.W.L.R. 649. See also *Veselinovic* v. *Thorley* [1988] 1 Qd.R. 191; *Government Insurance Office of N.S.W.* v. *Planas* [1984] 2 N.S.W.L.R. 671; *McCamley* v. *Cammell Laird Ltd* [1990] 1 W.L.R. 963, 967.

90 See e.g. *Sharman* v. *Evans* (1977) 13 A.L.R. 57, 87 *per* Murphy J.

91 *Atiyah's Accidents* p. 183.

there are outer limits beyond which awards would be thought clearly unjustifiable.[92] The limits seem to be set by reference to the general or average wealth of society rather than with reference to the position of the particular plaintiff.[93] Thus, awards for non-pecuniary loss are increased broadly in line with inflation; judicial experience is usually thought very important in assessing them;[94] and in England, where juries are very rarely used in personal injury actions, jury assessment of such damages is thought appropriate only in cases where there is no body of judicial expertise.[95]

There is an argument for saying that since non-pecuniary loss is basically incapable of being expressed in money, damages for such loss are not compensatory. Either they are provided by way of consolation to enable the plaintiff to find alternative sources of satisfaction or they are designed to punish the defendant.[96] In theory Australian law does not award damages to provide solace; and although punitive damages can be awarded in personal injury actions,[97] the facts of most personal injury actions would not justify an award of punitive damages. There is no way of conclusively resolving this dispute because whether damages for non-pecuniary loss are compensatory or not depends on whether one accepts that non-pecuniary losses are 'really losses', and this is a matter purely of definition. To call such damages punitive is usually just to say that they ought not to be awarded.

In light of the difficulty of putting monetary values on non-pecuniary losses it might be thought that more important than the question of how much to award is the question of who should decide how much to award. This is why the courts lay considerable emphasis on achieving a certain uniformity in awards; this maintains the credibility of the judiciary as decision makers in this area. The counsel of moderation in the assessment of damages for non-pecuniary loss also plays a part in legitimizing the judicial decision-making process.

(b) Pain and suffering[98] The only points to note about this head of damages are the following: first, pain and suffering is not considered to be

---

92 For relevant statutory limitations see Commonwealth Employees Rehabilitation and Compensation Act 1988 (Cwth) s. 45(4); Motor Accidents Act 1988 (N.S.W.) s. 79 (*Southgate* v. *Waterford* (1990) 21 N.S.W.L.R. 427; *Dell* v. *Dalton* [1991] Aust. Torts Reports 81-112) and Workers Compensation Act 1987 (N.S.W.) s.151G; Wrongs Act (S.A.) s.35a(1)(a),(b) (*Packer* v. *Cameron* (1989) 54 S.A.S.R. 246; *Percario* v. *Kordysz* (1989) 54 S.A.S.R. 259) and Workers Rehabilitation and Compensation Act 1986 (S.A.) s.54(4); Transport Accident Act 1986 (Vic.) s.93 (7)(b) ('pain and suffering'); Limitation Act 1935 (W.A.) s.38(3) (asbestos-related cases). See generally N. Mullaney (1990) 17 *M.U.L.R.* 714.

93 *Gardner* v. *Dyson* [1967] 1 W.L.R. 1497, 1501 *per* Salmon L.J.; *West* v. *Shephard* [1964] A.C. 326, 356 *per* Lord Devlin.

94 But see Mullaney (1990) 17 *M.U.L.R.* 714, 714-17.

95 *Hodges* v. *Harland & Wolff Ltd* [1965] 1 All E.R. 1086.

96 See particularly Windeyer J.'s judgment in *Skelton* v. *Collins* (1965-6) 115 C.L.R. 94.

97 *Lamb* v. *Cotogno* (1987) 74 A.L.R. 188; *Coloca* v. *B.P. Australia Ltd* [1992] Aust. Torts Reports 81-153. But see Motor Accidents Act (N.S.W.) s.81A and Workers Compensation Act 1987 (N.S.W.) s.151R. See also Handford (1991) 21 *U.W.A. L.R.* 63, 65-7.

98 This includes 'harassment', 'vexation', 'distress', 'worry' and other such mental states.

periodic (it is not, for example, calculated on a *per diem* basis); secondly, damages for pain and suffering are assessed purely subjectively—they are awarded for actual awareness of pain; thirdly, this head covers awareness of loss of amenities and of loss of expectation of life.[99]

(c) Loss of expectation of life[100] Damages under this head compensate for loss of the prospect of a predominantly happy life.[101] They are awarded when the plaintiff's life expectancy has been reduced by the accident. The amount awarded is small and conventional in the sense that, unlike the other heads of non-pecuniary loss, it varies little from case to case;[102] except that slightly less may be awarded in the case of very young children (because of the uncertainties of the future[103]) or (perhaps) in the case of very old people, or where the court thinks that the victim's way of life was unlikely to (or, perhaps, ought not to) produce a predominance of happiness over unhappiness.[104]

This is the only head of damages which can be called damages for deprivation of life, and the fact that the sum is small and conventional perhaps shows the law's dislike for the task of valuing life. From one point of view, it is illogical that less should be awarded if the plaintiff is prematurely deprived of all his faculties than if, for example, he loses a leg. The uncertainties of the future do not seem an adequate explanation for the parsimony of the law under this head. It arises from the unwillingness to inquire how happy a particular individual would have been and probably also from a realization that this sum operates very often as a solace for relatives. It has been suggested, therefore, that this head of damages be abolished and replaced by an award for loss of society recoverable at the suit of bereaved relatives.[105]

(d) Loss of amenities Under this head compensation is awarded for loss of enjoyment of life during the rest of the plaintiff's expected lifetime. In other words, the plaintiff is compensated for the frustration and deprivation involved in not being able to do those things he could do before the accident. There are two main strands in the current judicial approach to this head.[106] The first is the conceptual or objective strand. This attempts to rank injuries on a sort of scale of seriousness and to award damages proportional to the injury on the basis of a tariff. It is not the case, however, that in this approach the injury is in some way 'valued' independently of its effect on the plaintiff. One of the reasons why the loss of a leg, for example, attracts more compensation than the loss of a toe is that the former usually has more serious consequences for the plaintiff than the latter. Furthermore, if because of some personal characteristic the

---

99 *Thurston* v. *Todd* (1966) 84 W.N.(Pt.1)(N.S.W.) 231, 242 *per* Jacobs J.A.
100 O. Kahn-Freund (1941) 5 *M.L.R.* 81.
101 *Flint* v. *Lovell* [1935] 1 K.B. 354.
102 *Benham* v. *Gambling* [1941] A.C. 147.
103 *Yorkshire Electricity Board* v. *Naylor* [1967] 2 All E.R. 1, 10 *per* Lord Guest.
104 *Burns* v. *Edman* [1970] 2 Q.B. 541.
105 This has been done in England: Administration of Justice Act 1982 (U.K.), s.1.
106 A.I. Ogus (1972) 35 *M.L.R.* 1.

impact of a particular injury is significantly greater on the plaintiff than it would be on the 'average' plaintiff he can be awarded more under this head.[107] For example, the loss of an arm or a leg would justify a higher award to a pianist or an athlete respectively than to a plaintiff who engaged in no activity depending to an unusual extent on the use of the lost limb. But the fact that the plaintiff was particularly rich or poor is not, in itself, a reason for awarding more or less under this head.[108] Suggestions have been made[109] that if, for example, the plaintiff was a cripple before the accident his damages might be less than if he was whole; and that if the plaintiff is very young or very old this might make the quality of his loss of enjoyment less and so justify a lower award.

The second strand is the personal or subjective approach.[110] Here the relevant issue is the effect of the injury on the plaintiff's psyche: loss of happiness is the relevant loss. The most important application of this reasoning is to deny recovery under this head by a permanently unconscious plaintiff.[111] It is important to be clear that the unconscious plaintiff is denied recovery not only for pain and suffering but also for loss of amenities. The strongest argument for the rule is that since enjoyment of life is not something on which monetary value can be put, damages for the loss of it are given essentially as a solace or consolation rather than as compensation for a loss suffered. If the plaintiff is not conscious no amount of money will or is needed to console him. Any damages awarded will benefit relatives either by way of consolation or as pure windfall. The argument put in favour of awarding such damages is that the fact of unconsciousness does not deny the reality of the deprivation in an objective sense. To refuse to award such damages would be to treat the victim as if he were already dead.

It is apparent that there could be borderline cases in which it would be very difficult to determine the level of the plaintiff's awareness of his lot. There is authority for the proposition that the amount awarded for loss of amenities should take account of the degree of the plaintiff's awareness of his situation; and even that a plaintiff's damages under this head could be reduced if his injuries had induced a euphoric state of mind.[112] Clearly, such an approach would require courts to make very difficult judgments about the plaintiff's mental state, and it could be applied in only a very rough sort of way.

A third possible approach to this head of loss, besides the objective and the subjective, can be called the functional approach. This approach is based on the idea that damages under this head are to provide consolation

---

107 On the relevance of the sex of the plaintiff to the assessment of damages for cosmetic injuries see *Ralevski* v. *Dimovski* (1987) 7 N.S.W.L.R. 487; *Del Ponte* v. *Del Ponte* (1987) 11 N.S.W.L.R. 498; *G.I.O.* v. *Burbury* (1989) M.V.R. 189.

108 *Fletcher* v. *Autocar & Transporters Ltd* [1968] 2 Q.B. 322, 341.

109 In *Andrews* v. *Freeborough* [1967] 1 Q.B. 1, 14 *per* Willmer L.J.; 21, 23 *per* Winn L.J.

110 The most thorough exposition of this approach is the judgment of Diplock L.J. in *Wise* v. *Kaye* [1962] 1 Q.B. 638.

111 *Skelton* v. *Collins* (1965-6) 115 C.L.R. 94. The English rule is different: *Wise* v. *Kaye* [1962] 1 Q.B. 638; *West* v. *Shephard* [1964] A.C. 526.

112 *Dundas* v. *Harbour Motors Pty Ltd* [1988] Aust. Torts Reports 67,453.

or alternative sources of satisfaction for the victim. In this view the damages are not awarded to compensate for past loss so much as to enable the plaintiff to find new sources of enjoyment in the future. Such authority as there is in the cases is against the adoption of this approach, apparently because it implies a need to inquire into how the plaintiff will use his damages and to make judgments about what sort of alternative activities it would be reasonable to expect the defendant to pay for.[113] On the other hand, it would be possible to adopt a tariff approach classifying injuries according to their severity in terms of the amounts of money which might reasonably be needed to provide alternatives to the enjoyment the plaintiff has lost as a result of the injury. Whether such a tariff would differ significantly from the tariff used under the objective approach is hard to say. At all events, the existence of a tariff which sets the quantum of the damages very largely turns the issue of 'objective or functional' into one of purely theoretical justification for recovery, and deprives it of most of its practical significance to the question of the proper measure of damages.

A couple of miscellaneous points should be made. First, damages under this head are not calculated by the multiplier method; or, in other words, not on a *per diem* or *per annum* basis.[114] Secondly, under this head damages can be awarded for such things as loss of enjoyment of sexual activity;[115] the loss of a holiday due to injury;[116] the extra risk and anxiety inflicted on a woman with conscientious religious objections to artificial contraception by an accident which would make childbirth both difficult and dangerous for her;[117] the loss by an Aboriginal, as a result of brain damage, of rank and chances of advancement in the hierarchy of his tribe.[118]

8. Itemization of Damages and Overlapping

Itemization of awards of general damages into their constituent heads used to be frowned upon.[119] The theoretical reason was that damages were to be awarded in a lump sum and it was the lump sum which had to be fair and reasonable. A fair and reasonable amount would not be produced simply by adding up the amounts awarded under each head.[120] Itemization could lead to overlapping between different heads of compensation and hence to double compensation.

---

113 *Lawrence* v. *Mathison* (1982) 11 N.T.R. 1, 10 *per* Muirhead J.

114 *Andrews* v. *Freeborough* [1967] 1 Q.B. 1, 13 *per* Willmer L.J.; cf. *McLean* v. *Walker* [1979] 2 All E.R. 965, 970.

115 e.g. *Hills* v. *Transport Commission* Tas.S.R. 154; *Hodges* v. *Harland & Wolff* [1965] 1 All E.R. 1086.

116 *North* v. *Thompson* [1971] W.A.R. 103.

117 *Walker-Flynn* v. *Princeton Motors Pty Ltd* [1960] S.R.(N.S.W.) 488.

118 *Napaluma* v. *Baker* (1982) 29 S.A.S.R. 192; *Dixon* v. *Davies* (1982) 17 N.T.R. 31.

119 e.g. *Fletcher* v. *Autocar and Transporters* [1968] 2 Q.B. 322, 336 *per* Lord Denning M.R.; *Travaglia* v. *Club Motor Insurance Agency Pty Ltd* [1968] Qd.R. 352.

120 *Arthur Robinson (Grafton) Pty Ltd* v. *Carter* (1967-8) 122 C.L.R. 649, 654-5 *per* Barwick C.J.

Particular examples of overlapping can be identified from the cases. First, there can be overlapping between different heads of pecuniary loss. Thus, if damages are awarded both for loss of earnings and for cost of care the court should not compensate twice for basic living expenses which were incurred as much before the accident as after it.[121] A related point is that there must be deducted from any damages for loss of earnings or profits the costs of making those earnings or profits.[122]

Secondly, there may be overlapping between heads of pecuniary and non-pecuniary loss. In *Fletcher* v. *Autocar and Transporters*[123] it was held by a majority that if the plaintiff spent some of his income on pleasurable activities, and if he is being compensated for the loss of that pleasure by an award of damages for loss of amenities, his award for loss of earnings should be reduced by the cost of the activities because the plaintiff could not have had both the pleasure and the cost of deriving it. Lord Denning M.R. developed the theme in *Smith* v. *Central Asbestos Ltd* where he said that a high award for loss of earnings might reduce the award for pain and suffering and loss of amenities because it would be a comfort to the plaintiff to know that his economic losses are being fully compensated.[124] On the other hand, it has been said that since damages for pecuniary and non-pecuniary loss are calculated on different principles and serve different purposes, there is no possibility of overlap.[125] They compensate for different losses; and since there is such a large element of arbitrariness in damages for non-pecuniary loss, it is very difficult to say that a plaintiff has ever been overcompensated by an award of such damages.

Thirdly, there is some possibility of overlap between heads of non-pecuniary loss. For example, the plaintiff should not be awarded, under the head of loss of amenities, for anguish caused by awareness of his condition since this is taken into account in assessing damages for pain and suffering.

The ban on itemization has been largely lifted.[126] It is never wrong, and often convenient, to itemize; assessment of damages is a matter for calculation, not intuition. But it is not an error of law not to itemize, and simple aggregation of items is to be avoided. The ultimate duty is still to award a lump sum which is reasonable.[127] Itemization has been encouraged by the need to divide damages into pre- and post-trial components for the purposes of awarding interest; by the fact that pecuniary and non-pecuniary losses are differently calculated; and by the desire of appeal courts to exercise careful control over decisions of trial courts on assessment of damages.[128]

---

121 See p. 492 above.
122 *Sharman* v. *Evans* (1977) 138 C.L.R. 563, 577 *per* Gibbs and Stephen JJ.
123 [1968] 2 Q.B. 322.
124 [1972] 1 Q.B. 244; cf. *Henley* v. *Commane* [1971] Tas.S.R. 180.
125 *Sharman* v. *Evans* (1977) 138 C.L.R. 563, 578-9 *per* Gibbs and Stephen JJ.
126 *Gamser* v. *Nominal Defendant* (1977) 136 C.L.R. 145; *Lai Wee Lian* v. *Singapore Bus Service (1978) Ltd* [1984] A.C. 729.
127 *Masson* v. *Crook* (1979) 22 S.A.S.R. 473.
128 See, for example, *Keefe* v. *R.T. & D.M. Spring Pty Ltd* [1985] 2 Qd.R. 363; *Lloyd* v. *Faraone* [1989] W.A.R. 154, 164 *per* Malcolm C.J.

9. Collateral Benefits and Off-setting[129]

The question to be considered here is whether sums which the plaintiff receives from third parties on account of his accident should be set off against his damages so that the defendant has to pay less. Such sums may accrue from one of three sources: statutory provision (e.g. social security payments); contract (e.g. sick pay or the proceeds of insurance policies); or benevolence (which may take the form of gratuitous payments or services).

The starting point for consideration of the question is that the plaintiff is only to be compensated. Collateral benefits should not be ignored in assessing the plaintiff's damages for the sake of punishing the defendant. But this concession does not take matters very far because much depends on how we define the loss for which compensation is to be given. There are two basic approaches to this question. The traditional approach involves drawing a distinction between payments which reduce the plaintiff's loss and which must be set off, and payments which do not. Three ways of drawing this distinction appear from the cases. The first asks whether the benefit resulted directly from the accident (in which case it will be set off)[130] or, contrariwise, was the product of 'thrift and foresight' on the part of the plaintiff (as in the case of the proceeds of insurance policies,[131] or of benevolence on the part of third parties[132]), or of some other independent source.[133] A way this question is sometimes put is to ask whether the payment was *res inter alios acta,* which, loosely translated, means whether the payment was any of the defendant's business. The distinction is a difficult one to draw consistently and its application leads to considerable apparent anomalies. For example, if the plaintiff receives contractual sick pay 'as part of his ordinary wages' this is set off against his damages on the ground that it reduces his loss.[134] But if he receives sums from a contributory disablement pension fund set up by his employer these will not be set off because they partake of the nature of insurance.[135] This would appear to be the case even if membership of the pension fund was compulsory (and so not a matter of thrift or foresight) since, in the words of Lord Reid in *Parry* v. *Cleaver,* the proceeds of the pension would be the fruit of money set aside in respect of past work rather than, in effect, wages for contemporaneous work.[136] Finally, if the

---

129 J.G. Fleming (1966) 54 *California L.R.* 1478; *Atiyah's Accidents* pp.398-409.

130 e.g. *Colledge* v. *Bass Mitchells & Butlers Ltd* [1988] I.C.R. 125.

131 *Bradburn* v. *Great Western Railway Co.* (1874) 10 L.R. Ex. 1; *Oakley* v. *McIntyre* [1984] Tas.S.R. 44. But the plaintiff must have paid or contributed to the premiums: *McCamley* v. *Cammell Laird* [1990] 1 W.L.R. 963, 970.

132 The *Donnelly* v. *Joyce* principle (see p. 494 above) falls under this head: *Griffiths* v. *Kerkemeyer* (1977) 139 C.L.R. 161, 166-7 *per* Gibbs J.

133 e.g. a matrimonial relationship as in the case of maintenance payments: *Leak* v. *Gronert* [1966] S.A.S.R. 120; or an order under the Testators Family Maintenance Act: *Deering* v. *Norton* (1970) 92 W.N.(N.S.W.) 437.

134 *Graham* v. *Baker* (1961) 106 C.L.R. 340. The fact that the employer takes out insurance to cover the payments does not alter the situation: *Hussain* v. *New Taplow Paper Mills* [1988] A.C. 514.

135 *Parry* v. *Cleaver* [1970] A.C. 1.

136 ibid., 16.

employer voluntarily and gratuitously pays the employee while he is away from work, the sums are not set off.[137]

From one point of view, the plaintiff's position is the same in each of these three situations and yet his legal right to obtain damages differs significantly. It is hard to see that the sick pay is any more the defendant's business than the insurance or benevolence. They are all the result both of the accident and of another factor. Perhaps an accurate description of what the courts have tried to do was given by Sholl J. in *Johns* v. *Prunell*:

> the law seems to me to have endeavoured to form a kind of moral judgment as to whether it is fair and reasonable that the defendant should have the advantage of something which has accrued to the plaintiff by way of recoupment or other benefit as a result of the defendant's infringement of the plaintiff's rights . . . it is difficult to achieve wholly logical results.[138]

The second way of distinguishing between benefits which reduce the plaintiff's loss (and so must be set off) and benefits which do not is to ask whether the provider of the benefit intended it to be additional to any damages which the payee might recover (in which case, the benefit will be set off) or, on the contrary, whether the payment was made in anticipation of reimbursement out of any damages recovered.[139]

The issue of the intentions of the giver presents difficulty where the giver is an institution, and so the third way of drawing the distinction is a modification of the second to meet this situation: was the purpose of the payment, objectively judged, to provide the plaintiff with a sum additional to any damages he might receive?[140] In cases where the benefit is provided under statute this question resolves itself into a question of statutory interpretation.[141] A statute may, of course, contain express provision about offsetting, but in the absence of such provision the court has to decide for itself whether any particular benefit ought to be ignored or taken into account. Thus it has been held that a war pension paid under the Repatriation Act 1920–59 (Cwth) is not to be set off;[142] nor is an invalid pension paid under the Social Security Act 1947 (Cwth)[143] or under the Defence Forces Retirement Act (Cwth);[144] nor is a widow's

---

137 *McMahon* v. *Juranovich* (1961) 78 W.N.(N.S.W.) 519; *Johns* v. *Prunell* [1960] V.R. 208; *Beck* v. *Farrelly* (1975) 13 S.A.S.R. 17.

138 [1960] V.R. 208, 211.

139 *National Insurance Co. of New Zealand Ltd* v. *Espagne* (1960-1) 105 C.L.R. 569, especially 573 *per* Dixon C.J.; *Berriello* v. *Felixstowe Dock & Railway Co.* [1989] 1 W.L.R. 695.

140 *Wellington* v. *State Electricity Commission of Victoria* [1980] V.R. 91 (property damage case).

141 *Keating* v. *Cochrane* (1959) 77 W.N.(N.S.W.) 35, 37 *per* Else-Mitchell J. The interaction of workers' compensation legislation with the common law rules of employers' liability is particularly complex and beyond the scope of this book.

142 *Zielke* v. *Voak* [1961] Qd.R. 440.

143 *National Insurance Co. of New Zealand* v. *Espagne* (1960-1) 105 C.L.R. 569; *Redding* v. *Lee* (1983) 57 A.L.J.R. 393; see also *Muscat* v. *Statewide Industries Ltd* [1988] 1 Qd.R. 637.

144 *Donaldson* v. *Korostovetz* [1980] Qd.R. 294.

pension paid under Commonwealth legislation.[145] Domiciliary care allowance is not set off against damages representing the value of gratuitous nursing services.[146] It has also been held that medical, hospital or nursing benefits paid under the National Health Act 1956 (Cwth),[147] or the Health Insurance Act 1973 (Cwth),[148] whether past or future, are not to be set off. But social security legislation tends to be subject to frequent amendment, and so the question of whether any particular benefit should be set off may be given a different answer at different times. For example, since 1987 the Social Security Act 1947 (Cwth) has provided that unemployment benefit is not payable during any period in respect of which an award of damages for loss of earning capacity is received; and that a person who has received benefits in respect of any such period may be required to repay them. So despite earlier authority that unemployment benefit received up to the date of trial was to be set off,[149] it now appears that both unemployment benefits received and the expectation of future benefits should be ignored in assessing damages for loss of earning capacity.[150] On the other hand, for example, an award of compensation under the Criminal Injuries (Compensation) Act 1970 (W.A.) is set off against damages in tort.[151]

All of these three approaches treat the issue of off-setting essentially in terms of the rights and obligations *inter se* of three parties. Thus the relationships of the parties with one another are relevant. In the discussion so far it has been assumed that the defendant and the payer were different. Where the payer of the benefit is also the defendant (usually the employer of the plaintiff) there is probably a strong presumption in favour of off-setting, unless it is very clear that the defendant intended his payment to be additional to any damages which he might be liable to pay. Where the payer is a third party the question of off-setting is only one relevant issue. The other is whether the third party should be entitled to recoupment against the defendant if his payment is set off against the plaintiff's damages or if the plaintiff does not bring an action; or from the plaintiff if it is not set off. In the latter case the payer would be entitled to recoupment only if the plaintiff had made a legally binding promise to repay out of any damages received. As against a defendant, the third party's rights would depend on his having a right to be subrogated to the plaintiff's cause of action against the defendant, whether contractual or statutory or recognized by the common law. Where the third party is an insurer it will sometimes have such a right (but not, significantly, in respect of personal accident insurance). But rights of subrogation are administratively costly

145 *Glover* v. *Evans* (1981) 34 A.C.T.R. 24; *Lindquist* v. *Maier* [1980] Qd.R. 203.

146 *Wann* v. *Fire & All Risks Insurance Co. Ltd* [1990] 2 Qd.R. 596.

147 *Datson* v. *Handley* (1979) 28 A.L.R. 618. The value of free board and lodging in hospital is not set off either: *Jensen* v. *Burnham* [1966] Q.W.N. 51; cf. *Daish* v. *Wauton* [1972] 1 Q.B. 262 now reversed by Administration of Justice Act 1982 (U.K.), s.5.

148 *Oakley* v. *McIntyre* [1984] Tas.S.R. 44.

149 *Redding* v. *Lee* (1983) 57 A.L.J.R. 393.

150 *Dabinett* v. *Whittaker* [1989] 2 Qd R. 228 *per* Andrews C.J. and Thomas J.; see also *Muscat* v. *Statewide Industries* [1988] 1 Qd R. 637. Sickness benefit was repayable even before 1987, and so was to be ignored in assessing damages. See also *Russell* v. *Craddock* [1985] 1 Qd.R. 377.

151 *Moignard* v. *Marriott* [1976] W.A.R. 83.

to enforce, and in some cases it may be cheaper overall for the insurer to bear the loss. So motor accident insurers often short-circuit the process by entering into 'knock-for-knock' agreements by which they promise not to exercise rights of subrogation against parties insured with the other. Where the third party is not an insurer, the enforcement costs of subrogation, even if the right existed, would often make the right of little or no value.

The other way of viewing the collateral benefits issue is in much wider social terms: if the plaintiff receives the monetary 'value' of his loss more than once, from whatever sources, he has been over-compensated. Thus 'collateral' benefits should always be set off; otherwise resources are wasted. In this approach, the important issue is how to rank sources of payment so as to decide which should constitute the primary source of compensation. Two factors might be thought relevant here. One is the administrative cost of repayment, recoupment or subrogation as means of preventing over-compensation. This consideration would dictate that the temporally first source of compensation should bear the cost. On this basis, for example, pre-trial social security payments would always be set off against damages and the state would never have a right of recourse against the defendant.

The other relevant factor is that by far the majority of sources of compensation are funded by insurance, whether in the form of third-party liability insurance or private first-party insurance or social security schemes funded by taxation. In deciding which insurance fund is to bear the cost it will be relevant to ask who makes up the class of premium payers, because we may want to require a particular activity to bear the costs it generates. If the classes of premium payers for two types of insurance are large enough, the common members may be so numerous that it makes very little difference in practice which fund bears the cost. In our society, for example, the overlap between taxpayers and third-party insurance-premium payers is so large that, in effect, 'the public' pays whether the compensation is in the form of an insurance payment or of social security payments. So, in many cases the exact source of the compensation does not matter; what matters is that the plaintiff should only recover once. Of course, the ban on double recovery does not mean that the plaintiff may not appropriately in some cases recover from two sources. For example, if the plaintiff receives partial compensation in the form of social security payments it would be thought indefensible by many that he should not be entitled to recover for the balance of his loss from an insurer.

The essence of this loss allocation approach is social, whereas the other approach looks at the rights of individuals. From this latter point of view it seems unfair that if, for example, a plaintiff has taken out an insurance policy which entitles him to compensation regardless of someone else's fault, he should not keep that amount as well as his fault-based compensation. The advantages and disadvantages of these two approaches have been extensively discussed and are beyond the scope of this work. Suffice it to say that the cases support the first approach while the opinion of most academic writers and law reformers, both official and unofficial, favours some form of the second approach.

IV: ACTIONS ARISING OUT OF INJURY TO ANOTHER PERSON

As a general rule one person may not recover damages for the effects on him of injury to or the death of another person. In this section and the next we will examine exceptions to this general principle. As we noted earlier, loss arising out of injury to or the death of another person is purely economic loss; but the main objections to recovery for such economic loss are overcome in this context by definition of a limited class of specific persons who may recover for such loss.

There are two actions for loss arising out of injury to another: the action for loss of services (*actio per quod servitium amisit*), and the action for loss of consortium (*actio per quod consortium amisit*). At common law, a husband can bring both actions if his wife is injured (but a wife cannot bring the actions if her husband is injured); and an employer can bring an action for loss of an employee's services. Both are based on the idea that the plaintiff has some rights over the person injured, and in this way the actions are totally archaic. In New South Wales and Tasmania statute now provides that neither spouse can sue in respect of loss of the other's services or society;[152] but an injured person can recover damages for loss of ability to perform housekeeping functions.[153] The husband's right of action has also been abolished in Western Australia.[154] Employers can no longer bring an action for loss of services in New South Wales.[155]

1. THE ACTION FOR LOSS OF AN EMPLOYEE'S SERVICES

The action will lie wherever the plaintiff and the injured person are in the relationship of master and servant, although it does not matter that there is no contract of service between the parties.[156] It is not restricted to cases in which the servant is a menial or domestic servant but extends to any type of worker who would in the world of private individuals be called a 'servant',[157] even if the degree of control which the employer can exercise over the worker is slight.[158] But it does not apply to employees who hold

152 Law Reform (Marital Consortium) Act 1984 (N.S.W.); Common Law (Miscellaneous Actions) Act 1986 (Tas.) s.3. The Married Persons (Equality of Status) Act 1989 (N.T.) may indirectly have the same effect by treating married persons as if they were unmarried.

153 See p. 492 above.

154 Law Reform (Miscellaneous Provisions) Act 1941 s.3 (inserted in 1986). The Australian Law Reform Commission (ALRC 32) has suggested a similar reform for the A.C.T.

155 *Swan* v. *Williams (Demolition)* (1987) 9 N.S.W.L.R. 172; see also Employees Liability Act 1991 s.4.

156 *Commissioner for Railways (N.S.W.)* v. *Scott* (1958-9) 102 C.L.R. 392; *The Commonwealth* v. *Quince* (1943) 68 C.L.R. 227.

157 See below p. 700 for a definition of this term.

158 *Marinovski* v. *Zutti Pty Ltd* [1984] 2 N.S.W.L.R. 571 ('de facto' managing director of a company).

public offices,[159] such as police constables or service personnel,[160] who exercise an element of discretion in performing their duties, or probably to high public servants.[161]

Damages are recoverable for pecuniary loss actually sustained through loss of the employee's services. So an employer can recover hospital and medical expenses, and amounts paid as 'accident pay'.[162] Since the employer would have had to pay wages even if the employee had not been injured, ordinary wages paid during disability are not the measure of the plaintiff's loss. The cost of substitute labour, if reasonably incurred, could provide a measure of the loss. But if other employees have pitched in and done the injured employee's work at no extra cost to the employer then the latter has suffered no loss.[163] In exceptional cases where the injured employee was irreplaceable, the employer might recover for profits lost or losses incurred as a result of the tort.[164]

There is a good argument for abolishing the employer's right to sue in respect of loss of an injured employee's services. The employer's costs arising from the injuries are most easily met either by first-party insurance or by the passing-on of the costs in the form of higher prices for goods and services. In this way the cost is spread widely throughout the community, saving litigation and administrative costs. Especially where the injury is caused by a road accident—so that the defendant is insured—there is little point in incurring the expense of shifting the loss from the employer to the driver, because, both being able to spread the loss, much the same group of the general population will bear the loss in either event. This is not true of actions in respect of loss of household services, which will normally have to be absorbed by the close family circle if they are not met by an insured defendant.

2. Actions[165] for Loss of Domestic Services and Consortium[166]

Except in South Australia where s.33 of the Wrongs Act 1936 gives the wife a statutory right of action, this action will, as we have noted, lie only at the suit of a husband, not at the suit of a wife.[167] Nor can a wife circumvent this rule by claiming breach of a duty owed directly to her.[168]

---

159 *Attorney General for New South Wales* v. *Perpetual Trustee Co. Ltd* (1951-2) 85 C.L.R. 237; [1955] A.C. 457.

160 *The Commonwealth* v. *Quince* (1943) 68 C.L.R. 227.

161 *A-G* v. *Wilson & Horton Ltd* [1973] 2 N.Z.L.R. 238, 249 *per* Turner P.

162 *Sydney City Council* v. *Bosnich* [1968] 3 N.S.W.R. 725.

163 For these propositions see *A-G* v. *Wilson & Horton* [1973] 2 N.Z.L.R. 238.

164 *Marinovski* v. *Zutti Pty Ltd* [1984] 2 N.S.W.L.R. 571, 575-6 *per* Hutley J.A.

165 Technically, the action is for loss of consortium, and loss of servitium is a head of damages available in this action: *Harris* v. *Grigg* [1988] 1 Qd.R. 514.

166 P. Brett (1955) 29 *A.L.J.* 321; 428; A.C. Riseley (1981) 7 *Adelaide L.R.* 421; P. Handford (1979) 14 *U.W.A.L.R.* 79.

167 *Wright* v. *Cedzich* (1929-30) 43 C.L.R. 493; *Marx* v. *A-G* [1974] 1 N.Z.L.R. 164; *Best* v. *Samuel Fox & Co. Ltd* [1952] A.C. 716.

168 *Harris* v. *Grigg* [1988] 1 Qd.R. 514; *Marx* v. *A-G* [1974] 1 N.Z.L.R. 164.

The reason for this rule is historical—only the husband had rights in a spouse. But the refusal of modern courts to extend the action to the wife is a rejection of this outdated view of marriage and has arisen from a feeling that this anomalous action should not be extended any further than authority demands. The action is one for loss of the domestic services and society; thus, except in very special circumstances[169] a husband could not recover loss of business profits as a result of injury to his wife who was his partner or employee.[170] A husband can recover costs of medical treatment and convalescence and travelling expenses to see his wife if they were incurred in reasonable mitigation of his loss of consortium,[171] and wages lost or chances of advancement forgone by giving up work to look after the wife.[172]

The husband's action is independent of the wife's (although derived from it) and his recovery is not defeated or limited by contributory negligence on the part of the wife (unless she was acting as his agent).[173] The action can be built not only on to a wife's common law action for physical injuries but also on to a statutory action for nervous shock.[174] Damages for loss of consortium may be recovered only in respect of the period when both spouses are alive[175] and during which the marriage lasts.[176]

Damages can be recovered for loss of services and consortium even if the loss is only partial.[177] The husband can recover not only expenses incurred in replacing the wife's services or mitigating his loss of consortium but also for the intangible loss of his wife's society, companionship and service in the home, even where the husband has not incurred any expense in making good this loss. Some aspects of services and consortium are not easily replaceable (if at all) by the expenditure of money, and a plaintiff is not to be denied damages merely because he chooses to put up with his loss.[178] But a husband cannot recover for the distress he endures at seeing his wife in her injured condition,[179] or for the loss of the 'spiritual' as opposed to the 'temporal' aspects of the relationship,[180] or that the fact that the wife performs all the services she did before, but now 'with a

---

169 e.g. *Behrens* v. *Bertram Mills Circus Ltd* [1957] 2 Q.B. 1.

170 *Kirkham* v. *Boughey* [1958] 2 Q.B. 338; *Plover* v. *Giampolo* [1965] V.R. 275; *Dahm* v. *Harmer* [1955] S.A.S.R. 250.

171 *Hunter* v. *Scott* [1963] Qd.R. 77.

172 *Keally* v. *Jones* [1979] 1 N.S.W.L.R. 723, 742-3 *per* Hutley J.A.

173 *Curran* v. *Young* (1965) 112 C.L.R. 99; *Porcheddu* v. *Hagan (No. 1)* [1965] Q.W.N. 6; *Anderson* v. *Blazeley* [1966] Tas.S.R. 281. But see *contra Meadows* v. *Maloney* (1973) 4 S.A.S.R. 567 and *Hasaganic* v. *Minister of Education* (1973) 5 S.A.S.R. 554 applying Wrongs Act 1936, s.27a(9), with which compare Law Reform (Miscellaneous Provisions) Act 1956 (N.T.), s.17; Law Reform (Miscellaneous Provisions) Act 1955 (A.C.T.), s.17.

174 *State Railway Authority of N.S.W.* v. *Sharp* [1981] 1 N.S.W.L.R. 240.

175 *Sloan* v. *Kirby* (1979) 20 S.A.S.R. 263 (Wrongs Act, ss.33 and 34 do not alter this).

176 *Parker* v. *Dzundza* [1979] 1 N.S.W.L.R. 723.

177 *Toohey* v. *Hollier* (1954-5) 92 C.L.R. 618; *Birch* v. *Taubmans Ltd* [1957] S.R.(N.S.W.) 93; *Pickering* v. *Ready Mixed Concrete (Queensland) Pty Ltd* [1967] Q.W.N. 45.

178 *Keally* v. *Jones* [1979] 1 N.S.W.L.R. 723.

179 *Markellos* v. *Wakefield* (1974) 7 S.A.S.R. 436.

180 *Birch* v. *Taubmans* [1957] S.R.(N.S.W.) 93.

scowl rather than a smile'.[181] And since marriage is 'for better or for worse' a husband may be entitled only to modest damages for the fact that he now has to do more around the house.[182] Moreover, the principle in *Griffiths* v. *Kerkemeyer*[183] does not entitle him to damages representing the value of gratuitously rendered replacement services.[184]

Consortium 'in its fullest sense implies a companionship between each of them, entertainment of mutual friends, sexual intercourse—all those elements which, when combined, justify the old common law dictum that a man and his wife are one person'.[185] It goes without saying that the task of putting a value on the intangible elements of consortium is an extraordinarily artificial and difficult one. So compensation, it is said, should be reasonable, although not nominal or purely conventional.

Should the action for loss of consortium be abolished altogether? There is a strong argument, based on modern views of the nature of marriage and the respective roles of the partners to it in running the household, for doing away with compensation for loss of consortium as defined in the previous paragraph. It seems fair that a spouse should be able to recover expenses incurred by him or her and be compensated to some extent, at least, for losses suffered in looking after the other spouse. But such recovery can be fitted under other heads which we have already examined and has nothing to do with consortium as such. Recovery for loss of household services should be by the person who can no longer render them. There is no reason why the action should not be abolished entirely.

V: ACTIONS ARISING OUT OF THE DEATH OF ANOTHER PERSON

1. Fatal Accidents

In each State and Territory there are statutory provisions which enable dependants of a person killed by the tort of another to recover for loss to them arising out of the death.[186] Such actions are often referred to generally as actions under Lord Campbell's Act after the United Kingdom Act on which all the Australian provisions are modelled. The basic provision is much the same in all jurisdictions, and provides, in effect, that where the death of a person is caused by a wrongful act, neglect or default such as would, if death had not ensued, have entitled the person

---

181 *Keally* v. *Jones* [1979] 1 N.S.W.L.R. 723, 746 *per* Samuels J.A.

182 *Bagias* v. *Smith* [1979] F.L.C. 78,497, 78,510 *per* Hutley J.A.

183 (1977) 139 C.L.R. 161.

184 *Johnson* v. *Kelemic* [1979] F.L.C. 78,487; but see *Bertram* v. *Kapodistrias* [1984] V.R. 619.

185 *Crabtree* v. *Crabtree (No. 2)* [1964] A.L.R. 820 cited in *Rozario* v. *Fernandez* (1977) 16 A.L.R. 445.

186 Wrongs Act 1958 (Vic.) ss.15-22; Compensation to Relatives Act 1897 (N.S.W.); Wrongs Act 1936-75 (S.A.) Part II; Common Law Practice Act 1867-70 (Qld) ss.12-15C; Fatal Accidents Act 1934 (Tas.); Fatal Accidents 1959-84 (W.A.); Compensation (Fatal Injuries) Act 1974 (N.T.); Compensation (Fatal Injuries) Act 1968 (A.C.T.).

injured to maintain an action and recover damages in respect thereof, then the person responsible can be sued notwithstanding the death. This provision is an exception to a basic common law rule that the death of a person gives rise to no cause of action.[187]

(a) **The condition of the dependants' action** The dependants' action is independent of that of the deceased, but the requirement that the deceased, had he lived, would have been entitled to sue is a condition precedent of the dependants' action. The words 'wrongful act, neglect or default' include a breach of contract.[188] The condition is only satisfied if the deceased was in a position to sue at the date of his death;[189] if the deceased's claim was statute-barred at that date the dependants have no action unless the limitation period could have been extended in the discretion of the court.[190] If the deceased before his death brought an action and recovered damages, this would probably bar an action by his dependants.[191] In all jurisdictions except New South Wales and the A.C.T., contributory negligence on the part of the deceased has the effect of reducing the damages payable to the dependants in the same proportion as it would reduce the damages paid to the estate of the deceased suing on the deceased's cause of action after his death.[192] In the A.C.T. contributory negligence of the deceased is ignored;[193] this is also the basic position in New South Wales,[194] but not in motor accident and work accident cases[195] which, in practice, are the majority.

The statutes make the dependants' action conditional on death of the deceased caused by a wrongful act, neglect or default. In *Haber* v. *Walker*[196] it was held by majority that this means that all that need be shown is that there was a direct casual link between the wrong and the death. It is not necessary for the death to have been foreseeable. The disagreement on the issue arises out of crucial unclarity in *Chapman* v. *Hearse*[197] as to whether causation or foreseeability is the test, and this issue is not yet resolved in most jurisdictions.

---

187 *Burgess* v. *Florence Nightingale Hospital for Gentlewomen* [1955] 1 Q.B. 349.

188 *Woolworths Ltd* v. *Crotty* (1942) 66 C.L.R. 603.

189 *British Electric Railway Co.* v. *Gentile* [1914] A.C. 1034.

190 *Crawford* v. *Hydro-Electric Commission* [1963] Tas.S.R. 83.

191 *Pickett* v. *British Rail Engineering Ltd* [1980] A.C. 136, 148 *per* Lord Wilberforce; 152 *per* Lord Salmon; 162 *per* Lord Edmund-Davies. Cf. *Nominal Defendant (Qld)* v. *Taylor* (1982) 41 A.L.J.R. 244.

192 Wrongs Act 1958 (Vic.) s.26(4); Wrongs Act 1936-75 (S.A.) s.27a(8); Law Reform (Tortfeasors Contribution etc.) Act 1952 (Qld) s.10(4); Tortfeasors and Contributory Negligence Act (Tas.) s.4(4); Law Reform (Contributory Negligence & Tortfeasors' Contribution) Act 1947 (W.A.) s.4(2); Compensation (Fatal Injuries) Act 1974 (N.T.) s.11. This applies also where the deceased is killed partly by the fault of his agent: *Perrotta* v. *Cavallo* [1971] S.A.S.R. 163.

193 Compensation (Fatal Injuries) Act 1968 (A.C.T.) s.11 (substituted 1991).

194 Law Reform (Miscellaneous Provisions) Act 1965 (N.S.W.) s.10(4). The Victorian Chief Justice's Law Reform Committee suggested adoption of a similar provision: Report on Survival of Causes of Action (1982), para. 13.

195 Motor Accidents Act 1988 s.75; Workers Compensation Act 1987 s.151N(5).

196 [1963] V.R. 339.

197 (1961) 106 C.L.R. 112.

(b) The claimants The class of claimants is defined in each of the statutes and varies from jurisdiction to jurisdiction. In general terms the class consists of members of the immediate family of the deceased[198] and the action is most often brought on behalf of the spouse and children of the deceased. There is only one cause of action in respect of any death and it is brought on behalf of all the eligible beneficiaries by the deceased's personal representative or, in the absence of such, by the persons beneficially interested. If the executor brings no action within six months of the death the dependants can sue themselves. Members of the class of beneficiaries can be bound by any out-of-court settlement to which they give their assent.

Several of the statutes allow as claimants persons to whom the deceased stood *in loco parentis*. This phrase refers to a position where a person not only assumes the obligation of making financial provision for another but also actually takes on the role and duties of a parent—there must, in effect, be a foster relationship.[199] The phrase creates a concept of notional parenthood, of de facto incorporation into a family irrespective of ties of blood, marriage or adoption and regardless of legitimacy.[200]

The action must be commenced within three (in Victoria, six) years of the death (subject to any relevant provision for the extension of the limitation period) and the pleadings cannot be amended after the expiry of the period so as to add new claimants. Negligence on the part of any of the beneficiaries which contributed to the death of the deceased will affect the defendant's liability to him;[201] but since the remedy in damages is given to each of the dependants individually, negligence by one of them does not affect the rights of the others.[202]

(c) Assessment of damages The statutes say very little about the damages recoverable.[203] The court may award such damages as it thinks proportioned to the injury resulting from the death to each of the beneficiaries respectively. Costs not recovered from the defendant are deducted from the lump sum so calculated, and the single amount is then apportioned between the claimants in such shares as the court thinks fit. This means

---

198 But in Victoria the class of claimants includes all 'dependants': Wrongs (Dependants) Act 1982. Illegitimate and adopted children are specifically included in some jurisdictions. In New South Wales they may claim by virtue of the Children (Equality of Status) Act 1976: *McIntosh* v. *Williams* [1979] 2 N.S.W.L.R. 543. In many cases they would be covered by the *in loco parentis* provision on which see below. De facto husbands and wives are specifically provided for in some jurisdictions: Compensation to Relatives (De Facto Relationships) Amendment Act 1984 (N.S.W.); Wrongs Act 1936-75 (S.A.) s.20(4); Fatal Accidents Act 1985 (W.A.) 1959-84 s.6(1) and Sch.2(h); Compensation (Fatal Injuries) Act 1974 (N.T.) s.4(3) (this Act also allows the parties to a traditional Aboriginal marriage to claim); Compensation (Fatal Injuries) Act (A.C.T.) s.4(2)(h). Otherwise they have no claim. Separated spouses have a claim if they can establish loss.

199 *Nash* v. *Commissioner for Railways* [1963] S.R.(N.S.W.) 357; *Hunt* v. *National & General Insurance Co. Ltd* [1974] Qd.R. 157.

200 *Nash* v. *Commissioner for Railways* [1963] S.R.(N.S.W.) 357, 362.

201 *Kain & Shelton Ltd* v. *Virgo* (1965) 97 C.L.R. 230.

202 *Dodds* v. *Dodds* [1978] 2 All E.R. 539.

203 See generally *Horton* v. *Byrne* (1957) 30 A.L.J. 583.

that the share a claimant receives may not be proportional to the injury he suffers. This occurs most notably where the claimants are a spouse and children of the deceased, when the lion's share of the award is often apportioned to the parent who has the responsibility of looking after the children.[204]

The basic principle on which damages are awarded is that the dependants are to be compensated for pecuniary loss resulting from the death[205]—either the loss of actual pecuniary advantages or prospective pecuniary advantages, of which there was a reasonable expectation at the date of the death.[206] The loss must be referable to the relationship between the claimant and the deceased which gives rise to the claim. In *Burgess* v. *Florence Nightingale Hospital for Gentlewomen*[207] a husband and wife were professional dancers. The wife died as a result of the negligence of a surgeon and the husband, unable to find a suitable partner, lost income. The couple had been dancing partners long before they married, and it was held that the loss of income was referable not to their relationship as husband and wife but to their business relationship. On the other hand, the husband was allowed to recover on account of the fact that while the wife was alive they were living together and their living expenses were less than twice those of one living separately. The sharing of living expenses was referable to the marriage.

The multiplier method involving a discount for contingencies and early receipt is used here as well as in personal injury actions.[208] Damages for loss of dependency are calculated in one lump sum using a multiplier determined with reference to the date of death, not the date of trial.[209] But the damages are then divided into pre- and post-trial components[210] and

---

204 *Gullifer* v. *Pohto* [1978] 2 N.S.W.L.R. 353,359; *Mackenzie* v. *McNamara* [1970] 3 N.S.W.R. 421.

205 *Franklin* v. *South Eastern Railway Co.* (1858) 3 H. & N. 211; 157 E.R. 448. But there is a ceiling on damages in asbestos-related cases in Western Australia: Fatal Accidents Act 1959 s.7(4). If the deceased was killed by the second of two successive torts, the first of which reduced his ability to provide for his dependants, the tortfeasor responsible for the death would only be liable to pay damages for that reduced ability to provide: C. Phegan (1985) 34 *I.C.L.Q.* 470, 480-1. In the normal case, very little would be awarded for loss of a child; but see E. Quah and W. Rieber (1989) 9 *Int.J. of Law & Economics* 165.

206 *Taff Vale Railway Co.* v. *Jenkins* [1913] A.C. 1; *Chief Commissioner for Railways & Tramways (N.S.W.)* v. *Boylson* (1915) 19 C.L.R. 505.

207 [1955] 1 Q.B. 349. Cf. *Foodlands Association Ltd* v. *Mosscrop* [1985] W.A.R. 215; *Swan* v. *Williams (Demolition)* (1987) 9 N.S.W.L.R. 172.

208 *Nance* v. *British Columbia Electric Railway Co.* [1951] A.C. 601.

209 *Graham* v. *Dodds* [1983] 1 W.L.R. 808. But in exceptional cases, events occurring between the death and the date of trial can affect the multiplier: *Corbett* v. *Barking, Havering and Brentwood Health Authority* [1991] 2 Q.B. 408. The multiplicand, too, can be calculated in light of events occurring between death and trial.

210 *Australian Telecommunications Commission* v. *Parsons* (1985) 59 A.L.R. 535.

interest may be awarded only on the former.[211] Although *Todorovic* v. *Waller*[212] does not concern the appropriate discount rate for fatal accident cases, it is likely that the High Court would favour adopting the same discount rate for both personal injury and fatal accident cases, if only for the sake of uniformity and simplicity. The equivalent of the *Gourley* rule[213] for fatal accident cases is that the loss of dependency is to be assessed with reference to the deceased's income net of tax.[214]

In relation to the discount for vicissitudes, there are two relevant sets of vicissitudes: those which might have affected the deceased had he lived, and those which have affected or might affect the dependants. For example, the fact that the deceased spent time in gaol is relevant as showing that he might not always have been in a position to provide for his family;[215] and if the deceased provided for his family out of the proceeds of crime they may be denied recovery for loss of dependency.[216] Where the plaintiff and the deceased separated before the latter's death, the chance that they would have been reconciled if the deceased had lived is relevant to the assessment of damages.[217] A contingency which is ignored both in this area and in that of loss of consortium is the possibility of divorce.[218] The law makes the rather outdated assumption that most marriages are life-long unions. But this attitude is probably justified, in the absence of specific evidence that the marriage was likely to have broken up if the deceased had not died, by the speculative and unpleasant nature of any other approach.

The fact that a widow(er) or a bereaved de facto spouse has remarried or entered a new, de facto relationship[219] between the death and the trial has to be taken into account in assessing future pecuniary loss, to the extent that this reduces the claimant's loss of dependency.[220] Even if the claimant has not remarried or entered a new, de facto relationship before the trial, his or her prospects of remarriage or entering a new, de facto relationship

---

211 *State Government Insurance Office (Qld)* v. *Biemann* (1984) 154 C.L.R. 539. But in the earlier case of *Ruby* v. *Marsh* (1975) 132 C.L.R. 642 the High Court held that the Victorian legislation governing the award of interest required interest to be awarded on the whole of the lump sum; and the Victorian Full Court has applied this decision, and distinguished *Biemann* as applying to the Queensland legislation: *Wright* v. *West Australian Trustee Executor and Agency Co. Ltd* [1987] Aust. Torts Reports 68,849.

212 (1982) 150 C.L.R. 402.

213 See p. 488 above.

214 *Lincoln* v. *Gravil* (1954) 94 C.L.R. 430.

215 *Langlands* v. *Shepherd* (1964) 82 W.N.(Pt.1)(N.S.W.) 65; *Sinclair* v. *Bonnefin* (1968) 13 F.L.R. 164. The same consideration may be relevant in a personal injuries claim: *Meah* v. *McCreamer* [1985] 1 All E.R. 367.

216 *Burns* v. *Edman* [1970] 2 Q.B. 541.

217 *Davies* v. *Taylor* [1974] A.C. 207.

218 Also ignored is the fact that before the death of a spouse or partner, the couple had decided to have children: *Malone* v. *Rowan* [1984] 3 All E.R. 402.

219 *A.A.Tegel Pty Ltd* v. *Madden* (1985) 2 N.S.W.L.R. 591 (foreshadowed in *Budget Rent-a-Car Systems Pty Ltd* v. *Van Der Kemp* [1984] 3 N.S.W.L.R. 303); but contrast *Australian Telecommunications Commission* v. *Parsons* (1985) 59 A.L.R. 535.

220 *Willis* v. *The Commonwealth* (1946) 73 C.L.R. 105; *Fuller* v. *Clarkson* [1961] S.A.S.R. 340; *Hollebone* v. *Greenwood* (1968) 71 S.R.(N.S.W.) 424. Similarly, if a child claimant is adopted between the death of its parents and the trial, this is taken into account in assessing loss of dependency: *Watson* v. *Willmott* [1991] 1 Q.B. 140.

after judgment have to be taken into account.[221] The ultimate question is whether the remarriage or the new, de facto relationship is likely, as a matter of fact, to make the spouse and any children better or worse off or no better or worse off than before the deceased's death. The question is not what the claimants have a legal right to expect from the second spouse, but what, in fact, they have a reasonable expectation of receiving.[222] It has been pointed out that assessing the prospects of a new relationship may require a high degree of speculation, and despite the fact that statistical tables of rates of remarriage may be available, courts have expressed distaste at the element of personal evaluation involved.[223] Also, taking account of a new relationship actual or prospective is likely to be a disincentive to the formation of such a relationship and to encourage underestimation by the bereaved spouse of the prospect in order to attract a higher award.

In *Carroll* v. *Purcell*[224] it was held that although prospects of remarriage, or, in other words, the widow's revived capacity to marry, ought to be taken into account, her capacity to earn should be ignored. The reason for this approach was a view that the capacity to work is one which the widow enjoyed equally whether her husband was alive or dead and so his death did not revive it. And if the need, for example, to look after children meant that she could not work before, her husband's death will not alter this. By parity of reasoning, sums actually earned by a wife after her husband's death are not set off against her damages.[225]

Although only pecuniary loss is recoverable under the legislation, the notion of pecuniary loss is given a quite wide interpretation. It has long been established, for example, that a spouse can recover not only for the loss of actual monetary contributions which the other spouse made to their joint expenses, but also for loss of gratuitously rendered domestic services.[226] Such damages may be awarded even if the lost services have been replaced gratuitously by a third party, or even if they are not replaced at all but performed by those who have lost them.[227] Children have a right

221 *Carroll* v. *Purcell* (1961-2) 35 A.L.J.R. 384. Evidence that a widow has married since the trial may be admitted on appeal: *Government Insurance Office of New South Wales* v. *Maher* (1981) 55 F.L.R. 187.

222 *Hollebone* v. *Greenwood* (1968) 71 1 S.R.(N.S.W.) 424; *Allen* v. *The Commonwealth* (1980) 24 S.A.S.R. 581; *Australian Telecommunications Commission* v. *Parsons* (1985) 59 A.L.R. 535.

223 *Public Trustee* v. *Paniens* (1971) 1 S.A.S.R. 297.

224 (1961-2) 35 A.L.J.R. 384.

225 *Burley* v. *Trewartha* (1976) 13 S.A.S.R. 514.

226 *Berry* v. *Humm* [1915] 1 K.B. 627; *Wilson* v. *Rutter* (1956) 73 W.N.(N.S.W.) 294. But if the surviving spouse supported the deceased spouse financially, the cost of this support is to be set off against the value of the services lost: *Nguyen* v. *Nguyen* (1989) 169 C.L.R. 245, 257 *per* Deane J.

227 *Nguyen* v. *Nguyen* (1989) 169 C.L.R. 245. According to one view, the value of the services lost must be assessed in the light of whether it would be reasonable to expect those deprived to look after themselves in future (Deane J. at pp. 169-70; and see p. 493 above); but another view is that if a person would not have looked after himself if the service provider had not died, then he should be compensated for the loss of services (Dawson, Toohey and McHugh JJ. at p. 176). For more detail on valuation of gratuitous third-party or self-provided services see *Nguyen* v. *Nguyen* [1992] 1 Qd.R. 405.

to recover not only for such loss of their mother's services as their father can replace himself or by hiring a domestic helper, but also for loss of the intangible benefits such as their mother's care, encouragement and help rendered to them while she was alive.[228] Such intangibles, it can be argued, do have a pecuniary value in that they affect the child's material future by contributing to the child's moral, psychological and educational upbringing. Where the child claimants are illegitimate the mother, not being a legal wife, cannot claim, except in those jurisdictions which make specific provision for her (that is, New South Wales, South Australia, Western Australia, the Northern Territory and the Australian Capital Territory). But it has been held that, at least to the extent that if the mother is not supported she will not be able to look after the children as well as before, an amount representing the de facto wife's loss of support should be included in the children's damages.[229]

The above principles set the limits of the non-tangible losses arising out of the death of another for which compensation can be awarded at common law. Damages cannot be awarded for grief or sorrow at the loss of another.[230] Nor can damages be awarded for pecuniary loss resulting from emotional suffering, because such pecuniary losses do not result directly from the death. However, in South Australia[231] and the Northern Territory[232] there are statutory provisions allowing the award of a sum by way of *solatium*. *Solatium* compensates for any loss or injury which does not fall within the meaning of pecuniary loss; where pecuniary loss ends, *solatium* begins.[233] So a parent can recover for the fact that many hopes and expectations were invested in a deceased child.[234] In awarding *solatium* the court takes account of the degree of the defendant's negligence and the degree of suffering experienced by the claimant (although an emotional claimant should not necessarily get any more than a stoical one).[235] A widow(er)'s prospects of happiness in a second marriage are also relevant.[236] The nature of the relations between the claimant and the deceased can be a ground for reducing the award[237] or, in South Australia, refusing to make one at all.[238] The wealth or standing of the claimant is irrelevant.[239] In South Australia there are statutory limits on the amount which can be awarded. It has been held that under the Northern Territory

228 *Fisher* v. *Smithson* (1978) 17 S.A.S.R. 223; *Hay* v. *Hughes* [1975] Q.B. 790; *Regan* v. *Williamson* [1976] 1 W.L.R. 305. The same applies to the loss of a father: *Jacobs* v. *Varley* (1976) 9 A.L.R. 219, 234-5 *per* Murphy J. See also *Spittle* v. *Bunney* [1988] 1 W.L.R. 847 on relevance of age of child to valuing parent's services.

229 K. v. *J.M.P. Co. Ltd* [1976] Q.B. 85; *Johnson* v. *Ryan* [1977] 1 N.S.W.L.R. 294; *Radovanovic* v. *Motor Vehicle Insurance Trust* [1980] W.A.R. 105.

230 *Blake* v. *Midland Railway Co.* (1892) 18 Q.B. 93; *Public Trustee* v. *Zoanetti* (1945) 70 C.L.R. 266, 276 *per* Dixon J.

231 Wrongs Act 1936-75 (S.A.), ss.23a and 23b.

232 Compensation (Fatal Injuries) Act 1974 (N.T.), s.10(3)(f).

233 *Jeffries* v. *Commonwealth of Australia* [1946] S.A.S.R. 106.

234 *Taverner* v. *Swanbury* [1944] S.A.S.R. 194.

235 ibid.

236 *Rafferty* v. *Barclay* [1942] S.A.S.R. 194.

237 *Taverner* v. *Swanbury* [1944] S.A.S.R. 194.

238 Wrongs Act (S.A.), s.23c(2).

239 *Rafferty* v. *Barclay* [1942] S.A.S.R. 147.

Act the court's discretion is not to be limited by analogous reference to these statutory limits.[240]

Various of the statutes make explicit provision for the recovery of other heads of damage, such as medical expenses and burial or funeral expenses, incurred by the claimants. Funeral and other expenses are only recoverable to the extent that they have been actually incurred.[241]

As a general rule, benefits accruing to the claimants from the death of the deceased have to be set off against the loss suffered by them as a result of the death in assessing their damages.[242] As in the case of losses, so here the question is whether an actual benefit has been received or whether there was, at the date of the death, a reasonable expectation of benefit flowing from the death.[243] The benefit must result from the death.[244] But the requirement of causal link has been interpreted broadly. Thus, actual remarriage is treated as a benefit resulting from the death rather than as a result of the actions of the widow(er) and her (or his) new spouse. On the other hand, a spouse's ability to go out and work after the deceased's death is not treated as a benefit flowing from the death;[245] more curiously, neither are actual earnings. Damages awarded under legislation providing for the survival of causes of action to the estate of a deceased person must be taken into account in assessing damages in a fatal accidents action to the extent, at any rate, that they arise out of the death.[246] Damages in respect of the period between the accident and the death do not so arise.

To be set off, a benefit must be referable to the relationship between the claimant and the deceased on which his claim is founded. The question whether, for example, the profits of a partnership hotel business are referable to the relationship of husband and wife or to a business relationship is one of fact.[247]

As in the case of personal injury actions, so here the common law notion of reasonable expectation of pecuniary benefit does not require charitable relief or generosity to be off-set.[248] The theoretical reason for this seems to be that charity results from the generosity of the giver, not the death, and that in most cases a dependant will have no reasonable expectation of charity. The same principle applies to gratuitous services as much as to monetary payments.[249] It would seem that if a casual nexus between the death and the charity or a reasonable expectation of its receipt

---

240 *Cook* v. *Cavenagh* (1981) 10 N.T.R. 35.

241 *Breeze* v. *Edwards* (1963) 81 W.N.(Pt.1)(N.S.W.) 12; *Adams* v. *Dillon* [1962] Tas.S.R. 310.

242 *Nance's* case [1951] A.C. 601; *Public Trustee* v. *Zoanetti* (1945) 70 C.L.R. 266, 276 *per* Dixon J.

243 e.g. *Mockridge* v. *Watson* [1960] V.R. 405.

244 *Carroll* v. *Purcell* (1961-2) 35 A.L.J.R. 384; *McCullagh* v. *Lawrence* [1989] 1 Qd.R. 163.

245 See p. 513 above.

246 *Davies* v. *Powell Duffryn Associated Collieries Ltd* [1942] A.C. 601.

247 *Henry* v. *Perry* [1964] V.R. 174.

248 *Wilson* v. *Rutter* (1956) 73 W.N.(N.S.W.) 294.

249 *Hay* v. *Hughes* [1975] Q.B. 790.

could be shown, charitable payments or services might be taken into account.[250]

The general common law principle that benefits accruing from the death are to be set off has been so heavily modified by statute that it is probably accurate to say that there is a general statutory principle against off-setting. All the statutes provide that the proceeds of insurance policies shall not be set off. Whether a pension scheme falls within the description of 'a contract of assurance or insurance' depends on the nature of the scheme. The fact that it is contributory or not, voluntary or not, is relevant but not conclusive.[251] In several jurisdictions the proceeds of superannuation funds are not to be set off;[252] and in some, social security benefits are to be ignored.[253] In a few, gratuities are specifically exempted from set-off. Provisions such as these are intended to benefit the plaintiff, and so payments falling within them are not ignored in calculating the claimant's loss of dependency. For example, if the deceased received a pension or some other payment before his death, the loss of the benefit of this to the claimant by his death is relevant to the assessment of the loss.[254]

2. Survival of Actions

The basic rule at common law was that the personal representatives of a deceased person could neither sue nor be sued for any tort committed by or against the deceased.[255] This general rule has now been significantly modified by statute in all Australian jurisdictions.[256] The basic provision is that on the death of a person all causes of action subsisting against or vested in him survive against his estate or, as the case may be, for the benefit of his estate. Certain causes of action do not survive because they are considered to be too personal to the deceased: actions for defamation,[257] seduction or inducing one spouse to leave another, or damages claims for

---

250 *Mockridge* v. *Watson* [1960] V.R. 405; *Papowski* v. *The Commonwealth* [1958] S.A.S.R. 293.

251 *Parker* v. *The Commonwealth* (1965) 112 C.L.R. 295.

252 The provision applies to statutory as well as voluntary superannuation schemes: *Peipman* v. *Turner* (1961) 78 W.N.(N.S.W.) 362.

253 Some forms of social welfare which partake of the nature of charity might not be set off if the chance of receiving them is unpredictable: *Parker* v. *Willmott* (1983) 1 S.R.(W.A.) 412. The argument against deducting social security benefits from damages is that to do so relieves the tortfeasor of liability at the expense of the public purse: *Lincoln* v. *Gravil* (1954) 94 C.L.R. 430 *per* Webb J. (dissenting). But if the benefits have already been received the public purse is not relieved unless the recipient is under a duty to repay them if he recovers damages.

254 *Watson* v. *Dennis* (1969) 88 W.N.(Pt.1)(N.S.W.) 491; *Vaughan* v. *Olver* [1977] Qd.R. 1; *Wright* v. *Dwyer* [1977] Tas.S.R. 131 (N.C.2).

255 The Latin maxim was *actio personalis moritur cum persona.*

256 Law Reform (Miscellaneous Provisions) Act 1944 (N.S.W.) s.2; Administration and Probate Act 1958 (Vic.) s.29; Common Law Practice Act 1867-1981 (Qld) s.150; Survival of Causes of Action Act 1940 (S.A.); Law Reform (Miscellaneous Provisions) Act 1941 (W.A.) s.4; Administration and Probate Act 1935 (Tas.) s.27; Law Reform (Miscellaneous Provisions) Act (N.T.) Part II; Law Reform (Miscellaneous Provisions) Ordinance 1955 (A.C.T.) Part II.

257 Except in Tasmania. See also Defamation Act 1974 (N.S.W.) s.46.

adultery. A claim under a survival statute is not a new cause of action created by the Act; it is a cause of action existing independently of the Act which is preserved from the extinction which the death of the deceased would otherwise have brought about.[258]

There are limitations on the damages recoverable in such actions.[259] Exemplary damages are excluded even where it is the victim rather than the tortfeasor who has died. There is a distinction between cases where the death of the victim of the tort was caused by the tort and cases where it was not. In the former case the damages are to be assessed without reference to any loss or gain to his estate consequent upon the death, except that a sum in respect of funeral expenses may be included. This provision precludes off-setting of incidental gains such as pensions, superannuation benefits or insurance moneys, and is presumably meant to bring actions under this legislation in respect of the death of a person into the line with actions under the fatal accidents legislation. But in such cases, damages cannot be recovered for the deceased's pain and suffering, for bodily or mental harm suffered by him or for the curtailment of his expectation of life. This provision is designed to ensure that the estate recovers only for loss suffered by those left behind as a result of the deceased's death. It is not clear why this provision should not extend to cases where the death occurred independently of the tort, and in some jurisdictions this is the case.[260]

It will be recalled that it was decided in *Skelton* v. *Collins*[261] that damages for loss of earning capacity are to be calculated on the basis of the victim's pre-accident rather than his post-accident life expectancy. In other words, damages may be recovered for loss of earnings in the lost years if the defendant's tortious act reduces the victim's life expectancy. The High Court has held that the right to recover such damages survives to the estate in the absence of statutory provision to the contrary.[262] This interpretation of the survival of actions legislation creates the possibility that a defendant might be liable twice over to different plaintiffs in certain circumstances. For this reason, the effect of the High Court's decision has been reversed by statute in most jurisdictions.[263] In some jurisdictions the new provision applies whether or not the death was caused by the tort.[264] If it was caused by the tort, damages for loss of support will be recoverable by qualified relatives under fatal accidents legislation. In cases where the

---

258 *Richters* v. *Motor Tyre Service Pty Ltd* [1972] Qd.R. 9.

259 But basic principle is that the estate can recover such damages as the deceased plaintiff could have recovered had he lived. This includes damages for gratuitous services: *Harper* v. *Phillips* [1985] W.A.R. 100. Re asbestos-related cases in W.A. see Law Reform (Miscellaneous Provisions) Act 1941 s.4(2)(ca).

260 Qld, S.A., W.A. and Tas.

261 (1966) 115 C.L.R. 94.

262 *Fitch* v. *Hyde-Cates* (1982) 150 C.L.R. 482; cf. *Gammell* v. *Wilson* [1982] A.C. 27.

263 N.S.W. Act s.2(a)(ii); Qld Act s.150(2)(d)(ii) (see also Succession Act 1981 (Qld) s.66(2)(d)(ii)); Survival of Causes of Action Amendment Act 1982 (S.A.); Administration and Probate Act 1958 (Vic.) s.29(2)(c)(ii); Law Reform (Miscellaneous Provisions) Amendment Act 1982 (W.A.); Administration and Probate Amendment Act 1983 (Tas.) cf. Administration of Justice Act 1982 (U.K.) s.4(2).

264 Qld, S.A., W.A. and Tas.

death was not caused by the tort, the common law principle that vicissitudes materializing between the date of the tort and the trial must be taken into account in assessing damages would produce the same result as the statutes.

It is worth noting that a group which will sometimes suffer badly by abolition of survival of the head of damages of loss of earnings for the lost years are third-party creditors of the estate. The interests of such creditors are ignored because of the fear that, since the survival of actions allows recovery for economic loss consequential on the death of another, if third-party creditors were let in, there would be no way of limiting the class of potentially affected parties.

It should be noted that it is specifically provided that a cause of action under fatal accidents legislation survives for or against the estate of a deceased person. However, in South Australia the Wrongs Act provides that the causes of action for *solatium* provided by the Act do not survive.[265]

All of the statutes except that in Queensland impose time limits for the bringing of survival actions, but they are quite liberal. This is clearly of importance where the deceased is the tortfeasor.[266] The statutes also provide that where the tortfeasor dies before or at the same time as the damage caused by the tort occurs, there is deemed to exist against him such cause of action in respect of his tort as would have existed if he had died after the damage had been suffered. So, if the tortfeasor dies in the same accident as the deceased victim, the latter's dependants can sue the estate of the tortfeasor.[267]

VI: PERSONAL INJURY, DEATH AND FINANCIAL LOSS

There is one strand in the above discussion of damages recoverable in actions arising out of personal injury and death which deserves a little more discussion. It concerns the extent to which proof of financial loss is a precondition of the recovery of damages. The heads of damages which we have called damages for non-pecuniary loss do not compensate for financial loss, and the plaintiff need not prove any financial loss in order to recover under these heads. At the other extreme is loss of earning capacity: here damages can be awarded only if and to the extent that the plaintiff can prove that the loss of capacity has been, or will likely be, productive of financial loss. A person is not entitled to compensation for the loss of a capacity to earn which he has never exercised and will never exercise.

But there are heads of damages which, as it were, fall between these two extremes. Take, first, damages for gratuitous services rendered to the

265 Section 23c(3).
266 On the power of the court to extend the period see Limitation (Amendment) Act 1990 (N.S.W.); Limitation of Actions (Personal Injury Claims) Act 1983 (Vic.), s.10.
267 *Partridge* v. *Chick* (1950-1) 84 C.L.R. 611.

plaintiff.[268] By definition, these do not compensate the plaintiff for financial loss he has suffered because he has not paid for the services; furthermore, damages can be recovered even if the plaintiff is under no obligation, either legal or moral, to pay for the services, and the law imposes no obligation to use the damages to pay the service provider. Moreover, damages may be awarded under this head representing the 'value' of the services, even if the service provider has suffered no financial loss in providing them. So it was suggested above that the reason why damages are awarded under this head is to ensure that the defendant's activity bears all of the 'costs' it generates: this notion of 'cost' recognizes that services may be of economic importance even if they are rendered for no financial return and at no financial cost.

Secondly, consider damages for loss of the ability to perform unpaid domestic services. Once again, this loss may not be productive of financial loss if the services are replaced gratuitously by a third party; or if they are not replaced because the beneficiaries of the services do without them or do for themselves what was previously done for them. It is generally agreed that the fact that the services are gratuitously replaced by a third party provides no reason not to compensate for their loss. The reasons for this conclusion are the same as we have just considered in relation to services gratuitously provided to an injured plaintiff. It is also generally agreed that the mere fact that the services are not replaced at a financial cost provides no reason not to compensate for their loss. Once again, the basis of this approach appears to be that the lost services were economically valuable, even though not financially rewarded, and that this value represents a cost which the defendant's activity ought to bear; and that it represents a loss to the beneficiaries of the services.

Consider, finally, claims in respect of loss of unpaid domestic services brought by the beneficiaries of the services either in an action for loss of consortium or in a fatal accidents action. As under previous heads, damages can be awarded for such loss even if the services are gratuitously replaced by a third party. But in respect of these claims there is a view which says that damages for the loss of unpaid domestic services should not represent the full value of those services (whether they are replaced or not) if and to the extent that it would be reasonable to expect the beneficiaries of the services to do without or to look after themselves. In other words, although the fact that loss of unpaid domestic services is not productive of financial loss does not, in itself, provide a reason not to compensate for it, nevertheless to the extent that replacing the services at a cost would be thought unreasonable, to that extent also compensation will not be given for unreplaced services. But this view is not universal, and we have seen that a majority of the High Court in a fatal accident case appear to have taken the view that a person ought to be compensated to the full extent of his loss of domestic services as a result of a tort.[269]

---

268 What follows applies to the common law rules unmodified by statute.
269 See n. 227 above.

VII: DAMAGES FOR DAMAGE TO PROPERTY AND ECONOMIC INTERESTS

1. DISCOUNT RATE

We have seen that the High Court in *Todorovic* v. *Waller* fixed the discount rate for personal injury actions at 3 per cent.[270] The earlier case of *Barrell Insurances Pty Ltd* v. *Pennant Hills Restaurants Pty Ltd*[271] involved a claim for damages for economic loss caused by the failure of a broker to keep the plaintiff's workers' compensation policy current. A majority of the High Court settled on a discount rate of 2 per cent. *Barrell* was distinguished or doubted by the judges in *Todorovic*, and it is perhaps likely that when the issue arises again the High Court will, in recognition of the essentially arbitrary nature of the choice of any particular figure, adopt 3 per cent as the rate for cases of economic loss for the sake of uniformity.

2. TAX ON THE AWARD

The rule in *Gourley's* case[272] applies to cases not involving personal injury to the same extent and in the same way as it applies to personal injury actions.

3. DATE FOR ASSESSMENT OF DAMAGES

There has been much discussion in recent cases involving damage to buildings[273] about the proper date at which to assess damages in cases where the cost of repair has risen because of inflation between the date of the damage and the date of the trial.[274] Two separate questions become entangled in the cases.[275] The first concerns mitigation of damages: ought the plaintiff be limited to recovering damages for losses suffered up to the date when he ought reasonably to have had the repairs done? The second concerns pre-trial inflation: if the cost of doing those repairs rises because of inflation between the date when the plaintiff ought reasonably to have had the repairs done and the date of judgment, who should bear the cost of that inflation? Should the plaintiff's damages be assessed according to costs and prices at the 'mitigation date' or should the defendant be required to pay damages assessed in currency values at the date of judgment?

---

270 See p. 489 above.
271 (1981) 145 C.L.R. 625.
272 See p. 488 above.
273 But this issue can arise in other types of case as well. See, for example, *Koutsonicolis* v. *Principe* (1987) 48 S.A.S.R. 328; *Rentokil Pty Ltd* v. *Channon* (1990) 19 N.S.W.L.R. 417.
274 See P. Cane (1984) 10 *Mon.L.R.* 17, 17-23.
275 Different issues arise in cases where a solicitor is sued for negligent failure to bring litigation to a proper conclusion. Here, the rule is that damages are to be assessed as at the date the action failed: *Johnson* v. *Perez* (1988) 166 C.L.R 351; *Nikolaou* v. *Papasavas* (1988) 166 C.L.R 394.

We have already discussed some of the relevant cases in the context of remoteness of damage,[276] because a common third strand in these cases is that the plaintiff argues that he was justified in delaying the doing of repairs because he was short of money, with the result that any additional loss attributable to his impecuniosity is not too remote to be recovered. The position is somewhat confused by failure in the cases to distinguish clearly between these separate strands, but the position appears to be as follows. If the plaintiff ought, in the light of all relevant factors, including his financial position, to have taken action to mitigate his loss, then the date at which he ought to have acted will be the latest date for determining the losses for which he is to be compensated. But in assessing damages for these losses, the plaintiff is entitled to cast the burden of inflation on the defendant and have his damages assessed in currency values as at the date of trial.

4. Damage to and Destruction of Chattels

The leading case concerning the measure of damages for destruction of chattels is *The Liesbosch*.[277] The basic measure of damages in the case of a profit-earning chattel is its value to the owner as a going concern at the time and place of its loss.[278] In assessing the profit-earning value of a chattel it is necessary to capitalize its future engagements to present value; but this sum is not merely added to the market value of the chattel, since the earning of profits would preclude sale. If the plaintiff is no longer in the line of business for which the chattel is designed, so that the chattel has no profit-earning value for him, some other measure, such as resale value, would be appropriate.[279] Similarly, if for some reason, such as a slump in the market, a profit-earning chattel was not in profitable use, market value would be the proper measure.[280]

If (as will often be the case) the plaintiff intends to replace (or has replaced) the chattel, the appropriate measure of damages will be the cost of purchasing a replacement, not resale value. The plaintiff is also entitled to recover the cost of the replacement exercise including transporting of the replacement to the site where it is to be used, any costs of adaptation, insurance, interest, overheads and so on. Also, the plaintiff can recover any losses on contracts in hand when the chattel was destroyed, subject to his having reasonably mitigated those losses. If the chattel is not replaceable in the market, the plaintiff might be awarded the cost of having a replacement made. This measure might be appropriate, for example, in cases of destruction of buildings by fire.[281]

In the case of non-profit-earning chattels, the basic measure of damages is market value, which, in this context, will usually mean the cost of

---

276 See pp.471-2 above.
277 [1933] A.C. 449.
278 *Electricity Trust of S.A.* v. *O'Leary* (1986) 42 S.A.S.R. 26.
279 *Mizza* v. *H.W. McKay-Massey Harris Pty Ltd* (1935) 37 W.A.L.R. 87.
280 *The Liesbosch* [1933] A.C. 449, 464.
281 *Harbutt's Plasticine Ltd* v. *Wayne Tank & Pump Ltd* [1970] 1 Q.B. 447.

buying a replacement of equivalent quality.[282] If the plaintiff, albeit in reasonable mitigation of his loss, buys a new chattel to replace an old one, he can only recover the cost of purchasing an aged chattel.[283] Even if the chattel was not itself a profit earner, its destruction may produce loss of income or other consequential loss. The plaintiff could recover damages for loss of use measured probably by the cost of hiring a replacement until steps could be taken to purchase a replacement. Recovery for other items of consequential loss would depend on application of the rules of remoteness of damage.

The most commonly adopted measure of damages for damage to chattels is the cost of repairs. The plaintiff can recover the reasonable cost of repairs even if he does them himself.[284] But the cost-of-repairs measure is subsidiary to the diminution-in-value measure: the plaintiff is entitled to the difference between the value of the chattel before the accident and its value immediately after the accident.[285] So a plaintiff may recover diminution in value even though it is greater than the cost of repairs; he is not required to repair rather than sell, nor need he establish that selling was the more reasonable course of action in the circumstances.[286] If he does repair, any residual diminution in value after the repairs have been done can be recovered in addition to the cost of repairs.[287] If repairs are uneconomic, that is, if they will cost more than the market value of the goods, then the case will be treated as one of constructive total loss, and market value, in the sense of replacement cost, will be the proper measure.[288] Similarly, if the cost of repairs is greater than the diminution in value, then, in normal circumstances, depreciation will be the proper measure. But if the chattel is in some way unique or has special or peculiar value for the owner which is not reflected in its market value, he may be allowed to recover the cost of repair even if this exceeds the diminution in market value.[289]

A plaintiff whose goods are damaged can also recover for consequential loss. In the case of a non-profit-earning chattel this will usually take the form of loss of use, and the appropriate measure will be the cost of hiring

---

282 e.g. *Millar* v. *Candy* (1981) 38 A.L.R. 299; cf. *Phillips* v. *Ward* [1956] 1 W.L.R. 471.
283 *Hoad* v. *Scone Motors Pty Ltd* [1977] 1 N.S.W.L.R. 88.
284 *Price* v. *Commissioner of Highways* [1968] S.A.S.R. 329; *Commonwealth Railways Commissioner* v. *Hodsdon* (1970) 16 F.L.R. 437.
285 *Dryden* v. *Orr* (1928) 28 S.R.(N.S.W.) 216.
286 *Davidson* v. *J.S. Gilbert Fabrications Pty Ltd* [1986] 1 Qd.R. 1; Derrington J. disagreed on this last point.
287 ibid.; *Eastern Construction Co. Pty Ltd* v. *Southern Portland Cement Ltd* (1961) 78 W.N.(N.S.W.) 293.
288 *Van der Wal* v. *Harris* [1961] W.A.R. 124; *Dominion Mosaics & Tile Co. Ltd* v. *Trafalgar Trucking Co. Ltd* [1990] 2 All E.R. 246.
289 *Anthoness* v. *Bland Shire Council* [1960] S.R.(N.S.W.) 659.

an alternative while repairs are done.[290] If the chattel is a profit-earning one, the measure of the plaintiff's damages will be loss of profits[291] or, alternatively, interest on the value of the chattel during the period it was out of operation.[292]

What if the repairs add to the pre-accident value of the chattel? Must the plaintiff make allowance for this? Most of the cases on this question concern damage to land or structures on land and will be considered below. One might have thought that since the defendant is liable for any residual diminution in value after repairs have been done, it would follow that the plaintiff would have to make an allowance for any residual increase in value, and there is authority to this effect.[293]

5. DAMAGE TO REAL PROPERTY

The basic measure of damages for damage to land (for example, by removal of lateral or subjacent support) is diminution in value. But the cost of restoration may be recoverable provided it is not disproportionate to the value of the land.[294] It may be that cost of restoration would be more readily awarded in cases of damage to buildings as opposed to the soil itself.[295] It will usually be reasonable for a plaintiff to reduce his loss by repairing a building[296] or constructing a replacement, whether to mitigate loss of profits or to restore a family home to habitability.[297] The cost of repair will not necessarily be disproportionate to the value of the land or building just because it is greater than the diminution in value (or even if

---

290 *R.* v. *Owners of S.S. Argyllshire, The Argyllshire* [1922] St.R.Qd. 186; in some cases it might be reasonable for the plaintiff to buy a temporary replacement: *Reid* v. *Brown* (1952) 69 W.N.(N.S.W.) 131. There are cases in which damages for loss of use of a non-profit-earning chattel have been awarded even though the plaintiff did not hire a substitute: *The Mediana* [1900] A.C. 113; *The Chekiang* [1926] A.C. 637; *Birmingham Corporation* v. *Sowersby* [1970] R.T.R. 84; cf. *Nauru Local Government Council* v. *New Zealand Seamen's Industrial Union of Workers* [1986] 1 N.Z.L.R. 466 (actionable deprivation of use).

291 *Price* v. *Commissioner of Highways* [1968] S.A.S.R. 329; *Zappulla* v. *Perkins* [1978] Qd.R. 92.

292 *Jillett* v. *Hungerford* [1956] Q.W.N. 14. Analogous issues arise in cases where, as a result of the defendant's tort, the plaintiff is deprived of the use of money; as to which see *Hungerfords* v. *Walker* (1989) 84 A.L.R. 119; *Boden* v. *Gordon* [1985] 1 Qd.R. 483.

293 *Eastern Construction* v. *Southern Portland Cement* (1961) 78 W.N.(N.S.W.) 293.

294 *Jones* v. *Shire of Perth* [1971] W.A.R. 56; *Hansen* v. *Gloucester Developments Pty Ltd* [1992] 1 Qd.R. 14. But restoration must be legally possible, unless the plaintiff owns other property which, by restoration, could provide a substitute for the damaged property; in which case, damages not exceeding the cost of restoring the damaged property could be awarded to enable restoration of the alternative: *Ward* v. *Cannock Chase District Council* [1986] Ch. 546.

295 *Clearlite Holdings Ltd* v. *Auckland City Corporation* [1976] 2 N.Z.L.R. 729; *Taylor* v. *Auto Trade Supply Ltd* [1972] N.Z.L.R. 102.

296 As a general rule, it is more likely to be reasonable to repair buildings than chattels because, in the case of real property, selling the damaged premises and buying a substitute is often not a realistic option.

297 *Livingstone* v. *Raywards Coal Co.* (1880) 5 App. Cas. 25 (profits); *Evans* v. *Balog* [1976] 1 N.S.W.L.R. 36 (family home).

the diminution in value is nil).[298] If the plaintiff intends to continue occupying the building then awarding the cost of repair may be the only way of fairly compensating him.[299] In fact, it may be that the proper approach to proportionality is simply to ask whether in all the circumstances it was reasonable for the plaintiff to repair the building. If the plaintiff's intention is simply to sell the property after repairing it, the proper measure would be the diminution in the sale value as a result of the tort.

In some cases, buying a substitute building might be a reasonable way of mitigating the loss; and, if so, the court may award the cost of the new building even if that exceeds the pre-tort value of the damaged premises.[300] The plaintiff may also recover for consequential losses, such as loss of profits in the case of a commercial building or farming land, or the cost of alternative accommodation in the case of a dwelling.

In rare cases neither the diminution-in-value nor the cost-of-restoration measures may be appropriate. For example, in *Genders* v. *South Australian Railways Commissioner*[301] the defendant negligently caused a fire on arable land belonging to the plaintiff. It was held that the *prima facie* measure of damages was the extra cost of clearing the land as a result of the fire. Again, in *Williamson* v. *Commissioner for Railways*[302] where grass on the plaintiff's grazing land was destroyed, the *prima facie* measure was the cost of buying fodder or the cost of agistment.

If the cost of reinstatement is awarded, the plaintiff can recover, in addition, for any residual diminution in value. But what if the expenditure on reinstatement increases the value of the property? Does the plaintiff have to make allowance for the increase (for 'betterment' as it is often called)? There are authorities both ways on this point.[303] The best approach is to ask in every case whether the plaintiff had any real choice whether to repair in such a way as would improve the property. If the repairs which had to be done to repair the damage caused by the defendant's tort necessarily involved improvement, either because of legal requirements as to how the property was to be repaired, or because the repairs could not physically be done without improving the property, no allowance for the improvement should be made—unless, perhaps, the plaintiff's only interest in the property is commercial, so that he can and will recoup the value of the improvement on resale.[304]

---

298 But suppose, for example, that the building was on land zoned for high-rise development: the building would have no real value, but the cost of repairing it would be substantial. In such case, repairing might be held to be unreasonable.

299 *Evans* v. *Balog* [1976] 1 N.S.W.L.R. 36.

300 *Dominion Mosaics & Tile Co. Ltd* v. *Trafalgar Trucking Co. Ltd* [1990] 2 All E.R. 246.

301 [1928] S.A.S.R. 272.

302 [1960] S.R.(N.S.W.) 252.

303 Yes: *Bushells Pty Ltd* v. *Commonwealth* [1948] St.R.Qd. 79; *Robinson* v. *Sherwood* (1925) 28 W.A.L.R. 21; *Hargrave* v. *Robinson* (1953) 70 W.N.(N.S.W.) 50; *Westwood* v. *Cordwell* [1983] 1 Qd.R. 276. No: *Adams* v. *Mayor of Brunswick* (1894) 20 V.L.R. 455; *Rockhampton Harbour Board* v. *Ocean Steamship Co. Ltd* [1930] St.R.Qd. 343.

304 Similar principles regarding 'betterment' can be relevant in other types of case as well. See, for example, *Hardware Services Pty Ltd* v. *Primac Association Ltd* [1988] 1 Qd R. 393, 401.

Finally, the plaintiff can recover the cost of taking measures to protect his land, structures or chattels from damage if, were they damaged, the defendant would be liable for that damage.[305]

All these principles must be read subject to the possibility that the plaintiff may have only a limited interest in the land: the plaintiff will be entitled to recover damages only to the extent that *his* interest has been damaged. For example, a reversioner can recover only if the property has suffered some permanent damage.[306]

6. Economic Loss Resulting from Damage to Another's Property

It will be recalled that in *Caltex* v. *Dredge 'Willemstad'*[307] the High Court held that in certain circumstances a plaintiff could recover damages for economic loss suffered as a result of damage to property belonging to another. It has been argued that the damages recoverable under this principle are normally restricted to expenses actually incurred, and do not extend to profits not realized.[308] But this is not an appealing distinction because it is apt to operate quite fortuitously.

7. Financial Losses Resulting from Negligent Statements or Financial Services

As we have already seen, the basic rule is that professionals can be sued concurrently in tort and contract. It is also the case that misrepresentations which induce contracts often give rise to rights of action in both tort and contract.[309] The rules for assessing damages in tort and contract are, in some respects, different. Suppose that A, as a result of negligent professional advice from B, invests $X with the hope of making a profit of $Y, but ends up losing all his money; and suppose that if he had not made this investment, he would have made a different investment on which he would have made a smaller profit of $Y–Z. Whether A frames his action in tort or contract, he will be able to recover his lost capital of $X. He may under certain circumstances also recover the profit of $Y–Z, which he would have made on the alternative investment, whether he frames his action in tort or contract. But it is only if he frames his action in contract that he will have any chance of recovering the expected profit of $Y on the investment he actually made. However, even by suing in contract he may not be able to recover that expected profit, unless B is held to have *warranted* that A would make a profit of $Y. If B only undertook to take

305 *New Zealand Forest Products Ltd* v. *O'Sullivan* [1974] 2 N.Z.L.R. 80. Because such damages represent purely economic loss, they would probably not be recoverable in England unless *Hedley Byrne* principles were satisfied on the facts.

306 This issue most often arises in nuisance actions; see p. 605 below.

307 (1976) 136 C.L.R. 529.

308 R. Hayes (1979) 12 *M.U.L.R.* 79; for a detailed reply see P. Cane (1980) 12 *M.U.L.R.* 408.

309 e.g. *Esso Petroleum Ltd* v. *Mardon* [1976] Q.B. 801.

care to see that A would realize a profit of $Y, then the most A can recover, even if he frames his action in contract, is $X plus (Y−Z).

Thus, as a general proposition, it is probably true to say that the test for assessment of damages for breach of a contractual duty of care is the same as the test for assessment of damages for breach of a tortious duty of care.[310] It is only if the plaintiff can satisfy the court that the defendant warranted by his contract that the former would reap a specified profit that there will be any advantage to him, so far as assessment of damages is concerned, in framing his action in contract rather than tort. In fact, many actions against professionals are simply framed as actions for 'professional negligence' without specifying whether the action is one in tort or contract or both.

In this section, we are basically concerned with cases in which, as result of bad advice or the inadequate performance of financial services (that is, services other than those involving the production of buildings or chattels, which are dealt with below), a person invests or expends money, or makes a loan, or purchases property at an overvalue;[311] or in which, alternatively, a person, as a result of reliance on another to protect his financial interests, fails to take steps to protect himself.

A straightforward example of the latter type of case is that of the insurance broker who negligently fails to renew the plaintiff's policy or to inform the plaintiff that it has not been renewed. In such a case, the measure of damages is the sum the plaintiff would have received under the policy if it had been in force.[312] He may also recover for consequential losses.[313] There are a number of cases in which auditors have been sued for negligent failure to discover defalcations by an employee of the plaintiff. Here the measure of damages is the money which would have been saved if the defendant had not been negligent. So, if the plaintiff can show that, if the defendant had made a proper report or made his suspicions known when they formed, the employer would have been alerted to the defalcations and could have taken steps to put an end to them, then the auditor will be liable for amounts lost after the date when, if the auditor had done his job properly, the employer would have known of the irregularities.[314]

---

310 Cf. *Boden* v. *Gordon* [1985] 1 Qd R. 482, 490 *per* Macrossan J.

311 In most cases, the plaintiff will be led to make a contract. If the defendant is the other party to the contract, the plaintiff may be able to rescind the contract as well as claim damages in tort.

312 *Cherry* v. *Allied Insurance Brokers Ltd* [1978] 1 Lloyd's Rep. 274. See also *Lewis* v. *Tressider Andrews Associates Pty Ltd* [1987] 2 Qd.R. 533 (broker negligently places business with a financially unsound insurer). If an insurance broker undertakes to arrange new insurance but tortiously fails to do so, the measure of damages depends on whether, and at what cost, appropriate cover was available; and if it was not, on how the plaintiff would have reacted to this fact if the broker had told him: *Norwest Refrigeration Services Pty Ltd* v. *Bain Dawes (W.A.) Pty Ltd* (1984) 157 C.L.R. 149; *Cee Bee Marine Ltd* v. *Lombard Insurance Co. Ltd* [1990] 2 N.Z.L.R. 1.

313 *Osman* v. *J. Ralph Moss Ltd* [1970] 1 Lloyd's Rep. 313.

314 *New Plymouth Borough Council* v. *R.* [1951] N.Z.L.R. 49; *Hardie (Qld) Employees Credit Union Ltd* v. *Hall, Chadwick & Co.* [1980] Qd.R. 362.

Another common type of case is where a solicitor negligently handles an action for damages[315] with the result that the case never comes to trial; perhaps he fails to commence the action before the expiry of the limitation period, or fails to keep the action going with the result that it is struck out for want of prosecution. In such cases the court, in assessing the damages, has to take into account not only what the plaintiff would have recovered if he had been successful but also his chances of success. If the plaintiff would certainly have won, he can recover everything he would have recovered in the action; if there was only a chance he would have won, he will recover an amount proportional to that chance.[316] If a solicitor negligently settles a claim when pressing on with it would have been the reasonable thing to do, the measure of damages is the difference between the settlement figure and the damages the plaintiff would probably have received if the action had proceeded.[317]

These cases against solicitors are particularly interesting and important because they throw doubt on two commonly asserted propositions about the assessment of damages in tort. The first such proposition is that damages for expected gains not realized cannot be recovered in a tort action; and the second is that damages for loss of a chance cannot be recovered in tort in cases where all that has been lost is the chance. Damages for chances of future income lost as a result of personal injury or property damage are, of course, recoverable in tort. In these solicitor cases, the plaintiff is awarded damages for loss of the chance of recovering damages in litigation even though this is the only loss he has suffered, and he is awarded damages for the gain he expected to make by the litigation; he is not limited to recovering wasted investment in the form of any amounts paid to the solicitor for his services.[318] The usual assumption on which such damages for gains not realized are awarded is that if the plaintiff had known that the solicitor he had engaged would not conduct his case efficiently, he would and could have hired another solicitor who would have done the job properly and recovered damages for him. But there are exceptional cases where damages for gains not realized can be recovered even though this assumption does not hold.[319]

The proposition that damages may sometimes be recovered in tort for gains not realized is also borne out by cases where a person is led, as a result of negligent advice or the negligent performance of a service, to

---

315 The damages recoverable will be different if the action is, for example, one for an injunction; see, for example, *Heywood* v. *Wellers* [1976] Q.B. 446 (action against solicitor in contract).

316 *Tutunkoff* v. *Thiele* (1975) 11 S.A.S.R. 148; *Appo* v. *Barker* (1981) 50 F.L.R. 298; it is also relevant that the tortfeasors might not have been able to satisfy any judgment given against him: *Perri* v. *Zaitman* [1984] V.R. 314; and that the plaintiff might have settled out of court for a lesser sum than the court would have awarded: *Dolman* v. *Penrose* (1983) 34 S.A.S.R. 481.

317 *Thompson* v. *Howley* [1977] 1 N.Z.L.R. 16.

318 cf. *Murray* v. *Lloyd* [1989] 1 W.L.R. 1060 (loss of chance to become a statutory tenant); *Waribay Pty Ltd* v. *Minter Ellison* [1992] 2 V.R. 391.

319 *Ross* v. *Caunters* [1980] Ch. 297.

make a loan or invest money which is then lost. In such cases the plaintiff can, of course, recover the amount of the principal sum lost as a result of the tort (after making allowance for all receipts and for expected future payments discounted to present value).[320] In cases where a person buys property in reliance on a negligent survey or valuation, this basic rule entitles him to recover the difference between the value of the property[321] and the price paid.[322] But in exceptional cases it may be proper to award the cost of making good the unreported defects in the property.[323] Damages may also be awarded for consequential losses such as interest payments not made by the debtor,[324] as well as vexation, distress and inconvenience suffered as a result of the tort.[325]

In addition, however, if certain conditions are satisfied, a plaintiff who makes a bad investment may also recover damages representing gains which he did not realize because of the negligence.[326] The conditions are that the plaintiff must prove that if he had not entered the transaction he did enter as a result of the defendant's negligence, he would have entered some other transaction; and that he would have made a gain as a result of that alternative transaction (the likely amount of that gain will determine the quantum of the damages under this head). In other words, if these conditions are satisfied, the plaintiff can recover in tort damages for gains not realized calculated on an 'alternative investment' basis.[327] On the other hand, if, but for the defendant's negligence, the plaintiff simply would not have made an investment,[328] then all he is entitled to recover in tort is the money he lost on the investment he made; the same is true if,

---

320 How much this is will depend on whether, if the tort had not occurred, the plaintiff would have invested less or not invested at all.

321 This is normally assessed as at the date of purchase; but not always: *Naughton* v. *O'Callaghan* [1990] 3 All E.R. 191.

322 *Phillips* v. *Ward* [1956] 1 W.L.R. 471; *Perry* v. *Sidney Phillips & Son* [1982] 1 W.L.R. 1297, 1302. Consequential losses are also recoverable: *Brickhill* v. *Cooke* [1984] 3 N.S.W.L.R. 396.

323 P.A. Chandler (1990) 106 *L.Q.R.* 196.

324 e.g. *Crowder* v. *Horgan* (1901) 3 W.A.L.R. 31; *Holmes* v. *Walton* [1961] W.A.R. 96; *Baxter* v. *F.W. Gapp & Co. Ltd* [1939] 2 K.B. 271; *London & South of England Building Society* v. *Stone* [1983] 1 W.L.R. 1242; *Trade Credits Ltd* v. *Baillieu Frank Knight Pty Ltd* (1985) 12 N.S.W.L.R. 670; *Swingcastle Ltd* v. *Gibson* [1990] 1 W.L.R. 1223. This would also be the basic measure of damages in cases where creditors sue mortgagees or receivers/liquidators for negligence in exercising powers of sale.

325 *Brickhill* v. *Cooke* [1984] 3 N.S.W.L.R. 396; *Campbelltown C.C.* v. *Mackay* (1988) 15 N.S.W.L.R. 501.

326 *State of South Australia* v. *Johnson* (1982) 42 A.L.R. 161, 170; *Gates* v. *City Mutual Life Assurance Society Ltd* (1986) 63 A.L.R. 600; *Esso Petroleum Ltd* v. *Mardon* [1976] Q.B. 801; *G. & K. Ladenbau (U.K.) Ltd* v. *Crawley & de Reya* [1978] 1 All E.R. 682; *County Personnel (Employment Agency) Ltd* v. *Alan R. Pulver & Co.* [1987] 1 All E.R. See also D.W. McLauchlan (1987) 6 *Otago L.R.* 370.

327 An analogous type of case would be one where a person does not make an investment because of negligent advice against it. Here, if the plaintiff could prove that he would have made the investment if properly advised, he may recover damages for gains not realized from the investment.

328 This was the situation in *Kyogle Shire Council* v. *Francis* (1988) 13 N.S.W.L.R. 396.

but for the negligence, the plaintiff would have made the investment he did but on terms more advantageous to himself.[329]

What can never be recovered in a tort action is what might be called damages calculated on a 'successful investment' basis; that is, a tort plaintiff cannot recover the gains he expected to realize from the investment he actually made. But, as we have noted, 'successful investment' damages may not be recoverable in a contract action, either; unless the defendant warranted that the investment would yield a particular return, the plaintiff will be restricted to recovering his loss on the investment made[330] or damages calculated on the alternative investment basis.

8. Defective Products and Premises

This topic deserves separate treatment only because there is a divergence in the law between England and Australia which ought to be explained. If a defect in tangible property causes personal injury, or damage to or the destruction of tangible property other than the defective property itself (whether belonging to the owner of the defective property or to anyone else), then principles we have already discussed concerning assessment of damages for personal injury and property damage apply. The question to be considered here is when damages can be recovered representing the amount by which the defect reduces the value of the defective property below what was paid for it, or representing the cost of repairing or replacing the defective property. We are not concerned here with how to choose between the diminution-in-value measure and the repair or replacement measure; this has already been considered above. Rather we must consider the question of when damages assessed on either measure are recoverable in tort by someone who owns defective property. In a sense, this is an issue of liability, not of assessment of damages; but the two issues are closely related, and some discussion of the matter here is justified.[331]

In England, the basic rule is that cost of repairing or replacing defective property is not recoverable in tort because it is purely economic loss; *a fortiori* damages could not be recovered representing the amount by which the defective property was worth less than equivalent non-defective property. This rule applies to the tort liability of any party involved in the construction of buildings or the manufacture of chattels, including builders, architects, designers and engineers, and public authorities

---

329 If, despite the negligence, he would have made the investment on the same terms, he will recover nothing in tort but may recover nominal damages in contract: *Hanflex Pty Ltd* v. *N.S. Hope & Associates* [1990] 2 Qd.R. 218. Where the defendant is the other party to a contract which the plaintiff was induced to enter, and the plaintiff rescinds the contract, this by itself may support the conclusion that, but for the tort, he would not have entered any similar contract, or that he would have entered some alternative similar contract. If he affirms the contract, then the only proper conclusion would normally be that, but for the tort, he would have made the contract but on different terms.

330 e.g. *Hayes* v. *Dodd* [1990] 2 All E.R. 815.

331 The whole issue is more fully considered in Ch. 15 below.

exercising powers of supervision. But in Australia and New Zealand the recoverability of such damages seems to depend on the same rules as govern liability for economic loss in other contexts.[332] And in circumstances where such damages are recoverable, the rules considered above concerning the choice between the diminution-in-value measure and the repair or replacement measure, concerning liability for consequential losses (such as loss of profits or the cost of procuring a temporary alternative or for residual diminution in value[333] and betterment) would apply here too. The usual measure of damages in respect of a defective building would be the cost of removing the defect and repairing any damage it had caused,[334] provided repairing the building was the reasonable thing to do.[335] In some cases an award of the cost of buying a substitute would be appropriate.[336] As in other contexts, where a defective house is built as a result of reliance on bad advice or incorrect information, it will be relevant to the measure of damages to ask how the plaintiff would have acted had he known the truth.[337]

---

332 See pp. 354-63 above.
333 *Bowen* v. *Paramount Builders Ltd* [1977] 1 N.Z.L.R. 394.
334 *Mt Albert Borough Council* v. *Johnson* [1979] 2 N.Z.L.R. 234; *Junior Books Ltd* v. *Veitchi Co. Ltd* [1983] 1 A.C. 520.
335 *Carosella* v. *Ginos & Gilbert Pty Ltd* (1981) 27 S.A.S.R. 515 (reversed on the facts (1983) 57 A.L.J.R. 315).
336 e.g. *Batty* v. *Metropolitan Property Realisations Ltd* [1978] Q.B. 554.
337 See, for example, *Wollongong City Council* v. *Fregnan* [1982] 1 N.S.W.L.R. 244.

13

DEFENCES TO TORTS INVOLVING NEGLIGENCE

I: CONTRIBUTORY NEGLIGENCE[1]

1. THE QUALIFICATIONS IN ALFORD V. MAGEE

The basic rule at common law was that if negligence on the part of the plaintiff was a factual and legal cause of his injuries or contributed to them the defendant had a complete defence and the plaintiff recovered nothing, no matter how great a contribution to the injuries the defendant's negligence made. The harshness of this rule for the plaintiff was mitigated by principles which were discussed at length by the High Court in *Alford* v. *Magee.*[2] The basic idea behind the qualifications to the common law rule was that there are cases in which there is so substantial a difference between the position of the plaintiff and that of the defendant at the material time that (although the accident could not have happened if the plaintiff's conduct had not been negligent) it would not be fair or reasonable to regard the plaintiff as in any real sense the 'author of his own harm'.

The High Court gave four illustrations of such situations: The first was where the defendant had, but the plaintiff had not, a real opportunity, of which the reasonable person would have availed himself, of avoiding the accident. The second was where the defendant's negligent conduct was substantially later in point of time than the plaintiff's negligence and avoided its consequences. The classic example of this situation is *Davies* v. *Mann*[3] where it was held that the defendant was liable in respect of a

1 This defence is expressly mentioned in some of the occupiers' liability statutes: Wrongs Act 1957 (Vic.) s.14D; Occupiers' Liability Act 1985 (W.A.) s.10; Occupiers' Liability Act 1962 (N.Z.) s.4(8). But the defence is available to a claim under such a statute even if not specifically mentioned. Special considerations may affect the application of the defence to claims against auditors and other persons with investigatory responsibilities; *re* auditors see P.S. Marshall and A.J. Beltrami [1990] *L.M.C.L.Q.* 416.

2 (1951-2) 85 C.L.R. 437.

3 (1842) 10 M. & W. 547; see also judgment of Bollen J. in *March* v. *E. & M.H. Stramare Pty Ltd* (1989) 50 S.A.S.R. 588.

collision between the defendant's waggon and a donkey tethered at the roadside by the plaintiff, even assuming that the plaintiff had been negligent in tethering the donkey where he did. By the exercise of reasonable care the defendant, coming along later, could have avoided the collision.

The third illustration given by the High Court is where the defendant has an advantage over the plaintiff in that he was master of the situation and chose to run a risk. In *Wilson* v. *Murray*[4] A collided with the rear of B's car at night. A and B stood behind the two cars near the centre of the road to warn oncoming traffic. A was looking down rolling a cigarette when a motor cycle doing 30–40 m.p.h. (50–65 k.p.h.) appeared around a bend. B warned A then ran for cover. A was struck by the cycle and killed. The majority held that there was no evidence on which the jury could find A to have been contributorily negligent and so no occasion arose to apply any qualification. Menzies J., who dissented, discussed the present qualification and thought that it could not be said that the cyclist was in any sense master of the situation arising out of an unexpected obstruction upon a wet road at night with poor visibility when his cycle skids as he brakes to avoid the obstruction; especially when the dead man was standing in the middle of the road for the very purpose of warning oncoming traffic of the obstruction and had been warned of the approach of the cycle. In order to apply the 'master of the situation' qualification it would be necessary to be able to specify what action the defendant could have taken to get rid of the consequences of the plaintiff's negligence.

The final qualification arises where the defendant had such an advantage over the plaintiff that he ought to have been master of the situation but unreasonably failed to take advantage of his superior position.

A question which has caused considerable difficulty is whether the qualifications in *Alford* v. *Magee* are still relevant now that contributory negligence is a ground of apportionment of damages rather than a complete defence.[5] The dominant view seems to be that they are no longer relevant.[6] In support it is said that since the general rule that contributory negligence defeats a cause of action has been abolished, so must have been the *Alford* qualifications to it.[7] The *Alford* qualifications were not rules of causation—they did not mean that the plaintiff's negligence had not

---

4 (1962) 110 C.L.R. 445.

5 The apportionment legislation is as follows: Law Reform (Miscellaneous Provisions) Act 1965 (N.S.W.) Part III; Wrongs Act 1958 (Vic.) Part V; Wrongs Act 1936-75 (S.A.) s.27a; Law Reform (Tortfeasors' Contribution, Contributory Negligence and Division of Chattels) Act 1952 (Qld) Part III; Tortfeasors' and Contributory Negligence Act 1954 (Tas.) s.4; Law Reform (Contributory Negligence and Tortfeasors' Contribution) Act 1947 (W.A.) s.4; Law Reform (Miscellaneous Provisions) Act 1956 (N.T.) Part V; Law Reform (Miscellaneous Provisions) Ordinance 1955 (A.C.T.) Part V.

6 See e.g. *March* v. *Stramare* (1991) 171 C.L.R. 506, 513-14 *per* Mason C.J.; 522 *per* Deane J; *Chapman* v. *Hearse* (1961) 106 C.L.R. 112, 123; *Anderson* v. *Eric Anderson Radio & T.V. Pty Ltd* (1965) 114 C.L.R. 20, 47 *per* Windeyer J. See also N. Burbank (1952) 26 *A.L.J.* 167; J.P. Bourke (1953) 27 *A.L.J.* 477; G.H.L. Fridman (1953) 27 *A.L.J.* 451; J.F. Keeler (1967) 41 *A.L.J.* 148.

7 *Winter* v. *Bennett* [1956] V.L.R. 612.

contributed to the accident—but rather rules about allocation of responsibility which only applied once contributory negligence had been established. The legislation now governs apportionment and so the qualifications must have been superseded.[8] Another argument in favour of this result is as follows: there is English authority for the view that the apportionment legislation only applies if the plaintiff was partly at fault; so the legislation does not allow the plaintiff to be awarded full damages.[9] Since the application of an *Alford* v. *Magee* qualification would lead to this result, the qualifications cannot have survived the legislation.

On the other hand, the apportionment legislation does not explicitly prevent the court awarding the plaintiff full damages under the legislation even if he was partly at fault (or awarding no damages even if the defendant was partly at fault). So the *Alford* qualifications could be seen as providing illustrations of when a court would be justified in not reducing the plaintiff's damages at all even though the damage was partly his own fault. This seems to have been the position taken by the Tasmanian Full Court in *Smith* v. *McIntyre*.[10] One of the factors relevant to apportionment is the relative causal contribution of the acts of the two parties to the damage; the *Alford* qualifications spell out when the defendant's act can be treated as being the wholly predominant causal factor.

The best approach to the *Alford* qualifications is to treat them as no more than illustrations of situations where, although the plaintiff was partly at fault, his fault played only a minor role in causing the loss. The important thing is that the question of contributory negligence should be dealt with broadly and flexibly on the facts of individual cases. So the fact that the plaintiff's and defendant's acts are separated in time, or that one party had, at a particular moment, an advantage of knowledge or appreciation of the danger resulting from the negligence of the other, will be relevant both to the question of causation (should the plaintiff's fault be treated as partly a *cause* of his loss?) and to that of apportionment (if the loss was partly the result of the plaintiff's fault, how should this affect the damages recoverable by him?) but will be conclusive of neither. No rules can be laid down as to the effect of these matters,[11] and the *Alford* qualifications should not be treated as such.

---

8 *Evans* v. *Parberry* (1969) 92 W.N.(N.S.W.) 146.

9 *Pitts* v. *Hunt* [1990] 1 Q.B. 302. Conversely, it does not allow the plaintiff to be denied any damages. Cf. *March* v. *Stramare* (1991) 171 C.L.R. 506, 524 *per* Deane J.; 528 *per* McHugh J.

10 [1958] Tas.S.R. 36. See also *Elms* v. *Commissioner for Railways* [1965] Qd.R. 471 *per* Lucas J.; *Kammerman* v. *Baster* (1981) 28 S.A.S.R. 571.

11 *Admiralty Commissioners* v. *Owners of S.S. Volute; The Volute* [1922] 1 A.C. 129; *Sigurdson* v. *British Columbia Electric Railway Co. Ltd* [1953] A.C. 291.

2. What is Contributory Negligence?

Contributory negligence, like actionable negligence, is failure to take reasonable precautions against foreseeable risks of injury.[12] But unlike actionable negligence, contributory negligence consists primarily of failure to take care for one's own safety rather than a breach of a duty of care owed to another.[13] So a plaintiff can be held contributorily negligent even though he took all reasonable care for the safety of others. But breach of a duty of care owed to another may constitute contributory negligence,[14] and a finding of no contributory negligence negatives both failure of care for oneself and for others.[15] Of course, breach by a plaintiff of a duty owed to the defendant will also open him to a cross-claim for any injury inflicted as a result on the defendant.

The defence of contributory negligence has to be specifically pleaded.[16] Although contributory negligence is strictly a plea in mitigation of damages rather than a defence, the onus of establishing it still rests on the defendant.[17] Negligence is a fairly vague concept as applied to plaintiffs.[18] But the significant risk calculus is sometimes applied *mutatis mutandis* to plaintiffs, especially in cases where the plaintiff was faced with a risk or emergency created by the defendant to which it was necessary to react quickly.[19] Whether the plaintiff has been negligent is always a question of fact;[20] but in New South Wales, in certain situations a finding of contributory negligence is required by statute.[21] Further, as in the case of actionable negligence, the fact that the plaintiff's act is a breach of the law does not necessarily mean that he is guilty of contributory negligence.[22]

Once it has been decided that the plaintiff behaved negligently it must then be shown that the damage he suffered was partly the result of his own negligence.[23] The negligence must, of course, be a factual cause of the

12 *Jones* v. *Livox Quarries Ltd* [1952] 2 Q.B. 608, 615 *per* Denning L.J.; all that need be foreseeable is the type of injury suffered: *Hanly* v. *Berlin* [1975] Qd.R. 52.

13 *Jones* v. *Livox Quarries* [1952] 2 Q.B. 608; *Nance* v. *British Columbia Electric Railway Co.* [1957] A.C. 601; *Froom* v. *Butcher* [1976] Q.B. 286.

14 *Nance's* case [1957] A.C. 601; *Noall* v. *Middleton* [1961] V.R. 285; a typical example is negligence which contributes to a head-on collision.

15 *Noall* v. *Middleton* [1961] V.R. 285.

16 *Christie* v. *Bridgestone Australia Pty Ltd* (1983) 33 S.A.S.R. 377; *Brown* v. *Heathcote C.C. (No. 2)* [1982] 2 N.Z.L.R. 618.

17 *Hercules Textile Mills Pty Ltd* v. *K. & H. Textile Engineers Pty Ltd* [1955] V.L.R. 310.

18 *Sungravure Pty Ltd* v. *Meani* (1963-4) 110 C.L.R. 24, 33 *per* Windeyer J.

19 *Caterson* v. *Commissioner for Railways* (1972) 128 C.L.R. 99 especially 111-12 *per* Gibbs J.; *King* v. *Commissioner of Railways* [1971] Qd.R. 266.

20 e.g. *Cashmore* v. *Chief Commissioner for Railways & Tramways (N.S.W.)* (1915) 20 C.L.R. 1; *Roeder* v. *Commissioner for Railways (N.S.W.)* (1938) 60 C.L.R. 305.

21 Motor Accidents Act 1988 s.74(2).

22 *Sibley* v. *Kais* (1967) 118 C.L.R. 424. See also *Westwood* v. *Post Office* [1974] A.C. 1.

23 In all jurisdictions but W.A. the apportionment provision applies where a person suffers damage partly as a result of his own fault and partly as a result of the fault of another. In W.A. the legislation refers to the 'event which caused the damage'. This phraseology causes difficulty in cases where, for instance, the plaintiff's injuries are partly attributable to failure to wear a seat-belt or a crash-helmet: such negligence does not contribute to the accident but only to the injuries. But in *Motor Vehicle Insurance Trust* v. *Wilson* [1976] W.A.R. 175 the Full Court held that the word 'event' refers to the injuries, not to the accident, and so a plaintiff could be held contributorily negligent for riding with a driver he knew to be drunk.

loss. This formed the basis of some early decisions in which it has been held that failure to wear a seat-belt was not contributory negligence; there was held to be no evidence that the injuries would have been avoided or reduced if a seat-belt had been worn.[24] Also, the negligence must be a legal or attributive cause of the damage.[25] Foreseeability is relevant to legal causation but is not decisive of it. In *Jones* v. *Livox Quarries* Denning L.J. said that the negligence of the plaintiff in riding on the tow-bar of a vehicle would be a cause of injury to him whether he was thrown off the tow-bar or crushed when another vehicle collided with it.[26] But there would be no (attributive) causal link between his injuries and his negligence if he was shot by a negligent sportsman and the bullet would not have hit him if he had been in the cab rather than on the tow-bar.

Contributory negligence may consist of conduct which contributes to the accident, such as stepping out on to a busy road without looking.[27] Another type of contributory negligence consists in conduct which contributes to the plaintiff's injury but not to the accident, such as failure to wear a seat-belt or a crash helmet.[28] In *Froom* v. *Butcher*[29] the English Court of Appeal suggested that if wearing a seat-belt would have prevented the plaintiff's injuries entirely his damages should be reduced by 25 per cent but if the belt would only have reduced the injuries the reduction should be 15 per cent. In South Australia, s.35a(1)(i) of the Wrongs Act 1936 provides for a reduction of 15 per cent or more depending on the extent to which the proper use of a seat-belt would have reduced or lessened the severity of the plaintiff's injuries.[30]

Another type of contributory negligence involves direct causal contribution neither to the accident nor to the injuries, but rather allowing or helping a situation to arise in which injuries are foreseeable or putting oneself in a position where injuries are foreseeable.[31] The latter arises

---

24 *Tonkes* v. *Hodgkinson* (1970) 90 W.N.(Pt.1)(N.S.W.) 753; *Woodward* v. *Porteous* [1971] Tas.S.R. 386 (N.C. 25).

25 *Fitzgerald* v. *Penn* (1954) 91 C.L.R. 268; *Tucker* v. *Tucker* [1956] S.A.S.R. 297.

26 [1952] 2 Q.B. 608, 616.

27 N. Gravells (1977) 93 *L.Q.R.* 581; just as it is negligent to drive when one's faculties are impaired by alcohol or drugs, so it can be negligent for a pedestrian to do some things while intoxicated: *Kilminster* v. *Rule* (1983) 32 S.A.S.R. 39.

28 As to the wearing of other protective clothing see *Kirk* v. *Nominal Defendant (Qld)* [1984] 1 Qd.R. 592. It might be argued that treating failure to wear a seat-belt as contributory negligence is not obviously desirable. Education and the making of the wearing of seat-belts compulsory has probably had the effect of raising usage to as high a level as can be achieved. The law of tort is probably not needed to encourage use of seat-belts. And since the defendant will be insured and the plaintiff is unlikely to have any insurance to cover anything but his medical and hospital expenses, a finding of contributory negligence will, in serious cases at least, leave loss on shoulders not well able to bear the burden. On the other hand, it might be thought unfair that a plaintiff who neglects his own safety should be entitled to recover in full, even if it is not easy to say that he was morally blameworthy in not looking after himself: *Pennington* v. *Norris* (1956) 96 C.L.R. 10, 16.

29 [1976] Q.B. 286; in Qld it has been held that there is no standard percentage: *Hallowell* v. *Nominal Defendant* [1983] 2 Qd.R. 266.

30 Concerning the relationship between s.35a and s.27a. see *Carroll* v. *Lewitzke* (1991) 56 S.A.S.R. 18.

31 For both types see *Owens* v. *Brimmell* [1977] Q.B. 859; *Duncan* v. *Bell* [1967] Qd.R. 425.

typically where a passenger gets into a car with a person whom he knows or ought to realize[32] is not in a fit condition to drive (normally by reason of alcoholic or drug-induced intoxication).[33] This form of the defence has replaced the defence of *volenti non fit injuria* in most[34] situations,[35] the disadvantage of the latter defence from the plaintiff's point of view being that it relieves the defendant of any liability to pay damages to the plaintiff.[36] A person might be held to have allowed or helped a dangerous situation to arise if, for example, he accompanies another on a drinking spree which both diminishes the driver's capacity to drive and robs the plaintiff of the capacity for clear thought and judgment on the issue of the advisability of allowing himself to be driven by the defendant.[37] But a plaintiff may not be held negligent just because he allowed himself to get too drunk to judge the driver's state if he had no reason to think the driver would not remain sober;[38] otherwise a person could never safely arrange for another to drive him home in order that he could enjoy an evening's drinking.

We have seen already[39] that in judging whether a child plaintiff has been contributorily negligent the courts have applied a more generous and subjective test than when deciding whether a child has been guilty of actionable negligence.[40] There are examples of a similar leniency to adult plaintiffs. This is particularly true in two areas which we will consider later, namely actions against employers for breach of their common law duties and actions for breach of statutory duties. But it may also be true in motor accident cases (probably because the defendant will be insured and so better able to bear the loss) especially where, for example, the defendant is driving a heavy goods vehicle and the plaintiff a motor cycle[41] or where the plaintiff is a pedestrian.[42]

3. The Apportionment Legislation[43]

(a) Fault In all jurisdictions except Western Australia, the apportionment provisions apply where a person suffers damage as a result partly of

---

32 What a drunken passenger ought to realize is judged according to the standard of the sober passenger: *Morton* v. *Knight* [1990] 2 Qd.R. 419.
33 For South Australia see Wrongs Act 1936 ss.35a(1)(j) and 35a(4).
34 But not in all cases: *Morris* v. *Murray* [1991] 2 Q.B. 6.
35 A defence of contributory negligence can succeed even if the plaintiff was not *volens* to the risk: *Dodd* v. *McGlashan* [1967] A.L.R. 433.
36 Another way of dealing with such cases is in terms of standard of care, as to which see p. 424 above and p. 451 below.
37 Here a *volenti* defence would fail because of lack of ability of the plaintiff to make a free choice to accept the risk.
38 *Banovic* v. *Perkovic* (1982) 30 S.A.S.R. 34.
39 See p. 422 above.
40 cf. *Gough* v. *Thorne* [1966] 1 W.L.R. 1387.
41 *Cocks* v. *Sheppard* (1979) 25 A.L.R. 435, 334 *per* Murphy J.; cf. *Watt* v. *Bretag* (1982) 56 A.L.J.R. 760 *per* Murphy J.
42 *Pollard* v. *Ensor* [1969] S.A.S.R. 57; *Evers* v. *Bennett* (1982) 31 S.A.S.R. 228, 234.
43 See n. 5 above. As to the relationship between apportionment for contributory negligence and contribution between tortfeasors in cases where there are two or more defendants see *Fitzgerald* v. *Lane* [1989] A.C. 328 and p. 738 below.

his own fault and partly of the fault of another. The definition of the word 'fault' raises a number of issues. First, in all jurisdictions except New South Wales fault includes breach of statutory duty. In New South Wales (except in work injury cases[44]) contributory negligence is not available as a defence to an action for personal injuries 'founded on a breach of statutory duty imposed on the defendant for the benefit of a class of persons of which the person so injured was a member at the time the injury was sustained'.[45] This provision was designed primarily to protect employees in actions for personal injuries against their employers from being held negligent by reason of breach of a provision designed for their own safety. But now work injury cases form an exception to the general rule so large that the the provision is of little practical importance.

Secondly, opinions (and judgments) differ on the issue of whether the legislation applies only to claims in tort, or whether it also applies to some contractual claims.[46] It seems that contributory negligence is not available at common law as a defence to an action for breach of contract,[47] and whether the legislation applies to claims in contract is technically a question of interpretation of the words of the relevant provisions, and in particular of the word 'fault'. The question is of particular importance in cases where a defendant can be sued concurrently in tort and contract. In such cases, if the legislation does not apply to actions in contract, a defendant's liability may differ according to whether the plaintiff brings his claim in tort or contract, even though the substance of his claim is the same regardless of the form it takes. It seems that the legislation was drafted with actions in tort only in mind, even though, at that time, concurrent actions in tort and contract in respect of personal injuries could be brought, for instance, against occupiers of land by contractual entrants and by employees against employers. Developments in the law governing liability in tort for purely economic loss and the recognition of a general rule allowing concurrent claims in contract and tort in respect of such loss, which have occurred since the apportionment legislation was drafted, have made the question of the scope of the legislation a very live issue.

A view which is gaining increasing acceptance is that if a breach of

---

44 Workers Compensation Act 1987 s.151N(3) and (4).

45 Statutory Duties (Contributory Negligence) Act 1945 s.2. It has been held that liability under s.2(2) of the Damage by Aircraft Act 1952 (which is strict) is not liability for breach of statutory duty, and that the apportionment legislation applies to it: *Southgate* v. *Commonwealth of Australia* (1987) 13 N.S.W.L.R. 188.

46 Restricted to claims in tort: *Belous* v. *Willetts* [1970] V.R. 45; *A.S. James Pty Ltd* v. *Duncan* [1970] V.R. 705; *Harper* v. *Ashton's Circus Pty Ltd* [1972] 2 N.S.W.L.R. 395; *Arthur Young & Co.* v. *W.A. Chip & Pulp Co. Pty Ltd* [1989] W.A.R. 100. See generally J. Swanton (1981) 55 *A.L.J.* 278. Covers claims in contract: *Queen's Bridge Motors & Engineering Co. Pty Ltd* v. *Edwards* [1964] Tas.S.R. 93; *Smith* v. *Buckley* [1965] Tas.S.R. 210; *Bains Harding Construction & Roofing (Australia) Pty Ltd* v. *McCredie Richmond & Partners Pty Ltd* (1988) 13 N.S.W.L.R. 437; *Rowe* v. *Turner Hopkins* [1980] 2 N.Z.L.R. 550; *Forsikringsaktieselskapet Vesta* v. *Butcher* [1989] A.C. 852 (C.A.).

47 *Belous* v. *Willetts* [1970] V.R. 45; *Read* v. *Nerey Nominees Pty Ltd* [1979] V.R. 47; *Harper* v. *Ashton's Circus* [1972] 2 N.S.W.L.R. 395.

contract would also be actionable in tort (as will normally be the case in relation to breach of a contractual duty of care), then the legislation applies to a claim in contract in respect of that breach. Whatever the arguments against recognizing contributory negligence as a defence to a wrong actionable only in contract,[48] they must have much less force where the breach of contract would also be actionable as a tort to which the apportionment legislation applies. Why should a plaintiff be able to deprive the defendant of a defence simply by a choice as to the form in which he pleads his case?

Thirdly, so far as it relates to the plaintiff's acts or omissions, the word 'fault' refers to conduct which would, apart from the legislation, give rise to a defence of contributory negligence. At first sight this might be thought to preserve the *Alford* v. *Magee* qualifications, but perhaps this is so only if those qualifications are treated as going to causation as opposed to apportionment of damages. The other issue raised by these words is whether the legislation applies to torts to which, before the legislation, contributory negligence was not a defence.[49] In *Venning* v. *Chin*[50] the Full Court of South Australia held that it did apply to an action for negligent trespass to the person.[51]

In Western Australia the apportionment provision applies to 'any claim for damages founded on an allegation of negligence'. This formulation might well exclude actions in respect of intentional or strict liability torts; and it has been held that the Western Australian provisions do not apply to contract claims even if the breach of contract would also be actionable in tort.[52]

There are two issues of principle underlying the question of the scope of the apportionment legislation. First, it is often argued that a defence of contributory negligence ought only to be available in cases where the liability of the defendant depends on proof that he was negligent. Where the defendant can be liable even if he was not negligent, or where he can be held liable only if it can be proved that he acted with the intention of injuring the plaintiff, it may seem unfair to the plaintiff that negligence on his part should justify a reduction of his damages. On the other hand, it might be thought desirable to use the defence of contributory negligence to give plaintiffs an incentive to take care of themselves regardless of the basis of the defendant's liability. Secondly, in cases where the same act amounts to two different legal wrongs (such as a tort and a breach of contract) it might be thought undesirable that a plaintiff, by choosing to treat the act as one wrong rather than the other, should be able to deprive the defendant of a defence which he would have if the act had been treated

48 See English Law Commission Working Paper No. 114 *Contributory Negligence as a Defence in Contract* (1990).
49 The same issue arises in relation to breach of contract given that contributory negligence is probably not a defence to a contract claim at common law.
50 (1974) 10 S.A.S.R. 299.
51 See *Hoebergen* v. *Koppens* [1974] 2 N.Z.L.R. 597.
52 *Arthur Young* v. *W.A. Chip & Pulp Co.* [1989] W.A.R. 100.

differently.[53] This argument is particularly strong in cases where the reason why the act constitutes one legal wrong is exactly the same as the reason why it constitutes another legal wrong, as in the case where the same negligent act is actionable as a breach of a tortious duty of care and as a breach of a contractual duty of care.

In all jurisdictions except New South Wales, Victoria and Queensland, 'fault of a person' is defined to include the fault of any person for whom that person is vicariously liable. At common law this was known as the doctrine of identification and it has been held that this provision is simply declaratory of the common law.[54]

(b) Apportionment The plaintiff's damages are to be reduced to such extent (less than 100 per cent)[55] as the court thinks just and equitable having regard to his share in the responsibility for the damage.[56] This provision gives the judge or jury which does the apportionment a very wide discretion,[57] the exercise of which an appeal court will interfere with only in exceptional cases, such as misdirection of the jury, error of law by the judge or gross disproportion between the plaintiff's degree of responsibility and the percentage reduction of the damages.[58] The decision of a jury on apportionment is even less likely to be interfered with than that of a judge;[59] and a decision for which reasons are given is more easily overturned than one for which they are not.[60] Although apportionment is a jury question,[61] lack of evidence relevant to apportionment is no ground for not making an apportionment;[62] the court must do the best it can, for example, by apportioning 50-50.[63]

Responsibility for the damage is judged by two criteria: the degree of departure of the plaintiff's action from the standard of the reasonable person[64] and the relative causal contribution of the plaintiff's negligence

---

53 There are other differences between tort and contract liability (for instance, regarding limitation periods and remoteness and assessment of damages) which raise the same issue.

54 *Milkovits* v. *Federal Capital Press of Australia Pty Ltd* (1972) 20 F.L.R. 311; *Doyle* v. *Pick* [1965] W.A.R. 95.

55 *Pitts* v. *Hunt* [1990] 1 Q.B. 302. But it is not clear whether this represents the law in Australia.

56 D. Payne (1955) 18 *M.L.R.* 344.

57 Limited, however, in N.S.W. by Workers Compensation Act 1987 s.151N(2).

58 *Pennington* v. *Norris* (1956) 96 C.L.R. 10; *Muller* v. *Evans (No. 2)* [1982] Qd.R. 209; *Smith* v. *McIntyre* [1958] Tas.S.R. 36 (judge); *Zoukra* v. *Lowenstein* [1958] V.R. 594 (jury); *Taylor* v. *Miller* [1969] V.R. 987.

59 *Podrebersek* v. *Australian Iron & Steel Pty Ltd* (1985) 59 A.L.R. 529.

60 *Winter* v. *Bennett* [1956] V.L.R. 613; *Pollard* v. *Ensor* [1969] S.A.S.R. 57.

61 *Madalaine Textile Manufacturing Co. Pty Ltd* v. *Merrylands Bus Co. Ltd* [1969] 2 N.S.W.R. 573.

62 *Bird* v. *Ward* [1954] V.L.R. 20.

63 *Smith* v. *McIntyre* [1958] Tas.S.R. 36.

64 *Not* moral blameworthiness: *Pennington* v. *Norris* (1956) 96 C.L.R. 10; *Melbourne & Metropolitan Tramways Board* v. *Postneck* [1959] V.R. 39; J.P. Bourke (1956) 30 *A.L.J.* 283.

to the damage.[65] In relation to the first, a literal reading of the legislation might suggest that it would only be necessary to look at the plaintiff's actions in order to decide on the appropriate reduction of damages, but it has been said that the relative departure of the plaintiff and the defendant from the standard of the reasonable person should be considered.[66]

The idea of attaching numerical values to degrees of negligence is a vague, if not meaningless, one; but the idea of comparing departures from different standards of care appropriate to the different situation of each of the parties is even more difficult. What, for example, will the court do if it decides that the defendant fell short of his standard by 30 per cent and the plaintiff of his by 20 per cent? On the other hand, it is of course relevant to deciding how responsible a plaintiff has been for his injuries to know that, for example, he was seeking to avoid a hazardous situation created by the defendant. The whole concept of apportionment is so vague that it can only be understood in a very loose way.

Comparison of the positions of the two parties is more useful for giving effect to value judgments than for judging degrees of fault. So, for example, the courts tend to be more generous to pedestrians or cyclists as against drivers of cars or heavy vehicles because of the incidence of insurance and the relative potential of the parties to inflict (as opposed to cause the infliction of) damage, even though pedestrians and cyclists can often by stupidity or heedlessness cause accidents which would probably otherwise not occur.[67]

As for relative causal contribution, this too is a difficult notion. Even if the idea of attributive causation could be reduced to common-sense formulae it is highly doubtful that the idea of relative causation could be given any but a policy-oriented content.

II: VOLENTI NON FIT INJURIA[68]

The difference between the defence of *volenti non fit injuria* and the defence of consent to an intentional tort is that the latter involves assent to the infliction of injury whereas the former involves only assumption of the risk of injury. Perhaps the most significant factor in the modern

---

65 *Melbourne Tramways* v. *Postneck* [1959] V.R. 39; *Smith* v. *McIntyre* [1958] Tas.S.R. 36; *Taylor* v. *Miller* [1969] V.R. 987. *Davies* v. *Swan Motor Co. Ltd* [1949] 2 K.B. 291; *Froom* v. *Butcher* [1967] Q.B. 286; *Winter* v. *Bennett* [1956] V.L.R. 612; *Podrebersek* v. *Australian Iron & Steel* (1985) 59 A.L.R. 529.

66 *Karamalis* v. *Commissioner of South Australian Railways* (1977) 15 A.L.R. 629; *Taylor* v. *Miller* [1969] V.R. 987.

67 J.A. Redmond (1957) 31 *A.L.J.* 520.

68 This defence is expressly mentioned in some occupiers' liability statutes: Occupiers' Liability Act 1985 (W.A.) s.5(2); Occupiers' Liability Act (N.Z.) s.4(7). But the defence is, in theory at least, available to a claim under such a statute even if it is not expressly mentioned. The defence is *not* available in N.S.W. in motor accident cases (Motor Accidents Act 1988 s.76; see also ss.74(2)(b) and 74(6)) or in employment injury cases (Workers Compensation Act 1987 s.151O); but in cases where the defence would have been available but for its abolition, the court must apportion the damages on the basis of contributory negligence.

development of the law governing this defence was the introduction of apportionment of damages for contributory negligence. Knowledge of the risk[69] is an element both of contributory negligence and of assumption of risk. But a plea of *volenti* will succeed only if the plaintiff actually knew of the risk,[70] whereas a plea of contributory negligence can succeed if the plaintiff ought to have known of the risk but was not actually aware of it. And since assumption of risk is a complete defence, courts have tended to tighten the other requirements of the defence of *volenti* in order to exclude its operation as frequently as possible and thus leave the court free to award the plaintiff a proportion of his damages. So whereas in *Insurance Commissioner* v. *Joyce*[71] it was not thought to make much difference whether cases where gratuitous passengers accepted lifts with drunken drivers were analysed in terms of assumption of risk or in terms of contributory negligence, this is clearly not now the case.

1. Volenti and Standard of Care

We have already examined Dixon J.'s theory of variable standards of care, the mixed reception it received in *Nettleship* v. *Weston*,[72] and its re-affirmation in *Cook* v. *Cook*.[73] Under the variable standards of care approach it does not matter that the plaintiff did not know and fully appreciate the nature of the risk he was running; all he needs to have known (or have had reasonable means of knowing) are the facts giving rise to the risk, and he does not need to have been aware of the riskiness of the situation.[74] This is in marked contrast to the *volenti* defence which requires that the plaintiff both knew the facts constituting the danger and fully appreciated the danger inherent in them. It is not true, as Dixon J. seems to have thought in *Insurance Commissioner* v. *Joyce*,[75] that it did not much matter in practice whether standard of care or *volenti* reasoning was adopted.

The other important element of the variable standard of care approach is that, on the whole, a plaintiff is required to accept a lower standard of care only if it was by his free choice that he was confronted with the risk. Once again, however, the plaintiff need not have consented to endure the exact risk, because he may, through ignorance, not have known what the exact risk was. He need only have consented to be in the situation or relationship which gave rise to the risk. By contrast, a plea of *volenti* will succeed only if the plaintiff can be reasonably treated as having accepted the risk which actually materialized.

Nevertheless, there is considerable similarity between the cases dealt with in terms of standard of care and those dealt with in terms of *volenti*.

---

69 The plaintiff must be '*sciens*'.
70 *Scanlon* v. *American Cigarette Co. (Overseas) Ltd.* [1987] V.R. 289.
71 (1948) 77 C.L.R. 39.
72 [1971] 2 Q.B. 691.
73 (1986) 68 A.L.R. 353; and see p. 424 above.
74 See particularly *Wooldridge* v. *Sumner* [1963] 2 Q.B. 43, 68-70 *per* Diplock L.J.
75 (1948) 77 C.L.R. 39, 59-60.

The difference, it seems, lies in this, that in the former type of case the law is prepared to make a relatively general value judgment about the standard of care required and to enforce it at the expense of the plaintiff. But where the law can see no redeeming feature in the defendant or his activity then it is only prepared to find against the plaintiff if the plaintiff has himself in effect exonerated the defendant in advance. But it is not easy to understand why all cases in which the court thinks that the plaintiff's conduct is partly responsible for his loss should not be dealt with in terms of contributory negligence; the only difficulty with doing so is that, according to one view, the apportionment legislation does not allow the plaintiff to be awarded nothing or the defendant to be held fully liable. But there must be few cases in which, on the facts, this limitation would be a significant handicap to dealing with the case fairly.

2. Volenti and Exclusion of Liability

Related to the standard of care cases are others where there has been some communication between the plaintiff and the defendant to the effect that the former accepts the risk of injury by the defendant's negligence and (usually by implication) agrees not to sue the defendant in the event of such injury. For example, in *Bennett* v. *Tugwell*[76] the plaintiff was held to have agreed to assume the risk of injury as a result of having travelled frequently as passenger in a car in which there was a clearly visible notice on the dash-board saying: 'Warning. Passengers travelling in this vehicle do so at their own risk'. The notice had been affixed by the driver of the car, the son of its owner, who thought, incorrectly, that his father's insurance did not cover the plaintiff. If he had known it did cover passengers, he would not, he said, have wanted to deprive the plaintiff of his remedy. The plaintiff thought that the notice meant that he could not sue the son but that he could sue the insurance company. These misunderstandings were held to be irrelevant: the test of exemption from liability was said to be objective and unaffected by the actual subjective beliefs of the parties.[77]

Similarly, it has been held that since an occupier of premises is usually free to exclude visitors from his land, he is also free to attach conditions to their entry including a condition that the visitor accepts risks attendant on his entry and will not sue the occupier in respect of injury suffered on the premises.[78] The test of whether the visitor is bound by the condition is

76 [1971] 2 Q.B. 267.

77 At the time this case was decided insurance against liability to passengers was not compulsory in Britain. It is compulsory now under the Road Traffic Act 1988; and s.149 of that Act provides that any agreement or understanding purporting to negative or restrict the liability of the driver is ineffective. It was the absence of compulsory insurance which gave rise to the uncertainty about the insurance position and led the son in this case to post the notice. But, of course, a driver might want to exclude his liability even though he is insured if the making of claims on his insurance will affect the premium charged.

78 *Ashdown* v. *Samuel Williams & Sons Ltd* [1957] 1 Q.B. 409; *White* v. *Blackmore* [1972] 2 Q.B. 651.

not whether he was aware of its existence and had read its terms but whether the occupier had taken reasonable steps to bring it to his notice at or before the time of entry,[79] so that the visitor was in a position to decide not to enter if he did not wish to accept the condition. In *Burnett* v. *British Waterways Board*[80] the plaintiff was a lighterman who was injured when manoeuvring a barge into the defendant's lock. A notice outside the lockmaster's office said that the Board's facilities were used at the user's own risk. The plaintiff gave evidence that he had read the notice as a young apprentice but did not think it applied when he had his accident. It was held that the plaintiff was not bound by the notice because the nature of his job gave him no real choice not to enter the area of the lock.

If there is a contractual relationship between the plaintiff and the defendant, the terms of that contract may exclude the liability of one of the parties to it for tortiously inflicted injuries. And according to one view, a person ought not to be bound by an express exclusion of liability unless it is embodied in a contract.[81] But it is clear from the above cases that liability in tort may be excluded on the basis of actual or implied or constructive knowledge of a notice or condition excluding liability, coupled with behaviour which the law is prepared to treat as objectively signifying agreement to that notice or condition, even if there is no contract between the parties.[82] The defence of exclusion of liability differs from that of *volenti* in that it is objectively based, and the knowledge and acceptance which it requires is not of the risk but of a stipulation that the defendant is not to be liable if a risk, whatever it might be, does materialize.

Some judges have expressed the view that it is only if the facts can support a finding of an express or implied agreement (but not necessarily amounting to a contract) to waive any claim for negligence that the defendant will be able to escape liability.[83] This approach would rule out a defence in any circumstances where there had been no communication between the parties on the issue of liability prior to the occurrence of the accident. To rule out a defence in the absence of agreement to waive liability is in one sense to deny that a defence of *volenti* exists (although this is not always recognized in the cases) because it amounts to saying that assumption of risk is not the basis of the defence but rather agreement to waive liability. Thus, the defence is really exclusion of liability, not assumption of risk. Further, on this approach, an agreement to waive liability could not be spelled out of merely accepting a lift with a drunken

79 The same principle applies to notices in cars: *Birch* v. *Thomas* [1972] 1 All E.R. 905.

80 [1973] 1 W.L.R. 700.

81 Lord Denning M.R. dissenting in *White* v. *Blackmore* [1972] 2 Q.B. 651; L.C.B. Gower (1956) 19 *M.L.R.* 532; (1957) 20 *M.L.R.* 181.

82 In Australia, if the owner of a car chose to post a notice to the effect that passengers travelled at their own risk, it appears that the relevant legislation would not render the notice ineffective unless it was part of a contract between the parties; and in some States even then only if the contract was one for conveyance for reward.

83 *Nettleship* v. *Weston* [1971] 2 Q.B. 691, 701 *per* Lord Denning M.R.; *Dann* v. *Hamilton* [1939] 1 K.B. 509, 518 *per* Asquith J.; *Morrison* v. *Union Steamship Co. of N.Z. Ltd* [1964] N.Z.L.R. 468, 474ff *per* Turner J.; W.L. Morison (1953) 1 *Syd.L.R.* 77.

driver (for example) because there would have been no prior communication between the parties on the issue of liability. At all events, Australian courts have generally not adopted this approach.[84]

Finally, it should be noted that in England the Unfair Contract Terms Act 1977, which imposes limits on the freedom of contracting parties to exclude their contractual liability by terms in the contract, also limits the effectiveness of non-contractual exclusion notices such as we have been considering above. There is obviously a case for such legislation in Australia.[85]

3. Assumption of Risk

In cases dealt with in terms of standard of care the burden of establishing the appropriate standard is on the plaintiff. In cases where the defendant pleads an agreement to waive liability, the burden of establishing that agreement will be on him. Where assumption of risk is pleaded the defendant must prove[86] that the plaintiff was aware of the facts constituting the danger,[87] that he fully appreciated the danger inherent in the factual circumstances,[88] and that he encountered or submitted himself to the danger freely and willingly.

The view has been taken that the requirement that the plaintiff fully appreciate the danger would rule out a successful defence of *volenti* in any negligence action because the unplanned and unintended nature of the consequences of negligent conduct make it impossible to appreciate fully the risks inherent in negligent conduct in advance of their occurring.[89] *Volenti* is not based on foreseeability of risk but on subjective awareness and appreciation of risk.[90] But the point needs to be refined a little. If one takes the example of negligent driving, there may be cases in which the relevant negligence is complete at the time the passenger enters the car. It is negligent to drive a car with a headlight not working, and if the passenger knows of the defect when he enters the car he cannot complain of any injury resulting from the lack of a headlight.[91] But if one gets into a car with a drunken driver, although it is negligent for the driver to drive in a drunken state, it is much harder than in the case of the lack of a headlight to anticipate exactly what the results of the negligence will be.

---

84 *Roggenkamp* v. *Bennett* (1950) 80 C.L.R. 292; *Sara* v. *G.I.O. of N.S.W.* (1968) 89 W.N.(Pt.1)(N.S.W.) 203, 206-8 *per* Walsh J.A.; *Ranieri* v. *Ranieri* (1973) 7 S.A.S.R. 418. See also R.A. Blackburn (1951) 24 *A.L.J.* 351. But contrast *Wilkinson* v. *Joyceman* [1985] 1 Qd.R. 567.

85 N.C. Seddon (1981) 55 *A.L.J.* 22.

86 *Insurance Commissioner* v. *Joyce* (1948) 77 C.L.R. 39; *Parker* v. *Lane* [1958] S.A.S.R. 260.

87 See e.g. *Sloan* v. *Kirby* (1979) 20 S.A.S.R. 263; *Perry* v. *G.I.O. of N.S.W.* (1956) 73 W.N.(N.S.W.) 1; *Dodd* v. *McGlashan* [1967] A.L.R. 433; *O'Shea* v. *Permanent Trustee of New South Wales Ltd* [1971] Qd.R. 1.

88 *Heard* v. *N.Z. Forest Products Ltd* [1980] N.Z.L.R. 329, 341 *per* Gresson P.

89 *Wooldridge* v. *Sumner* [1963] 2 Q.B. 43.

90 *Scanlon* v. *American Cigarette Co. (Overseas) Pty Ltd* [1987] V.R. 289.

91 *Gent-Diver* v. *Neville* [1953] Q.S.R. 1; *Beck* v. *Mercantile Mutual Insurance Co. Ltd* [1961] S.A.S.R. 311.

At all events, Australian courts have not taken the view that the exact nature of the risk of negligent conduct cannot be sufficiently appreciated in advance to found the defence of *volenti.*[92] But the plaintiff must have known of the defendant's drunkenness, for example, and have thought that this rendered him incapable of driving carefully.[93] Such knowledge may be proved by direct evidence of the plaintiff or others or implied from the facts, but a finding of knowledge cannot be based on the judgment that the plaintiff ought to have realized that the defendant was drunk.[94] This is the very difference between a plea of *volenti* and one of contributory negligence.[95] Thus, if the plaintiff was himself so drunk that he could not assess the risk, a plea of *volenti* could not succeed against him.[96] But the mere fact that the plaintiff was drunk, while relevant to the question of appreciation of risk, is not conclusive of it because the plaintiff may not have been so drunk that he could not see the danger;[97] it will just be harder to establish *volenti* against a drunk plaintiff.[98]

The plaintiff must have accepted the risk freely and willingly if a defence of *volenti* is to succeed.[99] It was at one stage held that rescuers could be met by a plea of *volenti,*[100] but now they are treated as not having acted freely and willingly but under the pressure of a sense of moral duty; or instinctively, in the heat of the moment.[101] Again, the lack of truly free acceptance of risk underlies the unwillingness to allow a plea of *volenti* by an employer to succeed against his employee in respect of risks encountered at work. The willing acceptance may only apply to certain of the risks encountered by the plaintiff. So a passenger who assumes risks flowing from the lack of a headlight does not thereby assume the risk of unrelated negligence on the part of the driver: the driver must take all reasonable care given the lack of a headlight.[102] Again, a visitor may have accepted risks arising from the normal operation of trains on the defendant's land but not risks arising from their negligent operation.[103]

---

92 *Roggenkamp* v. *Bennett* (1950) 80 C.L.R. 292.

93 *O'Shea* v. *Permanent Trustee Co.* [1971] Qd.R. 1; *Dodd* v. *McGlashan* [1967] A.L.R. 433. But in South Australia, the defence of *volenti* is not available in motor accident cases where the driver was under the influence of alcohol or drugs; such cases must be dealt with in terms of contributory negligence: Wrongs Act 1963 s.35a(1)(j) and (4).

94 See cases in previous note.

95 *Heard* v. *N.Z. Forest Products* [1980] N.Z.L.R. 329, 357 *per* North and Cleary JJ.

96 *Dixon* v. *King* [1975] 2 N.Z.L.R. 357.

97 e.g. *Morris* v. *Murray* [1991] 2 Q.B. 6.

98 *Jansons* v. *Public Curator of Queensland* [1968] Qd.R. 40.

99 The estate of a prisoner of sound mind who commits suicide in prison can be met with defence of *volenti*; otherwise if the prisoner was not of sound mind, and the prison authorities knew this and were, therefore, under a duty to protect the prisoner from himself: *Kirkham* v. *Chief Constable of Manchester* [1990] 2 Q.B. 283.

100 e.g. *Stevens* v. *McKenzie & Sons* (1899) 25 V.L.R. 115; *Evenden* v. *Shire of Manning* (1930) 30 S.R.(N.S.W.) 52.

101 *Haynes* v. *Harwood & Son* [1935] 1 K.B. 146; *Ward* v. *T.E. Hopkins & Son Ltd* [1959] 3 All E.R. 225.

102 *Gent-Diver* v. *Neville* [1953] Q.S.R. 1; *Beck* v. *Mercantile Mutual* [1961] S.A.S.R. 311; cf. *Kent* v. *Scattini* [1961] W.A.R. 74; *Ranieri* v. *Ranieri* (1973) 7 S.A.S.R. 418.

103 *Slater* v. *Clay Cross Co. Ltd* [1956] 2 Q.B. 264.

The requirement of free and willing acceptance is sometimes put in terms of whether the risk was one which no reasonable person would have taken. If so, willing acceptance can be inferred provided the plaintiff did not act under compulsion.[104] But if the plaintiff was, for example, confronted by the urgent need to get a child to hospital then it might be said both that he acted under the pressure of emergency in accepting a lift from an intoxicated driver and that, under the circumstances, it could not be said that no reasonable person would have done the same. But this way of putting the matter really renders the defence of *volenti* indistinguishable from contributory negligence since the question ceases to be whether the plaintiff accepted the risk and becomes whether the reasonable person would have accepted the risk. It is, of course, possible in any case to ask an objective question—'did the plaintiff act reasonably in exposing himself to the risk?'—rather than a subjective one—'did he freely expose himself to it?'. But if this is done it is difficult to justify depriving the plaintiff of all his damages rather than apportioning them between the plaintiff and the defendant.

When *volenti* and contributory negligence were both complete defences, the theoretical difference between them was not of great importance; but now that only the former is a complete defence, some special justification is needed for dealing, under the rubric of *volenti*, with cases which could be dealt with more generously to the plaintiff in terms of contributory negligence. If there has been no express or implied agreement not to sue, then even if we view the situation strictly in terms of fault, there seems little reason to treat a plaintiff more harshly for being subjectively aware of a risk than for being in a position where he ought to have been objectively aware of it. The defendant has no more reasonable expectation of not being sued in the former situation than in the latter. In other words, there is an argument for saying that only an agreement not to sue makes a moral difference to the defendant; the difference between the plaintiff's subjective and objective 'state of mind' is of no concern to the defendant.

III: ILLEGALITY[105]

Confusion about the proper role of tort law—is it to compensate plaintiffs? or to give effect to judgments about fault by compensating plaintiffs in appropriate circumstances? or to deter culpable conduct?—comes to a head in this area. The situation is made more complicated by an overlay of public policy about the extent to which the courts would lower their prestige and credibility if they were to 'help' criminals by awarding them damages.

---

104 *Standfield* v. *Uhr* [1964] Qd.R. 66; *Tingle* v. *J.B. Hinz & Sons* [1970] Qd.R. 108; *King* v. *Commissioner for Railways* [1971] Qd.R. 266.

105 W.J. Ford (1977-8) 11 *M.U.L.R.* 32 and 164; J. Swanton (1981) 9 *Syd.L.R.* 304; N. H. Crago (1963-4) 4 *M.U.L.R.* 534.

The basic question is about the extent to which a plaintiff should be penalized because at the time when he was injured he was acting illegally—either in breach of a statute or perhaps contrary to common law. A number of basic problems have troubled the courts. The first concerns the extent to which the civil law ought to be used as an adjunct to or a reinforcement for the criminal law. The argument that it should be so used is a two-edged sword where both the plaintiff and the defendant were acting illegally at the time of the injuries. To deny compensation to the plaintiff *might* deter him from criminal activity, but relieving the defendant of liability for his tort could hardly have a deterrent effect on him. A second point is that much modern 'criminal' legislation is in fact only regulatory; it is very often designed to co-ordinate human behaviour for the sake of efficiency or to set safety standards to protect people from their own carelessness or stupidity.[106] Little, if any, moral censure will attend breach by injured persons of many such laws; and so while deterrence of breach by means, for example, of a fine may be desirable, the unpredictable and usually much more serious sanction of the denial of a civil remedy may seem an unnecessary and unduly harsh sanction. Thus, in a number of recent English cases the question of whether a plea of illegality should succeed has been said to depend in part on whether the 'public conscience' would be 'affronted' or the 'ordinary person shocked' if the plaintiff were allowed to recover.[107]

A third point relates to the allocation of resources: if a choice has to be made between allowing the plaintiff to recover from the defendant's insurer or, on the contrary, leaving him in the position that he needs to rely on social security benefits, it is by no means obvious that any good purpose is served by denying recovery against the defendant. A fourth problem concerns the relationship between the illegal act and the tort. In the formulation adopted above, the issue was put in terms of whether the plaintiff was acting illegally *at the time* the injuries were suffered. But it has usually been felt that to justify a denial of recovery there would need to be a closer nexus between the injury and the illegality. At various times and by various judges this nexus has been put in terms of whether the illegal act was the legal cause of the injury, or whether the injury was a foreseeable consequence of the illegality, or whether there was a direct

106 It now seems clear that breach of safety regulations by an injured person will not as such normally lead to denial of recovery even if the breach was the direct cause of the injuries; *a fortiori* if the defendant was concurrently in breach of relevant safety regulations: *Gala* v. *Preston* (1991) 100 A.L.R. 29.

107 e.g. *Kirkham* v. *Chief Constable of Manchester* [1990] 2 Q.B. 283; *Saunders* v. *Edwards* [1987] 1 W.L.R. 1116; *Pitts* v. *Hunt* [1991] 1 Q.B. 24, 45-6 *per* Beldam L.J.; but note the reservations of Dillon L.J. at p. 56. See also *Rance* v. *Mid-Downs Health Authority* [1991] 1 Q.B. 487 (public policy would not allow P to sue for loss of a chance to have an illegal abortion). Cf *Gala* v. *Preston* (1991) 100 A.L.R. 29, 64-5; Brennan J.'s idea that recovery should be denied when to allow it would 'impair the criminal law's normative influence' (49) may be seen as embodying ideas similar to those adopted in these cases. Of course, this approach offers little or no guidance as to the resolution of particular cases. In *Fletcher* v. *National Mutual Life Nominees Ltd* [1990] 1 N.Z.L.R. 97 a negligent breach of trust was held not to be an illegal act in the relevant sense.

relation (but not necessarily a causal link)[108] between the illegality and the injury. None of these formulae seems now to be crucial.

The basic common law principle appears to be that the fact that the plaintiff was acting illegally at the time the injuries were suffered provides no answer to a claim for damages. This principle can be explained by a number of quite straightforward propositions.

(i) If the plaintiff alone was acting illegally and this illegality consisted of the breach of a statutory duty or regulation,[109] the question is whether the statute, as a matter of interpretation, was intended to deprive a party in breach of it of a civil remedy.[110] Of course, unless the statute in question contains explicit reference to civil liability, the question of the intention of the statute will be answered by a value judgment by the court as to whether the plaintiff ought to be denied damages. The basic principle by itself gives very little guidance as to the proper resolution of individual cases.

The degree of connection between the illegality and the injury will be relevant to the question of the impact of the regulation on civil liability. In *Matthews* v. *McCullock of Australia Pty Ltd*[111] the plaintiff was injured due to the defendant's negligence when riding a motor cycle while disqualified from holding a licence. It was held that since the only connection between the illegality and the injury was that the plaintiff would not have been in a position to be injured if he had not breached the statute by riding without a licence, he could not be denied recovery. The illegality was merely a necessary condition of the injury. Similarly, in *Mills* v. *Baitis*[112] the plaintiff was allowed to recover damages for loss of wages suffered as a result of the defendant's negligence even though those wages were earned carrying on business as an automotive engineer in a residential zone in contravention of planning regulations. On the other hand, in *Meadows* v. *Ferguson*[113] it was held that since the plaintiff's lost earnings were attributable to his employment as a clerk in an illegal bookmaking establishment, he could not recover.

It is clear, however, that even the fact that the illegal act is the direct cause of the injury will not necessarily bar the plaintiff's recovery.[114] But if the purpose of the regulation is not to protect a person from his own carelessness but to impose strict obligations for the protection of a group including the plaintiff, then the result may be different.[115]

(ii) Sometimes the fact that the plaintiff acted illegally will be relevant to the issue of whether he was contributorily negligent.[116]

---

108 *Smith* v. *Jenkins* (1969) 119 C.L.R. 397, 434 *per* Walsh J.

109 Where the crime is a common law one, the question would have to be framed in terms such as the seriousness of the offence.

110 (1938) 60 C.L.R. 438.

111 [1973] N.S.W.L.R. 331; cf. *Andrews* v. *Nominal Defendant* (1965) 66 S.R.(N.S.W.) 85.

112 [1968] V.R. 583; cf. *Le Bagge* v. *Buses Ltd* [1958] N.Z.L.R. 630.

113 [1961] V.R. 594; cf. *Burns* v. *Edman* [1970] 2 Q.B. 541; *Richters* v. *Motor Tyre Service Pty Ltd* [1972] Qd.R. 9. See also *Thackwell* v. *Barclays Bank p.l.c.* [1986] 1 All E.R. 676.

114 *Henwood* v. *Municipal Tramways Trust (S.A.)* (1938) 60 C.L.R. 438.

115 *Christiansen* v. *Gilday* (1948) 48 S.R.(N.S.W.) 352.

116 *Henwood* (1938) 60 C.L.R. 438; *Jackson* v. *Harrison* (1978) 138 C.L.R. 438, 453 *per* Mason J.

(iii) Again, in some cases the fact that the plaintiff acted illegally might be relevant to the question of whether he voluntarily assumed the risk of injury. This might be of particular relevance in connection with some intentional torts. For example, if the plaintiff is a thief who is injured when the householder, who is the victim of the criminal activities, takes action in self-defence which is beyond the bounds of reasonableness, a court might have little sympathy for the plaintiff's claim in battery.[117]

(iv) Where the plaintiff and the defendant are jointly involved[118] and co-operating in illegal activity[119] the rule appears to be that this will bar the plaintiff from recovery (leaving aside the question of statutory interpretation)[120] only if the nexus between the act of negligence and the illegal activity is such that the standard of care owed in the particular circumstances could only be determined by taking into account the illegal nature of the activity in which the parties were engaged.[121] So if a thief is injured when a companion plants explosives to blow a safe in an allegedly negligent way, the court will not inquire into whether the burglar alarm had sounded or whether the police were on their way or whether the furtive nature of the occasion made it inappropriate to apply to the defendant a standard of care which would be appropriate to a lawful activity. The reason for this approach appears to be one of public policy, but it is not clear what the policy is: it may be that if the courts were to engage in such inquiries this would lower the respect felt for the courts; or some vague feeling that if things go wrong in the course of criminal activities, even if by the negligence of one of the criminals, the criminals deserve everything they get. To this extent the compensatory aim of the law is subordinated to other values. This is not altogether surprising, because even when no-fault systems of motor accident compensation are adopted there is often much dispute as to whether persons

---

117 *Murphy* v. *Culhane* [1977] Q.B. 94, 98 *per* Lord Denning M.R.

118 Even if only minimally: *Holland* v. *Tarlinton* (1989) 10 M.V.R. 129.

119 A problem in this type of case is that while denial of damages to the plaintiff *might* be seen as a discouragement to illegal activity, relieving the defendant of liabilty might equally be seen as an encouragement.

120 A statute might expressly provide that persons who contravene it should be denied a remedy in damages: *Gala* v. *Preston* (1991) 100 A.L.R. 29, 33, 45.

121 *Jackson* v. *Harrison* (1978) 138 C.L.R. 438; *Progress & Properties Ltd* v. *Craft* (1976) 135 C.L.R. 651; cf. *Ashton* v. *Turner* [1980] 3 All E.R. 890; *Smith* v. *Jenkins* (1970) 119 C.L.R. 397 as interpreted in *Gala* v. *Preston* (1991) 100 A.L.R. 29. The majority in *Gala* clothed their conclusion in the superfluous and unhelpful language of 'proximity', but the proposition in the text captures the majority's underlying reasoning (at pp. 36 and 37). Only Brennan and Toohey JJ. adopted a principle significantly different from the proposition in the text. In the recent English case of *Pitts* v. *Hunt* [1991] 1 Q.B. 302 one judge adopted this approach but the other two did not. One judge said that there was a close nexus between the illegality (riding a motor cycle under the influence of alcohol) and the plaintiff's injuries. In most Australian jurisdictions such facts could have been dealt with in terms of *volenti*, but this was not possible in this case because this defence is ruled out by statute in motor accident cases in England: Road Traffic Act 1988 s.149. The test in the text is not appropriate to cases where, for example, a person is induced to enter an illegal transaction by an unrelated fraudulent misrepresentation: see, for example, *Shelley* v. *Paddock* [1980] Q.B. 348; *Saunders* v. *Edwards* [1987] 1 W.L.R. 1116. In these cases a version of the 'close nexus' test was applied: the loss was the direct result of the misrepresentation, not the illegality.

involved in criminal activities should be entitled to claim. The alleviation of need and suffering regardless of fault is clearly an important part of our morality, but it is unlikely that all elements of personal responsibility will ever be eliminated from popular views about the proper way to deal with non-criminal injuries.

IV: EXCLUSION OF LIABILITY

As we have seen, liability for tortious negligence may be excluded by contract terms[122] or, in some cases, by non-contractual disclaimers.[123] The basis on which such provisions operate is that the plaintiff has, by expressly or impliedly agreeing to the exclusion, bound himself not to sue the negligent party. It is also clear that in cases where a defendant is concurrently liable in tort and contract, any relevant term in the contract limiting or excluding the contractual liability will be effective to limit or exclude the concurrent tortious liability.[124] More difficult are cases in which either the plaintiff or the defendant, but not both, is a party to a contract containing an exclusion clause. Such cases often arise out of building contracts where, for example, P employs C to build a building and C sub-contracts some of the work to D. Suppose that P sues D in tort for negligence in performing the work and that there is an exclusion clause in the contract between P and C covering liability for the loss caused by D. Can D plead the exclusion clause against P? If the exclusion clause purports to be for the benefit of both C and D, there is English authority to the effect that D can do so on the basis that it would not be just or reasonable in those circumstances to impose tort liability on D at the suit of P.[125] There is no direct authority on whether D could plead against P an exclusion clause in a contract between P and C which purported only to protect C.

Suppose, however, that the relevant exclusion clause is not in the contract between P and C but in the contract between C and D. Could D plead that exclusion clause against P? This case is more difficult than the former because here D is trying to *burden* P with a provision contained in a contract to which P is not a party; whereas in the former case, D was attempting to take the *benefit* of a provision in a contract to which he was not a party but to which the burdened person was a party. The English cases dealing with this situation are not easy to interpret, but much would seem to depend on whether or not P knew of the exclusion clause at the time he contracted with C.

Statutory provisions designed to exclude liability for negligence are rare. As we will see later, statutory authorization (which may be express or

---

122 As to the interpretation of such provisions see J. Swanton (1989) 15 *U.Qld.L.J.* 157.
123 The latter, like contractual exclusion clauses, are interpreted strictly against the person seeking to rely on them: *Burke* v. *Forbes S.C.* (1987) 63 L.G.R.A. 1.
124 *Coupland* v. *Arabian Gulf Petroleum Co.* [1983] 3 All E.R. 226.
125 *Norwich C.C.* v. *Harvey* [1989] 1 W.L.R. 828; *Pacific Associates Ltd* v. *Baxter* [1990] 1 Q.B. 993.

implied) is a defence to a claim in nuisance; and liability for nuisance is, in essence, based on negligence. But if the defendant could have avoided the nuisance by exercising reasonable care, the defence is unlikely to be available. As a general principle, courts are unwilling to interpret statutory provisions which do not unambiguously exclude liability for negligence as doing so; and legislatures are unwilling to attempt to exclude liability for negligence.[126] One area in which legislatures have seen fit to exclude liability, *inter alia,* for negligence is that of the supply of blood and blood products which are liable to be contaminated with HIV virus which can lead to AIDS. For example, the Blood Contaminants Act 1985 (S.A.) excludes all civil liability of donors, suppliers and transfusers of contaminated blood or blood products provided prescribed procedures are followed in the taking of the blood. But a supplier of blood who has reasonable cause to suspect that it or products made from it may be contaminated must take all reasonable steps to ensure that the blood or the products are not used for transfusion purposes. There are similar provisions in other jurisdictions.[127] However, although the literal terms of these provisions exclude liability for negligence in the acquisition of blood, the statutes also aim to prescribe procedures for the taking of blood which, if properly followed, could not, as a matter of fact, give rise to allegations of negligence.

In England the efficacy of contractual exclusions clauses and non-contractual disclaimers is considerably limited by legislation[128] but there is no equivalent legislation in any Australian jurisdiction.[129]

126 See, for example, Transplantation and Anatomy Act 1983 (S.A.) s.36(1).

127 Human Tissue Act 1983 (N.S.W.) s.21DA; Blood Transfusion (Limitation of Liability) Act 1986 (Tas.); Blood Donation (Limitation of Liability) Act 1985 (W.A.); Blood Donation (Acquired Immune Deficiency Syndrome) Ordinance 1985 (A.C.T.).

128 Unfair Contract Terms Act 1977.

129 See generally J. Jackson (1991) 65 *A.L.J.R.* 507.

14

EMPLOYERS' LIABILITY

I: GENERAL COMMENTS

Like the rules of occupiers' liability, the law governing the duties of employers to protect their employees[1] from suffering personal injury at work was well developed before the decision in *Donoghue* v. *Stevenson*[2] and, as a consequence, the structure of the law in this area has remained to some extent unaffected by that case. There was a time when the liability of the employer was very considerably qualified by the doctrine of 'common employment', according to which an employer could not be held *vicariously* liable to any of its employees for injuries caused by the negligence of fellow employees. This doctrine has now been abolished by statute.[3] But an important by-product of the doctrine was the rule that the employer's obligations are personal to itself and cannot be discharged simply by appointing a competent manager or other employee to perform its duties.[4] We will examine this principle in more detail in due course.

---

1 'Employee' in this context primarily means 'servant' as opposed to 'independent contractor' (see p. 700 below), and this is the meaning it has in this chapter. But employers do owe a duty of care to independent contractors. However, because the employer has less control over what an independent contractor does and how, when and where it is done, the duty of the employer to the independent contractor is, in general terms, less demanding than the duties to servants. One particular aspect of the employer's duty to independent contractors is the duty to co-ordinate their work where several independent contractors are employed. See *Stevens* v. *Brodribb Sawmilling Pty Ltd* (1985-6) 160 C.L.R. 16.

2 [1932] A.C. 562.

3 Workers Compensation Act 1987 (N.S.W.) s.151AA; Employers and Employees Act 1945 (Vic.); Wrongs Act 1936-75 (S.A.) s.30; Law Reform (Abolition of the Rule of Common Employment) Act 1951 (Qld); Employers' Liability Act 1943 (Tas.); Law Reform (Common Employment) Act 1951 (W.A.); Law Reform (Miscellaneous Provisions) Act 1955 (A.C.T.) s.21; Law Reform (Miscellaneous Provisions) Act (N.T.) s. 22.

4 *Wilsons & Clyde Coal Co. Ltd* v. *English* [1938] A.C. 57.

The rationale of the employer's liability in tort[5] is its *control* over the employee's conditions of work. The employee is in a relationship of dependence with his employer, who, despite the power of modern unions and the plethora of legislation governing working conditions, is still, in practice, often in a position to dictate to the worker what he will do, how, where, when and under what conditions. Another justification for employers' liability is a loss-allocation argument: the employer is in a much better position than his employees both to take steps to ensure that avoidable accidents do not occur and to insure against the risks which his employees face.

As is well known, the cost, in both financial and human terms, of industrial accidents is very high. The greatest sufferers tend to be those who are in the weakest position *vis-á-vis* their employers: women, part-time workers, the non-unionized and recently arrived or non-English-speaking migrants. The tort system of compensation based on negligence (and breach of statutory duty) is, in this area, as in others, a complex, inefficient and slow method of compensating the victims of industrial injuries and diseases. In an attempt to meet some of these difficulties all Australian jurisdictions have a system, which operates in parallel with the common law, of statutory workers' compensation.[6] Very loosely, this is a system of strict employers' liability for accidents occurring in and arising out of the course of employment. The employee does not have to prove that the accident was caused by anyone's fault, and the compensation is provided out of the proceeds of a (compulsory) insurance policy taken out by the employer to cover his liability. The system of workers' compensation has certain advantages over the common law system: the issues raised in litigation are less complex in that the employee does not have to prove fault; compensation for financial loss can be awarded in periodical form; compensation for non-pecuniary loss is awarded according to a fixed tariff by type of injury, thus doing away with much argument over the 'proper' amount of the award.

On the other hand, by no means all those in paid employment are covered by the workers' compensation statutes. Secondly, the total compensation available under the legislation is often less than that which a worker could recover at common law, so that although workers' compensation payments will usually be set off against common law damages, there may be financial advantage for an injured worker, especially one whose injuries are serious and lasting, in suing at common law. For these reasons, the common law of employers' liability is of continuing importance.

5 And in contract to the extent that it depends on terms implied by law. In some circumstances, policy considerations may negate any duty of care on the part of the employer towards employees: *Hughes* v. *National Union of Mineworkers* [1991] 4 All E.R. 278.

6 For a short account see R.P. Balkin and J.L.R. Davis, *Law of Torts* (Sydney, 1991) pp. 401-4.

II: THE GENERAL NATURE OF THE EMPLOYER'S DUTIES

The duty of the employer is usually divided into three: to provide safe tools and equipment, a safe place of work and a safe system of work. The last of these is a residual category, but out of it a fourth particular duty has crystallized: the duty to employ competent fellow employees. The employer's 'duties' do not determine the standard of care which the employer must discharge; the standard of care required of the employer is always the same: to use such care as is reasonable in the circumstances to ensure that its employees are not injured. Nor do the 'duties' serve to limit the circumstances in which the employer can be held liable: the employer is under a general duty to take reasonable care to carry out its operations so as not to subject those employed by it to unnecessary risks.[7] Unnecessary risks are those which could be avoided by the exercise of reasonable care. The importance of stressing this general duty is to avoid technical arguments by employers to the effect that the facts of the case before the court do not fit exactly into any one of the particular 'duty categories'. In fact the particular duties are just examples or manifestations of the employer's general duty; the law of employers' liability is the application to a specialized area of ordinary negligence principles.[8] The major respect in which the employer's position is special is that because of its control over conditions of work and in recognition of the relationship of dependence between it and its employees, the employer will in many situations be under a duty not just to refrain from causing injury but to take positive steps to prevent injury occurring.

There is, of course, a contract of service between employer and employee, and originally the duties of the employer and their limits were explained in terms of the express or implied provisions of the contract. But in the more modern cases the duties of the employer are usually seen as being tort-based rather than contract-based;[9] and an employee can sue his employer for personal injuries concurrently in tort and contract.[10] This emphasis on tort has led to at least one expression of doubt as to whether an employee could expressly agree with his employer to work in unsafe conditions;[11] and it makes it unlikely that a court would hold that a contract of service contained an implied term to this effect, especially in the light of the very restrictive attitude which has been taken to the defence of *volenti non fit injuria* in this context.[12] As far as employees are

---

7 *Wilson* v. *Tyneside Window Cleaning Co.* [1958] 2 Q.B. 110; *Turner* v. *State of South Australia* (1982) 56 A.L.J.R. 839.

8 There has been a trend over the years to make the standard of care required of employers higher and higher; but it has been said that the courts ought not to turn common law employers' liability into strict liability, given the existence of strict liability workers' compensation schemes: *Mihaljevic* v. *Longyear (Australia) Pty Ltd* (1985) 3 N.S.W.L.R. 1, 10 *per* Kirby P.

9 *Toth* v. *Yellow Carriers Ltd* (1969) 0 W.N.(Pt.1)(N.S.W.) 378; *Davie* v. *New Merton Board Mills Ltd* [1959] A.C. 604, 619 *per* Viscount Simonds; 642 *per* Lord Reid.

10 *Matthews* v. *Kuwait Bechtel Corporation Ltd* [1959] 2 Q.B. 57.

11 *Imperial Chemical Industries Ltd* v. *Shatwell* [1965] A.C. 656, 674 *per* Lord Reid.

12 See p. 567 below. But see *Johnstone* v. *Bloomsbury Health Authority* [1992] 1 Q.B. 333.

concerned, the main advantage of tort over contract would probably be the greater generosity of remoteness of damage rules in tort. Contract might have an advantage depending on how the uncertainties concerning the availability of contributory negligence as a defence to a claim in contract are resolved.[13]

As mentioned above, the doctrine of common employment has been abolished by statute. Before its abolition a technique was developed for ameliorating its harsh effect: the doctrine was held only to protect the employer from vicarious liability for what were called 'casual' acts of negligence done by his employees. Casual negligence was negligence committed in the course of performing acts other than acts done for the purpose of fulfilling any of the employer's duties which are personal to himself. The employer could not escape liability for negligence in the performance of the fourfold duty by employing a competent servant (or, of course, an independent contractor[14]) to do what was necessary to discharge its duties; and this was so despite the fact that the only practicable way of endeavouring to perform the duties might have been to employ a competent person to do it.[15] With the abolition of the doctrine of common employment the distinctions between personal and vicarious liability of the employer, and between casual acts of negligence by fellow-employees and acts of negligence done in performing tasks delegated to employees but personal to the employer, have ceased to be of any great importance. The employer is liable not only for unsafe systems adopted by employee-supervisors appointed to ensure the safety of the workplace, but also for unsafe practices adopted by ordinary employees in performing their allotted tasks.[16] The employer can also, of course, be held liable if he himself has been negligent in performing any of his duties. The point about the non-delegability of the 'personal' duties is that the employer is liable for their breach whether he was personally negligent or not, provided someone for whom he is responsible *was* negligent.

But there may be limits to the extent to which the employer is liable for negligence by employees in the performance of the personal duties. In *Witham* v. *Shire of Bright*[17] Sholl J. held that where an employer employs a competent person to do a job and delegates entirely to him the manner of the doing of that job, and the employee is injured by his own carelessness in the doing of it, he cannot sue the employer. It may be, too, that if the performance of a job required a great deal of adjustment to the particular circumstances in which it fell to be done, so that the worker had of necessity to be given considerable freedom to temper the circumstances

---

13 See further p. 537 above.

14 *Jones* v. *Tivoli Collieries Pty Ltd* [1966] Qd.R. 140; *Davie* v. *New Merton Board Mills* [1959] A.C. 604.

15 *Kodak (Australasia) Pty Ltd* v. *Retail Traders Mutual Indemnity Association* (1942) 42 S.R.(N.S.W.) 231, 235-6.

16 *Katsilis* v. *Broken Hill Pty Co. Ltd* (1978) 52 A.L.J.R. 189,201-2; *Hamilton* v. *Nuroof (W.A.) Pty Ltd* (1956) 96 C.L.R. 18, 25; *Turner* v. *State of South Australia* (1982) 56 A.L.J.R. 839, 842-3.

17 [1959] V.R. 790.

and his working method to his own safety, the employer would not be held liable if the employee was injured in doing the job.

The other important limitation on the liability of the employer for breach of the personal duties is contained in *Davie* v. *New Merton Board Mills.*[18] There the plaintiff was injured when a piece of metal flew off a negligently manufactured tool. The defendant employer had bought the tool from a reputable dealer who had bought it from a reputable supplier. It was argued on behalf of the plaintiff that the defendant was liable for the negligence of the manufacturer; but the House of Lords held that since the employer had not in any sense delegated the task of manufacturing the tool to the manufacturer, nor had there been any relations between them at any stage, the employer could not be held liable. He could have been required to pay damages if the tool had been made by a servant or independent contractor, or perhaps even an independent manufacturer if the employer had in some sense delegated to it the task of providing the tools, for example by providing the design to which the tools were to be made; but none of these conditions was satisfied in the case before the court. The employer could also have been held liable if there had been any indication before the accident that the tool was defective.[19]

It might be thought that *Davie* v. *New Merton* involves a rather unfortunate and unnecessary limitation on the employer's liability. Wherever the employer purchases its tools and plant, the employee is still injured by a failure to provide safe equipment, and the employer is in a good position to absorb the loss. Also, it is much easier for the employee to enforce a liability against the employer than against a third-party manufacturer. As far as the employee is concerned, the details of the arrangements under which the employer acquires tools and plant should be treated as *res inter alios acta.* The force of such arguments has been recognized in England, where the effect of *Davie* has been reversed by statute in the Employers' Liability (Defective Equipment) Act 1969.

III: SCOPE OF EMPLOYMENT

Although the obligations of the employer to employees are not dependent for their existence on the contract of employment, the contract can be of importance in defining when the relationship of employer and employee is in existence and so when the employer's duties are operative. In *A.C.I. Metal Stamping & Spinning Pty Ltd* v. *Boczulik*[20] the plaintiff fell in a hole on a path while walking from her place of work to a bus stop at night. The factory stood in a large field surrounded by highways. There was no evidence that the defendant owned the path. It was held that the plaintiff was using the path in the course of her employment and so could

---

18 [1959] A.C. 604.
19 *Taylor* v. *Rover Company Ltd* [1966] 1 W.L.R. 1491.
20 (1964) 110 C.L.R. 372; see also *Milligan* v. *L.J. Hooker Ltd* (1966) 85 W.N.(N.S.W.) 160.

recover damages from her employer. Kitto J. pointed out that the concept of course of employment is not a narrow one.[21] The course of employment extends beyond the period of the working day to every situation in which the employer sustains the character of employer towards the employee. This means that while an employee may go somewhere or do something by virtue of being an employee of his employer, a duty will only rest on the latter if and when the employee is acting as such. So, for example, if an employer as such acquires a free theatre ticket for an employee or arranges for an employee to use a short-cut to work, the employee in going to the theatre or using the short-cut will be where he is by virtue of being the defendant's employee, but he will not be normally acting as an employee while there; rather he will be acting as a member of the public. When the employee makes a journey, the relevant question is not in what character he is making the journey, but whether the master is employer in relation to that journey. This is not the case when the worker is simply going to and from work, but it may be if the employee is on an errand for the employer.

In *A.C.I.* v. *Boczulik* the workplace was surrounded by land owned by third parties, and so there was an implied term in the contract of employment that the employer would arrange access to the factory for the employee. This meant that at the time the employee was using the arranged access the employer was under a duty for her safety. The crucial difference between this and the case of a short-cut was that here, unless access was arranged, the employee could not have got to work without trespassing and so could not have performed her contractual obligations. So the access became, in effect, an extension of the employer's premises. If the servant had used some route other than the arranged one she would not have been in the course of her employment in using the route.

IV: THE EMPLOYER'S FOUR DUTIES

1. Safe Tools and Equipment

In *Foufoulas* v. *F.G. Strang Pty Ltd*[22] the plaintiff was injured when he lost his balance while unloading bales of wool. The usual method of doing the job was to use a single-pronged hook provided by the worker. The plaintiff had tried to organize a strike over the use of the hooks, which he considered dangerous, but had failed. He argued that the job should have been done mechanically or that a double-pronged hook ought to have been provided by the employer. It was held that the plaintiff could not recover: he had been employed to do a particular job in a particular way and even if it was dangerous, there is no duty on an employer not to employ people to do a dangerous job. Furthermore, since

21 But it is probably not as wide in this context as in the context of the vicarious liability of an employer to third parties; for example, the employee may not be as 'free' to ignore prohibitions in this context without affecting the employer's liability.

22 (1970) 123 C.L.R. 168.

the usual practice was for the worker to supply his own hook, the plaintiff could have used a two-pronged hook if he had wanted to.

The nub of this decision seems to have been that the plaintiff was really trying to impose on the employer a duty to offer certain working conditions to prospective employees before a contract of employment was even made. The employer's duties only apply once the employment relationship has come into existence. There is also a strong undertone of freedom of contract in the judgments: the plaintiff need not have taken the job, and although, once an employment relationship exists, the courts are very unwilling to hold that an employee has consented to take risks associated with the work, they are apparently not as unwilling to find consent where the plaintiff knew the risks when he took the job. This difference of approach is perhaps a little unrealistic. If it is unfair to expect an employee either to accept a risk or resign then, especially in times of high unemployment, it may also be unfair to expect a job applicant, who may be experienced in no other work, either to accept a risk or remain unemployed.

On the other hand, the decision does recognize that an employer may be under a duty not only to provide safe tools and equipment but even, where it has not provided the tools, to take reasonable steps to ensure the safety of its employees if it becomes aware they are using unsafe tools. Furthermore, in some cases, if the job which the employer takes on workers to do or the situation into which it intends to send its employee is dangerous enough, then it may be under a duty not to ask anyone in its employ to do the work. But this principle would probably apply only in very extreme cases.

Often the use of unsafe machinery will involve a breach of statutory duty by both the employer and the employee. In *Czislowski* v. *Read Press Pty Ltd*[23] it was held that if the only reason why the employer was in breach of statutory duty was that the employee was in breach then (while an action might lie for breach of statutory duty) the employer could not be held liable in negligence. For the employer to be liable in negligence it would have to be shown that it had been additionally at fault in some way, such as by failure to give proper instructions or supervision, or by employing an inexperienced worker, or by having in the past acquiesced in a wrong way of working. In this case, in the light of the seriousness of the likely injury, the defendant had been negligent in not ensuring that the guard was in use and in acquiescing in its past non-use. Further, the defendant should have put pressure even on experienced workers to use the guard and, since the use of the guard was so unattractive to the workers, it should have devised a form of protection which they would have been more willing to use. The plaintiff was also held to have been contributorily negligent.

---

23 [1968] Qd.R. 129.

2. Safe Workplace

The employer must take reasonable care to ensure that the workplace is a safe place having regard to the nature of the work to be done there. Thus the concept of safety is relative to the type of activity the employer conducts; and the lack of safety must be the result of some lack of care on the part of the employer or someone for whom he is responsible.[24]

As we have already seen, the employer's duty to provide safe premises can extend to places which the employer does not own and over which it has only limited control, such as the access path in *A.C.I.* v. *Boczulik.*[25] A leading case on this point is *Wilson* v. *Tyneside Window Cleaning Co.*[26] in which an experienced window cleaner was injured when a rotten window frame by which he was supporting himself gave way. It was held that the plaintiff's employer was under a duty to him even though he was not working on the employer's premises. But even though the employer owes a duty in respect of other people's premises, the steps which the duty requires will be very different from those required in respect of its own premises, because the employer will usually have very little control over the premises of others. If a plumber or electrician sends a worker to an ordinary private home, it could not be expected to inspect the premises beforehand to ensure that they are safe. But if it sends him to a very dilapidated building to work, it may be under some duty to make a preliminary reconnaisance. What is required must be judged according to the facts and circumstances of the particular case and the extent of the employer's reasonable knowledge of the state of the premises to which the worker is being sent.[27]

A question which sometimes arises in this context, as well as in relation to the other duties of the employer, is whether the risk which the employee faced was one which was inherent in the nature of the work the employee was engaged to do. This is very much tied up with the question of whether the plaintiff was *volens* to the risk, and we will consider it again in that context. However, even apart from this question, it is sometimes said than an employee cannot complain of risks which are part of the very nature of the work. The concept of inherent risks is a difficult one, since danger as often resides in the way or circumstances in which something is done as in the activity itself. The proper interpretation of the idea of inherent risks seems to be that an employee cannot succeed against an employer in respect of risks which the exercise of reasonable care could not eliminate from the work and which the employee must guard against himself.[28]

---

24 *Laubscher* v. *Mt Isa Mines Ltd* (1967-8) 41 A.L.J.R. 125; *New South Wales Fresh Food & Ice Ltd* v. *Graham* [1963] S.R.(N.S.W.) 244. *Query* whether an employer could be held liable for not prohibiting smoking in the workplace to a worker who contracted cancer from other workers' smoke. It is unclear whether the *Scholem* case (*Sydney Morning Herald* 28 May 1992) goes this far or only requires proper ventilation.

25 (1964) 110 C.L.R. 372.

26 [1958] 2 Q.B. 110; cf. *Sinclair* v. *William Arnott Pty Ltd* (1964) 80 W.N.(N.S.W.) 798.

27 *Smith* v. *Austin Lifts Ltd* [1959] 1 W.L.R. 100, 117 *per* Lord Denning.

28 *Knight* v. *Robert Laurie Pty Ltd* [1961] W.A.R. 129, 132 *per* Hale J.

3. Competent Fellow Employees

This duty is really only of practical importance in cases where the plaintiff has been injured by conduct beyond the course of the employee's employment with the result that the employer cannot be fixed with vicarious liability. The duty is a quite limited one. Clearly, if the employer's business involves danger if workers do not exercise care and competence, or if, for its successful and safe conduct, it requires the exercise of special skill or the use of special knowledge, the employer could be held to be in breach of its duty if it (or its delegate) negligently appointed a worker who lacked the requisite degree of skill or competence with the result that injury was caused to another employee.[29] Similarly, if it came to the employer's attention that someone in its employ was incompetent or lacking in the required skills, it could be held liable if it failed to do something to remedy the situation before injury was caused.[30] But defects in human beings are not as easily detected and dealt with as defects in inanimate objects, and this must inevitably affect the degree of perspicacity and anticipation of trouble which could be expected of an employer in this respect.

An employer might also be under a duty to dismiss an employee who demonstrated a propensity for deliberate misconduct or violence towards fellow employees. The ultimate question is whether the employer ought to have foreseen that the conduct of the unruly employee might present a danger to fellow employees.[31] The employer could not be expected to go beyond a reprimand on the first report of trouble; even less so if all that the employer was told was that the employee had allegedly threatened violence—then the appropriate thing to do might be to investigate the matter. On the other hand, repeated reprimands might not be an adequate step in relation to an employee who had displayed dangerous propensities over a long period.[32] Considerable latitude in personnel matters must be left to the employer, especially since trouble can be the result of personality problems or racial animosities which require delicate handling. Nor are employers entirely free agents in the matter of hiring and firing, since unions can exercise considerable influence through the threat of industrial action, and it has been said that the common law should not allow itself to be used to foment or aggravate industrial unrest.[33]

In the case of the appointment of persons to jobs requiring the exercise of mental or intellectual abilities or requiring high levels of probity or judgment, the notoriously difficult nature of the task of determining in advance whether a particular person will turn out to be a good appointment must mean that actions alleging negligence in such appointments will very rarely succeed.[34]

---

29 *Vallender* v. *Victorian Railways Commissioners* (1896) 22 V.L.R. 141.
30 *Kodak* v. *Retail Traders etc. Association* (1942) 42 S.R.(N.S.W.) 231, 236.
31 *Smith* v. *Crossley Bros* (1951) 95 Sol.Jo. 655; *Smith* v. *Ocean Steamship Co. Ltd* [1954] 2 Lloyd's Rep. 482.
32 *Hudson* v. *Ridge Manufacturing Co. Ltd* [1957] 2 Q.B. 348.
33 *Antoniak* v. *Commonwealth* (1962) 4 F.L.R. 454.
34 *Carpenter's Investment Trading Co. Ltd* v. *Commonwealth of Australia* (1952) 69 W.N.(N.S.W.) 174.

4. Safe System of Work

The employer's duty[35] is to take reasonable care to see that the working practices, systems and arrangements in its establishment are reasonably safe.[36] The employer should provide proper and adequate means of carrying out the work without unnecessary risk, warn of unusual or unexpected dangers, and instruct in the performance of the work where instruction might reasonably be thought to be necessary to protect workers from the risk of injury.[37] Employers are also required to take into account the possibility that workers may act carelessly or inadvertently and thus create dangers against which precautions need to be taken.[38] In deciding whether the employer has discharged this duty, the court must take account of its power to 'prescribe, warn, command and enforce obedience to' its commands.[39] The employer's duty to take precautions, to warn and to instruct is not necessarily limited to dangers of which the employer is aware but the employee is ignorant.[40] The greater the danger and the easier the precautions, the greater the burden on the employer to warn and instruct employees how to protect themselves against it and to take positive steps itself to eliminate unnecessary risks, even if they are obvious. The fact that an employee knows of a danger *might* relieve the employer of liability if the only duty were to warn; but often the duty will go beyond this and require the employer to provide a system of work which minimizes or eliminates the risk.[41]

On the other hand, an employer will be negligent only if it fails to take precautions against a foreseeable risk, and it has been said that in judging whether a defendant ought to have taken precautions, employers are not to be treated as persons possessing superhuman qualities of imagination and foresight;[42] and that while any employer would envisage that in the course of performing almost any type of factory work an employee might, for example, sustain muscular strain or other physical lesion, one should not jump from that statement to a conclusion that the employer was negligent.[43]

Also relevant in judging what precautions the employer should take is the degree of skill and experience of the worker in dealing with the type of danger in question. The mere fact that the employee is skilled will not necessarily relieve the employer of the duty to do something, because accidents can happen even to the most highly trained and experienced worker, who may need to be reminded periodically of the risks of the work

---

35 Which is 'not a low one': *Bankstown Foundry Pty Ltd* v. *Braistina* (1986) 160 C.L.R. 301.

36 *Karatzidis* v. *Victorian Railways Commissioners* [1971] V.R. 360.

37 *Akkari* v. *Western Australian Government Railways Commission* [1968] W.A.R. 182; *O'Connor* v. *Commissioner for Government Transport* (1958) 100 C.L.R. 225.

38 *Bus* v. *Sydney County Council* (1989) 167 C.L.R. 78.

39 *McLean* v. *Tedman* (1984) 155 C.L.R. 306, 313.

40 *Raimondo* v. *State of South Australia* (1979) 23 A.L.R. 513.

41 *Turner* v. *State of South Australia* (1982) 56 A.L.J.R. 839; *McLean* v. *Tedman* (1984) 155 C.L.R. 306.

42 *Rae* v. *Broken Hill Pty Co. Ltd* (1957) 97 C.L.R. 419.

43 *Quintano* v. *Cable Makers of Australia Pty Ltd* [1966] 2 N.S.W.R. 496.

and of the need to guard against them.[44] But the more inexperienced and the less skilled the worker the more the employer must do to protect him;[45] and the more experienced he is, the more he can be left to get on with the job by himself.[46] Provided the employee takes reasonable care for his own safety, he is entitled to assume that the employer's system of work will provide him not with perfect but with reasonable protection in the light of both the likelihood and the gravity of the risk.[47] The duty of the employer is also related to the degree of pressure under which the employee works.[48]

What is the employer's duty towards an employee who is more than normally susceptible to the risks involved in the activity? Is the employer under any obligation to take special measures to protect the hypersensitive worker? One thing is reasonably clear: if a worker insists on doing a job for which he is not fit, his employer is under no obligation to dismiss him for his own good or to find other work for which he is fit.[49] But what if the worker is required in the course of his employment to do a task which involves for him a greater risk of injury or a risk of a greater injury than it involves for other workers? In *Paris* v. *Stepney Borough Council*[50] a one-eyed worker lost the sight in his good eye when a piece of metal flew off the chassis of a vehicle he was repairing. It was held that even assuming that the employer was under no duty to provide protective goggles for ordinary two-eyed workers, it ought to have provided a pair for the plaintiff, whom it knew to have only one eye, because the consequences of the loss of an eye would be much graver for him than for the ordinary worker. It may be that this principle only applies where the employer knows or had means of knowing of the plaintiff's peculiar weakness or susceptibility.[51]

Perhaps the most difficult problem which arises in actions in which failure to provide a safe system of work is alleged is that of proving that some alternative system was practicable and reasonable and that it would have prevented the injury. The onus, of course, rests on the plaintiff, and in some cases courts have been particularly harsh on plaintiffs in requiring a high standard of probative material on this issue. There is an element of risk in most industrial operations, even the simplest, and it is not enough for the plaintiff to show the existence of the risk. He must also show that it was capable of reduction or elimination by some practicable precaution or safeguard without unduly impeding the employer's business.[52] Sometimes an alternative system may be identifiable without the benefit of

---

44 *Perkovic* v. *McDonnell Industries Pty Ltd* (1987) 45 S.A.S.R. 544.
45 *McInerney* v. *Schultz* (1981) 27 S.A.S.R. 215.
46 *Akkari* [1968] W.A.R. 182; *Raimondo* (1979) 23 A.L.R. 513.
47 *Carlyle* v. *Commissioner for Railways* (1954) 54 S.R.(N.S.W.) 238.
48 *Sroka* v. *Park Ridge Private Hospital* (1981) 28 S.A.S.R. 15; cf. *General Cleaning Contractors Ltd* v. *Christmas* [1953] A.C. 180.
49 *Crisa* v. *John Shearer Ltd* (1981) 27 S.A.S.R. 422, 435; *Uehlin* v. *Standard Telephones & Cables Pty Ltd* (1964) 80 W.N. (N.S.W.) 1600.
50 [1951] A.C. 367; cf. *McInerney* v. *Schultz* (1981) 27 S.A.S.R. 215.
51 *Brkovic* v. *Clough (J.O.) & Son Ltd* (1983) 49 A.L.R. 256.
52 *Retsas* v. *Commonwealth* (1976) 50 A.L.J.R. 104, 106 *per* Barwick C.J.; *Vozza* v. *Tooth & Co. Ltd* (1964) 112 C.L.R. 316, 318.

specific or expert evidence,[53] but in many cases, without the aid of such evidence, the court will not be able to pronounce upon whether reasonable precautions were possible.[54] Where it is alleged that the employer failed to take some proper safety measure, the court will not speculate or grope in the dark to satisfy itself, in the absence of technical evidence, as to what the employer ought to have done.[55] It is not to be assumed that some precaution can and should be taken against every risk with which a worker can be confronted in the industrial setting.[56] There are still such things as unavoidable risks (although advances in technology may render preventable risks which were once unavoidable).[57] It is to be remembered, too, that there is a statutory system of no-fault workers' compensation which provides for cases in which the employer was not at fault.[58] Indeed, this may be one of the most potent of the unexpressed factors which have led the courts to adopt such a hard line on proof in this area. This suggestion gains in plausibility when one remembers that the common law offers more generous compensation in serious cases than the statutory scheme.

However, principles of proof are always uttered in a particular context with the aim of justifying the result reached, and cases can be pointed to in which the desire to find, or to leave open the possibility in the right case of a finding, for a plaintiff, has produced somewhat different principles. Thus it is clear that, despite all the above, the principle of *res ipsa loquitur* can be appealed to in employers' liability cases;[59] and that common knowledge *can* sometimes justify a finding of negligence even in an industrial context.[60] It has even been said that it is not always for the employee to prove, but sometimes for the employer to disprove, that some reasonably practical alternative system could have been adopted and would have been safe. While in some cases an employee may not get far with a bare allegation of unsafe system, in other cases it may be enough for the plaintiff to say, 'this is dangerous and there must be some other way of doing it which can be found, and it is not for me to devise it or say what it is'.[61] But even if no alternative way of doing the job can be envisaged, the employer may be held in breach of duty if the risk of injury was so great that the particular system of work should be abandoned.[62]

---

53 e.g. *Tressider* v. *Australian Stevedoring and Lighterage Co. Pty Ltd* [1968] 1 N.S.W.R. 566.

54 *Da Costa* v. *Australian Iron & Steel Pty Ltd* (1978) 20 A.L.R. 257, 266 *per* Mason J.; *Bressington* v. *Commissioner for Railways* (1974) 75 C.L.R. 339.

55 *Power* v. *Snowy Mountains Hydro-Electric Authority* [1957] S.R.(N.S.W.) 9.

56 *Australian Iron & Steel Ltd* v. *Krstevski* (1973) 128 C.L.R. 666, 667 *per* Barwick C.J. and Menzies J.

57 *Mihaljevic* v. *Longyear* (Australia) (1985) 3 N.S.W.L.R. 1, 18 *per* Mahoney J.A.

58 e.g. *Foufoulas* v. *F.G. Strang Pty Ltd* (1970) 123 C.L.R. 168, 174 *per* Barwick C.J.; *Quintano* v. *Cable Makers of Australia Pty Ltd* [1966] 2 N.S.W.R. 496; *Mihaljevic* v. *Longyear (Australia) Pty Ltd* (1985) 3 N.S.W.L.R. 1, 10 *per* Kirby P.

59 *Australian Iron & Steel* v. *Krstevski* (1973) 128 C.L.R. 666.

60 *Tressider* v. *Australian Stevedoring and Lighterage* [1968] 1 N.S.W.R. 566.

61 *McInerney* v. *Schultz* (1981) 27 S.A.S.R. 215.

62 *Condo* v. *South Australia* (1987) 47 S.A.S.R. 584, 593 *per* Bollen J.

In *Rae* v. *B.H.P.*[63] Kitto J., who dissented on the facts, said that while the issue of negligence should not be decided with the benefit of hindsight,[64] this principle does not help employers more than other types of defendants. The question is not whether the employer ought to be blamed for what happened, but whether he did or did not comply with an objective standard of care. This contrast between moral and legal obligations is echoed in the views of Murphy J.[65] to the effect that there are good reasons of social policy to impose quite strict liability on employers. Furthermore, as 'community expectations' of safety become more and more demanding, the duties imposed on employers (and others, such as occupiers of land to which the public has access) may become correspondingly more stringent.[66]

Several other matters of proof require mention. First, we have already examined in general terms (in Chapter 10) the relevance of an allegation in a negligence action that the defendant failed to comply with common practice in its industry. This type of allegation is made very frequently in employers' liability actions. A plaintiff who can establish such a departure from accepted practices is in a strong position. Conversely, a plaintiff who seeks to argue that, although the defendant complied with common practice, it ought to be held liable because the common practice is unsafe, bears a heavy onus since a court will usually find it difficult to condemn as unreasonably unsafe procedures widely adopted throughout an industry.[67] This is particularly so in relation to industries which employ modern technology, which are usually run by people of long practical experience, and in which health and safety are regulated by detailed legislative provisions enforced by constant official supervision.[68]

Secondly, plaintiffs in actions against employers often seek to adduce evidence that the employer has introduced, after the accident, a precaution which, if it had been introduced earlier, would have reduced or eliminated the risk of injury. The basic rule is that such evidence is not admissible to prove negligence at the time of the accident, but that it is admissible to show that some precaution was practicable before the accident.[69] The sense behind this rule is that it may only have been the occurrence of the accident itself which could have alerted the employer to the likelihood or seriousness of the risk which made it unreasonable not to guard against it.

---

63 (1957) 97 C.L.R. 419, 426-7.

64 But where an employee's injury is the result of a defect in equipment acquired from a third party, the date for judging whether the employer was negligent may be later than that for judging whether the supplier was negligent: *Cross* v. *TNT Management Pty Ltd* (1987) 46 S.A.S.R. 105.

65 e.g. in *Raimondo* (1979) 23 A.L.R. 513. See also *Brady* v. *Girvan Bros Pty Ltd* (1986) 7 N.S.W.L.R. 241, 245 and *Western Suburbs Hospital* v. *Currie* (1987) 9 N.S.W.L.R. 511, 518 *per* Kirby P.

66 *Bankstown Foundry* v. *Braistina* (1986) 160 C.L.R. 301, 308-9 *per* Mason, Wilson and Dawson JJ.; 314 *per* Brennan and Deane JJ.

67 *General Cleaning Contractors Ltd* v. *Christmas* [1953] A.C. 180, 192 *per* Lord Reid; 195 *per* Lord Tucker; *Morris* v. *West Hartlepool Steam Navigation Co. Ltd* [1956] A.C. 574 *per* Lord Reid.

68 *Great Western Consolidated Gold Mines N.L.* v. *Downey* (1957) 31 A.L.J. 470.

69 *Davis* v. *Langdon* (1911) 11 S.R.(N.S.W.) 149.

Or again, the precaution may not have been introduced for safety reasons but, for example, to improve productivity.[70] On the other hand, although the onus of proving the practicability of some precaution, in the light of the likelihood and seriousness of the risk and the advantages and countervailing disadvantages of the suggested precaution, rests on the plaintiff, this onus may be relatively easily discharged. If he proves the installation of some precaution after the accident and the defendant gives no evidence to suggest that the precaution was inordinately expensive or in any other way disadvantageous, then the tribunal of fact is entitled to infer that the advantages of the system the defendant has since adopted were not outweighed by its disadvantages and, therefore, hold that it was unreasonable not to adopt it earlier.[71]

Finally, a couple of points about causation. We discussed in Chapter 11 cases in which courts have attempted to grapple with difficulties resulting from lack of knowledge of how particular diseases and medical conditions are caused. Such difficulties often arise in employers' liability cases, and so that earlier discussion is particularly relevant here.

Another commonly occurring issue of causation in the context of safe systems of work is whether, even if the defendant had provided some safety device, the employee would have used it. The onus on this point is on the plaintiff, and since what the plaintiff has to prove is hypothetical—if a safety device had been provided he would have used it—in theory the onus is a very heavy one. But in practice it may not be quite so heavy.[72] In *McWilliams* v. *Sir William Arrol & Co. Ltd*[73] the issue was whether, if a safety belt had been provided, the deceased steel erector would have worn it. Lord Reid said that where the provision of a safety device is common practice or required by regulation, then the court would start with the presumption that it was reasonable to use it and that the deceased was a reasonable person. The plaintiff could then normally discharge the onus merely by proving the circumstances which led to the accident. Only if the defendant could produce evidence to shake this presumption would the plaintiff be in difficulties. It would not necessarily be enough for the defendant to show that common practice among workers generally was against using the device, because one would assume that the plaintiff, being reasonable, did not follow the unsafe practice. Furthermore, since an employer is under a duty to take reasonable steps (such as warning, instructing and commanding) to ensure that employees work safely, he might have to show that such steps would have been resisted by employees.[74] But in *McWilliams* there was evidence that the deceased personally normally did not wear a belt and shared the common view that it was in certain circumstances unsafe to do so.

---

70 *Pitsiavas* v. *John Lysaght (Australia) Pty Ltd* [1962] N.S.W.R. 1500, 1503 *per* Herron A.C.J.

71 *Nelson* v. *John Lysaght (Australia) Pty Ltd* (1974-5) 132 C.L.R. 201, 214-15 *per* Gibbs J.

72 It was discharged in *Bux* v. *Slough Metals Ltd* [1973] 1 W.L.R. 1358.

73 [1962] 1 All E.R. 623; cf. *Duyvelshaff* v. *Cathcart & Ritchie Ltd* (1973) 1 A.L.R. 125.

74 *McLean* v. *Tedman* (1984) 155 C.L.R. 306, 314.

In *Qualcast (Wolverhampton) Ltd* v. *Haynes*[75] Lord Denning said that if it can be shown that after the accident the employee went back to work and failed to use the safety device which he argued his employers should have provided, or, if they had provided it, should have advised or instructed him to use, this is good evidence that he would not have used the device even if it had been provided or he had been instructed to use it, if provided. Especially in the case of experienced workers, the argument that the worker would probably not have used a provided device even if instructed to do so, if successful, is likely to merge with or be treated as the same as the argument that the employer was under no duty, having provided the safety equipment, to take steps to exhort or advise its use.

But it is not always the case that evidence that the plaintiff would not have used a provided device, even if exhorted to do so, will be fatal to his case. In *Mt Isa Mines Ltd* v. *Bates*[76] the defendant, instead of replacing a faulty drill, gave the plaintiff safety glasses to wear to protect him from bits of metal liable to fly off it. Because of the humid climate the goggles were prone to fog up and so the plaintiff would not wear them. It was held that the failure of the plaintiff to wear the glasses was foreseeable and causally irrelevant, and that the defendant had been negligent in not avoiding the risk by making an inexpensive and known modification to the machine the employee was using.

V: DEFENCES

1. Contributory Negligence

In *Caswell* v. *Powell Duffryn Associated Collieries Ltd*[77] Lord Wright said that it was important to adapt the standard of contributory negligence[78] to the facts:

> . . . and to give due regard to the actual conditions under which men work in a factory or mine, to the long hours and the fatigue, to the slackening of attention, which naturally comes from the constant repetition of the same operation, to the noise and confusion in which the man works, to his pre-occupation in what he is doing at the cost perhaps of some inattention to his own safety.[79]

This approach has been recently reaffirmed by the High Court.[80] On the other hand, in *Sungravure Pty Ltd* v. *Meani*[81] Windeyer J., while accepting

---

75 [1959] A.C. 743, 762.
76 [1972-3] A.L.R. 635.
77 [1940] A.C. 152, 178-9.
78 I. Fagelson (1979) 42 *M.L.R.* 646.
79 cf. *Kakouris* v. *Gibbs, Burge & Co. Pty Ltd* [1970] V.R. 502, 508; affirmed (1970) 44 A.L.J.R. 384; cf. *Fennell* v. *Supervision and Engineering Services Holdings Pty Ltd* (1988) 47 S.A.S.R. 6, 17 *per* Von Doussa J.
80 See especially *Podrebersek* v. *Australian Iron & Steel Pty Ltd* (1985) 59 A.L.R. 529; *Bankstown Foundry Pty Ltd* v. *Braistina* (1986) 160 C.L.R. 301, 310 *per* Mason, Wilson and Dawson JJ.
81 (1964) 110 C.L.R. 24.

the sentiment embodied in Lord Wright's statement, asserted that it did not contain a rule of law peculiarly applicable to industrial cases: whether a party has been negligent or contributorily negligent is always a question of fact, and it is not only in the factory that people are faced with pressures or emergencies which prevent their actions in response being classified as negligent. The most that can be said, therefore, is that the realities of the factory environment will in many cases provide good reason not to castigate the plaintiff's lack of care for his own safety as unreasonable.

Murphy J. took a rather different line on the issue of contributory negligence in the industrial context. His view was that the rules of contributory negligence do nothing to improve safety in factories or to encourage employees to be more careful; their only effect is to reduce the amount of compensation an injured employee receives, and to relieve industry of some of the costs of its activities, thus providing producers (and consumers) with a hidden subsidy. Given this, and that working conditions are very largely under the employer's control, plus the degree of inattention to one's own safety that comes of being absorbed in one's work, his Honour thought that a plea of contributory negligence should only succeed if the employee put himself in a position of danger with full appreciation of the risk;[82] and the plea should not succeed if what the employee did was done to advance the interests of his employer.[83] This approach might be thought to turn contributory negligence into *volenti non fit injuria*; and, for this reason, it is unlikely to be explicitly accepted by other judges of the High Court. On the other hand, the approach in recent cases to the issue of contributory negligence perhaps suggests that Murphy J.'s views are, in effect, not so far from the present law as they at first seem. At all events, it seems clear that in cases where the job involves very serious risks, such as the shunting operations which were the subject of *Commissioner for Railways* v. *Halley*,[84] the mere fact that the plaintiff knew of the risks might not satisfy the knowledge requirement of the defence of contributory negligence because, in such cases, an employer has a duty to warn his employees repeatedly of the risks.

2. Volenti Non Fit Injuria

In the light of the general difficulty in modern law of making a successful plea of *volenti*, and of the greater difficulty in industrial cases than in some other cases of making a successful plea of contributory negligence on the facts, it is not surprising that it is very difficult for an employer successfully to plead *volenti* against an employee. It is worth recalling here the distinction made earlier between express or implied agreements to accept a risk and not to sue if it materializes, and *volenti* in the purer

---

82 e.g. *Bassanese* v. *Freightbases Pty Ltd* (1981) 26 S.A.S.R. 508 (affirmed (1982) 29 S.A.S.R. 300).

83 In traditional theory, the fact that the employee was acting to advance his employer's interests would not be decisive in this way, but just one factor to be taken into account: *Knight* v. *Robert Laurie Pty Ltd* [1961] W.A.R. 129, 133 *per* Hale J.

84 (1978) 20 A.L.R. 409.

sense, which requires no prior communication or dealing between the parties. In the employer–employee context, there will always have been some prior dealings between the parties, so that the question to be asked in this context is usually said to be whether the employee expressly or impliedly agreed to take the risk upon himself. It is not enough that the plaintiff knew that the work he was doing was dangerous and nevertheless went ahead and did the work; he must have voluntarily undertaken himself to accept and carry the risks which might flow from a breach by his employer of the latter's duty towards him.[85]

At one time it used to be said that since an employee is free to stipulate a higher wage (or for some other benefit) in return for doing a more dangerous job, acceptance of the negligently created risks of the job could be inferred from failure to do so.[86] But it is not clear that this conclusion would be drawn today,[87] partly, no doubt, because it assumes a much more direct relationship between the level of wages and the riskiness of the job than seems to exist. Of course, it is possible that an employee would agree to accept the consequences of his employer's breach of duty, but unless there was an express agreement to this effect, an agreement would only be implied if it could be shown that the employee knew that injury was an *inevitable* result of his continuing to work in the conditions involving the risk.[88] The mere fact that an employee knows that his job involves the possibility of injury as a result of his employer's negligence will not usually help the employer, since in such a case the continuance of the employee in the job would very often not be the result of free choice but of some pressure 'whether social, economic or simply habit'.[89]

At all events, cases in which an employee agrees to accept risks created by his employer's breach of duty to provide safe tools, premises or system of work are likely to be very rare. Much more common will be cases where an employee, in return for a high wage or for some other benefit,[90] takes on a job which is quite dangerous no matter how much care the employer takes.[91] It is clear that in such a case, in the absence of any breach of duty by the employer, the employee could not complain if he was injured as a result of a risk of his job materializing. An employer is under no duty not to employ people to do a job which is dangerous despite all reasonable care being taken by him.[92] The reason the employer is not liable in such a

---

85 *Hewertson* v. *Courtaulds (Australia) Ltd* [1957] S.R. (N.S.W.) 398; *Cianciarulo* v. *H.P. Products Pty Ltd* [1959] V.R. 170.

86 *Smith* v. *Baker & Sons* [1891] A.C. 325, 362-3 *per* Lord Herschell; *Bowater* v. *Rowley Regis Corporation* [1944] K.B. 476.

87 *Imperial Chemical Industries Ltd* v. *Shatwell* [1956] A.C. 656, 674 *per* Lord Reid.

88 *Smith* v. *Baker* [1891] A.C. 325, 361-2 *per* Lord Herschell; *Cianciarulo* v. *H.P. Products* [1959] V.R. 170, 171 *per* Sholl J.

89 *I.C.I.* v. *Shatwell* [1965] A.C. 656, 686 *per* Lord Pearce; cf. Lord Hodson at 681; *Cianciarulo* v. *H.P. Products* [1959] V.R. 170, 171 *per* Sholl J.

90 Such as in *Johnstone* v. *Bloomsbury Health Authority* [1992] 1 Q.B. 333.

91 See *Cvetkovic* v. *Princes Holdings* (1989) 51 S.A.S.R. 365 (plaintiff's job held not to be such).

92 *Bowater* v. *Rowley Regis* [1944] K.B. 476; *James* v. *Wellington City Council* [1972] N.Z.L.R. 978, 982 *per* Richmond J.; *Hasaganic* v. *Minister of Education* (1973) 5 S.A.S.R. 554; *Charlesworth* v. *Ramsay* [1966] 1 N.S.W.R. 65; *Johnstone* v. *Bloomsbury H.A.* [1992] 1 Q.B. 333.

case is that there was no negligence *vis-á-vis* the creating of the risk; it is not that the plaintiff accepted it.

In short, then, the defence of *volenti* will not be relevant to any case where a risk is not the result of breach of duty by the employer. Where the employer has been negligent then a plea of *volenti* will probably succeed only if the employee has expressly agreed not to sue or if he went into a job knowing that injury was the inevitable result of the employer's breach of duty.

Finally, there is one situation in which the defence of *volenti* is clearly available. In *I.C.I.* v. *Shatwell*[93] the plaintiff and his brother, who were both employees of the defendant and experienced in the use of explosives, deliberately agreed with each other to ignore certain safety regulations when testing some detonators. The plaintiff was injured in a consequent explosion. The statutory regulations were imposed solely on the workers, and the defendant was not in breach of them. Nor was the employer personally in breach of any common law duty, since even before the regulations were made the company had taken all reasonable steps to alert employees to the risks of the job and to ensure that they adopted safe systems of work. But the defendant was vicariously liable for the deliberate breach of both statutory and common law duties by the plaintiff's brother. It was held that the plaintiffs freely accepted the risk involved in their joint illegal behaviour and that the defendant was entitled to rely on the defence of *volenti* because it had been in no way at fault; and that the sole cause of the accident had been the joint wrongdoing of the plaintiff and his brother. The defendants were therefore held not liable.

93 [1956] A.C. 656.

15

PRODUCTS AND PREMISES

In this chapter we will consider certain matters relevant to liability for injury and damage caused by products (that is, chattels) and premises (that is, realty) which have not yet been discussed. It has become popular in recent years to treat liability for injury and damage caused by products as a separate area of the law, but as far as common law liability in tort is concerned, it is really only an application of negligence principles, and this is, perhaps, reflected in the relative paucity of case law concerned specifically with liability for defective products. In America there is an enormous volume of case law on this topic, and this is explained partly by the fact that common law principles have there been developed to impose what is called 'strict liability' on manufacturers. Certain steps were taken in this direction in Australia by statutory enactments; and in 1989 the Australian Law Reform Commission made quite radical proposals for a regime of strict liability for injuries caused by products.[1] But the Industry Commission reported adversely on these proposals,[2] and the Federal government decided not to adopt them. Instead, it decided to follow the model provided by a European Communities Directive on strict liability for injury and damage caused by products, and in June 1992 Federal Parliament enacted a new Part VA of the Trade Practices Act.

There has been a lot of litigation in recent years concerning loss caused by defects in buildings, especially against local authorities in respect of the exercise of statutory powers to regulate building work; but there has been considerably less of such litigation in Australia than in many other common law jurisdictions. Much of the litigation was sparked off by the decision of the House of Lords in *Anns* v. *Merton L.B.C.*;[3] but the relevant parts of this decision have now been reversed by the House of Lords,[4] and it is widely expected (perhaps wrongly) that the volume of such litigation will decrease in jurisdictions which adopt the new line.

---

1 A.L.R.C. 51; V.L.R.C. 27 (1989).
2 Report No. 4 on *Product Liability* (1990).
3 [1978] A. C. 728.
4 *Murphy* v. *Brentwood D.C.* [1991] 1 A.C. 398.

I: PRODUCTS

1. General Introduction

One of the earliest techniques for the protection of consumers[5] who acquired dangerous or shoddy goods was the implication into contracts of sale made by commercial sellers[6] of warranties that the goods were fit for the purpose for which they were intended and that they were of merchantable quality. The English Sale of Goods Act 1893, on which the Sale of Goods legislation of all Australian jurisdictions is based, put this implication on a statutory footing, but the relevant provisions were only an enactment into statutory form of common law rules which had been in existence for many years. There is now an enormous body of case law surrounding these provisions, and although the most common type of action in contract for breach of these warranties concerns defects of quality which inflict financial loss on the purchaser, damages are also recoverable for personal injuries or property damage resulting from dangerous defects which are attributable to a breach of one or both of the warranties.

The warranties implied into contracts for the sale of goods have three main shortcomings as 'consumer protection' devices. The first is that, as originally enacted (and as they still stand in many jurisdictions), the warranties could be excluded either by express provision to that effect contained in the contract or by inclusion in the contract of a provision inconsistent with the warranties. In New South Wales s.61(1) of the Sale of Goods Act 1923 renders void any provision in or applying to a contract for a consumer sale (that is, a sale of goods commonly bought for private use or consumption to a person not buying or holding himself out as buying them in the course of a business) which purports to exclude or restrict the operation of the warranties as to fitness and quality. There is a similar provision in South Australian and Commonwealth legislation.[7]

The other main shortcomings of the Sale of Goods Act warranties arise from the fact that they are contained in a contract of sale. In the typical and most common case, this contract of sale will not be between the manufacturer and the ultimate consumer but between the consumer and a wholesaler or a retailer who may in turn have purchased the goods from a

---

5 The word 'consumer' is tricky: in modern usage it tends to refer to private individuals; but the Sale of Goods Act warranties enure to the benefit of all purchasers of goods whether acting in the course of business or not. There is an argument for saying that the sort of protection provided by implied contractual warranties or by the law of tort is less needed by commercial than by non-commercial buyers, and that the law of contract and tort ought to be more solicitous of private buyers than of commercial buyers, at least in respect of property damage and economic loss. This is because commercial buyers are more likely to be able to bargain for express contractual protection than non-commercial buyers, and if they do not do so the law may be justified in assuming that they were happy to bear any loss which might be suffered if the goods were of substandard quality.

6 That is, sellers acting in the course of business. In practice, the most important effect of this limitation is that that sales of second-hand goods by private (that is, non-commercial) vendors do not attract the statutory warranties.

7 Consumer Transactions Act 1972 (S.A.), s.10; Trade Practices Act 1974 (Cwth), s.68.

wholesaler. In the law of contract the doctrine of privity of contract provides, subject to certain limited exceptions (some common law and some statutory), that only the actual parties to a contract may sue or be sued for breach of the terms of the contract. This means that the purchaser of the goods has contractual rights only against the person from whom he purchased them, usually a wholesaler or a retailer. He will have no rights in contract against dealers further up the chain of distribution and supply or against the manufacturer. This situation can usefully be referred to as 'vertical privity'. This inability to sue anyone but the immediate seller may not particularly worry the purchaser if the seller is a substantial corporation well able to meet the claim. In fact, in many cases larger distributors might be substantially more able financially to meet such claims than smaller manufacturers from whom they acquire the goods they sell. An action in contract also has the great advantage that liability for breach of warranty is strict and does not depend on proof of negligence by the purchaser.[8]

But vertical privity can create difficulties. The party with whom the purchaser contracted may not be as substantial financially as the manufacturer or some intermediate supplier, and may not be worth suing. Secondly, if the last seller is successfully sued by the purchaser, the former will normally have a contractual right to sue its supplier (if any) for breach of warranty and recover as an indemnity the amount it has had to pay the purchaser; and so on up the chain of distribution and supply to the manufacturer. This is a cumbersome and expensive way of bringing home to the manufacturer liability for having marketed defective goods; and the process can break down.[9]

More difficult than the position of the purchaser is that of persons who have suffered loss as a result of the manufacturer's marketing of a defective product but who are not in contractual privity even with the last seller. The classic example of this situation, which might usefully be described by the phrase 'horizontal privity', is *Donoghue* v. *Stevenson*.[10] There, it will be recalled, the plaintiff was a woman who allegedly suffered personal injury and nervous shock when she drank ginger beer from a bottle which had been bought for her by a friend and in which, so it was alleged, were the decomposed remains of a snail. A very common example of the horizontal privity problem arises when members of the family of a person who has purchased a defective product are injured by it. Persons thus injured do not have a claim in contract against anyone. It was unsuccessfully argued in *Donoghue* v. *Stevenson* that such persons could not sue the manufacturer in tort either, because in such a situation the manufacturer owed a duty of care only to persons with whom it was in

---

8 Although the concepts of merchantability and fitness for purpose raise questions of judgment and degree similar to those inherent in the concept of negligence: K.C.T. Sutton *Sales and Consumer Law in Australia and New Zealand* 3rd edn. (Sydney, 1983) pp. 182, 201-15.

9 e.g. *Lambert* v. *Lewis* [1982] A.C. 225 (wholesale supplier unidentifiable; retailer wants to sue the manufacturer for an indemnity). The chain may also break down where one of the parties in it is bankrupt or protected from liability by an exclusion clause.

10 [1932] A.C. 562.

contractual privity. This argument embodies what has become known as the '(privity of) contract fallacy', and its rejection forms the foundation of the modern law of liability in the tort of negligence for defective products. And, of course, the decision to allow third parties, such as Mrs Donoghue, to sue the manufacturer in tort also enables the person who purchases the product from a distributor to sue the manufacturer in tort if he suffers injury as a result of a defect in it.[11]

Allowing purchasers and others to sue the manufacturer of a defective product in tort should not, however, be seen just as a way of overcoming legal difficulties generated by the doctrine of privity. There are good arguments for making manufacturers pay for losses caused by their products which have nothing to do with the doctrine of privity: such liability may give manufacturers an incentive to produce safer and better products; and, anyway, it is important that the price of a product should reflect not only the cost of producing it, but also the cost of any injuries or damage suffered in the course of its proper and normal use. These arguments justify allowing recovery not only by consumers of products but also by intermediate suppliers of the product.

From the plaintiff's point of view, the chief disadvantage of the law of tort in these situations is that to succeed the plaintiff must prove that the manufacturer breached the duty of care owed to all those whom it ought reasonably to have foreseen might be injured by the product or whose property might be damaged by it. Even with the assistance of the principle of *res ipsa loquitur* it may be difficult for the plaintiff to prove that the manufacturer was negligent in manufacturing or marketing the product. Difficulties of proof may vary according to the precise content of the allegations of negligence made by the plaintiff. First, the most straightforward cases in this respect are those involving allegedly negligent failure to give proper warnings or instructions which, if they had been given, would have enabled the plaintiff to avoid injury or loss. In such cases there will often be no dispute about what warnings or instructions were given, and the only question will be an evaluative one of whether better warnings or instructions ought to have been given.

Secondly, the plaintiff may allege that the loss was the result of a defect in the product which arose from some malfunction (whether human or mechanical) in the production process which resulted in the product not meeting the design specification or standard of quality intended by the manufacturer and which could have been avoided by the exercise of reasonable care (let us call this an allegation of 'production-negligence'). Such a malfunction may affect only one or a relatively small number of individual products. The snail in the ginger beer bottle in *Donoghue* v. *Stevenson* is an example. Cases of this type often present problems of proof similar in nature to those raised by normal road or industrial

---

11 It should be noted, however, that the position of the purchaser is different from that of the 'stranger third party' exactly by reason of the fact that the former is in contractual privity with the vendor and so could, in theory at least, obtain a remedy by suing in contract (provided the statutory warranties of quality apply). See J. Stapleton (1991) 107 *L.Q.R.* 249 esp. pp. 273-4.

accidents caused by a momentary lapse of care. It is in cases such as this that the doctrine of *res ipsa loquitur* is of most help.

Thirdly, the plaintiff may allege that the relevant negligence affected the *design* of the product or of the production process. Whereas in the case of production-negligence the design is accepted as safe and the plaintiff's case is that the product did not conform to the design, in 'design-negligence' cases the plaintiff accepts that the product conformed to the design but argues that the design was unsafe or defective. Courts are somewhat unwilling to decide whether the design of a product was negligent. There are, perhaps, three reasons for this unwillingness.[12] One is the difficulty of proving in many cases that it would have been practicable for the manufacturer to design its product or its production line in some different way which would have eliminated the defect in the design of the product. On the other hand, there are cases in which courts have been prepared to hold the design of a product to have been negligent. For example, in *O'Dwyer* v. *Leo Buring Pty Ltd*[13] the court did not hesitate to hold that the design of the stopper of a bottle of sparkling wine was negligent. Such a case may be explicable on the basis that the design issue involved was a straightforward one—the danger was obvious and the remedy simple.

A second difficulty in design-negligence cases is that if the court decides that the defendant ought to have introduced some precaution into a large system or production line, or that it ought to have designed a product differently, it is going well beyond the limits of the case before it. It is not just deciding that the defendant was negligent in causing one accident, but it is also setting a certain level of accidents as the acceptable level for the defendant's activity as a whole. This might have serious repercussions not only for the economics of the activity carried on by the defendant but also for society as a whole, since the result of the decision may be that the supply of goods or services provided by the defendant diminishes or dries up. The impact may be even greater if the defendant is just one of a number of persons engaged in the same activity and taking the same precautions. Such judgments about the proper level of accidents and precautions involve complex questions of economic and social policy concerning the desirability of particular activities. Courts often feel ill-equipped and unwilling to deal with such issues.

Furthermore, design 'defects' are often the result of conscious design decisions which take account of cost, efficiency and other factors. The tort of negligence is aimed primarily at providing compensation for injury inadvertently caused. No social or economic arguments can be adduced in favour of inadvertence; but such arguments can often be adduced in favour of conscious design choices which allow for a certain probability

12 *Atiyah's Accidents* pp. 55-9; J.A. Henderson (1973) 73 *Columbia L.R.* 1531; (1978) 56 Nth Carolina L.R. 625; Bruce Lemer (1982) 20 *O.H.L.J.* 250.

13 [1966] W.A.R. 67. Other examples are *Suosaari* v. *Steinhardt* [1989] 2 Qd.R. 477 (design of a trailer) and *Flynn* v. *Commonwealth of Australia* (1988) 6 M.V.R. 186 (design, construction and installation of a median strip). See also *Parsons* v. *John Holland-Christiani and Nielson Joint Venture* [1991] 1 Qd.R. 137 (design of barrier not negligent).

of mishaps. It is clearly the case that we do not always consider the fact that some activity (e.g. driving) causes injury or death as a reason for not engaging in it; and sometimes we are even prepared to see those injured left without compensation. Much depends on the value we put on the activity. Some products are so beneficial[14] that we are prepared to use them even if users sometimes suffer injury or damage in the process.

A third issue raised by negligence in design is that of custom and common practice. To what extent ought a defendant be entitled to plead that it took the same precautions as everyone else and therefore that it was not negligent? If a large number of manufacturers design their products in the same way as the defendant, a decision against it will have serious repercussions for the industry or profession as a whole. Similar issues arise in relation to statutory standards of product safety, of which there are many. While failure to comply with such standards will provide very strong proof of negligence, a court would perhaps be unwilling to hold a manufacturer who had complied with all the prescribed standards to have been negligent because it did not take some further precaution.

Fourthly, the plaintiff may allege that the loss was the result of what is often called a 'development risk'. In design-negligence cases the plaintiff's case assumes that the defect was known, or at least knowable, at the time of production, and that an alternative safe design was available. On the other hand, in cases where the plaintiff alleges negligence in developing the product, these assumptions may be the subject of dispute. The problems associated with 'development-negligence' claims are dramatically illustrated by the aftermath of the thalidomide tragedy of the early 1960s when thousands of children were born with defects, many very serious, as a result of the administration of a particular drug to their mothers during pregnancy. One of the major problems facing the children in their actions against the drug companies was that of showing that the companies had been negligent in not discovering the deforming effect of the drug before it was put on the market, and in not warning against its use by pregnant women. We shall discuss later the liability of manufacturers to test their products to discover defects in them.

Two techniques, both involving the imposition of strict liability, have been used to overcome problems of proving fault on the part of a manufacturer. In South Australia and the Australian Capital Territory and at the Commonwealth level[15] legislation has been enacted imposing what are usually called 'manufacturer's warranties'. The South Australian legislation applies to retail sales of manufactured goods normally sold for less than $10 000. The Commonwealth and A.C.T. legislation applies to consumer sales, that is, sales to persons not buying in the course of a business, of goods normally bought for private use or consumption. The various statutes differ in detail but share two characteristics relevant to the present discussion. The first is that they impose on the manufacturer

---

14 But on a crucial ambiguity in the notion of benefit see J. Stapleton (1986) 6 *O.J.L.S.* 392, 405-6.

15 Manufacturers Warranties Act 1974 (S.A.); Law Reform (Manufacturers Warranties) Act 1977 (A.C.T.); Trade Practices Act 1974 (Cwth), Part V, Div. 2A.

(broadly defined) in favour of the purchaser the same warranties of quality as the Sale of Goods legislation imposes on the seller, and they make them enforceable as if they were contained in a contract between the 'manufacturer' and the purchaser. The legislation is thus aimed at the problem of vertical privity,[16] and because the 'manufacturer's' obligations take the form of a warranty, its liability for breach of the obligation is strict. The statutes do not do anything to overcome the problem of horizontal privity, and therefore only cover part of the ground dealt with by *Donoghue* v. *Stevenson.*

The second important feature of the statutes is that they impose on the 'manufacturer' liability for statements as to quality made in advertising material. It is very difficult, either in contract or tort, to bring home liability for such statements: in contract because it has to be proved that the statement was meant to have force as a contractual warranty of quality or that it was a misrepresentation of fact (as opposed to a promise) which would be likely to induce a reasonable person to contract; and in tort because of the need to establish a special relationship under *Hedley Byrne* v. *Heller* principles—the fact that the advertising material is not normally directed at any particular individual or group would make this difficult.[17]

In New South Wales[18] the court has power, in an action in contract by the purchaser against the seller for breach of warranty, to add the manufacturer as a party if it appears that the goods were defective at the time of delivery to the purchaser and so not of merchantable quality, and to order him to repair or to pay the cost of repairing the goods. Unlike the provisions considered above which effect a limited abrogation of the rules of privity of contract, this is only a procedural provision, but within its limited sphere of operation and subject to the discretion of the court, it achieves a similar end to the legislation already noted.

The other technique for avoiding the shortcomings of negligence liability as a consumer protection device is to impose strict *tortious* liability on 'manufacturers'. This does not involve use of the language of warranties but simply the imposition on the manufacturer of liability, regardless of fault, for the marketing of a defective product. This is the technique which has been adopted in England as required by a European Community directive,[19] and in the new Part VA of the Trade Practices Act. We will discuss this Act in more detail later.

---

16 It is worth noting that the statutes also overcome the problem which faced the retailer in *Lambert* v. *Lewis* (above n. 9): sellers who are sued for breach of contractual warranties of quality are given a statutory right to recover an indemnity from the manufacturer if the latter could be sued by the purchaser for breach of a manufacturer's warranty, regardless of whether the seller has a contractual right of indemnity against the manufacturer.

17 See *Lambert* v. *Lewis* [1982] A.C. 225, 264 *per* Stephenson L.J.

18 Sale of Goods Act 1923 s.64(5).

19 Consumer Protection Act 1987 (U.K.) Part I.

2. THE DONOGHUE V. STEVENSON PRINCIPLE

Besides the 'neighbour principle' which we have already discussed, Lord Atkin laid down in *Donoghue* v. *Stevenson* a narrower principle relating to the liability of manufacturers in the following terms:

> a manufacturer of products, which he sells in such a form as to show that he intends them to reach the consumer in the form in which they left him with no reasonable possibility of intermediate examination, and with the knowledge that the absence of reasonable care in the preparation or putting up of the products will result in an injury to the consumer's life or property, owes a duty to the consumer to take that reasonable care.[20]

(a) The duty of care *Donoghue* v. *Stevenson* establishes, therefore, that there is a duty relationship between manufacturers and those who use or consume their products, whether or not those consumers are in a contractual relationship with the manufacturer. Using our earlier terminology, we could say that there is a relationship of proximity between the manufacturer and the consumer.

The manufacturer can be held liable for defects which arise either out of the preparation or the packaging of the goods. The term 'manufacturer' is understood broadly. For example, a flooring contractor who purchases chemical substances which it then combines to produce a flooring material which it lays in the plaintiff's premises is a manufacturer in the relevant sense.[21] But the *Donoghue* principle is not confined to manufacturers in this sense; it applies also to repairers;[22] and to second-hand dealers who are under a duty to take reasonable care to detect defects in the products they sell which they are in a position to spot. Distributors of products are also under a duty.[23] In fact, the *Donoghue* principle covers everyone in the chain of manufacture, distribution and supply.

The common law of negligence is not only concerned with allocating responsibility for defects in products (as is typically the case with strict liability schemes), but more broadly with providing remedies for acts of negligence in performing any of the processes or acts which go to make up the activities of producing, distributing and marketing 'goods' (which term includes not only consumables such as food and clothing, but also every type of vehicle, tool and implement and even items incorporated into buildings, such as windows and lifts[24]) and which cause physical injury or damage or, to some extent, economic loss, to people consuming or using goods, or to bystanders. Nor, unlike Sale of Goods legislation, does the common law discriminate, in terms of duty of care, between commercial and non-commercial manufacturers and sellers; although the

---

20 [1932] A.C. 562, 599.

21 *Junior Books Ltd* v. *Veitchi Co. Ltd* [1983] 1 A.C. 520.

22 *Haseldine* v. *Daw* [1941] 2 K.B. 343. In the rest of this section we shall use the word 'manufacturer' as a convenient shorthand to include repairers and other persons who make physical changes to the product after its original manufacture.

23 *Watson* v. *Buckley, Osborne, Garrett & Co. Ltd* [1940] 1 All E.R. 174; *Fisher* v. *Harrods Ltd* [1966] 1 Lloyd's Rep. 500.

24 *Haseldine* v. *Daw* [1941] 2 K.B. 343.

standard of care owed by a non-commercial defendant would, no doubt, often be lower than that which would be owed by a commercial defendant in similar circumstances.

Neither does the common law discriminate between claimants in the way that legislative schemes of strict liability often do. The common law is prepared to help anyone, whether individual or large corporation, who suffers negligently inflicted injury or damage. On the other hand, modern legislative concern with products liability tends to be directed more specifically at protecting people who buy things normally put to personal use and who do so otherwise than in the course of business. Whereas everyone, it seems to be thought, deserves protection against negligence, the extra burden of strict liability can really only be justified to protect those who are particularly vulnerable in the market-place. While this may be reasonable in respect of economic loss or property damage, it seems less justifiable so far as personal injury is concerned. This distinction is observed in s.75AD of the Trade Practices Act as amended in 1992 which allows anyone to recover for personal injury caused by defective products, but only allows individuals to recover for property damage.

In the discussion so far it has been assumed that the defendant received value for the goods, not necessarily from the plaintiff but from someone. But does a person who makes a gift or gratuitous loan of a chattel owe a similar duty of care to the recipient or to those whom he ought reasonably to foresee will use or come into contact with the chattel? Or does the law expect the donee neither to look a gift horse in the mouth nor complain if, as well as having rotten teeth, it kicks and bites? Certainly, given that a gratuitous adviser can be liable for negligent advice causing economic loss,[25] there seems no reason why a gratuitous supplier of goods should not, in suitable circumstances, be held liable for physical damage.[26] The requirement of value is a vestige of the contract fallacy. Of course, just as in the context of statements, the exact circumstances would be important in determining the content of the duty; so a donor or gratuitous bailor would not always be expected to take as much care as a person who receives value. But there is no reason why the standard of care expected of a distributor or retailer should vary according to whether the goods were sold or given away free as a 'loss-leader' or why a manufacturer should be treated differently when it gives goods away as a promotional special or introductory offer.

(b) The standard of care There is no need here to repeat any of the general discussion of standard of care to be found in Chapter 10. It is only necessary to deal with a few points of particular relevance to liability for defective products.

(i) Products dangerous per se: Courts have often been tempted to draw a distinction between more and less dangerous products in terms of whether the product is inherently dangerous (or dangerous *per se*) or only 'potentially

---

25 *Hedley Byrne* v. *Heller* [1964] A.C. 465.
26 *Pivovaroff* v. *Chernabaeff* (1978) 21 S.A.S.R. 1.

dangerous'. An inherently dangerous thing is something which, if left unguarded, may at any moment cause damage. Such things are, for example, loaded guns (at least if they are left lying about in a condition in which they may go off if handled), sticks of phosphorus, explosives, hatchets and unsheathed swords. These are things which cannot be handled without serious risk. On the other hand, in the case of things potentially dangerous, the source of danger is not essential to the ordinary character of the thing; if there is negligence or some mischance or misadventure, injury might be caused, but otherwise the thing itself presents no danger. Things which have been held not to be dangerous in themselves include a shanghai,[27] a spray-painting gun,[28] an ordinary domestic boiler (even without a safety valve)[29] and a domestic lawn mower.[30]

The original relevance of the distinction between things dangerous *per se* and things only potentially dangerous was that a person who manufactured or sold a product dangerous in itself owed a duty of care to all who might foreseeably be injured by it even if the plaintiff had no contract with the defendant. Since *Donoghue* v. *Stevenson*, where the distinction was rejected by Lord Atkin, repeated attempts to revive it (presumably with a different significance—perhaps that liability for things dangerous *per se* ought to be strict) have failed, and now the accepted view is that the idea of things dangerous in themselves makes little sense because whether a thing is dangerous or not depends as much on the person using it and the circumstances of its use as on the nature of the thing itself. So now products are all seen as lying somewhere on a single scale of dangerousness, and the standard of care required is proportional to the degree of risk of injury to users of the product.

(ii) Foreseeability of risk: This point follows on from the last. Many products can be used for a variety of purposes. Some uses will be intended by the manufacturer; there may be others which were foreseen or reasonably foreseeable, but not intended by the manufacturer; there may be yet others which were not be reasonably foreseeable. Some uses will be reasonable, but others may be unreasonable, and a person using the product in such a way may not be taking due care for his own safety. The duty of the manufacturer is to design and produce its products so that they are safe for all reasonable and intended, foreseen or reasonably foreseeable uses.[31] The test of whether a use is reasonable and reasonably foreseeable must be seen from the user's point of view: the manufacturer must make the product safe for all uses which, from the user's point of view, seem usual or not wholly improper. It is only if a person uses a product in an unreasonable and unforeseeable way, or for an unreasonable and unforeseeable purpose, that he will be held contributorily negligent.

27 *Smith* v. *Leurs* (1945) 70 C.L.R. 256, 259 *per* Latham C.J.
28 *Imperial Furniture Pty Ltd* v. *Automatic Fire Sprinklers Pty Ltd* [1967] 1 N.S.W.R. 29 *per* Jacobs J.A.
29 *Ball* v. *London County Council* [1949] 2 K.B. 159.
30 *Todman* v. *Victa Ltd* [1982] V.R. 849.
31 *Suosaari* v. *Steinhardt* [1989] 2 Qd.R. 477.

On the other hand, a manufacturer is not required to design its product in such a way as to remove dangers which may develop as a result of ordinary wear and tear, or to remove the need for ordinary maintenance;[32] although the manufacturer should, no doubt, provide instructions as to maintenance and warn of dangers which may develop with use and how to recognize their presence.

(iii) Date for assessing negligence: We have touched on this matter before, but it deserves to be mentioned briefly again because it is of great importance in product liability cases. Two principles need to be enunciated: the first is that, except in relation to the duty to warn users of dangers or defects in products and the duty to withdraw dangerous products from the market, the question of whether the manufacturer was negligent or not is to be judged at the date of manufacture and not at some later date when standards of safety or quality applicable to a particular product may have risen.[33] This principle is particularly important in design-negligence and development-negligence cases. An important issue which arises when regimes of strict product liability are being considered is whether this principle ought to be carried over into the strict liability regime or whether, by contrast, the safety and quality of products ought to be judged according to standards prevalent at the date on which the injury or loss was suffered. We will return to this issue later.

The second principle is that, except in relation to the duty to warn of defects or dangers and the duty to withdraw products from the market, the question of whether a manufacturer was negligent or not must be judged at a time when the product was in its physical control. This principle may be seen as concerning causation rather than the issue of negligence, because if the condition of the product which gives rise to the claim came about after the product left the manufacturer's physical control, it will not usually be possible for the plaintiff to prove that the condition of the product was the result of the manufacturer's negligence.

(iv) The duty to warn: Sometimes the manufacturer need only warn of the dangerous quality of the product (for example, 'Highly Inflammable') without instructing the purchaser as to appropriate safeguards in the use of the material. This will be particularly so where the product is likely to be used in a wide variety of circumstances and situations so that it would be impractical for the manufacturer to give directions to cover them all. In other cases, if the danger will only manifest itself in particular circumstances or adequate knowledge of it can be communicated only by giving directions for use and as to particular safeguards, then more detailed warnings will be required. Clearly, the identity of the expected users is very relevant: warnings adequate to alert a skilled worker to the dangers of a product might be quite inadequate if the product is to be put on to the

---

32 *Bull* v. *Rover Mowers (Australia) Pty Ltd* [1984] 2 Qd.R. 489.

33 e.g. *Cross* v. *TNT Management Pty Ltd* (1987) 46 S.A.S.R. 105.

'do-it-yourself' market.[34] The main function of a warning is to counteract the appearance of safety for certain uses which most products carry with them.

A duty to warn may arise in respect of dangers of which the manufacturer was not and could not reasonably have been aware before the product left its control. But sometimes it will not be enough for the manufacturer to warn of a danger in a product. If the danger is great and users of the product are not in a position to protect themselves properly from it, the manufacturer may be required to withdraw products which have already been put into the stream of commerce and to modify the product to make it safe before marketing it again.[35] For example, it would not be enough for a chair manufacturer to market a chair with a warning attached that it was liable to collapse if sat upon by a person weighing more than 76 kilograms; his duty in such a case would be to alter the design of the chair so as to make it stronger. But there may be many cases in which it would be hard to locate the line between the duty to warn and the duty to modify.[36]

Even if it is held that the manufacturer ought to have given some warning or instruction as to use which he did not give, it is still for the plaintiff to prove that the warning would have been heeded and that, if it had been, the injury would not have been suffered. Where the difference between the terms of the warning given (if any) and those of the warning which ought to have been given are very great, then the required causal inference will be relatively easy to draw if, as is likely, the court is prepared to assume that the plaintiff, in the absence of specific evidence to the contrary, would have reacted reasonably to the warning. But where the difference is slight, it might be difficult for the court to conclude that the proper warning would have been efficacious.

(v) The duty to test: We have already mentioned in relation to drugs the question of the extent to which the law requires manufacturers to test their products for adverse effects before marketing them. Clearly, if there is a well-recognized testing procedure which a manufacturer has failed to follow it could easily be held negligent. But even applying the negligence calculus, it may be difficult to say that the defendant ought to have done more tests: the precautions which ought to have been taken to detect potential danger are related to the seriousness and likelihood of the risk, and often this is not known until it materializes. The risk may be foreseeable in the attenuated sense in which the law uses that term, yet it may not be reasonable to expect the manufacturer to have done the amount of testing which would have been necessary to reveal the danger.

---

34 *Norton Australia Pty Ltd* v. *Streets Ice Cream Pty Ltd* (1969) 120 C.L.R. 635; see also *Todman* v. *Victa* [1982] V.R. 849.

35 *Thompson* v. *Johnson & Johnson Pty Ltd* [1991] 2 V.R. 449, 490-1.

36 Cigarettes are a very difficult case: is it negligent to market them at all, given their dangers, or only to market them without suitable warnings? See, for example, *Scanlon* v. *American Cigarette Company (Overseas) Pty Ltd* [1987] V.R. 281.

It would seem from such cases as there are on the duty to test[37] that the law is sometimes prepared to impose a duty of positive action, that is, a duty to take steps to discover the dangers inherent in the use of a product. Because the time for assessing negligence is the date of the allegedly negligent act, a defendant could not be liable for a design defect or a development defect which was discovered after the goods left its hands unless it could be said that its research and development activities ought to have revealed the defect before the products left the factory. But it is clear from the cases that a manufacturer may have a duty to warn of dangers in using its products or to stop manufacturing or supplying products, or to withdraw products already supplied to distributors, on the basis of advances in knowledge after the date of manufacture, for breach of which damages may be awarded. In other words, the time for assessing negligence depends on what the alleged act of negligence is. The liability of the manufacturer for the existence of defects is limited to the period of its control over the products. But its liability for negligent failure to warn, stop production, or withdraw products can extend well beyond the time when the products leave the factory.

(c) **Intermediate inspection** According to the *Donoghue* principle, the causal chain between the defendant's negligence and the plaintiff's injury will only be regarded as unbroken if, after the product left the control of the defendant, there was no reasonable possibility of inspection by the plaintiff or some third party which could have revealed the defect and enabled the plaintiff to avoid damage or injury. The relevance of intermediate inspection is that it can alert the plaintiff to the danger; on the whole the *Donoghue* principle only imposes liability for latent defects.[38] If the plaintiff knew or ought to have known of the danger before he used the product, he could not bring liability for injuries home to the defendant unless he was not free to remove or avoid the danger or it was not reasonably practicable to do so.[39] For example, a tenant who knows of a danger in the premises may be expected to do no more than tell the landlord of it. The proper test is not whether there was the opportunity for intermediate inspection; the causal chain will be broken only if it was reasonable for the defendant to act on the basis that the opportunity would probably be taken advantage of;[40] and only, of course, if the inspection which it was reasonable to anticipate was such as would have revealed the defect in the article.[41]

---

37 e.g. *Vacwell Engineering Co. Ltd* v. *B.D.H. Chemicals Ltd* [1971] 1 Q.B. 88; *Wright* v. *Dunlop Rubber Co. Ltd* (1972) 13 K.I.R. 255.

38 *Murphy* v. *Brentwood D.C.* [1991] 1 A.C. 398.

39 *Rimmer* v. *Liverpool C.C.* [1985] Q.B. 1; *Denny* v. *Supplies & Transport Co. Ltd* [1950] 2 K.B. 394. Note that a manufacturer can apparently escape liability if it reasonably expected that the defect would be *discovered*, even if it was not reasonable to expect that something would be done to protect the plaintiff from injury or damage. See further C.J. Miller and P.A. Lovell *Product Liability* (London, 1976) pp. 285-6.

40 *Rutherford* v. *A-G* [1976] 1 N.Z.L.R. 403, 413.

41 *Herschstal* v. *Stewart & Ardern Ltd* [1940] 1 K.B. 155; *Jull* v. *Wilson and Horton* [1968] N.Z.L.R. 88; *Griffiths* v. *Arch Engineering Co. (Newport) Ltd* [1983] 3 All E.R. 217.

A few examples will illustrate the operation of the principle. Clearly, in *Donoghue* v. *Stevenson*[42] the nature of the receptacle which contained the ginger beer was intended to, and did, prevent inspection of the contents before consumption. *Grant* v. *Australian Knitting Mills*[43] shows that even if the packaging of a product physically allows inspection, if the manufacturer intended the product to reach the consumer in the state in which it left its factory, and there is no evidence of tampering by some third party or the plaintiff, then the manufacturer will be liable for undiscovered defects. A second-hand car dealer may well not be able to plead reasonable probability of inspection if the defect is one which a mechanic could easily have spotted and it has no reason to expect that the purchaser will have the car checked before using it.[44] Similarly, a car mechanic cannot normally expect the owner to spot defects in repairs done by the mechanic unless the defect is obvious to the untrained eye.[45] But an owner who sells a car at auction 'as seen and with all its faults and without warranty' may well be entitled to assume that the purchaser will have the car examined before driving it any distance.[46] Distributors may have a duty to inspect, failure to perform which will break the chain of causation between the manufacturer's conduct and the plaintiff's injury.[47] If the person to whom the product is supplied is highly experienced in the use of the product, this will justify the supplier in relying to some extent on an examination of the product by the user and an awareness of pitfalls in its use. And if the product is one which can be used in a wide variety of ways and in many different circumstances, the manufacturer will be entitled to expect that the user will take some pains to ensure the suitability of the product for the intended application.[48]

The intermediate examination principle seems to go to the issue of causation,[49] although there is some authority for treating it as relevant to duty.[50] Either way, it seems that failure to inspect by the plaintiff is not a ground for apportionment of damages for contributory negligence. If the defendant can rely on the probability of intermediate inspection by the plaintiff, this means either that the injury was not 'partly his fault' but entirely the fault of the plaintiff, or that the injury was not 'caused' by his fault. Contributory negligence in this area applies to the way the plaintiff uses the product. This all-or-nothing interpretation of the intermediate examination principle is out of step with the modern way of dealing with negligence on the part of the plaintiff under the apportionment legislation.

---

42 [1932] A.C. 562.

43 [1936] A.C. 75.

44 *Andrews* v. *Hopkinson* [1951] 1 Q.B. 229.

45 *Stennett* v. *Hancock* [1939] 2 All E.R. 578.

46 *Hurley* v. *Dyke* [1979] R.T.R. 265.

47 e.g. *Kubach* v. *Hollands* [1937] 3 All E.R. 917; *Watson* v. *Buckley* [1940] 1 All E.R. 174.

48 *Norton* v. *Streets Ice Cream* (1969) 120 C.L.R. 635; *Gledhill* v. *Liverpool Abbatoir Utility Co.* [1957] 1 W.L.R. 1028.

49 *Grant* v. *Australian Knitting Mills* [1936] A.C. 85, 104; *Voli* v. *Inglewood Shire Council* (1963) 110 C.L.R. 74, 87-8 *per* Windeyer J.

50 *Daley* v. *Gypsey Caravan Co. Pty Ltd* [1966] 2 N.S.W.R. 22; *Jull* v. *Wilson* [1968] N.Z.L.R. 88; *Cathcart* v. *Hall* [1963] N.Z.L.R. 333.

There is something to be said for abolishing the separate relevance of intermediate examination by the plaintiff and simply treating it as relevant to contributory negligence and hence to apportionment of damages. Where a third party negligently fails to inspect, there is a certain amount of authority that the manufacturer may, in suitable circumstances, be held jointly liable; but the predominant English approach is that negligent failure to inspect breaks the chain of causation and absolves the manufacturer of liability.[51]

(d) Other issues of causation and proof The mere fact that a person is injured while using a defective product does not show that the defect caused the injury or that the defendant is responsible for it.[52] Where there is a number of possible causes of the injury it is, of course, for the plaintiff to prove that it was the defect for which the defendant was responsible which in fact caused the injury. But the plaintiff can rely in appropriate cases on the principle of *res ipsa loquitur.*[53] If the defendant argues that its system of manufacture is foolproof and the court accepts this, then it will have answered the case against it (assuming the defect to be a production defect). But if all the defendant can establish is that its system is the safest and most efficient available, and is forced to concede the possibility of negligence on the part of an employee, then it is not up to the plaintiff to point out who the negligent employee was. Even though millions of items may have been produced without mishap, if a defective item is produced even though the system of manufacture was properly supervised and was designed to be foolproof, the proper inference, in the absence of evidence to the contrary from the defendant, is that someone for whom the defendant is responsible was negligent.[54]

An inference of negligence on the part of the manufacturer will be more easily drawn in some cases than in others. The inference was easy in *Donoghue* v. *Stevenson* because of the nature of the alleged defect and of the container. If a soft-drink bottle explodes it may be harder to find for the plaintiff against the manufacturer in the absence of evidence from the plaintiff and intermediate handlers negativing negligence on their part. In *Fletcher* v. *Toppers Drinks Pty Ltd*[55] it was said that common experience supports an inference that if a bottle explodes some time after being sold by a retailer, the cause is likely to be the responsibility of the manufacturer. Handling by a retailer might cause immediate bursting but is unlikely to cause bursting an hour after purchase. So an inference of negligence by the defendant manufacturer was open on the facts.

Where the doctrine of *res ipsa loquitur* is available to the plaintiff, the common law in effect imposes liability without proof of fault (or 'strict liability') on the manufacturer because it will usually be very difficult for

---

51 Miller and Lovell *Product Liability* pp. 284-90.

52 e.g. *Hunnerup* v. *Goodyear Tyre & Rubber Co. (Australia) Pty Ltd* (1974) 7 S.A.S.R. 215, especially 226-7.

53 e.g. *Tarling* v. *Noble* [1966] A.L.R. 189.

54 *Grant* v. *Australian Knitting Mills* [1936] A.C. 85; *Martin* v. *Thorn Lighting Industries Pty Ltd* [1978] W.A.R. 10; *Hill* v. *James Crowe (Cases) Ltd* [1978] All E.R. 812.

55 [1981] 2 N.S.W.L.R. 911.

the latter to adduce evidence strong enough to rebut the presumption of negligence and to lead the court to hold that the plaintiff has not discharged the burden of proof resting on him. But *res ipsa loquitur* is unlikely to be of much assistance to a plaintiff in cases of design-negligence or development-negligence, as opposed to cases of production-negligence, unless the defect in the design was of an extreme nature; if a new chair collapses when sat on by a person weighing 65 kilos, a court might well be prepared to infer negligence from this fact alone. But many cases of design-and development-negligence will be much less straightforward than this.

(e) **Damages recoverable**[56] Lord Atkin's statement in *Donoghue* v. *Stevenson* refers only to injury to person or property other than the defective item itself; and it was, for a long time, assumed that damages could not be recovered in tort representing either diminution in the value of a defective chattel resulting from its defectiveness, or the cost of remedying a defect in a chattel or repairing damage to a chattel caused by a defect in it. However, all of these assumptions were upset by the decision of the House of Lords in *Anns* v. *Merton L.B.C.*[57] As a result of that case, it seemed clear that if a defect in a product caused physical damage to the product itself identifiably separate from the defect, the cost of repairing that damage (and forestalling further damage) could be recovered. It also seemed that 'preventive damages' could be recovered representing the cost of repairing a defect which had not yet caused damage either to the product itself or to any other thing or person, but which almost certainly would cause some such damage in the near future if the defect was not repaired.[58] Even if damage was unlikely to occur for some time, if it was certain to occur sooner or later then such damages could be recovered.[59] The plaintiff could also recover for consequential losses, such as loss of profits or the cost of obtaining a substitute while the product was repaired.[60] Another significant development occurred in *Junior Books Ltd* v. *Veitchi Co. Ltd*,[61] which supported the proposition that in certain circumstances damages could be recovered representing the cost of repairing or replacing a defective product (and for consequential economic losses) even if the defect in the product threatened no injury or damage to

56 See also p. 529 above. With the substitution of the word 'premises' for 'product' or 'chattel' the discussion in this section is also relevant to the section below on damages recoverable in actions in respect of defective premises. But is the law right to treat chattels and real property in the same way? Should it, for example, reflect the fact that the contractual remedies available to the purchaser of chattels are usually much better than those available to a purchaser of real property? Or that purchasers of second-hand buildings, (although not of new buildings) usually have the property surveyed before the contract is made? Or that purchasers of some second-hand chattels (notably cars and ships) sometimes have them inspected by an adviser before purchase? See J. Stapleton (1991) 107 *L.Q.R.* 249 esp. pp. 276-7.

57 [1978] A.C. 728. See also P. Cane (1979) 95 *L.Q.R.* 117.

58 *Rutherford* v. *A-G* [1976] 1 N.Z.L.R. 403.

59 *Batty* v. *Metropolitan Property Realizations Ltd* [1978] Q.B. 554.

60 *Rivtow Marine* v. *Washington Ironworks* (1974) 40 D.L.R. (3d) 530.

61 [1983] 1 A.C. 520.

persons or other property but only caused the product to deteriorate sooner than a sound product would have done. This decision seemed to run counter to a traditional dogma of the common law, that a complaint by a purchaser to the effect that what he had acquired was worth less than what he paid for it, could not be made in a tort action but only in a contract action.

After some initial uncertainty, it became generally accepted that the loss for which all of the above propositions allowed recovery was purely economic; so, in Australian terms, the recoverability of damages for such losses in any particular case depended, in part at least, on there being a sufficiently close relationship of proximity between the plaintiff and the defendant.

So far as English law is concerned, the above propositions derived from *Anns* v. *Merton L.B.C.* are no longer good law. The decision of the House of Lords in *D. & F. Estates Ltd* v. *Church Commissioners*[62] supports the proposition that damages may be recovered in a tort action for loss caused by a defective product only if that loss is personal injury or damage to tangible property other than the product itself (or is consequential upon such loss); and that damages may not be recovered in respect of the defect or of damage to the defective product itself. On the other hand, the decision in *Junior Books* v. *Veitchi* seems to remain good law in England on the basis that it supports recovery for purely economic loss caused by a defective product if the loss was suffered as a result of reliance by the plaintiff on express or implied statements of the defendant (concerning the quality, safety or suitability of the product), provided there was a very close relationship of proximity between the parties, such as might exist where the product was custom-made for the plaintiff, but which would not exist as between a manufacturer and a person who bought its product just on the basis of media advertising by the former.[63]

The justifications for this change of direction by the House of Lords are not entirely clear. The decision in *D. & F. Estates* rests on a reassertion of the distinction between physical loss and damage (and economic loss consequential upon it) on the one hand and purely economic loss on the other; but this distinction is itself suspect, at least so far as damage to tangible property is concerned.[64] There is, furthermore, a good case to be made for allowing recovery of the cost of forestalling expected future damage or loss, at least in cases where the probability of such loss occurring is high. Perhaps the main foundation of the new approach is a desire to reduce the role of tort law as a means of providing compensation for negligently caused economic loss and to encourage the use of contractual arrangements to protect economic interests; if people want to protect their financial interests, they should bargain and pay for protection

62 [1989] A.C. 177; Cane (1989) 52 *M.L.R.* 200.
63 See also *Muirhead* v. *Industrial Tank Specialties Ltd* [1986] Q.B. 507.
64 See Cane *Tort Law and Economic Interests* (Oxford, 1991) pp. 12-15.

in advance rather than look to the law of tort to provide it after the event.[65] The reader might discern similarities between this approach and the economic policies dominant in both Australia and the United Kingdom during the 1980s, which stressed individual initiative and the superiority of the market to other techniques, such as social welfare programmes, for providing financial benefits.

The accidents of litigation have not given Australian courts much opportunity to grapple with the issues raised by the recent English cases. The basic position here seems to be that damages for purely economic loss are recoverable provided there is a sufficient relationship of proximity between the parties; and that reliance by the plaintiff on the defendant is not the only source of such proximity. For example, in *Suosaari* v. *Steinhardt*[66] a farm-worker was injured when using a badly designed trailer bought by his employer from the defendant manufacturer. The farmer was held liable to the worker for providing unsafe equipment; but the manufacturer was also held liable to the farmer for supplying a negligently designed trailer and thus causing the farmer economic loss consisting of his liability to pay damages to the worker. There was, the court said, a sufficient degree of proximity between the manufacturer and the farmer to support the claim for economic loss.[67] The damages payable to the worker were divided 60:40 between the manufacturer and the farmer.

A similar situation was dealt with by the House of Lords in *Lambert* v. *Lewis*,[68] in which the House left open the question of whether a party in the chain of distribution (a retailer, for example) could recover in tort from another party higher in the chain with whom *he* had no contract (the manufacturer, for example) an indemnity in respect of damages he had had to pay to the plaintiff in contract for defects which were the result of negligence on the part of the manufacturer. This question would almost certainly now be answered negatively by an English court, but Australian law might support a different result if there was a sufficient relationship of proximity between the two parties. The existence of a right of action in tort between parties in the same chain of manufacture and supply could serve to overcome certain difficulties (caused, for example, by the disappearance or insolvency of a party intermediate in the chain between the retailer and the manufacturer)[69] in bringing a chain of contract actions; and such a right would not, it might be thought, impose on the manufacturer a liability which it ought not in justice to be required to bear. On the other hand, it might be argued that it is one thing

---

65 *A fortiori*, if P could sue D in contract, or could sue C in contract instead of suing D in tort, there is an argument for saying that P should not be allowed to sue D in tort. So far as the former possibility is concerned, English law (anomalously, perhaps) allows concurrent actions in contract and tort in many situations.

66 [1989] 2 Qd.R. 477.

67 ibid., p. 487.

68 [1982] A.C. 225.

69 There are many different reasons why a person who has a right of action in contract against A might choose to sue B in tort instead. For more detailed discussion see Cane *Tort Law and Economic Interests* (Oxford, 1991) pp. 336-44.

to allow the purchaser of a defective product to recover in tort from the manufacturer for economic loss resulting from the defect, but quite another to allow a supplier of the product to do so; perhaps such indemnity actions should be dealt with solely in terms of contract law.

3. Trade Practices Act (Cwth), Part VA

The law of products liability has received much attention from law reform bodies in Europe and Australia in the last twenty years or so. But whereas reform of the law of occupiers' liability, for example, has been in the direction of assimilating the special rules into the main body of negligence law, the tendency in respect of products liability has been towards the introduction of stricter forms of liability. A watershed was the thalidomide tragedy of the 1960s, which generated an enormous amount of publicity and sympathy for its victims, and alerted policy makers and politicians to the potential of drugs and other mass-produced items to cause widespread injury and loss. That incident was also important because it highlighted the fact that negligence and causation could be difficult to prove; and the fact that litigation can take a long time, cost a lot of money and generate considerable anxiety and insecurity in the victims of personal injury, especially if they are faced with a large corporate defendant who has the incentive and the resources to prolong the litigation and settlement process as much as possible.

In 1989 the Australian Law Reform Commission made radical proposals for reform of product liability law, perhaps the most radical feature of which was the definition of the causal factor which would attract liability: not 'a defect in a product', but 'something that the goods did'. (Loss caused by other factors, such as the plaintiff's own conduct, was not to be compensatable.) In other words, the A.L.R.C. did not propose liability for loss caused by *defective* products but liability for loss caused by *products*. In this respect, the proposed liability was very 'strict'.[70] But the strictness of the proposed liability was softened by the recognition of several 'defences': it was proposed that the amount of compensation could be reduced (up to 100 per cent) if the risk of the loss was increased by some (unreasonable) act of the user of the product or by (unreasonable) advice as to the use of the goods; and that no liability would arise if the loss was caused by the product acting in a way which could not, *by any means*, have been discovered at the time of its supply to a user. The liability proposed by the A.L.R.C. would have rested not only on manufacturers but also, for example, on designers and assemblers, and even on carriers and warehousers. Loss recoverable under the proposals included purely economic loss[71] and non-pecuniary loss, as well as personal injury and

70 But the proposals were still, in a sense, fault-based: see Industry Commission (Report No. 4), *Product Liability* (1990) p. 22.

71 But only (1) if suffered by a person with a possessory or proprietary interest in the loss-causing goods, or (2) if the loss consisted of the cost of meeting a liability to pay compensation to a person who suffered personal injury or property damage caused by goods.

property damage. The proposals did not apply to a building as such (although they did apply to goods incorporated into a building) or to services which do not result in the production of 'goods'.

These proposals were underpinned by two main policy objectives: to reduce the cost of enforcing liability (that is, of making and resolving product liability claims); and to ensure that the cost of compensating for losses caused by products was borne by manufacturers and (through them) by those who use the products. In theory, if such cost is not reflected in the price of goods, then 'too many' of such goods will be produced and purchased, thus resulting in 'too many' product-caused losses; moreover, producers will have insufficient incentive to produce goods which cause fewer losses. The validity of much of the argumentation in support of the proposals depended on the truth of assertions about the economic effects of the law as it stood at the date of the proposals and about the likely economic effects of the proposed rules. The Industry Commission, in its report on the proposals, pointed out that such assertions were very difficult to test, and that it was hard to be sure whether the proposals 'would promote better outcomes in respect of the production, purchase and use of goods'.[72] There is little point here in detailing the Industry Commission's reactions to the A.L.R.C. proposals. The overall conclusion was that the proposals should not be implemented because any economic benefits they might have produced would be too small to justify the upheaval that introduction of the proposals would have caused. Instead, the Commission suggested that consideration be given to more limited reform, the main points of which would have been as follows:

(a) that there should be a single legal regime to deal with product-caused injuries (as opposed to the current amalgam of statutory rules and common law rules of tort and contract liability);
(b) that the rules governing the payment of compensation should make no distinction between owners of goods and non-owners of goods (such as members of the owner's family or bystanders);
(c) that product misuse should be taken into account in all cases, whether or not the misuse could be described as 'unreasonable';
(d) that a development risk defence and a defence of assumption of risk should be available;
(e) that loss caused by deterioration in a product should attract liability only if (as under the present law) it was the result of a defect in the product.

The Commission also thought that consideration could be given to placing the burden of proof in product liability actions on the defendant. As we shall see, some of these points have been taken up but others, most notably the first, are still just aspirations.

A consequence of the Industry Commission's criticisms of the A.L.R.C. proposals was that the Federal government decided not to implement them. Instead, in June 1992 Federal Parliament enacted a new Part VA of the Trade Practices Act, modelled on an E.C. directive on liability for

72 Industry Commission (1990) p. 10.

defective products. Because of constitutional limits on the legislative powers of the Commonwealth, the Act imposes liability only in respect of goods supplied *commercially* by a *corporation*. The Act imposes liability for loss[73] suffered by anyone[74] (except the defendant manufacturer) as a result of injury to or the death of an individual caused by a defect in goods. It also imposes liability for loss suffered by a person (other than the defendant manufacturer) which is caused by a defect in goods and which results from damage to or destruction of goods (other than the defective goods) which are used by that person for non-commercial purposes and which are of a type ordinarily acquired for non-commercial purposes (s.75AF). Loss suffered as a result of damage to or destruction of non-commercial land, buildings or fixtures is also recoverable (s.75AG).

The liability rests primarily on the manufacturer of the defective goods. 'Manufacturer' is defined widely to include, for example, a manufacturer of component parts; a corporation which holds itself out as manufacturer, or which puts its own brand name on goods manufactured by someone else; and certain importers of goods.[75] Also, any corporate commercial supplier is deemed to be a manufacturer if it is requested to reveal the identity of a manufacturer of the goods unknown to the plaintiff, but fails after a reasonable time to comply with the request (s.75AJ). Furthermore, if the only reason why the goods were defective is that they complied with a *mandatory* Commonwealth standard, then the Commonwealth can be held liable instead of the manufacturer.[76] But goods are not defective simply because any such mandatory standard was not the safest possible standard at the time the goods were supplied by the manufacturer (s.75AC(4)). Moreover, it is a defence to a claim against a manufacturer that the goods were defective only because they complied with a mandatory standard (whether or not a Commonwealth standard) (s.75AK(1)(b)).

Goods have a defect if 'their safety is not such as persons generally are entitled to expect' (s.75AC(1)). In judging the safety of goods, relevant factors include their packaging, any instructions or warnings given as to the use of the goods, and the reasonably foreseeable uses of the goods (s.75AC(2)). The issue of safety is to be decided with reference to the time the goods were supplied by the manufacturer. There are a number of defences to a claim under the legislation (s.75AK): there is no liability if the defect did not exist at the time the manufacturer supplied the goods; a component manufacturer is not liable if the defect is attributable to the

---

73 But not if the loss is covered by State or Territory workers' compensation legislation: s.75AI.

74 Including, for example, relatives who suffer economic loss: s.75AE. In this respect, Part VA is very wide. The legislation also empowers the Trade Practices Commission to commence actions on behalf of injured persons who have consented in writing to such an action: s.75AQ.

75 Trade Practices Act s.74A; see s.75AB.

76 Section 75AL. The Industry Commission (Report on *Product Liability*, p. 65) recommended such a provision.

manufacturer of the finished product;[77] and there is a so-called 'state of the art' or 'development risk' defence which allows a defendant to argue that the state of scientific or technical knowledge at the time the goods were supplied was not such as to enable the defect to be known.[78] If the loss was caused partly by a defect in goods and partly by an act or omission of the plaintiff (whether unreasonable or not), the damages *must* be reduced to take account of the plaintiff's causal contribution to the loss (s.75AN). Furthermore, one of the factors to be taken into account in judging defectiveness would allow a court to hold that goods were not defective simply because they were unsafe if used in an unreasonable way or for an unreasonable purpose (s.75AC(2)(e)).

Any contract term purporting to exclude, restrict or modify the statutory liability is void (s.75AP). The statutory liability is additional to any other relevant liability under State, Territory or Commonwealth law (s.75AR).

The new provisions present a host of difficulties and complications which it would be inappropriate to discuss here. But it is worthwhile noting several general points about the liability imposed by Part VA. First, it is often said of the directive on which the Part is based that it introduced a regime of 'strict liability' alongside the common law which, of course, nominally imposes liability for negligence. But, as we have seen, the effect of the doctrine of *res ipsa loquitur* is that the common law imposes liability which is, in effect, strict at least in production-negligence and simple design-negligence cases. On the other hand, the definition of 'defect' in the Act is such that in cases of a sort to which the doctrine of *res ipsa loquitur* would not apply at common law, the standard of liability under the Act is, to all intents and purposes, indistinguishable from common law negligence.[79] The availability of the state-of-the-art defence, which prevents the imposition of liability for risks which were undiscoverable at the time of manufacture,[80] and the fact that defectiveness under the Act is to be judged at the time the goods left the control of their manufacturer, further reduce any difference between the standard of liability under the Act and common law negligence. One important result of this is that at least one of the frequently stated aims of reform in this area is unlikely to be realized: that is, the aim of reducing the time and cost involved in resolving product liability claims by reducing the complexity of the issues of liability and causation presented by such claims.

77 But the manufacturer of the finished product can be liable, along with the component manufacturer, for defects attributable to the component manufacturer. At common law, the manufacturer of a product is not liable for defects in components manufactured by someone else unless the product manufacturer is vicariously liable for the negligence of the component manufacturer, or the former was negligent in choosing or failing properly to supervise or check the work of the latter. Concerning vicarious liabilty, see *Peake* v. *Steriline Manufacturing Pty Ltd* [1988] Aust. Torts Reports 80-154.

78 *Query* by any means or by any reasonable means?

79 J. Stapleton (1986) 6 *O.J.L.S.* 392; C. Newdick (1987) 104 *L.Q.R.* 288. The burden of proving that the loss was caused by a defect in goods rests, under the Act, on the plaintiff, although there is a rather meaningless provision designed to encourage courts to draw inferences in favour of plaintiffs.

80 C. Newdick [1988] *C.L.J.* 455.

The only respect in which the Act imposes any significant measure of strict liability is that it allows claims to be made against persons other than the manufacturer, who may in no real sense be responsible for the condition of the product. But, of course, such persons can be liable only if the product was defective, so that although the liability is strict as far as they are concerned, it is not strict in any absolute sense.

The second general point worth noting is that the Act applies only to 'goods'; it does not apply to services such as the giving of financial advice. The reasons for this are explicable in historical terms, but it is very difficult to find any principled reason why liability for defective goods should be subject to a different legal regime from that dealing with liability for defective services.[81] Even more anomalously, the Act does not draw a clear distinction between goods and services, because complaints that goods are defective are normally, at bottom, complaints that someone has performed some service (such as designing the product or supervising the production line) defectively.[82]

Thirdly, by creating a special regime of liability for product-caused injuries, the Act creates an anomaly between one class of injured persons and other classes (such as those injured by negligent driving). Why do victims of product-caused injuries deserve to be treated differently and in some respects better than those injured in other ways? This question is but one aspect of a much wider question about the way society deals with disability and misfortune not only through the tort system of compensation but also, for example, through social security systems. It is not easy to think of any reason why product-caused injuries deserve special treatment even within the law of tort, let alone within the wider context of accident compensation.[83] In the case of road accidents, we can at least justify special compensation schemes by pointing out that road accidents have, for a long time, been perceived as a major social problem, and that the way the tort system deals with them is highly inefficient and scandalously expensive; but it does not seem that product-caused injuries are perceived in a similar way, and a consultant appointed by the Industry Commission estimated that the number of product-caused accidents which would warrant legal actions would be only 500 per year under the law as it was in 1990.[84] If this estimate is anything like accurate, it seriously weakens any case for preferential treatment of victims of product-caused injuries.

81 There is a proposal for an EC directive on liability for services under which liability is fault-based but the burden of proof is on the defendant.

82 J. Stapleton (1989) 9 *Tel Aviv Univ. Studies in Law* 147 and in P. Cane and J. Stapleton eds *Essays for Patrick Atiyah* (Oxford, 1991) pp. 258-70.

83 See generally *Atiyah's Accidents* esp. pp. 552-4.

84 Industry Commission Report p. 39.

II: DEFECTIVE PREMISES

1. LIABILITY

Here we are concerned with the liability of non-occupiers to occupants and visitors for defects in premises.[85] Occupiers' liability was considered in Chapter 9. Defective premises need to be considered separately from defective products because there are some special rules peculiar to liability for defects in real property; and because, as we have seen, recent law reform activity[86] has been much more concerned with defective products than with defective premises. Even before *Donoghue* v. *Stevenson* it was decided that the landlord of unfurnished premises owed no duty of care in tort in respect of the state of the premises either to the tenant or to other users of the premises.[87] This rule was left untouched in *Donoghue* v. *Stevenson*, and was later extended to cover the position of a vendor *vis-à-vis* the purchaser and third parties;[88] and of a builder who builds on his own land and then sells the house—such a 'speculative builder' enjoyed the immunity which attached to the owner. But a builder who built for another on the latter's land could be sued in tort for negligence in doing the work.[89] The basis of the immunity of the lessor and vendor was probably the idea, strong in relation to the sale or lease of land, that the purchaser or lessee has ample opportunity to examine the property and he should avail himself of it; and that he only has himself to blame if the premises are defective.[90] The law thus drew a sharp distinction between chattels and real property in this respect: as we have seen, the common law principle of *caveat emptor* ('let the buyer beware') is considerably modified by statute in relation to goods but not in relation to land, and the law of tort mirrored this difference.[91]

The position now is that the owner-builder (or lessor-builder) does not enjoy the owner's (or lessor's) immunity but is under the same duty as a

---

85 Liability in tort is supplemented and to some extent rendered redundant in some jurisdictions by legislation which provides for the implication of warranties into contracts for the construction of dwellings or establishes a scheme of insurance against bad workmanship by builders, or both. See Builders Licensing Act 1971 (N.S.W.) Part VI; Housebuilders Registration and Homeowners' Protection Act 1979-82 (Qld) Part V; Local Government Act 1958 (Vic.) Part XLIX, Div. 1A; Defective Houses Act 1976 (S.A.).

86 Especially in Australia. For the U.K. see Defective Premises Act 1972.

87 *Cavalier* v. *Pope* [1906] A.C. 428; the immunity exists even in respect of defects not discoverable by the tenant on reasonable inspection. Should it? *Cavalier* v. *Pope* is no longer law in South Australia: *Parker* v. *South Australian Housing Trust* (1986) 41 S.A.S.R. 493.

88 *Bottomley* v. *Bannister* [1932] 1 K.B. 458.

89 *Sharpe* v. *E.T. Sweeting & Son Ltd* [1963] 1 W.L.R. 665; *Bowen* v. *Paramount Builders (Hamilton) Ltd* [1977] 1 N.Z.L.R. 394.

90 In relation to real property, no distinction is drawn between commercial and non-commercial sellers (nor, of course, between commercial and non-commercial buyers). Indeed, the commercial/non-commercial distinction, whether in relation to sellers or buyers, has never been developed by the common law but is a product of legislative intervention. There are no statutory equivalents of Sale of Goods legislation in respect of land.

91 See J. Stapleton (1991) 107 *L.Q.R.* 249 at pp. 249-52.

contracting builder, that is, the ordinary duty of reasonable care.[92] Also subject to ordinary negligence rules are developers,[93] architects[94] and engineers.[95] A builder (etc.) can also be held liable for failure to investigate the state of neighbouring land to ensure that, if it provides support to the land on which the building is being done, it is stable and that the support it provides is adequate.[96] A builder (etc.) may be responsible not only for the structure itself but also for other aspects of the site and its preparation which affect the safety of the house. Local authorities might, in certain circumstances, be held liable for defective premises if the authority is negligent in carrying out (or failing to carry out) an inspection of the premises to ensure that they comply with building regulations;[97] or in approving building plans which do not comply with regulations or which subject the house to risk of damage of which the council is or should be aware;[98] or in requiring a house to be built in a way which does not comply with regulations or subjects the house to a risk of damage.[99]

Despite these extensions of liability in negligence for loss and damage caused by defects in premises, the immunity of the owner or lessor who is not also a builder apparently remains intact, except in South Australia.[100]

2. DAMAGES RECOVERABLE

Obviously a person who suffers personal injury or damage to property (other than the defective premises) as a result of a defect in premises can recover damages for that loss. But what of the premises themselves? In England, as we have seen, the general rule now is that damages may not be recovered in tort in respect of damage to defective premises caused by the defect, nor in respect of the defect itself, because such loss is said to be purely economic. There may, however, be exceptions to the general rule in cases where the plaintiff suffers loss as a result of detrimental reliance on the defendant, or in some cases where the loss suffered consists of the cost of meeting a legal liability to a third party injured by the defect in the

92 *Anns* v. *Merton L.B.C.* [1978] A.C. 728; *Batty* v. *Metropolitan Property Realizations Ltd* [1978] Q.B. 554; *Rimmer* v. *Liverpool C.C.* [1985] Q.B. 1; *McNerny* v. *Lambeth L.B.C.* (1988) 21 Housing L.R. 188. In this sentence, the word 'builder' includes 'designer' and any other person whose negligence is responsible for the defective state of the premises. An owner who subdivides land and offers the blocks for sale can also be liable: *Gabolinscy* v. *Hamilton City Corporation* [1975] 1 N.Z.L.R. 150. Re the duty of the building contractor see *A.C. Billings Ltd* v. *Riden* [1958] A.C. 241.

93 *Batty* [1978] Q.B. 554; *Mt Albert Borough Council* v. *Johnson* [1979] 2 N.Z.L.R. 234.

94 *Voli* v. *Inglewood Shire Council* (1962-3) 110 C.L.R. 74; *Clayton* v. *Woodman & Son (Builders) Ltd* [1962] 2 Q.B. 533; *Clay* v. *A.J. Crump & Sons Ltd* [1964] 1 Q.B. 533.

95 *Carosella* v. *Ginos & Gilbert Pty Ltd* (1981) 27 S.A.S.R. 515.

96 *Batty* [1978] Q.B. 554.

97 *Sutherland S.C.* v. *Heyman* (1984-5) 157 C.L.R. 424. The position in England now is that a local authority could only be sued in respect of personal injury (or, perhaps, damage to property other than the defective premises) if caused by a latent (that is, undiscoverable) defect: *Murphy* v. *Brentwood D.C.* [1991] 1 A.C. 398.

98 *Wollongong C.C.* v. *Fregnan* [1982] 1 N.S.W.L.R. 244; *Brown* v. *Heathcote C.C.* [1987] 1 N.Z.L.R. 720; *Rothfield* v. *Manolakos* (1989) 63 D.L.R. (4th) 449.

99 *Wollongong C.C.* v. *Fregnan* [1982] 1 N.S.W.L.R. 244.

100 *Parker* v. *South Australian Housing Trust* (1986) 41 S.A.S.R. 493.

premises, or where the defect is in some good (such as a boiler) incorporated into the building by an independent contractor.[101]

But in Australia, the recoverability in the common law of tort of damages for economic loss caused by defective buildings depends on the rules governing recovery for purely economic loss generally. The rules about assessment of damages in this context were discussed in Chapter 12.

101 For more detailed discussion see Cane *Tort Law and Economic Interests* (1991) pp. 511-18. Important in justifying this approach is the regime of protection for the acquirers of defective *dwellings* contained in the Defective Premises Act 1972 (U.K.) and the insurance schemes which back it up. The absence of an equivalent scheme in New Zealand has, conversely, been used to justify the more generous New Zealand common law rules, at least in respect of private dwellings (as opposed to commercial buildings): J. Smillie [1990] *N.Z.L.J.* 310; C.S. Withnall (1990) 7 *Otago L.R.* 189; articles by S. Todd and C. Brown & B. Feldthusen in *Negligence after Murphy* v. *Brentwood D.C.* (Auckland, 1991).

16

NUISANCE

There are two types of nuisance:[1] public and private. They are different in many ways and require separate consideration. We will deal first with private nuisance.

I: PRIVATE NUISANCE

A private nuisance is an unreasonable interference with the use and enjoyment of land.[2] This interference may take the form of physical damage to property, such as the killing of trees by noxious fumes,[3] or the breaking of windows by escaping golf balls,[4] or the damaging of stock in a shop by the penetration of dust;[5] or the flooding of land and deposition of debris by the blocking of a watercourse.[6] Or it may consist of interference with the comfort or 'amenities' of the inhabitants of the property

1 R. Buckley *The Law of Nuisance* (London, 1981).
2 *Oldham* v. *Lawson (No. 1)* [1976] V.R. 654, 655 *per* Harris J.
3 *St Helen's Smelting Co.* v. *Tipping* (1865) 11 H.L.C. 642.
4 *Lester-Travers* v. *City of Frankston* [1970] V.R. 2.
5 *Harris* v. *Carnegies Pty Ltd* [1917] V.L.R. 95.
6 *Thorpes* v. *Grant Pastoral Co. Pty Ltd* (1954) 92 C.L.R. 317.

by such things as noise,[7] smoke, smells,[8] vibration,[9] glare[10] and so on. Or, finally, it may consist of personal injury to the inhabitants, for example from escaping cricket or golf balls, or of damage to their health, for example from noxious fumes.

Generally speaking, the term 'nuisance' denotes a state of affairs that is either continuing or recurrent[11] but this is not always the case since, for example, it has been held that the isolated escape of tangible things causing physical damage can constitute a nuisance.[12] The importance of the element of continuance is probably related to the type of damage inflicted. If the damage is physical then the law is likely to be prepared to award damages even if it is the result of an isolated incident. But if the damage consists of interference with comfort or amenities then the law is less likely to award damages or, more especially, an injunction if, for example, the noise or smell complained of occurs only infrequently.[13] At the same time, while the immediate cause of the damage may be an isolated incident, the underlying cause in a nuisance action will usually be some continuing state of affairs. For example, in *British Celanese* v. *Hunt*[14] the escape of foil was the result of a continuing situation in which the defendant stored the foil on its land. It is not, however, every

---

7 *Oldham* v. *Lawson* [1976] V.R. 654; *Vincent* v. *Peacock* [1973] 1 N.S.W.L.R. 466.

8 *Bamford* v. *Turnley* (1860) 3 B & S. 66. It is beyond the scope of this book to discuss statutory schemes for the control of various sorts of environmental pollution, such as oil pollution, water and air pollution and pollution by noise and smells. The typical scheme lays down standards and empowers a statutory authority to police them. There may also be statutory compensation provisions: e.g. Marine Pollution Act 1987 (N.S.W.) s.51. In practice the best first step might be to seek to persuade an authority to exercise its powers; but since such authorities typically have a wide discretion to decide how they will act in the face of breaches of statutory standards, recourse to the law of nuisance may be necessary in the end. The common law of nuisance is, however, only part of a larger legal framework for controlling and protecting land use and is very much a last resort. On pollution control see G.M. Bates *Environmental Law in Australia* (1983) Ch. 9. Building and zoning regulations are also important in this context; but the law of nuisance still has a role to play here because the fact that the particular use to which a person puts land complies with planning law does not mean that it cannot constitute a nuisance.

9 *Sturges* v. *Bridgman* (1879) 11 Ch.D. 852.

10 *Bank of New Zealand* v. *Greenwood* [1984] 1 N.Z.L.R. 525.

11 *Hargrave* v. *Goldman* (1963) 110 C.L.R. 40, 59 *per* Windeyer J.

12 *British Celanese Ltd* v. *A.H. Hunt (Capacitors) Ltd* [1969] 1 W.L.R. 659. There are some terminological difficulties here. A cause of action for damages in nuisance is not complete until damage has been suffered (but if the plaintiff seeks an injunction, he need only show that damage is likely in the future: see p. 616 below). Often the word 'nuisance' or the term 'actionable nuisance' is used to refer to such damage, which may be isolated (as often in the case of physical damage) or continuing (as often in the case of amenity damage). On the other hand, the term 'nuisance' is also used to refer to the state of affairs which gives rise to the damage, and looked at in this way even isolated damage-causing incidents usually arise out of a continuing state of affairs. But the state of affairs does not give rise to a cause of action for damages until damage is suffered. It is, strictly, only a potential nuisance. Finally, the word 'nuisance' is often used in a colloquial sense to refer to interferences with use and enjoyment whether unreasonable (and so actionable) or not.

13 See e.g. *Bamford* v. *Turnley* (1860) 3 B. & S. 66, 79 *per* Pollock C.B.; *Spencer* v. *Silva* [1942] S.A.S.R. 213; *Dunstan* v. *King* [1948] V.L.R. 269.

14 [1969] 1 W.L.R. 659.

continuing state of affairs causing physical damage which the law perceives of as giving rise to a nuisance. For example, an unroadworthy car can be described colloquially as a nuisance but any action for physical damage resulting from the state of the car would be brought in negligence, not in nuisance. The relationship between negligence and nuisance is one of the most obscure topics in the modern law of torts, and we shall return to it later.

1. UNREASONABLENESS

(a) Triviality Whether an interference with the use and enjoyment of land is unreasonable depends on a variety of factors. To start with, an interference will not be unreasonable if it is trivial in nature. Personal injury is probably never trivial enough to be dismissed entirely;[15] property damage might be so slight as to be insignificant.[16] But most importantly, not every interference with comfort and convenience will qualify as a nuisance. The matter has to be judged according to the standards of reasonable people. The question is whether the inconvenience ought to be considered as more than fanciful, more than one of 'mere delicacy or fastidiousness according to plain and sober and simple notions, not merely according to elegant or dainty modes and habits of living'.[17] So it has been said, for example, that to amount to a nuisance, noise must be unusual or excessive.[18]

(b) Give and take The common law subscribes to a morality of 'give and take, live and let live',[19] at least to the extent that the interference is of a relatively trifling nature and is the result of the ordinary use of land.[20] When people live in close proximity to one another they have to be prepared, to some extent, to allow others to do things which annoy them at times when they would prefer to be left in peace and quiet if they, in turn, want to be able to behave in a way which might annoy their neighbours and at a time when their neighbours would prefer they did not.

(c) Hypersensitivity The question of reasonableness is to be judged according to the standards of the normal person; an abnormally sensitive

---

15 But see *Stormer* v. *Ingram* (1978) 21 S.A.S.R. 93 (bees flying into and stinging people not in the ordinary course sufficient to amount to a nuisance).

16 ibid.

17 A loose quotation from *Walter* v. *Selfe* (1851) 4 De G. & Sm. 315; 64 E.R. 849, 852 *per* Knight-Bruce V.C.

18 *Spencer* v. *Silva* [1942] S.A.S.R. 213, 219 *per* Mayo J.; *McKenzie* v. *Powley* [1916] S.A.L.R. 1, 17 *per* Murray C.J.

19 *Bamford* v. *Turnley* (1860) 3 B. & S. 66, 84 *per* Bramwell B.; cf. *Bayliss* v. *Lea* [1962] S.R.(N.S.W.) 521. See also *Clarey* v. *Principal and Council of the Women's College* (1953) 90 C.L.R. 170.

20 e.g. *Pittar* v. *Alvarez* (1916) 16 S.R.(N.S.W.) 618; *McKenzie* v. *Powley* [1916] S.A.S.R. 1; *Painter* v. *Reed* [1930] S.A.S.R. 295. There are obviously value judgments involved in deciding what is an ordinary use of land.

plaintiff is not entitled to relief by reason of his sensitivity.[21] The classic illustration of this proposition is *Robinson* v. *Kilvert*[22] where heat emanating from the defendant's premises caused the plaintiff's store of brown paper to be spoiled by drying out. It was held that the plaintiff could not recover in nuisance: the defendant's activity was a lawful one and was not 'noxious' in the sense that it incommoded the workpeople on the plaintiff's premises. But the mere fact that the plaintiff or his activity is more sensitive than some other activity will not necessarily bar his recovery. Sensitivity is a relative thing, and some judgment has to be made about how great the plaintiff's deviation from the norm must be to justify denial of recovery. Judgments of hypersensitivity also involve an evaluation of the social desirability of the plaintiff's activity, and such evaluations can change over time. For example, in 1965 in England it was decided that television broadcasting was a hypersensitive activity which should not be protected by the law of nuisance from occasional, even if recurrent and severe, electrical interference.[23] On the other hand, in Canada in 1978 it was decided that television broadcasting was an activity deserving of such protection and not abnormally sensitive.[24]

If, however, the plaintiff can establish that, ignoring the sensitivity of his land use, the defendant's actions nevertheless constituted a nuisance, he can recover damages in respect of all the loss suffered, even if it was suffered only because the use was hypersensitive, to the extent that it is not too remote in law. The test of remoteness in nuisance, as in negligence (where the same rule about sensitivity applies), allows recovery for all loss of a foreseeable kind, even if its exact extent or manner of occurrence was unforeseeable.[25] There is also authority for the proposition that if the conduct of a hypersensitive activity is interfered with deliberately or maliciously, this may constitute a nuisance.[26]

(d) Locality The unreasonableness of an interference has to be judged according to the locality in which it occurs. Thus, for example, the inhabitants of an industrial area cannot expect the fragrances of a sweet-smelling orchard.[27] It has been said that what would be a nuisance in Belgravia (or Toorak or Killara) would not necessarily be so in Bermondsey (or Richmond or Redfern).[28] A person must endure noises and other interferences which are an ordinary incident of life in his locality; otherwise a person could, by using land for a purpose incompatible with established uses, put an end to those established activities. On the other

---

21 *Munro* v. *Southern Dairies Ltd* [1955] V.L.R. 332, 355 *per* Sholl J.; *Pelmothe* v. *Phillips* (1899) 20 L.R.(N.S.W.) 58.

22 (1889) 41 Ch.D. 88.

23 *Bridlington Relay Ltd* v. *Yorkshire Electricity Board* [1965] Ch. 436.

24 *Nor-Video Services Ltd* v. *Ontario Hydro* (1978) 84 D.L.R. (3d.) 221. See further R. Kidner [1989] *Conv.* 279.

25 *The Wagon Mound (No. 2)* [1967] 1 A.C. 617; cf. *McKinnon Industries Ltd* v. *Walker* [1951] 3 D.L.R. 577.

26 *Hollywood Silver Fox Farm* v. *Emmett* [1936] 2 K.B. 468.

27 *Shoreham-by-Sea U.D.C.* v. *Dolphin Canadian Proteins Ltd* (1971) 71 L.G.R. 261.

28 *Sturges* v. *Bridgman* (1879) 11 Ch.D. 852, 865; *Bamford* v. *Turnley* (1860) 3 B. & S. 66, 79 *per* Pollock C.B. (Grosvenor Square and Smithfield Market).

hand, the fact that a locality is industrial does not mean that the introduction of some new device such as a steam hammer, making sleep impossible where it was not before, is not a nuisance.[29] But a plaintiff who argues that a factory which has been operating without nuisance for a long time has become a nuisance by the introduction of new machinery 'imposes upon himself (to say the least) an arduous task'.[30]

However, the nature of localities can and does change—for example, from predominantly residential to predominantly industrial; or residential areas may grow and encroach on industrial areas which were formerly isolated from housing. The principles of nuisance could in theory be used either to hinder or to facilitate changes in the character of neighbourhoods, and ultimately the court will have to decide which of two competing land uses ought to be encouraged and which discouraged.[31] In practice, such issues of change of land use are usually regulated by planning legislation, and the law of nuisance is largely confined to resolving land use conflicts which arise out of the diversity of contiguous land use permitted by planning schemes.

(d) Time and duration Another factor relevant to unreasonableness is the time of day at which the interference occurs. In *Daily Telegraph Co. Ltd* v. *Stuart*[32] mechanical drills which generated much noise were used on a building site almost continuously between 9.00 a.m. and 5.00 p.m., Monday to Saturday. The court awarded an injunction limiting the hours during which the drills could be operated. Related is the question of the duration of the interference. In *Munro* v. *Southern Dairies*[33] it was said that loss of a single night's sleep from the noise of a dairy could amount to a substantial interference. On the other hand, in *Andreae* v. *Selfridge & Co. Ltd* Lord Greene M.R. said that 'when one is dealing with temporary operations such as demolition and rebuilding everybody has to put up with a certain degree of discomfort because operations of that kind cannot be carried on at all without a certain amount of noise and a certain amount of dust'.[34] Clearly, before a court would award an injunction to restrain a particular activity it would want to be sure that the interference created was likely to be repeated with some frequency.[35]

(e) Nature of activity Also relevant is the nature of the defendant's activity. We have already noted the importance of this in the context of abnormal sensitivity, in applying the locality principle and in deciding what is an ordinary use of land. In *Lester-Travers* v. *City of Frankston*[36] Anderson J. thought that since the playing of golf was not a trade and since it did not have to be carried on in the particular neighbourhood,

---

29 *Polsue & Alfieri Ltd* v. *Rushmer* [1907] A.C. 121.
30 *Gaunt* v. *Fynney* (1872) L.R. 8 Ch.App. 8, 12 *per* Lord Selborne L.C.
31 *Sturges* v. *Bridgman* (1879) 11 Ch.D. 852, 865-6.
32 (1928) 28 S.R.(N.S.W.) 291; cf. *Abbott* v. *Arcus* (1948) 50 W.A.L.R. 41.
33 [1955] V.L.R. 332.
34 [1938] Ch. 1, 5; cf. *Harrison* v. *Southwark & Vauxhall Water Co.* [1891] 2 Ch. 409.
35 *Shoreham-by-Sea U.D.C.* v. *Dolphin Canadian Proteins* (1971) 71 L.G.R. 261.
36 [1970] V.R. 2.

then if it could not be done without interfering with the comfort of neighbours and threatening bodily harm and property damage, it ought not to be played there at all. On the other hand, at least some English judges have shown considerable tenderness towards cricket clubs whose grounds were so close to houses or roads that escaping balls could do damage.[37]

(f) **Precautions** Finally, it is relevant to ask whether the defendant has taken all reasonable precautions to reduce the interference to a minimum.[38] If he has not, then the court can, by awarding damages or issuing an injunction, encourage the taking of those precautions. On the other hand, the fact that all reasonable precautions have been taken will not necessarily prevent an activity constituting a nuisance if it nevertheless causes a substantial interference. In this respect, liability in nuisance is stricter than that in negligence. As in negligence, the reasonableness of precautions depends on their practicability and expense; practicability is to be judged initially according to the state of technology at the time the nuisance is alleged to have been first created, but since nuisance is a continuing tort and every new substantial interference creates a fresh cause of action,[39] a defendant may be liable for failure to incorporate new precautions into an activity when they become available.

(g) **Proof** Some nuisances are easier to establish than others. Physical damage is quite straightforward but interference with comfort and amenities, being more subjective, is more difficult to prove. Some sort of objective measurement of noise is possible, but assessment of the unpleasantness of smells is heavily dependent on judgments about the credibility of the witnesses and their sensitivity to smells.[40]

(h) **Type of damage** There is old authority for the proposition that the reasonableness of an interference, especially in terms of the locality principle, is only relevant where the damage inflicted is injury to amenities and not where the plaintiff suffers physical injury or property damage.[41] When this rule was laid down it seems to have been designed to mark the seriousness of material damage: people who live in urban areas have to put up with a certain amount of discomfort or annoyance from their neighbours, but they are not expected to tolerate physical damage to their property. The force of the distinction was heightened by the fact that liability in nuisance for physical damage did not depend on proof that the defendant had been negligent, that is, that he had failed to take reasonable

37 *Bolton* v. *Stone* [1951] A.C. 850; *Miller* v. *Jackson* [1977] Q.B. 966.

38 *Painter* v. *Reed* [1930] S.A.S.R. 295; *Lester-Travers* v. *City of Franskton* [1970] V.R. 2; *Shoreham-by-Sea U.D.C.* v. *Dolphin Canadian Proteins* (1971) 71 L.G.R. 261.

39 *Manson* v. *Shire of Maffra* (1881) 7 V.L.R.(L) 364.

40 *Baulkham Hills Shire Council* v. *A.V. Walsh Pty Ltd* [1968] 3 N.S.W.R. 138.

41 *St Helen's Smelting Co.* v. *Tipping* (1865) 11 H.L.C. 642. For a modern application of the rule see *Halsey* v. *Esso Petroleum Co. Ltd* [1961] 1 W.L.R. 683.

precautions against injury; the liability was strict.[42] Today, however, it seems that liability for physical damage in nuisance depends on proof of negligence[43] and this has rather diminished the force of the distinction. It may be just as onerous to have to prove negligence as to have to prove unreasonableness of user.

(i) Unreasonableness and public interest We have seen that judgments of the social value of activities or, in other words, of the public interest, are often involved in the issue of unreasonableness. More particularly, the locality principle often comes down to a question of public interest, because the interferences to which town-dwellers are subject are often produced by business and industry which benefits the whole population.[44] On the other hand, it seems clear that once it has been decided that the defendant has created a nuisance, it is no answer to say that the public as a whole benefits from the activities.[45] Nuisance is an essentially local thing, and if a defendant causes substantial interference with the use and enjoyment of a neighbour's land, he cannot plead the importance of the activity to others living out of the physical range of the activities. In this respect the law of nuisance serves a quite different end from much planning legislation, which attempts to control land use over a much larger area.

2. Motive

Certain interferences with the use and enjoyment of land (for example, the extraction of water flowing under the land in undefined channels)[46] attract no liability even if done in order to injure the landowner.[47] This may be so even if the extraction causes the land to subside.[48] On the other hand, it appears that an interference which is not unreasonable (and therefore not a nuisance) judged by the above criteria may become such if it is done with the intention of inflicting injury on the plaintiff. In *Hollywood Silver Fox Farm* v. *Emmett*[49] the plaintiff bred silver foxes; silver fox vixens are very sensitive during the breeding season, and if disturbed are likely to refuse to breed, or to miscarry or kill their young. The defendant, an adjoining landowner, maliciously caused his son to discharge guns on the defendant's own land as near as possible to the breeding pens in order to injure the plaintiff. Clearly the defendant was

---

42 P.S. Atiyah (1980) 23 *J. of Law & Econ.* 191; cf. *Halsey* v. *Esso* [1961] 1 W.L.R. 683, 691 *per* Veale J.

43 See pp. 619-22 below.

44 See *Hole* v. *Barlow* (1858) 4 C.B.N.S. 334, 345 *per* Willes J.

45 *Bamford* v. *Turnley* (1860) 3 B. & S. 66, 84-5 *per* Bramwell B.; *Munro* v. *Southern Dairies* [1955] V.L.R. 332.

46 *Stephens* v. *Anglian Water Authority* [1987] 1 W..R. 1381; *Xuereb* v. *Viola* [1990] Aust. Torts Reports 81-012.

47 G.H.L. Fridman (1958) 21 *M.L.R.* 484; Cane *Tort Law and Economic Interests* (1991) pp. 280-2, 283-4.

48 ibid.; but see *Perth Corporation* v. *Halle* (1911) 13 C.L.R. 393, 399.

49 [1936] 2 K.B. 468.

entitled to shoot on his own land and the hypersensitivity of the plaintiff's activity might have prevented the amount of noise made constituting a nuisance. But it was held that since the defendant had acted maliciously he could be held liable. It is possible to argue that in this case the noise would have been a nuisance even if innocently made; but in *Christie* v. *Davey*[50] it was specifically held that making a noise in order to vex and harass one's neighbour could constitute a nuisance even if no action would have lain if the noise had been made innocently.

It is not clear whether the principle in these cases applies where the defendant's malicious acts are done in response to a nuisance committed against him. In *Fraser* v. *Booth*[51] the plaintiff was held not liable to be enjoined from letting off fire crackers and directing water at pigeons in flight, the keeping, breeding and training of which by the defendant constituted an actionable nuisance. But in *Stoakes* v. *Brydges*[52] a householder was held liable for phoning a noisy milkman's employer in the middle of the night as retaliation.

3. Interests Protected

Most of the cases we have considered so far have concerned interference with the use of the plaintiff's land by some physical emanation of a damaging kind from the defendant's premises. But the tort of nuisance is not limited to such situations. It has been held, for example, that the existence of a brothel in proximity to dwelling houses[53] or the presence of a bookshop selling hard-core pornography and showing pornographic films[54] could constitute a nuisance. Less dramatically, it has been held that the siting of a public convenience in relation to private dwellings can constitute a private nuisance.[55] In *Kent* v. *Cavanagh*[56] Fox J. was not prepared to rule out the possibility of a building which is unsightly or aesthetically displeasing or unduly prominent being a nuisance. The law is venturing into rather deep water when it attempts to protect aesthetic values varying, as they do, so much from person to person.

There is no right at common law to an unobstructed view from one's premises:[57] obstruction of a view, in itself, cannot constitute a nuisance. But if a person unlawfully builds a structure which obstructs the view then damages may be recoverable.[58] The law also recognizes a right not to

50 [1893] 1 Ch. 316.
51 (1950) 50 S.R.(N.S.W.) 113.
52 [1958] Q.W.N. 5. See also *Alma* v. *Nakir* [1966] 2 N.S.W.R. 396.
53 *Thompson-Schwab* v. *Costaki* [1956] 1 W.L.R. 335.
54 *Laws* v. *Florinplace* [1981] 1 All E.R. 659.
55 *Miller* v. *Shoalhaven Shire Council* [1967] 2 L.G.R.A. 46.
56 (1973) 1 A.C.T.R. 43 (Black Mountain Tower in Canberra). But in *Bathurst City Council* v. *Saban (No. 2)* (1986) 58 L.G.R.A. 201, 206 Young J. said that 'unsightliness alone does not constitute a nuisance'.
57 *Phipps* v. *Pears* [1965] 1 Q.B. 76; building regulations concerning the height and placement of buildings play an important part here.
58 *Campbell* v. *Paddington Corporation* [1911] 1 K.B. 869; in this case the stand erected by the defendant was a public nuisance, and hence unlawful, by reason of being an obstruction of the highway.

have the light coming into one's premises unduly obstructed. To be actionable an obstruction of light must be serious enough to render occupation of the premises uncomfortable according to ordinary standards and, in the case of business premises, to prevent the plaintiff carrying on business as beneficially as before the obstruction.[59] A landowner has no right not to be observed in the use of premises even if they are used for commercial purposes which may be injured by the observation. In *Victoria Park Racing & Recreation Grounds Co. Ltd* v. *Taylor*[60] the defendant, without the plaintiff's permission, broadcast descriptions of races taking place on the plaintiff's land which he observed from adjoining land. Attendances at the races fell off. By majority a claim in nuisance was dismissed. Latham C.J. said that 'the law cannot by injunction in effect erect fences which the plaintiff is not prepared to provide'.[61]

Picketing may constitute a private nuisance if it interferes with a person's use and enjoyment of his property.[62] In *Thomas* v. *National Union of Mineworkers*[63] Scott J. went further and held that workers who had to run the gauntlet of fifty to seventy unruly pickets to get to work might sue for 'unreasonable harassment' which the judge put forward as a new head of tortious liability analogous to private nuisance. Given that there was no interference with any property rights of the workers it is difficult to see how harassment is analogous to private nuisance, and this aspect of the decision has been criticized.[64]

It does not seem that this pattern of included and excluded interests is based on any set principles; it is simply the result of *ad hoc* value judgments.

4. Who Can Sue?[65]

A nuisance is an interference with the use and enjoyment of land, and so the plaintiff must have an interest in or appropriate rights over the land.[66] The basic interest which gives a right to sue is possession. Possession must be distinguished from mere occupation: a person who occupies property merely as licensee (including, for example, members of the family of a lessee of land who are not themselves parties to the lease) may not bring an action.[67] The distinction between possession and occupation

---

59 *Colls* v. *Home and Colonial Stores Ltd* [1904] A.C. 179; *Carr-Saunders* v. *McNeil* [1986] 1 W.L.R. 922.

60 (1937) 58 C.L.R. 479.

61 (1937) 58 C.L.R. 479, 494.

62 See pp. 623-4 below.

63 [1986] Ch. 20.

64 A. Davidson (1988) 18 *U.W.A.L.R.* 138, 153-6; (1989) 19 *U.W.A.L.R.* 201, 212.

65 G. Kodilinye (1989) 9 *L.S.* 284.

66 Damage is actionable in nuisance only if it results from interference with some right over land: *Elston* v. *Dore* (1983) 57 A.L.J.R. 83; *Tate & Lyle Industries Ltd* v. *Greater London Council* [1983] 2 A.C. 509.

67 *Oldham* v. *Lawson (No. 1)* [1976] V.R. 654; *Malone* v. *Laskey* [1907] 2 K.B. 141.

can, however, be fine[68] and it seems difficult to reconcile all the cases with one another in strictly technical terms. A more promising approach would be to try to relate the 'title' the plaintiff must have to the interests which the law of nuisance protects. If the damage in issue is physical damage to property then the person with the right to sue ought to be the person with the obligation to repair or the burden of repairing the property. A licensee will rarely be in this position. On the other hand, even a mere occupant, or a person in unlawful possession (such as a squatter) might suffer damage of a sort compensatable in the tort of nuisance.[69] Where the damage is personal injury or interference with comfort or amenities there seems no technical reason[70] why any occupant should not recover, since in these cases the plaintiff recovers not for damage to the property or diminution in its value but for diminished enjoyment of it.

The cases on the rights of reversioners fit into this pattern. A person whose only interest in the property is to have it back when someone else's interest comes to an end can only sue for nuisance committed before his interest matures if the nuisance adversely affects the reversionary interest because it involves some permanent or long-term damage to the property.[71] Conversely, if there is a continuing nuisance then a party with an interest in the property may be able to recover for loss caused by it, even if the nuisance began before he acquired the interest.[72]

The technicalities surrounding the right to sue in private nuisance spring from the original nature of the tort as a protection for rights in land. But a more appropriate rule in modern law would be that if damage is suffered in the course of the use and enjoyment of the land, then the person who actually suffers that loss ought to be entitled to recover for it in nuisance regardless of his exact legal interest in the land.

5. Who Can Be Sued?

Most private nuisances arise out of the use by the defendant of his land, but since nuisance is a tort involving interference with the use of land rather that a tort arising out of the unlawful use of land, acts can constitute a nuisance even if they are not done by the defendant on his land. Thus in *Halsey* v. *Esso Petroleum Co. Ltd*[73] Neale J. said that the

68 See *Vaughan* v. *Shire of Benalla* (1891) 17 V.L.R. 129; *Ruhan* v. *Water Conservation and Irrigation Commission* (1920) 20 S.R.(N.S.W.) 439; *South Australia Co.* v. *Port Adelaide Corporation* [1914] S.A.L.R. 16.

69 See cases in previous note; and cf. *Paxhaven Holdings Ltd* v. *A-G* [1974] 2 N.Z.L.R. 185.

70 Although there may be reasons of policy why persons in unlawful occupation or possession should not receive the aid of the law of nuisance, in respect of amenity damage anyway.

71 *Simpson* v. *Savage* (1856) 1 C.B.(N.S.) 347; *Thompson* v. *Sydney Municipal Council* (1938) 14 L.G.R. 32.

72 *Masters* v. *Brent L.B.C.* [1978] 2 All E.R. 664; *Taylor* v. *Auto Trade Supply Ltd* [1972] N.Z.L.R. 102 *contra.*

73 [1961] 1 W.L.R. 683; cf. *Kidman* v. *Page* [1969] Qd.R. 53, 60 *per* Stanley J.; *Vincent* v. *Peacock* [1973] 1 N.S.W.L.R. 466.

use of heavy trucks on a public highway outside the defendant's terminal could amount to a private nuisance to neighbouring residents. A defendant can also be held liable in respect of a nuisance created by him *on the plaintiff's land* even if he has the plaintiff's permission to enter and so is not a trespasser.[74]

Where the nuisance does emanate from private property, the basis of the defendant's liability is control over what happens on the land.[75] Thus the owner of leased premises is not, *as such*, liable for nuisance arising out of disrepair of the premises.[76] But he will be liable if he knew or ought to have known that the nuisance was already on the land at the date of the lease;[77] or if he was under a contractual obligation to repair the premises;[78] or if such an obligation can be implied into the lease; or if the landlord has reserved in the lease the right to enter and repair;[79] or if such a right can be implied into the lease.[80] In all these cases the landlord has a sufficient degree of control over the premises to do repairs. But the fact that the landlord is liable does not mean that the tenant may not also be liable if the latter has convenanted to repair;[81] or if the tenant notices that the premises are in disrepair and need urgent attention but the landlord is abroad or cannot be contacted.[82] In all these cases the rule appears to be that the landlord will be liable only if he knew or ought to have known of the state of the premises. This rule applies whether the nuisance is public (in the form of premises on the highway falling into disrepair) or private. The only authority to the contrary is *Wringe* v. *Cohen*,[83] which seems out of step with the modern trend to assimilate nuisance to negligence in respect of the infliction of physical damage.

An independent contractor who is on land neither as occupier nor possessor but merely as licensee can be liable for nuisances created by him on the land by virtue of his control over the activities being conducted there,[84] that is, by virtue of the fact that he created the nuisance.[85] The control test is applied, at least in cases of positive creation of a nuisance, to the creation and not to abatement of the nuisance. In *Fennell* v. *Robson*

---

74 *Paxhaven Holdings Ltd* v. *A-G* [1974] 2 N.Z.L.R. 185; *Clearlite Holdings Ltd* v. *Auckland City Corporation* [1976] 2 N.Z.L.R. 729.

75 *Eastern Asia Navigation Co. Ltd* v. *Fremantle Harbour Trust Commissioners* (1950) 83 C.L.R. 353.

76 *Braine* v. *Summers* (1881) 7 V.L.R.(L) 420; *Williamson* v. *Friend* (1901) 1 S.R.(N.S.W.) 133.

77 Cases in previous note; *Cull* v. *Green* (1924) 27 W.A.R. 62 (public nuisance); cf. *Sampson* v. *Hodgson-Pressinger* [1981] 3 All E.R. 710. This is so even if the landlord takes from the tenant a covenant by the latter to repair: *Brew Bros Ltd* v. *Snax (Ross) Ltd* [1970] 1 Q.B. 612.

78 *Williamson* v. *Friend* (1901) 1 S.R.(N.S.W.) 133.

79 *Wilchik* v. *Marks* [1934] 2 K.B. 56.

80 *Mint* v. *Good* [1951] 1 K.B. 517 (public nuisance).

81 *Brew Bros* v. *Snax* [1970] 1 Q.B. 612.

82 *Wilchik* v. *Marks* [1934] 2 K.B. 56.

83 [1940] 1 K.B. 229; see further p. 629 below.

84 *Clearlite Holdings Ltd* v. *Auckland City Corporation* [1976] 2 N.Z.L.R. 729; *Kraemers* v. *A-G of Tasmania* [1966] Tas.S.R. 113.

85 This was the explanation preferred by Samuels J.A. in *Fennell* v. *Robson Excavations Pty Ltd* [1977] 2 N.S.W.L.R. 486.

Excavations[86] the contractor was held liable even though the danger created by the excavation did not materialize until six months after the work was complete, by which time the contractor had left the land and had lost any power to enter and abate the nuisance.

In non-repair cases the relevant control resides not over creation but over abatement of the nuisance. This is true, too, of the liability of an occupier for adoption or continuance of a nuisance created by another, for example, a tenant or a trespasser or a predecessor in title.[87] An occupier adopts (i.e. actively makes use of) or continues (i.e. passively tolerates) a nuisance, so far as the law is concerned, if he knows or ought to know of its existence and fails to take reasonable steps to bring it to an end. Liability for adoption or continuance is, therefore, essentially liability for negligently allowing a nuisance to remain on the land.[88] In other words, liability for adoption or continuance of nuisance is a form of liability for nonfeasance.

Sometimes liability can be imposed on a defendant for the creation of a nuisance by someone else over whom he has control,[89] independently of adoption or continuance of the nuisance by the defendant. Liability can accrue for allowing crowds to gather on one's land even if they are total strangers. The possibility of suing the 'controller' obviates difficulties of proof and enforcement which would arise if actions were brought against individual troublemakers. On the other hand, it has been held that a person who merely encourages another to do acts which constitute a nuisance does not thereby incur liability for nuisance.[90] A landlord is not, by and large, personally liable for nuisances created by his tenants. In *Smith* v. *Scott*[91] a local authority placed in a house next to the plaintiff's tenants who were known to be unruly and likely to commit a nuisance. It was held that the authority could not be liable unless it had authorized the nuisance or unless the creation of a nuisance was, to the authority's knowledge, so highly likely that the authority must be taken impliedly to have authorized it. On the other hand, it has been held that an occupier of land may be liable for nuisances created by independent contractors working on the land, or by persons using the land with the occupier's permission, if their authorized activities create a 'special risk of nuisance';[92]

---

86 ibid.; cf. *Thynne* v. *Petrie* [1975] Qd.R. 260.

87 *Sedleigh-Denfield* v. *O'Callaghan* [1940] A.C. 880; *Torette House Pty Ltd* v. *Berkman* (1939-40) 62 C.L.R. 637; *Cartwright* v. *McLaine & Long Pty Ltd* (1979) 24 A.L.R. 97 (public nuisance); *Burchett* v. *Commissioner for Railways* [1958] S.R.(N.S.W.) 366.

88 *Montana Hotels Pty Ltd* v. *Fasson Pty Ltd* (1986) 69 A.L.R. 258.

89 e.g. *Stewart* v. *Enfield M.C.* (1915) 15 S.R.(N.S.W.) 204; *Matheson* v. *Northcote College Board of Governors* [1975] 2 N.Z.L.R. 106; contrast *Hall* v. *Beckenham Corporation* [1949] 1 K.B. 716.

90 *Casley-Smith* v. *F.S. Evans & Sons Pty Ltd* (1988) 67 L.G.R.A. 108, 141.

91 [1973] Ch. 314; cf. *Winter* v. *Baker* (1887) 3 T.L.R. 569.

92 *De Jager* v. *Payneham and Magill Lodges Hall Incorporated* (1984) 36 S.A.S.R. 498 (hall hired for weddings and other functions which created noise nuisance). The liability is primary, not vicarious, and is noteworthy because, although it is liability for the acts of another, it is strict in the sense that it is no defence that the occupier took all possible precautions to prevent the nuisance occurring. The stress in *Smith* v. *Scott* (previous note) on 'authorization' suggests that the liability contemplated in that case would be vicarious.

or if the nuisance was an 'ordinary' or 'natural' or 'necessary' consequence of the permitted activity.[93]

It is not clear that all of these decisions are consistent with one another, and the general issue of nuisance liability for the acts of third parties would benefit from detailed attention by an appellate court. The basic issue underlying these cases concerns when one person should be under an obligation to take positive steps to prevent another creating a nuisance. It is clear that in certain circumstances a landowner can be liable in nuisance (and negligence) for failure to prevent physical damage to neighbouring property by the operation of natural forces on his land.[94] But where the immediate cause of the nuisance is human conduct of a third party, more difficult issues arise.[95] Should a landowner be expected to exercise more control over the conduct of persons whom he allows on to his land than we expect to be exercised in cases where the relationship of occupier and visitor does not exist?

6. DEFENCES

(a) Prescription A private nuisance can be legalized 'by prescription' if it continues for a certain period, provided the party suffering it was in a position either physically to prevent it or to sue on it but refrained to do either.[96] This defence is of very little importance in Australia because the right to commit a nuisance can only be acquired by prescription if it could, in land law, amount to an easement which could be acquired by prescription. Under the Torrens system in most States (as well as in New Zealand) easements cannot be acquired in this way.[97]

(b) 'Coming to the nuisance' It is no defence for the defendant to say that the plaintiff brought his trouble upon himself by moving into premises so close to the defendant's activities that he would inevitably be affected by the defendant's activities where no one had been affected before.[98] However, this statement of the position rather disguises the significance of the rule. It is not the case that as a result of the rule a plaintiff can, for example, by setting up a dwelling in an industrial area, force factories to close down. Any question of defence to nuisance only arises if there is a nuisance, and this depends partly on whether the activities carried on in a locality are unreasonable given the nature of the locality. So if the character of a locality is well fixed and established it cannot be rendered unlawful by a person simply deciding to pursue some incompatible activity in the area. Today, of course, incompatibility of use is regulated chiefly by zoning laws, but these tend to be directed primarily

93 *Tetley* v. *Chitty* [1986] 1 All E.R. 663
94 See p. 383 above.
95 Cf. p. 385 above.
96 *Sturges* v. *Bridgman* (1879) 11 Ch.D. 852.
97 See E.A. Francis *Torrens Title in Australasia* (Sydney, 1972) Vol. 1 pp. 530-3. *Re* the position in Victoria see *Stoneman* v. *Lyons* (1975) 133 C.L.R. 550.
98 *Miller* v. *Jackson* [1977] Q.B. 966.

at preventing the introduction of potentially nuisance-creating activities into nuisance-sensitive areas, whereas the coming-to-the-nuisance rule is concerned conversely with the introduction of sensitive uses into areas devoted to potentially nuisance-creating activities.

The other situation covered by the rule is one where a sensitive use, such as residence, by reason of urban growth encroaches on an area formerly isolated and devoted to a potentially nuisance-creating activity. Zoning and planning regulations are also designed to prevent this sort of situation. But mistakes can be made, and this is where the law of nuisance may become relevant. In *Miller* v. *Jackson*[99] a playing-field on which cricket was played in the summer was surrounded by fields until 1970, when a row of houses was built adjacent to it. Despite a high wall, balls hit beyond the boundary fell into the rear gardens of the houses and on to or against the buildings. Clearly the planning authority made a mistake in allowing houses to be built so close to the playing-field, and the common law of nuisance was the only available mechanism by which an *ad hoc* rectification of the mistake could be achieved. The inhabitants wanted the cricket club to find another ground, and two of the three judges held that the defendant could not plead that the plaintiff had come to the nuisance. But in the result a majority refused to grant an injunction and awarded a modest sum of damages to cover all past and future loss. The other main actor in this drama, the developer who built the houses, was, of course, absent from the proceedings. One might think, however, that its position would be relevant if, as a result of their proximity to the ground, the houses were worth less than what the purchaser paid for them. Whether the purchasers should be able to recover against the developers (and whether, in turn, the developers would have a claim against the planning authority) are most difficult questions, but they do serve to show how nuisance problems often implicate more persons than just the immediate landowners.

(c) **Statutory Authorization** A plea of statutory authorization[100] is in substance a plea of public interest. Sometimes the interests of private individuals in the use and enjoyment of their land have to be subordinated to the wider interests of the public. For example, the inhabitants of an area may have to put up with a certain amount of noise and smells from an oil refinery which would, without the statutory authorization, amount to a common law nuisance, for the sake of providing the community with what the legislature has decided are necessary supplies of fuel products.[101] The law of private nuisance is designed primarily to circumscribe the activities of private citizens, and there are many essential and desirable public works which would be practically impossible if they had to be performed within the strictures imposed by the law of nuisance.

The basic principle is that a nuisance is authorized by statute if it is an

99 [1977] Q.B. 966.
100 S. Kneebone (1986) 10 *Adel. L.R.* 472.
101 *Allen* v. *Gulf Oil Refining Ltd* [1981] A.C. 1001.

inevitable consequence of[102] an activity which is expressly or impliedly authorized by statute. In determining whether an activity is authorized, statutes have to be interpreted in a commonsense way. For example, a statute which expressly authorizes the *construction* of an oil refinery must be taken as impliedly authorizing the *operation* of that refinery if the obvious intent of the legislature is not to be defeated.[103] But a statute will not be read as authorizing unnecessary acts.[104]

It is for the defendant to establish that the nuisance was inevitable.[105] But when will a nuisance be treated as 'inevitable'? To answer this question, it is necessary to draw a distinction between provisions which require a specified activity to be carried on and provisions which permit but do not require a specified activity to be carried on. In the former type of case, any nuisance which results from the conduct of the activity will be authorized unless it is the result of negligence on the part of the person conducting the activity.[106] In such cases there is no separate requirement of inevitability; the requirement that the activity be carried on renders its consequences inevitable, provided they could not have been avoided by the exercise of reasonable care. In the latter type of case, by contrast, the basic presumption is that the legislature intended the activity to be carried on without creating a nuisance. In such cases, therefore, the defendant must show not only that it acted without negligence, but also that that which the legislature authorized could not be done without creating a nuisance.[107] However, it is not clear how literally the phrase 'could not be done without creating a nuisance' is to be taken. In *Allen* v. *Gulf Oil*[108] Lord Edmund-Davies said that to prove inevitability the defendant would have to show that the injury could not have been avoided no matter how much was spent on precautions. The problem created by this interpretation is that it could effectively prevent authorized activities being carried on at all. By contrast, in *Carmichael* v. *Sutherland S.C.*[109] Helsham J. seems to have equated inevitability with the results of taking reasonable care, not in conducting an activity but in deciding whether to engage in the activity, or where, when, how and so on. In this view, inevitability is a relative concept, to be judged in the light of the current state of technology, the location of the activity and the expense of precautions, all viewed in the light of the interests of the defendant and the plaintiff and taking into

---

102 Or 'necessarily incidental to': *Howard* v. *Bega Municipal Council* (1916) 16 S.R.(N.S.W.) 138.

103 *Allen* v. *Gulf Oil*; cf. *Fullarton* v. *North Melbourne Electric Tramway & Lighting Co.* (1916) 21 C.L.R. 181; *Archibald* v. *Cabramatta and Canley Vale M.C.* (1930) 10 L.G.R. 23.

104 e.g. *Rudd* v. *Hornsby Shire Council* (1975) 31 L.G.R.A. 120.

105 *Manchester Corporation* v. *Farnworth* [1930] A.C. 171, 182 *per* Viscount Dunedin; *Casley-Smith* v. *F.S. Evans & Sons Pty Ltd* (1988) 67 L.G.R.A. 108, 138-9.

106 e.g. *R.* v. *White* (1910) 12 W.A.L.R. 31; cf. *Hammond* v. *Vestry of St Pancras* (1874) L.R. 9 C.P. 316; *Tock* v. *St John's Metropolitan Area Board* (1989) 64 D.L.R. (4th) 620, 629.

107 *Metropolitan Asylum District (Managers of)* v. *Hill* (1881) 6 App.Cas. 193; *McDonald* v. *Shire of Coburg* (1866) 13 V.L.R. 268; *Nalder* v. *Commissioner for Railways* [1983] 1 Qd.R. 260.

108 [1981] A.C. 1001, 1015.

109 (1972) 25 L.G.R.A. 434, 444; see also *Rudd* v. *Hornsby S.C.* (1975) 31 L.G.R.A. 120, 137; *Manchester Corporation* v. *Farnworth* [1930] A.C. 171.

account the social importance of their respective land uses. According to this interpretation, a nuisance might not be inevitable even if the authorized activity was conducted with all reasonable care if, for example, it could have been sited in a place where it would not have caused a nuisance. But the converse is not true: if an activity has been negligently conducted, any nuisance produced by it cannot be inevitable.

If we accept that a nuisance will be treated as inevitable if it could not have been avoided by the exercise of reasonable care, then it would be simpler to equate the defence of statutory authorization with a plea of no-negligence either in deciding on works or in executing them, whichever is appropriate. If the works executed were required by statute the defendant would need to show that they were done carefully. If the defendant was given by the statute some element of choice as to what to do or how to do it, then the authorization defence would entail a plea of no-negligence both in deciding what to do and in doing it. If the defendant were a public authority it might also be able to plead policy immunity from having the reasonableness of its actions judged by a court.[110] Such a plea would arise more usually in relation to the process of deciding what to do than in relation to the execution of the decision.

The discussion so far has assumed that the statute in question says nothing explicitly about the liability of the undertaker of the authorized activity. But a statute may contain a provision (a 'nuisance clause') which expressly imposes or preserves liability for nuisance. According to the House of Lords, such a provision does not impose liability for the consequences of the conduct of a required activity provided it was carried on without negligence; but under such a provision a defendant will be liable for a nuisance resulting from the conduct of a permitted (but not required) activity even if it acted without negligence.[111] In this context, 'without negligence' means 'with all reasonable regard and care for the interests of other persons'. Under a nuisance clause, therefore, a defendant can be liable even for nuisances which are unavoidable by taking reasonable care in planning and executing authorized works.[112]

Some statutes make express provision for the payment of compensation to persons injured by the conduct of authorized activities. If there is such a provision and the defendant's conduct falls within its terms, the plaintiff will be entitled only to such compensation as the provision specifies. But if the defendant's conduct is not covered by the compensation provision, then it may be liable at common law unless the nuisance created was an inevitable consequence of doing that which the legislature had authorized[113] (assuming the statute does not contain a nuisance clause).

The basic issue underlying these rules is that of who should bear the

---

110 Chapter 20 below.

111 *Department of Transport* v. *North West Water Authority* [1984] A.C. 336, 334, 359-60.

112 But there is some authority the other way: e.g. *Fullarton* v. *North Melbourne etc. Co.* (1916) 21 C.L.R. 181, 188 *per* Griffith C.J.; *Powrie* v. *Nelson City Corporation* [1976] 2 N.Z.L.R. 247.

113 *Dubois* v. *District Council of Noarlunga* (1959) 59 L.G.R.A. 53; *Foxlee* v. *Proserpine Shire River Improvement Trust* (1989) 67 L.Q.R.A. 395; *Rushcutters Investments Pty Ltd* v. *Water Board* (1989) 68 L.G.R.A. 128.

cost of inevitable adverse consequences of socially desirable activities. The common law places this cost on the victim and leaves it to the legislature to shift the cost on to the undertaker either by the use of a nuisance clause or a compensation clause. It can be argued, however, that although people who suffer for the sake of socially desirable activities should not be able to prevent such activities proceeding (by obtaining an injunction), they should be entitled to be compensated by those who benefit, even if the injury was a necessary concomitant of the authorized activity. The Supreme Court of Canada has recently moved in this direction by holding that a plea of statutory authorization cannot succeed in cases where the nuisance-causing activity was permitted but not required.[114] This distinction between permitted and required activities is embedded in Australian law, but it can be criticized on the ground that the beneficiaries of an activity should pay the costs of nuisances generated by it even if the activity was mandatory.[115] Of course, it would still be open to the legislature to provide expressly that there should be no liability for nuisance and, in doing so, to decide the extent to which individuals should be expected to bear loss for the sake of some wider interest.

7. Remedies

(a) Abatement The law in certain circumstances gives the plaintiff a right of self-help called abatement, that is, the right to take steps to put an end to the nuisance even though such steps might amount to a legal wrong (such as trespass).[116] If, in order to abate the nuisance, the plaintiff needs to enter the defendant's land, he must usually give notice to the defendant of his intention to enter. But notice of intention to abate may not be necessary if the plaintiff can abate without entering the defendant's land (for example, lopping off the overhanging branches of a tree)[117]; or if the defendant was the original creator of a nuisance consisting of the placing of 'filth' on his land, or if there is such an immediate danger to health or safety that it is unsafe to wait until notice is given, or if the nuisance is the result of default by the defendant in performing a legal duty to remove the 'filth'.[118] A right of abatement arises even before damage has been suffered (that is, it is available as a preventive measure).

The law does not favour abatement in preference to legal action, and if it involves entering the land of another it requires strong justification.

---

114 *Tock* v. *St John's Metropolitan Area Board* (1989) 64 D.L.R. (4th) 620.

115 cf. judgment of La Forest J. in *Tock* (1989) 64 D.L.R. (4th) 620. This judge would, in effect, abolish the defence of statutory authorization.

116 But rebuilding a bridge which a landowner had allowed to fall into disrepair would not qualify as abatement: *Campbell Davys* v. *Lloyd* [1901] 2 Ch. 518. Nor would replacing clay pipes with plastic ones to prevent damage by nuisance-creating tree roots: *Young* v. *Wheeler* [1987] Aust. Torts Reports 68,966. The right to abate cannot justify assaulting someone in an attempt to bring to an end an obstruction of access to land: *Richter* v. *Risby* (1987) 27 A. Crim. R. 68.

117 *Lemmon* v. *Webb* [1895] A.C. 1. But see *Jamieson's Towing & Salvage Ltd* v. *Murray* [1984] 2 N.Z.L.R. 144.

118 *Jones* v. *Williams* (1843) 11 M. & W. 176.

Once a right of abatement has been exercised, there can be no action in respect of damage allegedly arising thereafter from the nuisance.[119] The fact that the plaintiff in a nuisance action could have abated the nuisance is no ground for refusing to award an injunction.[120] Abatement is classified as a 'remedy' because it involves the doing of acts which would be unlawful if not sanctioned by the law. In this way, it differs from simply settling a claim in nuisance without recourse to the courts.

(b) Injunctions

(i) *Availability*: The injunction is the primary remedy for nuisance in English law. The injunction may be either prohibitory (or 'negative') or mandatory. As the names suggest, a prohibitory injunction orders the defendant to cease doing something while a mandatory injunction orders him to do some positive act. Usually a prohibitory injunction will simply order the defendant to refrain from causing a nuisance, and it will then be up to him to modify his operations in whatever way is necessary to achieve this end, or to bring them to an end if this is not possible. It is no answer to a claim for an injunction for the defendant to say that he will have to cease his activity in order to comply with it. On the other hand, it is open to him, once the injunction has been granted, to seek to buy it off by bargaining with the plaintiff for a release from it in return for a payment of money.[121] In some cases the injunction may be more detailed. For example, it may specify hours when mechanical drills may be used on a building site;[122] or restrict the opening hours of a playground and the age of the children who might use it;[123] or specify the number and type of meetings which a speed-boat club could hold on a particular lake.[124] There is a general principle governing the award of injunctions that the injunction should tell the defendant clearly what must be done to comply with it, and that it must be capable of being easily policed; the very precise and detailed terms of the above injunctions achieve this end.

---

119 For the last two sentences see *Traian* v. *Ware* [1957] V.R. 200. The latter sentence does not represent the view of Scrutton L.J.: *Job Edwards Ltd* v. *Proprietors of Birmingham Navigations* [1924] 1 K.B. 341, 356. Wood J. in *Young* v. *Wheeler* [1987] Aust. Torts Reports 68,966, 68,971 said that damages may possibly be recovered for loss suffered before the abatement (approved in *City of Richmond* v. *Scantlebury* [1991] 2 V.R. 38). There is conflicting authority on the question of whether the plaintiff can recover costs of abatement already incurred: in *Tate & Lyle Industries Ltd* v. *Greater London Council* [1983] 2 A.C. 509 the plaintiff was compensated for the cost of abatement, but Wood J. *Young* v. *Wheeler* (above) said that such costs are irrecoverable. In *Proprietors of Strata Plan 14198* v. *Cowell* (1989) 24 N.S.W.L.R. 478, 487 Hodgson J. said that the costs of abatement could be recovered if they were incurred in reasonable mitigation of loss. The cost of abatement in the future may be recovered by claiming damages in lieu of an injunction: *Barbagallo* v. *J. & F. Catelan Pty Ltd* [1986] 1 Qd.R. 245, 269 *per* Thomas J. See also *City of Richmond* v. *Scantlebury* [1991] 2 V.R. 38.

120 *Lawlor* v. *Johnston* [1905] V.L.R. 714.

121 See e.g. *York Bros (Trading) Pty Ltd* v. *Commissioner of Main Roads* [1983] 1 N.S.W.L.R. 391, 402 (public nuisance).

122 *Daily Telegraph Co. Ltd* v. *Stuart* (1928) 28 S.R.(N.S.W.) 291.

123 *Dunton* v. *Dover District Council* (1977) 76 L.G.R. 87.

124 *Kennaway* v. *Thompson* [1981] Q.B. 88.

Where the plaintiff has established that the defendant has unreasonably interfered with the use and enjoyment of his land and that the interference is likely to be repeated, he is *prima facie* entitled to an injunction to restrain this interference with his rights.[125] But a court will not impose on anyone an obligation to do something which is impossible or unlawful or cannot be enforced.[126] This principle might seem to conflict with the statement made earlier that it is no answer to a claim for an injunction for a defendant who is creating a nuisance to say that he will have to cease his activity if the injunction is granted. The reconciliation of the two principles seems to lie in recognizing implicit underlying value judgments. If the defendant's activity is of sufficient social importance the court will want to preserve the activity, but in other cases it may be willing to see it disappear, at least from the place where the defendant is conducting it.

The court also has power in exceptional cases[127] to award damages for future loss in lieu of an injunction,[128] whether negative or mandatory. Unless the plaintiff claims damages in lieu, it is for the defendant to establish that they ought to be awarded in preference to an injunction.[129] The function of such damages is to compensate the plaintiff for all the future effects of the nuisance; once they have been paid, the defendant has the right to continue the nuisance-creating conduct; he has, in effect, been allowed to buy the right to commit the nuisance. There are two basic conditions for an award of damages in lieu of an injunction: that damages will be an adequate remedy, and that to award an injunction would be unfair to the defendant.[130] Damages will be adequate if the injury to the plaintiff's rights is small, can be estimated in money and can be compensated for by a small monetary payment.[131] The fact that the plaintiff has, before seeking an injunction, accepted monetary payments will go a long way to establishing that damages are an adequate remedy.[132]

As for unfairness to the defendant, in *Sampson* v. *Hodson-Pressinger*[133] the first defendant was the tenant of a flat which had a tiled terrace above the kitchen, bathroom and sitting room of the flat below. The noise created by use of the terrace was held to be a nuisance actionable at the suit of the lower tenant. But as the terrace had been created by the landlord it was held that it would be unfair to award an injunction against the tenant, especially since something could apparently be done to abate the

125 *Morris* v. *Redland Bricks Ltd* [1970] A.C. 652,664; *Pride of Derby & Derbyshire Angling Association Ltd* v. *British Celanese Ltd* [1953] Ch. 149, 181 *per* Evershed M.R.; *Kennaway* v. *Thompson* [1981] Q.B. 88.

126 *Pride of Derby etc.* v. *British Celanese* [1953] Ch. 149; *Vincent* v. *Peacock* [1973] N.S.W.L.R. 466.

127 *Shelfer* v. *City of London Electric Lighting Co.* [1895] 1 Ch. 287; *Kennaway* v. *Thompson* [1981] Q.B. 88.

128 Such damages are sometimes called 'equitable damages' because the injunction was a remedy originally only available in the courts of equity.

129 *McKinnon* v. *Walker* [1951] D.L.R. 577.

130 *Shelfer* v. *City of London Electric Lighting Co.* [1895] 1 Ch. 287.

131 *Shelfer.*

132 But see *McKinnon Industries* v. *Walker* [1951] D.L.R. 577.

133 [1981] 3 All E.R. 710.

noise nuisance, and the plaintiff was willing to accept damages. Delay on the part of the plaintiff in seeking an injunction can justify a refusal to award it, but perhaps only if the defendant did not know that what he was doing was a nuisance but the plaintiff did, and then stood by and let him do it and incur expense.[134] The defendant might by his own behaviour disentitle himself from seeking damages in lieu of an injunction, for example, by acting in reckless disregard of the plaintiff's rights.[135]

The mere fact that the conditions for the award of damages are not met, however, does not necessarily mean that an injunction will be awarded. In every case the court has a discretion whether or not to award an injunction, and if the defendant has not acted unfairly or in an unneighbourly spirit, or if there was a genuine dispute as to whether his actions amounted to a nuisance, or if the plaintiff has in some way acquiesced in what the defendant was doing, the court might exercise its discretion not to award an injunction.[136]

In *Miller* v. *Jackson*[137] Lord Denning M.R. and Cumming-Bruce L.J. held that the decision whether to award an injunction or damages in lieu depended on a balancing of the interests of the two parties and of the public interest. The reference to the public interest was rejected by the Court of Appeal in *Kennaway* v. *Thompson*,[138] which reaffirmed that an injunction was to be refused only in exceptional circumstances and that the public interest was not relevant. However, in practice this difference of approach may not be of much importance. In *Miller* v. *Jackson* the public interest was that of the villagers as a whole, whose interest was probably seen as much the same as that of the cricket club—that cricket should continue to be played. In *Kennaway* the court took account of the interests of the club, which no doubt included the interests of all those who followed its activities, whether as members or not.

(ii) *Postponement of injunction:* An injunction may be awarded to take effect immediately, or its operation may be deferred, usually subject to an undertaking by the defendant to pay damages for any injury inflicted during the period of the suspension. If no such undertaking is required, the plaintiff will have to bear any intervening damage as a sort of payment for the injunction when it comes into force. The purpose of a deferment is usually[139] to enable the defendant to find ways of conducting its operations without committing a nuisance.[140] It is for the defendant to satisfy the court that a deferment ought to be granted.[141]

(iii) *Interlocutory and* quia timet *injunctions:* In certain circumstances

---

134 *Lawlor* v. *Johnston* [1905] V.L.R. 714.

135 *Shelfer* [1895] 1 Ch. 287; *John Trenberth Ltd* v. *National Westminster Bank Ltd* (1980) 39 P. & C.R. 104 (trespass); *Pugh* v. *Howells* (1984) 48 P. & C.R. 298.

136 *Fishenden* v. *Higgs & Hill Ltd* [1935] All E.R. 435.

137 [1977] Q.B. 966.

138 [1981] Q.B. 88.

139 But for a different reason for postponement see *Taylor* v. *City of Perth* (1988) Aust.Torts Reports 80-191.

140 *Stollmeyer* v. *Trinidad Lake Petroleum Petroleum Co. Ltd* [1918] A.C. 485.

141 *Pride of Derby etc.* v. *British Celanese* [1953] Ch. 149.

an interlocutory injunction may be awarded. This is a temporary injunction which restrains the defendant pending conclusive settlement of the rights of the parties at a full trial.[142] (An injunction which finally settles the rights of the parties is called a final or perpetual injunction.) Students are referred to specialized works on equitable remedies for more details.[143] Sometimes a court will award what is known as a *quia timet* injunction. A cause of action in nuisance for damages is not complete until damage has been suffered, but in certain exceptional circumstances an injunction can be awarded in anticipation of damage being inflicted in the near future. Because damage has not yet occurred, *quia timet* injunctions are often mandatory in form requiring the defendant to take steps to prevent damage occurring.[144] But *quia timet* injunctions can be negative in form.[145] A *quia timet* injunction may be awarded either before any injury at all has been inflicted on the plaintiff, or where the plaintiff has exhausted his rights of action in respect of an injury already inflicted but he anticipates more injury in the future.[146] Damages may be awarded in lieu of a *quia timet* injunction;[147] such damages are primarily, but not exclusively, designed to cover the cost of abating the nuisance,[148] but such damages may not be an adequate substitute for an injunction if, for example, the injunction is mandatory and the plaintiff has no right to go on to the defendant's land and do the remedial works himself.

In order to obtain a *quia timet* injunction the plaintiff must normally prove that there is an imminent danger of injury of a substantial kind or that the apprehended injury, if it comes, will be irreparable,[149] although it has been said that neither of these requirements is crucial or indispensable.[150] The cost of satisfying the injunction is also relevant, especially where it is mandatory. If the defendant has acted unreasonably or wantonly towards a neighbour, he may be ordered to do work even if the cost is out of all proportion to the benefit to the plaintiff. But if the defendant has acted reasonably though wrongly, cost is important because no legal wrong may ever occur, or not on the scale anticipated; but if it does, the plaintiff will have all his legal and equitable rights in respect of it. The court can consider requiring the defendant to do works which may lessen rather than eliminate the danger. The injunction should be in very clear terms so that the defendant knows what has to be done. It is no good ordering him to *ensure* that no damage will occur if no one knows what would have to be done to achieve this.[151]

---

142 The leading case is *American Cyanamid Co.* v. *Ethicon Ltd* [1975] A.C. 396.
143 I.C.F. Spry *Equitable Remedies* 4th edn (London, 1990) pp. 437ff.
144 e.g. *Hooper* v. *Rogers* [1975] Ch. 43; cf. *Grocott* v. *Ayson* [1975] 2 N.Z.L.R. 586.
145 e.g. *Grasso* v. *Love* [1980] V.R. 163.
146 *Morris* v. *Redland Bricks Ltd* [1970] A.C. 625.
147 By this route, damages can be recovered before any loss has been suffered: *Barbagallo* v. *Catelan* [1986] 1 Qd.R. 245.
148 As to what would happen if the plaintiff did not use the damages for this purpose, see *Barbagallo* v. *Catelan* [1986] 1 Qd.R. 245, 259 *per* McPherson J.
149 *Fletcher* v. *Bealey* (1885) 28 Ch.D. 688; *Grasso* v. *Love* [1980] V.R. 163; *Morris* v. *Redland Bricks* [1970] A.C. 625.
150 *Grocott* v. *Ayson* [1975] 2 N.Z.L.R. 586.
151 For all this see *Morris* v. *Redland Bricks* [1970] A.C. 625.

(iv) *The price of an injunction:* Finally, it is worth noting that whereas the defendant is often required to 'purchase' the right to commit a nuisance by paying damages, Anglo-Australian courts have not so far adopted the course followed by one American court of requiring the plaintiff to compensate the defendant for having to give up a nuisance-creating activity. In *Spur Industries Inc.* v. *Del E. Webb Dev't Co.*[152] the defendant set up a cattle-feeding operation well outside city limits. The plaintiff bought up nearby land for development as a retirement village and sought to enjoin the defendant's operation. It was held that the defendant had committed a nuisance; but since the plaintiff had brought into a previously agricultural area a residential population to the foreseeable detriment of the defendant, the plaintiff was required to indemnify the defendant for the reasonable cost of moving or closing down. The plaintiff took advantage of the availability of large tracts of cheap land and should in fairness buy the defendant out. This is a good compromise solution (suitable for some cases) to the problem of plaintiffs coming to the nuisance. If a defendant conducting a socially desirable activity can be expected to compensate the plaintiff out of his profits, why should a plaintiff who comes to the nuisance not do the same?

(c) **Damages** We have just considered in some detail the award of (equitable) damages for future loss in lieu of an injunction. Besides such damages, a court in a nuisance action may also award damages (often called 'common law damages') for past loss, either alone, if the nuisance has ceased, or together with an injunction or damages in lieu if it is continuing. A cause of action in nuisance for common law damages is not complete until damage has been suffered, and in the case of continuing nuisances, each new and separate infliction of damage gives a fresh cause of action.[153] Common law damages compensate only for loss already suffered; there is authority for the view that an award of such damages cannot include the cost of abating the nuisance,[154] and the defendant, by paying them, does not acquire the right to continue the nuisance-creating conduct. By contrast, an award of equitable damages can, as we have seen, include the cost of abatement and can compensate the plaintiff for all the future effects of a continuing nuisance.

Because nuisance is an interference with the use and enjoyment of land, doubts have from time to time been raised as to the existence of a right of recovery for certain losses, such as personal injury[155] and nervous shock.[156] However, the position now appears to be that provided the loss suffered was a foreseeable result of the nuisance, it is recoverable. So, for example, damages may be recovered for damage to chattels[157] and for loss of profits

152 (1972) 494 P. 2d 700.
153 *Manson* v. *Shire of Maffra* (1881) 7 V.L.R.(L.) 364.
154 See p. 613 above.
155 M. Davies (1990) 20 *U.W.A.L.R.* 129.
156 *Evans* v. *Finn* (1904) 4 S.R.(N.S.W.) 297.
157 *Howard Electric Ltd* v. *A.J. Mooney Ltd* [1974] 2 N.Z.L.R. 762.

which would otherwise have been earned from use of the land;[158] as well as for consequential pecuniary[159] and non-pecuniary[160] loss.

Often a nuisance will diminish the value of property. In strict theory, diminution in value is not *per se* a nuisance, but a consequence of the interference with use and enjoyment which constitutes the nuisance. So diminution in value is not compensated for as such, but can provide evidence of the seriousness of the nuisance and hence of the appropriate measure of damages.[161] The question of diminution in value is to be looked at as it would present itself to the hypothetical prudent purchaser (or tenant) capable of appreciating the effect of the nuisance on the value of the property and what the position would have been if the nuisance had not been committed.[162] In some cases, of course, the property may already have been sold or leased at the lower figure. The lower rent would normally fix the quantum of the injury to a lessor's reversionary interest. A vendor, although having no interest in the land as at the date of trial entitling him to sue in nuisance, *ex hypothesi* had such an interest at the date the nuisance caused the diminution in value giving rise to the cause of action, and so could recover.

In this context, it is worth specifically noting that damages for purely economic loss are recoverable in an action for private nuisance; and the plaintiff apparently is not required to satisfy the rather stringent conditions for the recovery of damages for such loss which apply to actions in negligence. The rationale for this difference of approach would appear to lie in the fact that a private nuisance is an interference with *rights* over land, and that once such an interference has been established, the damage caused by the nuisance merely quantifies the interference. But the difference is apt to create anomalies, since many fact situations could give rise to actions in negligence *and* nuisance.

In cases where the nuisance causes interference with comfort and amenities but no diminution in the value of the plaintiff's land, the task of assessment of damages is extremely difficult and has been analogized to calculating damages for loss of the amenities of life in a personal injury action. So the sum awarded should be moderate and represent reasonable compensation judged in the light of the interests of both of the parties.[163]

Despite a contrary view,[164] there is some authority for the proposition that aggravated damages may be awarded in a nuisance action if, for example, the defendant removes lateral support from the plaintiff's land for his own financial aggrandisement.[165]

---

158 *Campbell* v. *Paddington Corporation* [1911] 1 K.B. 869; *Trappa Holdings Ltd* v. *District of Surrey* (1978) 78 D.L.R. (3d) 107; *Page Motors Ltd* v. *Epsom & Ewell B.C.* (1982) 80 L.G.R. 337.

159 *Barbagallo* v. *Catelan* [1986] 1 Qd.R. 245, 248 *per* McPherson J.

160 *Barbagallo* v. *Catelan* [1986] 1 Qd.R. 245, 263 *per* Thomas J.

161 *Soltau* v. *De Held* (1851) 2 Sim. (N.S.) 133, 158; *McKenzie* v. *Powley* [1916] S.A.L.R. 1.

162 *Owen* v. *John L. Norris Holdings Pty Ltd* [1964] N.S.W.R. 1337.

163 See generally *Bone* v. *Seale* [1975] 1 W.L.R. 797; *Oldham* v. *Lawson (No. 1)* [1976] V.R. 654.

164 *Oldham* v. *Lawson (No. 1)* [1976] V.R. 654, 658-9.

165 *Minter* v. *Eacott* (1952) 69 W.N. (N.S.W.) 93; see also *Municipal Council of Willoughby* v. *Halstead* (1916) 22 C.L.R. 352.

8. Nuisance and Negligence

The relationship between nuisance and negligence is one of the most obscure issues in the modern law of torts. In the first place, negligence and nuisance are said to be two separate torts, which perhaps means no more than that there are identifiably distinct and different sets of rules recognized by the law which may apply to the same, or very similar, fact situations, but which focus on different elements of those fact situations in deciding whether the defendant ought to be held liable. The two sets of rules are not mutually exclusive; so a defendant may be held liable in both negligence and nuisance on the same facts.[166] Further, in some cases it is possible to say that if an action in negligence would fail, so would an action in nuisance.[167] Indeed, courts have become unwilling to distinguish clearly between nuisance and negligence.[168] One clear difference between negligence and nuisance is that the plaintiff in nuisance does not have to prove that the defendant owed him duty of care.[169] On the other hand, the idea of reasonableness which lies at the heart of the tort of nuisance is very similar to the concept of reasonableness in negligence. Both essentially involve a cost-benefit analysis. The main difference is that in negligence the question is whether particular *acts* of the defendant were reasonable, whereas in nuisance the question is whether the defendant's activity—his use of land—was reasonable. In negligence actions the courts are somewhat unwilling to pronounce upon the reasonableness of complete systems and activities. There is no obvious reason for this difference of approach.

More difficult is the question of the role that negligence, in the sense of a failure to take reasonable precautions against foreseeable risks of injury, plays in the tort of nuisance. The question being asked here is not whether a defendant liable in nuisance may also be liable, on the same facts, in negligence; he clearly may be liable in both torts. Rather, the question is whether the plaintiff in nuisance ever has to establish that the defendant was negligent in order to succeed, or whether the defendant ever has to disprove negligence in order to escape liability. There are authorities which support answering this question in the negative.[170] The force of these authorities is, however, by no means clear. In *The Wagon Mound (No. 2)*[171] it was said that the test of remoteness in nuisance is foreseeability. The liability of a landlord for nuisances on the demised premises at the time they were let or for nuisances developing later depends on knowledge or means of knowledge on the part of the landlord and failure by him to exercise this control over the premises to abate the nuisance; except, perhaps, in the case of man-made premises on the highway falling into

166 e.g. *Miller* v. *Jackson* [1977] Q.B. 966, 985-6 *per* Geoffrey Lane L.J.
167 *Bolton* v. *Stone* [1951] A.C. 850, 860 *per* Lord Porter; 868 *per* Lord Reid.
168 *Miller* v. *Jackson* [1977] Q.B. 966, 985-6; *Leakey* v. *National Trust* [1980] Q.B. 485.
169 *Spicer* v. *Smee* [1946] 1 All E.R. 489, 493.
170 e.g. *Paxhaven Holdings* v. *A-G* [1974] 2 N.Z.L.R. 185; *Clearlite Holdings* v. *Auckland City Corp.* [1976] N.Z.L.R. 729 (on which see Todd *et al. Law of Torts in New Zealand* (Sydney, 1991) pp. 420-1; *Hargrave* v. *Goldman* (1963) 110 C.L.R. 40, 62 *per* Windeyer J.; *Don Brass Foundry Pty Ltd* v. *Stead* (1948) 48 S.R.(N.S.W.) 482, 483 *per* Jordan C.J.
171 [1967] 1 A.C. 617.

disrepair.[172] Liability for the adoption or continuance of nuisances created by another depends on knowledge or means of knowledge and failure to do anything to abate the nuisance.[173] Liability in public nuisance for damage caused by trees overhanging the highway depends on proof of negligence;[174] the same rule applies in private nuisance, both to overhanging of branches and encroachment by roots.[175] Not only will the occupier who has a naturally occurring nuisance on his land not be held liable in the absence of negligence, but also the question of negligence will, in some cases at least, be judged taking his physical and financial resources into account.[176] We have also seen that a defendant who pleads statutory authorization will have to prove, at least, that the nuisance was not the result of negligence on its part. Finally, it will be recalled that one of the factors relevant to unreasonableness of user is the question of whether the defendant took reasonable care to reduce the interference with the plaintiff's use and enjoyment of his property to a minimum.[177]

What are we to make of this collection of cases and rules? Some people, attempting to find a general principle, have argued that whereas liability for failure to abate a nuisance created by another or by forces of nature depends on negligence, liability for creation of a nuisance is strict (that is, not dependant on proof of negligence). The cases provide some support for this proposition,[178] but it is not easy to see, as a matter of principle, why the creator should be in a worse position than the non-abator of a nuisance, except, perhaps, that the latter is guilty only of nonfeasance.

It may be significant that all the cases in which negligence has been held to be an essential element in the tort of nuisance involved claims for damages for injury to property or personal injury. In modern law there are few cases, in theory at least, in which damages for physical injury or

---

172 See p. 606 above.

173 See p. 607 above.

174 *British Road Services Ltd* v. *Slater* [1964] 1 W.L.R. 498; *Caminer* v. *Northern & London Investment Trust* [1951] A.C. 88; *Noble* v. *Harrison* [1926] 2 K.B. 332.

175 *Solloway* v. *Hampshire County Council* (1981) 79 L.G.R. 449. But contrast *Davey* v. *Harrow Corporation* [1958] 1 Q.B. 60; H. Street [1982] *Conv.* 294.

176 *Leakey* v. *National Trust* [1980] Q.B. 485; cf. *Goldman* v. *Hargrave* [1967] 1 A.C. 645. But as to liability for escape of naturally occurring water see J.G. Fleming *Law of Torts* 7th edn (1987) pp. 400-1.

177 But there are cases in which the question of reasonable care is irrelevant. Damage caused by removal of lateral or subjacent support to land is actionable without proof of negligence: *Pantalone* v. *Alaouie* (1989) 18 N.S.W.L.R. 119; *Fennell* v. *Robson Excavations Pty Ltd* [1977] 2 N.S.W.L.R. 486; *Thynne* v. *Petrie* [1975] Qd.R. 260; *Byrne* v. *Judd* (1908) 27 N.Z.L.R. 1106; *Bognuda* v. *Upton & Shearer Ltd* [1972] N.Z.L.R. 741; *A-G* v. *Whangarei City Council* [1987] 2 N.Z.L.R. 150. The right of support relates to the land itself and not to buildings on it, but if the land would have subsided even if there had been no building on it, compensation can be awarded for damage to the building as well as to the land: *Pantalone* v. *Alaouie* (above); *Bognuda* v. *Upton & Shearer* (above) p. 760 *per* Turner P. In New Zealand, at least, where subdivision of sloping sites is common, the subdivider is not strictly liable for subsidence where it is clear that sections in a subdivision have been created by excavation: *Blewman* v. *Wilkinson* [1979] 2 N.Z.L.R. 208.

178 See e.g. *Richmond C.C.* v. *Scantlebury* [1991] 2 V.R. 38, 40.

damage are recoverable in the absence of negligence.[179] When the question is whether damages ought to be awarded in respect of the infliction of physical damage, the courts tend to look at the particular acts which caused the damage and ask whether they were negligent. In cases involving continuing interference with comfort and amenities, on the other hand, or cases in which there is a continuing threat of injury to a person, property or financial interests, the law is not concerned only or primarily with providing compensation for injuries already inflicted by negligent acts or omissions, but with regulating the behaviour of the parties in the future and resolving conflicting land-use claims.[180] The law of negligence is, of course, concerned with deterring future negligent conduct, but this concern is only incidental to the main function of compensation. In nuisance, by contrast, striking a reasonable balance between the rights of the parties in the use of their land is of the very essence of the tort. So the court's concern tends not to be with defining adequate precautions but with deciding what is a reasonable amount of interference. It is then left to the defendant to achieve the prescribed level of non-interference as best as he can. In other words, whereas the tort of negligence is concerned primarily with the past and with defining adequate precautions against injuries defined in terms of what has actually been inflicted, the tort of nuisance is concerned primarily with the future and with defining what would be a fair and acceptable level of 'injury' to expect the plaintiff to tolerate. To this issue negligence is not relevant because once the acceptable level of interference has been set, it is no defence for the defendant to say that he has taken all reasonable precautions to avoid any greater interference. And while what is practicable by way of precautions is relevant to deciding what level of interference is acceptable, it is not conclusive of this issue.

The fact of the matter appears to be that if a claim for damages for past injury, especially if it is personal injury or damage to property, is framed in nuisance it is likely to be assimilated to a claim in negligence and the court will see the relevant issue in terms of reasonable precautions to avoid injury. The plaintiff will claim damages for past injury if he thinks that the risk of his suffering further damage as a result of the activities of the defendant is so low that he does not want an injunction or that he could not satisfy the court that there was a significant probability of repetition of the injury. But if he is concerned about the future, he will frame his case in nuisance in order to be able to claim an injunction,[181] and then the court is likely to decide the case in terms of fair distribution

---

179 See *Read* v. *J. Lyons & Co. Ltd* [1947] A.C. 156, 170-1 *per* Lord Macmillan. But contrast *Hiap Lee (Cheong Leong & Sons) Bricklayers Ltd* v. *Weng Lok Mining Co. Ltd* [1974] 2 *Mal. L.J.* 1 and cases on removal of support discussed n. 177 above. Statutes may also impose strict liability for physical damage: e.g. Damage by Aircraft Act 1952 (N.S.W.). See further J.G. Fleming *Law of Torts* 7th edn (Sydney, 1987) p. 306.

180 For this distinction see e.g. *French* v. *Auckland City Corporation* [1974] 1 N.Z.L.R. 340, 351 *per* McMullin J.

181 It is simply assumed that injunctions are not available in negligence actions: *Miller* v. *Jackson* [1977] Q.B. 966, 980 *per* Lord Denning M.R. But as to this see Cane *Tort Law and Economic Interests* (1991) p. 99.

of the benefits and burdens of land use rather than in terms of reasonableness of precautions. Where the concern is with the past the question of what the defendant ought reasonably to have done will be decided quite narrowly with reference to the particular damage-causing incident. But when the concern is with the future the question of reasonableness is asked with reference to the activity which the defendant is conducting on his land which gives rise to the continuing interference with the neighbour's use of his land. The contrast can be seen by comparing *Bolton* v. *Stone*,[182] in which the risk of the plaintiff being injured again in the future was very small, with *Miller* v. *Jackson*,[183] where the repetition of damage was almost inevitable. The former case was treated as a negligence case, the latter as a nuisance case.

In practical terms, the upshot of this difference of approach would seem to be that a defendant might be held liable for a continuing interference even though it could not be eliminated by the exercise of reasonable care, whereas if the interference was an isolated incident he would only be liable if it was the result of negligence. The fact of repetition might be thought to justify a stricter form of liability simply because something which a person might be reasonably expected to tolerate if done once can become intolerable if repeated.

It might be noted in passing that the distinction between liability for failure to take reasonable precautions against injury and liability for infliction of an unreasonable level of interference with the use of land helps to resolve a perennial question as to whether contributory negligence is a defence to an action in nuisance. If the nuisance action is based on negligence there is no reason why it should not be a defence. But if the basis of liability is fairness in the distribution of the benefits and burdens of conflicting land uses, there is no reason why contributory negligence, any more than coming to the nuisance (which is based on a similar idea), should, as such, be an answer. The question is not whose fault the injury is, but whether in fairness it ought to be allowed to continue and who ought to be required to bear the cost of it. The conduct of the plaintiff is relevant to the question of fairness; but just as the defendant cannot escape liability simply by showing that he took all reasonable care, so the fact that the plaintiff in some sense brought the injury on himself should not have the result that he must bear the cost of that injury.

II: PUBLIC NUISANCE

1. What is a Public Nuisance?

'A public nuisance is a nuisance so widespread in its range or so indiscriminate in its effect that it would not be reasonable to expect one person to take

182 [1951] A.C. 850.
183 [1977] Q.B. 966.

proceedings on his own responsibility to put a stop to it, but that it should be taken on the responsibility of the community at large'.[184]

This can be done by means of a 'relator action' in which the Attorney-General, on the relation of some private individual, seeks an injunction to restrain the nuisance.[185] A public nuisance is also a crime for which the perpetrator can be prosecuted.[186] Many prosecutions for public nuisance are now brought under statutory provisions and prosecutions at common law are quite rare.

There are, in effect, two varieties of public nuisance, although both varieties may be relevant in the same case. The first involves a large number of private nuisances, such as where the operations of a quarry cause nuisance by noise and dust to neighbouring landowners over a considerable area[187] or where neighbours of a farm are affected by smells produced by the manufacture of compost.[188] Since an injunction to restrain the nuisance would enure for the benefit of all the affected landowners, it is not fair to expect one of them to bear all the cost and effort of obtaining it, and so the law allows the Attorney-General (or perhaps some other representative body, such as a local authority) to bring a sort of class action on behalf of all those interested. The second variety of public nuisance involves interference with some public right or with the use of some public place. The most common example of such a nuisance is obstruction of a highway or of a public waterway; but other examples include filling the air with unpleasant or noxious smells or fumes,[189] polluting of rivers so as to kill fish or render the water unfit for drinking,[190] discharging oil into the seas in such circumstances that it is likely to be carried on to the shore,[191] causing dust from quarrying to descend on users of the highway,[192] failing to keep premises on the highway in a good state of repair.[193]

It has also been held that picketing commercial premises with associated obstruction, coercion and intimidation of, and threats of physical violence

---

184 *A-G* v. *P.Y.A. Quarries Ltd* [1957] 2 Q.B. 169, 191 *per* Denning L.J. Reynolds J.A. offered a useful definition in *R.* v. *Clifford* [1980] 1 N.S.W.L.R. 314, 318-19: 'an act not warranted by law the effect of which is to endanger the life, health, property, morals or comfort of the public'. The reference to 'morals' should probably be taken as referring to cases in which premises used, for example as brothels or sex shops, are cause for complaint.

185 See p. 626 below.

186 See generally J.C. Smith & B. Hogan *Criminal Law* 6th edn (London, 1988) pp. 794-8.

187 *A-G* v. *P.Y.A. Quarries* [1957] 2 Q.B. 169.

188 *Baulkham Hills S.C.* v. *Domachuk* (1988) 66 L.G.R.A. 110.

189 *R.* v. *White and Ward* (1757) 1 Burr. 333.

190 *R.* v. *Medley* (1834) 6 C. & P. 292.

191 *Southport Corporation* v. *Esso Petroleum Co. Ltd* [1954] 2 Q.B. 182, 197 *per* Denning L.J.; see also e.g. Marine Pollution Act 1987 (N.S.W.) esp. s.51. Such statutory schemes of pollution control (which are beyond the scope of this book) are in practice much more important than the law of nuisance in controlling pollution. Nuisance is a last resort for private individuals.

192 *A-G* v. *P.Y.A. Quarries* [1957] 2 Q.B. 169.

193 *Cartwright* v. *McLaine & Long Pty Ltd* (1979-80) 143 C.L.R. 549.

to, those wishing to enter the premises can be a public nuisance.[194] It can be a public nuisance for the owner of a vacant land to allow filth and refuse to remain on the land even if it was put there by strangers;[195] or for the authority which owns a public park to interfere substantially with it in a way deleterious to its use as a park.[196] It can be a public nuisance to make a bogus telephone call warning of the presence of explosives in a building;[197] and the law of public nuisance can be, although in practice rarely is, used to prosecute those involved in civil disorder.[198] On the other hand, it has been held that the law of public nuisance cannot be used to control what another may build on land by reference to its beauty or lack of it or its incompatibility with the historical quality or natural character of the neighbourhood.[199] It has also been held that it is not a public nuisance to deposit material in a bay in such a way as to interfere with fishing.[200]

As in the case of private nuisance, one person may be liable in public nuisance for the acts of others. So, it has been held that whoever has charge of a highway is bound to prevent its use in such a way as to create a public nuisance.[201]

The main significance of the distinction drawn earlier between the two varieties of public nuisance lies in the question of proof. In an action in respect of a large number of private nuisances it would have to be proved (unless the application was for a *quia timet* injunction) that all the affected parties had suffered actual damage, because an action in private nuisance is not complete until damage occurs. On the other hand, interference with the use of a public place or with some other public right is actionable (at the suit of the Attorney-General) without proof of actual damage to particular individuals: the inconvenience, danger to health, or whatever, which constitutes the nuisance is all that need be shown.

2. THE PUBLIC OR A SECTION OF THE PUBLIC

How many people have to be affected before it can be said that the nuisance is one interfering with the comfort or convenience of a class of the public and so actionable as a public nuisance? No conclusive answer can be given to the question since it is all a matter of degree.[202] It is also tied up with the question of whether the effect on the affected members of

194 *Bird* v. *O'Neal* [1960] A.C. 907.
195 *A-G* v. *Tod Heatley* [1897] 1 Ch. 560.
196 *Kent* v. *Johnson* (1972) 21 F.L.R. 177.
197 *R.* v. *Madden* [1975] 3 All E.R. 155.
198 e.g. *R.* v. *Clarke (No.2)* [1964] 2 Q.B. 315; see G. Flick *Civil Liberties in Australia* (Sydney, 1981) pp. 93-100.
199 *Kent* v. *Johnson* (1972) 21 F.L.R. 177, 212.
200 *Ball* v. *Consolidated Rutile Ltd* (1990) Aust. Torts Reports 81-023.
201 *A-G* v. *Brisbane City Council, ex parte Pratt* (1987) 63 L.G.R.A. 294. But merely selling liquor to people who then engage in offensive behaviour would not incur liability: *Teamay* v. *Severin* (1988) 94 F.L.R. 47.
202 *A-G* v. *Abraham & Williams Ltd* [1949] N.Z.L.R. 461, 498-9 *per* Hutchinson J. For illustrative decisions see *R.* v. *Lloyd* (1802) 4 Esp. 200; 170 E.R. 691; *R.* v. *Madden* [1975] 3 All E.R. 155.

the public has to be actual or only potential. For example, if noxious fumes escape from a factory on to a highway in the middle of the night when very few people are about, does the lack of bystanders prevent the escape being a public nuisance? Denning L.J. in *P.Y.A Quarries* suggests not. His Lordship said that the obstruction of a public footpath could be a public nuisance even if it was seldom used except by one or two householders, because the obstruction affects everyone indiscriminately who *may wish* to walk along it.[203]

3. UNREASONABLENESS

Where the public nuisance at issue consists of a large number of private nuisances, then obviously the rules of private nuisance which we have already discussed are relevant to deciding whether private nuisances have been committed. But some of those rules are also relevant to the other variety of public nuisance. In particular, an interference with a public right will be a nuisance only if it is unreasonable.[204] This has to be judged in the light of all the circumstances of the case; if the defendant is a private individual pursuing his own interests then those interests have to be weighed against the inconvenience to the public which his activity causes;[205] and if the defendant is a public body executing public works, such as the erection of a communications tower, the public interest in the building of the tower has to be weighed against the degree of public inconvenience caused by it.[206]

To constitute a public nuisance, the thing must be a nuisance (in the popular sense) to all persons (or, at least, a representative cross-section of people)[207] who come within the sphere of its operation. For example, smoke or noxious fumes or an obstruction on the highway is more or less an inconvenience or danger to all within its reach even though some may be affected more by it than others. But, whereas the pealing of church bells may be an intolerable intrusion on the peace and quiet of someone who lives next to the church, it may be no inconvenience and indeed a positive pleasure to persons who live further away.[208] This does not mean, of course, that the bells may not constitute a private nuisance to the next-door neighbour, but only that they are not a public nuisance.[209]

The more limited in duration and the more trivial in nature an interference with the rights of the public the less likely it is to be a public nuisance.[210] For example, it is not every obstruction of the highway which amounts to unreasonable user: to leave a vehicle parked in a wide street

203 [1957] 2 Q.B. 169, 191.
204 See e.g. *R.* v. *Clarke (No. 2)* [1964] 2 Q.B. 315; *Grand Central Car Park Pty Ltd* v. *Tivoli Freeholders* [1969] V.R. 62; *York Bros (Trading) Pty Ltd* v. *Commissioner for Main Roads* [1983] 1 N.S.W.L.R. 391.
205 *Trevett* v. *Lee* [1955] 1 All E.R. 406.
206 *Kent* v. *Johnson* (1972) 21 F.L.R. 177, 220 *per* Smithers J.
207 *A-G* v. *P.Y.A. Quarries* [1957] 2 Q.B. 169, 184 *per* Romer L.J.
208 cf. *A-G* v. *Sheffield Gas Consumers Co.* (1853) 3 De G.M. & G. 304; 43 E.R. 119.
209 *Soltau* v. *De Held* (1851) 2 Sim.(N.S.) 133.
210 *Harper* v. *G.N. Haden & Sons Ltd* [1933] Ch. 298.

for a short time might not be a nuisance, whereas if the same were done in a very narrow street it might be;[211] it would not normally be a nuisance to stand and talk to a friend on a footpath for a reasonable time; or to park a vehicle in order to deliver goods to premises on the highway. In the context of civil liberties, since the normal use of the highway is to pass and repass, a static meeting on the highway is more likely to be a public nuisance than would a procession. It can be a nuisance to attract a crowd on the highway which congregates and ceases to use the highway for the purposes of passage.[212]

The frequency with which a 'nuisance' occurs is, of course, relevant to its actionability. But any appreciable interference with the public use of a highway causing inconvenience to many can be a public nuisance even if it occurs only once.[213]

4. Remedies

(a) Abatement In an old Victorian case[214] Higinbotham J. said that any person whose right of user of a highway or navigable river is obstructed by a public nuisance has a right to remove the obstruction. But in an even older New South Wales case[215] it was said that a private individual cannot, of his own authority, abate a public nuisance on the highway unless it does him a special injury. Even then, he can only interfere with it to the extent necessary to enable him to exercise the right of passing along the highway; and he cannot justify doing any damage to the property of the person who has improperly placed the nuisance in the highway if, by avoiding it, he might have passed on with reasonable convenience.

(b) Injunctions The Attorney-General is entitled to an injunction to restrain a public nuisance. He may do so either of his own motion ('*ex officio*') or at the request (or 'on the relation') of a private individual affected by the nuisance ('*ex relatione*'). In seeking the injunction the Attorney-General acts in the public interest and for the vindication of

---

211 *A-G* v. *Sheffield Gas* (1853) 43 E.R. 119, 132-3 *per* Lord Cranworth L.C. This situation is, of course, primarily dealt with, at least in cities, by parking control regulations.

212 See further *Silservice Pty Ltd* v. *Supreme Bread Pty Ltd* (1950) 50 S.R.(N.S.W.) 127; *Lyons, Sons & Co.* v. *Gulliver* [1914] 1 Ch. 361; *Dwyer* v. *Mansfield* [1946] K.B. 437; *Fabbri* v. *Morris* [1947] 1 All E.R. 315. There are problematic cases which might be interpreted as suggesting that picketing may be tortious even though not unreasonable in the sense normally found in public nuisance cases if it involves obstruction of the highway and 'besetting' (i.e. interfering with other people's freedom of movement in such a way as to cause them to fear for the safety of themselves or their property: but *query* whether besetting in this sense could ever be other than unreasonable in its usual sense.). See A. Davidson (1988) 18 *U.W.A.L.R.* 138, 149-53; (1989) 19 *U.W.A.L.R.* 201, 207-18. See also *Animal Liberation (Vic) Inc.* v. *Gasser* [1991] V.R. 51. The most vigorous judicial denial of this suggestion is that of Lord Denning M.R. in *Hubbard* v. *Pitt* [1976] Q.B. 142, 177.

213 *Lloyd* v. *Blake* (1917) 4 L.G.R.(N.S.W.) 19; *A-G* v. *P.Y.A. Quarries* [1957] 2 Q.B. 169, 191 *per* Denning L.J.

214 *Fergusson* v. *Union Steamship Co. of N.Z. Ltd* (1884) 10 V.L.R.(L) 279.

215 *Alexander* v. *Mayor of Sydney* (1861) 1 S.C.R.(N.S.W.) 26 (Appendix); see also *Campbell Davys* v. *Lloyd* [1901] 2 Ch. 518.

public rights and so the court will refuse relief only in exceptional circumstances.[216] A private individual who is entitled to claim damages for public nuisance according to the principles to be discussed in the next section may also seek an injunction without the aid of the Attorney-General. As in the case of private nuisance, there is a discretion not to award an injunction if damages in lieu would be an adequate remedy;[217] but in the case of public nuisance, since the Attorney-General is not entitled to damages, the question has to be asked with reference to the complainants on behalf of whom the Attorney-General is acting. There is authority for the proposition that a court is less likely to exercise its discretion to award damages in lieu of an injunction where the nuisance is public than where it is private.[218] But an injunction will not be awarded if the injury is merely temporary, or, even if it is likely to be repeated, it is trifling in nature.[219]

The court will not by injunction order the doing of that which is physically impossible, but the fact that compliance with the injunction may be very difficult or expensive for the defendant is no ground not to award it, although it may be a reason to postpone its operation to give the defendant a chance to find ways to abate the nuisance.[220] But if he cannot do so then he must cease his activity.

As in private nuisance, public interest considerations are not relevant to the decision whether or not to award an injunction. So the fact that if a cattle saleyard (which constitutes a public nuisance because its sanitary state breeds smell, flies and mosquitoes) closes down, this will have a detrimental effect on the operation of a nearby abattoir, an undertaking of great economic importance to the area, is no reason not to grant an injunction even if the saleyard is located in a suitable place and no other alternative site had been found despite repeated efforts.[221] Only if the section of the public whose rights have been interfered with by the nuisance are the very same people who have benefited from the nuisance-creating activity would a plea of public interest have any chance of success.[222]

(c) **Damages** In order to recover damages for public nuisance an individual must show that he has suffered some special or particular damage over and above that suffered by members generally of the class or section of the public interference with whose rights constitutes the public

---

216 *A-G* v. *Harris* [1961] 1 Q.B. 74.

217 *A-G* v. *Sheffield Gas* (1853) 43 E.R. 119, 125 *per* Turner L.J.

218 *York Bros* v. *Commissioner of Main Roads* [1983] 1 N.S.W.L.R. 391.

219 ibid.; *A-G* v. *Cambridge Consumers Gas Co.* (1868) L.R. 4 Ch. App. 71; *A-G* v. *Mosman Council* (1910) 11 S.R.(N.S.W.) 133.

220 *A-G* v. *Colney Hatch Lunatic Asylum* (1868) L.R. 4 Ch.App. 146; *A-G* v. *Tod Heatley* [1897] 1 Ch. 560; *A-G* v. *Abraham & Williams* [1949] N.Z.L.R. 461.

221 *A-G* v. *Abraham & Williams* [1949] N.Z.L.R. 461; cf. *York Bros* v. *Commissioner of Main Roads* [1983] 1 N.S.W.L.R. 391, 396.

222 *Abraham & Williams* [1949] N.Z.L.R. 461, 487 *per* Gresson J.

nuisance.[223] What is special damage?[224] Injury to person or chattels[225] clearly qualifies, as does loss of custom[226] and depreciation in the value of land.[227] Consequential economic loss can also be special damage.[228] Special damage need not be pecuniary. Delay and inconvenience over and above that suffered by members of the public generally will suffice.

In most of the older cases it is said that for compensation for special damage to be recoverable, the damage must be a *direct* result of the nuisance. However, in *The Wagon Mound (No. 2)*[229] it was held that the rule of remoteness of damage in both public and private nuisance is foreseeability, and it has been specifically said that the old statements about special damage have to be read in this light.[230]

5. Defences

Little need be said here. Statutory authorization is clearly a defence[231] and the applicable principles are the same, *mutatis mutandis*, as those we have already discussed in the context of private nuisance.[232] It seems, too, that coming to the nuisance is no defence.[233] A right to commit a public nuisance cannot be acquired by prescription because a public nuisance is a crime.

6. Public Nuisance and Negligence

As already noted, the rule of remoteness of damage in public nuisance is foreseeability. There are also some cases in which it is clear that liability in public nuisance is based on negligence, so that, to succeed, the plaintiff will have to prove that the defendant was negligent. This is true in relation to natural nuisances, such as trees overhanging the highway.[234] Liability for personal injury caused by the escape on to the highway of cricket and golf balls is based on negligence.[235] There is also considerable

---

223 *Teamay* v. *Severin* (1988) 94 F.L.R. 47.

224 G.H.L. Fridman (1951-3) 2 *W.A. Ann. L.R.* 490; G. Kodilinye (1986) 6 *L.S.* 182.

225 e.g. *The Wagon Mound (No. 2)* [1967] 1 A.C. 617; *Halsey* v. *Esso Petroleum Co.* [1961] 1 W.L.R. 683.

226 *Smith* v. *Warringah Shire Council* [1962] N.S.W.R. 944.

227 *Walsh* v. *Ervin* [1952] V.L.R. 361.

228 e.g. *Blundy Clark & Co. Ltd* v. *London & North Eastern Railway Co.* [1931] 2 K.B. 334. But *query* whether liability for purely economic loss in public nuisance is subject to the same proximity rules as recovery for such loss in the tort of negligence: *Ball* v. *Consolidated Rutile* [1990] Aust. Torts Reports 67,797, 67,816-7.

229 [1967] 1 A.C. 617.

230 *Smith* v. *Warringah S.C.* [1962] N.S.W.R. 944, 949 *per* Hardie J.

231 e.g. *Kenthurst Investments* v. *Wyong Shire Council* (1964) 10 L.G.R.A. 307.

232 *East Fremantle Corporation* v. *Annois* [1902] A.C. 213; *O'Brien* v. *Board of Land & Works* (1880) 6 V.L.R. 204; *Hancock* v. *Midland Junction Corporation* (1926) 28 W.A.L.R. 91; *York Bros* v. *Commissioner of Main Roads* [1983] 1 N.S.W.L.R. 391.

233 *A-G* v. *Abraham & Williams* [1949] N.Z.L.R. 461.

234 *Caminer* v. *Northern & London Investment Trust* [1951] A.C. 88; *Noble* v. *Harrison* [1926] 2 K.B. 332; *British Road Services Ltd* v. *Slater* [1964] 1 W.L.R. 498.

235 *Bolton* v. *Stone* [1951] A.C. 850; *Castle* v. *St Augustine's Links Ltd* (1922) 38 T.L.R. 615.

authority for the view that liability for damage to person or property caused by vehicles on the highway, whether stationary or in motion, depends on proof of negligence.[236] Moreover, in *The Wagon Mound (No. 2)* Lord Reid said that foreseeability of risk is always an element in nuisance claims arising out of the creation of dangerous situations on highways or navigable waterways.[237]

In one area at least it appears that a defendant can be liable in nuisance, both public and private, regardless of whether he knew or had means of knowing that there was a risk of injury; that is, in the case of premises adjoining the highway falling into disrepair through neglect of a person responsible for their state of repair.[238] The rule does not apply, however, where the nuisance is created by the act of a trespasser or by unobservable operation of natural forces such as subsidence. In *Cartwright* v. *McLaine & Long*[239] the plaintiff suffered personal injury when he slipped on oil which had flowed on to the footpath from under a pile of rubbish in a disused and derelict service station on adjoining land. Gibbs A.C.J. was prepared to assume, without deciding, that *Wringe* v. *Cohen* was good law in Australia, but said that it had to be restricted in its operation to cases where nuisance is caused by the defendant's failure to repair premises for the repair of which he is responsible. Stephen J. (with whom Aickin J. agreed) was not even prepared to assume that *Wringe* v. *Cohen* represented the law. Murphy J. took a quite different line, saying that liability ought to be strict without proof of negligence, for social policy reasons: those who store or use dangerous substances should bear the risk of injury or damage caused by them. It is certainly ironic that in these days of widespread insurance and the prevalence of loss-spreading ideas, the trend in the law relating to the liability of occupiers of premises to the public should be away from strict liability. Public liability insurance is relatively cheap and quite common (perhaps almost universal among business concerns). The arguments of social policy in such a situation certainly seem to favour Murphy J.'s approach.

On the whole, then, it would seem that so far as liability for damages in public nuisance is concerned, the law either already does require, or is tending towards requiring, the plaintiff to prove that his injury or damage was foreseeable and that the defendant failed to take reasonable precautions to prevent it. So far as injunctions are concerned, if the public nuisance is one consisting of a large number of private nuisances the relevance of negligence is, as we have already seen, a matter of difficulty.[240] If the nuisance is one involving an interference with public rights negligence is probably irrelevant: the basis of the action is an interference with rights, not causation of damage.

---

236 *Blackburn* v. *Woollongong Municipal Council* (1917) 4 L.G.R. 5; *Mitchell* v. *Tsiros (No. 2)* [1982] V.R. 301; *Maitland* v. *Raisebeck* [1944] K.B. 689; *Everitt* v. *Martin* [1953] N.Z.L.R. 298.

237 [1967] 1 A.C. 617, 639-40.

238 *Wringe* v. *Cohen* [1940] 1 K.B. 229; applied in *Heap* v. *Ind, Coope & Allsopp Ltd* [1940] 2 K.B. 476 and *Mint* v. *Good* [1951] 1 K.B. 517.

239 (1979-80) 143 C.L.R. 549.

240 See pp. 619-22 above.

17

LIABILITY FOR DANGEROUS THINGS ESCAPING FROM LAND

I: THE PRINCIPLE IN RYLANDS V. FLETCHER

Separate treatment of liability for the escape of dangerous things from land stems from the decision in *Rylands* v. *Fletcher*,[1] although it appears that at the time the case was decided it was perceived as involving no more than a slight extension of existing principles to cover a case of infliction of material injury to property as the result of an isolated incident, as opposed to a continuing situation, occurring on the defendant's land. The escape of noxious or annoying things from the defendant's land is the central case of nuisance; and, in the words of Windeyer J. in *Benning* v. *Wong*, Rylands v. *Fletcher* involved 'a special form of the ancient cause of action for nuisance'.[2] However, a separate and distinct body of rules has grown up around *Rylands* v. *Fletcher*, although their exact status in the law is very unclear. Windeyer J. in *Benning* v. *Wong* referred to them variously as constituting a 'separate chapter in the law of torts', and a 'rule, doctrine or principle, whatever you choose to call it'. Perhaps 'principle' is a suitably neutral term.

The accepted formulation of the principle is that of Blackburn J. in *Rylands* v. *Fletcher* in the Court of Exchequer Chamber:

> The person who, for his own purposes, brings on his land and collects and keeps there anything likely to do mischief if it escapes must keep it in at his peril, and if he does not do so he is prima facie answerable for all the damage which is the natural consequence of its escape. He can excuse himself by showing that the escape was owing to the plaintiff's default; or perhaps that the escape was the consequence of *vis major*, or the act of God.[3]

The reference to the defendant acting 'at his peril' suggests that Blackburn J. saw the liability as being liability for the creation of risks which materialize to the plaintiff's damage rather than liability for causing

1 (1866) L.R. 1 Ex. 265; (1868) L.R. 3 H.L. 330.
2 (1969) 122 C.L.R. 249, 296.
3 (1866) L.R. 1 Ex. 265, 279-80.

damage by fault. On this basis, liability under *Rylands* v. *Fletcher* is often treated as a form of strict liability.[4] As we have seen, the tendency in modern law is to impose liability for the infliction of personal injury and property damage only if the plaintiff can prove negligence on the part of the defendant. On the other hand, as Windeyer J. pointed out in *Benning* v. *Wong*,[5] the imposition of liability for risks is particularly appropriate when insurance is common, and it only seems fair that those who create and benefit from the creation of risks ought to bear the costs of injuries inflicted when those risks materialize.

We will consider the various elements of Blackburn J.'s statement in order.

1. For his Own Purposes

There is little authority on the exact meaning of this phrase. In *Kiddle* v. *City Business Properties Ltd*[6] it was held that the plaintiff could not recover, without proof of negligence, in respect of escape of water into his shop from a blocked gutter which served both the plaintiff's and his landlord's (the defendant's) premises. Where a person rents a building or part of a building which shares common drainage with adjacent premises the water carried by those drains is there with his consent and for the benefit of both parties. Again, in *Dunne* v. *North Western Gas Board*[7] it was held that a nationalized gas undertaking does not store gas in its pipes for its own purposes but for the common benefit of the whole public. However, this view was rejected by Windeyer J. in *Benning* v. *Wong*[8] and Barwick C.J.[9] omitted any reference to this requirement in his formulation of the *Rylands* v. *Fletcher* principle.

As a matter of principle the requirement would seem designed to ensure that the person who bears the financial burdens of an activity is the person who reaps the financial rewards. The person who reaps the financial rewards of supplying gas is the supplier, and of renting premises, the landlord. The entrepreneur is also in a better position than his customer to procure insurance against the risks attendant on his activity or to spread the costs generated by those risks, and will, as a general rule, be financially better off than his clients. So perhaps the rule ought to be that as against the plaintiff, a defendant will only be treated as not acting for his own purposes if he is the servant or agent of the plaintiff.

---

4 S. Stoljar (P.D. Finn, ed. *Essays on Torts* (Sydney, 1989) Ch. 11) argues that *Rylands* liability is liability for negligence but that the burden of proof on the issue of negligence rests on the defendant. On this apporach, a plea in terms of the principle in *Rylands* is akin to a plea of *res ipsa loquitur* in a negligence action.

5 (1969) 122 C.L.R. 249, 304.

6 [1942] 1 K.B. 269; cf. *A. Prosser & Son Ltd* v. *Levy* [1955] 1 W.L.R. 1224; *British Office Supplies (Auckland) Ltd* v. *Auckland Masonic Institute and Club* [1957] N.Z.L.R. 512; *Martin's Camera Corner Pty Ltd* v. *Hotel Mayfair Ltd* [1976] 2 N.S.W.L.R. 15, 27 *per* Yeldham J. *contra*.

7 [1964] 2 Q.B. 806.

8 (1969) 122 C.L.R. 249, 300-1. But Menzies and Owen JJ. took the view adopted in *Dunne*.

9 (1969) 122 C.L.R. 249, 255.

In relation to accumulations by a third party, a defendant occupier will be held responsible if the person who brought the things on to the land was the defendant's servant or independent contractor or if the defendant authorized the accumulation or acquiesced in or adopted it.[10] The landowner will not be liable for accumulations by a person who merely has permission to enter, at least if the accumulation was made under statutory authority and the landowner has no right to object to it.[11]

2. Things Brought on to the Land and Collected and Kept There

The defendant can be liable not only for obvious accumulations, such as the building of a reservoir or the storing of inflammable materials, but also for such things as the erection of a flagpole[12] or the manufacture of explosives[13] or the planting of a tree, the roots of which eventually encroach on to a neighbour's land,[14] or the erection of high voltage wires.[15] On the other hand, the defendant will be liable only if the things brought on to the land are under his control. So a landlord is not liable under *Rylands* v. *Fletcher* for the behaviour of unruly tenants.[16] There is authority for the propositions that a school board is not responsible under *Rylands* v. *Fletcher* for the trespassing of its pupils from school premises and that prison authorities cannot be held strictly liable for the escape even of dangerous prisoners.[17] There is a real sense in which school and prison authorities have control over their charges, and the basis of the rule may be that running schools and prisons is an ordinary and natural use of land or that human beings cannot be said to be dangerous if not confined.

3. His Land

The defendant need not be the owner of the land on which the things are collected in order to be subject to liability for their escape. It is sufficient if he has a licence or other right to enter the land and bring things there.[18] The basis of the liability is control (to the complete exclusion of the plaintiff, but not necessarily of others) of the accumulation of dangerous things on the land. A landowner who has such control may be liable even

---

10 See fn. 18 below.
11 *Burchett* v. *Commissioner for Railways* [1958] S.R.(N.S.W.) 366.
12 *Shiffman* v. *Venerable Order of the Hospital of St John of Jerusalem* [1936] 1 All E.R. 557.
13 *Read* v. *J. Lyons & Co. Ltd* [1947] A.C. 156.
14 *McKail* v. *Hamilton* [1948] A.L.R.(C.N.) 214.
15 *Fullarton* v. *North Melbourne Tramway & Lighting Co. Ltd* (1916) 21 C.L.R. 181.
16 *Smith* v. *Scott* [1973] Ch. 314. Anyway, the landlord is not in control of the land when it is the subject of a lease. It would be otherwise if the defendant remained in control of the land and the unruly occupants were only licensees: *A-G* v. *Corke* [1933] Ch. 89.
17 *Matheson* v. *Northcote College Board of Governors* [1975] 2 N.Z.L.R. 106.
18 *Rainham Chemical Works Ltd* v. *Belvedere Fish Guano Co.* [1921] 2 A.C. 465; *Casley-Smith* v. *F.S. Evans & Sons Pty Ltd* (1988) 67 L.G.R.A. 108; but contrast *Pett* v. *Sims Paving & Road Construction Co. Pty Ltd* [1928] V.L.R. 247.

if he did not himself bring the things on to the land, if he 'acquiesced in or adopted' the situation.[19] Conversely, a landowner will not be liable if he has no control over what is done on the land. Liability can arise for things done on a highway.[20] So, it was no bar to liability in *Benning* v. *Wong*[21] that the gas company had no title to the public street where its pipes lay because it had exclusive control of the pipes in which the gas ran.

4. WHO MAY SUE?

It is not necessary for the plaintiff to be an occupier of neighbouring land in order to have title to sue.[22] In *Shiffman* v. *Order of St John*[23] the plaintiff was a member of the public using a public place. In *Charing Cross Electricity Co.* v. *Hydraulic Power Co.*[24] the plaintiff was another licensee permitted to lay cables under the highway; the cables were damaged when one of the defendant's water mains burst.

5. ANYTHING LIKELY TO DO MISCHIEF IF IT ESCAPES

At various times it has been suggested that the law recognizes a category of things which are hazardous in themselves (*per se*) and that liability for damage caused by such things is strict. But there is no rule of strict liability for damage arising out of the use of ultra-hazardous things or the creation of ultra-hazardous situations. In general, liability rests on proof of negligence, subject to the principle that the more dangerous the thing or activity the more careful the defendant must be.[25] *Rylands* v. *Fletcher* liability is not liability for things dangerous *per se* but for things dangerous if they are not confined. This is clearly true of things like water, gas or explosives, but not of people such as pupils or prisoners.[26]

6. NON-NATURAL USER[27]

Blackburn J. said in the Court of Exchequer Chamber that liability would be strict only if the things brought on to the land were not naturally there. This is almost tautologous since it covers not only bringing new things on to land but also accumulation of things there anyway (such as water) in greater quantities or concentrations than those in which they naturally

---

19 *Casley-Smith* v. *Evans* (1988) 67 L.G.R.A. 108.

20 *Rigby* v. *Chief Constable of Northamptonshire* [1985] 1 W.L.R. 1242.

21 (1969) 122 C.L.R. 249; cf. *Charing Cross Electricity Supply Co.* v. *Hydraulic Power Co.* [1914] 3 K.B. 772.

22 cf. *British Celanese Ltd* v. *A.H. Hunt (Capacitors) Ltd* [1969] 1 W.L.R. 959; W.A. West (1966) 30 Conv. 95.

23 [1936] 1 All E.R. 557.

24 [1914] 3 K.B. 772.

25 *Read* v. *Lyons* [1947] A.C. 156; *Adelaide Chemical & Fertilizer Co. Ltd* v. *Carlyle* (1940) 64 C.L.R. 514, 522-3 *per* Starke J.

26 *Matheson* v. *Northcote College* [1975] 2 N.Z.L.R. 106, 117 *per* McMullin J.

27 A.L. Goodhart (1930-32) 4 *C.L.J.* 13; G.H.L. Fridman (1956) 34 *Can B.R.* 810; F.H. Newark (1961) 24 *M.L.R.* 557; D.W. Williams [1973] *C.L.J.* 310.

occur. In the House of Lords, Lord Cairns added that the defendant would not be liable strictly if the things were brought on 'in the ordinary course of the enjoyment of land' or in 'the natural use of land'.

The leading authority on the requirement of 'non-natural user' is *Rickards* v. *Lothian*[28] in which damage was caused to property of the plaintiff located on the second floor of a building leased to the defendant as the result of continuous overflow of water from a lavatory basin on the top floor of the building. Lord Moulton said that to attract liability under the *Rylands* v. *Fletcher* principle the use of land must be:

> some special use bringing with it increased danger to others and must not be merely the ordinary use of land or such use as is proper for the general benefit of the community . . . the provision of a proper supply of water to various parts of a house is not only reasonable but has become, in accordance with modern sanitary views, an almost necessary feature of town life.[29]

Several points emerge from this decision. First, views about what uses of land are ordinary can change as society develops. For example, in *Benning* v. *Wong* Windeyer J. said that if he had 'only to apply literally Lord Moulton's words, I would have thought that putting gas mains under streets was today a natural and ordinary use of land'.[30] Again, in *Read* v. *Lyons* Lord Macmillan said that he would 'hesitate to hold that in these days and in an industrial community it was a non-natural use of land to build a factory on it and conduct there the manufacture of explosives'.[31]

Secondly, naturalness is to be judged not just according to current community standards but also with reference to the place where the land is. Thus, in towns ample supplies of running water are essential for hygienic sanitation. In fact, the test of non-naturalness of user in this context is similar to the test of unreasonableness of user in nuisance.[32] The principle in *Rylands* v. *Fletcher*, like the tort of nuisance, is concerned with incompatibility of land uses. Ironically, however, whereas in nuisance questions of location and 'live and let live' are irrelevant where the damage inflicted is material, they are relevant in *Rylands* v. *Fletcher* even though it does not apply to mere interference with the enjoyment or amenities of land. The explanation for this may be that whereas in nuisance liability for material damage rests, in effect, on negligence, liability in *Rylands* v. *Fletcher* is somewhat stricter in that it attaches *prima facie* to the causation of damage regardless of negligence. The notion of non-naturalness of user serves to introduce questions of reasonable conduct to soften this strictness.

Thirdly, the requirement that the use be one bringing with it increased danger assumes that a certain level of danger is acceptable and perhaps

---

28 [1913] A.C. 263; *Municipality of Kingborough* v. *Bratt* [1959] Tas.S.R. 173.
29 [1913] A.C. 263, 280.
30 (1969) 122 C.L.R. 249, 302.
31 [1947] A.C. 156, 174.
32 Motive may be relevant to non-naturalness: *Pratt* v. *Young* (1952) 69 W.N.(N.S.W.) 214; *Shire of Glenelg* v. *Grills* [1907] V.L.R. 673, 685 *per* Cussen J.; adequacy of precautions is also relevant: *Mason* v. *Levy Autoparts of England Ltd* [1967] 2 Q.B. 530.

inevitable in the ordinary affairs of life and must be mutually accepted by all. So a use will not be non-natural simply because it is dangerous. It has to be unusually dangerous.

This social and relative approach to non-naturalness makes clear the nature of *Rylands* v. *Fletcher* liability as a mechanism for allocating the risks of physical injury generated by contiguous land uses to the party whom it is conceived, as a matter of fairness, ought to bear them. Examples of uses which have been held to be non-natural are: the digging of excavations (in which water collected) as part of the building of a railway;[33] the attraction of animals *ferae naturae*[34] on to one's land;[35] the installation of a large pipe for the purpose of confining and discharging a mountain watercourse in a settled area;[36] damming a stream, thus raising the water table with the result that salt was deposited on the surface of the land;[37] allowing a large number of caravan dwellers with habits offensive to those of fixed abode to congregate on a quite small piece of land;[38] the supply of electricity to trams through wires stretched on poles in public streets;[39] the planting on suburban land of a large forest tree likely to grow large and encroach on neighbouring land.[40] The following have been held not to be non-natural uses: the introduction of water irrigation on to farming property in an irrigated area;[41] the use of land for the manufacture of flour,[42] or for mining or farming,[43] or for welding,[44] or as school premises;[45] the laying of bitumen paving;[46] 'to put pipes on or leading to land for the purposes of bringing water to it, of providing a normal reticulation for domestic purposes, of conveying away wastes and sullage and perhaps even of sewage, and even of draining it with pipes of conventional design, manufacture and capacity';[47] the installation of ordinary domestic electrical wiring;[48] the bringing of water on to land for industrial purposes;[49] the manufacture of electrical and electronic components in a factory on an industrial estate and the bringing and storing of metal foil on the premises.[50]

---

33 *Peers* v. *Victorian Railways Commissioners* (1893) 19 V.L.R. 617.
34 See p. 648 below for the meaning of this term.
35 *Pratt* v. *Young* (1952) 69 W.N.(N.S.W.) 214. In New South Wales, A.C.T. and South Australia *Rylands* v. *Fletcher* does not apply to damage caused by any animal: see p. 647 below.
36 *Municipality of Kingborough* v. *Bratt* [1957] Tas.S.R. 173.
37 *Glasson* v. *Fuller* [1922] S.A.S.R. 148.
38 *A-G* v. *Corke* [1933] Ch. 89.
39 *Fullarton* v. *North Melbourne Electric Tramway etc. Co.* (1916) 21 C.L.R. 181.
40 *McKail* v. *Hamilton* [1948] A.L.R.(C.N.) 214.
41 *Bayliss* v. *Lea* [1962] S.R.(N.S.W.) 521.
42 *Wise Bros Pty Ltd* v. *Commissioner of Railways* (N.S.W.) (1947) 75 C.L.R. 59.
43 *Peers* v. *Victorian Railways Commissioners* (1893) 19 V.L.R. 617.
44 *General Jones* v. *Wildridge* [1988] Tas.S.R. (N.C. 12).
45 *Matheson* v. *Northcote College* [1975] 2 N.Z.L.R. 106.
46 *Pett* v. *Sims Paving* [1928] V.L.R. 247.
47 *Municipality of Kingborough* v. *Bratt* [1957] Tas.S.R. 173; cf. *Torette House Pty Ltd* v. *Berkman* (1939-40) 62 C.L.R. 637.
48 *Colls* v. *Home & Colonial Stores Ltd* [1936] 3 All E.R. 200.
49 *Kara Pty Ltd* v. *Rhodes* [1966] V.R. 77.
50 *British Celanese* v. *Hunt* [1969] 1 W.L.R. 959.

There are numerous cases in which *Rylands* v. *Fletcher* principles have been invoked in respect of the escape of fire. The principles are modified in that where the fire starts in inflammable materials brought on to the land, what escapes is the fire, not the inflammable materials;[51] in other cases the fire is lit by the landowner to burn off scrub or stubble naturally occurring on the land, and what is introduced are the materials with which to start the fire which escapes.[52] In the first type of case, non-naturalness will reside, if at all, in the quantity of combustible materials stored, the way they were stored and the neighbourhood in which they were stored.

In the case of deliberately lit fires the question of non-naturalness has to be decided on all the circumstances of the case: the degree of hazard to others involved in the use of the fire; the extent of the damage it is likely to do and the difficulty of controlling it depending on the climate, the character of the country and natural conditions.[53] In fact the test of non-naturalness in these cases is, as elsewhere, just another application of the basic idea of reasonableness underlying the law of nuisance: is the use of fire an accepted incident of some ordinary purpose to which the land is reasonably applied by the occupier, and has the occupier used reasonable precautions in its use? Thus it may be non-natural user to burn off stubble or scrub or to use fire to rid land of vermin in the hot, dry and windy conditions of an Australian or New Zealand summer,[54] or to maintain a refuse dump in such a way that it constitutes a fire risk.[55] The risk of the spread of fire introduced for ordinary domestic purposes such as cooking and heating is, as a general rule, one which all members of society must mutually accept.[56] But even a domestic fire may be used in such a way as to be non-natural: the test of non-naturalness in respect of domestic fires usually predicates the use of a fireplace, a stove or some other container calculated to prevent escape.[57] And whereas it may be ordinary and natural to smoke cigarettes in a house, to do so while hurrying about doing household chores quickly so as to be able to go out to the cinema may be non-natural.[58]

All this having been said, it must now be noted that there is some doubt as to the status of the non-naturalness requirement in Australia, at least as it was formulated by Lord Moulton in *Rickards* v. *Lothian*. In his statement of the *Rylands* v. *Fletcher* principle in *Benning* v. *Wong*[59] Barwick C.J. made no mention of the requirement. Windeyer J. reverted to the formulation of Blackburn J. by holding that, at least as far as gas in

51 *Mason* v. *Levy Autoparts of England Ltd* [1967] 2 Q.B. 530.
52 See e.g. *Cottrell* v. *Allen* (1882) 16 S.A.L.R. 122; *Craig* v. *Parker* (1906) 8 W.A.L.R. 161.
53 *Hazelwood* v. *Webber* (1934) 52 C.L.R. 268; *Smith* v. *Badenoch* [1970] S.A.S.R. 9; *New Zealand Forest Products Ltd* v. *O'Sullivan* [1974] 2 N.Z.L.R. 80.
54 Cases in previous note; *Triplett Pastoral & Development Co. Pty Ltd* v. *Cleave and Saggers* [1973] W.A.R. 173. Also relevant is how far from buildings the fire is lit: *McCarty* v. *Leeming* [1937] S.A.S.R. 432, 439 *per* Cleland J.
55 *Casley-Smith* v. *F.S. Evans & Sons Pty Ltd* (1988) 67 L.G.R.A. 108.
56 *Whinfield* v. *Lands Board* (1914) 18 C.L.R. 606.
57 *McCarty* v. *Leeming* [1937] S.A.S.R. 432.
58 *Robert* v. *Czycyerskyz* [1961] W.A.R. 175.
59 (1969) 122 C.L.R. 249.

pipes was concerned, the user of the land to carry the pipes was non-natural because gas in pipes was not naturally found on the land. At the same time his Honour thought that gas pipes would not be a non-natural use according to Lord Moulton's formula.

7. ESCAPE

There will be no liability under *Rylands* v. *Fletcher* unless there has been an escape[60] of the things accumulated, or of fire or of debris, produced, for example, by an explosion, from land[61] under the control of the defendant to land over which he had no control.[62] The plaintiff does not have to prove that the escape was the result of negligence, nor is it a defence for the defendant to show that he took all reasonable care to prevent the escape. Thus the occupier will be answerable for the negligent acts of an independent contractor causing the escape.[63]

8. ALL THE DAMAGE THE NATURAL CONSEQUENCE OF THE ESCAPE

Two issues arise here: what types of damage are recoverable; and what is the rule of remoteness? In relation to the first question, if the plaintiff is the occupier of land he can recover for damage to the land (such as the destruction of pasture or trees by water or fire), for damage to chattels on the land, such as animals or vehicles, and for economic loss consequential on such damage.[64] There is also good authority for saying that an occupier can recover for personal injuries suffered on the land.[65] The position is less clear as regards a claimant who has no interest in land. This is really the same question as whether such persons have standing to sue at all, and it now appears to be widely assumed that they do. There are cases which allow recovery for chattels located on the highway,[66] and which suggest that the plaintiff whose chattels are damaged can recover even though he is not the occupier of adjoining land or of any land.[67] There are several cases which support recovery for personal injuries not suffered as a consequence of the occupation of land to which dangerous

---

60 *Query*: as opposed to a deliberate release? See *Rigby* v. *Chief Constable of Northamptonshire* [1985] 1 W.L.R. 1242, 1255.

61 There is no strict liability for escape of fire from a chattel, such as a car, not on land of the defendant: *Mayfair Ltd* v. *Pears* [1987] 1 N.Z.L.R. 459.

62 *Read* v. *Lyons* [1947] A.C. 156.

63 *Rylands* v. *Fletcher* (1866) L.R. 1 Ex. 265.

64 Including the cost of averting damage resulting from the escape of fire or other dangerous things: *New Zealand Forest Products Ltd* v. *O'Sullivan* (1974) 2 N.Z.L.R. 80.

65 *Benning* v. *Wong* (1969) 122 C.L.R. 249, 255 *per* Barwick C.J.; 318 *per* Windeyer J.; *Hale* v. *Jennings Bros* [1948] 1 All E.R. 579; *Read* v. *Lyons* [1947] A.C. 156, 173 *per* Lord Macmillan *contra.*

66 *Halsey* v. *Esso Petroleum* [1961] 1 W.L.R. 683.

67 *British Celanese* v. *Hunt* [1969] 1 W.L.R.; *Charing Cross Electric* v. *Hydraulic Power* [1914] 3 K.B. 772.

things have escaped.[68] Provided the plaintiff has a right to be where he is, whether as occupier, licensee or member of the public, he may recover for personal injuries suffered. Such a plaintiff could also recover for consequential economic losses; but it is unlikely that a defendant could be held liable, in the absence of proof by the plaintiff of negligence on the former's part,[69] for purely economic loss resulting from damages to a third party's land or chattels, even where the third party had an action, not dependent on proof of negligence, under the *Rylands* v. *Fletcher* principle.

What is at stake here is whether *Rylands* v. *Fletcher* is to be seen as just a special application of nuisance principles, that is, as a weapon in the armoury of those with interests in land to enable them to protect their rights; or whether it is to be seen as embodying a wider principle of strict liability for dangerous things. There are contradictory indications in the cases relevant to this issue. The idea of non-natural user has been developed in such a way as to inject elements of negligence into *Rylands* v. *Fletcher* and, as we will see later, some of the defences available to the defendant have the same effect. On the other hand, statements can be found to the effect that the prevalence of insurance makes strict liability an appropriate way of spreading the cost of injuries resulting from dangerous activities. In some areas of the law, notably products liability, strict liability is currently popular, and the Pearson Royal Commission in England suggested the extension of strict liability into a number of areas, as well as the establishment of a general principle of strict liability for the conduct of ultra-hazardous activities.[70] The basic difficulty with any such general principle is to define ultra-hazardousness without reference to the way in which the activity is carried on; and such reference tends to smuggle negligence back in.[71] At all events, if a general principle of strict liability is thought desirable, it would be better for a properly thought out and comprehensive scheme to be introduced by legislation rather than leaving the development of the principle to the courts by extension of *Rylands* v. *Fletcher*. There is certainly no clear justification for allowing recovery for property damage without proof of negligence just because it results from an escape of dangerous things accumulated on land. Further, legislative proposals for strict liability often do not allow recovery for damage to chattels unless this is consequential on or associated with personal injury (e.g. damage to clothing).

As for the rule of remoteness, Blackburn J. spoke of all natural

---

68 *Fullarton* v. *North Melbourne etc. Co.* (1916) 21 C.L.R. 181; *Benning* v. *Wong* (1969) 122 C.L.R. 249, 319-20 *per* Windeyer J.; *Shiffman* v. *Order of St John* [1936] 1 All E.R. 557; *Perry* v. *Kendricks Transport Ltd* [1956] 1 All E.R. 154.

69 And subject, of course, to the requirement of proximity.

70 Report of Royal Commission on Civil Liability and Compensation for Personal Injury, Cmnd. 7054 (1978) Vol. 1, esp. Ch 31.

71 The Pearson Commission sought to deal with this problem by suggesting statutory specification of activities included in the strict liability regime. But this would not overcome the difficulty inherent in specifying in advance activities which are ultra-hazardous without reference to particular circumstances.

consequences of the escape, but also of natural and anticipated consequences. The judgment of Windeyer J. in *Benning* v. *Wong* is even more equivocal. His Honour suggests that liability rests on causation and reinforces this by saying that the defences of act of God and act of stranger are based on a break in the chain of causation between accumulation and injury.[72] On the other hand, his Honour also says that these defences are 'essentially pleas of no negligence' (that is, unforeseeability of damage and no carelessness on the part of the defendant)[73] and that recovery for damage depends on being able to say that it was reasonably foreseeable that if the accumulated thing escaped it would be likely to do damage. This last is a very minimal requirement: the defendant need not have been able to foresee the type of damage but just damage. In most cases this would impose no real limit on liability at all. The best that can be said on this issue is that the law is unclear as between foreseeability and causal directness as the rule of remoteness. This is related to the general ambivalence of the law about the proper role of strict liability.

Finally, there is some authority for a rule that the plaintiff may not recover under *Rylands* v. *Fletcher* if he suffers damage from conducting on his land a hypersensitive activity.[74]

II: LIABILITY FOR FIRE

As we have seen, a defendant can be held liable for the escape of fire[75] under *Rylands* v. *Fletcher* principles.[76] If the conditions of liability under these principles are not satisfied, the plaintiff will have to prove negligence on the part of the defendant or someone for whose acts he is responsible in order to succeed. Because of the great potential dangers involved in the use of fire, the standard of care required of the defendant is very high.[77]

Section 86 of the Fires Prevention (Metropolis) Act 1774, which is probably part of the law of all Australian jurisdictions except New South Wales (and, *query*, the Northern Territory),[78] excludes liability of an occupier of premises for fires which accidentally begin on his premises and spread to other property. The plaintiff must prove that the fire did not

---

72 (1969) 122 C.L.R. 249, 306-7.
73 (1969) 122 C.L.R. 249, 306.
74 *Eastern and South African Telegraph Co.* v. *Cape Town Tramways* [1902] A.C. 381.
75 On the difficult history of liability for fire see A.I. Ogus [1969] *C.L.J.* 104.
76 There is no strict liability for fire outside *Rylands* v. *Fletcher: Hazelwood* v. *Webber* (1934) 52 C.L.R. 268; *Holderness* v. *Goslin* [1975] 2 N.Z.L.R. 46.
77 *Pett* v. *Sims Paving* [1928] V.L.R.; *McCarty* v. *Leeming* [1937] S.A.S.R. 432; *Preston Erections Pty Ltd* v. *Rheem Australia Pty Ltd* (1978) 21 A.L.R. 379, 387 *per* Murphy J.
78 *Re* New South Wales see *Hazelwood* v. *Webber* (1934) 52 C.L.R. 268. In Queensland (*Abel Lemon & Co. Pty Ltd* v. *Baylin Pty Ltd* (1985) 63 A.L.R. 161), South Australia (*Young* v. *Tilley* [1913] S.A.S.R. 87) and Western Australia (in *Robert* v. *Czycyerskyj* [1961] W.A.R. 175, D'Arcy J. assumed the section was in force in W.A. without actually deciding the point) the Act was received as part of the reception of imperial statute law. See also Local Government (Consequential Amendments) Act 1962 (Tas.), s.37; Supreme Court Act 1958 (Vic.), s.68; Careless Use of Fire Act 1936 (A.C.T.). The Act is also in force in *New Zealand: New Zealand Forest Products* v. *O'Sullivan* [1974] 2 N.Z.L.R. 80.

begin accidentally.[79] The phrase 'accidentally begins' refers to a fire that begins by inevitable accident as distinct from one caused intentionally or by the negligence of someone for whom the occupier was responsible.[80] The Act does not provide a good defence when the conditions of liability under *Rylands* v. *Fletcher* principles are satisfied.[81] Where a fire begins accidentally but then by negligence spreads and causes damage, the Act provides no defence. This circumvention of the words of the Act is rather clumsily reconciled with its terms by drawing a distinction between the initial fire and the conflagration which causes the damage. So the Act provided no defence in *Musgrove* v. *Pandelis*[82] where a fire which began accidentally in a carburettor of a vehicle parked in a garage spread as a result of failure of the chauffeur to turn off the petrol tap. Again, the Act was of no assistance to the landowner in *Goldman* v. *Hargarve*[83] whose less-than-entirely-successful attempts to extinguish a fire begun by a bolt of lightning were not adequate to prevent it rekindling itself some days later and damaging the plaintiff's property.

III: DEFENCES

The defences to a *Rylands* v. *Fletcher* claim can be conveniently divided into two groups: those which relate to the accumulation and those which relate to the escape. Into the former category fall consent and statutory authority and into the latter act of God and act of a stranger. We will consider these defences in turn.

1. CONSENT

Where the plaintiff has consented to the accumulation, the balance of benefits and burdens arising from it can be presumed to be at least evenly balanced so far as the plaintiff is concerned; and so it is no longer fair that the defendant should be liable strictly for damage caused by his activity.[84] Consent can be constructive: the plaintiff may not have explicitly agreed to accept the burdens inherent in a situation, but if he has willingly enjoyed the benefits he may be required to accept the burdens, unless he can prove negligence. For example, in *Kiddle* v. *City Business Properties*[85] it was held that a tenant of part of a building could not recover for water damage caused by overflow from a blocked gutter shared with his landlord

---

79 *Young* v. *Tilley* [1913] S.A.S.R. 87; *How* v. *Jones* [1953] S.A.S.R. 82; *Robert* v. *Czycyerskyj* [1961] W.A.R. 175; *General Jones* v. *Wildridge* [1988] Tas.R. (N.C. 12).

80 *Filliter* v. *Phipard* (1847) 11 Q.B. 347; *Goldman* v. *Hargrave* [1967] 1 A.C. 645; *New Zealand Forest Products* v. *O'Sullivan* [1974] 2 N.Z.L.R. 80.

81 *Musgrove* v. *Pandelis* [1919] 2 K.B. 43.

82 [191] 2 K.B. 43.

83 [1967] 1 A.C. 645.

84 *A-G* v. *Cory Bros & Co. Ltd* [1921] A.C. 521,539 *per* Viscount Finlay.

85 [1942] 1 K.B. 269; cf. *Peters* v. *Prince of Wales Theatre (Birmingham) Ltd* [1943] 1 K.B. 73.

without proof of negligence, since the gutter was there with the consent and for the benefit of both of them. The onus of proof on the issue of consent is probably on the defendant.

2. Statutory Authority

As we noted in the chapter on nuisance, a legislative authorization of an activity (in this context, an accumulation of dangerous things) also changes the balance of benefits and burdens by leading to a presumption that what the defendant is authorized to do is in the public interest. We have seen that a plea of statutory authorization in answer to a claim in private nuisance will succeed only if the defendant can prove that the damage was an inevitable result of performing authorized acts or was inflicted despite the exercise by him of all reasonable care in performing authorized acts. It is not clear whether the effect of a plea of statutory authorization in a *Rylands* v. *Fletcher* action is the same.

The difficulty arises from the fact that whereas in nuisance the ultimate question is whether the statutory provision covers the damage inflicted (damage being the gist of an action in nuisance), in *Rylands* v. *Fletcher* it is possible to argue that the proper question is whether the accumulation is authorized by statute; if so, the principle in *Rylands* v. *Fletcher* is inapplicable and the question of whether the defendant is liable for the injury inflicted will depend on whether it was negligently inflicted. On the other hand, if principles analogous to those of private nuisance are applied to *Rylands* v. *Fletcher*, the question will be whether the injury inflicted was the result of negligence in making or maintaining the accumulation. Thus both approaches in the end lead to an inquiry about negligence; the crucial difference between them is seen as lying in the question of where the burden of proof on the issue of negligence lies. On the nuisance approach the defendant must prove that it took all reasonable care. On the first approach, since *Rylands* v. *Fletcher* principles do not apply to statutorily authorized accumulations, it is said that it is for the plaintiff to prove negligence, not for the defendant to disprove it. There is authority for each of these approaches.[86]

The crux of the approach which treats statutory authorization as ousting the principle in *Rylands* v. *Fletcher* seems to be the idea that to allow a plea of no-negligence in answer to a *Rylands* v. *Fletcher* claim would be virtually to defeat the purpose of the rule. Further, to overcome this by imposing strict liability for the escape of things stored under statutory authority would impose an excessive burden on statutory undertakers. But neither of these propositions is necessarily acceptable. Dealing with the latter first, while it would be no doubt oppressive to impose strict liability in nuisance on statutory undertakers for the laying of pipes and the charging of them with water or gas (hence the statutory authorization),

86 Onus on plaintiff: Menzies & Owen JJ. in *Benning* v. *Wong* (1969) 122 C.L.R. 249; *Dunne* v. *North Western Gas Board* [1964] 2 Q.B. 806. Onus on defendant: Barwick C.J. & Windeyer J. (dissenting) in *Benning* v. *Wong; Fullarton* v. *North Melbourne etc. Co.* (1916) 21 C.L.R. 181; *Matheson* v. *Northcote College* [1975] 2 N.Z.L.R. 106.

it does not follow that it is oppressive to hold the undertaker strictly liable for personal injury (and perhaps property damage) inflicted by the escape of water or gas. Since the public at large reaps the benefit of the provision of essential commodities and services, there is no reason why it should not, and good reason why it should, bear the cost of personal injuries (and perhaps property damage) caused by that provision. This is best achieved by imposing liability on the undertaker, who can then pass on the cost to consumers in higher prices. The principle that the undertaker may plead lack of negligence is, on this view, an unnecessary concession. In both nuisance and *Rylands* v. *Fletcher* a distinction could be drawn between the activity and damage caused by it, and the principles of statutory authorization applied only to the former, strict liability being imposed for the latter.

As for the first point, to allow a plea of no-negligence does not necessarily defeat the purpose of a strict liability rule, although it does, undoubtedly, water it down. It is often extremely difficult to prove a negative—the absence of negligence, even though the statutory undertaker will have much better access to the relevant information than the plaintiff. Thus in practice the liability will often be strict while in theory it is hybrid—negligence is relevant but the onus rests on the defendant.

At all events, if *Rylands* v. *Fletcher* is seen as a form of nuisance, there seems little reason to treat them differently so far as the defence of statutory authorization is concerned. This was the approach of Barwick C.J. and Windeyer J. in *Benning* v. *Wong*, who interpreted a plea of statutory authorization to a claim under *Rylands* v. *Fletcher* as a plea of no-negligence. On the other hand, if we wish to take seriously the role of strict liability as a mechanism for allocating the risks of activities which benefit the public to the public as a whole, there is an argument for treating both nuisance and *Rylands* v. *Fletcher* in the same way by disallowing the plea of no-negligence and simply asking whether the activity which caused the damage was, as conducted, authorized by statute. In cases where the statute gave the undertaker a degree of choice or discretion in the performance of his functions, the court would have to decide, according to principles concerning the exercise of statutory discretion, whether the undertaker had acted within the limits of that discretion. If it had, no action would lie; but if it had not, it would be liable regardless of negligence.

3. Act of the Plaintiff

Where the escape is caused solely by an act of the plaintiff he would clearly have no cause of action. But what if it is caused partly by his fault? Should contributory negligence be a defence? Only if the defendant had also been negligent would the apportionment legislation apply. But if the function of strict liability is to allocate and spread the cost of risks fairly there seems no reason why fault of the plaintiff should be available either as a complete or a partial defence[87]—the fact that the plaintiff was at fault

87 See *Martin's Camera Corner* v. *Hotel Mayfair* [1976] 2 N.S.W.L.R. 15, 27 *per* Yeldham J.

does not mean that he has benefited from the defendant's activity. On the other hand, to the extent that fault is introduced as a relevant factor in *Rylands* v. *Fletcher* cases, the defendant ought to be allowed to plead the plaintiff's fault at least in mitigation of damages (that is, in cases where he, too, was at fault).

4. ACT OF A STRANGER

If the escape is the result of the intentional and unforeseeable acts of a third party the defendant can escape liability.[88] We could view this rule as based on principles of causation—the voluntary (that is, intentional) act of the third party breaks the chain of causation between the accumulation and the damage. However, the defence seems to be seen as embodying a plea of no-negligence, the onus of proving that the acts of the third party could not have been foreseen and that the reasonable person could not be expected to have taken precautions against them resting on the defendant.[89] An alternative way of viewing the defence is to say that a stranger is a person whom the defendant has no legal right to control or, in other words, a person for whose acts he is not vicariously liable.[90] A way of combining these two approaches is to say that if the defendant could not be expected to have foreseen and taken precautions against the intervention of the third parties, he will be liable for their acts only if the third parties were persons whom he had a right to control.[91]

5. ACT OF GOD

If the escape was caused by the operation of an act of God on the defendant's accumulation, the defendant can escape liability. An act of God is a natural event which no one could reasonably be expected to foresee or take precautions against.[92] Thus the defence amounts to a plea of no-negligence. The onus of establishing that the event was an act of God rests on the defendant. Whether an occurrence is an act of God is a question of fact which depends on local conditions.[93]

---

88 *Rickards* v. *Lothian* [1913] A.C. 263.

89 *Benning* v. *Wong* (1969) 122 C.L.R. 249, 306 *per* Windeyer J.; cf. *Emanuel* v. *Greater London Council* [1971] 2 All E.R. 835; *Eriksen* v. *Clifton* [1963] N.Z.L.R. 705.

90 *Holderness* v. *Goslin* [1975] 2 N.Z.L.R. 46.

91 *Perry* v. *Kendricks Transport* [1956] 1 All E.R. 154, 159-60 *per* Jenkins L.J. Conversely, if the acts of the third party were clearly ones for which the defendant is vicariously liable, the question of whether they were foreseeable need not be considered.

92 *Nicols* v. *Marsland* (1876) 2 Ex.D. 1; *Commissioner of Railways (W.A.)* v. *Stewart* (1936) 56 C.L.R. 520, 528-9 *per* Latham C.J.

93 *Lucas* v. *Commissioners for Railways* (1890) 24 S.A.L.R. 24.

IV: RYLANDS V. FLETCHER AND NEGLIGENCE

It is clear that elements of fault are contained in the principles of *Rylands* v. *Fletcher* liability.[94] Non-naturalness of user depends to some extent on whether the defendant took all reasonable care in conducting his activity, although a user may in theory be non-natural even if he did. A plea of statutory authorization has the effect either of ousting the operation of *Rylands* v. *Fletcher* principles and putting the plaintiff to proof of negligence or of allowing the defendant to exonerate himself by proving that he took all due care to prevent the damage. The pleas of act of God and act of a stranger seem to amount in most cases to pleas of no-negligence.

The effect of the introduction of these elements of fault is to shift the focus of the tort from the accumulation and the risks created by it and from the question of who, as a matter of fair distribution of benefits and burdens, ought to bear the costs generated by those risks, to the way in which the escape and the injury came about: was it anyone's fault? This change of focus has more or less destroyed *Rylands* v. *Fletcher* as a source of strict liability, and further witnesses the dominance of negligence as a principle of liability in the modern law of tort.[95]

94 G.H.L. Fridman (1956) 34 *Can. B.R.* 810.
95 P. Cane (1982) 2 *O.J.L.S.* 30, 53-4.

18

LIABILITY FOR ANIMALS

Rules of law concerned exclusively with liability for injury and damage done by animals have existed for many centuries. The explanation for this is largely socio-economic. In medieval England, which was, of course, an agricultural community, very little land was securely fenced, and as a result the interests of crop growers and cattle raisers frequently came into conflict. Hence arose the rules of cattle trespass governing liability for damage to land and crops done by wandering animals. Injury to persons by animals is also likely to have been more common in an agricultural community where people and animals in large numbers lived in close proximity to one another, where animals were probably less closely controlled than they are today and where dogs, for example, were often kept not as pets but for purposes which required their being trained to take hostile action. Hence arose rules imposing strict liability for personal injuries inflicted by dangerous animals.

The lack of fencing also accounts for the old rule that landowners are immune from liability for injury or damage done by domesticated animals straying from land adjoining the highway on to the road. Because there was very little fast or vehicular traffic on the roads (and so the exercise of a little care could prevent collisions), the risk of straying animals was considered to be one which road users had to accept. At first sight this rule might seem in conflict with strict liability for cattle trespass, but the two are compatible: the owner of crops can do little or nothing (given that fencing is not expected) to protect static crops effectively from wandering animals, whereas human users of the highway can take evasive action.

Besides these special rules governing liability for animals, damage caused by animals could in the right circumstances also be actionable in other torts, such as *Rylands* v. *Fletcher*, nuisance and negligence (including the rules governing the liability of occupiers and employers). In the modern law of animals two broad questions are prominent. One is the extent to which liability for animals ought to be strict or should, on the other hand, be made to depend on proof of negligence. The other is the extent to which there ought to be special rules governing liability for animals. Liability for animals, based as it is ultimately on control, can be analogized to liability for acts of human third parties, and this latter is dealt with by adaptation of general torts, not by categories of special rules. It may be, however, that given the relative lack of control which is customarily exercised over animals as compared with children or prisoners (for example), and given the wide variety of circumstances in which animals are kept—sometimes in large numbers (usually in rural areas) for commercial reasons and sometimes in small numbers (often in urban areas) as pets or for security reasons—it might be thought that some special rules would be appropriate. We will return to these questions later.

I: CATTLE TRESPASS

The tort of cattle trespass is related to ordinary trespass; so the rules about title to sue in trespass apply also to cattle trespass. For example, the occupier of land can recover for personal injuries inflicted on him by straying cattle, but anyone else on the land could not.[1] But the two torts do not cover exactly the same ground. Cattle trespass only applies if cattle stray on to neighbouring land, not if they are driven there by their owner; in the latter case an ordinary action of trespass would lie. Trespass to person or goods is not, as such, actionable in cattle trespass; cattle trespass is basically trespass to land.[2] The rules of cattle trespass do not apply to cattle which are being driven along the highway and which stray on to property adjoining the highway. If the property owner is to recover damages he must prove negligence because, it is said, the wandering of cattle which are being driven along the highway is one of the inevitable risks of owning land adjacent to the highway which the frontager must accept. On the other hand, if cattle trespass applies, liability is strict in the sense that the plaintiff need not prove lack of reasonable care.[3]

Because cattle trespass originated to protect crops, the question of whether the rules apply to a particular animal depend on the propensity of animals of the type in question to damage such things, not on their tendency, for example, to chase other animals.[4] On the other hand, the tort only applies to animals which the law classifies as not dangerous to people—animals *mansuetae naturae*, and not to animals which are classified as dangerous to people—animals *ferae naturae*, or animals which, although not classified as dangerous, have, to the knowledge of the owner, a dangerous propensity in cases where the damage done is a manifestation of that propensity. In other words, cattle trespass and the *scienter* action, which we will consider below, are mutually exclusive.

---

1 *Wormald* v. *Cole* [1954] 1 Q.B. 614.
2 *Manton* v. *Brocklebank* [1923] 2 K.B. 212; *Edwards* v. *Rawlins* [1924] N.Z.L.R. 333.
3 For all of these propositions see *Tillett* v. *Ward* (1882) 10 Q.B.D. 17; *Bourchier* v. *Mitchell* (1891) 17 V.L.R. 27; *Rayner* v. *Shearing* [1926] S.A.S.R. 313.
4 *Buckle* v. *Holmes* [1926] 2 K.B. 125.

Damages for cattle trespass can be recovered in respect of all the natural and probable consequences of the trespass. Originally the damages recoverable in cattle trespass were confined to damage to the surface of the land trespassed upon and to depasturing of crops. But this was gradually extended to cover infection of cattle by trespassing stock and injury to animals of the occupier. Cattle trespass also covers personal injury to the occupier of the land trespassed upon. But in the case at least of injury to people (and possibly also of injury to animals)[5] cattle trespass is not the appropriate action if the injury is the result of the display by the trespassing animal of a known dangerous propensity. So if a straying animal, known to be vicious, attacks the occupier, *scienter* would be the appropriate action; but if it just knocks the occupier over while blundering about, cattle trespass is appropriate.[6] These distinctions do the law little credit, and led Hodson L.J. in *Wormald* v. *Cole* to suggest that all personal injury to the occupier should be actionable in cattle trespass provided it was a direct result of the trespass and regardless of whether it was viciously inflicted.[7]

Besides a remedy in damages, a landowner who finds cattle trespassing on his property often has a statutory right to impound the cattle. The landowner also has a common law self-help remedy called 'distress damage feasant'. This right to detain the cattle until the plaintiff pays damages may not be exercised until the owner of the cattle has had a reasonable opportunity to remove them.[8] Distress may only be made if the animal is actually in the process of doing damage or has done damage and has to be distrained to prevent it doing more.

The law of cattle trespass is very technical and abounds with restrictions and qualifications which are of very little, if any, apparent value. The New South Wales Law Reform Commission[9] was most impressed by the fact that a non-occupier could not recover for personal injuries; and the fact that cattle trespass does not apply to the case of animals wandering off the highway on to adjoining land. The Commission recommended the abolition of the tort of cattle trespass and of the remedy of distress damage feasant (which recommendations were implemented in ss.4 and 5 respectively of the Animals Act 1977 (N.S.W.)) in favour of applying the ordinary rules of negligence.[10] The tort has also been abolished, by implication, in South Australia by s.17a(1) of the Wrongs Act. But there may well be an argument for retaining strict liability in at least some cases of straying by animals, especially if the owner is a commercial enterprise and so in a good position to bear or insure against the loss. In New South Wales, the A.C.T. and apparently in South Australia, damage by straying

5 *Lee* v. *Riley* (1865) 18 C.B.(N.S.) 722.
6 *Wormald* v. *Cole* [1954] 1 Q.B. 614; but see *Mark* v. *Barkla* [1935] N.Z.L.R. 347.
7 [1954] Q.B. 614, 633.
8 *Goodwyn* v. *Chevely* [1859] L.J. Ex. 298.
9 L.R.C. 8 (1970).
10 The tort and the remedy have also been abolished in the A.C.T.: Civil Liability (Animals) Act 1984 ss.4,5.

animals is not now actionable in *Rylands* v. *Fletcher* either,[11] although it might still be actionable in nuisance. But it is by no means clear that liability for damage to person or property done by animals would be strict in nuisance. It is somewhat curious at a time when 'strict' liability for product-caused injuries has just been introduced that liability for animals should be reformed so as to turn on negligence rather than strict liability. Why this indiscriminate 'tenderness' for animal owners?

II: LIABILITY FOR DANGEROUS ANIMALS: THE SCIENTER ACTION

1. Types of Animals

The law classifies animals into two groups: those which are dangerous to people—*ferae naturae,* and those which are not dangerous to people—*mansuetae naturae*. Animals are classified not according to their individual training and habits but according to the general habits of the species to which they belong.[12] Examples of animals *ferae naturae* are elephants,[13] dingoes,[14] lions,[15] gorillas and tigers;[16] examples of animals *mansuetae naturae* are horses,[17] cattle,[18] camels,[19] bees,[20] dogs and cats,[21] goats,[22] and kangaroos.[23] The classification of animals is a question of law for the judge. But it is not a question on which evidence may be called; the judge takes judicial notice of the characteristics of the species in question. This means that the categories into which the law divides animals are not very detailed because judicial notice can only be taken of matters of common knowledge. So no distinction is drawn, for example, between Indian and African elephants.[24] And since what is relevant are species characteristics, no distinction is drawn between wild and circus elephants, for example.[25] Animals which are classified as *mansuetae naturae* may be so classified

11 Animals Act 1977 (N.S.W.), s.9; Civil Liability (Animals) Ordinance 1984 s.7; Wrongs Act (S.A.) s.17a(10)(a) preserves actions in nuisance; but is *Rylands* v. *Fletcher* a form of nuisance?

12 *Behrens* v. *Bertram Mills Circus Ltd* [1957] 2 Q.B. 1 (circus elephant *ferae naturae* even though 'no more dangerous than a cow'); *Filburn* v. *People's Palace & Aquarium Co. Ltd* (1890) 25 Q.B.D. 258.

13 ibid.

14 *Fischer* v. *Stuart* (1979) 25 A.L.R. 336.

15 *Trethowan* v. *Capron* [1861] V.R. 460, 462 *per* Adam J.

16 *Buckle* v. *Holmes* [1926] 2 K.B. 125, 128 *per* Bankes L.J.

17 e.g. *Manton* v. *Brocklebank* [1923] 2 K.B. 212.

18 In the narrow sense; 'cattle' in the term 'cattle trespass' is wider, but only animals *mansuetae naturae* fall within it.

19 *McQuaker* v. *Goddard* [1940] 1 Q.B. 687; *Nada Shah* v. *Sleeman* (1917) 19 W.A.L.R. 119.

20 *Stormer* v. *Ingram* (1978) 21 S.A.S.R. 93.

21 *Trethowan* v. *Capron* [1961] V.R. 460, 463.

22 *R.* v. *Drinkwater* (1981) 27 S.A.S.R. 396.

23 *Lake* v. *Taggart* (1978) 1 S.R.(W.A.) 89.

24 *Behrens* v. *Bertram Mills Circus* [1957] 2 Q.B. 1.

25 ibid.

either because experience has shown that by their nature they are harmless to people (e.g. rabbits) or because the animals have become harmless by cultivation and breeding (e.g. sheep, horses, oxen and dogs).[26]

2. STRICT LIABILITY

Liability for injury or damage done by an animal *ferae naturae* which escapes from the control of its keeper is said to be strict. The keeper is liable for all the natural consequences of the escape even if he took all reasonable care to prevent the escape. This is so whether or not he realized that the animal was dangerous: since it is by common knowledge dangerous, the keeper ought to have realized this too. To this extent liability for damage done by dangerous animals is not strict but is based on foreseeability of injury, the infliction of injury being in the ordinary nature of the animal in question.

This rule of 'strict liability' also applies to any particular animal *mansuetae naturae* which the defendant actually knew[27] to have a propensity to injure humans. The plaintiff must prove both that the animal had a vicious propensity and that the defendant actually knew this. Proof of the latter may be very difficult, especially where the claim of knowledge is based on very few incidents.[28] Sometimes the knowledge of a third party is, as a matter of law, attributed to the defendant. This is so if the defendant has delegated full custody and control of the animal to another who knows of the propensity. Where this is not so, but the third party has general control of the animal or of the premises on which it is kept, it is a question of fact (not a matter of law) whether the third party's knowledge has been communicated to him.[29] In neither case need the third party be a servant of the defendant.

Proof of vicious propensity does not require proof that the animal has injured anyone in the past; it is enough to prove that it has manifested a tendency to attack humans.[30] Nor is it necessary to prove the exact way (e.g. kicking, biting) in which the animal was liable to do injury.[31] But it is not enough to show a tendency to attack other animals.[32] The drawing of this distinction can create great difficulties for the plaintiff, as in *Eather* v. *Jones*.[33] There the animal, a horse, had chased another horse on which the plaintiff was riding and had bitten the plaintiff when he put out his hand in an attempt to protect himself. It was held that the plaintiff had failed to prove that the horse had a propensity to injure humans because the incident was consistent with a propensity to attack other animals, the

26 *Filburn* v. *People's Palace* (1890) 25 Q.B.D. 258.
27 Hence the name of the action: *scienter*, Latin for 'knowingly'. The early writs were directed at one who knowingly kept (*scienter retinuit*) a dangerous animal.
28 e.g. *Eather* v. *Jones* [1974] 2 N.S.W.L.R. 19; affirmed (1975) 49 A.L.J.R. 254.
29 *Crittendon* v. *Brenock* [1949] V.L.R. 366.
30 *Worth* v. *Gilling* (1866) L.R. 2 C.P. 1; *Crittendon* v. *Brenock* [1949] V.L.R. 366.
31 *Fitzgerald* v. *E.D. & A.D. Cooke Bourne (Farms) Ltd* [1964] 1 Q.B. 249, 260 *per* Willmer L.J.
32 *Eather* v. *Jones* [1974] 2 N.S.W.L.R. 19; (1975) 49 A.L.J.R. 254.
33 ibid.

injury to the plaintiff being incidental. Murphy J., who dissented, thought that it should be enough for the plaintiff to prove a propensity to attack other animals and an attack causing him injury. There certainly seems to underlie the distinction between a propensity to injure humans and to injure animals a questionable idea that animals make conscious choices about who or what to attack. If no such assumption is made then there seems little reason to discriminate between attacks directed at humans and attacks on animals which just happen to injure humans. After all, the horse in *Eather* v. *Jones* apparently had a propensity to attack animals without regard to whether a human might get in the way. Why should it not be enough for the plaintiff to show either a propensity to attack humans or to attack other animals in circumstances which might injure a human?

At all events, a strong insistence on clear proof of a vicious propensity towards humans and of actual knowledge of the propensity really empties of any practical importance the theory that liability in a *scienter* action for damage done by animals *mansuetae naturae* is strict. It is true that the plaintiff does not have to prove that the plaintiff failed to take reasonable care, but in a negligence action the principle of *res ipsa loquitur* would apply to a case in which an animal known to be vicious (or, indeed, an animal *ferae naturae*) attacked a human being, and this renders the distinction between *scienter* and negligence of academic importance only. This may be why in some cases *scienter* and negligence are virtually equated.[34] In this light, a plaintiff has very little incentive to sue in *scienter* rather than negligence, since in the latter he need only show that the defendant ought to have known of the animal's vicious propensity.[35]

3. RECOVERABLE DAMAGE

Since what attracts strict liability is the propensity to injure a person, it might be thought that recoverable damage would be restricted to the direct and natural consequences of the 'exercise' of such a propensity, namely personal injury. The question was discussed by Devlin J. in *Behrens* v. *Bertram Mills Circus*[36] where the plaintiff was injured when a circus booth was brought down by an elephant chasing a dog which had barked at it. The elephant was classified as *ferae naturae,* but it was argued that since the damage here was not the result of a vicious attack on a human the defendant ought not to be liable. However, Devlin J. held that there was no illogicality in saying that liability was strict only for damage done by vicious animals to human beings, but at the same time imposing liability for all damage which was the direct result of an escape of the animal from the control of its keeper whether or not the result of a vicious attack on a human. But Devlin J. thought that this harsh rule should perhaps only apply to animals *ferae naturae,* and not to animals

34 e.g. *Cox* v. *Burbridge* (1863) 13 C.B.(N.S.) 430; cf. *Matheson* v. *G. Stuckey & Co. Pty Ltd* [1921] V.L.R. 637.
35 *Southall* v. *Jones* (1879) 5 V.L.R.(L) 403.
36 [1957] 2 Q.B. 1.

mansuetae naturae with a known vicious propensity. In the latter case liability should accrue only for damage resulting from a vicious attack on a human.

There is a conflict in the law here. It has been said that the *scienter* action was an attempt by medieval courts to develop a workable rule of thumb to ascertain when the defendant was at fault: fault was presumed from knowledge of vicious propensity.[37] And we have already noted the lack of practical difference between *scienter* and negligence. In this light there is an argument for restricting liability for damage done by an animal *mansuetae naturae* with a known vicious propensity to the foreseeable consequences of a vicious attack. The position in relation to animals *ferae naturae* is more difficult. Since the criterion of dangerousness is propensity to attack people, and since an individual animal may be *ferae naturae* even if as docile and tame as an animal *mansuetae naturae*, it is difficult to see the justice of a general rule of liability for all damage done by such an animal. On the other hand, even 'harmless' animals *ferae naturae* can have a potential for doing much damage to chattels and other animals; for example, the sheer bulk of an elephant makes it a danger in an urban environment. Even some animals *mansuetae naturae*, such as rabbits, have a great potential for damaging land and crops. It seems clear, therefore, that the criterion of dangerousness to people is a strait-jacket which prevents a proper consideration of the problems associated with the keeping of animals.

4. Reform

One response to the need for greater flexibility is that adopted in New South Wales, South Australia and the A.C.T., where the *scienter* action has been abolished and replaced by the ordinary rules of liability in negligence and nuisance.[38] While this no doubt achieves flexibility, it does so at the cost of the element of strict liability which it might be thought worthwhile to retain and even to strengthen in some cases. For example, there does seem to be a good argument for imposing strict liability on circus owners of at least some species of animals. Circuses usually operate in urban areas where an escape is potentially very dangerous, and the circus proprietor is in a good position to insure against injury and damage. No doubt, in a negligence action a very high standard of care would be imposed in such cases, but the issue of negligence still has to be resolved, and this takes time and money; further, the circus proprietor who is in the better position to bear the loss may escape liability, even under strict standards of care. Animal transporters should perhaps also be subject to strict liability.

---

37 G. Williams *Liability for Animals* (London, 1939) p. 273.

38 Animals Act 1977 (N.S.W.) s.7; Wrongs Act (S.A.) s.17a(1),(9),(10)(a); Civil Liability (Animals) Ordinance 1984 (A.C.T.) s.6.

5. SCIENTER AND RYLANDS V. FLETCHER

Two final matters need to be discussed in relation to the common law. In *Rylands* v. *Fletcher*[39] Blackburn J. linked liability for dangerous animals with liability for the escape of dangerous things. This suggested the idea that a defendant could only be required to compensate for damage caused by a dangerous animal if the animal escaped from land controlled by the defendant on to land not in his control. But in *Higgins* v. *William Inglis & Son Pty Ltd*[40] it was held that liability in no way depends on proof of escape, but merely on keeping the animal after acquiring knowledge of its mischievous habits. Thereafter the owner keeps the animal 'at his peril' whether or not it escapes from confinement. In that case the plaintiff was injured by a bull which he was inspecting in its pen at a sale yard. It is clear, therefore, that even if *scienter* and *Rylands* v. *Fletcher* come from the same juristic stem, they are different branches of strict liability.

6. DEFENCES TO A SCIENTER CLAIM

What defences are available to a *scienter* action? In *Higgins* v. *Inglis*[41] it was held that at common law contributory negligence as such was not a defence to a *scienter* claim; the only defence was that the plaintiff was the sole cause of his own injury by, for example, teasing or baiting the animal.[42] It followed from this that the apportionment legislation did not apply to a *scienter* claim because where the injury was only partly the plaintiff's fault, that fault would not fall within the statutory definition of fault, namely such as would, apart from the Act (that is, at common law), have given rise to a defence of contributory negligence.

Volenti is clearly available as a defence to a *scienter* claim, although here, as elsewhere, it is very difficult to establish.[43] In *Rands* v. *McNeil*[44] it was held that an employer is not strictly liable to an employee for injury suffered while handling dangerous animals in the course of his employment. The employer only has a very high duty of care not to expose his employee to unnecessary risks. In England, the effect of *Rands* v. *McNeil* has been reversed by s.6(5) of the Animals Act 1971 (U.K.) which provides that where a person employed as a servant by a keeper of an animal incurs a risk incidental to his employment, he shall not be treated as accepting it voluntarily. In Australia the position is unclear, but would appear to be that a *scienter* action could be brought by an employee against his employer but that *volenti* would be available as a defence, subject to the

39 (1866) L.R. 1 Ex. 265.

40 [1978] 1 N.S.W.L.R. 649; cf. *Dorman* v. *Horscroft* (1980) 24 S.A.S.R. 154; *Christian* v. *Johanesson* [1956] N.Z.L.R. 664; *Rands* v. *McNeil* [1955] 1 Q.B. 253 *contra*; question left open in *James* v. *Wellington City* [1972] N.Z.L.R. 978.

41 [1978] 1 N.S.W.L.R. 649; cf. *Dorman* v. *Horscroft* (1980) 24 S.A.S.R. 154.

42 cf. *Simpson* v. *Bannerman* (1932) 47 C.L.R. 378 *per* Starke J.; *Behrens* v. *Bertram Mills* [1957] 2 Q.B. 1, 19-20 *per* Devlin J.; *Dorman* v. *Horscroft* (1980) 24 S.A.S.R. 154; *James* v. *Wellington City* [1972] N.Z.L.R. 70.

43 *Behrens* v. *Bertram Mills* [1957] 2 Q.B. 1, 20-1; *Dorman* v. *Horscroft* (1980) 24 S.A.S.R. 154; *James* v. *Wellington City* [1972] N.Z.L.R. 70.

44 [1955] 1 Q.B. 253.

strictures on that defence in the employment context. In South Australia s. 17(a)(5) of the Wrongs Act provides that 'it shall not be presumed' that an employee has accepted risks attendant upon working with animals. The force of this provision is unclear because the law never applied such a presumption.

It is not clear whether it is a defence to a *scienter* claim that the plaintiff was a trespasser. Starke J. in *Simpson* v. *Bannerman* said it was, at least where the injury is done by an animal *mansuetae naturae* with known vicious propensities.[45] This defence in effect allows a landowner to keep an animal, such as a dog, for security purposes.[46] What if a landowner kept a vicious animal *ferae naturae* for such purposes? A court might require him to give some warning of the presence of the animal. Indeed, there seems no reason why this should not be required in the first case also.

In *Behrens* v. *Bertram Mills*[47] Devlin J. said, *obiter*, that act of a stranger was no defence to a *scienter* claim. As for act of God, in *Nicols* v. *Marsland*[48] Bramwell J. said that act of God would be no defence to an action in respect of damage done by an animal *ferae naturae*; but in *Baker* v. *Snell*[49] it was held that act of God might be a defence to a *scienter* claim. As we have seen before, if these defences are allowed they inject an element of fault into action, and it is worth asking whether and to what extent the law governing liability for animals ought to be pushed in the direction of negligence and away from strict liability.

III: SCIENTER AND STATUTORY LIABILITY FOR DOGS

Dogs have been singled out for special statutory treatment. The reason, no doubt, is that they are common in urban areas and do in fact quite frequently attack humans and other animals.[50] All Australian jurisdictions except Queensland have legislation imposing liability for damage or injury caused by dogs. Such liability is additional to any liability arising at common law (such as for negligence or trespass). The widest of these provisions are derived from the English Dogs Act of 1906, and provide that the owner of a dog shall be (or 'is') liable for damage or injury done (or 'caused') by the dog without proof of vicious propensity or negligence

---

45 (1932) 47 C.L.R. 378, 384; cf. *Wilkins* v. *Manning* (1897) 13 W.N.(N.S.W.) 220; see Wrongs Act (S.A.) s.17a(6)(b).
46 cf. *Trethowan* v. *Capron* [1961] V.R. 460.
47 [1957] 2 Q.B. 1.
48 (1875) L.R. 10 Ex. 255, 260.
49 [1908] 2 K.B. 825.
50 *Liability for Injuries Caused by Dogs* N.S.W.L.R.C. 52 (1988) p. 32.

on the part of the owner.[51] These provisions are potentially extremely broad in their effect; at the very least they would not apply where the defendant could justify or excuse the intentional infliction of harm. Self-defence might, in certain circumstances, provide such a justification. In *Wilkins* v. *Manning*[52] it was held that it was a defence that the plaintiff was a trespasser on the owner's property. In *Trethowan* v. *Capron*[53] Adam J. denied this broad proposition but thought that a trespasser could not recover if the defendant kept the dog merely to guard and protect his property. It has been held that if the plaintiff's trespass is merely technical (for example, resting his arm on a fence) he will not be disentitled to recover by reason of it.[54]

Contributory negligence is apparently a good defence,[55] as perhaps is *volenti*,[56] and a plea that the plaintiff, by provoking the dog, was the cause of his own injuries.[57] Another difficulty in the legislation is the proper interpretation of the phrase 'injury (or damage) done (or caused) by a dog'. It has been held that this phrase is not to be read narrowly as limited to injury done by 'canine acts' nor to injury done by direct physical contact between the dog and the person, property or animal injured or damaged. The word 'done', where used, is to be equated with the word 'caused'. So the owner of a dog can be held liable if a person falls when stepping out of the way of an oncoming dog even if the dog does not come into contact with him;[58] or if a dog runs on to a highway and a car collides with it.[59]

The relevant provision in Victoria is somewhat narrower than the provisions we have been considering so far.[60] While it dispenses with the need to prove *scienter* or negligence in much the same terms as the basic provision, it only applies to cases where damage is caused by a dog which rushes at, attacks, worries or chases a person or any horse, cattle, sheep or poultry. Thus the provision rules out the widest interpretations of causation adopted under the more general provisions. The A.C.T. provision is more detailed again.[61] It only applies where a dog attacks a person and injures his person or property; or where a person reasonably fears an attack and as a result suffers personal injury; or where a domestic or farm animal is injured or killed by an attack. Certain defences are

---

51 Law Reform (Miscellaneous Provisions) Act (N.T.), s.32 ('loss, damage or injury as a result of the actions of the dog'); Dog Control Act 1979 (S.A.), s.2; Law of Animals Act 1962 (Tas.), s.15; Dog Act 1976 (W.A.), s.46 as amended by Dog Amendment Act 1987 s.38 (but liability for damage caused by dogs straying on to the highway is based on negligence: Dog Amendment Act 1983 (W.A.) s.3). 'Owner' usually includes the keeper or person in control of the dog.

52 (1897) 13 W.N. (N.S.W.) 220; cf. *Chittenden* v. *Hale* [1933] N.Z.L.R. 836; *Christian* v. *Johanesson* [1956] N.Z.L.R. 664; *Knowlson* v. *Solomon* [1969] N.Z.L.R. 686.

53 [1961] V.R. 460.

54 *Rigg* v. *Alietti* [1982] W.A.R. 203.

55 See New Zealand cases in fn. 52 above; *Irving* v. *Slevin* (1982) 30 S.A.S.R. 66.

56 *Chittenden* v. *Hale* [1933] N.Z.L.R. 836.

57 *Knowlson* v. *Solomon* [1969] N.Z.L.R. 686.

58 *Twentieth Century Blinds Pty Ltd* v. *Howes* [1974] 1 N.S.W.L.R. 244.

59 *Martignoni* v. *Harris* [1971] 2 N.S.W.L.R. 102.

60 Dog Act 1970 (Vic.), s.22.

61 Dog Control Act 1975 (A.C.T.), s.40.

provided: that the plaintiff was a trespasser or was contributorily negligent or provoked the dog; or that, in case of injury to a farm or domestic animal, the animal provoked the dog on the defendant's property. The A.C.T. Ordinance does not expressly dispense with the need to prove negligence, but the phrase 'is liable' probably achieves this effect.

The New South Wales provisions are also limited to dog attacks.[62] They impose liability for injury to or death of persons and damage to clothing, and for injury to or death of animals, as a result of dog attacks. The Act does not regulate situations which fall under the rules of occupiers' liability (in other words, to attacks which take place on land occupied by the dog's owner or on which the dog is ordinarily kept); so far as injury to persons is concerned, such cases are regulated by ss.8 and 10 of the Animals Act 1977, which basically make the common law rules of occupiers' liability the governing regime. The exclusion of cases covered by occupiers' liability rules is part of the policy given effect to in the Animals Act 1977 of abolishing special rules regulating liability for animals. The Animals Act also abolishes *scienter*, and so the provisions of the Dog Act do not contain words dispensing with the need for proof of *scienter*. The Dog Act provisions do not apply where the attack by the dog is an immediate response to human provocation or an attack by the injured animal. Section 20C provides that the legislation allowing apportionment for contributory negligence applies to the statutory action.

The New South Wales Law Reform Commission has recommended the repeal of s.20 of the Dog Act.[63] In its place would be put a much wider provision which would impose strict liability for all harm caused by a dog while outside its owner's property. The new provision would not be limited to 'dog attacks', and it would allow recovery for all personal injury (including nervous shock) and property damage. Contributory negligence and intentional cruelty or provocation by the victim would be available as defences. The reasons given for this proposal are that dogs 'by their mere presence in public places[64] . . . present a special risk to the community'; and that the imposition of strict liability is desirable in terms of the loss-allocation and harm-prevention goals of the law of tort.[65] However, inconsistently with these two latter reasons, the Commission also recommends that the ordinary law of occupier's liability (that is, negligence) should apply to harm caused by dogs on the owner's property.[66] One cannot help observing that the law of liability for personal injuries (and, to a lesser extent, property damage) is in an incoherent state: such liability depends, basically, on proof of negligence; but in selected areas

---

62 Dog Act 1966 (N.S.W.), ss.20-20C; but liability for damage caused by dogs straying on to the highway does not fall within these provisions: Dog (Amendment) Act 1977 (N.S.W.) s.2.

63 N.S.W.L.R.C. 52 (1988).

64 But strict liability would apply to harm caused anywhere outside the owner's property.

65 N.S.W.L.R.C. 52 (1988) pp. 80-1.

66 This proposal was partly an answer to an outrageous argument that property owners have a 'right to keep a watchdog', and that they should be immune from liability for harm done by a dog kept on the owner's property regardless of negligence.

negligence liability has been replaced by strict liability or by statutory no-fault compensation.

IV: LIABILITY FOR NEGLIGENCE

The owner or keeper of a dog can be liable in negligence as well as in *scienter*.[67] If the animal is *ferae naturae* the standard of care required will be very high, just as the standard of care required of those who use or keep dangerous chattels is very high. Where the animal is *mansuetae naturae* the main special factors relevant to determining the standard of care and the question of remoteness of damage are the fact that the animal is capable of spontaneous action and the issue of *scienter*. Since the action is one in negligence, not *scienter*, proof of *scienter* is not indispensable, but it will be difficult for a plaintiff to prove negligence or to establish that his damage was not too remote unless he can show that the animal had some particular propensity and that the defendant knew or ought to have known of the propensity.[68] This shows the closeness of *scienter* and negligence which we noted above. It has, on the other hand, also been said that, whereas the place where the incident happened is irrelevant in a *scienter* action, it is very relevant in a negligence action to deciding whether the defendant ought to have taken greater precautions.[69]

The question of the relevance of the ability of an animal to take spontaneous action was discussed in *Aldham* v. *United Dairies (London) Ltd*[70] where Lord Greene M.R. said that damage caused by an animal which escapes might not be attributable to the negligence of the defendant in letting it escape. If a horse is negligently released and it gallops off and knocks someone down this would be a result of the negligence. But if a horse having no known vicious propensities 'celebrates its freedom' by biting a passer-by, this would not be the result of the negligence but a spontaneous act of the horse for which its release merely gave it the opportunity. Ignoring the difficulty and unreality of seeking to discern an animal's intentions or motivations, it is clear from this that the question of knowledge of vicious propensities is relevant here too. Du Parcq L.J. made this even clearer by saying that negligence could not be established merely by proof that a defendant failed to provide against the possibility that a tame animal of mild disposition will do something contrary to its ordinary nature. For a defendant to be liable it would have to be shown that the conduct of the animal was foreseeable on the basis of its past conduct.

---

67 *Fardon* v. *Harcourt-Rivington* (1932) 48 T.L.R. 215, 217 *per* Lord Atkin.

68 *Galea* v. *Gillingham* [1987] 2 Qd.R. 365; *Carroll* v. *Rees* (1985) 2 M.V.R. 423. See generally *Draper* v. *Hodder* [1972] 2 Q.B. 556; cf. Wrongs Act (S.A.) s.17a(2)(a); but see sub-s.(3).

69 *Fitzgerald* v. *Cooke Bourne* [1964] 1 Q.B. 249, 257 *per* Willmer J.

70 [1940] 1 K.B. 507; see also judgment of Lord Du Parcq in *Searle* v. *Wallbank* [1947] A.C. 341.

V: THE RULE IN SEARLE V. WALLBANK

An important limitation on the liability of an owner or keeper of animals, not only in negligence but also in any relevant tort, is the rule that has become known as the rule in *Searle* v. *Wallbank*,[71] to the effect that an owner or occupier of land adjoining the highway is immune from liability for injury or damage caused on the highway by animals *mansuetae naturae* and not known to be dangerous, which stray on to the road because the defendant's land is not fenced or the fence is not kept in repair or a gate is left open. The rule, as we have noted, is traceable back to days when there was little traffic on highways and when land was rarely fenced. Thus the social conditions which gave rise to the rule have all but disappeared, and occur only in a few places today. Further, it is very strange that if an animal strays on to neighbouring land and does property damage there can be strict liability for cattle trespass, but that if an animal strays on to the highway and causes personal injury there cannot even be liability for negligence, let alone strict liability. The scales of justice are in this situation, it might be thought, weighted unduly in favour of the landowner, especially since not only does the landowner owe no duty of care to the road user, but also the motorist does owe the landowner a duty of care not to injure his animals.[72]

It is important to be clear about the exact scope of the rule in *Searle* v. *Wallbank*. It does not apply where an animal is brought on to the highway and left unattended there;[73] or where sheep are being driven along a stock route which crosses a highway on to which they are allowed to stray;[74] or where cattle are being driven along a highway;[75] or where a person is walking a dog on the highway.[76]

The status of the rule in *Searle* v. *Wallbank* in Australia was for a time a matter of controversy. The question was resolved by the High Court in *State Government Insurance Commission* v. *Trigwell*.[77] Strictly, the case only decides that the rule in *Searle* v. *Wallbank* is part of the law in South Australia, because part of the ratio of the decision is that the rule was received into the colony upon its settlement. But it probably will be treated as of general application. The main interest of the case is that it does not support the view that the rule in *Searle* v. *Wallbank* ought to be the law.[78] The main reason why the court refused to depart from *Searle* v. *Wallbank* was that it considered that the issues relevant to what the law ought to be were so complex that the court was not a suitable body to decide whether the law ought to be reformed. The proper avenue for reform was wide-ranging investigation and inquiry leading to legislation.

---

71 [1947] A.C. 341.
72 *Warren* v. *Anderson* (1958) 75 W.N.(N.S.W.) 494.
73 *Aldham* v. *United Dairies* [1940] 1 K.B. 507; *Dorsett* v. *Adelaide Corporation* [1913] S.A.S.R. 71; *Tucker* v. *Hennesy* [1918] V.L.R. 56; *Lind* v. *Stump* (1916) 12 Tas.S.R. 74.
74 *Hill* v. *Clark* (1969) 91 W.N.(N.S.W.) 550.
75 *Griffith* v. *Turner* [1955] N.Z.L.R. 1035.
76 *Pitcher* v. *Martin* [1937] 3 All E.R. 918.
77 (1978) 142 C.L.R. 617.
78 M. Atkinson (1982) 9 *Syd. L.R.* 541.

The implausibility of this argument is, as Murphy J. (dissenting) made clear in his judgment, that many law reform agencies have recommended the abolition of the rule in *Searle* v. *Wallbank*. Of course, if law reform agencies recommend complicated reforms it may be beyond the capacity of a court to give effect to them. But here, simple abolition of the *Searle* rule was well within the bounds of proper judicial action.

It may be that the real reason why the court did not simply reject the *Searle* rule is that the judges thought that this was not a sufficiently subtle solution to the complexities of the problem. This conjecture is supported by the fact that Mason J. suggested the possibility of a different rule for urban and rural areas, a matter not considered by any Australian law reform agency. As we have noted, too, there might be an argument for considering strict liability in certain situations which fall under the *Searle* rule. However, abolition of the rule in *Searle* v. *Wallbank* and use of the ordinary rules of negligence has been recommended in Queensland. The rule has been abolished by statute in New South Wales, Western Australia and the A.C.T. in favour of the rules of negligence.[79] In Western Australia abolition of the rule has been accompanied by guidelines for determining the issue of negligence.[80] The rule has also been abolished in South Australia, Tasmania and Victoria.[81]

In *Searle* v. *Wallbank* it was recognized that the rule of no-liability is not unqualified; in special circumstances the rule might not apply. It does not apply where the defendant knew that the animal had a propensity to behave dangerously on the highway.[82] A propensity common to all animals of a particular group could not be called a special or peculiar circumstance or characteristic.[83] A special proclivity towards straying cannot be a special characteristic since straying is the very characteristic with which the *Searle* rule is concerned. To be special a characteristic must incline the animal towards vicious or dangerous (even if frolicsome) behaviour on the highway. This is because the basis of the liability is not the mere obstructive presence of the animal on the highway but a propensity to act dangerously when there. If an animal had a tendency to jump over fences or hedges at or on to passers-by, this might be a special circumstance;[84] so might a tendency of a dog to shoot out into the road more like a missile than a dog,[85] or to rush madly about the road.[86] But if

79 Animals Act 1977 (N.S.W.) s.7(2)(b) (see also Dog (Amendment) Act 1977 (N.S.W.) s.2); Civil Liability (Animals) Act 1984 (A.C.T.) s.6.

80 Highways (Liability for Straying Animals) Act 1983 (W.A.). Negligence liability is now the *only* form of liability available in respect of damage done by animals straying on to the highway: P. Clarke (1985) 34 *I.C.L.Q.* 786, 796. There is also a monetary ceiling on such liability. See also Dog Amendment Act 1983 (W.A.) s.3.

81 Wrongs Act 1936 (S.A.) s. 17a; Animals Act 1962 (Tas) s. 19(1) (inserted in 1985); Wrongs Act 1958 (Vic.) s. 33. It may be that the rule still operates in relation to public nuisance in South Australia, Victoria and South Australia: Clarke (1985) 34 *I.C.L.Q.* 786, 789-90.

82 cf. *Simeon* v. *Avery* [1959] N.Z.L.R. 1345; *Graham* v. *Royal National Agricultural and Industrial Association of Queensland* [1989] 1 Qd.R. 624.

83 ibid.

84 For all of these propositions see *Brock* v. *Richards* [1951] 1 K.B. 529 *per* Evershed M.R.

85 *Ellis* v. *Johnstone* [1963] 2 Q.B. 8, 26 *per* Donovan L.J.

86 *Hughes* v. *Williams* [1943] K.B. 574, 576 *per* Lord Greene M.R.

the only thing normally to be expected of the animal was that it would cause a blundering obstruction on the road, this would not constitute special circumstances.[87]

There is some support in Lord Du Parcq's judgment in *Searle* v. *Wallbank* for a broader exception to the landowner's immunity in the following terms: 'an owner might be liable on the ground of negligence if he could be shown to have failed in his duty to take reasonable care'.[88] Taken literally, this is not an exception to the immunity but a negation of it. In Australia Mason J.'s judgment in *Trigwell*[89] is firmly against any exception to the *Searle* rule except that based on peculiar propensity.

VI: COMPREHENSIVE REFORMS

The only Australian jurisdictions to attempt an overall reform of the law of animals are New South Wales, South Australia and the A.C.T. The basic aim of the New South Wales Animals Act was to abolish all special rules relating to civil liability for damage and injury caused by animals (the provisions of ss.20-20C of the Dog Act 1966 being the only such provisions remaining), and to make liability depend on the ordinary rules of relevant torts: negligence (including occupiers' liability), nuisance and trespass. The application of the rule in *Rylands* v. *Fletcher* to animals has been abolished by s.9 of the Act. The main substantive provision is s.7, which abrogates all common law rules which 'related exclusively to liability for damage caused by an animal'. Liability for damage caused by an animal now depends on so much of the law as is not abrogated. Section 8 provides that liability for dangers on premises, whether arising out of the state of the premises or current operations, associated with the presence of an animal, is to be governed by occupiers' liability rules. The effect of the Civil Liability (Animals) Act 1984 (A.C.T.) is broadly the same.

The South Australian legislation (Wrongs Act s.17a) makes liability depend on the law of negligence and nuisance. In addition, s.17a(8) provides that where 'a person incites or knowingly permits an animal to cause injury he shall be liable in trespass'. In sub-ss.(2), (6) and (7) the Act lists certain factors relevant to assessing the standard of care in negligence. Other provisions of the section have been referred to, where relevant, in the course of this chapter.

The main question worth asking about these reforms is whether the basic approach of abolishing special rules relating to animals is necessarily the best one. The main effect of the legislation will no doubt be to make liability for animals in the normal case depend on negligence, and there must be some doubt whether consideration ought not to have been given to the imposition of strict liability in some cases at least.[90] One attraction

---

87 ibid.

88 [1947] A.C. 341, 359.

89 (1978) 142 C.L.R. 617. There is some support in *Batival a* v. *West* [1970] 1 Q.B. 716 for an exception where the presence of a docile animal on the highway was a result of a foreseeable reaction to extraneous circumstances.

90 G. Kelly (1972) 46 *A.L.J.* 123.

of negligence liability is that it is very flexible and relieves the legislature of the need to make hard and possibly politically contentious decisions as to where the burden of animal-related accidents should lie: the courts are left to work this out on a case-by-case basis. But the attraction of the easy answer needs to be resisted if the real difficulties of this area of the law are to be resolved.

In 1977 the Queensland Law Reform Commission in a Working Paper recommended the enactment of an Animals Act along the lines of the English Animals Act 1971.

19

THE ACTION FOR BREACH OF STATUTORY DUTY

I: THE NATURE OF THE ACTION

The fact that a defendant has committed a breach of duty imposed by a statute or by statutory regulations can figure in the reasoning in a common law tort action in a number of ways. First, breach of a statutory duty may provide evidence of negligence. We examined this in Chapter 10. Secondly, in actions against public authorities the duties, as well as the powers, of the authority, which it has by virtue of a statute under which it operates and which, taken together, constitute the statutory scheme which governs its activities, can be used to define to whom and in what respects the authority is under a common law duty of care.

A third way in which statutory duties can be relevant in a tort action is the subject of this chapter. Even apart from founding an action in negligence on a breach of statutory duty, it is possible in some cases to found an action simply on the breach of that duty regardless of whether or not that breach constitutes negligence. Liability for breach of statutory duty is distinct from liability for negligence in that a defendant may be liable for breach of statutory duty even though he is held not liable in negligence, or could also be held liable in negligence;[1] and in that a claim for breach of statutory duty ought to be pleaded separately from a claim in negligence.[2] There is a theory adopted in the United States which says that the action for breach of statutory duty is really a negligence action in which the statute specifies the standard of care and in which breach of the statute is deemed to be 'negligence *per se*' regardless of whether the conduct of the defendant would justify a verdict against him in an

1 *London Passenger Transport Board* v. *Upson* [1949] A.C. 155; cf. *Downs* v. *Williams* (1971) 126 C.L.R. 61, 74-5 *per* Windeyer J.

2 *Murfin* v. *United Steel Companies Ltd* [1957] 1 W.L.R. 104.

ordinary negligence action.[3] But this theory has been rejected in Anglo-Australian law.[4]

There is another important indication of the distinctness of the action for breach of statutory duty from the tort of negligence: an injunction may be available to restrain a threatened breach of statutory duty, whereas injunctions are usually assumed never to be available in negligence actions. Most of the discussion in this chapter is couched in terms of actions for damages, but many of the principles which govern the availability of such actions also apply, *mutatis mutandis*, to claims for an injunction.[5]

II: WHEN WILL AN ACTION FOR DAMAGES LIE?[6]

It is not for every breach of statutory duty or for breach of every statutory duty that an action for damages will lie at the suit of an injured party. The first part of this proposition is directed to determining exactly to whom,

---

3 The Canadian Supreme Court has gone even further towards assimilating breach of statutory duty and negligence: except in the case of industrial safety legislation (where breach of the statutory standard is, *per se*, negligent), the statutory standard is only one factor to be taken into account in deciding whether the defendant has acted negligently. *Canada* v. *Saskatchewan Wheat Pool* (1983) 143 D.L.R.(3d) 9; A. Brudner (1984) 62 *Can. B.R.* 668; G.H.L. Fridman (1984) 16 *Ottawa L.R.* 34.

4 See e.g. *Graham* v. *C.E. Heinke & Co. Ltd* [1958] 1 Q.B. 432, 436 *per* Donovan J.; *Downs* v. *Williams* (1971) 126 C.L.R. 61.

5 But there is an important distinction between actions for damages and actions for an injunction: damages are recoverable only in actions brought by private individuals. On the other hand, an injunction to restrain breach of a statutory duty may be awarded not only at the suit of a private individual (in respect of a statutory duty held to be enforceable in tort at the suit of private individuals) but also (in respect of statutory duties which are not privately enforceable) at the suit of the Attorney-General, either acting in his own name (*ex officio*) or at the request (or 'on the relation') of a private individual (*ex relatione*). The Attorney-General is always entitled to enforce duties owed to the public. Actions by or in the name of the Attorney-General are more often brought to enforce statutory prohibitions (or, in other words, to enforce public rights) than to restrain breach of statutory duties owed only to the public. It will be recalled that the Attorney-General can also sue to restrain a public nuisance (that is, an interference with right of the public). But whereas a private individual can sue for public nuisance in his own name provided he has suffered *special damage*, this is not (as we will see) enough to entitle a private individual to sue in tort for breach of statutory duty. Injunctions are also available to restrain wrongs which do not amount to torts but which are recognized in public law as amounting to illegal conduct. Breach of a statutory duty resting on a public authority could amount to such conduct; and in this context, an individual can be awarded an injunction if he has a 'special interest in the subject matter of the action' (see M. Allars *Introduction to Australian Administrative Law* (Sydney, 1990) pp. 288-93). This test of eligibility for an injunction is much less demanding than the tort rules considered in this chapter. But damages cannot be awarded in lieu of an injunction to restrain breach of a statutory provision which does not, according to the rules to be considered in this chapter, give a private right of action: *Wentworth* v. *Woollahra Municipal Council* (1982) 149 C.L.R. 672. See generally P.D. Finn (1983) 57 *A.L.J.* 493 and 571.

6 G. Williams (1960) 23 *M.L.R.* 233; G.L. Fricke (1960) 76 *L.Q.R.* 240; A.M. Linden (1966) 44 *Can. B.R.* 25.

by whom and in respect of what types of damage the duty is owed, and will be considered a little later. The latter part of the statement is directed to the more general question of whether the breach of the statutory duty in question can form the basis of an action for damages by anyone. So, for example, it has been held that a private individual cannot recover damages from another private individual for failure to comply with planning legislation;[7] and that a company cannot sue in respect of breaches by its directors of statutory duties of trust and fidelity.[8]

The type of statutory duty which is most consistently held not to give a private right to sue for damages is that designed for the regulation of traffic. Whether the duty relates to the safety of vehicles[9] or to safety in driving,[10] the basic approach of the courts is that as a general rule breach of traffic regulations is not actionable as such by private individuals. Rather, breach of traffic regulations is usually only relevant in deciding whether the defendant has been negligent.[11] Perhaps the best explanation for this approach is the recognition that sometimes, because of the infinite variety of situations which can arise on the highway, compliance with a traffic regulation can be the worst thing to do. In other words, there is a sense in which traffic regulations are only *prima facie* rules of conduct which may need to be adjusted to meet particular situations. It must be admitted, however, that this rationale is stronger for regulations concerning driving than for regulations concerning safety of vehicles.

There are some cases in which non-industrial legislation has been held to give a private cause of action for damages: for example, a provision requiring the shoring up or underpinning of buildings on adjoining land while excavations are being carried out;[12] a provision requiring local authorities to take out insurance against personal injury to volunteer firefighters;[13] and a provision requiring a local authority to keep fire hydrants in effective working order.[14] But the vast majority of successful actions for breach of statutory duty arise out of provisions designed to ensure the safety and protect the health of workers in factories and other industrial settings. In fact, although in theory the question of whether a private cause of action lies falls to be decided in relation to each statutory provision separately, it is now beyond doubt, for example, that provisions requiring the fencing of dangerous machinery generally give rise to a cause of action.[15] Indeed, it is probably not going too far to say that if a provision requires an employer to take specific precautions for the protection of employees, or even, perhaps, if it just requires in general terms that all reasonable steps be taken to secure their health and safety,[16] then

---

7 *Grand Central Car Park Pty Ltd* v. *Tivoli Freeholders Ltd* [1969] V.R. 62.
8 *Castlereagh Motels Ltd* v. *Davies-Roe* (1967) 67 S.R.(N.S.W.) 279.
9 *Hopewell* v. *Baranyay* [1962] V.R. 311.
10 *Tucker* v. *McCann* [1948] V.L.R. 222.
11 *Abela* v. *Giew* (1964) 65 S.R.(N.S.W.) 485.
12 *Anderson* v. *Mackellar C.C.* (1968) 87 W.N.(Pt.2)(N.S.W.) 308.
13 *Owen* v. *Shire of Kojonup* [1965] W.A.R. 3.
14 *Maceachern* v. *Pukekohe Borough* [1965] N.Z.L.R. 330.
15 *Downs* v. *Williams* (1971) 126 C.L.R. 61, 75 *per* Windeyer J.
16 e.g. *Crisa* v. *John Shearer Ltd* (1981) 27 S.A.S.R. 422.

in the absence of some good reason to the contrary, the provision will be held to give a private cause of action.[17]

When a court is confronted with a particular provision, how does it decide whether or not it gives rise to a private action? The main difficulty in answering this question arises from the fact that it is only relatively rarely that the provision on which the plaintiff seeks to base his action says one way or the other whether an action for damages for breach is available. In fact, while examples can be found in which explicit provision has been made for an action,[18] there is apparently no case in which explicit provision has been made to the effect that no action for damages can be brought. This surprising reticence on the part of the legislature was commented upon by Lord Du Parcq, in *Cutler* v. *Wandsworth Stadium Ltd*,[19] who said: 'There are no doubt reasons which inhibit the legislature from revealing its intention in plain words. I do not know and must not speculate what those reasons may be'.

A possible explanation of the continuance, although not of the initial adoption, of this practice of silence is that the legislature has discerned the principles upon which the courts decide whether an action will lie and approve of these principles. But since the courts often stress how much depends on the exact provisions of the particular enactment, the legislature might be equally justified in taking the view that the reaction of the courts could never be predicted in advance. A slightly more plausible version of the argument might say that since the only type of statutory duties which the courts consistently hold to be actionable by private individuals are duties to secure industrial safety, and since such duties are very rarely held not to give rise to an action, the legislature must be taken to be happy that only such regulations should be predictably actionable. Fleming's view is that 'the legislature's silence on the question of civil liability . . . points to the conclusion that it either did not have it in mind or deliberately omitted to provide for it'.[20]

The fact of the matter may be that political considerations frequently militate against the simple expedient of inserting a clause providing for actionability. There may very often be some lobby group prepared to accept the regulation of their activities by a system of fines, but which has sufficient influence to persuade the government not to increase the burden on them by providing for actionability. Another factor may be that since liability for breach of statutory duty will often be stricter than liability in negligence, the still-predominant philosophy of fault may count against actionability. At all events, despite Lord Du Parcq's plea in *Cutler* that the legislature should make its intention in this matter more plain, there has been no significant change in drafting practice.

There are important issues of legal and social policy at stake here. Actions for damages for breach of statutory duty brought by individuals can be seen as an alternative to other methods of enforcing compliance

---

17 *Darling Island Stevedoring and Lighterage Co. Ltd* v. *Long* (1956-7) 97 C.L.R. 36, 49-50 *per* Williams J.

18 Trade Practices Act 1974 (Cwth), s.82(1); Consumer Affairs Act 1972 (Vic.), s.61(1).

19 [1949] A.C. 398.

20 *Law of Torts* 7th edn (1987) p. 114.

with statutes, such as licensing, criminal prosecutions and other public regulatory techniques. Opinions differ as to the relative efficacy of the various available enforcement techniques. But apart from questions of efficacy, private enforcement by means of actions for damages may be identified with a desire to reduce the intervention by the state (in the guise of public regulatory agencies) in social and economic life. One feature of market-oriented politics of the 1980s was a commitment to 'pushing back the frontiers of the state', and one way of doing this is to reduce government regulation of private activity and to encourage individuals to take a greater part in ensuring that businesses, in particular, act in socially desirable and responsible ways. During the 1980s in the U.K. a considerable number of statutory provisions were enacted in areas such as competition law and consumer protection law which, by expressly allowing actions for breach of statutory provisions, were designed to facilitate private policing of statutory prohibitions and duties. The use of private litigation in this way has, for a long time, been much more common in the U.S. than in Australia or the U.K. This is partly the result of procedural factors, such as the more ready availability of class actions in the U.S.;[21] but it is also partly the result of a greater commitment in the U.S. to private litigation as a means of social change.

Many of the U.K. statutory provisions dating from the 1980s allow actions in respect of purely economic loss; whereas the courts have, traditionally, been particularly unwilling to interpet statutes which do not expressly provide for a damages action as impliedly doing so in cases where the loss likely to be suffered is purely economic. More generally, Australian and English courts have been unwilling, outside the area of industrial safety, to interpret statutes as impliedly providing for damages actions even where the damage likely to be suffered was personal injury or property damage. But there is really no evidence that courts have seriously addressed the policy issues raised in the previous paragraph.

The classic Australian statement of the way the courts approach the issue of actionability is that of Dixon J. in *O'Connor* v. *S.P. Bray Ltd.*[22] His Honour pointed out that the traditional doctrine is that the question of whether breach of a statutory duty is actionable at the suit of a private individual depends on the intention of the legislature and the construction of the statute.[23] And since statutes rarely say anything explicit on the matter, the intention of the legislature, assuming it had an intention in the matter, must be gathered from considering the provision in question in the light of the contents and purpose of the statute as a whole.[24] But because the legislature will very often have given no thought to the question of actionability, even this wider inquiry will often be a 'fatuous'

---

21 For Australian developments in this respect see Federal Court of Australia Act 1991 noted by R. Baxt (1992) 66 *A.L.J.* 223.

22 (1937) 56 C.L.R. 464.

23 cf. *Whittaker* v. *Rozelle Wood Products Ltd* (1936) 36 S.R.(N.S.W.) 204; *Phillips* v. *Britannia Hygenic Laundry* [1923] 2 K.B. 832.

24 cf. *Sovar* v. *Henry Lane Pty Ltd* (1967) 116 C.L.R. 397, 405 *per* Kitto J; *Tassone* v. *M.W.S. & D.B.* [1971] 1 N.S.W.L.R. 207, 211-12.

one,[25] and in the end the question will be answered not by reference to the meaning or contents of the statute but by the application of presumptions, by recourse to policy arguments based on the nature and purpose of the provision, or by giving to the statute a certain complexion 'upon very general considerations without either the authority of a general rule of law or the application of any definite rule of construction'.[26]

The most important point which Dixon J.'s statement makes is not that principles cannot be found in the cases by which the courts say they are guided, for there clearly are quite a few such principles; it is, rather, that none of these principles are conclusive of anything. The courts can and do pick and choose among them and manipulate them to reach results on grounds not usually expressed, even if they exist. With this in mind let us examine the principles which emerge from the cases. First, let us deal with the presumptions of interpretation of which Dixon J. spoke. In *O'Connor* v. *Bray*[27] itself Dixon J. put forward such a presumption: where a provision prescribes a specific precaution for the safety of others in a matter where the person upon whom the duty laid is, under the general law of negligence, bound to exercise due care, the duty will give rise to a correlative private right of action unless from the nature of the provision, or from the scope of the legislation of which it forms part, a contrary intention appears.

This suggested presumption immediately raises a number of difficulties. In the first place, while it may be an accurate reflection of the practice of the courts in relation to duties concerned with industrial safety, it is clearly quite inaccurate so far as concerns traffic regulations, many of which are directed to the safety of road users as well as to the orderly use of the roads. Secondly, the presumption applies to provisions which prescribe a specific precaution for the safety of others. This requirement of a specific or definite duty can be found also in cases not concerned with safety regulations.[28] On the other hand, a provision requiring an employer to take all reasonable precautions to ensure the health and safety of workers can give rise to a civil cause of action.[29] The true position appears to be that while it may be easier to engraft a civil action on to a specific provision, the fact that a provision is general will by no means prevent it being actionable. Perhaps more important than the degree of particularity would be the area the duty was concerned with. Breach of industrial safety regulations is much more likely to be held actionable than breach of other types of statutory provisions, whether or not the duty in question is particular.[30]

Dixon J.'s presumption operates where the statutory duty is parallel to a common law duty of care. This does not apparently mean that a statutory duty will be actionable under the presumption only if breach of

---

25 *Haylan* v. *Purcell* (1949) 49 S.R.(N.S.W.) 1, 4 *per* Davidson J.
26 cf. *Australian Iron & Steel Ltd* v. *Ryan* (1956-7) 97 C.L.R. 89, 98 *per* Kitto J.
27 (1937) 56 C.L.R. 464.
28 e.g. *Cutler* v. *Wandsworth Stadium* [1949] A.C. 398 *per* Lord Reid.
29 *Crisa* v. *Shearer* (1981) 27 S.A.S.R. 422; cf. *Kirkpatrick* v. *Lewis Construction Pty Ltd* [1964] V.R. 515.
30 Witness cases in the previous note.

it would also put the defendant in breach of a common law duty of care. If this were the case, there would be no point in founding the action on the statutory duty. The presumption must allow an action for breach of a duty which is stricter than a duty of care. What it seems to mean is that actionability will be presumed in situations where the common law recognizes a duty relationship, such as employer and employee.[31] The difficulty is that there is clearly a common law duty between drivers and road users and yet very rarely are traffic regulations actionable. Another problem relates to the principle that an action for breach of statutory duty is more readily allowed where there is no other adequate remedy.[32] Thus one suggested explanation, although not a very good one, of the difference between industrial safety regulations and traffic regulations is that there is an adequate common law remedy for the injured road user in the form of an action for damages for negligence.[33] (The injured worker, of course, has equally good remedies at common law.) Dixon J.'s principle, on the other hand, seems to allow an action more easily in just those cases where there is an action at common law in the area dealt with by the statutory duty.[34] Once again the true position appears to be that the fact that there are no common law rules of liability in the same area as the statutory duty is ambiguous as to whether the statutory duty will be held actionable.

There are certain other presumptions of interpretation recognized by the courts. One is that if a statute creates an obligation but provides no means of enforcing it, then 'the legislature is to be taken as intending the ordinary result; and the proper remedy for breach of the statute is an action for damages'.[35] But this rule, too, is not universally valid, and there may be cases, more particularly in relation to the duties of public bodies, where a duty is meant to be enforced, if at all, through the political process and not at the suit of individuals. Another presumption is that where a statute creates an obligation and provides a remedy (usually a fine) for its non-observance, that remedy is the only remedy,[36] and this presumption would be strengthened if a special tribunal were established to hear complaints under the legislation.[37] But a more accurate statement of the law appears to be that there is no presumption either way of general application.[38] The fact that the statute provides for a fine is one relevant factor to be weighed in the balance with other points. Thus, it is sometimes asked whether the remedy provided in the statute is adequate. However, from the injured party's point of view a fine is always an inadequate 'remedy' because the plaintiff does not get the proceeds of the fine which, anyway, will usually bear no relationship to the seriousness of his loss. Thus, we can find it said that a statutory remedy will be

31 *Sovar* v. *Lane* (1967) 116 C.L.R. 397, 404 *per* Kitto J.
32 e.g. *McCall* v. *Abalesz* [1976] Q.B. 585.
33 *Dennis* v. *Brownlee* [1963] S.R.(N.S.W.) 719; *Phillips* v. *Britannia Hygenic Laundry* [1923] 2 K.B. 832.
34 cf. *Anderson* v. *Mackellar County Council* (1968) 87 W.N. (Pt.2) (N.S.W.) 308.
35 *Phillips* v. *Britannia Hygenic Laundry* [1923] 2 K.B. 832, 838 *per* Bankes L.J.
36 cf. *Haylan* v. *Purcell* (1949) 49 S.R. (N.S.W.) 1.
37 *Martin* v. *Western District of Australasian Coal etc. Union* (1934) 34 S.R.(N.S.W.) 593.
38 *Groves* v. *Lord Wimborne* [1898] 2 Q.B. 402, 415 *per* Vaughan Williams L.J.

inadequate where the provision is designed to protect individuals in a particular class.[39] Conversely, a penalty will be adequate where the purpose of the statute is to protect the public as a whole, not individuals.[40] This reasoning is clearly circular.

It would seem, therefore, that by far the most important consideration is one usually only mentioned in passing in the cases, namely whether 'convenience and policy' favour a remedy in damages and whether it is likely that the legislature would have intended to impose on the defendant the sort of burden which would arise from recognition of a right of civil action.[41] Unfortunately, however, this recognition does not get us very far either, because there is very little discussion of policy in the cases, and it is not easy to discern the policy motivations of the courts. Only a few general statements are possible: for some reason the courts think that industrial safety legislation ought to give rise to actions whereas road safety legislation ought usually not to. Another tendency in the cases is perhaps to allow actions more readily where the injury is physical than where it is economic. This trend is not very easy to confirm because of the relative dearth of cases involving economic loss. But such a trend would not be surprising. Statutory duties are often stricter than a duty of care, and the courts might feel that economic interests by and large only deserve protection against negligence. Finally, it may be suggested, in accordance with general principle, that courts are less willing to allow actions in respect of nonfeasance than of misfeasance.[42]

The last consideration which is very commonly stated in the cases is whether the statute was intended to protect individuals or whether, on the contrary, it was meant only to protect the public as a whole. This is sometimes put by asking whether or not the statute is designed to create duties to a specific class of individuals;[43] but it has been frequently said that there is no need to be able to pick out a protected class: the duty may be of such importance that each individual member of the public is protected. The proper question is whether the duty is owed to individuals

---

39 *Martin's* case (1934) 34 S.R.(N.S.W.) 593; *Haylan* v. *Purcell* (1949) 49 S.R.(N.S.W.) 1.

40 *Wright* v. *T.I.L. Services Pty Ltd* (1956) 56 S.R.(N.S.W.) 413, 416 *per* Owen J; *Whittaker* v. *Rozelle Wood Products* (1939) 36 S.R.(N.S.W.) 204.

41 See e.g. *Martin's* case (1934) 34 S.R.(N.S.W.) 593; *Haylan* v. *Purcell* (1949) 49 S.R.(N.S.W.) 1.

42 So, for example, a statutory duty may not be held actionable if to do so would be to impose a duty to control another: *Chordas* v. *Bryant (Wellington) Pty Ltd* (1989) 91 A.L.R. 149; *Ticehurst* v. *Skeen* (1986) 3 M.V.R. 307,314. See also *Meade* v. *Haringey L.B.C.* [1979] 1 W.L.R. 637 esp. *per* Rees J.; *Dawson* v. *Bingley U.D.C.* [1911] 2 K.B. 149. But if nonfeasance by a public authority amounts to breach of a statutory duty, an aggrieved individual may be able to seek the public law remedy of mandamus (or, perhaps, a mandatory injunction) to enforce the duty. It is not clear what the rule of eligibility for the award of such a remedy would be (see M. Allars *Introduction to Australian Administrative Law* (1990) p. 286), but it is probably less demanding than the rules governing the availability of tort actions for breach of statutory duty. But damages would not be available in such an action.

43 e.g. *Abela* v. *Giew* (1964) 65 S.R.(N.S.W.) 485; *Haylan* v. *Purcell* (1949) 49 S.R.(N.S.W.) 1.

or only to the public in aggregate.[44] Whichever way this requirement is put, it is not a test of actionability but simply a restatement of the question of whether the statute grants to any individual a civil cause of action for damages.

Statutory duties resting on public authorities are particularly prone, because of their often political (or discretionary) content or social-planning purposes, not to be actionable by private individuals.[45] So, for example, no private action lies for breach of a planning authority's duties under planning legislation;[46] or for failure to supply (and, perhaps, maintain) sufficient sewerage facilities;[47] or for failure by a fire authority to 'take all practicable measures for preventing and extinguishing fires';[48] or for failure by the police to enforce the law;[49] or (at least if there is an alternative statutory remedy in the form of a ministerial default power, which is the most common alternative remedy in statutes imposing duties on public authorities) for failure to provide public housing to individual applicants.[50] No action will lie at the suit of a private individual for breach of the duty of gaol authorities, owed to the Crown, to keep prisoners in safe custody. Liability would accrue only if a common law duty could be established by proof of special knowledge on the part of the gaoler of the propensity of the prisoner to escape and to damage.[51] The political nature of a duty can also sometimes make it unenforceable *against* a private individual. For example in *Lonhro Ltd* v. *Shell Petroleum Co. Ltd*[52] it was held that breaches of orders establishing trade sanctions against Rhodesia would not sound in tort.

III: DELEGATED LEGISLATION

Statutory duties may be contained either in primary (or 'parliamentary') legislation or in secondary (or 'delegated') legislation, that is, legislation made by an official, typically a Minister, to whom Parliament has delegated some of its law-making functions. The powers of a delegate are

---

44 e.g. *Phillips* v. *Britannia Hygenic Laundry* [1923] 2 K.B. 832, 841 *per* Atkin L.J.; *Whittaker* v. *Rozelle Wood Products* (1939) 36 S.R.(N.S.W.) 204, 208.

45 But even if a particular duty resting on a public authority is privately actionable, the particular breach in question may not be actionable: see p. 688 below.

46 *Miller & Croak Pty Ltd* v. *Auburn Municipal Council* [1960] S.R.(N.S.W.) 398; *Attorney-General* v. *Birkenhead Borough* [1968] N.Z.L.R. 383.

47 *Robinson* v. *Workington Corporation* [1897] 1 Q.B. 619; *Carden* v. *Ku-ring-gai Municipal Council* (1932) 10 L.G.R. 162; cf. *Arpedco Pty Ltd* v. *Beaudesert Shire Council* [1977] Qd.R. 351.

48 *Board of Fire Commissioners* v. *Rowland* [1960] S.R.(N.S.W.) 322; *Bennett & Wood Ltd* v. *Orange City Council* (1967) 67 S.R.(N.S.W.) 426; *R. & W. Vincent Pty Ltd* v. *Board of Fire Commissioners of New South Wales* [1977] 1 N.S.W.L.R. 15.

49 *Ticehurst* v. *Skeen* (1986) 3 M.V.R. 307: a statutory duty may be merely descriptive or declaratory of an authority's responsibilities and not meant to be enforceable at all except through the political process.

50 *Southwark L.B.C.* v. *Williams* [1971] Ch. 734.

51 *Thorne* v. *Western Australia* [1964] W.A.R. 147.

52 [1982] A.C. 173.

always limited, and their extent is defined by the terms of the statute which gives the delegate the power. If legislation made by the delegate is beyond his powers it will be invalid.[53] The importance of this in the present context is that it may be relevant to the question of whether a regulation made by a delegate confers a right of action to ask whether the delegate had power to make regulations conferring a right of action or whether the only power was to provide for the imposition of fines.

At first sight this might appear to provide a helpful way of approaching the difficult issue of actionability. Unfortunately, however, this approach is infected with just the same uncertainty as that which involves considering the actual terms of the regulation. Thus in *Haylan* v. *Purcell*[54] Street J. said that if a delegate is to have the power to create new causes of action then the statute conferring the regulation-making power would be expected to confer this power specifically and not just to confer a power to impose fines; normally new causes of action can only be created by regulations made by Parliament. However, it was held in *Darling Island Stevedoring* v. *Long*[55] that the fact that the regulation-making power expressly confers authority to provide for the imposition of fines does not necessarily mean that the delegate has no power to create new causes of action. Whether this is so depends on exactly the same question as governs whether a parliamentary statute creates a new cause of action, namely whether the provision was intended for the protection of individuals. Just as industrial safety regulations are invariably interpreted as creating causes of action, so a power to make such regulations would be interpreted as including a power to create new causes of action. Conversely, since traffic regulations do not create new causes of action, a power to make traffic regulations does not include a power to create new causes of action.[56]

IV: THE SCOPE OF THE DUTY

Once it has been established that the duty is one which is actionable in tort, it is necessary to determine the exact scope of the duty. Unless the duty is one owed to every member of the public, it will first be necessary to determine whether the plaintiff is a person to whom the duty is owed. For example, it has been held that the duty to fence dangerous machinery extends to every person employed on the premises where the machine is, whether they are employees of the occupier or of an independent contractor.[57] On the other hand, it has been held that a duty to fence a machine to protect passers-by does not impose a duty to fence internal

53 See e.g. *Utah Construction Pty Ltd* v. *Pataky* [1966] A.C. 629.
54 (1949) 49 S.R.(N.S.W.) 1.
55 (1956-7) 97 C.L.R. 36.
56 *Tucker* v. *McCann* [1948] V.L.R. 222.
57 *Quilty* v. *Bellambi Coal Co. Pty Ltd* (1967) 67 S.R.(N.S.W.) 193; *Massey-Harris-Ferguson (Manufacturing) Ltd* v. *Piper* [1956] 2 Q.B. 396.

parts of the machine to protect workers using it;[58] but that it does protect an employee who is using a machine with the permission of his employer outside working hours.[59]

It must also be established that the type of injury suffered by the plaintiff was the type the provision was directed at preventing or, in other words, within the risk against which the provision was directed.[60] For example, it has been held that the duty to fence does not apply where the injury is caused not by the worker coming into contact with the machine but by contact between the machine and a tool being used by the worker, with the result that his hand is thrown against the machine.[61] By interpreting the scope of statutory provisions restrictively in this way the courts can limit the potentially very heavy liability imposed by safety provisions. It is probably going too far to suggest that by means of this 'fine tuning' the courts are giving effect to any more specific policy objective than not demanding too much of employers. And there are, anyway, differences of opinion on the proper approach to the interpretation of safety regulations. In *F.E. Callow (Engineers) Ltd* v. *Johnson*[62] Lord Hailsham, while of the view that such restrictions on liability could only be removed by legislative provisions, was not prepared to extend the gap in the statutory protection which his Lordship thought the restrictions had created.[63]

Finally, it must be shown that the defendant is a person on whom the provision casts an obligation. For example, in *Darling Island Stevedoring* v. *Long*[64] it was held that a provision imposing duties in connection with loading operations on the 'person in charge' did not impose any obligation on the stevedoring company but only on its employee who was supervising the operations. Similarly, in *Harrison* v. *National Coal Board*[65] it was held that duties imposed on a shot-firer were not obligations of the employer.

58 *Wenck* v. *Morris' Woollen Mills (Ipswich) Pty Ltd* [1974] Qd.R. 142.

59 *English* v. *Comalco Products Pty Ltd* [1972] Qd.R. 52.

60 *Gorris* v. *Scott* (1874) 9 Ex.D. 125.

61 *Sparrow* v. *Fairey Aviation Co. Ltd* [1964] A.C. 1019.

62 [1971] A.C. 335; cf. *Wearing* v. *Pirelli Ltd* [1977] 1 All E.R. 339 *per* Lord Edmund-Davies.

63 Similar ambivalence can be seen in cases concerning the strictness of the duty to fence dangerous machinery: this duty has always been treated as very strict (see e.g. *Bouronicos* v. *Nylex Corporation Ltd* [1975] V.R. 120); but machinery is only treated as dangerous if it constitutes a foreseeable cause of injury to somebody acting in a way which a human being might be expected to act in circumstances which might reasonably be expected to occur: *Close* v. *Steel Company of Wales* [1962] A.C. 367. Cf. *Waugh* v. *Kippen* (1986) 160 C.L.R. 156.

64 (1957) 97 C.L.R. 36.

65 [1951] A.C. 639.

V: THE REQUIRED STANDARD OF CONDUCT

Ultimately, the standard of conduct required of a person on whom a statutory duty is placed depends on the terms of the provision imposing the duty. And just as questions of purpose, convenience and policy are often decisive in determining whether an action for damages for breach of statutory duty is allowed, such considerations also enter into the question of the strictness of the statutory standard. This, at least, is the only possible explanation of some apparently conflicting decisions.[66]

Sometimes the statutory duty is, in so many words, a duty of reasonable care ('shall take all reasonable precautions'), and in such cases the statutory standard of care will be the same as the common law standard. On the other hand, if the statute specifies a particular precaution which the employer must take or a particular standard it must attain then the statutory, and not the common, law measure covers the situation and precludes any further discussion of what is reasonable and practicable in the circumstances.[67] It is not entirely clear where the onus of proof in cases of the first type lies. The House of Lords has held that a duty to keep the workplace safe 'so far as is reasonably practicable' casts the burden of proving that no further precaution was reasonably practicable on the defendant.[68]

A difficult question arises in some cases from the fact that a statute will state an obligation in unqualified terms but then provide for a defence to a criminal prosecution for breach of obligation in terms such as that the defendant took all reasonable precautions to avoid committing the offence.[69] The difficult issue is whether the provision of such a defence to a criminal prosecution should be interpreted as indicating an intention that a defendant in a civil action should be allowed to plead reasonable care. If he can make such a plea, the position of the defendant in such an action would be very little different from that of the defendant in many negligence actions, where in practical terms the defendant must adduce evidence to establish that he took reasonable care. In *Sovar* v. *Lane*[70] it was held that the distinction between a criminal prosecution and a civil action is so clear that only a very special context could justify holding that an Act which made express provision for a reasonable care defence to a criminal prosecution, but was silent regarding such a defence to a civil action, meant to extend the benefit of the defence to civil actions. Taylor J. in dissent argued, however, that since the legislature had not expressly provided for a civil action, it was not surprising that the statute was silent on the issue of defences to civil actions, and that the benefit of the defence ought to apply to the latter. This argument suggests that a distinction

66 e.g. *Galashiels Gas Co. Ltd* v. *O'Donnell* [1949] A.C. 275; *Austral Bronze Co. Pty Ltd* v. *Ajaka* (1970) 44 A.L.J.R. 52.

67 *Smith* v. *Elliott Bros Pty Ltd* (1980) 26 S.A.S.R. 138.

68 *Nimmo* v. *Alexander Cowan & Sons Ltd* [1968] A.C. 107; cf. *Australian Oil Refining Pty Ltd* v. *Bourne* (1979) 54 A.L.J.R. 192, 194 *per* Murphy J.

69 The standard of care is the same in the civil as in the criminal proceedings: *Waugh* v. *Kippen* (1986) 160 C.L.R. 156.

70 (1967) 116 C.L.R. 397.

should perhaps be drawn between statutes which do and those which do not provide expressly for civil actions. The *American Restatement of Torts (2d)*[71] takes the position that in the former case the court should apply the statutory standard for prosecutions (whatever it might be) in the civil action, but that in the latter case it need not adopt the statutory standard for criminal prosecutions as relevant to civil actions: conduct may be excused for the purposes of civil actions but not for the purposes of criminal prosecutions or vice versa.[72] This approach seems to be the converse of Taylor J's: his Honour seems to have thought that the absence of express provision for a civil action was an argument in favour of accepting the statutory standard in a civil action.

It might be better, however, if the issue were resolved in more overtly policy-oriented terms. For example, the Consumer Protection Act 1987 (U.K.) provides for civil actions for breach of regulations concerning the safety of goods and makes a reasonable care defence available in criminal prosecutions. If the safety of consumers is thought to justify a regime of strict civil liability then there would be an argument for saying that no reasonable care defence should be recognized in civil actions based on the statute. There is no good reason of logic or policy why a defendant should not be held strictly liable in a civil action for breach of duty for which he could not be convicted in a criminal prosecution. More generally, there is much to be said for more explicit reference to policy in all cases where the statutory provisions are opaque on the question of civil actions; only by this means can a more rational and less *ad hoc* approach to the action for breach of statutory duty be achieved.

VI: CAUSATION

The plaintiff must, of course, establish a causal link between his injury and the defendant's breach of duty. We have already (in Chapter 11) looked at the general approach of the courts to questions of causation, and in Chapter 14 we considered some particular issues which may arise in actions by employees against their employers. Here we need only consider a couple of points especially relevant to actions for breach of statutory duty.

The question of attributive causation in actions for breach of statutory duty is often closely tied up with the question of whether the plaintiff's injury falls within the risk at which the provision was directed. In fact the two questions may be seen just as different formulations of the same inquiry. But factual causation can also be related to the scope of the duty. For example, in *Phillips* v. *Britannia Hygenic Laundry* Bankes L.J. pointed out that while a regulation requiring cars to have rear red lights may be designed for the safety of the car itself or of cars overtaking it, the requirement of a red light could not be directed at the safety of a

---

71 Section 286, comments c and d.
72 ibid., s.288A, comment b.

pedestrian passing in front of the car, nor could the lack of a light be the cause of his injury.[73] On the other hand, if the plaintiff can prove a breach of duty and injury of a type which breach of the provision might be expected to cause (and so against which it is probably directed) this may be enough to justify an inference, in the absence of any sufficient reason to the contrary, that in fact the accident was caused by the breach.[74]

A particular problem of causation arises where the duty which has been breached requires that some piece of machinery or equipment or some vehicle only be operated by a licensed operator. Licensing provisions are usually designed to ensure that those who use dangerous equipment are competent and qualified to use it. This causes difficulty because there is no necessary connection between lack of a licence and incompetence: an operator may be perfectly competent even though he has no licence; the accident might be the result of negligence rather than incompetence. This problem is to some extent overcome because the courts are quite ready to infer incompetence from the lack of a licence, and to infer that the incompetence was the cause of the injury. It would then be for the defendant to show that the cause was something other than incompetence, such as a latent defect in the machine or equipment;[75] or negligence on the part of the operator, although this will not help the defendant unless the plaintiff has failed to make a claim in negligence as well as breach of statutory duty.[76]

Another important causal problem arises in cases where the plaintiff is an employee who is injured partly as a result of a breach of statutory duty by the employer and partly by his own breach of duty. In some cases an employee in breach of duty will be held to have been contributorily negligent, and we will consider that shortly. But there are cases where the employer can escape liability entirely on causal principles. This may happen where the duty which the employee has breached is different from and in some sense independent of that which the employer has breached.[77]

More frequent are cases in which a statutory duty rests concurrently on employer and employee but the only reason why the employer is in breach of statutory duty is because of the employee's actions. The basic principle was recognized in *Stapely* v. *Gypsum Mines Ltd*, namely that an employer can be held vicariously liable to an employee for breaches of duties resting concurrently on the employer and another employee.[78] This rule has not, however, been found entirely palatable where a plaintiff seeks to hold the employer liable in respect of the employee's own breach of duty. It has been held that where the employer's liability is purely vicarious, where the *only* reason why the employer is in breach of duty is that an employee has acted in breach of duty, the employee's breach will be treated as the

73 [1923] 2 K.B. 832, 840.
74 *Betts* v. *Whittingslowe* (1946) 71 C.L.R. 637, 649 *per* Dixon J.
75 *John Pfeiffer Pty Ltd* v. *Canny* (1981) 36 A.L.R. 466, 475 *per* Mason J.
76 As in *Leask Timber & Hardware Pty Ltd* v. *Thorne* (1961) 108 C.L.R. 33. See also *Schlederer* v. *The Ship Red Fin* [1979] 1 N.S.W.L.R. 258.
77 e.g. *Sherman* v. *Nymboida Collieries Pty Ltd* (1963) C.L.R. 580.
78 [1953] A.C. 663; cf. *Imperial Chemical Industries Ltd* v. *Shatwell* [1965] A.C. 656; see also P.S. Atiyah (1965) 43 *Can. B.R.* 609.

sole cause of his injuries and this causal argument will provide the employer with a complete answer to the employee's claim for damages.[79] The employer's breach will be treated as causally irrelevant, but only if the employer has not been at fault in any way which is independent of or goes beyond the fault of the employee, such as lack of proper supervision or instruction,[80] or the employment of inexperienced workers or faulty equipment, or acquiescence in past breaches by employees.[81] The principle seems to spring out of a certain moral indignation that a blameless employer should have to pay damages to an employee who 'has no one to blame but himself' for his injuries.

The onus of proof that the employee was the sole cause of the injuries is on the employer; the employee need only prove a breach of statutory duty resulting in injury to himself. He does not have to establish that the employer could or should have taken some steps to ensure compliance with the duty by himself;[82] and the employer's defence is not that it was not in breach but that its breach was causally irrelevant. The same principle applies to cases where an employer has delegated to an employee the task of fulfilling its common law duties of care, and the employee is injured solely as a result of his own negligence; the employer is in breach of its duty, which is non-delegable, but it has a causal defence.

VII: DEFENCES

We have already discussed general limitations on the operation of the defences of contributory negligence and *volenti non fit injuria* in actions by employees against their employers. Here we will mention a few points particularly relevant to actions for breach of statutory duty.

1. Contributory Negligence

Contributory negligence is available as a defence to an action for breach of statutory duty in all Australian jurisdictions except New South Wales (where it is available in work-injury cases but not others).[83] The apportionment provisions apply to such actions. There is an argument for saying that in cases where reasonable care is relevant neither as an element in the plaintiff's case nor (as a defence) to the defendant's case, the aim of imposing the statutory obligation (that is, to protect the plaintiff) is interfered with if fault on his part is a ground for reduction of damages.

---

79 *Ginty* v. *Belmont Building Supplies Ltd* [1959] 1 All E.R. 414 as explained in *Ross* v. *Associated Portland Cement Ltd* [1964] 2 All E.R. 452, 455 *per* Lord Reid; cf. *Sheen* v. *Fields Ltd* (1984) 58 A.L.J.R. 93.

80 See *Boyle* v. *Kodak Ltd* [1969] 1 W.L.R. 661.

81 *Ginty* [1959] All E.R. 414; *Shedlezki* v. *Bronte Bakery Pty Ltd* (1969) 92 W.N.(N.S.W.) 151.

82 *Boyle* v. *Kodak* [1969] 1 W.L.R. 661.

83 Statutory Duties (Contributory Negligence) Act 1945 (N.S.W.) as qualified by Workers Compensation Act 1987 s.151N(3),(4).

Once it has been decided that an action for damages was intended, it seems at odds with the compensatory aim of the provision to penalize the plaintiff for his fault. On the other hand, it might be argued that if contributory negligence on the part of the plaintiff were not a defence, the persons to whose protection statutory provisions are directed would have no incentive to take care for their own safety. This argument, of course, makes challengeable assumptions about the deterrent effect of the contributory negligence rules. Finally, in loss-allocation terms, the defendant will very often be in a much better position to bear the loss than the plaintiff. At all events, there is no doubt that contributory negligence is available as a defence in all cases of breach of statutory duty.[84]

As we have already seen, the duties of employers, both common law and statutory,[85] are said to be owed to the careless as well as to the careful, and so considerable allowances have to be made to the plaintiff in applying the contributory negligence rules.[86] Certainly it is not open to an employer who has, for example, failed to fence a dangerous machine, to tell an employee repeatedly to be careful of the danger thus created and then plead contributory negligence when by his own forgetfulness or inadvertence the employee is injured.[87] When the accident which happens is the very thing which the provision was designed to prevent (for example, the insertion of a hand into a moving machine), the fact that it happened through the carelessness of the plaintiff provides the defendant with no defence.[88] The provision is designed to prevent the untoward consequences of just such carelessness. One situation in which the plaintiff could, despite these strictures, be held guilty of contributory negligence is where he has done some deliberate act in defiance of a danger of which he was aware and which he consciously invited. But it appears that there is no rule that only deliberate stupidity can amount to contributory negligence in employer's liability and breach of statutory duty cases. The ultimate question remains whether, in the light of all the circumstances, the plaintiff failed to take reasonable care for his own safety.

2. Volenti Non Fit Injuria

Theoretically, *volenti* is available as a defence to an action for breach of statutory duty. But the defence will not normally be available where the risk to which the plaintiff consents is the very risk against which the provision is designed to protect.[89] In *Imperial Chemical Industries* v. *Shatwell* Lord Reid left open the question of whether an employee could

---

84 *Piro* v. *W. Foster & Co. Ltd* (1943-4) 68 C.L.R. 313.

85 According to Cox J. in *Kondracuik* v. *Jackson Morgan & Sons* (1988) 47 S.A.S.R. 280, 284-5, it is no harder for an employer to establish contributory negligence in an action for breach of statutory duty than in an action for breach of a common law duty of care.

86 *Caswell* v. *Powell Duffryn Collieries Ltd* [1940] A.C. 152.

87 *Piro* v. *Foster* (1943-4) 68 C.L.R. 313; *Dunlop Rubber Australia Ltd* v. *Buckley* (1952) 87 C.L.R. 313.

88 *Davies* v. *Adelaide Chemical & Fertilizer Co. Ltd* (1947) 74 C.L.R. 541.

89 *Wheeler* v. *New Merton Board Mills Ltd* [1933] 2 K.B. 669.

expressly contract not to sue for breach of statutory duty;[90] the likely answer is 'no'. That case illustrates one of the few situations in which a defence of *volenti* might succeed. The deceased and his brother were shotfirers employed by the defendant. The deceased was killed in an explosion caused when, by mutual agreement, the two brothers were testing a circuit in a way which involved a breach of statutory duty. The dependants of the deceased sued the defendant on the basis of its vicarious liability for the breach of duty by the surviving brother. The defendant pleaded *volenti* and it was held that the plea succeeded. The deceased had done a deliberate act in breach of statutory duty in full knowledge of the risk. Moreover, the defendant had been in no way at fault because it had fully instructed its employees on the impact of the regulations and the need to comply with them. It would have been different if the brothers had collaborated carelessly, but here they had deliberately agreed together to take a known risk.

3. Illegality

It is clear that the fact that the plaintiff was himself in breach of statutory duty and thus had acted illegally provides, *per se*, no defence to an action for breach of statutory duty.[91] Otherwise there would be little room for the operation of the other defences since very many breaches of statutory duty are offences. Further, the fact that the plaintiff was trespassing when injured is as such irrelevant to the defendant's liability for breach of statutory duty.[92] It may even be irrelevant to the question of contributory negligence.[93]

---

90 [1965] A.C. 656, 674.
91 *National Coal Board* v. *England* [1954] A.C. 403.
92 *Westwood* v. *Post Office* [1974] A.C. 1.
93 ibid.

20

TORT LIABILITY OF PUBLIC AUTHORITIES[1]

The discussion of this topic in a torts textbook is made somewhat difficult because it is not easy to understand the present law without an appreciation of some of the finer points of administrative law. An attempt will be made to expound these points where relevant, but those readers with a detailed knowledge of administrative law may well find the result dissatisfying at least so far as concerns its administrative law aspects.

The term 'public authorities' as used in the title of this chapter has no precise meaning. It refers at least to departments of the governments of the Commonwealth and the States. These are often referred to as 'the Crown in right of the Commonwealth' and 'the Crown in right of Victoria' (for example).[2] The 'Crown' originally enjoyed immunity from liability in tort, but legislation has now largely removed that immunity.[3] The term 'public authorities' also embraces local governmental authorities; and the principles discussed in this chapter are relevant to a wide range of other governmental agencies and corporations which perform public functions but which are not part of the central core of executive government.

In this chapter we are primarily concerned with the application of the ordinary rules of tort law to the acts of public authorities. But there is one tort, which is usually referred to as 'misfeasance in a public office', which

---

1 See generally M. Aronson and H. Whitmore *Public Torts and Contracts* (Sydney, 1982) Ch. 2.

2 The term 'the Crown' is an historical hangover which reminds us of the British origins of the Australian governmental system and of the monarchical origins of the British governmental system.

3 See Aronson and Whitmore *Public Torts and Contracts* Ch. 1. It is not clear to what extent the legislation makes the Crown liable to be sued for breach of statutory duty: see *Downs* v. *Williams* (1971) 126 C.L.R. 61. Despite the legislation, some immunities remain, such as the immunity of governments from liability for the negligence of judges, as to which see p. 400 above. As to the vicarious liability of governmental bodies for acts of their officials, see p. 703 below; and as to the vicarious liability of the Crown see P.W. Hogg *Liability of the Crown* (2nd edn, Sydney, 1989) pp. 86-97. Concerning the personal liability of Crown employees see *State of Western Australia* v. *Bond Corporation Holding Ltd* (1991) 5 W.A.R. 40, 61-9.

only applies to the acts of public authorities. This tort has already been discussed;[4] the point to note here is that it does not raise the issues dealt with in this chapter.

I: BASIC CONCEPTS

Several basic concepts lie at the bottom of the law in this area and it will be useful to introduce these in general terms to start with. The first is a distinction we have already come across, namely that between nonfeasance (or omission) and misfeasance. The distinction between misfeasance and nonfeasance is of particular importance as regards the liability of highway authorities for the state of the highway, but it is also of wider significance given that many negligence actions against public authorities arise out of situations where the authority had a statutory power to act but was under no statutory duty to act. If a person or body is under a duty to act then it can clearly be liable for failure to act; but it is not so clear to what extent a body ought to be liable for the exercise or non-exercise of its powers.

The second important idea to understand is the distinction between powers and duties. The statutory functions of public authorities are of two types: those cast in mandatory terms, i.e. duties, and those cast in permissive terms, i.e. powers. A duty is a black and white thing: once the content of the duty has been determined and the conduct of the duty-bearer described, then it can be said either that the authority has breached its duty or that it has not. Conduct in breach of a duty is illegal. In the case of a power, on the other hand, since it confers on the power-holder a choice whether or not to act in a particular way, it is not possible to say that acting or failing to act in that particular way is necessarily illegal: it may be, but this will depend on the limits, if any, which are put on the choice in terms of the reasons and motives for, and the circumstances of, its exercise or non-exercise in that particular way.

It can be seen to follow from this distinction between powers and duties that whereas the power-holder has a certain freedom in deciding what to do, the duty-bearer never has any such freedom. The question of what a duty requires of the duty-holder in any particular situation will always be for some other person or body to decide. In the case of a power, on the other hand, the external control will only extend so far as setting outer limits on the options between which the power-holder is free to choose. This picture is, however, slightly complicated by the fact that an authority may have a duty coupled with a power.

The third basic concept of which it is necessary to have some understanding is the doctrine of *ultra vires*. If in exercising a statutory power a power-holder makes a choice which falls outside the limits which the law imposes on his freedom of choice, he is said to have acted '*ultra vires*' (literally 'beyond the power') or 'illegally'. Decisions within power are '*intra vires*'. The limits which the law imposes on the exercise by public

---

4 See p. 237-9 above.

authorities of statutory powers are encapsulated in a number of grounds of illegality.[5] The main remedy for illegal exercise of a power is to have the decision 'quashed', that is, deprived of legal effect, and to require the authority to make it again, but this time observing the limits laid down by the court. The reason why the authority is given another chance to decide the issue rather than allowing the court to make the decision is that the role of the court is merely to set the limits of the authority's choice. It is for the authority to decide, within those limits, what it will do. This is a basic principle of distribution of constitutional power between the various organs of government.

Damages is not a remedy available for illegality (in the sense of *ultra vires*) as such.[6] The position presently taken by the law is that an award of money compensation can be obtained in respect of a public authority's *ultra vires* action if there is a statutory provision for compensation or if the authority's *ultra vires* action also constitutes a private law wrong such as a breach of contract or a tort. The main question with which we are concerned in this chapter is the extent to which the law of tort can be used as an avenue for obtaining an award of monetary compensation for damage suffered as a result of *ultra vires* action. The law of tort cannot be used to provide compensation for *intra vires* action. Judicial remedies, including damages, are, at common law, only available against public authorities in respect of illegal (*ultra vires*) acts.

In at least some tort actions against public authorities the fact that the damage was inflicted as a result of the exercise of a power could create considerable problems of causation. As we have seen, in order to be able to say that a tortious act caused damage to the plaintiff, it has to be established that the damage would not have occurred but for the negligent act. Suppose that a plaintiff alleges that because of the *ultra vires* (and tortious) failure of a planning authority to grant planning permission he has suffered economic loss. It may well be that even if the authority had acted *intra vires* (within its power) it would still have refused the permission and thus still inflicted the damage. But it is not open to the court to say how the authority would have acted if it had not exceeded its powers, and so it may be impossible for the plaintiff to establish a causal link between his damage and the authority's illegal act.

II: THE GENERAL POSITION

1. THE DEVELOPMENT OF THE LAW

The development of the law in this area culminating in the judgment of Lord Wilberforce in *Anns* v. *Merton L.B.C.*[7] shadowed certain developments in public law. In very broad terms, from about the middle of the

5 For a discussion see M. Allars *Introduction to Australian Administrative Law* (Sydney, 1990) pp. 165-277.

6 e.g. *Navarro* v. *Spanish-Australian Club of Canberra A.C.T. Inc.* (1987) 87 F.L.R. 390.

7 [1978] A.C. 728; *Fellows* v. *Rother D.C.* [1983] 1 All E.R. 513; P.P. Craig (1978) 94 *L.Q.R.* 428; C.S. Phegan (1976) 22 *McGill L.J.* 605; N. Seddon (1978) 9 *F.L.R.* 326.

nineteenth century up until about 1970 the prevailing, although not universally predominant, idea was that so far as the civil (or private law) liability of public authorities was concerned, the proper approach was simply to apply to the actions of individual public officials or corporations the same rules as applied to the activities of private citizens, without making any concessions or modifications by reason of the fact that the defendant was a public official, except to the extent that such modifications were required by statute. This approach was an outworking of one aspect of the set of constitutional ideas often referred to by the term 'the rule of law'. It was adopted in the legislation which abolished the historically based common law immunity of the 'Crown' from actions in tort.[8] All the relevant statutes aimed to assimilate the position of the Crown in respect of liability in tort 'as nearly as possible' to that of an ordinary citizen.

This approach finds clear expression in the leading nineteenth-century cases. Thus in *Mersey Docks Trustees* v. *Gibbs*[9] Blackburn J. said that in the absence of contrary indication the legislature must be taken as intending that statutory bodies, in exercising their statutory functions, should have the same duties, and that their funds should be subject to the same liabilities, as the general law would impose on a private person doing the same things. When the same judge reached the House of Lords he said in *Geddis* v. *Proprietors of Bann Reservoir* that 'no action will lie for doing that which the legislature has authorized if it be done without negligence, although it does occasion damage to anyone; but an action does lie for doing that which the legislature has authorized if it be done negligently'.[10] Statements of this basic rule can be found a century later.[11] While neither of these nineteenth-century cases concerned governmental bodies in the core sense, they have since been taken as establishing the basic rule governing the tort liability of public authorities.

The approach of assimilating the liability of public authorities to that of private individuals really only works well so long as government is not seen as having too many peculiarly governmental functions. It is only possible to treat the government as a private citizen when it is doing things which private citizens also do. But more importantly, perhaps, the growth of the philosophy and practice of social welfare, and increasing state intervention in and regulation of numerous areas of social life and economic activity, have led to a significant shift in the way we perceive the relationship between the individual and the state. On the one hand we have, of necessity, become much more prepared to accept curtailment of the interests of the individual for the sake of wider social interests which the government supposedly represents and which it is its job to further and protect. On the other hand, although to a much lesser extent, we have come to expect government, in return for the grant of power over us which we have made, to exercise that power with especial regard for and

---

8 See n. 3 above and accompanying text.
9 (1866) L.R. 1 H.L. 93, 110.
10 (1878) 3 App. Cases 430, 455-6.
11 See e.g. *Caledonian Collieries Ltd* v. *Speirs* (1956) 97 C.L.R. 202, 220.

sensitivity to the interests of individuals. We have come to recognize that government is indeed very different from the citizens it governs.

The need to give government special leeway in furthering the public interest, and at the same time the need to impose special limitations and burdens on government in the exercise of its extensive powers, were perhaps recognized in the statutory phrase 'as nearly as possible',[12] but the implications of the recognition have never been worked out in statutory form. The common law's response to the need (as expounded by Lord Wilberforce in *Anns*) is somewhat one-sided. The law grants to public authorities an immunity from liability in tort[13] if it appears that in order to judge the tortiousness of the defendants' behaviour the court would have to pass judgment on the reasonableness of the authority's assessment of 'policy' (or 'planning')[14] matters, which the court considers to be beyond its competence or constitutional province to pronounce upon, provided only that the authority has acted *intra vires*. But if an authority's decision on policy matters is *ultra vires*, an action for negligence may be allowed.

It should be noted that this immunity only applies to decisions on policy matters and not to decisions on matters which raise no issues of policy beyond the competence of the court. Decisions which raise no such policy issues are now called 'operational' decisions. In respect of such decisions public authorities are subject to the law of tort in the same way as a private individual. The basic idea underlying the distinction between policy and operational decisions is that in matters of public policy, public authorities must be given considerable freedom of action, and that it is not for judges, who are unelected and not even indirectly answerable to the electorate, to tell public bodies, which are either elected or answerable to an elected body, what they should do in the public interest and to award damages against them if they cause loss by failing to do it.

2. The Tort of Negligence

This immunity in respect of *intra vires* policy decisions was developed mainly in the context of the tort of negligence;[15] it received its first important modern consideration in the judgment of Lord Diplock in *Dorset Yacht Co.* v. *Home Office*,[16] and was expounded in greater and more authoritative detail by Lord Wilberforce in *Anns* v. *Merton L.B.C.*[17] But the idea of a policy immunity was not an entirely new one. In 1880 it was held in a New South Wales case that no action would lie in respect of the government's failure to spend money (allocated by Parliament for the repair of a bridge) on its intended purpose.[18] It was also held in an early

12 See *Davidson* v. *Walker* (1901) 1 S.R.(N.S.W.) 196, 212 *per* A.H. Simpson J.

13 *Anns* strictly only concerned actions in negligence, but the principle it contains is applicable to other torts as well.

14 In this context, the term 'planning' is not confined to land use planning.

15 S. Todd (1986) 102 *L.Q.R.* 370; A. Rubinstein (1987) 13 *Mon. L.R.* 75.

16 [1970] A.C. 1004, 1067-8.

17 [1978] A.C. 728.

18 *Wakely* v. *Lackey* (1880) 1 L.R.(N.S.W.) 274.

case that no action would lie for negligence in respect of the choice of site and method of construction of a lock up, the noise from which disturbed neighbours. The government, it was said, had to possess a large degree of immunity from liability in respect of the exercise of its important executive functions.[19] In *Local Board of Health of City of Perth* v. *Maley*[20] it was held that, provided the board exercised its discretionary power to build such drains as it thought necessary honestly and bona fide, a private individual would have no right to complain if the drainage system inflicted damage on him; the board had to consider the interests of all and keep within a budget. The germ of the idea of an immunity for policy decisions can also be found in *Sheppard* v. *Glossop Corporation*[21] where the plaintiff suffered injury as a result of the fact that the defendant had decided for reasons of economy to turn street lights in its area off at 9 p.m. A main ground of the decision was that although Lord Blackburn's rule would apply if the council, for example, erected a lamp post and left it unprotected in the middle of the road or close by the highway so as to be a danger to passers-by,[22] or if it allowed gas from a lamp to escape into someone's house, it would not apply to a discretionary decision as to how long to keep lamps alight, or to a decision to remove a lamp post or to supply gas to some lamps but not to others.

In *Anns* v. *Merton L.B.C.*[23] the Council had a statutory power to inspect the foundations of houses in course of construction to ensure that they complied with building regulations. The House of Lords was asked to decide whether the Council could be subject to liability in negligence on the assumption (i) that no inspection had taken place, and (ii) that an inspection had taken place but had been negligently performed. It was held that a duty could arise on either hypothesis subject to the policy immunity and the principle of *ultra vires*. This meant that an authority could be liable for failure to inspect at all,[24] provided the decision not to inspect (or the failure to decide whether or not to inspect) was an *ultra*

---

19 *Davidson* v. *Walker* (1901) 1 S.R.(N.S.W.) 196.

20 (1904) 1 C.L.R. 702.

21 [1921] 3 K.B. 132. But for a different interpretation of this case see A. Rubinstein (1987) 13 *Mon. L.R.* 75, 83.

22 cf. *Bird* v. *Pearce* [1979] R.T.R. 369.

23 [1978] A.C. 728. As we saw in Chapter 9, Lord Wilberforce's two-stage approach to finding a duty of care has been disapproved by the House of Lords in more recent cases, and, to the extent that the case recognized liability for the cost of repairing defective premises, it has now been overruled: *Murphy* v. *Brentwood D.C.* [1991] 1 AC 398. But that part of the judgment of Lord Wilberforce which discusses the doctrine of *ultra vires* and the policy/operational distinction has not yet been repudiated.

24 If this were not so, authorities would be sorely tempted to do nothing in order to avoid the risk of liability for negligent intervention (cf. p. 384 above for a similar issue in a private law context). Another way of limiting liability for negligent intervention is to hold that an authority which intervened could only be liable if it increased an existing danger or created a new one, but not if the only result of its negligence was failure to remove an existing danger or to prevent the creation of a new danger by a third party. This was the approach taken in *East Suffolk Rivers Catchment Board* v. *Kent* [1941] A.C. 74 (applied in *Administration of the Territory of Papua & New Guinea* v. *Leahy* (1960-1) 105 C.L.R. 6). But it seems that the result and reasoning in *East Suffolk* could not survive adoption of the principle in *Anns*.

vires exercise of the power to decide as a matter of policy when and if to inspect. This reasoning was adopted in the Canadian case of *City of Kamloops* v. *Nielsen*[25] in which the council decided to exercise its discretion not to enforce an order requiring a builder to stop building work until he fulfilled a condition as to the foundations; it was found that one of the reasons why the council had decided not to enforce the stop-work order was that the building owner was an alderman and the builder's father. So the decision not to enforce the order was *ultra vires*, and a subsequent purchaser of the house was awarded damages for the cost of repairing the house and consequential economic loss.

It is clear, therefore, that an authority may have a common law duty to take care in taking action, or in deciding whether or not to take action, even though it has no statutory duty to take action. The first part of this proposition is simply a restatement of Lord Blackburn's rule and imposes liability on ordinary negligence principles for operational negligence. The second part allows imposition of liability for *ultra vires* decisions not to act made on policy grounds. But if such a decision was *intra vires* the defendant would enjoy immunity from liability.

We can summarize so far by saying that if in the exercise of statutory power a public authority makes a decision on grounds of public policy, the reasonableness of which the court feels it is not in a position to assess, and that decision is *intra vires*, no action in negligence will lie in respect of it. But if the decision is *ultra vires*, an action in negligence may lie if the other conditions for such an action are satisfied. If the exercise of power complained of raises no issues of policy which the court feels unable to adjudicate upon in a negligence action, it will be called 'operational' and will be actionable according to ordinary negligence rules.

Australian courts have not found much occasion to consider in detail the law as expounded by Lord Wilberforce.[26] But the policy/operational distinction was accepted as a useful one by Gibbs C.J. and Mason J. in *Sutherland S.C.* v. *Heyman*;[27] and something like it played an important part in the reasoning of Brennan J. in the *San Sebastian* case.[28] On the other hand, Mason J. in *Heyman*[29] said that there was 'no compelling reason for confining . . . a duty of care to situations in which a public authority . . . [acts] in excess of power or authority', that is, *ultra vires*. This *dictum* seems to contemplate the possibility of a tort action even in respect of *intra vires* decisions. On the contrary, however, it can be asked why an action for negligence (which would require the court to decide whether the authority had exercised its powers reasonably) should *ever* be allowed in respect of policy decisions (even if *ultra vires*). How does the fact that an authority has acted *ultra vires* make it any more appropriate

---

25 (1984) 10 D.L.R. (4th) 641.

26 The policy/operational distinction has been adopted in New Zealand (e.g. *Craig* v. *East Coast Bays C.C.* [1986] 1 N.Z.L.R. 99) and in Canada: *City of Kamloops* v. *Nielsen* (1984) 10 D.L.R. (4th) 641.

27 (1984-5) 157 C.L.R. 424, 442, 458, 469. See also *F.S. Evans & Sons Pty Ltd* v. *Delaney* (1984) 58 L.G.R.A. 405, 410-11 *per* King C.J.

28 (1986) 68 A.L.R. 161, 183.

29 (1974-5) 157 C.L.R. 424, 458.

that a court should decide whether it has acted unreasonably? Is it not for the authority to decide what it is reasonable to do in the circumstances?

There are two possible ways of overcoming this difficulty. One is to say that an action for negligence in respect of an *ultra vires* policy decision could succeed only if the ground on which the decision was *ultra vires* entailed that it was also negligent. For example, one ground of *ultra vires* is that a public authority's decision was *so unreasonable* that no reasonable authority could have made it. This test of unreasonableness is stricter than that applied in the tort of negligence in the sense that it is harder to say that a decision is unreasonable in the former than in the latter sense. So if a decision is held to have been unreasonable in that stricter sense, it will also be unreasonable in the less strict negligence sense.

Another way around the difficulty is to say that policy decisions are not actionable in tort at all even if they are *ultra vires*. This seems to have been the approach taken by Lord Keith, speaking for the Privy Council on appeal from the New Zealand Court of Appeal, in *Rowling* v. *Takaro Properties Ltd*[30] when he said that the policy/operational distinction was 'expressive of the need to exclude altogether those cases in which the decision under attack is of such a kind that a question whether it has been made negligently is unsuitable for judicial resolution'. When his Lordship's opinion is read as a whole, what he seems to have meant by this is that a negligence action will not lie in respect of a policy decision if the allegation of negligence relates to the *substance* of the decision; in other words, if the plaintiff alleges that the decision was an unreasonable one to make. But if the plaintiff alleges that the decision-making *procedure* was negligent, the court may adjudicate on such an allegation even if the decision in question raises policy issues. This was the situation in *Takaro* itself in which the allegation was, in essence, that the Minister had been negligent in not taking legal advice before reaching his decision not to grant consent to the purchase by a Japanese corporation of shares in a New Zealand land development company (which was accepted to be a policy decision).

Lord Keith's opinion in *Takaro* also places a very important qualification on that part of Lord Wilberforce's account which suggests that operational decisions are actionable in negligence according to ordinary principles. In a number of recent decisions the Privy Council and English courts have laid down restrictive duty-of-care principles governing the actionability in negligence of operational decisions of public authorities. In other words, it is not every instance of operational negligence by public authorities which will be actionable in tort: in addition to negligence there must also, of course, be a duty of care.

There are a number of grounds on which a duty of care may be held not to exist.[31] An action in tort will not lie (or, in other words, a duty of care will not be owed) if, first, there was available to the plaintiff a suitable

30 [1988] A.C. 473, 500-3.

31 For more detailed discussion see Cane *Tort Law and Economic Interests* pp. 255-62.

alternative avenue of redress for his grievance;[32] or if, secondly, the purposes which the functions being exercised by the defendant were designed to achieve did not require, for their proper fulfilment, that injured individuals be allowed to sue for damages;[33] or if, thirdly, the statute under which the defendant was acting was not designed to protect the plaintiff against losses of the sort suffered by him.[34] Fourthly, the courts are unwilling to impose tort liability on public authorities if they think that the fear of such liability might lead authorities to be over-cautious in exercising their powers or unhelpful to citizens who seek their advice or assistance.[35] Finally, if the plaintiff's claim is in respect of economic loss, or if he alleges that the defendant ought to have done something in exercise of its powers which it did not do,[36] then the general bias in the law of tort against compensating for economic loss and for failure to take positive action respectively will militate against the success of the claim.

None of these factors is peculiar to actions against public authorities,

---

32 *Jones* v. *Department of Employment* [1989] Q.B. 1 (applied in *Coshott* v. *Woollahra M.C.* (1988) 14 N.S.W.L.R. 675; *Mills* v. *Winchester Diocesan Board* [1989] Ch. 428; *Hill* v. *Chief Constable of West Yorkshire* [1989] A.C. 53. Cf. the idea that a tort action will not be allowed if the plaintiff could protect himself by contract, as to which see p. 362 above.

33 *Yuen Kun Yeu* v. *Attorney General of Hong Kong* [1988] A.C. 175; cf. *Minories Finance Ltd* v. *Arthur Young [a firm]* [1989] 2 All ER 105. Another way of putting this is to say that there must be a sufficient relationship of proximity between the plaintiff and the defendant: *Hill* v. *Chief Constable of West Yorkshire* [1989] A.C. 53. See also *Clough* v. *Bussan* [1990] 1 All ER 431; but contrast *Ticehurst* v. *Skeen* (1986) 3 M.V.R. 307.

34 *Governors of Peabody Foundation Fund* v. *Sir Lindsay Parkinson & Co. Ltd* [1985] A.C. 210. These last two considerations are directly analogous to requirements for the actionability in tort of breaches of statutory duty, whether the duty is owed by a private citizen or a public authority (but there is some Australian authority against drawing such an analogy: *Sutherland S.C.* v. *Heyman* (1984-5) 157 C.L.R. 424, 436 *per* Gibbs C.J., 459 *per* Mason J.; but contrast 482 *per* Brennan J. and 509 *per* Deane J.). Technically, they are issues of statutory interpretation which can only be decided in relation to particular statutory provisions. But reasonable people can usually disagree about the right answer to contested questions of statutory interpretation; and the willingness of a judge to decide these issues in favour of the plaintiff will undoubtedly be influenced by the judge's general views about the desirability or otherwise of making public authorities pay for losses caused by the exercise of their statutory powers. English courts are currently much less willing to allow tort actions against public authorities than New Zealand courts. See, for example, *Craig* v. *East Coast Bays C.C.* [1986] 1 N.Z.L.R. 99; *Stieller* v. *Porirua C.C.* [1986] 2 N.Z.L.R. 84. In *Anns* it was held that an owner or occupier could recover from a local authority the cost of remedying a defect in a building if the defect presented a danger to the health or safety of occupants. In *Peabody* this was restricted so that only an endangered occupant (and not a non-occupying owner) could recover. Finally, in *Murphy* v. *Brentwood DC* [1991] 1 A.C. 398, it was held that local authorities could not be held liable for the cost of forestalling personal injury. This narrowing down of liability was not the result of interpretation of significantly different statutory provisions but of a change in attitude to the desirability of local authority liability.

35 *Calveley* v. *Chief Constable of Merseyside* [1989] A.C. 1228; cf. *Hill* v. *Chief Constable of West Yorkshire* [1989] A.C. 53. We have already seen this argument used in the context of the tort liability of doctors and other professionals: p. 428 above.

36 As will very often be the case in actions against regulatory authorities: e.g. *Yuen Kun Yeu* v. *Attorney-General of Hong Kong* [1988] A.C. 175.

but they provide the courts with a powerful armoury of weapons with which to repel actions against public authorities, if the court is minded so to do. Moreover, while these factors have been enunciated in cases concerning operational negligence, they apply equally, of course, to cases in respect of policy decisions.

Two other points were made by Lord Keith in *Takaro* which deserve mention here, because they increase even further the difficulty of bringing a successful claim of negligence against a public authority. The first is that according to Lord Keith it would be very difficult to castigate an error of law made by a public authority as negligent because reasonable people can often disagree about the right answer to a contested question of law. The importance of this point arises from the fact that many of the heads of *ultra vires* are based on misinterpretations of statutory provisions, that is, on errors of law. Secondly, Lord Keith said it would be very difficult to identify cases in which it could be said that failure to take legal advice before exercising a statutory power would be negligent. Conversely, it has been held that a public authority can normally repel a claim of negligence in the exercise of a statutory power by showing that it took legal advice about the extent of its powers before acting.[37]

3. The Role of the Policy/Operational Distinction in Other Torts

Although the policy/operational distinction was developed in the context of the tort of negligence, the basic principle underlying it is theoretically applicable to other torts as well. Consider trespass first. In the nineteenth-century case of *Cooper* v. *Wandsworth Board of Works*[38] the board demolished part of the plaintiff's house in execution of a demolition order made under statutory powers. The plaintiff sued the board in trespass, and the order was held to be *ultra vires*; so the demolition was unlawful and trespassory. If the order had been *intra vires*, the demolition would have been lawful because done under statutory authority. In terms of the policy/operational distinction, the decision to issue the demolition order could probably be classified as a policy decision, and according to this view the case neatly illustrates the principle that *ultra vires* policy decisions may be actionable in tort. On the other hand, suppose that a road (for the building of which land has been duly acquired) is carelessly sited so that it encroaches on a person's private property: this might be classified as an 'operational trespass' which would be actionable without any reference to the doctrine of *ultra vires*.

A similar analysis applies to the tort of nuisance. As we have seen, if a nuisance is created by acts done in exercise of statutory powers, the creator of the nuisance will be able to plead the defence of statutory authorization provided the nuisance was an inevitable consequence of the performance

37 *Dunlop* v. *Woollahra M.C.* [1982] A.C. 158.
38 (1863) 14 C.B.N.S. 180.

of authorized acts and that the defendant was not negligent.[39] In the final analysis, it is reasonably accurate to say that a plea of statutory authorization will not succeed unless the defendant can show that it did not act negligently. But if the question is whether the defendant acted negligently in exercising its statutory powers, the same considerations which have led courts to be wary of answering this question in a negligence action would apply here, too. This analysis would also seem to be applicable to actions brought under the rule in *Rylands* v. *Fletcher*.[40]

Finally, let us consider the tort of breach of statutory duty. At first sight, the *Anns* approach would appear to be of no relevance to this tort because the logic of being under a duty is that the duty-bearer has no choice as to whether or not to do what it has a duty to do; so no question of judicial review of its choices should arise. But the matter is slightly more complicated than this because although a statute may provide that an authority has a duty to do X, it may not specify what X is in sufficient detail or with sufficient precision to relieve the authority of the need to make choices as to what its statutory duty requires it to do in particular circumstances. For example, the duty in issue in *Meade* v. *Haringey L.B.C.*[41] was a duty to provide sufficient schools. The question in the case was whether a decision to close schools during a strike by cleaners was a breach of this duty. The English Court of Appeal said that the decision whether to close the schools was within the area of discretion left to the authority to exercise on policy grounds. In other words, the authority had a power (to decide what amounted to sufficient schooling) coupled with a duty (to provide such schooling); and so the court would only intervene if the authority had acted *ultra vires* in deciding to close the schools.

In *Anns* terms, breaches of such vague and imprecise statutory duties can be either at the policy level or at the operational level. If the duty in question were one to ensure that school buildings were reasonably safe, for example, a court might well hold that failure to do so which resulted in personal injury to a student was an operational breach, and so actionable regardless of whether the authority's decision not to take appropriate safety precautions was *ultra vires* or not.[42]

4. Application of the Policy/Operational Distinction

(a) General points It has been argued that the policy/operational distinction is unnecessary, at least in respect of negligence and nuisance, because the concept of unreasonableness which lies at the bottom of these torts is flexible enough to allow the considerations which gave rise to the policy/operational distinction to be taken into account.[43] For example, in *Page Motors Ltd* v. *Epsom and Ewell B.C.*[44] the council delayed for

---

39 See p. 609 above.
40 See p. 641 above.
41 [1979] 1 W.L.R. 637.
42 See *Reffell* v. *Surrey County Council* [1964] 1 W.L.R. 358 and Cane [1981] *P.L.* 11.
43 S.H. Bowman and M.J. Bailey [1986] *C.L.J.* 430.
44 (1982) 80 L.G.R. 337.

some years in executing an eviction order against gypsies who were camping on a field near the plaintiff's automotive garage and deterring customers. The plaintiff sued the council for nuisance, and it was argued (in effect) that the council's decision to delay in enforcing the eviction order had been taken for sound policy reasons and so was not actionable unless *ultra vires*. The court rejected this argument and said that the only issue in the case was whether the council had, in the terms of ordinary nuisance principles, unreasonably interfered with the plaintiff's use of its land. But in answering this question the court took into account in favour of the defendant the very matters of policy which the defendant referred to in its argument.

In the final analysis, it probably does not matter much whether we adopt something like the policy/operational distinction and limit the application of tort law to public authorities; or whether, on the other hand, we simply take relevant policy matters into account in deciding whether a public authority has acted tortiously. Either course involves a recognition that public authorities may deserve some immunity from the ordinary application of the law of tort because their responsibilities to the public may require them sometimes to inflict injury on private individuals for which it would not be appropriate to compensate through the law of tort. Of course, this leaves open the question of whether some other avenue for obtaining compensation (such as a no-fault statutory compensation scheme) ought to be provided. It is important to understand that the arguments used to justify the policy immunity do not also justify a conclusion that individuals should not be compensated for loss inflicted by policy decisions; they only justify that conclusion that compensation should not be given through the common law of tort.

'Matters of policy' often, in the final analysis, come down to decisions about the allocation of limited resources between competing activities for which a defendant authority is responsible. An authority will often want to argue that the only way it could have prevented the loss suffered by the plaintiff was by spending money which it had already allocated to some other activity which, in its view, was more deserving (in policy terms) of support.[45] This sort of argument is particularly controversial because it is not normally open to the defendant in a negligence action to argue that it could not afford to take reasonable precautions against risks of injury or loss; but it is also the case, of course, that private individuals, as much as public authorities, have limited resources. It might be thought that although some policy choices made by public authorities ought not to be actionable in negligence, choices turning just on whether to use funds for one purpose rather than another should not be protected by such an immunity;[46] otherwise, a public authority could always defend a claim of negligence by arguing that it had exhausted its budget. However, decisions about the use of money usually reflect political priorities, so that the

45 See fn. 48 below.

46 See A. Rubinstein (1987) 13 *Mon. L.R.* 75 esp. 117-18; for an inconclusive judicial discussion see *Cekan* v. *Haines* (1990) 21 N.S.W.L.R. 296.

distinction between such decisions and other policy decisions really makes little sense.

This might suggest that the issue of resources has no independent force but is subsidiary to the underlying issues in any particular case. If the court thinks that the plaintiff's loss ought, in principle, to be compensatable in a tort action, then although it might take the fact of limited resources into account in deciding what precautions to avoid the loss ought to have been taken by the authority, it will not allow the authority to plead lack of resources as a justification for not taking those precautions; in other words, the court would apply ordinary negligence principles.[47] But if the court thinks that the authority's decision ought not to be challengeable in a tort action, one way of expressing this is to say that it involved the allocation of scarce resources.[48]

(b) Classifying decisions as policy decisions Whatever the current status in Australian law of the policy/operational distinction, it must be said that it is a distinction impossible to draw in the abstract because it depends on whether the court decides that the decision in question raises policy issues which it is not prepared to adjudicate upon according to the ordinary rules of negligence. So the best way to approach the distinction is by looking at concrete examples.

We have already looked at some cases in which alleged negligence of public bodies has been held to be immune from attack for policy reasons. There are a few other cases which throw some light on the way the courts will approach the question of classifying decisions as turning on matters of policy or not. It seems that there would have to be a fairly close relationship between the alleged policy considerations and the challenged decision or action. For example, in *Evans* v. *Finn*[49] an action was brought in respect of a military rifle range, the escape of bullets from which constituted a danger to life and limb. It was held that the mere fact that the range had been established for military purposes, and could hence be said to fall under the umbrella of the Crown's prerogative powers of waging war, did not put the Crown in any better position than a private citizen so far as liability in tort was concerned. There was no evidence that any good military purpose required that the rifle range be set up in such a way that it constituted a danger to neighbours. This case would suggest that the onus will be on the defendant body to establish the matters necessary to make out a policy immunity, although in none of the modern cases has the question of the location of the onus of proof on the question of the policy nature of the decision been discussed. Most courts have simply assumed that it is for the court itself to assess whether policy is involved. However, of the modern cases, *Dorset Yacht Co.* v. *Home Office*[50] would seem to provide the best basis for an argument that the

---

47 See, for example, *Knight* v. *Home Office* [1990] 3 All E.R. 237, 243.
48 The suggestion made in this paragraph is supported by *Just* v. *British Columbia* (1990) 64 D.L.R. (4th) 689.
49 (1904) 4 S.R.(N.S.W.) 297.
50 [1970] A.C. 1004.

defendant must establish that the case is a proper one for according the immunity.

An interesting case on the classification point is *Takaro Properties* v. *Rowling*[51] which was heard on a motion to strike out, *inter alia,* a cause of action alleging negligence against a Minister for his admittedly *ultra vires* refusal of consent for the taking up by a Japanese corporation of shares in the plaintiff company. Both Woodhouse J. and Richardson J. thought that it might be relevant to classifying the decision as a policy one to ask whether it was made by a high- or low-ranking official.[52] If it was made by the Minister, this might indicate that it was a decision raising important issues of policy; but if it was left to a minor official this might indicate that it only involved the application of already settled policies. This by itself would not, however, take matters far enough because if the minor official faithfully applied the policy guidelines, any challenge to his decision would be, in effect, a challenge to those policy guidelines. Only if the challenge to the minor official's decision was based just on a failure to apply the guidelines properly would the action have no policy ramifications.

Several of the relevant cases concern the running of prisons. *Dorset Yacht Co.* v. *Home Office*[53] supports the proposition that policy decisions such as whether to establish a system of open Borstals, and possibly decisions about whether to send particular prisoners to open institutions, would enjoy immunity from challenge in a negligence action if *intra vires.* In *L.* v. *Commonwealth*[54] it was said that although, for policy reasons, no liability would arise merely from the (*intra vires*) failure of prison authorities to provide an adequate prison, the officers in charge of the prison have an obligation, so far as is possible, to keep remand and unsentenced prisoners separate and apart from convicted or sentence-serving prisoners. In that case the plaintiff, a remand prisoner, was sexually assaulted by sentence-serving prisoners with whom he was made to share a cell for the night. On the other hand, in *Booth* v. *Dillon (No. 2)*[55] the question was whether certain matters fell within the jurisdiction of the Ombudsman who has power to investigate matters of administration. 'Matters of administration' in this context is loosely synonymous with 'operational matters' in the *Anns* sense. The Ombudsman conducted an investigation into action taken to ensure that certain prisoners at Pentridge were not subjected to sexual assaults. The action involved increasing the prison staff and seeking funds to convert dormitory accommodation into single cell accommodation. It was held that the Ombudsman had gone beyond his jurisdiction because the sleeping arrangements of prisoners and the provision of funds for the particular

---

51 [1978] 2 N.Z.L.R. 314. When this case reached the Privy Council, it was accepted that the decision involved matters of policy. See p. 685 above.

52 cf. *Just* v. *British Columbia* (1990) 64 D.L.R. (4th) 689.

53 [1970] A.C. 1004.

54 (1976) 10 A.L.R. 269.

55 [1976] V.R. 434.

purposes of a government department were matters of policy, not administration. The issue of sleeping arrangements raises questions about the appropriate method of treating offenders.[56]

In *Vicar of Writtle* v. *Essex County Council*[57] a boy on remand, who was a known fire-maker, was put into an open community home but the house parent was not told of his pyromaniac propensities. In the middle of the day the boy wandered out of the house and set fire to a nearby church. It was held that while the local authority had a very wide statutory discretion as to the proper way to deal with children in its care, with which the court would not interfere if it was properly exercised, the authority had at the same time a duty to take reasonable care in exercising control over the boy to whom it stood *in loco parentis*. The failure of the council's social worker to disclose the boy's known propensity was not a bona fide exercise of the discretion vested in the authority. The authority had no discretion not to reveal such information, but a duty to make it known. In other words, there was no possible argument which could be said to support the decision not to disclose the information and so justify a policy immunity for that decision.

Three other cases deserve mention.[58] In one it was held that decisions by the Commonwealth government under the Air Navigation Act as to what types of equipment to approve and as to what steps to take in relation to types of equipment when doubts arose as to their suitability were discretionary (i.e. policy) decisions rather than operational ones. This was because although safety is an important purpose of the Act, it is not the sole purpose. Other aims are that air services should be developed and operated regularly, economically and efficiently. The balancing of these aims is a matter of policy.[59]

In another case a local authority failed to warn an applicant for a building permit that the house as planned would be subject to flooding. The council in fact did not know of the danger and had taken no steps to ascertain whether such a danger existed. Instead it had an arrangement with the Drainage Board under which the latter examined all applications

---

56 Along similar lines, it was held in *Skuse* v. *Commonwealth* (1985) 62 A.L.R. 108 that security arrangements at courthouses raised policy issues about law and order and the administration of justice.

57 (1979) 77 L.G.R. 656.

58 In order of discussion they are: *Sasin* v. *Commonwealth* (1984) 52 A.L.R. 299; *Brown* v. *Heathcote C.C.* [1982] 2 N.Z.L.R. 584 (affirmed on different grounds by PC [1987] 1 N.Z.L.R. 720); *Minister for Environmental Planning* v. *San Sebastian Pty Ltd* [1983] 2 N.S.W.L.R. 268 (affirmed by HC (1986) 68 A.L.R. 161; but only Brennan J. addressed the issue currently under discussion).

59 In *Rigby* v. *Chief Constable of Northamptonshire* [1985] 1 W.L.R. 1242 it was held that a decision not to acquire a type of C.S. gas canister the use of which entailed a lesser fire risk than the use of another type of canister, which the police already had, was a policy decision; but that a decision to use the more dangerous type of canister without fire-fighting equipment being available was an operational decision. But *query* whether the police, in deciding to use the canister, were not balancing the need to apprehend the criminal against the risk of fire damage in a way consistent with their discretionary power to enforce the law. *Rigby* was distinguished in *Hughes* v. *National Union of Mineworkers* [1991] 4 All ER 278 (Chief Constable not liable for injuries suffered by police engaged in riot control).

for building permits in respect of matters within its statutory remit. It was held that the council's decision to leave matters of flooding and drainage to the board was an *intra vires* policy decision, and so it could not be sued in negligence for failing to warn of the danger of flooding. It was also held that it was a matter of policy for the board to decide whether it would assume a consultancy role for the council. But once the board had decided to take on the job of giving advice about building applications, the giving of advice was an operational matter and the board was under a duty to take care in giving advice.

The third case concerned alleged negligence in the preparation and publication of an outline plan for the development of a large area of inner Sydney. It was also argued that the planning authority had been negligent in not abandoning the plan when its defects became known. The case raised many issues, one of which was whether the authority could be sued in negligence at all. Hutley J.A. said that the authority enjoyed immunity from action in respect of the preparation and publication of broad social plans because even if there were standards by which such plans could be judged they were not suitable for judicial evaluation. Glass J.A. thought that the publication of the plan was an operational not a policy act, but that the decision whether to abandon or persevere with the plan was a matter of policy.

(c) Negligence in reaching a policy decision As we have already noted, Lord Keith in *Rowling* v. *Takaro Properties*[60] seems to have taken the view that even if the substance of policy decisions could not form the basis of a negligence claim, the process by which such decisions were made might found a negligence action. In *Takaro* itself, the allegation of negligence was, in essence, that the Minister ought to have taken legal advice before reaching his decision. The Privy Council held that his failure to take legal advice was not unreasonable in the circumstances; but Lord Keith went further and said that it would be difficult to identify cases in which it could be said that failure to take legal advice would be negligent. Conversely, however, it seems clear that if an authority *does* take legal advice about the legality of what it proposes to do before making a policy decision, it is very unlikely to be held to have acted negligently.[61]

(d) Examples of operational negligence There are a number of cases in which public authorities have been held liable for negligent misstatements: for example, to the effect that development consent had been granted;[62]

---

60 [1988] A.C. 473.

61 *Dunlop* v. *Woollahra M.C.* [1982] A.C. 158.

62 *Hull* v. *Canterbury M.C.* [1974] 1 N.S.W.L.R. 300. Rather problematic is *Smith* v. *Shire of Murray* (1985) 54 L.G.R.A. 246 in which it was held that the granting of planning permission which the defendant had no power to grant amounted to a negligent misrepresentation to the effect that the plaintiff was entitled to use the land as he wished. This decision in effect awards damages for loss suffered as a result of *ultra vires* action which Anglo-Australian law does not, in theory, allow.

that a proposed development involved no impermissible change of use;[63] that a truck was roadworthy;[64] that land was immediately suitable for the breeding of lambs and the production of wool;[65] that land was unaffected by road-widening proposals;[66] that premises intended for use as a milk-bar and coffee lounge business met all health requirements.[67] Liability has also been imposed for negligence in issuing a land title search certificate which failed to reveal that the land was subject to a charge, with the result that the chargee's security was destroyed.[68]

Then there is a body of cases in which public authorities have been held liable for negligence in performing their supervisory functions in respect of the building of premises in their area: for example, passing a building application without warning of the danger that the building would be subject to slippage and even requiring it to be built where the risk of slippage was greater than necessary;[69] issuing a building permit without giving an adjoining owner the required opportunity to object,[70] or without noticing defects in the plans;[71] failure, when inspecting foundations before they were covered up, to notice that they did not comply with building regulations;[72] approving plans for the construction of a house without noticing that the foundations were inadequate;[73] failure, when examining the plans for a public hall, to notice that the proposed stage did not comply with by-laws.[74]

Prison authorities can be held liable for negligent failure to supervise prisoners properly so as to prevent injury or damage to third parties,[75] or for putting a remand prisoner in the same cell as a long-term prisoner who might take advantage of him in some way.[76] A social welfare authority has been held liable for failure to warn the person in charge of an open prison of dangerous propensities of a child put into his charge,[77] and police have been held liable for failure to tell prison authorities of the suicidal tendencies of a person committed to their custody.[78]

---

63 *G.J. Knight Holdings Pty Ltd* v. *Warringah S.C.* [1975] 2 N.S.W.L.R. 795.
64 *Rutherford* v. *Attorney-General* [1976] 1 N.Z.L.R. 403.
65 *State of South Australia* v. *Johnson* (1982) 42 A.L.R. 161.
66 *Shaddock* v. *Parramatta C.C.* (1981) 150 C.L.R. 225; but see now Environmental Planning and Assessment Act 1979 (N.S.W.), s.149.
67 *R.A. & T.J. Carll Ltd* v. *Berry* [1981] 2 N.Z.L.R. 76.
68 *Ministry of Housing and Local Government* v. *Sharp* [1970] 2 Q.B. 223. But see now Local Land Charges Act 1975 (U.K.) s.10.
69 *Wollongong C.C.* v. *Fregnan* [1982] 1 N.S.W.L.R. 244; cf. *Brown* v. *Heathcote C.C.* [1987] 1 N.Z.L.R. 720.
70 *Craig* v. *East Coast Bays C.C.* [1986] 1 N.Z.L.R. 99.
71 *Stieller* v. *Porirua C.C.* [1986] 1 N.Z.L.R. 84.
72 *Mt Albert Borough Council* v. *Johnson* [1979] 2 N.Z.L.R. 234; *Young* v. *Tomlinson* [1979] 2 N.Z.L.R. 441; *Commonwealth* v. *Turnbull* (1976) 13 A.C.T.R. 14.
73 *Carosella* v. *Ginos & Gilbert Pty Ltd* (1981) 27 S.A.S.R. 515.
74 *Voli* v. *Inglewood S.C.* (1962-3) 110 C.L.R. 74.
75 *Dorset Yacht Co. Ltd* v. *Home Office* [1970] A.C. 1004.
76 *L.* v. *Commonwealth* (1976) 10 A.L.R. 269.
77 *Vicar of Writtle* v. *Essex County Council* (1979) 77 L.G.R. 656.
78 *Kirkham* v. *Chief Constable of Manchester* [1990] 2 Q.B. 283.

III: THE SPECIAL POSITION OF HIGHWAY AUTHORITIES

1. THE NONFEASANCE RULE

The law governing the liability of highway authorities developed before the rules we have been considering. The basic common law rule is that bodies responsible for highways are only liable for misfeasance[79] and not for nonfeasance. This applies not only to the maintenance of highways already constructed but also to the construction of new highways or the extension or improvement of existing ones.[80] One explanation for this rule is the law's general reluctance to impose a duty to take positive action. Another justification for the rule might be that it must, as a matter of policy, be left to highway authorities to decide how much to spend on road construction and repair and which roads to repair. It has also been argued that authorities whose area of responsibility is large and served by a widespread road system need special consideration because of the administrative and financial difficulties of their position, the possibility of a flood of claims, and the desirability of encouraging a high degree of self-help among road users.[81] However, these factors would not justify a blanket immunity from liability for non-repair but only a rule that they should be taken into account in deciding what the authority ought reasonably to have done.

It may be, however, that the rule is not based on rational argument but is just the result of historical accident:[82] in some of the earliest English cases arising out of non-repair of highways, the duty to repair rested on all the inhabitants of an area or county through which the road went. For procedural reasons these groups of inhabitants, not being legal persons, could not be sued. By the time responsibility for highways became vested in incorporated local authorities which could be sued, the rule of no-liability for non-repair may have become too entrenched to be dislodged. At all events, there are several qualifications to the basic rule which serve to limit the scope of its operation.

In the first place, the rule of no liability for nonfeasance only applies to highway authorities[83] and not, for example, to drainage or tramway authorities. More problematically, where (as is often the case) a highway authority also has other functions, the rule only applies to things done by the authority strictly and exclusively[84] in its capacity as highway authority. It is difficult to construct any rational criterion for deciding whether a

79 e.g. *Marr* v. *Holroyd M.C.* (1986) 3 M.V.R. 235.

80 *Miller* v. *McKeon* (1906) 3 C.L.R. 50. For a recent application of the rule see *Hill* v. *Commissioner for Main Roads* (1988) 6 M.V.R. 158.

81 G. Sawer (1955) 18 *M.L.R.* 541.

82 But see G. Sawer (1966) 2 *N.Z.U.L.R.* 115.

83 Or, more accurately, public authorities with 'highway functions': *McDonogh* v. *Commonwealth* (1985) 73 A.L.R. 148, 158-9 *per* Neave J.

84 *Buckle* v. *Bayswater Road Board* (1937) 57 C.L.R. 259, 273 *per* Latham C.J. So the rule would not apply, for example, to the building of a drain for both road and drainage purposes.

particular act is done by an authority in one capacity or another. Secondly, the nonfeasance rule applies only to

> the actual roadway itself and such artificial structures in and about the roadway as can fairly be considered 'part of the road' or 'made for road purposes' . . . Bridges, drains and culverts, which are essential parts or accessories of a roadway, are generally considered as falling within the purview of the [nonfeasance] rules.[85]

Thirdly, the nonfeasance rule applies only to 'mere' or 'pure' nonfeasance. Actionable negligence can, as we have seen, consist of either acts or omissions; not all omissions are non-actionable. So a highway authority can be liable for creating a danger and then failing to take any action to remove it or warn of its presence.[86] If a highway authority obstructs a highway or does anything to make it dangerous, it is under a duty to take positive steps to remove the obstruction or danger.[87] And if a highway authority, instead of refraining from action, takes positive action in relation to the highway,[88] it is under a duty to take care to ensure that it does everything reasonably necessary to ensure that its activities do not cause damage or injury.[89]

But these principles are not peculiar to highway authorities; they are an application of more general rules. The one respect in which the position of highway authorities is peculiar is that they can, according to the

---

85 *Gorringe* v. *Transport Commission (Tas.)* (1950) 80 C.L.R. 357, 379 *per* Fullagar J.; cf. McTiernan J. in *Buckle* v. *Bayswater Road Board* (1936) 57 C.L.R. 259, 300: the rule does not apply to structures which are 'appurtenant or subservient to the road but not a component part of the road structure'. See also G. Sawer (1938) 12 *A.L.J.* 231. This limitation may simply be another version of the first limitation: *Murphy* v. *The Murray Roads Board* (1906) 8 W.A.L.R. 45 explaining *Borough of Bathurst* v. *McPherson* (1879) 4 App. Cas. 256 which is the source of the limitation. It is usually put in terms that the nonfeasance rule does not apply to 'artificial structures', and some judges have attempted to define 'artificial' analytically by reference to the nature of the structure itself; but given that 'the whole of any well made road is artificial' (see *Crouch* v. *Huon Municipality* (1912) 8 Tas. S.R. 107), a functional approach in terms of the road itself and accessories to it seems clearer, even if no easier to apply. Trees are particularly difficult to deal with on the analytical approach: cf. *Hams* v. *City of Camberwell* [1946] A.L.R. (C.N.) 568 and *Donaldson* v. *Sydney M.C.* (1924) 24 S.R. (N.S.W.) 408 with *Bretherton* v. *Hornsby S.C.* [1963] S.R. (N.S.W.) 334.

86 *Bird* v. *Pearce* [1979] R.T.R. 369; *Desmond* v. *Mount Isa City Council* [1991] 2 Qd.R. 482.

87 *Sydney Municipal Council* v. *Bourke* [1895] A.C. 433; *Invercargill Corporation* v. *Hazlemore* (1905) 25 N.Z.L.R. 194.

88 The cases present a confused picture on the question of whether inadequate repair or maintenance which does not make a highway any *more* dangerous than it previously was can constitute 'positive action' for this purpose: see N.S.W.L.R.C. 55 pp. 13-18; Fleming *Law of Torts* 7th edn, p. 405: 'The execution of *superficial* repairs . . . does not attract liability, unless it increased the risk of accidents' (emphasis added). However, even if, in theory, such inadequate maintenance or repair cannot attract liability, in practice a judge who is minded to impose liability in a particular case can usually find in the facts sufficient new danger to justify holding for the plaintiff even if only because inadequate repair or maintenance may create a deceptive appearance of safety.

89 *Buckle* v. *Bayswater Road Board* (1937) 57 C.L.R. 259; *South Australian Railways Commissioner* v. *Barnes* (1927) 40 C.L.R. 179, 186 *per* Isaacs J.; *Baxter* v. *Stockton-on-Tees Corporation* [1959] 1 Q.B. 441; *Marr* v. *Holroyd M.C.* (1986) 3 M.V.R. 235.

traditional authorities, never be liable for pure nonfeasance. In *Anns* v. *Merton L.B.C.*,[90] as we have seen, it was held that pure nonfeasance by a public authority might be actionable in negligence if its failure to act was the result of an *ultra vires* failure to give proper consideration to the question of whether it should take some action. And this is the case even if such consideration would require the assessment of policy matters. Since all the major cases concerning the liability of highway authorities pre-date *Anns* it may well be that the earlier cases must now be read subject to this decision.

There is no good reason why highway authorities should be treated differently from any other public authority so far as liability in tort is concerned, and this would suggest that the simplest way to reform the law would be to abolish the nonfeasance rule and leave the liability of highway authorities to be assessed according to the general law already discussed.

2. REFORM PROPOSALS

The Western Australian Law Reform Commission has recommended that the nonfeasance rule be abolished.[91] The Commission decided not to impose a duty to take care to keep highways in good repair but rather a duty of care to avoid risks of injury to road users. Thus it would be open to a highway authority to discharge its duty by warning, fencing or closing roads as well as by repair, according to what was reasonable in all the circumstances. The Commission also recommended that certain factors relevant to the issue of negligence be specifically stated, but subject to the normal rule that all circumstances of the case be taken into account. The only factor which causes difficulty is that which requires the financial and other resources of the authority to be taken into account. There is a danger that this would always leave it open to the authority to argue that it lacked funds to do the necessary repairs or take the necessary precautions. But there is an argument for saying that such a resources argument should rarely be relevant in cases involving failure to remove dangers from the highway or to guard against them. The real question is not whether the authority had the funds but whether the decision about how much money to allocate to various purposes is one which should be left to the uncontrolled discretion of the authority. When the issue is the physical safety of road users it should be for the court to decide whether the authority can plead lack of resources.[92] The Western Australian Commission favoured placing the onus of proof of negligence on the plaintiff.

The South Australian Law Reform Committee[93] has recommended that the position of highway authorities be dealt with as part of a wider reform

90 [1978] A.C. 728.

91 Report No. 62 (1981).

92 The South Australian Law Reform Committee (25th Report, 1974) recommended that the defence of bona fide policy decision to expend resources on other things should be available to all public authorities except highway authorities (p. 19, para. 2).

93 ibid.

of the law relating to nonfeasance by public authorities. It has also recommended that the law be amended power by power rather than by a general statute, on the theory that each power needs separate consideration if the law is to deal properly with nonfeasance in different contexts. This approach seems hopelessly piecemeal. It would be better to have a general framework which the courts could apply to particular instances.

In 1987 the New South Wales Law Reform Commission[94] recommended simply that the nonfeasance rule be abolished in respect of claims for personal injury and death, and that claims against highway authorities (and other authorities responsible for the maintenance of structures forming part of or on the highway) should be brought under that state's now-defunct no-fault transport accident compensation scheme.

IV: SPECIFIC STATUTORY IMMUNITIES

This is a somewhat technical topic and resolves itself ultimately into questions of statutory interpretation. So only a couple of examples will be given to illustrate the points at issue.[95]

Some statutes contain provisions expressly designed to protect public officials from liability for the 'bona fide exercise of statutory powers'.[96] In *Board of Fire Commissioners of N.S.W.* v. *Ardouin*[97] an action was brought in connection with the negligent driving of a fire engine on its way to the scene of a fire. Dixon C.J. said that the protective clause did not cover the negligent driving of fire engines to fires.[98] It mainly concerned interference with or infliction of damage on persons or property in the course of fighting a fire. The driving of a fire engine involved no exercise of a 'power' to which the protective clause could attach. If a fire officer decides to interfere with property in order to fight a fire, the section protects the decision to do the act, the decision how to do it, and the doing of it, from action in negligence. Also protected are decisions that it is safe to leave the scene of a fire because the fire has been extinguished.[99]

Statutes also sometimes contain provisions governing the assessment and payment of compensation for damage and injuries inflicted by the exercise of statutory powers. In *Murtagh* v. *Coleraine Sewerage Authority*[100] it was held that such a provision did not rule out a common

---

94 N.S.W.L.R.C 55.

95 For a somewhat more detailed account see Aronson & Whitmore *Public Torts and Contracts* pp. 162-74.

96 e.g. s.69B(1) of the Police Act 1937 (Qld). See also Police Service Act 1990 (N.S.W.) s.112.

97 (1952-3) 109 C.L.R. 105.

98 Nor does it protect the fire authority from vicarious liability for negligence of its employees as a result of which another employee is injured: *Soanes* v. *Plessing* [1985] 2 Qd.R 55. Cf. *McEvelly* v. *Minister of Health* (1984) 2 S.R. (W.A.) 215.

99 *R. & W. Vincent Pty Ltd* v. *Board of Fire Commissioners of N.S.W.* (1977) 1 N.S.W.L.R. 15. Cf. *Ticehurst* v. *Skeen* (1986) 3 M.V.R. 307, 319-20.

100 [1969] V.R. 306; cf. *Gifford* v. *Minister for Water Supply, Sewerage & Drainage* (1953) 55 W.A.L.R. 94.

law action for personal injuries suffered by a plaintiff when he fell into a trench dug by the defendant in the street. Once again, it seems that the provision is treated as primarily designed to deal with cases of damage to property inflicted as an integral part of, and for the purposes of, the execution of the authority's powers. In relation to such damage it appears that such a provision rules out a common law action for negligence in all cases except those in which the injury is inflicted by the doing of *ultra vires* unauthorized works.[101] These cases establish for this type of compensation clause much the same ambit as the above type of protective clause has.

This similarity of approach is desirable and fits in quite neatly with the *Anns* scheme where there is no such relevant statutory provision. Negligent driving of fire engines or negligent failure to fence trenches is operational negligence in *Anns* terms and so actionable. The statutory power defines the limits of the 'policy' or 'discretionary' or 'emergency' defence or immunity available to the authority and if the authority exceeds these powers by not exercising them bona fide or by doing something it has no power to do, then its action, though in purported exercise of its powers and so in the 'policy' or 'discretionary' or 'emergency' area, is *ultra vires* and so a proper subject for an action in negligence. Otherwise, the statutory compensation provisions alone will be relevant.

101 *Ex parte Metropolitan Water, Sewerage and Drainage Board; re Roberts* (1932) 33 S.R.(N.S.W.).

21

VICARIOUS LIABILITY

Vicarious liability is a form of strict liability in the sense that the person held vicariously liable may not have been personally at fault. So, for example, the vicarious liability of a master for the negligence of servants should be distinguished from the master's personal liability for failure to employ competent workers.[1] At one time the so-called doctrine of common employment protected masters from actions by their servants seeking to make the master vicariously liable for certain acts of fellow-servants, but this has now been abolished by statute.[2]

I: RELATIONSHIPS IMPORTING VICARIOUS LIABILITY

The first requirement for the imposition of vicarious liability is that there be in existence as between the defendant and the wrongdoer one of a number of specified relationships. We will examine these relationships in turn.

1. Master and Servant[3]

Servants are usually distinguished from independent contractors because whereas the *prima facie* rule is that a master is vicariously liable for the tortious acts of servants, the basic rule is that an employer is not vicariously liable for torts committed by independent contractors.[4] The distinction between servants and independent contractors can be relevant not only to

1 For a discussion of this duty see p. 560 above. See also *Wilsher* v. *Essex Area Health Authority* [1987] Q.B. 730.
2 See p. 552 above.
3 The term 'servant' is a technical one with no pejorative implication. The word 'employee' is often used as a synonym as in the context of employers' liability.
4 G. Williams [1956] *Camb. L.J.* 180; J.A. Jolowicz (1957) 9 *Stanford L.R.* 690.

questions of the liability of employers to third parties injured by workers but also to such questions as a worker's entitlement to workers' compensation[5] or to long-service leave;[6] an employer's liability for payroll tax[7] or to make social security contributions;[8] or to provide a safe system of work.[9] As we will see, the decision as to whether or not a worker is a servant depends very much on all the facts and circumstances of particular cases, and one might have thought that the issue would depend at least to some extent on the reason why the distinction between servants and independent contractors was important in the particular case.[10] For example, the policies relevant to deciding whether an injured person ought to be compensated are different from the policies relevant to when payroll tax ought to be paid, and this difference might be relevant to whether a worker is classed as a servant or an independent contractor. The courts, however, do not openly acknowledge such policy issues, and a uniform set of principles has been developed governing the question of whether a worker is a servant in whatever context it might arise. The principles are, however, very open-textured (that is, they do not dictate a result) and it may well be that policy factors can be found to underlie decisions in particular cases.

(a) The control test One way of putting the distinction between servants and independent contractors is to say that the former are employed under a contract of service whereas the latter are employed under a contract for services. Somervell L.J. said of this distinction in *Cassidy* v. *Ministry of Health* that one perhaps cannot get much beyond this: 'Was his contract a contract of service within the meaning which an ordinary person would give to the words?'[11] But this is of no help because the difficult cases are those in which the contract speaks with two voices. Again, in *Stevenson, Jordan & Harrison Ltd* v. *Macdonald and Evans* Denning L.J. said that it 'is often easy to recognize a contract of service when you see it, but difficult to say wherein the difference [between it and a contract for services] lies.'[12]

A particularly detailed attempt to define the peculiar characteristics of a contract of service is that of Mackenna J. in *Ready Mixed Concrete (South East) Ltd* v. *Minister of Pensions*.[13] A contract of service exists, his Lordship said, if three conditions are fulfilled: first, that the worker agrees that, in consideration of a wage or other remuneration, he will provide his own work and skill[14] in the performance of some service for his master. If

---

5 *Zuijs* v. *Wirth Bros Pty Ltd* (1955) 93 C.L.R. 561; *Hatzimanolis* v. *A.N.I. Corporation Ltd* (1992).
6 *A.M.P. Society* v. *Chaplin* (1978) 18 A.L.R. 385.
7 *F.C.T.* v. *Barrett* (1973) 129 C.L.R. 395.
8 *Ready Mixed Concrete (South East) Ltd* v. *Minister of Pensions and National Insurance* [1968] 2 Q.B. 497.
9 *Bertram* v. *Armstrong & De Mamiel Constructions Pty Ltd* (1978) 23 A.C.T.R. 15.
10 cf. H. Collins (1990) 10 *O.J.L.S.* 353.
11 [1951] 2 K.B. 343, 352-3.
12 [1952] 1 T.L.R. 101, 110-1.
13 [1968] 2 Q.B. 497.
14 *Humberstone* v. *Northern Timber Mills* (1949) 79 C.L.R. 389, 404 *per* Dixon J.

the worker is free in a more than limited or occasional way to delegate the performance of the contract to another, the contract will not be one of service.[15]

Secondly, the worker must agree, expressly or impliedly, that in performance of the contract services he will be subject to the control of the employer to a sufficient degree to justify a finding that a master–servant relationship exists. The classic formulation of the required degree of control is that the employer must be in a position not only to tell the worker what to do but also to tell him how to do it. In many cases where the employee is doing a job which requires the exercise of a skill which the employer does not possess, the latter will not personally be in a position to tell the worker how to do his job, although he may employ skilled supervisors who can do so on his behalf. But the test is not whether the employer *can* tell the worker how to do the job but whether he is *entitled* to do so and, ultimately, whether he has the power of dismissing the worker for failure to observe instructions.[16] On the other hand, it is clear that control is only one relevant factor.[17] For example, in *Queensland Stations* v. *F.C.T.*[18] the question was whether a drover was a servant: by agreement the drover was to drove certain cattle to a destination, obey and carry out instructions and devote the whole of his time, energy and ability to droving the stock. His remuneration was a fixed sum per head of cattle delivered. He was required to find his own workers, plant, horses and rations and to pay all wages. It was decided that the last features of the situation outweighed the reservation of a right to control which would, anyway, be difficult to exercise over a drover by the very nature of the work, especially since the drover might be droving animals belonging to more than one owner at one and the same time.

A particular application of the control test is found in cases involving the hiring or transfer of workers by one employer to another. The *prima facie* rule is that the general (or lending) employer is master and the burden on him of establishing that the borrower (or particular employer) is in fact the master is a very heavy one.[19] The ultimate question is which

---

15 e.g. *A.M.P. Society* v. *Chaplin* (1978) 18 A.L.R. 385.

16 *Zuijs* v. *Wirth Bros* (1955) 93 C.L.R. 561; *Queensland Stations Pty Ltd* v. *F.C.T.* (1945) 70 C.L.R. 539; *Humberstone* v. *Northern Timber* (1949) 79 C.L.R. 389; *A-G for N.S.W.* v. *Perpetual Trustee Co.* (Ltd) (1951-2) 85 C.L.R. 237, 251-2 *per* Dixon J. It should be noted that the basis of vicarious liability under the control test is not failure by the employer to exercise control. Rather, the degree of control is relevant to the nature of the employment relationship and it is this which determines whether the employer is vicariously liable.

17 *Stevens* v. *Brodribb Sawmilling Co. Pty Ltd* (1985-6) 160 C.L.R. 16.

18 (1945) 70 C.L.R. 539. Contrast *Gilchrist, Watt & Cunningham* v. *Logan* [1927] St.R.Qd. 185 and *F.C.T.* v. *Barrett* (1973) 129 C.L.R. 395.

19 *Mersey Docks & Harbour Board* v. *Coggins & Griffiths (Liverpool) Ltd* [1947] A.C. 1; cf. *Century Insurance Co. Ltd* v. *Northern Ireland Road Transport Board* [1942] A.C. 509; *Kondis* v. *State Transport Authority* (1984) 154 C.L.R. 672.

employer has the authority to tell the worker how to do the job,[20] although many other factors are relevant: the fact that the general employer selected the worker; the questions of who is the paymaster, who can dismiss, how long the alternative service lasts, what machinery is employed. The ultimate question is one of degree: how much control was transferred to the particular employer.[21] The rule that the general employer is *prima facie* responsible is said to be justified by the avoidance of uncertainty not only as to whom the plaintiff should sue, but also as to which employer is responsible for insuring the employee in respect of health, unemployment and accident. Presumably, too, the general employer will usually be in a better position to assess the risks involved in the use of the equipment (if any) he is lending or hiring out and so in a better position than the particular employer to insure against these risks.

But the particular employer *may* be held to be the master, as in *McDonald* v. *The Commonwealth*[22] where the lending employer did not know even the general nature of the work the hired employee would be doing or where it was to be done: the employee was under the instructions of the the particular employer's foreman for any purpose that arose incidental to the work the foreman was carrying out. If the servant is lent to perform a specified task the lender is well placed to assess the risks inherent in the task and to insure against them; but not if the task is unspecified. So the plaintiff does run the risk of suing the wrong employer, a difficulty which could be alleviated by holding both employers responsible *vis-á-vis* the plaintiff and then leaving them to sort out their relative share of responsibility according to the degree of control transferred.[23]

A special application of the control test is the rule that an employer is not vicariously liable for the acts of employees who exercise 'independent discretions',[24] that is, who perform tasks not by virtue of authority arising out of the relationship of employer and employee but arising out of the fact that they hold a public office either by statute or at common law.[25]

---

20 ibid.; *Steel Structures Ltd* v. *Rangitikei County* [1974] 2 N.Z.L.R. 306.

21 *McDonald* v. *The Commonwealth* (1945) 46 S.R.(N.S.W.) 129.

22 ibid.

23 But it has been expressly held that this result is not possible under the law as it presently stands: *Oceanic Crest* v. *Pilbara Harbour Services* (1986) 160 C.L.R. 626.

24 The words 'function', 'duty' and 'responsibility' are all used as substitutes for 'discretion' in this phrase. Of course, the rule only applies to acts done in the course of exercising the discretion and not to other acts of the officer done in the course of employment. It may not apply where the acts were done not only in exercise of an independent discretion but also by way of purportedly discharging a duty of care resting on the employer: *Skuse* v. *Commonwealth* (1985) 62 A.L.R. 108, 121 *per* Lockhart J.

25 *Oriental Foods (Wholesalers) Co. Pty Ltd* v. *Commonwealth* (1983) 50 A.L.R. 452. So if the employee's authority derives from his employment by the Crown the rule does not apply: *Ramsay* v. *Larsen* (1964) 111 C.L.R. 16. See generally S. Kneebone (1990) 16 *Mon. U.L.R.* 184.

Examples are magistrates;[26] police officers;[27] navigation pilots;[28] an officer in charge of a legal aid office;[29] customs officers;[30] commissioners of taxation.[31] Such public officers are usually employed by public authorities, but the rule that the employer is not vicariously liable for the torts of persons exercising public functions also applies to private employers.[32]

The exact basis of the independent discretion rule is not clear. In some cases, such as that of magistrates, the absence of vicarious liability may be a function of the fact that the employee is meant, as a matter of *constitutional* law and theory, to act independently in exercising his functions. More generally, the rule may be seen as following from the basic public law principle that an officer with public functions must exercise those functions personally and not delegate them to someone else or allow someone else to tell him how to exercise them. In some cases the question of vicarious liability has been rested on the criterion of whether, in the exercise of his functions, the employee is in fact subject to the direct control of the employer;[33] but another view is that the crucial factor is not absence of factual control but of the right to control.[34] It is not even clear whether the basis of the rule is that a public officer is not a *servant* of the employer in the relevant sense, or whether the employer is not vicariously liable for his torts despite the fact that he is a servant.[35]

At all events, if we adopt a functional approach to vicarious liability and view it as a technique for allocating losses so as to maximize the chance that injured plaintiffs will be compensated in the most economically efficient way, there seems very little justification for the rule. In

26 *Thompson* v. *Williams* (1915) 32 W.N.(N.S.W.) 27.

27 *Enever* v. *R.* (1906) 3 C.L.R. 969; *Irvin* v. *Whitrod (No. 2)* [1978] Qd.R. 271; *Thorne* v. *State of Western Australia* [1964] W.A.R. 147. The rule as it applies to police has been reversed by statute in some jurisdictions: Australian Federal Police Act 1979 (Cwth) s.64B; Police Act 1937-78 (Qld), s.69B; Police Regulation Act 1952 (S.A.) s.51a; Police Administration Act 1979 (N.T.), s.163; Crown Proceedings Act 1950 (N.Z.) s.6; Police Act 1964 (U.K.), s.48 (discussed in K. Williams [1989] *New. L.J.* 1664). See also M.R. Goode (1975) 10 *M.U.L.R.* 47; S. Churches (1978-80) 6 *U. Tas. L.R.* 294.

28 *Oceanic Crest Shipping Co.* v. *Pilbara Harbour Services Pty Ltd* (1986) 160 C.L.R. 626; by statute the pilot is treated as the employee of the ship being piloted and not of the harbour authority which engages the pilot.

29 *Field* v. *Nott* (1939) 62 C.L.R. 660.

30 *Baume* v. *Commonwealth* (1906) 4 C.L.R. 97.

31 *Clyne* v. *Deputy Commissioner of Taxation (N.S.W.)(No. 5)* (1982) 13 A.T.R. 677. But schoolmasters do not exercise independent discretion (*Ramsay* v. *Larsen* (1964) 111 C.L.R. 16; *Geyer* v. *Downs* (1977) 138 C.L.R. 91); nor does a comptroller of prisons (*Thorne* v. *W.A.* [1964] W.A.R. 147).

32 *Oceanic Crest* (1986) 160 C.L.R. 626, 637-8 *per* Gibbs C.J.; 650 *per* Wilson J.; 681-2 *per* Dawson J. But Brennan and Deane JJ. dissented and held that the rule should not apply to a private employer of a navigation pilot. See also *Jobling* v. *Blacktown Municipal Council* [1969] 1 N.S.W.R. 129 and Crown Proceedings Act 1972 (S.A.) s.10(2) which was given a wide interpretation in *DeBruyn* v. *South Australia* (1990) 54 S.A.S.R. 231. The rule has been reversed both in relation to the Crown and other employers by Law Reform (Vicarious Liability) Act 1983 (N.S.W.) ss.7,8; see also Law Reform (Miscellaneous Provisions) Amendment Act 1983 (N.S.W.). Cf. Crown Proceedings Act 1947 (U.K.) s.2(3).

33 *Thorne* v. *W.A.* [1964] W.A.R. 147.

34 *Oceanic Crest* (1986) 160 C.L.R. 626, 682-3 *per* Dawson J.

35 For the latter view see *Oceanic Crest* (1986) 160 C.L.R. 626, 639 *per* Gibbs C.J.

Oceanic Crest v. *Pilbara Harbour Services*[36] both Gibbs C.J. and Wilson J. expressed dissatisfaction with the current state of the law, and Brennan and Deane JJ. held, in dissent, that a private employer of a navigation pilot should be vicariously liable for the latter's torts. There is also a good argument for reversing the rule as it applies to public employers. There is no reason why the public as a whole should not bear the cost of wrongful action by a public official even if the official is not subject to direction by the Crown but is exercising an independent discretion; or even if, technically, the employee is an officer not a servant. It seems very strange to argue that a public employer should not be vicariously liable for the torts of a public officer because the officer, in performing his functions, was serving the public, not his employer: after all, his employer in some sense *is* the public.

To return to Mackenna J.'s exposition in *Ready Mixed Concrete* v. *MoP*, the third condition for the existence of a contract of service is that the terms of the contract, other than those specifying the work to be done, the remuneration and matters relevant to control, should be consistent with the contract being a contract of service. The judge gave examples to illustrate this negative condition. So if a person contracts to build for another, himself providing at his own expense the plant and materials, this is a building contract, not a contract of service, even if the builder accepts a high degree of control; otherwise if a labourer contracts to work for a builder under the latter's control and to provide his own tools. The fact that the labourer provides his own tools does not prevent the contract being one of service. Again, if a party agrees to carry another's goods in his own vehicle, this is a contract of carriage, even if the carrier accepts a high degree of control, because carriage is the crux of the contract; otherwise if, for example, a salesman agrees to work for another and provides his own car.[37]

The upshot of all this is that control (in the sense of the right to control) is one, but only one, factor relevant to classifying particular employment relationships. This broad weighing and balancing approach has received recent support from the High Court.[38]

In many cases the parties to a contract will not have given any thought, when drafting the contract, to the question of what sort of relationship their contract created. But often contracts are drafted with the specific intention of regulating the tax position of the employee or the obligations of the employer towards workers by constituting the worker a self-employed independent contractor. Sometimes the contract will expressly declare that the worker is an independent contractor. The basic rule is that such declarations are not conclusive of the relationship between the parties. If the court decides that as a matter of fact the relationship is one

36 (1986) 160 C.L.R. 626.

37 Also relevant are matters such as the nature of the worker's obligation to work (e.g. must he work exclusively for the employer?), whether the hours and place of work are specified by the employer, the provision for holidays, whether taxes are deducted from his remuneration. See *Stevens* v. *Brodribb Sawmilling* (1985-6) 160 C.L.R. 16, 24 *per* Mason J.; 36-7 *per* Wilson and Dawson JJ.

38 *Stevens* v. *Brodribb Sawmilling* (1985-6) 160 C.L.R. 16.

of master and servant then a declaration to the contrary will be of no avail.[39] But if, on the basis of the facts other than the declaration, the court cannot decide what the relationship is, the declaration can be taken into account. The same basic principle applies to contracts designed to change the status of an employee from that of servant to that of independent contractor.[40]

In *Ferguson* v. *John Dawson & Partners (Contractors) Ltd*[41] Megaw and Browne L.JJ. inclined to the view that declarations in a contract as to the status of the employee should be totally ignored even if the declaration is part of a genuine attempt to stipulate the employee's status. The attitude of the courts to this question may well depend on the exact facts of the case. In *Ferguson* v. *Dawson* the worker was suing his employer for breach of statutory duty; he was working 'on the lump', a system under which the employer did not deduct tax from the worker's wages and did not pay social security contributions in respect of the worker. By and large such arrangements are socially undesirable because they encourage tax evasion by the labourers and leave them insufficiently protected so far as health and safety are concerned (because health and safety regulations often do not cover independent contractors). The reality of the situation was that the employer was in a good position to take proper steps to protect the safety of the workers whether or not they were technically self-employed, and it was this social reality which is reflected implicity in the decision that the worker was a servant. In *Massey* v. *Crown Life Insurance*[42] the issue was rather different: the manager of a branch office of the company brought an action for unfair dismissal when the company terminated an agreement, sought by the plaintiff, the object of which was to change his status from that of employee to that of self-employed agent. Here, as a matter of policy, there was very little reason why, having sought the tax advantages of being self-employed, the plaintiff should be allowed to bring an action predicated on his being a servant.

(b) The organization test In order to deal with some of the inadequacies of the control test Lord Denning in *Stevenson* v. *Macdonald*[43] put forward the idea that under a contract of service a person 'is employed as part of the business and his work is done as an integral part of the business, whereas, under a contract for services, his work, although done for the business, is not integrated into it but is only accessory to it . . .'.[44] This test seems to assume that the employer has a core organization over which he

---

39 *A.M.P. Society* v. *Chaplin* (1978) 18 A.L.R. 385; *Ready Mixed Concrete* v. *MoP* [1968] 2 Q.B. 497.

40 *Massey* v. *Crown Life Insurance Co.* [1978] 2 All E.R. 576.

41 [1976] 3 All E.R. 817.

42 [1978] 2 All E.R. 576.

43 [1952] 1 T.L.R. 101; cf. Stephen J. in *F.C.T.* v. *Barrett* (1973) 129 C.L.R. 395, 402. See also *Bank voor Handel en Scheepvart N.V.* v. *Slatford* [1953] 1 Q.B. 248, 295 *per* Denning L.J. ('part and parcel of the organization').

44 One view of this test is that it is subsidiary to the control test: an employer is entitled to control integrated workers to an extent that he cannot control non-integrated workers: *Stevens* v. *Brodribb Sawmilling* (1985-6) 160 C.L.R. 16, 27 *per* Mason J. But here it is treated as an independent test.

has a high degree of control and that on occasion, or perhaps regularly, he supplements that core with workers over whom he exercises considerably less control. The test would not be of much use where there is no evidence as to the organization of the defendant's business[45] or if the business was not organized in this two-tier way. Further, there are cases, of which *Massey* v. *Crown Life* is a clear example, where the legal status of the worker may bear no relation to his degree of integration into the workforce: in *Massey* the change of status entailed no change in the organizational relationship between the company and the plaintiff. The thrust of the organization test seems to be based on a distinction between selling a commodity—one's own labour—for a fixed price, and conducting a business in order to generate maximum profits. But this distinction is by no means a clear-cut one since the idea of who owns what depends largely on where the power of control over the thing in question lies. So in the end the distinction inherent in the organization test is just a restatement of the very question in issue: was the worker selling service or services?

At all events, the organization test has been recently rejected by the High Court.[46]

(c) The independent business test In *Lee Ting Sang* v. *Chung Chi-Keung*[47] the Privy Council had to decide whether a construction worker who was part of a large pool of casual labourers who worked on a job-by-job basis for a number of different employers was a servant for the purposes of entitlement to compensation under workers' compensation legislation. In considering this issue the board rejected the organization test because it seemed to contemplate that only persons on an employer's permanent staff would be servants, whereas the Privy Council believed it to be socially desirable that casual building workers should be protected by the workers' compensation statute. The test adopted by the Privy Council looked not to the nature of the employer's business or to the degree of control exercised by him over his workers, but rather to the economic status of the worker: was he a 'skilled artisan earning his living by working for more than one employer as an employee' (in which case he would be a servant) or was he 'a small businessman venturing into business on his own account as an independent contractor with all its attendant risks'? Was he or was he not 'performing services as a person in business on his own account'?[48] If so, he was an independent contractor; if not, he was a servant.

This is an intuitively appealing and commonsense approach: the phenomenon of a person starting his working life as part of someone else's business and then leaving to go into business on his own account is a common and easily understood occurrence. By running a business rather than working for a business a person usually hopes to increase his

45 e.g. *Bertram* v. *Armstrong* (1978) 23 A.C.T.R. 15, 19.
46 In *Stevens* v. *Brodribb Sawmilling* (1985-6) 160 C.L.R. 16.
47 [1990] 2 A.C. 374.
48 cf. *Ellis* v. *Wallsend District Hospital* (1989) 17 N.S.W.L.R. 553, 598 *per* Samuels J.A.: was the doctor 'engaged on his own business or the hospital's'?

freedom of action and his income: independent contractors typically benefit relatively more from the sale of their labour than do servants. It may, therefore, seem only fair that a person who goes into business on his own account should take responsibility for his own safety and security, and not expect someone else to be burdened with liability for his torts.

But the Privy Council's approach is also an attempt to deal with an important social problem, namely that of disintegration in the labour market. For a variety of reasons many people work on a piece-rate basis, often part-time, often at home and often for more than one employer. Some of those reasons are self-regarding, but often people are forced into such arrangements because there is no other work available for which they are qualified, or because the industry in which they are qualified to work operates mainly or exclusively on this basis. As compared with permanent employment, such arrangements typically provide many more benefits to employers (chiefly in the form of reduced costs) than to workers, who are often poorly paid and may fall outside the letter of legislation which protects job security and the health and safety of employees. Under such circumstances it seems only fair that the common law should, by extending the notion of 'servant' to cover such workers, offer them such protection as it can and shift responsibility for the torts of such workers on to those who benefit most from their work.

It must be said, however, that none of these tests is ultimately very satisfactory because they all involve the weighing and balancing of incommensurable factors, but none of them provides any objective criterion of the strength of the various factors. In many cases this will not matter because most people would agree about the nature of the relationship in question. But in marginal cases, where reasonable people could disagree about the status of the worker, the lack of an objective criterion by which the strength of the various relevant factors can be measured means that the ultimate decision as to the nature of the employment relationship will almost inevitably rest on value judgments. And such value judgments are bound to be influenced by the relevance in the particular case of the distinction between servants and independent contractors. For this reason it is very strange that the courts, as we have noted, insist that the term 'servant' has a uniform meaning throughout the law.

2. Cases where Status of Employee is Irrelevant

There are a number of cases in which the status of the worker is irrelevant to the employer's vicarious liability. Whether the worker is a servant or an independent contractor, the employer will be liable for injury caused by negligence of the employee. These cases form exceptions to the basic rule that an employer is not liable for the negligence of independent contractors. Not all the cases are based on the same principle and so it is necessary to consider them in a number of groups.

(a) Strict liability Strict liability depends on the defendant being in control of a situation or state of affairs which creates or constitutes a risk of danger. If the risk materializes, the defendant is liable unless he can show that the causal chain between the risky situation and the damage was broken by the intervention of some unforeseeable (and hence uncontrollable) human or natural agency. The acts of a servant never break the causal chain, even if the servant is acting outside the course of his employment. An independent contractor's acts will break the causal chain if they are totally outside what could be anticipated. The rule is sometimes differently put by saying that if the contractor commits an act of 'casual' or 'collateral' negligence beyond the scope of what he was employed to do (i.e. beyond the scope of the risk which the employer must guard against and which the independent contractor is employed to obviate) then this will relieve the employer of liability.[49] So in *Emanuel* v. *G.L.C.*[50] Lord Denning said that an occupier could not be held liable for the negligent act of an independent contractor in starting a fire if, in so doing, the contractor was acting in a way alien to anything the occupier had permitted him to do or, in other words, if he was acting as a 'stranger'.

This principle of liability for all but acts of collateral negligence applies to all instances of strict liability recognized by the law (and, indeed, to all cases in which an employer can be liable for negligence of an independent contractor): the rule in *Rylands* v. *Fletcher,*[51] public nuisance,[52] private nuisance[53] and the escape of fire.[54] The policy rationale for the rule is that since the effect of strict liability is to impose the burden of insuring against the risk on the defendant, there is no good reason to relieve him of liability in cases which his insurance will cover simply because the risk materialized as the result of the act of an independent contractor (for example).

(b) Employers' duties An employer is vicariously liable for the negligence of anyone to whom he entrusts the job of doing acts designed to fulfil his duty to provide safe equipment, premises and system of work for his employees (that is, his servants).[55] However, if the employer reasonably delegates the task to a qualified employee and the employee is himself injured by his failure to fulfil the delegated task properly, the employee cannot recover against his employer. Nor can the employer be held liable to the servants of an independent contractor for negligence by the contractor to whom the task has been entrusted, provided those employees

---

49 For an example see Lord Denning's judgment in *Cassidy* v. *Ministry of Health* [1951] 2 K.B. 343, 364-5.

50 [1971] 2 All E.R. 835; cf. *Dobson* v. *Holderness* [1975] 2 N.Z.L.R. 749.

51 (1868) L.R. 3 H.L. 330; *Lamb* v. *Phillips* (1911) 11 S.R.(N.S.W.) 109.

52 *Halter* v. *Moore* (1864) 3 S.C.R.(N.S.W.) 5; *O'Brien* v. *Board of Land and Works* (1880) 6 V.L.R. 204; *Mint* v. *Good* [1951] 1 K.B. 517.

53 *Harris* v. *Carnegies Pty Ltd* [1917] V.L.R. 95; *Matania* v. *National Provincial Bank Ltd* [1946] 2 All E.R. 633.

54 Cases cited n. 50 above; *McInnes* v. *Wardle* (1931) 45 C.L.R. 548; *Balfour* v. *Barty-King* [1957] 1 Q.B. 496; *General Jones* v. *Wildridge* [1988] Tas.R. 164.

55 *Wilsons & Clyde Coal Co. Ltd* v. *English* [1938] A.C. 57; *Kondis* v. *State Transport Authority* (1984) 58 A.L.J.R. 531; *McDermid* v. *Nash Dredging & Reclamation Co. Ltd* [1987] A.C. 906.

are engaged on the delegated task or on related work.[56] The basic rule can, once again, be justified by the fact that the employer's insurance will probably cover injuries regardless of whether they result from personal negligence on the part of the employer or from negligence for which he is vicariously liable.

As we have seen, an employer also owes a duty of care to his independent contractors, which includes a duty to co-ordinate the activities of his contractors when he employs more than one.[57] It is not clear whether the employer could be held vicariously liable for the negligence of an independent contractor to whom he entrusted the performance of this duty.[58] But he may incur liability (which may be personal if he acts himself, or vicarious if a servant acts for him) if he does not take care to ensure that someone is responsible for co-ordinating the activities of several independent contractors or if he undertakes co-ordination himself but does so negligently.

(c) **Occupiers** Consider the common law first. Prior to the decision of the High Court in *Australian Safeway Stores Pty Ltd* v. *Zaluzna*[59] an invitor was liable to invitees for negligence of independent contractors giving rise to dangers in the condition of the premises for which, as invitor, the defendant would be liable under the rules of occupiers' liability.[60] This rule also applied to contractual entrants.[61] One view was that this rule only applied where the delegated task was of a non-technical or non-skilled nature.[62] This restriction has been questioned, and *Voli* v. *Inglewood Shire Council*[63] supports a narrower limitation to the effect that the occupier will escape liability in respect of skilled work only if he himself does not understand what is required and is unable to check what is proposed by the contractor or examine what is done. The occupier's liability for contractor's negligence did not operate in favour of licensees[64] but it may have operated in favour of entrants to whom the duty owed was at least that owed to an invitee, that is, persons entering as of public or statutory right.

As we have already seen, the result of *Zaluzna* has been to abolish the distinctions between different types of visitors. So the issue which will

---

56 *Witham* v. *Shire of Bright* [1959] V.R. 790.

57 *Stevens* v. *Brodribb Sawmilling* (1985-6) 160 C.L.R. 16.

58 See *Stevens* v. *Brodribb Sawmilling* (1985-6) 160 C.L.R. 16, 32-3 *per* Mason J. (depends on whether the employer assumed control of operations in such a way as to lead the various contractors to expect that he would co-ordinate their activities); 45 *per* Wilson and Dawson JJ. (employer vicariously liable for negligence of independent contractors in co-ordinating themselves); 47-8 *per* Brennan J. (employer can only be *personally* liable for negligent co-ordination or failure to co-ordinate).

59 (1987) 162 C.L.R. 479.

60 *Hislop* v. *Mooney* [1968] 1 N.S.W.R. 559.

61 *Frances* v. *Cockrell* (1870) L.R. 5 Q.B. 501; *Voli* v. *Inglewood Shire Council* (1962-3) 110 C.L.R. 74.

62 *Vial* v. *Housing Commission of New South Wales* [1976] 1 N.S.W.L.R. 388, 394-5 *per* Glass J.A.

63 (1962-3) 110 C.L.R. 74, 98 *per* Windeyer J.

64 *Morgan* v. *Incorporated Central Council of Girls' Friendly Society* [1936] 1 All E.R. 404.

now arise is whether an occupier, by virtue of being an occupier, should be vicariously liable for loss suffered by visitors as a result of dangers on the land caused by acts of independent contractors. Given the ready availability of cheap insurance against liability to visitors (household contents policies often include such cover), and given the special responsibility which the law places on occupiers in respect of the state of their premises, there seems no strong reason why the occupier should not be vicariously liable for negligence of independent contractors which results in dangers on the land.[65]

So far as statutory occupiers' liability is concerned, the U.K. and New Zealand statutes[66] in effect abolish occupiers' vicarious liability for independent contractors by requiring proof, in order to make an occupier liable, that the occupier was negligent in entrusting the work to a contractor or in selecting the contractor or in supervising the work. In place of the first of these requirements, the Western Australian statute requires proof that it was reasonable to have the work done.[67] The other statutes do not deal with the issue of vicarious liability.

(d) Hospitals[68] It has been said that where a hospital offers to provide full medical, surgical and nursing services for patients through the agency of doctors and nurses provided by it, then the hospital is liable for the negligence of doctors and nurses on their permanent or part-time staff whether the doctors are resident medical officers or honorary consultants, and whether any of the employees are servants or independent contractors. But the principle only applies to such services as the hospital provides directly to the patient. So if the doctor is chosen and employed by the patient and the hospital merely provides the doctor with the physical facilities necessary for the treatment administered, the hospital will not be liable for the doctor's negligence; but it will be liable for the negligence of persons providing services supplied by it to the patient (such as nursing).[69] This principle makes sense in loss allocation terms since the hospital, whether a state or private institution, is in a good position[70] to insure the patient against injury suffered in the course of receiving any of the treatment or services it provides under its roof.

---

65 cf. *Brown* v. *Josiah Wedgwood & Sons (Australia) Pty Ltd* (1989) 51 S.A.S.R. 81, 84 *per* Matheson J.

66 Occupiers' Liability Act 1957 (U.K.) s.2(4)(b); Occupiers' Liability Act 1962 (N.Z.) s.4(6).

67 Occupiers' Liability Act 1985 (W.A.) s. 6.

68 W.P. Whippy (1989) 63 *A.L.J.* 182; B. Chapman (1990) 28 *O.H.L.J.* 523 argues that strict hospital liability will reduce incentives to engage in defensive medicine and reduce the cost of compensating victims.

69 *Cassidy* v. *Ministry of Health* [1951] K.B. 343 *per* Denning L.J.; O. Kahn-Freund (1951) 14 *M.L.R.* 504; *Roe* v. *Minister of Health* [1954] 2 Q.B. 66, 82 *per* Denning L.J.; *Samios* v. *Repatriation Commission* [1960] W.A.R. 219; *Albrighton* v. *Royal Prince Alfred Hospital* [1980] 2 N.S.W.L.R. 542; *Ellis* v. *Wallsend District Hospital* (1989) 17 N.S.W.L.R. 553.

70 And in a better position than many of its employees, *pace* Samuels J.A. in *Ellis* v. *Wallsend District Hospital* (1989) 17 N.S.W.L.R. 553, 606.

An analogous case is *The Commonwealth* v. *Introvigne*[71] in which the plaintiff pupil was injured by the negligence of a teacher employed by the N.S.W. Government under an arrangement by which the N.S.W. Government ran A.C.T. schools. It was held that the Commonwealth was liable for the negligence of the teacher because it could not discharge its duty of care for the safety of children (who were required to be sent to school and were accepted into the school by the defendant) by delegating the job of providing education to another authority. Just as the patient will naturally look to the hospital if anything goes wrong in the course of the treatment provided by it, so parents will naturally look to the school authority responsible for their child's care and education if anything goes wrong at school.

(e) **Bailees** A bailee for reward is liable for the negligence or dishonesty of servants or agents to whom the bailed goods have been entrusted by the bailee for the very purpose of doing that which the bailee is under an obligation to do. Lord Denning's discussion of the matter[72] (with which neither of the other two judges were prepared to be associated) bears similarities to his discussion of the hospital's liability in *Cassidy* v. *Ministry of Health*[73] and *Roe* v. *Minister of Health*,[74] and it *may* be that where goods are entrusted to a bailee for reward (who has a duty to look after them) or to a person who is under a contractual duty to look after them, the custodian would also be liable if he delegated the performance of the duty to an independent contractor (for example, by depositing the goods in someone else's depository).

(f) **Property developers** In New Zealand, property developers are liable to purchasers of buildings in respect of negligence of independent contractors employed by the developer to construct the buildings.[75] But while acknowledging the desirability of this rule, the House of Lords has declined to adopt it,[76] despite the fact that under the Defective Premises Act 1972 (U.K.) a developer (and a local housing authority) which engages independent contractors to 'take on work for or in connection with the provision of a dwelling' is under the duty imposed by s.1(1) of that Act in respect of the fitness of the dwelling for human habitation.

(g) **Public authorities** There is authority for the proposition that public bodies cannot escape liability for tortious performance of statutory powers by delegating the execution of their functions to independent contractors.[77]

---

71 (1982) 56 A.L.J.R. 749.
72 In *Morris* v. *C.W. Martin & Sons Ltd* [1966] 1 Q.B. 716.
73 [1951] 2 K.B. 343.
74 [1954] 2 Q.B. 66.
75 *Mount Albert Borough Council* v. *Johnson* [1979] 2 N.Z.L.R. 234.
76 *D. & F. Estates Ltd* v. *Church Commissioners* [1989] A.C. 177.
77 *Darling* v. *Attorney-General* [1950] 2 All ER 793; *Murphy* v. *Brentwood D.C.* [1991] 1 AC 398 (C.A., reversed on unrelated grounds by H.L.) Cf. *Stevens* v. *Brodribb Sawmilling* (1985-6) 160 C.L.R. 16, 44 *per* Wilson and Dawson JJ.; *Casley-Smith* v. *F.S. Evans & Sons Pty Ltd* (1988) 67 L.G.R.A. 108.

This rule may be justified on the ground that if a public authority is given a function by statute, the authority is meant to be responsible for the performance of that function and should not be allowed to avoid responsibility by contracting it out. But this rationale would, perhaps, only apply to the performance of 'public functions' and not to a situation where a public authority is acting in the capacity, for example, of an ordinary employer or occupier of property.

The legal basis of the principles discussed in the last six sections is by no means clear. One theory is that in all these cases the law imposes on the employer a 'non-delegable' (or 'independent') duty of care,[78] that is, a duty which the employer cannot perform by delegating tasks to an independent contractor. Breach of such duties is sometimes said to justify the imposition of 'personal' as opposed to 'vicarious' liability. But it is important to distinguish between personal liability in the sense of liability for negligence of the employer in selecting or supervising the independent contractor, and liability for breach of a non-delegable duty, which is strict in the sense that it may be imposed even if the employer has not been negligent in any way. There is no suggestion in any of the cases considered above that the employer had been personally negligent.

Another theory is that the employer's duty is not a duty of care but a duty to see that care is taken. For example, in the case of hospitals the duty is to ensure that the patient receives reasonably competent treatment from all the people whom the hospital engages to look after him. This duty is not a duty of care but a duty to insure against the materialization of risks, that is, a strict duty; and it is not a ground of liability for the employer's own actions but a ground of liability for the actions of others. For example, if (under the pre-*Zaluzna* law) the occupier personally did the work himself then his liability to an invitee was based on a breach of a duty of care; but if he employed an independent contractor to do it and the contractor did it negligently, the occupier's liability was strict. Under this theory the employer's liability in these cases simply constitutes an exception to the rule of no vicarious liability for the negligence of independent contractors.

But whatever the conceptual basis of these exceptions to the basic rule of no-liability, they can best be explained by saying that liability is placed on the employer because the employer is well placed to insure against or to spread or absorb the costs of liability. It is more efficient, for example, for a hospital authority to take out insurance to cover negligence by all the persons working for it in the hospital than for each of those persons to take out insurance to cover themselves. Also, the courts seem to have shown a desire to place the liability where the plaintiff would naturally in the first instance look for compensation and redress, whether that be hospital, employer, property developer, school authority or public body with statutory functions and responsibilities. To adapt the words of

78 See especially the judgments of Lord Denning in *Cassidy* [1951] 2 K.B. 343 and *Morris* v. *Martin* [1966] 1 Q.B. 716; and of Samuels J.A. in *Ellis* v. *Wallsend District Hospital* (1989) 17 N.S.W.L.R. 553. See also *J. Swanton (1991) 4 J. of Contract Law* 183; (1992) 5 *J. of Contract Law* 26.

Mason J. in *Kondis* v. *State Transport Authority*,[79] it is reasonable to impose vicarious liability on hospitals (for example) because patients reasonably expect (and are dependent upon)[80] hospitals to provide careful treatment, and are justified in expecting them to take responsibility for injuries suffered by patients.

(h) Dangerous activities The leading case on this topic is *Honeywill & Stein Ltd* v. *Larkin Bros (London's Commercial Photographers) Ltd*[81] in which it was held that when a person employs another to do work of a dangerous character, this imposes on the employer a duty to take special precautions, and this duty cannot be delegated to independent contractors. This principle does not apply to the doing of things which are merely dangerous if done negligently; it only applies to activities which the law recognizes as (rather than activities which actually are) extra-hazardous in themselves,[82] such as the causing of fires or explosions. The duty imposed on the employer is not a duty of care but a duty to insure against the materialization of a risk. Further, it is a duty to insure against injuries caused by the acts of another: there is no *general* principle of strict liability for the conduct of extra-hazardous activities but only particular rules such as the principle in *Rylands* v. *Fletcher*; by and large the conduct of dangerous activities imposes on the person actually doing them only a duty of care, albeit a very high one. In fact, the principle in *Honeywill* is a straight exception to the rule of no vicarious liability for the acts of independent contractors.

The exact scope of this principle is by no means clear. It appears to apply to soldering work done on the highway,[83] to demolition or repair of premises immediately adjacent to the highway,[84] and to felling a tree on the highway.[85] It does not apply to ordinary plumbing work,[86] or to the transportation of chlorine or other dangerous goods by road, sea or air,[87] or to the demolition or erection of a building (necessarily involving an excavation) in the immediate proximity of the wall of an adjoining house.[88] At all events, the High Court has recently held that the *Honeywill* principle is not part of Australian law.[89]

---

79 (1984) 154 C.L.R. 672, 687. See *Ellis* v. *Wallsend District Hospital* (1989) 17 N.S.W.L.R. 553, 605-6 *per* Samuels J.A.

80 But the notion of dependency is tricky because patients are also, and more directly, dependent upon doctors, nurses and so on to provide careful treatment.

81 [1934] 1 K.B. 191.

82 As to the difficulty of this notion see p. 578 above and *Stevens* v. *Brodribb Sawmilling* (1985-6) 160 C.L.R. 16, 40 *per* Wilson and Dawson JJ.

83 *Halliday* v. *National Telephone Co.* [1899] 2 Q.B. 392.

84 *Walsh* v. *Holst & Co. Ltd* [1958] 1 W.L.R. 800.

85 *Witham* v. *Shire of Bright* [1959] V.R. 790.

86 *Torette House Ltd* v. *Berkman* (1939-40) 62 C.L.R. 637.

87 *Imperial Chemical Industries of Australia and New Zealand Ltd* v. *Murphy* (1973) 47 A.L.J.R. 122.

88 *Stoneman* v. *Lyons* (1975) 133 C.L.R. 550.

89 *Stevens* v. *Brodribb Sawmilling* (1985-6) 160 C.L.R. 16.

3. Principal and Agent[90]

In the law of contract, an agent is a person authorized (by a contract of agency) to enter contracts on behalf of another, who is called the 'principal'. In the law of tort the term 'agent' has a wider meaning: it is used to indicate that one person acts with the authority of another (the principal). An agent in this sense may be a servant or an independent contractor or neither.[91] Indeed, there may be no contract at all between principal and agent, but just authorization of one party to act on behalf of another.

Thus the concept of an agent overlaps with that of a servant or an independent contractor; servants and independent contractors are authorized to act on their employers' behalf in doing their jobs, and the scope of their authority depends on the express and implied terms of their contracts of employment. The basic rule is that a person is vicariously liable for the torts of an agent. Where it is sought to make an employer liable for the acts of a servant, the notion of agency would be useful only if the act in question was outside the scope of the servant's employment; although it may be that the scope of a servant's authority could be no wider than the scope of the employment.[92] In relation to independent contractors, the notion of agency might be used to create exceptions to the basic rule of no-liability:[93] if a person were held to be an agent, his status as a servant or independent contractor would be irrelevant. So the concept of agency could, in theory, be used to create another type of case where the status of the employee was irrelevant; although it has been pointed out that if applied generally, the rule of liability for torts of an agent would swallow up the rule of no-liability for torts of an independent contractor.[94]

The notion of agency based on authorization plays a role in the context of liability of the owner of a motor-car for negligence of the driver. In most Australian jurisdictions the owner of a car must, as a prerequisite of registration, take out a policy of insurance covering the liability of the owner and the driver (whether the latter is driving with the authority of the owner or not)[95] for personal injury or death caused by or arising out of the use of the motor-vehicle.[96] This provision by itself is wide enough to impose liability on the owner (and thus tap his insurance) whether or not the driver was the owner's common law agent. But in some jurisdictions

---

90 D.J. Stephens [1974] *C.L.P.* 59.

91 For example, partners. See Higgins and Fletcher *The Law of Partnership in Australia and New Zealand* (6th edn, K.L. Fletcher, Sydney, 1991) pp. 174-7.

92 See J. Swanton (1985) 16 *U.W.A.L.R.* 1, 16, 20-1. But if the defendant employer is in a contractual relationship with the plaintiff and the tort is committed by the defendant's servant or independent contractor in the course of fulfilling the defendant's contractual obligations to the plaintiff, the defendant might be liable in contract for loss suffered by the plaintiff in circumstances where he would not be vicariously liable according to tortious principles: see ibid., pp. 21-7.

93 As was done in *Colonial Mutual Life Assurance Society Ltd* v. *Producers and Citizens Co-operative Assurance Co. of Australia Ltd* (1931) 46 C.L.R. 41.

94 Swanton (1985) 16 *U.W.A.L.R.* 1, 18. See also fn. 92 above as to contractual liability.

95 An unauthorized driver may be a thief: *Marsh* v. *Absolum* [1940] N.Z.L.R. 448; or an authorized driver who, at the time of the accident, is exceeding his authority.

96 See generally M.G. Britts *Third Party Insurance in Australia* (Sydney, 1973).

there is a provision which deems the driver of a motor vehicle (whether with or without the authority of the owner) to be the agent of the driver for the purpose of the legislation.[97] Where insurance is not taken out by the owner, the injured person has recourse against a statutory fund. So there are very few cases in which a plaintiff will need to appeal to common law principles to establish the liability of the owner of a car for the negligence of the driver. The common law principles may be relevant where the plaintiff seeks to recover for damage to property or in the rare case where he wishes to sue someone other than the statutory principal (that is, the registered owner).[98]

Whether the driver of a vehicle is the common law agent of the owner is a question of fact;[99] but there is a presumption that this is so both in the case of commercial and private vehicles.[100] This presumption can be rebutted by evidence to the contrary.[101] The basis of a finding of agency in this context is that the driver was using the car wholly or partly for the purposes of the owner under the delegation of some task or duty; it is not enough that the owner had some interest or concern in the use of the car.[102] Nor will the mere fact that the owner has given the driver permission to use the car make the driver the owner's agent.[103] An agency relationship may sometimes arise between the driver of a car and someone who is not the owner. Thus, in *Greenwood* v. *The Commonwealth*[104] the defendant was held vicariously liable for the negligence of a naval rating who was using his own car to drive himself and a fellow rating from Melbourne to Sydney. They were on duty at the time and the driver was using his own car with his superior's permission.

4. OTHER RELATIONSHIPS

A person conducting a driving test is not vicariously liable for negligence of the driver; the exercise of control by the tester is inconsistent with the aim of the exercise.[105] Parents are not vicariously liable for the negligence of their children merely because of the parent–child relationship. The parent's liability is based on a failure to exercise proper control over the child. Failure to exercise proper control is also the basis of the liability of

---

97 As to cars owned by the Commonwealth see Commonwealth Motor Vehicles (Liability) Act 1959 s.5.

98 For an example of the latter see *Soblusky* v. *Egan* (1959-60) 103 C.L.R. 215.

99 *Fenn* v. *Sagar* (1955) 57 W.A.L.R. 12; J.A. Smillie (1969-70) 1 *A.C.L.R.* 67.

100 *Jennings* v. *Hannan (No. 2)* (1969) 71 S.R.(N.S.W.) 226. The presumption can be rebutted by evidence of the actual relationship between the driver and the owner: *Lansdown* v. *W.T.H. Pty Ltd* (1990) 10 M.V.R. 355.

101 *Christmas* v. *Nicol Bros Pty Ltd* (1941) S.R.(N.S.W.) 317.

102 *Morgans* v. *Launchbury* [1973] A.C. 127; but the purpose need not be commercial—it may be domestic or social: *Milkovits* v. *Federal Capital Press of Australia Pty Ltd* (1972) 20 F.L.R. 311.

103 *Carberry* v. *Davies* [1968] 2 All E.R. 817.

104 [1975] V.R. 859; cf. *Scarsbrook* v. *Mason* [1961] 3 All E.R. 767; contrast *Commonwealth of Australia* v. *Cocks* (1966) 115 C.L.R. 413.

105 *Fettke* v. *Bogovic* [1964] S.A.S.R. 119.

occupiers for the conduct of visitors to their premises;[106] and of gaolers for the conduct of prisoners.[107] Social services authorities are not vicariously liable for the torts of foster parents.[108] Where businesses are involved in joint ventures based on contractual arrangements between them, their close associations and common interest will not necessarily mean that one is vicariously liable for the acts of the other.[109]

II: NEXUS BETWEEN RELATIONSHIP AND ACT

Once it has been established that there is in existence between the defendant and the wrongdoer a relationship out of which vicarious liability can arise, it must then be established that the act of the latter was properly referable to that relationship. In the case of servants the question is whether the servant was acting in the course of his employment at the time the tort was committed; in the case of agents, the question, though the same in substance, is usually put in the form of whether the agent was acting within the scope of his authority.

1. SERVANTS

In relation to servants, the first question to ask is what the servant was employed to do. Then it is necessary to decide whether the tortious acts of the servant were outside the scope of that employment (in which case the employer will not be vicariously liable);[110] or whether, on the other hand, the employee, at the time of committing the tort, was doing authorized acts or acts which were an unauthorized mode or method of doing an authorized act (in which case the employer will be vicariously liable).[111] In this sense, negligence is always just an unauthorized mode of acting rather than an unauthorized act. Whether the servant was acting within the scope of the employment is a question of fact. A phrase sometimes used to describe action outside the course of employment is to say that the servant was on 'a frolic of his own'.[112]

It has been said that in determining whether the servant was acting in the course of employment, the allotted task should be described broadly

106 *Wilkinson* v. *Joyceman* [1985] 1 Qd.R. 567, 573 *per* Campbell C.J.

107 But see Law Reform (Miscellaneous Provisions) Act (N.T.) s.29A(3).

108 *S.* v. *Walsall Metropolitan Borough Council* [1985] 1 W.L.R. 1150.

109 e.g. *Misaka* v. *Wellington Publishing Co. (1972) Ltd* [1975] 1 N.Z.L.R. 10; *re* partners see *Butler* v. *Modrak* (1983) 49 A.C.T.R. 3.

110 *Greenwood* v. *Commonwealth* [1975] V.R. 859.

111 The mere fact that an employer permits employees to do a particular thing does not necessarily mean that in doing it they are acting in the course of their employment. They may, for example, be allowed to leave work early: *Hilton* v. *Thomas Burton (Rhodes) Ltd* [1961] 1 W.L.R. 705. If the employment merely provides the employee with the occasion to commit the tort, then it may be outside the course of employment: *Heasmans* v. *Clarity Cleaning Co.* [1987] I.C.R. 949 (telephone cleaner uses client's phones to make international calls).

112 *Joel* v. *Morison* (1834) 6 Car. & P. 502, 503 *per* Parke B.

rather than narrowly.[113] The choice between detailed and general characterization is always open, and a broad description is much more likely to produce a result favourable to the plaintiff than a narrow one. Thus, in *Century Insurance Co. Ltd* v. *Northern Ireland Road Transport Board*[114] a petrol tanker driver caused a fire when he lit a cigarette while delivering petrol into an underground tank. Despite the gross stupidity of the driver's action, it was characterized as merely an unauthorized way of doing the job of delivering petrol. This case makes it clear that the act the employee is performing can be in the scope of employment even though it is not for the employer's benefit.[115] Conversely, the fact that the servant thinks that he is acting for his master's benefit does not necessarily mean that he is acting in the course of employment.[116]

Apart from questions of deviation from specified routes of travel,[117] the question sometimes arises whether a particular trip or mode of travel is in the course of employment. Thus an employee will not usually be acting in the course of employment in getting to or from work, since his contractual duty will usually be to present himself at his place of work.[118] But if a servant has a *duty* to travel from A to B,[119] or a duty to transport fellow employees to work,[120] or if he is travelling *in his employer's time*[121] between workplaces, or from home to a workplace other than his regular workplace, or in the course of a peripatetic occupation, or to the scene of an emergency,[122] his trip may be in the course of employment. Return journeys are treated in the same way as the corresponding outward journeys.

In relation to torts not involving negligence, the basic question is whether the act constituting the tort was done in the course of the servant's employment. This will usually depend on whether the act itself or an act of that type was authorized expressly or impliedly,[123] or was reasonably incidental to some authorized act. Thus, in *Whitfield* v. *Turner*[124] the servant had authority to light a fire in an emergency to create a fire break. He lit a fire even though no emergency had arisen, and it spread. It was held that the type of act which the servant was authorized to do was the lighting of fires, and the fact that no emergency had arisen

---

113 *Ilkiw* v. *Samuels* [1963] 2 All E.R. 879, 889 *per* Diplock L.J.
114 [1942] A.C. 509.
115 But torts committed as a result of industrial action directed against the employer may well be outside the course of employment: *General Engineering Services Ltd* v. *Kingston and St Andrew Corporation* [1989] 1 W.L.R. 69.
116 *Kay* v. *I.T.W. Ltd* [1968] 1 Q.B. 140, 153 *per* Sellers L.J.
117 e.g. *Chaplin* v. *Dunstan* [1938] S.A.S.R. 245; *Harvey* v. *R.G. O'Dell Ltd* [1958] Q.B. 78.
118 *Nottingham* v. *Aldridge* [1971] 2 Q.B. 739; *Commonwealth* v. *Cocks* (1966) 115 C.L.R. 413.
119 *Greenwood* v. *Commonwealth* [1975] V.R. 859.
120 *Redpath* v. *Scott* (1946) 48 W.A.L.R. 1.
121 It would probably be enough if the employer set aside working time for the journey even if the employee did it in his own time and used the working time for his own purposes.
122 *Smith* v. *Stages* [1989] A.C. 928.
123 e.g. *Carrington* v. *A-G* [1972] N.Z.L.R. 1106.
124 (1920) 28 C.L.R. 97.

would not avail the defendant. This case shows that a broad view will be taken of the question of what acts have been authorized.

Particular difficulty may arise when the tortious conduct was wilful.[125] Why, it might be asked, should an employer be held liable for the deliberate torts of servants even if they are committed in the course of doing the employer's business? On the other hand, if we see the justification of vicarious liability as being to provide injured plaintiffs with a reliable source of compensation for losses arising out of the conduct of the employer's business, the fact that the servant's tort was wilful seems unimportant; it makes no difference to the plaintiff whether the tort was deliberate or not, and employing a violent or dishonest servant is just as much a foreseeable risk of doing business as employing a negligent one. A number of different situations can be usefully distinguished.

(a) Emergencies A servant may be impliedly authorized to do in an emergency acts (even deliberate acts) which would be beyond his authority if no emergency existed. In *Poland* v. *John Parr & Sons*[126] a carter, who had finished work and was about to go home, hit a boy whom he thought he saw stealing his master's goods. It was held that although the carter was not bound to act as he did, he was impliedly authorized to do so in order to protect his master's goods, and that he had not acted in excess of what the situation required so as to put his act into the unauthorized class. On the other hand, in *Keppell Bus Co. Ltd* v. *Ahmad*[127] the plaintiff had an altercation with a bus conductor; they tried to fight but passengers separated them. The conductor began collecting fares, and as he did so he swore at the plaintiff, who asked the conductor not to use abusive language. The conductor hit the plaintiff in the eye and caused the loss of the sight of the eye. It was held that no emergency existed to justify the use of violence on the part of the conductor and so the employer was held not vicariously liable for his acts.

(b) Illegal acts Often deliberate torts will be criminal as well as tortious. The fact that the servant's act was illegal (as well as tortious) will not necessarily take it out of the course of employment.[128] But if the illegal act is totally inimical to the purposes for which the employee has been hired (as, for example, where taxation officers had allegedly conspired to issue false assessments in order to injure the plaintiff,[129] or where police used menaces and excessive violence in dealing with a suspect,[130] or where firefighters enagaged in 'go-slow' industrial action as a result of which they arrived too late to extinguish a fire before substantial damage was

125 See generally Swanton (1985) 16 *U.W.A.L.R.* 1.
126 [1927] 1 K.B. 236.
127 [1974] 1 W.L.R. 1082.
128 e.g. *Macdonald* v. *Dickson* (1868) 2 S.A.L.R. 32.
129 *Carpenter's Investment Trading Co. Ltd* v. *Commonwealth of Australia* (1952) 69 W.N.(N.S.W.) 175.
130 *Lackersteen* v. *Jones* (1988) 92 F.L.R. 6.

done[131]), this may lead to the act being characterized as outside the course of employment.

The question of a master's liability for theft by a servant of property belonging to a third party is somewhat complex. If a master were negligent in employing a servant whom he ought to have realized might commit theft, he could, of course, be held personally liable for negligence. But in the absence of such personal negligence, a master is not vicariously liable just because a servant turns out to be dishonest. On the other hand, if the property of the third party has been entrusted to the employer for some purpose which imposes a duty to keep it safe, and the employer delegates this duty to a servant, then the former can be held liable for theft of the property by the latter. The employer would not be liable if some other employee to whom the property had not been entrusted had stolen it.[132] It is not clear what justifies this distinction: whether or not the servant had personal custody of the stolen proeprty, the theft is incidental to the conduct of the employer's business.

(c) Fraud Deliberate wrongdoing by an employee can be in the course of employment even if it is not done in any sense for the benefit of or to protect the interests of the employer. In *Lloyd* v. *Grace Smith & Co.*[133] the defendant firm's conveyancing clerk fraudulently induced a client to convey property to him under cover of authorizing the firm to sell the property on her behalf. It was held that the fraudulent act of the clerk was merely an unauthorized mode of doing the conveyancing he was employed to do and so was within the scope of his employment. The employee need not be authorized to do the very act complained of; he need only have authority, express or implied, to engage in the transaction or be held out as having authority to engage in the transaction in the course of which the fraud is committed.[134] The plaintiff need not be a client or customer of the employer. Provided the employee's authority, actual or ostensible, extends to dealing with third parties, the employer will be liable.[135] But if the employee's fraud is totally incompatible with the purpose for which he was employed, the employer may not be liable.[136]

Where the fraud of the servant consists of a misrepresentation, made in the course of an authorized transaction, that he has authority to do a particular thing, the employer will be liable only if he himself, by words or acts, held the servant out as having the authority to do that particular thing or it was a thing which an employee in his position would usually have authority to do.[137] In other words, fraudulent assertions of authority to do a particular act take the act outside the scope of employment. This rule is narrower than that applied in *Lloyd* v. *Grace Smith*, and its

131 *General Engineering Services* v. *Kingston Corporation* [1989] 1 W.L.R. 69.
132 *Morris* v. *Martin* [1966] 1 Q.B. 716.
133 [1912] A.C. 716.
134 *Barrow* v. *Bank of New South Wales* [1931] V.L.R. 323.
135 *Uxbridge Permanent Benefit Society* v. *Pickard* [1931] V.L.R. 323.
136 *Polkinghorne* v. *Holland* (1934) 51 C.L.R. 143; *Carpenter's Investment etc. Co.* v. *Commonwealth* (1952) 69 W.N.(N.S.W.) 175.
137 *Armagas Ltd* v. *Mundogas S.A.* [1986] A.C. 717.

justification appears to rest on the idea that a person should not rely on statements by a servant as to the scope of his authority unless there is some independent reason to think that the agent has the authority he claims to have. Statements of authority invite and require verification; whereas it may be less reasonable to expect a person to question a servant's authority when the servant has not raised the issue of authority explicitly but simply acts fraudulently in the course of an authorized transaction. On the other hand, it is not clear why the law should not adopt the attitude that a person is entitled to believe such an assertion of authority by a servant unless there is some good reason to suspect its truth.

(d) Personal motives Even the fact that the servant has acted out of personal resentment, ill-will or spite will not necessarily take his act outside the course of his employment. In *Petterson* v. *Royal Oak Hotel Ltd*[138] a barman refused a drink to a drunken customer; the customer threw a glass at the barman who, as the customer was leaving, as an expression of ill-will, threw a piece of glass back at him. The glass lodged in the eye of another customer, the plaintiff. It was held that even though the barman had acted out of spite, his act was just a negligent way of performing his duty of keeping order. This case may, however, be exceptional. In *Deatons Pty Ltd* v. *Flew*[139] a barmaid threw a glass at a customer in anger at his behaviour towards her. It was held that throwing beer glasses was not incidental to keeping order. The barmaid had acted purely for her own purposes and not even in supposed furtherance of her employer's interests. Acts, such as self-defence, done in the employee's own interest, can be in the course of employment, but they must be acts which are incidental to or arise out of the performance of the master's work. Here the barmaid's resentful behaviour was no part of what she was employed to do. In *Auckland Workingmen's Club and Mechanics' Institute* v. *Rennie*[140] the test was put in this way: was the employee impelled in his conduct, however mistakenly, by allegiance to the interests of his employer, or was he predominantly actuated by personal motives unconnected with the employer's business?

2. AGENTS

Analogous principles to these apply in the case of agents. Where the agency is non-contractual, the authorization on which the finding of agency is based expressly or impliedly defines the scope of the defendant's vicarious liability. In the case of contractual agents, the express and implied terms of the contract help to define the scope of the agent's authority. Also, in business contexts, those dealing with agents are entitled to assume that they have authority to do acts which agents in that context normally have ('usual authority') or which the principal has held

138 [1948] N.Z.L.R. 136.
139 (1949) 79 C.L.R. 370; cf. *Rutherford* v. *Hawke's Bay Hospital Board* [1949] N.Z.L.R. 400.
140 [1976] 1 N.Z.L.R. 278.

the agent out as having authority to do ('ostensible' or 'apparent' authority). The agent may be authorized to do specific acts or acts of a particular type; if the latter, the principal is liable if an act of that type is done mistakenly, negligently or wrongfully. But if, in the course of an authorized transaction, an agent fraudulently misrepresents that he has authority to do a particular act, and the principal has not held him out as having that authority, the principal will not be bound by that misrepresentation unless the act was one which an agent in his position would usually have authority to do.[141]

III: EXPRESS PROHIBITIONS

If the employer expressly prohibits his servant or agent[142] to do certain acts the question will be whether, in disobeying the prohibition, the employee was acting outside his employment or authority or was merely adopting an unauthorized mode of performing allotted tasks. The basic principle is that for the purposes of vicarious liability the exact terms of the employee's service or authority are not conclusive of the scope of the employment. The question is whether the act constituting the tort or out of which it arose was broadly[143] of the class which the employee was required or permitted to do.[144] Thus, in *Colonial Mutual Life Assurance Society* v. *Producers & Citizens Co-operative Assurance Co.*[145] the defendant company was held vicariously liable for defamatory statements made in the course of selling insurance, despite a term in the agency agreement between the salesman and his employer which required him not to make defamatory statements. It has long been recognized that the law's attitude to prohibitions is often prompted by a desire to give the plaintiff access to the financial resources of the employer.[146]

As a general rule, prohibitions on drivers from allowing other persons to drive their vehicles being used in the course of their employment only affect the mode of doing the job, not its scope. So, at least in cases where the employee remains in a position to exercise ultimate control by being in or near the vehicle while the unauthorized person is driving, the employer will be liable.[147]

Another line of cases involves situations where a driver, in disobedience of an express prohibition, allows a passenger to travel in the employer's vehicle while it is engaged on the employer's business. In *Twine* v. *Bean's Express Ltd*[148] the employer was held not liable on two grounds. The first

---

141 *Armagas Ltd* v. *Mundogas S.A.* [1986] A.C. 717.
142 *Re* agents see generally *Bonette* v. *Woolworths Ltd* (1937) 37 S.R.(N.S.W.) 142.
143 *Ilkiw* v. *Samuels* [1963] 2 All E.R. 879, 889 *per* Diplock L.J.
144 *Bugge* v. *Brown* (1919) 26 C.L.R. 110.
145 (1931) 46 C.L.R. 41; see also *Canadian Pacific Railway Co.* v. *Lockhart* [1942] A.C. 591.
146 See *Limpus* v. *London General Omnibus Co.* (1862) 1 H. & C. 526; cf. *London County Council* v. *Cattermoles (Garages) Ltd* [1953] 1 W.L.R. 997.
147 *Ilkiw* v. *Samuels* [1963] 2 All E.R. 879; *Black Range Tin* v. *Shoobert* [1973] W.A.R. 131.
148 [1946] 1 All E.R. 202; cf. *Kohler* v. *Howson* [1927] S.A.S.R. 341; F.H. Newark (1954) 17 *M.L.R.* 102.

was that, as against the employer, the passenger was a trespasser because he did not have the employer's permission to be in the vehicle; it was thought to follow from this that the employer owed no duty to the passenger and so could not be liable to him. This ground of decision is now suspect; it was rejected by Lord Denning M.R. in *Rose* v. *Plenty*[149] on the basis that it is no longer the law that occupiers owe no duty to trespassers on their premises; it is also suspect because it assumed that a master can be held vicariously liable only if he owes a duty to the plaintiff.[150] The second ground of the decision was that in giving the lift the driver was acting beyond the scope of employment. This seems now to be the proper explanation of the decision.[151] In *Rose* v. *Plenty*[152] the employee, a milk deliverer, contrary to express instructions, allowed a boy to help him with his rounds. This case is distinguishable on its facts from *Twine*, because in *Twine* the driver was giving the plaintiff a lift purely for his own purposes, whereas in *Rose* v. *Plenty* the boy was helping the employee do his master's work. But the difference of result probably also reflects an increasing desire on the part of the courts to tap third-party insurance funds for the benefit of injured plaintiffs.

But there are limits to the willingness of the courts to ignore prohibitions. In *Kooragang Investments Pty Ltd* v. *Richardson & Wrench Ltd*[153] a valuer employed by the defendant negligently prepared valuations for the plaintiff despite an express instruction not to work for the plaintiff. The valuer was a director of one of the companies in the group to which the plaintiff belonged; he used the group's offices to do the valuations but sent them out on the defendant's letterhead and signed them with its corporate name. There was no suggestion that the valuer had ostensible or apparent authority because the plaintiff did not know who the valuations had been prepared by. The only issue was whether making of the valuations was actually authorized. The Privy Council held that it was not, because the valuer had prepared the valuations in his own interest and without any connection with the defendant's business. The board was not prepared to apply the principle that a prohibition is of no avail if the acts are of the type which the employee is employed to do, because that principle, it was said, belongs to the law about ostensible authority, which only applies where the plaintiff has dealings with the employee.

This decision is consistent with the rule, noted above, concerning vicarious liability for misrepresentations of authority: the employer will only be liable if, in the circumstances, it was reasonable for the plaintiff to rely on the statement without checking its truth. A prohibition on doing acts of a particular class cannot be overcome by a misrepresentation by an employee that he has authority to do acts of that class, but only if the employer held the employee out as having appropriate authority or,

149 [1976] 1 W.L.R. 141.

150 See further p. 726 below.

151 See *Rose* v. *Plenty* [1976] 1 W.L.R. 141; *Joss* v. *Snowball* (1969) 72 S.R.(N.S.W.) 218; *Young* v. *Edward Box & Co. Ltd* [1951] 1 T.L.R. 789 *per* Denning L.J.

152 [1976] 1 W.L.R. 141.

153 [1982] A.C. 462.

perhaps, if an employee in the position of this one would usually have such authority.[154] As observed above, however, it is not clear why the law should place the onus of enquiry on the plaintiff in cases where an employee fraudulently claims an authority he does not have, but not in circumstances where he does an unauthorized and fraudulent act without making any claim of authority.

It would seem, therefore, that in all cases except those involving fraudulent misrepresentations of authority, the courts will take a wide view of the course of employment; only in extreme cases will disobedience of a prohibition be treated as taking an employee outside the course of employment. In fact it is probably true to say that the prohibition as such is irrelevant, in the sense that action in disobedience of a prohibition will only fall outside the course of employment if it would do so even if there were no prohibition.[155] If it falls within the course of employment then the prohibition will, once again, be irrelevant.

IV: THE ACT FOR WHICH LIABILITY IS IMPOSED

The third requirement for imposing vicarious liability is that some wrongful act has been done by the employee. The nature of this requirement has received most discussion in the context of the master–servant cases, but the discussion has ramifications for other areas.

In the first place, it seems clear that where the liability of the employer rests on breach of a strict personal duty (that is, where the liability is for the creation of risks, as in *Rylands* v. *Fletcher*) the liability is not vicarious at all. The employer is not made liable for the conduct of another, but for the creation of a risk which has materialized; the act of the employee is merely a link in the causal chain between creation of risk and damage. In other cases where the exact status of the employee is irrelevant the liability imposed seems, as was stated above, to rest on the same theoretical basis as liability for acts of servants.

Vicarious liability in the strict sense, that is, liability for the acts of servants and, in some cases, for independent contractors, is not a tort, because the employer is not made to pay damages in respect of his own acts but on account of the acts of another. What is not so clear is whether the employer's liability rests on the fact that the employee has committed a tortious act (so that the employer is made liable for the acts and the tort of another); or whether the liability rests on the fact that if the employer had done the acts which the employee did he would have committed a tort (so that the employer is made liable for the careless—or intentional—acts of another which, because of the duty resting on the employer, would have amounted to a tort if done by him). The second alternative is often

---

154 In *Kooragang* neither ostensible or usual authority could be pleaded because the plaintiff did not know who the valuer was.

155 This is true of *Kooragang*: even if there had been no prohibition, the rule in *Armagas* v. *Mundogas* (see p. 722 above) would have relieved the defendant of liability.

referred to as the 'master's tort' theory of vicarious liability.[156] In a sense, it is not a theory of vicarious liability at all, in that it rests on the breach of a duty personal to the employer. But it *is* a theory of vicarious liability in that the acts which constitute the breach were not done by the person whose duty has been broken.

The first view was adopted by the Court of Appeal in *Rose* v. *Plenty*.[157] It involves asking two questions: first, whether the employee committed a tort against the plaintiff; if he did, secondly, whether the employer ought to be made responsible for the tort of his employee. The other view was adopted in *Twine* v. *Bean's Express*[158] where it was held that because the employer of the driver who gave a lift to an unauthorized passenger owed no duty to the trespassing passenger, he could not be held liable for the driver's careless acts, which injured the passenger. It was also adopted in *Darling Island Stevedoring & Lighterage Co. Ltd* v. *Long*[159] where it was held that an employer is not vicariously liable for an employee's breach of a statutory duty imposed on the employee personally and not on the employer. A majority of the court said that the reason for non-liability was that the master himself owed no duty to the plaintiff of which the employee's acts could constitute a breach. Usually, it is said, the content of the duty of both employer and employee will be the same; but when they are not, the fact that the employee has committed a breach of his duty will not entail liability of the employer if the employee's act does not constitute a breach of the employer's duty.

The master's tort theory has also been adopted in cases where one spouse has been allowed to sue the other spouse's employer despite the fact that the other spouse could not be sued personally because of the common law rule (now largely, but not completely, abolished) that spouses cannot sue each other in tort;[160] and by Lord Denning in cases such as *Cassidy* v. *Ministry of Health*[161] and *Morris* v. *Martin*[162] where he wanted to render irrelevant the distinction between servants and independent contractors by imposing a personal duty on the employer. These uses of the theory seem to be very much a matter of expedience to produce a desired result; they do not rest on any firm principle. The theory might also provide a basis for denying liability in the employer in any case where the employer, to the plaintiff's knowledge, had prohibited the conduct which constituted the tort or in the performance of which the tort was committed.

The master's tort theory may, therefore, depending on the facts, make the employer liable when the employee would not be, or relieve the employer of liability despite the employee's liability. But in most cases the

156 G. Williams (1956) 72 *L.Q.R.* 522; J.J. Gow (1958) 32 *A.L.J.* 183.
157 [1976] 1 W.L.R. 141.
158 [1946] 1 All E.R. 202.
159 (1956-7) 97 C.L.R. 36; cf. *Ramsay* v. *Pigram* (1967) 118 C.L.R. 271, 276-8 *per* Barwick C.J.; 285 *per* Taylor J.; *L. Shaddock & Associates Pty Ltd* v. *Parramatta C.C.* (1981) 36 A.L.R. 385, 403 *per* Mason J.
160 *Waugh* v. *Waugh* (1950) 50 S.R.(N.S.W.) 210; *Broom* v. *Morgan* [1953] 1 Q.B. 597.
161 [1951] 2 K.B. 343.
162 [1966] 1 Q.B. 716.

two theories will produce the same result, since usually the employer's duty will be the same as the employee's. In one situation it is clear that the employer cannot be held liable if the employee would not be liable, and that is where the employer is the Crown.[163]

The choice between the two theories is basically a choice between viewing vicarious liability as a device for allocating losses to the party best able to bear them, and viewing it as based on traditional ideas of duty and responsibility. The former seems now to be the preferred view, and this should at least rule out application of the master's tort theory to relieve an employer of liability when his employee could be sued. At the same time, it might justify adoption of the master's tort theory when for some reason the servant could not be sued for his tortious acts. But the better way to justify this course might simply be to say that the employer should not be entitled to take advantage of defences personal to the employee.[164]

V: THE EMPLOYER'S INDEMNITY

The principle of vicarious liability is designed to provide the plaintiff with an additional source of compensation; it does not mean that the employee may not be sued, but just that the plaintiff may also have recourse against the employer. The common law implies into the employee's contract a term to the effect that the employee will perform his duties carefully. If the plaintiff sues the employer and the latter is held vicariously liable,[165] the employer may then sue the employee and recover damages for breach of contract constituting a complete indemnity in respect of the damages the employer has had to pay to the plaintiff.[166]

---

163 *Hall* v. *Whatmore* [1961] V.R. 225; *Parker* v. *Commonwealth of Australia* (1964) 112 C.L.R. 295; cf. Crown Proceedings Act 1947 (U.K.), s.2(1); Crown Proceedings Act 1950 (N.Z.), s.6(1). But the rule has been partially reversed in N.S.W.: see n. 164 below.

164 In N.S.W. an employer (including the Crown) can be held vicariously liable even if the employee enjoys a 'statutory exemption' from liability: Law Reform (Vicarious Liability) Act 1989 (substituting s.10 in Law Reform (Vicarious Liability) Act 1983).

165 If the employer is also personally liable the rule does not apply and the employer would be entitled, at most, to contribution under the legislative provisions considered in Ch. 22: *Canberra Formwork Pty Ltd* v. *Civil & Civic Ltd* (1982) 41 A.C.T.R. 1; but see *Davenport* v. *Commissioner of Railways* (1953) 53 S.R.(N.S.W.) 552.

166 *Lister* v. *Romford Ice & Cold Storage Co. Ltd* [1957] A.C. 555. In theory, the employer also has a claim under contribution legislation (see Ch. 22) concurrent with and additional to the contractual claim recognized in *Lister*, but the arguments against the latter apply equally to the former. Both claims have been abolished by legislation in N.S.W. (Employees Liability Act 1991). See also Insurance Contracts Act 1984 (Cwth) s.66 discussed in *Boral Resources (Qld) Pty Ltd* v. *Pyke* (1989) 93 A.L.R. 89. *Lister* has been overcome in S.A. (Wrongs Act 1936-75, s.27c) and the N.T. (Law Reform (Miscellaneous Provisions) Act s.22A). But none of these provisions apply where the servant's tort amounts to 'serious and [or] wilful misconduct'. As to wilful wrongs see *Davenport* v. *Commissioner of Railways* (1953) 53 S.R.(N.S.W.) 552.

This is so even if the employer has taken out insurance designed to indemnify the employee against liability incurred for acts done in the course of employment,[167] so that if the employee were sued he could call on the insurer to pay.[168]

Although this position is justified in terms of a strict enforcement of legal rights, it makes no sense in terms of loss allocation, at least where the employee is a servant as opposed to an independent contractor. The employer usually takes out insurance exactly to cover himself against liability for injury to third parties by negligence of his servants, and the costs of such negligence are thereby efficiently and widely spread. The employer has no interest in suing his servant, and the effect of this on industrial relations will usually be a positive disincentive to the enforcement of the employer's strict contractual rights. There seems little justification for allowing the insurer to enforce the employer's rights against an uninsured servant.[169] In practice, the employer's rights are probably very rarely pursued unless the servant was guilty of wilful wrongdoing. In *Morris* v. *Ford Motor Co. Ltd*[170] a majority of the English Court of Appeal held that a right of subrogation would arise only if expressly or impliedly provided for and that a right of subrogation could not be implied in an industrial setting.

---

167 In N.S.W., S.A. and the N.T. the employer is required to indemnify the employee against such liability. In Tas. the employer must take out insurance to cover the employee for liability to fellow-workers: Workers Compensation Act 1927, ss.34(1)(c) and 34(1A).

168 In N.S.W., S.A. and the N.T., if such insurance exists, and the employer is sued vicariously, he can call on the insurer to pay. This avoids circuity of action.

169 If the employee is held liable to his employer he cannot have recourse to any insurance designed to indemnify the employer for liability to the plaintiff. The insurer who has paid out to the employer in respect of his vicarious liability is subrogated to the rights of the employer to sue the employee under the contract of employment. But see *Commercial and General Insurance Co. Ltd* v. *G.I.O. of N.S.W.* (1973) 129 C.L.R. 374.

170 [1973] 1 Q.B. 792.

22

MULTIPLE TORTFEASORS AND CONTRIBUTION

I: MULTIPLE TORTFEASORS[1]

1. SOLIDARY LIABILITY

Sometimes the same damage to the plaintiff may be the result of tortious conduct by more than one person. The plaintiff is free to choose which of such persons to sue, and if he chooses to sue only one of them, he is entitled to judgment against that person for the full amount of any damages awarded.[2] Where a plaintiff sues more than one defendant in tort in respect of the same damage, and more than one are held liable, the plaintiff is entitled to judgment against each and every one for the full amount of the damages awarded whether their liability is joint[3] or several and concurrent.[4] This is sometimes expressed by saying that the liability of multiple tortfeasors is 'solidary' rather than 'proportionate'. It is not open to any of the defendants to argue, as against the plaintiff, that his contribution to the damage was smaller than that of others or that he was only partly responsible. Such arguments can only be put in contribution proceedings against the other defendants, the aim of which is to apportion the liability among the tortfeasors according to their relative responsibility. The plaintiff is entitled to recover the whole amount of the loss against any one or a combination of the defendants but may, of course, only

---

1 This word means 'a person who has committed a tort'. But it should be noted that a person vicariously liable for the tort of another may claim contribution or be subject to a claim for contribution even though the former has not committed a tort. The word 'tortfeasor' is used in this chapter to include a person vicariously liable for the tort of another; and the phrase 'commit a tort' and its cognates and the term 'tortious conduct' also include reference to being vicariously liable.

2 But the person sued may join other tortfeasors as parties to the action for the purpose of claiming contribution from them. In such circumstances, a claim for contribution will succeed only if the first defendant can prove that if the joined defendant(s) had been sued by the plaintiff he would have been held liable.

3 *Bell* v. *Thompson* (1934) 34 S.R.(N.S.W.) 431, 435 *per* Jordan C.J.

4 *Barisic* v. *Devenport* [1978] 2 N.S.W.L.R. 111, 116-7 *per* Moffitt P.

recover in total the full amount of the loss.[5] The fact that judgment has been given against several defendants for $X does not mean that the plaintiff may recover $X from each but only that he may recover $X in total from them in whatever way possible.

At common law the rule (known as the rule in *Brinsmead* v. *Harrison*)[6] was that a judgment against one of several persons *jointly* liable in tort was a bar to an action against any of the others for the same cause even if the judgment remained unsatisfied. This rule was designed to avoid multiplicity of actions. A release of one of several persons jointly liable in tort also operated to discharge them all; but a covenant not to sue one such person did not discharge the others, who could still be sued. Whether an agreement is a release or a covenant not to sue depends on the intention of the party granting the concession as gathered from interpretation of the document.[7] The rule in *Brinsmead* v. *Harrison* has now been abolished by statute,[8] but the rule that a release discharges all the tortfeasors still survives, although courts today might be unwilling to interpret a document as a release rather than a covenant not to sue.[9]

The provisions which abolish the rule in *Brinsmead* v. *Harrison* have been held to abolish the rule not only where the plaintiff obtains judgment against a defendant and then seeks to sue another defendant in a separate action, but also where a plaintiff sues several defendants in the same action and obtains judgment against one of them in the form, for example, of a consent order giving effect to an out-of-court settlement. At common law this would have barred recovery of judgment against the other defendant(s).[10]

Except in Victoria, where more than one action is brought in respect of the same damage, the judgment in the first of such actions[11] sets an upper limit on the amount which the plaintiff can recover in aggregate under all the judgments; and a plaintiff who brings more than one action may have to pay the costs of later actions unless the court is of the opinion that he had reasonable grounds for bringing the later action(s). This provision is designed to prevent unnecessary multiplication of actions and abuse of abolition of the rule in *Brinsmead* v. *Harrison*. The first part of the

---

5 *D'Angola* v. *Rio Pioneer Gravel Co. Pty Ltd* [1979] 1 N.S.W.L.R. 495.

6 (1871) L.R. 6 C.P. 584.

7 *Duck* v. *Mayeu* [1892] 2 Q.B. 511; *Cutler* v. *McPhail* [1962] 2 Q.B. 292. In Tasmania a release only discharges other tortfeasors if it specifically says so: Tortfeasors and Contributory Negligence Act 1954, s.3(3).

8 Refer to the legislative provisions listed in note 32 below.

9 *Bryanston Finance Ltd* v. *De Vries* [1975] Q.B. 703,732 *per* Lord Diplock.

10 *XL Petroleum (N.S.W.) Pty Ltd* v. *Caltex Oil (Australia) Pty Ltd* (1984-5) 155 C.L.R. 448; *Wah Tat Bank Ltd* v. *Chan Cheg Kum* [1975] A.C. 507; *Bryanston Finance* v. *De Vries* [1975] Q.B. 703.

11 At least in respect of compensatory, as opposed to exemplary, damages: *XL Petroleum* v. *Caltex* (1984-5) 155 C.L.R. 448, 469-70 *per* Brennan J.

provision has been abandoned in England,[12] and in Victoria,[13] the sanction in costs being thought sufficient to discourage multiple actions designed simply to try for a higher award rather than, for example, to find a solvent defendant if the first one sued is unable to satisfy the judgment.[14] Even if the subsequent action had this aim, the plaintiff would still have to give some good reason why he had not sued all the tortfeasors at once. Inability to identify or trace the other tortfeasors at the time of the first action might constitute such a reason.

This provision deals only with successive actions and does not deal with separate judgments given in the same action. Normally, where judgments are entered against more than one defendant in the same action, the judgments will be for the same amount. But they may differ if, for example, exemplary damages are awarded against one defendant but not against the other(s)[15] or if a consent judgment is awarded against one defendant but the court assesses the damages against the other(s). Consider the latter situation by way of illustration. If a plaintiff obtained a consent judgment against one defendant (D1) and then the court awarded judgment in a different and greater amount against another defendant (D2), then the plaintiff would be entitled to recover the greater of the two sums, but the liability of D1 (both to P and, by way of contribution, to D2) would be limited by the amount of the consent judgment. If the later judgment was less than the consent judgment, the liability of D2 to the plaintiff would be limited to the amount of the judgment against him, and any contribution awarded to D1 against D2 would be calculated on the basis of the judgment against D2.[16]

One effect of this system of solidary liability is to encourage plaintiffs to sue the tortfeasor who is most likely to be able to pay any damages awarded to the plaintiff; and so it increases the chance that plaintiffs will actually be compensated. Another related effect of the system is that the risk of a tortfeasor being insolvent or not worth suing is placed on other tortfeasors and not on the plaintiff. But the principle of solidary liability is open to criticism. In the first place, since the person most likely to be able to pay any compensation awarded is not necessarily the person best able to prevent losses of the type suffered by the plaintiff from occurring in the future, it may be argued that solidary liability is not the best way of achieving the loss-prevention aim of tort law. Secondly, it is often argued that solidary liability is unfair to defendants because it imposes on them liability disproportionate to fault. But the force of this objection is weakened by the existence of rights of contribution between tortfeasors

---

12 Civil Liability (Contribution) Act 1978 (U.K.), s.4.

13 But where the amount of the damages payable by a person from whom contribution is claimed is limited by statute or by agreement made before the damage occurred, or is to be reduced for contributory negligence, that person cannot be required to pay contribution greater than the amount of those damages as limited or reduced: Wrongs Act 1958 (Vic.) s.24(2A).

14 It is for the plaintiff in a subsequent action to prove that the first judgment remains unsatisfied: *Bryanston Finance* v. *De Vries* [1975] Q.B. 703.

15 *XL Petroleum* v. *Caltex* (1984-5) 155 C.L.R. 448.

16 *Bryanston Finance* v. *De Vries* [1975] Q.B. 703, 732-3 *per* Lord Diplock; see also *Caltex Oil* v. *XL Petroleum* [1982] 2 N.S.W.L.R. 852.

and by the fact that the relationship between liability and fault is, as we have seen, very loose throughout the law of tort.

Thirdly, the principle of solidary liability has come under attack in recent years on the basis that it is unfair that one tortfeasor should have to bear the full risk of the insolvency or impecuniosity of other tortfeasors. But given that, in general, tort law operates effectively as a mechanism for compensating for losses only as against insured defendants, any unfairness in this allocation of the risk of insolvency or impecuniosity seems tolerable. It is also asserted (without much evidence) that the rule has contributed to significant increases in the cost of liability insurance for certain groups of defendants, such as public authorities and professional advisers, who present particularly attractive targets for litigation. Objectors propose the introduction of proportionate liability: each tortfeasor would be liable only for a share of the plaintiff's loss proportionate to that tortfeasor's responsibility. But provided we accept that the main aim of the law of tort is compensation, and that tort liability coupled with a system of liability insurance is the best way to ensure that people who suffer loss are compensated for it,[17] then solidary liability coupled with rights of contribution seems better suited to achieving this aim than proportionate liability. This was the main consideration which led the New South Wales Law Reform Commission[18] to reject calls for proportionate liability.

2. Injury and Damage

Solidary liability arises only where more than one person is liable for the same damage. It is important to draw a distinction between the plaintiff's injury and the damage which it causes. A good illustration is *Performance Cars Ltd* v. *Abraham.*[19] The plaintiff's Rolls Royce was involved in two collisions, each one the fault of the driver of the other car. In the first collision the offside front wing and the bumper were damaged; in the second the car was dented at the rear. The court accepted that because of the nature of the car, the result of each collision required and justified a respray of the whole of the lower portion of the car. Thus, although each defendant inflicted a different *injury* on the plaintiff, the *damage* caused by each was the same, namely the cost of respraying the whole of the lower portion of the car. If the two collisions had occurred simultaneously, there would have been a right of contribution between the tortfeasors; but because the two collisions occurred successively, it was held that the first tortfeasor alone was liable for the damage.

However, as we saw in Chapter 11, the first of two successive tortfeasors may be liable for damage also caused by the second tortfeasor if some or all of the damage caused by the second is held to be a foreseeable

17 Of course, both of these assumptions can be attacked either generally or as they apply to particular areas of tort liability.
18 Report No. 65, 1990.
19 [1962] 1 Q.B. 33.

consequence of the first tort,[20] as where a person injured in a road accident receives negligent medical treatment. In such a case, the two tortfeasors will be liable '*in solidum*' (that is, 'solidarily') for some of the plaintiff's loss even though the damage caused by both torts represents only a portion of the damage inflicted by one or each of the tortfeasors individually.[21] But successive tortfeasors will not be liable *in solidum* if the second tort is causally unrelated to the first.[22] Nor will contemporaneous tortfeasors be liable *in solidum* if their torts cause distinct and different damage to the plaintiff.

3. Types of Multiple Tortfeasor

'Several concurrent tortfeasors' are persons who commit torts which are independent of one another but inflict the same damage on the plaintiff. What is meant by 'independent' will become clear when we have defined joint tortfeasance, since the terms 'several concurrent' and 'joint' are mutually exclusive. Perhaps the commonest case of several concurrent tortfeasors is where a passenger in a motor vehicle is injured in a collision caused by the negligence of both drivers.

When the torts of two persons causing the same damage to the plaintiff are related in certain ways, the tortfeasors are called 'joint tortfeasors'. In *The Koursk*[23] Bankes L.J. thought it unwise to attempt to define the necessary degree of connection between the torts, and that each case must depend on its own facts. Scrutton L.J. thought it helpful to ask whether the cause of action against the two tortfeasors is the same: cases where it is are where the two tortfeasors are principal and agent acting within the scope of authority, master and servant acting in the course of employment, and parties taking concerted action to a common end. In all these cases, since the plaintiff has proved negligence by one of the parties—the agent or servant or one of the 'conspirators'—then he does not have to prove negligence against the other but only that there was a nexus of service, agency or concerted action between them. Sargant L.J. made the same point by saying that in order to constitute joint tortfeasance there must be a concurrence in the act or acts causing damage, not merely a coincidence of separate acts which, by their conjoined effect, cause damage.

In *Brook* v. *Bool*[24] the defendant was the landlord of a shop on the ground floor of a house adjoining that in which he lived. The defendant

20 Or, in other words, if the first tort is held to be a joint cause in law of some of the damage caused by the second tort.

21 *Mahony* v. *Kruschich* (1985) 156 C.L.R. 522.

22 *Dillingham Constructions Pty Ltd* v. *Steel Mains Pty Ltd* (1974-5) 132 C.L.R. 323 as interpreted in *Mahony* v. *Kruschich* (1985) 156 C.L.R. 522.

23 [1924] P. 140.

24 [1928] 2 K.B. 578; cf. *Schumann* v. *Abbott* [1961] S.A.S.R. 149; contrast *Ruffino* v. *Grace Bros Pty Ltd* [1980] 1 N.S.W.L.R. 732.

had the right to enter the shop at the end of the day when the tenant left to ensure it was secure. The landlord and a lodger went in and were examining a gas pipe (which supplied a burner in the shop) with naked flames. The landlord examined the lower part and the lodger, a younger man, climbed on to the counter to examine the upper part. There was an explosion which damaged the plaintiff's stock. Salter J. held that there were three grounds on which the two could be held joint tortfeasors: the lodger was acting as the defendant's agent; he was acting under the defendant's control; and because the enterprise they were engaged upon was a joint one and the immediate cause of the explosion was an act done in pursuance of their concerted purpose.

II: CONTRIBUTION BETWEEN TORTFEASORS

1. The Right to Contribution

Note, first, that here we are concerned not with contractual rights of indemnity, such as that recognized in *Lister* v. *Romford Ice and Cold Storage Co. Ltd*[25] which we discussed in the chapter on vicarious liability,[26] or those we discussed in the context of products liability,[27] but with the right, independently of the agreement of the parties, of one person liable for damage[28] to require another person liable for the same damage to contribute to the damages awarded to the plaintiff or to indemnify the

25 [1957] A.C. 555. See also *T.A.L. Structural Engineers Pty Ltd* v. *Vaughan Constructions Pty Ltd* [1989] V.R. 545.

26 See p. 726 above.

27 See p. 572 above.

28 A person may be liable in tort for damage even though not a tortfeasor. We have already noted that a person vicariously liable for the tort of another is not a tortfeasor. See also *Mathieson* v. *Workers Compensation Board of Queensland* [1990] 2 Qd.R. 57: Board and Nominal Defendant (see also *Dunning* v. *Altmann* [1991] 2 VR 667) liable in tort for the purposes of contribution proceedings. But *Esdale* v. *Esdale* (1968) 88 W.N. (Pt. 1)(N.S.W.) 286 and *Hall* v. *Warren* [1964] Tas. S.R. 155 decide the contrary in respect of the Nominal Defendant. The S.A. legislation provides that a contribution claim can be made against an insurer or the Nominal Defendant in circumstances in which proceedings can be brought against such parties under the compulsory third-party motor vehicle insurance legislation (Wrongs Act 1936 s.26a). The Nominal Defendant (and the Queensland Workers Compensation Board) are like liability insurers; but an ordinary liability insurer has no right to claim contribution from other tortfeasors in its own name. Rather, it is entitled to be subrogated to the insured's right (if any) to claim contribution. Conversely, claims can usually not be made directly against liability insurers: they have to be made against the insured.

first person in full in respect of those damages.[29] As the name implies, the right to recover contribution is a right to recover *part* of the damages payable to the plaintiff. But the law does sometimes give a party a right to recover from another wrongdoer the *whole* of the damages payable by the former to the plaintiff, even in the absence of a contractual right of indemnity. The general principle is that where one person's liability is fault-based, but another person can be held liable even though in no way at fault, the latter is entitled to an indemnity from the former.[30]

At common law the general rule (known as the rule in *Merryweather* v. *Nixan*)[31] was that there could be no contribution between tortfeasors. All Australian jurisdictions have legislation which abolishes this common law rule, although it varies considerably in points of detail from one jurisdiction to another.[32] In what follows, the most important differences of detail are noted where they are relevant.

The relevant provision (in all jurisdictions except Victoria) reads:

> Any tortfeasor liable in respect of that damage [i.e. the damage caused by the tortfeasor who seeks contribution] may recover contribution from any other tortfeasor who is, or would if sued have been, liable in respect of the same damage, whether as a joint tortfeasor or otherwise, so, however, that no person shall be entitled to recover contribution under this section from any person entitled to be indemnified by him in respect of the liability in respect of which the contribution is sought.

---

29 In N.S.W. both the employer's contractual right to an indemnity recognized in *Lister* v. *Romford Ice* ([1957] A.C. 555) and his statutory right to claim contribution from the employee for whose tort he is liable have been abolished by Employees Liability Act 1991 s.3(1)(a) (which partly re-enacts a relevant provision of the Employees Liability (Indemnification of Employer) Act 1982 and partly gives effect to the decision in *McGrath* v. *Fairfield M.C.* (1984-5) 156 C.L.R. 672. A right of indemnity must be distinguished from an independent claim by A against B in tort (usually for breach of a duty of care owed by B to A) for damages representing the amount of damages which A is liable to pay to C. The possibility of such an action has been contemplated in three contexts: where a ship-owner is held vicariously liable for the negligence of a navigation pilot employed by a harbour authority with whom the ship-owner is not in contractual privity (see *Oceanic Crest Shipping Co.* v. *Pilbara Harbour Services Pty Ltd* (1985) 160 C.L.R. 626, 658-9 *per* Brennan J.); where a party in the chain of manufacture and supply of defective property seeks to pass liability further up the chain to a party with whom he is not in contractual privity (see *Lambert* v. *Lewis* [1982] A.C. 225, 278; but contrast *Southern Water Authority* v. *Carey* [1985] 2 All E.R. 1077, 1094); and where the acquirer of a defective building is held liable to a person who suffers injury as a result of the defect attributable to the negligence of a party with whom the acquirer is not in contractual privity (see *Murphy* v. *Brentwood D.C.* [1991] 1 A.C. 398, 475 *per* Lord Bridge; but note Lord Oliver's reservation at p. 489.)

30 e.g. *Pantalone* v. *Alaouie* (1989) 18 N.S.W.L.R. 119; *Sherras* v. *Van der Maat* [1989] 1 Qd.R. 114 (probably otherwise where both are liable without fault).

31 (1799) 8 Term Rep. 186; 101 E.R. 1337.

32 Reform (Miscellaneous Provisions) Act 1946 (N.S.W.), s.5; Law Reform (Tortfeasors Contribution, Contributory Negligence and Division of Chattels) Act 1952 (Qld) ss.5-9; Wrongs Act 1936-75 (S.A.) ss.24-7; Tortfeasors and Contributory Negligence Act 1954 (Tas.) s.3; Wrongs Act 1958 (Vic.) ss.23A-24AD; Law Reform (Contributory Negligence and Tortfeasors' Contribution) Act (W.A.) 1947 s.7; Law Reform (Miscellaneous Provisions) Act (N.T.) ss.13-14; Law Reform (Miscellaneous Provisions) Ordinance 1955 (A.C.T.) ss.10-13.

This provision has presented acute difficulties of interpretation.[33] The first difficult phrase is 'any tortfeasor liable'. These words refer to a tortfeasor whose liability has been ascertained; the liability may have been 'ascertained' by judgment of a court[34] including a consent judgment; or by an out-of-court settlement without the sanction of the court (often called in the cases 'accord and satisfaction').[35] It does not matter whether, in settling, a party seeking contribution has admitted liability or not.[36] But if a party settles an action, that party cannot recover contribution unless he proves that if the claim had been fought out he would have been held responsible in law and liable to pay in whole or in part for the damage. In the contribution proceedings, therefore, the party seeking contribution cannot maintain the attitude of refusing to admit liability.[37] In Victoria, a person who settles a claim is entitled to contribution provided he would have been liable if the 'factual basis' of the claim against him could be established. This provision differs from that in other jurisdictions in that a person may recover contribution even if he would not have been held liable by a court after a hearing.

The phrase 'any other tortfeasor who is . . . liable' is reasonably straightforward. It is now clear that if the injured party could not have recovered against the party from whom contribution is sought then the party seeking contribution has no claim against him. This rule used to be important when spouses were immune from liability in tort at the suit of each other. If a spouse was injured by the tort of the other spouse and a third party, the latter could not recover contribution from the former. There are provisions (now largely redundant) in some jurisdictions which give the third party a right to contribution in such a situation.[38]

Much greater problems arise out of the words 'or would if sued have been liable'.[39] These words contain no indication of the time at which the hypothetical action is to be treated as having been brought. For example,

---

33 *Bitumen and Oil Refineries (Australia) Ltd* v. *Commissioner for Government Transport* (1954-5) 92 C.L.R. 220, 211-12.

34 ibid.

35 Wrongs Act 1936 (S.A.) s.25(1)(ca)(i); *Stott* v. *West Yorkshire Road Car Co. Ltd* [1971] 2 Q.B. 651; *Bakker* v. *Joppich & Bitumax Pty Ltd* (1980) 25 S.A.S.R. 468. This rule is necessary so as not to discourage settlement of as many cases as possible without recourse to litigation.

36 *Stott* v. *West Yorks Road Car Co.* [1971] 2 Q.B. 651.

37 *Stott* [1971] 2 Q.B. 651, 656-7 *per* Lord Denning M.R.

38 S.A., Tas., N.T., A.C.T. The immunity has been abolished in most jurisdictions: Law Reform (Husband and Wife) Act 1968 (Qld); Wrongs Act 1936-75 s.32 (S.A.); Married Women's Property Act 1965, s.4 (Tas.); Marriage (Liability in Tort) Act 1968 (Vic.); Married Persons (Equality of Status) Act 1989 (N.T.); Married Persons (Torts) Act 1968 (A.C.T.). In N.S.W. (Married Persons (Property and Torts) Act 1901-64 s.16B) and W.A. (Motor Vehicles (Third Party Insurance) Act 1943-72 s.6A) the immunity has been abolished only in relation to road accidents. Compulsory third-party insurance policies must cover spouses, but in Tas. the amount of cover required in respect of members of the insured's family is limited: Traffic Act 1925, s.64. Non-compulsory insurance policies often exclude liability to members of the insured's family. The upshot of all this is that in N.S.W. and W.A. the immunity has some relevance in cases other than road accident cases.

39 Wrongs Act 1958 (Vic.) s.23B(1) does not contain these words. But 'liable' is defined in terms of liability 'which has been or could be established'.

suppose the plaintiff is injured by the joint negligence of A and B on 1 January 1993. In most jurisdictions the plaintiff must commence the action within three years of this date. Suppose next that the plaintiff sues A within the time allowed and recovers judgment on 20 January 1996. A then brings contribution proceedings against B. Would B have been liable if he had been sued? It all depends on when he is said to have been sued. If he had been sued at the same time as A was sued then he could have been held liable. But if he had been sued by the plaintiff at the date of the contribution proceedings the action would have been out of time and B could have not been held liable. So which of these dates, or of the other possible dates, is to be chosen? In *Brambles Construction Pty Ltd* v. *Helmers*[40] the High Court held that no specific time reference ought to be imported into the provision but that the words 'at any time' should be understood after the words 'if sued'.[41] It seems clear, however, that if the party from whom contribution is sought has been sued and found not liable because of effluxion of time, he would not be liable to pay contribution.[42] But this rule does not apply where the action against him has been dismissed for want of prosecution. He must have been sued to judgment and found not liable.[43]

It should be noted that the provisions we have been considering (except that in Victoria)[44] only allow contribution between persons liable in tort. The legislation does not allow a person liable in tort to recover contribution against a party liable (for example) in contract or under statutory warranties in consumer legislation, or vice versa. This is so even if the party held liable in contract could also have been held liable in tort.[45]

---

40 (1965-6) 114 C.L.R. 213. See also *Quinn* v. *Llesna Rubber Co. Pty Ltd* [1989] V.R. 347; *Moore* v. *Western Australian Government Railways Commission* (1990) 3 W.A.R. 409.

41 This decision has been given statutory force in the S.A. legislation by use of the words 'any other tortfeasor who is, or would at any time have been'; and by a provision to the effect that contribution proceedings against a party can be brought even after the expiry of the time within which the plaintiff could sue that party. In Tas., the time of the hypothetical action is fixed by the words 'at the time when the [injured person's] cause of action [against the person from whom contribution is sought] arose'; and the W.A.L.R.C. has recommended adoption of this provision: Report on Limitation and Notice of Actions (1982). The S.A. legislation specifically provides that a person may be liable to pay contribution even if the person injured has released him from liability for any part of the damage; and the Vic. legislation provides that a person may be liable to pay contribution even if he has ceased (for any reason other than effluxion of time) to be liable in respect of the damage.

42 cf. *Castellan* v. *Electric Power Transmission Pty Ltd* (1967) 69 S.R.(N.S.W.) 159; *Canberra Formwork Pty Ltd* v. *Civil & Civic Ltd* (1982) 41 A.C.T.R. 1. Wrongs Act 1958 (Vic.) s.23B(3) provides that contribution cannot be sought against a person who has ceased to be liable by virtue of the expiry of a period of limitation. The definition of 'liable' in s.23B(6) of the Act seems to require that if the person from whom contribution is sought has not already been held liable by a Vic. court, then contribution will not be available from him unless the relevant limitation period has not expired at the date when contribution is sought. If this is the correct interpretation of the provision, the Vic. statute is very much more protective of the person from whom contribution is sought than the provision in other jurisdictions as it has been interpreted by the High Court.

43 *Hart* v. *Hall & Pickles Ltd* [1969] 1 Q.B. 405.

44 Wrongs Act s.23A(1).

45 *Brown* v. *Sevrup Fisheries Pty Ltd* [1970] Tas.S.R. 1.

This is another respect in which the question of whether a client of a professional person who has a contract with the latter requiring the exercise of due care can also sue the professional in tort is relevant, although in this case it is of importance to a party who has no direct control over how the action is framed.

The last part of the provision we are presently considering disentitles a party from seeking contribution if the party from whom it is sought is entitled to be indemnified against liability by the party seeking it. Such a right to be indemnified may arise at common law or by contract. This provision is designed to prevent circuity of action.

2. THE ASSESSMENT OF CONTRIBUTION

All the statutes give the court a wide discretion to award such contribution as it considers to be 'just and equitable' ranging from nothing[46] to a complete indemnity.[47] This is why the claim made is always for 'contribution or an indemnity'. Except in Western Australia, a full indemnity is only recoverable by one wrongdoer against another when the first, though not at fault himself, is legally liable for the fault of the other; an indemnity cannot be recovered where both tortfeasors are independently at fault.[48] The Western Australian legislation provides that an indemnity may be recovered where the person claiming contribution was induced by fraud or misrepresentations, which he had no reason to believe to be false, to commit tortious acts; or where the act was not clearly tortious in itself and the person committing it had no knowledge at the date of the act of its true legal nature; or where the person's liability is purely vicarious.

The apportionment exercise in a negligence case requires an examination of the departure of each person from the standards of the reasonable person.[49] As in the context of apportionment of damages for contributory negligence, it is sometimes said that the court must consider the relative blameworthiness of the tortfeasors and the relative causal potency of their acts. These are very vague, even meaningless, concepts. The court's discretion is wide, and involves no question of principle or of positive findings of fact or law but only of proportion and balance, of the weighing of all relevant considerations.[50] If the party seeking contribution has settled the claim against him, it is open to the court to decide that he acted improvidently or unreasonably in agreeing to settle for as high a figure as he did, and to make an appropriate reduction in the contribution

46 cf. *Ballina S.C.* v. *Volk* (1989) 18 N.S.W.L.R. 1.

47 But a contribution to the costs of defending the action brought by the plaintiff against the person seeking contribution is not recoverable: *Hanson* v. *Matthew Bros Contractors Ltd* (1990) 55 S.A.S.R. 183.

48 *Sinclair* v. *William Arnott Pty Ltd* (1963) 81 W.N.(Pt.2)(N.S.W.) 204; or, *query*, where neither is at fault: *Sherras* v. *Van der Maat* [1989] 1 Qd.R. 114.

49 *Watt* v. *Bretag* (1982) 56 A.L.J.R. 760.

50 *Dare* v. *Dobson* (1959) 77 W.N.(N.S.W.) 227.

it requires from the other party; that is, to take a lesser figure as representing the plaintiff's entitlement to damages.[51]

Difficult questions of apportionment can arise where the liability of one of several tortfeasors falls for some reason to be reduced. In *Unsworth* v. *Commissioner for Railways*[52] the wife of the deceased brought an action in negligence against the plaintiff and the defendant. Damages were assessed at £5616. The defendant was held 85 per cent responsible and the plaintiff (for whose negligence the deceased was vicariously liable) 15 per cent. By statute the defendant's liability to the widow was limited to £2000, and the plaintiff was awarded as contribution 85 per cent of £2000, that is, £1700. He appealed, claiming to be entitled either to 85 per cent of the judgment or £2000. It was held by majority that the plaintiff could recover £2000 on the basis that the Commissioner's liability to contribute should be assessed independently of the statutory limitation and then, if necessary, reduced to take account of that limitation. But even so, the plaintiff may have ended up paying more than the 15 per cent of the damages which had been assessed as his just share. Nevertheless, the Victorian legislation expressly provides that a person's liability to contribute must not exceed any statutory (or contractual) limit on his liability to the injured person.[53]

Where a plaintiff who has been contributorily negligent sues several defendants in the one action, the basic position is that his damages are reduced for contributory negligence independently of any question of contribution between the tortfeasors.[54] The fact that the tortfeasors may be liable in different proportions does not affect the plaintiff, because the basic common law principle is that the plaintiff is entitled to judgment in full against all the tortfeasors, and it has been held that there is nothing in the legislation governing apportionment for contributory negligence which affects this basic rule. Suppose the plaintiff is held 20 per cent to blame, and one defendant is held 20 per cent and the other 60 per cent to blame. The plaintiff is entitled to judgment for 80 per cent of his loss against each defendant even though one will end up paying more than the other as between themselves. The only exceptions to this approach arise where not all of the tortfeasors are entitled to have their damages reduced for contributory negligence; for example, in a case where one defendant is liable for breach of a common law duty of care and the other for breach of a statutory duty in respect of which, in New South Wales, contributory

51 *Bitumen and Oil Refineries* case (1954-5) 92 C.L.R. 200; *Bakker* v. *Joppich* (1980) 25 S.A.S.R. 468. The Vic. legislation (Wrongs Act 1958 s.24(2B)) expressly gives the court this power; while the Tas. legislation requires the person seeking contribution to satisfy the court that the settlement figure was reasonable, and gives the court the power to fix the amount at which the claim ought to have been settled.

52 (1958) 101 C.L.R. 73.

53 Wrongs Act 1958 s.24(2A).

54 *Fitzgerald* v. *Lane* [1989] A.C. 328. The importance of this rule resides in the issue of who bears the risk of the insolvency of one of the defendants: the plaintiff or the co-defendant(s)? See N.S.W.L.R.C. Report No. 65 paras 18-27; J.G. Fleming (1988) 104 *L.Q.R.* 6.

negligence is no defence.[55] In such a case judgment might be entered against the various tortfeasors in different amounts. This can happen also, of course, in cases in which successive actions can be brought against different tortfeasors.[56]

3. Proposals for Reform

The existence of rights of contribution between tortfeasors can be criticized.[57] At first sight, contribution seems fair (why should one tortfeasor alone bear full liability for damage caused by several?) and, indeed, necessary to further the deterrent aim of tort law (without it some tortfeasors might go scot-free while others bore more than the losses attributable to their fault). However, in practice most tort defendants are insured against liability, and so most potential beneficiaries of contribution rights are insurers (who are subrogated to the insured defendant's rights of contribution). Because of the high cost of enforcing contribution rights, in practice contribution will usually only be sought against tortfeasors who are insured, and it is hard to see that society as a whole gains anything from such actions between insurers. It can be argued, therefore, that rights of contribution ought to be abolished.[58] We have already seen that the employer's right of indemnity against an employee for whose tort the former is vicariously liable has been abolished in some jurisdictions,[59] and there are wider limitations on the exercise of rights of subrogation by liability insurers (among others) in s.65 of the Insurance Contracts Act 1984 (Cwth). However, more wide-ranging reform is not on anyone's agenda at the moment, and so we are left with less radical reform which the New South Wales Commission is currently considering.

The South Australian Law Reform Commission[60] has recommended that the law in South Australia be amended as it has been in England[61] to allow a claim for contribution to be made where parties are liable for the same damage regardless of whether or not the liability of either or both arises in tort. The Commission has also made a recommendation about the sort of case in which contribution is sought against a party liable in contract whose liability is limited or excluded by a clause in the contract. Suppose the plaintiff's total loss is $10 000 and that each of two defendants is 50 per cent responsible; but that the liability of one is limited by contract to $4000. Who should bear the other $1000—the plaintiff or the

---

55 Statutory Duties (Contributory Negligence) Act 1945; but note Workers Compensation Act 1987 (N.S.W.) s.151N(3).

56 See generally *Barisic* v. *Devenport* [1978] 2 N.S.W.L.R. 111. In such situations it is theoretically possible that a defendant may be held liable to pay more to another defendant by way of contribution than he was held liable to pay the person injured. Wrongs Act 1958 (Vic.) s.24(2A)(b) is designed to prevent this happening by limiting a defendant's liability to contribute to the amount of his liability to the plaintiff.

57 A classic discussion of the pros and cons of contribution is the exchange between Fleming James and Charles Gregory in (1941) 54 *Harv. L.R.* 1156 ff.

58 See Cane *Tort Law and Economic Interests* (Oxford, 1991) pp. 449-56.

59 See p. 726 above.

60 S.A.L.R.C. No. 42 (1977).

61 Civil Liability (Contribution) Act 1978, s.4.

other defendant? The Commission opts for the latter. It is adamant that, at least in cases between commercial parties involving economic loss, the contract should set the limit. The Commission has also recommended that cases where the independent torts of two tortfeasors cause part of the overall damage of which the plaintiff complains, but not the same parts of that damage, contribution ought to be recoverable by each against the other.[62]

---

62 Such a provision would make contribution recoverable in a case like *Dillingham* (1974-5) 132 C.L.R. 323 (see p. 732 above).

23

LIMITATION OF ACTIONS

Considerations of fairness to the defendant and the orderly administration of justice demand that a time limit be put on the bringing of actions in the courts.[1] The passage of time makes it more and more difficult to establish accurately the facts of a case as memories fade and documents become difficult to locate and interpret; and potential defendants must not be left indefinitely in the position of being unable to organize their affairs without the fear of having their activities and finances disrupted by litigation. So the law has always imposed time limitations of one sort or another on intending litigants. In practical terms, questions of limitation are of very great importance; in a book of this character, however, the issue of limitation requires only brief consideration.

The 'limitation period' is the period of time during which the plaintiff must bring the action, and on the expiry of which the cause of action becomes barred, that is, ceases to be a cause of action on which he can sue. Periods of limitation are laid down by statute[2] and so an expired cause of action is often called 'statute-barred'. We have already mentioned the limitation periods for the bringing of actions for or against the estate of a deceased person (survival actions)[3] and will not discuss this further. The limitation periods of most concern here are as follows: in most jurisdictions

---

1 Or the amendment of pleadings in such a way as to raise new causes of action: *Hristeas* v. *General Motors Holdens Pty Ltd* [1968] V.R. 14; *Church* v. *Lever & Kitchen Pty Ltd* [1970] 3 N.S.W.L.R. 566; *Black* v. *South Melbourne Corporation* (1964-5) 38 A.L.J.R. 309 *per* Barwick C.J.

2 Limitation provisions are not, in any Australian jurisdiction, all contained in one statute. But in all jurisdictions there is a main limitation statute which deals with limitation periods for the great bulk of actions and regulates general questions relating to the limitation of actions. These general statutes are: Limitation Act 1969 (N.S.W.); Limitation of Actions Act 1974-8 (Qld); Limitation of Actions Act 1936-75 (S.A.); Limitation Act 1974 (Tas.); Limitation of Actions Act 1958 (Vic.); Limitation Act 1935-54 (W.A.); Limitation Act 1981 (N.T.); Limitation Act 1985 (A.C.T.).

3 See p. 518 above.

the period for most actions 'founded on tort' is six years.[4] But also in most jurisdictions actions for damages which consist of or include damages for personal injuries[5] or for loss of dependency (under fatal accidents legislation)[6] must be brought within three years. The limitation period for bringing contribution proceedings varies from jurisdiction to jurisdiction, but a commonly occurring provision gives the claimant for contribution two years from the date of the judgment or award against him or from the settlement with the injured party, or four years from the date when the injured party's cause of action against the person claiming contribution arose.[7]

A few other provisions deserve mention. All the statutes contain a provision which, subject to various qualifications and conditions, has the effect of extending the limitation period in favour of a person under a disability (the most common of which is being under age) at the time the limitation period begins to run, for the length of the period of the disability.[8] Another important provision says, in effect, that where a cause of action is based on fraud or mistake or where a cause of action has been fraudulently concealed, the period of limitation does not begin to run until the plaintiff has or could with reasonable diligence have discovered the fraud or mistake. In cases of fraudulent concealment, 'fraud' does not bear its common law meaning, that is, the making of a false statement knowing it to be false or recklessly as to its truth, but bears a much wider meaning of unconscionable conduct. A party can have fraudulently concealed a cause of action, even if he took no active steps to conceal it, if he knowingly committed a wrongful act and kept it secret.[9]

It is also worth noting that the statutes contain a provision governing cases involving successive wrongs to goods: where goods are converted or detained and before the plaintiff recovers them they are converted or detained again, giving rise to a further cause of action, this further cause of action must be sued on within six years of the accrual of the first cause of action.

In order to calculate the date of expiry of a limitation period it is, of course, necessary to know not just the length of the period but also when it begins. This is governed by the basic common law principle that the period begins to run when the cause of action accrues. Where the tort is

---

4 But three years in N.T. Concerning limitation of claims for damages under the Trade Practices Act 1974 (Cwth) see *Jobbins* v. *Capel Court Corporation Ltd* (1989) 91 A.L.R. 314.

5 Including damages for loss of consortium or servitium: *Opperman* v. *Opperman* [1975] Qd.R. 345. But in W.A. the period is six years, and in 1982 the W.A.L.R.C. recommended retention of this period subject to a discretion to waive it: W.A.L.R.C. Project 36 Part 1 (1982). In Vic. in 1983 the period was changed from three years to six: Limitation of Actions (Personal Injury Claims) Act 1983, s.3(c).

6 For A.C.T. see *Noja* v. *Civil & Civic Pty Ltd* (1990) 93 A.L.R. 224.

7 For provisions *re* limitation period for contribution proceedings in Vic. see Wrongs Act 1958, s.24(4); and for Tasmania see Tortfeasors and Contributory Negligence Act 1954, s.3(5).

8 *Re* postponement on grounds of impairment of mental condition see *Kotulski* v. *Attard* [1981] 1 N.S.W.L.R. 115.

9 *Gabolinscy* v. *Hamilton City Corporation* [1975] 1 N.Z.L.R. 150.

actionable *per se* (for example, trespass to land) the period begins to run when the wrongful act is done even though the damage, if any, does not occur or is not discovered until later. But where actual damage is the gist of the action, the basic rule is that the period does not begin to run until the damage occurs.[10]

It is not, however, always a simple matter to determine when the damage which forms the gist of the action (or the 'gist-damage', for short) occurred.[11] Three distinct problems arise. The first is the need to determine what the gist-damage is. In some cases this is obvious: in an action for personal injuries or for physical damage to property, the gist-damage will consist of physical changes to the person or property of the plaintiff (although in some cases it may be difficult to determine when such changes occur). Much more difficult are cases involving the acquisition of defective property. As we have seen, in England there can be no cause of action in tort in such cases unless and until the defective state of the property causes injury (that is, physical changes) to some person or damage (that is, physical changes) to some property other than the defective property itself. But in Australia, in theory at least, actions might lie[12] for (1) physical damage to the property itself;[13] or (2) for the cost of remedying the defect in order to remove a risk of injury or damage to persons or other property; or (3) for the cost of remedying the defect in order to restore the property to a sound state; or (4) for diminution in the value of the property attributable to the defect. In relation to (1) the gist-damage would occur when physical changes to the property first occurred; in relation to (2) the gist-damage would probably occur at the date when the property first presented a relevant risk; in relation to (3) and (4) it is unclear whether the gist-damage occurs when the defective property is acquired, or only at some later point when the defect becomes known.[14]

---

10 See e.g. *Gabolinscy* v. *Hamilton City Corporation* [1975] 1 N.Z.L.R. 150, 159-60; *Glasson* v. *Fuller* [1922] S.A.S.R. 148 (*Rylands* v. *Fletcher*).

11 J. Stapleton (1988) 104 *L.Q.R.* 213.

12 Limitation rules are concerned with defining the latest date on which an action can be brought; but, of course, the date the cause of action accrues defines not only the start of the limitation period but also the earliest date on which the plaintiff could bring an action.

13 There is considerable discussion in *Sutherland Shire Council* v. *Heyman* (1984-5) 157 C.L.R. 424 of the question of whether the defect itself constitutes physical damage or whether the loss suffered when a defective property is acquired is purely economic. It certainly seems strange to say that a defect is damage to the property, because to say that property has been damaged assumes that it has changed from its original state, whereas the original state of defective property is defectiveness. But perhaps it seems less strange to identify defect and damage in cases, such as *Junior Books Ltd* v. *Veitchi Co. Ltd* [1983] 1 A.C. 520, in which the defect causes the property to deteriorate and require replacement more quickly than it would otherwise have done. At all events, by 'physical damage' we mean physical changes to the property (and so not the defect itself); items (3) and (4) deal with the defect itself.

14 See *Sutherland Shire Council* v. *Heyman* (1984-5) 157 C.L.R. 424, 503-5 and *Hawkins* v. *Clayton* (1988) 164 C.L.R. 532, 587-8 *per* Deane J. who preferred the later date; *Hawkins* v. *Clayton* at pp. 600-1 *per* Gaudron J. (date when limitation period begins to run may depend on nature of interest infringed).

Also difficult are cases in which economic loss is suffered as a result of negligent financial advice or services. In *Forster* v. *Outred & Co.*[15] it was held that when a solicitor by negligence encumbers the plaintiff's property with a mortgage the loss occurs at the date the mortgage is executed and not when the plaintiff is called upon to pay under the mortgage. Similarly, it has been held that an insured suffers loss upon entering a voidable (re)insurance policy even though the (re)insurer does not discover the grounds of voidability until some time later.[16] The effect of these cases is to define the gist-damage as the *risk* of suffering economic loss as opposed to the loss itself. By contrast, in *Dove* v. *Banham's Patent Locks Ltd*[17] where the defendant installed a defective security door, it was held that actionable damage was not suffered until there had been a burglary.[18] In other words, the *risk* of suffering a loss was not actionable.

In *Hawkins* v. *Clayton*[19] the executor and beneficiary under a will suffered economic loss as a result of negligent delay by the testator's solicitor in informing him of the existence of the will and of the death of the testator. The majority judges who held that the solicitor owed the plaintiff a relevant duty of care also held that the limitation period did not begin to run until either the date the plaintiff was told about the will (Gaudron J.) or the date of his formal appointment as executor (Brennan and Deane JJ.). But only Gaudron J. reached this conclusion on the ground that not until that date did the plaintiff suffer loss. Both Brennan J. and Deane J. said, in effect, that although the loss occurred during the period of the solicitor's delay, the limitation period did not begin to run until the plaintiff was in a position to assert his rights against the solicitor because the *effect* of the solicitor's negligence had been to conceal the loss from the plaintiff.[20]

We can summarize so far by saying that the date of commencement of the limitation period in a tort action in respect of damage suffered cannot be ascertained until it is decided what the gist-damage is. This may be determined by the way the plaintiff defines the damage in the pleadings,[21] but it will also depend on what sorts of loss the court is prepared to allow to form the basis of a tort action. Most relevant in this context are the issues of whether purely economic loss resulting from the acquisition of

15 [1982] 1 W.L.R. 86; cf. *Moore & Co. Ltd* v. *Ferrier* [1988] 1 W.L.R. 267; *Bell* v. *Peter Browne & Co.* [1990] 3 W.L.R. 510; *Gillespie* v. *Elliott* [1987] 2 Qd.R. 509; *Deputy Commissioner of Taxation* v. *Zimmerlie* [1988] 2 Qd.R. 500.

16 *Iron Trade Mutual Insurance Co. Ltd* v. *J.K. Buckenham Ltd* [1990] 1 All E.R. 808; *Islander Trucking Ltd (in liq.)* v. *Hogg Robinson & Gardner Mountain (Marine) Ltd* [1990] 1 All E.R. 826.

17 [1983] 2 All E.R. 833.

18 cf. *Wright* v. *Borzi* [1979] Qd.R. 179.

19 (1988) 164 C.L.R. 532.

20 We saw above that limitation statutes postpone the start of the limitation period in cases of fraudulent concealment of the cause of action. The reasoning of Brennan and Deane JJ. effects a similar postponement in the case of negligent concealment. Such concealment may also occur in cases of negligent misrepresentation. Concerning this problem as it affects actions under the Trade Practices Act 1974 (Cwth) see *Jobbins* v. *Capel Court* (1989) 91 A.L.R. 314, 318.

21 *Crisp* v. *Blake* (1992) Aust. Torts Reports 81-158.

defective property is actionable; and of whether the risk of incurring a loss (or not making a gain) is actionable either before or after the event of which there was a chance has occurred.[22]

The second problem posed by the need to determine when the gist-damage occurred is that sometimes the plaintiff's damage occurs over a substantial period. The law does not, of course, say that the plaintiff can bring the action only after all the damage in respect of which he sues has occurred: such a rule would be unfair to plaintiffs, who need and deserve financial assistance in dealing with the past, present and future consequences of the defendant's tort, as well as to defendants who would, under such a rule, be forced to endure long periods of uncertainty. In fact, all that the law requires in order to give the plaintiff a right to sue and to start the limitation period running is a significant amount of damage, although just what this means is very unclear. Cases of traumatic injury (such as personal injury or property damage suffered in a road accident) are relatively easy: the injury inflicted at the time of the accident will usually be significant. In such cases the main difficulty is to assess what the future effects of the initial traumatic injury are likely to be, given that the common law requires damages to be assessed in one lump sum. Cases of tortiously caused illness or disease may be considerably more difficult because the symptoms of illnesses and diseases often develop from imperceptible beginnings and only reach their mature form after a considerable period of time.[23]

In *Cartledge* v. *E. Jopling & Sons Ltd*[24] the plaintiffs alleged that as a result of exposure to noxious dust over a period of years they had contracted a lung disease called pneumoconiosis. The medical evidence was that a person who inhaled noxious gas over a period of years could suffer substantial injury from pneumoconiosis before it could be discovered by any means known to medical science. The plaintiffs discovered that they had the disease between 1950 and 1955 and the writs were issued on 1 December 1956. But no breaches of duty after September 1950 could be discovered.[25] The plaintiffs argued that their cause of action did not arise until they discovered that they had the disease, or that if it did arise earlier a fresh cause of action arose when they made the discovery. The House of Lords held that the cause of action arose as soon as the breach of duty by the defendant caused personal injury to the plaintiffs beyond what could be regarded as negligible, even if that injury was unknown to and could not be discovered by the sufferer. The plaintiffs' claim was therefore statute-barred. Any further damage occurring after the date on which the cause of action originally accrued was part of the same cause of action and did not give rise to any further right which would 'reset the limitation clock' in the plaintiffs' favour. But the House of Lords in this case did not give any clear guidance as to when significant damage first occurs in a

---

22 On this issue see further p. 454 above.

23 See J. Stapleton *Disease and the Compensation Debate* (Oxford, 1986) Ch. 1 esp. pp. 26-9.

24 [1963] A.C. 758.

25 The limitation period was six years.

case where the early symptoms of a disease may be so slight as to be imperceptible. In practice, courts tend to avoid this difficult question by assuming that the first significant damage occurs contemporaneously with first exposure to the tortious source of risk.[26]

The principle that the plaintiff's cause of action accrues on the date the first significant damage occurs is the basis of the rule of assessment of damages that in personal injury actions the damages must be assessed once and for all in one lump sum and theoretically by reference to the date when the cause of action arose. This rule causes significant problems even in cases in which the act of negligence is momentary and causes traumatic injury, but it is even more inadequate to deal with cases of continuing breach of duty.

In *Cartledge* the continuing breach of duty on which the claim was founded had ceased more than six years before the writ was issued. If it had continued into the limitation period, so that it could be said that breaches of duty within that period had materially aggravated the plaintiffs' condition, then there is authority that they could have recovered damages for the whole of their loss attributable to the defendant's continuing breach of duty, even that which occurred outside the limitation period.[27]

The rule that any damage occurring after the date of accrual of the original cause of action is part of that cause of action is not universally applicable. For example, in cases of continuing nuisance each repetition of the nuisance which inflicts damage on the plaintiff gives rise to a separate cause of action at law in which damages can be awarded. In *Cartledge* Lord Pearce noted this difference between nuisance actions and personal injury actions[28] but gave no rationale for it. In an action under the Trade Practices Act 1974 (Cwth) concerning loss suffered by reliance on misleading statements, it was suggested that where a person acts on one occasion to his detriment in reliance on such a statement (for example, by purchasing property) and then on some later occasion acts again to his detriment in reliance on the same statement (for example, by buying other property), each act of reliance might give rise to a different cause of action.[29] Analogous reasoning could be applied to an action at common law in respect of misstatements.

More problematically, in some cases it may be possible to treat subsequent damage as giving rise to a fresh cause of action even in the absence of a new causal factor.[30] For example, in *Mount Albert Borough Council* v. *Johnson*[31] flats were built for a developer on filled land in 1965. In 1967 cracks appeared and remedial work was done. In 1968 the first purchasers of the flat in question sold it and in 1970 it was resold to Johnson. At the time of this last sale there was no sign of cracking, but

---

26 Stapleton *Disease and the Compensation Debate* p. 28.
27 *Clarkson* v. *Modern Foundries Ltd* [1958] 1 All E.R. 33; *Adams* v. *Ascot Iron Foundry Pty Ltd* (1968) 89 W.N.(Pt. 2)(N.S.W.) 37.
28 [1963] A.C. 758, 778-9.
29 *Jobbins* v. *Capel Court* (1989) 91 A.L.R. 314, 318-19.
30 *Bowen* v. *Paramount Builders Ltd* [1977] 1 N.Z.L.R. 394, 424 *per* Cooke J.
31 [1979] 2 N.Z.L.R. 234.

subsequently cracking more serious than the first appeared. The court held that the second lot of cracking was distinct from the first and created a new cause of action even though it was caused by the same acts of negligence as the first lot of cracking. But there is no discernible principle according to which damage can be divided up in this way; and the New Zealand approach is unlikely to be followed in Australia in this type of case.[32]

The third problem posed by the rule that a cause of action accrues when damage occurs is that sometimes damage is 'latent', that is, not discoverable by reasonable means at the date it first occurred. This problem was present in *Cartledge* where the House spoke of the 'secret onset' of the disease; and it is a feature of many cases in which the injury consists of an illness or disease. In *Cartledge* the plaintiffs urged the House of Lords to hold that the limitation period did not begin to run until the disease was discoverable by reasonable means, but the House declined this invitation.

The fact of the matter appears simply to be that the common law of limitation relating to personal injuries was originally developed with traumatic injuries in mind[33] and it has failed to adapt to cases of progressive disease. The law has now been updated in Victoria by the enactment of amendments to the Limitation of Actions Act 1958 which give effect to a distinction between accidents on the one hand and diseases and disorders on the other, and provide in the case of the latter that the limitation period does not begin to run until the plaintiff knows that he has the disease or disorder and that it is attributable to the wrongful act of some person.[34] There has also been a limited reform (to cover asbestos-related diseases) in Western Australia.[35]

The principle that the limitation period begins to run when the damage is suffered rather than when it could reasonably have been discovered has also been applied by the House of Lords to a case of damage to a building caused by defective design,[36] but the Law Lords expressed their dislike of the rule, preferring a rule based on discoverability of damage.[37] In the U.K. the Latent Damage Act 1976 created a rather complicated regime to deal with latent damage in cases not involving personal injury: the plaintiff can bring the action within six years of the date when the cause of action accrues, or within three years of the date when the plaintiff ought reasonably to have realized he had a cause of action, whichever date is the later; but an action may not be brought after fifteen years from the date of the alleged tort. So far as defective buildings are concerned, this legislation is now of little relevance because damages are not recoverable in respect of the defect itself or of damage to the

---

32 See *Sutherland S.C.* v. *Heyman* (1984-5) 157 C.L.R. 424, 490-2 *per* Brennan J.

33 cf. *Church* v. *Lever & Kitchen Ltd* [1970] 3 N.S.W.L.R. 566.

34 Limitation of Actions (Personal Injury Claims) Act 1983, s.3(b).

35 Acts Amendment (Asbestos Related Diseases) Act 1983 (W.A.); P. Handford (1991) 21 *W.A.L.R.* 63, 75-88.

36 *Pirelli General Cable Works Ltd* v. *Oscar Faber & Partners* [1983] 2 A.C. 1, discussed in detail by N. Mullaney (1991) 54 *M.L.R.* 216. See also S. Todd (1983) 10 *N.Z.U.L.R.* 311; C.J. Rossiter and M. Stone (1985) 59 *A.L.J.* 606.

37 See also *Askin* v. *Knox* [1989] 1 N.Z.L.R. 248.

defective building. But in Australia, where such damages are recoverable, the date-of-occurrence rule still applies.[38]

As we saw above, problems of latent damage may also arise in cases of negligent financial advice or services; for example, where a lawyer drafts a defective document. Here, too, the basic rule is that the limitation period begins to run when the first significant damage occurs, and this may, for example, be when the document is executed rather than when its defectiveness comes to light. The Latent Damage Act 1976 (U.K.) applies to such cases (provided the plaintiff sues the adviser in tort, not contract), but in Australia the date-of-occurrence rule still applies unless the effect of the defendant's tort is to conceal the cause of action for a period; in which case the limitation period will not begin to run until the facts giving rise to the cause of action come to light.[39]

Besides replacing the date-of-occurrence rule with a date-of-discoverability rule, another way of dealing with problems of latent damage (among other things)[40] is to enact provisions empowering the court to extend the limitation period; in some jurisdictions this has been one in respect of actions generally, but in others only in respect of personal injury actions. A common condition of the availability of an extension (but not in Tasmania or Victoria) is that a fact material to the cause of action (*simpliciter* or, in some jurisdictions, of a decisive character) was not known to the person claiming to have a right of action until a date not long before the expiration of the initial limitation period. The granting of an extension is always a matter for the court's discretion. The detailed provisions governing extension of the period are mostly of considerable complexity and vary markedly from jurisdiction to jurisdiction.

Consideration of the case law which has grown up around the extension provisions would be out of place in a book of this nature. It is simply worth noting that criticism has been directed at the complexity generated by statutory provisions designed to regulate in great detail the circumstances in which extensions may be granted.[41] Such provisions tend to encourage litigants to rely on technical points of interpretation at the expense of concentration on the issue of whether the plaintiff ought in fairness to be granted an extension. The extreme solution is to abolish fixed periods entirely and to leave the question of limitation completely within the discretion of the court. A middle way is to retain fixed periods but to couch the discretion to allow extensions in very broad terms.[42] The main objection to fixed periods is that in some cases they can be unfair to

---

38 For a discussion of options for reforming the law of limitation as it relates to latent damage, especially in building cases, see N. Mullaney (1991) 54 *M.L.R.* 349.

39 *Hawkins* v. *Clayton* (1988) 164 C.L.R. 539. This rule appears to be confined to cases in which the tort consists of non-disclosure (or concealment) of information. It would not apply to a case where a builder negligently lays inadequate foundations and then covers them up, because the covering up is not, in itself, tortious.

40 Latency of damage is not the only reason why plaintiffs sometimes fail to commence their actions within the limitation period. For this reason, extension provisions may be justifiable even in respect of cases to which a date-of-discoverability rule applies.

41 P.J. Davies (1982) 98 *L.Q.R.* 249.

42 As in S.A. (see *Napolitano* v. *Coyle* (1977) 15 S.A.S.R. 559) or even more markedly in Tas.

plaintiffs. Defendants, on the other hand, may dislike the greater element of uncertainty involved in wide discretions (although there is disagreement as to how serious a problem uncertainty is).

Another important issue is whether the question of limitation should be treated as going to the merits of the case or as a more technical device to bring order to the administration of justice. Proponents of the latter view support fixed periods; those who see the question of limitation as intimately tied up with the reasonableness of the behaviour of the litigants in conducting their respective cases favour discretionary provisions. Victorian legislation[43] provides for the retention of a fixed period of six years for personal injury and disease actions but in conjunction with a wide discretion to extend the period subject to the following guidelines as to its exercise: the length of and reasons for the plaintiff's delay; any prejudice to the defendant caused by the delay; the extent to which the defendant made relevant facts available to the plaintiff; the duration of any disability from which the plaintiff suffered; whether the plaintiff acted promptly once he knew that he might have a cause of action; any steps taken by the plaintiff to get medical, legal or other relevant advice and the nature of the advice received. Such a half-way house is perhaps a reasonable compromise between the interests of the litigants and the public interest in the orderly administration of justice.

43 Limitation of Actions (Personal Injury Claims) Act 1983, s.5 (substituting new s.23A in Limitation of Actions Act 1958). See also W.A.L.R.C. Report on Limitations (1982).

INDEX